IN FURTHER PURSUIT
OF TRIVIAL PURSUIT®

IN FURTHER PURSUIT
OF TRIVIAL PURSUIT®

(A fascinating, entertaining, informative reference book
embellishing the answers given in America's hottest new boardgame:
"Trivial Pursuit® " – Genus Edition.)

By Joseph A. DeBartolo

SARSAPARILLA LTD.
Chicago, Illinois

Sarsaparilla Ltd.
62 West Huron, Chicago, Illinois 60610

International Standard Book Number: 0-930281-00-4

First printing, September, 1984

Printed in the United States of America

DEDICATION

To Dad
…and his homemade, unpatented, electric hot dogger
…and the book he would have read.

EDITOR

Marianne Elizabeth DeBartolo

RESEARCHERS

GEOGRAPHY

Marijo Burke
Paul C. Burke

ENTERTAINMENT

Nancy (J.C.) Johnson
Cary A. Noehre

HISTORY

Bonnie E. Grove

ART AND LITERATURE

Monica David-Casey
Bill Eichengreen
Jerry Eichengreen

SCIENCE & NATURE

Maureen Burke Bench
Valentine Herdeg

SPORTS AND LEISURE

Timothy J. Landers

CONTRIBUTORS

Kathy Arrigo
Julie Casey
Robin Ellis

Margaret Haddix
Helen Nelson
Jeanne Radell

SPECIAL ASSISTANTS

Sean Michael Bench   Molly Maureen Bench

CONTENTS

A FEW OPENING REMARKS

This book might also have been titled "The Ultimate Argument Settler." Just how many times during the course of playing any edition of *Trivial Pursuit* ® have you or your friends come away as fully satisfied with the answers as given to the questions posed in the game? How many times did you want to know more?

In Further Pursuit Of Trivial Pursuit ® will increase discussion among players, settle a few disagreements, fascinate, entertain, amaze and educate you. Each fact has been thoroughly researched and our findings are presented here for your edification in an easy to use reference book.

During the thousands of hours required to complete this work, we were consistently impressed with the accuracy of the answers in the Genus Edition of *Trivial Pursuit*®. In very rare instances were there ever inaccuracies. However, in playing the game, just accepting the answers as given wasn't enough for us. We wanted to know more. We trust that you will too. We have answered the "why" for each question in each category. Or, embellished upon the answer as given. Some are more detailed than others, but each will add to your enjoyment of the game.

Answers are alphabetically arranged in accordance with the first word of each, not including the English articles, "A", "An", and "The." Such articles appear at the end of each answer. Numeric answers appear at the end of each section, following the letter Z.

GEOGRAPHY

A: **Acapulco**
Q: Where do divers leap from a 100-foot cliff into waters between the Quebrada rocks?
W: Acapulco is one of Mexico's chief Pacific Ocean ports. This popular winter resort lies on a beautiful bay 140 miles southwest of Mexico City. "Quebrada" is a Spanish word meaning "gorge" or "canyon." La Quebrada is a striking cliff formation on the ocean side of the western peninsula of Acapulco Bay. Daredevil divers perform outstanding feats from this 130 foot cliff. Not only do they have to plunge into a narrow crevice between the rocks, but they can only dive on the incoming tide!

A: **Adriatic, The**
Q: What sea separates Italy from Yugoslavia?
W: The Adriatic is a gulf or arm of the Mediterranean Sea. The Adriatic, about 480 miles long with an average width of 100 miles, is located at the back of the boot of Italy.

A: **Aegean, The**
Q: What sea sparkles between Asia Minor and Greece?
W: The Aegean is a gulf or arm of the Mediterranean Sea. It lies between Greece on its west and north, Turkey on the east, and the island of Crete to the south. It is about 400 miles long and more than 200 miles wide at its widest point. Asia Minor, the Asian portion of what is now Turkey, was called Anatolia in ancient times. It was the center of the Hittite empire, and it is believed that the people of this area may have played a major role in the shift from

gathering food to actually producing food… in the New Stone Age!

A: **Aer Lingus**
Q: What's the national airline of Ireland?
W: Aer Lingus flies nonstop from New York and Boston to Shannon and Dublin. Flights to and from many other cities in Europe are also available on this airline.

A: **Aeroflot**
Q: What is the largest airline in the world?
W: Aeroflot, the Soviet airline, operates 1,300 aircraft over about 560,000 miles of routes. It employs 500,000 people and carried 106 million passengers to 97 countries in 1981. If you're a heavy smoker, look for another airline. You may smoke on Aeroflot, but only after having been airborne for four hours!

A: **Afghanistan**
Q: What country ranks first in an alphabetical list?

W: Afghanistan is a kingdom of southern Asia that is almost as large as the state of Texas. In 1979 Afghanistan was invaded by Russian troops who began a long war began against Muslim rebel forces opposed to the pro-Soviet government.

A: **Afghanistan and Pakistan**
Q: What two countries share the Khyber Pass?
W: The Khyber Pass connects the northern frontier of West Pakistan with Afghanistan. The Kyber is one of the most famous mountain passes in the world: it was an important military point for hundreds of years since it connects the Indian Peninsula with Afghanistan. Through it have passed the Persians, Greeks, Mughals, Afghans, and Tatars.

A: **Africa**
Q: What continent pushes up the Atlas Mountains?
W: The mountains were named after Altas (Greek mythology). They extend for 1,200 miles along the coast of North Africa in the countries of Morocco, Algeria, and Tunisia. These mountains yield silver, antimony, lead, copper, iron, and marble.

A: **Africa**
Q: What continent is Sierra Leone in?
W: Sierra Leone is a British colony and protectorate on the western coast of Africa. It lies south of Guinea and north of Liberia. Freetown, the capital, is the most important seaport in West Africa. A group of Englishmen established a settlement here in 1787 for American blacks who had escaped to England and, after 1807, for other blacks rescued from slave ships.

A: **Africa**
Q: What's the second largest continent?
W: A continent is one of the seven great land masses of the world. Asia is the largest, Africa is second, and Antarctica is the smallest.

A: **Africa**
Q: What's the warmest continent?
W: Correct; however, Africa's climate is not *always* warm. The Nile has frozen over at least twice, 829 A.D. and 1010. Africa also has 13 square kilometers of glaciers on three of its highest mountain peaks.

A: **Africa**
Q: What continent is home to the largest number of countries?
W: The people of Africa may be divided into several broad groups based on race, language, and culture. Each group contains characteristics of other groups because the people of Africa have mixed together for thousands of years. Early explorers from Portugal, Spain, Germany, Italy, Great Britain, Belgium, and the United States invaded and settled in Africa, resulting in the large number of different countries. There are currently (1984) 55 countries in Africa. The next most "countried" continent is Asia with 39 and then North America, including Central America and the West Indies, with 37.

A: **Africa's**
Q: What continent's southern tip is Cape Agulhas?
W: That's right, it is not the Cape of

Good Hope! Cape Agulhas extends 65 kilometers farther south than Hope.

A: **Africa's**
Q: What continent's westernmost point is called Cape Verde?
W: Cape Verde is an extension of the west African country Senegal. Cape Verde Island is off the coast of Senegal.

A: **Akron, Ohio**
Q: What U.S. city is known as "The Rubber Capital of the World"?
W: Akron is the home of five of the largest tire and tube plants. It is the largest rubber manufacturing center in the world. Akron also has the world's largest fishing tackle industry and one of the largest cereal mills in the U.S.

A: **Alaska**
Q: What U.S. state has the longest border with Canada?
W: The Yukon Territory of Canada forms the eastern boundary of the state of Alaska for over 600 miles. The coastal section of British Columbia forms the southeastern boundary. One frequently forgets that Alaska is in the United States and, when this question is asked, tends to think only of the U.S. mainland.

A: **Alaska**
Q: What U.S. state has the smallest population?
W: Alaska ranks 50th in population among the states, with a 1980 census of 401,851. California ranks first, with a 1980 population of 23,667,902.

A: **Alaska**
Q: What U.S. state has the longest coastline?
W: Alaska's general coastline is 6,640 miles long, 5,580 on the Pacific and 1,060 on the Arctic Ocean. However, if you include the "shoreline" of mainland Alaska, its offshore islands, sounds, bays, rivers, and creeks, the length of land washed by tidewater measures 33,904 miles! Florida has the second longest coastline, at 1,350 miles.

A: **Alaska**
Q: What's the only U.S. state that borders on Canadian territory?
W: All of the other states border Canadian *provinces*. Alaska borders the Yukon Territory of Canada.

A: **Alaska**
Q: What state is Mount McKinley in?
W: Mount McKinley, in southcentral Alaska, is the highest point in the continent of North America at 20,320 feet. It is also the scenic site of the Denali National Park. The National Park was known as Mount McKinley until 1980 when Congress enlarged the park and renamed it Denali National Park.

A: **Alaska**
Q: What U.S. state is free of houseflies?
W: One would think that there would be no insects in Alaska because of its permafrost terrain; however, Alaska's terrain is like a giant sponge: it *freezes* solid in the winter, but in the summer its top layer thaws leaving shallow, stagnant water that becomes a haven for breeding insects. Mosquitoes are a common pest from May to August, but Alaska is fairly insect-free by September. The ordinary housefly cannot breed in the cold climate, and even those who make it by ship or plane die before reproducing.

A: **Alaska**
Q: What U.S. state would you find the Mount McKinley Station Hotel in?
W: The Station Hotel was located near Mount McKinley in Alaska; however, it burned down in the early 1970s! It was rebuilt and is now called the Denali National Park Hotel. It has a variety of accommodations, including renovated railroad cars!

A: **Alaska**
Q: What U.S. state receives the least sunshine?
W: Alaska receives the smallest amount of sunshine because it is located on the earth's surface farthest from the rays of the sun as it rotates around the earth. At Alaska's northernmost point the sun remains above the horizon for 2.5 months, from May to August. But from mid-November to late January, the sun never shows its face. Because of the slanting light in Alaska you will always have a shadow on a sunny day, i.e., the sun is never directly overhead in this state!

A: **Alaska**
Q: What was known as Russian America before 1867?
W: Alaska was owned by Russia. In 1867 U.S. Secretary of State William Seward was responsible for purchasing Alaska from the Russians for $7.2 million, or less than two cents per acre (Seward's Folly).

A: **Alaska**
Q: What U.S. state is known as "The Last Frontier"?
W: Alaska is known as the "Last Frontier" because it has vast regions not yet explored.

A: **Alaska, California, Hawaii, Washington**
Q: What four U.S. states have active volcanoes?
W: Our sources verify active volcanoes in Alaska (Gareloi erupted in 1982), Hawaii (Mauna Loa and Kilauea are erupting as we write), and Washington (Mt. St. Helens erupted in 1983). The only volcano in California is Lassen, which is dormant.

A: **Alaska Highway, The**
Q: What road links Dawson Creek, British Columbia, and Fairbanks, Alaska?
W: The U.S. built the 1,523 mile Alaska Highway from Fairbanks, Alaska, to Dawson Creek, British Columbia, as a military supply road during World War II. It was opened to civilian traffic in 1947 and links the road system of Alaska with those of the other states and Canada. Travelers may enjoy mountain beauty and glimpse wild life along the highway.

A: **Albania, Andorra, Austria**
Q: What three European countries begin with the letter A?
W: Albania, a Communist dictatorship, lies along the eastern shore of the Adriatic Sea, about 50 miles across the strait of Otranto from the heel of the boot of Italy. Yugoslavia lies to the north and east; Greece to the east and south. Andorra is one of the smallest countries in the world. It lies in the Pyrenees Mountains between France and Spain. Only a single automobile road connects the country with France and Spain. Austria is a medium-sized country in central Europe. It is a democratic republic and is geographically hemmed in by other countries.

A: **Albania's**
Q: What country's capital is Tirana?
W: Tirana is Albania's capital and largest city. It lies in the central part of Albania.

A: **Alberta**
Q: What Canadian province was named for a daughter of Queen Victoria?
W: Alberta is the second most westerly of Canada's provinces. It lies south of the Northwest Territory of Canada, west of the Province of Saskatchewan, and north of the State of Montana. It was named for Princess Louise Caroline Alberta.

A: **Alcatraz**
Q: What's the notable rocky island in San Francisco Bay?
W: San Francisco Bay was the location of Alcatraz, a federal prison. The prison was established in 1933 and abandoned in 1963. It used to house unusually dangerous criminals such as Al Capone, Alvin Karpis, Machine Gun Kelly, Doc Barker, and, lest we forget, Robert Stroud, "The Birdman of Alcatraz."

A: **Alexandria**
Q: What Egyptian city was founded by Alexander the Great in 331 B.C.?
W: Alexandria is the chief port and second largest city of Egypt. The city lies on the northwestern end of the Nile River Delta on a strip of land between the Mediterranean Sea and Lake Mareotis. The famous lighthouse known as the Pharos of Alexandria, one of the seven wonders of the ancient world, was located here. There are several "Alexandrian" cities in the U.S., including one in Louisiana, one in Virginia, and one in Minnesota.

A: **Amazon, The**
Q: What's the longest river in the Americas?
W: The Amazon is 3,912 miles long, its source is glacier-fed lakes in Peru; and its outflow is the Atlantic Ocean. It was named for the warlike women from Greek mythology - the Amazons - because the Spanish explorer Francisco de Orellana asserted he fought with them there. The longest river in the world is the Nile.

A: **Amazon, The**
Q: What's the longest navigable river in the world?
W: Many experts have disputed whether the Amazon or the Nile is the longest. However, because of the many sections of the Nile that are navigable for short stretches only, it has been accepted that the Amazon and its tributaries compose the longest navigable river.

A: **Amazon, The**
Q: What's the world's widest river?
W: It is so wide that from its mouth pours one fifth of all the moving fresh water on earth!

A: **America**
Q: What's named for Amerigo Vespucci?
W: Amerigo Vespucci explored the coasts of what are now Brazil, Uruguay, and Argentina in 1497 to 1503. The name was first applied by mapmakers to South America, but later it was applied to both con-tinents. Vespucci claimed to have discovered the continent of America in 1497. Columbus did not dispute this claim. In 1492 Columbus had no idea that he had discovered the Western Hemisphere; he thought the *islands* he explored were part of the Indies. He first set foot on the *mainland* in 1498.

A: **Amsterdam**
Q: What's the capital of the Netherlands?
W: Amsterdam is the capital and largest city of the Netherlands. Amsterdam lies well below sea level. A well-planned series of interconnected circular canals drain the city. These picturesque, tree-shaded waterways divide Amsterdam into numerous islands. About 400 bridges connect the islands, and nearly all the houses are built on wooden piles because the ground is soft and boggy.

A: **Amsterdam**
Q: Where is Dam Square?
W: Amsterdam is divided into two sections by the Amstel River. The first dam across the Amstel was constructed in 1270, and since that time Dam Square has been the heart of Amsterdam. Today Dam Square is a busy, spacious square on which the Royal Palace is located.

A: **Anchorage**
Q: What's the largest city in Alaska?
W: Anchorage is the largest city in Alaska, and the northern defense center of the United States. Fort Richardson houses the headquarters of the U.S. Army in Alaska, and the Alaskan Air Command has its headquarters at Elmendorf Air Force Base. The 1980 population of Anchorage was 173,017. The next largest place is the Kenai Peninsula borough with 25,282.

A: **Andes, The**
Q: What mountain range is traversed by the highest railroad in the world?
W: The Andes Mountains are the longest chain of mountains in the world. They stretch along the entire west coast of South America from Cape Horn to Panama, for a distance of 4,500 miles. Engineers find railroads much harder to build in the Andes than in the Rocky Mountains, because in the central Andes they have had to climb more than 10,000 feet to find a pass through which they could build railroad tracks. The highest standard gauge railway is on the Peruvian State Railways at La Cima, 15,806 feet above sea level!

A: **Angel Falls**
Q: What falls is near where Jimmy Angel crashed his plane in 1937?
W: Angel Falls is the highest waterfall in the world. It is located in southeastern Venezuela and is 1,000 feet higher than any other known falls. James Angel, an American aviator, discovered Angel Falls in 1935. Jimmy had earlier requested that upon his death he be cremated and his ashes scattered over the falls.

A: **Angel Falls**
Q: What's the world's highest waterfall?
W: The Salto Alto (Angel Falls) in Venezuela is the highest waterfall known. It is more than 15 times higher than Niagara Falls in New York.

A: **Antarctica**
Q: Where's Little America?
W: Little America was a base of operation for Commander Richard Byrd. It is on top of the Ross Ice Shelf in the Bay of Whales. Byrd made four expeditions to Antarctica: 1928, 1933, 1939, and 1947.

A: **Antarctica**
Q: What continent contains Queen Maud Land, Wilkes Land, and Byrd Land?
W: These three "lands" are divisions of the continent of Antarctica. Marie Byrd Land was named by Commander Richard Byrd for his wife.

A: Apennines, The
Q: What mountains form the spine of Italy?
W: The Apennines is the name of a mountain range that runs from the Gulf of Genoa to the toe of boot-shaped Italy. The mountains are made up chiefly of limestone and marble. The quarries near Carrara are noted for their pure white marble. One of the peaks of this mountain range is the famous volcano, Vesuvius.

A: Appalachians, The
Q: What mountain range extends from the Gulf of St. Lawrence to Alabama?
W: The Appalachian Mountains chain is the chief mountain system of eastern North America and the oldest mountains in the United States. The Appalachians are made up of smaller ranges: northern, central, and southern.

A: Arabian, The
Q: What sea is Bombay on?
W: The Arabian Sea is the part of the Indian Ocean that lies between Arabia and India. Bombay is the largest city in India and India's leading western seaport. Bombay lies on an island facing an excellent enclosed harbor 14 miles long and five miles wide. Cattle roam freely in the streets of Bombay because the Hindus consider them sacred.

A: Arabic
Q: What's the official language of Egypt, Tunisia and Morocco?
W: Egypt, Tunisia, and Morocco are countries of North Africa that border the Mediterranean Sea. The Arabic language became the language of Moslem culture from North Africa to the borders of India. Arabs are called "semites" because Arabic is a semitic language.

A: Arc de Triomphe, The
Q: What arch can you see from the Place de la Concorde?
W: The Arc stands at the head of the wide, tree lined avenue called Champs Elysees in Paris in the E'toile

(star) at which 12 avenues meet. The French placed the grave of their unknown soldier beneath the Arc after World War I. An eternal flame burns there in his honor.

A: Argentina
Q: What country contains South America's highest and lowest points?
W: The highest point is Mount Aconcagua (22,834 ft. above sea level); the lowest is the Valdes Peninsula (131 ft. below sea level). Do the people who live there have to swim to the grocery store?

A: Argentina
Q: What South American country took its name from the Latin for "silvery"?
W: Argentium is the Latin word for "silver." It was given to the region by early explorers who had hoped to find silver. It turned out that the rich, black soil proved to be more valuable than any precious metal.

A: Argentina
Q: Where are the pampas?
W: The pampas covers about one fifth of Argentina. This fertile grassy plain stretches some 300 miles northwest, west and south of Buenos Aires. Some of the richest soil in the Western Hempisphere lies in this region.

A: Argentina and Chile
Q: What two South American countries share the region of Patagonia?
W: The Plateau of Patagonia in the southern half of South America is shared by Argentina and Chile. A statue of Christ of the Andes, 26 feet high and made of granite, is located there and has the following engraved on its base: "Sooner shall the mountains crumble into dust than the Argentines and the Chileans break the peace to which they have pledged themselves at the feet of Christ the Redeemer."

A: Arizona
Q: What's the only U.S. state with a cactus as its state flower?
W: The State flower is saguaro (giant

cactus), and it's "bad medicine" to pick one. As a matter of fact, it's a violation of state law!

A: Arizona
Q: What is "The Grand Canyon State"?
W: The 200-mile-long gorge cut by the Colorado River gives Arizona the nickname of the Grand Canyon State. Arizona got its name from the Indian word Arizonac which means "small springs." The Painted Desert and The Petrified Forest are two other natural wonders of Arizona.

A: Arizona
Q: What U.S. state is due south of Utah?
W: Look at a map... there it is, right under Utah!

A: Arizona
Q: Where's the Petrified Forest?
W: The Petrified Forest is made up of tree trunks that were buried in mud and sand ages ago and that have turned to stone. Petrified forests have also been found in other states, especially New York, Wyoming, and California. The most famous, of course, is the one in northern Arizona.

A: Arizona
Q: What state can you walk to from Nevada across the Hoover Dam?
W: The Hoover Dam, located on the Colorado River in Nevada is one of several dams from which Arizona receives it hydroelectric power. It's awesome.

GEOGRAPHY

A: **Arkansas's**
Q: What U.S. state's name begins but doesn't end with the letter A?
W: Arkansas, called the "Land of Opportunity", became the 25th state in June 1836.

A: **Asia**
Q: What continent is home to half the world's people?
W: Asia has a larger area and more people than any other continent. About 60 of every 100 persons in the world live in Asia. The continent has the widest plains, the highest and broadest plateaus, and the lowest and highest points on the surface of the earth. The estimated population of Asia was 2.7 billion in 1980 vs. 0.39 billion in North America.

A: **Athens**
Q: Where's the famed Arch of Hadrian?
W: Hadrian, one of the "five good Emperors" of Rome, was one of the ablest of the Roman emperors. The Emperor Hadrian completed the great temple of Zeus, started over 600 years earlier, as the chief ornament of the new eastern suburb of Athens. He then constructed a gateway to this area that says on one side, "This is the Athens of Theseus, the old city" and on the other side "This is the city of Hadrian, not of Theseus."

A: **Athens's**
Q: What city's old quarter is called the Plaka?
W: Athenians refer to the section of the city clustered about the foot of the Acropolis as the "old city." This section is a remnant of the dreary days before the revival of Athens that began after the Greek revolution of 1835. The "new city" spreads in a great crescent about the "old city." Plaka is on the north slope of the Acropolis where small one-story houses are clustered up the hillside with many tiny "squares," once celebrated for their dancing, celebrations, and folk music.

A: **Atlanta**
Q: What southern U.S. state capital is said to have been named for the Western and Atlantic Railroad?
W: Actually Atlanta was originally known as Terminus. In 1843 it was chartered as Marthasville, in honor of the ex-governor's daughter. However, certain railroad men thought this was inappropriate for the future site of a great center. Mr. J. Edgar Thomson, chief engineer of the Georgia railroad, suggested the name Atlanta (feminine form of the masculine Atlantic). Although the legislature had just named it Marthasville, the prestige of the railroad was so great that the citizens gave in, and in the next legislative session the name of Atlanta was substituted on the 1845 Act of Incorporation.

A: **Atlantic, The**
Q: What ocean surrounds the Madeira Islands?
W: The Atlantic Ocean has a north division and a south division. The North Atlantic Ocean is east of North America and north of the Equator. The Madiera Islands are of volcanic origin and lie off the northwest coast of Africa. The South Atlantic is east of South America and south of the Equator.

A: **Atlantic, The**
Q: What ocean is almost exactly half the size of the Pacific?
W: The Atlantic Ocean is the second largest body of water in the world. Only the Pacific Ocean covers a greater area. The Atlantic was the first ocean to be crossed by ships and airplanes. The Pacific Ocean measures approximately 64.1 million square miles, whereas the Atlantic Ocean measures 33.4 million square miles.

A: **Atlantic, The**
Q: What ocean does Mauritania border?
W: The Atlantic Ocean forms the western border of this African nation. Mauritania is located on the northwest coast of Africa near Algeria, and its capital is Nouakchott with a population of 250,000.

A: **Atlantic, The**
Q: What ocean is zero degrees longitude, zero degrees latitude, found in?
W: The Equator is an imaginary line at zero degrees latitude. It divides the Atlantic into North and South. Zero degrees longitude is another imaginary line which runs through the North and South Atlantic at the extreme western edge of Europe and Africa.

A: **Atlantic, The**
Q: What ocean surrounds the Sargasso Sea?
W: The Sargasso Sea is an irregular, oval-shaped area of the North Atlantic Ocean. No land boundaries of any kind mark off this body of water from the rest of the open ocean. It is set apart only by the presence of marine plants, or seaweed, that float on the surface. It is an area of about 2,000,000 square miles, located roughly between the 20th and 40th parallels of north latitude and between the 35th and 75th meridians west of Greenwich.

A: **Atlantic City, New Jersey**
Q: Where would you find Caesars Boardwalk Regency Hotel Casino?
W: Atlantic City is one of the largest seaside resorts in the world. It is famous for its Boardwalk and is the home of the Miss America Beauty Pageant. Caesars is one of the many hotels, motels, and casinos now found on the Boardwalk.

A: Atlantic Ocean, The
Q: What body of water does the French resort of Biarritz lie on?
W: Biarritz, located on the Basque coast of France is one of the most elegant bathing resorts with several casinos, night clubs, and hotels. This location is very close to the borders of France and Spain.

A: Atlantic, Pacific, Indian, Arctic, The
Q: What are the world's four oceans?
W: Generally, we talk about five oceans of the world, not four. In order of their size, they are: the Pacific, the Atlantic, the Indian, the Antarctic, and the Arctic.

A: Atoll
Q: What is the geographical term for a ring-shaped coral island?
W: Tropical plants thrive on the thin layer of soil that forms on the coral ring, and it becomes a coral island. Atolls are found chiefly in the Pacific Ocean.

A: Augusta
Q: What's the easternmost U.S. state capital?
W: Augusta, Maine, is the easternmost U.S. state capital. There is also an Augusta in Arkansas, Illinois, Indiana, Kansas, Kentucky, Michigan, Missouri, Montana, New Jersey, Ohio, West Virginia, Wisconsin and Virginia.

A: Australia
Q: What country covers an entire continent?
W: Australia is both a country and one of the seven continents of the world. Sometimes called the "Island Continent," it is the smallest continent.

A: Australia
Q: What's the largest country entirely within the Southern Hemisphere?
W: The entire Australian continent and country is below the equator. A little known fact: 1974 reports show Australians consume 100 gallons of beer per person annually!!

A: Australia
Q: What country has the largest sheep population?
W: More sheep are raised in Australia than any other country. Wool, which accounts for over 50 percent of all Australian exports, is vital to the Australian economy. Australia supplies one third of the world's wool.

A: Australia
Q: What country would you be in if you wiled away time playing a didjeridoo in Wagga Wagga?
W: Wagga Wagga is a city north of Melbourne in southeastern Australia. It is a service center for the Riverina district, which produces wheat and sheep. A didjeridoo is a wind instrument of the Australian aboriginals made of bamboo or a hollow sapling about five feet long.

KANGAROO

A: Australia
Q: What country was originally known as Terra Australis Incognita?
W: Not necessarily "originally." It was called New Holland by the Dutch explorers in the late 1600s and New South Wales after the British explorer, James Cook in 1770. In the early 1700s there was much written about the possible commercial value of the south seas and "Terra Australis Incognita." These writings led to the British government financing Cook's expeditions. The words are from *terra*, land; *Australis*, southern; *incognita*, unknown.

A: Australia
Q: What continent has the lowest highest mountain?
W: Millions of years of rain, wind, and flowing water have worn down the surface of Australia. There are really no high mountains and most of the continent is flat. The mountains are not rugged but have rounded summits. The highest point is Kosciusko at 7,310, which is the lowest "high" point of any continent. The chain of mountains in southeastern Australia is called the Australian Alps.

A: Australia
Q: What country was called New Holland, Botany Bay, and New South Wales until 1820?
W: The continent was first called New Holland by the Dutch Explorers. In 1770 Captain James Cook, following along the Australian coast, claimed for England a great tract of land that he called New South Wales. Botany Bay is a circular area of the Pacific Ocean. It also was discovered by Captain Cook and was named Botany Bay because of the variety of plants growing on its shores.

A: Australia
Q: What country is bounded in part by the Indian Ocean and Coral and Tasman Seas?
W: The Indian Ocean is on the west and south of Australia. The Coral and Tasman Seas are arms of the South Pacific Ocean. The Coral Sea lies to the north and east, the Tasman to the south and west.

GEOGRAPHY

A: **Australia's**
Q: What country's flag is made up of the Union Jack and the Southern Cross?
W: Australia's flag is the British blue ensign with six stars on the field. The Union Jack is the national flag of the United Kingdom of Great Britain and is also called the Blue Ensign (Public Service Flag). Claimed by Britain in 1770, Australia was colonized beginning in 1788 with convicts (25 percent female).

A: **Austria**
Q: Where are Graz and Linz?
W: Graz is the second largest city of Austria. Linz is located on the Danube River and is the largest city in Austria.

A: **Austria**
Q: What's the only European country that uses schillings?
W: Notice how this is spelled with an *sch*. Several other countries use shillings spelled without the *c* after the *s*.

A: **Austria and Italy**
Q: What two countries do Tyroleans come from?
W: Tyrol originated as a family name. Tyrol is a beautiful country in western Austria and northern Italy. After World War I, Tyrol was divided into two parts. Northern Tyrol was given to Austria and Southern Tyrol came under the Italian rule.

A: **Austria and Italy**
Q: What two countries are linked by the Brenner Pass?
W: The Brenner Pass straddles the border between Austria and Italy at the east end of the Alps. The pass begins at Bolzano, Italy, and descends to Innsbruck, Austria. It is one the lowest passes through the main chain of the Alps.

B

A: **Baghdad**
Q: What is the capital of Iraq?
W: The capital and largest city of Iraq is Baghad. It is famous as the scene of the stories in "Arabian Nights." It lies on the Tigris River about 330 miles north of the Persian Gulf.

A: **Bahamas, The**
Q: What islands got their name from the Spanish "baja mar," meaning "shallow water"?
W: The Bahamas is a group of West Indian islands that stretch from southeast of Florida to northeast of Cuba. There are about 700 islands and 2,000 keys and reefs of rock and coral sand. Nassau is the capital and chief port. It was here that Columbus first stepped ashore in the Americas. The islands are separated from near-by lands by deepwater channels.

A: **Baja Peninsula, The**
Q: What separates the Gulf of California from the Pacific Ocean?
W: Baja, California, is a long narrow penisula that extends 810 miles from the northwestern corner of Mexico. This 30-to 150-mile-wide finger of land forms the western boundary of the Gulf of California.

A: **Baltic, The**
Q: What sea lies between Riga and Stockholm?
W: The Baltic Sea is a large inland sea or gulf of northern Europe. This sea separates the Scandinavian Penisula from the northern coast of Europe. Stockholm is the capital of Sweden; Riga is the capital of the Latvian Soviet Socialist Republic, incorporated into the USSR in 1940.

A: **Banff National Park**
Q: What was Canada's first national park?
W: Banff National Park is located in the Canadian Province of Alberta. The city of Banff lies at the southeastern end of the national park. At the Banff Indian Days, Indians dress up in costumes and pose for the tourists and sportsmen who visit Banff every year.

A: **Bangladesh**
Q: What country was formerly East Pakistan?
W: Bangladesh is located in south Asia on the north bend of the Bay of Bengal between India and Burma. Bangladesh was founded in 1979 following the Bengali revolt against Pakistan.

A: **Baton Rouge**
Q: What southern U.S. state capital took its name from the French for "red stick"?
W: Baton Rouge, the capital of Louisiana, means "red stick" in French. It stands on bluffs along the Mississippi. The city was named for a red cypress tree that marked a boundary between Indian trails. The present capitol building was erected in 1932 and is one of the tallest structures in the South.

A: **Battle Creek, Michigan**
Q: Where's the headquarters of Kellogg's?
W: Battle Creek is a famous health center and the breakfast food capital of the world. It lies in southern Michigan about 110 miles west of Detroit. John Harvey Kellogg, one of the originators of Battle Creek breakfast foods, pioneered in the development of the Battle Creek Sanitarium, now known as the Battle Creek Health Center.

A: **Bay of Bengal, The**
Q: What bay does the Ganges River flow into?
W: The Bay of Bengal is the northern part of the Indian Ocean. The "Ganges Plain" on the Bay, which includes the city of Calcutta, is the most populated region in the world.

A: **beaver, The**
Q: What's the official animal of Canada?
W: The beaver is a fur-bearing animal that lives in lakes and streams that run through the woods. It is well-known for its skills at building dams and cutting down trees. Beavers were once found in many wooded places in both the U.S. and Canada; however, they almost became extinct as a result of trappers. Today state and federal laws protect the animal.

A: **Belfast**
Q: What's the capital of Northern Ireland?
W: Belfast is the capital and largest city of Northern Ireland. It lies on Belfast Lough (bay) at the mouth of the River Lagan on the country's east coast.

A: **Belgian Congo, The**
Q: What's the former name of Zaire?
W: The Belgian Congo was the name of the Republic of Congo until the nation gained its independence in 1960. The original name was derived from the name of the Congo River which drains that country. Most of the people of Congo are African natives. In 1965 General Joseph Mobutu was named president; he later changed his name to Mobutu Sese Seko. On July 1, 1965, he changed the name of Leopoldville to Kinshasa and Stanleyville to Kisangani. He later changed Elizabethville to Lubumbashi. On October 27, 1971, the country of Belgian Congo changed its name to Zaire, and in 1972 Zairians with Christian names were ordered to change their names to ones of African origin.

A: **Belgium**
Q: What country's home to Sabena Airlines?
W: The full name is Sabena Belgian World Airlines. They fly to the Middle East, Africa, the Orient, and, of course, Europe.

A: **Belgium**
Q: What country contains the Waterloo battlefield?
W: Many countries have fought battles in Belgium because of its strategic location. The Battle of Waterloo monument is an artificial 148-foot-high pyramid that overlooks the 1815 battlefield, located 12 miles south of Brussels. On June 18, 1815, Napolean met his final defeat ending almost 23 years of constant warfare between France and other European powers.

A: **Belgium**
Q: What country do Walloons call home?
W: The Walloons, who live south of Brussels, speak a dialect of French called Walloon. Today the customs and language of the Celtic Walloons are much like those of the French.

A: **Belgium, the Netherlands, Luxembourg**
Q: What are the Benelux countries?
W: One of the red-letter days in Belgium history was in 1948 when the Benelux Union was formed with the Netherlands and Luxembourg. The name Benelux comes from the abbreviations of all three of the countries involved in the Union. This economic union allows free circulation of goods, persons, capital, and services among these nations. In 1970 the border controls between these countries were abolished. All three also participate in the European Common Market.

A: **Belgrade**
Q: What's the capital of Yugoslavia?
W: Belgrade is the capital and largest city of Yugoslavia. It is situated on the banks of the Danube River and is a railroad and river center.

A: **Belgrade**
Q: What capital city lies at the junction of the Sava and Danube rivers?
W: Armies have fought battles around Belgrade for hundreds of years because of its strategic location at the junction of the Sava and Danube Rivers. Belgrade became the seat of Tito's dictatorship over Yugoslavia.

A: **Bering Sea, The**
Q: What body of water does the Yukon River empty into?
W: The Bering Sea is a part of the North Pacific Ocean. It lies north of the Aleutian Islands between Alaska and Siberia and is named for the Danish explorer, Vitus Bering. The Yukon drains more than 330,000 miles of Canada (the Yukon Territory) and Alaska.

A: **Bermuda Triangle, The**
Q: What fabled area touches the coasts of Florida, Bermuda and Puerto Rico?
W: The Bermuda Triangle is a section of the North Atlantic Ocean (25 to 40 degrees north and 55 to 85 degrees west) where more than 50 ships and 20 planes have reportedly disappeared mysteriously. One of the best known disappearances is that of the U.S. nuclear submarine *Scorpion* in 1968, which was discovered on the ocean floor several months later.

A: **Bern**
Q: What's the capital of Switzerland?
W: Bern lies in the west central part of Switzerland. It became the capital in 1848. A medieval clock tower, the landmark of Bern, sounds the hours of the day at which time the clock displays a wooden rooster, a man in armor, dancing bears, and a man on a throne. The name Bern is a German word meaning bear. The bear appeared on the first known seal of Switzerland in 1224, and there is a bear pit in the city of Bern where bears have been kept since 1513.

A: **Big Ben**
Q: What London landmark has an 11-foot-long hand?
W: Big Ben is the great clock tower of the House of Parliament in London. It was installed during the time that tall, stout Sir Benjamin Hall served as Commissioner of Works. He was called Big Ben and members of

Parliament named the bell for him, but eventually the name came to indicate the clock itself.

A: **Big Sur**
Q: What's the spectacular California coastline south of Monterey?
W: Big Sur is a resort area known for its rugged beauty. The area referred to as "Big Sur" stretches approximately 75 miles along the Pacific coast from Carmel to San Simeon. It is edged by high ridges of the Santa Lucia Range and includes Los Padres National Forest. Big Sur is a favorite for those who love the rugged outdoors and for artists and photographers. Whether you plan to visit the beautiful state parks or stop for an Ambrosia-burger at Nepenthe, the well-known restaurant built on a bluff, allow plenty of time to drive the Big Sur region as the roads are very twisting and mountainous.

A: **bill, The**
Q: What arrives at your table in Madrid if you say, "La cuenta, por favor"?
W: What would arrive at your table would be your bill or check because of the meaning of the following words: *la* meaning "the", *cuenta* meaning "check," and *por favor* meaning "please."

A: **Black**
Q: What color are Venetian gondolas, except those of high public officials?
W: An old law requires that all Venetian gondolas except those of high officials be painted black. The gondola today still serves as tourists' favorite way of quiet sightseeing.

A: **Black Hills, The**
Q: What are the famed hills of South Dakota?
W: The Black Hills gained national fame when an expedition led by Colonel George A. Custer discovered gold in the region in 1874. The Mt. Rushmore Memorial, in the Black Hills, features granite carvings of Presidents Washington, Jefferson, T. Roosevelt, and Lincoln.

A: **Black, red, gold**
Q: What are the three colors on the West German flag?
W: The flag of both East and West Germany has three broad horizontal stripes, the top stripe being in black, the center in red and the bottom in gold. Since the 1830s these colors have been associated with the struggle for a united Germany.

A: **Black, Red, White, Yellow The**
Q: What four seas are named for colors?
W: The Black Sea is located to the north of Turkey. The Red Sea is an area of the Indian Ocean that separates the Arabian Penisula from northeastern Africa. The White Sea, which is called the Bloye More in Russian, is an area of the Artic Ocean. The Yellow Sea is an area of the Pacific Ocean extending inland for about 400 miles between the east coast of China and Korea.

A: **Black Sea, The**
Q: What body of water does the Danube River flow into?
W: The Danube River is one of the great waterways of Europe. The river runs east and south winding for 1,725 miles to its mouth in the Black Sea. The Black Sea is one of the three seas which border Turkey.

A: **Black Sea, The**
Q: What sea does the Crimean Peninsula jut into?
W: The Crimean Penisula is part of the USSR (Ukranian SSR) on the north side of the Black Sea into which it juts.

A: **Blarney Castle**
Q: What castle is "The Blarney Stone" found in?
W: The Blarney Stone is a stone in the Blarney Castle near Cork, Ireland. Legend has it that a person who kisses the Blarney Stone will be given the power of sweet, persuasive, wheedling eloquence.

A: **Blue**
Q: What's the most common color on the fields of U.S. state flags?
W: Twenty-eight states have a blue field, and many others have at least some blue on their flag. Ohio is the only flag with an unusual shape, a swallow-tailed pennant; the remainder are square or rectangular in shape.

A: **Blue, white, red**
Q: What three colors are on the French flag?
W: The French flag is often called the tricolor, meaning flag of three colors. Blue and red were the colors of Paris and white stood for the royal family.

A: **"Bluegrass State, The"**
Q: What's the nickname of Kentucky?
W: Kentucky is called the Bluegrass State because of the dusty blossoms of the grasses on its rolling meadows and pastures. Abraham Lincoln and Jefferson Davis, the opposing presidents in the Civil War, were both born in Kentucky, 100 miles apart. The Bluegrass Region lies in the north central part of the state.

A: **Bogota**
Q: What's the capital of Columbia?
W: Bogota is often called the Athens of America as it is the center of art and learning in Columbia. Columbia is located on the northwest side of South America. Bogota is located in the center of Columbia on a plateau 8,660 feet above sea level.

A: **Bolivia and Paraguay**
Q: What are the only two landlocked countries in South America?
W: Bolivia is blocked from the Pacific Ocean by Peru and Chile on the west and Brazil on the east. Paraguay is blocked off by Bolivia (north and west), Argentina (south and west), and Brazil on the east. All other countries are on the Atlantic or Pacific Oceans or on the Caribbean Sea.

A: **Bologna, Italy**
Q: Where was baloney first served?
W: Bologna is a city in northern Italy. It is an important industrial center manufacturing silks, velvets, and the famous bologna sausage. Its university, founded in 1088, is one of the oldest and most famous schools in the world.

A: **Bombay**
Q: What's the largest city in India?
W: *WRONG* by the *World Almanac* of 1984 it has 8.2 million people vs 9.1 million in Calcutta.

A: **Bonn**
Q: What's the capital of West Germany?
W: Bonn is the capital of West Germany and has been since 1949. It lies on the left bank of the Rhine River about 20 miles from Cologne. Bonn was founded by the Romans as a fortified encampment on the Rhine River. Bonn became the provisional capital when Germany was divided after World War II, and the former German capital of Berlin became the capital of East Germany.

A: **Bordeaux**
Q: What French district produces Graves, Medoc, and St. Emilion wines?
W: Bordeaux is the center of the wine-shipping trade of France. It is one of the commercial cities of the country. Villages nearby Bordeaux noted for their wines are Pessac for Graves, Blanquefort and Soulac for Medoc, and Cadillac for St. Emilion.

A: **Borsht**
Q: What soup is likely to be on the menu in Poland or Russia?
W: Borsht, or borsch, is a beet soup that may be served either cold or hot. Many nations have distinctive soups. In addition to the Russian–Polish borscht, there's Italy's minestrone; France's onion soup and bouillabaisse, and China's bird nest soup.

A: **Boston**
Q: Where is Beacon Street?
W: Beacon street is one of the wide avenues leading into the city of Boston. It is an area that combines the old and the new. The Massachusetts Statehouse is located on Beacon Street.

A: **Boston**
Q: What U.S. city has a gold-domed statehouse, originally covered with copper by Paul Revere?
W: The Massachusetts Statehouse located on Beacon Street in Boston is a gold-domed building designed by Charles Bulfinch, who was head of town government in Boston. This domed portion was constructed in 1795-1798 and houses the Senate and Hall of Representatives. After the Revolutionary War Paul Revere set up a rolling mill for the manufacture of sheet copper that was used in U.S. ships including the *Constitution* and for the dome of the Massachusetts Statehouse.

A: **Boston**
Q: Where is Faneuil Hall?
W: Faneuil Hall, originally built as a market by Peter Faneuil, is called the "Cradle of Liberty" as it was the scene of many meetings by the advocates of American freedom. The Hall now houses a museum of flags, photographs, and weapons of the Artillery Company of Boston. The upper level hall balcony is still used as a forum for public discussion.

A: **Boston**
Q: What U.S. city had the first subway?
W: Boston was the first U.S. city to have a subway, opening its line of 1.5 miles in 1897. The subway in New York City is the largest in the world. London was the first city in the world to have a subway.

A: **Boston**
Q: What city is *The Christian Science Monitor* based in?
W: The Christian Science Church and Publishing House is located on Copley Square in Boston. *The Christian Science Monitor* is published there and has a current circulation of 149,913. The paper was begun in 1908 by Mary Baker Eddy, founder of the Christian Science Church.

A: **Boston**
Q: What city does Beacon Hill light?
W: Beacon Hill, 110 feet high, is so called because it was once used as a beacon station from which to signal ships. On top of this hill is the Massachusetts Statehouse, its gilded dome visible for many miles. Beacon Hill has long been the home of many famous families.

A: **Boston Common**
Q: What's the oldest public park in the U.S.?
W: The Boston Common is located below the Massachusetts Statehouse on Beacon Hill in Boston. It is a popular city park that began as a cow pasture!

A: **Bowery, The**
Q: What is New York City's "Street of Forgotten Men"?
W: The Bowery is a district on New York City's Lower East Side, which includes a street with the same name. The Bowery was the theatrical center of New York from 1860 to 1875. In the 1880s it became peopled with the unemployed, the poor, and the homeless.

A: **Brandenburg Gate, The**
Q: What gate opens on East and West Berlin?
W: The Brandenburg Gate stands at the dividing line between East and West Berlin. East Germany's government restored the monumental war-scarred arch in 1957.

A: **Brasilia**
Q: What's the capital of Brazil?
W: Brazil is the largest county in South America. Brasilia, the capital of Brazil since 1960, lies inland about 500 miles north of Rio de Janeiro. Before 1960 Rio de Janeiro was the capital. The "Palace of Dawn" in Brasilia is the home of Brazil's president.

A: **Brazil**
Q: What country contains the easternmost point in South America?
W: Looks like Grande, Brazil, wins this one. Looking at a map it is at about 8 degrees latitude and 35 degrees longitude on the eastern edge of Brazil.

A: **Brazil**
Q: Where can you buy a cup of coffee with cruzeiros?
W: Cruzeiros are the monetary unit of Brazil. And it will take about 381 of them to buy coffee, at $1 (U.S.) per cup. In a year or so it may take over 700, since Brazil's rate of inflation has been close to 95 percent recently!

A: **Brazil**
Q: What's the fifth-largest country in the world?
W: Brazil is the fifth largest country in the world in land mass. Only Russia, Canada, China, and the U.S. are larger in area.

A: **Brazil**
Q: What country is home to Varig Airlines?
W: Varig Brazilian Airlines is South America's largest airlines and flies to every continent.

A: **Brazil**
Q: What's the only country crossed by both the equator and tropic of Capricorn?
W: The equator is an imaginary line at 0 degrees latitude. The tropic of Capricorn is an imaginary line at 23 degrees, 27 minutes south of the equator. The tropic of Capricorn crosses Brazil just south of Rio de Janeiro, while the equator crosses Brazil near the northeastern city Macapa. No other country in the world stretches between these two latitudes.

A: **Brazil, Columbia, Ecuador**
Q: What three South American countries does the equator cross?
W: The equator cuts across the northern portion of Ecuador on the Pacific Coast, the southern part of Columbia, and the northern section of Brazil on the Atlantic coast.

A: **Brazil's**
Q: What country's anthem begins: "From peaceful Ypiranga's banks"?
W: ...and it goes on "rang out a cry." One of the more interesting lines is "Oh, Brazil on you the sun of this New World shines down forever."

A: **Bread**
Q: What is Greek "pita"?
W: The Greek sandwich called a gyros is very hard to eat in your hands – sloppy too. This "pocket" bread holds the juices better!

A: **Brigham Young**
Q: What Mormon University is found in Provo, Utah?
W: Brigham Young University, founded in 1875, is a co-educational school and is controlled by the Church of Jesus Christ of Latter Day Saints (Mormons). But students of many faiths are accepted.

A: **Britain**
Q: What country boasts the most cars per mile of road?
W: And when you are sitting in the traffic jam, be sure you're on the *left* side of the road!

A: **Britain's**
Q: What country's flag is incorporated most often in others'?
W: The so-called cross of St. Patrick was incorporated into the well-known "Union Jack" in 1801. Many other flags from other countries, states, provinces, and cities incorporate the "Union Jack" into their colors. Here are just a few: Hong Kong, Australia, Tasmania, New Zealand, Fiji, Manitoba, Hawaii, Bermuda, Cayman Islands, and the Virgin Islands.

A: **British Airways and Air France**
Q: What two airlines fly the Concorde?
W: The supersonic BAC and Aero spatiale Concorde was first flown on March 2, 1969, with a capacity of 128 passengers. Air France and British Airways opened passenger service simultaneously with the first supersonic airliners on January 21, 1976.

A: **British Columbia, Alberta, Saskatchewan**
Q: What three Canadian provinces border Montana?
W: Montana is called the "Treasure State" because it is so rich in gold, copper, silver, and other minerals. In addition to bordering three Canadian provinces, it also borders three U.S. states: Idaho, Wyoming, and North Dakota.

A: **Broadway**
Q: What street contains "The Great White Way"?
W: Broadway is a key street in New York City and one of the most famous in the world. It runs the whole length of Manhattan Island. In midtown New York it becomes "The Great White Way" as it crosses Times Square at 42nd Street. This is the heart of the entertainment world with theaters, movie houses, and night clubs.

A: **Brooklyn**
Q: What part of New York City was called "broken land" by the Dutch?
W: Brooklyn is one of five districts, called boroughs, that make up New York City. Dutch pioneers founded the city in 1636. They named it Breuckelen, which means "broken land," after a town in Holland.

A: **Brussels**
Q: What city is home to the famed Manneke Pis fountain?
W: Brussels is the capital of Belgium. The Manneke-Pis fountain is a bronze statue of a boy urinating and is located near the Grand Palace in Brussels. The boy is dressed in special outfits for various holidays, including an American sailor suit on October 27th, United States Navy Day. It was constructed in 1619 and the boy is often referred to as "Brussel's Oldest Inhabitant."

A: **Buckingham Palace**
Q: Where does Queen Elizabeth II live when she's in London?
W: Buckingham Palace has been the house of England's kings and queens since 1837. It stands in the West End district of London and was once a private home. The Royal Standard flies from the mast when the queen is in residence.

A: **Buckingham Palace**
Q: What royal residence has 600 rooms?
W: Buckingham Palace today has 614 rooms, although it is alleged that no two people have ever arrived at the same number!

A: **Burma Road, The**
Q: What World War II road ran from Lashio, Burma, to K'un-ming, China?
W: The Burma Road from Lashio, Burma, to K'un-ming, China is a distance of 360 miles "as the crow flies." To cover this distance, the road curves and twists for about 700 miles through mountains and forests and across gullies and rivers. It was a highway of earth and crushed rock built to carry war supplies to Chinese troops by truck. About 160,000 Chinese and Burma laborers worked on the road under great hardship. The Burma Road became a symbol of Chinese resistance during World War II.

C

A: **C**
Q: What letter is on the hot-water tap in France?
W: *Chaud* is the French word for "hot"; *frois* is the French word for "cold."

A: **CCCP**
Q: What's Russian for USSR?
W: In the Russian alphabet the letters USSR are CCCP. This is the way that it appears on their postage stamp.

A: **Cairo**
Q: What's the largest city in Africa?
W: Cairo, the capital of Egypt, is located on the northeast corner of the continent of Africa. Its population in 1979 was estimated at 5.4 million.

A: **Cairo**
Q: What city rises at the head of the Nile River Delta?
W: Cairo, located in Egypt, lies at the head of the Nile River Delta and dates back 1,000 years. The Great Pyramids are at the southeastern edge of the city. Cairo has more registered historic landmarks (over 400) than any other African or Middle Eastern city.

A: **Calcutta**
Q: Where would you be if you landed at Dum Dum Airport?
W: Calcutta itself consists of North Dum Dum, South Dum Dum, and the Cantonment. The ammunition factory there made the first dumdum expanding bullet. The name "Dum Dum" was derived from "damdama," a raised mound or battery.

A: **California**
Q: What U.S. state has the most blondes?
W: That's probably why everyone is always smiling and having fun in all the travel brochures. And we're sure the sun makes the hair of even those who aren't blonde a lot lighter!

A: **California**
Q: What's the third-largest state in the U.S.?
W: Alaska ranks at the top of the list in size, while Texas follows close behind as number two. California is third.

A: **California**
Q: What U.S. state is most of Death Valley in?
W: Death Valley lies in east central California near the Nevada border. A group of pioneers traveling to the California gold fields in 1849 named the valley because many of their companions had died crossing this area. Death Valley became a national monument in 1973. It contains the lowest point in the Western Hemisphere.

A: **Canada**
Q: What's the U.S.'s biggest trading partner?
W: In 1982 exports to Canada totaled $33.7 billion and imports totaled $46.5 billion. Japan is the U.S.'s second biggest trading partner.

A: **Canada**
Q: What's the second largest country in the world?
W: The Soviet Union is the largest country in the world in land mass. Canada is second, and China ranks third.

A: **Canada**
Q: What country lies directly south of Detroit?
W: Detroit is located near the southeastern border of Michigan at a point where the Detroit River separates the United States from Canada. Windsor, Ontario, lies across the river from Detroit. The two cities are connected by a bridge and two tunnels beneath the river. Windsor is somewhat south of Detroit.

A: **Canada**
Q: What country has the most coastline?
W: Not only does Canada have the world's longest coastline, but also the world's longest unfortified border.

A: **Canada and the U.S.**
Q: What two countries lie on opposite sides of the Juan de Fuca Strait?
W: The Juan de Fuca Strait is a narrow body of water that separates Vancouver Island in Canada from the state of Washington. The Strait forms an important passageway through which ships pass to the Pacific Ocean from Seattle, Vancouver, and Victoria, British Columbia.

A: **Canada and the U.S.**
Q: What two countries are joined by the Ambassador Bridge?
W: The Ambassador Bridge is located between Detroit and Canada. It has a span of 1,850 feet and was completed in 1929.

A: **Canary Islands, The**
Q: What island group is Las Palmas a part of?
W: The Canary Islands are located in the Atlantic Ocean, west of Morocco. Las Palmas and Santa Cruz are thriving ports of these islands. The islands were so named because of the multitude of large dogs (canines) reportedly seen there in an expedition around the year 40 B.C.

A: **Canberra**
Q: What's the capital of Australia?
W: Canberra is located on the east coast of Australia. One of the strangest lakes of the World, Lake George located near Canberra, keeps disappearing and reappearing. No one has been able to determine why.

A: **Cape Cod**
Q: What resort peninsula curves 65 miles to its tip?
W: Cape Cod is a peninsula on the coast of Massachusetts, south of Massachusetts Bay. The peninsula is in the shape of a human arm. The land is 65 miles long and from one to 20 miles in width, covering approximately 600 square miles. One of the chief towns on the Cape is Hyannis Port, the home of the Kennedy family.

A: **Cape Kennedy**
Q: What's the former name of Cape Canaveral?
W: Cape Canaveral is an extension of an island off the east central coast of Florida and is the site of operations for the U.S. Space Program. Following the death of President John F. Kennedy in 1963, the Cape's name was changed to Cape Kennedy, but later reverted to its original Spanish name.

A: **Caribbean, The**
Q: What sea surrounds the Cayman Islands?
W: The Caribbean Sea – an important extension of the Atlantic Ocean – is enclosed by Central and South America and island groups of the West Indies. The Cayman Islands are a group of three islands in the northwest Caribbean Sea consisting of the Grand Cayman, Cayman Brac, and the Little Cayman. The islands were discovered by Columbus.

A: **Carson City**
Q: What's the capital of Nevada?
W: Carson City was originally named for the famous frontiersman, Kit Carson. Nevada is called the silver state because of the vast amounts of silver once mined in that area. Carson City has been the capital of the state since 1861 and is located 16 miles east of Lake Tahoe, at the extreme southeast corner of the state.

A: **Carson City**
Q: What U.S. state capital was named for Kit Carson?
W: Carson City was the site of a trading post in 1851. In 1858, it was platted and named for Kit Carson. It became a station for the Pony Express in 1860 and was made the seat of both county and territorial governments in 1861. Carson City was chartered as a city in 1875.

A: **Casablanca's**
Q: What seaport's name is Spanish for "white house"?
W: Casablanca is a seaport of Morocco on the Atlantic Coast. It is the most populous city and leading economic center of Morocco as well as its busiest port. In Spanish *Casablanca* means "white house." The city has been called this since the 16th century because most of its houses are white. The most popular of this city's beaches have "borrowed" names: Miami, Tahiti, and the Lido.

A: **Caspian Sea, The**
Q: What lake lies between the Soviet Union and Iran?
W: The Caspian Sea is a large lake or inland sea between Europe and Asia, nearly surrounded by Russian territory with the exception of Iran to the south. By means of river and canal there is water communication between the Caspian and the Black Sea, the Baltic Sea, and the White Sea.

A: Caspian Sea, The
Q: What's the largest lake in the world?
W: A lake is a body of water (salt or freshwater) surrounded by land. The Caspian *Sea* is the world's largest lake, even though it is called a sea. It is surrounded on three sides by the USSR and at the southern tip by Iran.

A: Champs Elysee, The
Q: What's the main boulevard of Paris?
W: Champs Elysee is an avenue in Paris. It extends from the Place de la Concorde to the Arc de Triomphe, a distance of one and a quarter miles, and is a famous public promenade. The Place de la Concorde was once the notorious Place de la Guillotine where Louis XVI, Marie Antoinette, and others lost their heads during the French Revolution.

A: Chancellor of the Exchequer
Q: What government position is held by the resident of 11 Downing Street, London?
W: The Exchequer is a department of the British Government Treasury that collects, manages, and disburses government funds. The Chancellor is actually the financial minister and is a cabinet member. He prepares the annual budget. Number 10 Downing Street is the official home of the Prime Minister… did you get caught on this one?

A: Chang
Q: What's the most common surname in the world?
W: Muhammed, according to some sources.

A: Channel Islands, The
Q: What island group contains Jersey, Guernsey, Sark, and Herm?
W: The Channel Islands are in an archipelago in the English Channel belonging to Great Britain, but only 10 to 30 miles off the west coast of France. The group consists of Jersey, Guernsey and its dependencies: Alderney, Brecghou, Great Sark, Little Sark, Herm, Jethou and Liho. The islands are celebrated for their cattle, a special breed now distinguished as Jerseys and Guernseys.

A: Charleston, South Carolina
Q: What southern U.S. city was named for King Charles II?
W: Charleston is the second largest city in South Carolina and an important Atlantic seaport. Known as Albemarle Point until 1671, it was renamed Charleston after King Charles II and later became the state capital in 1790.

A: Chesapeake Bay
Q: What bay divides Maryland's eastern and western Shores?
W: The Chesapeake Bay is the largest inlet of the Atlantic Ocean coastline. The first European settlement in the Bay area was Jamestown in 1607.

A: Cheyenne
Q: What's the capital of Wyoming?
W: Cheyenne, also the largest city in Wyoming, was named for the Cheyenne Indians by squatters moving into the area around 1867. The town was known as "Hell on Wheels" during the days of the vigilantes and the war between cattlemen and sheepmen.

A: Chicago
Q: Where is the Lincoln Park Zoo?
W: The Zoo is located at Fullerton Avenue near Lake Michigan, on the north side of Chicago. It covers 35 acres and is especially noted for its gorillas. The late 550-pound gorilla named Bushman is now stuffed and in Chicago's Field Museum.

A: Chicago
Q: Where are the Union Stockyards?
W: *Wrong*!! Well, they used to be. The stockyards opened in 1865 but went out of business in 1971. All that remains today is the stockyard gate, which has been declared a historical landmark. Now the only things being slaughtered in Chicago are politicians.

A: Chicago
Q: What's the largest U.S. city on the Great Lakes?
W: New York City is the largest U.S. city at 7.07 million in 1980. Chicago is second largest at 3.01 million. Los Angeles is the third largest at 2.97 million. P.S. Chicago is the only one on the Great Lakes!

A: Chicago
Q: Where's the Sears Tower?
W: The Sears Tower is the world's tallest *building*. It is 110 stories high (1,454 feet). It is made of galvanized steel and was completed in July 1974. The world's tallest *structure* is the 2,120 foot mast of Warszarva Radio at Konstantznow near Plock in Poland.

A: Chicago
Q: What U.S. city was called "The Birthplace of the Skyscraper"?
W: Forty-two buildings in Chicago are over 460 feet high. It's the home of three of the five tallest buildings in the U.S. and also the home of the world's tallest building, The Sears Tower, which stands 1,454 feet tall and has 110 stories. The first steel-framework skyscraper was built in 1884 in Chicago. The 1871 Chicago fire destroyed much of the city, and the high cost of land made upward extension desirable.

A: **Chicago**
Q: What city bills itself as "The First City of the Plain"?
W: Chicago has been immortalized by many poets primarily by Carl Sandburg in his "Chicago" and by William Mandy in "An Ode in Time of Hesitation-Chicago Sitteth at the Northwest Gates."

A: **Chicago**
Q: Where is the Loop?
W: The Loop, narrowly defined, is that section bounded by Lake, Wells, and Van Buren Streets and Wabash Avenue, above which the elevated trains into the city "loop" before beginning their return trip to the outlying areas.

A: **Chicago**
Q: What's "The Windy City"?
W: Chicago is often called the "Windy City" but no one knows who first coined the nickname. It may come from the strong gusts that blow across the city from Lake Michigan or it may also refer to the boastfulness of Chicagoans. A New York City newspaper editor made the nickname famous during the 1880s.

A: **Chicago's**
Q: What city's bus terminal boasts the world's busiest pay phone, at 270 calls a day?
W: Ma Bell, in her infinite wisdom of keeping many secrets would not confirm nor deny the accuracy of this claim. However, a spokesman for the company would say that there are 47 pay phones in the Greyhound station, and one of them was indeed the world's busiest.

A: **Chicken**
Q: What's "pollo" on a menu in Rome?
W: *Pollo* is the Latin term from which we derive the word, "poultry," meaning "all domestic fowl."

A: **Chile**
Q: What South American country took its name from the Inca for "cold winter"?

W: Another source indicates that Chile is thought to be derived from an Indian word that means "snow," or the Aymara word that means "place where the earth ends."

A: **Chile**
Q: What country can claim Magallanes, the world's southernmost city?
W: Magallanes is not really a city. It is a province! Its capital, Punta Arenas, is the southernmost city of the world.

A: **Chile and Ecuador**
Q: What two South American countries don't border Brazil?
W: Brazil, of course, is the largest country in South America. Because it is so large, most South American countries do border Brazil at some point. However, Chile and Ecuador on the west coast of South America do not touch the west borders of Brazil.

A: **China**
Q: What country are you in if you woo in the Wu dialect?
W: Wu is one the nine chief dialects into which the ancient Chinese language can be classified. Talking love would be "woo-ing" in Wu.

A: **China**
Q: What does a Sinophobic Russian fear?
W: Sino- is the prefix to designate China. Phobia is an unreasonable fear.

A: **China, India, the Soviet Union, and the U.S.**
Q: What four countries boast half of the world's population?
W: Well, almost half. Census records taken in July, 1982, give China an estimated 1,008,175,288 people, India approximately 713,000,000, the USSR 268,800,000 and the U.S. — fourth ranked — 232,000,000. The estimated world population is 4,677 million, and these four countries total 2,221.9

million. Add Japan at 118.6 million and you'll have slightly over half the world population!

A: **Chocolate**
Q: What product built Hershey, Pennsylvania?
W: The world's largest chocolate and confectionery factory was that built by Hershey Chocolate Company in Hershey, Pennsylvania in 1903-05. It has two million square feet of floor space. The town of Hershey grew up around the plant.

A: **Christopher Columbus**
Q: Who was the capital of Ohio named for?
W: Columbus was once the village of Franklintown. It was incorporated as a city in 1834 and is the capital of the state and the seat of Franklin County. It was planned in 1812 as a political center by the Ohio General Assembly and named for Christopher Columbus.

A: **City**
Q: What does the Greek word *polis* mean, as in Minneapolis?
W: As commonly used in the U.S., the word "city" merely means a relatively dense aggregation of population of considerable size in which the conditions of life can be described as urban in contrast with the rural life of the open country. To the student of Greek and Roman history, it included the walled town and the territory surrounding it — in other words, a city state.

A: **city hall, The**
Q: What's the *hotel de ville* in Lyon, France?
W: The word *ville* is French for city. Lyon is the second largest city in France and famed for its silk fabrics and haute cuisine.

A: **city hall, The**
Q: What's the *rathaus* in Frankfurt?
W: *Rathous* is the German name for any city hall.

A: **Claridge's**
Q: What's the most exclusive hotel on Brook Street in London?
W: Claridge's may be reached at 499-7070, once you arrive in London. You may wish to have the lunch or dinner buffet in their restaurant, Causerie, which we understand is a better bargain than the rooms!

A: **Cleveland**
Q: What city has a newspaper called *The Plain Dealer*?
W: Cleveland, Ohio, has the newspaper called *The Plain Dealer,* which was started in 1842. However, if you guessed McHenry, IL; North Vernon, IN; Wabash, IN; Almena, KS; Williamstown, NJ; or Kearny, NJ you are also correct as each of them has a paper called *The Plain Dealer* or *The Plaindealer.*

A: **Clock Tower, The**
Q: What tower is topped by Big Ben?
W: Big Ben is actually a great bell in the clock tower of Westminster Palace which is now occupied by the Houses of Parliament in London. Big Ben, named for Sir Benjamin Hall, the Commissioner of Works when the tower was constructed, has generally come to mean the clock as well as the bell.

A: **Coca-Cola**
Q: What company owns the world's second-largest truck fleet?
W: The largest trucking company in the U.S. is Consolidated Freightway, Inc. and is followed in rank by Associated Transport, Inc. The world's largest truck fleet belongs to the U.S. Postal Service, and Coca-Cola does have the second largest fleet of trucks.

A: **Coca-Cola**
Q: What's the largest-selling soft drink in Morocco?
W: Morocco has a population of approximately 22,300,000, of which about 1,371,000 live in Casablanca. Maybe all the Coke is consumed in Rick's Cafe Americain.

A: **Cognac, France**
Q: Where is the best brandy bottled?
W: The famed brandy named for this fair city is distilled from the wines of Charente and Charente-Maritime. The liquor Grand Marnier is also made in France in Cognac. The town of Cognac was chartered as a city in 1352.

A: **Cologne**
Q: What German city is famed for a scent it produces?
W: Cologne is on the Rhine River. Eau de Cologne was first made here about the beginning of the 18th Century and has spread the city's name throughout the world. The city was originally named Colonice Claudia Ara Agrippinensirum but later was shortened to Colonia.

A: **Columbia**
Q: What's the northernmost country in continental South America?
W: Columbia is the northernmost country in continental South America because a peninsula-like projection of land jutting into the Caribbean Sea is north of Venezuela.

A: **Columbia, The**
Q: What river does the Grand Coulee Dam dam?
W: The Grand Coulee Dam stands across the Columbia River about 90 miles west of Spokane, Washington. It is three times as large as the Great Pyramid of Egypt and is the second largest hydroelectric plant in the world.

A: **Colorado**
Q: What state has the highest overall elevation?
W: The approximate elevation of the state of Colorado is 6,800 feet, the highest of any state in the Union.

A: **Colorado, The**
Q: What river does the Hoover Dam dam?
W: The mighty Hoover Dam was known as Boulder Dam until 1947 when it was renamed for President Hoover. It controls the floods of the Colorado River and supplies domestic and irrigation water and electric power for a large portion of the Pacific southwest. Lake Mead is the water reservoir created by the dam.

A: **Colorado, The**
Q: What river flows through the Grand Canyon?
W: The Colorado River is cliff-bound nine tenths of its way and travels 1,000 miles through deep canyons. The Grand Canyon is the largest, deepest, and most spectacular of these. The first sighting of the Grand Canyon is credited to the Coronado expedition of 1540.

A: **Colosseum, The**
Q: What Rome ruin is inhabited by hundreds of cats?
W: Whoever found this question was really trivia-oriented. The Colosseum has been considered both a symbol of Rome's grandeur and one of the world's edifices. It was a kind of amphitheater and the scene of many combats, contests, and wild beast fights.

A: **Constantinople**
Q: What's the former name of Istanbul?
W: Istanbul, Turkey, formerly Constantinople and before that Byzantium, is the capital of Turkey. It was restored, enlarged, and renamed Constantinople after the emperor, Constantine I. One source has it that the city was always called Istanbul by the Turks, only outsiders called it Constantinople. When the post office started returning letters addressed to "Constantinople," people took the hint and began using the proper name of Istanbul!

A: **Continental Divide, The**
Q: What Rocky Mountain ridge separates North America's eastward and westward-flowing rivers?
W: The Continental Divide is the term applied to the line separating areas drained to opposite sides of a continent. In the U.S., it is often called the Great Divide and is the line separating the basins of streams draining to the Atlantic from those draining to the Pacific. Three national parks in the U.S. — Yellowstone, Glacier, and Rocky Mountain — lie across the Continental Divide.

A: **Continental shelf**
Q: What's the geographic term for the submerged fringe of a continent?
W: Continental shelf is the term used to describe that part of the ocean floor adjacent to continental shores and covered by water of shallow depth, less than 80 to 100 fathoms (480 to 600 feet). It is on the continental shelves that most of the world's best fishing grounds are located.

A: **Cook County**
Q: What county is Chicago in?
W: Chicago is the county seat of Cook County in northeastern Illinois.

A: **Copenhagen**
Q: Where are the famed Trivoli Gardens?
W: The Trivoli Gardens in Copenhagen is an amusement park which has been open since 1843. Copenhagen is the capital of Denmark.

A: **Copenhagen's**
Q: What city's harbor does *The Little Mermaid* grace?
W: *The Little Mermaid* is a statue of the famous Hans Christian Andersen character. It is located in a park called Langelinie where all of Copenhagen strolls on Sunday afternoons.

A: **Cuba**
Q: What's the largest island in the West Indies?
W: Cuba lies just south of the tropic of Cancer. The Florida Strait separates Cuba from the U.S.

A: **Cuba**
Q: What country has been called "The Queen of the Antilles"?
W: Antilles is another name for the West Indies, excluding the Bahamas, which separate the Atlantic Ocean from the Gulf of Mexico and the Caribbean Sea. Cuba is the largest of the West Indies islands and has thus been called "The Queen." When Columbus discovered Cuba in 1492, he said it was "the most beautiful land eyes ever beheld."

A: **Cyprus**
Q: What Mediterranean country is the only one in the world to display its map on its flag?
W: The Cyprus flag has a white background and its country is depicted in yellow. Crossed green leaves are pictured under the country's map.

A: **Czechoslovakia**
Q: What country does a true Bohemian live in?
W: A more exact answer to this question would be "Bohemia," which is one of three divisions of Czechoslovakia. Moravia and Slovakia are the other two.

A: **Czechoslovakia**
Q: What country forms all of Hungary's northern border?
W: Hungary is bounded on the south by Yugoslavia, on the southeast and east by Rumania, and on the northeast tip by the Ukranian S.S.R.

A: **Czechoslovakia's**
Q: What country's name is abbreviated CSSR?
W: After World War II, Czechoslovakia became a Communist police state, patterned after Russia. The abbreviation stands for the Czechoslovakia Soviet Socialist Republic.

A: **Dallas**
Q: What Texas city is said to have been named for James Polk's vice president?
W: George Mifflin Dallas was Vice President from 1845-49. He was also mayor of Philadelphia, U.S. District Attorney for eastern Pennysylvania, U.S. Senator, Attorney General of Pennysylvania, and minister to both Russia and Great Britain. The town of Dallas, Oregon, was also named after him.

A: **Dallas**
Q: Where is the famed Nieman-Marcus department store?
W: Actually, the posh store can be found in several cities, however it's corporate headquarters are in Dallas, and its first store was located there.

A: **Dallas**
Q: What U.S. city is known as "The Big D"?
W: There are many opinions about "The Big D" but the one we liked best was that it was a brand such as is used on cattle, i.e. "Circle D" or "Crossbar."

A: **Damascus**
Q: What's the capital of Syria?
W: Syria is about the size of North Dakota. It has an estimated population of 9,700,000. Damascus, the capital, has some 1,142,000 residents and contains some of the most ancient remains of civilization.

A: **Danube, The**
Q: What river does the Budapest Hilton afford a spectacular view of?
W: The Budapest Hilton is situated next to Fisherman's Bastion on Castle Hill. It has 323 rooms (all with bath), several restaurants, a night club, and a casino. Sound inviting? Here's the phone number for reservations: 853-500.

A: **Danube, The**
Q: What river flows through Vienna, Budapest, and Belgrade?
W: The Danube is the second river of Europe rising in the Black Forest of southwestern Germany. It flows from west to east for 1,760 miles and empties into the Black Sea. Cities through which the Danube River flows include Vienna, once the capital of the Holy Roman Empire, Budapest, which is the capital of Hungary, and Belgrade, chief city of Yugoslavia.

A: **Dartmouth**
Q: What college enlivens Hanover, New Hampshire?
W: This Ivy League school was founded in 1769.

A: **Death Valley**
Q: What sun-blasted, 140 mile long valley is just north of the Mojave Desert?
W: Death Valley a low desert in Inyo County in California, is noted for its large number of plant specimens. It was called Death Valley because its heat and lack of water claimed so many lives of the pioneers trying to cross it.

A: **Delaware**
Q: What U.S. state has the lowest highest elevation, at 60 feet?
W: *WRONG!* Florida actually has a lower highest elevation than Delaware. Florida is primarily a low-lying plain mostly under 100 feet above sea level and its highest point is 345 feet. Delaware's plain is rarely over 60 feet, but its highest elevation is 438 feet. Delaware does,

however, qualify as the lowest state in terms of average altitude.

A: **Delaware, The**
Q: What river forms the Pennsylvania-New Jersey border?
W: The Delaware, which starts in New York and flows 405 miles, also forms part of the border between New York and Pennsylvania, and Delaware and New Jersey.

A: **Denmark**
Q: What country produces Carlsberg, Tuborg, and Wiibroe beer?
W: There are currently five major breweries in Denmark. Carlsberg and Tuborg are the best known and were at one time independent companies; however they merged in 1969. Another Danish beer gaining in popularity is the Ceres Red Eric.

A: **Denmark**
Q: What country sold the Virgin Islands to the U.S. in 1917?
W: The U.S. originally purchased the islands for defense purposes. The first permanent settlement in the territory was by the Danes in 1672. The residents have been citizens of the U.S. since 1927.

A: **Denmark**
Q: What country administers Greenland?
W: Greenland is a province of Denmark even though it is separated from Denmark by 1,300 miles of ocean. Godthaab is Greenland's capital and largest town. Most of Greenland lies within the Arctic Circle.

A: **Denmark**
Q: What country consists mainly of the Jutland Peninsula?
W: Denmark consists of the peninsula of Jutland, which extends northward from Germany, and about 500 nearby islands.

A: **Denmark's**
Q: What country's flag has lasted the longest without change?
W: The Danes honor their flag as the world's oldest. It has flown since the 1100s and consists of a large white cross on a red field.

A: **Denmark's**
Q: What country's national folk hero is called Holger Danske?
W: This was one of the figures in Shakespeare's "Hamlet." His statue stands in Kronborg Castle north of Copenhagen, and he has pledged to come to life to protect Denmark.

A: **Des Moines**
Q: What's the capital of Iowa?
W: Des Moines is also the largest city in the state and has earned worldwide recognition as an insurance center. About fifty insurance companies have home offices in Des Moines.

A: **Dearborn, Michigan**
Q: Where is the Henry Ford Museum?
W: Dearborn is the fourth largest city in the state of Michigan. It lies along the River Rouge on the western outskirts of Detroit. The Henry Ford Museum exhibits man's progress in such fields as science, invention, handicraft, transportation, manufacturing, and agriculture.

A: **Devil's Island**
Q: What former penal colony lies off the coast of French Guiana?
W: Ila Du Diable, Devil's Island, in the Atlantic off the coast of Frech Guiana, is a small, palm covered isle where the French kept a few political prisoners. This was only a small part of French Guiana's system of prisons. Convicts and ex-convicts did most of the work of the colony until 1938 when France abolished the last penal settlement.

A: **Diamonds**
Q: What is Kimberley, South Africa, renowned for?
W: Ninety-five percent of the world's supply of diamonds comes from Africa. The Union of South Africa produces most of the jewelry diamonds (as opposed to industrial diamonds) at Kimberley. One can still see the Big Hole where diamond mining began, although it is no longer in operation. However, several of the newer mines can be viewed.

A: **dinar, The**
Q: What unit of currency will buy you dinner in Iraq, Jordan, Tunisia, and Yugoslavia?
W: In Iraq the dinar is a gold coin, while in Yugoslavia the dinar is a copper and nickel coin. The dinar was once the chief coin of Moslems and the territory they controlled. It's name, "dinar," comes from a silver Roman city coin, the denarius.

A: **Disneyland**
Q: What's found at 1313 Harbor Boulevard, Anaheim, California?
W: Disneyland, the famous amusement park created by Walt Disney, occupies approximately 160 acres of land in Anaheim, California, and draws over five million people a year to the city.

A: **Dogs**
Q: What kind of creatures are the Canary Islands named for?
W: The ancients named the Islands after the large dogs they found there. The Latin term for dog is *canis*.

A: **Dover**
Q: What's the capital of Delaware?
W: The state of Delaware ranks 49th in area of the fifty states and 47th in population, but it was the first of the original thirteen colonies to ratify the Constitution. John Dickinson, "Penman of The Revolution," called the state capital, Dover, his home. Not much of note has happened there since. What do you expect from a place whose state bird is the Blue Hen Chicken?

A: **Dublin**
Q: What capital city does the Liffey River flow through?
W: Dublin is also the largest city of the Republic of Ireland. It lies on the east coast of Ireland at the mouth of the Liffey River. The name Dublin comes from the Gaelic word, *dubh*, meaning "dark", and *linn*, meaning "pool." This name refers to the dark waters of the Liffey River which the Vikings used as a harbor.

A: **Dublin**
Q: What's the capital of Ireland?
W: Dublin is the capital of the Republic of Ireland in southern Ireland. It became a dominion in 1921 and later a republic. Northern Ireland chose to remain part of the United Kingdom. Dublin was first settled in the 1800s.

A: **Dublin's**
Q: What city's main thoroughfare is O'Connell Street?
W: O'Connell Street and Dublin, Ireland, are filled with statues of historic figures and make a fine walk for tourists.

A: **Dungarees**
Q: What overalls are named for Dungri, a suburb of Bombay?
W: Bombay and its environs are the center for the spinning and weaving of cotton. The word *dungri* is derived from the Bombay suburb where a coarse kind of blue cotton cloth was first manufactured. The town of Madras is also a name used to identify a commonly used cotton material (remember how it "bleeds"?).

A: **east, The**
Q: What coast of Australia is Sydney on?
W: Sydney, the oldest and largest city in Australia, was founded as a penal colony in 1788. The area where the city now stands was first discovered when Captain Arthur Smith, originally directed to Botany Bay and finding the area too exposed, looked farther north and came upon Port Jackson, now Sydney Harbor. The early settlement was constantly troubled by disputes between the free settlers, the convicts, and the soldiers sent to guard the prisons.

A: **East Berlin**
Q: What's the capital of East Germany?
W: East Berlin is controlled by 400,000 Soviet troops although it is declared to be a fully sovereign state. It is across the Berlin wall from West Berlin. Berlin as a united city was the capital of Germany before World War II. Once the country was divided, the capital of West Germany "temporarily" became Bonn.

A: **East Germany**
Q: Where are Leipzig, Dresden and Magdeburg?
W: Leipzig was home to Wagner, Bach, Schumann, and Mendelssohn. A cultural center until World War II, Dresden has heavy deposits of kaolin, or procelain clay, and produces much of the world's fine china. Magdeburg is a large manufacturing city with machine shops and a large synthetic oil plant.

A: East Indies, The
Q: What Indies constituted the Spice Islands?
W: These are the islands off the Malay Peninsula. They are the major source of spices for the world, hence the name. It is the largest group of islands in the world, extending in a belt along the equator for over 3,800 miles.

A: Easter Island
Q: What island is home to statues called Mauis?
W: These are eyeless statues weighing about 70 tons each. Scientists have been unable to determine who carved them. They were probably begun about 400 A.D. The island is located in the eastern Pacific Ocean about 2,300 miles west of Chile, of which it is a dependency.

A: Easter Island
Q: What island was first sighted from a Dutch ship on Easter Day, 1772?
W: Easter Island is also called Rapanwi. The first European to discover the island was the Dutch Admiral Jacob Roggeveen in 1722. He saw the people worshipping the sun in front of the statue. When the English explorer Captain James Cook arrived in 1774, he observed that the statues were no longer venerated and in fact had been deliberately knocked down.

A: Ecuador
Q: What country is named for a line of latitude that runs through it?
W: The equator runs through Ecuador, where most of the people are descendents of the Incas. The land was called Quito and had existed for 2,000 years before the Incas conquered it in the 1500s.

A: Ecuador
Q: What country do the Galapagos Islands belong to?
W: The Islands harbor many rare forms of wildlife and take their name from the giant 500-pound turtles that live there. The word *Galapagos*, is Spanish for turtle. The islands lie across the equator in the Pacific Ocean, 600 miles west of Ecuador.

A: edelweiss, The
Q: What's the national flower of Austria?
W: The edelweiss is grown wild in mountain regions. The word *edelweiss* is German, meaning "noble white."

A: Egypt
Q: What country lies beneath the High Aswan Dam?
W: Egypt's recorded history dating back to 3100 B.C. makes it the oldest of all modern countries. Greek and Roman tourists traveled to see its wonders more than 2,000 years ago. The Aswan Dam on the Nile River controls its flooding. It is a rock-filled dam completed in 1970. Creation of its reservoir, Lake Nasser, necessitated relocation of the ancient temple complex of Abu Simbel.

A: Egypt
Q: What country is home to the Bank of Alexandria?
W: Alexandria is the chief port and second largest city of Egypt. It is not only a vast Mediterranean port but also a delightful seaside resort with endless stretches of golden sands and perfect bathing beaches.

A: Egypt's
Q: What country's major seaport is Alexandria?
W: Alexandria lies on the northwestern end of the Nile River Delta on a strip of land between the Mediterranean Sea and Lake Mareotis. The Pharos of Alexandria lighthouse and watchtower, one of the seven wonders of the ancient world, was built on the island of Pharos about 240 B.C. Pharos is now a peninsula, not an island.

A: Egypt's
Q: What country's travel requirements include a $3 contribution to save Nubian monuments?
W: A departure tax of four Egyptian pounds (about $3) is assessed to cover the cost of repairing and preserving the ancient monuments.

A: Eiffel Tower, The
Q: What has 1,792 steps?
W: The Eiffel Tower was built when the French government was organizing the 1889 Centennial Exposition to celebrate the French Revolution. The glass cage elevators were developed by the Otis Elevator Company of the U.S.

A: Eight
Q: How many U.S. states border on the Great Lakes?
W: They are listed alphabetically: Illinois, Indiana, Michigan, Minnesota, New York, Ohio, Pennsylvania, and Wisconsin.

A: El Salvador
Q: What's the most densely populated country on the American mainland?
W: El Salvador lies on the west coast of Central America. The people of El Salvador speak Spanish. There are five million people in an area of 8,124 square miles, a density of 615 people per square mile. This really is nothing compared to the 47,258 people per square mile in the Portuguese province of Macao! We wonder where they find room to stand.

A: El Salvador
Q: What's the smallest country in Central America?
W: El Salvador is about the size of Massachusetts and has approximately 8,124 square miles.

A: Eleven
Q: How many points are there on the maple leaf on the Canadian flag?
W: This is true. All you have to do is find a picture of one and count the points. This flag was adopted by Canada in 1965; the maple leaf is its national emblem.

A: Elizabeth I
Q: What queen were the Virgin Islands named for in 1627?
W: *WRONG!* They were named by Christoper Columbus in 1493 in memory of St. Ursula and her 11,000 maidens, not for Queen

Elizabeth! Ursula was a British maiden who was martyred with her maidens by the Huns. The British Virgin Islands have been under the British flag since 1672.

A: **Elysee Palace, The**
Q: What's the official residence of the president of France?
W: The Palais del'Elysee (Elysian Palace) is the residence of the President of France. It stands northwest of the Place de la Concorde (Place of Peach) and is one of many famous buildings of France. Madame de Pompadour, Josephine, and Napoleon (before becoming emperor) lived at the Elysee Palace as well.

A: **Empire State Building, The**
Q: What stands on the site of New York's old Waldorf-Astoria Hotel?
W: On Dec. 21, 1928 the *New York Times* page 1 headline was "Waldorf-Astoria Sold, Fifty Story Building to be Erected." It ended up with 102 stories! This famed building, built in 1931, was once the tallest skyscraper in the world.

A: **Empire State Building, The**
Q: What Manhattan edifice has 10 million bricks in it?
W: This famed building also contains 6,500 windows, 1,860 steps to the 102nd floor, 350 miles of telephone and telegraph cable, and 60 miles of water pipes. During a storm, the building absorbs as many as 20 bolts of lightening, and the steel structure creaks slightly when heavy winds cause it to sway.

A: **England and Belgium**
Q: What two countries are joined by the Harwich-Ostende ferry?
W: The Harwich-Ostende ferry operates in the Strait of Dover which is a narrow channel that connects the North Sea with the English Channel and separates England and France at their closest points. Harwich is one of the best harbors on the east coast of England. Ostende, Belgium is the railroad "gateway to Europe."

A: **England and Scotland**
Q: What two countries did Hadrian's Wall separate?
W: Hadrian's Wall stretched about 73 miles between the estuary of the River Tyne to Solway Firth. Hadrian, one of the "fine, good Emperors of Rome" built the first wall between 122 and 127 A.D. as part of a general reorganization of frontier defense against the Caledonians. It is one of the largest Roman remains in Britain.

A: **English**
Q: What's the official language of Nigeria?
W: Nigeria is a West African nation in the British Commonwealth. More people live in Nigeria than in any other African country. English is the official language, however, there are about 400 other languages and dialects spoken in Nigeria.

A: **English**
Q: What's the principal language of Trinidad and Tobago?
W: The Republic of Trinidad and Tobago is located off the east coast of Venezuela. Port of Spain is its capital. While English is the official language, Hindi, French, and Spanish are also spoken.

A: **English**
Q: What's the second-most-spoken language on Earth?
W: More people speak a variety of Chinese as a native language than any other. One in every seven people worldwide speak English.

A: **English**
Q: What's the official language of Papua New Guinea?
W: Papua New Guinea is an island off the eastern Malay Archipelago north of Australia. In December 1973, Papua New Guinea achieved self-governing status.

A: **English and Afrikaans**
Q: What are the two official languages of South Africa?
W: Afrikaans is the language used by South Africans who are descendents of the Dutch. While English and Afrikaans are the official languages, the Bantu tongue predominates in terms of the number of people speaking one of these three.

A: **English and Maltese**
Q: What are the two languages of Malta?
W: Malta is an island in the Mediterranean and its local language is derived from the ancient Phoenician language. Maltese resembles Arabic with the addition of Italian words. English is the other official language.

A: **English Channel, The**
Q: What does the River Seine empty into?
W: The Seine is the second largest river in France. It flows through Paris in a northwesterly direction to the English Channel. Notre Dame is on an island in the Seine called the Ile de la Cite, where Paris began its history as the village named Lutetia.

A: **English Channel, The**
Q: What do the French call La Manche?
W: The French call the channel "La Manche" meaning "the sleeve" because of its shape. Geologists believe that England and France were connected by land at one time before the channel was formed.

A: **English, French, Spanish, Italian**
Q: What are the four most widely used languages in North America?
W: Defining North America as Mexico, the U.S., and Canada, and using the "mother tongue" as the definition of language, the approximate breakdown of these four languages is 70 percent English, 25 percent Spanish, 3 percent French and 2 percent Italian.

A: **Erie, Ontario, Michigan, Huron, Superior**
Q: What are the five Great Lakes?
W: The Great Lakes are the largest group of fresh water lakes in the world. Lake Michigan is the only one of the lakes that lies entirely within the U.S.

A: **Eros**
Q: What statue overlooks Piccadilly Circus?
W: Piccadilly Circus is the Times Square of London. Eros was the Greek name for the God of Love, whom the Romans called Cupid. His mother is Venus. He is usually depicted as a naked, winged infant armed with a bow and arrow that he shoots to inspire love. The Eros statue in Piccadilly Circus is made of bronze.

A: **Ethiopia**
Q: What is Abyssinia now called?
W: Ethiopia is an empire on the Red Sea in northeastern Africa. It is one of the world's oldest Christian countries. The name Ethiopia comes from the Greek, meaning "sunburned faces." The earliest recorded civilization of this country was known to the Egyptians as Punt. Abyssinia was the name applied to Ethiopia by Europeans, rather than a name the Ethiopians called themselves, as *abyssinia* comes from an arabic word meaning "confused, mixed or mongrel race."

A: **Eureka**
Q: What's the state motto of California?
W: Eureka is the name of a northern California port where its first settler, James Ryan, shouted "Eureka" as his ship drove onto the mud flats in Humboldt Bay. The other story about the source of this motto is of course, the gold rush. *Eureka* means "I have found it."

A: **Europe**
Q: What continent has the most people per square mile?
W: Europe has over 692 million people in four million miles or 173 persons per square mile. Asia is a close second with 162 people per one square mile. Europe is the second largest continent in terms of population but fifth of seven in land mass.

A: **Everglades National Park**
Q: What U.S. national park contains Gumbo Limbo Trail?
W: The Everglades is the largest remaining subtropical wilderness in the continental U.S. It is the third largest of the U.S. national parks. Branching off the main road in the Everglades are a variety of viewing areas, such as the Pa-hay-okee overlook, and a variety of trails, including the Gumbo Limbo which leads you through a tropical area so dense you can see only a few feet through the foliage.

F

A: **F**
Q: What letter appears on the cold-water tap in Spain?
W: In Spanish *caliente* (C) is "hot"; *frio* (F) is "cold."

A: **fez, The**
Q: What cap was first made in and named for a Moroccan city?
W: The *fez* is a brimless, cone-shaped red felt hat that was made only in Fes or Fez until the 19th century. It was the characteristic headgear of the Turks until abolished in 1925 by Kemal Ataturk.

A: **Fifth Avenue**
Q: What Manhattan thoroughfare was nicknamed "Millionaires' Row"?
W: As far as we can tell, this nickname goes back to the 1800s following the construction of Commodore Vanderbilt's Grand Central train shed. The new cut and tracks isolated the bulk middle-class housing to the east from the town palaces lining Fifth Avenue (so-called "Millionaires' Row") and related side streets as far north as 96th Street.

A: **Finland and Sweden**
Q: What two countries are separated by the Gulf of Bothnia?
W: The Gulf of Bothnia is the north arm of the Baltic Sea, which separates Finland and Sweden. Many sawmills occupy the coastline processing the trees of the hinterland, which was formerly called Bothnia, hence the Gulf's name. It is 450 miles long, but only 50 to 150 miles wide with many islands, thus making navigation difficult.

A: **Firenze**
Q: What do Italians call Florence?
W: Florence, Firenze in Italian, lies almost at the center of Italy. The impact of Florentine citizens on the world is still a matter of fascination for scholars, since from this small town, ruled for generations by the Medici family, came such notables as Leonardo da Vinci, Michelangelo, Dante, Machiavelli, Galileo, and Amerigo Vespucci, to mention a few!

A: **Five**
Q: How many dollars a day did Arthur Frommer say you could get by on in Europe in 1968?
W: He claimed this in his book *Europe on Five Dollars a Day*. In 1976, Simon and Schuster distributed Frommer's book entitled, *Europe on Ten Dollars a Day*. Inflation affects budget travel also because Frommer's 1981-82 book was *Europe on Twenty Dollars a Day*!

A: **Five**
Q: How many U.S. states border the Pacific Ocean?
W: Alaska, California, Hawaii, Oregon, and Washington.

A: **Five**
Q: How many U.S. states border the Gulf of Mexico?
W: Alabama, Florida, Louisiana, Mississippi, and Texas.

A: **Fleet Street**
Q: What London street is the home of British journalism?
W: Fleet Street has been called "the main artery of the Press." At one time or another, the offices of most major newspapers were on this street. It is presently the home of the *Daily Telegraph, Daily Express*, and many others. However, the grandaddy of them all, the *Times*, has moved to a new office on Gray's Inn Road.

A: **Florence**
Q: What city is home to almost half of Michelangelo's statues?
W: Michelangelo Buonarroti was an Italian sculptor, painter, architect, and poet of the High Renaissance. He created more than 20 sculptures, 10 of which can be found in Florence: Battle of the Centaurs, Madonna of the Steps, River God, Bacchus, Young David, Matthew, Victory, Deposition from the Cross, and the tombs of several Medici.

A: **Florida and Hawaii**
Q: What two states contain the farthest-separated points in the U.S.?
W: *Wrong!* It used to be Washington and Florida, but with the addition of Hawaii and Alaska, the farthest-separated points are Florida and Alaska.

A: **Florida**
Q: What U.S. state has the second longest coastline?
W: The second longest coastline is Florida with 1,350 miles, 580 on the Atlantic and 770 on the Gulf of Mexico. Alaska has the longest coastline, 6,640 miles with 5,580 on the Pacific

and 1060 on the Arctic. California is third with 840 miles on the Pacific.

A: **Florida's**
Q: What U.S. state's ocean shores have yielded the most sunken treasure?
W: Even the Florida Tourist Bureau is stumped about where this can be documented!

A: **forget-me-not, The**
Q: What is the state flower of Alaska?
W: Alaska has no official state name but it does have everything else. Besides the state flower forget-me-not, some other official "tidbits" include: motto: North to the Future; bird: willow ptarmigan; tree: Sitka spruce; song: Alaska's Flag. Don't worry-they'll get around to nicknaming the state someday. What else is there to do up there?

A: **Forty-eight**
Q: How many stars were on the U.S. flag in 1958?
W: Alaska was the 49th state, joining the Union in 1959. Hawaii, the 50th star, joined in 1959 as well. The 48th state was Arizona, which joined the Union in 1912.

A: **Forty-eight**
Q: How many stars did the U.S. flag have in 1912?
W: You actually have three correct answers here: 46, 47, *or* 48! On Jan. 1, 1912 it had 46; on Jan. 6th, New Mexico joined to make 47; and on Feb. 14, Arizona joined to make 48. Tricky!

A: **Four**
Q: How many U.S. state capitals are named for presidents?
W: Jefferson City, Missouri; Lincoln, Nebraska; Madison, Wisconsin; and Jackson, Mississippi.

A: **Four**
Q: How many official languages does Switzerland recognize?
W: This is the question which generated the idea for this book... the first time we played we wanted to know *which four!* The answer to our

question and yours is: 67 percent German, 20 percent French, 10 percent Italian, and about 3 percent Rhaeto-Romanic (Romansh). Romansh was added as the fourth official language by a federal popular vote in 1938.

A: **Four**
Q: How many U.S. states border Mexico?
W: Arizona, California, New Mexico, and Texas.

A: **Fourth**
Q: Where does the U.S. rank among world countries in area?
W: The USSR is the largest (2.5 times the area of the U.S.) with 8,649,490 square miles. Canada is second at 3,851,809; People's Republic of China is third at 3,691,521; and the U.S. fourth at 3,615,122. The next largest, in order, are Brazil, Australia, India, and Argentina.

A: **France**
Q: What does a gallophobic Englishman fear?
W: According to the dictionary, *gallophobic* is a hatred or dread of anything French.

A: **France**
Q: What's the largest country in Europe after the Soviet Union?
W: France ranks second in land mass in Europe with 210,040 square miles (four fifths the size of Texas). The Soviet Union is over 8.6 million square miles.

A: **France**
Q: What country has the highest per capita consumption of cheese?
W: France is also the second highest producer of cheese. The average American eats a half ton of cheese during his lifetime.

A: **France**
Q: Where are the Vosges Mountains?
W: The Vosges Mountains extend west of the Rhine River Valley in eastern France. These dome-shaped mountains form chains of granite in the south and of red sandstone in the north. In the southwest the mountains slope to valleys and lakes creating a favorite tourist area.

A: **France**
Q: What country administers the Caribbean hideaway of Martinique?
W: Martinique is a 431-square mile island in the Caribbean. It has participated in about 20 wars during its history. It was held by Britain from 1762 to 1763, then 1794 to 1802, and finally 1809 to 1814. It is now administered by France. The island suffers from some type of natural disaster every 4.5 years, from hurricanes to earthquakes! The most dramatic disaster was the 1902 explosion of Mt. Pelee, the island's only active volcano.

A: **France**
Q: Where would you be if your train's engine had S.N.C.F. painted on it?
W: S.N.C.F. stands for Societe Naionale des Chemins de Fer Francais, the one company managing French railroads. It was created in 1938, and the government holds a 51 percent share of ownership.

A: **France**
Q: What country owns Corsica?
W: Corsica is the fourth largest island in the Mediterranean. At the request of its citizens it became a French "department" in 1789 and now comprises two "departments" (states).

A: **France**
Q: Where is Normandy?
W: Normandy is a section of northern France located on the English Channel. Under William the Conqueror (1035-1087), it was the strongest fief (feudal estate) in France. It was from this strong point that William undertook to conquer England in 1066. Normandy was also the site of the Allied invasion of German-occupied France in June 1944.

A: **France and Italy**
Q: What countries does the Mont Blanc Tunnel?
W: The Mont Blanc Tunnel is a seven-mile-long automotive tunnel. The tunnel was a joint project of the French and Italians. The Italians began on their side in 1958, the French on their side in 1959. The tunnel goes under the highest mountain of the Alps, Mont Blanc, which is 15,771 feet high.

A: **France and Spain**
Q: What two countries is Andorra nestled between?
W: Andorra is 179 square miles. It is governed by an elected General Council that meets in secret twice a year. However, the real rulers are the President of France and the Spanish Bishop of Urgel. They have shared joint control since 1278! The fees for their services in 1975 were about $180 for the French president and $6.87 for the Bishop.

A: **France and Spain's**
Q: What two countries' coastlines border the Bay of Biscay?
W: The Bay of Biscay is an 86,000-square-mile inlet of the Atlantic Ocean, known for its rough seas, squalls, and storms. The French resort of Biarritz is on this Bay. Fishing is a principal industry with catches that include sardines, cod, tuna, anchovies, and lobster.

A: **Frankfort**
Q: What's the capital of Kentucky?
W: Frankfort has been the capital since 1792. The story goes that it was not named for the German town, rather for a local frontiersman, Stephen Frank, who was killed in an Indian skirmish at a nearby fording place known as "Frank's ford."

A: **French**
Q: What nationality is a Breton?
W: Celtic refugees, displaced from southern England by the influx of Anglo-Saxons, settled in northwestern France in the 5th and 6th centuries. They and their language are still known as Bretons.

A: **French**
Q: What's the most commonly-spoken language in Belgium?
W: Unless the French talk more than the Dutch, this answer is incorrect... Our sources say 56 percent speak Flemish (Dutch), 32 percent French, 1 percent German, and 11 percent are legally bilingual.

A: **French franc, The**
Q: What's the official currency of Monaco?
W: The French franc, *or* the Monegasque franc. Monegasque is also an ethnic group in Monaco constituting 15 percent of the population.

G

A: Ganges, The
Q: What river are the cities of Patna and Calcutta on?
W: The Ganges River, India, is 1,557 miles long (39th longest river in the world). Calcutta is the largest city in India and a major port – located 80 miles upstream from the Bay of Bengal. Patna is on the Ganges in northern India and is the site of many archaeological excavations, with finds dating back to about 600 B.C.

A: Ganges, The
Q: What's the sacred river of India?
W: The myth is that the Ganges, personified as a goddess, flowed only in heaven until she was brought to earth by a king in order to purify the ashes of his ancestors. The Hindus often cast their dead upon the river, believing they will go straight to heaven. Cremation temples have been built along the Ganges to assist families choosing this method of burial.

A: Garcia
Q: What's the most common Spanish surname?
W: Garcia is the name of a village in Spain. It is thought to be of pre-Roman origin and means "fox." It was formerly a first name but has become the most popular and widespread surname found thoughout Spain and all Hispanic regions.

A: Garden State
Q: What does it say on the bottom of the New Jersey license plates?
W: New Jersey was one of the 13 original U.S. states. It is called the "Garden State" because of its many prosperous truck farms. It is the 5th smallest state, 7,836 square miles, but very densely populated.

A: Gauchos
Q: What are South American cowboys called?
W: Gauchos were usually of mixed heritage – Indian and European. They hunted large herds of escaped cattle and horses, often selling them to European traders doing contraband business in hides and tallow. One of the more unusual "tools" used by the Gauchos were the bolas, leather cords with three iron balls or stones that they threw at the animal to entwine and immobilize its legs.

A: Georgia
Q: What U.S. state boasts Stone Mountain, the world's largest mass of exposed granite?
W: Stone Mountain, which stands 1,686 feet tall, is located near Atlanta in DeKalb county. It is known for the Confederate Memorial carved on the northeast wall. Work began on the memorial in 1917 but wasn't completed until 1967.

A: Georgia
Q: What's the largest U.S. state east of the Mississippi?
W: When Georgia was founded in 1732, it was even larger than today, as it then included much of what is now Alabama and Misissippi. Georgia, 58,876 square miles, is the largest state east of the Mississippi; Florida is second at 58,560; Michigan is third at 58,216.

A: Georgia
Q: What U.S. state contains the counties of Macon and Bacon?
W: Four other states have counties called Macon: Alabama, Illinois, Missouri, and North Carolina; however, no other state has a "Bacon." The only state with more counties than Georgia (Georgia has 159) is Texas with 254.

A: German
Q: What's the official language of Austria?
W: 95 percent of the Austrian population speaks German.

A: Gibraltar
Q: Where on the Iberian peninsula is the Trafalgar Graveyard?
W: On October 21, 1805, the famous naval Battle of Trafalgar took place on the west coast of Spain, in which Horatio Nelson, commander of the British Mediterranean Fleet defeated the combined French and Spanish Fleets. The Trafalgar Graveyard or Cemetery commemorates the many who died in that battle and other naval battles. It lies just beyond the Charles V Wall in Gibraltar.

A: Ginza, The
Q: What Tokyo street glitters with famed department stores and nightclubs?
W: Ginza is the main shopping street in Tokyo. Nihonbashi Street is the northern extension of Ginza that has the best department stores. A walk on the Ginza is popularly known as "Ginbura."

A: Glasgow
Q: What city does Prestwick Airport serve?
W: Prestwick is the international airport in Scotland. It is operated by the British Airport Authority and was opened in 1935. It is about 35 miles from Glasgow, Scotland's capital. Abbotsinch, the airport in Glasgow, is used for domestic services in the United Kingdom and for some flights to other European cities.

A: Gold
Q: What color is the hammer and sickle on the Soviet Union's flag?
W: The background is red, the star, the hammer, and the sickle are gold. The hammer and sickle symbolize the nation's industrial and agricultural workers, while the star represents the rule of the Communist Party.

A: **Granada, Spain**
Q: Where's the Alhambra Palace?
W: It was a palace and fortress of the Moorish monarchs, built between 1238 and 1358. The name, which means "red" in Arabic, is probably from the color of the bricks in the outer walls.

A: **Grand Canyon, The**
Q: What's the world's deepest land gorge?
W: The details on this one can fool you: Hell's Canyon of the Snake River in Idaho is the *deepest* in the U.S. at 7,900 feet. The deepest in the world was discovered in 1981 and is El Canon de Colca, Peru. The Grand Canyon in Colorado is the *largest*: 217 miles long, 600 feet to 18 miles wide at the brim, and 4,000 to 5,500 feet deep.

A: **Grand Canyon, The**
Q: What canyon cuts its way from Marble Gorge to the Grand Wash Cliffs?
W: The Grand Canyon is a gorge in the Colorado River where it flows across the northwest corner of Arizona. It extends from the mouth of the Little Colorado River to Grand Wash Cliffs near the Arizona Nevada boundary and includes Marble Canyon. In 1975, Congress nearly doubled the size of Grand Canyon National Park from 783,561 acres to 1,218,375. The Marble Canyon absorption adds the upstream 50 miles of the Grand Canyon with rapids and 3,000-foot canyon walls.

A: **Grand Canyon, The**
Q: What would you be exploring if you followed the Bright Angel Trail down to the Colorado River?
W: If you have a sense of adventure, take the two-day muleback trip from the South Run of the Canyon that begins on the celebrated twisted "Bright Angel Trail" at the west end of the Grand Canyon Village and goes into the Inner Gorge. The ride down, over switchbacks cut into the sheer cliffs, seems forbidding, but

those surefooted mules haven't lost a rider for over 50 years. After lunching at a cottonwood oasis, your trail will reach the level of the roaring Colorado River and crosses the narrow Kaibab Suspension Bridge. Advance confirmed reservations for muleback trips are necessary. Write Grand Canyon National Park Lodges, Grand Canyon, Arizona, 86023.

A: **Grand Central Station**
Q: What's the largest train station in the world?
W: If you are looking for it in New York City, it's at Park Avenue and 43rd Street. You can't miss it! It covers 48 acres and has two levels with 41 tracks on the upper level and 26 on the lower level. If you still can't find it, ask someone – about 180,000 people use it every day.

A: **Great Barrier Reef, The**
Q: What's the world's largest coral reef?
W: This coral reef is more than 1,250 miles long and is located off the northeast coast of Australia. It was first charted and successfully navigated by the English explorer James Cook in 1770.

A: **Great Barrier Reef, The**
Q: What natural breakwater lies off the northeast coast of Australia?
W: The Great Barrier Reef was formed over millions of years from the skeletons and skeletal waste of marine organisms. The waters are so clear that marine life can be observed to depths of 100 ft. The great clams of this area are famous – up to 4 feet wide and 200 pounds!

A: **Great Britain**
Q: What's the largest island in Eurpoe?
W: Great Britain is the eighth largest island in the world, 84,200 square miles. Greenland is the largest at 840,000 square miles.

A: **Great Pyramid of Khufu, The**
Q: Which is the only one of the Seven Wonders of the Ancient World still standing?
W: The Great Pyramid was finished in 2580 B.C. It was originally almost 481 feet high with a base of 756 feet. It has been estimated that it took about 4,000 people approximately 30 years to move 2,300,000 blocks of limestones into position. Of the other six wonders, at most, only fragments remain.

A: **Great Salt Lake**
Q: What's the largest lake in Utah?
W: The Salt Lake is the largest saltwater body in the Western Hemisphere. It is a remnant of the freshwater Lake Bonneville, which was about the size of Lake Michigan well over 10,000 years ago (Pleistocene Epoch).

A: **Great Wall of China, The**
Q: What's 50 feet high, 26 feet wide, and 1,500 miles long?
W: Our research indicates that the Great Wall has a main line length of 2,150 miles, ranging in height from 15 to 39 feet and in thickness up to 32 feet.

A: **Greece**
Q: What country has 100 lepta to the drachma?
W: Drachmas are the monetary unit of Greece. There are, about 50 drachmas to the dollar. So a shot of the liqueur ouzo would cost between 200 and 500 leptas in Greece!

A: **Greece**
Q: Where is Mount Olympus?
W: Mount Olympus, on the north eastern side of Greece, is the highest peak in Greece at 9,570 ft. Mount Olympus was thought to be the home of the gods and the site of the throne of Zeus.

A: **Greece**
Q: What country owns the island of Corfu?
W: The island of Corfu lies off the western coast of Greece and Albania in the Ionian Sea. Because of its strategic location between Italy and Greece, it had a long succession of "owners" including the Italians, French, Normans, Germans, and Greeks. It has been a Greek possession since 1944 and is said to have the most attractive countryside of the Greek Islands.

A: **Greece**
Q: What country is home to Olympic Airways?
W: Olympic Airways was formed in 1957, and it links Greek cities with five continents. The familiar five Olympic rings adorn the tail of their planes.

A: **Greece**
Q: What was the last country to join the European Economic Community?
W: Also known as the **Common Market**, the European Economic Community was established in 1957 by the Treaty of Rome to facilitate trade among members, coordinate transportation systems, assure mobility of labor, etc. France, Belgium, Luxembourg, the Netherlands, Italy, and West Germany were the first members. Denmark, Ireland, and the United Kingdom joined in 1973. Greece became the 10th full member on Jan. 1, 1981.

A: **Greece**
Q: What country is the Hellenic Republic?
W: The Greeks are called Hellenes in honor of Hellen, a king in Greek mythology. He was the grandson of Prometheus, who was a god of fire and was associated with the creation of man.

A: **Greece**
Q: Where's the Isthmus of Corinth?
W: In ancient times ships were dragged over the isthmus (piece of land) between the Gulf of Corinth (Ionian Sea) and the Sarconic Gulf. In 1882 the first ship canal was constructed.

A: **Greek islands**
Q: What are Kythnos, Siphnos, Seriphos and Mykonos?
W: If you want to be alone go to any of the first three listed here. They are part of the over 2,000 Greek Isles that are uninhabited. Mykonos is quite inhabited, and you will love the swimming and exploring in the Aegean Sea. Numerous windmills cover the island.

A: **Green, white, red**
Q: What are the colors of the Italian flag?
W: The flag is composed of three vertical stripes of equal size. This flag has a colorful history. In 1796, after being inspired by France's attempts to become liberated from Austrian rule, Bologna adopted a flag based on the French vertical tricolor but used green rather than the French blue, as a symbol of the rights of man to liberty and equality. The following year the Cisalpine Republic of Napoleon also adopted the green, white, and red tricolor. By 1848, it was generally accepted as a symbol of United Italy. When Victor Emmanuel of Sardinia became ruler in 1861, the tricolor became the national flag of Italy.

A: **Greenland**
Q: What's the world's largest island?
W: Greenland is the largest at 840,000 square miles. New Guinea, in the Pacific Ocean, is second at 306,000 square miles.

A: **Greenwich**
Q: Where is Britain's Royal Observatory?
W: *WRONG*! Not anymore! In 1423 Humphrey, Duke of Gloucester, built a watchtower on the north-facing hill above the Thames River in London. This later became the Royal Observatory under Charles II in 1675. Between the end of World War II and 1958, the functions of the Royal Observatory were gradually transferred to Herstmonceaux Castle in Herstmonceaux, Sussex, because the bright lights of London made Greenwich unsuitable for observing.

A: **Greenwich, England**
Q: What city is associated with the Prime Meridian, or zero degrees longitude?
W: Britain became the foremost maritime power of Europe during the 18th century, and its Admiralty was responsible for many developments in charting (map development) and improvements in navigation facilities. When the Admiralty proposed Greenwich as the prime meridian for longitude, the other nations agreed. The prime meridian is 0 degrees longitude, an imaginary line through both geographic poles and Greenwich.

A: **Gulf of California, The**
Q: What separates the Baja Peninsula from the Mexican mainland?
W: The Gulf of California is the third largest gulf in the world. Cortes conducted an expedition across this gulf to the Baja Peninsula in 1532. It was not until 1539 that it was proven that California was not an island.

A: **Gulf of California, The**
Q: What body of water does the Colorado River empty into?
W: The Colorado River begins in Rocky Mountain National Park in Colorado and flows 1,450 miles to the Gulf of California. There is also a Colorado River that begins in west Texas and empties into Matagorda Bay, Gulf of Mexico...so Matagorda Bay is also correct!

A: **Gulf of Mexico, The**
Q: What's the world's largest gulf?
W: The Gulf of Mexico, 582,100 square miles, is the largest. The Persian Gulf is second at 88,800 and the Gulf of California third at 59,100.

A: Gulf of Mexico, The
Q: What body of water receives the Rio Grande's flow?
W: The Rio Grand starts in San Juan County, Colorado and flows 1,885 miles to the Gulf of Mexico. It forms the natural border between Texas and Mexico.

A: Hague, The
Q: Where's the International Court of Justice?
W: The International Court of Justice is the principal judicial arm of the United Nations. The purpose is to provide a means for peaceful settlement of disputes between nations. Fifteen judges sit on the Court which is based in the Hague, capital of the Netherlands.

A: Haiti
Q: What country are you visiting if you land at President Duvalier Airport?
W: Dr. Francois Duvalier ("Papa Doc", M.D. from University of Haiti) was the President of Haiti from 1957 until his death in 1971. He was succeeded by his son, Jean-Claude.

A: Haiti and the Dominican Republic
Q: What two Caribbean countries share the island of Hispaniola?
W: Hispaniola Island is the second largest island in the Caribbean with 29,530 square miles; Haiti occupies the western third of the island. Cuba is the largest island, over 44,000 square miles.

A: Hamilton
Q: What's the capital of Bermuda?
W: Bermuda is a group of 360 small islands of coral formation. Twenty-one square miles in total and lying 580 miles east of North Carolina in the Atlantic Ocean, Bermuda is a British dependency. Hamilton was

founded in 1790 and succeeded the historic town of St. George as capital in 1815.

A: Hanging Gardens of Babylon, The
Q: Which of the Seven Wonders of the Ancient World was alive?
W: The gardens did not actually hang, but were terraced roof gardens, "up in the air," in the royal palace at Babylon. Estimated to have been built between 810 and 562 B.C., these gardens are believed to have been irrigated by pumps, and the "roofs" were so constructed as to keep water from seeping through the terraces.

A: Hartford, Connecticut
Q: What city is often called "The Insurance Capital of the World"?
W: The first Hartford fire insurance policy was issued Feb. 8, 1794, and insurance continues as a leading business in that city.

A: Hawaii
Q: Where are three quarters of the world's pineapples grown?
W: Pineapple is the king of fruits in Hawaii. It has been the second most important island crop, after sugar, since Jim Dole decided to can the fruit! In the late 1950s three quarters of the pineapple supply did come from Hawaii, but now it's down to about half. Hawaii does supply about 60 percent of the world's canned pineapple products.

A: Hawaii
Q: What's the southernmost state in the U.S.?
W: The southern tip of Texas and Florida are just north of 25 degrees north latitude. All of the Hawaiian Islands are south of 25 degrees north.

A: Hawaii
Q: What U.S. state doesn't have borders?
W: It's out there in the Pacific, not bordering any other state or country.

A: Hawaii
Q: What's the only U.S. state name that ends with three vowels?
W: Correct. And if you cared about that, we're sure you'll want to know how many end in two vowels: nine – California, District of Columbia, Georgia, New Jersey (remember the rule, "and sometimes *y*"?), Ohio, Pennsylvania, Tennessee, Virginia, and West Virginia.

A: Hawaii
Q: Which of the Hawaiian Islands has active volcanoes?
W: The island of Hawaii has the only active volcanoes in the Hawaiian Islands. At the time of writing, our source said the volcano Mauna Loa was last active in 1978; we are updating our sources – make it March, 1984! Kilauea is the other active volcano on the island of Hawaii, active in 1983 and in 1984! The entire state of Hawaii actually consists of the tops of a chain of submerged volcanic mountains that form eight major islands and numerous small islets.

A: Hawaii
Q: What's the wettest state in the U.S.?
W: Mount Waialeale, Hawaii is the rainiest spot in the world according to the National Geographic Society. It is on the island of Kauai and has an average annual rainfall of 460 inches.

A: Heathrow
Q: What airport is on the Piccadilly subway line?
W: It is also known as London Airport, so that guess is also correct!

A: Helena
Q: What's the capital of Montana?
W: The area was first visited by Lewis and Clark in 1805. In July 1864 gold was discovered in "Last Chance Gulch," now the main street. Helena is the seat of "Lewis and Clark County," and is located in the "Prickly Pear Valley" near the Mississippi.

A: **Helsinki**
Q: Which is farthest north – Helsinki, Oslo, or Stockholm?
W: Helsinki, capital of Finland, is at 60 degrees 10 minutes north latitude; Oslo, capital of Norway, is at 59 degrees 55 minutes north latitude; and Stockholm, capital of Sweden, is at 59 degrees 20 minutes north latitude.

A: **Helsinki**
Q: What Scandinavian city is called "The White City of the North"?
W: After Reykjavik, Iceland, Helsinki is the most northerly capital in the world. This fact combined with the physical appearance of the city (it is built largely of local light-colored granite) has led people to call it "The White City of the North."

A: **Himalayas, The**
Q: Where is the "Abominable Snowman" said to wander?
W: Other names include "Bearman" and Tibetan "Yeti." He is a mythical character believed to inhabit the Himalayas near the snow line. Reports state that "at certain gaits bears place the hindfoot partly over the imprint of the forefoot, thus making a very large imprint that looks very much like an enormous human footprint traveling in the opposite direction."

A: **Hindi**
Q: What's the official language of India?
W: Sixteen languages are spoken in India; however, Hindi is the official language and English is the "associate official" language. Some English words with Hindi origin are *guru*, *punch* (drink), *dungaree*, *loot*, *shampoo*, and *pajamas*.

A: **Hong Kong**
Q: What is Britain's possession on the Chinese mainland?
W: Hong Kong is a British Crown Colony in Asia. Acquired from China in 1841, Hong Kong Island itself is 35.5 square miles and the location of the capital Victoria. Of the colony's total 409 square miles, 335 square miles were leased from China in 1898 for 99 years. The total population is estimated at 5.1 million (1981) with less than 20,000 British and about 1 million refugees absorbed between 1949 and 1962.

A: **Hong Kong**
Q: What British colony has a famed jade market on Canton Road?
W: *WRONG*! If you are looking for this famed market, don't go to Canton Road. The open air market was moved by the City Services Department of Hong Kong some 250 meters from its original spot to the junction of Reclamation and Kansu Streets on March 12, 1984. However, when you do find it you may very well walk away with a bargain.

A: **Honolulu**
Q: What U.S. state capital has more than 30 Buddhist temples?
W: The Hawaii Tourist Bureau was positive that there were at least 30 temples, but to be sure of the exact number, someone in Hawaii would have to count them. We couldn't wait that long, so we are taking the word of the tourist office. After all, that's their business!

A: **Honolulu**
Q: What city boasts the only royal palace in the U.S.?
W: The Iolani Palace served as the capitol building until replaced in 1968. It now houses public offices.

The Palace or "Heavenly Hawk" is truly the only royal palace on American soil. The structure was completed in 1882, and shortly thereafter, King Kalakaua, the "Merry Monarch," moved in. He was the only king to occupy the Palace. You may tour the Palace on Wednesdays through Saturdays between the hours of 9 am and 2:15 pm.

A: **Honshu**
Q: What's the largest Japanese island?
W: Japan is comprised of four large islands and many smaller ones. Honshu (87,805 square miles) represents over 50 percent of the land mass of Japan. It is the seventh largest island in the world, 3,600 square miles larger than Great Britain.

A: **Horatio Nelson**
Q: What admiral stands over London's Trafalgar Square?
W: Horatio Nelson was a British naval commander born in 1758. He was killed in 1805 during the Battle of Trafalgar (Spain), but the Battle established Britain's naval supremacy. His 17-foot statue stands atop a 167-foot marble column in the Square.

A: **hospital, A**
Q: What's a "hotel-Dieu" in France?
W: The term refers to any hospital dating back to the Middle Ages. The most important feature of these structures (many of which still stand) is the vast hall with beds for the sick. The word *Dieu* means "God" in French; thus, the literal translation is "hotel of God."

A: **Houston**
Q: Which is farthest south – Houston, Jacksonville, or New Orleans?
W: Houston, Texas, is 29 degrees 45 minutes north latitude; Jacksonville, Florida, is 30 degrees 19 minutes north; and New Orleans is 29 degrees 56 minutes north.

A: **Houston Astrodome, The**
Q: What sports stadium has been billed as "The Eighth Wonder of the World"?
W: The seven manmade wonders of the ancient world are the Pyramids of Egypt, Hanging Gardens of Babylon, Colossus of Rhodes, Pharos of Alexandria, Temple of Diana at Euphesus, Mausoleum at Halicarnasus, and the Statue of Zeus at Olympia...pretty good company for the Astrodome! The Astrodome, the first domed stadium, has a seating capacity of 50,496. However, it is overshadowed in seating capacity by the Rose Bowl, JFK stadium, and many others.

A: **Hudson, The**
Q: What river is spanned by the George Washington Bridge?
W: The George Washington Bridge, built in 1931, is the fourth longest suspension bridge in the world at a span of 3,500 feet. It has two levels, 14 lanes of traffic, and connects New York City at 178th Street with Ft. Lee, New Jersey.

A: **Hudson, The**
Q: What river flows above the Holland Tunnel?
W: The Holland Tunnel is the third longest underwater vehicular tunnel in the world—8,557 feet. The longest is the Bart Trans-Bay Tubes located beneath the San Francisco Bay at 3.6 miles.

A: **Hudson Bay**
Q: What's the largest bay in the world?
W: The Hudson Bay, in east central Canada, is 281,900 square miles. It is larger in size than the Black Sea, the North Sea, the Baltic Sea, and the Persian Gulf. Henry Hudson was searching for a Northwest Passage from the Atlantic to the Pacific when he discovered what later became the Hudson River, Hudson Strait, and Hudson Bay.

A: **Hungary's**
Q: What country's people call their language Magyar?
W: Magyars were the nomadic tribes that came into the Carpathian Basin more than a thousand years ago.

A: **Hungary's**
Q: What country's capital was formed when Pest and Buda merged?
W: Budapest is the city divided by the Danube River into two sections, Buda and Pest. Buda has many hills and bluffs rising up from the Danube. Pest is flat and commercial. Many parts of Pest have been completely rebuilt since the 1940s.

A: **Hyde Park**
Q: What London park are the Kensington Gardens part of?
W: Hyde Park is the largest of the six Royal Parks in London. Kensington Gardens are contiguous with Hyde Park. In 1689, William III took 26 acres off the western end of Hyde Park to make a garden for Kensington Palace. These Gardens were not opened to the public until the mid-19th century. The Albert Memorial, a 175-foot structure with 175 sculpted figures, stands in Kensington Gardens.

A: **Iberian Peninsula, The**
Q: What peninsula do Spain and Portugal share?
W: Iberia is the ancient name of the peninsula occupied by Spain and Portugal. The term *Iberia* is still sometimes used in literature and by geographers to refer to the Iberian Peninsula.

A: **Iceland**
Q: Where is Loftleidir Airlines based?
W: Icelandic Loftleidi Inc. is a nonscheduled operator. It operates low cost flights in the northern hemisphere. Icelandair is the airline of Iceland with which we are all more familiar!

A: **Idaho, Illinois, Indiana, Iowa**
Q: What four U.S. states start with the letter I?
W: We checked all the rest and couldn't find any others. Did we miss some?

A: **Idlewild**
Q: What's the former name of John F. Kennedy Airport?
W: The New York International Airport located at Idlewild, New York, is now known as John F. Kennedy Airport. It is one of the largest and most modern commercial airports in the world.

A: **Illinois**
Q: What state can you see if you look east across the Mississippi from St. Louis?
W: And if you look west from East St. Louis, Illinois, you will see Missouri!

A: **Inca's, The**
Q: What civilization's legendary lost city can be seen at Machu Picchu?
W: Machu Picchu was once an Incan city. Its ruins lie 8,000 feet high amid the towering Andes Mountains. The Inca civilization was centered in the Andes Mountains of present-day Peru.

A: **India**
Q: Where is Darjeeling tea grown?
W: Darjeeling is the summer capital of the state of West Bengal in Eastern India. It lies on the lower slopes of the Himalayas, north of Calcutta. The well-known Darjeeling tea grows on hillsides around the city.

GEOGRAPHY

A: **India**
Q: What country is called Bharat in Hindi?
W: Hindi is the language spoken by more than two of every five persons in India, over 40 percent. Bharet is the official name for India in the Hindi language.

A: **Indian, The**
Q: What ocean does the Zambezi River empty into?
W: The Zambezi is the fourth largest river in Africa, about 1,600 miles long. It was first explored by David Livingstone of Stanley and Livingstone fame.

A: **Indian, The**
Q: What ocean surrounds the Maldive Islands?
W: The Maldive Islands are a group of 1,087 coral islands in the Indian Ocean, almost 400 miles southwest of Ceylon. About 200 of the islands are inhabited. The islands had been a British protectorate since 1887, but gained full independence in 1965.

A: **Indiana**
Q: What is "The Hoosier State"?
W: And if you can believe this – one story about how they adopted the name is that it comes from "Who's there?." Another story is that it indicates a kind of homespun wisdom, wit, and folksiness reminiscent of a less hurried and sophisticated period of American history.

A: **India's**
Q: What country's flag flies over the states of Mysore and Madras?
W: India is comprised of 22 states and nine union territories, and its geographic area is about one third the size of the U.S. Mysore is one of the states in India. Madras was also a state in India, but was renamed Tamil Nadu with Madras as its capital.

A: **Indonesia**
Q: What country does the tourist mecca of Bali belong to?
W: Bali is an island of 2,147 square miles located in the East Indies.

A: **Indus, The**
Q: What river was India named for?
W: The Indus River is the greatest river of West Pakistan. In ancient poetry of historic India, it was called "King River." The Indus rises in Tibet north of the Himalayas and empties into the Arabian Sea. The river drains an area larger than the combined areas of the states of Ohio, Indiana, Wisconsin, and Illinois. The word "India" evolved from the Sanskrit word *Sindhuh*, meaning "river."

A: **Intourist**
Q: What's the name of the Soviet Union's state-run travel agency?
W: Except for Sputnik, the Russian travel bureau that organizes youth travel on an exchange basis, and trade unions that arrange reciprocal tours for union functionaries only, Intourist is the only organization that deals with tourists inside Russia. Even the arrangements you make at home or elsewhere for your travel in Russia will eventually go through Intourist.

A: **Ireland**
Q: What country did the Romans call Hibernia?
W: Scholars believe that Julius Caesar gave the name Hibernia to Ireland. Hibernia is a variant of a Latin word meaning "winter."

A: **Ireland**
Q: Where is Bantry Bay?
W: Bays are defined as deep indentations of a shoreline and Ireland has many such indentations. Bantry Bay is located on the southwest coast of Ireland.

A: **Ireland**
Q: What's the largest country on the second largest of the British Isles?
W: The second largest island in the British Isles is Ireland, with approximately 32,599 square miles. The Irish Republic has 27,136 square miles, while Northern Ireland consists of 5,463 square miles.

A: **Israel**
Q: What country has the port of Haifa?
W: Israel is a republic in the Middle East. Its main port, Haifa, is the location of the famed Mount Carmel. Haifa is also the world headquarters of the Baha'i movement.

A: **Israel**
Q: What country is bordered by Lebanon, Syria, Jordan, and Egypt?
W: Israel faces Lebanon on the north, Syria on the northeast, Jordon on the south and southeast, Egypt on the southwest, and the Mediterranean Sea on the west. Israel was created on May 15, 1948 following the UN Partition of Palestine. It was the first Jewish state to be established in nearly 2,000 years.

A: **Israel and Jordon**
Q: What two countries border the Dead Sea?
W: Israel is on the west bank of the Dead Sea and Jordon lies on the east bank. The Dead Sea is a salt lake that lies 129 feet below sea level.

A: **Iraq**
Q: What country contains the greater lengths of the Tigris and Euphrates rivers?
W: Iraq is an Arab republic in southwestern Asia. Baghdad is the capital and largest city. Today the Euphrates and Tigris Rivers join at Al-Qurna, Iraq, about 120 miles from the Persian Gulf, to form a single river called the Shatt-al-Arab.

A: **Italian**
Q: What's the official language of the Most Serene Republic of San Marino?
W: San Marino, the smallest republic in the world, is located on the Italian Peninsula on the slopes of the Apennines Mountains. It is noted for its tourist trade and its many issues of colorful postage stamps.

A: **Italian**
Q: What nationality is a Sicilian?
W: Italy is a boot-shaped peninsula that juts into the Mediterranean Sea. Sicily, a triangular island, lies like a football just off the toe of the Italian boot and is one of the seven clearly marked national regions of Italy. Consequently, a Sicilian is also an Italian.

A: **Italy**
Q: Where's the Blue Grotto?
W: It's on the Isle of Capri. The Blue Grotto is a cave accessible only by boat. Sunlight entering through the water that fills most of the entrance produces an extraordinary blue light. Nearby are the other grottos: the Green Grotto, the Yellow Grotto, and the Pink and White Grotto, each so named because of the refraction of light from the walls and waters through the entrance.

A: **Italy**
Q: What country owns Elba, Capri and Ischia Islands?
W: Elba is a little island 18 miles long, 12 miles wide. Capri is even smaller, only four miles long and two miles wide and is the ancient home of the famed Blue Grotto. Ischia is more than twice the size of Capri but still small enough to enjoy if you don't mind bumping into hundreds of vactioners!

A: **Italy**
Q: Where's Lake Como?
W: Lake Como is bordered by towns like Como Bellagio and Colico. It lies in a setting of beautiful villas, lush foliage, and flowers. This lake, along with Garda, Maggiore, and Lugano, lies at the foot of the Alps.

A: **Italy**
Q: What country surrounds San Marino, the world's smallest republic?
W: San Marino covers only 23 square miles. It lies in northern Italy on the eastern slopes of the Apennines Mountains, overlooking the Adriatic Sea. The country issues many colorful postage stamps and is believed to be the world's oldest republic. Because of its hard to reach location, San Marino has resisted enemy invasions throughout the ages.

A: **Italy**
Q: What country brews Peroni beer?
W: Birra Peroni has been brewed in Italy since 1846. It is somewhat cloudy because of yeast, which is said to be a good sign, and has an above average body and flavor.

A: **Italy**
Q: What country consumes the most wine per capita?
W: *WRONG!* France is the leading consumer of wine, averaging .44 pints of wine per person per day. Maybe the Birra Peroni (discussed above) is replacing wine as the dinner drink in Italy!

A: **Italy**
Q: What country would you visit to ski in the Dolomites?
W: The Dolomites are a part of the Alps in northeastern Italy and the Austrian Tyrol. The main center of this tourist and mountain climbing region is Cortina d'Ampezzo. Another resort is Ortiser, which has a narrow gauge railroad.

A: **Italy**
Q: Where do you go to row on the Po?
W: The Po is one the chief rivers of Italy, whose primary value is that its waters irrigate the rich Po Valley. The Po ultimately flows eastward into the Adriatic Sea.

A: **It's the easternmost point in the U.S.**
Q: What's the distinction of West Quoddy Head, Maine?
W: Maine forms the northeastern tip of the U.S. West Quoddy Head is located on the southeast coast of Maine in the Grand Manan Channel that separates Canada and the U.S. West Quoddy Head is at 66 degrees 57 minutes west. The easternmost town is Eastport, Maine.

A: **It's the highest city in the U.S.**
Q: What's the claim to fame of Leadville, Colorado?
W: Leadville, Colorado, is often called "Cloud City" because it is the highest city in the U.S. The city was incorporated in 1878 and is located 10,200 feet above sea level. It was named Leadville because of the large quantities of lead ore in that area.

A: **It's the world's highest city**
Q: What's the claim to fame of Lhasa, Tibet?
W: It has an elevation of 12,087 feet above sea level.

A: **Ivanov**
Q: What's the most common Russian surname?
W: It translates to "son of Ivan" and comes from the Slavic "John." "Ivan Ivanov" is used in Russia as a term similiar to our "John Smith," typical American citizen.

A: **Iwo Jima**
Q: What Pacific island boasts Mount Suribachi?
W: Iwo Jima is the middle island of the three Volcano Islands or Kazan Retto in the northwestern Pacific Ocean. Iwo Jima is about five miles long and about two and one-half miles wide at its widest point. At the southern end is the 546-foot high cone of Mount Suribachi, a volcano. *Iwo Jima* means "Sulfur Island." The photo of the U.S. flag being raised on Iwo Jima is considered the best portrait of World War II and won a Pulitzer Prize for its portrayal of the War.

J

A: **Jakarta**
Q: What's the capital of Indonesia?
W: Djakarta (Jakarta) is also the chief port of Indonesia. Formerly called Batavia, *Djakarta* means "important city." The city was founded by the Dutch in the early 1600s and was the capital of the Netherlands East Indies under the Dutch.

A: **Japan**
Q: What country forms a 2,000-mile archipelago along the east coast of Asia?
W: Japan is an island country in the Pacific Ocean, lying along the eastern coast of Asia. Four large islands and many smaller ones make up the country. Only one fifth of the land is suitable for cultivation or urban development.

A: **Japan**
Q: What country is the world's largest exporter of frogs' legs?
W: We couldn't verify this one. We did find out, however, that fishing is second only to agriculture as Japan's most important food industry.

A: **Japan**
Q: What country suffers from the most earthquakes?
W: Each year there are about 1,500 earth tremors in the islands, but most of them cause little damage. In 1923, however, the earthquake in Tokyo and Yokohama and the fires that followed it killed about 100,000 people.

A: **Japan**
Q: What country did venetian blinds originate in?
W: This window blind made of slats was given the name venetian because of their wide use in Venice in the 1600s. Similar curtains had been developed earlier by the Japanese who used bamboo rods.

A: **Japan's**
Q: What country's currency is considered the most difficult to counterfeit?
W: Many different colors are used in painting all Japanese bank notes and the 5,000 and 10,000 yen notes are printed on watermarked paper that is sold only to the government printing office. Could be very hard to duplicate!

A: **Japan's**
Q: What country's people stand up for the anthem "The Reign of Our Emperor"?
W: Kimi-ga-yo (The Sovereigns Reign) is the national anthem of Japan.

A: **Jefferson City**
Q: What's the capital of Missouri?
W: Missouri is called the "Show me" state. Famous Missourians include: Harry Truman, Walt Disney, General Omar Bradley, General Pershing, and Mark Twain.

A: **Jerez**
Q: What Spanish city gave its name to sherry?
W: Sherry is a strong, light-colored wine of southern Spain. The city of Jerez is located on the southwest coast of Spain, on the Atlantic Ocean side of the Strait of Gibraltar.

A: **Jerusalem**
Q: What's the capital of Israel?
W: Jerusalem is a holy city of Jews, Christians, and Moslems, part of which is in Israel and part in Jordan. The New City of Jerusalem is the capital of Israel, and most of the inhabitants of the New City are Jews. The Old City belongs to the Hashemite Kingdom of Jordon. Two thirds of the Old City people are Moslems, while the remaining one third are Christians.

A: **Jerusalem**
Q: Where's the Wailing Wall?
W: The Wailing Wall, also called The Western Wall, is a high wall in Jerusalem and the only remains of the Second Temple of Jeruselem,

which was destroyed by the Romans in 70 A.D. It is about 160 feet long and about 60 feet high and dates from the second century B.C. In services at the Western Wall, the Jews recall their traditions and sufferances, while wailing and praying; thus, it was named the Wailing Wall. The control of the Wall was regained by the Jews from Jordan in the fighting of June, 1967.

A: **Johannesburg**
Q: What African city is built on gold?
W: This city is the largest city in the Union of South Africa. It lies in the Southern Transvaal Province in the heart of the Witwatersrand, the richest gold field in the world. Gold has made Johannesburg the most important industrial and commercial city in the Union.

A: **Johansson**
Q: What's the most common surname in Sweden?
W: Those names describing the bearer of the English equivalent of "son of John" also include Johanson and Jonsson in Sweden.

A: **John F. Kennedy Airport**
Q: What sits on a 5,000-acre landfill at the head of Jamaica Bay, near New York City?
W: The JFK Airport is the New York International Airport, formerly Idlewild.

A: **Johnson**
Q: What's the second-most common surname in America?
W: The most common, naturally, is Smith. There were 2,382,509 Smiths in the U.S. in 1973. What's in a name anyway?!

A: **July 4, 1776**
Q: What's inscribed on the tablet held by the Statue of Liberty?
W: The Statue of Liberty is located on Liberty Island in New York Harbor and is the largest statue ever made. France gave the statue to the U.S. in 1884 as a symbol of liberty and friendship. The woman holds a torch in her raised right hand and a

tablet bearing the date of July 4, 1776 in her left hand.

A: **Juneau**
Q: What's the northernmost U.S. state capital?
W: All of Alaska is north of 50 degrees north latitude. No other U.S. state lies this far north.

A: **K2**
Q: What's the second-highest mountain in the world?
W: It's also known as Godwin Austen and is located in Kashmir. Its 28,250-foot elevation is second only to Everest's 29,028, which is in Nepal-Tibet.

A: **Kabul**
Q: What's the capital of Afghanistan?
W: Afghanistan is located between Soviet Central Asia and the Indian Subcontinent. Kabul had a 1979 population of 891,750. In December, 1979, the USSR began a massive airlift into Kabul, and a Soviet-backed coup on December 27 ended the old regime. Fighting continued in 1983 as the Soviets found themselves engaged in a guerrilla war.

A: **Kampala**
Q: What's the capital of Uganda?
W: This capital city had a 1980 population of 458,000. The African nation of Uganda was controlled by General Idi Amin from 1971 to April, 1979, when rebels finally forced him from office.

A: **Kansas and Missouri**
Q: What two states have a Kansas City?
W: These cities are contiguous and are located on the Missouri River at the mouth of the Kansas River.

A: **Kentucky**
Q: What U.S. state is Mammoth Cave National Park in?
W: This national park is located in west central Kentucky. It was established in 1941 to protect an extensive system of limestone caverns of which over 150 miles on five levels have been explored. Mummified Indian bodies have been found in the caverns.

A: **Kentucky**
Q: What U.S. state is Fort Knox in?
W: The United States Bullion Depository at Fort Knox is 30 miles southwest of Louisville, Kentucky. It has been the principal federal depository of U.S. gold since December, 1936. The gold is stored in 446,000 mint bars of 400 troy ounces each.

A: **Kentucky**
Q: What state boasts the Duncan Tavern Museum, where Daniel Boone often drank?
W: The Duncan Tavern Museum is in Paris, Kentucky. Built in 1788, today it is an historical and genealogical library that houses, among other things, the original manuscripts of John Fox, Jr., author of *Little Shepherd of Kingdom Come*.

A: **Khartoum**
Q: What's the capital of the Sudan?
W: Khartoum became the capital of Sudan in 1830 and literally translated means "elephant's trunk"! Sudan, called Nubia in ancient days, is the largest country in Africa and lies on the Red Sea.

A: **Khartoum, Sudan**
Q: What national capital rises where the Blue Nile and White Nile Rivers converge?
W: Khartoum lies south of the junction of the Blue Nile and the White Nile. The town was originally an Egyptian army camp (1821).

A: **Kremlin, The**
Q: Where are 47 czars buried?
W: Our research indicates 46 tombs! They are buried at the Cathedral of the Archangel. And, as an interesting sidelight, each one's likeness is painted on the wall above his tomb! Now you can see just what Ivan the Terrible looked like!

A: **Kuwait**
Q: What desert country borders Saudi Arabia, Iraq and the Persian Gulf?
W: Kuwait is an independent Arab country on the Arabian Peninsula at the northern end of the Persian Gulf. Iraq borders Kuwait on the north and west, and Saudi Arabia lies to the south. Oil, first exported in 1946, is the fiscal mainstay of this tiny country.

A: LBJ Ranch, The
Q: What famed ranch can you see from the Ranch Road No. 1 near Stonewall, Texas?
W: U.S. Rt. 290 southeastward from Fredericksburg takes you straight to Stonewall. Once you are on Ranch Road No. 1 you will see the Ranch headquarters across the Pedernales River. Below the point where the Ranch Road exits to US 290 you can see LBJ's boyhood school in Albert, where they say he told his classmates "Someday, I'm going to be President of the United States."

A: "La Marseillaise"
Q: What's the national anthem of France?
W: A young captain of the engineers named Claude Joseph Rouget de Lisle wrote this song during the French Revolution. It is believed that he composed the words and the music in one night. France adopted the song as its national anthem in 1875.

A: La Paz, Bolivia
Q: What South American capital is the world's highest?
W: Sucre is the legal capital of Bolivia; La Paz is the administrative and de facto capital and the largest city of Bolivia. La Paz is 11,926 feet above sea level.

A: La Paz, Bolivia
Q: What South American city has the world's highest commercial landing field?
W: Kennedy International Airport is located five miles from La Paz (and you thought it was in New York!). El Alto airport at La Paz is 13,385 feet above sea level.

A: Lake Erie
Q: What lake is Buffalo on?
W: Lake Erie lies on the international border between the U.S. and Canada and is the farthest south of the five Great Lakes. Buffalo, New York, was where the first steamboat on the Upper Great Lakes was built; it was called "Walk-in-the-Water"!

A: Lake Erie
Q: Which of the Great Lakes does Pennsylvania border?
W: Lake Erie is the only Great Lake to border Pennsylvania, but Pennsylvania is not the only state to border Lake Erie. Others are Ohio, Michigan, and New York and the Canadian province of Ontario.

A: Lake Maracaibo
Q: What's the largest lake in South America?
W: Lake Maracaibo is the trade waterway and rich petroleum region of northern Venezuela. It is connected with the Caribbean Sea by a short channel and the Gulf of Maracaibo. The lake is important because of the large number of oil wells in it and on its shores.

A: Lake Michigan
Q: Which is the only one of the Great Lakes without an international border running through it?
W: It is the only one of the Great Lakes that is contained entirely within the continental U.S. The others are shared with Canada.

A: Lake Michigan
Q: Which of the Great Lakes shares its name with a U.S. state?
W: Lake Michigan is the largest body of fresh water in the U.S. It is the third largest of the Great Lakes.

A: Lake Michigan
Q: What lake is Sheboygan on?
W: Sheboygan is located on the western shore of Lake Michigan in Wisconsin, at the mouth of the Sheboygan River. Its Indian name means "rumbling underground" in reference to the falls upriver.

A: Lake Ontario
Q: What's the smallest of the Great Lakes?
W: When considering the area in square miles of water surface, that's correct: 7,550 square miles in Canada and the U.S. However, when considering total square miles of both surface water and the drainage basin in the U.S. and Canada, it's fourth in size of the five Great Lakes, slightly larger than Lake Erie.

A: Lake Ontario
Q: Which of the Great Lakes do all the others flow into?
W: Lake Ontario forms an important link in the St. Lawrence Seaway System. The system starts at the St. Louis River in Minnesota and flows through the Great Lakes. The St. Lawrence proper extends from the eastern exit of Lake Ontario.

A: Lake Superior
Q: What's the largest freshwater lake in the world?
W: It has an area of 31,700 square miles. It's dwarfed in comparison, however, to the largest saltwater lake, the Caspian Sea, which covers an area of 143,244 square miles.

A: Lake Superior
Q: What's the largest lake in the Americas?
W: Lake Superior is the largest and most inland of the five Great Lakes. It is part of the U.S.-Canadian border.

A: Lake Titicaca
Q: What South American body of water is known as "The Lake of the Clouds"?
W: Lake Titicaca lies at the highest level above the sea (12,507 ft.) of any large lake in the world. It is in a basin surrounded by two ranges of the Andes Mountains. The lake forms part of the boundary between Bolivia and Peru.

A: Lake Titicaca
Q: What's the highest navigable lake in the world?
W: Lake Titicaca lies across the border of Bolivia and Peru. It is both the highest lake in the world and the highest navigable lake. It has an area of 3,500 square miles, and steamboats regularly sail on it.

A: Lake Victoria
Q: What's the third largest lake in the world?
W: Care to know which is first? It's the Caspian Sea in the USSR and Iran. The largest freshwater lake in the world is Lake Superior and it's second largest among both salt – and freshwater lakes. Located on the border of Kenya, Uganda, and Tanzania, Lake Victoria is the largest lake in Africa, the second largest freshwater lake in the world, and the third largest lake overall in the world.

A: Lake Victoria
Q: What lake is the source of the White Nile?
W: The Nile River issues from the northern end of Lake Victoria at Jinja, Uganda. It merges with the Blue Nile near Khartoum, Sudan, and enters the Mediterranean Sea north of Cairo.

A: Lake Victoria
Q: What's the largest lake in Africa?
W: It's also the third largest in the world! Owens Falls Dam, built across the Nile in 1954, has raised Lake Victoria's level about three feet to an elevation of 3,723 feet above sea level. The lake was named in honor of Queen Victoria of Britain.

A: Lake Zurich
Q: What lake does Zurich overlook?
W: Zurich, the only large town on the lake, is located at the norwestern end in an alpine setting.

A: Las Vegas
Q: What U.S. city has the most chapels per capita?
W: It's better known for its gambling casinos and nightclubs, but it seems that every other 100 feet has a wedding chapel open 24 hours! Vegas became a boom town in the 30s during the construction of Hoover Dam and was a way station for the armed forces, as well.

A: Las Vegas
Q: Where did gangster Bugsy Siegel build the Flamingo Hotel in 1946?
W: In 1931,Nevada legalized gambling, and small casinos began to appear. The city's first big gambling casino opened in 1946. The Flamingo was the third hotel built on U.S. 91, now "The Strip." Benjamin "Bugsy" Siegel had three reasons to come to Vegas: he was wanted for murder in New York City, he was setting up a syndicate-backed book and wire service for people back home, and he was obsessed with the idea of a superluxurious hotel-casino far enough out to attract people from Los Angeles before they went somewhere else. It was a fantastically lavish olive-green castle.

A: Leaning Tower of Pisa, The
Q: What is predicted to topple over between 2010 and 2020?
W: If is often considered one of the seven wonders of the modern world. The tower tips so far to one side that it looks as though it would fall, but it has stood for hundreds of years. The ground began to sink after the first three stories of the tower were built, and the tower has continued to tip, about one foot in the last 100 years. Cement was poured into the soil beneath the tower to prevent further leaning.

A: Leaning Tower of Pisa, The
Q: What Italian landmark has 296 steps?
W: The Leaning Tower is 179 feet tall. The walls are 13 feet thick at the base and between 6 and 7 feet thick at the top. An inner staircase of 296 steps leads to the top.

A: Lebanon
Q: What's the only Arab country without a desert?
W: Lebanon is a small independent republic at the eastern end of the Mediterranean Sea. Beirut is the capital. Lebanon is made up of three geographic areas: a narrow coastal strip, the Lebanon Mountains, and a fertile inland plain called the Bekaa (note: no desert region).

A: leek, The
Q: What vegetable is the Welsh national emblem?
W: Leek is a vegetable that resembles the onion but has a mild flavor. It is related to onions, garlic, shallots, and chives. Leeks are not often grown in home gardens and have little commerical value; however, the Welsh like to eat them and have made the leek their national flower.

A: left, The
Q: What hand do Arabian desert nomads not eat with?
W: According to the Information Center in the Saudi Arabian Consulate Office in Washington, D.C. the nomads would only use the right hand to eat with. All motions are initiated with the right hand. The left hand is used for hygiene purposes.

A: Leningrad
Q: What Russian city used to be called St. Petersburg and Petrograd?
W: Leningrad has had three different names. Peter the Great founded it in 1703 as his capital and named it St. Petersburg. When Russia went to war against Germany in 1914, the name was changed to Petrograd, which means Peter's City, because the Russians wanted to eliminate the German ending -burg – When

Lenin, organizer of the Communist government in Russia, died in 1924, it was renamed in his honor.

A: **Leningrad**
Q: What Russian city boasts the Hermitage Museum?
W: Lengingrad has about 50 museums, but probably the best known is the Hermitage, famed throughout the world for its art masterpieces. It was founded by Catherine the Great as a court museum.

A: **Lesbonians**
Q: What are the residents of the island of Lesbos called?
W: The island of Lesbos is a part of the Grecian archipelago, which includes some islands formed by ancient volcanos and some by pure white marble. Be careful with its pronunciation.

A: **Library of Congress, The**
Q: What building built in 1800 contains 327 miles of book shelves?
W: These shelves hold perhaps the greatest collection of books in the world. The number of volumes exceed 79 million, and by 1982 its shelves extended to 532 miles!

A: **Libya's**
Q: What country's capital is Tripoli?
W: Libya is an independent kingdom on the coast of North Africa. It has three provinces: Tripoli, Cyrenaica, and Fezzan. Tripoli is on a rocky promontory overlooking the sea, due south of Sicily.

A: **Lido, The**
Q: What famed strip of land is a 15-minute boat trip across the Venetian Lagoon from Venice?
W: The Lido is a sandbar in the lagoon formed by the mouths of the Po and Piave rivers. This is a famous resort area where the water is very warm and so shallow you have to wade out one half mile before you can swim.

A: **Lincoln**
Q: Where is the University of Nebraska?
W: The "Cornhuskers" have been there since 1869. Great football country! Go Big Red!

A: **Lisbon**
Q: What capital city overlooks the Tagus River?
W: Lisbon is the capital and largest city of Portugal. It lies about two thirds of the way down Portugal's west coast overlooking a broad bay formed by the mouth of the Tagus River.

A: **Lisbon**
Q: Which is the farthest west — Dublin, Glasgow or Lisbon?
W: A look at the world map will show that Lisbon is closer to 10 degrees longitude than either Glasgow or Dublin. All three do lie between the prime meridian and 10 degrees west longitude.

A: **Lisbon and Madrid**
Q: What two Iberian cities does the "Lusitania Express" run between?
W: Lusitania was a country in western Hispania, an ancient territory that included the present-day Spain and Portugal. The Lusitania Express is a train that runs daily between Madrid and Lisbon. The night train, called the Lusitania Express, takes 12 hours to complete the trip but does offer sleepers and couchettes. The day train, called the Lisbon Express, takes only 10 hours.

A: **Little Rock**
Q: What U.S. state capital was once called La Petite Roche?
W: The French explorer Bernard de la Harpe, who explored the Arkansas River in 1722, named the river bluff La Petite Roche (Little Rock). Little Rock's nickname is the City of Roses because of the many roses raised there.

A: **Liverpudlian**
Q: What's the term for a resident of Liverpool?
W: Liverpool is the sixth largest city in England. A resident of Liverpool, in either Liverpool, England or Liverpool, Nova Scotia, Canada, is called a "Liverpudlian."

A: **London**
Q: What city boasts the Billingsgate fishmarket?
W: Only a few thousand people have homes in "The City," the oldest part of London since the land is too valuable to be used for dwellings. Smithfield, the London meat market, and Billingsgate, the fish market, stand in "The City." The abusive language that the fishmongers often use has come to be called "billingsgate."

A: **London**
Q: What city has the world's longest subway system?
W: The subway in London began operating in 1863 and has been extended and improved ever since. Some of its stations are 200 feet below ground and are reached by elevators and escalators. It is locally called "the tube" and currently has 260 miles of route. New York's subway has the most stations, and Moscow has the busiest system.

A: **London**
Q: What city gained renown for its pea-soup fogs?
W: It is estimated that a typical heavy London fog contains 820,000 dust particles per cubic inch. London fogs have been decreasing as more people are using gas and electricity for heating and power.

A: **London**
Q: Where is Euston Station?
W: Euston Station is the terminal of the London Midland Region train serving Liverpool and Manchester. It was rebuilt in 1963 to 1968, and the statue in the forecourt is of Robert Stephenson, one of the two people who designed the original station in 1836.

A: **London**
Q: Where is Kew Gardens?
W: Close, but not correct. Kew Gardens are located in the city of Kew near London. It is a botanical collection begun back in the 1600s. The garden's publications include "The Kew Bulletin" and "Index Kewensis," which maintain a record of all described higher plant species of the world.

A: **London**
Q: What city has a district called Elephant and Castle?
W: Elephant and Castle is a busy traffic center on the south side of the London Bridge. It was redesigned in 1957 to 1964 as two roundabouts with a shopping area. The name "Elephant and Castle" came from a former tavern in the area.

A: **London**
Q: Where is Drury Lane?
W: Drury Lane is part of the theater district and also the oldest theater in the city.

A: **London**
Q: Where is Bond Street?
W: Actually, there is "Old Bond Street" created by Sir Thomas Bond in 1686 from a muddy country lane. It leads out of Piccadilly to join "New Bond Street," built in 1700. It's there that the upper middle class built country houses to escape the smoke and noise of Westminster and the city. It has become one of the most famous shopping streets in the world.

A: **London**
Q: What major city is served by Gatwick Airport?
W: London is also served by Heathrow Airport.

A: **London**
Q: What city dug the first subway?
W: The first subway was dug in London in 1863. The people of London, however, use the term "subway" to refer to a pedestrian tunnel. They call their underground train "the tube."

A: **London**
Q: Where is the Admiralty Arch?
W: One passes under the Admiralty Arch to enter St. James Park and has a distant view of Buckingham Palace from the spot. The Arch was designed by Aston Webb as part of the national memorial to Queen Victoria.

A: **London and Edinburgh**
Q: What cities were joined by the "Flying Scotsman"?
W: The "Flying Scotsman" is a high speed train that covers nearly 400 miles in five hours. The trip from London through Newcastle upon Tyne to Edinburgh takes you through much rural scenery and past many historic sites.

A: **London and New York**
Q: What two cities did Freddie Laker first join with cut-rate flights?
W: Sir Freddie Laker's autobiography, "Fly Me, I'm Freddie," tells about the life and times of the man who broke the airline cartel and made air travel available to everyone. There was a six-year battle with British and American aviation authorities before Freddie was able to bring cheaper fares to trans-Atlantic flights.

A: **London Bridge**
Q: What's no longer falling down in Lake Havasu City, Arizona?
W: In the 1960s the New London Bridge in London was replaced, but its masonry facing was dismantled and shipped to the U.S. where it was re-erected in Lake Havasu City, Arizona, as a tourist attraction.

A: **"Lone Star State, The"**
Q: What's the nickname of Texas?
W: Texas is called the "Lone Star State" because of the single star in its state flag. Texas was ruled by Mexico until the Texas Revolution in 1836, it then became an independent country. In 1846 it became a state, but retained the single star in its state flag as representation of its former independence.

A: **Long Island**
Q: What's the biggest island in New York state?
W: Long Island is the largest at a length of 120 miles and a width of up to 40 miles. It lies between the Atlantic Ocean and Long Island Sound, as well as the East River and New York Bay. Staten Island is New York City's largest island.

A: **Los Angeles**
Q: Which is farthest east – Reno, Nevada, or Los Angeles, California?
W: Correct. Reno is at 119 degrees 48 minutes west, while Los Angeles is at 118 degrees 15 minutes west. Reno was named for General Jesse Lee Reno, a Union soldier killed in the Civil War. The full name of Los Angeles is *El Pueblo de Nuestra Senora la reina de Los Angeles*: "The Town of Our Lady the Queen of the Angels." It was called El Pueblo for many years.

A: **Louisiana**
Q: What U.S. state has an annual Gumbo Festival with a 4,000-gallon pot?
W: The festival is held in late October, just after Ohio's "Circleville Pumpkin Show," which boasts the largest pumpkin pie baked, a little over 260 pounds!

A: **Louvre, The**
Q: What's the largest museum in the world?
W: The Louvre in Paris covers 40 acres of land and holds eight miles of galleries. It was built as a fort in the 1100s. Among other works, it houses the Mona Lisa and Venus de Milo.

A: **Luxembourg**
Q: What Grand Duchy is bordered by Belgium, West Germany, and France?
W: Luxembourg is such a tiny country that you can drive in any direction from its center and reach a border within a half hour. That's small!

GEOGRAPHY

M

A: **Macy's, New York**
Q: What's the world's largest department store?
W: R.H. Macy and Co., Inc. is at Broadway and 34th street in New York City. The store covers 50.5 acres of floor space and employs 12,000 people who handle 400,000 items. The sales of the company and its subsidiaries in 1982 totaled almost $3 billion. Mr. Rowland Hussey Macy's sales on his first day, October 27, 1858, at his fancy goods store on 6th Avenue were recorded as $11.06. Talk about growth!

A: **Madagascar**
Q: What major island lies 250 miles off the southeastern coast of Africa?
W: Madagascar is the fourth largest island in the world after Greenland, New Guinea, and Borneo. It is situated in the Indian Ocean and is separated from Africa by the Mozambique Channel.

A: **Madame Tussaud's**
Q: What London museum features a Chamber of Horrors?
W: Madame Tussaud's, located on Marleybone Road in central London, has become known throughout the world for its waxworks of the famous. Almost every distinguished victim of the guillotine was molded by Madame Tussaud or her uncle. In the Chamber of Horrors, opened in 1980, special effects include the shadow of Jack the Ripper. It's no wonder that a nickname for Madame Tussaud is "Madame of the Macabre."

A: **Madrid's**
Q: What capital city's section centers on Puerta del Sol?

W: Madrid, capital of Spain, is characterized by two important thoroughfares that form a cross. The point where the two arteries intersect is called Plaza de las Cibeles. If you go west from Cibeles on the horizontal thoroughfare, Alcala, the first major square you reach is the Puerto del Sol. This is literally where Spain begins, because all principal highways going into northern, southern, eastern, and western Spain emerge from the "Kilometer O" point in the center of the square.

A: **magnolia, The**
Q: What's the state flower of Mississippi?
W: Actually the evergreen magnolia flower is the state flower of Louisiana and Mississippi. It has laurel-like leaves and large white or pink flowers. This type of magnolia often grows as high as 100 feet.

A: **Maine**
Q: What U.S. state borders only one other?
W: The only state that borders Maine is New Hampshire, to the west. It's bounded on the north and northwest by the Canadian province of Quebec, on the north and northeast by the Canadian province of New Brunswick, and on the south and southwest by the Atlantic Ocean.

A: **Mali**
Q: What country is Timbuktu in?
W: Timbuktu is a town of Mali, West Africa on the south edge of the Sahara Desert. The town is notable for its commerce and also as a center of Mohammedan learning. It is also the focus of caravan trade in West Central Africa.

A: **Manhattan**
Q: What borough forms the central core of New York City?
W: Manhattan is one of the five boroughs comprising New York City. The others are the Bronx, Brooklyn, Queens, and Staten Island. However, it is Manhattan that contains the main financial, commercial, and residential sections of the city.

A: **Maori, The**
Q: What Polynesian people inhabit New Zealand?
W: The explorers Tasman (1642) and Cooke (1769) have been credited with the discovery of New Zealand, a collection of islands in the southwest Pacific Ocean. The evolution of the Maori race is laced with legend. Students of the Maori race claim that the brown-skinned warriors came from a mystery-shrouded island named Haviiki in the North Pacific to take the land they called Hotearoa (The Land of The Long White Cloud), better known as New Zealand. After many battles with land hungry nations, the Maori managed to save themselves from extinction and emerge as a vital, virile people.

A: **Marble**
Q: What is the Taj Mahal made of?
W: The Taj Mahal, a mausoleum of white marble and alabaster, located in Agra, India, was built by the fifth Mogul emperor of Hindustan, Shah Jahan, between 1630 and 1652, as a burial place for his favorite wife, Mumtaz Muhall. It has often been described as the most beautiful 17th-century building in the world.

A: **Mariana Trench, The**
Q: What Pacific trench is the world's deepest at 36,198 feet?
W: Until 1959, the deepest point of Mariana Trench, located in the west Pacific, was recorded as 35,760 feet. In March 1959, the USSR research ship *Vityaz* claimed that at the longitude and latitude assigned to the deepest part of the trench (Challenger Deep) it was actually 36,198 feet.

A: **Marijuana**
Q: What is "ganja" in Jamaica?
W: Anyone who has been to Jamaica KNOWS that ganja is quite abundant there. In fact, there's a famous place on Negril Beach called Mrs. Brown's that serves "ganja" tea. But if you're caught in possession, watch out. The fine is several years of hard labor!

A: **Marseilles**
Q: What's the largest port in France?
W: Marseilles, located on the French Riviera, may only be the third largest city in France, but it is the premier port of the country. A crossroads of world traffic, the city is ancient, founded in the sixth century B.C. by Greeks from the city of Phocaea.

A: **Martha's Vineyard**
Q: What was once called Martin's Vineyard?
W: Martha's Vineyard, Massachusetts, is an island in the Atlantic Ocean. It is actually a terminal moraine formed at the end of the last great glacial period. We could find no record of its being known as "Martin's Vineyard." The first cartographic record of the island was made by Giovanni de Verrazano who named it Louisa, but the name did not stick. The naming of the island in 1602 is credited to Bartholomew Gosnold. He chose the name in honor of his youngest daughter, Martha, and of the many wild grapes he found growing on the island.

A: **Mason-Dixon line, The**
Q: What did Jeremiah Dixon and Charles Mason survey starting in 1763?
W: Obviously the Mason-Dixon line was named after its surveyors. It marked the boundary between Pennsylvania and Maryland and was regarded as the demarcation line between the North and South in the years leading up to the Civil War.

A: **Maxim's**
Q: What Paris restaurant is at 3 Rue Royal?
W: That certainly is the address for this famous Paris restaurant that has developed a global reputation. The decor is Art Noveau, the clientele is sophisticated, and the food is *tres bien*! We have it on good authority that some dishes to try are the duck with peaches specialty, *caneton nantais aux peches*, or *cuilles de bombes au raisins de muscat*.

A: **Mecca**
Q: Where is the Holy Kaaba?
W: The Kaaba, or inner sanctuary, is located in El Haram Courtyard of Mecca. It is a windowless, cube-shaped building believed to have been built by the Hebrew patriarch Abraham. In the southeast corner of the Kaaba is the Black Stone, supposedly given to Abraham by the Angel Gabriel.

A: **Mecca**
Q: What is the holy city of Islam?
W: Mecca, one of the two capitals of Saudi Arabia, is the birthplace of Mohammed and the most sacred of the Moslem Holy Cities. It is visited by tens of thousands of pilgrims annually.

A: **Mediterranean, The**
Q: What sea did the Romans call "mare nostrum"?
W: *Nostrum* is the Latin for "ours," *mare* is Latin for "sea." Some of the most ancient civilizations flourished around the Mediterranean. Carthage, Greece, Sicily, and Rome were rivals for dominance of its shores and trade. Under the Roman Empire it became virtually a Roman lake and was called "mare nostrum." Later, the Byzantine Empire and the Arabs dominated the Mediterranean.

A: **Mediterranean, The**
Q: What body of water is the old port of Marseilles on?
W: Marseilles has been called the most famous of Mediterranean port-towns, and claims an ancestry that few, if any, western ports can rival. Originally Greek, then Carthaginian, then Greek again, and for many centuries independent, it later became a principal port of the Roman Empire. It was annexed to the French monarchy in 1481.

A: **Mediterranean, The**
Q: What's the world's largest sea?
W: *Wrong*! According to the *1984 World Almanac and Book of Facts*, the South China Sea (1,148,500 square miles) and the Caribbean Sea (971,400 square miles) out rank the Mediterranean's 969,100 square miles.

A: **Mediterranean, The**
Q: What sea separates Naples and Algiers?
W: Naples is a seaport on the southwest side of Italy. Algiers is the capital of Algiers on the Mediterranean coast.

A: **Mediterranean Sea, The**
Q: What body of water does the Rhone River empty into?
W: The Rhone River starts in central Switzerland and flows 505 miles southwest to the Mediterranean, emptying near Arles, France.

A: **Mersey, The**
Q: What river runs through Liverpool?
W: The English Mersey is 70 miles long and empties into the Irish Sea. There is also an Australian Mersey which is 100 miles long and was named after the British River. Do you remember the famous song by Jerry and the Pacemakers, "Ferry 'cross The Mersey"?

A: **Mexico**
Q: Where is the Yucatan Peninsula?
W: It is located in the extreme southern end of Mexico. It juts into the Gulf of Mexico and the Caribbean Sea. It is as close to Cuba as Cuba is to the state of Florida.

A: **Mexico**
Q: Where's Tabasco?
W: Unless you're referring to the sauce commonly used in chili or on scrambled eggs, you'll find that State of Tabasco in southeast Mexico, just south of the Bay of Campeche. The state has an approximate population of 767,000. Tabasco is also the name of a 300-mile-long river in southeast Mexico.

A: **Mexico City**
Q: What's the largest city in Latin America?
W: The population of the metropolitan area of greater Mexico City in 1979 was published as 13,950,364. Next in line is Sao Paulo, Brazil, with a 1980 population of 7,033,529.

A: **Mexico City**
Q: What's the oldest capital city in the Americas?
W: The traditional date for the founding of Mexico City is 1325. In 1535, Mexico City became the capital of the viceroyalty of New Spain. In case you're wondering, the oldest capital city in the world is Damascus, the capital of Syria. It has been continuously inhabited since 2500 B.C.

A: **Miami**
Q: What U.S. city has been called Little Havana?
W: The Miami area has received well over 200,000 refugees since Castro's 1959 takeover of Cuba. The 1981 population of the city was 346,865, with 194,087 of Spanish origin.

A: **Miami Beach**
Q: What is Miami's most famous suburb?
W: Until 1912 the Miami Beach area was a mangrove swamp with coconut and avocado plantations. A bridge and causeway were then built, and the area was dredged to form an island with an eight mile beach. The city is now a year round resort and convention center.

A: **Michigan**
Q: What state is across the lake from Milwaukee?
W: Just look at a map of Lake Michigan and surrounding areas and you will discover that Grand Rapids, Michigan, is almost directly across the lake from Milwaukee.

A: **Milan**
Q: What Italian city is home to da Vinci's *The Last Supper*?
W: The famous painting entitled *The Last Supper* is painted on the wall of the refectory of Santa Maria delle Grazie on the Corso Magenta. The artwork is currently being restored after centuries of deterioration from damp weather and war.

A: **Minneapolis**
Q: Which is farthest north — Milwaukee, Minneapolis, or Toronto?
W: They're close but if you check your atlas, you'll discover that Minneapolis, at 45 degrees north beats Toronto at 43 degrees 42 minutes north, and Milwaukee at 43 degrees 3 minutes north. Details, details...

A: **Minneapolis and St. Paul**
Q: What are the Twin Cities?
W: Minneapolis was incorporated in 1856. Its name was derived from the Sioux word *minne* meaning "water" and the Greek word *polis* meaning "city." It has 22 lakes and lagoons within its limits. St. Paul is the capital of Minnesota. The city was known as "Pig's Eye" until 1841, because the first person to stake a claim there was Pierre "Pig's Eye" Parrant.

A: **Minnesota**
Q: What U.S. state boasts Leif Ericson Park?
W: This park is not a national park. It is located at 11th Avenue E. and London Road and is open to tourists daily from May through September. In the park is a half-sized reproduction of the sailing vessel Lief and his crew of Norsemen are said to have sailed to America in 997, long before Columbus! A Norwegian crew sailed this miniature boat (12 feet 4 inches long) from Bergen, Norway, to Duluth in 1927.

A: **Minnesota**
Q: What U.S. state is known as "The Land of 10,000 Lakes"?
W: Most of Minnesota was at one time covered with glaciers and the surface of the land today has been shaped by the movement and melting of those glaciers. Among the many remnants of the glaciers are the 10,809 lakes, hence the nickname.

A: **Minnesota**
Q: What's the northernmost U.S. state apart from Alaska?
W: The northern boundary with the Canadian provinces of Manitoba and Ontario includes a small hump that makes Minnesota the northernmost of the 48 continental states. Minnesota's northernmost point is Northwest Angle at 49 degrees 23 minutes north. The northernmost point in the U.S. is Point Barrow, Alaska, at 71 degrees 23 minutes north.

A: **Minnesota**
Q: What U.S. state is the home of the headwaters of the Mississippi River?
W: To be exact, the source of the Mississippi is Lake Itasca, Minnesota. The head of navigation is at St. Paul, Minnesota.

A: **Mississippi**
Q: What U.S. state are you visiting if you drive the Natchez Trail from Tupelo?
W: Actually you would be driving down the Natchez Trace Parkway. This is an old road, over 500 miles long, used in the early 19th century by traders returning from Natchez after having floated produce down the Mississippi River.

A: **Mississippi, The**
Q: What river flows between Minneapolis and St. Paul?
W: Correct, the mighty Mississippi flows between the Twin Cities. Do you think Minneapolis and St. Paul started out as Siamese twins?

A: **Mississippi, The**
Q: What's the longest river in the U.S.?
W: This isn't quite true. The Mississippi River is North America's largest river, but its tributary, the Missouri River, is the longest.

A: **Mississippi, The**
Q: What river is known as "The Father of Waters"?
W: Literally, Mississippi is an Ojibwa (Indian) term for "big" (*missi*) and "river" (*siippii*). The character and physical appearance of the Mississippi proper are in three stages. From the source to St. Paul it is a clear, fresh stream winding its way through low countryside dotted with lakes. From St. Paul to the mouth of the Missouri, it grows into the powerful, dominating river that led the Indians to name it the "Father of Waters." Its union with the Missouri changes the Mississippi River completely by adding enormous quantities of salt to the clearer waters.

A: **Missouri and Mississippi, The**
Q: What two rivers join forces on the outskirts of St. Louis?
W: A quick glance at a map will confirm that these great rivers converge just outside of St. Louis. Together they form a valley stretching from the Rockies in the west to the Appalachians in the east and drain a basin of over one million square miles, which amounts to about one eighth of the North American continent.

A: **Missouri and Tennessee**
Q: What two U.S. states border the most others?
W: The state of Missouri borders eight states: Arkansas, Tennessee, Kentucky, Illinois, Iowa, Nebraska, Kansas, and Oklahoma. Tennessee also borders eight states: Mississippi, Alabama, Georgia, North Carolina, Kentucky, Virginia, Missouri, and Arkansas.

A: **Monaco**
Q: What country has the world's highest population density?
W: Actually, the most densely populated territory in the world is the Portuguese province of Macao, on the southern coast of China. It has an estimated population of 293,000 (mid-1981) in an area of 6.2 miles, giving a density of 47,258 per mile. The Principality of Monaco, on the south coast of France, has a population of 27,000 (mid-1981) in an area of 470 acres, giving a density of 36,765 per square mile.

A: **Monaco**
Q: What principality derives its revenues from casinos instead of taxes?
W: The shipping magnate Aristotle Socrates Onassis owned "the" casino at Monte Carlo. Citizens of Monaco, although spared taxes because of the casinos, are forbidden to gamble at them.

A: **Monaco**
Q: What's the capital of Monaco?
W: The principality of Monaco has four towns: Monte Carlo, most famous for its casino; Monaco, the capital; La Condamine, with many fine restaurants and hotels; and Fontvieille, rapidly emerging as an industrial center. Not bad for a country of 11 square miles!

A: **Monaco**
Q: What maritime country has the shortest coastline, at three and a half miles?
W: Monaco lies on the northeastern end of the French Riviera surrounding a natural harbor on the Mediterranean coast.

A: **Mongolia**
Q: What country is Ulan Bator the capital of?
W: Ulan Bator had a 1981 population of 435,400. Mongolia is a vast plateau in eastern Asia largely occupied by the Gobi Desert. Under Genghis Khan and his grandson Kublai Khan (1200s) the Mongol Empire became the biggest land empire in history, extending from the Yellow Sea in eastern Asia to the borders of Europe. Mongolia, bordered by Russia on the north, set up a soviet-type government in the 1920s.

A: **Monrovia**
Q: What African capital is named for a U.S. president?
W: The capital of Liberia, with one of the best developed harbors on Africa's Atlantic coast, was founded in 1822 by the American Colonization Society that bought the freedom of many American slaves and helped them establish the Republic of Liberia. It was founded during the administration of President James Monroe for whom it was named.

A: **Montana**
Q: What U.S. state does the Continental Divide leave to enter Canada?
W: The Continental Divide separates the rivers flowing west to the Pacific from those flowing east. It is created by the Rocky Mountains. At the north, the Continental Divide goes through Montana and Glacier National Park to Canada.

A: **Montreal**
Q: What major city is on an island in the St. Lawrence River?
W: Montreal is often called the "Paris of the New World," 63 of every 100 people there speak French. In 1535 Jacques Cartier climbed the inactive volcano that the city now surrounds and named it Mont Real or Mount Royal. The city takes its name from the mountain. The present city proper occupies about one third of Ile de Montreal near the junction of the Ottawa and St. Lawrence Rivers.

A: **Montreal**
Q: What city is at the eastern end of the St. Lawrence Seaway?
W: Montreal, a French settlement for 120 years, fell to the British in 1769 during the French and Indian War. In 1775 American forces occupied the city but were forced to withdraw. The strategic location of Montreal at the junction of the Ottawa and St. Lawrence Rivers has made it the major seaport on the St. Lawrence.

A: **Moon**
Q: Where's the Sea of Tranquility?
W: The Sea of Tranquility was the ultimate target for touchdown of Apollo 11. It was missed by only four miles because of the existence of unexpected rocks at the scheduled touchdown point. The Sea of Tranquility was first thought to be a body of water; however, later it was learned that it was simply a large plain on the surface of the moon.

A: **Morocco**
Q: What African kingdom is ruled by Hassan II?
W: Morocco, in northern Africa, is only nine miles from Spain across the Strait of Gibraltar. Casablanca is its largest city. Almost all Moroccans are Berbers, Arabs, and Moors whose ancestors built the mighty Moorish Empire that ruled Spain, Portugal, and most of North Africa from the 700s to the 1400s. King Hassan II, current ruler of Morocco, was born July 9, 1929, and took office on March 3, 1961.

A: **Moscow**
Q: What city is home to Europe's tallest building?
W: The Moscow M. V. Lomonosov State University, with a height of 720 feet, is the tallest *building* in Europe, and ranks number 39 in the world.

A: **Moscow**
Q: Where is Gorki Park?
W: Gorki Park of Culture and Rest is the city's chief amusement park. It extends 4.5 miles along the Moscow River and was named for writer Maxim Gorki who is regarded as the foremost literary artist in the Soviet Union.

A: **Moscow**
Q: Where's the GUM department store?
W: GUM, also known as State Department Store, is Moscow's leading department store. GUM has a staff of well over 4,000.

A: **Moscow and Vladivostok**
Q: What two cities are at the ends of the Trans-Siberian Railway?
W: The Trans-Siberian Train takes eight days to travel the total length of this trip from western Moscow to the seaport of Vladivostok in the Soviet Far East. However, since Vladivostok is a military port with limited access, foreigners must board the train 50 miles farther north at Nakhodka.

A: **Mount Etna**
Q: What volcano showers ash on Sicily?
W: Mount Etna is on the east coast of the island of Sicily. Its name comes from the Greek phrase *Aitne* meaning "I burn." It last erupted in 1982.

A: **Mount Everest**
Q: What mountain is revered by locals as "Goddess Mother of the Earth"?
W: Mount Everest, an eastern Himalayan peak of 29,028 feet above sea level on the Tibet-Nepal border, was discovered to be the world's highest mountain in 1852 by the Survey Department of the Government of India. Although the mountain was named after the Surveyor General of India, Colonel Sir George Everest, the locals continued to call it Chomolungma or "Goddess Mother of the Earth." The Yeti or Abominable Snowman is said to inhabit the lower slopes.

A: **Mount Fuji**
Q: What's the most photographed, painted, and climbed mountain in the world?
W: Mount Fuji, perhaps the most beautiful mountain on Earth, is located in Japan, 50 miles southwest of Tokyo. Fuji, "the never dying mountain," is revered as a symbol of purity to many Japanese. As many as 200,000 people climb Fuji each summer. An almost perfect volcanic cone, it rises from a lake-studded plain to a 12,388-foot summit that is snowcapped nine months of the year. A Japanese proverb says, "He who climbs Fuji once is a wise man, he who climbs twice – a fool."

A: **Mount Fuji**
Q: What mountain can you view from the windows of a train called the "Bullet"?
W: The "Bullet" is so popular that there are posters showing it speeding past Mount Fuji in the Japan National Tourist Office located in Chicago. Actually, the "Bullet" is part of the Tokaido Sanyo Shin Kansen line; *Shin Kansen* is Japanese for "bullet train." The line runs between Tokyo and Hakata, and there are approximately 45 departures from Tokyo daily, running every 15 minutes.

A: **Mount Kilimanjaro**
Q: What African mountain is known as "The Mountain of the Cold Devils"?
W: This is only one of the nicknames for Africa's highest mountain. A possible explanation for the name is the incredible vertical progression of climate and vegetation ranging from equatorial to polar conditions, topped by an ice cap 200 feet thick. It's also called Ngaje Nga (*House of God*).

A: **Mount Kilimanjaro**
Q: What's the highest mountain in Africa?
W: Mount Kilimanjaro, located in Tanzania, reaches 19,340 feet. Next in line is Mount Kenya at 17,058 feet.

A: **Mount Kilimanjaro**
Q: What's the world's highest mountain that isn't part of a range?
W: There are peaks that are taller than Mount Kilimanjaro's Kibo Peak at an elevation of 19,340 feet, but they are all part of a range of mountains.

A: **Mount McKinley**
Q: What's the highest mountain in North America?
W: It certainly is. At 20,320 feet, Alaska's Mount McKinley is higher than Canada's Mount Logan, which reaches 19,850 feet.

A: **Mount McKinley**
Q: What's the highest mountain in the U.S.?
W: No other mountain in the U.S. can stand up to Alaska's Mount McKinley, which has an elevation of 20,320 feet. The only U.S. mountain that comes close is St. Elias, which stretches between Alaska and Canada at 18,008 feet.

A: **Mount St. Helens**
Q: What dropped 1,313 feet in 1980?
W: Mt. St. Helens erupted May 18, 1980. The blast blew off the the mountain's 9,677-foot summit, reducing it to a height of 8,000 to 8,300 feet, and opened a crater more than a mile long and 1,700 feet deep.

A: **Mount Vesuvius**
Q: What mountain erupted to destroy Pompeii?
W: In A.D. 79, after being dormant for centuries, Vesuvius erupted, burying the cities of Pompeii and Stabial. Pliny the Younger wrote an account of the eruption in two letters.

A: **Mount Vesuvius**
Q: What's the only active volcano on the European mainland?
W: The key word here is "mainland." Mount Etna, which last erupted in 1982, is on the island of Sicily and Mount Stromboli, which last erupted in 1975, is on the Strom-boli Island. Mount Vesuvius, with an elevation of 4,200 feet, is located southeast of Naples and is, in fact, the only active volcano on the European mainland.

A: **Mount Vesuvius**
Q: What volcanic peak can you see from Naples?
W: Vesuvius is an active volcano that rises above the Bay of Naples. The greatest attraction of Naples is the National Museum, full of Greek and Roman art. However, none of the exhibits is identified. Enough to drive a tourist crazy!

A: **Mount Whitney**
Q: What's the highest mountain in the 48 contiguous U.S. states?
W: Mount Whitney is the tallest peak in the 48 continental states but 29th highest in the U.S., Canada, and Mexico. The tallest peak is Mount McKinley in Alaska at 20,320 feet compared to Whitney's mere 14,494 feet.

A: **Munchen**
Q: What does a German call Munich?
W: Munich dates from 1158 and is considered a fun-loving city. Carnival time, called "Fasching" by the Bavarians, lasts from New Year's Eve until Mardi Gras!

A: **Munich**
Q: What's the capital of Bavaria?
W: Munich is also the beer capital of the world. The last two weeks of September are devoted to Oktoberfest when the big breweries erect tents on the fair grounds and the only measure of beer allowed is a one-liter mug, just over a quart!

A: **Munich**
Q: What German city do Italians call "The Monaco of Bavaria"?
W: The term "Monaco of Bavaria" refers to its fun-loving attitude and constant celebrations from "Fasching" through summer festivals to Oktoberfest.

A: **Muscovite, A**
Q: What's a resident of Moscow called?
W: Moscow is Moskva in Russian. In the 13th century it became the center of the newly formed Muscovy principality; thus the term "Muscovite." Moscow is located on the Moskva River and is the capital of the USSR.

N

A: **Nairobi**
Q: What Kenyan city is the safari center for east Africa?
W: Kenya is an east African republic, with Nairobi as its capital. Nairobi is in the heart of the safari area in east Africa. Some of the better known safari areas include Tsavo National Park, the largest game reserve in Kenya; Mt. Kenya National Park; and Aberdare National Park

A: **Nepal**
Q: What country is Mount Everest in?
W: Give yourself credit for Tibet or China as well! Mount Everest is on the undemarcated border of Nepal and Tibet (an autonomous ethnic region of China). The world's highest point, Mount Everest is 29,128 feet above sea level. The Tibetans call it Chomolungma, "Goddess Mother of the World."

A: **Nepal**
Q: What is Katmandu the capital of?
W: Nepal is a landlocked monarchy between China and India. Katmandu is its capital with a population of about 195,000. Founded in 723, and throughout most of its history isolated from the outside world, Katmundu is known to westerners as the jumping-off place for climbing expeditions in the Himalayas. It is the only place in Nepal with electricity!

A: **Netherlands, The**
Q: What country is home to Heineken beer?
W: There are five major breweries in Holland, but Heineken supplies nearly 40 percent of the beer consumed there. Heineken lager is the leading import in the U.S. and the standard by many tasters.

A: **Netherlands, The**
Q: What country produces the original Edam cheese?
W: Edam is a red-coated cheese produced in Edam, Netherlands.

A: **Nevada**
Q: What U.S. state records the least rainfall?
W: We couldn't confirm this. According to the *1984 World Almanac*, Nevada's normal annual preciptation is 8.47 inches. There are two states that record less: Arizona with 7.05 inches and New Mexico with 7.77 inches.

A: **Nevada**
Q: What U.S. state has sagebrush as its state flower?
W: Nevada was admitted to the Union in 1864 as the 36th state. Carson City is the capital. The name "Nevada" comes from the Spanish meaning "snow clad." It is the only state with sagebrush as its flower and is frequently called the "sagebrush state." Sagebrush has silver green leaves and large dusters of small white flowers.

A: **New Guinea**
Q: What's the second largest island in the world?

W: Greenland, Denmark is the largest island with a total area of 840,000 square miles. New Guinea, situated north of Australia in the Pacific Ocean, is 2nd largest with an area of 306,000 square miles.

A: **New Hampshire**
Q: What U.S. state is Dixville Notch in?
W: New Hampshire holds the earliest presidential primary in the nation, consequently it furnishes a "testing ground" for candidates.

A: **New Haven, Connecticut**
Q: What city is home to Yale University?
W: Yale was founded in 1701 and is the third oldest university in the U.S. Yale originally would only admit men until 1969 when the first women were allowed to attend. The movement leading to the founding of what was first called the Collegiate College of America was begun by ten ministers nine of whom were graduates of Harvard!

A: **New Mexico**
Q: What U.S. state does the Continental Divide enter Mexico from?
W: The continental divide is a fairly continuous ridge of mountain peaks that divide the continent's drainage into that flowing eastward to the Mississippi from that flowing westward to the Pacific Ocean. The divide runs along the crest of the Rocky Mountains and does enter Mexico from New Mexico.

A: **New Mexico**
Q: What U.S. state boasts the Carlsbad Caverns National Park?
W: This national park, so designated in 1930, is located in southeastern New Mexico. Beneath the park lies the largest underground chambers ever discovered; the explored area of the caverns is 23 miles long. Several million bats live in the cavern during the summer and pour from the entrances at dusk to forage for insects; the sight of these bats is why exploration was started in 1901.

A: **New Orleans**
Q: What city was the original Dixie?
W: New Orleans is the birthplace of Dixieland jazz. "Dixie," a term applied to the southern states, is believed to be derived from the Mason-Dixon Line that divided the North and the South during the Civil War. However, it may also be from *dixie*, a French word meaning "10"; a $10 bill was issued by a New Orleans bank prior to the Civil War with a large "Dix" on each side.

A: **New Orleans**
Q: What southern U.S. city has an exhibit of the original streetcar named Desire?
W: Building number 400 on Esplanade Avenue near Charbres in New Orleans is the U.S. Mint. The Jazz and Carnival Museum is on the second floor. In the rear courtyard you'll find the original "Streetcar Named Desire," which inspired the name of the Tennessee Williams play.

A: **New York**
Q: What city has the world's largest black population?
W: According to the 1980 census, the three cities with the largest black population were: New York City, 1,784,124; Chicago, 1,197,000; and Detroit, 758,939.

A: **New York**
Q: What city is sometimes called Gotham?
W: If you never heard of New York referred to as Gotham, don't feel bad. It took quite a lot of digging for us to find the answer! Actually a "Gothamite" is a humorous epithet for a New Yorker, first used by Washington Irving in his "Salmagunde" (1807), a collection of whimsical essays that mirrored the rise and fall of New York opinion on its social life, books, theaters, politics, and personalities. The real Gotham was an English village noted in stories for the blundering simplicity of its inhabitants. Allegedly, Gotham became the nickname of New York City because of its citizens alleged pretensions of wisdom.

A: **New York**
Q: What North American city has the longest subway system?
W: New York City's subway system has a total of 231.73 route miles and, as of 1979, 458 stations. Approximately 1,096,006,529 passengers rode the subway in 1979.

A: **New York**
Q: What's the only U.S. state that ends with a K?
W: No other!

A: **New York**
Q: What U.S. state are the Finger Lakes in?
W: The finger lakes are a group of narrow glacial lakes in west central New York between Syracuse and Genesco. The region located in north-south valleys has ten state parks and is noted for its scenery.

A: **New York**
Q: What city gets water through the Delaware Aqueduct?
W: The Delaware Aqueduct is a circular tunnel and part of the Delaware system that supplies water to New York City. It was constructed between 1937 and 1953 with extensions causing construction to continue until 1965. In some places it is as deep as 2,500 feet and as wide as 19.5 feet.

A: **New York City**
Q: Where's the 1,046-foot-high Chrysler Building?
W: Precisely, it's at the corner of 42nd Street and Lexington Avenue. (Remember when King Kong was its *major* tenant?) When it was first built in 1930, its height of 1,046 feet made it the tallest building in the world. But it was soon topped by the completion of the Empire State Building in 1931. Now the twin World Trade Center Towers are the highest in the City.

A: **New York City**
Q: What's "The Big Apple"?
W: There are several versions of why New York City is called "the Big Ap-ple." One associates the popular dance of the 1930s called the Big Apple with New York, which had been known for generations as the Big Town. Another version explains that colorful people in the entertainment world used the name as a way of saying "I'm playing New York City; I've made it to the big time – the Big Apple." A variation of the same theme goes: "There are many apples on the tree, but when you pick New York City, you pick the Big Apple."

A: **New York City**
Q: Where is the Guggenheim Museum?
W: To be exact, the Solomon R. Guggenheim Museum is located at 1071 Fifth Avenue. The ultra modern facade and interior created by Frank Lloyd Wright, is the center-piece for the modern works on display.

A: **New York City**
Q: Where was the 1939 World's Fair?
W: The most popular exhibit at the Fair was General Motors "Futurama" with predictions of America in the 60s: "...People won't care much for possessions, ...two month vacations, ...cars will be air conditioned and cost as little as $200." What, the car or the air conditioner? The 1939-40 and the 1964-65 World's Fairs were held at Flushing Meadow-Corona Park, which is a zoned city in the northern section of the borough of Queens, New York City.

A: **New York City**
Q: Where is Pennsylvania Station?
W: From 1910 to 1963 the imposing bulk of the old Pennsylvania Station stood at Madison Square Garden. Now "Penn Station" spreads out below street level, accommodating three railroads: Amtrak, New Jersey Transit, and the Long Island Railroad. About 600 trains are scheduled daily, entering or leaving New York through tunnels under the Hudson and East Rivers. Above ground, a new group of buildings includes a high-rise office building along Seventh Avenue, the round Madison Square Garden Sports Center, and other facilities.

A: **New York City**
Q: Where is Battery Park?
W: The Battery Park area, located in lower Manhattan, is where the city's history began. Within a small radius are some of the city's most historic sites. If you walk along the esplanade of Battery Park, you'll appreciate the strategic geographical situation of the city, which gave it a commercial advantage over all other cities. It is the same stroll that Wall Street tycoons take to help clear their heads and quiet their nerves when they are faced with multimillion dollar decisions.

A: **New Zealand**
Q: What country owns the Auckland Islands?
W: Auckland, the principal city of an

island nation, is a one-to-seven-mile wide isthmus located on New Zealand's North Island. The city is surrounded by Waitemata Harbor and the Hauraki Gulf. There are a number of islands in this gulf, but they are not called the Auckland Islands. Our sources refer to them as the Hauraki Gulf Islands.

A: **New Zealand**
Q: Where in the South Pacific can you have a pub lunch alongside the Avon River?
W: The renowned Avon River is more like a peaceful stream that meanders through the middle of the city of Christchurch in the Upper South Island. Office workers take noontime picnics along its banks and schoolboys on bicycles pause to fish from its bridges. It is also the site of the Town Hall, which houses a lovely restaurant.

A: **New Zealand**
Q: What country includes North Island, South Island, Stewart, and Chatham Islands?
W: New Zealand proper consists of North Island (44,281 square miles), South Island (58,093 square miles), Stewart Island (670 square miles), and Chatham (372 square miles). There are also many minor outlying islands, giving New Zealand a total square mileage of 10,736.

A: **New Zealand's**
Q: What country's capital is Wellington?
W: Wellington is New Zealand's capital and seat of government. It has often been called "New Zealand's Little Chicago" because of the sudden gusts of wind that blast at you as you round a corner. Like Chicago, Wellington has a solid reputation as a "Windy City."

A: **New Zealand's**
Q: What country's citizens are called Kiwis?
W: Actually, the New Zealanders' nicknamed themselves "Kiwis" after the flightless bird of their land. The nickname has nothing to do with the delicious fruit that is native to Asia.

A: **Niagara, The**
Q: What river is spanned by the Rainbow Bridge?
W: The Niagara River connects Lake Erie and Lake Ontario forming part of the boundary between New York and the province of Ontario. All the Great Lakes, except Lake Ontario, empty into this short stream, which is only 35 miles long. The Falls View Bridge, built in 1898, was replaced by Rainbow Bridge in 1941.

A: **Niagara Falls**
Q: What famed falls are split in two by Goat Island?
W: After dividing at Goat Island, the larger of the two streams (95 percent of the water) falls over a rocky ledge of limestone, the Horseshoe Falls on the Canadian Bank. The remaining water flows over the American Falls, which is receding at a rate of four to seven inches per year.

A: **Niagara Falls**
Q: Where did the Rainbow Bridge replace the Honeymoon Bridge?
W: Our research shows that the Rainbow Bridge replaced Falls View International Bridge, but don't doubt it was nicknamed "Honeymoon Bridge" since so many newlyweds went there! The Falls View International Bridge, built in 1898, crashed under the pressure of ice in 1938. The new bridge, the Rainbow Bridge, was completed in 1941.

A: **Nicaragua**
Q: What bordering country is due north of Costa Rica?
W: Nicaragua is the largest republic of Central America, stretching from the Caribbean to the Pacific Ocean.

A: **Nigeria**
Q: What's the most populous country in Africa?
W: According to a 1982 census, Nigeria's population is approximately 82,300,000 with a density of 216.09 per square mile. The only other African nation that comes close to that population and density is Egypt, with a 1982 census of 44,000,000 and a density of 115.90 per square mile.

A: **Nigeria's**
Q: What country's capital is Lagos?
W: Lagos was confirmed to be the federal capital of Nigeria in 1960. It is also the chief port as well as the major trade and industrial center of Nigeria.

A: **Nile, The**
Q: What river flows past the Temple of Karnak?
W: Thebes, capital of the ancient Egyptian empire, was about 419 miles south of Cairo on the Nile River. The modern town of Luxor occupies part of the site of this ancient city. Karnak is the most northerly part of what was Thebes and lies on the east bank of the Nile. The temple of Karnak has a vast pillared hall of 5,800 square yards and over 110 pillars, many 78 feet tall.

A: **Nile, The**
Q: What does the National Geographic Society call the longest river in the world?
W: The Nile shares with the Amazon River the distinction of maybe being the world's longest river. However, the National Geographic Society lists the length of the Nile as 4,145 miles and that of the Amazon as 4,000 miles.

A: **Nine**
Q: How many horizontal rows of stars are there on the U.S. flag?
W: Count them yourself sometime! There are five six-star rows and four five-star rows for a total of 50 stars.

A: **Nippon**
Q: What do the Japanese call Japan?
W: The Japanese call their country Nippon or Nihon, which means the "source of the sun." Westerners often call Japan "The Land of the Rising Sun."

A: **North**
Q: What direction does the Nile River flow?
W: The Nile River flows 4,145 miles. It is *not* the only river in the world that flows north, as there are several in North America!

A: North America
Q: What continent is Barbados considered part of?
W: Barabados is a member of the West Indies Federation, and Bridgetown is its capital. President Reagan was the first U.S. President to visit the island.

A: North America
Q: What continent is Jamaica considered part of?
W: North America includes Greenland, Canada, the United States, Mexico, Central America, and the islands of the West Indies, of which Jamaica is a part.

A: North Carolina
Q: What's "The Tar Heel State"?
W: There are two stories here! One claims it was nicknamed the "Tar Heel State" because the long-leaf pine forests of the coastal plains produce an abundance of rosin, turpentine, and tar, which explains only the "tar." Another source suggests the term is a derogatory one arising during the Civil War when a brigade of North Carolinians could not hold a certain hill and were laughed at for having forgotten to "tar their heels" that morning!

A: North Carolina
Q: What U.S. state contains Cape Hattaras?
W: Cape Hattaras is known as "the Graveyard of the Atlantic" because so many ships have been wrecked there by the rough seas and difficult currents.

A: North Dakota
Q: What U.S. state contains the geographic center of North America?
W: The geographic center of North America lies just southwest of Rugby, North Dakota.

A: North Dakota
Q: What's the most rural state in the U.S.?
W: Farms and ranches cover nearly all the state. Almost three fourths of the people live on farms or in small towns.

A: North Sea, The
Q: What sea separates Britain from Norway?
W: The North Sea is a wide arm of the Atlantic Ocean that lies between Great Britain and the continent of Europe. The harbors of many of the greatest seafaring nations such as England, Germany, Norway, the Netherlands, and Denmark, are on the shores of the North Sea.

A: Northern, The
Q: Which hemisphere has more countries, the Northern or Southern?
W: The equator crosses through the northern part of South America and the middle of Africa, and a glance at a world map will show that far more countries lie north of this line.

A: Northern Ireland
Q: What do Tyrone, Antrim, Down, Londonderry, Fermanagh and Armagh make up?
W: These are the six counties that make up Northern Ireland, which occupies one fifth of the island of Ireland. The people call themselves Orangemen or Ulstermen. The term Orangemen dates from the 1600s when many people in Northern Ireland supported William of Orange in a war against James II of England.

A: Northern Ireland
Q: What is Ulster?
W: Ulster was the old name for Northern Ireland before it separated from the rest of Ireland in 1920. The people of Northern Ireland, mostly Protestant, knew that freedom from British rule for all Ireland would make them a minority group, outnumbered by the large number of Roman Catholics in southern Ireland. They therefore chose to remain in the British Commonwealth. In fact, only six of the nine counties that made up Ulster are now in Northern Ireland.

A: Northwest Passage, The
Q: What were Baffin, Frobisher and Franklin looking for?
W: The clue to this one is probably "Baffin" since he now has an island named after him in northern Canada! These men were all looking for the Northwest Passage from the Atlantic to the Pacific. Sir Martin Frobisher sailed from England in 1576, and Baffin searched for the Passage from 1612 to 1616. Sir John Franklin finally proved the existence of the Passage in an 1845 expedition when he found the Canadian Arctic waterway.

A: Norway
Q: What country shares a 1,030-mile border with Sweden?
W: The Kjolen Mountains separate eastern Norway from Sweden, but they were almost one country in the 1800s! After Napoleon's defeat in 1814, the Treaty of Kiel gave Norway to Sweden; however, the Norwegians refused to become Swedish subjects and proclaimed Norway an independent nation.

A: Norway
Q: What's the northernmost Scandinavian country?
W: Norway is often called "The Land of the Midnight Sun." One third of the country lies north of the Arctic Circle, and from May through July the sun shines there at night as well as during the day. The most northern section of Norway lies at the top of Finland and Sweden.

A: Norway
Q: What country contains the largest icefield in Europe?
W: The total area of Norway covered by glaciers is 2,744 square kilometers. Here are the five largest: Jostedalsbreen at 486 square kilometers; Svartisen at 369 square kilometers; Folgefonni at 172 square kilometers; Blaamannsisen at 87 square kilometers; and Hardangerjoekulen at 78 square kilometers.

A: **Norway, Sweden, the Soviet Union**
Q: What three countries border Finland?
W: The Soviet Union comprises the entire eastern boundary of Finland, Sweden is the western land boundary, and Norway borders it on the top. The Finns call their country Suomi meaning "swamp," since about 60,000 lakes dot the countryside.

A: **Oahu**
Q: What island is Pearl Harbor on?
W: Pearl Harbor was the site of the Dec. 7, 1941, Japanese bombing of the United States' territory. The USS *Arizona*, which was sunk that day, remains in the harbor with a white concrete-shell structure spanning the sunken hull as a national memorial.

A: **Oahu**
Q: What island is Honolulu on?
W: Honolulu is the capital of Hawaii and is located on Oahu, the most populated island. Only three of every 100 people are pure Hawaiians, 37 are of Japanese ancestry, 23 are Caucasian, 12 are Philipino, seven are Chinese, and the remaining 18 a variety of a variety of other heritages.

A: **Occident, The**
Q: What's the opposite of the Orient?
W: That's exactly how Webster's Dictionary defines it. Technically, the Occident consists of the Western Hemisphere and Europe. The word Occident is derived from the Latin words *occidens* and *occidere* meaning "of the sun," that quarter of the sky in which the sun sets.

A: **Oklahoma**
Q: What U.S. state has the largest Indian population?
W: Oklahoma had 156,501 American Indians residing on or near federally recognized reservations in 1981. Arizona had the second largest Indian population at 152,145.

A: **Old Bailey, The**
Q: What famed London criminal court was once a feudal castle?
W: Central Criminal Court, or Old Bailey, is the chief criminal court for Greater London. Tours of the building, which incorporates a large section of the medieval wall of London and a Great Hall, are no longer given. *Bailey* is a term for an area between inner and outer city walls.

A: **Old Faithful**
Q: What erupts every hour at Yellowstone National Park?
W: For over 100 years, this geyser has been erupting as regularly as clockwork. Every hour for approximately five minutes, Old Faithful spews forth a scalding column of water, estimated at 150 feet high. An exploring party led by General Henry Washburn discovered the geyser in 1870 and named it for its uncanny punctuality.

A: **One**
Q: How many Canadian provinces border the Great Lakes?
W: The Great Lakes form the entire southern border of the Canadian province of Ontario.

A: **One**
Q: How many South American countries have Portuguese as their official language?
W: Brazil has Portugese as its official language. But how about Fang? That's one of the languages of Equatorial Guinea!

A: **One ruble**
Q: What do 100 kopecks make?
W: A kopeck is a small Russian coin worth about half a cent. A ruble is the unit of the Soviet money system and is divided into 100 kopecks.

A: **Oregon**
Q: What U.S. state is proud to call itself "The Beaver State"?
W: Oregon is also called the "Hard Case State," "Sunset State," and "Webfoot State." It has been known as the "Beaver State" because of the association of the little fur-bearing animal with the early history of the Oregon country, as well as because of the beaver's industry, ingenuity, and other admirable qualities.

A: **Oregon's**
Q: What U.S. state's highest point is Mount Hood?
W: Mount Hood, 11,235 feet high, is located in the Mount Hood National Forest in northwestern Oregon and includes a region of waterfalls.

A: **Organization of American States**
Q: What does OAS stand for?
W: The Organization of American States was formed in 1948 to promote cooperation among the 21 American Republics. It has acted as a consulting or mediating body in several cases of conflict within the region. Cuba has been excluded from participation in OAS activities since 1962.

A: Osaka, Japan
Q: What city staged Expo 70?
W: Japan's third largest city, Osaka has been called the "Chicago of Japan." Over 800 bridges cross the many canals, rivers, and arms of the sea that cut through the city. Osaka was badly damaged during World War II.

A: Oslo
Q: What's the capital of Norway?
W: Oslo, which covers a total of 175 square miles, is one of the biggest in area of the world capitals. Yet it remains underappreciated season after season. Oslo has been called the ideal city and the most underrated art center of modern Europe. Oslo's relative obscurity is caused by the western fjords near Bergen, which offer tourist competition that no other Scandinavian capital has had to endure.

A: Oslo
Q: What city would you visit to see the *Kon-Tiki* raft?
W: The *Kon-Tiki* raft is on display at the museum complex at Bygdoy, across the fjord from downtown Oslo. The *Kon-Tiki* is a balsa craft on which Norwegian explorer Thor Heyerdahl and five colleagues sailed 5,000 miles across the Pacific from Peru to Polynesia, on a historic 1947 journey lasting over three months.

A: Osterreich
Q: What does an Austrian call Austria?
W: It is a German word meaning "the eastern kingdom." By 1300, the House of Hapsburg had gained control of the Austrian lands, and the Hapsburgs added vast territories in all parts of Europe to their realm. World War I, which started after the assassination of Archduke Ferdinand the Hapsburg heir, destroyed the Austrian empire, and by 1918 it was reduced to its current small size.

A: Ouzo
Q: What's the most popular drink in Greece?
W: It is an anise flavored Greek liqueur. Anise is a plant, native to the Mediterrean region, with licorice flavored seeds.

A: Pacific, The
Q: What ocean is the Malay Sea considered part of?
W: This sea is a misnomer! After futilely searching through several atlases, we were beginning to think it didn't exist! One source listed it as having a base area of 3.2 million square miles, but it wasn't pictured on the map. We then discovered that the Malayan Sea is not considered a geographical entity, but a convenient term used for waters between the South Pacific and the Indian Ocean.

A: Pacific, The
Q: What surrounds Pitcairn Island?
W: Pitcairn Island is an isolated volcanic formation in the south central Pacific Ocean, 1,350 miles southeast of Tahiti. This island and three uninhabited islands make up the British Colony of Pitcairn Island.

Its population is descended from the mutineers of the British ship HMS *Bounty*.

A: Pacific, The
Q: What ocean does the Gulf of Panama lead into?
W: The Gulf of Panama is an inlet of the Pacific Ocean and borders the south side of the Isthmus of Panama. The Pearl Islands are located in the Gulf, and Panama City is the main urban center on the gulf shore.

A: Pacific, Atlantic, Indian, The
Q: What are the world's three largest oceans, in order of size?
W: Facts are facts. The areas of these massive oceans are: Pacific, 64,186,300 square miles; Atlantic, 33,420,000 square miles; and Indian 28,350,500 square miles.

A: Pacific's, The
Q: What ocean's area is 64,186,000 square miles?
W: *Wrong!* The Pacific Ocean's area is 64,186,300 square miles. (Details, details...!) Give yourself credit for a correct answer. What's 300 square miles among friends.

A: Palace of Versailles, The
Q: Where is the Hall of Mirrors?
W: The Palace of Versailles, southeast of Paris, was built by Louis XIV. *Galerie des Glaces* is the French term for the Hall of Mirrors where the Treaty of Versailles, ending World War I, was signed in 1919. The Hall of Mirrors was designed by Henry Monsart and decorated by Charles Le Brun. It is 243 feet long and illuminated by 17 great windows.

A: Panama
Q: What's the capital of Panama?
W: The Spaniards founded the city in 1519 on the site of an Indian fishing village. The name comes from an Indian word meaning "fishermen" or "plenty of fish." It was the starting point for expeditions to conquer the Incas of Peru.

A: **Panama**

Q: Where in the Americas is it only 47 miles from the Atlantic to the Pacific?

W: The Panama Canal was built across this narrow stretch of land thereby shortening the trip from New York to San Francisco by 5,200 miles. The canal cost $380 million, and during construction 211 million cubic yards of earth and rock were removed. Yellow fever, bubonic plague, and malaria were the greatest obstacles to its construction.

A: **Panama Canal, The**

Q: Where do you pass through the Pedro Miguel Lock?

W: These locks lower a vessel 30 feet in one step to the manmade Miraflores Lake. The ship sails 1.5 miles across the lake to the Miraflores Locks where it is lowered to the Pacific Ocean.

A: **Panama Canal, The**

Q: What canal does the Thatcher Ferry Bridge span?

W: The Thatcher Ferry Bridge was built in 1955 and connects Panama City and Balboa with the north side of the canal. This bridge links the Pan American Highway System with that of Canada and the U.S.

A: **Paris**

Q: Where is the Austerlitz train station?

W: Gare d'Austerlitz is the main railway terminal for Bordeaux, Bayonne, and Toulouse.

A: **Paris**

Q: What city is famed for its Rive Gauche?

W: The Rive Gauche, or the Left Bank, always fairly seedy, was nevertheless dear to many as the playground, classroom, and workshop of the 1920 to 1935 "lost generation."

A: **Paris**

Q: What city does Orly Airport serve?

W: Le Bourget and Orly are the two chief commercial airports of the city.

The United States Air Force also uses Orly Airport.

A: **Paris**

Q: What city was the first home to the Statue of Liberty?

W: The Statue of Liberty was designed and built in France. On July 4, 1884 the government of France presented it to the United States. Five months later it was dismantled and shipped in carefully numbered pieces aboard the warship *Isere*. What a puzzle! It was dedicated in the U.S. by President Grover Cleveland on October 28, 1886.

A: **Paris**

Q: Where are the Austerlitz and Victor Hugo subway stops?

W: The Victor Hugo stop is the last stop before Porte Dauphine. Gare d'Orleans Austerlitz is the metro stop at the main railway terminal. There is also an FDR stop on the Metro.

A: **Paris**

Q: What is "The City of Lights"?

W: Paris is also called "The Capital of the World" and "A Town Like a Woman with Flowers in Her Hair." It bears the nickname "The City of Lights" because it was here the intellectual enlightenment began in the days of Diderot and Voltaire. If you guessed Perth, in western Australia, to be "The City of Lights," you are also correct. This is the city that turned on all its lights to greet American astronauts in flight.

A: **Paris**

Q: What city contains the Quartier Latin?

W: The area just south of the Ile de la Cite has been called "the Latin Quarter" since the Middle Ages. At that time, the students and the teachers living there spoke to each other in Latin.

A: **Paris**

Q: Where did the Orient Express end its run from Istanbul?

W: The inaugural run of the Orient Express took place in October, 1883, when it set off from Gare de L'Est

with an extraordinary assortment of persons on board. The whole party traveled in the type of luxury that is inconceivable today.

A: **Paris**

Q: Where is the famed Crazy Horse Saloon, telephone number 255-6969?

W: According to the International Operator, the number for the Crazy Horse is 723-3232, maybe 255-6969 is a pay phone or an old number!

A: **Paris**

Q: Where is *Le Figaro* published?

W: In France, where the number of daily papers has declined since 1946. The press is controlled mainly by four groups, each centered on one of the largest dailies: *France Soir*, *Le Figaro*, *L'Aurou*, and *Le Parisien Libere*. The postwar French press is less open to political pressure and more informational than in prewar days.

A: **Paris**

Q: What European capital celebrated its 2,000th anniversary in 1951?

W: Early Paris goes back to the century before Christ, when Casear conquered it and its residents, a tribe called the Parisu. Gradually the name of this tribe replaced the earlier city name of Lutetia.

A: **Paris**

Q: What city's the end of the line leaving Nice on the Mistral?

W: The Gare de Lyon is the station in Paris where you will arrive if you take the Mistral train from Nice.

A: **Paris**

Q: What's the destination of the Arlberg Express, leaving Vienna every night at 8:10?

W: Paris is Europe's be-all and end-all rail terminus. The celebrated expresses going in every direction either begin, terminate, or pass through one of Paris' great railway stations, Gare du Nord, Gare de L'Est, Gare St.-Logare, Gare de Lyon, or Gare Austerlitz.

A: **Paris**
Q: Where is Harry's New York Bar?
W: A favorite watering hole for American ex-patriots for decades, this is also the birthplace of many a famous cocktail. The first Bloody Mary is said to have been stirred up here in 1921 and the first Sidecar in 1931. The Black Velvet and the White Lady were reportedly the best-loved drinks of composer George Gershwin. It was bartender Harry MacElhone who shook up these immortal concoctions.

A: **Paris**
Q: What European capital boasts the Luxembourg Garden?
W: Having decided to leave journalism behind and instead try to support his family by selling stories, Ernest Hemingway tried to fend off starvation by eating pigeons that he found in these gardens. Every afternoon at four, he discovered the gendarme on duty would disappear into a cafe for a glass of wine. It was easy enough for Hemingway, the hunter, to lure his unsuspecting prey; all it required was a pocketful of corn. He would snatch up the birds, twist their necks with one deft movement, toss them under a blanket in his son's baby carriage, and take them home to be cooked.

A: **Paris**
Q: Where is the Cordon Bleu School of Cooking?
W: The Cordon Bleu School of Cooking is located at 24 Rue du Champ de Mars in Paris. It is considered one of the top schools for French cooking and has been attended by many of the world's most famous chefs. Classes are offered in 12 week sessions, four times a year, and fees range from 3,000 to 7,000 francs according to 1982 statistics. It's no wonder that French food is so expensive!

A: **Paris's**
Q: What city's sewer tour gets no stars in the Michelin "Green Guide"?
W: Don't take this too literally. It is not a tour of Paris' sewage system, but rather a number of underground galleries that display various exhibits. Michelin does not consider this a star attraction.

A: **Park**
Q: What's the most common street in America?
W: According to the *Book of Lists-No.2*, Park tops the list of the most common street names in America. Another interesting fact: Main Street ranked number 32!

A: **Parthenon, The**
Q: What's the largest building on the Acropolis?
W: The Parthenon is the chief temple of the Greek goddess Athena on the hill of the Acropolis at Athens. Three other small buildings still survive: the Propylaeum, a gateway; the Erechtheum, a shrine to the agricultural deities; and the Temple of Athena Nike.

A: **"Passion Play, The"**
Q: What is staged at Oberammergau, West Germany, every 10 years?
W: According to tradition, the play has been presented every ten years since 1634. This is in fulfillment of a vow made after the village was spared an epidemic of plague.

A: **Pentagon, The**
Q: What's the largest office building in the world?
W: It's the headquarters of the U.S. Department of Defense. The buildings have three times the floor space of the Empire State Building, house more than 23,000 employees, and cover 3,707,745 square feet. War is BIG business!

A: **Persian Gulf, The**
Q: What body of water does the Euphrates River empty into?
W: The Euphrates River is 1,700 miles long and originates in Turkey. It crosses Syria and meets the Tigris River in southern Iraq to form the Shatt-al-Arab River which flows another 120 miles to the Persian Gulf. The ancient city of Babylon was located on the Euphrates.

A: **Persian Gulf, The**
Q: What body of water borders Saudi Arabia to the east?
W: The Persian Gulf is a shallow sea of the Indian Ocean. Iran forms the Gulf's entire eastern border and some of the northern border, while Kuwait and Iraq are on the northwest side of the Gulf. The Gulf is critical to the world distribution of oil from these Middle East countries.

A: **Peru**
Q: What country was the Bridge of San Luis Rey in?
W: All of you literary critics will know that *The Bridge of San Luis Rey* was a book written by Thornton Wilder in 1927. It is the story of Peru in the days when it was still a Spanish colony.

A: **Peru**
Q: Where are the Nazca Lines?
W: Nazca was an ancient civilization of the Nazca, Pisco, and Ica River valleys on the desert coast of south Peru. Although the Nazca people did not produce any notable buildings or villages, they excelled in the production of beautiful ceramics and textiles. Recent aerial exploration of the arid tableland surrounding the Palpa Valley has revealed a remarkable network of lines and trapezoids interspersed with animal figures of unmistakable Nazca origin. The animals were probably built to be seen by the sky gods, and the lines are believed to be related to observations in astronomy.

A: **Peru**
Q: What country contains the westernmost point in South America?
W: To be exact, the city is Negritos, Peru, located at 4 degrees 38 minutes south and 81 degrees 19 minutes west.

A: **Philadelphia**
Q: Where was the first zoo in the U.S.?
W: The first zoological garden in the U.S. was the Philadelphia Zoological Garden, which was under the management of the Zoological Society of Philadelphia, incorporated March 21, 1859. The garden was opened to the public July 1, 1874. Feature attractions were the bear pit and the lion house.

A: **Philadelphia**
Q: What's "The City of Brotherly Love"?
W: Philadelphia is a Greek word meaning "brotherly love." The city was named by William Penn, a Quaker, whose dream was to have this city be a place of complete religous and racial freedom and universal goodwill.

A: **Piccadilly Circus**
Q: What London traffic circle was "The Hub of the British Empire"?
W: Piccadilly Circus is the "Times Square of London" and features a statue of Eros in bronze. Unfortunately, it has become the center of London's drug scene and at night can be a rather frightening area in which to be. It is the traffic hub in the west end of London where several main streets meet.

A: **Pierre**
Q: What's the capital of South Dakota?
W: Pierre was named for Pierre Chouteau, an early fur trader. The first permanent settlers arrived in 1878, and the Chicago and Northwestern Railroad reached the settlement in 1880. The town prospered as a railroad center and became the state capital in 1889.

A: **Pittsburgh**
Q: What U.S. city is at the junction of the Allegheny and Monongahela rivers?
W: The Monongahela and Allegheny rivers join to form the Ohio River in southwestern Pennsylvania at Pittsburgh. The point at which they unite is called the Golden Triangle (business district), which now includes the Civic Arena.

A: **Pittsburgh**
Q: What U.S. city was named for a British prime minister?
W: The name of Pittsburgh comes from Fort Pitt, a British outpost that once stood on the site. The fort was named in honor of William Pitt, a British Prime Minister.

A: **Poland**
Q: Where would you be if you landed smack in the middle of Plock?
W: Plock is the largest town in central Poland on the Vistula River. It is the oldest community in Mazowsze, having served as the seat of Polish rulers from 1079 to 1138.

A: **Port-of-Spain**
Q: What city does the Trinidad Hilton overlook from a cliff on Belmont Hill?
W: Port-of-Spain is the capital and trade center of Trinidad and Tobago, West Indies. Its harbor accommodates large ships and serves as a naval base.

A: **Portugal**
Q: What country is home to the TAP airline?
W: Transportes Aeros Portugueses (TAP) is the national airline of Portugal. It flies to Africa, Europe, and the Americas.

A: **Portugal**
Q: What country owns the Azores?
W: The Azores are ten major islands in the North Atlantic 740 miles west of Cape Roca, Portugal. The navigator Goncalo Cabral claimed the Azores for Portugal in 1431; at that time no one lived there. The islands are named for the native hawks, azores.

A: **Portugal's**
Q: What country's most popular tourist area is called the Algarve?
W: The Algarve is located at the southern tip of Portugal and has ideal winter resorts with excellent swimming and fishing.

A: **Portuguese**
Q: What's the official language of Brazil?
W: In 1808 the king of Portugal, fleeing from Napoleon's army, moved the seat of government to Brazil! After his return to Portugal, his son proclaimed independence for Brazil and made himself emperor.

A: **Portuguese**
Q: What language does *obrigado* mean "thank you" in?
W: *Faz favor* is "please," and *bom dia* is "good morning."

A: **potato, A**
Q: What's a *kartoffel* in Hamburg?
W: Any way you slice it, the German word for potato is *kartoffel*. If you want fried it's *gebratena kartoffel*, mashed it's *gestampfte kartoffel*, and boiled would be *gekochte kartoffel*.

A: **Prague**
Q: What city would you visit to check out Wenceslaus Square?
W: Wenceslas Square is probably the best known landmark in Prague, the regal capital of Czechoslovakia. Actually Wenceslas Square is not a square at all, but a long broad boulevard sloping down from the National Museum to what was once the moat around the Old Town.

A: **Prime Minister of Canada, The**
Q: Who lives at 24 Sussex Drive, Ottawa?
W: The Prime Minister of Canada is selected by the governor-general, who follows the wishes of the majority in the House of Commons. He holds office only as long as he has the backing of this majority. When he loses it, he must either resign or appeal for the support of the people in a general election.

A: **"Prosit"**
Q: What do you say when you raise a glass at Munich's Oktoberfest?
W: You'll be able to use this phrase or the more common *Prost*, both mean "cheers", at Octoberfest, an annual event in Munich. Have a good time, if you go. *Prosit!*

A: **Pyrenees, The**
Q: What mountain range marks the border of France and Spain?
W: The Pyrenees chain is a barrier to overland commerce, so France and Spain have had to trade with each other chiefly by sea for many years. There are only two passes over the mountains suitable for roads, the Col de la Perche and the Col de Somport. In addition, today there are two railways that cross the Pyrenees between France and Spain.

A: **Quantas**
Q: What airline is Queensland and Northern Territory Aerial Services?
W: When this airline was incorporated in 1922, it flew only between Queensland and the northern territories of Australia. When the line began flying internationally, it merely took the initials of the above areas to come up the present name Quantas.

A: **Quantas**
Q: What's the national airline of Australia?
W: This international airline is symbolized by the koala bear. There are presently 15 flights per week between Australia and North America. For further information call 800-227-4500.

A: **Quebec**
Q: What's the northernmost Canadian province?

W: In addition to its ten provinces, Canada contains two territories: the Yukon and the Northwest Territories. The Northwest Territories extend much farther north than Quebec but the question asks about "provinces." Quebec extends from the New York border to past the 60 degree north latitude.

A: **Quebec**
Q: What's the largest province in Canada?
W: Quebec's total area is 594,860 square miles – 523,860 square miles of land and 71,000 square miles of fresh water. Next in size is Ontario, with a total area of 412,580 square miles. In terms of population, according to a January, 1983, census, Ontario ranked first with 8,753,600 people; Quebec was second with 6,477,800.

A: **Quebec City**
Q: What city incorporates the Plains of Abraham?
W: There is an interesting legend associated with the Ursuline Convent Chapel and Museum in this city. The museum, located at 12 Donnacona Street in Quebec City, houses the skull of General Montcalm. The story goes that after Montcalm died of wounds received during the battle with the English on the Plains of Abraham, his officers, fearing to alarm the people, dragged his body to the convent and hid it in a hole in the countryside where a British cannon ball had exploded. The burial was witnessed by a young schoolgirl who, some 70 years later, identified the burial site for local officials. They recovered the body and claimed it to be that of Montcalm.

A: **Quito**
Q: What's the capital of Ecuador?
W: Quito is about 114 miles from the Pacific coast and 170 miles northeast of Guayguil. The city lies almost on the equator just southeast of the volcano Pichincha.

A: **Rabat**
Q: What's the capital of Morocco?
W: No doubt about it. Rabat is located on the Atlantic coast, 57 miles northeast of Casablanca, at the mouth of the Bou Regreg, opposite Sale.

A: **Red**
Q: What color are the castellated walls of the Kremlin?
W: A kremlin is the fortified part of a Russian city. The best known kremlin is the Kremlin of Moscow. It is fortified by walls topped with towers. Its present walls have stood since 1492.

A: **Red**
Q: What color does the bride wear in China?
W: We went straight to the source on this one – a Chinese librarian who wore the traditional color on her wedding day. According to ancient Chinese tradition, red symbolizes hope, good fortune, happiness, and prosperity. Red is worn frequently on other happy occasions as well.

A: **Red Crescent, The**
Q: What is the Red Cross called in Arab countries?
W: The crescent is the emblem of Turkish nations. It is also symbolized by a red lion and sun in Iran. The Red Cross arose out of the work of the Swiss humanitarian Jean Henri Dunant, and the first societies came into being in 1864.

A: **Red Sea, The**
Q: What's the world's warmest sea?
W: The normal Red Sea temperature is 22 degrees Centigrade or 71.6 degrees Fahrenheit. The temperature of the water at the surface of the world's seas varies from -2 degrees Centigrade or 28.5

degrees Fahrenheit in the White Sea to 35.6 degrees Centigrade or 96 degrees Fahrenheit in the shallow areas of the Persian Gulf in summer. The highest temperature recorded in the ocean is 350 degrees Centigrade or 662 degrees Fahrenheit. (The world's original hot tub?)

A: **Red Sea and Mediterranean Sea, The**
Q: What two bodies of water does the Suez Canal connect?
W: The Suez Canal, 103 miles long, links the Mediterranean and Red Seas. It was built by a French Corporation somewhere between 1859 and 1869, but Britain obtained controlling interest in 1875. The last British troops were removed in 1959, and Egypt then nationalized the canal. In 1948, Egypt barred Israeli ships and cargoes destined for Israel. The canal was closed to all shipping after the 1967 Arab-Israeli War, but reopened in 1975.

A: **Red Square**
Q: What's the square in the center of Moscow?
W: Red Square faces the northeastern wall of the Kremlin (the fortified section of Moscow). It has many famous buildings including the Church of St. Basil. The square is one half mile long and some 450 feet wide.

A: **Republic of Singapore, The**
Q: What country bustles with the highest population density in Asia?
W: This isn't totally accurate. Macao, an enclave penisula and two small islands at the mouth of the Canton River in China, is the most densely populated territory in Asia — for that matter, in the world. It has an estimated population in 1981 of 293,000 in an area of 6.2 miles giving it a density of 47,258 per mile. Portugal granted autonomy to Macao in 1976 so it is a country. The Republic of Singapore has a population density of 10,700 per square mile.

A: **Reykjavik**
Q: What's the capital of Iceland?
W: Reykjavik is not only Iceland's capital, but also a cultural center as well. Still quite young as a town, it was a sleepy fishing village of 6,000 people at the turn of the century. It now houses more than 118,000 of Iceland's citizens.

A: **Reykjavik, Iceland**
Q: What's the world's northernmost national capital?
W: Helsinski is the second most northern national capital.

A: **Reykjavik, Iceland**
Q: What's the largest city between Ireland and Canada?
W: This must mean "in usual air flight patterns" because "as the crow flies," there is nothing but ocean between Ireland and Canada!

A: **Reykjavik, Iceland**
Q: What national capital is heated by underground hot-water springs?
W: Iceland is an island republic in the north Atlantic Ocean. Large snowfields, glaciers, volcanoes, a deeply indented coastline, and hot springs (which are used to heat homes) are features of the rugged island.

A: **Rhine, The**
Q: What's the longest river in Western Europe?
W: Culturally and historically it is one of the great rivers of Europe and the greatest European artery of waterborne traffic. The Rhine River flows 820 miles from east central Switzerland north and west to the North Sea, into which it drains from The Netherlands. It is navigable overall for some 500 miles.

A: **Rhode Island**
Q: What U.S. state is named for a Greek island?
W: Giovanni da Verrazano, an Italian sea captain in the service of France, may have given Rhode Island its name. He wrote that an island in the vicinity resembled the island of Rhodes. Some believe that Adriaen Block, a Dutch navigator named the region. In 1614 he referred to the island in Narragansett Bay as *Roodt Eyelandt*, meaning "Red Island" because of the fiery aspect of the shore caused by the red clay soil in the area.

A: **Rhode Island**
Q: What's the smallest state in the U.S.?
W: With a total area of 1,212 square miles, Rhode Island certainly is last on the list. The next smallest state is Delaware, with a total area of 2,057 square miles.

A: **Rhode Island and Providence Plantations**
Q: What U.S. state has the longest name?
W: Providence and other towns on the mainland were called Providence Plantations in their English Charter of 1603. "Rhode Island and Providence Plantations" is its official name, but due to its size it bears the nickname "Little Rhody."

A: **Rio de Janeiro**
Q: What was the capital of Brazil before 1960?
W: Brasilia became the capital of Brazil in April 1960. The city lies on a plateau in central Brazil with a man-made lake surrounding it on three sides. Brasilia is a completely new city, and plans call for it to have a population of 500,000.

A: **Rio de Janeiro**
Q: What South American city features the exclusive Copacabana Beach and Ipanema?
W: It served as Brazil's capital for nearly two centuries (1793-1960). The blue sky, dazzling white beaches, green parks, and gray mountains make Rio de Janeiro one of the most beautiful cities in the world.

A: **Rio de Janeiro**
Q: What South American city does an 82-foot statue of Christ overlook?
W: Christ the Redeemer sits atop Mt. Corcorado, which is 2,310 feet high, overlooking the city of Rio de Janeiro. The statue is 120 feet tall and weighs 700 tons. The head alone weighs 30 tons and each hand eight tons! The statue was designed by Frenchman Paul Landowski and dedicated in 1931.

A: **Riyadh**
Q: What's the capital of Saudi Arabia?
W: It is also the largest city in Saudi Arabia. Discovery of immense petroleum deposits in the 1930s generated great wealth and transformed the city from a small oasis of mud-brick dwellings to a modern, cosmopolitan city.

A: **Rochester, Minnesota**
Q: What city is home to the Mayo Clinic?
W: Three generations of the Mayo family pioneered in the practice of group medicine and established the renowned Mayo Clinic. William Mayo, father of the doctors who developed the large-scale practice, moved to Rochester in 1863. After caring for casualties from a disastrous tornado, he and his sons along with the Sisters of St. Francis planned St. Mary's Hospital. This is the hospital used by Mayo Clinic patients.

A: **Rock, The**
Q: What was the nickname of Alcatraz Prison?
W: Located on Alcatraz Island, across the bay from San Francisco, "the Rock" had one of the most forbidding and chilling reputations of any place on earth for 30 years. Its impenetrable isolation, the impossiblity of escape and the tales of hair-raising brutalizing behind its walls fed the legend. The prison was closed in 1963.

A: **Rockies, The**
Q: What mountain range is traversed by Kicking Horse Pass?
W: Kicking Horse Pass is located in the Canadian Rockies at the Alberta-British Columbia border. It's the highest point on the Canadian Pacific Railway. Believe it or not, it received its name from its discoverer James Hector in 1858 because he got kicked by his horse while crossing it!

A: **Romania**
Q: What country is Transylvania in?
W: Transylvania means "beyond the forest." It was originally independent and later a part of Hungary. After Austria-Hungary was defeated in World War I, the Romanians of the land proclaimed themselves part of Romania. Part of the land was regained by Hungary during World War II but the entire region was restored to Romania in 1947.

A: **Rome**
Q: What is "The Eternal City"?
W: This name for Rome goes back to the poets of antiquity — Vergil, Ovid and others — who felt that no matter how many other empires might rise and fall, Rome would go on forever. The phrase was popularized by Hall Caine's 1901 novel, *The Eternal City*, which deals with a utopian state in Rome.

A: **Rome**
Q: What city does Leonardo da Vinci Airport serve?
W: Where else would an airport named after the famous Italian artist be located? To be precise, the airport is about 21 miles from Rome, but buses operate regularly to and from the terminal. It takes about eight and one half hours to fly from New York to Rome.

A: **Rome**
Q: Where's the Bernini-Bristol Hotel?
W: The Bernini-Bristol is behind Bernini's Triton Fountain, from which it takes the first half of its name. The rooms are luxuriously updated, and the top two floors consist of kitchenette-equipped suites. The Bernini-Bristol is one of the best run hotels in Rome.

A: **Rome**
Q: What city is graced by the Arch of Titus?
W: Titus was a Roman emperor who sent aid to Campania after the eruption of Vesuvius destroyed Pompeii. He also helped rebuild Rome after the fire of 80 A.D. and later completed the construction of the Colosseum begun by his father.

A: **Rome**
Q: What European city would you visit to stroll on the Via Veneto?
W: Via Veneto is where you'll find Palazzo Margherita, which houses the U.S. Embassy. As you stroll down the final stretch of the street, you'll walk past swank hotels, tearooms, outdoor cafes, and chic shops. The street was once the headquarters of La Dolce Vita and the place to be seen in the Eternal City.

A: **Rome**
Q: Where's the Trevi Fountain?
W: The Trevi Fountain is the most imposing of all Rome's more spectacular fountains. It features a couple of lusty marble Tritons hauling a winged chariot ridden by Neptune, the God of the Sea. Legend has it that whosoever tosses a coin into the huge basin will return to toss another one. No one is sure how the tradition started but the fact is that the worldwide publicity given the custom by the movie *Three Coins in a Fountain* attracts a handsome amount of the currency of all nations for local charitable organizations!

A: **Rome's**
Q: What European city's subway system is called the Metropolitana?
W: The new Metropolitana has two lines from Termini Station: one to EUR district and the beach at Ostia, another to the Ostia Antica excavations. Fast and comfortable, this subway system can take you from one vital point of the city to another.

A: **Rotterdam**
Q: What European city has the world's busiest port?
W: Rotterdam, located in the Netherlands, is not only the world's busiest port, but also the largest artificial harbor at about 38 miles square. It handled 31,565 seagoing vessels, carrying a total of 250 million tons of cargo, and about 180,000 barges in 1982. It is able to handle 310 seagoing vessels simultaneously.

A: **running of the bulls, The**
Q: What takes place every July in Pamplona?
W: The Fiesta de San Fermin was described in Ernest Hemingway's novel *The Sun Also Rises*. The festival named after St. Fermin, the town's first bishop, starts on the 6th of July and continues through the 14th. The daily bullfights are preceded by the *encierro* of the bulls when they are driven through the streets behind crowds of skillfully dodging men and boys.

A: **Russian**
Q: What nationality says *spasibo* for "thank you"?
W: Although it may not be as universally known as *gracias* or *merci*, *spasibo* is the Russian word for "thank you." We would have spelled it for you in Russian but the majority of our readers would have said, "Ya ne paneemah yoo" – I do not understand!

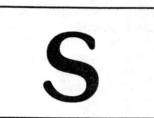

A: **Sahara, The**
Q: What desert has been called "The Garden of Allah"?
W: The Sahara is the world's largest desert and covers over 30 percent of the surface of Africa. Our hunch is that Allah is the only one who could grow anything there! (Allah is a Muslim term for God.)

A: **Sahara, The**
Q: What desert embraces the sunniest spot on earth?
W: The eastern Sahara gets an annual average of 4,300 hours of sunshine. St. Petersburg, Florida, recorded 768 consecutive sunny days from February 9, 1967, to March 17, 1969. The North Pole gets no sunshine for stretches of 186 days.

A: **Saigon**
Q: What was renamed Ho Chi Minh City in 1975?
W: Born into poverty, Ho Chi Minh spent his early years as a teacher, seaman, and laborer in France. As president of Vietnam during the first Indochina War (1946 to 1954), Ho sought negotiations with France and played an indirect role in the Geneva Accords (1954) that created two Vietnams.

A: **Salem**
Q: What's the capital of Oregon?
W: Its Indian name *Chemetka* means "place of rest" and was translated to the biblical name of Salem, from the Hebrew *shalom* meaning "peace."

A: **Salt Lake City**
Q: What city did the Mormons establish as their headquarters in 1847?
W: Salt Lake City is the headquarters of the Church of Jesus Christ of Latter-Day Saints. Members of this church, called Mormons, originally settled the area. About 65 out of every 100 of today's residents belong to the Mormon Church.

A: **Salzburg**
Q: What Austrian city was named for its mining and trading of salt?
W: Salzburg was first so called in the 19th century because of the large salt deposits in the area. This trade in salt with northern Italy gave impetus to the city's growth. This alpine town is probably best known as the birthplace of Mozart.

A: **San Andreas Fault, The**
Q: What extends more than 600 miles from northwestern California to the Gulf of California?
W: The Fault is a long crack in the earth's surface. It extends over 500 miles from the Gulf of California to Point Reyes and another 100 miles under the ocean. Movement along the Fault caused the earthquake that destroyed much of San Francisco in 1906.

A: **San Diego**
Q: What California city is home to the Scripps Institution of Oceanography?
W: Actually, the Scripps Institute is a graduate research institution in La Jolla, California. The institute is a part of the University of California, San Diego. Research projects include the topography and composition of the ocean bottom and the properties of water, waves, currents, tides, and marine biology.

A: **San Diego Zoo, The**
Q: What famed zoo is in California's Balboa Park?
W: One of the most magnificent aviaries in the world is in the San Diego Zoo in Balboa Park, where natural canyons have been roofed over. One canyon, used as a walk-through aviary, is 82 feet high, 150 feet long, and 70 feet wide.

A: **San Francisco**
Q: What U.S. city is "The Queen of the Pacific"?
W: Water nearly surrounds San Francisco: the Pacific Ocean to the west, San Francisco Bay to the east, and a one-mile-wide strait on the north. The city was the major Pacific coast port in the 1800s, but has been replaced by other ports in the Bay Area. It is also known as "America's Favorite City" (two million tourists per year), the "Most Asian City" (100,000 Orientals), the "City by the Bay," and the "City by the Golden Gate." It is the U.S. port of entry on the Pacific Coast.

A: **San Francisco**
Q: Where's the biggest Chinatown in the U.S.?
W: San Francisco's Chinatown, home for an estimated 25,000 of the city's 70,000 Chinese inhabitants, is actually the largest Chinese settlement outside of Asia.

A: **San Francisco**
Q: Where did cable car first roll down Clay Street in 1873?
W: Cable cars owe their existence to the soft heart and mechanical genius of a London-born engineer named Andrew Hallidie. In 1869, he watched a team of four overworked horses hauling a heavily laden horsecar up a steep San Francisco slope. Then and there, he decided to invent some contraption that would replace live horsepower with the mechanical kind. Years later, 1873, the first cable car, christened "Hallidie's Folly", made its maiden run from the top of Clay Street.

A: **San Francisco**
Q: What city has the two steepest streets in the U.S.?
W: Actually, San Francisco has the two steepest streets in the *world*! They are Filbert Street and 22nd Street, with gradients of 31.5 percent. San Francisco is also the home of the most crooked street in the world – the famous Lombard Street, which has eight consecutive 90 degree turns.

A: **San Francisco**
Q: What city was Fillmore West in?
W: The original Fillmore was a ballroom located on Fillmore Street near the Haight Ashbury area. In the days of "hippies and flower children," Rock promoter, Bill Graham, was responsible for setting up concerts, psychedelic light shows and album recordings at this ballroom. Graham opened a similar spot on 2nd Avenue in lower Manhattan, called the Fillmore East. He later took over a carousel on Market Street in San Francisco and dubbed it Fillmore West.

A: **San Francisco**
Q: What U.S. city was named for St. Frances of Assisi?
W: St. Francis founded the Franciscan Order of the Roman Catholic Church, though he himself was never an ordained priest! He was of a wealthy family, but gave up his wealth to live a life of poverty and service to the poor.

A: **San Francisco**
Q: Where is Nob Hill?
W: San Francisco's Nob Hill traces its name to the fabled courts of Kubla Khan and the language of the ancient Mogul Empire of India. A nabob, from the Hindustani *navah*, was originally a district ruler under the old Mogul regime. Later the word was applied to non-natives who came to India and became rich. Before the fire of 1906, the wealthiest of San Francisco aristocrats, many of whom had made their fortunes in trade with the Far East, built magnificent homes on the steep hill overlooking the bay. The area was so posh that it soon became known as Nabob Hill, only to be later shortened to its present name.

A: **San Francisco Bay**
Q: What bay does the Golden Gate Strait lead into?
W: The Golden Gate Strait lies to the north of San Francisco and connects the Pacific Ocean and San Francisco Bay. It is for this reason that San Francisco is often called "The City by the Golden Gate."

A: **San Simeon, California**
Q: Where is Hearst Castle, built by publisher William Randolph Hearst?
W: Hearst's ranch at San Simeon, 175 miles south of San Francisco, was one of the most lavish private dwellings in the U.S. The Estate included 240,000 acres of land, 50 miles of ocean frontage, four castles, and a priceless art collection. The Main Castle and 120 acres of surrounding land became a California state park in 1958.

A: **Sandals**
Q: What does the Statue of Liberty wear on her feet?
W: This statue measures 151 feet from her sandals to the top of her torch. The statue in her sandals stands on a granite and cement pedestal. The torch towers 305 feet above the base of the pedestal.

A: **Santiago**
Q: What's the capital of Chile?
W: Santiago is also the largest city in Chile. It serves as the commercial, industrial, and cultural center for the nation. Santiago's many large parks help make it one of the loveliest cities in South America.

A: **Sao Paulo**
Q: What is Brazil's largest city?
W: With a 1980 population of over seven million, Sao Paulo has top billing over Rio de Janeiro's five million.

A: **sausage, A**
Q: What's a "banger" in London?
W: There is something almost legendary about the English sausage or banger as it's usually called. Oxford sausages, which date back to the 18th century, are still sold in Oxford and are traditionally made from equal parts of veal and pork. Since they are skinless, they are very simple to prepare.

A: **Savile Row**
Q: What London street claims to be the world center for men's tailoring?
W: There's even one store that has a wooden horse, complete with saddle, to allow clients to check the fit of their riding attire!

A: **Schultz**
Q: What's the most common German surname?
W: *Schultz* means a village mayor or magistrate.

A: **Scotland**
Q: Where can you belt back a fifth of scotch on the Firth of Forth?
W: The Firth of Forth is the large mouth of the Forth River on the east coast of Scotland. The bay-like firth connects with the North Sea and forms one of the best natural harbors in Britain. The word, *firth*, comes from the language of Iceland. In Scandinavia, the word fiord, has a similar meaning. However, fiords always have high walls, and the walls of firths may be low.

A: **Scotland**
Q: What country was called Caledonia by the Romans?
W: The Romans called the people of the country "Picts" or "painted people" because they painted their bodies. The Roman emperor, Hadrian, built a wall from the Solway Firth to what is now Newcastle upon Tyne to keep the Picts under control.

A: **Seoul**
Q: What's the capital of South Korea?
W: At the end of World War II, United States troops occupied South Korea and Russian troops took over North Korea. In 1948, separate republics were set up, each claiming Seoul as its capital. The city changed hands several times during the war until U.S. forces won final possession in March, 1951.

A: **Seven**
Q: How many points are there on the Statue of Liberty's crown?
W: One observation platform in the crown has 25 windows and can accommodate 30 viewers at any one time.

A: **Seven**
Q: How many time zones are there in Canada?
W: Time calculations are reckoned from the meridian that passes through Greenwich, England. When it is noon on this meridian, it is midnight, exactly 180 degrees east or west, on the other side of the earth. Time advances one hour for each 15 degrees east of Greenwich and, in the same way, is one hour less for every 15 degrees west.

A: **Shanghai**
Q: What's the largest city in China?
W: The word *Shanghai*, which means "up from the sea," describes the city's location, as it is on the East China Sea coast between the Yangtze River and two bays. It is China's major seaport. The city had a 1981 population of 12 million.

A: **Shanghai**
Q: What's the largest city in the Communist world?
W: Shanghai, with a population of 12 million, is the largest city in the world as well as the largest in the Communist world. Calcutta is the second largest city in the world at 9.2 million. Peking is the third largest at 9.0 million and Moscow is fourth at 8.2 million.

A: **Shannon, The**
Q: What's the longest river in the British Isles?
W: Shannon is the main waterway of Ireland and the longest river in the British Isles.

A: **Shannon, The**
Q: What's the principal river of Ireland?
W: The Shannon rises in Cavan county and flows 230 miles southwest to the Atlantic Ocean.

A: **Sicily**
Q: What Italian island has been called "The Jewel of the Mediterranean"?
W: The eastern shore of Sicily has been famous for its beautiful sites since the days of ancient Greeks. It is a unique island in that you can ski a snowy slope and swim in the sea all in the same day.

A: **Sicily**
Q: What island is the boot of Italy kicking?
W: That's what it looks like, just look at a map.

A: **Sicily**
Q: What's the largest island in the Mediterranean?
W: It lies almost in the center of the Mediterranean, just off the southern tip of Italy. It is separated from Italy by the Strait of Messina.

A: **Sing Sing**

Q: What prison is found in Ossining, New York?

W: Ossining was originally the village of Sing Sing, named for the Sin Sinck Indians. In 1901 the name was changed to Ossining to avoid too close an identification with the prison! The prison is almost a city in itself, with its own school and factories. The construction of the building was started in 1825 with convict labor. Later the entire prison was reorganized, and a number of new buildings better suited to present-day prison methods were erected.

A: **Sir Walter Raleigh**

Q: Who was the capital of North Carolina named for?

W: Sir Walter Raleigh (he spelled his name Ralegh) was a soldier, explorer, writer, and businessman. When sentenced to death, he met his fate calmly. He joked with his executioner and even gave the signal for the axe to fall!

A: **Six**

Q: How many Australian states are there?

W: The capital of New South Wales is Sydney, the largest and oldest city in Australia. Melbourne, the second largest city is the capital of Victoria. Adelaide is the capital of the state of South Australia; Brisbane is the capital of Queensland; Perth is the capital of Western Australia; and Darwin the capital of the Northern Territory. There are the six states and their capitals, even more than you asked for!

A: **Smithsonian Institution, The**

Q: What was once called "America's Attic"?

W: James Smithson, a British scientist founded the Smithsonian Institution. He had never visited the U.S. but left $550,000 to the country in 1829 to establish an institution for the "increase and diffusion of knowledge among men." It was once called "America's Attic," but is now better organized so that throngs of tourists can easily view the treasures, trifles, and historical material displayed.

A: **Sofia**

Q: What's the capital of Bulgaria?

W: Early Sophia was a Roman city. The Huns invaded the city during the 400s and the Bulgarians occupied it 400 years later. Even later Sofia was under Turkish rule from 1382 to 1878. The town took its name from the sixth century Byzantine basilica called St. Sophia that is located in the town.

A: **Sorbonne, The**

Q: What's the leading university in Paris?

W: This famous institution of learning in Paris is the outgrowth of a medieval college of theology that was founded by Robert Sorbon in the 1200s.

A: **South Africa**

Q: Where's Soweto?

W: A group of towns inhabited by Africans (Bantu) is known as Soweto, which means southwestern townships. It covers an area of 26 square miles and is linked to Johannesburg by road and rail.

A: **South Africa**

Q: What country exports goods through the port of Durban?

W: The Republic of South Africa occupies the southern tip of Africa between the Atlantic Ocean on the west and the Indian Ocean on the east. The Port of Durban is located on the east coast on the Indian Ocean.

A: **South Africa**

Q: Where are the Transvaal and Orange Free State provinces?

W: The Republic of South Africa is the southernmost state on the African continent. It consists of four provinces: Cape of Good Hope Province (278,380 square miles), Transvaal (109,621 square miles), the Orange Free State (49,866 square miles), and Natal (33,578 square miles).

A: **South Africa**

Q: Where is Kruger National Park?

W: It is the world's largest wildlife sanctuary. Located northeast of Pretoria, the capital of the Republic of South Africa, Kruger National Park is 8,000 square miles inhabited by a variety of animals native to South Africa.

A: **South America**

Q: What continent does Lake Titicaca beautify?

W: Lake Titicaca is located in Bolivia and Peru. It is about half the size of Lake Ontario with a total area of 3,141 square miles. At an altitude of 12,507 feet, Lake Titicaca is one of the highest lakes in the world. Islands in the lake hold ruins of the ancient Incas.

A: **South Carolina**

Q: What U.S. state contains the resort of Myrtle Beach?

W: Myrtle Beach is in Harry County in South Carolina on the Atlantic Coast, between the ocean and the Intracoastal Waterway. It is a year-round resort named for the myrtle shrubs in that area.

A: **South Dakota**
Q: What state contains the geographic center of the U.S.?
W: The exact geographic center of the United States is 17 miles west of Castle Rock in the northwestern section of the state.

A: **South Dakota**
Q: What U.S. state is Mount Rushmore in?
W: Mount Rushmore National Memorial is a huge carving on the granite cliff in the Black Hills of South Dakota. Gutzon Borglum designed the memorial and supervised most of its work. After Borglum died in 1941, his son, Lincoln, completed it. And the four faces are…George Washington, Abraham Lincoln, Thomas Jefferson, and Theodore Roosevelt.

A: **South Pole, The**
Q: Where is Amundsen Scott Station?
W: Amundsen and Scott were South Pole explorers. Amundsen, the Norwegian, reached the Pole in 1911. He later disappeared while searching for a missing aviator in the Arctic. Scott was an English naval officer who reached the Pole in January, 1912, only to learn that Amundsen had beaten him to it. Scott's exploration party died on its return trip.

A: **South Pole, The**
Q: Which is colder, the North or South Pole?
W: The Polus Nedostupnosti, Antarctica, has an extrapolated annual mean temperature of -72 degrees F. Plateau Station, Antarctica has the coldest measured mean at -70 degrees F.

A: **Soviet Union, The**
Q: What country, after Canada and Mexico, is the closest to the U.S.?
W: At its westernmost point, the Alaska mainland lies only 54 miles from Russia. Alaska's Little Diomede Island lies only three miles from Russia's Big Diomede Island.

A: **Soviet Union, The**
Q: What country has the most time zones, with 11?
W: No other nation intersects eleven of the twenty-four world time zones. While citizens in the far eastern sections are greeting the dawn, their fellow citizens in Moscow, the capital located in the west, are sitting down to evening dinner!

A: **Soviet Union, The**
Q: What country is saddled with the ten coldest major cities?
W: According to our sources, Russia has only eight of the ten coldest cities in the world. The other two cities are Ulan-Bator, Mongolia, and Fairbanks, Alaska.

A: **Soviet Union, The**
Q: What communist country is closest to the U.S.?
W: While you probably guessed Cuba, this is wrong. The U.S. and the USSR are separated by only 54 miles at the Bering Strait, whereas Florida and Cuba are 112 miles from each other across the Straits of Florida.

A: **Soviet Union, The**
Q: What country borders the most others?
W: It's true that no other country is bounded by so many states. Norway, Finland, Poland, Czechoslovakia, Hungary, and Romania lie to the west; Turkey, Iran, Afghanistan, China, Mongolia, and the Democratic People's Republic of Korea lie to the south. The eastern and northern frontiers are bounded by seas.

A: **Soviet Union, The**
Q: What country owns October Revolution Island?
W: October Revolution, or in Russian Ostrovoktyabrskoi Revolyutsi, is the central island of the Severnaya Zemlya group in the Arctic Ocean.

A: **Soviet Union, The**
Q: What country has the most movie theatres?
W: That's correct, but how about these little known facts: San Marino has more movie theatres per total population than any other country in the world; one for every 1,512 inhabitants; Ascension Island has a record 733 movie seats for a population of 971; and Saudi Arabia (population 8.4 million) has *no* movie theaters!

A: **Spain**
Q: What country boasts the southernmost point in continental Europe?
W: A point near Gibraltar in Spain is the most southern tip of the European mainland. It is even farther south than any mainland areas in Italy and Greece.

A: **Spain**
Q: Where's the Costa del Sol?
W: *Costa del Sol* means "Coast of the Sun" and is 106 miles of coast in southern Spain along the Mediterranean. The City of Malaga lies in the center of the Spanish Riviera or Costa del Sol. Sheltered by the surrounding sierras, the area has a mild climate and is a popular resort. Several of the shallow beaches have pine woods reaching to the seashore. Only Sicily can equal the hours of sunshine in Malaga during the winter.

A: **Spain**
Q: What country covers more than 194,000 square miles of the Iberian Peninsula?
W: The Iberian Peninsula is occupied by the countries of Spain and Portugal. The Pyrenees Mountains form a land barrier to the north separating the Peninsula from the rest of Europe. The total area of Spain is 194,967 square miles including areas such as the Canary Islands. Portugal is 34,170 square miles.

A: **Spain**
Q: What country saw the origin of the term Holy Toledo?
W: This exclamation of surprise refers to Toledo, Spain, which became one of the great centers of Christian culture after its liberation from the Moors in 1085. Its 13th-century Gothic Cathedral, one of the largest in Europe, is the seat of the Cardinal Archbishop of Spain.

A: **Spain**
Q: What country did the fandango originate in?
W: The fandango is a folk dance of Spain done in triple time. It is probably of Moorish origin and was popular in Europe in the 18th century. Danced by couples, it begins slowly, and the rhythm is marked by castanets.

A: **Spain**
Q: What country produces Rioja wines?
W: The Riojas are one of the principal table wines of Spain and are produced in the region around Logrono in the northeast. Rioja resembles the French Bordeaux, though it is less delicate. Marques de Murrieta, Vina Alvina, and Motecello are among the better known brands.

A: **Spain and the U.S.**
Q: What two countries contain Sierra Nevada mountains?
W: Mount Whitney is the highest peak in the Sierra Nevada range in the U.S. These mountains were historically significant because of gold mining. In Spain the Sierra Nevada range is in the southeast near the Mediterranean coast. There is also a Sierra Nevada National Park in Venezuela, but it's in the Andes Mountains.

A: **Spain**
Q: What country's flag flies over the island of Ibiza?
W: Ibiza is one of Spain's 16 Balearic Islands. Actually Ibiza is the smallest and most southern of the "Balearic Big Three." The island has preserved many of its ancient customs and traditions. Until recent times, visitors to Ibiza were few and far between; however, the busy airport has put an end to this isolation.

A: **Spain's**
Q: What country's flag flies over the Canary Islands?
W: These islands, cones of ejection from volcanic eruptions millions of years ago, comprise two Spanish provinces.

A: **Spanish Steps, The**
Q: What Rome tourist attraction has 138 steps?
W: In Italian this is called the Scala Di Spagna. It is a dramatic late Baroque stepped passageway connecting two street levels. The steps ascend past the house in which Keats died, to the Church of Trinita dei Monti. Although suggested and partially paid for by French, they were named the Spanish steps because the Spanish Embassy moved onto the square in the 17th century.

A: **Sphinx, The**
Q: What figure sits on guard over the Great Pyramids?
W: Its head and body are carved from solid rock. The paws and legs are built of stone blocks. The face is believed to be a rendering of the Pharaoh who built it, but no one knows exactly who that might be.

A: **Sri Lanka**
Q: What country was formerly called Ceylon?
W: Sri Lanka was known as Ceylon until 1972. The name was changed shortly after the Sri Lanka Freedom Party formed an alliance with the Marxist Socialist parties and won a landslide victory over the United National Party, which was dominated by English-educated leaders. Sri Lanka, lying on the southeast coast of peninsular India, is considered an island state.

A: **St. Andrew**
Q: Who's the patron saint of Scotland?
W: Andrew, brother of St. Peter, was the first of Christ's apostles in the order of time. He is said to have preached the gospel in Asia Minor and Greece and to have suffered martyrdom by crucifixion. St. Andrew is considered the patron saint of Russia and Greece as well as of Scotland.

A: **St. Augustine, Florida**
Q: What's the oldest city in the U.S.?
W: It is located in northeastern Florida and was discovered in 1513 when Ponce de Leon was searching for the Fountain of Youth. It was eventually named St. Augustine by a Spanish admiral because he first sighted the coast on that Saint's feast day.

A: **St. Christopher**
Q: Who's considered the patron saint of travelers?
W: Not much is known about St. Christopher, the martyr. The famous legend connected with his name goes back to the sixth century. According to folklore, he lived beside a river and carried travelers over the ford; among his passengers one day was the child Jesus.

A: **St. George**
Q: Who's the patron saint of England?
W: There is reason to believe that St. George was a martyr who suffered at Drospolis in Palestine, probably before the time of Constantine; beyond this there seems nothing that can be confirmed with confidence. The East revered him in early times as a patron of soldiers, and he was known in England long before he was adopted as her patron in the Middle Ages. He was declared to be Protector of the Kingdom of England by Pope Benedict XIV.

A: **St. Louis**
Q: Where was Budweiser first brewed?
W: Anheuser-Busch is the world's largest brewer. Its beers include Budweiser, Busch Bavarian, and Michelob. Budweiser is made from the more expensive western two-row barley, rather than the common midwest six-row variety.

A: **St. Louis's**
Q: What U.S. city's skyline boasts the Gateway Arch?
W: St Louis is the largest city in Missouri. It lies on the west bank of the Mississippi River, about 10 miles south of where the Mississippi meets the Missouri River. The Gateway Arch, designed by the architect Eero Saarinen, is located on the river and rises 630 feet. St. Louis is often called the "Gateway Arch City" or the "Gateway of the West."

A: **St. Paul's Cathedral**
Q: What is London's largest cathedral, designed by Christopher Wren?
W: St. Paul's was begun in 1675 and completed during the reign of Queen Anne in 1710, when Wren was almost 80 years old. The Renaissance-style building is 520 feet long (the nave is 125 feet long), and the marvelous dome is 112 feet across; the top of the cross is 365 feet above the pavement of the church. The Whispering Gallery around the base of the dome is a source of fascination; it is 112 feet across, but words whispered on one side can be distinctly heard on the other.

A: **St. Peter**
Q: Who's buried beneath the altar of St. Peter's Basilica?
W: St. Peter's Basilica is the largest Christian church in the world. Michaelangelo took charge of its design and construction and worked on it for 18 years. The floor plan is in the shape of a cross. St. Peter, traditionally thought of as the first Bishop of the Church, is buried there.

A: **St. Peter's, Vatican City**
Q: What's the world's largest cathedral?
W: St. Peter's is indeed the largest *church* in the world, covering 163,200 square feet to Notre Dame's 64,100. However, it is incorrect to consider St. Peter's a *cathedral*, which means the Church of a Bishop. The Pope is also the Bishop of Rome, but as Bishop his official church is St. John Lateran. Thus, it is St. John Lateran that is technically the Cathedral of Rome, although it is so overshadowed by St. Peter's that no one ever calls it that. The world's largest cathedral is the cathedral church of the Diocese of New York, St. John the Divine, with a floor area of 121,000 square feet. The cathedral covering the largest area is that of Santa Maria de la Sede in Seville, Spain. It is 414 feet long, 271 feet wide, and 100 feet high to the vault of the nave.

A: **Stars and Stripes**
Q: What flag flies over Wake Island?
W: Wake Island is an unincorporated territory of the U.S., 2,300 miles west of Honolulu, with a total land area of three square miles. It was occupied by Japan during World War II and is now administered by the U.S. Air Force.

A: **Stonehenge**
Q: What famed English site is found on Salisbury Plain?
W: The attractive town of Salisbury lies in the valley of the Avon River in Wiltshire. Stonehenge, Britain's most important prehistoric monument, is a large oval of megalithic pillars and lintels, lying about nine miles north of Salisbury. Stonehenge is believed to be anywhere from 3,500 to 4,000 years old and is speculated to have been an astronomical observatory.

A: **Strait of Gibraltar, The**
Q: What neck of water do you cross in sailing from Malaga to Tangier?
W: Malaga is the birthplace of Pablo Picasso at No. 16, Plaza del la Merced. It is located on the Costa del Sol in southern Spain. Tangier, Morocco, is 17 miles across the strait from the tip of Spain and is an important port, trade, and tourist center.

A: **Strait of Gibraltar, The**
Q: What strait links the Mediterranean Sea and the Atlantic Ocean?
W: In ancient times this body of water was known as the Strait of Hercules. Only the existence of this strait keeps the Mediterranean from becoming a shrinking salt lake.

A: **Straits of Florida, The**
Q: What straits separate the Bahamas from Florida?
W: The Straits of Florida connect the Gulf of Mexico with the Atlantic Ocean. They extend between the Florida Keys on the north and Cuba and the Bahamas on the south and southeast. Ponce de Leon first recorded sailing through the straits in 1513.

A: **Sudan, The**
Q: What's the largest country in Africa?
W: With a total area of 967,491 square miles, the Sudan is definitely the largest nation in Africa. Sudan's area represents more than 8 percent of the African continent and almost 2 percent of the world's total land area.

A: **Suez Canal, The**
Q: What canal, spelled backward, is a Greek god?
W: We don't know of a God named Eire or Amanap, so we'll go with Zeus!

A: **Suez Canal, The**
Q: What manmade waterway is 100.76 miles long?
W: That's a fact all right! The canal extends 100.76 miles between Port Said in the north and Suez in the south, with dredged approach channels north of Port Said, into the Mediterranean, and south of Suez.

A: **Suez Canal, The**
Q: What canal does Port Said stand on?
W: Just look at a world map. Ships journeying southward through the Canal must pass through Port Said on the Mediterranean.

A: **"Sunshine State, The"**
Q: What's the nickname of Florida?
W: …and its state flower is the orange blossom; its state bird, the mockingbird. The state was named by Ponce de Leon on *Pacua Florida* meaning "Flowering Easter" (Easter Sunday) in 1513.

A: **Swaziland's**
Q: What country's anthem begins: "O God, Bestower of the blessings of the Swazi"?
W: It wasn't easy to find a copy of this song, but we did, and this is the first line. About 100 people entered the contest sponsored to compose a national anthem for Swaziland. Swaziland is a 6,704-square-mile country in southern Africa near the Indian Ocean coast.

A: **Sweden**
Q: What's the largest Scandinavian country?
W: The broadest definition of "Scandinavia" includes the countries of Sweden (179,896 square miles), Norway (125,057 square miles), Finland (130,119 square miles), Denmark (16,633 square miles), Iceland (39,769 square miles) and the Faeroe Islands (540 square miles). Sweden is definitely the largest.

A: **Switzerland**
Q: What country is the Helvetian Republic?
W: Swiss postage stamps and coins are marked Helvetia, the Latin name of the country.

A: **Switzerland**
Q: What country is the resort city of St. Moritz in?
W: St. Moritz is one of the highest villages in the Inn River Valley and has a magnificient view. Visitors come to St. Moritz from all parts of the world. Its fame dates back to the 1500's.

A: **Switzerland**
Q: What's the most mountainous country in Europe?
W: Switzerland is Europe's backbone, watershed, and most mountainous country. The mighty Alps cover 60% of Switzerland.

A: **Switzerland**
Q: Where does a car with a sticker bearing the letters CH come from?
W: *Confederatio Helvetico* is Latin for the Swiss Confederation.

A: **Switzerland**
Q: What European country numbers 26 cantons?
W: The cantons in Switzerland are somewhat like the states in the U.S. Each canton has its own constitution and local government and is divided into districts, which are divided into communities.

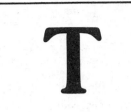

A: **Taipei**
Q: What's the capital of Taiwan?
W: Since 1949 Taipei has served as headquarters for the Chinese Nationalist government. Under nationalist rule business and industry have enjoyed a steady expansion in the city. Taipei is the home of the National Taiwan University.

A: **Taj Mahal, The**
Q: What is the claim to fame of Agra, India?
W: The Taj Mahal is one of the most beautiful and costly tombs in the world. The India ruler Shah Jehan ordered it built in memory of his favorite wife. Her title, Mumtaz-i-Mahal, which means "Pride of the Palace," gave the building its name. It was scheduled to be torn down in the 1830s so that its marble facing could be removed and shipped to London for sale at auction! Obviously, it was saved.

A: **Taj Majal, The**
Q: What are you forbidden to fly an airplane over in India?
W: The Consulate General of India Office explains it this way: there are no private airplanes owned by individual citizens, only those of flying clubs that are company-owned. Air lanes have been established that steer clear of the air space over the Taj Mahal.

A: **Tallahassee**
Q: What's the capital of Florida?
W: The capitol was completed in 1845 and was the only Confederate capital not captured by Union Forces during the Civil War. The city takes its name from a Creek Indian word meaning "old town."

A: **Tangier, Morocco**
Q: Where do Tangerines live?
W: Tangier ranks second to Casablanca among Morocco's seaports. From the sea the city looks like a great amphitheater with rows of white houses lining the hillsides.

A: **Tanzania**
Q: What country sprang from the union of Tanganyika and Zanzibar?
W: The United Republic of Tanzania is a sovereign state located in eastern Africa. It was formed in 1964 by the union of the Republic of Tanzanyika on the East African mainland with the offshore state of Zanzibar, comprised of the islands of Zanzibar and Pemba. The United Republic has a total population of 14 million, of whom 13.6 million live on the mainland and about .4 million on Zanzibar. The capital is the mainland port city of Dar es Salaam.

A: **Tasman Sea, The**
Q: What sea lies between New Zealand and Australia?
W: Just look at an atlas. The Tasman Sea is smack dab between New Zealand and Australia.

A: **Tasmania**
Q: What is Australia's island state?
W: The island state of the Commonwealth of Australia, Tasmania lies about 150 miles south of the State of Victoria. The state is comprised of a main island called Tasmania; Bruny Island; King and Finders Islands; numerous smaller islands off the coast of the main Island; and sub-Antarctic Macquarie Island, some 1,000 miles to the southeast.

A: **Tennessee**
Q: What state borders Alabama to the north?
W: Georgia is to the east, Mississippi to the west, and Florida and the Gulf of Mexico to the south. *Alabama* is Indian for "tribal town," and was later a tribe (Alabamas) of the Creek Confederacy.

A: **Texas**
Q: What U.S. state hosts the World's Champion Chili Cookoff every fall?
W: To be precise the event is held in Terlinqua, which is just west of Big Bend National Park on Camino del Rio. Each year, on the first Saturday in November, more than 5,000 spectators, contestants, and catcallers show up for this competition to see who makes the best bowl of the Texas state dish.

A: **Texas**
Q: What U.S. state was once an independent republic?
W: Texas is called the "Lone Star State" because of the single star on its flag. Once an independent nation, Texas kept its national flag when it became a state.

A: **Texas**
Q: What U.S. state lived under six flags?
W: The flags of the six nations were: Spain, France, Mexico, the Republic of Texas, the Confederate States, and the United States.

A: **Texas's**
Q: What U.S. state's biggest lake is Lake Sam Rayburn?
W: Sam Rayburn served as the Speaker of the U.S. House of Representatives longer than any other man. Rayburn was born in Tennessee and moved to Texas with his family at the age of five. He worked his way through East Texas College and law school at the University of Texas. Sam Rayburn Lake is in the eastern portion of Texas near the Louisiana border and is obviously named in his honor.

A: **Thailand**
Q: What country did Siam become?
W: Thailand is a country in southeast Asia. Its official name in the Thai Lanugage is *Muang Thai*, which means "Land of the Free." It was known as Siam until 1939.

A: **Thames, The**
Q: What river is Windsor Castle on?
W: Windsor Castle is the chief residence of the rulers of Great Britain. It stands at Windsor in Berkshire 21 miles west of London. William the Conqueror chose the site and built a stockade there in 1070. In the 1300s under Edward III it became a residence.

A: **Theodore Roosevelt**
Q: Who is the only president carved in Mount Rushmore wearing glasses?
W: Correct...but who are the other three? George Washington, Thomas Jefferson, and Abraham Lincoln.

A: **Three**
Q: How many U.S. states border California?
W: These three are Oregon, Nevada, and Arizona.

A: **Tiber, The**
Q: What river flows through Rome?
W: The Tiber River divides Rome into two unequal parts. The Vatican City, covering 108 acres stands on the right bank. Most of Rome is on the left bank. Ten bridges cross the Tiber within the city walls.

A: **Tibet**
Q: What Chinese region is nicknamed "The Roof of the World"?
W: The reason is that the valley bottoms of Tibet are often higher than the mountains of most countries! If one were to believe James Hilton, somewhere in the Karakorum Range is the Valley of the Blue Moon and, hidden by secret approaches, Shangri-La. The region around the North Pole is also sometimes referred to as the roof or top of the world.

A: **Tibet**
Q: What country is the Dalai Lama's palace in?
W: Tibet's religion is a type of Buddhism called Lamaism. There are two grand Lamas: the Panchen Lama is the leading spiritual authority and the Dalai or High Lama is looked upon as the ruler of the coun-

try and also as a spiritual leader. About one fifth of the population is monks or lamas. The Potala, the private monastery of the Dalai Lama, contains over 1,000 rooms and houses 300 lamas and numerous art treasures. In 1953 a communist government was installed by China, and after an unsuccessful Tibetan uprising in 1956, the Dalai Lama and 100,000 Tibetans fled to India.

A: *Tierra del Fuego*
Q: What's the name of the archipelago at the southern tip of South America?
W: *Tierra del Fuego* means "land of fire" and was so named because the Portuguese navigator Magellan saw a large number of fires burning there – it was the Indians trying to keep warm! Argentina owns the eastern part and Chile controls the western portion. Cape Horn is at the tip and was named by the Dutch sea captain William Schouten, not for its shape, but for his native city, Hoorn.

A: Tijuana, Mexico
Q: What foreign city is visited most by Americans?
W: Originating as a ranch settlement as part of a land grant in 1862, Tijuana was developed as a border resort with gambling casinos. It lies near the Pacific Ocean 12 miles south of San Diego. During the 20th century it emerged as the principal entry point to Mexico from California for tourists.

A: Times Square
Q: What's at the corner of Broadway and 42nd Street?
W: Times Square lies in the heart of the theater and entertainment district of New York City. Nearly every important play is performed in one of the nearby theaters.

A: Tokyo
Q: What city is served by Kagoshima Airport?
W: Kagoshima would be correct as well! Kagoshima Airport is 30 miles east of Tokyo, but only 21 miles from

Kagoshima. Tokyo International Airport is only 12 miles from Tokyo. About one million travelers pass through this city's airport each year.

A: Tokyo and Kyoto
Q: What two Japanese cities are spelled with the letters K,O,O,T and Y?
W: The only other thing these letters spell is Kooty!

SOUTH AMERICA
KEY TO RELIEF MAP

A: Tombstone, Arizona
Q: Where are the O.K. Corral and Boot Hill?
W: The city was named by Ed Schieffelin who discovered silver there in 1877, after he was told that all he would ever find there would be his tombstone. In 1881 the silver rush set in, followed by adventurers and outlaws including "Doc" Holliday and Johnny Ringo. The gun battle at the O.K. Corral was between the Earp and Clanton families. Boot Hill is the infamous cemetery that serves as the final resting place of many outlaws who came to Tombstone in the 1880s.

A: Toronto
Q: What Canadian city was Carling beer first brewed in?
W: Carling Black Label is a U.S. beer, but Carling Pilsner is Canadian. Carling Pilsner is considered an average light lager.

A: Toronto
Q: What city has the tallest building outside the U.S.?
W: The question is a matter of semantics. The world's tallest free-standing structure is Toronto's CN Tower, soaring 1,815 feet. The Sears Tower, at 1,454 feet, has been called the tallest building in the world. The tallest structure in the world is the guyed Warszawa Radio mast at Konstantynow in Poland (2,120 feet 8 inches).

A: Toronto
Q: What's the largest city in Canada?
W: This is a matter of semantics. According to *World Facts and Figures*, the 1976 census showed a population of 2.803 million for Toronto and adjacent suburbs. Montreal and its suburbs totaled 2.802 million. However, a 1981 report showed a population of 980,354 for Montreal alone and 599,217 for Toronto alone.

A: Tourism
Q: What is Spain's biggest source of income?
W: According to 1983 statistics by the Tourism Office of Spain, its visitors numbered 41.4 million and they spent 990 billion pesetas, which converts to $6.6 billion. That's a lot of pesatas!

A: Tourism
Q: What's Florida's biggest industry?
W: According to 1983 statistics by the Market Research Department of the State of Florida's Tourism Office, there were 38.9 million visitors to Florida who had total expenditures of $22.8 billion! We'd say tourism is big in Florida!

A: Tower Bridge, The
Q: What Thames River bridge is nearest the Tower of London?
W: Tower Bridge, with its twin towers and covered walkway, is the easternmost bridge across the Thames. It was constructed in 1894.

A: Tower of London, The
Q: Where in London are the crown jewels kept?
W: This building was originally constructed as a fortress in 1078 by William the Conqueror. It has since served as a zoo, a mint, a prison, a royal palace, and now, in Wakefield Tower, the home of the crown jewels.

A: Trafalgar Square
Q: What square is the geographical center of London?
W: The square has an imposing granite column with a statue of Horatio Nelson that rises 184 feet in the air. Seven major roadway arteries pump automobiles into the great paved space surrounding the square.

A: Trafalgar Square, London
Q: Where is Nelson's Monument?
W: Trafalgar Square was named in memory of Admiral Horatio Nelson in recognition of his great victory at Trafalgar. A fleet of 27 British ships defeated a combined Spanish and French fleet of 33 ships. Nelson was fatally wounded in the battle.

A: train, A
Q: What do you catch at a *stazione ferroviaria* in Italy?
W: The Ferrovie delle Stato is the state-owned railway known by its initials FS. *Stazione ferroviaria* means railroad station in the Italian language.

A: Trans-Siberian Railway, The
Q: What railroad has 97 stops on its 5,799-mile route?
W: The Trans-Siberian Railway is the longest railroad in the world. It stretches from Vladivostok to Moscow.

A: Trenton
Q: What state capital is ten miles from Princeton University?
W: In 1679 Mahlon Stacy, a Quaker, made the first permanent settlement in this area of what would become the state of New Jersey. In 1714 Stacy sold his plantation to William Trent, who later became chief justice of the colony. The name Trent Town, adopted in 1719, was later changed to Trenton.

A: Trevi Fountain, The
Q: What famed fountain was featured in the movie *Three Coins in the Fountain*?
W: The water from the Trevi Fountain was considered Rome's softest and best tasting. For centuries barrels of it were taken weekly to the Vatican and carried off by the jugful by expatriate English tea brewers. The worldwide publicity the fountain received in this movie has resulted in untold sums of all types of currency being collected from the fountain and donated to charitable groups in Rome!

A: Tropic of Cancer, The
Q: What tropic line passes through Taiwan?
W: The tropic of Cancer lies at 23 degrees 27 minutes north of the equator. The sun's rays are vertical on this imaginary line on the day of the summer solstice, June 21 or 22 of each year.

A: Tropic of Capricorn, The
Q: What tropic passes through Australia?
W: The tropic of Capricorn is at 23 degrees 27 minutes south of the equator. It passes through South America and Africa as well as Australia. At the tropic of Capricorn the sun is directly overhead at the winter solstice, Dec. 21 or 22 of each year.

A: Tropical Zone, The
Q: What zone lies between the tropics of Capricorn and Cancer?
W: In the tropics the sun at noon can be seen directly overhead twice each year. The suns rays never come from directly overhead in any region outside the tropics.

A: Truth or Consequences
Q: What New Mexico resort town was named for a radio game show?
W: Ralph Edward's radio and TV program offered to hold its tenth anniversary celebration in any city that would change its name to "Truth or Consequences." On March 31, 1950, the residents of Hot Springs, New Mexico, voted for the new name, and each April 1st the town holds a party with Ralph Edward and Bob Barker as guests!

A: Tunisia
Q: What country contains Africa's northernmost point?
W: Bizerte at 37 degrees 10 minutes north is the northernmost town.

A: Turkey
Q: What country would you have to visit to see the ruins of Troy?
W: There were nine Troys, dating from Troy I about 3000 B.C. through Troy IX during the Roman and Hellinistic Period. However, all of the Troys were located in the northwestern part of what is now Turkey.

A: Twelve
Q: How many avenues radiate from the Arc de Triomphe?
W: Arc de Triomphe de L'Etoile stands in the Etoile (star) at which 12 avenues meet in Paris. Its .name means "triumphal arch of the star."

A: Two
Q: How many stripes are there on Israel's flag?
W: The flag of Israel has a blue Star of David centered on a white background. A blue stripe runs across the top of the flag and another at the bottom. The design, based on a Jewish prayer shawl, was developed in America in 1891 and officially adopted by the new state of Israel in 1948.

U

A: U.S., The
Q: What country boasts the most dams?
W: The original face of the U.S. has been changed more by huge hydroelectric dams than is the case anywhere else in the world: from the 10,000 miles of shoreline created by the Tennessee Valley Authority dams to the large areas of now productive land created by the Bonneville, Hoover, and Grand Coulee Dams.

A: U.S., The
Q: What country is proud to claim Volcano National Park?
W: Both Kilauea and Mauna Loa are within this National Park on the "Big Island" of Hawaii.

A: U.S., The
Q: What country is the world's largest importer of cognac?
W: The U.S. may well import the most cognac, but its overall alcohol consumption of 9.0 liters per capita places it third in the rank of world nations. The Japanese consume 26.9 liters per capita, ranking them number 1.

A: U.S., The; and Britain
Q: What two countries have their flags flying over Caribbean Virgins?
W: The U.S. Virgin Islands include St. Croix, St. John, and St. Thomas Islands. They are the easternmost U.S. possessions. The British Virgin Islands include Anegada, Jost Van Dyke, Tortola, and Virgin Gorda Islands. Columbus discovered these islands and named them "St. Ursula and Her 11,000 Virgins."

A: U.S., The; and Soviet Union
Q: What two countries are separated by the Bering Strait?
W: In 1741, the Danish navigator Vitus Bering sailed between Alaska and northwestern Siberia, proving that Asia and America are separated by water. The Bering Sea (part of the North Pacific) and Bering Island are also named for him. At the strait, the U.S. and Russia are only 54 miles apart.

A: U.S.-Mexico border, The
Q: What international border is crossed the most?
W: We wanted to give you a number but it's unobtainable. Immigration Offices, where papers are checked, are 28 kilometers within the border of Mexico. Any crossing of the border up to that point is not recorded. It's a "free zone," so to speak.

A: Union Jack, The
Q: What flag flies over the fortress enclave of Gibraltar?
W: Gibraltar is a British Crown Colony that occupies a rocky peninsula on the southern shores of Spain and that is separated from the African Coast by the narrow Strait of Gibraltar. Often called the "key to the Mediterranean," the rock has been in British possession since 1704.

A: Union of Soviet Socialist Republics
Q: What does USSR stand for?
W: The name of the USSR in the Russian Language is Soyuz Sovietskikh Sotsialisticheskikh Respublik (SSSR). In the Russian alphabet these letters are CCCP.

A: United Nations, The
Q: What's headquartered on New York's East River between 42nd and 48th streets?
W: John D. Rockefeller donated the land for the building's site in Manhattan. The permanent Secretarial building was completed and occupied in 1951.

A: Unlimited
Q: What's the speed limit on German autobahns?
W: ...but a maximum of 130 kilometers per hour is recommended, seatbelts are compulsory, and children under 12 must ride in the back seat!

A: Urals, The
Q: What mountains separate Europe from Asia?
W: There's no doubt about it; the Ural Mountains are generally considered to be the boundary between Europe and Asia. It is a low range, little above 6,000 feet, with a general elevation of about 2,000 feet. In the center section, the range is divided into individual ranges.

A: Uruguay's
Q: What country's capital is Montevideo?
W: Montevideo is one of the great cities of South America. It is the chief port of Uruguay and is famous for its beaches and seaside resorts.

V

A: Vatican, The
Q: What's the largest one-person residence in the world?
W: The Vatican is the largest "one-person" residence on earth with 1,400 rooms and 200 staircases. However, it is not inhabited by only one person. The Pope and his papal court occupy an infinitesimally small part of the Vatican Palace; the rest is occupied by huge libraries, museums, and rooms with art and relics.

GEOGRAPHY

A: **Vatican City**
Q: What city is surrounded by Rome?
W: Vatican City covers 108 acres sprawled over a hill west of the Tiber River, separated by a wide high wall from the city of Rome that surrounds it.

A: **Vatican City**
Q: What's the world's smallest independent state?
W: Vatican City is the size of a golf course (approximately 1.6 sq. miles). The city became the smallest independent country in the world in 1929. Although there are roughly only 750 people who live in Vatican City, as the seat of the Roman Catholic Church its constituency consists of 550 million followers. The Vatican is an ecclesiastical paradise – there are no taxes!

A: **Venezuela**
Q: What country is Angel Falls in?
W: Angel Falls, the world's highest waterfall, drops 3,212 feet. The falls are over twice as high as the 1,472-foot Empire State Building in New York City.

A: **Venezuela's**
Q: What country's currency is the bolivar?
W: The bolivar is the standard coin of Venezuela, and it is made up of 100 centimos. The silver coin was named for Simon Bolivar, one of South America's greatest generals, who has been called "El Libertador" and "The George Washington of South America."

A: **Venice**
Q: What city would you be in if you were feeding the pigeons in the Piazza San Marco?
W: Some of the most famous buildings of Venice are on a square called the Piazza of San Marco in the heart of the city. This square was named for the patron saint of Venice, who was buried in Venice in A.D. 829.

A: **Venice**
Q: What European city is known as "The Bride of the Sea"?
W: This is from a medieval ceremony known as the "Marriage of the Adriatic" in which the Doge of Venice threw a ring into the sea to symbolize that the sea was subject to the republic of Venice as a wife is subject to her husband. The ceremony was held on Ascension Day each year from about 1000 to 1798.

A: **Venice**
Q: What Italian city marched its prisoners down the Bridge of Sighs?
W: Prisoners were marched from the Palazzo Ducale, the Doges' Palace, to the gloomy cells of Piombi Prison in Venice via the Bridge of Sighs that crossed the nearby canal. It way usually a one-way trip!

A: **Venice**
Q: Where does the Rialto Bridge span the Grand Canal?
W: The famous Rialto Bridge, a marble arch lined with a double row of shops on either side of a broad footway, was built from 1588 to 1591. Crossing the S-shaped Grand Canal of Venice, the Rialto Bridge connects Rialto, the center of commercial activity, and San Marco, the center of the city.

A: **Venice's**
Q: What city's main thoroughfare is the Grand Canal?
W: Although the Grand Canal is the high road of the city, one must cruise along its two-mile length by gondola. Measuring up to 230 feet across and never more than 17 feet deep, the Grand Canal winds like an inverted "S" through the whole of Venice.

A: **Vermont**
Q: What New England state doesn't border the Atlantic?
W: The New England states include Maine, New Hampshire, Vermont, Massachusetts, Rhode Island, and Connecticut. The area was named by Captain John Smith in 1614. Each of these states, except Vermont, does touch the Atlantic Ocean somewhere along its border.

A: **Verrazano-Narrows Bridge, The**
Q: What's the world's longest suspension bridge?
W: *Wrong!* It's the longest in North America. The longest in the world is the Humber Estuary Bridge in England with a span of 4,626 ft. New York's Verrazano-Narrows is 4,260 ft.

A: **Victoria Station**
Q: What London station do trains for Paris leave from?
W: These boat trains leave Victoria Station for both Dover and Folkestone on the British coast and cross the sea to Calais or Boulogne in France. The sea crossing takes about an hour and a half.

A: **Vienna**
Q: What city is *wiener schnitzel* named for?
W: Correct! *Wiener* is the German word for Vienna.

A: **Virginia**
Q: What U.S. state is George Washington's Mount Vernon in?
W: Mount Vernon was named for Admiral Edward Vernon, a commander in the British Navy under whom Lawrence, George Washington's half-brother, served.

A: **Volga, The**
Q: What's Europe's longest river?
W: There's no doubt about it; the Volga is Europe's longest river, winding 2,292 miles from northern Russia to the Caspian Sea.

A: **Volga's, The**
Q: What river's basin constitutes one third of the European Soviet Union?
W: The Volga, and its branches such as the Oka, the Kama and the Unzha Rivers, provide over 20,000 miles of water travel to a region of about 50 million people.

A: **Wall Street**
Q: What New York City Street is named for a barrier that once kept Indians at bay?
W: In 1653 Peter Stuyvesant build a wall or palisade on the northern boundary of the village. This wall ran the same way that Wall Street does now and is the origin of the present street's name.

A: **Washington**
Q: What state is Mount St. Helens in?
W: On May 18, 1980 Mount St. Helens, part of Washington's Cascade Mountains, began to erupt. The end result was $16 billion in damages and 57 deaths.

A: **Washington**
Q: What U.S. state includes the San Juan Islands?
W: The 170 or more islands that make up the San Juan Islands are centered in Puget Sound between Vancouver Island and Washington State. They were named by Spanish explorers. Friday Harbor is the center port—no relation to Robinson Crusoe that we know of!

A: **Washington**
Q: What's the capital of the District of Columbia?
W: The city and the District of Columbia have the same boundaries. George Washington chose the exact spot for the city in 1791. He then hired the famous French engineer Charles L'Enfant to draw plans.

A: **Washington**
Q: What's the most commonly-occurring place-name in the U.S.?
W: There are nine cities named Washington, including Washington Park, Illinois. By contrast there are only three Lincolns, and one town named after America's famous explorer Daniel Boone. There is also a Washington lily, a Washington palm, and a Washington pie, not to mention a Washington thorn, and a Booker T. Washington. The Washington apple is named after the state, so that doesn't count!

A: **Washington**
Q: What's the only U.S. state named for a president?
W: On March 2, 1853, the territory of Washington was named for George Washington, the first President of the U.S. No other state shares the distinction of being named for a past president.

A: **Washington, D.C.**
Q: What city is served by Dulles International Airport?
W: National Airport is across the Potomac from downtown Washington. Dulles International Airport was named after John Foster Dulles, Secretary of State under Eisenhower, and is located 15 miles from Washington, D.C. It was long underused because of this distance from the city.

A: **Washington Square**
Q: What square is considered the heart of Greenwich Village?
W: If you read a guide to New York City and look up the section on Greenwich Village, it will inevitably tell you to begin your tour at the Washington Square Arch, located at Fifth Avenue and Waverly Place. On the west bank is a statue of George Washington done by Alexander Stulenz Calder. Washington Square Park is a mecca for "villagers." You'll find ancient Sicilians playing chess; painters and composers from the lofts of So Ho south of the Park; children and their mothers from the expensive apartment buildings; and hippies, panhandlers, and college professors from New York University.

A: **Waterford**
Q: What Irish city is renowned for its crystal?
W: The Irish glass industry was nearly ruined by a 19th century British excise tax, but the industry has been revived and Waterford glass is again available. Phone (051) 3371 for the time of the next tour of the factory.

A: **Waterloo Station**
Q: What's the largest train station in Britain?
W: Waterloo is a terminal of the southern region where the boat trains from Southampton arrive. The station was rebuilt in 1912 to 1922.

A: **Wellington, New Zealand**
Q: What's the world's southernmost national capital?
W: It is over 40 degrees south of the equator. The next most southern capitals are Canberra, Australia; Buenos Aires, Argentina; Montevideo, Uruguay; Santiago, Chile; and Cape Town, South Africa.

A: **West Berlin**
Q: What city is served by Tempelhof Airport?
W: A memorial commemorating the great airlift of June 12, 1948 to October 6, 1949, can be seen at the Platz der Luftbrucke in front of Tempelhof Airport. Thirty-one American and 39 British airmen lost their lives flying in food and medicine during this Berlin Blockade.

A: **West Berlin**
Q: What Free World city is behind the Iron Curtain?
W: After World War II Berlin was divided into four sectors under the control of a four-power Kommandatura composed of U.S., British, French, and Soviet authorities. In June 1948, the Soviet General walked out and the Berlin Blockade began. West Berlin was isolated deep inside Soviet-occupied Germany. Although the blockade was lifted in September 1949, the city remains isolated.

A: **West Berlin**
Q: Where's Checkpoint Charlie?
W: It's the international frontier between East and West Berlin where foreigners with passports may cross at the corner of Friedrichstrasse and Zimmerstrasse.

A: **West Germany**
Q: What country borders Denmark to the south?
W: Denmark is actually a land extension of West Germany. West Germany is a Federal republic with Bonn as its capital. West Germany is over twice as large as East Germany and has three times as many people.

A: **West Germany**
Q: What country is home to the Dresdner Bank?
W: The Dresdner Bank A.G. is the second largest bank in West Germany, the largest being Deutsche Bank. The main branch of the Dresdner Bank is in Frankfurt. Like an address? 1 Juergen Ponto Platz, 6000 Frankfurt, a.M.1, West Germany. (The a.M. stands for "on the Mein River.")

A: **West Germany**
Q: What country is BRD?
W: The official name of West Germany is *Bundes Republic Deutschland* or Federal Republic of Germany.

A: **West Germany**
Q: What country is the largest per capita consumer of beer?

W: The West Germans win at .708 pints per person per day!

A: **West Germany**
Q: Where's the Black Forest?
W: Schwarzwald, or the Black Forest, is in southwestern Germany. It is densely covered with dark fir trees and the scene of many ancient German legends and fairy tales. The Rhine flows past it for 85 miles, and the Danube rises there. It is most famous for its cuckoo clocks. The well-known health spa Baden-Baden is there, and people come from all over to enjoy the health-giving mineral waters.

A: **Westminster Abbey**
Q: What British abbey contains Poet's Corner?
W: Burial in Westminster Abbey is one of the greatest honors England can give. Kings and Queens are buried in the Chapel of Henry VII. Statesmen and other great men of England are buried in other parts of the Abbey. The bodies of many of England's greatest poets lie in the Poet's Corner.

A: **White**
Q: What's the color of mourning in Moslem countries?
W: It is also the Chinese color for mourning, and white was worn by those who mourned Julius Caesar.

A: **White**
Q: What's the most common color of houses in North America?
W: Take a poll of the people you're playing this game with and you'll see!

A: **White House, The**
Q: Where does the phone ring if you dial 202-456-1414?
W: That's the number all right. Check it out for yourself by making a call!

A: **Windsor Castle**
Q: What's the largest inhabited castle?
W: Located at New Windsor, Berkshire, England, the royal residence of Windsor is indeed the largest inhabited castle in the world. Although there was a royal residence at Windsor in Saxon times, it was William I the Conqueror who developed the present site.

A: **Wine**
Q: What do the French "Appellation d'Origin Controlee" laws regulate?
W: This body legislates the production of the finest wines of France, not your everyday table wine. They control yield per acre, minimum alcoholic content in finished wine, the wine-making process, grape variety, and the region of origin.

A: **Wisconsin**
Q: What U.S. state borders Illinois to the north?
W: Illinois and Wisconsin are part of the East North Central States. Wisconsin and Illinois were part of the Northwest Territory, which also included Michigan, Indiana, and Ohio. These states all have universities that are members of the Big Ten Athletic Conference.

A: **World Trade Center, The**
Q: What New York City complex has 208 elevators and 43,600 windows?
W: Each of the two towers has over 4.3 million square feet of floor space! It was the tallest office building until the Sears Tower in Chicago reached the 104th floor on March 6, 1973!

A: **Wyoming**
Q: What U.S. state comes last in an alphabetical list?
W: From Alabama to West Virginia and Wisconsin, any way you look at it, Wyoming is last.

A: **Yangtze, The**
Q: What Chinese river is known as "The Child of the Ocean"?
W: The Chinese call the Yangtze the Great River; however, *Yangtze* itself does mean "Child of the Ocean."

A: **Yangtze, The**
Q: What's the longest river in Asia?
W: The Yangtze, winding 3,720 miles from its source in western China's Kunlun Range to the East China Sea near Shanghai, is the longest river in Asia and the third longest river in the world. The river cuts China into north and south and drains an area of 714,000 miles.

A: **Yellow, The**
Q: What river is known as "China's Sorrow" because of its flooding?
W: The Hwang Ho, or the Yellow River is called "China's Sorrow," "The Ungovernable," and "The Scourge of the Sons of Han" not only because it overflows its bank, but also because it completely alters its entire lower course! It has altered its outlet a dozen times or more in the last 4,000 years. Also the current is so swift that it is almost useless for large vessels.

A: **Yellowstone National Park**
Q: What park contains Firehole River and Fairy Falls?
W: Yellowstone was the first (1872) and is still the largest National Park in the U.S. The Firehole River was named for its valley, called Burnt Hole by early trappers because of a great forest fire that swept the area.

A: **Yellowstone National Park, Wyoming**
Q: Where's Old Faithful?
W: In a world where most things never stay the same, it's reassuring to know that for about five minutes every hour this old geyser erupts day in and day out. Yellowstone is the oldest National Park in the U.S. and the world's greatest geyser area.

A: **Yellowstone National Park's**
Q: What park's entrance is graced by the Roosevelt Arch?
W: Hiram Chittendon wrote a classic historical account of the park, built more than 400 miles of roads in the park, and built the Roosevelt Arch at the northern entrance. The Roosevelt Lodge Rough Rider Cabins offers tourist services and trips through the wilderness.

A: **Yiddish**
Q: What language is "klutz" an insult in?
W: Being called a "klutz" is certainly not a compliment. It's a Yiddish word that means a clod; a clumsy, slow-witted graceless person; or an inept blockhead.

A: **Yugoslavia**
Q: What country contains the medieval seaport of Dubrovnik?
W: Yugoslavia is located on the Adriatic Sea across from Italy. Dubrovnik is located on the southeastern edge of Yugoslavia.

A: **Yugoslavia**
Q: What country do Serbs, Croats, Slovenians, and Macedonians call home?
W: Yugoslavia is divided into six regions: Slovenia, Croatia, Bosnia, Serbia, Macedonia, and Montenegro. There are three

separate languages and several dialects. The country is as large as Wyoming but has 58 times as many people.

A: **Yukon**
Q: Where is Mount Kennedy?
W: At the height of the Klondike Gold Rush in 1898 an estimated 40,000 persons lived in the Yukon Territory in the northwestern corner of Canada. Today only about 12,000 live there!

A: **Zambezi, The**
Q: What river tumbles over Victoria Falls?
W: Victoria Falls, 354 feet high, was discovered by David Livingstone (or Spencer Tracy) in 1855 and named in honor of Queen Victoria. The falls are between Zambia and Zimbabwe. The Zambezi River is about a mile wide at this point, and the mist and steam can be seen for several miles. World travelers and explorers consider the Falls one of the seven natural wonders of the world.

A: **Zanzibar**
Q: What was known as the Spice Island?
W: Zanzibar is also known as the "Isle of Cloves." It lies 23 miles off the coast of Tanzania in the Indian Ocean. In 1964 the Republic of Tanganyika and the island Republic of Zanzibar joined into a single nation, the United Republic of Tanzania.

A: **Zimbabwe**
Q: What country comes last in an alphabetical list?
W: Any list of the nations of the world confirms the fact that Zimbabwe is last. However, this wasn't true prior to 1980 when this nation was known as Rhodesia!

GEOGRAPHY

A: **Zurich**
Q: What European city is considered the center of world banking and finance?
W: Zurich is the largest city in Switzerland and the industrial heart of the nation as well, although you would never know it because all the industries are electrified and their buildings look more like college dormitories or large hospitals! The amount of money in numbered bank accounts in Zurich is known only to the bank directors, and they aren't telling!

# #

A: **100**
Q: How many cents are there in a Bahamian dollar?
W: ...with lots of them you could probably buy your own island, as only 20 of the 700 islands are inhabited!

A: **102**
Q: How many floors are there in the Empire State Building?
W: It's located in New York City and is 1,250 feet high (1,472 with the TV tower). To get to the 102nd floor a visitor must climb 1,860 steps!

A: **132**
Q: How many rooms are there in the White House?
W: The White House is the official residence of the president of the U.S. It received the official name "White House" during the presidency of Theodore Roosevelt. It stands on 18 acres at 1600 Pennsylvania Avenue, Washington, D.C., and now consists of the original house and two additional wings connected by terraces. President Franklin Roosevelt added an indoor pool.

A: **212**
Q: What's the telephone area code for New York City?
W: There's no doubt about it, 212 is the Big Apple's area code.

A: **213**
Q: What's the telephone area code for Los Angeles?
W: Although Los Angeles is thousands of miles from the Big Apple, its area code is only one number away!

A: **312**
Q: What's the telephone area code for Chicago?
W: Any U.S. phone book showing area codes for major cities will confirm this!

A: **1600 Pennsylvania Avenue**
Q: What's the street address of the White House?
W: Some of the U.S.'s most important policies orginated in the Oval Office of this renowned building.

ENTERTAINMENT

A: A and M Records
Q: What record company was formed by Herb Alpert and Jerry Moss?
W: The "A" stands for Alpert and the "M" for Moss! The record company is located on the grounds of Charlie Chaplin's former studio.

A: Aaron
Q: What was Elvis Presley's middle name?
W: Elvis Aaron Presley was his real name. Elvis' twin, Jesse Garon, died at birth. Elvis, often referred to as the "King of Rock and Roll," died in 1977 at the age of 42.

A: "Abbey Road"
Q: What Beatles album cover shows Paul walking barefoot with his eyes closed?

W: This picture of Paul, in many persons' minds, helped to further the rumor that Paul was dead. A Volkswagen in the picture has the license plate number LMW281F, which people thought meant "Paul would have been 28 if he had lived."

A: "Abbey Road"
Q: What was the last album The Beatles recorded together?
W: This album was produced in 1969. Many people thought Paul McCartney had died previously (of course, an untrue rumor), and the cover of this album helped to further this rumor because it featured Paul walking barefoot with his eyes closed. Although this was the last album, the single "Let It Be" was released later.

A: Abilene
Q: What's the prettiest town that George Hamilton IV has ever seen?
W: Arthur Godfrey's "Talent Scout Show" was George's first professional job. He auditioned and was

originally signed to play a week. George later became a regular on the "Grand Ole Opry." "A Rose and a Baby Ruth" was his first major hit, and "Abilene," recorded for RCA, was his last major hit.

A: Academy Awards, The
Q: What was first presented at Hollywood's Roosevelt Hotel on May 16, 1929?
W: The governing body of the Academy Awards is the Academy of Motion Pictures Arts and Sciences. This group was organized in 1927, and in 1929 they presented the first Academy Awards for pictures from 1928. The Oscar statuette was designed in 1928 by MGM Art Director Cedric Gibbons.

A: "Across the Pacific"
Q: What Humphrey Bogart film poster is on the wall over Woody Allen's bed in *Play It Again, Sam*?
W: *Play It Again, Sam* was a play written by Woody Allen, which was later developed into a film. This

movie played off the nostalgia for old Humphrey Bogart movies.

A: **Adam, Hoss, Joe**
Q: What were the names of the three Cartwright sons?
W:
"Da-de-de-da-de-de-da-de-de-da-Bonanza..." Adam, Hoss and Little Joe lived with their father Ben on the Ponderosa for 11 years. "Bonanza" was broadcast almost every Sunday night. Adam was played by Pernell Roberts, Hoss by Dan Blocker, and Little Joe by Michael Landon.

A: **Addams family, The**
Q: Who did Lurch work for?
W: Lurch, played by Ted Cassidy, worked for Morticia (Carolyn Jones) and Gomez (John Astin) Addams. This show was based on Charles Addams' cartoon characters from the *New Yorker*. Lurch was the strong and silent type, but he was famous for the words, "You rang?"

A: **"African Queen, The"**
Q: What film featured the characters Charlie Allnut and Rosey Sayer?
W: Humphrey Bogart played Charlie Allnut, captain of the steam launch in *The African Queen*. Katherine Hepburn played Rosey Sayer, a shy spinster.

A: **Alan Brady**
Q: What role did Carl Reiner play on "The Dick Van Dyke Show"?
W: Playing the role of Dick Van Dyke's boss, Alan Brady, was only one of Carl Reiner's jobs on this hit show. Reiner was the creator of the series, and he seconded in the role of the producer/director/writer in various episodes.

A: **Albert Finney**
Q: Who played the title role in *Tom Jones*?
W: Tom Jones was Finney's most famous screen role. Recently he played Oliver Warbucks in *Annie*.

A: **Alec Guinness**
Q: Who won the 1957 best Oscar for his portrayal of Lieutenant-Colonel L. Nicholson?
W: Alec Guinness, better known as Obie Wan Kenobi (*Star Wars*) won an Oscar for his work as the stiff-ed-back British commander in the movie *The Bridge on the River Kwai*. The film won as Best Picture of the year.

A: **Alfred Hitchcock**
Q: Who appeared in more than 30 Alfred Hitchcock films?
W: Hitchcock loved to catch the public's attention as a personality. He worked at a time when most film directors stayed behind the camera, sight unseen. As a gimmick or trademark, Mr. Hitchcock always appeared in a scene in each of his films. His first signature appearance was in *The Lodger*.

A: **Alice Cooper**
Q: Who welcomed you to his nightmare?
W: Alice Cooper is the stage name of Vincent Furnier, a rock singer. "Welcome to My Nightmare" was an album produced by Cooper in the late 1970s for Atlantic Records. This album formed the basis for Cooper's Nevada casino appearances and an hour-long TV special.

A: **Alice's Restaurant**
Q: What's the most famous restaurant in Stockbridge, Massachusetts?
W: Alice's Restaurant was established by Alice May Brock in Massachusetts. Arlo Guthrie made it famous through a record and a movie. 'Cause we all know "you can eat anything you want at Alices's Restaurant."

A: *All About Eve*
Q: What 1950 film won seven Oscars, including best picture?
W: *All About Eve* starred Bette Davis as Margo Channing and co-starred Anne Baxter, Celeste Holm, George Sanders, and Gary Merrillo. *All About Eve* has the distinction of being the most nominated film (14 nominations). *Eve* won Oscars for Supporting Actor, Directing, Screenplay, Sound Recording, Costume Design, and Best Picture. That's six not seven!

A: *All the King's Men*
Q: What film did Broderick Crawford win the best actor Oscar for in 1949?
W: This movie depicted the rise and fall of Governor Willie Stark (Broderick Crawford) based on the career of Huey Long. *All the King's Men* also won Best Picture and Best Supporting Actress (Mercedes McCambridge).

A: **Allen Funt**
Q: Who hosted radio's "Candid Microphone" in 1947?
W: "Candid Microphone" was the father of Allen Funt's "Candid Camera." The first television version of "Candid Camera" was in fact called "Candid Microphone."

A: **"American Bandstand"**
Q: What TV show did Philadelphia kids Kenny Rossi and Justine Corelli regularly show up on?
W: The world's oldest teenager, Dick Clark, emceed this show starting in July 1956. Corelli and Rossi were the most popular dancing couple during the 1950s. The theme song for the show was "Bandsman Boogie," and the show's original host was Bob Horn.

A: **"American Pie"**
Q: What Don McLean song laments the day Buddy Holly died?
W: This song does lament the day Buddy Holly died, but it also goes deeper than that one verse. It tells the social and political history of a generation by following the rise and fall of rock 'n roll. Each verse deals with an episode in this history of rock 'n roll.

A: anchor, An
Q: What's tattooed on Popeye's arm?
W: What's more natural than an anchor for a sailor? Popeye was an animated cartoon character who started on the movie screen in the early 1930s. He was later brought to television. Popeye was known to be "strong to the finish 'cause I eat s me spinach."

A: *Anastasia*
Q: What movie told of Anna Anderson's claim to be a Russian czar's daughter?
W: The title role of Anastasia was played by Ingrid Bergman. She won the Film Critics Circle Award and the Oscar for her portrayal.

A: Andrews and Christie
Q: What two Julies won best actress Oscars for 1964 and 1965?
W: Julie Andrews won Best Actress in 1964 for her performance as Mary Poppins, a magical Nanny. Julie Christie won her Oscar in 1965 for her performance as an ambitious model in *Darling*.

A: Andrews Sisters, The
Q: What singing group consisted of Laverne, Maxine and Patty?
W: These three sisters appeared often on radio in the 1930s and 1940s working with such stars as Glenn Miller and Bing Crosby. They also worked with Leon Belasca's Band.

A: Animal acts
Q: What type of acts were barred from the Miss America contest in 1948?
W: The Miss America Pageant wasn't televised in 1948 so it wasn't viewer sensitivity they were worried about! All we can say is we wouldn't want to follow a "trained" act if we were contestants!

A: Ann Sheridan
Q: What Hollywood actress was the "Oomph Girl"?
W: Ann Sheridan won a beauty contest that got her a screen test and studio contract. Warner Brothers studios billed Miss Sheridan as the "Oomph Girl," but Miss Sheridan always claimed she couldn't figure out why.

A: Anne Bancroft
Q: Who portrayed Mrs. Robinson in *The Graduate*?
W: Anne Bancroft played opposite Dustin Hoffman in this film. (This was Dustin Hoffman's first major role.) Miss Bancroft, married to comedy actor/director Mel Brooks, won an Oscar in 1962 for her portrayal of Anne Sullivan in *The Miracle Worker*.

A: Anne Francis
Q: What beauty-marked blonde portrayed female TV detective Honey West?
W: Anne Francis has the distinction of being the first lady television private eye. John Ericson played Sam Bolt, Honey's partner. Remember her pet? An ocelot named Bruce.

A: Anthony Perkins
Q: Who portrayed baseball player Jimmy Piersall in *Fear Strikes Out*?
W: This film was Anthony Perkin's second film. He made this movie before he began specializing in portrayals of awkward, neurotic adolescents.

A: At the candy store
Q: Where did Betty meet the leader of the pack?

W: The "Leader of the Pack" was performed by the Shangri-Las in 1964. It was about the motorcycle craze of the 1960s, and became a number 1 hit. The Shangri-Las were two sets of twin sisters: Mary and Margie Ganser and Betty and Mary Weiss.

A: Audrey Meadows
Q: Who portrayed Alice Kramden on "The Honeymooners"?
W: This question actually has three answers! Audrey Meadows portrayed Alice Kramden from 1955 to 1956. Sheila MacRae played Alice in 1971. Pert Kelton originated the role of Alice Kramden when "The Honeymooners" was a sketch in Du-Mont's "Cavalcade of Stars."

A: "Auld Lang Syne"
Q: What was Guy Lombardo's theme song?
W: Before that his theme song was "Comin' thru the Rye." "Auld Lang Syne" was first broadcast from the Roosevelt Grill in New York.

A: "Avengers, The"
Q: What British TV series featured Emma Peel?
W: "The Avengers" first appeared on American TV in 1966 on ABC. Mrs. Peel (played by Diana Rigg) worked closely with John Steed (Patrick Macnee) as British secret agents.

B

A: **"Ballad of the Green Berets, The"**
Q: What 1966 hit was sung by Sergeant Barry Sadler?
W: Very appropriate that a Sergeant should sing the theme to a movie about a crack special forces unit of Green Berets. John Wayne, David Janssen, and Jim Hutton starred in the movie.

A: **"Band on the Run"**
Q: What Paul McCartney album cover did actor James Coburn appear on?
W: James Coburn was not the only actor on this cover. McCartney had several celebrities/friends dress in prison garb for this cover. In addition to Coburn, boxer John Conteh, actor Christopher Lee, TV interviewer Michael Parkinson, singer Kenny Lynch, and professional gourmet Clement Freud appeared in the photo.

A: **Barbara Hale**
Q: Who played Della Street on TV's original "Perry Mason"?
W: Barbara Hale played Perry Mason's devoted secretary Della Street from 1957 to 1966. Sharon Acker played Della Steet in the revival of Perry Mason in 1973.

A: **Barbara Stanwyck**
Q: Who played Victoria Barkley on "The Big Valley"?
W: Barbara Stanwyck was a major film star when she moved to TV's little screen. Miss Stanwyck has the reputation as the most professional actress in the business. "The Big Valley," a TV western, ran from 1965 to 1969.

A: **Barbara Walters**
Q: Who was the first woman to anchor a TV network evening newscast?
W: Barbara Walters joined ABC in October, 1976, to co-anchor the evening news with Harry Reasoner. She reportedly received $1 million to switch from NBC to ABC.

A: **Barbra Streisand**
Q: Who's the only person to have won Oscars for best actress and best song?
W: Barbra Streisand, a co-winner with Katherine Hepburn in 1968 for Best Actress, won her Oscar for her portrayal of Fanny Brice in *Funny Girl*. Her Oscar for best song was won in 1976. Paul Williams shares this Oscar with her for "Evergreen," from *A Star is Born*.

A: **Barbra Streisand and Katharine Hepburn**
Q: What two performers tied for the 1968 best actress Oscar?
W: This was the first time two people got exactly the same number of votes. Miss Hepburn received her Oscar for *A Lion in Winter*, Miss Streisand won for her performance in *Funny Girl*.

A: **Barney Rubble**
Q: Who's Fred Flintstone's best friend?
W: Barney Rubble and Fred Flinstone lived in the prehistoric city of Bedrock. This was the longest running animated series in prime time history. Barney Rubble's voice was provided by voice specialist Mel Blanc.

A: **Bashful**
Q: Which of the Seven Dwarfs comes first alphabetically?
W: Can you name the rest? Doc, Dopey, Grumpy, Happy, Sleepy, and Sneezy round out the seven.

A: **Basil Rathbone**
Q: Who portrayed Sherlock Holmes in 14 films between 1939 and 1946?
W: Basil Rathbone was the consummate and best known Holmes.

Rathbone felt his identification with Holmes led to the public overlooking his gifts as an actor. Rathbone's ever faithful assistant Dr. Watson was played by Nigel Bruce.

A: **bathroom, The**
Q: What room did W.C. Fields keep his library in?
W: Now why didn't we think of that! We do our best reading there!

A: **"Batman"**
Q: What TV series featured The Riddler, The Penguin, and The Joker?
W: "Holy Cow, Caped Crusader!" The Dynamic Duo fought many foes, and appearing as a guest villain on Batman became something of a status symbol. The Riddler was played by Frank Gorshin and John Astin, Burgess Meredith was the Penguin. Cesar Romero was the infamous Joker.

A: **Baxters, The**
Q: What family did Hazel work for?
W: Hazel may have worked for the Baxters but she was the "boss" of the house. This television show starred Shirley Booth as maid/housekeeper Hazel. George Baxter and Dorothy Baxter were played by Don Defore and Whitney Blake. Hazel was based on the *Saturday Evening Post* cartoons by Ted Key.

A: **Bea Arthur**
Q: Who played the title role in "Maude"?
W: "Maude" was a spinoff show from Norman Lear's "All in the Family." Maude Findley was Edith Bunker's cousin. Miss Arthur is a Tony Award-winning actress and has performed on Broadway, off and on for 25 years.

A: **Beach Boys, The**
Q: Who made the musical plea "Be True to Your School"?
W: Capitol Records released this song in November, 1963. The Beach Boys are best known for their California surfin' sound.

A: **Beach Boys, The**
Q: What group did the Wilson brothers form in 1961?
W: The Beach Boys was very much a family affair. Brian Wilson and his brothers, Dennis and Carl, formed the original group with cousin Mike Love and neighbor Alan Jardine.

A: **Beach Boys, The**
Q: What group founded Brother Records?
W: An interesting tidbit: Glen Campbell was a substitute in the group for a short time. And the Captain and Tennile were both once members of the Beach Boys.

A: **Beatles, The**
Q: What singing group was once known as The Quarrymen?
W: John Lennon at age 16 was the leader of a group called "John and the Quarrymen." He later added Paul McCartney (14), who in turn asked George Harrison (13) to meet John. Ringo was not a member of the group at this time.

A: **Beatles, The**
Q: Who sang about Desmond and Molly Jones?
W: The whole song is about how Desmond and Molly meet, fall in love, marry, build their "Home Sweet Home," raise two children, and take turns singing in the band. Oh, well...life goes on, Ob-la-di, Ob-la-da!

A: *Bedtime for Bonzo*
Q: What 1951 film featured Ronald Reagan raising a chimp?
W: Frederick de Cordova directed this light comedy with our then president-to-be. Mr. Reagan played a professor whose experiments with a chimp prove the importance of early environment on a child. Bonzo was the chimp.

A: **Bela Lugosi**
Q: Who was laid to rest in the black cape he wore on the silver screen?
W: Bela Lugosi played many roles in his long screen career. The role that brought him international stage and screen fame was *Dracula*. He was buried in the cape he wore in his movies.

A: *Bells of St. Mary's, The*
Q: What was the sequel to *Going My Way*?
W: Bing Crosby won an Academcy Award in *Going My Way*. He played this role again in *The Bells of St. Mary's* opposite Ingrid Bergman. He won an Oscar nomination for this portrayal.

A: *Ben Casey*
Q: Who worked in 56 West, Neurosurgical Ward, County General Hospital?
W: Vince Edwards will long be remembered as Ben Casey. Sam Jaffee and Bettye Ackerman also starred. This television show also has the honor of having a hit theme song.

A: *Ben Hur*
Q: What film holds the record for the most Academy Awards won, with 11?
W: In 1959 *Ben Hur* was nominated for 12 Academy Awards. *Ben Hur* won awards in the following categories: Best Picture, Best Actor, Best Supporting Actor, Best Director, Best Color Cinematography, Best Color Art Direction-Set Direction, Best Sound, Best Film Editing, Best Musical Score, Best Costume Design(color), and Best Special Effects.

A: **Benny Goodman**
Q: Who's "the King of Swing"?
W: Benny Goodman was an American jazz clarinetist, composer, and bandleader. He made his professional debut in 1921 at Central Park Theater in Chicago. Goodman helped to found and direct the important musical organization of the "swing" period. He was also the first white band leader to adopt and popularize an uncompromising jazz style.

A: **Bernard Schwartz**
Q: What's Tony Curtis' real name?
W: Bernard Schwartz was born June 3, 1925, in the Bronx, New York. A member of a notorious street gang at age 11, Bernard had his first taste of acting in a neighborhood settlement house. In his early years Tony had the "distinction" of playing most period roles (swashbucklers, caliphs) with a Bronx accent!

A: **Bert Lahr**
Q: Who portrayed The Cowardly Lion in *The Wizard of Oz*?
W: Bert Lahr starred in vaudeville and burlesque. He reigned as the comedy king of Broadway in the late 1920s and 1930s. Lahr is best remembered for his portrayal of the Cowardly Lion in *Oz* and his role as a hobo in *Waiting for Godot*.

A: **Bess Myerson**
Q: What former Miss America was a panelist on "I've Got a Secret"?
W: Miss Myerson was the first Miss America to win on the basis of skills, as well as the obvious attributes. She was a concert pianist. After working on "I've Got a Secret," she became New York's first Commissioner of Consumer Affairs.

A: **Bette Midler**
Q: What singer-actress got her start in a gays' bathhouse in New York City?
W: Continental Baths, a Turkish bathhouse in New York, served as the "launching pad" for her fame. Miss Midler was hired to entertain (musically only) the patrons. Soon the baths were "overflowing" with her newly acquired fans.

A: **Betty Grable**
Q: What actress was the top box office draw during World War II?
W: Betty (Legs) Grable lured millions of moviegoers into the theaters during World War II. She was acclaimed the G.I.s' favorite pinup. She starred in *Moon over Miami, A Yank in the R.A.F., Million Dollar Legs* and other films.

ENTERTAINMENT

A: Betty Grable
Q: What Hollywood actress was nicknamed "the Legs"?
W: Betty Grable always admitted "my legs made me." What a pair of legs! Three million photographs of Miss Grable, clad in a white bathing suit and displaying her curvaceous legs and winning smile, were distributed in the Armed Forces during World War II. Her legs were immortalized — she left prints of them in concrete at Grauman's Theater in Hollywood.

A: Bill Cosby
Q: Who created Weird Harold and Fat Albert?
W: Fat Albert and the Cosby Kids, an animated cartoon show, debuted in September, 1972, with Bill Cosby as the host. The characters were based on Bill Cosby's childhood friends, and Mr. Cosby also supplied the voices for some of his characters.

A: Bill Cosby
Q: Who was the first black to win a best actor Emmy?
W: Bill Cosby is a man of many "firsts." He was the first black performer to have a starring role in a dramatic series. He starred with Robert Culp in "I Spy." He might also have the distinction of being the only Emmy winner to hold a Ph.D. degree as well.

A: Bill Cosby
Q: Who was the first black to star in a regular dramatic TV series?
W: Bill Cosby starred in the TV series "I Spy," with Robert Culp. He later went on to star in "The Bill Cosby Show," "Fat Albert and the Cosby Kids," and numerous commericals.

A: Bill Dana
Q: What comedian opened his routines by saying, "My name is Jose Jimenez"?
W: Jose Jimenez was created on "The Steve Allen Show." Bill played this role on his own show and made guest appearances on "Make Room for Daddy."

A: Bill Haley and the Comets
Q: What group starred in the movie *Rock Around the Clock*?
W: This movie appeared in 1958. It was made to capitalize on the enormous popularity of Bill Haley and the Comets. Kind of like an early music video?

A: Billy Joe McAllister
Q: Who jumped off the Tallahatchee Bridge?
W: Billy Joe McAllister was the subject of Bobbie Gentry's song "Ode to Billy Joe." In 1976 a movie was made based on the song. Robby Bensen played Billy Joe, and Bobbie Lee Hartley tells the story.

A: Bing Crosby
Q: Who played Father O'Malley in the 1944 film *Going My Way*?
W: Bing won an Academy Award for his portrayal of Father O'Malley in *Going My Way*. He played this role again in *The Bells of St. Mary's* in 1945. Mr. Crosby is best remembered for his crooning and light comedies.

A: *Bismarck, The*
Q: What terror of the sea did Johnny Horton sing about?
W: The *Bismarck* was Germany's largest battleship in World War II. It was sunk off the coast of Brest, France, in 1941.

A: Black
Q: What's the only color Johnny Cash wears on stage?
W: Johnny wrote a song called "The Man in Black" in which he states his reasons for wearing only black. "The Man in Black" is also the title of his autobiography.

A: Black Hills of South Dakota, The
Q: Where did Rocky Raccoon live?
W: This song was written by Paul McCartney with help from John Lennon and Donovan. It was originally called "Rocky Sassoon," but the name was changed later. What earth shaking significance? None; they wrote it just for fun!

A: *Blue Angel, The*
Q: What German film launched the career of Marlene Dietrich?
W: Marlene Dietrich was a veteran of over a dozen films when she was "discovered" and given the role of Lola-Lola in *The Blue Angel*. This movie did lead to a contract for Miss Dietrich with Paramount Studios.

A: Blues Brothers, The
Q: What did Dan Akroyd and John Belushi quit "Saturday Night Live" to become?
W: Belushi and Akroyd were regulars on "Saturday Night Live" from its inception in 1975 until 1979 when they quit, citing other commitments to films and recordings. One of these films was *The Blues Brothers*, with the spectacular police car pileup in Chicago.

A: Bob Dylan
Q: Who began life as Robert Zimmerman?
W: Robert (Bob Dylan) Zimmerman was born in Duluth, Minnesota in 1941. He adopted the surname Dylan during his year at the University of Minnesota in 1959. It is believed that he adopted Dylan in imitation of the poet Dylan Thomas.

A: **Bob Dylan**
Q: Who made his electric debut at Newport on Aug. 24, 1965?
W: Bob Dylan's electric debut in Newport caused a furor among fans and critics alike. Although Dylan had in the past displayed talents in many styles of popular music, his fans were not ready for the electric guitars at the '65 Newport Folk Festival.

A: **Bob Fosse**
Q: Who directed *Cabaret* and *All That Jazz*?
W: Bob Fosse, director, choreographer, and dancer, won the Best Director Academy Award for his film version of the Broadway musical *Cabaret* in 1972. Fosse also did the choreography for that movie. *All That Jazz*, which Fosse directed in 1979, is supposedly semi autobiographical.

A: **Bob Hope**
Q: What comedian once boxed under the name Packy East?
W: Bob Hope, nee Leslie Townes Hope, boxed briefly as a teenager. He was also a newsboy and a soda jerk before trying his hand at show business. Bob Hope has performed in all media of entertainment. Mr. Hope has won five special Academy Awards for humanitarian action and contribution to the entertainment industry.

A: **Bob Hope and Bing Crosby**
Q: What movie actors, like Webster's Dictionary, were Morocco-bound?
W: These gentlemen were not only Morocco-bound but also Singapore-, Zanzibar-, Utopia-, Rio-, Bali-, and Hong Kong-bound, depending upon the "Road Show" movie at the time. Dorothy Lamour also went along for the ride.

A: **Bob Hope's**
Q: Whose theme song is "Thanks for the Memories"?
W: Bob Hope, because of his radio success, received a Hollywood invitation to appear in *The Big Broadcast of 1938*. In this comedy/variety film he sang "Thanks for the Memories" for the first time. It soon became his theme song.

A: **Bob Keeshan**
Q: What's Captain Kangaroo's real name?
W: Bob Keeshan created "Captain Kangaroo" in 1955 for children. Who could forget Mr. Green Jeans, Mr. Moose or Grandfather Clock! Bob Keeshan also played Clarabell the Clown on the "Howdy Doody Time" show before becoming the Captain.

A: **Bob Newhart**
Q: Who portrayed Major Major in *Catch-22*
W: Mike Nichols directed the movie, *Catch-22*. It was based on Joseph Heller's book by the same name. *Catch-22* was a black satirical comedy about war and what it means to the common man. Bob Newhart played Major Major, one of the lunatic characters in the story.

A: **Bob Newhart's**
Q: What comedian's mind is buttoned-down?
W: In the early 1960s, Bob Newhart had a couple of hit comedy albums, one of which was entitled "Buttoned Down Mind." As a result of those albums he was given a TV variety show in the fall of 1961.

A: **Bobby Darin**
Q: Who recorded the 1959 hit single "Mack the Knife"?
W: In the late 1950s Darin emerged as a highly successful nightclub and singing star. He won two Grammy Awards in 1960 for his rendition of "Mack the Knife." This single sold two million copies.

A: **Bobby Kennedy**
Q: Who's the fourth person mentioned in Dion Dimucci's song "Abraham, Martin and John"?
W: Bobby Kennedy was the fourth in the quartet of famous assassinations sung about in this song. Dion Dimucci is a former rock 'n roller (Dion and the Belmonts). He is now a born-again Christian and sings only gospel songs.

A: **Bobtail**
Q: What's the name of the horse in "Jingle Bells"?
W: Okay, start singing the song. Slow down after the first chorus into the first verse. Start saying the words after "laughing all the way." Here are the words: "Bells on *Bobtail* ring making spirits bright..." See, you knew the answer all along!

A: **Bonnie and Clyde**
Q: Who made their movie getaways to the song "Foggy Mountain Breakdown"?
W: The song "Foggy Mountain Breakdown" was performed by Flatts and Scruggs. They won the 1968 Grammy for Best Country Instrumental Performance for their work.

A: **Booker T.**
Q: Who did The M.G.s back up?
W: Booker T. Jones joined Steve Cropper, Lewis Steinberg and Al Jackson, Jr. of the Mar-Keys to become Booker T. and the M.G.s. Their first big hit: "Green Onions."

A: **Boris Karloff**
Q: Who played the monster in *Abbott and Costello meet Dr. Jekyll and Mr. Hyde*?
W: Boris Karloff was a master of the horror movie. His portrayal of the Frankenstein monster brought him international fame.

A: **Bowery Boys, The**
Q: What group included actors Leo Gorcey, Huntz Hall, and Gabe Dell?
W: The Bowery Boys, a group of wisecracking slum kids, started out as part of a Broadway hit play in 1937, *Dead End*. The cast of the play went to Hollywood and made the film version. The hoodlum screen team became known as the "Dead End Kids," later "The East Side Kids," and eventually the "Bowery (an area in New York City) Boys."

ENTERTAINMENT

A: *Breaking Away*
Q: What 1979 film pictured the townies against the gownies on bicycles?
W: This movie was based on a real event and the memories of the screenwriter's life in Bloomington, Indiana. The Little 500 bicycle race is an annual competition at Indiana University, patterned after the Indianapolis 500 auto race. In the movie a group of local boys ride in the race against the university students.

A: Bret and Bart
Q: What were the first names of the Maverick brothers?
W: Bret Maverick was played by James Garner, Brother Bart by Jack Kelly. Let's not forget the other Maverick relatives: Cousin Beauregard played by Roger Moore, and another *brother* Brent (Robert Colbert). The correct answer for this question should include Brent.

A: Brian Epstein
Q: Who managed The Beatles to superstardom?
W: In Hamburg in 1961, the Beatles recorded "My Bonnie." This recording came to the attention of Brian Epstein, a wealthy record store owner. Epstein found the Beatles back in Liverpool at the Cavern, a night spot. A perfectionist as a manager, Epstein died in 1968 of a drug overdose.

A: Brigadoon
Q: What mythical Scottish town appears for one day every 100 years?
W: *Brigadoon*, by Alan Lerner and Frederick Loewe, was a musical in 1947 and a movie in 1954. The play ran for 581 performances on Broadway with David Brooks, Marion Bell, and George Keane in the title roles. Gene Kelly, Cyd Charisse, and Van Johnson starred in the movie version.

A: Brigitte Bardot
Q: Who starred in Roger Vadim's *And God Created Woman*?
W: Brigette Bardot married Roger Vadim in 1952. In 1956 Vadim cast Bardot in the lead in his directorial debut *And God Created Woman*, a film that brought Bardot international fame. Bardot and Vadim were divorced in 1957.

A: British, The
Q: Who ran through the bushes where the rabbits couldn't go?
W: The line is from the song "The Battle of New Orleans." Johnny Horton recorded this Jimmy Driftwood song, and it became the number 1 song of the year.

A: Broderick Crawford
Q: Who starred in "Highway Patrol"?
W: Broderick Crawford, the only regular character on this show, played police chief Dan Matthews. Crawford was a film star before working in TV, and he won an Oscar for *All the King's Men*. Ten-four!

A: Brooke Shields
Q: What actress was the pretty baby on the Ivory Snow box at the age of 11 months?
W: From Ivory Snow to Calvin Klein...what a career!

A: Brooklyn
Q: What New York City borough was the setting for *Saturday Night Fever*?
W: *Saturday Night Fever*, John Travolta's first starring role, is a thoughtful study of a Brooklyn youth. Something tells us the movie would not have worked if filmed on Staten Island, so that must be why they chose Brooklyn!

A: Bud Collyer
Q: Who was the original host of "Beat the Clock"?
W: "Beat the Clock" started as a radio game show in 1949 with Bud Collyer as emcee, and it moved to TV in 1950. Bud Collyer also emceed the daytime version of "Beat the Clock." Interesting note: approximately 1,100 gallons of whipped cream were used on the show, an average of 3.5 gallons per week!

A: Buford Pusser
Q: What was the name of the Tennessee sheriff portrayed by Joe Don Baker in *Walking Tall*?
W: *Walking Tall* was based on the true-life experiences of Buford Pusser. Pusser, a Tennessee sheriff, took a stand against the hometown syndicate-owned gambling operations. For his stand against crime Buford was nearly beaten to death, and his wife was killed.

A: Bullet
Q: What was the name of Roy Roger's dog?
W: And what other animals were hangin' around the old Double R Bar Ranch? Roy's horse Trigger, Dale's horse Buttermilk, and Pat's jeep Nellybelle (well, Nelly seemed alive; at least it had a mind of its own!). "Happy Trails to You..."

A: Bulova
Q: What watch company sponsored the first TV commercial on July 1, 1941?
W: It cost only $9.00 for the commercial time!

A: Bunkers, The
Q: Who lived at 704 Hauser Street, Queens, New York?
W: Archie and Edith Bunker, played by Carroll O'Connor and Jean Stapleton, were stars of the sit-com "All in the Family." "All in the Family" changed the course of TV comedy by bringing a harsh sense of reality to TV. Truly, those were the days with "All in the Family" on TV.

A: Burt Bacharach
Q: Who wrote "The Look of Love" after viewing Ursula Andress?
W: Burt wrote and sang the song in the movie *The Boys in the Band* in 1978.

A: **Burt Reynolds**
Q: Who played the blacksmith on "Gunsmoke" from 1962 to 1965?
W: Burt Reynolds played half-breed Indian Quint Asper, the town blacksmith, for three seasons on "Gunsmoke." Reynolds has played many half-breed roles – in real life his paternal grandmother was a full-blooded Cherokee!

A: **Burt Reynolds**
Q: Who was the movies' biggest male box office attraction in 1980?
W: Burt also holds the award for top box office star for the years 1978 and 1979. Quigley Publications, which produces the list, asked film exhibitors in the U.S. to name the top box office stars. These polls made Burt a three time winner.

A: **Bus driver and sewer worker**
Q: What were the respective occupations of Ralph Kramden and Ed Norton?
W: Jackie Gleason and Art Carney played these roles on the TV show "The Honeymooners." Ralph and Ed were always trying to "get rich quick."

A: **Buster Keaton**
Q: What actor was known as "the Great Stone Face"?
W: Buster Keaton stood with Charlie Chaplin and Harold Lloyd as one of the three great clowns of the silent screen. Mr. Keaton established an unforgettable character – the sad and silent loner who perseveres against the world, thus earning the name "The Great Stone Face."

A: **Butterfly McQueen**
Q: Who portrayed Prissy, Scarlett O'Hara's high-strung maid, in *Gone With the Wind*?
W: Butterfly McQueen, born Thelma McQueen, was only 13 when she joined a theater group in Harlem. After dancing in the Butterfly Ballet in *A Midsummer Night's Dream*, she gained the nickname Butterfly. The role of Prissy was Miss McQueen's most memorable performance.

A: **Buttermilk**
Q: What beverage are the flies in in "Skip to My Lou"?
W: Young people in many 19th century midwestern communities were not allowed to dance. Thus play party was invented to take the place of sinful dancing. "Skip to My Lou" was a favorite play party. The third verse tells of those "flies in the buttermilk-two by two…"

A: **By drowning**
Q: How did My Darling Clementine die?
W: Well, if you know all the verses you know that Clementine died by "falling into the foaming brine," about verse three of the song.

C

A: **Callahan**
Q: What's Dirty Harry's last name?
W: Detective Callahan was played by Clint Eastwood. This role was originally offered to John Wayne. What two things are Harry noted for? A .44 magnum and his words "Go ahead, make my day."

A: **Camptown Racetrack**
Q: Where was a bobtail nag "runnin' a race with a shootin' star"?
W: Look, we'll just give you the verse as we found it – you figure it out! "Old Muley Cow came on to de track, Doo-dah! Doo-dah! De bobtail fling her o-ber his back, oh! doo-dah day! Den fly along like a railroad car, Doo-dah! Doo-dah! Runnin' a race with a shooting' star, Oh! doo-dah day!" This song was written by Stephen Foster.

A: **Captain Bligh**
Q: What role did Charles Laughton and Trevor Howard both play in the movies?
W: Trevor Howard played Captain Bligh in the 1962 version of *Mutiny on the Bounty*. Charles Laughton played Captain Bligh in 1935; this was one of his most memorable roles.

A: *Captain Blood*
Q: What 1935 film propelled Errol Flynn to fame?
W: Errol Flynn was lucky to get this role; originally Robert Donat was signed to the part. However, Jack Warner and Donat had a disagreement about payment, and Flynn got the role that made him a star.

A: **Captain James T. Kirk**
Q: Who was the commander of the Starship *Enterprise*?
W: Captain James T. Kirk is a character from the TV series "Star Trek" played by William Shatner. A few other little known facts: his service number was SC 937-0176, and the T. stood for Tiberius.

A: **Carly Simon**
Q: Who sang the theme song to *The Spy Who Loved Me*?
W: This was the theme song for the 1977 James Bond movie of the same name.

ENTERTAINMENT

A: **Carnegie Hall**
Q: Where did the Beatles perform their first U.S. concert?
W: In 1964 the Beatles made their U.S. debut tour. They appeared twice on the Ed Sullivan Show and performed in concert at such places as the Coliseum in Washington, D.C. and Carnegie Hall in New York City.

A: **Carole Lombard**
Q: What actress died Jan. 16, 1942, when her plane hit Table Mountain near Las Vegas?
W: The "Queen of Screwball Comedy" was a title lovingly given Carole Lombard by her fans and peers alike. Lombard had accepted the job of honorary National Chairman of a drive to sell war bonds in January, 1942. It was while serving in this job that she died in a plane crash on Table Mountain.

A: **Cary Grant**
Q: What actor did Mae West ask to "come up and see me sometime"?
W: Archibald Alexander Leach ran away from home at the age of 13 to join an acrobatic troupe as a song and dance man. He was signed by Paramount in the 1930s. Mae West chose him for her co-star in *She Done Him Wrong*, and it was in this movie she beckoned him to "come up and see me sometime." Actually Mae never said "Why don't you come up and see me sometime." She told Cary, "Why don't you come up sometime and see me." Oh, those details!

A: **Casablanca**
Q: What film was based on the play *Everybody Comes to Rick's*?
W: *Everybody Comes to Rick's* was written by Murray Burnett and Joan Alison. The screenplay of *Casablanca* was written by Havard Koch.

A: **Casper**
Q: Who's The Friendly Ghost?
W: Casper was created by Joe Oriola and Sy Reit. Casper, who has ap-

peared on TV and in a comic book series, debuted in a 1946 movie cartoon called "The Friendly Ghost."

A: **Castor Oyl**
Q: Who is Olive Oyl's brother?
W: Castor Oyl was one of the cartoon characters in Elzie Sezar's "Thimble Theatre" and was not a very nice person or brother in this strip. Popeye was also a "star" in this comic strip.

A: **cat, A**
Q: What did Peter Sellers use as an ink blotter in *The Wrong Box*?
W: Sellers played on oddball doctor in a scramble for an inheritance. Either Sellers was nearsighted or a cat hater or both in this film!

A: *Cat Ballou*
Q: What film did Lee Marvin win the 1965 best actor Oscar for?
W: Mr. Marvin had to work twice as hard for his Oscar in 1965. He played dual roles in *Cat Ballou*: one of an alcoholic gunfighter and another of an outlaw.

A: *Cat Ballou*
Q: What film featured a snarly character named Kid Shelleen?
W: Lee Marvin played twin brothers in this film. One brother was Kid Shelleen, the other Tim Strawn. The good twin, albeit a drunk, was called in to take care of the bad brother. Marvin won an Academy Award for his work in this film.

A: **Cat Stevens**
Q: Who sang the music in *Harold and Maude*?

W: Cat Stevens also wrote the music for *Harold and Maude*. *Harold and Maude* is kind of a cult movie; a comedy but also a social satire of the times.

A: **Cavern, The**
Q: What Liverpool nightclub spawned The Beatles?
W: The Beatles supposedly played at the Cavern 292 times (at least a plaque there claims that). The Beatles were discovered at the Cavern by manager-to-be Brian Epstein in 1961.

A: **Cecil B. DeMille**
Q: What director made one silent and one sound version of *The Ten Commandments*?
W: Cecil B. directed a silent version of *The Ten Commandments* in 1923, starring Theodore Roberts, Charles de Roche, Red La Rocque, and Richard Dix. It was not the Biblical epic the 1956 version was, because the 1923 movie gave the Biblical account and opposite it a modern story about two brothers upholding the commandments.

A: **Cecil B. DeMille**
Q: Who said: "Give me a couple of pages of the Bible, and I'll give you a picture"?
W: Interesting that Cecil B. should say this; his father was an Episcopalian clergyman. Many of Mr. DeMille's epic films followed the same formula: "explicit usual description of sin redeemed by verbal Christian ethic." Some historians call Mr. DeMille the founder of Hollywood.

A: **Champion**
Q: What was the name of Gene Autry's horse?
W: Champion co-starred with Gene Autry and Pat Buttram for six years. Each episode of "The Gene Autry Show" provided opportunities for Gene to sing, his sidekick Pat to get into trouble, and his horse Champion to show off the training that had made him a talented hunk of horse flesh.

A: **Channel Twelve**
Q: What channel did WJM-TV broadcast on?
W: Wondering what TV show WJM-TV was on? "The Mary Tyler Moore Show," with anchorman Ted Baxter, head newswriter Murry Slaughter, news producer Lou Grant, and, of course, assistant producer Mary Richards.

A: **Charles Bronson**
Q: What actor was the only member of *The Dirty Dozen* to survive?
W: Bronson played murderer Joseph Wladislaw, one of a group of 12 convicted GIs led by Lee Marvin, who must destroy a Nazi officers retreat in Nazi-infested France. Although Bronson was the only of the "dozen" to survive, naturally the two regular army personnel did too. Funny how that works.

A: **Charles Bronson**
Q: Who played The Tunnel King in *The Great Escape*?
W: Charles sure gets around. He was a member of both the Dirty Dozen and the Magnificent Seven. Bronson played a tunneling wizard, Velinski, in this movie based upon a true story.

A: **Charles Bronson**
Q: Who was a member of both The Dirty Dozen and The Magnificent Seven?
W: Charles is a real survivor! Although American, for many years he was the top box office star in Europe.

A: **Charles Laughton**
Q: Who defended Tyrone Power in *Witness for the Prosecution*?
W: Laughton's role as the brainy, bullying prosecutor in *Witness* is considered one of the high points in Laughton's career. Laughton played Sir Wilfrid Robarts.

A: **Charles Laughton**
Q: Who played the title role in the 1933 movie *The Private Life of Henry VIII*?

W: Laughton won his first Oscar for this movie. He was also given the first New York Film Critics Prize for the same role.

A: **Charlie Chaplin**
Q: Who was the "Little Tramp"?
W: the "Little Tramp" was introduced in the movie *Kid Auto Races at Venice*. Chaplin's "little tramp" was a mixture of two people Chaplin once knew: one a hobo he met in Los Angeles one evening, the other an old cabman he knew from home. Chaplin created his character while working for Sennett Studios.

A: **Charlie Chaplin**
Q: What actor signed Hollywood's first million-dollar contract?
W: Mr. Chaplin signed a contract with First National Studios in 1918 for more than a million dollars. All Charlie had to do was produce eight two reel films. Easy for a man who at one time had produced 35 films in a year.

A: **Charlie Chaplin**
Q: What comedian was Oona O'Neill married to?
W: Charlie Chaplin married Oona O'Neill when he was 57 years old. Oona resembled Chaplin's boyhood ideal – a girl named Hetty.

A: **Charlie Rich**
Q: What country and western singer is known as the "Silver Fox"?
W: Charlie Rich was the 1973 Album of the Year (CMA) winner. He was named the 1974 (CMA) Entertainer of the Year.

A: **Charlton Heston**
Q: Who played Moses in the 1956 film *The Ten Commandments*?
W: Heston started his career on Chicago radio. He performed on Broadway as a cast member in *Anthony and Cleopatra*, and made his film debut in 1950. He first played tough but realistic characters and eventually evolved into Hollywood's "Epic" hero. He won an Academy Award in 1959 for *Ben Hur*.

A: **"Chattanooga Choo Choo, The"**
Q: What train leaves Pennsylvania Station at a quarter to nine?
W: This song was recorded by Glenn Miller and Band on the RCA label. It went solid gold.

A: **Chester A. Riley**
Q: What radio, TV, and movie character did Jackie Gleason and William Bendix play?
W: In 1949, Jackie Gleason starred as the original Chester Riley in "The Life of Riley" on TV. The series was renewed four years later starring William Bendix.

A: **Chicago**
Q: What did Frank Sinatra call "my kind of town"?
W: Frank can't seem to pick one town to sing about. "Chicago" was his kind of town in 1957 on the Capitol record. He threw Chicago over for New York in 1980 for Reprise Studios.

A: **Chico, Harpo, Groucho, Gummo, Zeppo**
Q: Who were the five Marx brothers?
W: To movie audiences they may have been Chico, Zeppo, Harpo, Gummo and Groucho, but to Ma Marx they were Leonard (Chico), Herbert (Zeppo), Arthur (Harpo), Milton (Gummo) and Julius (Groucho). It is said they received their nicknames during a poker game.

A: *Chinatown*
Q: What film featured Jack Nicholson as a Los Angeles private eye?
W: Jack Nicholson played the role of J.J. Gettes in this Polanski directed whodunit. Faye Dunaway and John Huston also starred. Nominated for a number of Oscars, the movie was overshadowed by *The Godfather II* and won only one Oscar for the screenplay.

ENTERTAINMENT

ENTERTAINMENT

A: Chipmunks
Q: What were Alvin, Simon and Theodore?
W: The Chipmunks was a singing group featuring Alvin, Simon, and Theodore, who lived with Dave Seville. Ross Bagdasarian, the voice of David Seville (Dave Seville is also his professional name),also supplied the voices for the three chipmunks. Mr. Bagdasarian had a huge success with "The Chipmunk Song."

A: Christopher Lee
Q: Who portrayed Dracula in Hammer Studios' films?
W: Hammer Studios chose Christopher Lee to play the role of the creature in *The Curse of Frankenstein*. His good looks and his ability to appear sinister led him to the lead in *Dracula*, and he played this role many times.

A: Chuck Berry
Q: Who wrote "Roll Over Beethoven"?
W: Chuck Berry is known as one of the greatest rock 'n rollers, and he has been called the "greatest lyricist this side of Bob Dylan." He also wrote "Maybelline," "Rock 'n Roll Music" and "Johnny B. Goode." In 1972 he received his first gold record with the song "My Ding-a-ling."

A: Chuck Connors
Q: Who played Lucas McCain on "The Rifleman"?
W: Chuck Connors, a professional baseball player with the Chicago Cubs before becoming an actor, won critical acclaim for his role of Lucas McCain. After the "Rifleman" left TV, Mr. Connors starred in movies, westerns, and action films.

A: Cisco Kid, The
Q: Who rode Diablo?
W: The Cisco Kid, played on TV by Duncan Renaldo, rode the horse Diablo. His partner Pancho, played by Leo Carillo, rode Loco. After the show stopped production Renaldo toured with Diablo.

A: Cisco Kid, The
Q: What film role was portrayed by Cesar Romero, Gilbert Roland and Duncan Renaldo?
W: "Oh, Cisco!" "Oh, Pancho!" Of these three actors who played The Cisco Kid, Duncan Renaldo was the most famous. Renaldo played the Cisco Kid in films and on TV with Leo Carillo as his sidekick Pancho. Cesar Romero made six "Cisco" films from 1939 to 1941. Gilbert Roland acted in six films from 1946 to 1947. There was also a fourth Cisco: Warner Baxter played the Cisco Kid in the first sound feature in 1929 and won one of the first Academy Awards for his portrayal. Incidentally, "The Cisco Kid" was the first TV series to be filmed in color, years before color was used on TV.

A: *Citizen Kane*
Q: What won a 1972 poll as the best film ever made?
W: Orson Welles ("we'll sell no wine before its time") was the producer, director, and star of this film. Mr. Welles also co-wrote the screenplay with Herman J. Mankiewicz, and they won an Academy Award for their efforts.

A: Clara Bow
Q: What movie actress was known as "the It Girl"?
W: Clara Bow became a national screen star in Paramount's 1929 film version of Elinor Glyn's novel *It*. To many people Miss Bow personified the 1920s and her movie *It*, thus earning her the title "It Girl."

A: clarinet, The
Q: What musical instrument does Woody Allen play professionally?
W: Playing the clarinet is relaxation for Woody Allen. According to longtime friend Tony Roberts, Woody practices his clarinet everyday for an hour or more.

A: Clark Gable
Q: Who was known as "The King of Hollywood"?
W: Clark Gable was considered one of Hollywood's greatest stars. His considerable talent and personality earned him the title "the King." Of course, this acclaim came years after he was first turned down by Warner Brothers for having big ears.

A: Clark Gable
Q: What movie actor was married to Carole Lombard from 1939 to 1942?
W: In 1935 Lombard arrived at a party in an ambulance, and hired interns bore her into the house on a stretcher. Gable was also a guest at the same party. After such a grand entrance it was love at first sight. They were married in 1939.

A: *Class of '44*
Q: What was the sequel to "Summer of '42"?
W: *Summer of '42* dealt with a 15-year-old (Hermie) boy's coming of sexual age during the summer of 1942 in an island vacation community of New England. *Class of '44* picks up on Hermie and friends two years later graduating from high school and experiencing the real world.

A: *Claude Rains*
Q: Who portrayed Renaud in *Casablanca*?
W: Rains played opposite Humphrey Bogart, Ingrid Bergman and Paul Henreid in *Casablanca* and was nominated for an Oscar for his work in this film. In fact, Claude Rains was nominated four times for an Academy Award, yet he never won an Oscar. Mr. Rains held the honor of being the first British stage and film star to earn $1 million for a single role.

A: *Cleopatra*
Q: What 1963 Joseph L. Mankiewicz film cost $28 million?
W: This film version of *Cleopatra* starred Elizabeth Taylor, Richard Burton and Rex Harrison. This was an elaborate production, even though it wasn't very factually historic. It was nominated for the Best Picture Oscar.

A: **Cliff Arquette as Charley Weaver**
Q: Who used to read letters from Mama to Jack Paar?
W: Charley Weaver was a veteran of many great TV comedy shows. He is probably remembered best for his regular appearance on "Hollywood Squares." When asked on "Hollywood Squares," "Who played Helen in *What's the Matter with Helen*?, Dennis Weaver, Debbie Reynolds, or Shelly Winters?," Weaver answered, "Dennis Weaver, that's why they asked the question!"

A: **Clifton Webb**
Q: Who immortalized moviedom's Mr. Belvedere?
W: Clifton Webb seemed born to perform. He was a trained actor and dancer by the age of ten. At 17 he sang with the Boston Opera Company, and at 19 he became a leading ballroom dancer in New York. During his career he was nominated twice for an Oscar. Webb is best remembered for his role as the pompous but beloved babysitter Mr. Belvedere.

A: **Clint Eastwood**
Q: Who played Rowdy Yates on "Rawhide"?
W: Rowdy Yates was Gil Favor's second-in-command on "Rawhide." Rowdy eventually became a trail

boss. When this show was cancelled, Clint Eastwood went on to become an international star.

A: **Clipper**
Q: What was Sky King's nephew's name?
W: Who could forget the only western where wrongdoers were chased by an airplane instead of a horse! Sky King (Kirby Grant) lived on the Flying Crown Ranch with his niece Penny (Gloria Winters) and nephew Clipper (Ron Hagerty). He fought evildoers from the cockpit of his twin engine Cessna, the *Songbird*.

A: *Clockwork Orange, A*
Q: What was Stanley Kubrick's first film after *2001: A Space Odyssey*?
W: Mr. Kubrick's early movies were sprinkled with bitter cynicism and a "bleak view of the essential nature of man." These were the prevailing themes in *A Clockwork Orange*, which was voted the year's best by the New York Film Critics (1971). Kubrick was also voted Best Director by the same group.

A: *Coal Miner's Daughter*
Q: What film depicted the life of country singer Loretta Lynn?
W: The movie, released in 1980, featured Sissy Spacek as Loretta and Tommy Lee Jones as her husband Doolittle "Mooney" Lynn. The movie title was derived from Miss Lynn's most popular song and her best-selling autobiography.

A: **Cochise**
Q: What role did Michael Ansara play on TV's "Broken Arrow"?
W: The TV show "Broken Arrow" was based on the novel *Blood Brother* by Elliott Arnold. Cochise and Indian Agent Tom Jeffords worked together to fight renegades and dishonest whites threatening the Chiricahua Reservation.

A: **Colonel Tom Parker**
Q: Who was Elvis Presley's manager?

W: Elvis Presley was only a regional country artist when Tom Parker decided to manage him. He got disc jockeys above the Mason-Dixon line to play Elvis' records, and that's how history was made. Parker earned 25 percent of Elvis' income. Parker also managed Eddy Arnold, Hank Snow, Andy Griffith, and Gene Austin.

A: **Connie Frances**
Q: Who asked the musical question: "Who's sorry now?"?
W: Connie Francis started her musical career at the age of 11 with her first professional appearance, and MGM records signed her while she was still a teenager. For two years her recording career was not successful. Finally, at the suggestion of her father she recorded his favorite song "Who's Sorry Now," and it became a million seller.

A: **Constance**
Q: What was the Christian name of the title character in "Our Miss Brooks"?
W: "Our Miss Brooks" originated on radio. In the 1950s it ran simultaneously on radio and TV with virtually the same cast. Eve Arden immortalized the role of Constance Brooks.

A: **Cream**
Q: What group comprised Eric Clapton, Jack Bruce and Ginger Baker?
W: Clapton played guitar and sang lead vocal. Bruce was on bass and vocals; Baker was on the drums. Each came to Cream from other groups. Cream was a blues-based group with an accent on improvisational technique. They released their last record, "Goodbye," in 1969.

A: **Crystal Gayle**
Q: Who is Loretta Lynn's singing sister?
W: She was born Brenda Gail Webb, but changed her name to Crystal Gayle at her sister's suggestion. The name Crystal was inspired by a hamburger chain that was popular in the South – Krystal Burgers!

ENTERTAINMENT

ENTERTAINMENT

A: **Cutting heads off parking meters**
Q: What did Cool Hand Luke go to jail for?
W: *Cool Hand Luke*, directed by Stuart Rosenberg, starred Paul Newman in the title role. *Cool Hand Luke* is about a man alienated from the "establishment." For cutting heads off parking meters, Cool Hand got the penalty of two years on a chain gang (Read Co. No. 36). Kind of a stiff penalty!

A: **D.W. Griffith**
Q: Who directed *The Birth of a Nation*?
W: David Wark Griffith directed this Civil War epic without a script, improvising freely throughout. It was the first movie to be shown at $2 admission prices, and it eventually grossed over $50 million.

A: **dagger, A**
Q: What weapon is tattooed on Glen Campbell's arm?
W: He was the seventh son of a seventh son so everyone knew he would amount to something big. Campbell began his singing career at the age of four. Why a dagger on his arm? You'll have to ask him!

A: **Daisy**
Q: What's the name of Dagwood Bumstead's dog?
W: Daisy belonged to the Bumstead family. She had five puppies, one named Elmer. Currently she can be seen in the comic section of daily newspapers.

A: **Dan Rowan and Dick Martin**
Q: Who awarded the Flying Fickle Finger of Fate?

W: The Flying Fickle Finger of Fate was awarded on the TV show "Laugh-In." It was given for the current week's most embarrassing or unbelievable news story.

A: **Danny and the Juniors**
Q: What rock group struck gold with "At the Hop"?
W: First known as the Juvenairs, this group got together while still in high school. Danny Rapp was lead, Dave White first tenor, Frank Maffei second tenor, and Joe Terranova was baritone. Dick Clark suggested the name for their gold winning record "At the Hop." This group also wrote and recorded the classic "Rock and Roll is Here to Stay."

A: **Danny Kaye**
Q: Who played the title role in 1947's *The Secret Life of Walter Mitty*?
W: Danny Kaye is an actor, comic, and human being extraordinaire—Mr. Kaye has spent many years devoting his time and talent to UNICEF. Playing the title role in *Walter Mitty* gave Kaye an opportunity to display his talent of characterizing several personalities. In 1954 he was awarded a "special" Oscar.

A: **Darling**
Q: What film won Julie Christie an Oscar for her portrayal of an amoral model?
W: Julie Christie's work in *Darling* won her an Academy Award as well as the New York Film Critics Award and made her an international star. John Schlesinger had directed Miss Christie in an earler film and provided her with the tailor-made role in *Darling*. The movie *McCabe and Mrs. Miller* got her another Oscar nomination.

A: **Darth Vader**
Q: Who is Luke Skywalker's father?
W: Darth Vader is the name he took after being seduced by the dark side of the force.

A: **Dave Clark Five, The**
Q: What singing group felt glad all over?
W: They were one of the major rock groups of the 1960s. Dave Clark was an excellent athlete, and in order to raise the money to go to a tournament, he formed a five-man rock band. The group's music was so well received that they decided to continue working together. Their first gold song was "Glad All Over."

A: **Dave Garroway**
Q: Who was the original host of TV's "Today" show?
W: Dave Garroway was at one time a disc jockey and NBC page. In 1949 he brought to TV "Garroway At Large," a musical variety show. In 1952 he began his long run as the host of the "Today Show."

A: **David**
Q: What was Dr. Zorba's first name?
W: Dr. Zorba was a character of the popular medical show "Ben Casey." Sam Jaffe, who passed away in March 1984, played the role of David Zorba.

A: **David and Ricky**
Q: Who are the two sons of Ozzie and Harriet Nelson?
W: "The Adventures of the Nelson Family" debuted in 1952 and became one of TV's longest running sit-coms. This show was based on the real-life adventures of the Nelson family; even the house in the show was modeled on the Nelson's real home.

A: **David Bowie**
Q: What rock singer named his son Zowie?
W: Well, at least it's easy to remember!

A: **David Carradine**
Q: Who portrayed Woody Guthrie in the film *Bound for Glory*?
W: David Carradine is probably better remembered for his role as Caine in "Kung Fu," a popular TV show. Not only is he an actor, but he is also a singer and songwriter. He is the son of John Carradine, the actor.

A: **David Niven**
Q: Who portrayed the demolitions expert in *The Guns of Navarone*?
W: Mr. Niven could probably have portrayed any role in the *Guns of Navarone*. In his life time Mr. Niven has been a lumberman, laundry messenger, news reporter, gunnery instructor, bartender, wine representative, commando, and actor. He won an Oscar and a New York Critics Award for Best Actor in the film *Separate Tables*.

A: **David Niven**
Q: What actor was on stage when the 1974 Academy Awards were streaked?
W: As the streaker left the stage area Niven ad-libbed "The only way he could get a laugh was by showing his shortcomings." Quick thinking, David!

A: **"Day-O"**
Q: What's the more familiar name of "The Banana Boat Song"?
W: "Daylight's comin' and I want to go home."

A: **dead rat, A**
Q: What did Bette Davis serve up to Joan Crawford in *Whatever Happened to Baby Jane?*?
W: Bette Davis played a former child movie star who got her kicks by mentally torturing her crippled sister (Crawford). Victor Buono played a supporting role.

A: **Dean Martin**
Q: Who played Matt Helm in the movies?
W: Dean Martin and Jerry Lewis were a hit comedy team for ten years. When they broke up, few thought Dino would make it on his own. Mr. Martin did well as a singer, an actor and star of his own TV show. In the late 1960s he starred as Matt Helm in a number of films.

A: **Dean Martin and Jerry Lewis**
Q: What comedy team appeared on the first "Ed Sullivan Show" for $200?

W: The first telecast of the "Ed Sullivan Show" was produced on a small budget. Only $375 was set aside for talent. Martin and Lewis got most of that talent money, $200. Four other groups or people performed and shared the rest of the budget.

A: **"Death Valley Days"**
Q: What TV series did Ronald Reagan, Dale Robertson and Robert Taylor all host?
W: Let's not forget Stanley Andrews, ("The Old Ranger") who was the original host, or the last host, Merle Haggard. "Death Valley Days" was a Western anthology. Let's not forget the sponsor either – 20 Mule Team Borax!

A: **Debbie Reynolds**
Q: Who starred in *Singing in the Rain* and *The Singing Nun*?
W: These were the only two "singin" films Miss Reynolds played in, although she starred and sang in many musicals. She got her start in films after winning the Miss Burbank

Beauty Contest. Recently, Miss Reynolds has performed on Broadway in two hit shows.

A: **Debbie Reynolds**
Q: Who recorded the 1957 hit "Tammy"?
W: In 1957, Debbie played the title role in the movie *Tammy and the Bachelor*. She also sang the movie's theme song "Tammy."

A: **Deborah Kerr**
Q: Who did Burt Lancaster make love to on the beach in *From Here to Eternity*?

W: During her career, Deborah was nominated six times for the Best Actress Oscar, and in 1949, she was nominated for her role as an adultress in *From Here to Eternity*. She never won an Oscar. Miss Kerr retired from acting in 1969.

A: **"Defenders, The"**
Q: What TV show featured E.G. Marshal and Robert Reed as father-and-son lawyers?
W: "The Defenders" based on a story by Reginald Rose, was first shown as a two-part episode of "Studio One." The Prestons, a father-and-son lawyer team, worked jointly on cases each week.

A: *Deliverance*
Q: What film featured dueling banjos?
W: *Deliverance*, nominated for three Academy Awards, starred Jon Voight, Burt Reynolds, Ned Beatty, and Ronny Cox. Drew (Ronny Cox), a guitar player, strums up a "dueling" contest with a banjo playing youngster.

A: **Dennis Day**
Q: Who used to say: "Gee, Mr. Benny"?
W: Dennis Day appeared on the Jack Benny Show on an irregular basis. He also worked with Mr. Benny on his radio program.

A: **Dennis Hopper**
Q: Who directed and co-starred in *Easy Rider*?
W: Dennis Hopper directed, co-starred, and co-authored the hit movie *Easy Rider*. The film was made for less than $400,000 and grossed $16 million at the box office.

ENTERTAINMENT

A: **Dennis Weaver**
Q: Who played Chester on "Gunsmoke"?
W: Dennis Weaver played Chester Goode, Mr. Dillon's deputy, for nine years on "Gunsmoke." He is remembered for his pronounced limp, verbal twang, and mean pot of coffee.

A: **Desilu Studios**
Q: What production company did Lucille Ball and Desi Arnaz form?
W: Desilu, if you haven't guessed, stands for the creators, Desi Arnez and Lucille Ball. Originated in the 1950s, this company developed into one of the world's biggest TV businesses. Desi sold out to Lucy in 1960, and she later sold the business for a reported $10 million.

A: **Detroit Wheels, The**
Q: What backup group accompanied rock and roll singer Mitch Ryder?
W: Mitch Ryder and the Detroit Wheels (formerly known as Billy Lee and the Rivieras) took the music scene by storm in 1965 with their homegrown brand of rhythm and blues. They were the warm-up group for the Dave Clark Five and slated to sing just two songs. When they finished one and one half hours later, the Dave Clark Five didn't want to play!

A: **Diahann Carroll**
Q: Who was the first black star in a TV situation comedy?
W: The key word here is star. There were others who appeared in TV sit-coms but none who starred. Diahann Carroll played Nurse Julia Baker, widowed with a young son named Corie. Lloyd Nolan played her boss, Dr. Morton Chegley.

A: **diamond, A**
Q: What was "the Pink Panther" in *The Pink Panther*?
W: This diamond, containing an image resembling a panther, was owned by Princess Dola. The Phantom was trying to steal it. Inspector Clouseau, played by Peter Sellers, was trying, in his own bumbling way, to capture the Phantom.

A: **Diane Keaton**
Q: Who portrayed Michael Corleone's second wife in *The Godfather*?
W: Miss Keaton also played in the sequel *Godfather II*. In the early 1970s, she became a close companion of Woody Allen and played in a number of his films as well, winning an Academy Award for her work in Allen's *Annie Hall*. Diane Keaton's real name is Diane Hall.

A: **Dick Van Dyke**
Q: Who co-starred with Julie Andrews in *Mary Poppins*?
W: Dick Van Dyke was once an advertising agent. When his business folded he joined Phil Erickson in a nightclub pantomine act, which led to work in TV which, in turn, led to Broadway and, eventually, the movies. Van Dyke also starred for many years in his own TV series. He has won three Emmy Awards for his work.

A: **Dirk Bogarde**
Q: What actor died in *Death in Venice*?
W: Dirk Bogarde began his entertainment career on the London stage. He was spotted by Rank Studios and signed to a film contract. His performance in Visconti's *Death in Venice* is considered his best work.

A: **Disc jockey**
Q: What was Clint Eastwood's occupation in *Play Misty for Me*?
W: Jessica Walters' favorite request of disc jockey Eastwood was to "Play *Misty* for me. Eastwood makes the mistake of doing more than just playing requests for her and ends up with a psychotic on his hands.

A: **Dodge City, Kansas**
Q: What city was the setting for "Gunsmoke"?
W: Does it seem like all westerns take place in Dodge City? At one time Wyatt Earp, played by Hugh O'Brien, became Marshall in Dodge while on another TV channel we had Matt Dillon, portrayed by James Arness, as Marshall of Dodge City!

A: **Don and Phil**
Q: What were the first names of the Everly Brothers?
W: The Everly Brothers are considered one of the most important acts in the evolution of rock music. Their unique sounds and fine harmonies with rich acoustic guitar accompaniment and pronounced beat influenced many rock 'n rollers who followed them.

A: **Don Rickles**
Q: Who is Mr. Warmth?
W: Anyone who believes this is a "dummy"!

A: **Don Wilson**
Q: Who was the announcer on "The Jack Benny Show"?
W: There were two "regulars" on the Jack Benny Show who were with Jack throughout the show's run. "Rochester" was Benny's valet and Don Wilson appeared as his announcer and friend. Don Wilson also "appeared" on Benny's radio show.

A: **Donald Sutherland**
Q: Who portrayed the German spy "Die Nagel" in *The Eye of the Needle*?
W: This film was based on Ken Follet's bestseller. Sutherland is a super cool agent stranded on an island off the British coast. The film was directed by Richard Marquant and also starred Kate Nelligan.

A: **Donovan**
Q: Who sang "Mellow Yellow"?
W: Born Donovan Leitch in Glasgow, Scotland, he was first projected to stardom in the United Kingdom in early 1965. He wrote his first two hit records "Catch the Wind" and "Colours." Producer Mickie Most helped Donovan produce a number of semi-classical singles in 1966 to 1967; "Mellow Yellow" was one of them.

A: Dooley Wilson
Q: What actor sang "As Time Goes By" in *Casablanca*?
W: It's a good thing the question reads "sang" as reputedly Wilson couldn't play a note and the piano accompaniment was dubbed — so he couldn't "Play It Again." Sing it, yes; play it, no!

A: Dopey
Q: Which is the only one of the Seven Dwarfs without a beard?
W: Well, at least Snow White didn't have a hard time remembering his name. She could always nickname him "The Beardless One."

A: Dorothy and Lillian
Q: What were the first names of the Gish sisters?
W: Lillian and Dorothy Gish started in movies in 1912 under the wing of D.W. Griffith. The Gish sisters also were known stage performers. Although they often worked together, they were not an acting team.

A: Dorothy Lamour
Q: Who was "The Sarong Girl"?
W: If you were on "the Road" as much as Dorothy, you'd pack a wash and wear sarong, too. Dorothy Lamour was the actress who traveled with Bing Crosby and Bob Hope in their "Road" movies. Dorothy's trademark was the sarong in which she was so often clad as an exotic South Sea heroine.

A: Double Doody
Q: Who was Howdy Doody's twin brother?
W: Howdy and Double were twins born on Dec. 27, 1941 on a ranch in Texas. When they were six, a rich uncle died leaving them land in New York City. When Howdy became old enough he left Texas and traveled east to fulfill his dream of owning a circus. (Please keep in mind we are talking about puppets!)

A: Douglas Edwards
Q: Who preceded Walter Cronkite as anchorman on "The CBS Evening News"?
W: Douglas Edwards worked many years for a CBS affiliate station in New York. When CBS decided to produce a nightly network newscast, they chose to use Mr. Edwards' local show to become CBS's first network news show.

A: Dr. Galen Adams
Q: What character did Milburn Stone play on "Gunsmoke"?
W: Aside from James Arness' character, Matt Dillon, Doc Adams was the only other character to run the duration of this show. Doc, like many of the other residents of Dodge City, spent much of his nonworking time in The Long Branch Saloon.

A: *Dr. No*
Q: What was the first James Bond film?
W: This was the first of the James Bond films starring Sean Connery. Joseph Wiseman played the madman Dr. No, out to control the world. Ursula Andrews was Connery's love interest.

A: Dr. Zorba
Q: Who was Ben Casey's boss?

W: Dr. David Zorba, Ben Casey's boss and mentor, was played by Sam Jaffe. Mr. Jaffe passed away on March 24, 1984.

A: "Dragnet"
Q: What TV series changed the names to protect the innocent?
W: Here's "Just the facts, Ma'am — dum de dum dum...dum de dum dum *dum*...." Dragnet first began on radio in 1949 and moved into a television series in 1952. The show ran until 1959, was revived in 1967 and continued until 1970. Jack Webb played Detective Joe Friday and was also the director of the show. "And those are facts. No names have been changed because they are guilty on all counts."

A: Drums
Q: What instrument are you playing if you perform a rim shot?
W: A rim shot is when the drummer strikes the metal rim of his snare drum with one of the drumsticks.

A: Duke Ellington
Q: What bandleader had the themes "Satin Doll" and "Take the A Train"?
W: "I could never play anything I heard so I had to sit down and create something that fit under my fingers" once claimed Duke Ellington. So create he did, more than 900 published pieces including "Satin Doll" and "Take The A Train."

A: Dumbo
Q: Who was Mrs. Jumbo's son?
W: Dumbo was a cartoon character in a Disney feature. He had the unique ability to fly by using his large ears. Pretty good for an elephant!!

A: Dustin Hoffman
Q: Who portrayed Carl Bernstein in *All the President's Men*?
W: Wildwood Enterprises produced the true story about two reporters' investigation of a sensitive incident in contemporary political history. Robert Redford played Bob Woodward the other reporter who helped to bring the Watergate facts into the limelight.

ENTERTAINMENT

E

A: *Earthquake*
Q: What film was the first to feature Sensurround?
W: Sensurround is a trademark for a special effects system developed by Universal in 1974. It was made to enhance the impact of tremor scenes in *Earthquake*. Special equipment in the theaters vibrated air against the bodies and ears of the audience, creating the illusion of participation in an action-filled event.

A: Ed Ames
Q: Who threw a badly-aimed tomahawk on TV's "Tonight Show"?
W: Ed Ames played Mingo on the "Daniel Boone" television show. Mingo was an expert tomahawk thrower, but evidently Ed Ames was not!

A: Ed Sullivan
Q: Who made The Rolling Stones sing "Let's Spend the Night Together" as "Let's spend some time together"?
W: Their appearance on the Ed Sullivan Show in January, 1967 was the start of a bad year for the Stones. Conservative Sullivan censored their hit, and the Stones were hounded by the establishment by means of a series of drug busts that made big news.

A: Ed Wynn
Q: What comedian was "The Perfect Fool"?
W: Ed Wynn, father of actor Keenan Wynn, was billed as "the Perfect Fool" in several Ziegfeld Follies editions in 1914. A very successful vaudeville comic before the age of 18, Wynn also produced and wrote many of his own shows. He won an Emmy in 1949 and was nominated for an Oscar in 1959.

A: Eddie Fisher
Q: What singer has been married to Debbie Reynolds, Elizabeth Taylor and Connie Stevens?
W: Eddie Fisher was married to Debbie Reynolds when he became involved with family friend, Elizabeth Taylor. He divorced Miss Reynolds to marry Taylor. Taylor later divorced him to marry Richard Burton. Fisher later married and divorced singer Connie Stevens. Needless to say, Eddie "got around"!

A: Eddie Haskell
Q: What "Leave It to Beaver" character became a Los Angeles policeman in real life?
W: Anyone who has watched "Leave It to Beaver" can very vividly remember Eddie Haskell's slimy way of saying "Good Evening, Mr. and Mrs. Cleaver." The part of Eddie Haskell was played by Ken Osmond.

A: Edgar Bergen and Charlie McCarthy
Q: Who received the only Oscar made of wood?
W: Edgar Bergen won a "special" Oscar for the creation of his ventriloquist dummy and friend, Charlie McCarthy. So what was more appropriate than a wooden Oscar? Mr. Bergan passed away in 1978 and bequeathed Charlie to the Smithsonian Institute.

A: Edith Head
Q: Who's won the most Oscars for costume design?
W: Edith Head is Hollywood's best known and most successful designer. Miss Head has won a total of eight Academy Awards, the last for the costumes in the movie *The Sting*.

A: Edward Fox
Q: Who portrayed the title character in the film *The Day of the Jackal*?
W: Ed Fox is the brother of actor James Fox. He is known for his proficiency in playing cynical or cruel roles.

A: Edward G. Robinson
Q: Who portrayed poker shark Lancy Howard in *The Cincinnati Kid*?
W: "The Cincinnati Kid," played by Steve McQueen, was an itinerant card shark who traveled from one big game to the next, stopping occasionally to pick up a girl. He finally gets into the game of his life with Lancy Howard (Edward G. Robinson).

A: Edward R. Murrow
Q: Who was the first host of "Person to Person"?
W: "Person To Person" was a personal interview show during which Edward R. Murrow would visit two celebrities' homes via the magic of television. Charles Collingwood took over the show in 1959.

A: elephant, An
Q: What killed Chuckles the Clown?
W: Chuckles the Clown was a character on the "Mary Tyler Moore Show" played by Jerry Van Dyke. In Chuckles' final episode, the story line has him being crushed and killed by an elephant (offscreen), and upon their return to the newsroom from the burial service the WJM gang breaks up in laughter. Even in his passing on, Chuckles was a very funny fellow.

A: Elliott Gould
Q: Who portrayed private detective Philip Marlowe in Robert Altman's *The Long Goodbye*?
W: Philip Marlowe is a character created by Raymond Chandler. He was played on radio by Gerald Mohr, Howard Duff, and Van Heflin. On television he was portrayed by Philip Carey. In the movies Dick Powell, Humphrey Bogart, Robert Montgomery, George Montgomery, James Garner, and Robert Mitchum have all played Marlow.

A: Elmer Gantry
Q: What role did Burt Lancaster win the 1960 best actor Oscar for?
W: Lancaster, one of the first actors to become an independent pro-

ducer, was an acrobat, salesman, repairman, and soldier before accidentally being discovered and given an acting role.

A: **Elmer J. Fudd**
Q: Who is Bugs Bunny's archenemy?
W: For some unknown reason, Elmer Fudd has always wanted to "git dat cwazy wabbit." Elmer, who debuted in 1940, is a cartoon character whom Bugs Bunny is always putting one over on. Mel Blanc creates Elmer's voice.

A: **Elsa**
Q: What was the name of the African lioness in *Born Free*?
W: *Born Free* was a true story written by Joy Adamson about Elsa. Elsa was the winner of the 1967 and 1975 TV Patsy Award for her role in the movie *Born Free*.

A: **Elton John**
Q: Who was the first major rock star to perform in the Soviet Union, in 1979?
W: Elton John performed eight successful concerts in May, 1979, in the Soviet Union. The black market price for a ticket was as much as $300 (200 rubles). Although rock music is discouraged in the Soviet Union, young people can listen to rock on foreign radio broadcasts.

A: **Elton John**
Q: Who recorded "Captain Fantastic" and "The Brown Dirt Cowboy"?
W: This album is an autobiographical account in song about Elton John's and Bernie Taupin's early hardship. Captain Fantastic is Elton John and the "brown dirt cowboy" is Bernie Taupin.

A: **Elton John**
Q: Who named himself for Long John Baldry and Elton Dean?
W: Long John Baldry is a rhythm and blues singer whose backup group is the Blusology, of which Elton John was a part in the late 1960s. Elton Dean was a saxophonist in the same backup group. When Elton was trying to think of a new stage name, he combined the first names of Baldry and Dean. He made Elton John his legal name a few years later. His real name? It was Reginald Kenneth Dwight.

A: **Elvis Presley**
Q: What singer won the 1943 Alabama-Mississippi State Fair talent contest?
W: Elvis won the contest with the song "Old Shep." Elvis later recorded this song.

A: *Endless Summer, The*
Q: What film featured the search for the perfect wave?
W: This movie was a feature length documentary about the joys of surfing. Bruce Brown was the director, cinematographer, and writer.

A: **Ensign Pulver**
Q: What role did Jack Lemmon play in the 1955 film *Mr. Roberts*?
W: Jack Lemmon won an Oscar for Best Supporting Actor in this film, directed by John Ford and Mervyn LeRoy. The movie also starred James Cagney, William Powell, and Henry Fonda, repeating his Broadway role. This role was most recently played live on TV by Kevin Bacon.

A: **Ernest Borgnine**
Q: Who gained stardom with his 1955 portrayal of the title character in *Marty*?
W: Borgnine started his career in TV appearances, and in 1951 he made his film debut in *China Corsair*. Since he was mainly cast as a villain, it was very surprising when he got the title role in *Marty*. Mr. Borgnine won a Best Actor Oscar and various other awards for this portrayal.

A: **Ernest Borgnine's**
Q: Whose license plate reads: BORG 9?
W: Well this certainly makes sense if your last name is Borg*nine*. By the way Borgnine really is his family name; he was born Ermes Effron Borgnine.

A: **Errol Flynn**
Q: Who was Tasmania's most famous swashbuckler?
W: Errol Flynn was born in Hobart, Tasmania in 1909. Tall, athletic, and exceptionally handsome, Flynn starred in many costume adventure films and in fact performed many of his own stunts in his films. He was also reported to be a superior fencer.

A: **"Eve of Destruction"**
Q: What Barry McGuire hit was rock's first protest song?
W: "Protest rock" developed in the 1960s as part of the protest movements against Vietnam, prejudicial treatment toward blacks, and nuclear energy. Bob Dylan became the spearhead of the movement, and it was his "Blowin' in the Wind," a number 2 hit, that awakened and energized the movement. "Eve of Destruction" by Barry McGuire, number 1 in 1965, and "American Pie" by Don McLean are other examples of such protest songs.

A: **"Everybody's Talkin'"**
Q: What's the theme song for *Midnight Cowboy*?
W: The words and music were done by Fred Neil. The song was sung by Nilsson on the sound track to the movie.

A: "F Troop"
Q: What TV series featured Corporal Randolph Agarn, played by Larry Storch?
W: F-Troop was a sit-com on military life in the old west. This show also starred Forrest Tucker as Sergeant Morgan O'Rourke, Ken Berry as Captain Parmenter, Melody Patterson as Wrangler Jane, and Frank deKova as Chief Wild Eagle. Agarn and O'Rourke were always planning some get rich quick scheme while Parmenter was trying to outrun (marriage-wise) Wrangler Jane.

A: Fanny Brice's
Q: Whose life are the musicals *Funny Girl* and *Funny Lady* based on?
W: Fanny Brice was a noted stage and screen comedienne who earned radio fame with her portrayal of Baby Snooks. Barbra Streisand played Miss Brice in the films *Funny Girl* and *Funny Lady*.

A: Fanny Brice's
Q: What Ziegfeld Follies singer's career is recounted in *Funny Girl*?
W: Barbra Streisand played Fanny Brice in *Funny Girl* and won an Oscar for her portrayal. Miss Brice was a noted comedienne and a yearly favorite in Ziegfeld's Follies.

A: *Fantasticks, The*
Q: What long-running Broadway musical introduced the song "Try to Remember"?
W: As of May 2, 1983, *The Fantastiks* has had 9,416 performances. It is still running!

A: Fess Parker
Q: Who played Daniel Boone on TV?
W: Fess Parker gained fame playing Walt Disney's Davy Crockett, and became even more famous playing Daniel Boone for six years on NBC-TV. Prior to playing Daniel Boone, he starred in a number of western or pioneer type movies.

A: Fifty
Q: How many eggs did Cool Hand Luke bet he could eat in an hour?
W: *Cool Hand Luke* is a film about a man separated from the "establishment," and the title role was expertly played by Paul Newman. This was a serious film but it did have its comical moments such as the egg-eating bet.

A: Fifty cents
Q: How much are rooms to let, according to Roger Miller?
W: That's the price if you are "King of the Road." Roger Miller was very familiar with the situations he wrote about in this song. "King of the Road" was an international hit.

A: Fifty-four
Q: What was the number of Gunther Toody's patrol car?
W: Joe E. Ross played Gunther Toody in the TV sit-com, "Car 54, Where Are You?" He was partnered by Francis Muldoon, Fred Gwynne. Car 54 always seemed to run into more comedy than crime.

A: Figaro
Q: Who's the barber in *The Barber of Seville*?
W: The play *The Barber of Seville* was written by Beau Marchais. Three operas entitled *The Barber of Seville* were written, one each by Mozart, Rossini, and Paisiello.

A: *Finian's Rainbow*
Q: What 1947 musical introduced the song "How Are Things in Glocca Morra"?
W: The 1968 film version of this production was directed by Francis Ford Coppola and starred Fred Astaire and Petula Clark. *Finian's Rainbow*, a musical fantasy about racial injustice, was ahead of its time in the 1940s.

A: "Fire and Rain"
Q: What song put James Taylor in the limelight?
W: "Fire and Rain" made James Taylor's album "Sweet Baby James" a hit. The song "Fire and Rain" tells about James' heroin addiction, his stay in a mental institution and the suicide of a close friend.

A: "First Family, The"
Q: What Vaughn Meader LP was Number 1 on the charts in December, 1962?
W: "The First Family" was album of the year in 1962. It was also the Best Comedy Recording of the Year. The album was a parody on the then "First Family," the Kennedys.

A: Five
Q: How many seconds usually elapsed before the tape self-destructed on "Mission: Impossible"?
W: Dan Briggs and Jim Phelps must have had fantastic memories to remember all the instructions on the tape before it self-destructed. No instant replay! These gentlemen were the head of the Impossible Mission Force. Their assignment: to do jobs no other agency would accept.

A: Five golden rings
Q: What did my true love give to me on the fifth day of Christmas?
W: Not just five golden rings! There were also four calling birds, three French hens, two turtle doves, and a partridge in a pear tree.

A: Five miles
Q: How long is Camptown Racetrack?
W: Well, according to Pete Seeger in his book *American Favorite Ballads*, the Camptown Racetrack is two miles long. It must depend on the version you sing — Doo-dah! Doo-dah!

A: Five years
Q: How long was the TV mission of "Star Trek's Enterprise" to be?
W: All true "trekkies" know the opening monologue by heart: "Space, the final frontier. These are

the voyages of the starship *Enterprise*. Its five year mission, to explore strange new worlds, to seek out new life and new civilizations. To boldly go where no man has gone before."

A: **Flintstones, The**
Q: Who lives at 39 Stone Canyon Way?
W: Fred and Wilma Flintstone lived the town of Bedrock at the aforementioned address. The Flintstones, a parody on modern life, was an animated cartoon. Joining the Flintstones in their capers were their pet dinosaur Dino, daughter Pebbles, and neighbors Betty and Barney Rubble and their son Bamm Bamm.

A: **Flubber**
Q: What substance did Fred MacMurray invent in *The Absent-minded Professor*?
W: Ned Brainard (Fred MacMurray) invents a magic rubber that flies. He uses it to help his team win against Rutland. *Flying rubber.*

A: **Flying Purple People Eater, The**
Q: What had one eye, one horn, and flew in the 1958 hit by Sheb Wooley?
W: This song was Sheb Wooley's greatest hit. Wooley also composed the song.

A: **Ford Mustang, A**
Q: What kind of car did Bullitt drive?
W: Bullitt is the main character in a movie of the same name. Based on Robert Pike's novel *Mute Witness*, this movie was directed by Peter Yates on location in San Francisco and is best remembered for its spectacular car chase through San Francisco.

A: *Fortune Cookie, The*
Q: What film features Jack Lemmon and Walter Matthau trying to pull off an insurance fraud?
W: Walter Matthau won an Oscar for his performance in this Billy Wilder directed film. Lemmon is knocked down by a football player while doing his job, and money-hungry Matthau sees dollar signs.

A: **Four a.m.**
Q: What time did the Everly Brothers' Little Susie wake up?
W: "Wake up Little Susie" was the Everly Brothers' second number 1 hit on the Cadence label. There was some controversy about the lyrics: the president of Cadence, Archie Blyer, thought the lyrics were too suggestive.

A: *Four Horsemen of the Apocalypse, The*
Q: What 1921 film made Rudolph Valentino a star?
W: Screenwriter June Mathis insisted that Valentino be given the lead in this movie, and since she was very influential at the Metro studio, Valentino was given the part. The movie was a box office hit, and Valentino was a star.

A: **Four Seasons, The**
Q: What singing group was once known as The Four Lovers?
W: This group was formed in Newark, New Jersey as the Varietones. The became the Four Lovers in 1956 and made the charts with the song "Apple of My Eye." In 1961 they renamed the group the Four Seasons after a bowling alley in which they had played.

A: **Francis the Talking Mule**
Q: What was the name of Donald O'Connor's co-star in six films?
W: Chill Wills did all the talking for Francis in these six films. Francis won the first Patsy Award (Animal Oscar) in 1951. Francis spoke only in one movie without O'Connor, *Francis in the Haunted House*, with Mickey Rooney.

A: **Frank Sinatra**
Q: What singer starred on radio's "Your Hit Parade"?
W: "Your Hit Parade" was the Casey Kasen 1930s top 40 count down. Many talented singers, musicians and band leaders graced this show. Frank Sinatra teamed with Axel Stordahl to head the cast from 1947 to 1949.

A: **Frank Sinatra**
Q: What singer first appeared with The Hoboken Four?
W: Francis Albert Sinatra was born in Hoboken, New Jersey. His first break came in the late 1930s when he became a regular on the Major Bowes Talent Show. Mr. Sinatra is not only a renowned singer; he also won an Oscar for his performance in *From Here to Eternity*.

A: **Frank Sinatra**
Q: Who portrayed Maggio in the film *From Here to Eternity*?
W: Frank Sinatra won an Oscar for Best Supporting Actor for his role in this film. He really had to beg Columbia to cast him in this role, because earlier his vocal cords had ruptured and there was much concern about his voice.

A: **Frankie Laine**
Q: Who sang the theme song to "Rawhide"?
W: Frankie Laine's first big hit was "That's My Desire" in 1947. He has a long list of songs that were very successful, but he is probably best remembered for his rendition of "Rawhide." How did he hold that last note so long?

A: **Fred**
Q: What was the name of Baretta's cockatoo?
W: Fred was a 20-year-old Australian cockatoo, who was friend and pet to Tony (Robert Blake) Baretta of the TV show "Baretta". Fred's real name is Lala, and he was trained by Ray Berwick.

A: **Fred Allen's "Allen's Alley"**
Q: What radio show featured Senator Beauregard Claghorn?
W: Kenny Delmar, who portrayed Claghorn on Fred Allen's Show, modeled Claghorn after a Texas rancher he had once met. Delmar, as Claghorn, became a national sensation; he even cut two records as the Senator. Claghorn will be remembered for the words "That's a joke, son!"

ENTERTAINMENT

"A PIGSTY."

A: Freddie the Freeloader
Q: What was the name of Red Skelton's lovable hobo character?
W: Red Skelton was a huge star on radio before going to television where he portrayed the many different characters he had developed on his radio show. The major addition to his characters on the TV show was Freddie the Freeloader, a hobo who never spoke. Pretty tough to pull off on radio!

A: Fredric March
Q: Who played President Jordan Lyman in *Seven Days in May*?
W: Mr. March, considered one of the most subtle and sensitive actors in Hollywood, was the recipient of two Oscars. Also in this film were Burt Lancaster and Kurt Douglas, who played military officials scheming to overthrow the government.

A: *French Connection, The* and *French Connection II*
Q: What films featured the character Popeye Doyle?
W: Popeye was the code name for New York detective James Doyle, a character based on New York

policeman Edward Egan. Edward Egan himself appeared in *The French Connection* film, but not as himself.

A: *Fritz the Cat*
Q: What was the first X-rated animated cartoon movie?
W: "Fritz" was created by Robert Crumb. A sequel was made in 1974 called *The Nine Lives of Fritz the Cat*.

A: *From Here to Eternity*
Q: What 1953 film won Frank Sinatra a best supporting actor Oscar?
W: Winning this Oscar was a particularly high point in Frank Sinatra's career. In 1952 Sinatra's vocal cords suddenly hemorrhaged. He was dropped by his talent agency, and his career seemed finished. He worked on *From Here to Eternity* for only $8,000 — he really wanted that role — and winning the Oscar was the turning point in his career.

A: *From Here to Eternity*
Q: What film resurrected Frank Sinatra's career?
W: Sinatra had to beg Columbia to cast him in the role of Maggio in *From Here to Eternity*, and he agreed to play the role for only $8,000! His excellent work, however, did earn him an Oscar.

A: *From Russia with Love*
Q: What was the second James Bond novel to go before the cameras?
W: One year after *Dr. No* was released, James was back on the job *From Russia With Love*. Lotte Lenya was one of his nemeses in the film.

A: *Funny Girl*
Q: What Broadway play propelled Barbra Streisand to fame?
W: Barbra made her Broadway debut in 1962 in the musical *I Can Get It for You Wholesale*. The

musical bombed. In 1964 Barbra was chosen to play Fannie Brice in *Funny Girl* on Broadway, and her excellent performance in this play paved the way for her international stardom.

A: *Funny Girl*
Q: What was Barbra Streisand's first film?
W: Streisand, for her performance in *Funny Girl* tied with Katherine Hepburn for Best Actress in 1968.

G

A: Gabby Hayes
Q: Who played movie sidekick to Hopalong Cassidy, Gene Autry, Roy Rogers, and John Wayne?
W: Mr. Hayes was a vaudevillian before he became a famous movie sidekick. In the 1920s he began his film career playing villains in many John Wayne movies. In the 1930s he began playing comic sidekick to many western heroes.

A: Gale Storm
Q: Who played the title role on TV's "My Little Margie"?
W: For three years Gale Storm played the role of "My Little Margie," who was trying to save her widowed dad from the clutches of various women. "My Little Margie" went from TV to radio, running concurrently on both media from Dec. 1952 until Aug. 1955.

A: "Galloping Gourmet, The"
Q: What TV show was hosted by wine-nipping culinary artist Graham Kerr?
W: Graham Kerr is an international cooking expert who had an afternoon TV program. It was often rumored that there was more wine in the cook than in the food!

A: **Gardner McKay**
Q: Who starred in TV's "Adventures in Paradise"?
W: James A. Michener created "Adventures in Paradise" and sold the idea to television. He later dropped out of the project. Gardner McKay played the role of Captain Adam Troy, a Korean War veteran in search of cargo, passengers, and adventure.

A: **Garry Moore**
Q: Who was the original host of "I've Got a Secret"?
W: Garry Moore had a very successful variety show on TV for six years. After a two-year rest, he hosted a program featuring Durward Kirby and a variety of comedians and guests. In 1952 Moore began his career as a quiz show host on "I've Got a Secret."

A: **"Garry Moore Show, The"**
Q: What TV show propelled Carol Burnett to stardom?
W: From 1950 to 1951 Garry Moore hosted a live variety show on TV. In 1958 Garry revised and debuted a new variety show that ran successfully for six years. This show made a star of Carol Burnett and brought back Allen Funt's Candid Camera as a regular feature.

A: **Gary Cooper**
Q: Who played Billy Mitchell in *The Court Martial of Billy Mitchell*?
W: This film, released in 1955, was directed by Otto Preminger and had a star-studded cast including Charles Bickford, Ralph Bellany, Rod Steiger and Liz Montgomery. Cooper played a military general who was on trial and who in 1925 had predicted a Japanese attack on the U.S.

A: **Gary Cooper**
Q: Who played Will Kane in *High Noon*?
W: Cooper won an Academy Award—his second—for his portrayal of Will Kane in this movie.

A: **Gary Cooper**
Q: Who portrayed Beau Geste in the 1939 film?
W: This was the remake of the 1926 silent version of *Beau Geste* starring Ronald Colman. Robert Preston, Brian Donlevy, and Ray Milland all appeared in the remake.

A: **Gene Autry**
Q: Who built "Frosty the Snowman" into a 1952 hit?
W: Autry was not only an actor and singing cowboy but also a song writer who wrote some 200 popular songs. "Frosty" was not written by Autry, but he did sing it into a hit.

A: **Gene Autry**
Q: Whose theme song was "Back in the Saddle Again"?
W: Gene Autry and Ray Whitley wrote this song. It was the theme for Autry's TV show "Back in the Saddle Again" and the title of a book he wrote.

A: **Gene Barry**
Q: Who starred in the movie *The War of the Worlds*?
W: The radio version of this film touched off a minor panic when it was originally broadcast Oct. 30, 1938 by Orson Welles. The movie, although not panic inducing, was quite vivid with its dazzling special effects. Nothing compared to today's standards though!

A: **Gene Barry**
Q: Who portrayed TV's Bat Masterson?
W: This TV show was based in part on the exploits of William Bartley "Bat" Masterson, a debonair lawman, scout, and professional gambler who'd rather use his wits or cane instead of a gun.

A: **Gene Hackman**
Q: Who won the best actor Oscar for his portrayal of Popeye Doyle?
W: Gene Hackman was nominated twice before he finally won an Oscar. *The French Connection*, the film in which he starred as Popeye Doyle, also won an Oscar.

A: **Gene Kelly**
Q: What hoofer danced with a mouse in the film *Anchors Aweigh*?
W: It must be hard to choreograph for a mouse, but Mr. Kelly not only choreographed but danced with one in *Anchors Aweigh*. He received an Academy Award nomination for his work in this film.

A: **General Electric**
Q: What company sponsored TV's "College Bowl" quiz show?
W: General Electric has sponsored many shows on TV over the years. G.E. "College Bowl" matched 24 member varsity scholar teams against each other competing to answer liberal arts questions.

A: **General Tom Thumb**
Q: What 19th-century midget was exhibited throughout North America by Barnum and Bailey Shows?
W: This was the nickname for Charles Sherwood Stratton. General Tom Thumb was a dwarf (not a midget) standing 36 inches tall. In 1863 he married Lavinia Warren who stood 32 inches high and who also worked for Barnum. Tom died July 15, 1883.

A: **"Gentle on My Mind"**
Q: What was Glen Campbell's TV theme song?
W: John Hartford composed "Gentle on My Mind." He was a close personal friend of Glen Campbell and made frequent guest appearances on "Campbell's Goodtime Hour."

A: ***Gentlemen Prefer Blondes***
Q: What 1949 musical featured the song "Diamonds are a Girl's Best Friend"?
W: *Gentlemen Prefer Blondes* opened Dec. 8, 1949, at the Ziegfeld Theater and ran 740 performances. The cast included Carol Channing (she made the song "Diamonds..." famous), Yvonne Adair, and Jack McCauley. Marilyn Monroe played in the film version of this musical.

A: **George Burns**
Q: What comedian has played God in two movies?
W: George Burns played in many films prior to 1975. He made his screen comeback in 1975 with an Oscar-winning performance in *The Sunshine Boys.* In 1977 he played opposite John Denver in *Oh God!,* and a few years later he made a sequel entitled *Oh God, Book II.*

A: **George C. Scott**
Q: Who starred in *Islands in the Stream?*
W: This was the film version of a Hemingway novel about an island-dwelling sculptor and his three sons. It was directed by F. J. Schaffner and released in 1975. George wasn't nominated for any awards he could turn down.

A: **George Fenneman**
Q: What TV game show announcer brought on the star with, "Here he is, the one, the only — Groucho"?
W: Fenneman was Groucho's emcee on radio as well as on TV's "You Bet Your Life." Fenneman also hosted the quiz show "Anybody Can Play" and the comedy "Your Funny, Funny Films."

A: **George Gershwin**
Q: Who composed "An American in Paris"?
W: It was composed in 1928. A film starring Gene Kelly and Leslie Caron was built around Gershwin's jazz composition.

A: **George Gershwin**
Q: Who wrote "Rhapsody in Blue"?
W: "Rhapsody in Blue" was also the name of the film biography of George Gershwin who often worked with his lyricist brother Ira. "Rhapsody" was composed in 1924.

A: **George Gobel**
Q: Who's known as Lonesome George?
W: George Gobel adopted this nickname for himself. He starred in his own live variety TV series for six years.

A: **George Hamilton**
Q: Who portrayed Zorro in *Zorro, the Gay Blade?*
W: Hamilton played dual roles in this movie: Don Diego de la Vega, son of Zorro, and his own gay twin brother Bunny Wigglesworth.

A: **George Harrison**
Q: Who was the youngest Beatle?
W: Lennon was born Oct. 9, 1940; Starr was born July 7, 1940; McCartney was born June 18, 1942; and Harrison was born Feb. 25, 1943.

A: **George Jessel**
Q: Who was known as "The Toastmaster-General of the United States"?
W: He was an entertainer, singer, songwriter, actor, and producer who traveled extensively, entertaining and speaking on behalf of various causes. He won a special Oscar for his work. George was a compulsive teller of jokes and anecdotes, thus earning him the nickname "Toastmaster-General of the United States."

A: **George Lucas**
Q: Who wrote and directed *American Graffiti?*
W: George Lucas is a very talented director as well as a writer. While still a student at USC's Cinema School, he made several prize-winning films. Lucas' autobiographical *American Graffiti* thrust him into the front rank of directors, and his next film, *Star Wars*, did okay at the box office as well!

A: **George Reeves**
Q: Who played TV's Superman?
W: George Reeves made his movie debut in *Gone with the Wind*. He later became typecast as Superman and could not get other work. Reeves died in June 1959, two years after the cancellation of "Superman." The coroner's verdict was suicide.

A: **George Segal**
Q: Who played the owl in the film *The Owl and the Pussycat?*
W: Segal played Owl to Barbra Streisand's Pussycat in this 1970 film directed by Herbert Ross and based on a play of the same name.

A: **George Segal**
Q: Who played King Rat in the 1965 movie of the same name?
W: This James Clavell novel, adapted for film, dealt with the effects of a World War II Japanese prisoner of war camp on Allied prisoners.

A: **George Segal and Sandy Dennis**
Q: What performers appeared with Burton and Taylor in *Who's Afraid of Virginia Woolf?*
W: George Segal was nominated for an Oscar for his performance in this film, and Sandy Dennis won an Oscar for Best Supporting Actress. This was her first substantial screen role.

A: **Gerald Lloyd Kookson III, or Kookie**
Q: What was the name of the parking lot attendant on "77 Sunset Strip"?
W: Kookson was played by Edd Byrnes. Kookie, known for his wisecrack sayings, was a popular character on this detective show. Sayings such as "the ginchiest" (the greatest), "piling up the Zs" (sleeping), "a dark seven" (a depressing week) became well known. Byrnes, in his role as Kookie, recorded a hit song with Connie Stevens.

A: Gertrude and Heathcliffe
Q: What are the names of Red Skelton's two seagull friends?
W: Red did these "lame" birds in several of the opening monologues in his show that ran from 1951 to 1971. Yup, he did by George. "God Bless, Red."

A: *Gilbert and Sullivan*
Q: *Who wrote The Pirates of Penzance?*
W: Sir William Gilbert (librettist) and Sir Arthur Sullivan (composer) collaborated on the great Savoy Operas. The plot of *The Pirates of Penzance* was flavored with an adventure from Gilbert's own childhood.

A: Glenda Jackson
Q: Who played the title role in *The Romantic Englishwoman*?
W: Glenda Jackson was a prominent stage actress before starring in films. She won two Academy Awards for her work in *Women in Love* and *A Touch of Class*. She made the film *The Romantic Englishwoman* in 1975 with Michael Caine and Helmut Berger.

A: Glenn Ford
Q: Who portrayed golfer Ben Hogan in *Follow the Sun*?
W: Glenn Ford started his acting career early in stage plays at Santa Monica High School. After graduation he worked for various West Coast stage companies. Early in the 1940s he was a leading man in films, before he did a stint in the Army. After the service he became a leading man again in such films as *Follow the Sun*.

A: Glenn Miller Orchestra's, The
Q: What orchestra's theme song was "Moonlight Serenade"?
W: Glenn Miller was a trombonist, arranger, composer and band leader. His orchestra became one of the most popular "sweet" swing bands because of such songs as "Moonlight Serenade."

A: Glinda, The Good Witch of the North
Q: What role did Billie Burke play in *The Wizard of Oz*?
W: Miss Burke took her stage name from her father, William (Billie) Burke, a singing clown with Barnum and Bailey's Circus. She started her career on the London stage in 1903. She was married to the great Flo Ziegfeld, and was the star of many light comedies in the 1930s and 1940s. She was 54 years old when she played the part of Glinda.

A: *Godfather, The* and *The Godfather, Part Two*
Q: What film and sequal both won the Best Picture Oscar?
W: *The Godfather* won the Best Picture Oscar in 1972. Brando won the Best Actor Oscar, though he did reject the award. Two years later *Godfather II* won the Best Picture Oscar, Francis Ford Coppola received an Oscar for his direction, and Robert DeNiro received the award for Best Supporting Actor.

A: Goldie Hawn
Q: Who was the girl in Peter Seller's soup?
W: Peter Sellers starred in the film *There's a Girl in My Soup*. In the film Sellers, middle-aged, is trying to recapture his youth, but instead of finding his youth he finds Hawn!

A: *Gone with the Wind*
Q: What film made Hattie McDaniel the first black to win an Oscar?
W: This was not Miss McDaniel's only "first", she was the first black woman to sing on American radio as well. Hattie also starred in "Beulah" on radio and TV.

A: *Gone with the Wind*
Q: What premiered at Loew's Grand Theatre in Atlanta on Dec. 15, 1939?
W: Dec. 15, 1939, was declared a state holiday by the governor of Georgia because of the opening of this film. The film was re-released in 1967 with 70mm widescreen and stereophonic sound.

A: *Gone with the Wind*
Q: What movie ends with the line: "After all, tomorrow is another day"?
W: The original title of the book for this film was *Tomorrow is Another Day*. The title *Gone With the Wind* came from Ernest Dawson's poem "Cynara." The author, Margaret Mitchell, won a Pulitzer Prize for this work.

A: Good Ship "Lollipop", The
Q: What boat did Shirley Temple sing about in the 1934 film *Bright Eyes*?
W: This movie had Shirley orphaned and in the middle of a custody suit. Her singing always seemed to lift her spirits as well as those of everyone else!

A: Goodnight, Dick
Q: What was the proper "Laugh-In" response to: "Say goodnight, Dick"?
W: Must be an echo! Dan Rowan would always try to get Dick Martin to say "goodnight" to the TV audience. It never worked as Rowan expected!

A: Goons, The
Q: What British comedy team numbered Harry Secombe, Peter Sellers, Michael Bentine and Spike Milligan?
W: The Goons were a hit radio comedy group in England in the early 1950s. They were named after a character in the old Popeye cartoons. Milligan wrote the scripts and Sellers did most of the dialects for this BBC radio show.

A: Grace Kelly
Q: Who was the first actress to appear on a postage stamp?
W: Grace Kelly,   held the honor of being one of the first actresses to "grace" a postage stamp. This honor was bestowed on her after her marriage to Prince Rainier of Monaco. Princess Grace was tragically killed in a car crash in 1983.

A: *Grand Hotel*
Q: What 1933 box office smash starred Greta Garbo, John Barrymore, Joan Crawford and Wallace Beery?
W: Vicki Baum wrote the novel on which the movie was based. It is about a plush Berlin hotel where "nothing ever happens." Don't bet your money on that!

A: *Granny Smith, A*
Q: What kind of apple is on the Beatles' Apple label?
W: The Apple label was the Beatles' recording company. "Hey Jude" was the company's first single hit. A Granny Smith is a big green apple that appeared on the label of their albums.

A: *Grape Knee-High*
Q: What is Radar O'Reilly's favorite drink?
W: Radar was Colonel Blake's aide and company clerk in both the movie and hit television series *M*A*S*H*. His real name is Walter O'Reilly, but he was nicknamed "Radar" for his uncanny sense of knowing what was going to happen before it did. In both the movie and the TV series, Gary Burghoff played the part of the beloved company clerk and was known for never drinking anything stronger than Grape Nehi (not knee-high).

A: *Grease*
Q: What play holds the record for the longest run on Broadway?
W: On December 8, 1979, *Grease* set the long-run record for any Broadway show: 3,243 performances as of that date!

A: *Great Dictator, The*
Q: What 1940 Chaplin film satirized Hitler?
W: Charlie Chaplin poked fun at facism in this film in which he played the parts of both a Jewish barber and a surrealistic characterization of Hitler. This was Chaplin's last appearance as "the Little Tramp."

A: *Great Race, The*
Q: What movie had Professor Fate, played by Jack Lemmon, racing a Hannibal Twin 8?
W: Blake Edwards directed this wacky comedy about a cross-country race in which Tony Curtis and Natalie Wood also starred. The Hannibal 8 was a six-wheeled vehicle using Firestone No. 5 tires. Six different cars were built for the movie.

A: *Green*
Q: What color is Mr. Spock's blood?
W: Mr. Spock was the product of a truly mixed marriage. His father was Vulcan, his mother was human. Not only was his blood green but he had a complexion to match. This character on the television series was played by Leonard Nimoy.

A: *Greer Garson*
Q: Who portrayed Eleanor Roosevelt in *Sunrise at Campobello*?
W: Greer Garson returned to the screen after a five-year rest to play the role of Eleanor Roosevelt in this film. She received an Academy Award nomination for her work.

A: *Greer Garson's*
Q: Whose acceptance speech of more than 30 minutes prompted a time limit on Academy Award thank-yous?
W: If you thought the three hour 1984 Academy Awards program was long, you should have sat through Greer Garson's one-hour acceptance speech in 1942 for the Best Actress Award for *Mrs. Miniver*!

A: *Gregory Peck*
Q: Who played the title role in *The Man in the Gray Flannel Suit*?
W: N. Johnson directed Gregory Peck in this 1956 film based on a Sloan Wilson novel. Peck plays a Madison Avenue executive trying to get ahead.

A: *Greta Garbo*
Q: What was Greta Gustafsson's stage name?
W: Greta Garbo was born in a Stockholm slum. When she was noticed by director Mauritz Stiller, he lectured her on everything. Stiller was the one who changed her name from Gustafsson to Garbo.

A: *Groucho Marx*
Q: What cigar-chewing comedian observed: "You're only as old as the woman you feel"?
W: Groucho was ever the king of the quick answer. He was capable of voicing a responsible and original opinion on any given topic with a comic tone thrown in. When presented with a tree surgeon on his TV show, Groucho greeted him with, "Tell me, Doctor, did you ever fall out of a patient?"

A: *Groucho Marx*
Q: Who played Dr. Hugo Z. Hackenbush in the 1937 movie *A Day at the Races*?
W: The movie *A Day at the Races* was a sequel to the 1935 movie *A Night at the Opera*. It took 18 scripts to come up with the name Quackenbush for Groucho's character. Producers then found out there were 37 Dr. Quackenbushes in the continental U.S. ready to sue if their name were used for Groucho's character, a horse doctor. The name was quickly changed to Hackenbush.

A: *Groucho Marx*
Q: What actor said in *A Day at the Races*: "Either he's dead or my watch has stopped"?
W: Making a film in the 1930s was a trial and error ordeal. Filmmakers would take their movies to the stage live, then rework the lines and scenes until they got the right audience response. Only then did they film. In *A Day at the Races* they found that lines phrased as a question didn't get a laugh because people were waiting for a funny answer. Therefore, they changed "Is he dead or has my watch stopped?" to "Either he's dead or my watch has stopped."

A: *Guess Who's Coming to Dinner*
Q: What was Spencer Tracy's last film, in 1967?
W: Spencer Tracy received an Oscar nomination for *Guess Who's Coming to Dinner*, but he never found out that he did not win the award, as he passed away before the award ceremonies. He won two Oscars in his career.

A: **"Gunsmoke"**
Q: What was TV's top-rated series from 1957 to 1961?
W: "Gunsmoke" debuted on the small screen of television in September, 1955. John Wayne was first choice for the role of Marshall Matt Dillon but he suggested James Arness for the role. During its first season, the ratings were so poor that it didn't even rank among the top 15. Ratings for the second season far surpassed its previous year, bringing the show to eighth overall. After that, it remained on the top for four years.

A: **Gus**
Q: What was the name of the old fireman on "Leave it to Beaver"?
W: Beaver's buddy, Gus, was played by Bert Mustin in the TV series.

A: **Guy Lombardo**
Q: Who played the sweetest music this side of heaven?
W: Lombardo, Mr. New Year's Eve, was the leader of the Royal Canadians. Lombardo's rendition of "Auld Lang Syne" became a tradition. He used to say "When I die, I'm taking New Year's Eve with me."

A: **Guy Williams**
Q: Who played TV's Zorro?
W: Williams played Don Diego de le Vega, a California Robin Hood type. Zorro was created by Johnston McCulley in the story "The Curse of Capistrano." Williams also starred in "Lost in Space".

A: **Gypsy Rose Lee**
Q: What burlesque queen was the sister of actress June Havoc?
W: Her life story, *Gypsy* (adapted from the 1959 stage production), was made into a movie in 1962, starring Natalie Wood, Rosalind Russell, and Karl Malden. Both the play and the movie dealt with the early days of stripteaser Gypsy Rose Lee and the exploits of her ambitious mother.

A: **HAL 9000**
Q: What's the model name and number of the spacecraft's computer in *2001: A Space Odyssey*?
W: HAL 9000 is the computer of spaceship *Discovery-1*. It became operational at the Hall Plant, Urbana, Illinois on January 12, 1997. HAL is IBM stepped down one letter.

A: **Hal Holbrook**
Q: Who played Deep Throat in *All the President's Men*?
W: The 1976 film starred Dustin Hoffman and Robert Redford as two reporters from the *Washington Post* who discover the link between the White House and the Watergate burglars. Deep Throat was their secretive informer.

A: **Hal March**
Q: Who was the host of the "$64,000 Question"?
W: A Cadillac was the consolation prize for those who missed the big question on this game show. Dr. Joyce Brothers won $64,000 in the category of boxing. Jack Benny won $64.

A: **"Happy Birthday to You"**
Q: What song written by Mildred and Patty Hill is the most often sung?
W: "Happy Birthday to You" and "Auld Lang Syne" are probably the two most often sung songs. "Happy Birthday to You" is being sung somewhere every day...several times!

A: **"Happy Trails"**
Q: What was the theme song of Roy Rogers and Dale Evans?
W: "..to you, until we meet again." Roy (Leonard Slye) and Dale (Francis Octavia Smith) would ride off into the sunset together. Former theme songs were: "Smiles are Made Out of Sunshine" and "It's Roundup Time on the Double R Bar."

A: *Hard Day's Night, A*
Q: What was The Beatles' first film?
W: *A Hard Day's Night* opened in 1964. Other Beatle films included *Help*, 1965, which had the original title of *Eight Arms to Hold You*, *Yellow Submarine*, 1968, *Let It Be*, 1970, and *Magical Mystery Tour*, for television in 1967.

A: *Harry and Tonto*
Q: What film did Art Carney win the 1974 Best Actor Oscar for?
W: Carney won the Oscar for his role as Harry, an elderly New York resident who travels to Chicago after he is evicted. The film also starred Ellen Burstyn, Chief Dan George, and Larry Hagman.

A: **Harry Palmer**
Q: What spy did Michael Caine portray in three films?
W: Caine played spy Harry Palmer in *The Ipcress File*, 1965; *Funeral in Berlin*, 1967, and *Billion Dollar Brain*, 1967. James Bond had nothing to worry about!

ENTERTAINMENT

ENTERTAINMENT

A: **Harry Reasoner**
Q: Who co-anchored ABC's evening newscast with Barbara Walters?
W: In 1976, ABC attracted a great deal of attention by luring away Barbara Walters from NBC (for approximately $1 million) to co-anchor the evening news with Harry Reasoner. The match never really jelled and produced no change in the ratings.

A: **Hayley Mills**
Q: Who played twin sisters in *The Parent Trap*?
W: Mills play twin daughters of separated parents determined to bring the family back together. The film also starred Maureen O'Hara and Brian Keith as the parents.

A: **He had one arm**
Q: What was the distinguishing feature of Richard Kimble's quarry?
W: On the TV show *The Fugitive* the one-armed man's name was Johnson, the killer of Kimble's wife. Johnson was played by Bill Raisch. Kimble was played by David Janssen.

A: **He was drafted**
Q: Why did Birdie go bye-bye?
W: Conrad Birdie, played by Jesse Pearson, was a rock n' roll star in the 1963 movie *Bye Bye Birdie*. He visits the small town of Sweet Apple, Ohio, and lays waste to it with his hip cranking songs.

A: **He was a judge**
Q: What did Andy Hardy's father do for a living?
W: For most of the series, the judge was played by Lewis Stone. However, in the first picture, *A Family Affair*, Lionel Barrymore was Judge Hardy. Mrs. Hardy was played by Spring Byington and Fay Holden.

A: **Heartbreak Hotel**
Q: What's found on Lonely Street?
W: In January, 1956, Elvis Presley cut his first record for RCA. Within a month, "Heartbreak Hotel" shot up to number 1 on all the charts, where it stayed for eight weeks. It sold three million copies.

A: **Hearts**
Q: What was the shape of Lolita's sunglasses in the 1962 film?
W: Lolita was played by Sue Lyons. The film also starred Peter Sellers, Shelley Winters, and James Mason.

A: **Heidi Doody**
Q: What was Howdy Doody's sister's name?
W: Howdy's twin brother was named Double Doody. Other character's names from the children's television show, "Howdy Dowdy Time", were Mr. X, Ugly Sam, and Captain Scuttlebutt. The show's host was Buffalo Bob Smith.

A: **Helen Hayes**
Q: Who is considered the "First Lady of the American Stage"?
W: Other "firsts" include Norma Shearer, the "First Lady of the Screen," George Arliss, the "First Gentleman of the Screen," and Kate Smith, the "First Lady of Radio."

A: **Henry Blake**
Q: What character did McLean Stevenson play on TV's *M*A*S*H*?
W: The television show *M*A*S*H*, which stands for mobile army surgical hospital, began after the premiere in 1970 of the movie, which starred Donald Sutherland and Elliot Gould. The TV show also starred Gary Burghoff, who played Radar O'Reilly in both the show and the movie.

A: **Henry Fonda**
Q: Who played the president in *Fail Safe*?
W: In this 1964 film, an American atomic bomber is sent to destroy Moscow, and Fonda has to destroy New York in forced retaliation. The film also starred Walter Matthau and Larry Hagman.

A: **Herbie**
Q: What was the name of the Volkswagen in Disney's *The Love Bug*?

W: Herbie also appeared in the films *Herbie Rides Again*, *Herbie Goes to Monte Carlo*, and the short-lived television series "Herbie, The Love Bug." The number 53 was painted on both the hood and the side of the car.

A: *Here Comes Mr. Jordan*
Q: What film is Warren Beatty's *Heaven Can Wait* a remake of?
W: Both films follow the story of a young man who is killed and sent to heaven, only to find that he was supposed to live another 40 or 50 years. When the heavenly powers that be discover their error and try to replace him, they discover that his body has been cremated so they need to find him another body. The film, *Here Comes Mr. Jordan*, made in 1941, starred Robert Montgomery and Claude Rains.

A: **Herman**
Q: What was Mr. Munster's first name?
W: Fred Gwynne played the part of Herman, the Frankensteinish father of "The Munsters." The television series also starred Yvonne DeCarlo as Lily and Al Lewis as Grandpa.

A: **His right shoe**
Q: Where did Maxwell Smart hide his telephone?
W: Don Adams played the bumbling superspy, Maxwell Smart, in the television series "Get Smart," created by Buck Henry and Mel Brooks. Smart was an agent for C.O.N.T.R.O.L. and was well-known for his famous line "Sorry about that, Chief."

A: **His teeth**
Q: What did Walter Huston remove to perform in the movie *The Treasure of the Sierra Madre*?
W: Huston's portrayal of the old prospector, Howard, won him the Oscar for Best Actor in the 1948 film. Huston's son, John Huston, also won Oscars for the film in the categories of writing and directing. The film starred Humphrey Bogart.

A: **Hoagy Carmichael**
Q: Who wrote "Stardust"?
W: Hoagy, educated to be an attorney, made a name for himself when he wrote this famous song, which became an overnight success.

A: **holiday, A**
Q: What is life in the 1959 song "Primrose Lane"?
W: This song was also the theme song for the short-lived television series "The Smith Family," starring Henry Fonda and Ron Howard. The song was originally recorded in 1959 by Jerry Wallace.

A: **Holly Golightly**
Q: What character did Audrey Hepburn play in *Breakfast at Tiffany's*?
W: Hepburn was nominated as Best Actress for her portrayal of Holly. This 1961 film also featured George Peppard, Patricia Neal, and Martin Balsam.

A: **"Honeycomb"**
Q: What Jimmie Rodgers tune was Number 1 on the charts the week Sputnik I went up?
W: Sputnik I was the first space satellite in orbit, launched by the USSR on Oct. 4, 1957. The flight ended Jan. 4, 1958. The words and music to the song "Honeycomb" were written by Bob Merrill in 1954 and popularized by Rodgers in 1957. "Honeycomb" sold over a million copies.

A: **Hop Sing**
Q: Who was the Ponderosa's Chinese cook?
W: Hop Sing was the cook for the Cartwright clan on TV's "Bonanza." The character was played by actor Victor Sen Young.

A: **Hot Lips**
Q: What is Margaret Houlihan's nickname?
W: Major Margaret Houlihan, alias Hot Lips, was the head nurse at the 4077th M*A*S*H unit. The television character was played by Loretta Swit. Sally Kellerman played Hot Lips in the 1970 movie.

A: **House of the Rising Sun, The**
Q: What's been the ruin of many a poor boy in New Orleans?
W: This song was made popular by the Animals. Other hits by this group include "Don't Let Me Be Misunderstood," "We Gotta Get Out of This Place," and "Sky Pilot."

A: *How to Murder Your Wife*
Q: What 1965 film had Jack Lemmon portraying a cartoonist?
W: Lemmon portrayed a strip cartoonist accused of murder when his wife disappears. The film also starred Virna Lisi and Terry Thomas. Remember the Glopeta-Glopeta Machine?

A: **Howard Johnson's**
Q: What was the name of the space station restaurant in *2001: A Space Odyssey*?
W: ...but no HoJo Cola or clams! The hotel in the space station of the 1968 movie was actually the Hilton.

A: *Hud*
Q: What 1963 film did Patricia Neal win the Best Actress Oscar for?
W: *Hud* was one of several movies starring Paul Newman. Others include *Harper* in 1966, *Hombre* in 1967, and *The Hustler* in 1961.

A: **Humphrey Bogart**
Q: Who played private detective Philip Marlowe in the 1946 film *The Big Sleep*?
W: Howard Hawks directed the 1977 remake of this film starring Robert Mitchum and Sarah Miles, in which Lauren Bacall, Bogart's wife, was also featured.

A: **Humphrey Bogart**
Q: Who played William Holden's brother in *Sabrina*?
W: This 1954 film, directed by Billy Wilder and also starring Audrey Hepburn, received Oscar nominations for both writing and directing.

A: **Humphrey Bogart**
Q: Who was Lauren Bacall's first husband?
W: Bacall was Bogart's fourth wife. Together they made five films: *To Have and Have Not*, 1945; *Two Guys From Milwaukee*, 1946; *The Big Sleep*, 1946; *Dark Passage*, 1947; and *Key Largo*, 1948. The movie, *Melville Goodwin, U.S.A.* was scheduled to star both Bogart and Bacall; however, it was never filmed because of Bogart's death.

A: *Hunter, The*
Q: What was Steve McQueen's last film?
W: McQueen, in the 1960s and 1970s, most often played the tough, sexy, and determined leading man. He appeared in such films as *The Great Escape*, *The Cincinnati Kid* and *Bullitt*. In *The Hunter* McQueen played an aging modern day bounty hunter. McQueen died of cancer shortly thereafter.

A: *Hustler, The*
Q: What film did Paul Newman play Fast Eddie Felson in?
W: This 1961 film also starred Piper Laurie, George C. Scott, and Jackie Gleason. It was one of four "H" movies made by Newman, the others were *Hud*, *Harper* and *Hombre*.

A: *I Am Curious (Yellow)*
Q: What Swedish sex film caused a stir in 1969?
W: Compared to sex films of today, this flick would get a PG rating. The film deals with a female sociologist who is interested in class structure. The film surprisingly lacks many of the features of later sex flicks; no sadomasochism, no violence, no drugs. Just sex — any way, anywhere, and everywhere. The follow-up was titled *I Am Curious (Blue)*.

A: "I Love Lucy"
Q: What was TV's Number 1-ranked show from 1952 to 1955?
W: It debuted on October 15, 1951, and starred the married couple Lucille Ball and Desi Arnez as Lucy and Ricky Ricardo. The television series also starred Vivian Vance and William Frawley as Ethel and Fred Mertz. Lucy and Desi were married in 1940 and together formed the Desilu Television Company.

A: "I see nothing, I know nothing"
Q: What was Sergeant Schultz's standard cop-out?
W: John Banner played the jolly First Sergeant of Stalag 13 on the TV series "Hogan's Heroes." The show was a spoof on World War II prisoner of war camps. Banner later went on to pose for a U.S. Army recruiting poster.

A: Illya Kuryakin
Q: Who was Napoleon Solo's partner?
W: David McCallum played Illya Nickovetch Kuryakin, secret agent for U.N.C.L.E. in the TV series "The Man From U.N.C.L.E." The character Napolean Solo was played by Robert Vaughn.

A: Imperials, The
Q: What backup group accompanied singer Little Anthony?
W: The Imperials were one of the many rock n' roll groups of the 1950s and 1960s. Others include Sam the Sham and the Pharoahs, Wayne Fontana and the Mindbenders, and Booker T. and the M.G.s.

A: Impossible Missions Force
Q: What did TV's IMF stand for?
W: IMF was from the TV series "Mission Impossible," starring Steven Hill as Dan Briggs and later Peter Graves as James Phelps. This tape will self-destruct in 5 seconds…

A: In a newspaper ad
Q: Where does Alfred Hitchcock appear in *Lifeboat*?
W: Hitchcock has made cameo appearances in more than 30 of his 50 movies. He began this practice in the 1920s when he needed an extra, and it eventually became his trademark. He has never won an Oscar for Best Director.

A: In a plane crash
Q: How did Will Rogers, Carole Lombard and Mike Todd all die?
W: Rogers died August 15, 1935, Lombard on January 16, 1942, and Todd on March 22, 1958. Other famous persons also killed in plane crashes include Knute Rockne, Otis Redding, Rocky Marciano, Audie Murphy, and Jim Croce.

A: In a theatre
Q: Where is it bad luck to say "Macbeth"?
W: The "Macbeth Curse" dates back to the first performance in 1606. The boy actor who was to play Lady MacBeth was taken ill with a mysterious fever one hour before the performance was to begin. He died backstage in the middle of the play. There are many such "Macbeth Curse" stories throughout the years. To combat the curse after an actor says the word "Macbeth," he is to go outside the theater, turn around three times, expel intestinal gas, knock on the door, and beg to be readmitted to the theatre.

A: "In the Heat of the Night"
Q: What film won Rod Steiger the Best Actor Oscar in 1967?
W: Steiger won the Oscar for his portrayal of Police Chief Bill Gillespie. Sidney Poitier and Warren Oates starred with him in this film that won the Oscar for Best Picture.

A: "Indian Love Call"
Q: What song has someone calling you-ooo-ooo-ooo-ooo-ooo-ooo?
W: This song was sung by Nelson Eddy and Jeanette MacDonald in the 1936 movie *Rose Marie*. MacDonald also sang it at Jean Harlowe's funeral.

A: Ingrid Bergman
Q: What actress debuted in the 1938 film *Intermezzo*?
W: This film starred Leslie Howard as a married violinist who has an affair with his musical protege. Bergman went on to star in such classics as *Notorious* and *Casablanca*.

A: Ingrid Bergman
Q: Who played Ilsa Lund Laszlo in *Casablanca*?
W: Bergman, along with Humphrey Bogart, Claude Rains, Paul Henreid, Sydney Greenstreet, and Peter Lorre starred in this 1942 classic that won several Oscars, including Best Picture and Best Director.

A: *Inherit the Wind*
Q: What film dramatized the Scopes monkey trial?
W: Spencer Tracy starred in this 1960 film about a schoolteacher brought to trial for teaching the theory of evolution. Tracy was nominated for an Oscar for his portrayal of Scopes.

A: "Inka Dinka Doo"
Q: What was Jimmy Durante's theme song?
W: Durante's career theme song was first sung in the 1933 movie *Joe Palooka*.

A: **Ira Gershwin**
Q: Who wrote the lyrics to *Porgy and Bess*?
W: *Porgy and Bess* is the black opera about the inhabitants of Catfish Row, where a slum girl falls in love with a crippled beggar. The 1959 film featured Sidney Poitier, Dorothy Dandridge and Sammy Davis, Jr. The film won an Oscar for musical direction.

A: **Ireland**
Q: What was the setting of the John Wayne film *The Quiet Man*?
W: This 1952 film starred John Wayne as an Irish ex-boxer who retires to his father's homeland and looks for a wife. Maureen O'Hara and Barry Fitzgerald also starred in this movie, which won Oscars for direction and photography.

A: *Irma La Douce*
Q: What film featured Shirley MacLaine as a prostitute and Jack Lemmon as a pimp?
W: *Irma La Douce* was the 1963 movie in which Paris policeman Lemmon falls in love with prostitute MacLaine and becomes her pimp. The film won an Oscar for musical direction.

A: **Iron Curtain, The**
Q: What's the curtain in Alfred Hitchcock's *Torn Curtain*?
W: This 1966 film starred Paul Newman and Julie Andrews. It contains an ironic scene in which Newman kills a Nazi-type German by shoving his head into a gas-filled oven.

A: **Irving Berlin**
Q: Who wrote "God Bless America"?
W: This song was actually written in 1918 but was not sung until 25 years later when Kate Smith was given the exclusive rights to the song. She first sang it in 1943.

A: **Irving Berlin**
Q: Who wrote "White Christmas"?
W: Berlin's traditional Christmas song was first sung in the 1942

movie *Holiday Inn* by Bing Crosby, who also starred in the movie *White Christmas*. The song went on to be one of the biggest all-time hits.

A: *Is Paris Burning?*
Q: What film account of the liberation of Paris was written by Francis Ford Coppola and Gore Vidal?
W: This 1965 movie starred Leslie Caron, Gert Frobe, Charles Boyer and Yves Montand. It was nominated for an Oscar for Best Photography.

A: *It's a Mad, Mad, Mad, Mad World*
Q: What 1963 movie comedy had more than 50 stars in it?
W: Some of the more memorable players in this film were Spencer Tracy, Milton Berle, Phil Silvers, Terry Thomas, and Jonathon Winters. The story is about an assortment of people who are overcome by greed and their search of buried money.

A: **J.T. Hall**
Q: Who was Sergeant Bilko's colonel?
W: The TV series "Sergeant Bilko" was also called "The Phil Silvers Show" and "You'll Never Get Rich." The series starred Paul Ford as Colonel J.T. Hall and also featured Maurice Gosfield and Joe E. Ross.

A: **Jack Benny**
Q: What TV comedian demanded: "Now cut that out!"?
W: When Benny moved from radio to TV he brought along his entire entourage including Don Wilson, Eddie Anderson (Rochester), Dennis Day, and Mel Blanc. This cast, along with Benny's uncanny sense of comic timing, separated the show from all others of the same era.

A: **Jack Benny**
Q: Who was born in 1894 and died 80 years later at the age of 39?
W: Benny was a popular radio and TV comedian, famous for such lines as "Well," "Wait a minute," and "Now cut that out!" He was also famous for his running gag that he was never older than 39.

A: **Jack Hawkins**
Q: What actor led the attack on the bridge on the River Kwai?
W: The film, *The Bridge on the River Kwai*, also starring Alec Guinness and William Holden, won Oscars for Best Picture, Best Writing, Best Direction, Best Photography, Best Music, and Best Actor.

A: **Jack Lemmon**
Q: Who won the best actor Oscar for his role in *Save the Tiger*?
W: Lemmon won for his role as a middle-aged businessman who regrets the slack morality of modern America. The film was nominated for Oscars in Writing, and Best Supporting Actor (Jack Gilford).

A: **Jack Lemmon**
Q: Who portrayed Felix Unger in the film *The Odd Couple*?
W: Unger was the "cleanliness fanatic" photographer in the 1967 movie. Walter Matthau played opposite him as sportswriter Oscar Madison.

A: **Jack Lemmon and Lee Remick**
Q: Who portrayed the alcoholic couple in *The Days of Wine and Roses*?
W: Lemmon and Remick both received Oscar nominations for their portrayals in this 1962 movie that won an Oscar for the title song. Charles Bickford and Jack Klugman co-starred.

A: **Jack Nicholson**
Q: Who played J.J. Gittes in *Chinatown*?
W: Nicholson was nominated for an Oscar for this portrayal as Gumshoe J.J. Gittes in the 1974 film. Fay Dunaway and John Huston also starred in this film that received the Oscar for writing.

ENTERTAINMENT

A: Jack Paar
Q: Who walked off his TV show on Feb. 11, 1960, protesting censorship?
W: Paar wanted to tell a four-minute "toilet joke." It was cut by NBC. He returned to his show on March 7th after a trip to Hong Kong. His crying towel had dried out by then.

A: Jack Webb
Q: Who portrayed Sergeant Joe Friday?
W: Webb was the central character on the television series "Dragnet." His partners were officers Ben Romero, Ed Jacobs, Frank Smith, and Bill Gannon.

A: Jackie Coogan
Q: What child actor appeared in *The Kid*, Charlie Chaplin's first full-length film?
W: Coogan played the title role in the 1921 film. *The Kid* was proclaimed a classic and made Coogan a paltry $4 million. Later in his life, Coogan went on to play Uncle Fester on the television series "The Addams Family."

A: Jackie Gleason
Q: Who sang "My Gal Sal" as Joe the Bartender?
W: Gleason was known as the "Great One." Some of his other TV personalities included the Bachelor, Pedro the Mexican, and Rudy the Repairman. He was also the host of the 1961 TV quiz show "You're In The Picture."

A: Jackie Paper
Q: What's the name of Puff the Magic Dragon's human friend?
W: These characters are from the song made popular by Peter, Paul, and Mary. "Puff, the Magic Dragon" is considered by some to be a "sub-drug" song.

A: jacknife, A
Q: What kind of knife did Mack carry?
W: The song, "Mack the Knife" was made famous by both Ella Fitzgerald and Bobby Darin. Darin's release

sold over two million copies and was largely responsible for his success.

A: Jaclyn Smith, Kate Jackson, Farrah Fawcett-Majors
Q: Who played the original "Charlie's Angels"?
W: This television show of the mid-1970s featured three female cops who worked as private detectives for a never-seen boss, John Forsythe. Cheryl Ladd, Shelly Hack, and Tanya Roberts later replaced the original three.

A: James
Q: What was Dr. Kildare's first name?
W: Richard Chamberlain played the famous Dr. Kildare in the 1960s television series. An extremely dedicated doctor, Kildare never seemed to have the desire to do anything but cure disease. However admirable, the show seemed to follow a repetitive structure: each episode had three suffering patients, each with a different disease, while an in-house controversy raged between the doctors.

A: James Bond's
Q: What character's shoes have been filled by Roger Moore, George Lazenby, and David Niven?
W: The last two, but certainly not least, actors to portray Secret Agent 007 are Sean Connery and Roger Moore. Bond was created by Ian Fleming in earlier novels.

A: James Caan
Q: Who portrayed Sonny Corleone in *The Godfather*?
W: This film also starred Marlon Brando and Robert Duvall in the story of the rise and fall of the head of a Mafia family. Brando received his Oscar for Best Actor for his portrayal of Vito Corleone but refused to accept the award.

A: James Cagney
Q: Who portrayed Admiral William F. Halsey in *The Gallant Hours*?
W: This film also starred Dennis Weaver and Richard Jaeckel.

A: James Cagney
Q: Who portrayed George M. Cohan in 1942's *Yankee Doodle Dandy*?
W: Cagney won the Oscar for Best Actor for his portryal of Cohan. The film itself was nominated for several Oscars: Best Picture, Writing, Direction, Musical Direction, and Best Supporting Actor (Walter Huston).

A: James Dean
Q: Who died in a Porsche Spyder?
W: Dean was killed Sept. 30, 1955, when he ran into Donald Turnupseed on Highway 66 near Paso Robles, California. Written on the side of Dean's car was the number 130 and on the back were the words "Little Bastard."

A: James Garner
Q: Who played Bret Maverick?
W: This TV series of the late 1950s also starred Jack Kelly as Bret's brother, Bart. The two brothers roamed the West as drifting playboys who supported their gambling habits and expensive tastes with clever schemes and con games, usually at the expense of authority figures.

A: James Mason
Q: Who portrayed Field Marshal Erwin Rommel in *The Desert Fox*?
W: The film portrayed Field Marshal Rommel after his return from North Africa in defeat. Jessica Tandy, Cedric Hardwicke, and Luther Adler also starred.

A: Jason Robards
Q: Who portrayed *Washington Post* executive editor Benjamin Bradlee in *All the President's Men*?
W: This 1976 film starred Robert Redford and Dustin Hoffman as the *Washington Post* reporters, Woodward and Bernstein, who uncovered the Watergate scandel. Robards won the Oscar for Best Supporting Actor.

A: Jason Robards
Q: Who played President Monckton in *Washington: Behind Closed Doors*?
W: This movie was an ABC six-part mini-series depicting a political drama loosely based on John Ehrlichman's book *The Company*.

A: Jay Silverheels
Q: Who portrayed Tonto on TV?
W: Silverheels played the Lone Ranger's faithful Indian companion. On radio, Tonto was characterized by the voice of John Todd. In the movies, he was portrayed by Chief Thundercloud. Jay Silverheels was a Mohawk Indian and a one-time professional LaCrosse player in Canada.

A: *Jazz Singer, The*
Q: What was the first talking motion picture with the sound on film?
W: Al Jolson made his debut and starred in *The Jazz Singer* on Oct. 6, 1927. In the movie, Jolson says the famous line, "Wait a minute, wait a minute, you ain't heard nothing yet."

A: Jelly Roll
Q: What was the nickname of blues pianist Ferdinand Morton?
W: "Jelly Roll" Morton began his career playing the piano in city brothels and barrel houses. He was also known as the "father of jazz piano." His blues tunes include "The Original Jelly Roll Blues," "London Blues," "Sidewalk Blues," and "Dead Man Blues." He died in a sanatorium in Los Angeles in 1941.

A: Jellystone National Park
Q: Where does Yogi Bear live?
W: Jellystone National Park is the park where Yogi, who's "smarter than the average bear" and his little buddy, Boo Boo Bear, are on the constant prowl for "pic-a-nic" baskets while trying to dodge Ranger Smith.

A: Jerry Lewis
Q: What comedian emceed the 1955 Academy Awards?
W: Jerry Lewis, whose real name is Joseph Levitch, is a famed actor, comedian, and director. Since 1951, he has helped raise over $100 million to fight muscular dystrophy. On Sept. 5, 1976, Frank Sinatra brought Dean Martin, Lewis' one-time comedy partner, on stage at one of Jerry's muscular dystrophy telethons, ending a 20-year feud between Lewis and Martin.

A: Jerry Mahoney
Q: What was the name of ventriloquist Paul Winchell's most popular dummy?
W: Besides being a ventriloquist, Winchell is also an inventor and holds more than 30 patents, including one for a successful artificial heart. His other "dummies" are Knucklehead Smiff and Irving the Mouse. Winchell also does the voice of Tigger in Winnie The Pooh cartoons.

A: Jerry Mathers
Q: Who was the star of "Leave It to Beaver"?
W: The Beaver was the youngest member of the Cleaver clan, which also included father Ward, mother June, and brother Wally. Beaver's given name in the 1950s television series was Theodore.

A: *Jesus Christ Superstar*
Q: What Tim Rice and Andrew Lloyd Weber rock opera was turned into a film by Norman Jewison?
W: The production was called a "reverent rock opera." Although the theatrical version was phenomenally successful, the film version was not. The film was, however, nominated for an Oscar for musical direction.

A: jew's harp, The
Q: What instrument is pressed between the teeth and twanged with a finger?
W: The jew's harp, a musical instrument made of iron, is played by placing against the slightly separated front teeth its two parallel jaws, between which a steel tongue is made to vibrate by plucking a projecting bent piece with the finger. It produces "twanging" tones.

A: *Jezebel*
Q: What film had Bette Davis creating a scandal by wearing a daring red gown to a society ball?
W: This 1938 film featured Davis as Julie Morrison, a southern belle who stirs up trouble among the menfolk with her willfulness and spite, but makes amends when a plague strikes. Henry Fonda and George Brent co-starred. Davis won the Oscar for Best Actress that year.

A: Jill Clayburgh
Q: Who portrayed Carole Lombard in *Gable and Lombard*?
W: This disappointing 1976 film also starred James Brolin as Clark Gable. Allen Garfield co-starred as Louis B. Mayer.

A: Jim Backus
Q: Who is the voice of Mr. Magoo?
W: Mr. Magoo is the near-sighted cartoon character who made his debut in the UPA cartoon "Ragtime Bear" in 1949.

A: Jim Brown
Q: What former football star played opposite Raquel Welch in *100 Rifles*?
W: Brown played a black American sheriff in war-torn Mexico who became involved in a fight for vengeance with Welch after her father's death. Burt Reynolds and Fernando Lamas co-starred.

A: Jim Morrison
Q: What vocalist for the Doors died of a heart attack on July 3, 1971?
W: Morrison was the lead singer for the Doors. Their famous songs include "Touch Me," "People are

ENTERTAINMENT

Strange," and "Light my Fire." Morrison gave the group its name because "there are things that are known and things that are unknown in and between the doors." His death in 1971 from heart failure was a result of drug overdose.

A: Jimi Hendrix
Q: Who asked the musical question: "Have you ever been to electric lady land?"
W: Hendrix's third album was "Electric Ladyland." His American debut came at the Monterey Pop Festival in June 1967, where he played the guitar with his teeth and behind his back--and finished the set by burning it! Hendrix's other albums include "Are You Experienced" and "Axis: Bold as Love."

A: Jimi Hendrix
Q: Who asked the musical question: "Are you experienced?"?
W: Henrix's first album, "Are You Experienced," contained the singles "Purple Haze," "Hey Joe," "May This Be Love," "I Don't Live Today," and "The Wind Cries Mary." It's hard to believe that high-energy Hendrix set out to conquer America as the warm-up band for the Monkees!

A: Jiminy Cricket
Q: What character sang "When You Wish Upon a Star" in Disney's *Pinocchio*?
W: Jiminy Cricket was Pinocchio's friend and advisor. His voice is that of Cliff Edwards.

A: Jimmie Rodgers
Q: Who was known as "the Father of Country Music"?
W: Rodgers is also known as "the Singing Brakeman." He's one of the first three members elected to the Country Music Hall of Fame, along with Hank Williams and Fred Rose. He's renowned for his sad, lonesome yodels.

A: Jimmy Buffett
Q: Who kept searching for his long lost shaker of salt?

W: ...in the 1977 hit "Margaritaville." His first album was "A White Sport Coat and a Pink Crustacean." His second, and more popular album, was "Living and Dying in 3/4 Time," which featured the hit "Come Monday." He's also credited with the hit "Why Don't We Get Drunk and...."

A: Jimmy Stewart
Q: Who portrayed Charles Lindbergh in *The Spirit of St. Louis*?
W: The 1957 film about Lindbergh's famous flight, 3,600 miles nonstop from New York to Paris in 33.5 hours, also starred Murray Hamilton and Marc Connelly.

A: Jingles Jones
Q: Who called out: "Hey, Wild Bill, wait for me"?
W: Jingles Jones was Wild Bill Hickok's partner on the radio and TV series. He's played by Andy Devine whose real name is Jeremiah Schwartz. Jingles' horse is named Joker.

A: Joel Grey
Q: Who won the Best Supporting Actor Oscar for his portrayal of the Kit Kat Club emcee?
W: The Kit Kat Club was the 1931 Berlin nightclub setting where Sally Bowles (Liza Minnelli) sings. The film was released in 1972.

A: Johann Strauss Jr.
Q: Who was "the Waltz King"?
W: His nearly 200 waltzes, which are chains of lilting tunes, and his numerous polkas and other dances are remarkable for their subtle and brilliant scoring. "The Blue Danube" was his most famous waltz; other hits were "Wine, Women and Song," "Voices of Spring," and the "Emperor."

A: John Cameron Swayze
Q: Who was the anchorman of NBC's "Camel News Caravan"?
W: It quickly became the Number 1 news show for NBC, and remained so for seven years (1948 to 1954). In his reports, Swayze would suggest:

"Let's hopscotch the world for headlines" and then read a few bulletins taken from the wire services.

A: John Forsythe
Q: Who was the voice of the Angels' Charlie?
W: The mid-70s TV detective show (Charlie's Angels) featured three scantily clad beauties as private investigators who got their assignments over a speaker phone from Charlie. Although the plots were somewhat thin, so was the beachwear in which they often apperared. Forsythe never appeared on the show; just his voice was heard.

A: John Glenn
Q: What astronaut won $25,000 on "Name That Tune"?
W: At the time he was Marine Major John Glenn when he appeared on the late 1950s TV game show. He correctly identified 25 songs, including "Far Away Places."

A: John Lennon
Q: Who said: "We're more popular than Jesus"?
W: The late John Lennon caused quite a stir with that remark. It resulted in mass protests and the boycotting of Beatle records by religious groups.

A: John Mills
Q: Who won a Best Supporting Actor Oscar for his role as the village idiot in *Ryan's Daughter*?
W: Mills won for his performance as Michael in the 1971 film about a village schoolmaster's wife who fell for a British officer. *Ryan's Daughter* also starred Sarah Miles, Robert Mitchum, and Trevor Howard.

A: John Philip Sousa
Q: Who did Clifton Webb portray in *Stars and Stripes Forever*?
W: The 1952 film was about Bandmaster Sousa who wanted to write ballads and instead found success as a writer of marches. The film also starred Debra Paget and Robert Wagner.

A: John Philip Sousa

Q: Who was America's "March King"?

W: Sousa joined the Marines at 14, then joined their band. He became musical director for the U.S. Marine Band in 1880, and during his first tour of Europe the press began to call him "the March King". His first marches were "Review" and "Salutation."

A: John Wayne

Q: Who played Sergeant John M. Stryker in *The Sands of Iwo Jima*?

W: Wayne was nominated for Best Actor for his portrayal of the tough Marine sergeant who molds raw recruits into fighting men. Also starring in the 1949 film were John Agar, Adele Mara, and Forrest Tucker.

A: John Wayne

Q: Who turned down the lead in "Gunsmoke" for fear of being stereotyped as a cowboy?

W: Not too much irony there. "Gunsmoke" was the longest running TV Western, and Wayne introduced the first TV episode. Matt Dillon was played by William Conrad on radio and by James Arness on TV.

A: John Wayne

Q: Who played the Ringo Kid in the 1939 film *Stagecoach*?

W: This 1939 classic Western also starred Claire Trevor, Thomas Mitchell, George Bancroft, and John Carradine. It's the story about an assortment of Western characters who come under attack by an Indian war party.

A: John Wayne

Q: Who was born Marion Morrison?

W: Wayne was the famous western movie star who turned down the starring role in TV's "Gunsmoke" because he was afraid of being typecast as a cowboy! He won his only Oscar for his portrayal of Rooster Cogburn in *True Grit*. One of his favorite lines was "When the legend becomes fact, print the legend." He died of cancer on June 11, 1979.

A: Johnnie Ray

Q: Who recorded the 1952 hit single "Cry"?

W: Ray, who became partially deaf as a child, had his first big hit in "Cry". Influenced by gospel, and country and western music, he also recorded "Whiskey and Gin," "'Til I Say Goodbye," "Broken Hearted," and "Please, Mr. Sun." His style has been described as "a man in agony of suffering. He tears a passion to tatters and then stamps on the shreds. He clutches at the microphone and behaves as if he were about to tear it apart."

A: Johnny Carson

Q: Who hosted the TV game show "Earn Your Vacation"?

W: Carson began his career hosting game shows like "Earn Your Vacation" and "Who Do You Trust?" He then hosted "The Johnny Carson Show," a comedy/variety show in the mid-50s. He has been the host of the "Tonight Show" since Oct. 1, 1962.

A: Johnny Weissmuller

Q: Who played Tarzan in more films than anyone else?

W: Olympic medalist Weissmuller played the first "talking" Tarzan and went on to play the role in 12 more movies. His first was the 1932 *Tarzan the Ape Man* and his last was *Tarzan and the Mermaids*.

A: jolly swagman, A

Q: Who asked Matilda to go a-waltzing?

W: A "matilda" is not a girl, but a knapsack that "waltzes" or bounces as it is carried by a poor walking Australian worker or "swagman." In 1911 the song was published in *The Australian Students' Song Book*, and has become Australia's national song. It was a great favorite during World War II. How many of you sang this song through grade school and thought Matilda was a girl?

A: Jonathan Winters

Q: Who created Maudie Frickett?

W: Maudie Frickett was one of several of Winters' characters used in his comedy routines. Others were Maynard Fetlinger, Winslow G. Flydipper, Elwood P. Suggins, Chester Hunihugger, and Lance Loveguard--a "Hefty Bag" of characters.

A: Jose Feliciano

Q: Who sang the theme song for "Chico and the Man"?

W: The mid-70s TV comedy series starred Jack Albertson and Freddie Prinze. Ed Brown (Albertson) and his Chicano assistant Chico Rodrigues (Prinze) operated a run-down garage in a decrepit section of East Los Angeles.

ENTERTAINMENT

A: Jose Ferrer
Q: What actor defended the "Caine" mutineers?
W: Ferrer played Lieutenant Barney Greenwald in the 1954 film *The Caine Mutiny*. It was the story of jealousies and frustrations among the officers of a peacetime destroyer that come to a head when the neurotic captain (Humphrey Bogart) panics during a typhoon and is relieved of his post. The film also starred Van Johnson and Fred MacMurray.

A: *Judgment at Nuremberg*
Q: What 1961 film dramatized the Nazi war crimes?
W: Judgment at Nuremberg was a fictionalized version of the 1948 trial of the Nazi leaders for crimes against humanity. The film starred Spencer Tracy, Marlene Dietrich, Burt Lancaster and Richard Widmark. It was nominated for Best Picture.

A: Judy Carne
Q: Who was "Laugh-In's" sock-it-to-me girl?
W: The pilot for the series aired Sept. 9, 1967. The comedy series incorporated new videotape tricks and techniques, had a large crew of writers and performers, and provided viewers with familiar characters to guide them through it all. One character was Judy Carne, who often said "sock-it-to-me!" which was usually followed by her being doused with a bucket of water.

A: Judy Garland
Q: Who sang "You Made Me Love You" to a photo of Clark Gable in the film *Broadway Melody*?
W: Actually it was *Broadway Melody of 1938*. (There were also *Broadway Melodies* of 1929, 1936, and 1940.) It was the story of backstage problems that threatened the opening of a musical show and also starred Eleanor Powell, George Murphy, and Sophie Tucker.

A: Judy Garland's
Q: What actress's real name was Frances Gumm?
W: Garland starred in such classics as *The Wizard of Oz* and *A Star Is Born*. Judy was married 4 times: David Rose, Vincente Minnelli (their daughter is Liza Minnelli), Sid Luft, and Mark Herron.

A: Julie Andrews
Q: Who portrayed Eliza Doolittle in Broadway's original *My Fair Lady*?
W: The play was made into a film in 1964, and Audrey Hepburn played Eliza Doolittle in the film. It was actually a musical version of *Pygmalion*, the story of a flower girl trained by an arrogant elocutionist (Rex Harrison) to pass as a lady.

A: Jumbo
Q: What was the name of P.T. Barnum's giant elephant?
W: Barnum was the great American Showman. Jumbo was one of the many exhibits in his famous circus. Others were: General Tom Thumb, Siamese twins Chang and Eng, the Bearded Lady, the Wild Man of Borneo, and the Fiji Mermaid.

A: June Taylor Dancers, The
Q: What was the name of the dancing group on "The Jackie Gleason Show"?
W: Gleason's third wife is the sister of June Taylor. CBS axed Gleason's show in 1970 because the executives thought that it didn't appeal to the younger people of America. (The all-important buying audience of people 18 to 34 years old.)

A: Jupiter's
Q: What planet's moon was the destination in *2001: A Space Odyssey*?
W: *2001* was the 1968 science fiction film without death rays or monsters. The hero is Keir Dullea, and the villain is a super-computer named HAL. Directed by Stanley Kubrick, the film won an Oscar for special effects.

K

A: K-K-K-Katy
Q: What tune subtitled "The Stammering Song" was a World War I hit?
W: It was one of several humorous songs that poked fun at the soldiers "adventures" in France. Other such songs were "If He Can Fight Like He Can Love, Goodnight Germany," "Oh Frenchy!," and "How Ya Gonna Keep 'Em Down on the Farm, After They've Seen Paree?"

A: K.A.O.S
Q: What was the name of the evil organization on "Get Smart"?
W: This mid-60s comedy TV series starred Don Adams as Maxwell Smart, Agent 86. Barbara Feldon played "99." Smart worked for C.O.N.T.R.O.L. Smart's favorite lines were "Would you believe" and "Sorry about that, Chief."

A: Katherine Hepburn
Q: What actress has received the most Oscar nominations?
W: Furthermore, she's received the Oscar for Best Actress for her various roles in *Morning Glory*, *Guess Who's Coming to Dinner?*, *The Lion in Winter*, and *On Golden Pond*. She has received more Oscars than any other actress.

A: Katharine Ross
Q: Who portrayed Etta Place, companion to Butch Cassidy and the Sundance Kid?
W: This 1969 film starred Robert Redford and Paul Newman as the infamous outlaws. Ross played a schoolteacher who keeps the outlaws one step ahead of the law.

A: Kate Smith
Q: Who was renowned for her rendition of "God Bless America"?

W: Written by Irving Berlin in 1918, the song was thrown into a trunk until 20 years later. His profits from the song were donated to the Boy Scouts and Girl Scouts. Smith was originally given exclusive rights to sing the song.

A: **Kate Smith's**
Q: What singer's theme song was "When the Moon Comes over the Mountain"?
W: Sorry, Smith's theme song isn't "God Bless America," although she did a commendable job with it!

A: **Kay Kyser**
Q: Who emceed the radio quiz show "Kollege of Musical Knowledge"?
W: This was a popular radio quiz show in which Kyser would react to correct answers with "That's wrong, you're right!" and to wrong guesses with "That's right, you're wrong!" Funny, huh?

A: **Kellogg's**
Q: What company was the original sponsor of TV's "Superman"?
W: The "man of steel" debuted on TV April 15, 1953, and there were 108 TV episodes. George Reeves played Superman/Clark Kent. Opening narration: "Faster than a speeding bullet, more powerful than a locomotive, able to leap tall buldings in a single bound. Look! Up in the sky! It's a bird! It's a plane! It's Superman!" ...and millions of kids gobbled up all the cereal Kellogg's could make.

A: **Kermit**
Q: Who is Miss Piggy in love with?
W: She drools over every man she meets, but her heart belongs to Kermit. Kermit was the host of TV's "The Muppet Show," created by Jim Henson.

A: **Kermit**
Q: What frog emcees "The Muppet Show"?
W: He started as Kermit T. Frog, reporter on the TV series "Sesame Street." His voice is that of his creator, Jim Henson.

A: *Key Largo*
Q: What film pits Humphrey Bogart against gangsters in the Florida Keys?
W: The 1948 film also starred Lauren Bacall (Bogart's wife), Claire Trevor, Edward G. Robinson, and Lionel Barrymore. The film was directed by John Huston.

A: **Keystone Cops, The**
Q: What police force did Mack Sennett create?
W: Appropriately, or coincidentally enough, they worked for Keystone Pictures. Original members included: Slim Sumerville, Mack Riley, Edgar Kennedy, Bobby Dunn, Hank Mann, Georgie Jeske, and Charlie Avery.

A: **Kirk Douglas**
Q: Who portrayed Vincent Van Gogh in *Lust for Life*?
W: Douglas was nominated for an Oscar for his performance in this 1956 film. It also starred Anthony Quinn (as Gauguin) and James Donald.

A: **Kris Kristofferson**
Q: What singer made his film debut in *Cisco Pike*?
W: The 1971 film was about a former pop group dealer turned drug pusher who's blackmailed by a cop into selling heroin. It also starred Gene Hackman, Karen Black, and Harry Sean Stanton.

A: **Kristin Shepard**
Q: Who shot J.R.?
W: Kristin, played by Mary Crosby, was Sue Ellen's younger sister. The show caused a worldwide sensation. In Britain, the odds were 20 to 1 that J.R. shot himself! A record number of viewers tuned in to learn the answer. The show got a 53.3 rating and a 76 share making it the highest rated individual show ever on television. That's shop talk for "everybody tuned in"!

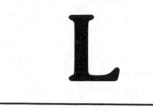

L

A: **Lamont Cranston**
Q: What was the secret identity of The Shadow?
W: "Who knows what evil lurks in the hearts of men? The Shadow knows!" "The Shadow" was first on radio in August 1930. Movie versions included: *The Shadow* (1939 serial), *The Shadow Returns* (1946), *Behind the Mask* (1946), and *The Missing Lady*. "The weed of crime bears bitter fruit – crime does not pay!" The Shadow – hmmmmm.

A: **Lana Turner**
Q: Who was "the Sweater Girl"?
W: Her full name is Julia Jean Mildred Frances Turner Shaw Crane Topping Barker May Easton Dante. She (obviously) was married eight times (twice to Stephen Crane). It was Lana's daughter Cheryl who killed Lana's boyfriend Johnny Stompanato with a butcher knife on April 4, 1958.

A: **"Lara's Theme"**
Q: What was the theme song to *Dr. Zhivago*?
W: The 1965 epic starred Omar Sharif, Julie Christie, Rod Steiger, and Alec Guinness. Sharif played a doctor caught up in World War I who was exiled from Moscow for writing poetry, forced into partisan service, and separated from his only love. "Lara's Theme" won the Oscar for Best Musical Score.

A: **Larry Hagman**
Q: What actor is Mary Martin's son?
W: He starred in "I Dream of Jeannie" with Barbara Eden and has found new popularity as the nasty J.R. Ewing on the TV series "Dallas."

A: **Larry Parks**
Q: Who played Al Jolson in *The Jolson Story*?
W: Parks was nominated for an Oscar for his portrayal of the great entertainer of the 1920s, whose success brings marital difficulties. Also starring in the 1946 film was William Demarest and Evelyn Keeyes. Jolson's singing voice was dubbed into the film.

A: **Las Vegas**
Q: What city is terrorized by Dracula in "The Night Stalker"?
W: This TV series starred Darren McGavin as a newspaper reporter who encounters vampires, werewolves, and slasher-types in modern-day Las Vegas.

A: **Lassie**
Q: What TV dog had successive masters named Jeff, Timmy and Corey?
W: Lassie was the famous collie that first appeared in Eric Knight's novel *Lassie Come Home*. All the Lassies have been male. He was the first animal to be named to the Animal Hall of Fame. However, Lassie was eliminated from competing for the Patsy award because he had already won too many.

A: **"Last Dance"**
Q: What Oscar-winning song was introduced in the film *Thank God It's Friday*?
W: This 1978 disco film dealt with the problems of a disc jockey in a Hollywood disco. It starred Valerie Landsburg, Terri Nunn, Donna Summer, and the Commodores.

A: *Last Tango in Paris*
Q: What 1972 Marlon Brando film was widely banned but not panned?
W: It was the story of a doomed love affair between a middle-aged man and a young French girl. The film won Oscar nominations for Best Actor (Brando) and Direction.

A: **Lauren Bacall**
Q: Who made her film debut opposite Humphrey Bogart in *To Have and Have Not* at age 19?
W: Bacall was married to Bogart and also starred with him in *Two Guys from Milwaukee* (1946), *The Big Sleep* (1946), *Dark Passage* (1947), and *Key Largo* (1948).

A: **Laurence Olivier and Michael Caine**
Q: Who were the stars of the film *Sleuth*?
W: This 1972 film was about a successful thriller writer who invents a murder plot that backfires on him. Caine and Olivier were the only two actors in the entire film, and both were nominated for Oscars for their performances.

A: **Lawrence Welk**
Q: Who has a license plate reading: A1ANA2?
W: Featuring his patented champagne music, Welk led a relaxed hour of dance music along with a talented crew of supporting players, including the singing Lennon sisters. He started every piece of music by chanting, "a-one and-a two..."

A: **Lee J. Cobb**
Q: Who portrayed Johnny Friendly in *On the Waterfront*?
W: Cobb was nominated for an Oscar in the 1954 film. The movie classic also starred Marlon Brando, Eva Marie Saint, Rod Steiger, and Karl Malden.

A: **left, The**
Q: Which hand did Charlie Chaplin carry his cane in?
W: That's so his right hand was always available to tip his hat. Chaplin was the greatest film comedian of all time whose secret of success was his originality. His more memorable pictures are *The Kid, The Gold Rush, City Lights,* and *Modern Times.*

A: **Leo**
Q: What's the name of the MGM lion?
W: Leo the lion is the trademark of MGM pictures. He was portrayed by three lions: Slats, Jackie, and Tanner (in color). He first roared July 31, 1928, for the debut of the movie *White Shadows of the South Seas.* The roar was heard via a phonograph record because it was a silent movie.

A: **Leo G. Carroll**
Q: Who played Cosmo B. Topper on TV's "Topper"?
W: Cosmo B. Topper was the central character of Thorne Smith's novel *Topper*. He was played on radio and in movies by Roland Young (three pictures). His wife, Henrietta, was portrayed on TV by Lee Patrick.

A: **Leonard Bernstein**
Q: Who wrote the music for *West Side Story*?
W: *West Side Story* is the 1961 musical "Romeo and Juliet" story in a contemporary setting. The songs, by Bernstein and Stephen Sondheim, included "Tonight," "Maria," "One Hand, One Heart," and "I Feel Pretty."

A: **Les Brown's**
Q: Whose orchestra was known as the Band of Renown?
W. "Sentimental Journey" was Brown and the Band's first best seller. The vocal rendition was done by Doris Day. The band was founded in 1938, and its theme songs included "Leap Frog" and "Sentimental Journey."

A: **Lesley Gore**
Q: Who sang the 1963 hit "It's My Party"?
W: "It's My Party" was about losing her boyfriend, and later that year she sang "Judy's Turn to Cry" in which her boyfriend came back. She was discovered by Quincy Jones who produced the "Party" songs, and her string of hits through 1967 include "She's a Fool" (1963), "Sunshine, Lollipops, and Rainbows" (1965), and "Young Love" (1966).

ENTERTAINMENT

A: **Liberace**
Q: What pianist countered his critics by noting: "I cried all the way to the bank"?
W: The flamboyant piano player, complete with candelabra, is probably laughing right now. He was once awarded $22,400 in damages because of what a London columnist had written about him (he donated the money to charity). He collects miniature pianos, of which he has over 1000. He's also known as "Mr. Showmanship" and has a Las Vegas salary of six figures.

A: **Liberace**
Q: What pianist always wanted you to meet his brother George?
W: His brother George, who studied violin and later taught at Northwestern University Conservatory, also played with various name bands during the big-band era. George was Liberace's *older* brother.

A: **Lieutenant Philip Gerard**
Q: Who chased Dr. Richard Kimble for four years?
W: In the TV series "The Fugitive," Dr. Kimble (David Janssen) was unjustly accused and convicted of murdering his wife, but was able to escape execution when the train he was on derailed. Kimble split his time between chasing the "one-armed man" who really killed his wife and avoiding Lieutenant Gerard (Barry Morse) who was obsessed with his capture.

A: *Life of Brian*
Q: What Monty Python movie was banned in Scotland?
W: The film was initially controversial because many people felt that it was sacrilegious because it was a comedy about a man mistaken for the Messiah. One scene featured three crucified men singing "Always Look on the Bright Side of Life."

A: **Limeliters, The**
Q: What folk group was Glenn Yarborough the lead singer for?
W: Also in the group were Leo Gottlieb (bass) and Alex Hassilev (guitar,

banjo). They debuted in 1959 and were best known for the 1961 hit "A Dollar Down." Yarborough went on to pursue a sucessful solo career including his hit "Baby, the Rain Must Fall."

A: **Linda Blair**
Q: Who played Regan MacNeil in *The Exorcist*?
W: Blair played little Regan MacNeil, who is possessed by the devil and turned into a hideous monster in the 1973 film. Blair's antics included turning her head a full 180 degrees and retching green vomit into the face of a priest. Yucko...Bucko...!

A: **Little Eva**
Q: Who asked you to do the "Loco-Motion" with her in 1962?
W: Born Eva Narcissus Boyde in 1944, she wanted to grow up to be a nurse or singer, but ended up babysitting for the songwriting team of Carole King and Gerry Goffin. She started singing around the house, and King and Goffin wrote "The Loco-Motion" for her. She released a few other songs, but "Loco-Motion" was her best.

A: **Little Susie**
Q: Who were the Everly Brothers trying to wake up?
W: Don and Phil Everly laid the groundwork for the countless other country rock groups of today. "Wake Up Little Susie" was a 1957 hit. Other Everly hits included "Bye, Bye, Love," "All I Have to Do is Dream," and "Cathy's Clown."

A: **Little White Dove**
Q: What was the name of the Indian maiden in Johnny Preston's hit "Running Bear"?
W: This 1959 song was made popular by Preston in a Mercury recording. The words and music were by J.P. Richardson.

A: **Lon Chaney**
Q: What actor was known as "the Man of a Thousand Faces"?
W: That's Lon Chaney, Sr. He was "the man of a thousand faces"

because he was often required to be made up into such characters as "the Hunchback of Notre Dame" and "the Phantom of the Opera." He was the son of deaf mutes. His son, Lon Chaney, Jr., achieved fame as "The Wolfman." The senior Chaney's 1957 film biography starred James Cagney.

A: **Lone Ranger, The**
Q: Who reared his horse to "The William Tell Overture"?
W: ...while giving the command, "High-ho Silver! Away!" The Lone Ranger was the secret identity of Texas Ranger John Reid whose faithful Indian companion was Tonto. The Lone Ranger was played most often in movies and on TV by Clayton Moore. Who was that masked man?

A: **Lone Ranger, The**
Q: Who did Clayton Moore portray in the movies and on TV?
W: To most people, he will always be *the* Lone Ranger. Atop his trusty steed Silver and alongside his Indian companion Tonto, he would seek out injustice and protect all that was good in America. He wore a blue shirt and pants, red kerchief, black mask (made from his brother's vest), and a white hat.

A: **"Lonely Bull, The"**
Q: What song propelled Herb Alpert and the Tijuana Brass to fame?
W: Albert added some intonations of Mexican mariachi music to Sol Lake's song called "Twinkle Star," recorded it, and titled it "The Lonely Bull." He went to Mexico and taped

crowd noises at the Tijuana bullfights and dubbed them in to complete the recording. Because Tijuana was the source of part of the Alpert song, the record was released under the group name "Tijuana Brass."

A: Longbranch, The
Q: What was the name of Kitty Russell's saloon on "Gunsmoke"?
W: The Longbranch Saloon, located on Front Street, was owned by Miss Kitty (Amanda Blake) on the TV series "Gunsmoke." The series also starred James Arness as Marshall Matt Dillon.

A: Los Angeles
Q: What city is the setting for the movie *Chinatown*?
W: *Chinatown*, set in 1937 Los Angeles, was the film in which a private eye takes a simple case and uncovers murder and scandal. Starring Jack Nicholson, Faye Dunaway, and John Huston and directed by Roman Polanski (who also has a bit part), the film won an Oscar for Best Screenplay.

A: *Los Angeles Tribune, The*
Q: What newspaper does Lou Grant work for?
W: Premiering in the fall of 1977, the TV series spinoff of "The Mary Tyler Moore Show" took a more dramatic approach to the news. The series also starred Mason Adams, Robert Walden, Linda Kelsey, and Daryl Anderson (as Animal). Ed Asner still played Lou Grant.

A: "Lost in Space"
Q: What TV series featured the line: "Warning, aliens approaching"?
W: It was spoken by Robot in the late-60s TV series about a typical American suburban family of the future who were launched into space and then immediately got lost. The Robinson family sailed around space in *Jupiter II*. (Warning, warning! Nausea approaching.)

A: Louis Armstrong
Q: Who was the singing trumpet player in the film *The Glenn Miller Story*?
W: This was the 1954 film about the life of bandleader Glenn Miller whose plane disappeared during World War II. It starred James Stewart, June Allyson, Harry Morgan, and Charles Drake. "Satchmo" Armstrong played himself, as he also did in the film *The Five Pennies*(1959). Armstrong was famous for his New Orleans jazz trumpet style.

A: *Love Me Tender*
Q: What was Elvis Presley's first film, in 1956?
W: It was the story of three brothers who fall out over some money that they've brought home from the Civil War. Presley sings four songs before being shot and then reappears in a ghostly form at the end. The film also starred Richard Egan and Debra Paget.

A: Lovin' Spoonful, The
Q: What group asked the musical question "Do You Believe in Magic"?
W: The lead singer was John Sebastian. Other hits of this group were "Daydream," "Younger Girl," "Darling Be Home Soon," "Darling Companion," and "Summer in the City."

A: LP selling a million copies, An
Q: What is a platinum record awarded for?
W: A platinum record is given for an LP which sells one million copies, a gold record is given for a single which sells one million copies, and a gold album is given for one million dollars in sales.

A: Lynn, Michael, Vanessa
Q: Who are the three acting Redgraves?
W: Sir Michael Redgrave is the father of Lynn and Vanessa. Michael is a tall distinguished British actor and former schoolmaster, who has appeared in *The Lady Vanishes* and *Thunder Rock*. Lynn has tended to play more comedic roles. She's appeared in *Tom Jones*, *Georgy Girl*, and *The Happy Hooker*. Vanessa, well-known for her espousal of causes, has appeared in *Camelot*, *Mary, Queen of Scots*, and *Julia*.

A: Lynn Redgrave
Q: Who played the title role in *Georgy Girl*?
W: Redgrave was nominated for Best Actress for her role in the 1966 film. She played a homely girl who has caught the eye of her boss but she leaves him to care for her friend's illegitimate baby. The film also starred James Mason and Charlotte Rampling.

M

A: Ma and Pa Kettle
Q: What film couple was portrayed by Majorie Main and Percy Kilbride?
W: The first Ma and Pa Kettle movie was *The Egg and I* in 1947. They played in a total of eight movies together as Ma and Pa Kettle.

A: Ma Barker
Q: What movie ma did Claire Trevor, Blanche Yurka and Shelley Winters all play?
W: Ma Barker was a real woman who was born Bonnie Clark. She was the reputed head of an outlaw gang that included her four sons. Shelley Winters played Ma in the 1970 movie *Bloody Mama*. Lurene Tuttel also played Ma Barker in *Ma Barker's Killer Brood* in 1960.

A: **Madame Butterfly**
Q: What operatic heroine commits suicide on her father's sword?
W: *Madame Butterfly* is an opera in three acts by Giacomo Puccini. It is based on a play by David Delasco that was derived from a short story by John Luther Long.

A: **Mae West**
Q: Who said: "When I'm good, I'm very good, but when I'm bad I'm better"?
W: Queen of the double entendre and innuendo, Mae West wrote her own lines and worked on the script and dialogue for most of her films.

A: **Mae West**
Q: Who said: "It's not the men in my life, it's the life in my men"?
W: She must have known some lively men in her time! In 1926 she produced and directed a play on Broadway called *Sex* for which she was brought up on charges of obscenity and jailed for ten days.

A: **Mafia**
Q: What word was intentionally omitted from the screenplay of *The Godfather*?
W: It did, however, appear in the 1974 sequel *Godfather II*. And the meaning of "Mafia": *Morte Alla Francia Italia Anelia* or "Death to the French is Italy's Cry."

A: **Major Bowes**
Q: Who preceded Ted Mack as host of radio's "Amateur Hour"?
W: Major Bowes was the founder and original host of the Amateur Hour; Ted Mack was his assistant. Major Bowes' "Amateur Hour" discovered/found Frank Sinatra in 1937.

A: **"Make Room for Daddy"**
Q: What TV series featured Uncle Tonoose?
W: Hans Conried, after making guest appearances in different roles on the show starring Danny Thomas, turned up as Uncle Tonoose in a fall 1958 telecast. He played this role from 1958 to 1971. Interesting note: the title "Make Room for Daddy" came from a phrase used in the real life Thomas household – whenever Danny returned home from tour his children had to switch bedrooms to "make room for Daddy"!

A: **Male**
Q: What sex have all TV Lassies been?
W: Now you may think that this is a straightforward answer to a simple question, except in all the "Lassie" shows, Lassie was supposed to be a female. Lassie performed a "miracle" on network TV; "she" gave birth to a litter of puppies. Neat trick – that's the magic of TV.

A: **Man of La Mancha**
Q: What Broadway musical was inspired by Cervantes's *Don Quixote*?
W: It was produced on Broadway by Selden and James, and the original cast included Richard Kiley and Irving Jacobson. The musical ran for 2,329 performances.

A: **Man with the Golden Arm, The**
Q: What film did Frank Sinatra portray a drug addict in?
W: In 1955, "Old Blue Eyes" was nominated for an Oscar as Best Ac-

tor for his dramatic performance in this film about a drug addict and his attempts to kick the habit.

A: **Man, Woman, Birth, Death, Infinity**
Q: What were the five opening words on "Ben Casey"?
W: This was one of the great medical dramas in television history. Vince Edwards, discovered by Bing Crosby, played Ben Casey. Sam Jaffe co-starred as Dr. David Zorba, Casey's mentor.

A: **Marcel Marceau**
Q: Who spoke the only word in Mel Brooks's *Silent Movie*?
W: Marcel Marceau is an internationally known mime. Mel Brooks, a comedian writer supreme, *would* have this twist in his film!

A: **Margot Kidder**
Q: Who played Lois Lane in the 1978 movie *Superman*?
W: Lois Lane was played by Margot Kidder in all three *Superman* movies. In *Superman I* Lois and Superman begin their love affair, and in *Superman III* they are married. Lois is notorious for two things: being a good reporter and trying to discover Superman's other identity.

A: **Marilyn Monroe**
Q: Who played Cherie in the movie *Bus Stop*?
W: This role was considered one of Miss Monroe's best. The film marked a turning point in her career as it re-established her as a talented artist and ended her 14-month absence from films.

A: **Marilyn Monroe**
Q: Who was the 1976 film *Goodbye Norma Jean* about?
W: She was born Norma Jean Mortenson on June 1, 1926, and went on to become Marilyn Monroe, Hollywood star. *Goodbye Norma Jean* takes a look at the adolescent Norma Jean and the road she took to become Marilyn Monroe. Misty Rowe starred as Norma Jean.

ENTERTAINMENT

ENTERTAINMENT

A: **Marilyn Monroe's**
Q: Whose figure did Walt Disney Studios use as a model for Tinker Bell?
W: Never before had the *Peter Pan* character Tinker Bell been shown. When Disney artists decided to sketch her, some decision had to be made about what she would look like. The final decision, Walt Disney claimed, was cemented by the popularity of Marilyn Monroe.

A: **Marlon Brando**
Q: Who portrayed U.S. Nazi leader George Lincoln Rockwell in *Roots II?*
W: Rockwell was the founder of the American Nazi Party in 1959. Many famous and infamous people were depicted in *Roots II*, and their roles were played by equally famous stars such as Marlon Brando.

A: **Marlon Brando**
Q: Who played Fletcher Christian in the 1962 film *Mutiny on the Bounty?*
W: Brando, who was dynamic, forceful, and highly successful in the 1940s and 1950s, made a string of unsuccessful movies in the 60's. *Mutiny-* was made during this period. Some critics argue that Brando did succeed in elevating "junk" to respectable heights andthe proof was *Mutiny*.

A: **Marlon Brando**
Q: What actor said in the movie *Superman*: "I have sent them you, my only son"?
W: Marlon Brando played Jor-el, Superman's scientist father, who saves his life by sending him to earth in a spacecraft. Brando earned $2.2 million for his brief portrayal. For that kind of money we'd send our daughter too!

A: **Marlon Brando**
Q: Who played Johnny in *The Wild One?*
W: Heroic individualism seemed to be Brando's personal trademark in his early career. This characterized the type of outsider character Johnny was in *The Wild One*. This film was banned in England for fear it would incite gangs to riot.

A: **Marlon Brando and George C. Scott**
Q: What two performers refused their Best Actor Oscars in the 1970s?
W: George C. Scott won the Oscar for *Patton* in 1970. He wasn't present for the presentation, and there is no evidence he returned for the Oscar. Scott maintained it was "degrading for actors to compete against one another." Marlon Brando became the second actor to turn down an Oscar. Winning for the *Godfather*, Brando sent a starlet, Maria Cruz, to refuse the Oscar for him.

A: **Marsha Mason**
Q: Who played the title role in *The Goodbye Girl?*
W: Miss Mason won an Academy Award nomination, her second, for her performance in *The Goodbye Girl*. She was married to playwright-screenwriter Neil Simon.

A: **Martin and Lewis**
Q: What comedy team's movies include *Hollywood or Bust* and *Living It Up?*
W: During an Atlantic City engagement in 1946, Martin met comedian Jerry Lewis with whom he formed a partnership. The Martin-Lewis team was one of the most phenomenal successes in show biz history — their partnership lasted through ten years and 16 films.

A: **Martin Balsam**
Q: What performer was the second to die in *Psycho?*
W: Balsam, a detective in *Psycho*, followed Janet Leigh to the Bates Motel where short work was made of him by Norman. He has kept busy as a screen character since his debut in *On the Waterfront* in 1954. He has won both Tony and Oscar Awards.

A: **Mary Hartman**
Q: Who lived at 343 Bratner, Fernwood?
W: Mary Hartman, star of "Mary Hartman, Mary Hartman", was a typical American housewife living in the small town of Fernwood, Ohio. Pigtailed and plain, her life was filled with one crisis after another. Louise Lasser, once the wife of Woody Allen, played Mary Hartman in this satirical soap opera.

A: **Mary Martin**
Q: What actress played Peter Pan on Broadway and TV?
W: Mary Martin was one of the major talents of the American musical stage. She also starred in several light films during her career, and later she appeared as a guest star. By the way, she's Larry "J.R. Ewing" Hagman's mother!

A: **Mary Pickford**
Q: Who was "the Girl with the Curl"?
W: Mary Pickford had a number of nicknames. Because of her head of golden curls, she was billed as "the Girl with the Curl" or "the Girl with the Golden Hair."

A: **Mary Pickford**
Q: What Canadian-born actress became "America's Sweetheart"?
W: Mary Pickford, born Gladys Smith, was forced at an early age to work to support her brother and sister. After several years in various road companies, she stormed into David Belasca's office at age 14 demanding a role in a play. He renamed her Mary Pickford. During her long career she played a variety of parts, but was best loved and remembered for her typical role as a sweet innocent little girl for which she was dubbed ''America's Sweetheart.''

A: *Mary Poppins*
Q: What movie originated the magic word ''supercalifragilisticexpialidocious''?
W: *Mary Poppins* was produced by the Disney Studios. This lengthy word was supposed to be the only word that could truly describe Mary.

A: **Mary Tyler Moore's**
Q: Whose legs were featured on TV's "Richard Diamond"?
W: Mary Tyler Moore's voice and legs were the only features revealed about her in "Richard Diamond." Her name was not even listed in the credits at the end of the show. Mary Tyler Moore was the first "Sam"; another actress, Roxanne Brooks, played the role for a year.

A: **M*A*S*H's**
Q: What TV show's song is "Suicide is Painless"?
W: "Suicide is Painless" was written by Johnny Mandel. Not only was it the theme for the TV show "M*A*S*H," it was also the theme for the movie "M*A*S*H." Remember the doctor who wanted to off himself?

A: **Maureen O'Sulivan**
Q: Who's Mia Farrow's mother?
W: Maureen O'Sullivan, best remembered as Jane to Johnny Weismuller's Tarzan, married writer-director John Farrow in 1936. She retired from the screen in 1942 to raise her growing family of seven children, one of whom was Mia.

A: **Max Von Sydow**
Q: Who played Christ in *The Greatest Story Ever Told*?
W: Max Von Sydow, born Carl Adolf Von Sydow, made his screen debut in 1949. He acquired a reputation for excellence on the Swedish stage and expanded into films in the late 1950s, under the guidance of Ingmar Bergman. His best remembered performance to date has been Christ in George Steven's *The Greatest Story Ever Told*.

A: **Maximilian Schell**
Q: Who won the 1961 Best Actor Oscar for his role in *Judgment at Nuremberg*?
W: Maximilian Schell is not only an Oscar-winning actor, but also a director, producer, and screen writer. Mr. Schell won an Oscar for his portrayal of an enigmatic defense attorney in *Nuremberg*. He has been nominated for Oscars on two other occasions.

A: **Maxwell**
Q: What is Corporal Klinger's first name?
W: Max Klinger (Jamie Farr), desperate to get out of the Army, resorted to wearing women's clothes to get out of Korea and the 4077th M*A*S*H* in one of TV's most popular shows. Max started as an aide to the doctors and finally became the company clerk in the TV series.

A: **Mayberry, North Carolina**
Q: What town did Andy Taylor and Barney Fife patrol?
W: Sheriff Andy Taylor was a widower with a young son and live-in aunt. Barney was Andy's cousin and deputy. Andy Griffith played Andy Taylor and Don Knotts played Barney Fife. Andy and Barney were found every week on "The Andy Griffith Show."

A: **Maynard G. Krebs**
Q: Who was Dobie Gillis' sidekick?
W: Maynard G. Krebs was a beatnik. To Maynard, *work* was a dirty word; Maynard and Dobie did their best to get by with a minimum of effort. Bob Denver, Gilligan of "Gilligan's Island," played Maynard.

A: **Mel Blanc**
Q: Who was the voice of Bugs Bunny, Sylvester, and Tweety Pie?
W: Mel Blanc's voice is one of the most famous in the world. He is the voice specialist behind some of the world's favorite cartoon characters, including Porky Pig and Daffy Duck. In addition, he was the voice of Twiki in *Buck Rogers in the 25th Century*. He is also a talented musician.

A: **Merle Haggard**
Q: What country and western singer is known as "the Okie from Muskogee"?
W: Merle Haggard was the son of Okie farmers. He is commonly identified with his song "Okie from Muskogee," which brought him to national attention in 1969.

A: **Meter maid**
Q: What is Lovely Rita's occupation?
W: Paul McCartney, amused by the American meter maids during a visit to the U.S., was inspired to compose the song "Lovely Rita The Meter Maid" that is a selection on the "Sergeant Pepper's Lonely Heart Clubs Band" album.

A: **Mia Farrow**
Q: Who did Frank Sinatra marry at the Sands Hotel, Las Vegas, in 1966?
W: Mia Farrow, daughter of director John Farrow and actress Maureen O'Sullivan, was 21 when she married "Old Blue Eyes." Frank was 30 years her senior. They were divorced in 1968. Farrow's career was spurred by her role of Alison MacKenzie in the TV soap opera "Peyton Place."

A: **Miami**
Q: What city was the setting for TV's "Surfside Six"?
W: "Surfside Six" was a cookie cutter copy of "77 Sunset Strip." Produced and shown on the same network as "Strip," Surfside Six was the Miami telephone exchange that included the number of the houseboat that served as both office and home to the detectives.

A: **Michael Anthony**
Q: Who delivered John Beresford Tipton's million-dollar checks?
W: Michael Anthony (Marvin Miller) was John Tipton's personal secretary who was instructed each week to present someone with a million-dollar check. John Tipton, like Charlie of "Charlie's Angels," was never seen on the show.

A: **Michael Landon**
Q: Who played the title role in *I Was a Teenage Werewolf*?
W: Eugene Maurice Orowitz picked a new name from the phone book when he decided to become a professional actor. That name, of course, was Michael Landon. Before making his movie debut in *I Was a Teenage Werewolf*, Mr. Landon had a number of minor roles in several TV dramas.

A: **Michael Stivic**
Q: Who is Archie Bunker's son-in-law?
W: In the TV series "All in the Family," Rob Reiner played Michael Stivic, also known as "Meathead." Unknown to many is the fact that Archie himself was called "Meathead" in high school!

A: **Mick Jagger**
Q: What rock star attended the London School of Economics for two years?
W: Fortunately for us he didn't graduate and studied rock 'n roll music full-time instead! Mick, along with Brian Jones, Keith Richard, Charlie Watts, Bill Wyman, and Ron Wood have all (at one time or another) been a member of the Rolling Stones.

A: **Mickey Mouse**
Q: Who was the first non-human to win an Oscar?
W: In 1932 Walt Disney received a special Academy Award for the creation of Mickey Mouse. Mickey is the most popular cartoon character ever. He debuted in *Plane Crazy* (silent) in 1928. He also made his first sound cartoon that same year, *Steamboat Willie*. In 1938 Mussolini banned all American cartoons from Italy...all except those featuring Mickey Mouse.

A: **Mickey Mouse Club, The**
Q: What TV club did Jimmie Dodd host?
W: "The Mickey Mouse Club" was a TV series that ran from 1955 to 1959. It featured Jimmie and the Mouseketeers and that unforgettable song: "M-I-C, see ya real soon, K-E-Y, why? Because we like you! M-O-U-S-E!"

A: **Mickey Rooney**
Q: Who portrayed Thomas Edison in the 1940 film *Young Tom Edison*?
W: This was the first of an MGM two-parter tracing Edison's first experiments. The second, *Edison the Man* starring Spencer Tracy, was released the same year. This film is often referred to as a "reasonably factual and absorbing junior biopic."

A: **Midnight Cowboy**
Q: What was the first X-rated film to win the Best Picture Oscar?
W: We didn't believe it either, but it *was* X-rated. Released through United Artists in 1969, it received Oscars for writing, Waldo Scott; and direction, John Schlesinger. *Midnight Cowboy* is the story of a slightly dim-witted Texan who comes to New York to offer his services as a stud for rich ladies. However, he ends up spending a hard winter helping a tubercular con man. The film starred Jon Voight as Joe Buck the cowboy, and Dustin Hoffman as Ratso Rizzo, the con man.

A: **"Mikado, The"**
Q: What Gilbert and Sullivan opera is about the emperor of Japan?
W: This is the story of a timid Japanese official who is appointed Lord High Executioner, only to discover his first intended victim is the Emperor's son who is traveling incognito. The 1939 film version starred Kenny Baker.

A: **Mike Nichols**
Q: Who directed *The Graduate*?
W: Nichols received the Oscar as Best Director for the film. Dustin Hoffman made his film debut as Benjamin Braddock, the college "graduate" who is led into an affair with the wife of one of his father's friends. Benjamin then falls in love with the woman's daughter. The film is a deft work of social satire and established Nichols as a cultural humorist in the tradition of Preston Sturges and Billy Wilder.

A: **Milton Berle**
Q: Who was "Mr. Television"?
W: Berle began as host of "Texaco Star Theater" in 1948. He hosted the "Kraft Music Hall" in 1958 and co-hosted "Jackpot Bowling" at one point. Berle was one of the first and most popular vaudeville performers to make the jump to television. "Uncle Miltie's" trademark was his frequent skits and sketches that required him to dress in drag.

A: **Mindbenders, The**
Q: What group backed up Wayne Fontana?
W: The Mindbenders were one of the many "and the" groups of the 1950s and 1960s. Others were Bill Haley and the Comets, Paul Revere and the Raiders, Sam the Sham and the Pharoahs, and Martha and the Vandellas.

A: **Minneapolis**
Q: What city was the setting for "The Mary Tyler Moore Show"?
W: Minneapolis-St. Paul was the location of WJM-TV, the TV station where Mary Richards (Moore) worked as an associate producer for the evening news. The program was the first hit in the new wave of sit-coms that effectively portrayed more contemporary attitudes of the early 1970s. The lead character was an intelligent, unmarried career woman who faced, often humorously, situations that real people often face.

A: *Misfits, The*
Q: What film was the last for Marilyn Monroe and Clark Gable?
W: Released in 1960, *The Misfits* was directed by John Huston. The film is tragic in several ways: it was Monroe's first and last important film; it was Clark Gable's last film before his death; it was Arthur Miller's first and last screenplay; and John Huston reportedly lost several thousand dollars at the gambling tables in Reno where the film was shot.

A: **Miss Frances**
Q: Who taught Ding Dong School?
W: Miss Frances was Dr. Frances Horwich (born Frances Rappaport), host of the TV series "Ding Dong School" from 1952 to 1956.

A: **Miss Jean Brodie's**
Q: What movie teacher's students were "la creme de la creme"?
W: This line is from the movie *The Prime of Miss Jean Brodie* released in 1969. This interesting but slackly handled and maddeningly played character drama resulted in an Oscar for Best Actress for Maggie Smith and an Oscar nomination for Best Song, "Jean" by Rod McKuen.

A: **Miss Landers**
Q: Who was Beaver Cleaver's schoolteacher?
W: Miss Landers was a character on TV's "Leave it to Beaver." Jerry Mathers played the Beaver, a young boy with an Alfred E. Neumanish grin and an appropriate set of dimples. Despite his adorable appearance, he actually engaged in normal preteen mischief, unlike most TV kids of the 1950s.

A: *Modern Times*
Q: What 1936 Chaplin film satirized the horrors of a mechanical age?
W: Among other things the film featured a "feeding machine", used as a timesaving device to keep factory workers working during lunch. *Modern Times* was rumored to be communistic in tone. Rumors of this sort grew in volume over the next decade and finally led to Chaplin's departure from the U.S. in 1952.

A: **Montgomery Clift**
Q: Who portrayed Matt Garth in *Red River*?
W: The 1948 film also starred John Wayne, Joanne Dru, and Walter Brennan as Groot. Howard Hawks directed *Red River*, a classic western that was nominated for an Academy Award for Best Original Story (Borden Chase). Unfortunately, it is one of those old movies that is usually broadcast between 2:00 and 4:00 A.M.!

A: **Montgomery Clift**
Q: Who portrayed Prewitt in *From Here to Eternity*?
W: Clift's performance as Robert E. Lee Prewitt won him an Academy Award nomination for this 1953 film. His co-stars, Burt Lancaster and Deborah Kerr, were also nominated. This film is famous for its classic love scene between Burt and Deborah where they make love on the beach while the waves come crashing in, getting sand in their swimsuits!

A: **Montgomery Scott, or Scotty**
Q: Who was the chief engineer of the Starship *Enterprise*?
W: James Doohan played Lieutenant Commander Montgomery Scott on TV's "Star Trek." When the series was cancelled by NBC in 1969, thousands of letters were sent in protest, including letters from the entire Princeton graduating class.

A: **Monty Hall**
Q: Who's the host of "Let's Make A Deal"?
W: It was the TV show where otherwise respectable citizens stood in line for hours in ridiculous costumes, hoping to be selected to wheel and deal their way to big bucks. Hall awarded them a small prize and then played on their natural greed in a series of valuable trades, offering visions of untold riches at the end if they would only deal the pittance they had for what lurked behind door number 1, door number 2 or door number 3.

A: **Moon River**
Q: What was the Oscar-winning theme song of *Breakfast at Tiffany's*?
W: Henry Mancini is credited for the music, Johnny Mercer is credited for the lyrics, and Andy Williams is credited for singing it so many times that nobody wants to hear it anymore!

A: **Morgenstern**
Q: What was Rhoda's maiden name?
W: Rhoda is from "The Mary Tyler Moore Show." She was Mary's upstairs neighbor, a New York City native, and a fast-talking putdown artist whose barbs were often self-directed ("Why am I eating this chocolate? I should just apply it to my hips!"). Rhoda looked to Mary as a close friend and confidante and the two shared their feelings on the hopes and frustrations of single life. Maybe they should have joined a video dating service!

A: **Morris the Cat**
Q: What veteran of TV commercials died at the tender age of 17?
W: Yes, the finicky cat of the "9-lives" cat food commercial is now down to eight lives. Morris was previously named Lucky because he was rescued as he was about to be put to sleep. He has since been replaced by a Morris clone that has the same voice and a similar appearance, but makes you wish they'd let the real Morris rest in peace.

A: **Mother's**
Q: What nighclub did Peter Gunn hang out in?
W: Mother's was Peter Gunn's (Craig Stevens) favorite nightclub. Mother was played by Hope Emerson and Minerva Urecal on the TV series. In the 1967 TV movie, *Gunn*, Mother was played by Helen Traubel. Every week Peter managed to pick up a different girl at Mother's. No wonder it was his favorite place!

A: **Motown**
Q: What Detroit-based record company was founded by Barry Gordy, Jr. in 1963?
W: Some of the Motown artists included: The Supremes, Four Tops, Temptations, Marvelettes, Diana Ross, Martha and the Vandellas, Marvin Gaye, Stevie Wonder, Gladys Knight and the Pips, Smokey Robinson, and some kid named Michael Jackson.

A: *Mouse That Roared, The*
Q: What movie has the tiny country of Grand Fenwick declaring war on the U.S.?
W: The 1959 film featured Peter Sellers, playing three parts, and Jean Seberg. Grand Fenwick is bankrupt and its minister decides to delare war on the U.S., be defeated, and receive Marshall Aid. (Could also be called *The Khomeini That Roared*, come to think of it.)

A: **Mouseketeers**
Q: What were TV's Doreen Tracy, Cheryl Holdridge, and Cubby O'Brien?
W: And do you remember Annette, Karen, Bobbie, Sharon, Tommy, and Darlene? How about their leader, Jimmie? Local children often took part in studio contests on "The Mickey Mouse Club." In 1957 a kid named Jerry Brown was a contestant; 17 years later he became Governor of California and a candidate for President of the U.S.

A: *Mousetrap, The*
Q: What play has recorded more performances than any other in British theater?
W: The play, written by Agatha Christie for Queen Mary, was originally titled *Three Blind Mice*. It now holds the record for the world's longest running play – its debut was November 25, 1952, and it is still running. You'd think the actors would be a little bored with it by now!

A: **Mr. B**
Q: What did Hazel affectionately call her boss?
W: Hazel was the maid of the Baxter family, including their little boy Harold, or "Sport," in the cartoon strip by Ted Key. The cartoons originally appeared in the *Saturday Evening Post*.

A: **Mr. Bojangles**
Q: What was the nickname of black dancer Bill Robinson?
W: Bill "Bojangles" Robinson is probably best remembered for his roles in *The Little Colonel* and *The Littlest Rebel*, starring opposite Shirley Temple, as a soft-shoed servant who dances his way into our hearts. Watching Bill Robinson in action was a pleasure and a joy.

A: **Mr. Spock**
Q: Who was half-man, half-Vulcan?
W: Spock's trademarks were pointed ears, logical thinking, and no outward displays of emotion. After the pilot episode of "Star Trek," creator Gene Roddenberry was told by the networks that, among other things, "the fellow with the funny ears has got to go."

A: **Mr. Spock**
Q: Who was second in command of the Starship *Enterprise*?
W: Leonard Nimoy played Commander Mr. Spock, First Officer of the Starship *Enterprise*, in the popular TV series "Star Trek." "Star Trek" is the most popular TV show in the world and has managed to survive a long and prosperous run.

Spock was half-man and half-Vulcan. The vulcans were an alien race motivated totally by logic; Spock was known for his calm analyses based on facts and precedent but not on normal human emotions.

A: **Mrs. Calabash**
Q: Who did Jimmy Durante bid goodnight after each performance?
W: "Good night, Mrs. Calabash, wherever you are," was the closing line of his TV shows. She was said to be Durante's first wife, Maude Jean Olson, who died in 1943. For 20 years Durante kept her identity a secret. Calabash was the name of a small town outside Chicago with which Jeannie and Jimmy fell in love.

A: *Mrs. Miniver*
Q: What 1942 film won Best Picture for its depiction of an English family during the Blitz?
W: MGM reached its peak as self-appointed publicist for Britain with *Mrs. Miniver*. Even Winston Churchill said its propaganda was worth many battleships. The film was supposed to portray a typical English couple during World War II, but it did not. The Minivers were nobler and nicer than any typical couple anywhere and well over the average income. However, it was a very effective movie. It swept the board in public and exhibitor polls as 1942's most popular picture, won cheers from critics, and earned seven Oscars from the Academy: Best Film, Best Actress (Greer Garson), Best Director (William Wyler), Best Supporting Actress, Best Script, Best Photography, and Best Producer.

A: **Mrs. Robinson**
Q: Who does Jesus love more than she will know?
W: This song has been associated with the film *The Graduate*, along with "The Sounds of Silence" and "Scarborough Fair," all by Paul Simon and Art Garfunkel.

A: **Muppets, The**
Q: What did Jim Henson create?
W: Besides Kermit the Frog and Miss Piggy, Henson is the creator of Big Bird, Cookie Monster, and Bert and Ernie of "Sesame Street." The program attempts to teach basic concepts of letters and numbers by using the technique of exciting, constant repetition pioneered by TV commercials. "Sesame Street" was and is entertaining, educational, and an instant success with adults as well as children.

A: **Murray Slaughter**
Q: Who was the head news writer for WJM-TV?
W: This character, played by Gavin MacLeod, delivered the traditional sit-com barbs, sharp one-liners, and putdowns, usually directed at Ted Baxter. Nevertheless, he departed from these often enough to develop his character beyond the quick-witted wisecracking types that were often found in other situation-comedies of the era.

A: *My Little Chickadee*
Q: What was the only film starring Mae West and W.C. Fields?
W: Considered a classic by many people, this 1939 film told the story of a shady lady and an incompetent cardshark who unmask a villain in the Old West. Not everyone liked it though: "A classic among bad movies...the satire never really gets off the ground. But the ground is such an honest mixture of dirt, manure, and corn that at times it's fairly aromatic." – Pauline Kael, 1968.

A: **"My Sweet Lord"**
Q: What George Harrison tune sounded too much like "He's So Fine" by The Chiffons?
W: Rumor has it George lost when he was taken to court over the matter. The songs do sound strikingly similar. After the Beatles broke up, Harrison started to explore the more spiritual side of music, incorporating sitar music into many songs.

N

A: **Nanoo-nanoo**
Q: How do you say goodbye in Orkan?
W: This expression is from the TV series "Mork and Mindy." Mork (Robin Williams) was a nutty alien from the planet Ork, who was sent on a long-term fact-finding mission to earth. He was very much like a little boy exploring a strange new world. Dressed in baggy jeans and suspenders, he innocently wandered into situations and each week learned some basic lesson in life. Some of his alien trademarks were drinking through his index finger, hanging upside down in a closet, and (at any moment) spouting lines from old movies, TV shows, and political speeches.

A: **Natalie Wood**
Q: Who played Maria in the film *West Side Story*?
W: The contemporary "Romeo and Juliet" tragedy concerning the doomed love of a white boy for a pretty Puerto Rican girl won a host of Oscars in 1961, including Best Picture, Supporting Actor, Supporting Actress, Direction, Screenplay, and Musical Score. Among the songs were: "Maria," "America," and "Tonight."

A: **"New York, New York"**
Q: What film introduced the song *New York, New York*?
W: Well, it certainly wasn't "Meet Me in St. Louis"! The 1977 film starred Robert DeNiro and Liza Minnelli and traced their careers (he a bitter jazz saxophonist with marital difficulties, she a rising singer) against the background of the changeover from big bands to bebop.

A: **Nellybelle**
Q: What was the name of Pat Brady's jeep?
W: Nellybelle was from the TV series "Roy Rogers," in which Pat Brady played Roy Rogers' comical sidekick who often got himself into trouble. The series also starred Dale Evans, Roy's second wife. "Whoooh, Nelly."

A: **Nigel Bruce**
Q: Who played Dr. Watson 14 times to Basil Rathbone's Sherlock Holmes?
W: Bruce played opposite Rathbone in such memorable films as: *The Hound of the Baskervilles*, *The Adventures of Sherlock Holmes*, *Sherlock Holmes Faces Death*, *Sherlock Holmes and the Spider Woman*, and *Sherlock Holmes and the Scarlet Claw*. Bruce's last film as Dr. Watson was *Dressed to Kill*.

A: **Nine**
Q: How many Oscars did *Gone with the Wind* win?
W: A still unbeaten record. Among the awards were: Best Picture, Actress (Vivien Leigh), Writer, Director,

ENTERTAINMENT

Photography, and Supporting Actress (Hattie McDaniel, the first black winner of an Oscar). Other records the film established were length (three hours, 42 minutes), and long runs (it played four years at London's Ritz, with long lines of people waiting outside even during the German air raids of World War II).

A: *North by Northwest*
Q: What film has Cary Grant being attacked from a biplane crop duster?
W: This 1959 film is classic Hitchcock and one of his best. Eva Marie Saint starred with rant in this comedy-thriller that climaxes on the face of Mt. Rushmore. Also in the film were James Mason, Leo G. Carroll, Edward Platt, and Martin Landau. The film received an Oscar nomination for Best Script (Ernest Lehman).

A: *North by Northwest's*
Q: What film's climax takes place on the face of Mount Rushmore?
W: This 1959 film starred Cary Grant and Eva Marie Saint. It was a classic Hitchcock comedy-thriller that does end on the face of Mount Rushmore.

A: **Nothing**
Q: What can stop the Duke of Earl?
W: This 1962 song was written by Earl Edwards, Bernie Williams, and Eugene Dixon. It was popularized by the Duke of Earl and by Gene Chandler, each in a best-selling Vee-Jay recording. Remember? "Duke, Duke, Duke, Duke of Earl..." Gene Chandler was known as the Duke of Earl in 1962, making personal appearances in a long flowing cape and a monocle singing the song "Duke of Earl."

A: **Nova Scotia**
Q: Where's the total eclipse of the sun in Carly Simon's "You're So Vain"?
W: The song was supposedly written with Warren Beatty in mind. Simon, married to James Taylor, also sang "Anticipation" and was paid $50,000 for its reuse in a catsup commercial. Talk about vain!

A: **Nun**
Q: What was the profession of the singer of the 1963 hit "Dominique"?
W: This event led to a 1966 MGM bomb called *The Singing Nun*, with Debbie Reynolds in the title role. Based on a true character, *The Singing Nun* is about a Dominican nun who befriends an underprivileged motherless youngster whose father is a drunkard and whose sister is a tramp. Soeur Sourire was the real singing nun, and she sang the songs for the film. Also starring were Ricardo Montalban, Greer Garson, Chad Everett, and (believe it or not) Ed Sullivan!

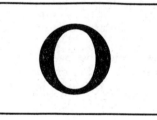

A: *Ocean's Eleven*
Q: What Las Vegas heist film featured the Rat Pack?
W: The Rat Pack included Frank Sinatra, Dean Martin, Peter Lawford, Sammy Davis Jr., Richard Conte, Caesar Romero, and Joey Bishop. The 1960 Warner Brothers film also starred Red Skelton and George Raft, appearing as themselves. The plot involved ten wartime buddies who conspire to rob five Las Vegas casinos on New Year's Eve.

A: **Oil drums**
Q: What do West Indian steel bands use as instruments?
W: The oil drum is the predecessor of the West Indian steel drum. It was developed in the 1940s and replaced the traditional carnival bamboo stick bands. The lid of a steel drum is hammered down to form a basin and then pitched to several musical tones. This "instrument" must have been discovered by a frustrated oil worker!

A: **Old Yeller**
Q: What did Tommy Kirk shoot because of hydrophobia?
W: The 1957 Walt Disney classic dealt with the bittersweet story of a boy's love for his dog. Anyone who doesn't want to cry at the end is un-American.

A: **Oliver Hardy**
Q: Who grouched: "This is another fine mess you've gotten me into"?
W: ...as said to Stan Laurel. Most of their comedies dealt with the two of them involved in an unpleasant situation. When disaster inevitably strikes, usually to Ollie's misfortune, he'd glare at the unharmed Stanley and recite "Here's *another* fine mess you've gotten me into."

A: **Olivia de Havilland**
Q: Who's the sister-actress of Joan Fontaine?
W: Olivia de Havilland is probably best known for her role as Melanie Hamilton in *Gone with the Wind*, for which she received an Oscar nomination. Joan Fontaine is best known for her role in *Rebecca*, for which she also received an Oscar nomination.

A: **Olivia de Havilland**
Q: Who portrayed the doomed Melanie in *Gone with the Wind*?
W: She played Melanie Hamilton who married Ashley Wilkes, much to Scarlet O'Hara's dismay. Olivia received an Oscar nomination for her role.

A: *On the Waterfront*
Q: What 1954 film featured the line: "I coulda been a contenda"?
W: This famous line was spoken by Marlon Brando who played Terry Malloy in the film. Longshoreman Malloy comes to realize that in order to stand upright as a moral being he must expose the gangster forces controlling the waterfront labor unions and inform on his former associates.

A: **One**
Q: How many grooves are there on each side of a 45 rpm record?
W: A real *long* one! The 45 rpm was introduced by RCA in 1949. In the 1950s the 45 became associated with rock 'n roll and was the medium for youth and their music. It was in the mid-50s that the 45 first surpassed the 78 rpm in sales.

A: *One Flew Over the Cuckoo's Nest*
Q: What film did Louise Fletcher win the Best Actress Oscar for?
W: Fletcher and Jack Nicholson both won Oscars for their portrayals in this 1975 film. Fletcher played the nasty nurse Ratched, opposite Nicholson's R.P. McMurphy. Fletcher appeared most recently in 1983,s *Brainstorm*.

A: *One Flew Over the Cuckoo's Nest*
Q: What film does Ken Kesey refuse to watch?
W: Kesey wrote the novel *One Flew Over the Cuckoo's Nest* in 1962. It was made into a movie in 1976 starring Jack Nicholson, who received the Best Actor Oscar for his portrayal of R.P. McMurphy.

A: *Ordinary People*
Q: What film marked Robert Redford's directorial debut?
W: This was the 1980 film for which Redford won the Oscar for Best Director. The movie, the story of a family's turmoil over the death of the elder son, starred Donald Sutherland, Mary Tyler Moore, Timothy Hutton, and Judd Hirsch.

A: **Orson Welles**
Q: Who produced and directed *Citizen Kane*?
W: Orson Welles was also the star of this 1941 classic. One of the greatest films of all time, *Citizen Kane* is the story (told in flashback) of the life of a newspaper tycoon and the effort to find out what his dying word (Rosebud) meant. The resemblance between Welles' Charles Foster Kand

and newspaper tycoon William Randolph Hearst fueled the nastiest controversy that had ever involved a motion picture company (RKO).

A: **Orson Welles**
Q: Who panicked America with his radio version of "War of the Worlds"?
W: On Halloween night 1938, Orson Welles and his "Mercury Theater of the Air"dramatized H.G. Welles' "War of the Worlds"so realistically and effectively that millions of Americans became frightened and thousands were panic-stricken. The broadcast described an invasion of Martians that threatened our whole civilization.

A: **Orson Welles**
Q: Who played Harry Lime in the movie *The Third Man*?
W: The 1949 film starred Joseph Cotton, who played a writer that goes to postwar Vienna to join his old friend Harry Lime who seems to have met with an accident...or has he?

A: **Oscar, An**
Q: What's ten inches tall, weighs seven pounds and is gold-plated?
W: If you guessed a miniature Mr. T doll, you're wrong. The Oscar statuette is gold-plated bronze, with a value of about $100. During World War II the statue was made of plaster. There is still some uncertainty as to the origin of the name. Some say that when Academy librarian Margaret Herrick first saw the statuette she exclaimed, "Why it looks just like my Uncle Oscar." A reporter overheard the remark, printed the story, and the name stuck. Others claim that Bette Davis nicknamed the figure after her husband, Harmon Oscar Nelson.

A: **Otto Preminger**
Q: What director portrayed the commandant of the POW camp in 1953's *Stalag 17*?

W: Preminger is better known for his directorial achievements including *Laura* (1944) and *Fallen Angel* (1945). He also directed *The Moon Is Blue* (1953), which was denied Production Code approval because it used the word "virgin,"and *The Man With the Golden Arm* (1956), which was also denied approval because it dealt with narcotic addiction.

A: **Otto Preminger**
Q: Who directed *Anatomy of a Murder*?
W: The 1959 film deals with a small town lawyer who successfully defends an Army officer accused of murdering a bartender who had assaulted his wife. The use of some "daring"words in this film caused controversy at the time.

A: *Our Town*
Q: What Thornton Wilder play was made into a movie with music by Aaron Copland?
W: Wilder also wrote the screenplay, and Copland was nominated for an Oscar for his music. The 1940 film retains the narrator and manages to make points of its own while absorbing the endearing qualities that made the play a classic.

A: **"Over There"**
Q: What George M. Cohan song was written to boost morale in World War I?
W: "Over There"was the first popular song played in St. Patrick's Cathedral in New York City. It was played at the funeral of George M. Cohan in 1941.

A: **Ozzie and Harriet Nelson**
Q: What was the first TV couple to share a bed on prime time?
W: ...and their hands were always on top of the covers! Ozzie and Harriet were on TV from 1952 to 1966 with David and Ricky, their sons. The show reappeared in 1973 without the sons as "Ozzie's Girls"instead of "The Adventures of Ozzie and Harriet." Ozzie died in 1975. Their full names were Oswald George Nelson and Harriet Hilliard Nelson.

ENTERTAINMENT

P

A: P.T. Barnum
Q: Who was known as "the Greatest Showman on Earth"?
W: P.T. Barnum's most famous exhibits in his circus included: General Tom Thumb, Jumbo the Elephant, the Siamese Twins (Chang and Eng), the Bearded Lady (Josephine Clofullia), Wild Man of Borneo, and the Fiji Mermaid.

A: Paladin
Q: Who was a knight without armor in a savage land?
W: Richard Boone played the mercenary gunfighter in the West of 1872 in the TV series "Have Gun Will Travel." From his business card, reading "Have Gun Will Travel, Wire Paladin, San Francisco," the gag arose that Paladin's first name was Wire. His logo was a chess knight.

A: Pancho
Q: Who was the Cisco Kid's faithful sidekick?
W: Oh, Cisco! Pancho was played by Leo Carillo in the TV series; Louis Sagin, Harry Lang, and Mel Blanc on radio; and Martin Garralaga, Chris-Pin-Martin, and Leo Carillo in the movies.

A: *Parallax View, The*
Q: What film opens with an assassin tumbling from the Seattle Space Needle?
W: Warren Beatty starred as a crusading journalist who tries to stop the systematic killing of the witnesses of a political assassination. The 1974 film is a stylish and persuasive political thriller with a downbeat ending: the villains win.

A: Paris
Q: What city is the setting for *Charade*?
W: In the 1964 film, a Parisenne finds her husband murdered. Four strange men are after her, and she's helped by a handsome stranger. *Charade* is effective both as a black romantic comedy and a macabre farce. It starred Audrey Hepburn and Cary Grant (who hides the fact that he's 60 by taking a shower fully clothed).

A: Pat Boone's
Q: Whose first hit song was "Ain't That a Shame"?
W: Fats Domino's rendition, which made it popular, was probably better remembered. It was one of the many popular songs of the 1950s.

A: Patti Page
Q: Who sang the theme to *Hush, Hush, Sweet Charlotte*?
W: Page is probably better known for her recording of "The Tennessee Waltz," which sold over two million records in its first year and seven million within a decade. Her other songs include "This Is My Song" and "That Doggie in the Window."

A: Patty Duke
Q: Who played Helen Keller in the 1962 film *The Miracle Worker*?
W: *The Miracle Worker* is the story of Helen Keller's childhood. She was taught by Anne Sullivan after being left blind, deaf, and mute after a childhood illness. Patty played the lead role of Anne Sullivan later in her career.

A: *Patty Duke*
Q: *Who won a Best Supporting Actress Oscar for the 1962 movie Miracle Worker?*
W: The film resulted in Academy Awards to Anne Bancroft as Best Actress for her portrayal of Anne Sullivan and to Patty Duke for Best Supporting Actress as Helen Keller.

A: Paul Anka
Q: Who wrote "Johnny's Theme" for the "Tonight" show?
W: "He-e-e-e-re's Johnny! Da, da, dat, da, da..." is played by Carl "Doc" Severinson's orchestra on the popular late night talk show. Paul Anka gets $30,000 a year for the theme.

A: Paul Lynde
Q: Who made the most appearances in the center square on "Hollywood Squares"?
W: Rumor has it that Lynde was very concerned about earthquakes in California so he asked some engineers to decide where the safest place for him would be if an earthquake occurred during the show. They told him that the center square was safest. It was supposedly written into his contract that he be allowed to sit in the center square!

A: Paul Whiteman
Q: What bandleader was known as "the King of Jazz"?
W: "The King of Jazz" premiered "Rhapsody in Blue," the theme music of his orchestra, at Carnegie Hall. Some of his most popular jazz hits were "Three O'Clock in the Morning," "When Buddha Smiles," and "China Bay."

A: Paul Whiteman's
Q: What orchestra premiered "Rhapsody in Blue" at Carnegie Hall?
W: "Rhapsody in Blue," the theme music of Paul Whiteman's orchestra, premiered Feb. 12, 1924. It was written by Ira Gershwin especially for Paul Whiteman. Whiteman, also known as "the King of Jazz," wanted to prove that jazz had a place in American popular music.

A: **Peace**
Q: What word did Dave Garroway sign off the "Today" show with each morning?
W: The program began in 1952, when daytime programming was exceedingly sparse. Some stations didn't sign-on until 10 A.M. The first broadcast was a hodgepodge of teletype machines, weather maps, clocks set to different times of various world cities, record players, newspapers, and the show's regular cast of Garroway, Jim Fleming, and Jack Lescoulie. Before long NBC "toned down" the show adopting a news review, features, and interviews format.

A: **Peach Melba**
Q: What peach dessert was named for an opera singer?
W: Mme. Nellie Melba is her full name. When she returned to her native Australia for the first time after achieving world renown, her rendition of "Home Sweet Home" (also to her own piano accompaniment) left few dry eyes at the opening concert.

A: **Peanut Gallery, The**
Q: Where did the kids sit on TV's "Howdy Doody Time"?
W: The TV series debuted on Dec. 27, 1947 and ran until 1960. It featured Buffalo Bob Smith, Howdy Doody, Clarabelle Clown, Chief Thundercloud, and Phineas T. Bluster. "Say kids, what time is it? It's Howdy Doody Time!"

A: **Penny**
Q: What was the name of Sky King's niece?
W: Sky King, "America's Favorite Flying Cowboy," was Texas Ranger Schyler King, pilot of the Twin Cessna *Songbird* who lived on the Flying Crown Ranch. King was played on TV by Kirby Grant and on radio by Jack Lester, Earl Nightingale, and Roy Engel. Penny was played on the TV Gloria Winters and on radio by Beryl Vaughn. Kirby Grant later married Gloria Winters.

A: **Pepe Le Pew**
Q: What's the name of Warner Brother's romantic skunk?
W: He's the French skunk of Warner Brothers cartoons. He made his debut in "Odor-Able Kitty," a 1944 cartoon, and his voice is that of Mel Blanc.

A: **Peppermint Lounge, The**
Q: What small New York City nightclub saw the origin of the twist?
W: The fad started there. The house band, Joey Dee (Joseph DiNicola) and the Starliters, recorded a number of twist records including "Peppermint Twist." Located in the Knickerbocker Hotel on West 45th Street, it was the setting of the 1961 movie *Hey, Let's Twist*.

A: **Perry Como**
Q: What singer was known as Mr. C.?
W: "Mr. C." was what Como's announcer, Frank Gallop, called him on his TV program.

A: **Peter Bogdanovich**
Q: Who directed *The Last Picture Show*?
W: He also co-wrote the 1971 film that dealt with teenage affairs in a small Texas town. Starring in the film were Timothy Bottoms, Cloris Leachman, Ellyn Burstyn, Ben Johnson, Jeff Bridges, and Cybill Shepherd.

A: **Peter Finch**
Q: Who was posthumously awarded the 1976 Best Actor Oscar for his performance in *Network*?
W: Finch played Howard Beale, a newsman who became a modern-day prophet denouncing the hypocrisies of our time (they let him say "bullshit" on the air). The film is also remembered for the phrase "I'm mad as hell, and I'm not going to take it anymore." The film also starred William Holden, Faye Dunaway, and Robert Duvall.

A: **Peter Gunn**
Q: What TV detective did Craig Stevens play?
W: Henry Kane created the detective, and Henry Mancini wrote the show's theme song that has sold over one million copies. Stevens also starred in the movie *Gunn* (1967). Pete's favorite nightclub? Mother's.

A: **Peter Lorre**
Q: Who portrayed Ugarte in *Casablanca*?
W: Lorre was at his fidgety best as the fugitive killer who tries to sell letters of transit that he has stolen. The classic 1943 film also starred Humphrey Bogart as Rick, and Ingrid Bergman as Ilsa.

A: **Peter, Paul and Mary**
Q: What names precede Yarrow, Stookey and Travers?
W: They were Peter Yarrow, Paul Stookey, and Mary Travers. Popular songs by this group include "If I Had a Hammer," "Blowin' in the Wind," and "Leaving on a Jet Plane."

A: **Peter Sellers**
Q: Who portrayed President Merkin Muffley in *Dr. Strangelove*?
W: Sellers also portrayed Group Captain Lionel Mandrake and Dr. Strangelove in the 1963 film. Sellers' triple-role won him an Oscar nomination. The whole title is actually *Dr. Strangelove; or How I Learned to Stop Worrying and Love the Bomb*. One of the more memorable scenes occurs when Slim Pickens yells "Ya-hoo!" as he rides the bomb a-l-l-l-l the way down.

A: *Petrified Forest, The*
Q: What movie established Humphrey Bogart as a tough guy?
W: However, some feel he was a tougher guy in *The Return of Dr. X*, in which he played a noted physician who was also a child murderer. Bogart's performance as Duke Montee in *The Petrified Forest* was his first substantial role. This 1936 film also starred Leslie Howard and Bette Davis.

A: **Pharoahs, The**
Q: Who backed up Sam the Sham?
W: Another of the many "and the" groups of the 1950s and 1960s. Others were Diana Ross and the Supremes, Wayne Fontana and the Mindbenders, and Smokey Robinson and the Miracles.

A: **"Phil Silvers Show, The"**
Q: What TV series featured Corporal Rocco Barbella?
W: The show made its debut during the 1955-56 season on CBS as "You'll Never Get Rich," later retitled "The Phil Silvers Show," but popularly known as "Sergeant Bilko." Silvers portrayed Master Sergeant Ernest Bilko, a sly con man who had nothing to do but eat, sleep, and gamble. He helped the GIs to pass away the time at an otherwise boring military base in Kansas while lining his own pockets in the process. The series also starred Paul Ford, Maurice Gosfield, Herbie Faye, Alan Melvin, Joe E. Ross, and Harvey Lembeck as Corporal Rocco Barbella.

A: **Philadelphia**
Q: What city did Dick Clark's "American Bandstand" originate in?
W: It was a local Philadelphia program for five years before its nationwide debut on ABC on Aug. 5, 1957. Dick Clark played the latest hit records while some high schoolers danced to the music. There were occasional appearances by guest performers who would lip-sync their own records instead of singing live.

A: **Philip**
Q: What's Columbo's first name?
W: Columbo was quietly added to the NBC mystery movie rotation ("McCloud" and "McMillan and Wife") in 1971 and slowly built a following. Though he appeared to be little more than a sloppy, seemingly bumbling policeman, Columbo (Peter Falk) was actually an alert, perceptive investigator.

A: **Pickfair**
Q: What was the name of Douglas Fairbanks and Mary Pickford's Hollywood mansion?
W: The Hollywood mansion was built by Fairbanks and Pickford after their marriage. A radio program, called "Parties at Pickfair", originated from their home.

A: **Plaster**
Q: What were Oscars made of during World War II?
W: During World War II the Motion Picture Academy was in deep financial trouble. The major motion picture studios provided most of the funding, and they were withdrawing their support because they did not always approve of the nominations or winners. Many expenses had to be trimmed, and the gold-plated Oscars were just not in the budget.

A: **Plastics**
Q: What industry was Benjamin Braddock advised to enter at his graduation party?
W: In the movie *The Graduate*, Benjamin (Dustin Hoffman) is the college graduate who returns home and finds he's unable to commit himself to anything. He has an affair with the wife of his father's friend and then falls in love with her daughter. The film also starred Anne Bancroft and Katharine Ross.

A: *Play Misty for Me*
Q: What film introduced the song "The First Time Ever I Saw Your Face"?
W: The 1971 shocker starred Clint Eastwood as a radio disc jockey who's pestered by a girl (Jessica Walter) who turns out to be homicidally jealous. The song was sung by Roberta Flack.

A: *Plaza, The*
Q: What New York City hotel was the backdrop to the climactic scene of *The Way We Were*?
W: This film starring Barbra Streisand and Robert Redford, dealt with the romance and marriage of an upper crust young novelist and a bluestocking Jewish girl. Of the film Stanley Kauffmann wrote, "Not one moment of the picture is anything but garbage under the gravy of false honesty." ("MemmmRieees"!)

A: **Pluto**
Q: What is Mickey Mouse's dog's name?
W: Pluto made his debut in the Disney cartoon "The Chain Gang" in 1930. In the first two cartoons he was called Rover. His voice was that of Jim MacDonald.

A: **Pool**
Q: What's the trouble right here in River City?
W: "Trouble starts with T, that rhymes with P, and that stands for pool!" This lyric is from a song in the 1962 film *The Music Man*, starring Robert Preston, Shirley Jones, and young Ronny Howard (with a lisp). Preston plays a bogus music professor whose presence in River City, Iowa changes the lives (for the better) of all who come in contact with him.

A: *Porgy and Bess*
Q: What musical is set in Catfish Row?
W: The 1959 film told the story of a poor slum girl who falls in love with a crippled beggar. It starred Sidney Poitier, Dorothy Dandridge, Sammy Davis, Jr., Pearl Bailey, and Diahann Carroll.

A: **Price-Waterhouse**
Q: What company tabullates the ballots in voting for the Academy Awards?
W: Price-Waterhouse is a public accounting firm that certifies the Academy Award and Emmy nominations, as well as totaling and verifying the votes.

A: **prima donna, The**
Q: What's the leading female singer in an opera called?
W: Another definition of "prima donna" is an extemely sensitive, vain, or undisciplined person. Not all Donnas are like that though.

A: **Princess Grace**
Q: Who has been the only princess on the board of Twentieth Century-Fox?
W: The former actress was also a voting member of the Academy of Motion Picture Arts and Sciences (Academy Awards). She was Grace Kelly before she married the Prince of Monaco.

A: **Private Dwayne Doberman**
Q: What dumb-but-loveable character did Maurice Gosfield play on "The Phil Silvers Show"?
W: "The Phil Silvers Show" is more popularly known as "Sergeant Bilko." Silvers played Bilko, a sly con man man who served in the Army on a military based filled with the most inept and disheveled Army outfit ever conceived. The name of the base was Fort Baxter.

A: *Producers, The*
Q: What film has Zero Mostel and Gene Wilder trying to mastermind a Broadway flop?
W: Mostel seduces old women to obtain finances for the play, sells 25,000 percent in the expectation it will flop (it's called *Springtime for Hitler*), and is horrified when it succeeds. This 1967 Mel Brooks film won him an Oscar for writing.

A: *Psycho*
Q: What film has Marion Crane stabbed to death in the Bates Motel?
W: Anthony Perkins (as Norman Bates) dresses up as his Mother and perforates Marion (Janet Leigh) while in the shower. *Psycho* is the grandfather of all the modern-day "slasher" films. When asked by the press what he used for blood in the bath, Hitchcock replied, "Chocolate sauce."

A: **"Que Sera, Sera"**
Q: What song is key to the climax of Alfred Hitchcock's *The Man Who Knew Too Much*?
W: Talk about your anticlimax! Doris Day and James Stewart (Doris did the singing) starred in the 1956 film. This film was actually a remake of his 1934 film of the same title. Most feel the original is far superior.

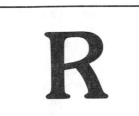

A: **R2-D2**
Q: Who is C3-PO's sidekick?
W: It looks like C3-PO (Anthony Daniels) and R2D2 (Kenny Baker) will be around for awhile. George Lucas has plans for nine *Star Wars* episodes (three trilogies), and the droids will be the only "actors" to bridge the three trilogies. The droids made their debut in 1977's *Star Wars* with Mark Hamill, Carrie Fisher, and Harrison Ford.

A: **Radio City Music Hall**
Q: What movie theater has sold the most tickets?
W: Radio City Music Hall was opened to the public in 1933. There are 6,200 seats in the hall, making it one of the largest theaters in the world. Since it's been open for over 50 years, with thousands of performances, it only stands to reason that it has sold the most tickets.

A: **Radio City Music Hall**
Q: What's the home of the Rockettes?

W: The Rockettes are dancers at the famous New York music theater. The Roxy theater, also in New York, has 30 dancers called the Roxyettes.

A: **"Raindrops Keep Fallin' on My Head"**
Q: What song was introduced in *Butch Cassidy and the Sundance Kid*?
W: This song was made popular by B.J. Thomas. The 1969 film starred Paul Newman as Butch and Robert Redford as Sundance. The song is heard in the scene in which Butch performs stunts on a bicycle to win the attention of the schoolmarm (Katharine Ross).

A: **Ralph Bellamy**
Q: Who portrayed Franklin Roosevelt in *Sunrise at Campobello*?
W: Bellamy repeated on screen the magnificent performance he had given on stage as FDR. The 1960 Warner Brothers film was concerned with the dark side of Roosevelt's life when he was stricken with polio. Greer Garson was not entirely at home as Eleanor and filling her mouth with a set of protruding teeth hardly helped.

A: **Ralph Kramden**
Q: What TV character said, "One of these days, Alice, pow, right in the kisser"?
W: Ralph is from the TV show "The Jackie Gleason Show." The "Honeymooners" was a domestic skit that appeared regularly on Gleason's show. The Kramdens' neighbors were Ed and Trixie Norton. Ralph is also known for saying (at the end of every skit), "Baby, you're the greatest."

A: **Ray Block**
Q: Who was Ed Sullivan's TV orchestra leader?
W: Ray was on the TV show "Toast of the Town," the longest running TV variety show, that played each Sunday night at 8 P.M. on CBS. The title was changed to "The Ed Sullivan Show" in 1955.

A: **Ray Bolger**

Q: Who played the scarecrow in *The Wizard of Oz*?

W: This film was the most expensive production in MGM's first 15 years, but the 1939 film has been piling up revenue ever since. Judy Garland played Dorothy, Jack Haley played Tin Man, Bert Lahr played Cowardly Lion, and Margaret Hamilton played the Wicked Witch of the West. Shirley Temple was MGM's first choice as Dorothy.

A: **Ray Walston**

Q: What red-haired actor portrayed the devil in *Damn Yankees*?

W: This 1958 Warner Brothers film starred Walston as the Devil who interferes in the fortunes of a failing baseball team. It also starred Tab Hunter and Gwen Verdon.

A: **Ray Walston**

Q: Who played the title role in "My Favorite Martian"?

W: Walston played the Martian character for three years. He was "Uncle" to earthling Tim O'Hara (Bill Bixby). While reporter O'Hara was on his way to cover a story, he stumbled across the stricken spaceship of "Uncle" Martin, and he took him home to recuperate. "Uncle" Martin could become invisible, and he was telepathic, had telekinetic powers, and was extremely intelligent. Some uncle – huh?

A: **Raymond Burr**

Q: Who played the heavy in Alfred Hitchcock's *Rear Window*?

W: James Stewart plays a news photographer confined to his apartment with a broken leg who sees Burr murder his wife in an apartment across the yard. One of Hitchcock's best, it has recently been re-released.

A: **Raymond Massey**

Q: Who portrayed Dr. Gillespie on "Dr. Kildare"?

W: This early-60s TV soap opera starred Richard Chamberlain in the title role. "Dr. Kildare" had a somewhat sugar-coated view of life with attractive people experiencing one dramatic crisis after another. It was interesting to watch the doctors practically kill each other arguing about how to save someone's life.

A: *Rebecca*

Q: What film starred Sir Laurence Olivier as the brooding ax de Winter?

W: This was a classic 1940 Hitchcock film that also starred Joan Fontaine. Fontaine played the naive young second wife of a Cornish landowner who is haunted by the image of his glamorous first wife, Rebecca. Olivier, Fontaine and Hitchcock all received Oscar nominations for the film.

A: **Red**

Q: What color upset the heroine of Hitchcock's *Marnie*?

W: Tippi Hedren played Marnie, who's sexually frigid because of a nightmare in her past. Directed by Hitchcock in 1964, the film also starred Sean Connery.

A: **"Red River Valley, The"**

Q: What was the theme song of the film *The Grapes of Wrath*?

W: Besides being the theme song of the 1940 movie, it was also the theme of the 1943 movie *The Ox-Bow Incident*, and the radio series "Our Gal Sunday."

A: **reel of film, A**

Q: What does Oscar stand on?

W: And we thought he stood on his feet! Oscar was designed by Cedric Gibbons. He holds a sword while standing on a reel of film. Oscar was first presented at the Academy Awards presentation at Hollywood's Roosevelt Hotel on May 16, 1929. The Academy will buy back any unwanted Oscar for ten dollars!

A: **Regis Philbin**

Q: Who was the announcer and sidekick on Joey Bishop's talk show?

W: Regis has an opening night to remember from the Joey Bishop Show. Not only was the show's premier guest (Governor Ronald Reagan) 14 minutes late, but Debbie Reynolds tackled Regis and threw him to the floor while giving a demonstration of how to help someone who was on fire. Regis was the announcer for the total run of the show, three years. He later became a "field interviewer" on the forgettable "Almost Anything Goes."

A: **Richard Beymer**

Q: Who starred opposite Natalie Wood in *West Side Story*?

W: Beymer played Tony in the popular 1961 musical. Beymer did his own acting, but the singing was dubbed.

A: **Richard Burton and Rex Harrison**

Q: Who played homosexual lovers in *Staircase*?

W: *Staircase* portrays the problems of two aging homosexual hairdressers (1969). Of the film one critic wrote, "The shape is smashed...no longer a graceful duet, it becomes a waddling tale, spattered with ugliness, that falls into the biggest sentimental trap for homosexual material: it pleads for pity." The film was directed by Stanley Donen, and the music was by Dudley Moore.

A: **Richard Crenna**
Q: Who portrayed Luke McCoy in "The Real McCoys"?
W: It became the first ABC show to reach the top ten, winning both urban and rural support. Urban viewers laughed at the out-of-place hillbilly ways of the McCoys, while rural viewers were amused by the clan's constant triumphs over the overly sophisticated city folk. Walter Brennan played Grandpaw Amos.

A: **Richard Harris**
Q: What actor made "MacArthur Park" a mega-hit?
W: The song was written by Jim Webb. In 1968, Harris recorded an album of Webb's songs, including the seven minute "MacArthur Park." The song was widely promoted by DJs and the album had over $1 million in sales within a few weeks.

A: **Rick's "Cafe Americain"**
Q: What was the name of Humphrey Bogart's club in *Casablanca*?
W: The 1942 film starrred Bogart, Ingrid Bergman, Claude Rains, Paul Henreid, Sidney Greenstreet, and Peter Lorre. Ronald Reagan almost had the role of Rick!

A: **Rin Tin Tin**
Q: What animal was voted most popular film performer of 1926?
W: Rin Tin Tin was the German shepherd, originally called "Rinty," who made films for Warner Brothers in the 1920s. The first film was *Where the North Begins*(1923). Rinty had four sons that became stars; Rinty number 4 became the star of the TV series "Rin Tin Tin." Rin Tin Tin the First died Aug. 10, 1932, in the presence of his master Lee Duncan and actress Jean Harlow, a neighbor. Yoah, Rinty!

A: **"Rin Tin Tin"**
Q: What TV series featured the character Rusty B Company?
W: Corporal Rusty was played by Lee Aaker. Rin Tin Tin was Private Rin Tin Tin on the show. He was the winner of the 1958 and 1959 TV Patsy Awards.

A: **Ringo Starr**
Q: Who replaced Pete Best?
W: Ringo (Richard Starkey) was the drummer of the rock 'n roll group the Beatles. Other members were John Lennon, George Harrison, and Paul McCartney. Previous members of the group had been Stu Sutcliffe, who died in Hamburg, Germany; Tommy Moore; Norman Chapman; and Pete Best.

A: **Ringo Starr**
Q: Who was the oldest member of The Beatles?
W: Paul McCartney was second oldest, followed by John Lennon and finally George Harrison. The Beatles had more number 1 records than any other artist or group: 20 songs. The earlier names of this group included Quarrymen, Johnny and the Moondogs, Silver Beatles, and The Rainbow.

A: **Rita Hayworth**
Q: Who starred as Gilda opposite Glenn Ford?
W: She "put the blame on Mame." This film is about a gambler (Ford) in a South American city who resumes a love-hate relationship with an old flame (Hayworth) who is now married to his dangerous new boss. This 1946 film also starred George acready and Steve Geray.

A: **River City**
Q: What town was the setting for *The Music Man*?
W: This 1962 film, starring Robert Preston and Shirley Jones, took place in River City, Iowa. Preston played a con man who persuades a small town to start a boys' band with himself as agent. The movie received an Oscar nomination for Best Picture.

A: *Road to Singapore, The*
Q: What was the first Crosby-Hope "Road" movie?

W: This was the first in the series of "Road" films for Hope, Crosby and Dorothy Lamour stretching from 1940 to 1962. They are (in chronological order): *Road to Singapore*, *Road to Zanzibar*, *Road to Morocco*, *Road to Utopia*, *Road to Rio*, *Road to Bali*, and *Road to Hong Kong*.

A: **Rob and Laura Petrie**
Q: What couple lived at 148 Bonnie Meadow Road, New Rochelle, New York?
W: The Petries were characters of the TV show "The Dick Van Dyke Show." It was an early-60s comedy show starring Dick Van Dyke, Mary Tyler Moore, Rose Marie and Morey Amsterdam. Van Dyke played a writer foe a TV comedy show.

A: **Robert Culp, Elliott Gould, Natalie Wood, Dyan Cannon**
Q: What four performers played the title roles in *Bob and Carol and Ted and Alice*?
W: Culp played Bob, Gould played Ted, Wood played Carol, and Cannon played Alice in the 1969 film about two California couples who try to liberate themselves from their old uptight attitudes by smoking pot and having extramarital affairs. It was a fine romantic comedy that reflected the attitudes of the sexual revolution. Gould and Cannon received Oscar nominations.

A: **Robert Duvall**
Q: Who portrayed the Corleone family lawyer in *The Godfather*?
W: Duvall played Tom Hagen in the 1972 Oscar-winning film that also starred Marlon Brando, Al Pacino, James Caan, and Diane Keaton. When, after ruling the New York Mafia for two generations, Vito Corleone dies of old age, his son (Pacino) reluctantly takes over the family "business." The movie received an Oscar for Best Picture.

ENTERTAINMENT

A: **Robert Shaw**
Q: What actor was stung in *The Sting*?
W: Shaw played Doyle Lonnegan, a big-time gangster who gets conned by Paul Newman and Robert Redford. The 1973 film won Oscars for Best Picture, Writing, Directing, and Music (Scott Joplin and Marvin Hamlisch). The theme song was "The Entertainer."

A: **Robert Young**
Q: Who played TV dad to Kathy, James, and Betty Anderson?
W: Young played the all-knowing, patient father. The show premiered Oct. 3, 1954, and the low ratings almost killed it in its first season. The Anderson kids were an adult's view of perfect children; they were never greedy, stupid, or mischievous, just unlucky.

A: *Robin and the Seven Hoods*
Q: What 1964 film introduced the song "My Kind of Town"?
W: And the song was sung by "old blue eyes" himself, Frank Sinatra. This spoof of the Robin Hood legend also starred Dean Martin, Bing Crosby, Sammy Davis, Jr., and Peter Falk. It was the first (and hopefully the last) musical-comedy gangster film. "My Kind of Town" was nominated for Best Song (Nelson Riddle, James Van Heusen, Sammy Cahn).

A: **Rochester**
Q: What was the name of Jack Benny's valet?
W: Rochester Van Jones, Benny's valet on radio and TV, was played by Eddie Anderson. He called Benny "Boss."

A: **Rock and roll**
Q: What term did disc jockey Alan Freed popularize?
W: Freed is given credit for coining the phrase. Freed called himself "Moondog" and broadcast over Cleveland radio station WJW in 1952. He moved to New York's WINS in 1955 and later starred with Rocky Graziano in the 1957 movie *Mr. Rock and Roll*.

A: **Rock Hudson and Doris Day**
Q: Who co-starred in *Pillow Talk*?
W: Rock and Doris co-starred in this 1959 romantic comedy about two people who can't stand each other, but end up falling in love via a telephone party line. The film is responsible for starting off the Hudson-Day partnership and a run of similar comedies that survived the 1960s.

A: *Rocky*
Q: What rags-to-riches film knocked out all competitors to win the 1976 Best Picture Oscar?
W: "Yo! Adrian! It's me, Rocky!" Sly Stallone starred as the slightly dim-witted Philadelphia boxer who made good. The film won Oscars for Direction (John G. Alvildsen) and Best Picture.

A: **Rod Serling**
Q: Who was the host of "Night Gallery"?
W: Serling hosted and wrote many of the episodes for the semi-popular TV series. It debuted during the 1970-71 season and consisted of six bizarre and often scary stories. Serling is much better known as the host of "The Twilight Zone."

A: **Rod Steiger**
Q: Who played Marlon Brando's brother in *On the Waterfront*?
W: Remembered for the line "I coulda been a contenda," this 1954 film also starred Karl Malden, Lee J. Cobb, and Eva Marie Saint. Steiger was nominateed for Best Supporting Actor for his performance.

A: **Rod Steiger**
Q: Who played the title role in *The Pawnbroker*?
W: Steiger was nominated for Best Actor for his portrayal of Sol Nazerman, a Jew in slummy New York who is haunted by his experiences in Nazi prison camps. Directed by Sidney Lumet, the film also starred Brock Peters and Geraldine Fitzgerald.

A: **Rod Steiger**
Q: Who portrayed W.C. Fields in the film *W.C. Fields and Me*?
W: Steiger's role as the famous alcoholic comedian was called a "stupid and pointless slander" by critic Judith Christ. The 1976 film also starred Valerie Perrine, John Marley, and Jack Cassidy as John Barrymore.

A: **Rodeo rider**
Q: What was Stony Burke's occupation?
W: Professional rodeo rider Stony Burke of the TV show "Stony Burke" (1962-63) wanted to win one thing: "the Golden Buckle." That's the award given to the world's champion saddle bronco rider. Jack Lord played Stony. The show lasted one season and Stony never got the award. Poor Stony!

A: **Roman Polanski**
Q: Who directed and made a cameo appearance in *Chinatown*?
W: This 1974 film starred Jack Nicholson, Faye Dunaway and John Huston. A Los Angeles gumshoe takes on a simple case and burrows into it until it leads to a murder and a public scandal. It won the Oscar for writing (Robert Towne). Polanski's scene consisted of cutting Nicholson's nose with a stiletto.

A: **Ron Ely**
Q: Who replaced Bert Parks as the host of "The Miss America Pageant"?
W: Bert Parks used to host game shows, early in his career, before becoming the popular host of the annual Miss America Pageant. His rendition of "There She Is, Miss America..." became somewhat of a tradition. It's rumored that Parks was replaced by Ely (TV's Tarzan) because Parks was too old.

A: **Ronald Reagan**
Q: Who called himself "The Errol Flynn of B Movies"?
W: President Reagan starred in such classics as *Bedtime for Bonzo* and

That Hagen Girl. His last movie was *The Killers* in 1964. He was married to Jane Wyman (1940 to 1948), then to Nancy Davis in 1952. He was also the MC for "G.E. Theater" and "Death Valley Days" on TV. He was governor of California from 1966 to 1974 and elected President in 1980.

A: Ronald Reagan
Q: Who played The Gipper in *Knute Rockne – All-American*?
W: The 1940 film starred Pat O'Brien as the legendary coach. Football enthusiasts from coast to coast were inspired by its reverential sentiments and supported it to box office success. The screenplay was based on private papers belonging to Mrs. Rockne and reports by intimate friends and associates.

A: Ronald Reagan
Q: Who signed Clark Gable's U.S. military service discharge?
W: Reagan signed the papers on June 12, 1944 in Culver City, California. Among his other accomplishments, Reagan emceed the first Patsy Awards and was president of the Screen Actors Guild. His autobiography is titled *Where's the Rest of Me?*.

A: Rooster Cogburn
Q: What character did John Wayne play in *True Grit*?
W: This 1969 film also starred Kim Darby and Glen Campbell. Wayne received his only Oscar for his performance as the "one-eyed fat man." The climactic scene is the classic image of Wayne confronting four outlaws in a glen, charging like a knight, reins in his teeth, with a gun and a repeating rifle blazing in each hand.

A: Rose Marie
Q: Who played Sally Rogers on "The Dick Van Dyke Show"?
W: Marie brought a sharp comic edge to her character on the show. Marie had begun her career as Baby Rose Marie singing on the NBC radio network when she was three years old.

A: "Rosebud"
Q: What was the name of Charles Foster Kane's sled?
W: "Rosebud" was Kane's dying word in the 1941 classic *Citizen Kane* and was also the frame of the whole film. The film also starred Joseph Cotton and Agnes Moorehead.

A: Rosemary
Q: Who coupled with the devil and gave birth to Andrew John?
W: This happened in the 1968 film *Rosemary's Baby*, starring Mia Farrow, John Cassavetes, and Ruth Gordon. The film was directed by Roman Polanski. Gordon won an Oscar for Best Supporting Actress. The film portrayed devil worshippers who invade the privacy of a young couple with designs on the pregnant wife! Less than a year later, Polanski's own pregnant wife – actress Sharon Tate – was murdered by a cult of similar characters (Manson Family) in the actor's home.

A: Route 66
Q: What was the favorite TV freeway of Martin Milner and George Maharis?
W: Route 66 is the U.S. highway from Chicago to Los Angeles and was the title of the theme song of the TV series "Route 66." The song was composed by Nelson Riddle.

A: Roy Bean
Q: What judge did Walter Brennan, Edgar Buchanan and Paul Newman all portray?

W: Newman appeared in the 1972 film *The Life and Times of Judge Roy Bean*. Brennan played Bean in *The Westerner*(1940). Buchanan played Bean in a TV series. In real life Roy's brother Josh Bean was the first mayor of San Diego, California. Roy Bean was "the law west of the Rockies."

A: Roy Coffee
Q: What sheriff patrolled Virginia City on "Bonanza"?
W: This western TV series about the Cartwrights, who lived on their ranch the Ponderosa, featured father Ben and his three sons, Adam, Hoss, and Little Joe. Although the brothers occasionally scrapped among themselves, they always pulled together to protect the ranch from corrupt and thieving outsiders.

A: Roy Scheider
Q: Who played the sheriff of Amity Island in *Jaws*?
W: Scheider played Chief Martin Brody in the 1975 thriller about a man-eating shark that munches on swimmers off the Long Island coast. The movie also starred Robert Shaw and Richard Dreyfuss and was directed by Steven Spielberg. It was nominated for Best Picture and won an Oscar for Best Musical Soundtrack (John Williams).

A: Royal Canadian Mounted Policeman
Q: What is Nelson Eddy's occupation in *Rose Marie*?
W: This is the 1936 story of a Canadian Mounty who gets his man and a lady (Jeanette MacDonald). It also starred James Stewart, Reginald Owen and David Niven.

A: "Rubber Soul"
Q: What Beatles album contains the song "Michelle"?
W: Between 1962, the year of "Love Me Do" their first hit, and 1967 the Beatles wrote 230 songs, almost one per week! They sold over 200 million records.

ENTERTAINMENT

A: **Rudolf Nureyev**
Q: Who defected from a Leningrad ballet troupe in 1961?
W: Nureyev was always an exceptional dancer but a "nonconformist." He was the principal dancer for three years with the Kirov Dance Company in Russia. After an outstanding personal success during his company's first trip to Paris in 1961, Nureyev was ordered back to Russia. Fearing official disapproval that might end his career, he defected and was given permission to stay in France.

A: **Rudy Vallee**
Q: What singer was known as "the Vagabond Lover"?
W: "Vagabond Lover" was Rudy Vallee's nickname from his theme songs "I'm Just a Vagabond Lover" (1929 movie) and "My Time Is Your Time." Vallee's real name was Hubert Prior Vallee.

A: **"Run for Your Life"**
Q: What TV series featured the Bonneville Salt Flats in its opening credits?
W: This TV series starred Ben Gazzara as Paul Bryan, an attorney that has an incurable disease and only a short time to live. He spends the time he has left trying to help others solve *their* problems. The series ran from Sept. 13, 1965, to Sept. 11, 1968.

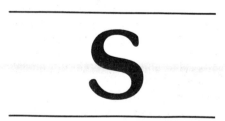

S

A: **Sal Mineo**
Q: Who played Gene Krupa in *The Gene Krupa Story*?
W: In the 1959 film Sal Mineo played a successful jazz drummer who, convicted of a drugs charge, falls from grace. It also starred Susan Kohner, James Darren, and Yvonne Craig.

A: **Sally Bowles**
Q: What character did Liza Minnelli play in the movie *Cabaret*?
W: This 1972 film takes place in the early 1930s when Berlin was a hotbed of vice and anti-Semitism. Bowles is a singer in the Kit Kat Club. Joel Grey and Michael York also starred and it was directed by Bob Fosse. The film won Oscars for Direction, Photography (Geoffrey Unsworth), Music (Ralph Burns), Best Actress (Liza Minnelli), and Best Supporting Actor (Joel Grey).

A: **Sally Kellerman**
Q: Who played Hot Lips Houlihan in the movie *M*A*S*H*?
W: The 1970 film was directed by Robert Altman. Other stars included Donald Sutherland (Hawkeye), Elliot Gould (Trapper John), Robert Duvall (Frank Burns), and Gary Burghoff (Radar). The movie was about surgeons at a Mobile Army Surgical Hospital in Korea who spend what little time they have chasing women and bucking authority. Kellerman was nominated for Best Supporting Actress for her portrayal.

A: **Sam**
Q: What role did Dooley Wilson play in *Casablanca*?
W: "Of all the gin joints and taverns all over the world, she walks into mine...Play it, Sam, you played it for her...you can play it for me." "It" refers to "As Time Goes By," the song that reminds Rick (Bogart) of his and Ilsa's (Ingrid Bergman) idyllic love affair in Paris.

A: **Sam Peckinpah**
Q: Who directed *The Wild Bunch*?
W: Possibly Peckinpah's best film, this mega-violent western starred William Holden, Ernest Borgnine, Robert Ryan, Edmond O'Brien, Warren Oates, and Strother Martin. In this 1969 film all the outlaws go out in a blaze of glory.

A: **Sammy Davis, Jr.**
Q: Who began his entertainment career as Silent Sam, The Dancing Midget?
W: Sammy was a member of the Will Mastin Trio. "Silent Sam, the Dancing Midget" was the creation of Davis' father who introduced him to show business. His first number 1 record was "The Candy Man." He also sang the theme song ("Keep Your Eye on the Sparrow") for the TV series "Baretta."

A: **Sammy Davis Jr.**
Q: Who played Sportin' Life in the film *Porgy and Bess*?
W: This 1959 film starred Sidney Poitier as Porgy and Dorothy Dandridge as Bess. It was directed by Otto Preminger and based on the play *Porgy* by DuBose and Dorothy Hayward.

A: **Sammy Davis Jr.**
Q: Who was the star of the 1965 Broadway hit *Golden Boy*?
W: *Golden Boy* was a narrative of a boy who becomes a prizefighter looking to get rich quick. Several changes had to be made from the premise of the all white cast of the 1939 movie and Clifford Odets' book. The cast of the stage play was all black.

A: **Sammy Spear**
Q: What orchestra leader did Jackie Gleason call "the Flower of the Music World"?
W: The Sammy Spear Orchestra, along with the June Taylor Dancers, appeared with Gleason throughout his career. They appeared on the "Cavalcade of Stars" and later on "The Jackie Gleason Show."

A: ***San Pablo*, The**
Q: What was the name of the U.S. Navy gunboat in the film *The Sand Pebbles*?
W: This 1966 film is about an American gunboat, patrolling the Yangtzee River in 1926, that gets involved with Chinese warlords. The movie starred Steve McQueen, Candice Bergen, Richard Attenborough, and Richard Crenna. It was nominated for Best Picture, Photography, Music, Best Actor (McQueen) and Best Supporting Actor.

A: **Sapphire**
Q: What was the name of Kingfish's wife?
W: Sapphire was the wife of George "Kingfish" Stevens from the radio and TV series "Amos 'n' Andy." She was played by Ernestine Wade on both radio and TV. "You old battleaxe!"

A: **Sarah Bernhardt**
Q: What actress was known as Divine Sarah?
W: Sarah Bernhardt was a celebrated French stage actress before she began her love-hate relationship with films. After her film debut in 1900 she declared she detested the medium, yet she agreed to play in another picture.

A: **Sardi's**
Q: Where do Broadway actors traditionally celebrate opening night?
W: Sardi's is the famous Broadway restaurant in New York where casts traditionally celebrate the opening night of a new Broadway play. Lot's of "rubber-necking" going on by the nonluminaries — folks like us!

A: **Scott Joplin**
Q: Who was called "the King of Ragtime"?
W: Joplin was the greatest creator of piano rags. He's believed to have written 500 compositions in all and not only rags, but also marches and waltzes. His first success was "Maple Leaf Rag."

A: **Scout**
Q: What was the name of Tonto's horse?
W: Tonto was the Lone Ranger's sidekick. In the movies Tonto, played by Chief Thundercloud, had horses named White Feller and Paint. On TV Tonto, played by Jay Silverheels, used a saddle, while on the radio version, Tonto originally rode double with the Lone Ranger on Silver!

A: **Sean Connery**
Q: What actor has a tattoo on his right wrist reading "Scotland Forever"?
W: Many thought that they were James Bond's tatooes, because he has two. Bond's other one says "Mum and Dad."

A: **Sergeant Preston of the Yukon**
Q: Who confronted criminals with the line, "I arrest you in the name of the Crown"?
W: The line originated on the Detroit radio station WXYZ in the series "Challenge of the Yukon." Sergeant Preston was played by Richard Simmons (no relation to the exercise guy), Paul Sutton, and Bruce Beemer.

A: **Sergeant York**
Q: What portrayal won Gary Cooper the 1941 Best Actor Oscar?
W: This is the classic story of Alvin York, who in 1918 singlehandedly captured 132 Germans. The film, directed by Howard Hawks, was something of an inspiration to enlisted men. For years the real life York refused to have his story dramatized. He agreed only after it was decided that he (York) could supervise every phase of the production and that Cooper would play the lead.

A: **Seven**
Q: How many times did Bing Crosby and Bob Hope hit the road in films?
W: They are in chronological order: *Road to Singapore*, *Road to Zanzibar*, *Road to Morocco*, *Road to Utopia*, *Road to Rio*, *Road to Bali*, and *Road to Hong Kong*.

A: *Sextette*
Q: What was Mae West's last film?
W: This 1978 film also starred Tony Curtis, Ringo Starr, Dom DeLuise, George Hamilton, Alice Cooper, Rona Barret, Walter Pidgeon, and George Raft. West plays a Hollywood film star whose honeymoon is interrupted by her previous husbands. The sight of 86-year-old West in her wedding dress and bleached blonde hair must be seen to be believed. One of West's better lines was, "I'm the type of girl who works at Columbia all day and Fox all night!"

A: **Shaggy Dog, The**
Q: What did Walt Disney turn Tommy Kirk into in 1959?
W: Kirk played a boy who turns into a big shaggy dog and catches some crooks. *The Shaggy Dog* starred Fred MacMurray, Jean Hagen, and Annette Funicello.

A: **"Shane, come back"**
Q: What's the last line of "Shane"?
W: This line was spoken by the character Joey Starrett (Brandon DeWilde). Alan Ladd played the title role in the 1953 film that also starred Jean Arthur, Van Heflin, and Jack Palance. Ladd played the mysterious stranger who helps a family of homesteaders.

A: **Sharks and Jets, The**
Q: What were the rival gangs in *West Side Story*?
W: In the 1961 musical reworking of the "Romeo and Juliet" story, we have the Sharks and the Jets instead of the Capulets and the Montagues. The Sharks consisted of newly arrived Puerto Ricans, and the Jets were white youths.

A: Shelley Fabares
Q: Who sang "Johnny Angel"?
W: Miss Fabares started her career as a professional dancer. Her big break came in 1953 after appearing on a Frank Sinatra TV special and after also appearing in several films. She played Donna Reed's daughter on the "Donna Reed Show." In 1962 she released her first major hit, which went all the way to number 1. That song was "Johnny Angel."

A: Shirley Bassey
Q: Who sang the title song to *Goldfinger*?
W: This 1965 James Bond movie starred Sean Connery as Bond. Bassey also sang the title song to *Diamonds are Forever*, the 1971 Bond film also starring Connery.

A: Shirley Jones
Q: Who played Mrs. Patridge on "The Partridge Family"?
W: This was a TV series about a musical group made up of members of a family. David Cassidy, Jones' real son, played Keith; Susan Day played Laurie; Danny Bonaduce played Danny; Jeremy Gelbwaks (and later Brian Forster) played Chris; and Suzanne Crough played Tracy.

A: Shirley MacLaine
Q: Who's Warren Beatty's sister?
W: She starred, among other films, in *Being There*, *Terms of Endearment*, and *Turning Point*. Her autobiography is titled *Out on a Limb*.

A: Shirley Temple
Q: What actress made a million by the age of ten?
W: Some interesting facts about Shirley: she was the youngest person to be listed in *Who's Who*. Her two stand-ins as a child actress were Marilyn Granas and Mary Lou Isleib. She was once married to John Agar. Shirley Temple Black later became the U.S. Ambassador to Ghana.

A: *Shootist, The*
Q: What was John Wayne's last movie?
W: Wayne ironically played an old cowboy dying of cancer (Wayne himself had cancer). The 1976 film also starred Lauren Bacall, James Stewart, Ron Howard, Richard Boone, John Carradine, Scatman Crothers, Harry Morgan, and Hugh O'Brien. It was directed by Don Siegel.

A: *Shot in the Dark, A*
Q: What was the sequel to *The Pink Panther*?
W: This 1964 sequel starred Peter Sellers as Inspector Clouseau. Other stars included Elke Sommer and George Sanders. It was written by Blake Edwards and William Peter Blatty, the theme music was by Henry Mancini, and it was directed by Blake Edwards.

A: Sid Caesar's
Q: What TV comedian's wife was played by Imogene Coca, Nanette Fabray, and Gisele Mackenzie?
W: Caesar appeared on one of the early "Texaco Star Theater" shows hosted by Milton Berle. He appeared with Coca on "The Admiral Broadway Revue" and "Your Show of Shows." After "Your Show of Shows" ended, Caesar reappeared in "Caesar's Hour." Janet Blair as well as Imogene Coca, Nanette Fabray, and Gisele MacKenzie appeared as his wife on "Your Show of Shows."

A: Sidney Greenstreet
Q: Who portrayed Casper Gutman in the 1941 film *The Maltese Falcon*?
W: *The Maltese Falcon* was based on the novel by Dashiell Hammett. The film, starring Humphrey Bogart as Sam Spade and Mary Astor as Brigid O'Shaughnessy, was written and directed by John Huston. It was nominated for Best Picture, Writing, and Best Supporting Actor (Greenstreet).

A: Sidney Poitier
Q: What actor came to dinner in *Guess Who's Coming to Dinner*?
W: In this 1967 film a well-to-do San Francisco girl announces that she is going to marry a black man, and her parents find that they are less broad-minded than they had thought. Poitier played John Prentice. Spencer Tracy and Katherine Hepburn played the parents. It was Spencer Tracy's last film.

A: Sidney Poitier
Q: Who was the first black man to win an Oscar?
W: And it was well-deserved! In *Lilies of the Field*, Poitier's role as a black itinerant workman who helps a group of nuns build a chapel was entertaining and inspiring.

A: Sidney Poitier
Q: Who won the Best Actor Oscar for *Lilies of the Field*?
W: Poitier won the Oscar for Best Actor for his portrayal of Homer Smith. He played a workman who helped a group of nuns build a chapel. The 1963 film also starred Lilia Skala.

A: silver bullet, A
Q: What symbolized justice and law to the Lone Ranger?
W: The Lone Ranger was the secret identity of Texas Ranger John Reid. His mask was made from his dead brother's vest. His horse's name was Silver, and his Indian companion was Tonto. Clayton Moore was most famous as the Lone Ranger on TV and in movies.

A: Simon and Garfunkel
Q: Who asked the musical question: "Where have you gone, Joe DiMaggio"?
W: The singing team of Paul Simon and Art Garfunkel has recently been reestablished. This line is from the song "Mrs. Robinson" in the movie *The Graduate*. Other songs by Simon and Garfunkel from the film include "Scarborough Fair" and "Sounds of Silence."

A: **Sing-A-Long Gang, The**
Q: What was the name of Mitch Miller's singers?
W: Remember "sing-a-long with Mitch"? Mitch Miller's Sing-a-long Gang consisted of 25 members.

A: **Sixty-four dollars**
Q: How much money did Jack Benny win on "The $64,000 Question"?
W: Sorry, Jack. The TV show ran from 1955 to 1958, was sponsored by Revlon, and emceed by Hal March. A new cadillac was the consolation prize for those who missed the $64,000 question. Psychologist Dr. Joyce Brothers won $64,000 in the category of boxing, and actress Barbara Feldon won in the Shakespeare category.

A: **Skitch Henderson**
Q: What orchestra leader did Doc Severinsen replace on the "Tonight Show"?
W: Johnny Carson replaced Jack Paar, who had replaced Steve Allen, as host of the popular late-night talk show. Jose Melis was Paar's bandleader before Henderson.

A: **Skull Island**
Q: What island was the jungle home of King Kong in the 1933 film?
W: ...or any island he wants! Skull Island was also the son of Kong's home. Skull Island is located 1,753 miles from DaKong, southwest of Sumatra in the Indian Ocean. Kong was brought to New York from the island aboard the ship *Venture*.

A: **Sky King**
Q: Who owned the Flying Crown Ranch?
W: The Flying Crown Ranch was Sky King's home, where he lived with his niece Penny and nephew Clipper, near the town of Grover.

A: **Sky King**
Q: Who was known as "America's Favorite Flying Cowboy"?
W: He was Texas Ranger Schyler King, pilot of the Twin Cessna

Songbird. He was played on TV by Kirby Grant and on radio, at different times, by Jack Lester, Earl Nightingale, and Roy Engel.

A: *Sleeper*
Q: What Woody Allen film featured an "orgasmatron"?
W: Allen played a health food store owner who is deep frozen after an operation and awakens 200 years in the future. Sex, as we know it, was considered primitive, so for emotional release a couple would step inside a phone booth for a few seconds of ecstasy.

A: **Sleeping Beauty**
Q: What is Princess Aurora's better known name?
W: Princess Aurora was Sleeping Beauty's name, she is also called Briar Rose. This character is from the fairy tale "Sleeping Beauty." A replica of her castle is the mainstay of Disneyland.

A: **Slim Pickens**
Q: What actor rode the bomb from a B-52 in *Dr. Strangelove*?
W: Pickens starred as Major T. J. "King" Kong, an air force pilot who yells "ya-hoo!" as he rides the big A-bomb al-l-l the way down—probably the most remembered scene in the whole film (1964). It also starred Peter Sellers, George C. Scott, and Sterling Hayden.

A: *Snow White and the Seven Dwarfs*
Q: What was Walt Disney's first full-length feature cartoon?
W: Released in 1937, it was a mammoth enterprise that no one in the business thought would work. The songs and the comic and villainous characters turned the film into a worldwide box office bonanza.

A: *Some Like It Hot*
Q: What 1959 film did Tony Curtis and Jack Lemmon appear in, in drag?
W: Curtis and Lemmon play two unemployed musicians who accidently witness the St. Valentine's Day Massacre and flee to Miami disguised as lady musicians. The film also starred Marilyn Monroe and George Raft and was directed by Billy Wilder. Lemmon was nominated for an Oscar for his performance as "Daphne."

A: *Songbird*
Q: What was the name of Sky King's Twin Cessna?
W: *Songbird* was Sky King's Twin Cessna airplane. The first *Songbird* was a Cessna T-50. The plane was kept at King's home, the Flying Crown Ranch.

A: **Sons of the Pioneers, The**
Q: What was the backup singing group for Roy Rogers?
W: The Sons of the Pioneers sang backup for the "King of the Cowboys." Roy made his debut in *The Old Homestead* as Len Slye, his real name. Later he used the pseudonym Dick Weston before Republic Pictures changed his name to Roy Rogers.

A: **Sophia Loren**
Q: Who won the Best Actress Oscar for her role in *Two Women*?
W: This 1960 film takes place during the Allied bombing of Rome. A woman (Loren) and her daughter travel south and have a hard time at the hands of invading soldiers. It was directed by Vittorio de Sica.

A: Sophie Tucker
Q: What singer was "the Last of the Red Hot Mamas"?Q: Who was "the Last of the Red Hot Mamas"?
W: The title of Tucker's autobiography is *My Time Is Your Time*. She was the first woman roasted by the Friar's Club.

A: "Sorry about that, Chief"
Q: How did Maxwell Smart apologize to Thaddeus?
W: This line is from the TV show "Get Smart" starring Don Adams as the bumbling, overconfident and klutzy Secret Agent 86. "Sorry about that, Chief" was his handy apology to his superior (Chief) after one of his major foul-ups.

A: *Sound of Music, The*
Q: What was the last Rodgers and Hammerstein musical?
W: This 1965 film starred Julie Andrews as a novice nun who becomes governess to the Trapp family, falls in love with the widowed father, and helps them all escape from the Nazis. Songs included "Edelweiss," "My Favorite Things," "Sound of Music," "Climb Every Mountain," "Sixteen Going on Seventeen," and "Do-Re-Mi."

A: "Sounds of Silence, The"
Q: What song opens *The Graduate*?
W: This 1967 film featured songs by Simon and Garfunkel. Other songs included "Mrs. Robinson," "Scarborough Fair," and "April Come She Will."

A: Soupy Sales
Q: What TV comedian worked with White Fang, Black Tooth, and Pookie the Lion?
W: All, along with "Hippy," were supporting puppets on the "Soupy Sales Show." The most that you could see of White Fang and Black Tooth was their arms.

A: *South Pacific*
Q: What Broadway show introduced the song "Some Enchanted Evening"?

W: In no other Rodgers and Hammerstein production did the music reflect the background and the characters as it did in *South Pacific*. Other songs were "I'm Gonna Wash that Man Right Outa My Hair," "Bali Ha'i," and "Happy Talk."

A: Spaghetti westerns
Q: What's the collective name for Italian-made western movies?
W: It was in spaghetti westerns that Clint Eastwood achieved popularity as "the man with no name" or the "drifter" in such films as *The Good, the Bad, and the Ugly, A Fistful of Dollars* and *For a Few Dollars More*. The term "spaghetti" was used because these films were made on location in Italy — sure looked like the U.S. West!

A: Speedy Gonzales
Q: Who is "the Fastest Mouse in All of Mexico"?
W: Si, Senor! Speedy, the Mexican mouse from Warner Brothers cartoons, lives in Guadalajara. The voice is that of Mel Blanc. In 1955 the cartoon "Speedy Gonzales" won an Oscar for Best Short Subject (how appropriate!).

A: Spencer Tracy
Q: What actor was awarded an Oscar engraved with the name of Dick Tracy?
W: At least they got the last name right. Tracy was nominated for an Oscar nine times. He won two years in a row for Best Actor for *Captains Courageous* (1937) and *Boys Town* (1938).

A: Spencer Tracy
Q: Who played the title role in the movie *Father of the Bride*?
W: Tracy was nominated as Best Actor for his portrayal of Stanley T. Banks. His superb portrait of frustrated dominance over a household in the throes of wedding fever was the centerpiece of this comedy. Elizabeth Taylor played the bride in this 1950 film.

A: Stanley Kubrick
Q: Who directed *Spartacus*?
W: Kubrick (who also directed *2001* and *A Clockwork Orange*) used *Spartacus* as a vehicle for what would soon emerge as his dominant theme: the lack of relationship between "the humanities" and true human feelings. The 1960 film starred Kirk Douglas and Laurence Olivier.

A: *Star is Born, A*
Q: What film ends with the line: "This is Mrs. Norman Maine"?
W: This classic 1937 film was remade twice. All three films have the same plot: a young actress marries a successful Hollywood star whose career wanes as hers becomes brighter. The first starred Janet Gaynor and Fredrick March, the second Judy Garland and James Mason, the third Barbara Streisand and Kris Kristofferson.

A: Stars and stripes
Q: What was painted on Peter Fonda's motorcycle helmet in *Easy Rider*?
W: Why do you think they called him "Captain America"? The 1969 film also starred Dennis Hopper and Jack Nicholson. Fonda and Hopper embark on a trip east to "find America."

A: Starship *Enterprise*, The
Q: What ship bears the identification number NCC 1701?
W: Federations United Starship, Constitution class, was from the TV series "Star Trek." Commanded by Captain James T. Kirk, the ship carried 430 crew members, measured 947 feet long and 417 feet wide, and had a gross weight of 190,000 tons.

A: Steve Allen
Q: Who did Louis Nye greet with: "Hi-ho, Steverino"?
W: Allen was the first host of the "Tonight Show." His announcer at the time was Gene Rayburn ("Match Game") and his bandleader was Skitch Henderson. Allen also hosted a Sunday night comedy show, competing against Ed Sullivan, that featured Nye, Don Knotts, Tom Poston, and Bill Dana.

A: Steve Allen
Q: Who portrayed Benny Goodman in "The Benny Goodman Story"?
W: Allen played Goodman, a clarinettist from the Jewish section of Chicago who became internationally famous. Also starring in this 1955 film were Donna Reed, Berta Gersten, and Harry James.

A: Steve Allen
Q: Who was the first host of the original "Tonight" show?
W: Allen was the first, Jack Paar the second, and Johnny Carson the third (and present). Groucho Marx introduced Carson on his first night as host, Oct. 1, 1962.

A: Steve Lawrence
Q: Who's Eydie Gorme's husband?
W: The two have been singing and living together for a long time. They appeared together as far back as Steve Allen's "Tonight" show in the mid-50s.

A: Steve McQueen
Q: Who played bounty hunter Josh Randall on TV?
W: McQueen played Randall in the TV series "Wanted-Dead or Alive." He called his 30-30 carbine "Mare's Laig," and the horse he rode was named Ringo.

A: Steve McQueen
Q: Who played the title role in *The War Lover*?
W: This 1962 film also starred Shirley Anne Field and Robert Wagner. McQueen played a Flying Fortress Commander based in East Anglia in 1943, who has the wrong ideas about women and war.

A: Steve McQueen
Q: Who portrayed the Cooler King in *The Great Escape*?
W: "Cooler King" Hilts was given that moniker because he spent a lot of time in "the cooler" (solitary) as punishment for attempted escapes. This 1963 film dealt with Allied prisoners' plan to escape from a German prison camp. The all-star cast included James Garner, Richard Attenborough, Charles Bronson, James Coburn, and David McCallum.

A: Steve McQueen and Ali McGraw
Q: What two performers got away in *The Getaway*?
W: McQueen plays a convict who leaves jail and promptly joins his wife (McGraw) in a bank robbery. Other stars included Slim Pickens and Sally Struthers. This 1972 film was directed by Sam Peckinpah.

A: Steven Spielberg
Q: Who directed *Close Encounters of the Third Kind*?
W: He directed this film in 1977. Other Spielberg films include *Jaws*, *Raiders of the Lost Ark*, and *E.T..*. *Close Encounters* stars included Richard Dreyfuss, Teri Garr, and Francois Trauffaut; special effects were by Douglas Trumbull. *Close Encounters* is a story about a series of UFOs that take Indiana by surprise. A workman is led by intuition and detection to the landing site that has been concealed from the public.

A: Steven Spielberg
Q: Who directed *Raiders of the Lost Ark*?
W: It was produced by George Lucas and starred Harrison Ford, Karen Allen, and John Rhys-Davies. Ford played Indiana Jones, an archaeologist who races against the Nazis to find the lost Ark of the Covenant.

A: "Strangers in the Night"
Q: What Sinatra hit did he "dooby dooby do" in?
W: "Old Blue Eyes" began his singing career with the Hoboken Four, after which he sang with Harold Arden, Harry James, and Tommy Dorsey orchestras and then on radio's "Hit Parade."

A: Stud Poker
Q: What game do Steve McQueen and Edward G. Robinson play in *The Cincinnati Kid*?
W: It was a hard-boiled drama about gamblers, directed with a keen eye for atmosphere and tension by Norman Jewison. In New Orleans in the late 1930s, stud poker experts competed for supremacy. The film also starred Karl Malden, Ann Margaret, Tuesday Weld, Joan Blondell, and Jack Weston.

A: Sue Ann Nivens
Q: Who was the star of WJM-TV's "The Happy Homemaker"?
W: Betty White played prissy Sue Ann Nivens, hostess of "The Happy Homemaker Show" on Minneapolis station WJM-TV on the TV series "The Mary Tyler Moore Show."

A: *Summer of '42*
Q: What 1971 film featured the characters Benjie, Oscy, and Hermie?
W: Benjie was played by Oliver Conant, Oscy by Jerry Houser, and Hermie by Gary Grimes. The film dealt with the growing pains of three sexually frustrated boys who are spending a summer holiday with their families off the coast of New England. It was Jennifer O'Neill's first starring role.

A: Sylvia
Q: What was Ed Sullivan's wife's name?
W: Sullivan hosted the longest running TV variety show, originally called "Toast of the Town." It played each Sunday night at 8 P.M. on CBS. The name was changed to "The Ed Sullivan Show" in 1955. Often mentioned, Sylvia was never seen on the show.

ENTERTAINMENT

A: **Surrender Dorothy**
Q: What did the Wicked Witch of the West write in the sky over the Emerald City?
W: Margaret Hamilton, as the witch, wrote this message in the sky with her broom outside the city of Oz in the 1939 movie *The Wizard of Oz*. Remember the ruby slippers?

A: **Suzanne Pleshette**
Q: Who portrayed the doomed schoolteacher in *The Birds*?
W: Pleshette played Annie Hayworth, the schoolteacher who befriends Melanie Daniels (Tippi Hedren) before becoming buzzard bait in the 1963 Hitchcock thriller. Rod Taylor starred as Mitch Brenner.

A: **Swee'pea**
Q: What's the name of Popeye's adopted son?
W: On radio he adopted a boy named Matey. Swee'pea's "mother" is Olive Oyl (Popeye's girlfriend). Popeye's first movie appearance was in a Betty Boop cartoon (1933) titled "Popeye the Sailor." He gets his strength from eating spinach (originally garlic).

T

A: **Tammy Wynette**
Q: Who stood at the top with "Stand by Your Man"?
W: Tammy Wynette, three times female vocalist of the year by the Country Music Association, has often been called the "first lady of country music." "Stand by Your Man" was recorded in 1969, sold two million copies, and is believed to be the largest seller by any woman country singer up to that time.

A: **Tarzan**
Q: What movie character was Elmo Lincoln the first to portray?
W: That's accurate, unless you count Gordon Griffith, who (at ten years old) played Tarzan as a boy in the same 1918 silent film. Other famous Tarzans were Johnny Weissmuller, Buster Crabbe, and Ron Ely (TV). Weissmuller's Tarzan yell was a recorded combination of a violin g-string, a hyena's howl, a dog's growl, and a camel's bleat.

A: **Tatum O'Neal**
Q: Who collected the 1973 Best Supporting Actress Oscar at age 10?
W: Tatum O'Neal, daughter of actor Ryan O'Neal, won the Oscar for her role as Addie Pray, the foul-mouthed, cigarette smoking little girl in Peter Bogdanovich's *Paper Moon*. She starred along with Daddy Ryan. Also starring were Madeline Kahn and John Hillerman. It was Tatum's film debut.

A: **Telstar**
Q: What satellite spawned a hit single?
W: Telstar-I was the first U.S. communications satellite (AT and T Company) to amplify radio and TV signals. It was launched July 10, 1962.

A: **Ten**
Q: How many lords a-leaping are there in the carol "Twelve Days of Christmas"?
W: It's the carol in which "my true love gave to me: a partridge in a pear tree, two turtle doves, three French hens, four calling birds, five golden rings, six geese a-laying, seven swans a-swimming, eight maids a-milking, nine ladies dancing, ten lords a-leaping, eleven pipers piping, and twelve drummers drumming.

A: **"Tennessee Waltz, The"**
Q: What song did Patti Page set people dancing to in 1951?
W: This ballad was recorded by Cowboy Copas in 1950 and by Patti Page in 1951. It became the top record in 1951. The song was originally offered to, but turned down by, Frank Sinatra. It became the official song of the state of Tennessee in 1965.

A: **tenor banjo, The**
Q: What musical instrument does George Segal play professionally?
W: Segal has played banjo on "The Tonight Show" several times, often with a small band featuring TV actor Conrad Janis ("Mork and Mindy") on trombone. Segal is better known for his movie roles. He's appeared in *Who's Afraid of Virginia Woolf?*, *The Owl and the Pussycat*, *A Touch of Class*, and *California Split*, in which he revives an old ragtime song "What You Goin' to Do When the Rent Comes Round?"

A: **Ted Baxter**
Q: Who was the only member of the WJM-TV news crew not fired in the last episode of "The Mary Tyler Moore Show"?
W: This early 1970s sit-com broke the mold with Mary's image as an unmarried career woman with a responsible job other than as secretary or teacher. Mary wanted to end the show while it was still popular, and there was some speculation as to how they would end it—such as Mary marrying Lou!

Instead, they gave the final episode the same ironic twist as all the others; a new owner buys the station and fires everyone…except Ted.

A: Tess
Q: What is the rain's name in the song "They Call the Wind Mariah"?
W: …the fire's Job. This song by Lerner-Loewe was from the 1969 musical *Paint Your Wagon*. It was sung by Harve Presnell.

A: "That Was The Week That Was"
Q: What TV show was informally known as TW3?
W: "*That Was The Week That Was*" has three sets of T and W words! The show premiered Dec. 1962 and marked a major step forward in British broadcasting, because it was the first show to poke fun at and actually ridicule politicians and officeholders. It premiered in America on Nov. 10, 1963, on NBC. The show was hosted by Henry Fonda.

A: That's all, folks
Q: What motto ended Merrie Melodies cartoons?
W: This was a movie cartoon series by Warner Brothers, as was also Looney Tunes. The title is similar to Disney's Silly Symphonies, which came first.

A: Theo
Q: What is Kojak's first name?
W: "Kojak" premiered Oct. 24, 1973. The pilot was the three-hour "The Marcus-Nelson Murders." It introduced Telly Savalas as Lieutenant Theo Kojak, a radiantly bald, fiercely independent Greek plainclothes detective on the New York City police force who fought the establishment he worked for—and lost. His portrayal of the confident bald man who brandished a lollipop instead of a cigar turned into a very unlikely sex symbol and attracted viewers that otherwise had only mild interest in cop shows.

A: Theodore
Q: What was Beaver Cleaver's first name?
W: The Cleaver family lived in a typical television suburban home in a quiet neighborhood with shady trees and nice front yards. Like every TV father of the time, Ward (Hugh Beaumont) disappeared between 9am and 5pm every day to an unknown job, though his real life's work seemed to be mowing the lawn and having weekly heart-to-heart talks with his sons. June (Barbara Billingsley) was a perfect TV mommy who wanted nothing more out of life than a clean carpet, whiter than white laundry, and a well-done roast. Beaver (Jerry Mathers), a cute little preteenager, was honestly trying to decipher the way the world worked and often turned to his brother Wally (Tony Dow) for advice. Wally usually responded with an exasperated "Aw, Beav!"

A: There's no place like home
Q: What phrase does Dorothy repeat as she clicks her ruby shoes to return to Kansas?
W: In *The Wizard of Oz* Dorothy repeats "There's no place like home," as she clicks the heels of her ruby slippers together three times in order to return to Kansas.

A: They played Scrooge
Q: What do actors Reginald Owen, Alastair Sim, and Albert Finney have in common?
W: Ebenezer Scrooge, the sad, stingy old man whose dead partner,

Jacob Marley, haunts him at Christmas, was played by Owen in *A Christmas Story* in 1938, by Sim in the 1951 movie *Scrooge*, and by Finney in the 1970 musical *Scrooge*.

A: They starred in *The Jazz Singer*
Q: What do Al Jolson, Danny Thomas, and Neil Diamond have in common?
W: Jolson starred in the 1927 film (which was also the first "talkie"). Thomas starred in the 1953 remake and Diamond in the 1980 remake. George Jessel played the jazz singer on Broadway. The jazz singer's name is Jack Robin, and in the first talkie Jolson says that well-known line, "Wait a minute, wait a minute, you ain't heard nothing yet!"

A: "The Thinker"
Q: What statue did Dobie Gillis mimic while contemplating life and love?
W: *The Thinker* (created by Rodin and called *Le Penseur*) was intended to have been Dante. When Dobie Gillis in the TV series "The Many Loves of Dobie Gillis" wants to think, he sits under this statue and asks the TV audience, "Now, I ask you…"

A: third of June, The
Q: What was another dusty delta day in "Ode to Billy Joe"?
W: This is the story-ballad from 1967 in which a preacher, Brother Taylor, sees Billy Joe and his girl throw an object whose identity remains a dark mystery, off the Tallahatchie Bridge. Bobbie Gentry recorded the seven-minute song in 1967.

A: Three
Q: How many finally made it to freedom in the movie *The Great Escape*?
W: This 1963 film was based on a true story of Allied POWs plotting to escape from a German prison camp. Of the 76 men who escaped, only three made it to freedom: Rocky Rockland, Jens Muller, and Bob Van Der Stok. The others were recaptured or killed.

A: **Three Stooges, The**
Q: What were Moe Howard, Larry Fine and Curly Howard better known as?
W: Originally in the 1920s they were known as "Ted Healy and His Stooges." Shemp Howard, another brother, replaced Curly Howard in 1947; Joe Besser replaced Shemp Howard in 1955; Joe DeRita (Curly Joe) replaced Joe Besser in 1958. Their first movie was *Soup to Nuts* in 1930.

A: **Thumper**
Q: What's the name of the rabbit in *Bambi*?
W: This 1942 Disney feature cartoon movie also featured Flower (the skunk). The voice of Thumper was Peter Behn.

A: **"Till Death Do Us Part"**
Q: What British TV series inspired "All in the Family"?
W: The BBC-TV series featured Alf and Elsie Garnett of London's East End. (The series did *not*, however, feature a son-in-law called "Kipper-head.")

A: **Tiny Tim**
Q: Who made it big with "Tiptoe Through the Tulips" in 1968?
W: "Tiptoe Through the Tulips" was "camp" performer and falsetto singer Herbert Buckingham Khaury's (Tiny Tim) biggest hit record. His first album was "God Bless Tiny Tim."

A: **Tiny Tim and Miss Vicki**
Q: What couple was married Dec. 17, 1969, on TV's "Tonight Show"?
W: Dozens of fresh tulips were brought in for this much-popularized ceremony (in honor of Tim's hit record "Tiptoe Through the Tulips"). Her full name is Victoria May Budinger, and they named their daughter "Tulip." They were divorced Oct. 24, 1977.

A: *Titanic*, **The**
Q: What ship sank in *A Night to Remember*?
W: This 1958 film was about the 1912 sea disaster when, on her maiden voyage, the *Titanic* struck an iceberg and sank. The "unsinkable" White Star liner hit an iceberg at 25 miles per hour and sank April 15, 1912. *Titanic*'s builder Thomas Andrews, John Jacob Astor, and author Jacques Futreller all perished along with 1,500 other passengers. In 1898, novelist Morgan Robertson wrote a story in which an 800-foot ocean liner hit an iceberg on her maiden voyage and sank; the vessel's name in that novel was the *Titan*.

A: **Title writing**
Q: What Academy Award category was abolished in 1929?
W: 1928 was the year that the "talkies" really became popular; thus there was no need for "title cards," which were necessary for communication in silent movies.

A: *To Catch A Thief*
Q: What film was Grace Kelly making in Monaco when she met Prince Rainier?
W: In the 1955 Hitchcock thriller, Cary Grant starred as a famous cat burglar (who has "retired" to the Riviera) that catches a thief who is imitating his old style. Filmed on location, one of the more memorable scenes is the love scene between Grant and Kelly; when they kiss passionately, fireworks go off outside.

A: **"Toast of the Town"**
Q: What was "The Ed Sullivan Show" originally called?
W: The TV show debuted June 20, 1948. Originally to be called "You're the Top," it was the longest running TV variety show in history. It played each Sunday night at 8pm on CBS. The title changed to "The Ed Sullivan Show" in Sept. 1955 and lasted until 1971. When the Beatles appeared in 1964, that particular show attracted 82 percent of the viewers.

A: **toga made of long beautiful hair, A**
Q: What do you wear to cause a gaga at the gogo?
W: This line is from "Lady Godiva" by Peter Asher and Gordon Waller (Peter and Gordon). It was released by Capitol Records in January 1967. The song is about the legendary lady and what might have happened if the ride had taken place in the modern days of the 1960s.

A: **Tom, Dick, Harry**
Q: What were the names of the three tunnels dug by the prisoners of war in the film *The Great Escape*?
W: They were dug by the POWs at Stalag Left North. Harry was the tunnel through which 76 men escaped; 50 were captured and executed in violation of the Geneva Convention. Tom from Hut 104 to the woods, Dick from the kitchen, and Harry from Hut 105, were all used for escape. Paul Brickhill's novel, on which the 1963 movie is based, mentions a fourth tunnel named George.

A: *Tom Jones*
Q: What movie featured Mrs. Waters and Tom sucking lobster claws and swallowing raw oysters?
W: This 1963 film starred Albert Finney and Susannah York. Finney's portrayal of the 18th century England foundling, who is brought up by a squire and (after many adventures) marries the squire's daughter, won him the Oscar for Best Actor.

A: **Tom Mix**
Q: What 1920's cowboy star rode Tony the Wonder Horse?
W: In the movies there were also Tony Jr., Tony I, Tony II, and Old Blue. Tom was a "real cowboy," born in 1880 and who died tragically in 1940.

A: **Tony Bennett**
Q: What singer was born Anthony Dominick Benedetto?
W: Tony appeared on TV for the first time in 1950 on "Arthur Godfrey's Talent Scouts Show." In 1962 he recorded his greatest hit song, "I Left My Heart in San Francisco," which sold three million copies and received two Grammys.

A: Tony Curtis
Q: Who portrayed Ferdinand Waldo Demara in *The Great Imposter*?
W: Demara was also known as Ben W. Jones, Assistant Warden; Brother John Payne, Trappist Monk; Dr. Cecil Boyce Hamann; Dr. Joesph C. Cyr, Surgeon; Dr. Robert Linton French; Martin Godgart, Latin teacher; and Dr. James Lore, Assistant at a boys' school. As Dr. Cyr he successfully operated on 19 South Korean soldiers in a single night aboard the Canadian destroyer HMCS *Cayuga*. After the incident he was called the Miracle Doctor.

A: Tony Curtis
Q: Who portrayed Ira Hayes in *The Outsider*?
W: Curtis played Ira Hayes, an American Indian, who becomes a war hero, but cannot reconcile himself to living in a white society.

A: Tony Curtis and Sidney Poitier
Q: What actors were chained together in the 1958 film *The Defiant Ones*?
W: Curtis played John "Joker" Jackson, and Poitier played Noah Cullen, two convicts (who hate each other) that escape from a chain gang. Curtis and Poitier each received Oscar nominations for their performances. It was the last film for Carl "Alfalfa" Switzer, one of the "Our Gang" kids.

A: Tony Dow
Q: Who portrayed Wally Cleaver?
W: The TV series "Leave It To Beaver" featured the Cleaver family. Theodore (Beaver) was played by Jerry Mathers; Wally by Tony Dow; Ward, the father, by Hugh Beaumont; and June, the mother, by Barbara Billingsley.

A: *Topkapi*
Q: What film featured Melina Mercouri, Maximilian Schell and Peter Ustinov as jewel thieves?
W: Mercouri played Elizabeth Lipp, Schell played Walter, and Ustinov played Arthur Simpson in the 1964 film in which international thieves try to rob the Istanbul Museum. Ustinov won the Oscar for Best Supporting Actor for his performance.

A: Topo Gigio
Q: Who used to ask: "Hey, Eddie, 'kees' me goodnight"?
W: Topo was referring to Ed Sullivan. Topo Gigio was the mechanical Italian mouse that spoke with a heavy accent as sort of a comedy routine with Ed Sullivan on his TV show. Topo's girlfriend is Rosy. Topo was featured in the 1965 movie *The Magic World of Topo Gigio*.

A: "Topper"
Q: What TV series featured Neal, a martini-drinking St. Bernard?
W: Neal drank dry martinis with an olive, up. Marion Kerby named him after her Uncle George. In the 1939 movie *Topper Takes a Trip*, the Kerbys' own a wire terrier named Mr. Atlas.

A: Tramp
Q: What was the name of the Douglas family's dog on "My Three Sons"?
W: As the pet dog on the series "My Three Sons", he has won the 1961, 1962, 1963, and 1964 TV Patsy Award. Tramp was also the name of the family dog on the TV series "Room for One More."

A: Trapp family, The
Q: What family was Julie Andrews governess to in *The Sound of Music*?
W: The Trapp family consisted of the Captain, Liesl, Louisa, Friedrich, Kurt, Brigitta, Marta, and Gretl.

A: *Treasure of the Sierra Madre, The*
Q: What film featured Bogey as Dobbs
W: Bogart played Dobbs, Walter Huston played Howard, and Tim Holt played Curtin in the 1948 film about three gold prospectors who come to grief through greed.

A: Treasury Department, The
Q: What government department did the Untouchables work for?
W: From 1959 to 1963 this TV series starred Robert Stack as Elliot Ness, Nicolas Georgiade as Enrico Rossi, Abel Fernandez as Bill Youngblood, and Paul Picerni as Lee Hobson. The role of Ness was first offered to Van Heflin and Van Johnson. In the silent movie *The Scarface Mob*, Elliot Ness marries Betty Anderson (Pat Crowley). His office number is 208, if you want to know!

A: Trevor Howard
Q: Who portrayed Captain Bligh in the 1962 film *Mutiny on the Bounty*?
W: It was a remake of the 1935 film about an 18th-century British naval vessel that sets off for South America, but during a mutiny the captain is cast adrift and the mutineers settle on the Pitcairn Islands. Marlon Brando played Fletcher Christian and overacts his final death scene.

A: Trixie
Q: What was Ed Norton's wife's name?
W: In "The Honeymooners" Jackie Gleason played Ralph Kramden, Art Carney played Ed Norton, Audrey Meadows played Alice Kramden, and Joyce Randolph played Trixie. "The Honeymooners" was a domestic skit that appeared regularly on "The Jackie Gleason Show." Famous lines from Ralph include: "One of these days, Alice ...POW!...right in the kisser!" and "Baby, you're the greatest!"

ENTERTAINMENT

A: **trombone, The**
Q: What instrument did Glenn Miller play?
W: Glenn Miler and his band were one of the great "swing" bands of the 1930s. Classic songs were "Moonlight Serenade," "In the Mood," "Chattanooga Choo Choo," and "The Little Brown Jug." Miller was aboard a single-engine plane, en route to an engagement during World War II, when his plane disappeared without a trace.

A: *Trouble with Harry, The*
Q: What Alfred Hitchcock film marked the debut of Shirley MacLaine?
W: The trouble with Harry is that he wouldn't stay buried. In the New England woods various circumstances cause various people to find and bury the same body.

A: *True Grit*
Q: What film did John Wayne win his only Oscar for?
W: This was the 1969 film which took place in the Old West and in which a young girl wanting to avenge the death of her murdered father seeks the aid of a hard-drinking old marshal. Wayne played Rooster Cogburn.

A: **trumpet, The**
Q: What instrument does Miles Davis play?
W: Davis' trumpet playing was sensitive, understated, and lyrical. It was the very essence of cool jazz. Between 1951 and 1960 Davis received top honors in polls conducted by *Down Beat*, *Metronome*, and *Playboy* magazines.

A: **Twenty-nine**
Q: What track does the "Chattanooga Choo Choo" leave Pennsylvania Station on?
W: This is from the famous Glenn Miller song. Other popular "swing" songs of the 1930s by Glenn Miller included "Moonlight Serenade" and "In the Mood."

A: **"Twist, The"**
Q: What was the only single to go to the top of the charts twice, in 1959 and 1961?
W: This song was made popular by Chubby Checker. The "twist" fad started in the Peppermint Lounge in New York.

A: **Two**
Q: How many years was Paul Bryan given to live on "Run For Your Life"?
W: The doctors told Bryan (Ben Gazzara) that he had two years to live on the TV series "Run for Your Life." (Even though the series lasted *three* years!)

A: **Tyrone Power**
Q: Who portrayed the emasculated Jake Barnes in *The Sun Also Rises*?
W: This 1957 film takes place in Paris after World War I. Power plays an impotent journalist who meets a nymphomaniac lady of title, and they and their odd group of friends have various saddening adventures around Europe. The film also starred Ava Gardner and Errol Flynn.

A: **U.N.C.L.E.**
Q: What organization did Illya Kuryakin work for?
W: David McCallum played the Russian agent in the TV series "The Man From U.N.C.L.E." He co-starred with Robert Vaughn (as Napoleon Solo) and Leo G. Carroll (as Alexander Waverly). U.N.C.L.E. stood for United Network Command for Law and Enforcement.

A: **U.N.C.L.E.**
Q: What organization did Mr. Waverly assign agents for?
W: Leo G. Carroll played Alexander Waverly, head of the United Network Command for Law and Enforcement.

A: **United Artists**
Q: What corporation was founded by Charlie Chaplin, Mary Pickford, Douglas Fairbanks, and D.W. Griffith in 1919?
W: Chaplin and Griffith wanted to make sure that their films would reach the screen exactly as they intended and to have total artistic control over all creative functions of their films, so (together with Pickford and Fairbanks) they founded United Artists.

A: **vast wasteland, A**
Q: What did FCC chairman Newton Minow declare TV to be on May 9, 1961?
W: Minow said, to a room filled with broadcast executives, "I invite you to sit down in front of your television set when your station goes on the air and stay there without a book, magazine, newspaper, profit-and-loss sheet, or ratings book to distract you, and keep your eyes glued to that set until the station signs off. I can assure you that you will observe a vast wasteland."

A: **Vera, Chuck, Dave**
Q: Who are the three grandchildren in The Beatles' hit "When I'm 64"?
W: It was one of many Beatle hits. Their first hit was "Love Me Do" in October 1962. The Beatles had more number 1 records than any other artist or group — 20.

A: **Veronica Lake**
Q: Who was "the Peekaboo Girl"?
W: Veronica Lake got her nickname from the 1942 movie *Star Spangled Rhythm*. Lake, Dorothy Lamour and Paulette Goddard performed "A Sweater, a Sarong, and a Peekaboo Song" dance number in the film.

A: **"Virginian, The"**
Q: What was the first TV western to run 90 minutes?
W: The TV series starred James Drury. His character was played in the movies by Dustin Farnum (1914), Gary Cooper (1929), and Joel McCrea (1945). He was the hero of a 1902 Western novel and was known only by that name. Famous line: "When you call me that, *smile!*"

A: **Vivien Leigh**
Q: Who won Oscars for her roles in *Gone with the Wind* and *A Streetcar Named Desire*?
W: Leigh won in 1939 for her portrayal of Scarlet O'Hara in *Gone with the Wind*, and in 1951 as Blanch DuBois in *A Streetcar Named Desire*.

A: **W.C. Fields**
Q: What comedian made his debut in *Pool Sharks* in 1915?
W: His real name is William Claude Dukinfield. Here are a few plumes from the Great One: "A woman drove me to drink, and I never had the courtesy to thank her!" and "What contemptible scoundrel stole the cork from my lunch?"

A: **W.C. Fields**
Q: Who asked aghast: "Who put the pineapple juice in my pineapple juice"?
W: W.C. Fields was a comedian famous for his love of liquor. He appeared in some films with child actor Baby LeRoy, who often "stole the scene" when they worked together. Fields once deliberately got the child drunk by spiking his orange juice with hard liquor. He then triumphantly bellowed, "Send him home! The kid's no trouper."

A: **W.C. Fields**
Q: Who declared: "I think I'll go out and milk the elk"?
W: This great film comedian began his career as a juggler. He starred in *The Bank Dick*, *My Little Chickadee*, *Tillie's Punctured Romance*, and *Never Give a Sucker an Even Break*. He has shown his disdain for children, dogs, bankers, and foreigners and shown his preference for gambling and booze.

A: **W.C. Fields**
Q: Who played Humpty Dumpty in the 1933 film *Alice in Wonderland*?
W: There were several "name" actors in cameo roles in the 1933 film. Some of them were Charlotte Henry as Alice (the role originally assigned to Ida Lupino), Gary Cooper as the White Knight, Edward Everett Horton as the Mad Hatter, Richard Arlen as the Cheshire Cat, and Cary Grant as the Mock Turtle.

A: **W.C. Fields**
Q: Who said: "A woman drove me to drink, and I never had the courtesy to thank her"?
W: This is from Fields' movie *Never Give a Sucker an Even Break*. Fields is asked, "You know, Uncle Bill, I've been thinking. Why didn't you ever marry?" He replies, "I was in love with a beautiful blonde once, dear. She drove me to drink. That's the one thing I'm indebted to her for."

A: **W.C. Fields**
Q: Who said: "What contemptible scoundrel stole the cork from my lunch?"?
W: Fields made his debut in *Pool Sharks* in 1915. He is remembered for other memorable lines such as "Anyone who hates children and dogs can't be all bad."

A: **"Wake Up, Little Susie"**
Q: What Everly Brothers song was banned in Boston?
W: "Wake Up, Little Susie" was initially controversial because Susie and her date were "sleeping" at the movie. Two of the Everly Brothers' songs, "Wake Up, Little Susie" and "Bye Bye Love" went gold in 1957.

A: **Wally**
Q: What was the name of Beaver Cleaver's brother?
W: Tony Dow played Wally Cleaver on the late-50s TV show, "Leave It to Beaver." Although the show focused on Beaver's problems, Wally had his also. His main problem was that he was old enough to be interested in girls, but too young to do anything about it. "Aaw, Beav!"

A: **Wally Cox**
Q: Who played Mr. Peepers?
W: Cox played Robinson J. Peepers, a quiet slow-tempered high school biology teacher in the small midwestern town of Jefferson City. The show was used as a replacement series by NBC in the 1952-53 season. The humor in "Mr. Peepers" developed from just slightly exaggerated situations that the soft-spoken Peepers encountered. The program also starred Tony Randall and Marion Lorne. At the end of the 1955 season, its last, the mild-mannered Peepers summoned the courage to ask the school nurse Nancy Remington (Patricia Benoit) to marry him.

ENTERTAINMENT

A: Walt Disney
Q: Who was the first voice of Mickey Mouse?
W: Disney was the first voice of the most popular cartoon character ever. Originally drawn by Ub Iwerks, Mickey was originally called "Mortimer Mouse." James McDonald did Mickey's voice after Disney. Mickey was the first "nonhuman" to win an Oscar.

A: Walter and John Huston
Q: What father and son won Oscars for *The Treasure of the Sierra Madre*?
W: Walter Huston starred in the 1948 film and won the Oscar for Best Supporting Actor for his portrayal of Howard, the old prospector. John Huston won two Oscars, one as writer, one as director. The film also starred Humphrey Bogart.

A: Walter Cronkite
Q: Who hosted "The Twentieth Century"?
W: Cronkite hosted this Sunday afternoon show that dealt with topical reports on news and sports.

A: Walter Matthau
Q: Who played the coach in the film *The Bad News Bears*?
W: Matthau played Morris Buttermaker, the beer-drinking ex-ballplayer who decides to coach a Little League team of tough kids. This 1976 film also starred Vic Morrow, Joyce Van Patten, and Tatum O'Neal.

A: Walter Winchell
Q: Who narrated "The Untouchables" for $25,000 an episode?
W: Walter Winchell, the New York newspaperman, was with the *New York Daily Mirror* for 34 years. He spoke at a rate of 197 words per minute.

A: "War of the Worlds"
Q: What Orson Welles radio play opened in the Meridian Room of the Hotel Park Plaza?
W: On Halloween night 1938, Welles and his Mercury Theater of the Air dramatized the H.G. Wells' fantasy so realistically that millions of Americans became genuinely frightened, and thousands were panic-striken.

A: Warren Beatty
Q: Who did Carly Simon allegedly have in mind when she wrote "You're So Vain"?
W: You're So Vain" was originally titled "Bless You, Ben" but Simon felt it was too sad so she scrapped the lyrics but kept the melody. When the song was first released, everyone wanted to know who it was about. A disc jockey in Los Angeles even ran a contest and had his listeners phone in their vote. Some of the finalists were Kris Kristofferson, Mick Jagger, and hubby James Taylor. She finally admitted some years later that it was Beatty.

A: Warren Beatty
Q: Who produced and starred in *Shampoo*?
W: This 1975 sex farce was also co-written by Beatty. He played George Roundy, a Beverly Hills hairdresser who seduces his most glamorous clients. The film also starred Julie Christie, Lee Grant, Goldie Hawn, and Jack Warden.

A: Wayne and Shuster
Q: What Canadian comedy team made the most appearances on "The Ed Sullivan Show"?
W: They appeared more than anyone on the longest running TV variety show. Originally called "Toast of the Town," "The Ed Sullivan Show" ran from 1948 to 1971. Between 1958 and 1971 Wayne and Shuster appeared 67 times. Sullivan liked them so much that he gave them carte blanche on their material, something he rarely did. Johnny Wayne and Frank Shuster were Canada's best loved comedy team. They did try to go it alone on their own comedy series in the U.S., but it failed.

A: "Wedding March, The"
Q: What march did Felix Mendelssohn compose?
W: "The Wedding March" is still the most popular song at weddings today. So he's the guy who aptly termed it a march!

A: "Welcome Back, Kotter"
Q: What TV show did John Sebastian sing the theme for?
W: In the show Gabe Kaplan played a young teacher who accepted a post at his old high school in Brooklyn, to teach a special remedial class of disruptive juvenile delinquents nicknamed the "sweathogs." The show also starred John Travolta, Robert Hegyes, and Ron Palillo.

A: "We'll Meet Again"
Q: What song is heard as the bombs go off at the end of *Dr. Strangelove*?
W: This 1964 film was directed by Stanley Kubrick. Slim Pickens rode the bomb cowboy-style all the way down. The film also starred Peter Sellers (in a triple role), George C. Scott, and Sterling Hayden.

A: West Virginia
Q: What state does John Denver call his mountain momma?
W: This is from Denver's song "Country Roads." His real name is Henry John Deutchendorf. His other popular songs are "Rocky Mountain High" and "Annie's Song".

A: "What's My Line?"
Q: What game show had Arlene Francis as a permanent panelist?
W: This TV game show ran from 1950 to 1965 and then in syndication from 1968 to 1973. Other panelists were Dorothy (no chin) Kilgallen, Bennet Cerf, and guests such as Steve Allen.

A: *What's New Pussycat*
Q: What film featured Woody Allen as the wardrobe man in a strip club?
W: Allen, who also wrote the screenplay for the 1965 film, played Victor Shakapopolis. It is a sex comedy about a fashion editor who becomes distracted by beautiful girls.

A: *What's Up, Tiger Lily?*
Q: What did Woody Allen call the Japanese gangster film he dubbed into English as a comedy?
W: A producer from American International Pictures offered Allen $75,000 to re-edit and write a new soundtrack for the Japanese "James Bond-type" movie in 1966. The movie tells the story of Phil Moscowitz and his search for a certain recipe for egg salad, because it is written that "he who has the best recipe for egg salad shall rule over heaven and earth." Allen and his crew dubbed gags over scenes of the Japanese gangsters.

A: "Whiter Shade of Pale"
Q: What song mentions one of the vestal virgins?
W: It was a hit in 1967 by the group Procul Harum. Unfortunately it was just about their only hit. Procul Harum is garbled Latin for "far from these things," and its members included Keith Reid, Matthew Fisher, Gary Brooker, and Robin Trower.

A: Wicked Witch of the East, The
Q: Which witch is flattened by a house in *The Wizard of Oz*?
W: It is from this witch that Dorothy removes the ruby slippers. The 1939 film starred Judy Garland as Dorothy, Jack Haley as the Tin Woodsman, Ray Bolger as the Scarecrow, Bert Lahr as the Cowardly Lion and Margaret Hamilton as the Wicked Witch of the West.

A: Will Rogers
Q: Who was credited with saying: "I never met a man I didn't like"?
W: Rogers was the most beloved figure of his time. He was a vaudeville performer, a silent and sound movie film star, a radio performer, and a newspaper columnist. Nearly five decades after his death people still recall his shy grin and easy manner. He's known for other quotes such as, "I'd rather be right than Republican," "Nobody but an Indian can pronounce *Oologah*" and "My ancestors didn't come on the Mayflower, but they met the boat."

A: William Boyd
Q: Who played Hopalong Cassidy?
W: The episodes were based on cowboy hero William Cassidy in novels written by Clarence E. Milford. Prior to choosing Boyd to play Cassidy (in the movie), James Gleason and David Niven were considered. Cassidy's horse was named Topper.

A: William Gilbert
Q: Who was Arthur Sullivan's collaborator?
W: The successful team of Gilbert and Sullivan is responsible for such stage classics as *H.M.S. Pinafore* and *The Pirates of Penzance*. Many other composers used Gilbert and Sullivan as models when writing musical theater in the late 1800s.

A: William Randolph Hearst's
Q: Whose life was the movie *Citizen Kane* based on?
W: The resemblance between Orson Welles' character Charles Foster Kane and newspaper tycoon William Randolph Hearst fueled the nastiest controversy that had ever involved a motion picture studio.

A: Wimpy
Q: Who was fond of saying: "I will gladly pay you Tuesday for a hamburger today"?
W: Wimpy (J. Wellington Wimpy) was Popeye's hungry friend who was always munching on a hamburger. Wimpy was played on radio by Charles Lawrence.

A: *Wings*
Q: What was the first film and only silent movie to win the Best Picture Oscar?
W: It starred Charles "Buddy" Rogers and Clara Bow. Gary Cooper also appeared in the movie. It beat *The Last Command*, *The Racket*, *Seventh Heaven*, and *The Way of All Flesh* to take the Best Picture award for 1928.

A: Wishbone
Q: What was the name of the cook on "Rawhide"?

W: This TV western series starred Steve Raines as Quince, Clint Eastwood as Rowdy Yates, and Paul Brinegar as Wishbone. "Rawhide" was one of the many westerns that emphasized the strong, silent types. Others were: "Wanted: Dead or Alive," "Lawman," and "The Texan."

A: "Wizard, The"
Q: What Bally pinball machine appeared in the movie *Tommy*?
W: This was the 1975 film of a deaf, mute, and blind kid who sure played a mean pinball. The music is by Pete Townsend and the Who. Also starring were Roger Daltray, Ann-Margret, Oliver Reed, Elton John, Eric Clapton, and Keith Moon.

A: WJM-TV
Q: What TV station did Mary Richards work for?
W: This was a fictional TV station (Channel 12) set in Minneapolis on the TV series "The Mary Tyler Moore Show". The six clocks in the newsroom were, left to right, for each of these cities: Tokyo, Los Angeles, Chicago, Minneapolis-St. Paul, New York, and London.

ENTERTAINMENT

A: **Wolfgang Mozart**
Q: Who composed "Twinkle, Twinkle, Little Star" at the age of five?
W: "Twinkle, Twinkle, Little Star" was adapted from Mozart's original theme by Ben Oaklan, and the words were written by Herb Magidson in 1936. It was introduced in the motion picture *Hats-Off*.

A: **Wolfman Jack**
Q: What's the pseudonym of disc jockey Robert Smith?
W: Wolfman Jack's program is syndicated to 1,453 radio stations, give or take a few. It began on radio station XERP in Mexico.

A: **Wolverton Mountain**
Q: Where does Clifton Clowers live?
W: This is from the song "Wolverton Mountain." The words and music were done by Merle Kilgore and Claude King.

A: **Woody Allen**
Q: What comedian was born Allen Stewart Konigsberg?
W: Woody was born in 1935. He became an American nightclub comedian, playwright, and filmmaker. Filmmaking credits include *Annie Hall*, *Manhattan*, *Bananas*, and *Zelig*. Some of his more chaotic appearances have been in *What's New Pussycat*, *Casino Royale*, *What's Up Tiger Lily*, and *Take the Money and Run*.

A: **Woody Guthrie**
Q: Who wote more than 1,000 songs, including "This Land is Your Land"?
W: He used personal experiences to write and sing songs about the depression, injustice, poverty, dust storms, intolerance, exploitation, migrant workers, unionization, and fascism. He wrote 1,000 or more songs about what he had seen or experienced in waterfront cafes, dives, Hoovervilles, and migrant camps. Some of his other songs were "So Long, It's Been Good to Know Ya," "Union Maid," and "Hard Traveling." His autobiography, *Bound for Glory*, was made into a movie.

A: **Xavier Cugat**
Q: What bandleader always carried a chihuahua under his arm?
W: The "Rhumba King", as he is dubbed by his adoring public likes to collect chihuahuas. If you collect 'em you have to keep them somewhere! Cugat started his career as a concert violinst with Enrico Caruso. Before becoming a band leader, he was a cartoonist.

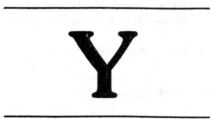

A: **"Yellow Rose of Texas, The"**
Q: Who beat the belles of Tennessee?
W: The song was first published in 1853. The author is identified simply as "J.K." The song, popular as a Confederate marching song, was successfully revived in 1955 and became a best-selling recording.

A: *Yellow Submarine*
Q: What Beatles movie featured the Blue Meanies?
W: This cartoon movie featured the speaking and singing voices of the Beatles. The Lonely Hearts Club Band was engaged in a war between the folks of Pepperland and the Blue Meanies. Old Fred was the Lord Admiral of Pepperland and the captain of the yellow submarine. The crew consisted of the Beatles and Jeremy Hillary Boob. The story was written by Erich Segal.

A: **Yoda**
Q: What's the name of Luke Skywalker's troll-like advisor in *The Empire Strikes Back*?
W: Yoda was a creation of Jim Henson and Frank Oz (of the Muppets). Yoda also made an appearance in *Return of the Jedi*. Yoda, at one time a great Jedi knight, was Obi-Wan-Kenobi's teacher.

A: **Yogi Bear**
Q: Who's smarter than the average bear?
W: Yogi, a cartoon bear, whose voice is that of Daws Butler, lives in Jellystone National Park. His hobby is stealing "pic-a-nic" baskets. His little sidekick is Boo Boo Bear (whose voice is that of Don Messick). Yogi was featured in a Hanna-Barbera cartoon from 1958 to 1960.

A: **You ain't heard nothin' yet, folks**
Q: What were the first words spoken on a film sound track?
W: These words were spoken by Al Jolson in the 1927 film *The Jazz Singer*, the first talkie. The whole line is "Wait a minute, wait a minute, you ain't heard nothin' yet!."

A: **You ate it, Ralph**
Q: What TV commerical line followed: "I can't believe I ate the whole thing"?
W: This Alka Seltzer commerical starred Milton Ross, an overstuffed man who states, "I can't believe I ate the whole thing." His wife yells, "You ate it, Ralph."

A: **Yukon King**
Q: What was the name of Sergeant Preston of the Yukon's lead dog?
W: Yukon King was Sergeant Preston's Alaskan husky in the TV series "Sergeant Preston of the Yukon." On radio it was known as "Challenge of the Yukon". King was raised by a wolf named Three Toes.

Z

A: Zero
Q: How many instruments accompany someone singing "a cappella"?
W: *A capella* is defined as "in the church or chapel style," which is without instrumental accompaniment.

A: zipper, A
Q: What runs up and down on the Rolling Stones' "Sticky Fingers" album cover?
W: The album was a grand celebration of jet-set debauchery and chic demonic postures. A rather prominent zipper is pictured on an unidentified bod in tight jeans on the album cover.

A: Zorro
Q: What was the secret identity of Don Diego de la Vega?
W: Zorro was a California Robin Hood type created by Johnston McCulley in the story "The Curse of Capistrano," retitled "The Mark of Zorro." In the movies he was played by Douglas Fairbanks, Sr., Tyrone Power, and Clayton Moore. On TV he was played by Guy Williams. The name means "fox" in Spanish. In the novel Zorro carves the letter "Z" on the cheeks of his foe; this was toned down in movies and on TV. Bernardo, his deaf-mute servant, was the only person to know of Zorro's identity.

A: Zsa Zsa Gabor
Q: Who had the 1936 Miss Hungary title taken away from her because she was underage?
W: The minimum age was 16 and Zsa Zsa was only 15. Had she won she would have been awarded $1,000, ten new dresses, and a trip to France to compete for Miss Europe. When the judges learned her age, she was then declared first runner-up and was awarded a bottle of perfume.

A: Zsa Zsa Gabor
Q: Who has sisters named Eva and Magda?
W: Their mother's name is Jolie. Zsa Zsa is famous for having several husbands, and Eva is remembered as Mrs. Douglas on TV's "Green Acres."

A: Zsa Zsa Gabor
Q: Who said: "I've never hated a man enough to give him his diamonds back"?
W: It seems as if she has trouble hating men, period. Her husbands include: Burhan Belge, Conrad Hilton (of Hilton Hotels), George Sanders, Herbert L. Hutner, and Joshua Cosden.

# #

A: 23rd, The
Q: What century was the setting for TV's "Star Trek"?
W: "Star Trek" was the science fiction Hugo award-winning TV series created by Gene Roddenberry. It starred William Shatner (Captain Kirk), Leonard Nimoy (Mr. Spock), DeForest Kelley ("Bones" McCoy), and James Doohan (Scotty). The series lasted from 1966 to 1969. When it was canceled by NBC, thousands of letters were sent in protest, including letters from the entire Princeton graduating class.

A: 44 Magnum
Q: What kind of gun does the movies' Dirty Harry pack?
W: Clint Eastwood played the San Francisco plainclothes cop Harry Callahan who packs a .44 Colt Magnum and who is famous for his "feel lucky, punk?" speech in the movie *Dirty Harry*. The role was originally to be played by Frank Sinatra; however, Sinatra hurt his wrist and was unable to take the role.

A: $100
Q: How much was the secret word worth on Groucho Marx's "You Bet Your Life"?
W: $100 was the prize won by the pair of contestants one of whom said the secret "word" held by the duck on "You Bet Your Life." Each contestant won $50. "It's a common word, something you see everyday…"

A: 555
Q: What's the most common telephone exchange number on TV?
W: This is a neutral and official exchange established by phone companies and is often used for fictitous numbers.

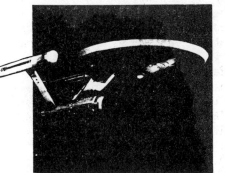

A: 1962
Q: What year was the setting for *American Graffiti*?
W: "Where were you in '62?" The 1973 George Lucas film takes place in 1962 California where four young men, two of whom were about to leave for college, gather for a night's girl-chasing and police-baiting. It starred Richard Dreyfuss, Ron Howard, Paul LeMat, and Charles Martin Smith.

A: ***2001: A Space Odyssey***
Q: What film featured the line: "Open the pod bay door, Hal"?
W: "Hal" is the H A L 9000 computer of spaceship *Discovery I* in the 1968 film. It became operational at the Hall Plant, Urbana, Illinois, on Jan. 12, 1997. Hal's voice is that of Douglas Rain. HAL stands for Heuristic and Algorithmic (two learning systems). HAL is IBM stepped down one letter alphabetically!

A: ***"2001" A Space Odyssey***
Q: What 1968 film featured music from Richard Strauss' "Also Sprach Zarathrustra"?
W: It was the most striking part of the musical score. The film's message: "From ape to modern space mankind has striven to reach the unattainable."

A: **4077th, The**
Q: What MASH unit does Hawkeye Pierce operate in?
W: The inspiration for the Mobil Army Surgical Hospital unit in the TV series M*A*S*H* was the actual 8055th MASH unit in Korea.

A: **5,000-watt station in Fresno, California; A**
Q: Where did it all begin for Ted Baxter?
W: "It all began at a 5,000 watt radio station in Fresno, California" was always Ted Baxter's opening line when he'd start to overdramatize his career. It was his first broadcasting job, but he never said what station it was. Ted Baxter (Ted Knight) was the egotistical newscaster on the TV series "The Mary Tyler Moore Show."

A: **$64,000**
Q: How much did Dr. Joyce Brothers win answering questions on "The $64,000 Question"?
W: The TV show ran from 1955 to 1958. Dr. Brothers' winning category was boxing. Barbara Feldon also won $64,000 in the category of Shakespeare. Jack Benny only won $64! The story has it that Joyce chose boxing because of its relatively short history, which meant she could study the category more fully than any of the others.

HISTORY

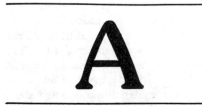

A

A: **A-bomb on Nagasaki**
Q: What did "Bock's Car" drop in 1945?
W: Nagasaki was the second target of the atomic bomb. "Bock's Car" was the B-29, piloted by Major Charles Sweeney, that dropped the bomb on Aug. 9, 1945.

A: **Aaron Burr**
Q: What U.S. vice-president killed Alexander Hamilton in a duel?
W: Burr was the victim of Hamilton's animosity three times. On the last occasion when Burr felt specific charges were denigrating his character, he demanded an explanation. Not satisfied with the response from Hamilton, Burr challenged Hamilton to a duel in Weehawken, New Jersey on July 11, 1804, in which Hamilton was killed.

A: **Abbie Hoffman**
Q: Who called himself an orphan of America at the Chicago Seven trial?
W: Feb. 20, 1970: Jerry Rubin, Tom Hayden, Rennie Davis, David Dellinger, Lee Weiner, John Froines, along with Hoffman were convicted of a conspiracy to cross state lines to incite a riot at the Democratic National Convention of 1968.

A: **Abdication**
Q: What was the one-word headline of *The London Star* on Dec. 10, 1936?
W: Edward VIII abdicated the English throne to marry American-born divorcee Mrs. Wallace Warfield Spencer Simpson and was succeeded by his brother, George VI.

A: **Abraham Lincoln**
Q: What U.S. president declared: "The ballot is stronger than the bullet"?
W: The full quote made in 1863 is, "Among free men there can be no successful appeal from the ballot to the bullet; and those who take such appeal are sure to lose their cause and pay the costs."

A: **Abraham Lincoln**
Q: What U.S. president was known as "the Rail-splitter"?
W: Lincoln gained what education he could while his family moved from Kentucky to Indiana and then to Illinois. While studying law he worked in a store, managed a mill, surveyed, and split rails.

A: **Abraham Lincoln**
Q: Who was the first U.S. president born outside the original 13 states?
W: He was born on Feb. 12, 1809, in Kentucky (Hardin County, now Larue). Kentucky was added to the Union June 1, 1792, making it the 15th state.

A: **Abraham Lincoln**
Q: Who was the tallest U.S. president?
W: In Lincoln's own words "...it may be said I am, in height, 6ft.-4in. nearly; lean in flesh, weighing on an average 180 pounds; dark complexion, with coarse black hair and gray eyes."

A: **Abraham Lincoln's**

Q: What president's ghost is said to haunt the White House?

W: Lincoln took his dreams seriously, often discussing them with his wife. On the day of his assassination he discussed one dream with his cabinet, in which he had seen himself sailing "in an indescribable vessel and moving rapidly toward an indistinct shore". The week before his assassination he had a dream in which he walked through the White House trying to locate the source of some sobbing. In the East Room he found a casket draped in black, and when he asked who was dead, the guard replied "The President". Several have "seen" his ghost. A maid of Eleanor Roosevelt related that she saw Lincoln sitting on the edge of a bed taking his shoes off. Queen Wilhelmina of The Netherlands also "saw" him during a state visit in 1945.

A: **Abraham Lincoln's**

Q: Whose funeral train traveled from Washington, D.C., to Springfield, Illinois?

W: Lincoln died on April 15, 1865. The funeral train brought the body to rest in Oak Ridge Cemetery near Springfield, Illinois.

A: **Abscam**

Q: What FBI operation sent agents disguised as Arabs fishing for crooked congressmen?

W: After a two year undercover operation called ABSCAM (for Arab scam), public officials were implicated on Feb. 2, 1980.

A: **Adam Clayton Powell**

Q: What U.S. Congressman said: "Keep the faith, baby"?

W: Powell, a Congressman from Harlem, was convicted of libel in a very publicized suit, during which he would not appear in court. Because of the warrants out for his arrest, he could not campaign; however, he was re-elected by a ten to one majority. He was known as "Black Moses" and was quoted in 1962 as being the "most misunderstood public figure in America."

A: **Adams, Harrison, Johnson, Roosevelt**

Q: What four surnames have been shared by more that one U.S. president?

W: John Adams was the second President; his son John Quincy Adams was the sixth. William Henry Harrison was the ninth President; Benjamin Harrison the 23rd. Andrew Johnson was the 17th President; Lyndon B. Johnson the 36th. Theodore Roosevelt was the 23rd President; Franklin D. Roosevelt the 26th.

A: **Adlai Stevenson**

Q: What Democratic nominee did Dwight Eisenhower defeat both times he was elected president?

W: In 1952 it was Ike's 442 electoral votes to Stevenson's 89; in 1956 Ike had 457 electoral votes to Stevenson's 73. Ike won nearly 58 percent of the popular vote in 1956.

A: **Adlai Stevenson**

Q: Who did the talking for the U.S. at the United Nations during the Cuban Missile Crisis?

W: On Oct. 22, 1962, Kennedy served notice that the U.S. was willing to risk war. From August to November of 1962 the U.S. blockaded Cuba; the blockade was lifted November 20, 1962.

A: **Admiral Horatio Nelson**

Q: Who was known as "the Hero of Trafalgar"?

W: On Oct. 21, 1805, Admiral Pierre de Villeneuve (French) lost 18 ships; Nelson lost none, but he was killed in action. The battle gave the British control of the seas for a century. Nelson's statue stands in Trafalgar Square, London.

A: **Admiral Robert E. Peary**

Q: Who allegedly led the first expedition to reach the North Pole?

W: On April 7, 1909 Peary discovered the North Pole. Dr. Frederick Cook claimed he had reached the pole a year earlier. The dispute was finally resolved in December 1909 in an official report issued by the University of Copenhagen, after which Peary received his just reward.

A: **Adolf Eichmann**

Q: Who lived in a house on Garibaldi Street in Buenos Aires?

W: Eichmann was the man who planned and organized the extermination of the Jews during World War II. He was captured May 11, 1960 in Argentina by Isser Harel, the head of Israeli Secret Services. Eichmann's Argentine identification card read "Ricardo Klement, single, a mechanic by trade, born at Bolzano of a German mother".

A: **Adolf Hitler**

Q: Who danced a jig at Compiegne, France, in 1940?

W: The Fuhrer was celebrating the signing of the armistice on June 25, 1940 and therefore, the fall of France. Hitler's forces broke through the west's defenses on May 10, 1940. Hitler was not always so happy though. He at one point suffered a sudden loss of confidence at a crucial moment and imposed a two-day halt on the advance just as his spearhead pierced the French defense and had an open path in front of it. One story reports he did not dance a jig, but merely gave a little jump of pleasure and the media "looped" it to look like a jig!

A: **Adolf Hitler**
Q: Who said: "The victor will never be asked if he told the truth"?
W: He's also known for such witty remarks as, "The broad mass of a nation will more easily fall victim to a big lie than to a small one." In addition, he is quoted as saying, "I go the way that Providence dictates with the assurance of a sleepwalker" and "It is the last territorial claim which I have to make in Europe," referring to the Sudetenland.

A: **African slaves**
Q: What did Englishman John Hawkins begin selling to New World colonists in 1562?
W: Sir John Hawkins was an English sea captain who, backed by certain English financiers, set forth in 1562 with 100 men in three small ships to round up 300 blacks from Sierra Leone. He then sailed to Hispaniola and exchanged them for colonial produce. A year later he embarked on a second voyage with 170 men and four ships again to capture as many natives as he could carry. He proceeded to peddle them in the Spanish Islands, then returned home with his gold and silver. On his third voyage, after again exchanging his cargo of blacks for more gold, silver and other valuables, his ships were attacked by a Spanish fleet of 13 vessels. The Spaniards captured his treasures, and Hawkins barely escaped with his life. This incident discouraged English slave trade for nearly a century to follow.

A: **Ajax**
Q: What cleaned like a white tornado?
W: This is from a television commerical in which Ajax was compared to a "white tornado"

A: **Al Capone**
Q: What Chicago citizen once declared: "Public service is my motto"?
W: "Citizen" Capone was born in Naples in 1899. The scarfaced public servant started out on a crooked path as a boy. He quit school after fourth grade and organized a gang of other boys that terrorized others and collected protection money from local grocers in exchange for not pummeling their produce. He eventually went on to take over bootlegging, prostition, and gambling in Illinois and he laid the foundations for the nationwide syndicates as we know them today.

A: **Al Capone's**
Q: What gangster's business card read: "Second hand furniture dealer"?
W: Al ran speakeasies and was implicated in several brutal murders. He was indicted in 1931 by a federal grand jury for income tax evasion and sentenced to 11 years in prison. In 1939 he was released with a case of syphilis. He died in 1947. Anyone who approached his business was told "we ain't open today"! He stocked the storefront at 2220 S. Wabash Street with junk and never tried to sell any of it.

A: **Alamo, The**
Q: What are Texans told to remember?
W: In 1835 the people of Texas revolted against the Mexican government, in an effort to become part of the U.S. The heroic defense of the old fort the Alamo at San Antonio by 183 Texans under W.B. Travis inspired successful efforts at resistance for 13 days. When all but six had been killed, Mexicans took the place by storm and the survivors were shot. The war cry of Texas became, "Remember the Alamo".

A: **Alaska**
Q: What did the U.S. buy for $7.2 million in 1867?
W: On Mar. 30, 1867, Secretary of State Seward bought Alaska from the Russians for less than two cents per acre – $7.2 million. Alaska natives were never consulted about the Seward's Folly!

A: **Alexander Haig**
Q: What non-president said: "I'm in control now, here at the White House"?
W: This misguided quote of Haig's was made on the occasion of President Ronald Reagan's being shot outside a Washington hotel. Haig came under much pressure for assuming that he had the reigns of power. Could it have been that no one ever explained the succession to Mr. Haig of power to the presidency?

A: **Alexander Haig**
Q: Who was Richard Nixon's chief of staff during the final days of Watergate?
W: When Watergate was coming to a head, Haig (for months) regarded himself as a "surrogate" president. All types of decisions were being left up to Haig, not Nixon. With Nixon so preoccupied with saving his own skin, it was Haig who ran the store. He decided what to take to the president and what decisions to make himself. It was to Haig that Nixon finally confessed, "Well, I screwed it up good, real good, didn't I"?

A: **Alexandre Eiffel**
Q: What French engineer built a tower for the 1889 Paris Exposition?
W: The structure is 984 feet high; 1,056 ft. including the television tower. Eiffel, a French engineer born in Dijon, gained his reputation as a bridge builder. The tower cost $1 million to build.

A: **Alf Landon**
Q: What Republican did Franklin Roosevelt beat in the 1936 presidential election?
W: In one of the greatest landslides in American history, FDR carried every state in the Union except Maine and Vermont. Final electoral tally was 523 to 8. The popular vote saw a record plurality of nearly 11 million.

HISTORY

A: **Alger Hiss**
Q: What U.S. state department official was charged with spying for the Soviet Union in 1949?
W: The House Un-American Activities Committee was given film, which had been concealed in a pumpkin in Whittaker Chambers' Maryland pumpkin patch. Chambers claimed Hiss had given him the filmed documents about a communist conspiracy in Washington. The jury believed Chambers and Hiss went to prison for perjury. Congressman Richard M. Nixon forced the confrontation between Chambers and Hiss leading to this perjury charge.

A: **Amelia Earhart**
Q: Who was the first woman to receive the Distinguished Flying Cross?
W: She flew alone from Harbor Grace, Newfoundland to Ireland in approximately 15 hours on May 20-21, 1932.

A: **American GIs**
Q: Who were "overpaid, oversexed, and over here"?
W: The term G.I. was first used in World War II as an abbreviation for "General Issue", a term for clothing and equipment issued to service men. It came into general use to describe the men as well.

A: **Anastasia**
Q: What daughter of Czar Nicholas II is said to have escaped death in the Russian Revolution?
W: Anastasia was said to have escaped the July 16, 1918 execution of her family. After living under cover for many years, she was believed to have married an American and moved to the U.S. Since 1920 several women have claimed to be Anastasia, legal heir to the Romanov fortune held in Swiss banks; however, none of these claims has proven to be legitimate.

A: **Anastasio Somoza**
Q: What Nicaraguan strongman was overthrown by the Sandinista guerrillas?
W: Somoza was president of Nicaragua from 1937 to 1947 and again from 1950 to 1956. He strongarmed his way into office despite charges from the Organization of American States investigations reigned as dictator until Sept. 21, 1956 when he was shot. His son Luis succeeded him to the presidency.

A: **"Anchors Aweigh"**
Q: What's the U.S. Navy hymn?
W: "'Eternal Father'' is also sometimes referred to as the navy hymn. "Anchors Aweigh" was first published in 1906. The words were written by A.H. Miles and R. Lovell, the music was composed by Charles A. Zimmerman. The Marine's Hymn is "From the Halls of Montezuma" and the field artillery march is "Caissons Go Rolling Along".

A: *Andrea Doria*, **The**
Q: What ship collided with the Swedish liner *Stockholm* on July 26, 1956?
W: A survivor, Linda Morgan the "Miracle Girl", was aboard the *Andrea Doria* when that ship collided with the *Stockholm*. She was found alive on the *Stockholm* when the ships separated and the *Andrea Doria* sank.

A: **Andrew Johnson**
Q: Who succeeded Abraham Lincoln as president?
W: Johnson became President after Lincoln's assassination in 1865. He served until Ulysses Grant was elected in 1868.

A: **Andrew Johnson**
Q: Who was the only U.S. president to be impeached?
W: Not exactly right. Johnson was impeached by the House, but not the Senate. Johnson's impeachment was for attempting to remove his disloyal Secretary of War, in defiance ot the Tenure of Office Act that required senatorial concurrence for such dismissals. The House impeached him for this and other reasons; however, in the Senate, the impeachment proceeding fell one vote short of the two thirds required for conviction.

A: **Andrew Young**
Q: Who was Jimmy Carter's controversial ambassador to the United Nations?
W: The outspoken Young made a series of controversial comments that periodically resulted in embarrassment to former President Carter. Often releasing statements that were in direct opposition to U.S. foreign policy, Young eventually resigned his post, more to Carter's disgrace than to his own. He once referred to Ayatollah Khomeini as a "misunderstood saint".

A: **Andy Warhol**
Q: What pop artist did writer-actress Valerie Solanis shoot with a .32-caliber pistol?
W: Solanis was the founder of S.C.U.M.(Society of Cutting Up Men). She would talk constantly about the complete elimination of the male sex, saying that the result would be an "out of sight, groovy, all female world". She once presented a film script, entitled *Up Your Ass*, for consideration to Warhol. Warhol was shot twice June 4, 1968, by Solanis, with bullets through his stomach, liver, spleen, esophagus, and both lungs. He did survive after five hours of extensive surgery.

A: **Anne Boleyn's**
Q: Which of Henry VIII's wives' last words were: "...my neck is very slender"?
W: Anne Boleyn was the second wife of Henry VIII and mother of Queen Elizabeth I. Anne was originally a maid-in-waiting to Queen Catherine, who was divorced by Henry to make way for Anne. After three years as Queen, Anne was beheaded on a charge of treason.

A: Anne Frank
Q: Who hid in a house at 263 Princengracht, Amsterdam, for two years?
W: Anne Frank, who was Jewish, is known for her revealing diary written while in hiding in the attic of that house during the Nazi occupation of Holland.

A: Anne Morrow
Q: Who married Charles Lindbergh?
W: In 1929, the same year Lindbergh was employed as a technical advisor in aeronautics to the Department of Commerce, he married Anne Morrow. She was the daughter of Dwight Morrow, U.S. Ambassador to Mexico

A: Anne Sullivan
Q: Who was Helen Keller's teacher?
W: Anne Sullivan was an American educator born in Feeding Hills, Massachusettes. She was admitted to Perkins Institute for the blind, since her eyes had been seriously weakened by a childhood infection, underwent a series of operations that partially restored her sight. She learned the manual alphabet and taught by the touch method. In 1905 she married John Macy.

A: Annie Oakley
Q: What cowgirl did Sitting Bull call "Little Sure-shot"?
W: Annie Oakley could shoot a cigarette out from her husband's lips at 30 feet or a dime held between his fingers and thumb. She joined Buffalo Bill's Wild West Show in 1885. During the first year with the show, Sioux Chief Sitting Bull became a true fan. He adopted her as his daughter into the Sioux nation and gave her the nickname "Little Sure-shot".

A: Annie Oakley
Q: What Ohio farmgirl once shot a cigarette from the mouth of Kaiser Wilhelm?
W: Born Phoebe Anne Oakley Mozee, she learned to handle a gun at the age of nine. Her husband was

vaudeville actor Frank E. Butler. The Wild West Show traveled throughout Europe, but Buffalo Bill became jealous of all the attention Annie received, so Annie and Frank went out on their own. In Germany Annie received even more publicity when the Crown Prince insisted she shoot a cigarette from his mouth – this young man grew up to be Kaiser Wilhelm.

A: Apartheid
Q: What's the name of South Africa's racial policy?
W: Any black or colored person is required to carry a number of passes and identifications. One can be thrown in jail without trial if he or she can't produce the required pass. Only members of the white minority (17.5 percent) can run for office or vote in parliamentary elections.

A: Appian Way, The
Q: What was the best chariot route from Rome to Brindisi?
W: It is also the oldest Roman road, originally laid by Appius Claudius from Rome to Capua and afterward extended to Brundisium.

A: Archduke Francis Ferdinand
Q: Who was assassinated at Sarajevo to spark World War I?
W: He was shot by Gavrilo Princip, a high school student, in 1914. Gavrilo and two friends were plotting the assassination when they were overheard by an officer of the Serbian Military Intelligence. They were given guns and grenades by the "Black Hand", a Serbian terrorist group trying to recapture Serbian land seized by other countries. During the Archduke's parade to the city, a grenade was thrown, but a policeman, not the Archduke, was injured. Gavrilo thinking "mission accomplished", went for coffee. From the restaurant he saw the Archduke in his car going to the hospital to see the injured policeman! Gavrilo walked up to the car and shot the Archduke.

A: Argentina
Q: Where did Israeli agents grab Adolf Eichmann?
W: Eichman was arrested by the Allies in 1945, then escaped to Argentina. He was located by Israeli agents in 1960 and tried and hanged in Israel for his role in the mass extermination of the Jews in Germany.

A: *Arizona*, The
Q: What U.S. battleship remained in commission after being sunk?
W: The *Arizona* was sunk on Dec. 7, 1941, (the "Day of Infamy") in Pearl Harbor. Nearly half of the 2,403 Americans killed that day were lost on the *Arizona*. The ship struck by a bomb on her forecastle that penetrated through to the forward magazine, blew up in a sheet of flames. The ship still lies at the bottom of Pearl Harbor and remains in commission as a memorial to the losses America suffered at Pearl Harbor.

A: Arizona, Alaska, Hawaii
Q: What were the last three U.S. states to join the Union?
W: Arizona was admitted as a state on Feb. 14, 1912. Alaska was admitted Jan. 3, 1959; and Hawaii became the 50th state on Aug. 21, 1959.

A: Arlo Guthrie
Q: Who yelled over the microphone at Woodstock: "The New York Thruway is closed, man!"?
W: That's because lots of people were still trying to get to the New York State Rock n' Roll Festival held Aug. 15-17, 1969, on a Bethel, New York, dairy farm. It was financed by John Roberts. Also appearing at the festival were Joe Cocker; Jimi Hendrix; and Crosby, Stills and Nash. The festival was the subject of a documentary movie in 1970.

A: Arthur Miller
Q: What playwright was married to Marilyn Monroe?

HISTORY

W: Arthur Miller was married to Marilyn Monroe from 1956 to 1962. Her other husbands were James Dougherty, 1942 to 1946; and Joe Dimaggio in 1954, for nine months. Miller's plays included *Death of a Salesman* and *The Crucible*, and the screenplay *The Misfits* that he wrote for Marilyn in 1961.

A: "As The World Turns"
Q: What CBS soap opera was interrupted by the bulletin of John F. Kennedy's assassination?
W: It was interrupted by the following news bulletin delivered by Walter Cronkite: "In Dallas, Texas, three shots were fired at President Kennedy's motorcade in downtown Dallas. The first reports say President Kennedy has been seriously wounded by this shooting."

A: **Associated Press, The**
Q: What's the world's largest news agency?
W: The Associated Press unofficially began in May 1848 when representatives of the six major New York dailies met and agreed to form a cooperative, owned by member newspapers, for gathering news. Up until that time the papers had been highly competitive, trying to get the news first, and it became very difficult with only one telegraph wire available for all the New York newspapers.

A: **Atlantic Ocean, The**
Q: What body of water were Ridgway and Blyth the first to row across?
W: *Wrong!* The first transatlantic trip by rowboat was actually accomplished by George Harpo and Frank Samuelson, who left Battery Park, New York, on June 6, 1896, and reached the Scilly Isles off England 54 days later.

A: **attack on Pearl Harbor, The**
Q: What began with the code signal: "Climb Mount Niitaka"?
W: On Dec. 7, 1941, Japanese planes swept in without warning over Oahu and attacked (7:55 A.M.). The bulk of the U.S. Pacific fleet was moored in Pearl Harbor at the time. Losses included 19 naval vessels, 188 aircraft, 2,280 military personnel killed, 1,109 wounded, and 68 civilians killed. On Dec. 8 the U.S. declared war on Japan.

A: **Attica State Prison**
Q: What was stormed by 1,500 state troopers, sheriff's deputies and guards on Sept. 13, 1971?
W: The inmates held the prison for four days and pressed their grievances. Thirty-one prisoners and nine hostages were killed during the retaking. A state appointed committee placed responsibility for the tragedy on Governor Nelson Rockefeller, prison officials, and conditions within the prison system.

A: **Attila**
Q: Who was king of the Huns from 406 to 453?
W: Attila was also called the "Scourge of God". He attacked the Roman provinces in 433 A.D.

A: **Audie Murphy**
Q: Who was the most decorated U.S. soldier of World War II?
W: Murphy was both a soldier and later an actor. Enlisting in the Army in June 1942 when he was 17, he was wounded three times and received a total of 24 medals, his last being the Congressional Medal of Honor. His others include the Distinguished Service Cross, Silver Star with Oak Leaf Cluster, and the Bronze Star. Toward the end of the war in Europe, he single-handedly held off

A: **Australia**
Q: What country accepted 75,000 convicts between 1790 and 1840?
W: The English explorer Captain James Cook explored the east coast of Australia in 1770, when the continent was inhabited by a variety of different tribes. Within years England claimed the entire continent and used it as a penal colony until immigration increased in the 1850s.

a German force of six tanks and some 250 men on June 26, 1945.

A: **Aug. 6, 1945**
Q: What date was Hiroshima bombed?
W: The first atomic bomb used in warfare was dropped on the city of Hiroshima, and an area of 4.5 square miles (60 percent of the city) was wiped out. Two days later another bomb was dropped on the seaport of Nagasaki.

A: **Axis Sally**
Q: Who was the German counterpart to Tokyo Rose?
W: Mildred E. Gillars was the real name of the German "Axis Sally". Rita Louise Zucca was the Italian "Axis Sally". Mildred studied music at Ohio Wesleyan University and went to Germany in the 1920s to further her music education. She was hired by the Germans to broadcast propanganda along with music from a Berlin studio. After the war she was arrested by American authorities, tried, and sentenced to twelve years in prison. She received her bachelors degree in 1973 at the age of 73.

B

A: Baby Face
Q: What was Dillinger gang member George Nelson's nickname?
W: Born Lester Gillis in Chicago, Illinois, in 1908, he was the most bloodthirsty, deathseeking bandit of the public enemy era. He was never called "Baby Face" to his face. After he robbed a Chicago jewelry store in 1931 and was caught a few days later, he was sentenced to from one year to life in Joliet Prison, but escaped on Feb. 17, 1932 and hooked up with Dillinger in 1934. In 1934, Gillis killed FBI agent, Carter Baum, and Gillis himself was killed on Nov. 27, 1934 in one of the wildest gun battles in crime history. It also resulted in the death of two FBI agents. His bullet-ridden body was found on a deserted road in Niles, Illinois, there was a total of seventeen slugs in the body.

A: Baltimore and Ohio
Q: What did the B and O Railroad's initials stand for?
W: It was the first steam railroad, carrying both freight and passengers in 1830.

A: Barbara Bach
Q: Who did Ringo Starr marry in 1981?
W: Bach is a model and movie actress who is most remembered as the shapely Russian agent in the James Bond film, *The Spy Who Loved Me*. She and Starr appeared together as cave dwellers in the prehistoric comedy *Caveman*.

A: Barbara Hutton
Q: Who was "the Poor Little Rich Girl," granddaughter of F.W. Woolworth?
W: Hutton changed husbands as often as her wardrobe. Often depressed, she was plagued by failed marriages. Her first of seven marriages was in June, 1933, to a sheepherder. She retired to the exclusive Beverly Wilshire Hotel in Los Angeles, where she died on May 12, 1979 at the age of 66, still very rich, but never really happy.

A: Barry Goldwater
Q: Who declared in 1964: "Extremism in the defense of liberty is no vice"?
W: ...and "moderation in the pursuit of justice is no virtue." Goldwater was a conservative Republican who ran for president in 1964. He believed in "peace through strength." (Sound familar?) The motto of the Strategic Air Command is "Peace is Our Profession", and Goldwater wanted to "make sure that they have the tools to practice that profession."

A: Barry Goldwater
Q: Who did *The Los Angeles Times* endorse in the 1964 presidential election?
W: Goldwater was the Republican nominee for the office of president in 1964. He was elected to the Senate from the state of Arizona in 1952 and was re-elected in 1958. Goldwater is most remembered for his ultra-conservative views, and he's quoted as once saying "extremism in defense of liberty is no vice."

A: Barry Goldwater
Q: Who used AuH_2O as an election slogan?
W: AuH_2O is the chemical symbol for gold (Au) and water (H_2O).

A: Bastille, The
Q: What was stormed in Paris in 1789?
W: Paris mobs stormed the Bastille, the symbol of Royal Power, on July 14, 1789. It was the beginning of the French Revolution that lasted ten years. The Bastille was King Louis XVI's prison for aristocrats, and when it was stormed only seven prisoners were found inside: four forgers, two madmen, and one Irish Lord imprisoned for 30 years for debts.

A: Battle of the Bulge, The
Q: What was the last major German counteroffensive of World War II?
W: This battle took place in December 1944. It was Hitler's plan to split the Western Allies by ramming two panzer armies through the Ardennes to Antwerp. After the loss of his mobile reserve and some hundreds of tanks and self-propelled guns and the virtual destruction of the Luftwaffe, who lost more than 1,000 aircraft, Hitler was never again able to seize the initiative on a strategic level.

A: Battle of the Little Big Horn
Q: What battle was a horse named Comanche the only losing survivor of?
W: And in recognition of this feat, upon his death Comanche was stuffed and placed in a museum on the site of the battle!

A: Battle of Midway, The
Q: What 1942 naval engagement saw the sinking of four Japanese aircraft carriers?
W: The epic battle took place June 4, 1942. The four carriers that sank were the *Akogi*, the *Kaga*, the *Soryu*, and the *Hiryu*. The U.S. carrier, *Yorktown*, was also sunk. The Japanese also lost 330 aircraft and a heavy carrier, but the U.S. lost only one carrier and 150 aircraft. This battle was the scene of the most extraordinarily quick change of fortune known in naval history.

A: Battle of New Orleans, The
Q: What battle of the War of 1812 was fought after the Treaty of Ghent was signed?
W: The Treaty of Ghent, which was signed on Dec. 24, 1814, ended the War of 1812; however word must not have reached Andrew Jackson for he continued to fight! He was victorious over the British at New Orleans on Jan. 8, 1815.

A: Battle of the Somme, The
Q: What World War I battle saw 60,000 troops killed on the first day?

W: The British lost over 400,000, the French 200,000, and the Germans about 450,000, all with no strategic results from July through November.

A: **Bay of Pigs, The**
Q: Where did the 2506 Brigade come ashore on April 17, 1961?
W: Cuba was invaded by an estimated 1,200 anti-Castro exiles aided by the U.S.; the invasion failed when President Kennedy refused it air support under Soviet and Latin American pressure.

A: **Bay of Pigs fiasco, The**
Q: What did John F. Kennedy consider his greatest blunder in office?
W: On April 17, 1961, 1,200 Cuban refugees landed at the Bay of Pigs in an attempt to "liberate" Cuba; all were killed or captured within three days. They had been trained and armed in Guatemala by the CIA since May 1960. It was Kennedy's apparent ineptitude in the handling of the Bay of Pigs invasion that encouraged the Soviets to test his resolution by moving missles to Cuba.

A: **bayonet, The**
Q: What rifle accessory originateed in Bayonne, France in 1641?
W: The bayonet, a dagger that fits over the barrel of a rifle, comes from Bayonne, France, where the weapons were first made about 1640.

A: **Beaver pelts**
Q: What were "harry bank notes" in the fur trade?
W: It should be "hairy"! Trappers used the pelts at trading posts and with the Indians to purchase anything they needed.

A: **Bebe Rebozo**
Q: Who provided a Key Biscayne, Florida, refuge for Richard Nixon?
W: After the April 30, 1973 resignations of Ehrlichman and Haldeman, Nixon had gone into a deep depression. He flew, alone, to Key Bis-

cayne on May 3, 1973 for a rest. This was not out of character for Nixon to avoid both his wife and staff. He would sometimes sit silently for hours on end with his friend, Rebozo.

A: **Belgium**
Q: What country's been the site of the most European battles?
W: This territory, because of its strategic position and its agricultural wealth, has been coveted and fought over by all the nations of western Europe. Its history has been colored by the rivalry of German and Celtic peoples who have occupied it, by their religious differences, and by the conflict of agricultural interests to the south and the commerical interests of the north.

A: **bell tower, A**
Q: What was the Leaning Tower of Pisa originally used as?
W: The Tower is 179 feet high and built entirely of white marble with walls 13 feet thick at the base. Its construction was begun in 1174, and it was originally intended as a bell tower for the white marble cathedral nearby. Within the past century the inclination of the tower has increased one foot. It should fall over early in the next century according to recent calculations.

A: **Benito Mussolini**
Q: What Italian leader had a lifelong fear of the evil eye?
W: He feared someone putting a curse on him. The evil eye is principally a Sicilian and Mesopotamian Indian superstition. In Sicily, any person or animal is considered vulnerable to the evil eye, and many people wear protection amulets or charms to nullify its effects.

A: **Benito Mussolini**
Q: What World War II leader dallied with Clara Petacci?
W: Mussolini and Petacci were caught and shot on April 28, 1945, by a band of partisans near Lake Como. Their bodies were exhibited, hung by their heels, in a Milan square. Petacci had been Mussolini's mistress for several years.

A: **Benito Mussolini**
Q: Who replaced the assassinated Giacomo Matteotti in 1924?
W: Mussolini headed the Fascist march on Rome, which led to his appointment as Prime Minister. He exercised dictatorial powers for the next 21 years but was assassinated in 1945.

A: **Berlin**
Q: What city did Adolph Hitler plan to rename Germania?
W: Berlin, the largest city in Germany, grew not because it was on an important trade route, but because those in power decided to make it grow. Hitler was one of those leaders.

A: **Berlin Wall, The**
Q: What was erected overnight in August 1961?
W: Erected on Aug. 13, 1961, it is 26.5 miles long and runs through the city. It was built to stem the flood of refugees from the East seeking freedom in the West; 200,000 fled during 1961 before the Wall was erected.

HISTORY

A: Bernadette Devlin

Q: What Irish activist became the youngest woman ever elected to the British Parliament in 1969?

W: In the spring of 1969, at the age of 21, Devlin was elected to Parliament. She epitomized the economic-social-political protest movement of Northern Ireland. She spent her days and nights on the barricades in August of 1969 as the Federation of Northern Ireland's Catholics finally burst into active protest. Devlin had become a force to reckon with as she was able to rally and lead her disinherited countrymen.

A: "Big Bertha"

Q: What long-range World War I German cannon was named for Bertha Krupp?

W: Alfred Krupp was a German ironmaster. He supplied artillery to almost every European nation and was the recipient of many foreign decorations. "Big Bertha," named for Bertha, Krupp's daughter, was the railroad-mounted 38/21 cm. gun used by the Germans in World War I to bombard Paris from a distance of over 60 miles.

A: Big Mac, A

Q: What was described as: "Two all-beef patties, special sauce, lettuce, cheese, pickles, onions and a sesame seed bun"?

W: This little ditty ran as a commercial for the giant burger chain, McDonald's, during the 1970s.

A: Billy Carter

Q: Who told a Senate committee: "Billy Carter is not a buffoon, a boob or a wacko"?

W: Even though he did appear to be all of these things, Billy's antics were found to be entertaining during his brother's presidency. However, his redneck jargon evolved into rude anti-Semitic remarks, and he also had an open relationship with some of the officials of the Libyan government. Once, while waiting for his Libyan friends at an Atlanta airport, he casually urinated against a wall. Billy, who initially provided some comic relief as Jimmy's colorful brother, eventually became more of an embarrassment.

A: Billy Graham

Q: Who said: "There is nothing in the Bible that says I must wear rags"?

W: Graham was right; Job, the world's richest man in Biblical times himself gave credit to God for his good fortune and blamed the devil for his losses. Job never gave up his faith and was later rewarded again by God.

A: Billy Mitchell

Q: What U.S. general was court-martialed for criticizing American air power?

W: The trial began Oct. 28, 1925, lasted three weeks, and resulted in five years suspension from rank, command and pay. Mitchell publicly stated that the destruction of a Navy dirigible *Shenandoah* was the result of incompetence, criminal negligence, and poor administration of our national defense by the Navy and War Departments.

A: Billy the Kid

Q: What was the infamous pseudonym of William Bonney?

W: William H. Bonney, born in New York City in 1859, had killed several men before he was 16 years old. In 1878 he led a gang in the Lincoln County Cattle War and later killed a sheriff. He was captured and sentenced to death, but escaped. He was later trapped and shot by Sheriff Pat F. Garrett in 1881.

A: Billy the Kid

Q: Who killed one man for each of the 21 years he lived?

W: Billy got an early start, killing his first man before he reached his teens. He was gunned down himself by Sheriff Pat Garrett in 1881.

A: "Birdman of Alcatraz", The

Q: What was the nickname of convict Robert F. Stroud?

W: Stroud, an inmate of Alcatraz prison, spent much of his time writing scientific books on bird diseases. His first two birds were sparrows called Peray and Runt. He also bred canaries and became an authority on bird diseases. Another name Stroud answered to was Prisoner Number 594. He died in 1963 at the Medical Center for Federal Prisoners in Springfield, Missouri, after spending 54 of his 73 years in prison, the last 42 years in solitary confinement.

A: *Bismarck*, The

Q: What was the name of Germany's largest World War II battleship?

W: The *Bismarck* displaced 52,600 tons. It was mounted with eight 15-inch guns and was capable of a speed of 35 miles per hour.

A: *Bismarck*, The

Q: What ship sank the British battleship *Hood*?

W: In May, 1941, two British cruisers along with the battleship *Prince of Wales* and battle cruiser *Hood* made contact with the *Bismarck* off the coast of Iceland. The cruiser *Hood* was destroyed in the battle that ensued.

A: Black Death, The; or the Black Plague

Q: What disease plagued Europe, Africa, and Asia in the 14th century?

W: Seventy-five million people died between 1347 and 1351 of this disease—half the population! Endemic to rodents and transmitted by fleas to humans, it is believed that the introduction of the domestic cat played a major role in the abatement of this disease. Hooray, Morris!

A: Bobby Kennedy

Q: What Kennedy was married to Ethel?

W: Robert Kennedy married Ethel Skakel in June of 1950. Robert was 24 and Ethel was 22 when they married. She is the daughter of self-made millionaire George Skakel and is the sixth of seven children. Together, Robert and Ethel had 11 children. At one point Ethel considered becoming a nun instead of marrying.

HISTORY

A: **Bobby Kennedy**
Q: Who left three PT boat tie clasps on top of the Yukon's Mount Kennedy in 1965?
W: The Canadian government named the 14,000-foot-high peak after the late John F. Kennedy. It was the tallest unclimbed peak in North America, and the National Geographic Society proposed that the remaining Kennedy brothers be the first to climb it. Bobby decided to climb it alone, because his brother Ted could not climb with his bad back. Bobby was accompanied by Barry Prather and James Whittaker. Once at the top, he left the tie clasps, crossed himself, stood for a moment of silence, and started on his way down. He was terrified of heights.

A: **Bobby Kennedy**
Q: Who was John F. Kennedy's attorney general?
W: Bobby became attorney general in 1961 and directed much of his effort toward James Hoffa and organized crime. He continued in this position when Lyndon Johnson became President until Katzenbach was appointed.

A: **Bobby Kennedy**
Q: Who won the 1968 California Democratic primary?
W: Kennedy captured 174 delegates' votes for the Democratic nomination in this primary. Everyone there was convinced that Kennedy would go on to Chicago and win the Democratic Convention nomination. He was assassinated that evening in the Ambassador Hotel in Los Angeles.

A: **body, The**
Q: What has to be produced in a writ of "habeas corpus"?
W: This Latin term is an injunction, meaning "have thou the body." An act passed by Parliament during the reign of Charles II, 1679, it provided that any person held too long without a hearing can claim a writ of habeas corpus be issued in his behalf in order to force accusers to show cause why he should be detained in custody longer.

A: **Boeing 727, A**
Q: What did the mysterious D.B. Cooper jump out of?
W: Cooper is the "successful" skyjacker who parachuted from the Boeing 727 airliner with $200,000 in 1971. Some of the money was found on the ground but no other clues were discovered as to D.B.'s whereabouts.

A: **bombing of Hiroshima, The**
Q: What prompted the co-pilot of the *Enola Gay* to enter only "My God" in his log?
W: Captain Robert Lewis, the co-pilot noted that the bright blue sunlit sky turned darkly yellow and a churning cloud of smoke spurted upward for 50,000 feet after the atomic bomb was dropped on Hiroshima. The cloud rose so high that its heat condensed water vapor. Actually Captain Lewis is quoted as saying, "My God, what have we done?"

A: **Bonnie and Clyde**
Q: What gangster couple was riddled with 104 bullets?
W: On Wenesday May 23, 1934, six lawmen fired into their car from all directions. Bonnie was hit over 50 times; Clyde, although closer to the source of fire, had only 27 bullet holes. A little overkill, don't you think?

A: **Boston Strangler, The**
Q: What was Boston resident Albert DeSalvo also known as?
W: Boston was terrorized by a killer whose insanity was equaled by his cunning. He could apparently materalize within locked apartments and not only kill but do fearful things to the women he killed—yet not leave a single clue. DeSalvo sexually molested and then strangled to death 13 women in an 18-month period. The women's ages varied greatly, ranging from 19 to mid-80's.

A: **Bouvier**
Q: What was the maiden name of John F. Kennedy's wife?
W: Jacqueline Lee Bouvier was born in New York in 1929 and married JFK in 1953 in a brilliant society wedding in Newport, Rhode Island.

A: **Boys Town**
Q: What boys' school was founded by Father Edward Joseph Flanagan in 1922?
W: Boys Town is the self-contained community of underprivileged and homeless boys in Omaha, Nebraska. Father Flanagan's motto was "There is no such thing as a bad boy." Our research has Boys Town founded on Dec. 1, 1917.

A: **Breadfruit trees**
Q: What cargo was the *Bounty* carrying when the mutiny occurred?
W: On April 28, 1789, the day of the mutiny, the HMS *Bounty* was returning home after having been in Tahiti for almost six months. The mission there was to obtain plantings of the breadfruit tree for West Indies plantation owners who were seeking a cheap food supply for their native workers.

A: **Bridey Murphy**
Q: What jig-dancing Irish girl did Colorado housewife Ruth Simmons become when hypnotized?
W: Dr. Morey Bernstein conducted hypnosis sessions with Virginia Tighe in 1952, during which she claimed she was a girl named Bridey Murphy living in Ireland in 1806. Tighe's pseudonym was Ruth Simmons.

A: **Brigham Young**
Q: What Mormon leader was said to have had 27 wives?
W: He was selected to be the Mormon leader after Joseph Smith's murder in 1844. Young endorsed Smith's teaching of polygamy. Boy, did he—he had 27 wives and 48 children!

A: **Britain**
Q: What was the third country to get the bomb?
W: In order to give force to its own foreign policy initiatives and in order to advertise to the world that Britain was still a great power, the Churchill government announced that Britain

would follow the American and Russian example and build its own hydrogen bomb as well. Such a weapon was successfully tested in 1957.

A: **Britain**
Q: What country was the target of Germany's planned but canned Operation Sea Lion?
W: "Since England, in spite of her military hopeless position, shows no signs of coming to terms, I have decided to prepare a landing operation against England" (Hitler, June 1940). The invasion never came. Hitler repeatedly postponed the date for several reasons, chiefly because of the strong resistance of the British air-fighter command. Operation Sea Lion eventually evolved into the Battle of Britain. The Battle of Britain was a defensive victory: it halted the enemy in its tracks, helped to strengthen English resolution during the years of war that lay ahead, and led to Germany's ultimate defeat.

A: **Britain, China, France, the USSR and U.S.**
Q: What are the five permanent members of the United Nations Security Council?
W: The Security Council has 15 members, five permanent and ten temporary members elected by the General Assembly for two-year terms, with different regions of the world in rotating representation.

A: **Britain, France, the Soviet Union, and U.S.**
Q: What four countries occupied Germany after World War II?
W: On May 8, 1945, Germany surrendered unconditionally to Allied and Soviet military commanders, and on June 5, the four-nation Allied Control Council became the de facto government of Germany.

A: **British**
Q: What nationality were the 123 people who died in the Black Hole of Calcutta?
W: The Black Hole of Calcutta was a small cell, intended for two or three men, in the East India Fort William. The fort was stormed June 20, 1756. The guards drove all the white inmates of the fort, 146 men, into the almost airless room where they were left overnight to suffocate. Only 23 survived.

A: **Bruno Richard Hauptmann**
Q: Who was executed for the kidnaping and murder of Charles Lindbergh Jr.?
W: Lindbergh's first son, Charles Augustus Lindbergh, Jr., was born in 1930, and kidnapped and killed in 1932. Publicity about the kidnapping was heated, and the public put pressure on the police to find the hero's baby's killer. Circumstantial evidence led to Hauptmann being executed.

A: **Bruno Richard Hauptmann**
Q: Who was the accused in "the Trial of the Century", which opened Jan. 1, 1935?
W: It was said that Hauptmann was framed and the evidence against him poorly collected and presented.

A: **buck stops here, The**
Q: What motto did President Harry Truman keep on his desk?
W: Everybody probably got this one. Less well-known is the motto that graced his desk when he was a Senator, a quote from Mark Twain: "Always do right. This will gratify some people and astonish the rest."

A: **Buddha**
Q: What man has the most monuments erected to him?
W: Buddha is the sacred name of Siddhartha Gautama. *Buddha* means "the Enlightened One" in Sanskrit. The aim of Buddhism is to achieve Nirvana, where desire, passion, and the ego are extinguished and the individual achieves the end of suffering. Today there are almost 250 million Buddhists in the world, almost all of whom live in Asia. No one knows for certain how many monuments are erected.

A: **Buffalo**
Q: What city was President William McKinley shot in?
W: The President was shaking hands with a line of well-wishers in the Temple of Music at the Pan American Exposition in Buffalo, New York. He was shot by a 28 year-old ex-factory worker and farmhand, Leon Czolgosz. The President died eight days later.

A: **Buffalo Bill**
Q: What was William F. Cody's better known name?
W: He was a genuine 19th century buffalo hunter, U.S. Army scout, and Indian fighter. In eight months he slaughtered 4,280 head of buffalo. That's a lot of buffalo chips!

A: **Bull**
Q: What was Admiral William F. Halsey's nickname?
W: "Bull" Halsey was so named because he was the symbol of dogged determination in his command of the fleet attacking Japan. By stating his purpose to be "to ride the Japanese emperor's white horse", he dramatized the main objective of the American naval forces, the capture of Tokyo.

A: **Bulls and bears**
Q: What animals do you find in the stock market?
W: Bullish market means upward movement; a bull bucks up. A bearish market means a downward movement; a bear pounces down on his prey.

A: **Bust size**
Q: What measurement did Marie Antoinette and Jayne Mansfield share?
W: They share a few other attributes also. Both were beautiful women, had celebrity status, and were decapitated in death. Antoinette was beheaded on the guillotine and Mansfield died in an auto accident.

HISTORY

A: **BVDs**
Q: What garment was named for Bradley, Voorhees, and Day?
W: BVDs are the pseudonym for men's underwear. It's also a brand name. The name is taken from the first initials of Bradley, Voorhhees, and Day.

A: **By drinking poison hemlock**
Q: How did Socrates commit suicide?
W: Socrates was condemned to death by a jury of 501 male citizens, all over the age of 30. Guilty – 281, not guilty – 220. Upon sentencing the jurors became incensed at his plea to be maintained at public expense in the Prytaneum for the rest of his life. Socrates did not really commit suicide since he was sentenced to die by drinking a cup of hemlock. This vote was 361 to 140.

A: **By hanging**
Q: How did Judas Iscariot commit suicide?
W: Jesus predicted that one of the disciples would betray him. Judas Iscariot did so by pointing Jesus out to Roman soldiers, by kissing Jesus, for 30 pieces of silver. Judas later hanged himself.

A: **By mail order**
Q: How did Lee Harvey Oswald purchase his rifle?
W: Oswald ordered the rifle under the name "A. Hidell." It was a Mannlicher-Carcano 6.5mm. He sent in a coupon from the American Rifleman and a money order for $21.95 to Klein's Sporting Goods, Inc., in Chicago. In return, the rifle bearing serial number C2766 and a four-power telescopic sight was shipped to the Dallas post office box number 2915 on March 20. The box was rented in Oswald's name.

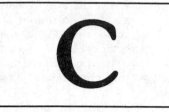

C

A: **Cadillac, A**
Q: What make was Al Capone's favorite bulletproof car?
W: Al's various business interests made him a few enemies. For protection while traveling, Capone always used a black, custom-built bulletproof Cadillac with a trusted, armed driver and a few "soldiers" along for the ride.

A: **Cadillac, The**
Q: What car was named for the founder of Detroit?
W: Antoine de la Mothe Cadillac, a French colonial governor in North America, was the founder of Detroit.

A: **California Gold Rush, The**
Q: What started in 1849 when gold was discovered at Sutter's Mill?
W: Pick, shovel, and tin pan were all that were required. People came from Great Britain, France, Spain, Holland, Germany, China, and all over. For some reason, the Japanese were indifferent. Over 80,000 people/prospectors came to California during the years of 1848 and 1849. The Rush was sufficient to cause more intricate social, economic, and political problems than had confronted any former frontier settlements in the history of the U.S.

A: **Caligula**
Q: What Roman emperor made his horse a senator?
W: Caligula was Emperor of Rome from 37 to 41 A.D. He was raised in a military camp where soldiers named him *Caligula*, which means "Little Boots." One of his more absurd actions was having his horse raised to the consulship. He was assassinated by his soldiers. Caligula, not the horse!

A: **Call girl**
Q: What was the occupation of Mandy Rice-Davies?
W: Marilyn "Mandy" Rice-Davies was the 16-year old roommate of Christine Keeler, a prostitute who caused the toppling of the Tory Government in 1963 and endangered the national security of Britain. Keeler's affair with Lord John Dennis Profumo, War Minister of the Government, was brought to public attention, and it was later revealed that a Russian naval attache, Ivannov, had asked Keeler to find out from Profumo when nuclear warheads would be delivered to West Germany. Both of the prostitutes testified at the trial.

A: **Calvin Coolidge**
Q: Who was the only U.S. president born on July 4?
W: He was born on July 4, 1872 in Plymouth, Vermont. After his Presidency, Cool Cal lived quietly in Northampton, Massachusetts, until he died there on Jan. 5, 1933.

A: **Cambodia**
Q: What country was the target of the U.S. 1969 Secret War?
W: In 1969 the U.S. military, under orders from President Nixon and his adviser Henry Kissinger, began a major bombing campaign in eastern Cambodia, an event that was kept secret from the U.S. Congress and the public. In 1970 the U.S. and South Vietnam began a massive invasion across Cambodia's border, officially aimed at communist "sanctuaries."

A: **Camelot**
Q: What Broadway show was identified with the Kennedy years?
W: Along with his elegant wife, Jacqueline, JFK breathed new life into the ancient myth of Sir Arthur's Camelot, ushering in an unprecedented era of culture and sophistication in the White House.

A: **Canterbury Cathedral**

Q: What cathedral was Thomas a Becket murdered in?

W: Thomas a Becket was chancellor of England and archbishop of Canterbury under Henry II. After a falling out with the King he fled England and remained in exile for six years. Upon his return to England, the conflict with Henry was renewed and Thomas was murdered in the cathedral on Dec. 29, 1170. Thomas was canonized by Pope Alexander III in 1173.

A: **Carol Burnett**

Q: What entertainer won a defamation suit against the *National Enquirer* in 1981?

W: A Los Angeles jury ruled in favor of Carol Burnett in her suit for libel against the *National Enquirer*. The paper was ordered to pay $1.6 million to Burnett for printing a damaging gossip item that they knew to be untrue.

A: **Carrie Nation**

Q: What six-foot temperance advocate wielded her hatchet on saloons?

W: Carry Nation became well-known for her violent attempts to stop the sale of alcoholic liquors. She began in 1890 by praying outside saloons and later began to smash them with stones and then with hatchets. She closed the saloons of her own town and then destroyed saloons in chief Kansas cities.

A: **Cash**

Q: What did the C stand for in chainstore founder J.C. Penney's name?

W: Penney, born on a farm near Hamilton, Missouri, began his mercantile career in a Hamilton store, then found employment in a dry goods stores in Colorado and Wyoming. Soon he had three stores of his own...now there are 1,600. No joke, his full name was John "Cash" Penney!

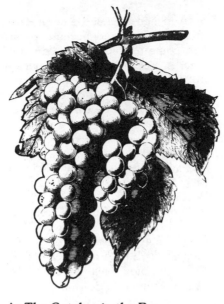

A: *The Catcher in the Rye*

Q: What book was Mark David Chapman carrying when he shot John Lennon?

W: On Dec. 8, 1980, Chapman waited for John Lennon and Yoko Ono to return home. At 11 P.M. he stepped out of the darkness, said "Mr. Lennon," and fired his revolver five times. Four bullets struck his victim. When the police arrived, Chapman was reading *Catcher in the Rye*, by J.D. Salinger.

A: **Cecil Rhodes**

Q: Who founded the DeBeers Mining Company and used his wealth to give a scholarship at Oxford University?

W: Rhodes was a British colonial statesman and financier. He went to Cape Colony in South Africa in 1871 and entered a diamond-mining enterprise at Kimberly. By 1888 he had obtained virtual control of the diamond industry. He became premier of the Cape Colony in 1890, ruling as an autocrat. Determined to extend British power, he organized The British Africa Co. to exploit the territory, which in 1893 was finally acquired by war and named Rhodesia. He left the bulk of his fortune for the founding of Anglo-American scholarships at Oxford. Winners are known as Rhodes Scholars.

A: **Cesar Chavez**

Q: Who founded and was first president of the United Farm Workers?

W: Cesar Chavez organized farm workers into an effective union, the United Farm Workers, an affiliate with the AFL-CIO. From 1966 until 1978 he organized nationwide boycotts of grapes, wine, and lettuce to force California growers to sign contracts with the UFW.

A: **Channel Islands, The**

Q: What part of Britain was occupied by the Germans in World War II?

W: These islands were the only British territory to suffer German Occupation during World War II.

A: **Chaps**

Q: What did cowpunchers use to protect their legs?

W: They are strong leather riding breeches or overalls which have no seat. Wonder why they have no seat?

A: **Charles De Gaulle**

Q: What French leader wondered: "How can you govern a nation that has 350 kinds of cheese?"

W: De Gaulle was the organizer of the French Resistance during the German occupation of France in World War II. He became Premier of France in 1958 and helped draw up a new constitution that was approved by popular vote. He became President of the Fifth Republic in December 1958.

A: **Charles (Chinese) Gordon**

Q: What British general was killed at Khartoum after an 18-month siege of the city?

W: Charles George Gordon, a British soldier, was called the "Chinese Gordon" or "Gordon Pasha" because of his distinguished service in China and Egypt. He was sent by the British government in the 1880s to help the khedive withdraw troops from the Sudan. He gallantly defended Khartoum but was killed two days before a British relief party came within sight of the city.

HISTORY

A: Charles Lindbergh
Q: Who was the leading spokesman for the America Firsters?
W: The American First Committee was a group established in 1940 to obstruct America's participation in World War II. In a speech delivered in New York in April 1941, Lindbergh explained "the Committee has been founded to give voice to the people ...who must do the paying and fighting and the dying if this country enters the war."

A: Charles Lindbergh
Q: Who was "The Lone Eagle"?
W: Lindbergh reached Paris 33 hours, 29 minutes after taking off from Roosevelt Field, Long Island, New York. This 3,600 mile first solo transatlantic flight was a triumph as Lindy averaged 107.5 miles per hour.

A: Charles Lindbergh, Jr.
Q: Who was kidnapped on the night of March 1, 1932?
W: Charles Augustus Lindbergh, Jr., was born in 1930, and kidnapped and killed Mar. 1, 1932, reportedly by Bruno Richard Hauptmann.

A: Charles Lindbergh Jr.'s
Q: Whose kidnapping was termed "the Crime of the Century"?
W: Because of Charles Lindbergh's popularity and worldwide exposure as an aviator, this dastardly crime made headlines around the world.

A: Charles Manson
Q: What mass murderer recorded an album called "Life"?
W: Charles Manson and three of his followers were found guilty of first-degree murder in the 1969 slaying of actress Sharon Tate and six others. This album was released by ESP Records in the 1960s, but is no longer in print.

A: Charlie McCarthy
Q: What dummy received an honorary degree from Northwestern University?
W: Edgar Bergen was a graduate of Northwestern University. He had

been invited to make a commencement address, and because people had come to think of his "dummy" Charlie McCarthy as a real person, the university bestowed the honorary degree upon *McCarthy*. Charlie was originally carved by Charlie Mack, a woodcarver.

A: Che Guevara
Q: What Argentine revolutionary fought with Castro and died in Bolivia?
W: Ernesto Che Guevara, originally trained as a doctor, and Castro fought the guerilla campaign that toppled the Batista regime in Cuba in 1958. He died while directing guerrilla movements in Bolivia.

A: Che Guevara's
Q: Whose body was displayed by the Bolivian army in 1967?
W: In 1967, Che Guevara was directing a guerrilla movement in Bolivia. He was captured and executed by the Bolivian army, and his body was put on public display.

A: Chesterfield
Q: What British peerage gave its name to an overcoat, a sofa and a cigarette?
W: This was the name of the fourth Earl of Chesterfield. His name is given to a kind of straight coat of any length that boasts a velvet collar. The couch is designed with upright arms that are almost the same height as the back. And we all know the cigarette! Chesterfield also wrote many letters to his son, which were the "Emily Post" standards of etiquette in that day.

A: Chicago
Q: Where was the 1968 Democratic National Convention?
W: The opening date was Aug. 26th. Humphrey/Muskie were the choice of that year's delegates. The Convention was marred by demonstrations of some 5,000 young people ranging from supporters of peace candidate Senator Eugene McCarthy to "Yippies." Unable to get into the Convention, they started a riot in the

Chicago streets that was seen by 50 to 80 million people on the tube.

A: *Chicago Daily Tribune*, The
Q: What was that newspaper Harry Truman was holding in that picture?
W: In the evening edition of Nov. 2, 1948, the *Tribune* printed the following headline "Dewey Defeats Truman." The victorious Truman waved this edition to the crowd from a train platform the next day. More recently, the *Sun-Times* (July 17, 1980) announced the Republican ticket as "Reagan and Ford" for the 1980 race. Well, everyone's entitled to one mistake!

A: Chicago Seven, The
Q: What group included Abbie Hoffman, Jerry Rubin and Tom Hayden?
W: Also included were: Rennie Davis, David Dellinger, Lee Weiner, and John Froines. These men were tried in Chicago shortly after the 1968 Democratic National Convention for "crossing state lines to incite a riot."

A: China
Q: What country lifted a ban on Aristotle, Shakespeare and Dickens on Feb. 11, 1978?
W: China had had a ten year ban on 70 renowned classical and modern international writers.

A: China
Q: What country was the scene of the Boxer Rebellion of 1900?
W: This was the patriotic, anti-foreign demonstration in China in 1900, which was led by the Chinese secret society called "The fist of righteous harmony", or "Boxers." The rebellion was directed against the aggressive attitude of European powers.

A: China
Q: What was the fifth country to get the bomb?
W: In order the countries are: 1)U.S. 1945, 2)USSR 1949, 3)Great Britain 1952, 4)France 1960, and 5) China 1964.

A: China and Japan
Q: What two Asian countries went to war on July 7, 1937?
W: From 1932 to 1937 Japan engaged in economic and political penetration of North China. In 1937 the Japanese troops invaded the northern provinces, and the Chinese resistance led to full-scale, although undeclared, war.

A: China and Japan
Q: What two countries were known as "the Yellow Peril" in the 1890s?
W: This phrase has come to have two meanings. The German Kaiser used it to describe the fear that overpopulation in China and Japan would endanger the western world. Another definition related the term to the fear of Japanese imperialism.

A: Ch'ing Dynasty, The
Q: What was China's last imperial dynasty?
W: The Ch'ing Dynasty was founded by the Manchus and lasted from 1644 to 1911.

A: *Christina*, The
Q: What was the name of Aristotle Onassis's yacht?
W: The yacht was named after Onassis' daughter Christina. It was a famous entertainment site for such notables as Princess Grace and Prince Ranier, Maria Callas (opera singer and former paramour of Onassis), Winston Churchill, Princess Radziwill (Jacqueline Kennedy's sister), and Jacqueline Kennedy, who eventually married Onassis.

A: Christopher Columbus
Q: What explorer was nicknamed "Iberia's Pilot"?
W: The original inhabitants of the Spanish peninsula, which was known to the Greeks and Romans as Iberia, were a primitive race called Iberians. Columbus started his voyage of discovery, which laid the foundation for Spain's vast empire in the three Americas, under the protection of Queen Isabella of Spain.

A: Christopher Columbus
Q: What Italian explorer is buried in the Dominican Republic?
W: Christopher died in 1506. In 1515 his remains were transferred from Valladolid, Spain, to Seville, Spain. Then in 1542, his remains and those of his son were taken to Hispaniola and placed first in the Cathedral of Santo Domingo, then in a tomb in this cathedral. In 1948 construction began on the Columbus Memorial Lighthouse, which is designed to be the last resting place of Columbus.

A: Christopher Columbus
Q: Who discovered Jamaica?
W: Original settlers were the Arawak Indians, who were later wiped out by the Spanish who came to the island searching for gold not long after it was discovered by Columbus.

A: Clarence Darrow
Q: Who defended John T. Scopes?
W: In 1925, John T. Scopes, a Tennessee schoolteacher, was tried for violating the law that forbade the teaching of Charles Darwin's Theory of Evolution. Famous criminal lawyer Clarence Darrow conducted the defense for a trial that became a public confrontation between a fundamentalist interpretation of the Bi-

ble and more liberal views. Scopes was found guilty, but his conviction was overturned by the State Supreme Court.

A: Clark Gable
Q: What actor and World War II airman had a $5,000 bounty put on his head by Hermann Goering?
W: In 1942 the plane on which Gable's wife, Carol Lombard, was returning from a War Bond drive crashed. The bereaved Gable joined the Air Force shortly after. He rose in rank to major and received the Distinguished Flying Cross and Air Medal for flying bombing missions over Germany, much to Herman Goering's dismay.

A: Clay Shaw
Q: What New Orleans businessman went to trial accused of conspiring to kill John F. Kennedy?
W: Abraham Zapruder's amateur film introduced the possibility of a second assassin. It was later used in the Clay Shaw trial in New Orleans. Shaw was suspected of conspiring with Lee Harvey Oswald in the assassination of President Kennedy.

A: Clementine
Q: What was Winston Churchill's wife's name?
W: Clementine Churchill was born Clementine Hozier on April 1, 1885, in London, England. She was wed to Winston Churchill in St. Margaret's Cathedral on Sept. 12, 1908.

A: Cleopatra
Q: What Egyptian sovereign married two of her brothers?
W: Cleopatra became queen of Egypt when she was 17 and, as was the custom, married her brother, Ptolemy XIII. She was ousted from Egypt two years later but was restored to the throne by her lover Julius Caesar after the Battle of Alexandria, in which her enemy brother-husband was killed. She took as a husband her younger brother, Ptolemy XIV, a union which, like the first, was probably not consummated.

HISTORY

A: **Cleopatra**
Q: Who was known as "the Serpent of the Nile"?
W: Cleopatra is painted as "the Serpent of the Nile", a femme fatale. Called the "harlot queen of incestous Canopus," she committed suicide rather than be carried off in humiliation by Octavian. Tradition says that she had an asp brought secretly to her in a basket of figs. She placed the snake on her arm and died of its bite.

A: **Cleopatra**
Q: Who was the last ruler in the Egyptian dynasty of the Ptolemies?
W: Although Cleopatra was the name of several Macedonian queens of Egypt, the most famous Cleopatra lived from 69 to 30 B.C. She was the last of the line of the Ptolemies, who had ruled Egypt for almost 300 years. She inherited the throne in 51 B.C. when her father, Ptolemy XI, died.

A: **Clyde Barrow**
Q: Who was Bonnie Parker's partner?
W: They made up the bank robbing team of Bonnie and Clyde. On Wednesday May 23, 1934, lawmen fired on their car and killed the pair.

A: **Colonel Harland Sanders**
Q: What restaurateur kicked the bucket in 1980?
W: Colonel Harlan T. Sanders was the famous goateed and mustachioed founder of Kentucky Fried Chicken. An honorary colonel in the Kentucky Guard, he made a cameo appearance in the 1967 Jerry Lewis movie *The Loud Mouth*.

A: **Columbia**
Q: What university was laid siege to in 1968's Battle of Morningside Heights?
W: On April 22, 1968, 300 students barricaded the office of the Dean to protest construction of a gymnasium, which they claimed was a rascist move to deprive blacks of a recreation area, and to protest the Univer-
sity's participation in the Institute for Defense analyses. The University temporarily closed as students took over control of two more buildings.

A: **Committee for the Re-election of the President**
Q: What did Richard Nixon's CREEP stand for?
W: Nixon supporters established the Committee to Re-elect the President, or CRP, with Attorney General Mitchell in charge. Nixon critics called this committee "CREEP."

A: **Confederacy, The**
Q: Which side did Britain support in the U.S. Civil War?
W: Britain gave minimal support to the South because Britain needed cotton. Britain also allowed the Confederacy to build six warships in its shipyards. Britain and France refused to intervene unless the South could show that it could win a final victory.

A: *Constitution*, **The**
Q: What warship was nicknamed "Old Ironsides"?
W: "Old Ironsides" was the nickname of the USS *Constitution*, which was launched at Boston on Sept. 20, 1797. It acquired the name because enemy cannonballs seemed to bounce off her sides, even though the sides of the ship were only made of oak wood!

A: **Cooking**
Q: What was the chuckwagon used for on cattle drives?
W: A chuckwagon is a food wagon that carries provisions and cooking equipment around to cowboys and harvest hands.

A: **Cooperative for American Relief Everywhere**
Q: What does C.A.R.E. stand for?
W: C.A.R.E. is a U.S.-based international agency founded in 1945. Funded primarily by private contributions, it distributes food, tools, building materials, and medical care in 38 war-torn and developing countries.

A: **corncob pipe, A**
Q: What kind of pipe did General Douglas MacArthur smoke?
W: Most intellectuals thought MacArthur was a ham; they considered his ornate hat, sunglasses, and corncob pipes props. It is almost impossible to find unposed pictures of him.

A: **Corregidor, the Philippines**
Q: Where did General Douglas MacArthur return to?
W: Corregidor is an island at the entrance to Manila Bay in the Philippines. Ships formerly stopped at the island to have their papers checked and corrected. *Corregidor* is Spanish for "corrector."

A: **Crazy Horse**
Q: Who was Sitting Bull's right-hand man?
W: Famed Sioux warrior and Indian Chief, Crazy Horse led the resistance to the U.S. government's forced settlement of the Sioux on the Pine Ridge reservation. After surrendering at Fort Robinson, Crazy Horse was imprisoned. While attempting to escape he was stabbed in the back and killed. Crazy Horse fought with Sitting Bull at Custer's Last Stand.

A: **Crimean War, The**
Q: What war did Florence Nightingale tend the troops in?
W: In 1814 the *Times*, London, sent out the first war correspondent to cover the Crimean War. The

eyewitness accounts of the poorly dressed, hungry, ill-supplied British troops led the *Times* to try to get Government help. When those efforts failed, the paper started a relief fund that brought in 25,000 pounds sterling and spurred Florence to go to Crimea with 38 nurses.

A: **crossbow, The**
Q: What weapon did the crossed slits in English castles accommodate?
W: The crossbow, a popular weapon of the Middle Ages, is a short, stiff bow set across the end of a stock. The archer draws the bow's string back and hooks it on a "nut." He then shoots by pulling a trigger that releases the nut. The advantage of the crossbow is that it could be cocked and held ready prior to shooting.

A: **Crusades, The**
Q: What was the series of campaigns to wrest the Holy Land from the Muslim Turks?
W: The Crusades lasted almost 200 years. Some of its leaders over this period of time were Godfrey of Bouillon, Conrad III, Louis VII, Frederick II, Philip Augustus, Richard the Lion-Hearted, Louis IX, and Edward I.

A: **Cuban Missile Crisis, The**
Q: What prompted the installation of the Hot Line?
W: The installation of the Hot Line was prompted by several days in 1962 when the world stood on the brink of nuclear war. Because Cuban leaders were convinced that the U.S. was planning to attack Cuba, they asked Russia for aid. Russia responded by sending materials to set up missile sites. When the U.S. discovered this they ordered a blockade to halt further shipment of arms. The tense situation was resolved when Russia agreed to Kennedy's demand to return home in exchange for a U.S. pledge not to attack Cuba.

A: **Czechoslovakia**
Q: What country did Russian troops invade in 1968?
W: In 1968 a liberalization movement swept Czechoslovakia, and a succession of leaders attempted to democratize the nation, promising reforms. Russia brought pressure on the new government, and the year was marked by student riots and workers' protests against the USSR. In July, Soviet-bloc forces invaded and occupied Prague, proceeding to force the submission of Dubcek's regime and a return by the Czechs to Communist principles.

D

A: **Daniel and Philip Berrigan**
Q: What two brothers led the draft file-burning Catonsville Nine in 1968?
W: Brothers Daniel and Philip Berrigan, both peace activists and priests, were the first Roman Catholic clerics to receive federal sentencing for peace agitation in the U.S.

A: **Daniel Ellsberg**
Q: Who leaked the Pentagon Papers to the *New York Times*?
W: The Pentagon Papers were documents on the U.S. involvement in Vietnam, which were taken from the Pentagon files in Washington during the Kennedy and Johnson administrations. The government tried to block their publication. Ellsberg was charged with espionage, conspiracy, and theft, but a mistrial was declared and charges dropped.

A: **Daniel Schorr**
Q: What newsman did CBS fire for leaking a CIA report to *The Village Voice* in 1977?
W: The CIA report was to become known as the Pentagon Papers.

A: **David**
Q: What was Dr. Livingstone's first name?
W: That's right, but he will always be remembered as Dr. Livingstone...I presume! Livingstone was an explorer and missionary whose discoveries in Africa greatly advanced geographical knowledge.

A: **David Ben-Gurion**
Q: Who was Israel's first prime minister?
W: Ben-Gurion was prime minister of Israel from 1948 until his retirement in 1963, with the exception of two years during that period. He guided Israel's spectacular course through the Arab Wars to a position of respected strength.

A: **David Eisenhower II**
Q: Who was Camp David named for?
W: It was previously named Shangri-La by FDR. President Dwight David Eisenhower renamed the camp after his grandson, David. Used as a residence and vacation getaway, it was also the scene of numerous high level meetings.

A: **David Livingstone**
Q: Who discovered Victoria Falls?
W: In 1840 Livingstone was sent to southern Africa by the London Missionary Society. He crossed Africa from the Zambezi to the Congo. From 1854 to 1856 he made his way from Luanda to Quelimane, following the course of the Zambezi River, and discovered Victoria Falls.

A: **Davy Crockett coonskin caps**
Q: What were millions of kids wearing on their heads in 1955?
W: David Crockett was a U.S. frontiersman and political figure who was killed in the Texan defense of the Alamo. Crockett was known by his furry cap made of raccoon skins with a raccoon tail trailing down his neck. After the Disney movie about Davy Crockett, U.S. kids wanted caps like their hero. The 1955 version of the classic cap was made of synthetic fur, unlike the original.

HISTORY

A: Dead Sea Scrolls, The
Q: What did a shepherd boy discover at Qumram, Jordan, in 1947?
W: The Dead Sea Scrolls are the remains of a collection of Hebrew and Aramaic documents discovered near the Dead Sea in the spring of 1947. A young Bedouin shepherd uncovered them when he threw a stone into a cave in the cliffs along the Dead Sea and heard the shattering of a jar, found to contain several leather scrolls. More scrolls and fragments were discovered in 11 caves in the vicinity.

A: Dean Rusk
Q: Who was John F. Kennedy's secretary of state?
W: He was appointed by Kennedy in 1961 and continued as Secretary of State during President Lyndon Johnson's term of office.

A: Declaration of Independence
Q: What document did Button Gwinnett sign on the upper left-hand side?
W: In 1776 Gwinnett was chosen by the Georgia Council of Safety as a delegate to the Continental Congress, which resulted in his signing the Declaration of Independence. His autograph is sought after, not only because he was one of the signers of the Declaration of Independence, but also because his signature is so rare. One of his autographs was sold at an auction in 1927 for $51,000.

A: Deep Throat
Q: Who was Bob Woodward's secret Watergate contact?
W: "Deep Throat" was *Washington Post* reporter Bob Woodward's name for his secret source during the Watergate investigation. They met in the garage of a Washington building. Hal Holbrook played the part of "Deep Throat" in the 1976 movie *All the President's Men*.

A: Denim jeans
Q: What kind of pants were first worn during the California Gold Rush?
W: When a gold miner friend of his

complained about the quality of work trousers, Levi Strauss had a pair of pants made for him from tent canvas. Realizing the large market, Strauss settled in San Francisco to manufacture the pants, which the miners called "Levis."

A: Detroit
Q: What city saw 42 die and $44 million in property damage in the summer riots of 1967?
W: In July 1967, the National Guardsmen and the U.S. Army were called into Detroit to restore order when rioting broke out in a chiefly black section of the city. Rioters burned buildings, looted stores, and shot at policemen and firemen. The riots, which lasted a week, resulted in over 40 deaths.

A: Dial
Q: What soap was touted as being "for people who like people"?
W: Dial had the face or dial of a clock on its wrapper. Supposedly it kept you clean-smelling for 24 hours...no matter what! This line is from one of their commercials, "Aren't you glad you use Dial? Don't you wish everyone did?"

A: Dick Tuck
Q: What Democratic prankster waved the train out of the station while Richard Nixon spoke from the caboose?
W: Numerous "dirty" stories were

circulating about Nixon and his staff. Dick Tuck was not a fan of Nixon's and made a fool of him at every opportunity at any cost. It was rather ironic that Dick Tuck's operations were considered good clean fun and activities from others (close to Nixon) were considered vicious espionage.

A: Dien Bien Phu
Q: Where did the French meet their Waterloo in Vietnam?
W: The Battle of Dien Bien Phu was the climactic contest in France's eight-year struggle to retain its colonial empire in Indochina. The battle resulted in more than 15,000 French casualties. This defeat ended French colonial rule in Vietnam, Laos, and Cambodia.

A: Dinah Shore
Q: Who advised listeners to "see the U.S.A. in your Chevrolet"?
W: In the early 1950s Dinah Shore starred in "The Chevy Show", a 15-minute, twice-a-day program that became a weekly one-hour show in 1956. She advised her audience to "see the U.S.A. in your Chevrolet" and finished each show by blowing a big kiss. (MMMWAHH!)

A: Dionne Quintuplets, The
Q: What five young ladies were born on May 28, 1934?
W: On May 28, 1934 the birth of the Dionne quintuplets in northern Ontario made headlines throughout the world. Because the Dionnes had an income of barely $100 a month, the Canadian Prime Minister made the quints wards of the state, establishing a trust fund of $1 million for them. They were not to be raised by their parents, but in a nine-room nursery on the Dionne farm, and they became North America's "number one peep show." After seven years the parents regained custody, but they treated the quints harshly and forced them to remain isolated behind a barbed wire fence surrounding the Dionne farm.

HISTORY

A: **Displaced person**
Q: What does D.P. stand for?
W: · This term especially refers to Europeans, but others also, who are removed from their homeland as a slave laborer or driven from their homeland by an invasion.

A: **Dixville Notch**
Q: What New Hampshire hamlet rises early to vote first in U.S. presidential elections?
W: The New Hampshire presidential primary is the first to be held each election year and has often forecast national trends or perhaps influenced important political decisions.

A: **Donald Duck**
Q: Who's the idol of the German Organization of Non-Commercial Supporters of Donaldism?
W: In 1943 Donald Duck, in an anti-Nazi film called *Der Fuehrer's Tale*, won an Oscar for Best Cartoon Short Subject. In 1978 a member of the Helsinki Youth Committee tried to get the cartoon character's comic books banned. Hans Von Starch launched a counterattack. He was President of the Donald Duck Club of Western Europe.

A: **Douglas MacArthur**
Q: What general first commanded United Nations forces in the Korean War?
W: MacArthur became U.N. Commander in Korea when the North Korean Communists invaded South Korea in 1950. After Chinese Communists entered the war on the side of the North Koreans, MacArthur wanted to attack the Chinese mainland. This action was forbidden by MacArthur's superiors because they feared it would increase the risk of a world war.

A: **Dr. Benjamin Spock**
Q: What pediatrician led the National Committee Against the Vietnam War?

W: After campaigning for Lyndon Johnson, Dr. Benjamin Spock became very concerned about the escalation of the Vietnam war and he began to lead peace demonstrations. His association with antiwar movements during the 1960s led to his arrest and conviction for violating selective service laws by encouraging drafted men to resist conscription.

A: **Dr. Benjamin Spock**
Q: Who told mothers how to raise their babies, then told the babies how to evade the draft?
W: Dr. Benjamin Spock is famous both for his book on child care, *The Commonsense Book of Baby and Child Care*, and for his leadership in the peace movement. His interest in the anti-nuclear and anti-war movements culminated in 1972 when he ran for president as a candidate of the People's Party.

A: **Dr. Pepper**
Q: What soft drink first appeared in the Old Corner Drug Store in Waco, Texas, in 1885?
W: A young man working in a Virginia drugstore concocted countless mixtures to impress the owner's daughter. The owner, named Dr. Pepper, fired the young man, who then moved to Waco, Texas and continued to improve his drink. A patron of the old drugstore, A.S. Lazenby, was also a beverage chemist and began research on "Dr. Pepper" at his Artesian Bottling Works. In 1885, he put "Dr. Pepper" on sale at soda fountains in and around Waco. The perfect formula has stayed the same throughout the years. Incidentally, the young man went back to Virginia and won the girlfriend's heart.

A: **Dr. Timothy Leary**
Q: Who suggested: "Turn on to the scene; tune in to what's happening. Drop out"?
W: It is more popularly written, "turn on, tune in, drop out." Drugs played a big part in Leary's life and

philosophy. Before Professor Timothy Leary "turned on", he attended the U.S. Military Academy at West Point where he studied for 18 months.

A: **Draft cards**
Q: What did it become illegal to burn on Aug. 31, 1965?
W: Draft cards represent conscription, compulsory enrollment of personnel for service in the armed forces. During the Vietnam War, conscription became a highly controversial issue. It was abolished by Congress in 1973. During demostrations in 1965, "draft card" burning was outlawed.

A: **Dunkirk**
Q: What French port did 200,000 British troops flee on June 4, 1940?
W: During World War II, Dunkirk was the site of a massive evacuation of about 350,000 English, French, and Belgian soldiers in the face of the May-June 1940 German onslaught. The city sustained severe damage and was occupied by the Germans for five years.

A: **Dutch, The**
Q: What settlers were the forebears of the Boers of South Africa?
W: In 1652 the Dutch East India Company sent colonists to South Africa. These colonists and their descendents were known as the *Boers*, a Dutch word meaning "farmer."

A: **Dwight Chapin**
Q: What appointments secretary to Richard Nixon went to jail?
W: Dwight Chapin, Nixon's appointments secretary was charged with perjury as a result of his false grand jury testimony about the activities of Donald Segretti, a young west coast lawyer he had hired to perform various acts of political espionage against the Democrats.

HISTORY

A: Dwight Eisenhower
Q: What U.S. president did actor Robert Montgomery coach for TV?
W: Eisenhower once said, "I can think of nothing more boring, for the American Public, than to sit in their living rooms for a whole half an hour looking at my face on their TV screens." Ike had Montgomery coach him to help him appear more comfortable and less boring while giving TV speeches.

A: Dwight Eisenhower
Q: Who was the first U.S. president to hold a televised news conference?
W: Eisenhower held the first presidential news conference to be recorded by both newsreels and television on Jan. 19, 1955. Reporters questioned him about Red China and Formosa, national security, the imprisonment of American fliers, trade with the Communists, and other subjects.

E

A: Earl
Q: What's Jimmy Carter's middle name?
W: James Earl Carter, Jr., was born in 1924 at Plains, Georgia. He became the 39th President of the U.S.

A: Earl Warren
Q: What chief justice headed the commission that declared: "Lee Harvey Oswald...acted alone"?
W: Despite the fact that certain pieces of information surrounding the assassination of President Kennedy remained questionable in many minds, the presidential commission, headed by Chief Justice Earl Warren, came to the unanimous conclusion that the assassination had been accomplished by Lee Harvey Oswald "acting alone."

A: Eat meat on Friday
Q: What could Roman Catholics do in good conscience for the first time on Dec. 5, 1966?
W: Before this date it was considered a sin to eat meat on Fridays. Eating meat on Friday is still prohibited during the Lenten Season, from Ash Wednesday until Easter Sunday.

A: Eddie Fisher
Q: Who did Elizabeth Taylor divorce ten days before marrying Richard Burton?
W: Eddie Fisher divorced Debbie Reynolds to marry Taylor in 1959. In 1964, Taylor left Fisher to marry her *Cleopatra* co-star, Richard Burton. Fisher, oddly enough, had been best man at Taylor's wedding to Mike Todd, her husband before Fisher.

A: Edmund Hillary
Q: Who snapped the picture of Tenzing Norkay atop Mount Everest?
W: Sir Edmund Hillary was born in 1919 in New Zealand. He was a mountaineer, author, and lecturer. In the British expedition led by Sir John Hunt in 1953, Hillary succeeded in reaching the summit of Mt. Everest, the world's highest peak. In recognition of his accomplishment, he was knighted by Queen Elizabeth II.

A: Edmund Muskie
Q: Who was Hubert Humphrey's 1968 vice-presidential running mate?
W: They lost to Nixon/Agnew by only about one half million popular votes but they only had 191 electoral votes to Nixon and Agnew's 301 electoral votes.

A: Edward VIII
Q: What 20th-century monarch reigned only 325 days?
W: Edward VIII succeeded to the throne of England upon the death of his father, George V, Jan. 20, 1936. He abdicated the throne in favor of his brother, the Duke of York, on Dec. 10, 1936, in order to marry the American divorcee Wallis Warfield Simpson.

A: Edward VIII and Wallis Warfield Simpson's
Q: Whose courtship was called the love story of the century?
W: We just told you about the conditions surrounding this "beautiful gesture of love"! (Read the previous response.)

A: Egypt
Q: What country did the Battle of El Alamein take place in?
W: El Alamein was a decisive World War II battle in North Africa between the British Eighth Army and the German and Italian troops. El Alamein was a turning point in the war because it saved the Suez Canal for the Allies and facilitated their landings in North Africa.

A: Egypt
Q: Where did the deposed Shah of Iran finally find refuge?
W: Some 90 people, including 63 Americans, were taken hostage at the American Embassy in Tehran, Iran, on Nov. 4, 1979 by followers of the Ayatollah Khomeini. They demanded the return of the former Shah, Mohammed Reza Pahlavi, who was undergoing medical treatment in New York City. The Shah left the U.S. and was sheltered in Panama before finally going to Egypt where he died.

A: Egypt's
Q: What country's air force was destroyed on the ground on the morning of June 5, 1967?
W: Egypt was brought into the war between Israel and the Arab States during the so-called "Six Day War", when the Israeli air force attacked and destroyed the Egyptian air force while it was still on the ground.

A: Eighty-seven
Q: How many years are there in four score and seven?
W: A score equals 20, plus seven equals 87. It adds up!

A: El Dorado
Q: What was "the City of Gold" sought by Spanish explorers?
W: In the 16th and 17th centuries, El Dorado, a legendary country abounding in gold, was rumored to exist in South America. Beginning around 1530, a long series of expeditions were organized by Europeans to search for El Dorado. Although El Dorado was never found, the expeditions resulted in the exploration of much of northern South America.

A: Elba
Q: What island was Napoleon's first home in exile?
W: In 1814 Napoleon's commanders insisted that he give up the throne. Louis XVIII was crowned king while Napoleon was made ruler of the tiny island of Elba off the coast of Italy. Although his exile from France was supposed to last forever, Napoleon escaped from Elba less than a year later. Louis XVIII fled Paris when Napoleon was hailed as emperor by his followers.

A: Elephant Man, The
Q: What's the better known identity of John Merrick, the noble ogre of Victorian England?
W: John Merrick lived in England from 1863 to 1890. He was found on exhibition at a freak show by Sir Fredrick Treves, a lecturer on anatomy at a medical college. The British public provided funds to set up a home for the Elephant Man in the back of the hospital. He attracted much attention and was even visited by the Queen. He died in his sleep in his hospital home in 1890, when one night the weight of his head, while in a prone position, crushed his neck.

A: Eleven
Q: How many fingers did Anne Boleyn have?
W: On her left hand Anne Boleyn had a sixth finger that she hid in her dress folds. To those who did not approve of her, it was a mark of the devil. It was also rumored that she had three breasts. If the King's charges of adultery and incest failed, he intended to use the sixth finger and third breast to accuse her of being a witch.

A: Eleven
Q: How many Israeli athletes were killed at the Munich Olympics?
W: In 1972 political tension threatened to disrupt the Summer Games in Munich, West Germany. Eight Arab terrorists attacked the Israeli team quarters, killing two and taking nine others as hostages. Several hours later a gun battle with the German police resulted in the death of all the hostages, five terrorists, and a West German policeman.

A: Elizabeth I
Q: What daughter of Henry VIII and Anne Boleyn became queen of England?
W: Elizabeth I reigned from 1558 to 1603. She ascended to the throne at the age of 25.

A: Elizabeth I
Q: Who was England's "Virgin Queen"?
W: Elizabeth I was the Queen of England from 1558 to 1603. She is famous for the glamor of her court, the success of her policies, and her long-preserved virginity. Elizabeth's authoritative leadership, England became a major European leader with a prospering commerce and a great naval force.

A: Elizabeth I
Q: Who was Good Queen Bess?
W: Elizabeth I, who became a living legend, was called "Good Queen Bess" by the majority of her subjects. They recognized that she made England's well-being the chief aim of her life and because of this she managed to gain and hold the love of her subjects to the end of her long life.

A: Elizabeth II
Q: Who succeeded George VI to the British throne?
W: Elizabeth II, who celebrated her 31st anniversary as Queen in 1983, came to the throne at the age of 25, upon the death of her father George VI. She is married to Philip Mountbatten, Duke of Edinburgh, and has four children; Charles (Prince of Wales), Princess Anne, Prince Andrew, and Prince Edward.

A: Elizabeth II
Q: Who was the first British monarch to visit New Zealand?
W: Queen Elizabeth II has traveled widely. Following her coronation, Elizabeth and her husband Prince Philip made an extensive tour of British Commonwealth countries, including New Zealand.

A: Elizabeth Taylor's
Q: Whose husbands have included Conrad Hilton, Jr., and Michael Wilding?
W: Her husbands include: Conrad N. Hilton, Jr. 1950; Michael Wilding with whom she had two sons; Mike Todd, whom she married in 1957 and with whom she had one daughter; Eddie Fisher, 1959; Richard Burton, 1964; John Warner…

A: Elvis Presley
Q: Who received his U.S. army discharge on March 5, 1960?
W: By the time of Elvis' discharge from Fort Dix, New Jersey, he had been promoted to sergeant and put in charge of a three-man reconnaissance unit. During his train ride home to Memphis, the stations in every town were mobbed with fans. Elvis rode on the back of the train and waved, smiled, and signed autographs.

HISTORY

HISTORY

A: **England**
Q: Where was the Liberty Bell made?
W: The Liberty Bell was cast in England in 1752 for the Pennsylvania Statehouse. It was cracked and twice recast before being hung. It was rung to signal the adoption of the "Declaration of Independence." It cracked when it was rung for the funeral of Chief Justice John Marshal, July 8, 1835. Another little bit of trivia: Pennsylvania is misspelled on the bell!

A: **England's**
Q: What country's sailors were known colloquially as lime-juicers?
W: In the "olden days", England's sailors were given a daily ration of lime juice to prevent scurvy while aboard ship during long periods, as fresh fruit was not otherwise available. This is also where the term "limeys" comes from. They were also given a daily ration (a "grog" or "tot") of rum.

A: *Enola Gay*, **The**
Q: What famed plane was piloted by Colonel Paul Tibbets Jr.?
W: The B-29 that was piloted by Colonel Paul Tibbets, Jr., dropped the bomb on Hiroshima, and was named the *Enola Gay* for the colonel's mother, Enola Gay Haggard.

A: *Enola Gay*, **The**
Q: What was the name of the B-29 that dropped the bomb on Hiroshima?
W: It was named for the pilot's mother, Enola Gay Haggard.

A: **Entebbe**
Q: What airport saw Israeli commandos free 103 hostages on July 4, 1976?
W: On July 4, 1976, Israeli airborne commandos attacked Uganda's Entebbe Airport and freed the 103 people that had been held hostage by Palestinian terrorist hijackers of an Air France plane. Killed in the rescue were the terrorists, a score of Ugandan soldiers, two hostages, and one rescuer.

A: *Enterprise*, **The**
Q: What was the name of the first nuclear-powered aircraft carrier?
W: This *Enterprise* was commissioned in 1961. It preceeded the "Star Trek" TV series USS *Enterprise* by five years.

A: **Erwin Rommel**
Q: Who commanded the German forces in North Africa during World War II?
W: Among other roles, Rommel was a German general, a member of the Nationalist Socialist Party, and a bodyguard for Hitler. He commanded Hitler's headquarters staff in Austria, Sudetenland, and Prague, as well as the occupations in the Polish campaign. He fought in Africa from 1941 to 1943. Hitler eventually had him killed.

A: **"Et tu, Brute?"**
Q: What were the alleged last words of Julius Caesar?
W: Fearing that Caesar would become an absolute king, many whom he had earlier pardoned conspired to murder him. The conspirators, led by Brutus and Cassius Longinus, stabbed him on the Ides (15th) of March, 44 B.C. As he fell Caesar addressed Brutus, "Et tu, Brute?" or "Even you, Brutus?" The people, instead of rejoicing at Caesar's death, were enraged, and Brutus fled from Rome. Soon after, he and Cassius were defeated at Philippi by Antony and Octavia. Feeling their cause was lost, Brutus fell upon his sword and died.

A: **Ethel and Julius Rosenberg**
Q: Who were the first U.S. civilians to be executed for espionage?
W: Julius Rosenberg, a member of the Communist Party, and his wife, Ethel, were accused of furnishing vital information about the atomic bomb to Soviet agents in 1944 and 1945. They were convicted under the Espionage Act of 1917 and on April 5, 1951, were sentenced to death. They were executed in 1953.

A: **Eugene McCarthy**
Q: Who won the 1968 Oregon Democratic primary?
W: Eugene McCarthy was a U.S. Senator from Minnesota from 1959 until 1971 and an unsuccessful presidential candidate in 1968. Because of his strong opposition to the U.S. involvement in Vietnam, he attracted much student support and won important primary elections in New Hampshire, Wisconsin and Oregon.

A: **Eva Braun**
Q: Who did photographer Heinrich Hoffmann introduce to Adolf Hitler in 1929?
W: Eva Braun was a shop assistant to Hoffman. He introduced her to Hitler, and she entered Hitler's household in 1936. On April 29, 1945, Hitler and Braun were married, and the following day they committed suicide in an underground shelter

A: **Exxon**
Q: What's the largest corporation in America?
W: Exxon operates in over 100 countries throughout the world. Although ownership figures are not available, it is believed that control is concentrated in the Rockefeller family.

A: **Ezra Pound**
Q: What U.S. poet was indicted for treason for broadcasting Fascist propaganda in World War II?
W: American poet Ezra Pound was a supporter of the Italian dictator Benito Mussolini. Pound remained in Italy during World War II and made more than 300 broadcasts over Rome radio. In 1945 he was indicted for treason by the U.S. and was arrested and placed in a prison camp for U.S. Army criminals at Pisa.

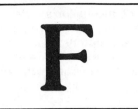

F

A: F. Lee Bailey
Q: Who defended The Boston Strangler?
W: Albert H. DeSalvo, widely known as the "Boston Strangler", killed 13 women in Boston between June 1962 and January 1964. He was represented by F. Lee Bailey, also known for defending Dr. Sam Sheppard and Patricia Hearst. There was no direct proof that DeSalvo was the Boston Strangler until he made a confession relating details that no one but the murderer could have known.

A: F. Lee Bailey
Q: Who made his name defending Dr. Sam Sheppard?
W: Because he was an authority on polygraphy, F. Lee Bailey was called into his first major case, that of Dr. Samuel Sheppard of Cleveland, who had been convicted in 1954 of murdering his wife. Bailey argued that pretrial publicity may have influenced the jury. In a retrial, Sheppard was acquitted, and Bailey became one of the country's leading trial lawyers.

A: Faisal
Q: What Saudi Arabian king was assassinated by his nephew in 1975?
W: Faisal, who was king of Saudi Arabia from 1964 to 1975, became an important world leader because of his control over his country's vast oil resources. In 1975 he was assassinated by one of his nephews—shot in the face three times. Faisal used government profits from oil for such things as expansion of public education and industrialization projects.

A: Fanne Fox
Q: Who was Wilbur Mill's favorite stripper?
W: Fanne Fox was the stripper who was found with Arkansas Democratic Representative Wilbur Mills in the Washington Tidal Basin in 1974. As a result of this incident, Mills resigned as Chairman of the House Ways and Means Committee.

A: Fifteen
Q: How many stripes did the flag first called the Star-Spangled Banner have?
W: It was first termed the *Star Spangled Banner* by Francis Scott Key in a poem he started on Sept. 13, 1814, to commemorate his seeing the flag flying over Fort McHenry in Baltimore during the American defense of the fort against the British in the War of 1812. The two additional stripes to the flag were in recognition of admission of Vermont and Kentucky to the Union.

A: Fifteen cents
Q: How much did a McDonald's hamburger cost in 1963?
W: In 1963 the price of the original hamburger, fifteen cents, was used as a special promotion! Twenty years later the special promotion was up to 39 cents! Where's the beef?

A: Fifth, The
Q: What ammendment to the Constitution did the Hollywood Ten invoke before the House Committee on Un-American Activities?
W: The Hollywood Ten were witnesses who invoked the fifth Amendment before the House Committee on Un-American Activity. The ten were fired by their studios, fined, sentenced to a year in jail, and prohibited from working in Hollywood for more than a decade.

A: Fiorello H. LaGuardia
Q: What New York City mayor was known as "the Little Flower"?
W: The nickname was taken from his first name. He fought civic corruption, supported labor, fostered civic improvement, and brought about a revision of the city character. He was a colorful figure with a flair for the dramatic. He once assigned an escort of Jewish police to a visitng Nazi delegation, and during a coal strike, he ordered the heat turned off in the room where the negotiators bickered.

A: Fiorello H. LaGuardia
Q: Who was elected mayor of New York City in 1933?
W: In 1933 LaGuardia unseated Tammany Hall in New York City's mayoral election. Twice re-elected, and serving 12 years as mayor, he began slum clearance and low cost housing projects; battled gangsters and official corruption; and built recreational facilities, health clinics, roads, and bridges, and LaGuardia Airport.

A: fish, The
Q: What creature was the early symbol for Christ?
W: The symbol was apparently chosen because Jesus instructed the Apostles, who were fishermen, "to fish for men" or, in other words, to convert men to Christianity. It was used as a signal by early Christians to avoid being discovered and persecuted.

A: Five
Q: How many Ringling brothers were there?
W: The world famous Ringling Brothers and Barnum and Bailey Circus was founded by the American Ringling brothers; Albert, Otto, Alfred, Charles, and John, who started out in 1884 from Baraboo, Wisconsin, with a well-run wagon show.

A: Flak jackets
Q: What jackets protect you from "flieger abwehr kanonen"?
W: *Flak* is from *Flieger Abwehr Kanonen*, meaning an "aircraft defense gun." The jackets were of cloth-covered heavy metal and were used during World War II by fliers and gunners to protect against shrapnel wounds.

A: Fletcher Christian
Q: Who led the settlers of Pitcairn Island?
W: Pitcairn, discovered by Robert Pitcairn, is a mountainous volcanic island in the South Pacific. In 1790, it was selected by Fletcher Christian and eight other mutineers from the ship *Bounty* as their refuge.

A: Florence Nightingale
Q: Who was "The Lady of the Lamp"?
W: Florence Nightingale, the founder of the nursing profession as we know it today, was one of the greatest women of England's Victorian age. British soldiers, wounded in the Crimean War, called her "Lady with the Lamp" when she walked the halls of the hospital at night. The "light" from the lamp has come to mean care for the sick, concern for the welfare of the ordinary soldier, and freedom for women to choose their own work.

A: Fly around the world
Q: What was Amelia Earhart trying to do when she disappeared in 1937?
W: Amelia was an American aviatrix born in Atchison, Kansas, in 1898.

She was the first woman to cross the Atlantic Ocean in an airplane. Her last flight was in July 1937.

A: Ford's Theatre
Q: What theatre was Abraham Lincoln in when shot?
W: It's in Washington D.C. Lincoln was shot on April 14, 1865 by actor John Wilkes Booth while Lincoln was attending a play entitled *Our American Cousin*.

A: Forty-nine
Q: How many states did Richard Nixon carry in 1972?
W: Richard Nixon carried 49 states with a total of 520 electoral votes in 1972. McGovern received 17 electoral votes and carried Massachusetts and Washington, D.C. One delegate cast his vote for John Hospers of the Libertarian party.

A: Four
Q: How many children does Queen Elizabeth II have?
W: They are Prince Charles (heir apparent), Princess Anne, Prince Andrew, and Prince Edward.

A: Four
Q: How many died at Kent State?
W: Four college students were shot and killed by the Ohio National Guard on May 5, 1970, at Kent State. Their names were Keith Gordon, Jeff McCracker, Talia Balsam, and Jane Fleiss.

A: Four
Q: How many eyes are there on a U.S. one-dollar bill?
W: On the front the two eyes belong to George Washington. On the back of the bill one eye tops the pyramid and one eye peers from the eagle's head.

A: Four
Q: How many Nixon-Kennedy debates were there?
W: Nixon and Kennedy took part in a unique series of four televised debates, whose audience included

most of the nation's voters. These debates marked the first time in American history that presidential candidates argued issues face-to-face in front of the entire nation.

A: Four
Q: How many people were executed for Abraham Lincoln's assassination?
W: A nine-man military commission tried eight accused conspirators in the Lincoln assassination, with the result that four were sentenced to death; George Atzerodt, for planning to murder the vice president; David E. Herold, for helping Booth escape; Lewis Paine, for attempting to kill the Secretary of State; and Mrs. Mary E. Surratt, the owner of a Washington boardinghouse, for helping the plotters.

A: Four
Q: How many times was Franklin Roosevelt elected president?
W: He was elected first in 1932, then in 1936, 1940, and 1944.

A: Four
Q: How many U.S. presidents have been assassinated?
W: Abraham Lincoln, 1865; James A. Garfield, 1881; William McKinley, 1901; and John F. Kennedy, 1963. Presidents elected in a zero year, since 1840, have died while in office but not all were assassinated nor did they necessarily die during their first term. The exception, so far, is President Ronald Reagan.

A: France
Q: What country did Morocco, Tunisia and Algeria fight to win their independence from?
W: France emerged from World War II weakened but determined to retain her empire. Initially surrendering control of Morocco and Tunisia, France held tenaciously to Algeria because of the large French population there. Algeria was regarded administratively as part of France.

A: **France**
Q: What country first claimed the Mississippi River in 1682?
W: In the late 17th century, the Frenchmen Jacques Marquette, Louis Joliet, and LaSalle explored the Mississippi River from the north. LaSalle claimed the whole valley for France when he reached the mouth of the river in 1682.

A: **France and Spain**
Q: What two European countries entered the War of American Independence against the British?
W: In 1775, the 13 American colonies rebelled after Britain taxed the colonies indirectly by imposing a tax on tea. France and Spain joined the rebelling colonies. The war closed with the Treaty of Versailles of 1783 and resulted in the independence of the American colonies. Britain acquired several West Indies islands, Spain recovered Florida and Minorca, and France secured Pondicherry and Chandernagore in India.

A: **Francis Scott Key**
Q: Who first called the U.S. flag the Star-Spangled Banner?
W: At the sight of the American flag flying over Fort McHenry the morning after bombardment in 1814, Key wrote a poem on the back of an envelope in which he referred to the flag as the Star-Spangled Banner.

A: **Francis Scott Key**
Q: Who wrote "The Star-Spangled Banner"?
W: Key was being detained on one of the British ships during the bombardment of Fort McHenry in 1814. The morning after, he wrote the words, as a poem, on the back of an envelope. The words were then printed on handbills, handed out, and published in Baltimore. Key wrote no other noteworty verses.

A: **Francisco Franco**
Q: Who emerged from the Civil War as Spain's leader?
W: Franco, dictator of Spain from 1936 until his death in 1975, came to power shortly after the start of the Spanish Civil War. The regime of "El Caudillo" was similar to a Fascist dictatorship, in that he held complete control of Spain; acting as Chief of State, prime minister, commander-in-chief, and leader of the Falange, the only political party permitted in Spain.

A: **Francisco Pizarro**
Q: What Spaniard conquered Peru in 1533?
W: Francisco Pizarro, the Spanish conquistador who secured Peru for Spain, reached an agreement with the Spanish King that gave the king all of Peru, its subjects, and its wealth. In return, Pizarro was made a knight of Santiago and Governor and Captain General of the conquered lands.

A: **Frank Sinatra**
Q: What singer paid a $240,000 ransom to free his kidnaped son?
W: On Dec. 8, 1963, a couple of hours before Frank, Jr. was to do his show at Harrah's Lake Tahoe Casino, Nevada, at 9:30 P.M., a "room service" impersonator knocked on the door and stated he had a package. The man walked in, placed a package on the table, and then produced a revolver. Frank, Sr., flew down to Reno and issued a statement that "I'd give the world for my son." (Frank, Jr., and his companion only had $12 in their wallets.) About 19 to 20 hours after the kidnapping, Sinatra got a call stating his son was in good shape and commanding the father to raise $240,000 in "used money" and prepare to deliver it to the kidnappers in Los Angeles. Frank, Jr.'s troubles, however, were not over. He had to help the FBI find his abductors and to help dispel growing suspicion that the kidnapping was a publicity hoax. He said he spent most of his time in the trunk of a car, riding for about 485 miles. The kidnapping team of Irwin and Amsler were able to produce $239,832.29 of the money after Irwin notified the FBI that he wanted to give himself up. Barry Keenan, who had masterminded the kidnapping, turned out to have been a classmate of Nancy Sinatra at University High School in Beverly Hills.

A: **Frank Sinatra**
Q: Who gave Marilyn Monroe a white poodle named Mafia?
W: Sinatra gave Monroe a poodle to keep her company. The name "Mafia" was a joke because of Sinatra's bad publicity—namely his alleged connection with the mob.

A: **Franklin Roosevelt**
Q: What U.S. president established the National Foundation for Infantile Paralysis?
W: This foundation grew out of the Warm Springs Foundation, organized by Roosevelt and incorporated on July 8, 1927, to sponsor patient care and research in the field of infantile paralysis. Roosevelt was a victim of infantile paralysis (polio).

A: **Franklin Roosevelt**
Q: Who called Dec. 7, 1941, "a date which will live in infamy"?
W: When President Roosevelt addressed Congress the day after the attack on Pearl Harbor by the Japanese, he said that Dec. 7, 1941 was "a date which will live in infamy." The U.S. then declared war against Japan. Four days later Germany and Italy declared war on the U.S., and the U.S. reciprocated.

HISTORY

A: **Franklin Roosevelt**
Q: Who delivered fireside chats?
W: The "Fireside Chat" was a gimmick of Louis Howe, who was in charge of public relations and fund raising for Roosevelt, in an effort to exploit FDR's audio appeal. These chats were friendly neighbor to neighbor reports on state affairs delivered from the Executive Mansion or Hyde Park, the Roosevelt home.

A: **Franklin Roosevelt**
Q: Who did Giuseppe Zangara try to assassinate in Miami on Feb. 15, 1933?
W: Guiseppe Zangara, a bricklayer, made an attempt on the life of President Roosevelt in 1933, but instead killed Anton Cermak, Mayor of Chicago who was with the President.

A: **Franklin Roosevelt**
Q: Who launched "the New Deal"?
W: The "New Deal" was a reform program described by President Roosevelt as a "use of-the authority of the government as an organized form of self-help for all classes and groups and sections in our country." It sponsored programs such as the Civil Works Administration, the Civilian Conservation Corps, and the Works Progress Administration.

A: **Franklin Roosevelt**
Q: Who said: "This generation of Americans has a rendezvous with destiny"?
W: This was part of his speech delivered June 27, 1936, in which he accepted renomination of the Democratic Party for the presidency.

A: **Franklin Roosevelt**
Q: Who was the first U.S. president to appear on TV while in office?
W: Roosevelt was the first President to appear on television when he spoke on April 30, 1939, at the opening ceremonies of the New York World's Fair. It was televised by NBC.

A: **French Foreign Legion, The**
Q: What fighting unit is headquartered in Corsica?

W: The Legion is a unit of the French Government but consists of volunteers. Although Frenchmen are forbidden to join the Legion, some enlist by giving false nationalities. Most units are located in Corsica, the French Territory of Afars and Issas, the Malagasy Republic, and the Pacific Islands controlled by France.

A: **Friday**
Q: What day of the week was John F. Kennedy assassinated on?
W: JFK was assassinated at Dallas, Texas, November 22, 1963. Enough said.

A: **Friedrich Nietsche**
Q: What philosopher was hailed by Hitler and Mussolini as the prophet of authoritarianism?
W: Nietsche was the German philosopher who initiated "morals of masters", the doctrine of perfectability of man through forcible self-assertion and glorification of the superman or over-man.

A: **Fugitive Nazis**
Q: What does Simon Weisenthal hunt?
W: Weisenthal has been very successful in finding instigators of the Holocaust. He has turned in many, from the lowest ranking to the highest, including Adolf Eichmann.

A: **Fulgencio Batista**
Q: What Cuban leader did Fidel Castro overthrow in 1959?
W: Castro engaged in revolutionary activities against the Batista regime. After many nonviolent attempts, Castro used guerrilla tactics to overthrow Batista. Castro made himself dictator in 1959.

G

A: **G. Gordon Liddy**
Q: Who served the longest jail term as a result of Watergate?
W: Liddy was sentenced to a term of from six to eight months to not more than 20 years in jail for his involvement in the Watergate scandel and his refusal to answer questions in front of a grand jury. He was convicted in connection with the break-in at the office of Daniel Ellsberg's psychiatrist and found guilty of contempt of Congress for refusing to testify before a congressional committee. After serving five years in prison, Liddy's sentence was commuted by President Carter in 1978.

A: **Gamal Abdel Nasser**
Q: Who led the coup that deposed King Farouk in 1952?
W: Nasser led the revolt that overthrew King Farouk in 1952 and established Egypt as a republic. Nasser served as Prime Minister from 1954 until he was elected President of Egypt in 1956, but he resigned after Egypt lost the Six Day War of 1967. The Egyptian National Assembly refused to accept his resignation and massive public support led him to stay in office and become both President and Prime Minister. He died suddenly in September 1970.

A: **Gamal Abdel Nasser**
Q: Who was the first president of Egypt?
W: Well, not exactly. The monarchy of Egypt was abolished in 1953 with General Muhammad Naguib becoming first president of the new republic. In 1954, Colonel Gamal Abdel Nasser forced Naguib out of office and became President.

A: Gary Gilmore
Q: Who was executed by firing squad in Utah in 1977?
W: Gilmore was the convicted murderer who was executed in front of a firing squad in Utah on Jan. 17, 1977. He was the first person to have been executed in the U.S in ten years.

A: General Curtis E. LeMay
Q: Who was George Wallace's running mate in 1968?
W: Partly because of his strong support of the U.S. military role in the Vietnam War, in 1968 Lemay became a vice-presidential candidate on the American Independent Party ticket headed by Alabama Governor George C. Wallace. After their defeat, LeMay retired again to private life.

A: General Douglas MacArthur
Q: Who challenged Truman's conduct of the Korean War and was fired for it?
W: MacArthur was born in Arkansas in 1880. In 1950, when South Korea was invaded by North Korean communists, General MacArthur was placed in command of the opposing forces - the first commander in chief under the flag of the United Nations. In 1951, President Truman removed him for making public statements critical of Washington policy. In 1952 he accepted chairmanship of the board of Remington Rand.

A: General Douglas MacArthur
Q: Who said: "Old soldiers never die; they just fade away"?
W: In April, 1951 President Truman relieved MacArthur of his Far Eastern commands because he violated an order of public silence that had been imposed on him. MacArthur returned home and defended his policies in a memorable address before a joint meeting of Congress. His speech included this famous reference to a military ballad.

A: General Dwight Eisenhower
Q: Who commanded the Allied landing at Normandy on D-Day?
W: General Eisenhower, 34th President of the U.S., was born in Denison, Texas, in 1890. After the reconquest of French Africa and the invasion of Sicily and Italy during World War II, he was recalled to London. There he organized and later directed the invasion and reconquest of France in 1944. The scope of this sea-air-land operation known as "D-Day" was unprecedented in military history.

A: General George S. Patton, Jr.
Q: Who was ordered to apologize for slapping Private Paul G. Bennett in the face?
W: "Old Blood and Guts" Patton was relentlessly hard driving and combative. He received unfavorable publicity for slapping an exhausted combat soldier in a hospital. He later publicly apologized.

A: General William Westmoreland
Q: Who commanded U.S. forces in Vietnam from 1964 to 1968?
W: Westmoreland was born in 1914 in Spartanburg County, South Carolina. He was Commander of the U.S. forces in South Vietnam, and in 1968 became the Army Chief of Staff.

A: George
Q: What was Christine Jorgensen's first name before the 1952 sex change?
W: Christine George Jorgensen became the world's first sex-change girl. The *New York News* marked the homecoming of Christine in the following manner: "Christine Jorgenson, the lad who became a lady, arrived home from Denmark yesterday, lit a cigarette like a girl, husked 'hello', and tossed off a Bloody Mary like a guy, then opened her fur coat. Jane Russell has nothing to worry about."

A: George III
Q: Who was the king of England when the American Revolution broke out?
W: George III, the longest reigning of male British monarchs, saw a great expansion of Britain's commercial empire during his rule, despite the loss of the American colonies. He viewed the concession of U.S. independence in 1783 with such loathing that he considered abdicating his throne.

A: George Lincoln Rockwell
Q: Who founded the American Nazi Party?
W: George Lincoln Rockwell founded the American Nazi Party in 1959. He was portrayed by Marlon Brando in the film *Roots II*.

A: George S. Patton Jr.
Q: What U.S. general died Dec. 10, 1945, when his jeep collied with a truck?
W: *WRONG!* Patton actually died on Dec. 21, 1945. In Germany on Dec. 9, 1945, a Signal Corps truck collided with the Cadillac in which General Patton was a passenger in what appeared to be a minor accident. The only injury was to Patton who proved to have a broken neck. He remained in the hospital paralyzed until his death on Dec. 21, 1945. General Patton is buried in the American Military Cemetery in Hamm, Luxembourg. On a white cross, identical with others in the cemetery, is this epitaph: "General Third Army, California. Dec. 21, 1945."

A: George S. Patton, Jr.
Q: What U.S. general was known as "Old Blood and Guts"?
W: General George Scott Patton, Jr., "Old Blood and Guts", was so called because of his tough-minded, outspoken manner. He even wore ivory-handled revolvers on his hips.

A: George Wallace
Q: Who did Arthur H. Bremer try to assassinate on May 15, 1972?
W: In 1972 Wallace sought the presidency for the second time; however, he abandoned the campaign after a would-be assassin (Arthur H. Bremer) wounded him and left him partially paralyzed. Wallace returned to his position as Governor of Alabama.

A: George Wallace
Q: Who finished third in the 1968 U.S. presidential election?
W: In 1968 Wallace ran for president on the American Independent Party ticket. He was defeated and returned to his home state of Alabama where he was re-elected governor in 1970. He ran for the presidency again in 1972.

A: George Wallace
Q: Who said: "Segregation now, segregation tomorrow, segregation forever"?
W: At his inauguration in 1963, Alabama Governor George Wallace pledged: "Segregation now, segregation tomorrow, segregation forever." He became a hero to opponents of integration when he stood in the doorway at the University of Alabama, opposing the enrollment of two black students. Despite Wallace's stand, many Alabama schools became integrated during Wallace's first term.

A: George Washington
Q: Who became president of the U.S. in 1789?
W: He was inaugurated on April 30, 1789, in New York, the temporary national capital, after having presided over the Constitutional Convention and yielding to the universal de-

mand that he serve as first President. Thomas Jefferson was the first President to be inaugurated in Washington, D.C.

A: George Washington
Q: Who laid the cornerstone of the U.S. Capitol?
W: In 1792, the competition for design of the Capitol was won by a West Indian doctor, William Thornton, who had lived in Philadelphia for a time but had no architectural experience. The cornerstone was laid by George Washington on Sept. 18, 1793.

A: George Washington
Q: Who was the only U.S. president never to live in Washington, D.C.?
W: During his term as president, Washington lived on an estate in Mount Vernon, Virginia, since the White House wasn't completed until 1800. Washington, D.C., was named after him. John Adams, the second U.S. president, moved to the White House during his first term in office, and all other presidents since have resided there.

A: George Washington
Q: Whose likeness is depicted on the Purple Heart?
W: The Order of the Purple Heart is a military decoration awarded to U.S. armed forces personnel who are wounded in combat. George Washington's likeness is depicted on the Purple Heart because it was this Order that in 1932 superseded the Badge of Military Merit established by George Washington in 1782 to honor soldiers for extraordinary bravery.

A: Georges Pompidou
Q: Who succeeded Charles De Gaulle as president of France?
W: Pompidou served as president from 1969 to 1974, succeeding DeGaulle who had served from 1959 to 1969. When DeGaulle's proposals for reform were rejected in a national referendum in April 1969, he retired from office. Georges Pompidou was then elected President of France.

A: Georgi Malenkov
Q: Who succeeded Joseph Stalin as Russian premier?
W: Malenkov was the head of aircraft and tank production for Russia during World War II. He served as Deputy Premier for the USSR from 1946 until 1953, then as Premier from 1953 to 1955.

A: Gerald Ford
Q: What U.S. President pardoned Tokyo Rose?
W: Tokyo Rose was the nickname given by U.S. troops in the Pacific to at least a dozen women who broadcast enemy propaganda and music to them from Japan. During World War II, one of these women, Ivaikuki Toguri d'Aquino, a U.S. citizen, was convicted of treason. Imprisoned until 1956, she steadfastly claimed to have worked under duress. On Jan. 19, 1977, President Ford granted her a pardon.

A: Gerald Ford
Q: What U.S. president was the target of two assassination attempts in 17 days?
W: Ford survived unharmed in a series of assassination attempts right after he announced his candidacy for the 1976 election for president. He was the first U.S. president to serve without being voted into office. He became vice president by appointment after Spiro Agnew resigned and then succeeded Nixon, who resigned as a result of Watergate.

A: Gerald Ford
Q: Who did Sara Jane Moore try to assassinate?
W: On Sept. 22, 1975, Gerald Ford escaped this assassination attempt in San Francisco. Sara fired one shot from a .38 caliber pistol that was deflected. This was the second attempt on his life that month.

A: Gerald Ford
Q: Who did Squeaky Fromme try to assassinate?
W: Sept. 5, 1975, Squeaky Fromme pointed, but did not fire, a .45 at President Ford in Sacramento. This was the first of two attempts to be made on his life in 17 days.

A: Gerald Ford
Q: Who said: "Our long national nightmare is over"?
W: This quote was part of Ford's inaugural address on Aug. 9, 1974, after he succeeded Richard Nixon as President of the U.S.

A: Gerald Ford
Q: Who succeeded Spiro Agnew as U.S. vice-president?
W: Ford was House Minority Leader under Richard Nixon and was appointed vice president after Agnew resigned. Ford was nominated in October and took office on Dec. 6, 1973, as the 40th vice president of the United States.

A: Gerald Ford
Q: Who was the first U.S. president to appear on TV's "Meet the Press"?
W: He was the first president to appear on "Meet the Press," but the ninth vice president to assume the presidency without being elected to the office.

A: Gerald Ford
Q: Who was the only U.S. president and vice-president never elected to either office?
W: Gerald Ford was appointed vice-president in 1973 after Spiro Agnew resigned. On Aug. 9, 1974 he took over for Nixon as 38th President of the United States.

A: Gerald Ford and Robert Dole
Q: What presidential ticket was dubbed Bozo and the Pineapple?
W: The media bestowed these nicknames. Ford's frequent "accidents" earned him the nickname "Bozo," and Dole's nickname became "Pineapple" after the Dole pineapple company.

A: German
Q: What was Queen Victoria's mother tongue?
W: Victoria, born in England in 1819, was the granddaughter of King Charles III who had succeeded to the British throne even though he was from Hanover, Germany (there was a union between Great Britain and Hanover at that time). When Victoria's uncle King William IV died, the thrones of Britain and Hanover were divided because the laws of Hanover prevented succession by a woman. Victoria became Queen of Great Britain.

A: Germany
Q: What country did Lord Haw Haw broadcast propaganda for in World War II?
W: Lord Haw Haw was the nickname of Irish-American William Joyce, who broadcast propaganda for the Germans during World War II. He was tried, convicted of treason, and hanged on Jan. 13, 1946.

A: Germany
Q: What country claimed the first U.S. warship sunk in World War II?
W: *Reuben James*, a U.S. destroyer completed in 1920, became the first American warship to be sunk during the war when she was torpedoed on Oct. 31, 1941 by the German submarine U-562. The attack occurred while the *Reuben James* and four other destroyers were escorting a British convoy about 600 miles west of Ireland. She sank in five minutes with the loss of 115 officers and men. A popular song was written about the tragedy.

A: Geronimo
Q: What Indian leader surrendered to General George Crook?
W: Geronimo led the Apaches in their war against the whites. Geronimo surrendered to Crook in January 1884, but took flight from the San Carlos reservation in May 1885. Crook went after him again in what was known as the Geronimo Campaign, and Geronimo surrendered again in March 1886. A rumor spread that the Indians were to be murdered, so Geronimo fled once more! In September 1886, he surrendered a third time to Brigadier General Nelson A. Miles, who had replaced Crook.

A: Geronimo
Q: Who was the last of the Apache warrior chiefs?
W: Geronimo is the Spanish form of the English name Jerome. The name was given to Goyathlay, meaning "one who yawns" by the Mexicans. Geronimo's courage and determination were responsible for keeping the Apaches from having to surrender their Arizona homeland to the U.S. until 1886. After his surrender and imprisonment, he was placed under military confinement and settled down at Fort Sill, Oklahoma. There he adopted Christianity and became a prosperous farmer. He went on to become a national celebrity, appearing in the St. Louis World's Fair and Theodore Roosevelt's inaugural procession.

A: Gestapo
Q: What's the infamous contraction of *Geheime Staatspolizei?*
W: The Gestapo was originally formed by Hermann Goering as a political police unit in the state of Prussia. It gradually came under the control of Heinrich Himmler and in 1936 Hitler decreed the Gestapo to be a national secret police and forbade judicial appeals against its decisions.

HISTORY

A: *Golden Hind*, **The**
Q: What ship did Sir Francis Drake circle the world in?
W: Sir Francis Drake is best known for his circumnavigation of the world, a feat that had been accomplished only once before by Ferdinand Magellan. Although Drake began his journey with five ships, by the time he reached the Pacific, he was left with only one ship, the *Golden Hind*.

A: **Good Friday**
Q: What religious holiday was Abraham Lincoln assassinated on?
W: John Wilkes Booth, an actor and Southern sympathizer, shot Abraham Lincoln on Good Friday, April 14, 1865, at Ford's Theater in Washington, D.C. It was the first assassination of a President.

A: **Grace Kelly's**
Q: What former movie star's children are Prince Albert and Princess Caroline?
W: Grace Kelly, who for five years was one of Hollywood's most beautiful and successful actresses, was for 26 years the wife of His Serene Highness Prince Rainier III of Monaco. As a Grimaldi (Rainier's family name), she was a member of Europe's oldest royal family. Grace and the Prince had three children: Princess Caroline, born in 1957; Prince Albert, born in 1958; and Princess Stephanie, born in 1965.

A: **Great Train Robbery, The**
Q: What British heist did Ronald Biggs mastermind?
W: The Great Train Robbery occurred on Aug. 8, 1963, when 12 masked Englishmen converged on a preselected site near Cheddington, England, and switched the railroad signals on the Glasgow-London mail train. The thieves fled with $7,368,715, but were later caught. Less than $1 million has been recovered.

A: **Great War, The**
Q: What was World War I known as before World War II?
W: It was the largest war the world had seen up to that time. Rivalries among Germany, France, Great Britain, Russia, and Austria-Hungary led to the devastation.

A: **Guess Who, The**
Q: What rock group raised a ruckus at the White House by singing "American Woman"?
W: The Guess Who group was one of Canada's top bands. In the early 1960s Chad Allan and Randy Bachman formed the first Guess Who lineup. They had their own Canadian TV Show called "Where It's At."

H

A: **H.R. Haldeman**
Q: Who was Richard Nixon's first chief of staff in the White House?
W: Harry Robbins Haldeman was President Nixon's White House Chief of Staff from 1969 to 1973. He was given a four-year sentence for conspiracy, obstruction of justice and perjury in the Watergate coverup, but was paroled after serving 18 months.

A: **Hail to the Chief**
Q: What song is traditionally heard when the president of the U.S. arrives on the scene?
W: About 1812, a New York publisher, John Poff, issued a song "Hail to the Chief". The words were from Sir Walter Scott's "The Lady of The Lake", and the music was by James Sanderson.

A: **Haile Selassie**
Q: What emperor was known as "the Lion of Judah"?
W: Haile Selassie became emperor of Ethiopia in 1930 and was overthrown by military leaders in 1974. He worked for economic and social reforms such as making slavery punishable by law. Selassie claimed to be descended from King Solomon and the Queen of Sheba. Although the Lion of Judah was one of Selassie's official titles, he was also called "The Conquering Lion" because of an adversary's description that he had jaws like a lion.

A: **Haiphong**
Q: What major North Vietnamese port was mined by the U.S.?
W: Haiphong is a city and major port in northern Vietnam on the Song Koi Delta. Haiphong was heavily damaged in U.S. bombing raids during the Vietnam War, and in 1972 its harbor was mined.

A: **Hanging Gardens of Babylon, The**
Q: What botanical marvel did Nebuchadnezzar build?
W: The Hanging Garden of Babylon were probably built by King Nebuchadnezzar after he married a mountain princess. It is believed that he built them to make her feel at home.

A: **Harold**
Q: Who was the last Anglo-Saxon king of England?
W: Harold was the son of Godwin, Earl of Wessex, and served as chief minister to his brother-in-law, Edward the Confessor. Upon Edward's death, Harold secured his own election as king. He was killed in the Battle of Hastings in 1066, when William the Conqueror and the Normans invaded England.

BABY BOOMER® is the registered trademark of Baby Boomers of America, Inc.

CODE CARD

Trivial Pursuit®

	GENUS EDITION	BABY BOOMER® EDITION	ALL-STAR SPORTS EDITION	SILVER SCREEN EDITION	YOUNG PLAYERS™ EDITION
⬤	SPORTS & LEISURE	R.P.M.	NUMBERS	PORTRAYALS	GAMES & HOBBIES
⬤	SCIENCE & NATURE	LIVES & TIMES	BASEBALL	PRODUCTION	NATURAL WORLD
⬤	ART & LITERATURE	PUBLISHING	BASKETBALL	ON SCREEN	ART & CULTURE
⬤	HISTORY	NIGHTLY NEWS	CATCH ALL	OFF SCREEN	SCIENCE & TECHNOLOGY
⬤	ENTERTAINMENT	STAGE & SCREEN	FOOTBALL	TITLES	GOOD TIMES
⬤	GEOGRAPHY	TELEVISION	NICKNAMES	SETTINGS	PEOPLE & PLACES

BABY BOOMER® is the registered trademark of Baby Boomers of America, Inc.

Trivial Pursuit®

CODE CARD

	GENUS EDITION	SILVER SCREEN EDITION	ALL-STAR SPORTS EDITION	BABY BOOMER® EDITION	YOUNG PLAYERS™ EDITION
⬤	GEOGRAPHY	SETTINGS	NICKNAMES	TELEVISION	PEOPLE & PLACES
⬤	ENTERTAINMENT	TITLES	FOOTBALL	STAGE & SCREEN	GOOD TIMES
⬤	HISTORY	OFF SCREEN	CATCH ALL	NIGHTLY NEWS	SCIENCE & TECHNOLOGY
⬤	ART & LITERATURE	ON SCREEN	BASKETBALL	PUBLISHING	ART & CULTURE
⬤	SCIENCE & NATURE	PRODUCTION	BASEBALL	LIVES & TIMES	NATURAL WORLD
⬤	SPORTS & LEISURE	PORTRAYALS	NUMBERS	R.P.M.	GAMES & HOBBIES

BABY BOOMER® is the registered trademark of Baby Boomers of America, Inc.

A: Harold Macmillan
Q: What British prime minister was at the podium of the United Nations when Nikita Khrushchev banged his shoe?
W: Khruschev went to the United Nations in September 1960 to personally offer his plan for the reorganization of the United Nations. His plan included moving the headquarters to Switzerland and replacing the secretary-general with a three-man commission. He laughed and shouted during the speeches and pounded his shoe on the desk during Macmillan's address.

A: Harry Truman
Q: Who said: "In the memory of our fallen president, we shall not fail"?
W: Truman made this statement as part of a radio broadcast to the U.S. Armed Forces six days after the death of Franklin Roosevelt on April 12, 1945.

A: Harvard
Q: What university dismissed Timothy Leary for involving students in drugs?
W: Timothy Leary was a professor at Harvard when he became a leader in the drug and protest culture of the 1960s. He was dismissed as a result of his activist participation.

A: Harvard
Q: What's the oldest university in the U.S.?
W: That's correct: it was founded Oct. 28, 1636. Harvard was named for John Harvard, a Puritan minister, who founded the college with an initial endowment of 400 pounds sterling and 300 books.

A: hat, A
Q: What is Bella Abzug's sartorial trademark?
W: A lawyer by profession, Bella Abzug became nationally prominent in the early 1970s as an advocate of women's rights and as a leader of the House of Representatives antiwar group. Her large, floppy hats became a trademark during her congressional terms.

A: Hatfield-McCoy feud, The
Q: What feud ended with a marriage in Kentucky on March 21, 1891?
W: The Hatfields and the McCoys were the two famous feuding hillbilly families. The Hatfields lived in Mingo County, West Virginia, while the McCoys resided in Pike County, Kentucky. Their feud finally ended with the inter-family marriage of Aaron Hatfield and Sophia McCoy on March 21, 1891, but only after 150 family members had been killed.

A: He became Pope John Paul II
Q: What happened to the Archbishop of Krakow in 1978?
W: Pope John Paul II was born Karol Wojtyla, Jr., 1920, in the town of Wadowice, Poland. In 1938, at the age of 18, he moved to Krakow to begin the study of Polish literature at the Jagiellonian University. In 1942, Karal became a student of theology and was ordained on Nov. 1, 1946. Later in 1958, he was named an auxilary bishop of Krakow and finally a cardinal in 1967. He became Pope in 1978.

A: He committed suicide
Q: What did Hermann Goering do three hours before he was to be executed?
W: Herman Wilhelm Goering was second only to Adolf Hitler in the German National Socialist regime. He was captured by the Allies in 1945 and tried as a major war criminal at Nuremburg. Although he was condemned to be executed, he cheated the hangman by poisoning himself.

A: He discovered the Watergate break-in
Q: What's the claim to fame of night watchman Frank Wills?
W: Frank Wills was the night watchman at the prestigious Watergate office complex, which at the time housed the Democratic National Committee's Headquarters. Wills, while making his rounds, spotted some tape covering the locks on the doors inside the office complex. He proceeded to call the police, and within minutes five men were arrested inside the Democratic office.

A: He filmed John F. Kennedy's assassination
Q: What's the claim to fame of Abraham Zapruder?
W: Zapruder was a bystander who filmed the assassination of JFK on Nov. 23, 1963, in Dallas, Texas with an 8-millimeter Bell and Howell camera. He sold the film to Time-Life for $25,000, but donated the money to Fireman's and Policeman's Benevolent Fund.

A: He was captain of the *Titanic*
Q: What was the claim to fame of Captain Edward J. Smith, who died on April 15, 1912?
W: Captain Smith was the captain of the supposedly unsinkable White Star liner, the *Titanic*, which struck an iceberg on her maiden voyage and sank in April 1912. Besides Smith, the Titanic builder, Thomas Andrews, and over 1,500 other passengers died.

A: He was the first black justice
Q: What's the distinction of U.S. Supreme Court Justice Thurgood Marshall?
W: In 1965 President Lyndon B. Johnson appointed Marshall Solicitor General of the United States. In 1967 Johnson nominated Marshall to the Supreme Court, making him the first black Supreme Court Justice.

A: **Heinrich Himmler**
Q: Who headed the Gestapo?
W: Himmler was one of the most powerful figures in Germany's National Socialist leadership. He commanded both the SS and the Gestapo. When captured at the end of the war, Himmler committed suicide.

A: **Hemorrhoids**
Q: What was Jimmy Carter operated on for while serving as President?
W: Other famous hemorrhoid sufferers included Karl Marx, Earl Warren, Gerald Ford, and Elizabeth Taylor. What a pain...

A: **Henry VIII**
Q: Who was the second son of Henry VII and Elizabeth of York?
W: ...and just who were his wives? (1) Catherine of Aragon, the widow of his brother Arthur; (2) Anne Boleyn, mother of Elizabeth I; she was beheaded for adultery; (3) Jane Seymour, mother of Edward VI; she died; (4) Anne of Cleves; they were divorced; (5) Catherine Howard, beheaded for adultery; and (6) Catherine Parr, who survived him. He was King of England from 1509 to 1547.

A: **Henry Cabot Lodge**
Q: Who was Richard Nixon's running mate in 1960?
W: Henry Cabot Lodge was the Ambassador to the United Nations at the time of his nomination, and John Kennedy had beat him in a Massachusetts Senate race in 1952. Little known fact: Kennedy and Nixon were both first elected to Congress in 1946, and Nixon was only four years older than Kennedy, but the campaign slogan for Nixon-Lodge was ''Experience Counts''...for what?

A: **Henry Hudson**
Q: What English explorer was set adrift by his mutinous crew near the bay that bears his name?
W: Because Hudson's party could not find the outlet from Hudson Bay

in 1610, they spent the winter there. In the spring the crew mutinied, and Hudson and a few remaining men were set adrift in a small boat.

A: **Henry Hudson**
Q: Who was the first European to sail into New York harbor?
W: In search of the Northwest Passage to the East Indies, Hudson sailed into New York Harbor and continued up the Hudson River as far as Albany. New York Harbor is an inlet of the Atlantic Ocean at the mouth of the Hudson River.

A: **Henry Kissinger**
Q: Who declared: "Peace is at hand"?
W: On Oct. 26, two weeks before the 1972 presidential election, Kissinger made this announcement regarding Vietnam negotiations. However, it was January 1973 before the "Agreement on Ending the War" was signed.

A: **Henry Kissinger**
Q: Who did Richard Nixon tender his resignation to?
W: In 1973 Kissinger was appointed Secretary of State; he was the first Jewish and foreign-born citizen to hold that post. On Aug. 9, 1974, Nixon resigned as President of the United States because of the Watergate investigation. He tendered his resignation to Kissinger as Secretary of State.

A: **Henry Kissinger**
Q: Who was awarded the 1973 Nobel Peace Prize with Le Duc Tho?
W: Kissinger, along with Le Duc Tho, the North Vietnamese negotiator, was awarded the Nobel Peace Prize for their roles in the disengagement of U.S. troops from South Vietnam. Tho declined the prize!

A: **Henry Kissinger**
Q: Who knelt in prayer with Richard Nixon in the final hours of Watergate?
W: According to Nixon's recent inter-

view, this is not accurate; nevertheless, as Kissinger was leaving the room where they met, Nixon did say he thought they ought to pray over their dilemma.

A: **Henry Kissinger**
Q: Who said: "Power is the ultimate aphrodisiac?"
W: This line is quoted from the *New York Times* on Jan. 19, 1971.

A: **Henry M. Stanley**
Q: Who did the *New York Herald* send looking for African explorer David Livingstone?
W: In 1871 Stanley was sent by the *New York Herald* to Africa to search for the noted missionary-explorer, David Livingstone, who had not been heard from for several years. After an arduous eight-month journey, Stanley found him, and together they explored Lake Tanganyika and the Ruiszi River. Stanley later discovered the source of the Nile.

A: **Hermann Goering**
Q: Who built and commanded Nazi Germany's Luftwaffe?
W: Goering joined the army in 1912 and during World War I won great distinction as an air fighter. In 1922 he became an organizer of Hitler's Storm Troopers. He later became Minister of Aviation and developed the largest air force in the world.

A: **Hertz**
Q: Who put you in the driver's seat?
W: Hertz Car Rental Agency, owned by the RCA Corporation, has been a competitor with Avis Car Rental for the number 1 place in the car rental business. Remember the commercials with people being floated into a car?

A: **"High Hopes"**
Q: What was John F. Kennedy's 1960 campaign song?
W: "High Hopes" from the movie *A Hole in the Head* won an Oscar for Best Song in 1959.

A: *Hindenburg,* **The**
Q: What blew up at Lakehurst, New Jersey, on May 6, 1937?
W: The *Hindenburg* was a German dirigible. Its explosion, cause unknown, took the lives of 36 of the 97 passengers.

A: *Hindenburg,* **The**
Q: What ill-fated craft was captained by Ernst Lehmann?
W: Herb Morrison, of Chicago's WLS radio, was broadcasting the landing and reported the crash live over the air. This was the first record-ed news broadcast.

A: **Hiroshima**
Q: What city was destroyed by "Little Boy"?
W: The Uranium-235 Bomb, known as "Little Boy," was 14 feet long, five feet in diameter, and weighed 10,000 pounds. It was loaded aboard the *Enola Gay,* a B-29 piloted by Colonel Paul W. Tibbets, Jr. Between 80,000 and 200,000 people were killed at Hiroshima.

A: **His head**
Q: What did Sir Walter Raleigh lose in 1618?
W: Upon his return to England from South America, Raleigh was sentenced to death for disobeying orders of King James I not to invade Spain. He met his fate calmly, joking with the executioner.

A: **His mother and wife**
Q: What two relatives did Theodore Roosevelt lose on St. Valentine's Day, 1884?
W: On February 14, 1884, Roosevelt's wife, Alice, died, two days after the birth of a daughter. On the same day, Roosevelt's mother, Martha, died of typhoid fever.

A: **Homosexuality**
Q: What was the love that dared not speak its name in Victorian England?
W: In 1698 homosexuality was relatively commonplace throughout England. In a letter to a friend, Elizabeth, Duchess of Orleans, wrote that "nothing is more ordinary in England than this unnatural vice." The age of sexual repression and moral hypocrisy began in England in 1837 as Victoria ascended the throne. Privately, it was said that Victoria was sexually liberated and that it was her husband, Albert, who was the prude.

A: **Horatio Nelson**
Q: Who said: "England expects every man will do his duty"?
W: This quote, made at the Battle of Trafalgar on Oct. 21, 1805, was first reported as, "Say to the fleet, England confides that every man will do his duty." It was said by Horatio Nelson who led the British fleet and was killed in that battle.

A: **House of Commons, The**
Q: What's the only house in England that the Queen may not enter?
W: The House of Commons seats members from England, Scotland, Wales, and Northern Ireland and has control over all financial legislation. The King or Queen is not allowed to enter the House, but there is a special room for other members of the Royal Family, from which they can watch the proceedings.

A: **Howard K. Smith**
Q: Who moderated the first Kennedy-Nixon TV debate?
W: Howard K. Smith was probably the number 1 TV and radio analyst of our time. He usually broadcast from the political conventions as well.

A: **Hubert Humphrey**
Q: Who was Lyndon Johnson's vice-president?
W: Hubert Horatio Humphrey was the 38th vice-president of the U.S. under President Lyndon Johnson. After four years as vice president, he was nominated for the presidency in 1968 but because of his defense of the Vietnam War, he was narrowly defeated by Richard Nixon in the November election.

A: **Huey Long**
Q: Who did Dr. Karl Austin Leiss assassinate in Baton Rouge in 1935?
W: Huey Pierce Long, the "Kingfish", governed Louisiana in a dictatorial fashion. He then served in the Senate and was considered a possible third-party candidate for the 1936 presidential election. On Sept. 8, 1935, however, he was shot by an assassin and died two days later.

A: **Humphrey Bogart**
Q: What actor was a seventh cousin of the Princess of Wales?
W: The cousin was Queen Mary Diana-Alexandria. Some of Bogart's pictures are *Casablanca* and *The African Queen*, for which he received an Oscar in 1951.

A: **Hundred Years War, The**
Q: What was the longest war in history?
W: And it lasted even longer than its name! It is the name given to the series of wars between England and France from 1337 to 1453. It was caused in part by the claim of British kings to the French throne.

A: **Hungary**
Q: What country was the victim of a Russian invasion in 1956?
W: In October 1956, a popular revolt against the government flared into revolution. Imre Nagy, who was returned to power against the wishes of Moscow, announced Hungary's withdrawal from the Warsaw Pact and the Soviets entered Budapest on November 4, 1956

HISTORY

A: "I Wish I Was in Dixie Land"
Q: What was the martial song of the Confederacy in the U.S. Civil War?
W: That's right...but did you know that it was written by a Northerner, Dan D. Emmett for a minstrel show (shows where white men in black-face makeup sang and danced)? The song, written in 1859, was claimed by both the North and the South, but during the Civil War it became the song of the Confederacy. The most likely source of the name "Dixie" is believed to be from the Mason-Dixon line, which geographically divided the South and the North. However, there is also another story about the currency issued in New Orleans with the French word *Dix* meaning "ten" on it, and how this came to be a nickname for New Orleans, and later the South.

A: Idi Amin
Q: What 20th-century African leader gave himself the title Conqueror of the British Empire?
W: Idi Amin ruled as military dictator of Uganda from 1971 to 1979, when he was overthrown. English is the official language of Uganda because it was an English colony from 1894 to 1914.

A: Idi Amin
Q: Who seized power from Milton Obote in 1971?
W: In 1966 Idi Amin helped Prime Minister Milton Obote overthrow Kabaka Mutea II, President of Uganda. In 1971 Amin ousted Obote from the presidency and proclaimed himself head of state.

A: Idi Amin
Q: What African leader wished Richard Nixon a speedy recovery from Watergate?
W: Idi Amin's mood fluctuations caused his activities to range from settling the Entebbe hijacking situation to having a person killed because he spoke poorly of Amin. This witty statement was a jab at Nixon's failings.

A: Income-tax evasion
Q: What was Al Capone finally imprisoned for in 1931?
W: Capone was indicted by a Federal Grand Jury and sentenced to 11 years in prison. He was released in 1939 with advanced syphilis and died in 1947.

A: India
Q: What country tested its first nuclear bomb in 1974?
W: In May 1974, India became the world's sixth nuclear power by exploding an underground nuclear device in the Thar Desert in Rajastham State. The U.S. was the first country to get the bomb, and was followed by the USSR, Great Britain, France, and China.

A: Indira Gandhi
Q: Who was the first female prime minister of India?
W: Indira was the daughter of Jawaharlah Nehru. She took a prominent part in the movement for independence in India and in the political party known as the Indian National Congress. She became the minister of information and broadcasting, and upon Shastri's death in 1966, she became the prime minister.

A: Indira Gandhi
Q: Who succeeded Shastri as Indian prime minister?
W: Indira Gandhi was elected prime minister after Shastri's death in 1966. Her father, Nehru, had been the first prime minister of India following independence in 1947.

A: I.N.R.I.
Q: What four letters were placed on the cross on which Christ was crucified?
W: The Romans nailed Christ to a cross, and they wrote "*I*esus *N*azarenus *R*ex *I*udaeorum" or "Jesus of Nazareth, King of the Jews" on the top. The inscription was written in Latin, Greek, and Hebrew.

A: International Red Cross, The
Q: What organization was given the only Nobel Peace Prize awarded during World War I?
W: In 1917 the International Committee of the Red Cross of Geneva, Switzerland, was given the Nobel Peace Prize for implementing the principles of humane warfare. There were no awards for peace given from 1914 to 1916 nor in 1918. The International Red Cross also received the only peace award given between 1939 and 1944.

A: Interpol
Q: What's the International Criminal Police Organization better known as?
W: Interpol is a mutual assistance organization of police forces. It was founded in Vienna in 1923 and now has a membership of 126 countries. Each member nation maintains a domestic clearinghouse that processes data on international criminals, especially those involved in smuggling, counterfeiting, and narcotic trade.

A: Ireland
Q: Where did Wrong-Way Corrigan land?
W: On July 17, 1938, Douglas Corrigan took off from New York's Floyd Bennet Airfield for the west coast. Corrigan's plane swept off in a wide arc out over the Atlantic and he landed 24 hours later at Dublin's Baldonnel Airport. He blamed the mistake on the fog, a faulty compass, and the lack of a radio!

A: Iron Age, The
Q: What age followed the Bronze Age?
W: The Iron Age marks the period in the development of technology in which the working of iron came into general use, replacing bronze as the basic material for implements and weapons. This is the last stage of the archaeological sequence known as the three age system: Stone Age, Bronze Age, and Iron Age.

A: Israel
Q: What country offered Albert Einstein its presidency in 1952?
W: Einstein had a vital interest in human affairs and a deep compassion for people who were politically or economically depressed. He supported Zionism and was offered the presidency of the state of Israel in 1952. He declined, saying he was not fit for the position.

A: It sank the *Lusitania*
Q: What was the infamous feat of Germany's U-20 submarine?
W: The *Lusitania* was torpedoed and sunk on May 7, 1915, by Germany's U-20 submarine off Old Head of Kinsdale, Ireland. The lives of 1,198 people were lost in this voyage from New York.

A: It was hit by a B-25 bomber
Q: What happened to the 79th floor of the Empire State Building on July 28, 1945?
W: The Empire State Building, a 102-story New York skyscraper, was for many years the world's tallest building. In 1945 a B-25 army bomber crashed into the building between the 78th and 79th floors, killing 14 people. The impact ripped the elevator cables and the two passengers aboard fell from the 75th floor to the subbasement. Neither was killed because of safety devices that had recently been installed.

A: It was lost at sea
Q: What happened to the U.S. nuclear submarine *Thresher* in 1963?
W: The *Thresher* was lost at sea on April 10, 1963 in the North Atlantic, 220 miles off Cape Cod. The *Thresher's* entire crew was lost during this test run. A malfunction and leak in the hull sent the submarine to extreme depths, crushing the hull. On May 21, 1968, the *Scorpion*, also a U.S. nuclear submarine, suffered the same fate.

A: Italy
Q: What country did the Allies invade in World War II's Operation Avalanche?
W: Operation Avalanche was the World War II code name for the Allied invasion of Italy.

A: Italy
Q: What country declared war on both Germany and the Allies in World War II?
W: On June 10, 1939 Italy declared war on both England and France. On June 22, 1941 it declared war on Russia and on December 11, 1941 it declared war on the U.S. By 1943 Italy was on the brink of defeat. The Italians signed an armistice and the new government, headed by Premier Marshall Pietro Badoglios, declared war on Germany on Oct. 13, 1943.

A: Italy
Q: What country did Victor Emmanuel III reign over as its last king?
W: Victor Emmanuel III became king of Italy after the assassination of his father Humbert I in 1900. People despised him because he refused to proclaim martial law to stop Mussolini's march on Rome in 1922. The King made no protest when Italy became a fascist dictatorship. In a 1946 election the Italian people voted to abolish the monarchy.

A: ITT
Q: Who did Dita Beard work for?
W: On March 17, 1972, Dita Beard, a Capitol Hill lobbyist denied writing a memo linking International Telephone and Telegraph (ITT) to the Republican Party that resulted in a favorable anti-trust settlement for ITT.

J

A: J. Paul Getty
Q: What oil tycoon left more than $1 billion when he died in 1976?
W: J. Paul Getty became one of the richest men in the world. He made his fortune in the petroleum business and his empire included Getty Oil Company, Skelly Oil Company and many smaller firms. His fortune may actually have totaled as much as $4 billion.

A: J. Paul Getty
Q: What oil tycoon once said: "A billion dollars isn't worth what it used to be"?
W: In 1957 Jean Paul Getty, who may have been worth $4 billion, sadly philosophized that "a billion dollars isn't worth what it used to be." He was born in Minneapolis on Dec. 15, 1892, and died on June 6, 1976.

A: Jack the Ripper
Q: Who killed five London prostitutes in 1888?
W: "Jack the Ripper," the London murderer of five prostitutes, was never apprehended. His five victims were Mary Anne "Polly" Nichols, "Dark" Annie Chapman, Elizabeth "Long Liz" Stride, Catherine Eddows, and "Black Mary" Jane Kelly.

A: Jack Ruby
Q: Who owned the Carousel Club and the Vegas Club in Dallas?
W: Jack Ruby killed Lee Harvey Oswald, alleged assassin of President John F. Kennedy, on Nov. 24, 1963.

A: Jack Ruby
Q: Who shot Lee Harvey Oswald?
W: Jack Ruby shot Lee Harvey Oswald, John F. Kennedy's alleged assassin, in a Dallas police station as a traumatized America watched on

HISTORY

television. It was never learned if Oswald was part of a plot. Ruby died of cancer after being imprisoned.

A: Jacqueline Kennedy
Q: Who gave a TV tour of the redecorated White House?
W: Jackie Kennedy thought that beauty and dignity were a necessary part of the White House and should be preserved. She restored it to the "Virginia" manner and in the summer of 1963 gave a tour on TV.

A: Jacqueline Kennedy
Q: Who lit the Eternal Flame on John F. Kennedy's grave?
W: Kennedy was buried with full military honors on November 25, 1963, at Arlington National Cemetery. At the close of the funeral service, Mrs. Kennedy lit an "eternal flame" at the President's grave.

A: James
Q: What's the most common Christian name of U.S. presidents?
W: And they were James Madison, James Monroe, James Polk, James Buchanan, James Garfield, and James Earl (Jimmy) Carter.

A: James I of England
Q: Which King James said: "He was a very valiant man that first adventured on eating oysters"?
W: No earlier reference can be found for this saying than that attributed to King James I of England. Although it is often attributed to Jonathan Swift, he did not write it until many years after James I.

A: James Earl Ray
Q: Who shot Martin Luther King Jr.?
W: Martin Luther King, Jr., was shot April 4, 1968, at a motel in Memphis, Tenn

A: James Meredith
Q: What black student integrated the state university at Oxford, Mississippi, in 1962?
W: Meredith was the first black to attend the University of Mississippi. He tried to register in the fall of 1962, accompanied by federal marshalls, but

was denied access by state officials. Rioting broke out in protest of his registering, but he succeeded and federal troops were stationed at the school until he graduated in 1963.

A: Jane Russell
Q: Whom did Howard Hughes design a cantilevered bra for?
W: During the filming of the movie *The Outlaw*, Hughes was trying to find a way to display Jane Russell's generous endowment. Hughes relied on his knowledge of aerodynamics and stress to design a bra that, at a pull of a string, would accentuate her already large breasts.

A: Jane Wyman
Q: Who was Ronald Reagan's first wife?
W: *Brother Rat*, filmed in 1938, was the first film that Reagan and Wyman did together. Over the next couple of years they fell in love and were married in Glendale, California, on Jan. 26, 1940. They were divorced July 18, 1949.

A: Japan and the U.S.
Q: What two countries fought the Battle of the Coral Sea?
W: The Battle of the Coral Sea was in part an attempt to neutralize the remaining American carrier fleet. The Japanese proposed to do this by expanding their defense perimeters in the area of the Coral Sea and Midway Island. The Battle was considered a draw with each side losing one carrier apiece: the U.S. lost the *Lexington and the Japanese the Shokaku*. The U.S. could be consoled that the Japanese didn't capture Port Moresby, thereby cutting off the supply lines from Pearl Harbor to Australia.

A: Japanese surrender in World War II, The
Q: What was signed aboard the *Missouri*?
W: The Japanese surrendered to allied forces led by General Douglas MacArthur aboard the battleship *Missouri* on Sept. 2, 1945.

A: Jawaharlal Nehru
Q: What Indian statesman coined the term the "Third World"?
W: Jawaharlal Nehru was India's first prime minister and served from 1947 until his death in 1964. He worked to establish a democracy and to increase living standards.

A: Jefferson, Lincoln, T. Roosevelt, Washington
Q: What four presidential likenesses are carved in Mount Rushmore?
W: Mount Rushmore National Memorial is a huge carving on a granite cliff in the Black Hills of South Dakota. It rises 5,752 feet above sea level and more than 500 feet above the valley. The memorial was designed by Gutzon Borglum. Work began in 1927 and was finally completed by Borglum's son in 1941.

A: Jerry Brown
Q: What California governor said: "Inaction may be the highest form of action"?
W: Edmund Gerald Brown became governor of California in 1975. He campaigned for the 1976 Democratic presidential nomination but was defeated. In 1978 he was re-elected governor, and in 1980 he was again an unsuccessful candidate for the Democratic presidential nomination.

A: Jim Garrison
Q: What New Orleans D.A. claimed: "My staff and I solved the assassination weeks ago"?
W: In 1967 New Orleans' district attorney Jim Garrison accused Mr. Clay Shaw of being part of a conspiracy to kill President Kennedy. Garrison subpoenaed a copy of the Zapruder film of the assassination, and it was as a result of this action that investigators have had a copy of the film available to view. President Johnson had issued an Executive Order that the two government copies of the film be locked in the National Archives until the year 2039.

A: Jimmy Carter
Q: What U.S. president pardoned Patricia Hearst?
W: Patty Hearst was kidnapped on Feb. 4, 1974 by the Symbionese Liberation Army. She was later identified by the FBI as taking part in a San Francisco holdup. On Sept. 18, 1975, the FBI captured Patricia and charged her with bank robbery. She was released from prison under executive clemency on Feb. 1, 1979.

A: Jimmy Carter
Q: Who was the first U.S. president born in a hospital?
W: James Earl Carter, Jr. was born on Oct. 1, 1924, at Americus and Sumter County Hospital in Americus, Georgia. He was also the first president to graduate from the U.S. Naval Academy, to be sworn in using his nickname, to appoint three women to the Cabinet, and to visit black Africa while in office.

A: Jimmy Hoffa
Q: What labor leader was last seen in the parking lot of a Michigan restaurant?
W: James Hoffa, former president of the Teamster's Union, disappeared in 1975. He is officially listed in police files as "Missing Person 753425." Hoffa was preparing to make a bid to regain the presidency of the Teamsters Union when he disappeared.

A: Joan Crawford
Q: What Hollywood actress became a member of the Pepsi-Cola board of directors?
W: Joan Crawford replaced her husband as a member of the board of directors of Pespsi-Cola when he died in 1959. In the 1930s Crawford had done advertisements for Coca-Cola!

A: Joan of Arc
Q: Who commanded the French forces at the Battle of Orleans?
W: Joan of Arc is a French national heroine and beloved saint of the Roman Catholic Church. She liberated the city of Orleans from the

English by excellent military strategy and personal bravery and led the French army to victory in 1429.

A: Joan of Arc
Q: Who was "the Maid of Orleans"?
W: Joan of Arc was a simple peasant girl who led the French army to victory at the seige of Orleans in 1429. Through excellent military strategy and bravery, she liberated Orleans from the English.

A: John
Q: What king was forced to witness the signing of the Magna Carta in 1215?
W: John was King of England from 1199 to 1216. He made himself so unpopular that the barons became determined to limit his power and establish their privileges. John compromised and met them in the meadow at Runnymede where he signed The Magna Carta, which became the basis of English constitutional freedom.

A: John Adams
Q: Who was George Washington's vice-president?
W: John Adams also became the second president of the U.S. He was

one of the delegates to the Continental Congress in 1774, one of the signers of the Declaration of Independence, and one of the men who he helped to draw up the Treaty of Paris.

A: John Anderson
Q: Who finished third in the popular vote in the 1980 U.S. presidential election?
W: Anderson, the independent candidate, received 5,719,437 popular votes and zero electoral votes.

A: John Brown
Q: Who led the raid on Harper's Ferry in 1859?
W: John Brown was an American abolitionist who incited the slaves to rebel in 1859. This rebellion eventually led to the outbreak of the Civil War. Brown's attempt to take the U.S. arsenal at Harper's Ferry was defeated, and he was hanged.

A: John Dean III
Q: Who was the star witness at the Senate Watergate hearings?
W: John Dean III, former presidential counsel, was the chief witness against Nixon in the hearings. He admitted he played a major role in the cover-up and said Nixon knew of his plans. He served a prison term of four months.

A: John Dean III
Q: Who warned: "There's a cancer growing on the presidency"?
W: On March 21, 1973, Dean told Nixon that there was a "cancer growing on the presidency" and that he doubted whether continued perjury and payoffs could sustain the attempted cover-up.

A: John Dillinger
Q: Who was America's first Public Enemy No. 1?
W: John Herbert Dillinger, 1903-1934, was one of the most infamous criminals in U.S. history. He organized a gang of skillful robbers and led them in many daring robberies. He was finally gunned down by law officers outside the Biograph Theater in Chicago.

A: **John Dillinger**
Q: What gangster was gunned down by the law officers outside the Biograph Theater?
W: John Dillinger, one of the most notorious bank robbers in U.S. history, and his gang robbed 11 banks of over $318,000 in 1933 and 1934. The FBI enlisted the help of Anne Daye, a friend of Dillinger to set up the confrontation at the Biograph in Chicago.

A: **John Hancock**
Q: Who passed the quill with the remark: "There, I guess King George can read that"?
W: John Hancock was president of the Continental Congress that drew up the Declaration of Independence for the U.S. during the reign of King George III of England. John's is the most prominent signature on the document.

A: **John Hancock's**
Q: Whose is the largest signature on the Declaration of Independence?
W: Hancock was the first to sign the Declaration of Independence, and the only one to actually sign it on July 4, 1776; most of the rest signed August 2 when the majority of the 56 were present.

A: **John F. Kennedy**
Q: Who said: "Ich bin ein Berliner"?
W: In an address at City Hall in West Berlin on June 26, 1963, Kennedy said: "All free men, wherever they live, are citizens of Berlin. And therefore, as a free man, I take pride in the words 'Ich bin ein Berliner'"(I am a Berliner).

A: **John F. Kennedy**
Q: Who was the first Roman Catholic U.S. president?
W: That's right, although he was not the first Catholic to run for that office. Alfred E. Smith ran and lost to Herbert Hoover in 1928.

A: **John F. Kennedy**
Q: Who visited his Dunganstown, Ireland, relatives in 1963?
W: Kennedy visted New Ross and spoke at the quarry from which his great-grandfather Patrick Kennedy had left for America more than a century earlier. If Patrick had not left New Ross, Kennedy told them, "I would be working over there at the Albatross Company", and he pointed at a fertilizer plant across the river. His family's old homestead was in nearby Dunganstown.

A: **John F. Kennedy**
Q: Who was the first navy veteran to become president of the U.S.?
W: At the outbreak of World War II, JFK enlisted in the U.S. Navy. He was a lieutenant in the southwest Pacific and saved the lives of three crew members. For this heroic deed he was awarded the Navy and Marine Corps Medal and the Purple Heart.

A: **John F. Kennedy**
Q: Who was the first U.S. president born in the 20th century?
W: JFK was born in 1917 in Brookline, Mass. The most immediate preceding president, Eisenhower, was born Oct. 14, 1890.

A: **John F. Kennedy's**
Q: What presidential administration challenged Americans to explore "the New Frontier"?
W: The first mention of the New Frontier was made during Kennedy's acceptance speech at the 1960 Democratic Convention. The New Frontier represented the frontier of the 1960s and all the challenges that loomed ahead.

A: **John F. Kennedy's**
Q: Whose last words were: "My God, I'm hit"?
W: During a visit to Dallas, Texas, on Nov. 22, 1963, he was struck by an assassin's bullet while riding in a motorcade. He died almost immediately.

A: **John F. Kennedy's**
Q: What U.S. president's news conferences were called the best matinee in town?
W: President Eisenhower conducted afternoon interviews, but they were recorded and played later on TV. Kennedy was the first to be televised live. During his first televised news conference, Jan. 25, 1961, he answered 31 questions in 38 minutes.

A: **John F. Kennedy and Richard Nixon**
Q: What two later presidents were first elected to Congress in 1946?
W: Kennedy began his political career in 1946 when he ran for and won a seat in the U.S. House of Representatives. Nixon also was elected to the House in 1946 and was re-elected in 1948. Nixon gained prominence as the House Un-American Activities Committee member who forced the showdown that resulted in the Alger Hiss perjury conviction.

A: **John Lindsay**
Q: Who preceded Abraham Beame as mayor of New York City?
W: John Lindsay was mayor of New York City from 1966 to 1973. In 1969 Linday was defeated for renomination in the Republican Party primary election, but ran as the Liberal and Independent candidate and was re-elected!

A: **John Paul I**
Q: Who succeeded Pope Paul VI?
W: John Paul I served as Pope of the Roman Catholic Church for only 34 days. He was the first Pope to use two names, which he took from his two predecessors, John XXIII and Paul VI.

A: **John Paul I**
Q: What pope died 33 days after his election?
W: John Paul I served as Pope of the Roman Catholic Church for only 34 days. He was elected Pope on Aug. 26, 1978 and died of a heart attack on Sept. 28, 1978.

A: **John Profumo**
Q: What British war secretary resigned on June 5, 1963, amid a sex scandal?
W: John Profumo, a British Secretary of State for War, resigned after his association with call girl Christine Keeler became public. To make the situation even worse, she was also sleeping with a Soviet naval attache!

A: **John D. Rockefeller**
Q: Who was the first U.S. billionaire?
W: In 1870 Rockefeller became president of the Standard Oil Company. By enlarging this enterprise, driving out or absorbing rival companies, and establishing the Standard Oil Trust, he secured a virtual monopoly in the petroleum refining business. By the time of his retirement he had accumulated over a billion dollars

A: **John T. Scopes**
Q: Who taught the theory of evolution in 1925, contrary to Tennessee law?
W: John Scopes was defended by Clarence Darrow, a famous American lawyer and lecturer who was a bitter foe of organized Christianity.

A: **John the Baptist**
Q: Who baptized Christ?
W: John the Baptist baptized Christ in the River Jordan at Christ's request. John said Christ should baptize him. Afterward, God's spirit came down from the heavens in the form of a dove: Matthew 3:16.

A: **Johnny Carson**
Q: Who said: "Ronald Reagan doesn't dye his hair; he bleaches his face"?
W: Many comedians have poked fun at the president accusing him of using makeup for the cameras and dying his hair. Reagan claims he does not dye his hair, and his associates insist he has a naturally ruddy complexion.

A: **Joseph Goebbels**
Q: Who was Hitler's Minister of Enlightenment and Propaganda?
W: In 1929 when the Nazis were an important minority party in Germany, Hitler assembled men who would help him rise to power. Paul Joseph Goebbels was one of these men and the chief Nazi propagandist; he founded and edited the party paper, *Der Angriff*. Under Hitler, he became Minister of Propaganda and ardently supported Hitler's anti-Semitic policy. At the fall of Berlin he committed suicide.

A: **Joseph P. Kennedy**
Q: Who was the U.S. ambassador to the Court of St. James at the outbreak of World War II?
W: Joseph Kennedy served as U.S. Ambassador to Great Britain from 1937 to 1940.

A: **Joseph P. Kennedy, Jr.**
Q: What member of the Kennedy clan was killed in World War II?
W: Joseph Kennedy, Jr., oldest of the Kennedy children, was a U.S. Navy pilot. Kennedy and his co-pilot were killed when their plane exploded in flight, after taking part in a hazardous mission against German rocket bases.

A: **Joseph Stalin**
Q: Who was Svetlana Aliluyeva's father?
W: Svetlana fled to the U.S. in the 1960s. She was one of two children born to Stalin and his second wife.

A: **Joseph Stalin**
Q: Who won the Russian power struggle to succeed Lenin?
W: Stalin led Lenin's armies. After Lenin's death he used his position as General Secretary of the Communist Party to increase his personal power. Stalin became Premier of Russia in 1924 and served until his death in 1953.

A: **Joseph Stalin, Franklin Roosevelt, Winston Churchill**
Q: What three leaders met at the Yalta Conference?
W: On Feb. 4, 1945, leaders of the "Big Three" Allied nations met at the Livadia, a famous Black Sea resort. The leaders issued a statement on Feb. 11, 1945, of plans to occupy Germany and set up a new Polish government. Preliminary plans for a world peace organization were included, which would be considered by an assembly of the United Nations on April 25, 1945, at San Francisco.

A: **Josephine**
Q: Who was Napoleon's first wife?
W: She was empress of France until he divorced her in 1809 and married Marie Louise. Josephine had previously been married to Vicomte Alexandre Beauharnias, with whom she had two children.

A: **Juan Carlos of Spain**
Q: What king boycotted Prince Charles' wedding?
W: Juan Carlos did not attend the wedding in protest over the decision to have Prince Charles and Princess Diana board the yacht for their honeymoon from Gibraltar on the southern coast of Spain. Spain has long demanded Britain's withdrawal from Gibraltar, which Britain has held since the early 18th century as a colony and naval base.

A: **Juan Ponce de Leon**
Q: Who tramped through Florida looking for the Fountain of Youth?
W: Ponce de Leon was the Spanish explorer who discovered Florida. Indians told him of an island named Bimini that supposedly contained a marvelous fountain that could restore youth to older persons. Ponce de Leon explored much of the Florida coast but found no such fountain.

HISTORY

A: **Judy Garland**
Q: Who was Liza Minnelli referring to when she said: "When she was sad, she was sadder than anyone"?
W: Judy Garland was Liza's mother. It is felt that Liza could make this statement because her life paralleled her mother's in many ways. Both women had brilliant careers, spectacular successes, and tragic failures in both their professional and personal lives.

A: **Julian Bond**
Q: What black was nominated for vice president at the 1968 Democratic National Convention?
W: Julian Bond, a black civil rights leader and a Democratic member of the Georgia House of Representatives from 1965 to 1975, became a member of the Georgia Senate in 1975. Bond's name was placed in nomination for vice president, but he was too young to qualify.

A: **Julius Caesar**
Q: Who said: "Veni, vidi, vici"?
W: "I came, I saw, I conquered" was Caesar's brief but meaningful message dispatched to the Roman Senate, reporting victory at Zela in northwestern Turkey, in 47 B.C. The Senate made him ruler of the Mediterranean world, marking the end of the Roman Republic. Thereafter, Caesar was dictator.

A: **Julius Hoffman**
Q: Who was the judge in the Chicago Seven trial?
W: Antiwar activists went on trial in Chicago as leaders of the 1968 Democratic National Convention demonstrations. William Kunstler, attorney for the Chicago Seven, asked for a mistrial because of the incriminating manner in which Hoffman read the charges. Twenty more motions for mistrial were filed, but at the end of the five month trial, all defendants were cleared of conspiracy charges. Although five were found guilty of crossing state lines to incite a riot, the convictions were overturned in 1972 by the U.S. Court of Appeals.

A: **July 4**
Q: What month and day did Thomas Jefferson, John Adams and James Monroe all die on?
W: John Adams, second president, died on July 4, 1826, in Quincy, Massachusetts. Thomas Jefferson, third president, died on July 4, 1826, at Monticello, his Virginia home. James Monroe, fifth president, died on July 4, 1831, in New York City.

A: **Karl Marx**
Q: Who called religion the opium of the people?
W: Karl Marx, one of the founding fathers of Communism, is regarded in most Communist countries as one of the greatest thinkers of all times. He wrote on social classes, the relationship between economy and state, and the principles that underlie a political system. He believed that relgion was both the symptom of a deep social malaise and a protest against it and that religion stood in the way of curing social evils because it tended to justify them.

A: **Karl Marx**
Q: Whose epitaph reads: "Workers of all lands unite..."?
W: This is a line from *The Communist Manifesto* written in 1848 by Karl Marx and Friedrich Engles: "Let the ruling classes tremble at a communist revolution. The proletarians have nothing to lose but their chains. They have the world to win. Working men of all countries unite!"

A: **Karl Marx and Friedrich Engels**
Q: What twosome penned *The Communist Manifesto* in 1848?
W: *The Communist Manifesto* is a presentation of the authors' political and historical theories and is considered a systematic statement of the theories that became known as Marxism.

A: **Kenya**
Q: What country did the Mau Mau uprising take place in?
W: The Mau-Mau movement sought an end to white domination in Kenya by using terrorism. The brutal Mau Mau uprising generated brutal white retaliation and lasted from 1952 to 1959. Its outcome was greater black participation in the government and independence from Britain under Jomo Kenyatta in 1963.

A: **Khrushchev's shoe pounding**
Q: What caused an adjournment of the 25th anniversary session of the United Nations General Assembly?
W: Khrushchev, in the fall of 1960 (actually the 15th anniversary of the UN), appeared before the U.N. General Assembly to propose a restructuring of the organization. He laughed and talked during the speeches and pounded his shoe on his desk during an address by Harold Macmillan.

A: **Kilroy was here**
Q: How did shipyard inspector James J. Kilroy designate equipment as being satisfactory?
W: The words first appeared in World War II. The theory is that Kilroy was an infantry soldier who got tired of hearing the Air Force brag that it was always first on the spot. "Kilroy" specialized in showing up in outrageous places such as the top of the torch of the Statue of Liberty.

A: **King Hussein of Jordan**
Q: Who is American-born Queen Nur married to?
W: King Hussein was married to Elizabeth (Lisa) Halaby in June 1978. They have two children.

A: **King Juan Carlos**
Q: Who did Franco designate as his successor in 1969?
W: In July 1969 Generalissimo Francisco Franco, then head of state, designated Prince Juan Carlos as the future king. When Franco died in 1975, Carlos assumed the throne. He promised to establish representative government and to dismantle Franco's repressive institutions.

A: *King Kong*
Q: What was Hitler's favorite movie?
W: Hitler's adolescence lasted until his death. His favorite composer was Wagner, his favorite movie *King Kong*.

A: **Klondike Gold Rush, The**
Q: What gold rush was started by Skookum Jim, Tagish Charlie, and George Carmacks?
W: On Aug. 17, 1896, George Carmacks, his Indian wife Kate, and her relatives, found a large quantity of gold in the gravel of a creek in the Klondike, a region in the Yukon Territory.

A: **Knossos**
Q: What Cretan city was excavated by Sir Arthur Evans?
W: Knossos was the chief center of the Menoan civilization that flourished on Crete from about 3000 to 1100 B.C. In 1900 Evans, a British archaelogist, began the excavation of a palace at Knossos.

A: **Konrad Adenauer**
Q: Who was West German chancellor from 1949 to 1963?
W: Under his leadership, West Germany gained its sovereignty, made an economic comeback, and built its military power. Adenauer was 73 years old when he started his 14 years as Chancellor.

A: **Korean War, The**
Q: What began on June 25, 1950?
W: The war began when troops from Communist-ruled North Korea invaded South Korea. The war was a major challenge for the United Nations which had been born only five years earlier.

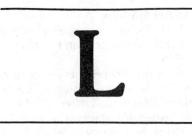

A: **Lauren Bacall**
Q: Who's Leslie Bogart's mother?
W: Leslie's father was Humphrey Bogart. She also has a brother Stephen.

A: **Lawrence of Arabia**
Q: What was the pseudonym of Thomas Edward Lawrence?
W: Lawrence was a British soldier and writer. When World War I started, he was working as an archaeologist for the British government. He was sent to Egypt on military business and later, as a colonel, became devoted to Arab causes and was a leader of daring guerilla raids. He refused all honors, but the Arabs hailed him as a hero.

A: **Leaving the scene of an accident**
Q: What was Ted Kennedy convicted of in the Chappaquiddick incident?
W: In 1969 Kennedy's automobile plunged from a bridge on Chappaquiddick Island in Massachusetts. His passenger, Mary Jo Kopekne, a staff worker for Robert Kennedy, was killed.

A: **Le Bourget, Paris**
Q: What airfield did Charles Lindbergh land at to end his historic solo transatlantic flight?
W: Lindbergh was actually the 81st person to fly across the Atlantic Ocean, but he was the first to do it alone.

A: **Lech Walesa**
Q: What unemployed electrician rallied Polish workers under the Solidarity banner?
W: Lech Walesa, leader of the Polish Solidarity Labor Union, endured an 11-month interment following the imposition of martial law and the outlawing of Solidarity in Poland in Dec. 1981

A: **Lee Harvey Oswald**
Q: Who allegedly killed officer J.D. Tippitt?
W: After President Kennedy was killed, Oswald allegedly killed police officer J.D. Tippitt. Following a ten-month investigation, a presidential commission reported that Oswald, acting alone, killed both Kennedy and Tippitt.

A: **Lee Harvey Oswald**
Q: Who was booked with mugshot No. 54018?
W: He was booked for the assassination of President John F. Kennedy on Nov. 22, 1963, in Dallas, Texas.

A: **Lee Harvey Oswald**
Q: Who was captured in the third-last row of the Texas Theatre?
W: Oswald was captured by police in a Dallas movie theater about 90 minutes after the President had been shot. He was armed with a revolver.

A: **Lee Harvey Oswald**
Q: Who was the victim of the first murder seen live on TV?
W: While being transferred to the Dallas County Jail, Oswald was shot in the basement of the Dallas police department by Jack Ruby.

HISTORY

A: left, The
Q: Which eye did Moshe Dayan wear a patch over?
W: These famous people also only had one eye: Rex Harrison, stage and screen actor; John Ford, Irish-American film director famous for his westerns; and Horatio Nelson, British naval wizard and national hero.

A: left, The
Q: Which foot did Neil Armstrong first put down on the moon?
W: On July 20, 1969, Neil Armstrong, commander of the Apollo 11 Mission, set foot on the moon. This was one small step for man and one giant step for mankind!

A: Leo Ryan
Q: What U.S. Congressman was murdered at the airstrip near Jonestown, Guyana?
W: In November 1978 U.S. Representative Leo Ryan led a group of Americans to investigate charges that members of the Peoples' Temple, a cult of U.S. origin, were being held against their will. Ryan and others were killed by a gunner as they were about to depart with a group of defectors.

A: Leon Trotsky
Q: Who was assassinated in Mexico City on Aug. 20, 1940?
W: Trotsky's real name was Lev Davidovich Bronstein. He was a leader of the 1917 Russian revolution and Stalin's chief rival for power. Under Lenin he was commissar of foreign affairs and of war. Dismissed from office in 1925 when Stalin emerged as victor, he was exiled and remained the leader of anti-Stalinist opposition abroad until he was assassinated Aug. 20, 1940.

A: Leonid Brezhnev
Q: Who succeeded Nikita Khrushchev as first secretary of the Communist Party?
W: Brezhnev was also premier of the USSR from 1960 to 1964.

A: Lester Maddox
Q: What future Georgia governor chased three blacks from his diner in 1964?
W: After the Civil Rights Act of July 2, 1964, which integrated all public accommodations, Lester Maddox, who owned a restaurant in Atlanta, chased blacks away with a pistol and supplied his patrons with ax handles. His actions began a political career that made him Governor of Georgia in 1966.

A: Liberia
Q: What African country was founded by freed American slaves in 1847?
W: In the early 1800s the American Colonization Society worked in the U.S. to take freed blacks back to Africa. The Society bought land from tribes in Liberia and started a settlement there. In the 1840s disputes arose between black settlers and the Society, and the settlers declared their independence in 1847.

A: Liberty Bell, The
Q: What developed a crack in 1835 while tolling the death of U.S. Chief Justice John Marshall?
W: That happened on July 8, 1835. Here's a little more trivia for you: the word *Pennsylvania* is misspelled on the bell!

A: Lieutenant William Calley's
Q: Whose court-martial opened at Fort Benning, Georgia, on Nov. 12, 1970?
W: On March 29, 1971, Calley was convicted of the premeditated murder of 22 South Vietnamese at My Lai on March 16, 1968. He was sentenced to life imprisonment on March 31st, but the sentence was reduced to 20 years on Aug. 20, 1971.

A: Life imprisonment
Q: What was Rudolph Hess' sentence at the Nuremberg trials?
W: The Nuremberg trials were a series of 13 trials held in Nuremberg, Germany, from 1945 to 1949. In these trials leaders of Nazi Germany were accused of crimes against international law. On Oct. 1, 1946, Hess was one of 19 found guilty. Twelve received death sentences, three got life imprisonment, and four were given lesser prison terms.

A: Life insurance
Q: What's the only kind of insurance not written by Lloyd's Association?
W: The Lloyd's Association of Underwriters, familiarly known as Lloyd's of London, received its name from the fact that when it was a loosely formed group of marine underwriters, they were in the habit of meeting in a London coffee shop established in 1688 by Edward Lloyd. As an association Lloyd's does not write insurance; it is merely an exchange, and each member does business on his own account or in partnership with other members. The members, working in groups, write virtually every conceivable kind of insurance except life insurance.

A: life jacket, A
Q: What was a Mae West on a World War II battleship?
W: Mae West was a full-breasted female actress. The typical life jacket, when inflated, gave the appearance of a full-breasted woman, hence a "Mae West."

A: Lightning war
Q: What does *blitzkreig* mean?
W: Blitzkrieg was a type of fast-moving warfare developed by the Germans in World War II.

A: lights went out, The
Q: What happened at 16 minutes and 11 seconds past 5 P.M. EST on Tuesday Nov. 9, 1965?
W: A massive electric power failure blacked out most of the northeastern U.S. and two Canadian provinces on this night. The rumor that there was a "baby boom" cannot be documented, since only one hospital in New York City reported a large increase in the number of births nine months later.

A: Lillian Carter
Q: Who said: "...When I look at my children, I say, 'Lillian, you should have stayed a virgin'"?
W: Nice, mom, real nice! Miss Lillian, as she was called, was by far the best loved of the Carter family. She was very outspoken and often quoted!

A: Linda Ronstadt
Q: Who is Jerry Brown's favorite singer?
W: Jerry Brown is former governor of California and a prominent California politician. Linda Ronstadt is a prominent popular singer whom he dated. Remember their trip to Africa?

A: Lindy Hop, The
Q: What dance was named for aviator Charles Lindbergh?
W: That's correct, but more importantly he was awarded the Medal of Honor, and he won the 1954 Pulitzer Prize for his autobiography, *The Spirit of St. Louis*. The Lindy Hop, was a favorite teenagers' dance and assumed to be named after him.

A: Liverpool
Q: What British city did Adolph Hitler study art in?
W: In 1907 Hitler went to Vienna to be an art student. He took the entrance exam of the Academy of Fine Arts, but failed. He failed a second time a year later. However, he earned a little money selling painting scenes of Vienna.

A: Lizzie Borden
Q: Who was acquitted of giving her parents a total of 81 blows with an ax?
W: According to the *New York Times*, the controversy about Miss Borden's guilt or innocence was cited as the cause of 1,900 other marital disputes that ended in divorce!

A: London
Q: What city was the site of the first meeting of the United Nations General Assembly?
W: The first meeting of the United Nations General Assembly was held in London on Jan. 10, 1946.

A: London
Q: What European city is Karl Marx buried in?
W: Karl Marx was the originator of the Communist philosophy. He died and was buried in London on Mar. 14, 1883.

A: London School of Economics, The
Q: What London school did John F. Kennedy attend?
W: Joseph Kennedy wanted the best for his son JFK, so he was sent to Choate, Harvard, then to the London School of Economics. At 29 JFK was successful in his try for Congress from the east Boston district.

A: Lord Cornwallis
Q: What British commander surrendered to George Washington at Yorktown in 1781?
W: On Sept. 28, 1781 at Yorktown, Virginia, Washington surrounded Cornwallis' army. October 6 brought Washington's attack, resulting in Cornwallis' surrender of his 8,000-man army.

A: Los Angeles
Q: What city was Bobby Kennedy assassinated in?
W: Bobby was shot June 5, 1968, at the Hotel Ambassador in Los Angeles, after celebrating his presidential primary victory that day in California. He was shot by Sirhan Bisharu Sirhan, a Jordanian who was convicted in 1969 and sentenced to death.

A: Los Angeles
Q: What city was John F. Kennedy nominated for president in?
W: He was nominated on the first ballot after defeating his chief rivals for the nomination, Hubert Humphrey of Minnesota and Lyndon Johnson of Texas, in all the primaries. Kennedy embarked on the "New Frontier" in his acceptance speech for the nomination, after

balancing the Democratic ticket with Lyndon Johnson as his running mate.

A: lost or overdue ship, A
Q: What does Lloyd's Lutine Bell announce?
W: In normal times unusual events, such as a lost or overdue ship, are announced by the ringing of the Lutine Bell, which hangs in the tower in "Lloyd's Rooms" (meeting place for members of Lloyd's of London). The bell was salvaged from the British ship *Lutine* that was wrecked off the coast of the Netherlands in 1799.

A: Louis
Q: What was the most common Christian name of French monarchs?
W: There have been 17 kings named Louis from King Louis I through King Louis XVIII with the exception of Louis XVII, son of Louis XVI and Marie Antoinette; who died in prison without ever ruling. King Louis XIV of France was the longest reigning monarch in European recorded history – 72 years!

A: Louisiana Purchase, The
Q: What was Uncle Sam's biggest real estate deal?
W: The Louisiana Territory, 100 million acres, was purchased in 1803 at a cost of $15 million. At the time of the purchase Napoleon was first consul in France and Thomas Jefferson was president of the U.S. Today a moderate-sized parcel of land in Manhattan may sell for more than that amount!

A: **Luci Baines Johnson**
Q: Who married Patrick Nugent on Aug. 6, 1966?
W: The Nugents were married in the Shrine of the Immaculate Conception in Washington, D.C. Luci was the first daughter of a president to marry while her father was president since Eleanor Wilson's marriage in 1914.

A: **Lurleen Wallace**
Q: Who succeeded George Wallace as governor of Alabama in 1966?
W: George Wallace's wife, Lurleen, ran for governor in 1966. At that time Alabama law prohibited George Wallace from serving two terms in a row. Mrs. Wallace won the election but died in office in 1968.

A: *Lusitania*, **The**
Q: What ship was torpedoed and sank off the coast of Ireland on May 7, 1915?
W: The ship sank with 1,198 passengers. Its final message, found in a bottle, read "Still on deck with a few people. The last boats have left. We are sinking fast. Some men near me are praying with a priest. The end is near. Maybe this note will…," and there it ended.

A: **Lynda Bird Johnson**
Q: Who did Charles Robb marry on Dec. 9, 1967?
W: Lynda married Charles in the East Room of the White House.

A: **Lyndon Johnson**
Q: What U.S. president graduated from Southwest State Teachers College in 1930?
W: Johnson entered Southwest State Teachers College in February of 1927. He worked his way through college as a janitor and graduated in 1930. He also attended Georgetown University Law School, receiving his degree in 1935.

A: **Lyndon Johnson**
Q: What U.S. president was castigated for picking up his pet beagles by the ears?
W: President Johnson's beagles, named Him and Her, were born June 27, 1963.

A: **Lyndon Johnson**
Q: Who counted himself out on March 31, 1968?
W: President Johnson shocked the nation by announcing on March 31, 1968, that he would not run for re-election. He said he was withdrawing in the name of national unity, after increased criticism of his Vietnam involvement.

A: **Lyndon Johnson**
Q: Who phoned three Dallas lawyers trying to locate a copy of the presidential oath of office?
W: Johnson wanted to take the oath of office before leaving Dallas on the day of Kennedy's assassination because he was concerned about the rules of succession if something should happen to him during the flight back to Washington.

A: **Lyndon Johnson**
Q: Who sought to create the "Great Society"?
W: During Johnson's full term the economy boomed. In May 1964 Johnson stated, "we have the opportunity to move not only toward the rich society but upward to the Great Society." The term "Great Society" caught on and was used to describe many of his domestic programs. Johnson sought to continue Kennedy's leadership by pledging reform in the areas concerning social welfare, health and education, and for blacks and families below the poverty level.

A: **Lyndon Johnson**
Q: Who told the U.S. Congress: "All I have I would have given gladly not to be standing here today"?
W: These words were spoken by Johnson in his first address to Congress as President on Nov. 27, 1963, five days after Kennedy's assassination.

A: **Lyndon Johnson's**
Q: Whose first presidential order was: "Let's get this goddamn thing airborne"?
W: Three minutes after being sworn in as the 36th President of the United States on the presidential air force jet, Johnson gave this, his first, order as President, "Now let's get airborne."

A: **machine gun, The**
Q: What was called a "Chicago piano" by gangsters in the 1930s?
W: The city of Chicago had an unsavory reputation as a city of gangsters. When the machine gun became available, it was soon obtained by gangsters in Chicago and across the nation. Because the staccato sound of the machine gun was reminiscent of similar sounds reproduced on a piano, the machine gun was frequently referred to as the "Chicago Piano."

A: **machine gun, The**
Q: What was the favorite weapon of George Kelly and Kate Barker?
W: Kate Barker (also known as Ma Barker) gave the gun to Machine Gun Kelly as a present. Kelly never killed anyone or even fired his weapon in anger. Kate Barker had a flair for promotion. She made George practice with the machine gun by shooting walnuts off fence posts. Kate would pass out cartridge cases in underworld dives, saying, "Have a souvenir of my husband, Machine Gun Kelly." Kelly eventually went on to join some local gangs and took part in some small-time holdups. After pulling off his one major big money kidnapping, he and Ma were caught.

A: Madame Tussaud's
Q: What museum did Marie Grosholtz open on London's Baker Street in 1834?
W: She learned the art of wax modeling from her uncle Philippe Curtius, and upon his death in 1794 she inherited his two wax museums. In 1802 she took her two sons and her collection of wax models to England, touring the British Isles for 33 years before establishing a permanent home on Baker Street in London.

A: Mahatma Gandhi
Q: What Asian leader was known as "the Little Brown Saint"?
W: His bestowal of his wealth upon the poor, his deep religious fervor, his earnest endeavors at uplifting the oppressed classes, and his eloquent preaching won him the surname "Mahatma" (Great Soul) and the reputation of a saint.

A: Mahatma Gandhi
Q: What leader was cremated on the banks of the Ganges River on Jan. 31, 1948?
W: Gandhi was assassinated by a nationalist fanatic. A Hindu, editor of an extremist newspaper who had denounced Gandhi for his appeasement of the Moslems, burst through a crowd as Gandhi emerged from a prayer session. After receiving Gandhi's blessing, the man assassinated him.

A: Mahatma Gandhi
Q: Who led the All-India Congress Party in seeking independence from Britain?
W: As a result of his passive resistance, strikes and riots broke out in India, so Gandhi was imprisoned (1922 to 1924). He was later released and became president of the Indian National Congress.

A: Malcolm X
Q: What Black Muslim leader was assassinated on Feb. 21, 1965?
W: Born Malcolm Little on May 25, 1925, he changed his name to Malcolm X in 1952 and adopted the name El Hajj Malik El-Shabazz. Although a Muslim, he was assassinated in Harlem by two Black Muslims.

A: Manfred von Richthofen
Q: Who was the top air ace of World War I?
W: In combat from 1915 to 1918 for Germany, von Richthofen claimed 80 victories (he shot down 79 British planes and one Belgian plane). He was known as the Red Baron or Red Knight because of the color of his plane.

A: Manhattan Island
Q: What did Peter Minuit buy for the equivalent of $24?
W: It was named after the Manhattan Indians who occupied it until 1626. They sold it to the Dutch for $24 worth of kettles, axes, and cloth. Such a deal...!

A: Manhattan Project, The
Q: What was the code name for the development of the A-bomb?
W: President Roosevelt initiated this project in utmost secrecy without Congressional approval. He recruited top scientists in the country to perfect the bomb at a cost of $2 billion.

A: Manifest Destiny
Q: What was the 19th-century term used by the U.S. to justify expansion?
W: The term was first used in 1845 by John L. O'Sullivan in an article on the annexation of Texas. People who believed in manifest destiny maintained that the U.S. should rule all of North America.

A: Manson Family, The
Q: Who murdered Leno and Rosemary LaBianca on Aug. 10, 1969?
W: Charles Manson and his followers also killed movie actress Sharon Tate and six others. Manson was the leader of a pseudo-religious cult with headquarters at a ranch near Los Angeles.

A: Mao-Tse-Tung
Q: Who made Chinese film actress Chiang Chin his fourth wife?
W: Chiang Chin, a Chinese political leader, was married to Mao-Tse-Tung from 1939 to 1976. Under her leadership, many popular Chinese dramas were written to favor Mao's government policies.

A: March 15, or the Ides of March
Q: What date in 44 B.C. was Julius Caesar assassinated?
W: He was assassinated by Brutus, Cassius, and others who regarded his dictatorial powers as a hindrance to the restoration of the Republic of Rome.

A: March 17
Q: What date is St. Patrick's Day?
W: St. Patrick's Day is celebrated on March 17th in honor of the patron saint of Ireland, who died on March 17, about 461 A.D. This holiday has been observed in America since colonial days.

A: Margaret Thatcher
Q: Who is nicknamed "The Iron Lady"?
W: British Prime Minister Margaret Thatcher, earned her nickname in Moscow because of her warnings of Soviet expansionism and military might.

A: Margaret Thatcher
Q: Who was the first woman elected to lead a European democracy?
W: In 1975 she became the first woman to head a British party when she was elected to the Conservative Party. She went on to become Prime Minister of Great Britain in 1979 and is the first woman ever to hold the office.

A: Margaret Trudeau
Q: Who described Fidel Castro as "the sexiest man I ever met"?
W: Margaret Trudeau was the wife of Pierre Trudeau, Prime Minister of Canada. Margaret became a part of the "jet set" after she left Trudeau.

HISTORY

A: Maria Callas
Q: What opera singer said: "First I lost my weight. Then I lost my voice. Now I've lost Onassis"?
W: Maria Callas was born in New York in 1923 and was both a U.S. and Greek citizen. She became one of the world's greatest and most flamboyant opera singers because of her singing and acting abilities and her fiery temperament. Her relationship with Onassis ended when he married Jacquelyn Kennedy. Callas died in 1977.

A: Marie Antoinette
Q: What victim of the French Revolution was known as "the Widow Capet" and "the Baker's Wife"?
W: Marie Antoinette was the queen of France who died on the guillotine on Oct. 16, 1793, during the French Revolution after being found guilty of treason. She was called "Widow Capet" by the revolutionists.

A: Marie Curie
Q: Who's the only woman to have won two Nobel Prizes?
W: In 1903 she and her husband shared the Nobel Prize for Physics with Henri Becquerel for their investigation of radioactivity. In 1911 Marie was awarded a second Nobel Prize, this time for her discovery of radium and polonium.

A: Marilyn Monroe
Q: Who sang "Happy Birthday" to John F. Kennedy at his 45th birthday celebration at Madison Square Garden?
W: The rumor that Marilyn was having an affair with the Attorney General Robert Kennedy, and probably had one with President John Kennedy earlier, is almost undisputed now.

A: Marina
Q: What was the first name of Lee Harvey Oswald's wife?
W: She was the daughter of a Russian KGB (intelligence) officer!

A: Marshall McLuhan
Q: Who coined the term "the Global Village"?
W: "Global Village" refers to the fact that electronics have made it possible to share information instantly with everyone and that each event is related to all other events. McLuhan, who got his Ph.D. in rhetoric at Cambridge, also coined these terms and slogans: "the medium is the message," "mixed media," and "hot and cold media."

A: Marshall Plan, The
Q: What plan to rebuild Europe was unveiled on June 5, 1947?
W: Announced by Secretary of State General George Marshall at commencement exercises at Harvard, this was a plan to restore European economics. Seventeen countries were involved in the plan, known formally as the "European Recovery Program." Four years, and $12.5 billion later, a firm European economic recovery was underway.

A: Martha
Q: What was the name of former U.S. attorney general John Mitchell's wife?
W: Martha Beall Jennings married John Newton Mitchell on Dec. 30, 1957. They had one child Martha Elizabeth who was born Jan. 10, 1961.

A: Martin Luther King, Jr.
Q: Who declared: "I have a dream"?
W: In a mass civil rights demonstration in 1963, King spoke to more than 300,000 people in the shadow of the Lincoln Memorial in Washington, D.C. He spelled out his objectives with rare spiritual power for a nationwide television audience.

A: Martin Luther King, Jr.
Q: Who declared: "I have been to the mountaintop"?
W: This was part of a speech that King presented to the Mason Street Temple the evening before his assassination on April 4, 1968. The speech contained a passage bordering on prophecy: "We've got some difficult days ahead, but it really doesn't matter with me now. Because I've been to the mountaintop. I won't mind. Like anybody, I would like to live a long life... But I'm not concerned about that now..."

A: Martin Luther King, Jr.
Q: Who was assassinated on April 4, 1968?
W: King was shot by James Earl Ray in Memphis, Tennessee. Ray pleaded guilty to murder and was sentenced to 99 years in prison.

A: Martin Luther King, Jr.
Q: Who wore mugshot number 7089 after his 1956 arrest during the Montgomery bus boycott?
W: The purpose of King's boycott of public buses was to protest racial segregation. A year of economic pressure was crowned with success when the U.S. Supreme Court ruled that racial segregation in intrastate as well as interstate transportation was unlawful.

A: Martin Luther King, Jr.'s
Q: Whose epitaph reads: "Free at last, free at last, thank God Almighty, I'm free at last"?
W: King, shot to death on April 4, 1968, in Memphis, Tennessee, is buried near Ebenezer Baptist Church in Atlanta. The words carved on his tombstone are from a spiritual.

A: *Mary Celeste*, **The**
Q: What ship was found mysteriously abandoned four weeks after leaving Boston for Genoa in November 1872?
W: The *Mary Celeste* left Boston in November 1872, and four weeks later it was found in the Atlantic, all sails set and the entire crew missing.

A: **Mary Jo Kopechne**
Q: Who drowned at Chappaquiddick on July 18, 1969?
W: A car driven by Senator Edward Kennedy plunged off a bridge into a tidal pool on Chappaquiddick Island, Martha's Vineyard, Massachusetts on that night. The body of Mary Jo, a 28-year-old secretary, was found drowned in the car.

A: **Mary Quant**
Q: What English designer created the Chelsea Look?
W: Mary Quant was a British fashion designer who in the 1960s created the miniskirt. Her trademark is the five-petaled daisy. Her best known fashions were similar to the outfits worn to dancing class by little girls: short pleated skirts, white anklets, and black patent anklestrap shoes.

A: **Mary, Queen of Scots**
Q: Who inherited the throne of Scotland at the age of six days?
W: Mary was born in 1542, the only child of King James V of Scotland, and became queen when she was one week old, upon the death of her father. She was crowned in 1543 and actively ruled the Scots from 1561 until her abdication in 1567. Imprisoned by her cousin Elizabeth I, who found her guilty of plotting to kill her, Mary was beheaded in 1587.

A: **Mason-Dixon line, The**
Q: What line divided the North and South in the U.S. Civil War?
W: The Mason-Dixon line was the boundary between Pennsylvania and Maryland. It was surveyed by Charles Mason and Jeremiah Dixon from 1763 to 1767.

A: **Massachusetts**
Q: What was the only state George McGovern carried in the 1972 presidential election?
W: Here's the vote count: McGovern 1,332,540; Nixon 1,112,078. George took a beating across the U.S. and finally ended up with only 17 electoral votes, the lowest since Alf Landon received eight in 1936 when he ran against FDR.

A: **Mata Hari**
Q: What was the operative name of Dutch-born World War I spy Geertruida Zelle?
W: She was a most notorious spy and accomplished mistress. Born Margaretha Geertruida Zelle in Holland, she worked as a spy for the Germans while posing as an exotic dancer in Paris.

A: **Mata Hari**
Q: What woman was Germany's most famous World War I spy?
W: It has been estimated that 50,000 Allied Soldiers died because of her activities. She slept with men for state secrets as well as for money. She died before a French firing squad.

A: **May 8, 1945**
Q: What date was V-E Day?
W: The surrender of the German forces was signed on May 4, 1945. Later an additional document was signed with more ceremony at Eisenhower's headquarters at Reims. At midnight on May 8, 1945, the war in Europe was officially over.

A: *Mayaguez*, **The**
Q: What ship was captured by the Cambodians in 1975 and retrieved at the cost of 38 U.S. Marines?
W: In the rescue operation U.S. Marines attacked Tang Island and bombed the air base. Cambodia surrendered the ship and the crew. The U.S. lost 15 men in battle and 23 in a helicopter crash.

A: *Mayflower*, **The**
Q: What famed ship did Christopher Jones captain?
W: The *Mayflower* sailed from Plymouth, England, on Sept. 16, 1620, with 102 passengers and reached the Cape Cod coast 66 days later. Christoper Jones, quarter owner of the ship, served as master. Contrary to popular belief the Pilgrims did not land at Plymouth Rock; in fact, they did not reach Plymouth Rock until Dec. 21, 1920, more than a month after they landed at Cape Cod.

A: **McDonald's**
Q: What chain did Ray Kroc build?
W: Ray Kroc's McDonalds began with a hamburger stand in Des Plaines, Illinois, on April 15, 1955. As of January 1978 there were 4,612 McDonald's throughout the world. Ray Kroc was originally a salesman for a malted milk multi-mixer company. He bought the name "McDonald's" from two brothers, Maurice and Richard McDonald, who had a thriving assembly line hamburger stand in San Bernardino, California.

A: **Melvin Belli's**
Q: What defense lawyer's clients included Lenny Bruce and Jack Ruby?
W: Lenny Bruce was a stand-up comic who was arrested many times for his "blue" acts. Jack Rudy was the nightclub owner who shot Lee Harvey Oswald, JFK's assassin.

A: **Memphis**
Q: What city was Martin Luther King, Jr. assassinated in?
W: Dr. King, at the age of 39, was assassinated on April 4, 1968, in Memphis, Tenn. James Earl Ray, an escaped convict, pleaded guilty to the slaying and was sentenced to 99 years in prison.

A: **Men Walk on Moon**
Q: What was the *New York Time's* headline for Monday July 21, 1969?
W: Could you think of a more important headline for that morning? Neil Armstrong, commander of the Apollo 11 mission, became the first man to set foot on the moon on July 20, 1969.

HISTORY

A: **Menachem Begin**

Q: What Israeli prime minister spent two years in a Russian concentration camp?

W: Begin completed law school in Warsaw. He fled to Vilna, Lithuania, in 1939 when the Germans invaded Poland. He was arrested by Soviet secret police for Zionist activities and was sentenced to eight years. However, he was released in 1941 following the Soviet-Polish exile agreement.

A: **Menachem Begin and Anwar Sadat**

Q: Who were the co-winners of the 1978 Nobel Peace Prize?

W: Begin and Sadat shared the 1978 Nobel Prize Prize for their efforts to end the Arab-Israeli conflict.

A: **Menachem Begin, Jimmy Carter, Anwar Sadat**

Q: What three leaders signed the Camp David Accords?

W: In September 1978, Begin, Carter, and Sadat held discussions that resulted in a major agreement that included plans for Israeli's gradual withdrawal from occupied Arab lands. The treaty was signed in 1979.

A: **Mexico**

Q: What country did Fidel Castro organize his 26th of July Movement in?

W: "July 26" (1953) became the rallying name for the entire revolutionary movement between Cuba and the Caribbean dictators.

A: **MGM Grand, The**

Q: What Las Vegas hotel burned in November 1980 with the loss of 84 lives?

W: This fire caused cities all over the country to review their fire codes, especially in high-rise buildings with limited escape routes.

A: **Mickey Mouse**

Q: What was the D-Day invasion password?

W: The Allied Forces invaded Europe at Normandy on D-Day June 6, 1944. Dwight David Eisenhower was Supreme Commander of the forces.

A: **middle class, The**

Q: What class is categorized as the bourgeoisie?

W: The middle class is a group of people between the upper class and lower class in a society. The term "middle class" came into general use during the early 1800's in Europe and was referred to in French as the "bourgeoisie."

A: **Mike Romanoff**

Q: What colorful Hollywood restaurateur claimed to have killed Rasputin?

W: Mike Romanoff, a self-proclaimed Russian prince, was a restaurant owner and a good friend of many actors and actresses. Rasputin was a favorite at the court of Czar Nicholas II, the last Russian czar (whose family name was Romanov). Rasputin was reportedly killed by a group of conspirators in 1916.

A: **Milhous**

Q: What's Richard Nixon's middle name?

W: Nixon was born Jan. 9, 1913 in Yorba Linda, California. He was the second of five sons of Francis Anthony Nixon and Hannah Milhous Nixon.

A: **Minoan civilization, The**

Q: What Bronze Age civilization emerged on the Greek island of Crete about 2500 B.C.?

W: The Minoan civilization was one of the four cultures that flourished on the islands and shores of the Aegean between 3000 and 1100 B.C. The Minoan culture arose on Crete and is known for its skilled artists and architects.

A: **Modeling**

Q: What was Suzy Parker doing to earn $100,000 in the early 1950s?

W: Suzy, born Cecilia Parker on Oct. 28, 1933, in San Antonio, Texas, was a top model of the 1950s for Conover Modeling Agency. Her tall figure and prominent cheek bones brought her to Hollywood in the late 1950s, but she failed to make it despite good opportunities starring opposite Gary Cooper and Cary Grant. She's married to Actor Bradford Dillman.

A: **Mohammed**

Q: Who was the founder of Islam?

W: Mohammed was born in 570 A.D. and died in 632. He was one of the most influential men of all time. He felt himself to be God's prophet and taught that there was only one God. He preached against the injustice of the wealthy classes of Mecca and tried to help the poor.

A: **Monaco**

Q: What principality has the house of Grimaldi ruled since the Middle Ages?

W: Monaco, an independent principality for over 300 years, has belonged to the house of Grimaldi since 1297, except during the French Revolution. The Prince of Monaco was an absolute ruler until the 1911 Constitution.

A: **Monte Carlo**

Q: Where did Joseph Jagger break the bank in 1886?

W: Monte Carlo, a town in the state of Monaco on the Riviera, nine miles from Nice, France, has been famous as an international gambling center since the 1800s. Aristotle Onassis owned the casino.

A: **Montgomery and Rommel**
Q: What two commanders directed the forces in the Battle of El Alamein?
W: Sir Bernard Montgomery, British soldier, drove the Nazi General Erwin Rommel's forces from Egypt at the Battle of El Alamein in 1942.

A: *Monitor,* **The; and** *Merrimac*
Q: What two vessels fought the first sea battle between iron-covered ships?
W: The *Monitor* and *Merrimac* fought a famous naval battle in the American Civil War. The battle focused worldwide attention on the importance of armor-plated ships.

A: **Moral Majority**
Q: What organization was founded by the Rev. Jerry Falwell?
W: Jerry L. Falwell, a Baptist clergyman, was born in Lynchburg, Virginia in 1933. He founded the group in 1979 and has been president of the Moral Majority since then. It is said that this group was very influential in getting Ronald Reagan elected president of the United States in 1980.

A: **Mormonism**
Q: What religious movement did Joseph Smith found?
W: On April 6, 1830, Joseph Smith founded the Church of Latter-Day Saints at Fayette, New York. This group is more commonly known as Mormons. Smith had a vision in which God and Christ appeared to him, after which he founded the movement as a church representing the restored authority of God on earth.

A: **Moses**
Q: What prophet led the children of Israel to the Promised Land?
W: Moses was the principal leader and teacher of the Israelites. He led his people out of slavery in Egypt to their homeland in Canaan.

A: **Mother Teresa**
Q: Who founded the Order of the Missionaries of Charity in Calcutta in 1948?
W: Twenty years prior to the founding of her order, Mother Terese had taught affluent Indian girls at St. Mary's School in Calcutta, within sight of a major slum. Responding to the call from God, she established an order of nuns devoted to helping the diseased and dying of the slums.

A: **Mount Ararat**
Q: Where is Noah's Ark thought to have landed?
W: Mount Ararat, originally in Armenia, is now in Turkey. According to legend the water receded enough for Noah to land on the mountaintop on April 15, 2348 B.C.

A: **Mrs. John B. Connally**
Q: Who said: "You can't say Dallas hasn't been nice to you today"?
W: John Kennedy smiled and said, "No, you can't." One minute later, at 12:30 P.M., the first bullet struck the president.

A: **Mrs. O'Leary's**
Q: Whose cow was considered to have started the Chicago Fire of 1871?
W: The fire was probably started by Mr. O'Leary's pipe that set the barn on DeKoven St. on fire. But it's probably easier to lay blame on a cow!

A: **Muhammad Ali**
Q: Who claims to be the most recognized person in the world?
W: Muhammad Ali became the first heavyweight boxing champion to win the title three times. He also became one of the most colorful and controversial champions in boxing history by bragging about his ability.

A: **Munich**
Q: Where did Hitler's 1923 Beer Hall Putsch take place?
W: In November 1923, Hitler tried to seize the Bavarian government in Munich in what became known as the Beer Hall Putsch, or Revolution of 1923. His attempt failed; if he had succeeded, he would have had an opportunity to attack the national German government in Berlin. Some of his followers were killed, and he and his assistant, Rudolph Hess, were imprisoned. Hitler was sentenced to five years in prison, but was released after nine months.

N

A: **Napoleon**
Q: Who was Corsica's most famous son?
W: Corsica is an island in the Mediterranean Sea. Napoleon was the son of a poor clerk in the royal district court. Carlo Buonaparte did not live to see his son ascend to his throne.

A: **Napoleon**
Q: Who said: "Soldiers win the battles and generals get the credit"?
W: And believe it or not, he's also given credit for another saying, "An army marches on it's stomach"! Another famous quote: "When I see an empty throne, I feel the urge to sit on it."

A: **Napoleon**
Q: Who was nicknamed "the Little Corporal"?
W: Napoleon I, who crowned himself Emperor of the French and created an empire that covered most of western and central Europe, was nicknamed "le Petit Caporal" because of his courage and short stature.

A: **Napoleon himself**
Q: Who crowned Napoleon emperor of France?
W: Napoleon also placed his brothers and sisters on their thrones; in all they became one emperor, three kings, a queen and two duchesses in seven different countries.

A: Nationalists, The
Q: Which side won the Spanish Civil War, the Nationalists or Republicans?
W: In July 1936 Spanish army units proclaimed revolution against Spain's government. Rebel leaders chose General Francisco Franco as their leader, and they became known as the Nationalists. Forces that fought to save the Republic were known as Republicans. By 1937 the Nationalists held the upper hand in Spain and Entered, one of the last republican strongholds, was captured in 1939.

A: neck brace, A
Q: What did Teddy Kennedy wear around his neck at Mary Jo Kopechne's funeral?
W: The doctor ordered a neck support for injuries sustained in the car accident in which he had been driving and in which Mary Jo had been killed. Ted was accompanied by his wife to the funeral, which was held in Ms. Kopechne's hometown in Pennsylvania.

A: Nehru jacket, The
Q: What 1960's fashion fad was inspired by an Asian leader's garb?

W: Jawaharlal Nehru was prime minister of India from 1947 until his death in 1964, 17 years later. The jacket, however, turned out to be a short-lived faddish loser.

A: Nelson and Bunker Hunt
Q: What two brothers lost a billion trying to corner the silver market in 1980?
W: Nelson and Bunker Hunt, sons of oil tycoon H.L. Hunt, attempted to corner the silver market. This led to an investigation by the Security Exchange Commission.

A: Nelson Rockefeller
Q: Who was Gerald Ford's vice president?
W: Former New York governor, Nelson Rockefeller, was sworn in as vice president on Dec. 19, 1974. He was appointed vice president by Gerald Ford, who had himself been appointed vice president by Richard Nixon. Rockefeller was the second vice president chosen under the 25th Amendment procedure.

A: Nelson Rockefeller
Q: Who was the richest man to be vice president of the U.S.?
W: Rich is a matter of opinion and degree. But since part of the Rockefeller fortune was his, it is not felt that Rockefeller had to worry about cashing his paycheck as vice president of the U.S.!

A: Neville Chamberlain
Q: What British prime minister claimed: "Hitler has missed the bus"?
W: Chamberlain did so in a speech delivered in the House of Commons on April 4, 1940.

A: Neville Chamberlain
Q: Who swapped the Sudetenland for "peace in our time"?
W: In an address from 10 Downing Street, London on Sept. 30, 1938, after returning from the Munich Conference, Chamberlain said: "For the second time in our history, a British Prime Minister has returned from Germany bringing peace with honor. I believe it is peace in our time... Go

home and get a nice quiet sleep." Sudetenland is a region located on the slopes of the Sudetes Mountains in Czechoslovakia. The Munich Agreement of 1938 (Munich Conference) gave Sudetenland to Germany (Hitler). Chamberlain truly believed that it was given in exchange for "peace in our time."

A: Neville Chamberlain
Q: Who did Winston Churchill succeed as British prime minister at the outbreak of World War II?
W: Neville Chamberlain, a Conservative, served as Prime Minister from 1937 to 1940. His government took Britain into World War II, and he was forced to resign in 1940.

A: New York
Q: What city became the U.S. federal capital in 1789?
W: The first Congress met at Federal Hall in New York City, with regular sessions beginning April 6th. Washington was inaugurated in New York City on April 30, 1789. New York had become the temporary capital in January 1785 and served as capital until Washington, D.C. was ready in 1800.

A: New York
Q: What state did Bobby Kennedy represent as a U.S. senator?
W: It was believed that Robert Kennedy moved to New York state and established residency so he could run for the Senate. After all, his brother had Massachusetts!

A: New York City
Q: Where did George Washington make his first inaugural address?
W: Washington was inaugurated April 30, 1789, at Federal Hall in New York City.

A: New Zealand
Q: What country was Sir Edmund Hillary born in?
W: Edmund Hillary was born in Auckland, New Zealand in 1919. On May 29, 1953 he became the first of the two men to reach the top of Mt. Everest and return.

A: **New Zealand**

Q: What country was the scene of the Maori wars?

W: The Maori wars arose out of a land conflict between the Maori tribe and the white settlers of New Zealand. The warfare was intently fought over a period of ten years between 1860 and 1870. These wars made way for many reforms that gave the Maori tribe their basic rights.

A: **Ngo Dinh Diem**

Q: What South Vietnam president was assassinated by his generals in 1963?

W: Ngo Dinh Diem, the son of a government official, was born in central Vietnam in 1901. He worked for Vietnam's independence from France and opposed control by Communist leaders. He was elected president of South Vietnam in 1955 and served until he was killed by army officers in 1963.

A: **Niccolo Machiavelli**

Q: Who said: "The end justifies the means"?

W: Niccolo Machiavelli was an Italian statesman and student of politics, who was in favor of a Republican form of government. Elizabethan literature associates him with the evil one, or the devil. He was in favor of a Republican form of government.

A: **Nicholas II**

Q: Who was the last czar of Russia?

W: Nicholas II, last czar of Russia, ruled from 1894 to 1917. Although charming and well-intentioned, he was described as being politically weak and unreliable.

A: **Nikita Khrushchev**

Q: What deceased Russian leader said: "We will in my lifetime rule the world by invitation"?

W: Khrushchev rose through the ranks of the Communist Party in Russia to become the most powerful man in the party and in Russia. He became Premier in March 1958. He sincerely believed that countries would ask to be part of Russia.

A: **Nikita Khrushchev**

Q: Who gave John F. Kennedy a dog named Pushinka?

W: Khrushchev sent the dog to Kennedy as a gift after their June 1961 meeting in Vienna. Pushinka was a direct offspring of Streika, who was the first dog in space.

A: **Nina**

Q: What was Nikita Khrushchev's wife's name?

W: Khrushchev met his second wife, Nina, at a worker's school where she was a teacher. They were married in 1924 and had one son and two daughters.

A: **Nipper**

Q: What was the name of the dog in RCA Victor's trademark?

W: Nipper was born in Bristol, England, in 1884. He became the symbol for the following companies: Gramophone Company, Victor Talking Machine Company, and, finally in 1929, the RCA Victor Company.

A: **Noah**

Q: Who made a boat out of gopher wood?

W: Noah, according to the Bible, was the only righteous, God-fearing man of his time. Genesis 6:9 tells that he was chosen by God to keep his family and two of every animal alive during the Great Flood. To accomplish this, God instructed him to build an ark of gopher wood 450 feet long.

A: **Nobody**

Q: Who won the 1942 Nobel Peace Prize?

W: Nobel Peace Prizes were not announced in 1939, 1940, 1941, 1942, or 1943. The 1944 Nobel Peace Prize was awarded to the International Red Cross for war relief.

A: **Normandy**

Q: Where were Omaha, Juno, and Gold Beaches?

W: On D-Day, June 6, 1944, the Allied invasion of France began at 1:30 A.M. when a massive airdrop was made behind Hitler's coastal defenses. Some five hours later the Allied assault troops landed on five bullet-swept beaches. The five beaches were the Utah, Omaha, Gold, Juno, and Sword.

A: **Normandy Invasion, The**

Q: What invasion was code named Operation Overlord?

W: In 1943 Allies set up a planning staff for the invasion of Normandy. Operation Overload was the code name for the invasion plan. Dwight D. Eisenhower was commander of the force.

A: **North Atlantic Treaty Organization**

Q: What does NATO stand for?

W: This organization was created by the North Atlantic Treaty, signed April 4, 1949, and went into effect Aug. 24, 1949. Member countries are Belgium, Canada, Denmark, France, Iceland, Italy, Luxembourg, the Netherlands, Norway, Portugal, United Kingdom, United States, Greece, Turkey, West Germany and Spain. It is basically a collective defense agreement among these nations in opposition to Soviet influence in Europe.

A: **North Pole, The**

Q: Where did explorer Robert Peary claim he arrived on April 6, 1909?

W: He began his trip March 1, 1909, from Cape Columbia, Ellesmere Island. Supported by Matthew Henson and four Eskimos with dog teams and sleds, they reached 90 degrees north latitude and stayed 36 hours. Cook's claim to have reached there in 1908 is generally discredited.

A: **Not guilty**

Q: What was the verdict in the trial of Lizzie Borden?

W: Lizzie Borden was tried and acquitted for the murders of her stepmother, Sarah A. Morse, and her father, Andrew Jackson Borden. They were killed on Aug. 4, 1892, in Fall Rivers, Massachusetts.

HISTORY

A: O.K. Corral, The
Q: Where were Billie Clanton and the McLowery brothers gunned down?
W: ...in Tombstone, Arizona, by the Earp brothers. Actually the battle was fought in a nearby alley. Today fiberglass life-size figures stand where they did.

A: O.K. Corral, The
Q: Where were the Earp boys involved in a shoot-out on Oct. 26, 1881?
W: Tombstone now has "Helldorado Days" in October when the town's residents relive the gunfights and hangings of earlier days. The life-size figure of Wyatt Earp will fire at you for a quarter!

A: Oct. 29, 1929
Q: What date was Black Tuesday?
W: *That* was the date of the Stock Market Crash of 1929. This complete collapse shattered the entire economy of the U.S. Stock losses from then through 1931 are estimated at $50 billion.

A: Office of Strategic Services, The
Q: What was the predecessor to the Central Intellgience Agency?
W: The Office of Strategic Services(OSS) was the secret intelligence agency for the U.S. during World War II with William J. Donovan as its director. The agency, developed to carry out the many espionage activities required during the war, was dissolved in 1945, and its functions were continued by both the State and War Departments until 1947 when the C.I.A. was formed.

A: Oil
Q: What business was the source of John D. Rockefeller's fortune?
W: John D. Rockefeller, who at the time was a bookkeeper for a produce commission house, encouraged his employer to refine kerosene from oil in 1862, three years after the first oil well was drilled in Pennsylvania by Edwin Drake. By 1867 Rockefeller was the major owner of the firm that grew into Standard Oil Trust. Exxon Corporation is a direct descendent of the Standard Oil Company of Ohio. By 1978 Standard Oil, combined with other Rockefeller companies, controlled about 85 percent of the country's oil industry. Gosh, J.D. was probably bigger than J.R. in Dallas!

A: Oklahoma
Q: What state did Anita Bryant represent in the 1959 Miss America contest?
W: But she lost to Mary Ann Mobley, Miss Mississippi.

A: One
Q: How many ballots did it take John F. Kennedy to win the 1960 Democratic presidential nomination?
W: Kennedy won every presidential primary contest in which his name was entered. He won the general election by less than 150,000 popular votes out of the 70 million votes cast.

A: One
Q: How many Israeli commandos died in the Entebbe raid?
W: Only one Israeli commando was killed in the rescue mission of a hijacked Air France airliner at Entebbe, Uganda, on July 4, 1976. Also killed in the rescue were the terrorists, a score of Ugandan soldiers, and two hostages.

A: orange, The
Q: What's Anita Bryant's favorite kind of fruit?
W: Anita Bryant is a noted entertainment personality. She was born in Barnsdall, Oklahoma, on March 25, 1940. She also gained fame doing TV commercials for orange juice!

A: Otto von Bismarck
Q: Who was "the Iron Chancellor", unifier of Germany?
W: Otto von Bismarck was a Prussian statesman who united the German states into one empire. He said that problems must be settled by "blood and iron" instead of speeches and resolutions. He served as chancellor of the German Empire from 1871 to 1890.

A: *Our American Cousin*
Q: What play was Abraham Lincoln watching when he was assassinated?
W: Lincoln attended a performance of *Our American Cousin* at Ford Theater in Washington on April 14, 1865. A shot rang out through the theater a few minutes after 10 P.M. Lincoln had been shot in the head; he died at 7:22 A.M. on April 15.

A: Oval Office, The
Q: What's been called the innermost sanctuary of American power?
W: The Oval Office is the main office of the president of the United States. As such, it is the room in which all types of domestic and foreign policies are discussed and thus one of the innermost sanctuaries of American power.

A: Oval Office bugging, The
Q: What revelation did Alexander Butterfield make to the Senate Watergate committee?
W: Alexander Butterfield is a business executive and retired government official. From 1969 to 1973 he was a deputy assistant to Richard M. Nixon as well as a secretary to the Cabinet. Butterfield told the Senate Watergate Committee that his boss, President Nixon, taped meetings that took place in the Oval Office.

P

A: **P.T. Barnum**
Q: What circus owner is credited with saying: "There's a sucker born every minute"?
W: Could be. Our sources give credit for the saying to Chicago gambling czar Michael Cassius McDonald.

A: **P.T. Barnum's**
Q: What showman's last words were: "How were the receipts today at Madison Square Garden?"?
W: Barnum entered show business by exhibiting Joyce Heth, the "161-year-old colored nurse of George Washington." She actually died in 1836 at the age of 80. In 1881 he merged his "Greatest Show on Earth" circus with the circus of J.A. Bailey to form the famous Barnum and Bailey Circus. Barnum is credited with turning tent carnivals into the modern three ring circus. He was thought to be the living example of the Horatio Alger hero.

A: **Pacific, The**
Q: What ocean was Amelia Earhart flying over when she disappeared?
W: In July 1937, along with navigator Fredrick Noonan, Earhart attempted a round-the-world flight. Their plane mysteriously disappeared after take-off in New Guinea.

A: **Pancho Villa**
Q: What Mexican leader was shot dead in 1923?
W: Pancho Villa was a Mexican bandit and revolutionary leader. On March 9, 1916 he raided the town of Columbia, New Mexico and killed 16 persons. He agreed to retire from politics and was granted a pardon and a ranch near Parral, Chihuahua. He was assassinated on his ranch.

A: **Papa Doc**
Q: What was the nickname of former Haitian leader Francois Duvalier?
W: Francois Duvalier was president of Haiti from 1957 until his death in 1971. He was a physician and authority on voodoo. He ruled as a dictator and allowed no one to oppose him.

A: **Parkland Hospital, Dallas**
Q: Where did John F. Kennedy, Lee Harvey Oswald, and Jack Ruby all die?
W: Kennedy and Governor John Connally were taken there after they were shot on Nov. 22, 1963. Oswald was taken there after he was shot by Ruby two days later. Ruby was taken there in 1966.

A: **Pasta**
Q: What food did Marco Polo introduce into Italy from the court of Kubla Khan?
W: According to legend, Marco Polo brought a pasta recipe with him from Asia in 1295. It quickly became a major element in the Italian diet, and its popularity spread throughout Europe.

A: **Pat Garrett**
Q: Who killed Billy the Kid?
W: Garrett gunned down Billy in 1861, but the law was a little slow in catching up with Billy who had already killed 21 men!

A: **Pat Paulsen**
Q: Who launched his ill-fated drive for the White House on "The Summer Smothers Brothers Show"?
W: Singers-comedians Tom and Dick Smothers were born on Governors Island where their father Major Thomas Smothers was stationed. In World War II their father died on a Japanese prisoner of war ship en route to Japan. Pat Paulson was a noted personality in the entertainment industry. He was born in South Bend, Washington. Pat was not a serious candidate, although he did go out on the campaign trail for awhile. He started his campaign because so many people were complaining that they had no one to vote *for*, only someone they wanted to vote against

A: **Patricia Hearst**
Q: Who became Tania?
W: Tania is the name that Patty referred to herself as when she was part of the Symbionese Liberation Army (SLA).

A: **Patricia Hearst**
Q: Who was kidnapped on Feb. 4, 1974?
W: She was kidnapped in Berkeley, California by the Symbionese Liberation Army (SLA), whose leader was Donald "Field Marshall Cinque" De Freeze, an escaped convict. She was captured by the FBI on Sept. 18, 1974, and convicted for bank robbery on Mar. 20, 1976.

A: **Patrick Henry**
Q: Who said: "Give me liberty or give me death"?
W: Although a great American political leader, Patrick owned 65 slaves at the time of his death!

A: **Paul McCartney**
Q: Who did Linda Eastman marry on March 12, 1969?
W: Paul McCartney was one of the Beatles, a famous rock group from England. McCartney was born in Liverpool June 18, 1938. He married Linda Eastman on March 12, 1969.

A: **Paul Revere**
Q: Who galloped from Boston toward Lexington on an April night in 1775?
W: Revere also designed the first issue of Continental currency, the first seal of the colonies, and the state seal used by Massachusetts.

HISTORY

A: **Paul Revere**
Q: Who made George Washington's false teeth?
W: Paul Revere was a multi-talented craftsman. He learned his father's trade of silversmithing but had to supplement his income by doing copper engravings and drawing political cartoons. He also tried his hand at dentistry but didn't continue at this for too long.

A: **Payola**
Q: What was a U.S. Senate committee probing when Dick Clark testified on April 29, 1960?
W: Some 207 disc jockeys in 42 cities received over $260,000 in payments to play certain records on the air. The inventor of the term "rock 'n roll," Allen Freed, was among those indicted. *Payola* was the term used to describe this payoff.

A: **Pearl Harbor**
Q: What attack did Isoroku Yamamota plan and lead?
W: On Dec. 7, 1941 at 7:45 A.M., Japanese aircraft launched a full attack on Pearl Harbor, Hawaii. Nineteen vessels were sunk or damaged, but the 26-year-old battleship *Arizona* was the only one lost. The others were salvaged, and most were restored to active service. This attack was the immediate cause of the U.S. involvment in World War II.

A: **Pepsi-Cola**
Q: What was the first U.S. consumer product sold in the Soviet Union?
W: This was not easy to verify, but we did! In Russian the word is spelled NENCN-KONA.

A: **Pepsi-Cola's**
Q: What company's stock exchange listing is abbreviated to PEP?
W: Pepsi-Cola is the largest American soft drink company, and it is abbreviated PEP on the exchange. In 1960 annual consumption of soft drinks in the U.S. was over 190 bottles per person!

A: **Peter Lawford**
Q: What actor married John F. Kennedy's sister?
W: Patricia Kennedy was married to Peter Lawford from 1954 to 1966.

A: **Pierre Salinger**
Q: Who was John F. Kennedy's press secretary?
W: Pierre Salinger is now the ABC correspondent for its Paris bureau.

A: **Pigasus**
Q: What was the name of the pig the Yippies nominated for president in Chicago in 1968?
W: This is in fact the prankish name of the Yippees' nominee for the presidency in 1968. A play on words of Pegasus, the mythical winged horse?

A: **Pinkerton's**
Q: What detective agency's motto is: "We never sleep"?
W: Allan Pinkerton, founder of the agency, grew up in a slum in Glasgow, Scotland. He left school at age eight and eventually made his way to Chicago where he became a barrel-maker (cooper). He lived in West Dundee, Illinois where he uncovered a counterfeiting ring, and served as deputy sheriff of both Kane and Cook Counties of Illinois before he founded the detective agency in the early 1850s.

A: **Pirates**
Q: What are Barbary corsairs?
W: Barbary States is the name formerly given to the countries along the coast of North Africa, from Egypt to the Atlantic Ocean. From about 1515 to 1816, Barbary pirates (corsairs) from these states attacked the ships of other nations in the Mediterranean waters and plundered their cargo.

A: **Pius XII**
Q: What pope was crowned on March 12, 1939?
W: We assume the Pope liked basketball, since the Harlem Globetrotters once performed their circle drill for 45 minutes with Pope Pius XII in the center of the circle. They were accompanied by the Brother Bones version of "Sweet Georgia Brown." There is no truth to the rumor the Pope blocked Meadowlark Lemon's slam dunk!

A: **Plymouth**
Q: What was the *Mayflower's* last port of call before setting sail for America?
W: In the 14th and 15th centuries, Plymouth was the port of embarkation for English troops about to fight in the Hundred Years War. Plymouth was the first English town to be incorporated by an act of Parliament in 1439 when it got its name; formerly called Sudtone. In July, 1588, the English fleet sailed from Plymouth to meet and defeat the Spanish Armada, which established British supremacy on the high seas.

A: **Pocahontas**
Q: What Indian maiden rescued Captain John Smith and later married John Rolfe?
W: She saved Smith's life after he had been captured by a tribe of Indians. Just as he had placed his head on the sacrificial stone to await death, Pocahontas flung herself down, embraced Smith's head, and successfully implored her father, Powhatan — leader of the tribe — to spare him. Later she fell in love with and married John Rolfe, a distinguished settler.

A: **Poland**
Q: What country did Germany invade on Sept. 1, 1939?
W: The liquidation of Polish Jewry began at this time. The Jewish population was 2,750,000 before World War II, 80 times larger than today. Two notorious concentration camps — Auschwitz near Krakow and Majdanek near Lublin — existed in Poland. The "campaign" was short. Part of Poland was incorporated into Germany while the rest became a "general government" where unwanted Poles were sent and recruited for slave labor in German factories.

A: **Politburo, The**
Q: What's the supreme policy-making bureau of the Soviet Communist Party?
W: The party, which first came into being in October 1917 with Lenin, Trotsky, Stalin, and Zinoviev as members, was formed to direct the Bolshevik seizure of power. It passed in and out of power over the years. In April, 1966, the Party's 23rd Congress revived the Politburo with Leonid Brezhrev as First Secretary.

A: **Pontius Pilate**
Q: What Roman governor tried Christ?
W: Actually, Pilate did not try Christ. Pilate was the highest Roman authority in the city of Jerusalem. He wasn't convinced that what Christ had done warranted such a severe sentence and wasn't anxious to see it carried out. The Sanhedrin, the highest Jewish authority, however, brought political pressure, and in the end Pilate turned Jesus over to his Jewish persecutors, saying, "I find in him no fault at all".

A: **Pony Express, The**
Q: What delivery service operated between Missouri and California starting in 1860?
W: The Pony Express was a private company that only survived for 18 months, at which time it was made obsolete by the first transcontinental telegraph line. Usual delivery time between Missouri and California was eight days, although the fastest trip was seven days, seven hours.

A: **Pope, The**
Q: Who wears the Fisherman's Ring?
W: The ring depicts St. Peter as a fisherman and has the reigning Pope's name inscribed around the border. The ring is broken in public after each Pope's death

A: **Pope John XXIII**
Q: What was Angelo Giuseppe Roncalli better known as?
W: He served as Pope from 1958 to 1963.

A: **Pope John Paul II**
Q: Who exclaimed, after being shot: "Why did they do it?"?
W: On May 13, 1981, Pope John Paul II and two bystanders were shot and wounded in St. Peter's Square, Rome by Mehmet Ali Agca, an escaped Turkish murderer.

A: **Pope Paul VI**
Q: Who was the first Pope to visit Africa?
W: Pope Paul VI made a pilgrimage to Uganda in 1969.

A: **Potatoes**
Q: What crop failure caused the Irish Famine?
W: During the 1700s the rulers of many European governments ordered the potato to be planted because of its food value. It soon became an important crop, especially in Ireland where it replaced wheat as the staff of life. During the 1840s the late blight disease of the potato wiped out the crop in Ireland two years in a row. The famine that resulted changed the course of Irish history.

A: **Poverty**
Q: What did Lyndon Johnson declare war against on Jan. 8, 1964?
W: Johnson's War on Poverty directed national attention to the problem of hunger and want in the midst of plenty. He also brought about the first large scale federal commitment to halt the process of big city decay.

A: **President and Mrs. Ulysses Grant**
Q: Who's buried in Grant's tomb?
W: During the Civil War, Grant demanded that his meat be cooked black as the sight of blood and red meat made him queasy. He was a devoted family man who was very dependent on his wife, although they were separated for a time which caused him to drink excessively.

A: **president, The; and vice president**
Q: What two U.S. public officials aren't allowed to travel together?
W: This is a custom rather than a law. It makes perfect sense as the vice president is to assume the duties of the president should the president be unable to continue in that position. Should fate allow neither the president nor his vice president to execute their duties, the speaker of the house steps into the White House.

A: **Prince Charles**
Q: Who was the first member of Britain's royal family to graduate from a university?
W: Prince Charles is the first heir to the British throne to attend school outside the palace grounds. All previous heirs were taught privately by tutors. Charles was born in 1948 and installed as Prince of Wales in July 1968.

A: **Princess Anne**
Q: Who is Captain Mark Phillips married to?
W: Princess Anne was born to Queen Elizabeth II of England on Aug. 15, 1950. She married Captain Mark Phillips on Nov. 14, 1973.

A: **Princess Elizabeth**
Q: Who married Lieutenant Philip Mountbatten on Nov. 20, 1947?
W: Princess Elizabeth became Queen Elizabeth II. She succeeded her father, George VI, who died on Feb. 6, 1952.

A: prison, A
Q: What purpose did the Bastille serve before it was stormed on July 14, 1789?
W: After it was stormed by 20,000 angry people seeking arms, the prisoners were freed, three officers were butchered, three were strung up on lampposts, and the Bastille governor was struck on the head with a pitchfork. The mob also murdered the Mayor of Paris. In his diary for this day, the King entered one word *Rien*, meaning "nothing – nothing worth saying."

A: Prohibition
Q: What did the only repealed amendment to the U.S. Constitution deal with?
W: The longest legal prohibition of alcohol was 26 years in Iceland, from 1908 to 1934. U.S. prohibition lasted 14 years. The 18th Amendment was ratified on Jan. 16, 1919; it was repealed by the 21st Amendment which went into effect on Dec. 5, 1933. The booze flowed that day for sure!

A: Prohibition Ends At Last
Q: What was the headline of the *New York Daily Mirror* on Dec. 6, 1933?
W: The 18th Amendment (prohibition of liquor) was repealed by the 21st Amendment, effective Dec. 5, 1933, ending almost 14 years of being dry.

A: Prostitution
Q: What was the occupaton of Jack the Ripper's five victims?
W: Other similarities between victims: all five were grabbed from behind and had their throats slit, an attempt was made to mutilate all of their bodies, every killing happened on either the first or last weekend of the month in the early morning, and none were sexually assaulted.

A: *Pueblo*, The
Q: What ship did Lloyd M. Bucher command?
W: Bucher was commander of this electronics surveillance ship when it was captured by North Korea on Jan. 23, 1968. In his youth Bucher was Mayor of Boys Town and he appeared as an extra in the 1957 movie *Hellcats*. The film was being made aboard the submarine to which he was assigned at the time, the USS *Besugo*.

A: Pyrenees, The; and Alps
Q: What two mountain ranges did Hannibal and his elephants march through in 218 B.C.?
W: Hannibal was the Carthaginian general who was to go to battle with the Romans. Hannibal, with 40,000 troops and a number of elephants, crossed the Pyrenees into Gaul. From there he proceeded across the Alps into northern Italy.

A: Quakers
Q: What are adherents to the Society of Friends called?
W: There are 1,184 churches in the U.S. that are part of the Society of Friends: Evangelical Friends Alliance, Friends General Conference, and Friends United Meeting. There are about 126,000 members of this religious group. A few celebrated Quakers: Betsy Ross, Johns Hopkins, Walt Whitman, Herbert Hoover, James Michener, and Richard Nixon.

A: *Queen Elizabeth*, The
Q: What ocean liner burned and sank in Hong Kong harbor?
W: The *Queen Elizabeth* was launched in 1938.

A: "Queen Elizabeth", The
Q: What was the largest passenger liner ever built?
W: Actually this should be the *Queen Elizabeth II*, which has since been retired to Port Everglades, Florida, and is now a tourist attraction. It is not to be confused with the *Queen Elizabeth* which was launched in 1938 and sunk in Hong Kong harbor! *Queen Elizabeth II* was launched in 1967.

A: Queen Elizabeth II
Q: What woman was *Time's* Man of the Year for 1952?
W: Queen Elizabeth II actually became the Queen of England while in Aberdare National Park in Kenya in 1952. She arrived there as a princess, but during her stay her father George VI died, and she left a day later as queen.

A: Queen Elizabeth II
Q: Who is Britain's Defender of the Faith?
W: The Church of England is Protestant Episcopal. The Queen is its temporal head, with right of appointment for archbishops, bishops, and other offices. There are two provinces each headed by an archbishop: York and Canterbury.

A: *Queen Mary*, The
Q: What ocean liner was retired in 1967 and became a hotel at Long Beach?
W: The *Queen Mary* is the Cunard Ocean Liner now moored at Pier J in Long Beach, California. It was purchased for $3 million in 1967.

A: Queen Victoria
Q: What British monarch reigned the longest?
W: Queen Victoria reigned from 1837 to 1901 as the longest reigning monarch. Here's the shortest: Lady Jane Grey who ruled for nine days in 1553.

A: Queen Victoria
Q: Who was the wife of Prince Albert of Saxe-Coburg-Gotha?
W: Prince Albert was Queen Victoria's first cousin. They married in 1840 and had nine children. He died in 1861 and she went into a seclusion that did not end until the 1880s.

R

A: **Radio Corporation of America**
Q: What does RCA stand for?
W: The company was formed on Oct. 17, 1919. NBC is a subidiary, and RCA also owns Hertz, Random House Publishing, Ballantine Books, Banquet Foods, and more. We think RCA stands for big bucks!

A: **Ralph Nader**
Q: Who sued the Dannon yogurt company for using a character named Ron Raider for promotion?
W: At one time Nader challenged the safety of General Motors' Corvair. A scandel developed when GM denied the charges and hired a private detective to "smear" Nader. After this Nader became America's leading "consumer advocate". He also investigated conditions in nursing homes and drug companies that used the elderly for drug research, to mention only a few of his causes!

A: **Rancho del Cielo**
Q: What's the name of Ronald Reagan's 688-acre California spread?
W: The Rancho del Cielo spread contains a small ranch house built on the property in 1881. It is located in the Santa Ynez Mountains, just north of Santa Barbara. The Reagans bought it in 1974.

A: **Raoul**
Q: What's Fidel Castro's brother's name?
W: Raoul is one of Fidel's strongest allies. He remains second in command of the Cuban government and is clearly slated to succeed Fidel.

A: **Rasputin**
Q: Who was "the Mad Monk"?
W: Rasputin was the Russian mystic who spent his life diverting his followers' religious fervor into sexual channels. This "savior and healer" seduced hundreds of women. He was in particular favor at the court of Nicholas II for his help in treating Nicholas' son's hemophilia.

A: **RCA Victor's**
Q: What company's trademark was "His Master's Voice"?
W: The RCA Victor's dog's name was Nipper. He was the terrier listening to the old phonograph. Nipper was first the symbol of the Gramophone Company, then the Victor Talking Machine Company, and finally RCA Victor in 1929. The phonograph to which Nipper is listening is an Edison.

A: **Red**
Q: What color was Judas Iscariot's hair?
W: Judas Iscariot was the apostle who betrayed Jesus Christ to his enemies for 30 pieces of silver. He identified Jesus to the arresting soldiers by kissing him. His hair was red! Other famous redheads were General George Custer, Mark Twain, and Harold "Red" Grange. Lizzie Borden was another infamous redhead!

A: **Red**
Q: What color were most 19th-century American schoolhouses painted?
W: It was customary, especially in New England and other northeastern sections of the country to paint frame schoolhouses red, not because it was the preferred color but because red paint was cheaper than any other kind obtainable.

A: **Red Baron, The; or The Red Knight**
Q: What was the nickname of German flying ace Manfred von Richthofen?
W: He had more victories than any other World War I air ace: 79 British planes and one Belgian plane. He was nicknamed the Red Baron because of the color of his plane.

A: **Red Brigades, The**
Q: What group kidnaped and murdered Italian Premier Aldo Moro?
W: The Red Brigades are terrorists that operate in Italy.

A: **Red Cross, The**
Q: What international organization was founded by Clara Barton?
W: Clara Barton was the president of the American Red Cross for 23 years after she founded it. The International Red Cross was founded by Jean Henri Dunant, a Swiss philanthropist, and is based in Geneva Switzerland.

A: **Reformation, The**
Q: What was the name of the Protestant revolt against the supremacy of the Pope?
W: Martin Luther preached that only faith could lead to salvation, without the mediation of clergy. He attacked the authority of the Pope, rejected priestly celibacy and recommended individual study of the Bible. His 95 theses led to his excommunication from the church in 1520.

A: **Reverend Jim Jones, The**
Q: Who founded the People's Temple Commune?
W: Jim Jones founded a commune in Guyana, on the north coast of South America. U.S. Representative Leo J. Ryan was ambushed and killed as he and others were leaving following an investigation of alleged mistreatment of Jones' followers. This triggered a mass suicide-execution of 911 cultists on Nov. 18, 1978.

A: **Reverend Sun Myung Moon**
Q: Who founded the Unification Church?
W: The Unification Church is often criticized because of the overpowering hold it maintains over its members. The Reverend Moon received international publicity recently by performing a wedding ceremony for hundreds of couples at the same time. He was also sentenced to prison for tax evasion in 1984.

HISTORY

A: **ribbon reading "E pluribus unum," A**
Q: What's in the eagle's beak on the Great Seal of the United States?
W: It means "Out of many, one," and appears on the Great Seal of the United States that was adopted on June 20, 1782. The U.S. national motto is "In God We Trust."

A: **Richard Daley**
Q: Who declared: "As long as I am mayor, there will be law and order in Chicago"?
W: Violence broke out at the Democratic National Convention from August 25 to 29, 1968. Approximately 60 million TV viewers watched Chicago police club a crowd of 5,000 demonstrators into submission. That's law and order alright!

A: **Richard Nixon**
Q: Who declared: "I am not a crook"?
W: Perhaps not, but he had several of them (later convicted) working for him! A few Watergate names: James McCord, Jr.; E. Howard Hunt, Jr.; G. Gordon Liddy; John Mitchell; John Dean; H.R. Haldeman; and John Ehrlichman. Nixon called himself a "non-crook" in a press conference on Nov. 11, 1973.

A: **Richard Nixon**
Q: Who declared: "The White House has had no involvement whatever in this particular incident"?
W: This is a quote from Richard Nix-

on after the Watergate incident in which five men were arrested on June 17, 1972, for breaking into the offices of the Democratic National Committee in the Watergate office complex in Washington, D.C. President Nixon was denying any knowledge of the event with this statement.

A: **Richard Nixon**
Q: Who ordered the Saturday Night Massacre?
W: John Dean had told the Senate Investigating Committee that criminal activities had taken place in the Oval Office, and Alexander Butterfield then told the Committee that White House conversations had been taped. Under Senate pressure, Nixon appointed Archibald Cox to investigate all aspects of Watergate. Nixon wanted the tapes to himself so he ordered Cox to "cease and desist" in his efforts to obtain the tapes. When Cox refused, Nixon ordered him fired, but before this was done Attorney General Elliot Richardson and Deputy Attorney General William Ruckelshaus both resigned rather than fire Cox. The term "Saturday Night Massacre" refers to this evening when two of Nixon's top aides resigned and Cox was fired.

A: **Richard Nixon**
Q: Who was the first U.S. president to visit Moscow?
W: Richard Nixon went to Moscow in May of 1972. It was the first visit by a president of the U.S. At its conclusion the U.S. and Soviet Union announced a major advance in nuclear arms limitation, bilateral trade accords, and plans for joint scientific and space ventures.

A: **Richard Nixon's**
Q: Whose name, apart from astronauts', is on the Apollo 11 moon plaque?
W: Nixon was president in 1969 when the Apollo 11 landed on the moon. The plaque bears this message: "Here men from the planet earth first set foot upon the moon July 1969 A.D."

A: **Richard Nixon and Nikita Khrushchev**
Q: Who argued it out in the Kitchen Debate?
W: In 1959 as he was preparing to run for president in 1960, Vice President Nixon, eager to establish a reputation as a statesman, traveled to Moscow to open a U.S. exhibition in a Moscow park. While touring the exhibit of an American model kitchen with Soviet Premier Khrushchev, Nixon couldn't resist engaging in a shouting match with Khrushchev in front of the world press.

A: **Riddle**
Q: What was Jimmy Hoffa's middle name?
W: Call Ripley, Believe it or Not. Hoffa's middle name is/was Riddle. Where are you, Jimmy? Will the real James Riddle Hoffa please call home. Here's another weird middle name: Joe E. Brown's middle name was Even!

A: **Robert Baden-Powell**
Q: What British colonial officer founded the Boy Scouts in 1907?
W: He was a retired British officer and part-time writer. He took 25 boys on a camping trip to Brownsea Island and returned to establish this new youth group for boys. He headed the Boy Scouts until 1937.

A: **Robert Frost**
Q: What poet read at John F. Kennedy's inauguration?
W: Because of the blinding winter sun, Frost had difficulty reading the poem he had written for the occasion. He eventually gave up and recited another poem he knew by heart.

A: **Robert McNamara**
Q: Who was Lyndon Johnson's secretary of defense?
W: That's who was Secretary of Defense when Johnson took over the unexpired term of JFK, and he remained with Johnson until 1968 when Clark M. Clifford became Johnson's Secretary of Defense.

A: Roman Catholicism
Q: What religion did Adolf Hitler profess?
W: Hitler claimed he learned "the use of terror from the Communists, the use of propoganda from democracies, and the use of slogans from the Catholic Church."

A: Roman Empire, The
Q: What empire ruled England in A.D. 120?
W: The boundaries of the Roman Empire changed many times during its 1,300 year history. At its greatest, in A.D. 117, the Roman Empire stretched from northern Britain to the shores of the Red Sea and the Persian Gulf.

A: Romanov
Q: What was the surname of Nicholas II, last czar of Russia?
W: Nicholas II was forced to abdicate by the revolution that followed Russian losses to Germany in World War I. The Czar, the Empress, the Crown Prince, and the Czar's four daughters were murdered by the Bolsheviks on July 16, 1918.

A: Rome
Q: What city did Emperor Augustus claim he found brick and left marble?
W: Augustus became the first Roman Emperor in 27 B.C. Rome reached its greatest glory during his reign and the period became known as the Augustan Age. Many roads, bridges, aqueducts and beautiful buildings were built in Rome under Augustus. He boasted that he "found Rome brick and left it marble".

A: Romulus and Remus
Q: Who were the legendary founders of Rome?
W: According to legend the city of Rome was founded by Romulus and Remus in 753 B.C.

A: Ron Ziegler
Q: What presidential press secretary dismissed Watergate as a third-rate burglary attempt?
W: President Nixon's press secretary, Ron Ziegler, attempted to minimize the significance of the Watergate break-in by likening it to a minor burglary.

A: Ronald Reagan
Q: Who blundered in 1975, saying, "The United States has much to offer the Third World War"?
W: As a candidate for president in 1975, Reagan was speaking about the "Third World" and inadvertently added "war" after the term!

A: Ronald Reagan
Q: Who married actress Nancy Davis?
W: They married March 4, 1952, and seven and one-half months later daughter Patti was born. Nancy Davis' full name is Anne Frances "Nancy" Robbins Davis Reagan.

A: Ronald Reagan
Q: Who said: "Honey, I forgot to duck"?
W: That's what he said to his wife Nancy after he was shot in the left lung outside a Washington hotel by John Hinckley, Jr. on Mar. 30, 1981.

A: Ronald Reagan
Q: Who said: "I hope you doctors are all Republicans"?
W: Before surgeons were to remove the .22-caliber bullet from his left lung after he was shot by John Hinckley, Jr., in 1981, Ronnie cracked this one liner.

A: Ronald Reagan
Q: Who was the first incumbent U.S. president to survive being shot?
W: One might have thought President Gerald R. Ford in 1975; however, in the first attempt by Squeaky Fromm no shot was fired; in the second attempt by Sara Jane Moore the shot was deflected. Reagan was shot in the left lung on Mar. 30, 1981.

A: Ronald Reagan
Q: Who was the first union president to occupy the Oval Office?
W: Reagan at one time was president of the Screen Actors Guild.

A: Ronald Reagan
Q: Who was the oldest U.S. president inaugurated?
W: Reagan was 69 when first inaugurated in 1981. William H. Harrison was next oldest at time of inauguration at 68, but he died in office a few months later. Reagan is the oldest president ever to have served in that office.

A: rose's, The
Q: What flower's petals does the British royal family use as confetti?
W: The rose has become a symbol of fragrance and beauty. The royal family throws rose petals at public functions, parades, and weddings in much the same manner as tickertape or confetti is thrown in the U.S.

A: Roy Bean
Q: What barroom judge called himself the "Law West of the Pecos"?
W: In real life Roy's brother Josh was the first mayor of San Diego. Judge Roy Bean was a saloon keeper and justice of the peace on the west Texas frontier where the Pecos and Rio Grande Rivers join. Judge Bean held court at one end of the bar and often relied on his six-guns to maintain order. He became noted for his colorful decisions and for his boast that he was the only "Law West of the Pecos".

A: **Rudolf Abel**
Q: What Russian master spy lived in the U.S. under the name Emil Goldfus?
W: In 1962 Abel was released from an Atlanta prison, in which he had been imprisoned for spying, in exchange for Francis Gary Powers, an American spy plane pilot shot down over the Soviet Union. Abel still works in the Soviet Secret Service.

A: **Rudolf Abel**
Q: What Russian spy was exchanged for U-2 pilot Francis Gary Powers in 1962?
W: Abel, a former KGB director in the U.S., was serving a 30-year sentence for spying. Powers, an Amercan shot down over the Soviet Union, could have been sentenced to death but was given ten years in prison. After two years of top secret negotiations, the exchange was made.

A: **Rudolf Hess**
Q: Which of Hitler's deputies parachuted into Scotland to negotiate peace terms?
W: On May 10, 1941, Hess secretly flew to Scotland to negotiate a peace between Germany and Britain. His proposals met with no response. He was held as a prisoner of war throughout World War II, which caused Hitler much embarrassment. Hess was tried at Nuremburg and convicted.

A: **Rudolf Hess**
Q: Who was Spandau Prison's last inmate?
W: After 1946 the Spandau Prison, on the Wilhelmstrasse of West Berlin, housed the Nazi war criminals sentenced by the Allies in the Nuremburg War Crimes Trial of 1945 and 1946. Hess, who had been second in line of Hitler's succession, was tried at Nuremburg, convicted, and given a life sentence.

A: **Rudolph**
Q: What is Gerald Ford's middle name?

W: But did you know that he was renamed after his stepfather Gerald R. Ford? He was the only son of Leslie and Dorothy Gardner King. His parents were divorced two years after his birth; his mother remarried and Jerry was renamed. Actually at birth his name was Leslie Lynch King, Jr., so if you guessed Lynch you're correct too!

A: **Rudolph Valentino's**
Q: Whose funeral was attended by more than 100,000 in New York City in 1926?
W: Valentino emigrated from Italy to the U.S. at age 18, under the name Rudloph Alfonzo Rafaelo Pierre Filbert Guglielmi di Valentina d'Antonguolla. The silent film sex symbol brought out the ladies, even at his funeral. He died of peritonitis caused by a bleeding ulcer.

A: **Runnymede**
Q: What English meadow saw the signing of the Magna Carta?
W: The Magna Carta was a compromise by King John with 40 English barons who were angry that their privileges and rights had been taken away. The Magna Carta served as the blueprint for English Common Law.

A: **Russia**
Q: What country did the houses of Rurik and Romanov rule?
W: Rurik established himself as ruler at Novgorod in 862 A.D. The Romanov House ruled from 1682 with Peter I (known as Peter the Great) to 1917 with Nicholas II, the last czar of Russia.

A: **Russia**
Q: What did Winston Churchill describe as "a riddle, wrapped in a mystery, inside an enigma"?
W: This statement was prefaced by, "I cannot forecast to you the action of Russia…" It was from a radio broadcast made by Churchill on Oct. 1, 1939.

A: **S**
Q: What did Harry S Truman's middle initial stand for?
W: A family disagreement on whether his middle name was Shippe or Solomon, after the names of his two grandfathers, resulted in his using only the middle initial without a period following the "S."

A: **Salvador Allende**
Q: What Chilean president was killed in a 1973 coup d'etat?
W: The overthrow of Allende was financed through the CIA. Allende was the last democratically elected president in Chile.

A: **Salvation Army, The**
Q: What army was founded by William Booth and his wife Catherine?
W: The Salvation Army was founded in London in 1865. Active in 70 countries and territories and with more than 16,300 corps and outposts, it operates as a religious and charitable organization. All officers must pledge total abstinence from intoxicating liquors, drugs, and tobacco.

A: **Salvation Army's, The**
Q: What army's motto is Blood and Fire?
W: The Salvation Army cooperates with local authorities and makes all of its resources available to all members of the community in times of emergency and disaster.

A: **Sam Houston**
Q: Who was the first president of independent Texas?
W: Texas was admitted to the Union in 1845 after Sam Houston defeated Santa Anna of Mexico, and independence was proclaimed.

A: **San Clemente, California**
Q: Where was the western White House?
W: During the Nixon Administration, San Clemente served as the western White House.

A: **San Francisco**
Q: What city shook for 47 seconds on April 18, 1906?
W: At 5:13 A.M., the quake overturned stoves, spilled out coal, and caused wooden buildings to collapse.
   The fires burned out after three days, but 315 people died and 514 blocks of buildings, including more than four square miles in the center of the city, were destroyed.

A: **San Juan Hill, Cuba**
Q: Where did Teddy Roosevelt lead the Charge of the Rough Riders on July 1, 1898?
W: San Juan Hill is near Santiago, Cuba. The Rough Riders made their famous charge on foot, under the command of Theodore Roosevelt, during the Spanish-American War.

A: *Santa Maria*, **The**
Q: What was the name of Christopher Columbus' flagship?
W: On Columbus' first voyage with the *Santa Maria* he did not discover America; rather he found the Bahamas and Cuba.

A: **Sargent Shriver**
Q: Who ended up on the ticket with George McGovern in 1972?
W: After backing Thomas Eagleton "1000 percent" as his running mate, George dropped Tom and enlisted the Sarge!

A: **Sargent Shriver**
Q: Who was the first director of the Peace Corps?
W: By Executive Order, President Kennedy created the Peace Corps on March 1, 1961. Over 1,000 volunteers were on the job in the West Indies and Africa by September, 1961, when Congress appropriated $40 million for the program. It was placed under the direction of R. Sargent Shriver, Kennedy's brother-in-law.

A: **SAVAK**
Q: What was Mohammed Reza Pahlavi's secret police called?
W: SAVAK has never given an account of its activities. Under the Shah there were an estimated 60,000 SAVAK agents and even more informants than agents. All of Iranian society was infiltrated by this secret police, and SAVAK was also active abroad keeping tabs on Iranian students in other countries.

A: **scar, A**
Q: What does Richard Nixon have on the left side of his scalp, from forehead to neck?
W: The scar is the result of an accident when he was three years old. He fell from a carriage and cut his head on the wheels. The accident almost killed him and left him permanently subject to motion sickness.

A: **Scarface**
Q: What was Al Capone's nickname?
W: The most famous U.S. gangster of the 20th century was the head of the Chicago syndicate. At the age of 28 he was believed to gross over $105 million a year from his operations. He finally went to prison for income tax evasion! He got his scar as a youth in a barroom fight with Frank Galluccio, another bad guy.

A: **Scotland Yard**
Q: What was built on the site of an unsolved London murder?
W: Scotland Yard police force for London was established in 1829. It keeps records on all known criminals in the country and guards royalty, cabinet members, and foreign visitors. Unlike the FBI, it has no national status and power. For example, it cannot interfere with cases outside London unless specifically invited by local police.

A: **Seagram**
Q: What is the world's largest distilling company?
W: The Seagram Company Ltd. of Canada is the world's largest, with sales totaling over $2.8 billion in 1982.

A: **Seattle**
Q: Where was the 1962 World's Fair?
W: The Space Needle, Seattle's most famous landmark, is the 605-foot tower constructed for the fair. It's the third tallest structure in the state.

A: **Senator Sam Ervin Jr.**
Q: Who was chairman of the Senate Select Committee that tried to get to the bottom of Watergate?
W: On May 17, 1973, Senator Sam Ervin, a Democrat from North Carolina, convened the Watergate hearings before live TV cameras.

A: *Sequoia*, **The**
Q: What was the presidential yacht for both Franklin Roosevelt and Richard Nixon?
W: The yacht was sold during the Carter administration.

A: **Sergeant Alvin York**
Q: Who captured 132 Germans in the Battle of the Argonne in 1918?
W: York was a former Tennessee fox hunter, who single-handedly shot and killed 28 Germans, thus persuading the other 132 to surrender during World War II. York is probably the most famous of all Medal of Honor winners.

HISTORY

A: **Seven**
Q: How many years are there in a French president's term?
W: Charles de Gaulle was elected in 1959 as the first president of the newly formed Fifth Republic to serve a seven year term as president. Since then Georges Pompidou, Valery Giscard d'Estsing, and Francois Mitterand have been elected to fill seven year presidential terms.

A: **Shah Mohammed Reza Pahlavi**
Q: Who was the last to sit on "the Peacock Throne"?
W: By law the "Peacock Throne" (symbol of the Iranian Monarchy) could not be assumed until the king had a male heir. Pahlavi, after three marriages, finally produced a male heir. Since Pahlavi fled Iran, however, he was technically the last to sit on "The Peacock Throne." Pahlavi was overthrown by the Ayatollah Ruhollah Khomeini, leader of the Iranian revolution of 1979.

A: **Shangri-La**
Q: What was the original name of the U.S. presidential retreat Camp David?
W: Camp David was named for Dwight Eisenhower's grandson. The retreat's previous name of Shangri-La was selected by Franklin Delano Roosevelt.

A: **She was the first woman atop Everest**
Q: What is woman climber Junko Tabei's claim to fame?
W: In 1971 this 35-year-old Japanese housewife became the first woman to climb Everest. That same year the British conquered the southwest face of the mountain, and China claimed that an expedition scaled Everest, reportedly without oxygen masks.

A: **Shirley Chisholm**
Q: Who was the first black woman elected to the U.S. Congress?
W: Shirley was elected to represent the Bedford-Stuyvesant and Bushwick districts of Brooklyn, New York in 1968. She retired from public office in 1982.

A: **silent majority, The**
Q: What majority did Richard Nixon say elected him?
W: The "great silent majority" was first referred to by Richard Nixon in a speech given on Nov. 3, 1969.

A: **Silver**
Q: What's Bunker Hunt's favorite precious metal?
W: In 1980 Nelson and Bunker Hunt attempted to corner the silver market. This led to a Security Exchange Commission investigation of the sons of oil tycoon H.L. Hunt.

A: **Silversmith**
Q: What was Paul Revere's occupation?
W: True, and he later owned a copper manufacturing business. But he is, of course, best remembered for his ride on the night of April 18, 1775, warning of the British invasion of the American colonies.

A: **Simon Bolivar**
Q: Who was known as "the Liberator of South America"?
W: In Rome, 22-year old Bolivar vowed to free his native Venezuela and other colonies in South America from Spanish rule. Eventually, he liberated Venezuela, Columbia, Ecuador, Bolivia (named after him), and Panama. He fought 200 battles and had 200 mistresses. A busy man!

A: **Sioux, The**
Q: What Indian tribe defeated Custer at the Battle of the Little Big Horn?
W: The advancement of gold seekers into the Black Hills of Montana provoked the uprising of the Battle of Little Big Horn led by Sioux Chieftain Crazy Horse.

A: **Sir Edmund Hillary**
Q: What former beekeeper scaled Mount Everest?
W: On May 29, 1953, the New Zealander, at the age of 34, became the first man to sit literally on top of the world. He scaled Mount Everest, at over 29,000 feet, the highest point on earth. The expedition was led by John Hunt. Actually two men, Hillary and Tenzing made it to the top. They stayed 15 minutes at the summit. Seems like a long hike for such a short stay!

A: **Sir Walter Raleigh**
Q: What English explorer discovered and named Virginia?
W: Raleigh led the expedition of 1584. Virginia was named by Raleigh in honor of Queen Elizabeth, the Virgin Queen of England.

A: **Sir Walter Raleigh**
Q: What 17th-century explorer was buried with a pipe and a box of tobacco?
W: Raleigh also left instructions for his coffin to be "lined throughout with the wood of my old Havana cigar-boxes".

A: **Sirhan Sirhan**
Q: What assassin is due for release on Feb. 28, 1986?
W: Sirhan shot Robert F. Kennedy in Los Angeles on June 5, 1968, while Kennedy was campaigning for the Democratic presidential nomination.

A: **Six**
Q: How many U.S. Marines raised the flag over Iwo Jima?
W: Iwo Jima, an island in the western Pacific, was the scene of a fierce battle between U.S. and Japanese troops that resulted in 22,000 Japanese troops killed or captured and 21,000 U.S. casualties. The picture of Marines raising the U.S. flag on Feb. 19, 1945, has been widely reprinted.

A: **Six-Day War, The**
Q: What war lasted from June 5 to June 11, 1967?
W: Israel's victory over Egypt in the Six-day War changed the boudaries of Israel to include Jordan's west bank, the City of Jerusalem, and the Sinai Peninsula.

HISTORY

A: sixth, The
Q: What floor did Lee Harvey Oswald allegedly shoot from?
W: Oswald is allegedly the man who shot John F. Kennedy from the sixth floor of the Texas School Book Depository in Dallas, Texas on Nov. 22, 1963.

A: Sixtus
Q: What is Edmund S. Muskie's middle name?
W: Edmund Sixtus Muskie served as governor of Maine from 1954 to 1958. He ran for vice president with Hubert Humphrey in 1968 and unsuccessfully campaigned for the Democratic nomination for president in 1972.

A: skull and crossbones, The
Q: What are emblazoned on the Jolly Roger?
W: The Jolly Roger is a black flag with white emblems associated with pirates. Pirates flew no other flag than the Jolly Roger, except to deceive others.

A: Slavery
Q: What did Abolitionists try to end?
W: Between the 15th and 19th century an estimated 15 million Africans were forcibly transported to the Americas. The Abolition Movement lasted from about 1783 to 1888 in western Europe and the Americas and was responsible for creating the climate necessary to end transatlantic slave trade. The Abolition Movement and other concerns led to the U.S. Civil War, which resulted in the emancipation of almost four million slaves.

A: Smirnoff
Q: What company supplied the imperial Russian court with vodka from 1886 to 1917?
W: Vodka is the fiery Russian beverage distilled from potatoes or fermented mash of rye, barley, and corn. Vodka is not flavored and has no taste of its own. The Pierre Smirnoff Company of Moscow, Russia, was the purveyor of vodka to the czars from 1886 to 1917. It is now produced in 30 other countries.

A: Snickers
Q: What chocolate bar created by Frank Mars and his wife is often called a Milky Way with peanuts?
W: Snickers is a chocolate candy bar made of milk chocolate, nougat, caramel, and peanuts. A Milky Way could be described the same way, but omitting the peanuts.

A: son of a gun, A
Q: What do you call a boy born between cannons on a British warship?
W: "Son of a gun" is an epithet of contempt. It was originally applied to boys born afloat when wives accompanied their husbands to sea. One admiral declared that he was actually cradled under the breast of a gun carriage. The phrase occurred as early as 1708.

A: Son of Sam
Q: What was the notorious pseudonym of David Berkowitz?
W: David Berkowitz killed six victims and wounded seven in eight known attacks. Most of his victims were pretty, young women who were also good students. He killed them with a .44 magnum. At first he explained the killings as being the result of his being demonically possessed, but later changed his explanation to "some unknown but consumate urge to kill."

A: South Pole, The
Q: What did Roald Amundsen reach first?
W: Amundsen was a Norwegian explorer. He set out in 1911 on a voyage to the Antarctic, and on Dec. 14th he succeeded in reaching the South Pole. The English explorer Robert Falcon Scott was also exploring in the area, but credit is given to Amundsen for being first to the South Pole.

A: Soviet Union, The
Q: What country imposed the Berlin Blockade in 1948?
W: The USSR began a land blockade of Berlin on April 1, 1948, but discontinued it on Sept. 30, 1949, after British and U.S. planes had successfully lifted 2,343,315 tons of food and coal into the city.

A: Soviet Union, The
Q: What country suffered the most combat deaths in World War II?
W: Twelve million Russians died in combat, in executions, and as prisoners. More than 20 million Russians died of starvation and disease.

A: Soviet Union, The
Q: What country was Kim Philby really working for?
W: Philby, who was educated at Cambridge, rose to one of the top spots in British intelligence. He eventually became a British liaison to the CIA, where he was privy to some of the most important American secrets. All this time he was working for the KGB! He defected to the Soviet Union in 1963.

A: **Spain**
Q: What country did Bing Crosby die in?
W: Bing Crosby was one of the most popular singers and motion picture stars in the U.S. During the 1930s he made the "crooning" style of singing famous in all parts of the world. He won an Academy Award in 1944 as a singing priest in *Going My Way*. He died on a golf course in Spain in 1977.

A: **Spain's**
Q: What country's flag was Christopher Columbus sailing under when he discovered America?
W: Columbus was an Italian navigator who prevailed upon Ferdinand and Isabella of Spain to bear the expense of an expedition of discovery. He set out on his first voyage in 1492. In 1498, on his third voyage, he landed on the lowlands of South America. He died in Spain in 1506.

A: **Spanish-American War**
Q: What war featured the rallying cry: "Remember the *Maine*"?
W: Feb. 15, 1898, the U.S. battleship *Maine* exploded in Havana Harbor; 260 enlisted men and officers died. This led to the U.S. Congress declaring war on Spain on April 25. The slogan was, "Remember the *Maine*! To hell with Spain!"

A: **Spanish Armada, The**
Q: What fleet set sail in 1588 to invade England?
W: The word *armada* actually means any fleet of armed ships, but the term nearly always refers to the Invincible Armada that Philip of Spain sent against England in 1588. England's stunning victory over the Spanish Armada elevated England to a first class naval power.

A: **Spanish Civil War, The**
Q: What civil war was fought between 1936 and 1939?
W: The Spanish Civil War was fought between the Republicans and Nationalists in Spain. The Nationalists were seeking to destroy the newly elected government that had expelled the monarch and threatened the traditional values. This war was complicated by the intrusion of outside forces such as Italy and other Nazis who joined the Nationalists and Russia who supported the Republicans. In March 1939, the Republicans surrendered and Spain settled into the dictatorship of Franco leader of the Nationalists.

A: **Spartacus**
Q: Who led the revolt of Roman slaves and gladiators in A.D. 73?
W: Close, it was 71 B.C., not A.D. 73. Spartacus was the most famous of all Roman gladiators, but he won his historical fame as the leader of a great slave uprising, rather than in the arena. He was captured by the Romans while serving as a soldier and was sold as a slave, to be made a gladiator. He escaped and raised his own army of rebel slaves.

A: **Spencer**
Q: What was the Princess of Wales' maiden name?
W: Lady Di is now the wife of Prince Charles of England.

A: **Spiced ham**
Q: What two words did the meat product Spam take its name from?
W: Spam was a "popular" meat ration served to serviceman in World War II. It was contained in a can so it was easily preserved and transported to all parts of the world and to servicemen everywhere. It is made of pork shoulder and ham.

A: **Spiro Agnew**
Q: What U.S. vice president once declared: "If you've seen one slum, you've seen them all"?
W: Spiro Agnew was Richard Nixon's vice president. On Oct. 10, 1973, he resigned after charges of tax evasion.

A: **Spiro Agnew**
Q: Who nominated Richard Nixon for president in 1968?

W: He then accepted the offer of the vice-presidency. Spiro resigned on Oct. 10, 1973, after pleading no contest to charges of tax evasion on payments made to him by Maryland contractors while he was governor of Maryland.

A: **Spiro T. Agnew**
Q: What U.S. vice-president said: "Some newspapers dispose of their garbage by printing it"?
W: Spiro Agnew was former governor of Maryland and vice president under Richard Nixon. Under pressure from the press about the charges of tax evasion, he was quoted as making the above statement to the papers. Agnew was sentenced to three years probation and a $10,000 fine.

A: **spurs, The**
Q: Where on a cowboys's attire would you find jinglebobs, a heel chain, and a rowel?
W: The spurs, also called grappling irons, were held in place by two chains under the instep and a spur leather shield laid over the instep of the boot. The rowels were sharp-toothed wheels inserted into the shank of the spur. Although the cowboy used spurs for clinging to the horse, the spurs also had a fashionable quality. The shank of the spur was turned down in order for the wheel to roll across the ground noisily. The noise was further enhanced by letting one of the chains drag or by adding pear shaped pendants to the wheel's axle.

A: **St. Helena**
Q: What island did Napoleon die on?
W: After his defeat at Waterloo in 1815, Napoleon was exiled to St. Helena, where he died six years later.

A: **St. Patrick**
Q: Who is known as "the Apostle of Ireland"?
W: Like the legendary apostle of Ireland who was supposed to have expelled all snakes from Ireland and

used the shamrock to explain the Trinity, the historical Patrick was not lacking in color. The British Patrick was captured by Irish pirates and enslaved for six years. After securing his freedom, he entered the priesthood. In 435, he was appointed the second bishop to the Irish and concerned himself with abolishing paganism, idolatry, and sunworship.

A: **St. Paul's Cathedral**
Q: What cathedral were Prince Charles and Lady Diana married in?
W: Not since Arthur Tudor married Catherine of Aragon in 1501(she later became the first wife of Henry VIII) had a Prince of Wales been married in St. Paul's. Traditionally, British royalty prefer the more intimate Westminster Abbey that seats 2,000 to St. Paul's Cathedral that accomodates 2,500.

A: **St. Valentine**
Q: What Catholic bishop was killed in Rome on Feb. 14, 270 A.D.?
W: There were two Valentine's martyred on that date. Neither the Roman priest nor the Bishop of Terni were connected with courting couples or lovers. This connection may stem from the Roman festival of Lupercalia that took place in mid-February.

A: **St. Valentine's Day Massacre, The**
Q: What happened on Feb. 14, 1929?
W: Seven members of the Bugs Moran gang were gunned down in a Chicago warehouse by four men, two dressed as policemen who were actually agents of Al Capone and who were never caught. No arrests were ever made.

A: **Stanley and Livingstone**
Q: Who met at Ujiji, Africa, in 1871?
W: Sir Henry Morton Stanley, a reporter from the New York *Herald*, was sent to Africa to find the missionary-explorer David Livingstone. On Nov. 10, 1871, this famous line "Dr. Livingstone, I presume?" was

spoken by Sir Henry Morton Stanley. Together they explored Lake Tanganyika and the Ruiszi River. Stanley discovered the source of the Nile and from 1874 to 1877 explored the Congo River Basin.

A: **Steven Weed**
Q: Who was with Patricia Hearst the night she was kidnaped?
W: Patty was kidnapped on Feb. 4, 1974 from her Berkeley residence. Steven, as Patty's live-in fiance, was the one who let the kidnappers in and was beaten up by them for his efforts. Not long after the story of the kidnapping broke, a memo at the San Francisco *Examiner* (owned by her father) requested that her living arrangements not be mentioned. Steven Weed wrote two books: *My Life with Patty Hearst* and *My Search for Patty Hearst*.

A: **Stokely Carmichael**
Q: Who popularized the slogan: "Black Power!"?
W: Carmichael made his black power speech in 1966 at a Mississippi black voters registration march. He and Martin Luther King, Jr. were called in to lead the march when James Meredith was injured in an attempted assassination. Carmichael spoke to the receptive crowd: "The only way we gonna stop them white people from whippin' us is take over. We been saying freedom for six years and we ain't got nothin'. What we gonna start saying now is black power... Ain't nothin' wrong with anything all black 'cause I'm all black and I'm all good... And from now on when they ask you what you want, you know what to tell them." The crowd shouted "Black Power! Black Power!"

A: **Stonewall**
Q: What was the nickname of U.S. Civil War general Thomas Jackson?
W: Stonewall Jackson was a West Point Graduate, and in 1861 he became a Brigadier General in the Confederate forces. The firm stand of his brigade at Bull Run won him the nickname "Stonewall." He was

accidently shot by his own men, pneumonia set in, and he died in 1863.

A: **Strange**
Q: What is former U.S. defense secretary Robert S. McNamara's middle name?
W: That's certainly a "strange" name! Although an unusual name, he came by it honestly through his mother Clara Nell (nee Strange).

A: **Strategic Arms Limitation Treaty**
Q: What does SALT stand for?
W: SALT is a series of negotiations between the U.S. and the Soviet Union to place limitations on their arsenals of nuclear weapons. SALT I provided quantitative control of nuclear arms. SALT II was concerned with qualitative controls. SALT III provided temporary bans on deployment of missile launchers.

A: **Students for a Democratic Society**
Q: What did SDS stand for?
W: Yes, it does. Tom Hayden, now husband of Jane Fonda, founded this organization in 1961 while a student at the University of Michigan. The group helped shape "the Movement" to replace the American political system with "participatory democracy"

A: **Studio 54**
Q: What disco was Jimmy Carter's aide Hamilton Jordan accused of using cocaine at?
W: Jordan, Jimmy Carter's Chief-of-Staff, was accused of sniffing coke at this "hip-chic" disco's downstairs playroom. The charge was investigated under the 1978 Ethics in Government Act at a cost to the taxpayers of $121,000. Jordan, who maintained his innocence throughout, was vindicated by the investigation.

A: **Susan B. Anthony**
Q: What American feminist went bust as a silver dollar?
W: It was the first silver dollar to go "bust." Try to find one these days. Hint: look for the oddly shaped "quarter" with the picture of the lady on it.

A: **Sweden**
Q: What country did King Gustav V reign over from 1907 to 1950?
W: Gustav V was the Swedish king who succeeded to the throne in 1907. A highly popular monarch, he succeeded in maintaining neutrality through the two World Wars.

A: **Switzerland**
Q: What landlocked European country remained neutral in both World War I and World War II?
W: In 1919, Geneva, Switzerland, was chosen as the site for the headquarters of the League of Nations and was granted special concessions concerning its status of neutrality. Although neutral, Switzerland is in armed readiness to defend itself against any aggressor.

A: **Symbionese Liberation Army, The**
Q: What group kidnapped Patricia Hearst?
W: When the ransom, a multi-million dollar food program for the poor, was not expedited quickly by her father, publisher Randolph Hearst, Patty changed her name to Tania and joined the SLA.

A: **Symbionese Liberation Army**
Q: What terrorist group was headed by Donald DeFreeze?
W: DeFreeze, AKA "Field Marshall Cinque", was an escaped convict and a onetime informer for the Los Angeles police.

A: **Taj Mahal, The**
Q: What mausoleum did Mogul Shah Jahan build to the memory of his favorite wife?
W: The Taj Mahal, meaning "Chosen One of the Palace," is a white marble mausoleum built at Agra, India in memory of Jahan's wife Mumtaz Mahal. She died in childbirth after being at Jahan's side from 1612 to 1631. More than 20,000 men were occupied for 20 years in its construction.

A: **tank, The**
Q: What fighting machine was originally code named a "cistern" or "reservoir"?
W: It was originally an armored motor car equipped with machine guns, first used by the British as a surprise to the enemy in September 1916 during World War I. Light tanks weigh under 25 tons, medium tanks are 25 to 40 tons, and heavy tanks are over 40 tons.

A: **teddy bear, The**
Q: What children's toy was named for Theodore Roosevelt?
W: This child's toy first appeared in a Brooklyn candy store. Morris Michtom and his wife created the bear with movable limbs and promoted it by displaying the bear with a copy of the famous Benyman cartoon of Roosevelt refusing to shoot a bear cub on a hunting trip in Mississippi in 1902. A label proclaimed the toy "Teddy's Bear."

A: **Teddy Kennedy**
Q: Who said: "The work goes on, the cause endures, the hope still lives and the dream shall never die"?
W: "For me a few hours ago this campaign came to an end" preceded the above statement which was part of Ted's speech at the 1980 Democratic Convention where Jimmy Carter was nominated.

A: **Telephone operator**
Q: What onetime occupation did Amanda Blake, Pat Nixon and Aristotle Onassis share?
W: As a poor foreigner on his own in Buenos Aires, Aristotle Onassis, then from Turkey, worked for 25 cents per hour as a telephone operator. He learned the language by eavesdropping on calls. Pat Nixon is former President Nixon's wife. Amanda Blake is a noted entertainment personality born in Buffalo, New York, on Feb. 20, 1931; she played Kitty in the long running TV series "Gunsmoke."

A: **Tenerife, Canary Islands**
Q: Where did two jumbo jets collide in 1977, killing 579?
W: During a steadily worsening fog at the Tenerife's Los Rodeos Airport on Sunday, Mar. 27, 1977, a KLM aircraft collided on its takeoff with a Pan Am 747 that was still on the runway.

A: **Texas School Book Depository, The**
Q: What building did Lee Harvey Oswald allegedly shoot John F. Kennedy from?
W: Reportedly the shooting was from the sixth floor. Oswald was employed there from Oct. 15, 1963 until his arrest in November of 1963.

A: **Thames, The**
Q: What river is Pocahontas buried along?
W: Her personal name was really Matoaka, daughter of Powhatan. Pocahontas means "playful one," a term used for several of Powhatan's daughters. Pocahontas, the Indian woman who aided peaceful relations between colonists and her people, died in England of smallpox after a successful tour with her husband, John Rolfe, in 1616. She was renamed Rebecca when she moved to England.

A: **Theodore Roosevelt**
Q: Who was called "the Hero of San Juan Hill"?
W: Lieutenant Colonel Theodore Roosevelt with the aid of the Rough Riders, the first volunteer cavalry, charged and took San Juan Hill in America's war with Spain for Cuba's freedom. This victory was a boost in his political career.

A: **Theodore Roosevelt**
Q: Who was nicknamed "the Cowboy President"?
W: Teddy was a rancher in North Dakota from 1884 to 1886. Thus, the nickname.

A: **Theodore Roosevelt**
Q: Who was the first U.S. president to travel in a car, plane and submarine?
W: In 1902, Roosevelt rode in a purple lined Colombia Electric Victoria automobile. In 1905, he went along with "the plunger" to a depth of 20 feet below the surface of the ocean for 55 minutes. Following these two events he then, in 1910, flew as a passenger in an airplane.

A: **Theodore Roosevelt**
Q: Who was the youngest person to become U.S. president?
W: At inauguration Teddy Roosevelt was 42 years old. Sorry folks, John F. Kennedy was 43!

A: **They married Marilyn Monroe**
Q: What did Arthur Miller and Joe DiMaggio have in common?

W: Miller was married to her from 1956 to 1962. Joe had a brief stint at the plate – nine months in 1954.

A: **They were crucified with Christ**
Q: What was the unfortunate claim to fame of two thieves named Dismas and Gestas?
W: From the Bible: "...and they crucified two robbers with him; one on his right and one on his left."

A: **They were fifth cousins**
Q: What was the family relationship between Theodore and Franklin Roosevelt?
W: The distant relative shared by Theodore and Franklin was Nicholas Roosevelt, a New York politician from early in the 18th century. Eleanor Roosevelt was also the niece of Theodore Roosevelt.

A: **They were sunk at Pearl Harbor**
Q: What did the fighting ships *Arizona, Oklahoma*, and *Utah* have in common?
W: The Japanese hit Pearl Harbor at 7:45 A.M. on Dec. 7, 1941. By 10 A.M. these three ships, along with 15 others, were sunk or badly damaged. The attack brought the U.S. into World War II.

A: **Third Reich, The**
Q: What phrase did the Nazis adopt in the 1920s to label their new order?
W: The Third Reich was the name given to Hitler's Nazi regime in Germany from 1933 to 1945, as successor of the medieval Holy Roman Empire (The First Reich) and the German empire of 1871 to 1918 (The Second Reich).

A: **Thirteen**
Q: How many were in attendance at the Last Supper?
W: Here are those who were present: Bartholomew, James the Less, Andrew, Judas Iscariat, Peter, John, James the Elder, Thomas, Philip, Matthew, Thaddeus (Jude), Simon, and Jesus Christ.

A: **Thirteen**
Q: What's the usual age for a Jewish boy to celebrate his bar mitzvah?
W: At this age, he is considered an adult and responsible for his moral and religious duties. The ceremony is a conferring of this status. In Hebrew the term *bar mitzvah* means "son of command."

A: **Thirty-five**
Q: How old do you have to be to become president of the U.S.?
W: "...and been fourteen years a resident within the U.S." See Article II, Section 1 of the Constitution for more.

A: **Thomas Eagleton**
Q: What running mate did George McGovern back 1,000 percent?
W: McGovern dropped his first choice for vice-president, Eagleton, for Sargent Shriver. But he did say that he was behind him 1,000 percent didn't he?

A: **Thomas Jefferson**
Q: Who took 18 days to write the Declaration of Independence?
W: The document was drawn up by a committee of the Second Continental Congress consisting of Thomas Jefferson, John Adams, Roger Sherman, Robert Livingstone, and Benjamin Franklin. The committee to draft the declaration was appointed on June 11, 1776, and the draft was reported out of committee on June 28, 1776. Jefferson was credited with doing the vast majority of the writing.

A: **Thomas Jefferson**
Q: Who was "the Father of the Declaration of Independence"?
W: On July 4, 1776, representatives of 13 British colonies in North America adopted an eloquent statement setting forth the reasons for declaring their independence from Britain. Thomas Jefferson, a member of the committee given the task of preparing the draft is credited with writing most of the statement, and thus is known as "the Father of the Declaration of Independence."

HISTORY

A: **Thomas Jefferson**
Q: Who was the first president inaugurated in Washington, D.C.?
W: In 1790 Congress agreed to locate the capital on the Potomac. George Washington had already been inaugurated in New York. Work on the White House and Capitol were not completed until October 1800, at which time John Adams took up residence. Jefferson was the first President to be inaugurated (1801) after the buildings were constructed. The very first presidential mansion was located at One Cherry Street in New York City.

A: **Three**
Q: How many hostages were killed in the Entebbe raid?
W: Entebbe Airport is a major stop between Europe and South Africa. In 1976 PLO terrorists hijacked a French plane and held the 100 passengers hostage. Most of the passengers were Israelis. After a week of siege, Israeli commandos staged a daring raid and freed all the hostages, except three who were killed in the crossfire.

A: **Three Wise Men, The**
Q: Who were Gaspar, Melchior and Balthasar?
W: According to western church tradition, Gaspar is represented as a king of India, Melchior as a king of Persia, and Balthasar as a king of Arabia. They offered gifts of gold, frankincense, and myrrh to the baby Jesus.

A: *Titanic*, **The**
Q: What was the sister ship of the *Olympic*?
W: Although the *Titanic* sank in 1912, the *Olympic*, her sister ship, continued to make voyages. In 1920 Cary Grant came to America for the first time aboard the *Olympic*. Charlie Chaplin returned to Europe on the *Olympic* in August 1921.

A: **Tokyo Rose**
Q: What was the infamous pseudonym of broadcaster Iva Toguri d'Aquino?
W: The U.S.-born Toyko Rose was convicted of treason in 1949 for her propaganda broadcasts from Japan to U.S. troops in the South Pacific during World War II. She received a ten-year sentence with a $10,000 fine.

A: **Tom Hayden**
Q: What member of the Chicago Seven did Jane Fonda marry?
W: Tom Hayden organized the Students for a Democratic Society, participated in the Mississippi Civil Rights Movement, and also ran, unsuccessfully, for the U.S. Senate in 1976. Hayden is currently active in the campaign for economic democracy with wife Jane Fonda.

A: **Tower of London, The**
Q: What fortress was built by William the Conqueror to protect London?
W: William the Conqueror ordered the erection of fortifications on the north bank of the River Thames — immediately after his occupation in 1066 — to control access to the Pool of London, the capital's major port area.

A: **Tower of London, The**
Q: What 11th-century London fortress has been a palace, prison, mint and observatory?
W: William I began the building of the White Tower in 1078 as a royal palace. Later kings made more additions. From the 15th to 18th centuries, many princes and nobles were executed or imprisoned in the Tower. The Crown Jewels are now kept in the Tower along with a collection of armor from various periods. The building has housed the royal mint, and the Tower Observatory was located at the top of one of the turrets until the Royal Observatory was constructed in Greenwich in 1675.

A: **Treaty of Versailles, The**
Q: What peace treaty ended World War I?
W: The Treaty signed at Versailles went into effect Jan. 10, 1920. It was an agreement between the Allies and Germany providing for the drastic reduction in Germany's naval and military forces, confiscation of Germany's overseas colonies, and the payment by Germany of large reparations to various members of the Allies

A: **Treaty of Versailles, The**
Q: What treaty did Hitler break in 1935?
W: The Treaty of Versailles, which ended World War I, went into effect on Jan. 10, 1920. Hitler was opposed to the Treaty and broke it when he annexed Austria and Czechoslovakia and invaded Poland in 1939, thereby precipitating World War II.

A: **Treaty of Versailles, The**
Q: What was signed on June 28, 1919?
W: This Treaty signaled the end of World War I. The U.S. Senate never ratified treaty. George Clemenceau was Chief of State in France and made a powerful contribution to the Allied victory in World War I. He presided over the Paris Peace Conference that resulted in the Treaty of Versailles and the Covenant of the League of Nations. The signing of the Treaty occurred in the Hall of Mirrors, where in 1871 William I had himself proclaimed German emperor — Clemenceau's idea of poetic justice!

A: **Tricia and Julie**
Q: What are the names of Richard Nixon's two daughters?
W: Patricia was born Feb. 21, 1946, and later married Edward Cox on June 12, 1971 at a White House wedding. Julie Nixon was born July 5, 1948, and married Dwight David Eisenhower, grandson of President Eisenhower, on Dec. 22, 1968.

A: **Trinity Site, New Mexico**
Q: Where did the first atomic bomb explode?
W: The first atomic bomb was exploded on July 16, 1945. This plutonium weapon was named "Trinity" and was exploded in a desert near Alamogordo, New Mexico. The following month, the untested uranium 235 bomb was dropped on Hiroshima.

A: **Trygve Lie**
Q: What Norwegian was the United Nations' first secretary-general?
W: Trygve was a statesman and officer of the Norwegian Labor Party for 18 years. He served in the Norwegian government from 1935 to 1945, four years as foreign minister. He was chosen secretary general of the UN in 1946 and re-elected in 1950.

A: **Tudor**
Q: What royal house did Henry VIII belong to?
W: This royal house ruled from 1485 to 1603. The first sovereign was Henry VII, descended from Owen Tudor, followed by Henry VIII, Edward VI, Mary, and Elizabeth, the last of the line.

A: **Turkey**
Q: What meat complemented sweet potatoes and peas in the first TV dinner?
W: The first TV dinner appeared in 1954 and was manufactured by C.A. Swanson and Sons.

A: **turkey, The**
Q: What bird did Benjamin Franklin advocate as the U.S. national symbol?
W: Franklin thought the turkey more respectable than the bald eagle. He felt the bald eagle had a bad moral character since it frequently steals foods from other animals.

A: **Tutankhamen's**
Q: Whose tomb was opened by Howard Carter and Lord Carnarvon?
W: George Herbert, fifth Earl of Carnarvon, was an ardent collector of antiquities. He sought Carter out to supervise excavations in the Valley of the Tombs of Kings in Egypt. The tomb was discovered by this group in 1922 with the mummy and all of the wealth buried with it still intact. King Tutankhamen was King of Egypt from 1361 to 1352 B.C. He died at the age of 18 and is chiefly known for the fact that his tomb was discovered intact, having somehow escaped the plundering that emptied the others.

A: **Twenty-first, The**
Q: What amendment to the U.S. Constitution ended prohibition?
W: It ended the prohibition of the manufacture and sale of alcoholic beverages in the U.S., which had lasted from 1920 to 1933. The Prohibition Amendment to the Constitution had been the 18th Amendment.

A: **Twenty-one**
Q: How many Johns have been Pope?
W: From Pope John I (523-526 A.D.) to Pope John XXIII (1958-1963). Depending upon the references you check and confusion over John XVI, antipope, and/or John XX who never was (number skipped to correct an earlier error?), this answer appears correct.

A: **Twenty-one**
Q: How old was Princess Elizabeth when she married Prince Philip?
W: She was born April 21, 1926, and married to Prince Philip on November 20, 1947. She became Queen Elizabeth II.

A: **Twiggy**
Q: What was the nickname of model Leslie Hornby?
W: Twiggy, the British model, appeared in the movie *The Boyfriend*. Twiggy was called "Sticks" during her schooldays, but was given the name "Twiggy" by her boyfriend and promoter Justin de Villeneuve.

A: **Twiggy**
Q: Who did Mary Quant call "the knock-out beauty of our time"?
W: A poll conducted in England found the most commonly thought of beautiful women in the world included: Twiggy, Elizabeth Taylor, Sophia Loren, Racquel Welch, and Brigette Bardot. Mary Quant is a London clothes designer and was the mother of the miniskirt.

A: **Two**
Q: How many days after John F. Kennedy's assassination was Lee Harvey Oswald shot?
W: Oswald was shot by Jack Ruby, a local nightclub owner two days after the assassination in the basement of the Dallas police station. Millions were witnesses to this shooting on television.

A: **Two**
Q: How many U.S. presidents were assassinated during Queen Victoria's reign?
W: Victoria reigned from 1837 to Jan. 22, 1901. Abraham Lincoln and President Garfield were both shot and killed during her reign. President McKinley was shot on Sept. 6, 1901 and died on September 14, less than eight months after the death of Queen Victoria. Had the Queen lived out the year, three presidential killings would have taken place during her reign as Queen.

HISTORY

A: U Thant
Q: Who preceded Kurt Waldheim as United Nations secretary-general?
W: The Burmese U Thant was the first non-European secretary of the United Nations. He held the office from November 1961 to December 1971. He attempted to bring peace in the 1967 Arab-Israeli War and end fighting in Vietnam. His efforts led to the Paris peace talks.

A: U Thant
Q: Who was secretary-general of the United Nations during the Cuban Missile Crisis?
W: The Cuban Missile Crisis of 1962 ended when Moscow agreed to dismantle its missile bases in Cuba in return for the U.S.'s promise not to invade Cuba. U Thant served as secretary-general from 1961 to 1971.

A: U-2 Incident, The
Q: What incident caused the canceling of a summit conference between Eisenhower and Khrushchev?
W: On May 5, 1960, CIA pilot, Francis Gary Powers, in a U-2 reconnaissance plane, had the misfortune of flying over Russia and getting shot down. The Soviets sentenced him to ten years in prison for violation of their air space. Khrushchev cancelled the scheduled meeting, and Eisenhower switched from plane to satellite reconnaissance of the Soviet Union. Powers was released in 1962 in exchange for the Soviet spy, Rudolf Abel, who had been captured in 1957 in the U.S.

A: Underground Railroad, The
Q: What escape route did abolitionist John Brown run?
W: The Underground Railroad saw some 50,000 fugitive slaves escape to the North during the Civil War. John Brown tried to move more of the Southern slaves by raiding a federal arsenal for weapons to arm them for a rebellion. He was hanged in 1859.

A: Union Pacific, The
Q: What was the first railroad to cross the U.S.?
W: Two companies started to build the transcontinental line, the Union Pacific from the east and the Central Pacific from the west. The Union Pacific had the advantage of relatively flat land to cross and a good supply line with the east. The Union Pacific was also said to have been sustained by whiskey as most of its workers were Irish, while the Central Pacific workers consumed large quanities of tea as most of them were of Chinese origin. On May 10, 1869, the two companies met at Promontory Point in Utah. The Union Pacific train made it to California three days later.

A: University of California at Los Angeles, The
Q: What university fired Angela Davis?
W: Angela was the self-avowed Communist who was also black, beautiful, and brilliant. She was the third woman placed on the FBI wanted list and was captured two months later in a New York City motel. After a three-month trial for her connection with the murder of a judge and three prison inmates during an attempt to free Soledad Brother "George Jackson" of California, she was acquitted.

A: *Unterseebot*, or undersea boat
Q: What does the U stand for in U-boat?
W: During World War I, German and Austrian submarines were called *unterseebots*, and were designated by a *U* followed by a number.

A: Urban terrorist
Q: What employment did Patricia Hearst claim when booked?
W: Patty, kidnapped from her Berkeley, California, apartment, joined the Symbionese Liberation Army, which had been her kidnapper. She was captured by the FBI on Sept. 18, 1975, and was indicted and found guilty of bank robbery in 1976. She is now out of prison and married.

A: U.S., The
Q: What country received all the Nobel Prizes awarded in 1976?
W: In physics, Burton Richter, Samuel Ting; chemistry, William Lipscomb; physiology-medicine, Baruch Blumberg and Daniel Gajdusek; literature, Samuel Bellow; and economics, Milton Friedman.

A: U.S., The; and Rhodesia
Q: What are the only two countries to have declared independence from Britain?
W: We all know the U.S. declared itself independent of Britain in 1776. On Nov. 11, 1956, Prime Minister Ian D. Smith announced his country's unilateral declaration of independence from Britain. Britain termed the act illegal and demanded voting rights be broadened to provide for the eventual rule by the majority Africans. On April 18, 1980, Rhodesia(Zimbabwe) finally achieved its independence.

A: U.S. Civil War, The
Q: What war did Johnny Reb and Billy Yank fight?
W: The "Brother's War" may have preserved the Union, but it caused a hatred that endured for decades. It was 20 years before a Democrat entered the White House again and almost fifty years before a southern-born man, Woodrow Wilson, was elected President.

A: U.S. Civil War, The
Q: What war saw the most Americans die?
W: During the Civil War, the Union Army lost more men as a result of disease than as a result of battle. It figures that more Americans were killed during this war – we were killing each other! Even though the Vietnam War was longer, more Americans were in fact killed during the Civil War.

A: Valery Giscard d'Estaing
Q: Who did Francois Mitterand succeed as president of France?
W: On May 10, 1981, France elected Francois Mitterand, a Socialist candidate, president in a stunning victory over Valery Giscard d'Estaing.

A: Vasco Balboa
Q: What Spanish soldier of fortune led the party that discovered the Pacific Ocean?
W: He was a Spanish explorer who was the first European to set eyes upon the Pacific Ocean on Sept. 25 to 27, 1513. He was also Governor ot Darien on the Isthmus of Panama. Balboa was known for leading gold and slave hunting expeditions into the area's Indian chiefdoms.

A: Victoria Cross, The
Q: What's Britain's highest military decoration?
W: Queen Victoria created this decoration to recognize the bravery and courage of the British soldier who suffered so during the Crimean War in 1854.

A: *Victory*, The
Q: What was Horatio Nelson's most famous ship?

W: The *Victory* was Nelson's flagship during the Battle of Trafalgar on Oct. 21, 1805. He was killed aboard the ship.

A: Vidkun Quisling
Q: Who betrayed Norway to the Nazis?
W: *Quisling* became a word that is still used today as a synonym for traitor. Vidkun Quisling was convicted of treason and shot at the end of World War II.

A: Vietnam War, The
Q: What was "the Living Room War"?
W: This term was coined by Michael Arlen in his *New Yorker* article entitled "Living Room War." He states that at one point 60 percent of Americans got their information on the Vietnam War from television. Don't you remember the war "scores" each evening on the nightly news?

A: Vietnam War, The
Q: What's the longest war in U.S. history?
W: The Vietnam War lasted nine years, from 1964 to 1973. It was the longest war in American history by one year. The Revolutionary War lasted eight years – 1775 to 1783. Over 57,000 U.S. soldiers died in Vietnam and 303,000 were wounded. Many of you will probably question the accuracy of the term "war," as the Vietnam "Conflict" was never officially declared a "war" by Congress. In which case, give yourself credit for answering "American Revolution"!

A: Vietnam War's, The
Q: What war's peace talks were delayed by an argument over the shape of the table?
W: The peace talks in Paris were stalled for one week while the North Vietnamese argued over the shape of the table and seating at that table where the talks would take place.

A: Virgin Mary, The
Q: What woman has the most monuments erected to her?
W: Mary is the Patron Saint of all Catholics, and the Patron Saint of the United States. As the Mother of Jesus, we have to believe that she probably does have the most statues erected to her, although we couldn't find even an approximate number.

A: Virginia
Q: What state is John F. Kennedy buried in?
W: He's buried at Arlington National Cemetary in Arlington, Virginia.

A: Venice
Q: What was Marco Polo's hometown?
W: This merchant and adventurer was born in 1254 in Venice.

HISTORY

A: Wallis Warfield Simpson
Q: Who did Edward VIII call "the woman I love"?
W: Edward VIII gave up the throne of England to marry this twice-divorced American woman. It was considered the "love story of the century."

A: Walter Cronkite
Q: Who announced John F. Kennedy's assassination on CBS-TV?
W: The bulletin about Kennedy's having been shot was made by Walter Cronkite during the soap opera "As the World Turns." This report stated that he was believed to be seriously injured, not that he had died.

A: Walter Cronkite
Q: Who delivered his last newscast on March 6, 1981?
W: Cronkite always ended his newscast with "And that's the way it is." After nearly 20 years of reporting, he retired on Mar. 6, 1981. CBS gave him the microphone he had used when covering his first Democratic Convention in 1952.

A: War of American Independence, The
Q: What war followed "the Shot Heard Round the World"?
W: The Revolutionary War began on April 19, 1775, when Colonial troops fought British soldiers at Lexington, Massachusetts. The basis for the conflict was that the colonists felt they were being overtaxed by the British.

A: War of the Roses, The
Q: What war was fought by the houses of York and Lancaster?
W: This war was fought between two royal houses for possession of the English throne. The war was named for the insignia each adopted: Lancaster chose the red rose, the house of York the white rose.

A: Warren Report
Q: What 26-volume work of 1964 cost $76?
W: The Warren Report was commissioned by President Lyndon Johnson to investigate the assassination of President John F. Kennedy. The investigation took the better part of a year, and the fist copies of the report were released to the public just 80 hours after LBJ received it. Printers worked around the clock to accomplish this, and copies were immediately airlifted all over the world.

A: wart, A
Q: What unsightly feature did Abraham Lincoln have on his face?
W: A wart is a rough growth on the surface of the skin. They are caused by viruses, not by touching toads!

A: Washington, D.C.
Q: Where was Resurrection City erected in 1968?
W: The idea of Resurrection City was conceived by Martin Luther King, Jr., in 1967 and originally planned for April 1968. Although King was assassinated in April 1968, nevertheless the "Poor People's Campaign," whose purpose was to pressure Congress to enact antipoverty legislation, was officially opened May 12, 1968, by Coretta King. An encampment of canvas and plywood, called Resurrection City, U.S.A., was constructed near the Lincoln Memorial on a 16-acre site in West Potomac Park in Washington, D.C. Three thousand demonstrators converged on the area, and over 50,000 were present at the Solidarity Day March on June 19th. The campaign ended June 24, 1968.

A: Waterloo
Q: Where did Napoleon suffer his final defeat?
W: This was the final battle of Napoleon's struggle to rule Europe. The defeat was so crushing that the term is used to designate any great reversal, "he met his Waterloo." Actually the battle occurred several miles from the town of Waterloo.

A: way of sorrows, The; or "Via Dolorosa"
Q: What route did Christ carry the cross on?
W: Christ was forced to carry the cross to Calvary. He became so exhausted as he traveled the street, called the "Way of Sorrows," that Simon of Cyrene helped carry the cross part of the way. This walkway can still be traveled in Jerusalem.

A: We
Q: What's the first word of the text of the U.S. Constitution?
W: From the Preamble:"We the people of the United States…"

A: Weimar Republic, The
Q: What was the name of the German republic that preceded Hitler's regime?
W: The Republic of Germany, 1919 to 1933, adopted the Weimar Constitution, tried to meet reparation payments, and elected Friedrich Ebert and General Paul von Hindenburg as presidents. It was so named because it met at Weimar, a city now in southwestern East Germany.

A: Westminster Abbey
Q: What building are British monarchs crowned in?
W: Parts of this London church, with cozy seating for 2,000, dates back to the 13th Century. It's the coronation place of royalty and the burial place of England's luminaries.

A: When
Q: What's the first word of the text of the Declaration of Independence?
W: "When in the Course of human events…"

A: whip, The
Q: What member of a political party enforces discipline?

W: A whip is a member of a legislative body, such as the U.S. Congress or the British Parliament, charged by his party with enforcing party discipline and insuring attendance.

A: **Whiskey-a-Go-Go**
Q: What Los Angeles discotheque was the first in the U.S.?
W: It's on Sunset Boulevard in Hollywood and was opened in 1963 by Elmer Valentine who was a former Chicago policeman.

A: **Wild Bill Hickock**
Q: Who was shot in the back during a poker game in Deadwood, Dakota Territory?
W: Wild Bill had the reputation of being "the fastest gun in the west," and for awhile he demonstrated his skill for audiences of "Buffalo Bill's Wild West Exhibition." While playing poker at Deadwood in 1876, he was shot in the back and killed by Jack McCall, who was later convicted and hanged.

A: **William Calley**
Q: Who was the only person convicted in the My Lai Massacre?
W: In 1970, Calley was charged with the slaying of civilians at My Lai, Vietnam, in the massacre of March 1968. His trial ran from Nov. 12, 1970, to March 28, 1971, ending in a verdict of guilty. He was sentenced by court martial to life imprisonment, but there was such a public outcry that his sentence was reduced to 20 years.

A: **William Jennings Bryan**
Q: Who was the prosecuting attorney in the Scopes monkey trial?
W: William Jennings Bryan represented the prosecution, and Clarence Darrow spoke for the defense in this trial of a schoolteacher who taught evolution in his classroom, which was contrary to state law.

A: **William Kunstler**
Q: Who defended the Chicago Seven?
W: The Chicago Seven were seven men, including Abbie Hoffman, Jerry Rubin, and Tom Hayden, who were tried for "crossing state lines to incite a riot" during the Democratic National Convention in 1968 in Chicago. The judge was Julius Hoffman.

A: **William McKinley**
Q: What U.S. president was assassinated in 1901?
W: On Sept. 14, 1901, William McKinley became the third president to be assassinated in office. He was shot in Buffalo, New York, by Leon F. Czolgosz, an anarchist.

A: **William Miller**
Q: Who was Barry Goldwater's 1964 vice-presidential running mate?
W: William E. Miller didn't add much strength to the ticket, which was crushed by Lyndon Johnson and Hubert Humphrey. Goldwater and Miller lost by almost 16 million popular votes and over 430 electoral votes.

A: **William Penn**
Q: Who founded Philadelphia, Pennsylvania?
W: William Penn acquired the Province of Pennsylvania in 1681 from King Charles II as a place where his fellow Quakers could enjoy freedom of worship and a chance to govern themselves. Penn sent his cousin William Markham to take charge of affairs of government and lay out the city of Philadelphia, named by Penn for "brotherly love."

A: **William Proxmire**
Q: What U.S. senator gives out the Golden Fleece Awards?
W: William Proxmire is a Senator from Wisconsin, who gives the award for the best example of waste in government. He was born in Illinois to a Lake Forest doctor whose patients included Jack Benny and Adlai Stevenson.

A: **William Rogers**
Q: Who was Richard Nixon's first secretary of state?
W: William P. Rogers, from New York, served as Nixon's Secretary of State from 1969 to 1973, when Henry Kissinger took over the position.

A: **William the Conquerer**
Q: Who led the victorious forces at the Battle of Hastings?
W: William was the first Norman king of England; he inherited Normandy, on the French coast, at the age of eight. His army defeated Harold, a brother-in-law of King Edward, who had died, at the Battle of Hastings. William was crowned King of England on Christmas Day in 1066.

A: **Willy Brandt**
Q: What mayor welcomed John F. Kennedy to West Berlin?
W: Brandt was elected Mayor of West Berlin in 1957 and showed great moral courage during the Berlin Crisis of 1961. He welcomed Kennedy on June 26, 1963, and Kennedy went on to make this notable quote in his address given at city hall in West Berlin: "All free men, wherever they live, are citizens of Berlin. And therefore, as a free man, I take pride in the words 'Ich Bin Ein Berliner'."

HISTORY

A: **Windsor**
Q: What's the house name of the British royal family?
W: The name "House of Windsor" was adopted July 17, 1917, during World War I to replace the family name of Saxe-Coburg-Gotha that was abandoned because of its German origin. The ruling sovereign under the House of Windsor have been George V, Edward VIII, George VI, and Elizabeth II.

A: **Winston Churchill**
Q: Who said: "I have never promised anything but blood, tears, toil and sweat"?
W: This was Churchill's first statement as prime minister to the House of Commons on May 13, 1940.

A: **Winston Churchill**
Q: Who was made the first honorary citizen of the U.S.?
W: On April 9, 1963, Churchill was accorded the unique distinction of having an honorary U.S. citizenship conferred upon him by an act of Congress.

A: **Winston Churchill**
Q: Who was the first British prime minister to serve under Queen Elizabeth II?
W: Churchill's second term as prime minister started in October 1951. He was the prime minister at the time of Queen Elizabeth II's coronation on June 2, 1953.

A: **Winston Churchill and Franklin Roosevelt**
Q: What British prime minister and U.S. president were seventh cousins once removed?
W: Through his maternal grandmother's family, President Franklin D. Roosevelt was a seventh cousin once removed to Winston Churchill. Here's a great one: Churchill was also related to George Washington — eighth cousins six times removed!

A: **Winston Churchill's**
Q: What British prime minister's mother was born in Brooklyn, New York?
W: Churchill's father was Lord Randolf Churchill. His mother, Jennie Jerome, was the daughter of a New York financier and race enthusiast, Leonard W. Jerome.

A: **Winston Churchill's**
Q: Whose 1965 state funeral was the first ever attended by a reigning British monarch?
W: Churchill's death at his London home on Jan. 24, 1965, was followed by a state funeral at which the whole world paid tribute. He was laid to rest in the family graveyard in Bladon Churchyard, Oxfordshire.

A: **With white smoke**
Q: How is the election of a new Pope announced to the world?
W: Cardinals vote by secret ballot in the Sistine Chapel. Immediately following the vote, the ballots are burned in a stove in the chapel and the smoke passes up a pipe through a window enabling the crowd assembled in St. Peter's Square to know how the voting has gone. When no candidate receives the required number of votes, the ballots are burned with wet straw so that the smoke appears black. When a new pope is elected, the ballots are burned with dry straw, so that the smoke appears white.

A: **Wood**
Q: What were George Washington's false teeth made of?
W: Fashioned by none other than Paul Revere!

A: **Wood**
Q: What were the sides of the U.S. fighting ship nicknamed "Old Ironsides" made of?
W: The USS *Constitution*, nicknamed "Old Ironsides," was one of the first frigates built for the U.S. Navy. The bolts fastening its wooden timbers and the copper sheathing on the bottom were made by Paul

Revere. First launched in 1797, it remains on the list of commissioned vessels of the U.S. Navy.

A: **Woodrow Wilson**
Q: Who's the only president buried in Washington, D.C.?
W: He's buried in Washington National Cemetery.

A: **Woodstock Music Festival, The**
Q: What began Aug. 15, 1969, on Max Yasgur's dairy farm?
W: The Woodstock Music and Art Fair was a rock festival staged near Bethel, New York. A crowd of 300,000 attended, many of whom camped at the farm for the entire festival.

A: **World Trade Center, The**
Q: What 110-story building was George Willig fined $1.10 for climbing in May 1977?
W: Willig "scaled" the South Tower of the World Trade Center on May 27, 1977, in only 3.5 hours! He earned the nickname "Spiderman" as a result of this achievement.

A: **World War I**
Q: What conflict was known as "the War to End All Wars"?
W: The U.S. tried to remain neutral in the early years of World War I, but when German submarines began sinking unarmed passenger ships, America joined the Allies "to make the world safe for democracy."

A: **World War I**
Q: What prompted Britain's royal family to change its name?
W: In 1917 during World War I the name Windsor — taken from Windsor Castle, the royal residence since William I — replaced the family name of Saxe-Coburg-Gotha, which was abandoned because of its German origin.

A: **World War I**
Q: What war did the Wanna-Go-Home Riots occur after?
W: The War ended in 1918, but many soldiers were stationed in foreign countries until 1923 as part of the occupational forces.

A: **World War I**
Q: What war ended the Austro-Hungarian monarchy?
W: The Austo-Hungarian monarchy, which lasted from 1867 to 1918, was eliminated after World War I and divided into the independent states of Austria, Hungary, Czechoslovakia, Poland, and Yugoslavia.

A: **World War I**
Q: What war ended with an armistice signed at the 11th hour of the 11th day of the 11th month?
W: The signing of the armistice was actually in a railway car at 5 A.M. The Armistice, however, specified that all fighting was to cease at 11 A.M. that day.

A: **World War II**?
W: What did America Firsters want to keep out of?
W: The America First Committee was a group established in September 1940 to obstruct America's participation in World War II. Charles A. Lindbergh became an important spokesman for the group.

A: **World War II**
Q: What war did the Potsdam Conference follow?
W: The Potsdam Conference was held at Potsdam, near Berlin, to fix occupation zones, assess quotas for reparation, and set up administration of enemy territories.

A: **World War II**
Q: What war did the U.S. Army commission its first black general in?
W: Benjamin Oliver Davis was the first black U.S. Army general in 1940. His son Benjamin Oliver Davis, Jr. was the first black graduate of West Point and later the first black general in the Air Force in 1954.

A: **World War II**
Q: What war was waged by 57 countries?
W: World War II killed more persons, cost more money, and affected more people than any war in history.

It brought far-reaching changes and was fought in almost every part of the world.

A: **Wyatt Earp**
Q: Who had four brothers named Morgan, James, Virgil, and Warren?
W: Virgil became town marshall of Tombstone, Arizona in 1879. Wyatt became his deputy. Their legendary enforcement of the law led to the infamous gunfight at O.K. Corral. Later friends of the men killed at O.K. Corral crippled Virgil with a shotgun blast and killed his brother Morgan.

A: **Yasser Arafat**
Q: Who addressed the United Nations General Assembly with a gun in his belt?
W: On Nov. 13, 1975 Arafat, appearing at the UN podium wearing a gun, said he had come "bearing an olive branch and a freedom fighter's gun," and warned "do not let the olive branch drop from my hand." Arafat had been invited by the UN to a discussion of the status of the Palestinian people. As a result of the debate, a resolution was passed recognizing the Palestinians' right to nationhood and giving observer status to the PLO (Palestinian Liberation Organization) at the UN.

A: **Yellow**
Q: What color is the stripe on a Mountie's dress pants?
W: The dress of the Royal Canadian Mounted Police has several variations, but best known are the broad-brimmed hats, scarlet tunics, blue breeches with wide yellow stripe, brown top boots and spurs.

Oh, by the way, most of the horses have been replaced by motorized vehicles.

A: **Yippies**
Q: What were the members of the Youth International Party called?
W: The Yippies was a militant group of people opposed to the Vietnam War. Gary Hart, a presidential candidate in 1984, played on the title with his group of "Yuppies," a title for his constituency of young, urban, upwardly mobile people.

A: **Yom Kippur**
Q: What Jewish holiday is the Day of Atonement?
W: It is the most solemn of Jewish religious festivals, when one makes attonement for sins and restores an amicable relationship with God. The Day of Attonement is marked by abstention from food, drink, and sex.

A: **Yom Kippur**
Q: What Jewish holiday saw the start of the 1973 Mideast War?
W: This war was fought, as most of the wars in the Mideast are fought, because of religious differences.

A: **Yorkshire Ripper, The**
Q: What was the infamous pseudonym of Peter Sutcliffe?
W: Peter Sutcliffe was a truck driver from the West Yorkshire mill town of Bradford. He killed 13 Yorkshire and Lancashire women between 1975 and his capture in 1980.

A: **Yuri Gagarin**
Q: What Russian cosmonaut was killed in an air crash in 1968 while commanding a training unit?
W: He was the first man to travel into space on April 12, 1961. Gagarin orbited the earth once in a flight that lasted one hour and 18 minutes. He never went into space again, but took an active part in training other cosmonauts. Gagarin was killed, with another pilot, in the crash of a two-seat aircraft on what was called a routine training flight.

HISTORY

Z

A: **Zero**
Q: How many transatlantic trips did the *Titanic* make before sinking?
W: The Titanic went down four days after leaving its dock at Southampton, April 10, 1912, on its maiden voyage.

A: **Zero**
Q: How many witches were burned at the stake in Salem, Massachusetts?
W: Judge Jonathon Corwin held preliminary hearings during the witchcraft crisis that led to the condemnation of about 30 persons, mostly women. They weren't burned at the stake, but 19 were hanged and one was "pressed" to death under heavy weights.

A: **Zipper, The**
Q: What invention was named for the 1926 ad: "Zip, it's open, zip, it's closed"?
W: The zipper was actually patented as a "slide fastener" in 1896. It was invented five years earlier by Chicagoan Witcomb Judson. Until the 1930s the garment industry considered the zipper a passing fad.

A: **Zoot suits**
Q: What kind of suit did true hepcats wear in 1942?
W: The term and style were associated with jive elements (hepcats) during the late 1930s and early 1940s. The suit was of a brightly colored garish pattern or black with vertical strips, typically worn with a wide satin-finished bright and boldly patterned tie, a wide-brimmed hat, and knee-length key chain.

# #

A: **109**
Q: What was the number of John F. Kennedy's PT boat?
W: Kennedy barely escaped death himself when the PT l09 was sunk in the Solomon Islands by a Japanese destroyer. He was awarded the Navy and U.S. Marine Corps Medal for heroism for leading his men back to safety.

A: **115 years**
Q: How long did the Hundred Years' War Last?
W: The Hundred Years War lasted from 1338 to 1453!!

A: **444**
Q: How many days were the 52 American hostages held in Iran?
W: The siege of the American Embassy took place on Sunday morning, Nov. 4, 1979. The hostages were freed 444 days later on Inauguration Day, 1981, as Jimmy Carter left office and Ronald Reagan was sworn in.

A: **1066**
Q: When was the Battle of Hastings?
W: The Battle of Hastings resulted in the conquest of England by William, Duke of Normandy. It is ranked among the 15 battles that changed the course of history.

A: **1620**
Q: What year did the Pilgrims first land in America?
W: "Pilgrim" was the name given to the small group of English people who set up Plymouth Colony on the shore of Cape Cod Bay in Massachusetts in 1620. One of their leaders, William Bradford, spoke of himself and his followers as "pilgrims and strangers upon the earth." The Pilgrims were part of the great body of Protestants called Puritans.

A: **1933**
Q: What year did Hitler become chancellor of Germany?
W: Hitler was the dictator of Germany from 1933 to 1945, when he committed suicide, as the Allies marched on Berlin. Hitler told the German people that "conquest is not only a right, but also a duty".

A: **1944**
Q: What year was Paris liberated?
W: Paris did not suffer much damage during World War II because they did not resist the German Occupation of June 1940. The city welcomed the Allied Forces in August 1944 with the greatest demonstration Paris had ever seen.

A: **1961**
Q: What year was the Berlin Wall erected?
W: The Berlin Wall was built by the Communist government of East Germany in 1961, because refugees were migrating to West Germany. By 1961 nearly three million people had left East Germany.

A: **1962 California gubernatorial, The**
Q: What election loss caused Richard Nixon to say: "You won't have Nixon to kick around any more"?
W: The quote continues: "Because, Gentlemen, this is my last press conference." This statement was reported to the press on Nov. 7, 1962.

A: **1965**
Q: What year did the lights go out?
W: A massive electric power failure blacked out most of the northeastern U.S. and parts of Canada on the nights of November 9 and 10, 1965. The story that there was a sharp rise in the birth rate nine months later appears to have no basis in fact, only one New York hospital reported a significant increase in births.

A: **1967**
Q: What year did the counter-culture celebrate its Summer of Love?
W: The "summer of love" was a hippie development that peaked in 1967 and promulgated hope that the world would change through love and "flower power." At the Monterey Pop Festival, even the police were persuaded to wear flowers on their helmets.

A: **30,000 feet over Missouri**
Q: Where was Richard Nixon when Gerald Ford became president?
W: Ford became President on Aug. 9, 1974, upon the resignation of Richard Nixon. Nixon left the White House in a helicopter to board a waiting jet. As Ford took the oath of office, Nixon was aboard the jet on his way to California. He and wife Pat Nixon rode in silence and in separate compartments on their way "home."

HISTORY

ART & LITERATURE

A: **A**
Q: What letter was the scarlet letter?
W: *The Scarlet Letter*, written by Nathaniel Hawthorne, tells the story of Hester Prynne, a young woman living among the Puritans during the 1650s. She is forced to wear a scarlet *A*, for adultery, after she is released from jail for having committed the crime of having a child out of wedlock.

A: **A**
Q: What's the first letter of the Russian alphabet?
W: Six letters are common to both English and Russian: A,E,K,M,O and T. The Russian alphabet, however, has 33 letters.

A: **A.A. Milne**
Q: Who created *Winnie-the-Pooh*?
W: Although best known for his books about Winnie-the-Pooh and Christopher Robin, inspired by his own son of the same name, Milne has also written comedies, mysteries, and a powerful plea against war – *Peace with Honour*.

A: **About**
Q: What does the Latin *circa* before a date mean?
W: Abbreviated ca, c., or C., this word is from the Latin *circum*, meaning "round about," which is from *circus*, meaning "circle." It is used before a date or year to indicate that the date given is the approximate time when something occurred; for example, what happened c. 1066.

A: **Achilles**
Q: Who was dipped in the River Styx?
W: He is said to have been dipped in the River Styx by Thetis and thus made invulnerable except for the heel by which she held him. He was killed by Paris with a poisoned arrow to the heel.(Hence, the expression "Achilles Heel").

A: **Adam**
Q: What Biblical figure is known as "the Father of the Human Race"?
W: Taken from the Phoenician or Babylonian origin, Adam means "man" or "mankind."

A: **Adele Davis**
Q: What U.S. nutritionist wrote *Let's Cook It Right* and *Let's Have Healthy Children*?
W: She also wrote *Let's Eat Right to Keep Fit* and *Let's Get Well*. After planning individual diets for more than 20,000 people who were suffering from almost every disease known, she gave up her consulting work to devote her time to her family, lecturing and writing.

A: **Adolph Hitler**
Q: Who was *Time's* Man of the Year for 1938?
W: Adolph Hitler was born April 20, 1889, the son of Alois Schickelgruber. Alois changed his name to

Hitler in 1876. Adolph was featured on the cover of the weekly news magazine *Time* as their Man of the Year for 1938. In 1939 he launched the attack against Poland that started World War II.

A: Adolph Hitler
Q: Who was cloned in *The Boys from Brazil*?
W: Ira Levin's 1976 novel was made into a movie in 1978. It was a story about a mad doctor in South America with a scheme to produce 94 copies of Adolph Hitler.

A: Aesop
Q: What Greek slave wrote fables?
W: Aesop, the creator of the fable in Greece, lived in the 6th century B.C. as a slave. His brief moral anecdotes, usually about animal life, were imitated in Rome, in the Middle Ages, in 17th century France, and in most recent times by James Thurber.

A: Aesop's
Q: Whose moral of the story was: "Don't count your chickens before they're hatched"?
W: "Don't count your chickens before they are hatched" is the moral of "The Milkmaid and her Pail," the story of the farmer's daughter who, while walking to the market with a pail of milk on her head, dreams about what she is going to do with the money she will get from the milk. But she flings back her hair and knocks over the pail, and her dreams are dashed!

A: "After all, tomorrow is another day"
Q: What's the last line of *Gone with the Wind*?
W: It's the last line spoken by Scarlet O'Hara in Margaret Mitchell's classic. Scarlett, a Georgia belle with an indomitable will to survive and a determination to save Tara, the family plantation, does anything to achieve her goals.

A: After Ford
Q: What does A.F. stand for after the date in Aldous Huxley's *Brave New World*?
W: This is the story of a world dominated by science in which individuality is forgotten – a world whose motto is "Community, Identity and Stability." Bernard Marx, a citizen of the world in the year 632 A.F., has emotions similar to those people who lived during Henry Ford's time.

A: *After the Fall*
Q: What Arthur Miller play recounts his marriage to Marilyn Monroe?
W: The 1964 play *After the Fall* includes a role allegedly suggested by Miller's wife, Marilyn Monroe. He scripted "The Misfits" in which his wife appeared.

A: Agatha Christie
Q: What English mystery writer said: "Give me a decent bottle of poison and I'll construct the perfect crime"?
W: Another related quote by Agatha Christie from *Life* on May 14, 1956, is "I specialize in murders of quiet, domestic interest. Give me a nice deadly phial to play with, and I am happy."

A: Agatha Christie
Q: Who's the most translated English author after Shakespeare?
W: The number of published works of Agatha Christie totals 87, 68 of which are novels. She is the most widely translated English author in the world with translations in 103 languages – 14 more than Shakespeare.

A: Agatha Christie's
Q: What British mystery writer's disappearance in 1926 prompted a nationwide search?
W: The death of her mother and the impending breakup of her own marriage resulted in Christie's amnesia. Her highly publicized disappearance in 1926 also resulted in increased book sales.

A: An alarm clock
Q: What did the crocodile swallow in *Peter Pan*?
W: Captain Hook tossed the alarm clock to the crocodile after it had eaten his hand. Now the Captain could hear the crocodile as it approached again for another snack.

A: Albert Speer's
Q: Whose diaries were published as *Spandau: The Secret Diaries*?
W: Albert Speer, Hitler's personal architect and confidante, was Reich Minister for Armaments and War Protection and the second most powerful man in Nazi Germany at the end of World War II. He was sentenced to 20 years imprisonment at Spandau. Notes from his 20 years were written on such items as tobacco wrappers, pages of calendars, and toilet paper.

A: Al Capp
Q: Who created *L'il Abner*?
W: *L'il Abner*, drawn by Al Capp, began as a daily strip in 1934 with the Sunday strip following in 1935. Capp's signature in the early daily episodes was "Al G. Cap"; the second *p* was added with the 25th episode. Now there's some obscure trivia.

A: Aldous Huxley
Q: Who has Miranda exclaiming: "Oh brave new world that has such people in it"?
W: *Brave New World*, Huxley's most celebrated work, is a bitterly satiric account of an inhumane society controlled by technology, in which art and religion have been abolished and human beings reproduce by artificial

fertilization. Huxley's distress about the modern world led him toward mysticism and use of hallucinatory drugs.

A: **Alexander Solzhenitsyn**
Q: What Russian writer was deported from the Soviet Union in 1974?
W: In *The Gulag Archipelago* he documents the oppression of the Soviet labor camp system. Following the release of this publication he was arrested, charged with treason, and exiled from the Soviet Union.

A: **Alex Haley**
Q: Who wrote *The Autobiography of Malcolm X*?
W: Malcolm X is the name adopted by Malcolm Little (1925-1965), a black nationalist and founder of the *Organization of Afro-American Unity*. His autobiography was told to and taken down by Alex Haley.

A: **Alex Haley**
Q: Who conducted the *Playboy* interview of U.S. Nazi leader George Lincoln Rockwell?
W: Haley is best known for his work *Roots: The Saga of An American Family*, which has been praised for its moving portrait of life under slavery. He received a Pulitzer Prize for *Roots*.

A: **Alfred E. Neuman**
Q: Who made his first appearance on the cover of *Mad* in 1956?
W: Alfred E. Neuman, *Mad* magazine's "What, me worry?" hero, first appeared on *Mad*'s cover issue No. 30, in 1956. The original drawing was on an undated, untraceable "comic" postcard many years before.

A: **Alfred Hitchcock's**
Q: Whose biography is titled *Hitch*?
W: English film director Alfred Hitchcock, born in 1899, was a master of suspense and mystery. He began his career as a title artist, eventually graduating to directing. All of his films are individualistic and often innovative. A characteristic of his films is his brief appearance in each.

A: **Alice**
Q: Who devoured a cake with the words "Eat Me" written on it in currants?
W: Upon spying a little glass box lying under the table, Alice opened it and found a very small cake, on which the words "eat me" were beautifully marked in currants. Because Alice had become so used to having unusual things happen, she was convinced that if she ate some of the cake she would grow either larger or smaller. She was quite surprised to find that she remained the same size.

A: **Alice**
Q: Who said: "I've had such a curious dream"?
W: *Alice in Wonderland*, written by Lewis Carroll, was set in Victorian England. Alice, an imaginative young English girl, falls asleep by the side of a stream in a meadow and dreams that she follows a rabbit down a hole. Many adventures in a wonderland inhabited by all kinds of strange characters follow.

A: **All for one, one for all**
Q: What was the motto of the Three Musketeers?
W: *The Three Musketeers*, written by Alexandre Dumas, is set in 1626. D'Artagnan, who has come to Paris to seek his fortune, becomes friends with Athos, Porthos, and Aramis, members of the King's Musketeers. He and his friends are induced to go to England to reclaim 200 diamond studs that the Queen has imprudently given her lover.

A: ***All the King's Men***
Q: What book, based on the life of Louisiana senator Huey Long, won Robert Penn Warren a Pulitzer Prize?
W: Warren, an American novelist, poet, and literary critic, won the 1947 Pulitzer Prize for his novel *All the King's Men*, which describes the rise and fall of a ruthless politician. Warren also won the 1958 Pulitzer Prize for Poetry for his collection entitled *Promises: Poems 1954-1956*.

A: **"Aloha"**
Q: What word is used in Hawaii as both a greeting and a farewell?
W: "Aloha" means love, greetings, welcome, and farewell. The Hawaiian alphabet has only 12 letters: A,E,H,I,K,L,M,N,O,P,U, and W. Every syllable and word ends with a vowel. Two consonants never occur without a vowel between them, and the accent on most words falls on the next to the last syllable.

A: **alphabet, The**
Q: What series of letters is named for the first two Greek letters?
W: The alphabet is the series of letters used in writing a language. The name means exactly what the term "ABC" means as a name for the 26 letters of the English alphabet: alpha is the first letter of the Greek alphabet and beta is the second.

A: **Alpha and omega**
Q: What are the first and last letters of the Greek alphabet?
W: Alpha is the first letter of the Greek alphabet; omega is the last. When alpha is mentioned with omega, it signifies the beginning and the end, the totality.

A: **Alvin Toffler**
Q: Who wrote *Future Shock*?
W: Toffler, American journalist and author, is best known for his works on sociology and futurology. His best-seller, *Future Shock*, is an important documentation of the increasing rate of change in most spheres of life in the 20th century and its resulting psychological trauma on civilization.

A: **Amazons, The**
Q: What race of warriors burned off their right breasts in Greek legend?
W: In Greek mythology, the Amazons were a race of female warriors said to have lived in Scythia, near the Black Sea. The word *Amazon* is derived from *a* meaning "without" and *mazos* meaning "breast," because of the fable that they cut off their right breasts to facilitate the use of the bow.

A: **Ambrosia**
Q: What was the food of the Greek gods called?
W: Ambrosia was a magical substance eaten by the gods of Greek and Roman mythology. Sometimes it was mixed with nectar as a drink. The gods kept their immortality by bathing in ambrosia or rubbing it into their skin. A human being who drank ambrosia became strong and immortal.

A: **ambulance, An**
Q: What does a CBer refer to as a "meat wagon"?
W: In the CB (citizen's band radio) dictionary, a school bus is referred to as a "baby buggy"; a police helicopter is a "bear in the sky," a hearse is a "box on wheels," an unmarked police car is a "brown paper bag," and a truck is a "kidney buster."

A: **Amen**
Q: What's the last word of the Bible?
W: The last book of the Bible is Revelation, and the last sentence is "The grace of the Lord Jesus be with all the saints. Amen."

A: *Amen*
Q: What Hebrew word means "so be it"?
W: Amen not only expresses a wish that requests in a prayer be granted, but also means that the statements made are true. The word comes from the Hebrew language and means "so be it" or "so it is."

A: **Amity Island**
Q: What island is the setting for Peter Benchley's novel *Jaws*?
W: *Jaws* is the story of a Long Island resort town called Amity that is attacked by the rare great white shark. It is also a tale of moral dilemma because the town fathers of Amity decide to cover up the shark attack for fear that news of the killer shark will ruin the summer tourist business. The movie *Jaws* was filmed on Martha's Vineyard.

A: **And**
Q: What word occurs 46,227 times in the Bible?
W: If you have the time to count them, go ahead. We hope you don't come up with 46,226 and have to start over!

A: **Andy Warhol**
Q: What painter popularized soup cans and Brillo soap pad boxes?
W: Andy Warhol, founder and major figure of the "pop art" movement, pioneered the development of a process whereby an enlarged photographic image is transferred to a silk screen that is then placed on a canvas and inked from the back. By using this technique, he was able to produce the mass media images of such items as Campbell's soup cans, Coca-Cola bottles, and Brillo soap pad boxes.

A: **Andy Warhol**
Q: Who put Marilyn Monroe's likeness on a series of silk-screen prints?
W: In 1960 Warhol produced the first of his paintings depicting enlarged comic strip characters such as Popeye and Superman. He also created a series of mechanical reproductions of celebrities including Elizabeth Taylor and Marilyn Monroe.

A: **Angels**
Q: What are cherubim and seraphim?
W: Seraphim, the plural of seraph, are angels of the highest order.

Cherubim, the plural of cherub, are one of an order of angelic beings ranking second to the seraphim. In art, the cherub is represented by a beautiful winged child.

A: *Animal Farm*
Q: What George Orwell novel features a pig named Napoleon?
W: George Orwell, English essayist and novelist, served in Burma with the Indian police, lived a vagrant life in England and Europe, and fought in the Spanish Civil War. *Animal Farm*, published in 1945, was a political fable satirizing the Communist regime in Russia.

A: **Anne, Charlotte, Emily**
Q: What were the names of the three Bronte sisters?
W: The three sisters and their brother, Branwell, spent most of their lives at their father's lonely parsonage, yet produced some of the most remarkable works in English literature. In 1846, they published *Poems by Currier, Ellis and Acton Bell*, pseudonyms they continued to use in their individual works.

A: **Anne Frank**
Q: Who wrote *The Diaries of Anne Frank*?
W: Anne Frank, a German-Jewish girl, wrote a vivid, tender diary while hiding from the Nazis during World War II. Her family hid in an attic during the Nazi occupation of the Netherlands, but after two years were betrayed and discovered. Anne died in the Nazi concentration camp at Belsen.

A: **Anne Hathaway**
Q: Who was William Shakespeare's wife?
W: Anne Hathaway married Shakespeare in 1582, when she was 26 years old and he was 18. They had three children, Susanna, Judith, and Hamnet. Her cottage home is kept as a memorial.

A: **Antonio**
Q: Who was the title character in *The Merchant of Venice*?

ART AND LITERATURE

W: Antonio was a character in several of Shakespeare's plays. In *The Merchant of Venice*, he was a merchant; in *Two Gentlemen from Verona*, he was the father of Proteus; in *The Tempest*, he was Prospero's brother; in *Twelfth Night*, Antonio was a sea captain; and in *Much Ado About Nothing*, he was the brother of Leonato.

A: **Aphrodite**
Q: Who was the Greek goddess of love?
W: Aphrodite, the daughter of Zeus and Dione, was the goddess of love and beauty. She is said to have been born of the foam of the sea. The word *aphrodisiac*, named after her, refers to a food or drug that arouses sexual desire or potency.

A: **Architecture**
Q: What's been called "the Mother of the Arts"?
W: Architecture is probably the oldest of the fine arts. Certainly it is the most useful and in some respects is a prerequisite for the other arts. Most early sacred texts associate buildings with deities. Architecture was not only considered the highest art form, to which other arts were adornments, but some buildings were viewed as representing another higher realm.

A: *Armada*
Q: What's the Spanish word for "navy"?
W: The Spanish Armada, a fleet of war vessels, was sent against England by Spain in 1588. Although it was called "the Invincible Armada," it was defeated by the English and almost entirely destroyed by storms.

A: *Armageddon*
Q: What Leon Uris novel dealt with the Russian capture of Berlin?
W: American novelist Leon Uris' best known work is *Exodus*, which tells about Jewish immigration into Palestine and the struggle to establish the State of Israel in the 1940s. Uris also wrote *Mila 18*, *Battle Cry* and *Armageddon*.

A: **arms, The**
Q: What's missing from the Venus de Milo?
W: The Venus de Milo, the last Hellenistic Aphrodite, is probably the most famous statue in the world. It has been accepted as the embodiment of the ideal of feminine beauty since its discovery on the island of Melos in 1820.

A: **Arthur Haley**
Q: Who wrote a novel about the closing of Runway 29 at Lincoln International Airport?
W: *Airport* is the fictional tale of Lincoln International airport, the "aviation crossroads of the world," an airport with outmoded operational areas, overtaxed air traffic control, and a career jinxed general manager. *Airport* is a behind the scenes story of seven eventful hours during a mid winter snowstorm and how airport personnel work around these problems.

A: **Arthur Miller**
Q: Who wrote *Death of a Salesman* in six weeks?
W: *Death of a Salesman* is about Willy Loman, a salesman whose escapist tendencies have blinded him to his real mediocrity. At age 63 when he is taken off salary and paid on commission only, the financial

distress of his family becomes acute. Willy, whose mind is failing, commits suicide to give his family the insurance money.

A: **Art Linkletter**
Q: Who wrote the 1957 best-seller *Kids Say the Darndest Things*?
W: Art Linkletter is best known as the TV host of "Art Linkletter's House Party" and "People Are Funny." His spontaneous wit and humor as he interviewed children have entertained millions and provided the basis for this book. His portraits on the $100 bill in the board game "Life" is the only real person's image used in the game.

A: **Athos, Porthos, Aramis**
Q: Who were the Three Musketeers?
W: Athos was the saintly member of the Three Musketeers who, when young, married a beautiful girl only to learn that she had been branded a thief. Porthos was noted for his great strength, vanity, and stupidity. Aramis joined the King's Musketeers after he giving up his intention of entering the priesthood as the consequence of fighting a duel.

A: **Atlanta**
Q: What Georgia town did Scarlett O'Hara condemn as being full of pushy people?
W: Because of Margaret Mitchell's novel, *Gone With the Wind*, Atlanta is known as the Civil War site of the Battle of Atlanta, an historical event that has reached mythical proportions. Atlanta was burned in 1864 by the Union's General Sherman.

A: *Atlas Shrugged*
Q: What Ayn Rand novel opens with the question: "Who is John Galt?"
W: Ayn Rand, a Russian-born American writer who originated a philosophy known as Objectivism, advocates capitalism in economics and individualism in ethics. Her novel *Atlas Shrugged* stated her philosophy that rational self-interest should be the basis of action and that self-fulfillment is an individual's moralAresponsibility, with production achievement the noblest activity.

A: **Audie Murphy's**
Q: What World War II hero's autobiography was titled *To Hell and Back*?
W: Audie Murphy won fame as the most decorated U.S. soldier of World War II. He received 24 medals from the U.S. government, three from France, and one from Belgium. He began his motion picture career about three years after being discharged from the Army in 1945. His films included *The Red Badge of Courage* and *To Hell and Back*.

A: **Auric**
Q: What is Goldfinger's first name?
W: In the movie *Goldfinger*, James Bond is pitted against his most famous adversary, the villainous Auric Goldfinger, and his assistant, the seemingly indestructible Oddjob. Aided by Pussy Galore, Bond thwarted Goldfinger from stealing all the gold in Fort Knox.

A: **Australia**
Q: What country is the setting for Colleen McCullough's *The Thorn Birds*?
W: *The Thorn Birds* is the story of the Clearys, who leave New Zealand to live on a vast Australian sheep station. The novel begins in 1915 and ends more than a half century later. The fortunes of the family are interwoven with the natural disasters of the land: the cycles of drought, fire, and torrential flood.

A: **Ayatollah Ruhollah Khomeini**
Q: Who was *Time's* Man of the Year for 1979?
W: The Ayatollah Khomeini became leader of Iran in 1979 by forcing the overthrow of the Shah and Prime Minister Shahpur Bakhtiar. In November 1979 militant students who invaded the U.S. Embassy and precipitated the "Iranian Hostage Crisis" received Khomeini's support. He imposed rigid censorship, executed members of the opposition, and banned western customs.

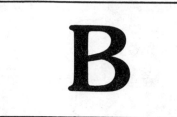

A: **Babe**
Q: What was Paul Bunyan's ox's name?
W: Just as heroes of old had their magic steeds and loyal companions, Paul had his giant blue ox, Babe. Babe, born in the "winter of the blue snow," measured 42 ax handles and a plug of Star chewing tobacco between the eyes.

A: *Barry Lyndon*
Q: What William Makepeace Thackeray novel was made into a film by Stanley Kubrick?
W: The character Barry Lyndon, the offshoot of a boozy Irish clan who aspires to the rank of gentleman, is an adventurer who purues Lady Lyndon, the most sought-after heiress in England. After acquiring great rank and fortune as a result of his marriage, he faces many personal tragedies, including the loss of his fortune, the collapse of his marriage, and the death of his child.

A: **Basketball**
Q: What kind of sports team was reunited in Jason Miller's *That Championship Season*?
W: This is the story of a reunion of a 1952 high school state championship basketball team 20 years later at the coach's house. The film won the New York Drama Critics Circle Award.

A: **Batman**
Q: What was Bruce Wayne's heroic identity?
W: When young Bruce Wayne's parents are killed by a gunman, he vows war on the underworld. He takes as his symbol a bat—the fearsome creature of darkness. Originally Batman is a somber, sinister hero. But after a year he adopts a young orphan, Dick Grayson, whose circus acrobat parents have been killed in a fall. They form the team of Batman and Robin.

A: **"Battle Hymn of the Republic, The"**
Q: What hymn did John Steinbeck get his title *The Grapes of Wrath* from?
W: "The Battle Hymn of the Republic" is the stirring popular hymn to the music of the song "John Brown's Body." Julia Ward Howe wrote it in 1861, after she visited the army campgrounds around Washington, D.C., during the civil war. Jane Russell Lowell, editor of the *Atlantic Monthly*, published the hymn and named it.

A: **Beatrix Potter**
Q: Who created Peter Rabbit?
W: Beatrix Potter was a British author and illustrator whose "Peter Rabbit" books became known in all parts of the world. Her first "Peter Rabbit" book grew out of letters she wrote in 1893 to a friend's invalid son.

A: *Beau Geste*
Q: What is the title of P.C. Wren's novel of the French Foreign Legion?
W: *Beau Geste*, a novel, play and motion picture, brought Percival Christopher Wren international attention. It is the romantic adventure story about life in the French Foreign Legion. Wren's first novels dealt with India, where he served in a government post for ten years.

A: **Beer**
Q: What is Nero Wolfe's favorite drink during office hours?
W: Nero Wolfe, created by Rex Stout, is perhaps the most eccentric of all detectives. He is only 5 feet, 11 inches tall, but he weighs a seventh of a ton. He is a gourmand and loathes unneccessary physical activity, although he once set out on an exercise program, throwing darts for 15 minutes each day. His hobby is growing orchids on the roof of his brownstone.

ART AND LITERATURE

A: **Before death**
Q: What does the Latin *ante mortem* mean?
W: *Ante* denotes "before," in regard to position, order, or time. *Morte* means "death, fatal or deadly." *Ante mortem* is often used as an adjective, such as an *ante mortem* statement.

A: **Belgian**
Q: What's the nationality of Agatha Christie's detective Hercule Poirot?
W: Hercule Poirot is a Belgian who was forced to flee to England after the German invasion of his homeland in 1914. He had served as a policeman with honor and distinction before retiring. After the war he remained in England as a "private inquiry agent".

A: **Belgium**
Q: What country claimed Rubens, Van Dyck and Bruegel as citizens?
W: The Flemish baroque painter Peter Paul Rubens was the most renowned northern European artist of his day. Flemish painter Peter Bruegel the Elder established the independence of landscape and genre subjects (scenes of everyday life) from traditional figural painting. Sir Anthony Van Dyck was noted primarily for his portraits and religious canvasses.

A: **Benjamin Franklin**
Q: Who published *Poor Richard's Almanac*?
W: Benjamin Franklin, U.S. statesman prominent in the struggle for independence from Britain, helped draft the Declaration of Independence. He published his *Poor Richard's Almanack* from 1732 to 1757. It contained his homey philosophizing and many of his quasi proverbial sayings.

A: **Betty Friedan**
Q: What suburban housewife and mother of three wrote *The Feminine Mystique*?
W: Betty Friedan is considered to be the founder of the Women's Liberation Movement in the U.S. She first gained fame from her 1963 book, *The Feminine Mystique*, in which she protested that society puts pressure on women to be housewives only and not to seek a career.

A: **Betty and Veronica**
Q: What two girls do Archie and Reggie run around with?
W: The cartoon strip Archie, created by Bob Montana, made its first appearance in December 1941. It features Archie, the "typical high school student"; his rival, Reggie; Jughead, who loves hamburgers more than girls; and Betty and Veronica, who vie for Archie's attention.

A: **Billie Holliday's**
Q: Whose biography is titled *Lady Sings the Blues*?

W: Jazz singer Billie Holliday first achieved fame in the 1930s with a series of recordings with Teddy Wilson's orchestra. Her influence on other vocalists is comparable with that of Louis Armstrong and Charlie Parker on other instrumentalists.

A: **Billy Carter**
Q: Who captured *Esquire's* Most Dubious Man of the Year award for 1980?
W: *Esquire*, a monthly magazine founded in New York in 1933, is noted for its humorous illustrations and its short stories, and more recently for its searching articles on various aspects of modern life and the arts. Because of his strange behavior and business dealings, Billy Carter, colorful younger brother of President Jimmy Carter, was featured in the magazine at the end of 1980.

A: **Black**
Q: What color was the Maltese Falcon?
W: In *The Maltese Falcon*, Sam Spade probes his partner's puzzling murder through dark streets and cheap rooms, dealing with eccentric criminals who pursue a black falcon statue said to be worth a fortune. The 1941 film version was directed by John Huston and starred Humphrey Bogart, Mary Astor, Sydney Greenstreet, and Peter Lorre.

A: **Blanch**
Q: What's the name of the Wizard of Id's wife?
W: *The Wizard of Id*, a cartoon strip, created by Johny Hart in collaboration with Brant Parker in 1964, features a cruel, greedy midget of a monarch whose greatest satisfaction in life lies in the exploitation of his subjects. He is flanked by his cowardly knight, Brandolph, and by the Wizard, a magician of dubious achievement.

ART AND LITERATURE

A: **Blonde**
Q: What color is Nancy Drew's hair?
W: Nancy Drew, created by Carolyn Keene, is a teenage detective heroine of 52 novels aimed at readers in the eight-to-thirteen age group. Highly intelligent and extraordinarily brave, Nancy solves crimes that generally take place in old dark houses, secret passages, and underground caves.

A: **Blue**
Q: What color eyes did the boys from Brazil have?
W: The 1976 best seller, *The Boys from Brazil*, by Ira Levin tells the story of a mad doctor in South America who has created clones of Adolph Hitler. Blue eyes and blonde hair are dominant characteristic traits of Germanic peoples, indicative of the "super" race Hitler was trying to produce.

A: **Bob Cratchit**
Q: Who was Tiny Tim's father?
W: Bob Cratchit is greedy Ebenezer Scrooge's destitute clerk in *A Christmas Carol*, written by Charles Dickens in 1843. Although overworked and underpaid, Cratchit still maintains his goodness and generosity. His long work hours are particularly necessary because his youngest son, Tiny Tim, a cripple, seems doomed to an early death unless there are improvements in the family fortune.

A: **Bob Woodward and Carl Bernstein**
Q: Who wrote *All the President's Men*?
W: These two young reporters for the *Washington Post* wrote of their day-by-day investigation of the Watergate scandal. It was made into a film in 1976 starring Robert Redford and Dustin Hoffman.

A: **Bonaparte**
Q: What name did Napoleon Bonaparte sign his letters?

W: Napoleon Bonaparte had many opportunities to sign his name! His biography, *Napoleon's Life*, comes from the essays and notes he wrote as a young man, his letters to family and loved ones, and the more than 30 volumes of letters, most of which he dictated, that depict his ruling of France.

A: **Bonn**
Q: What's the setting of John Le Carre's *A Small Town in Germany*?
W: The setting is Bonn, a small town elevated by the Cold War to the artificial status of a capital city. An aging second secretary has vanished from the British Embassy taking with him official files whose disclosure could ruin Britain's chances at the negotiating table. Investigator Alan Turner is sent to find him.

A: **book, The**
Q: Which came first, the book or the phrase "catch-22"?
W: Joseph Heller wrote *Catch-22* based on his experiences in the air force. The phrase "catch-22" – the system that traps all the participants, and especially the Assyrian hero Yossarian, into compliance in the crazy enterprise – entered the language after the book's publication.

A: **Books**
Q: What are catalogued under the Dewey decimal system?
W: The Dewey Decimal System is the most widely used method of classifying books in a library. It is named for its developer, Melvil Dewey. This system classifies books by dividing them into ten main groups, with each of these groups being represented by specific numerals.

A: **Books**
Q: What does a bibliophile enjoy?
W: Some book lovers, or "bibliophiles", collect worthy books to preserve them for posterity. Most of the large libraries of the 1500s,

1600s, and 1700s were brought together by bibliophiles with this purpose in mind.

A: **Bootlegger**
Q: What was the occupation of Jay Gatsby?
W: Jay Gatsby, the major character in F. Scott Fitzgerald's *The Great Gatsby*, is a fabulously rich racketeer in the 1920s. The son of poor parents from the Midwest, he spends much of his time trying to impress, and become accepted by, other wealthy people.

A: **Boris Pasternak**
Q: Who turned down the 1958 Nobel Prize for *Dr. Zhivago*?
W: Pasternak, Soviet poet and novelist, received international attention following the 1957 Italian publication of his novel *Dr. Zhivago*. Its publication, followed by the awarding of the Nobel Prize, caused him political difficulties, and even threats of deportation. As a result, he renounced the Nobel prize.

A: **Botticelli**
Q: What Italian artist painted *Birth of Venus*?
W: Sandro Botticelli, an Italian painter born in Florence, lived at the time of that city's greatest intellectual and artistic flowering. He is responsible for the thoughtful, but serene paintings of classical myths including *Birth of Venus* (sometimes jokingly referred to as "Venus on the halfshell"), *Pallas Subdueing a Centaur*, and *Venus and Mars*.

A: *Bounty,* **The**
Q: What was the name of Captain Bligh's ship?
W: The cruel Captain Bligh commanded the British war vessel, the *Bounty*, before the mutiny by the crew in 1787.

A: **brain, A**
Q: What was the scarecrow in *The Wizard of Oz* lacking?

W: Three companions join Dorothy in her venture to see the Wizard of Oz, each hoping that the Wizard might help him, too. A scarecrow lamented his lack of brains. Nick Chopper was turned into a tin man by the Wicked Witch and left without a heart. The lion is missing courage.

A: **Brazil**
Q: Where were the boys from in Ira Levin's 1976 novel?
W: The novel, The Boys from Brazil, tells the story of a mad doctor in Brazil who has created clones of Adolph Hitler. These boys possess the desired traits of the Germanic "super" race Hitler wanted to create: blonde hair and blue eyes.

A: **Bread**
Q: What's the staff of life mentioned in the Lord's Prayer?
W: The Lord's Prayer is the most widely recited Christian prayer. By tradition it is one of the three basic statements of Christian faith; the other two are the Apostles' Creed and the Ten Commandments. The Gospels tell that Jesus taught the prayer to his followers as the best way to pray to God.

A: *Bridges at Toko-Ri, The*
Q: What James Michner novel was filmed with William Holden, Mickey Rooney and Grace Kelly?
W: *The Bridges at Toko-Ri* was the 1954 film about the adventures of a pilot during the Korean conflict and the impact of the separation on his family.

A: *Bridge of San Luis Rey, The*
Q: What book did Thornton Wilder win the 1928 Pulitzer Prize for?
W: The plot:in 1714, a bridge in Peru breaks plunging five persons to their death. Brother Juniper views the accident as the judgment of God and investigates his theory. The threads of these mysteriously linked lives are finally drawn together on a mystical note, their deaths having occurred at a significant moment in each of their lives.

A: -**Bring on the Empty Horses**
Q: What was the seqel to *The Moon's a Balloon*?
W: These books by actor David Niven are autobiographic. *Go Slowly, Come Back Quickly* is his novel that was published in 1981.

A: **Bronte sisters, The**
Q: What sisters wrote under the pseudonyms Currer Bell, Ellis Bell and Acton Bell?
W: *Jane Eyre* was the principal novel of Charlotte Bronte, whose pen name was Currer Bell. *Wuthering Heights* was the principal novel of Emily, whose pen name was Ellis Bell. Acton Bell was the pen name for Anne, who wrote *Agnes Grey*.

A: **Broth**
Q: What did the old woman in the shoe give her children to eat?
W: After "she gave them broth without any bread, she whipped them all soundly and put them to bed".

A: **Bruno Richard Hauptmann's**
Q: What kidnapper's story was told in a book titled *Scapegoat* by Anthony Scaduto?
W: *Scapegoat: The Lonesome Death of Bruno Richard Hauptmann* is the story of the man who was convicted and executed for the 1932 kidnapping and murder of Charles and Anne Morrow Lindbergh's 20-month-old son. Hauptmann denied any connection with the kidnapping, but was convicted in a sensational trial and electrocuted. Some evidence suggests that Hauptmann was innocent.

A: **bugle, The**
Q: What musical instrument did Prewitt play in James Jones' *From Here to Eternity*?
W: James Jones is one of the most notable novelists of the World War II generation. He became famous overnight with *From Here to Eternity*, a powerful, often shocking picture of the lives of Hawaii-based U.S. Army personnel in the days preceding the attack on Pearl Harbor.

A: **bull terrier, retriever, cat, A**
Q: What are the three animals in Sheila Burnford's *The Incredible Journey*?
W: Pet animals in the 1961 novel by Sheila Burnford include Luath, the bull terrier; Tao, the Siamese cat; and Bodger, the retriever. These three house pets, who are left with a friend of the family while their owners are abroad, disappear into the Canadian wilderness. Their amazing trek back to their old home is their incredible journey.

A: **Bung**
Q: Who's the wine-swilling court jester of *The Wizard of Id*?
W: This inebriated jester was, along with the Wizard, the only man who could play tricks on the diminutive King of Id and get away with it. *The Wizard of Id* is a well-known comic strip.

A: **Burma**
Q: What country is the setting of *The Bridge on the River Kwai*?
W: The 1952 novel "The Bridge Over the River Kwai" was written by French author, Pierre Boulle. Most of his books are set amid the difficulties of war, international intrigue, and wilderness outposts in such places as Burma. His novels often satirize the British code of conduct or so-called heroism.

A: **Burt Reynolds**
Q: Who claimed his photograph in *Cosmopolitan* cost him an Academy Award?
W: Burt Reynolds was the first male to pose nude in a centerfold for

Cosmopolitan, a magazine primarily for women. Reynold's posed free for the April 1972 issue.

A: **Butcher, baker, candlestick maker**
Q: What were the occupations of the three men in the tub?
W: "Rub-a-dub-dub
Three men in a tub;
And who do you think they be?
The butcher, the baker,
the candlestick maker,
Turn 'em out, knaves all three!"

A: **Butterflies**
Q: What did the title character in John Fowle's *The Collector* collect?
W: *The Collector*, Fowle's first novel, was more sensational than those that followed. In it he attempts to probe psychologically what would induce a young man of one class to collect, imprison, and dissect the girl in another class that he thought he loved. It seems he wanted to expand his collection of beautiful butterflies.

ART AND LITERATURE

C

A: **C**
Q: What letter does a cedilla hang from?
W: The cedilla is a mark put under the letter *c* in some French words to indicate that it is to be sounded as an *s*.

A: **California**
Q: What state full of milk and honey was the destination in *The Grapes of Wrath*?
W: *The Grapes of Wrath*, by John Steinbeck, is the classic Pulitzer Prize-winning novel about a family's westward movement from Oklahoma and their battle with economic desperation. The Joads move west from a land of drought and bankruptcy to seek work as migrant fruit-pickers in California.

A: **California**
Q: What U.S. state is the most frequent setting of John Steinbeck novels?
W: John Steinbeck was born in Salinas, California, and some of the best scenes in his stories were set in Monterey County, where he spent most of his life. His literary reputation was established by *Tortilla Flat* and *In Dubious Battle*, both set in Monterey, California.

A: **Camelot**
Q: Where was King Arthur's court?
W: *Historia Regum Britanniae* (1135) was the earliest literature to romanticize Arthur. Arthur was the son of British King Uther Pendragon and Igraine. As king, Arthur makes many conquests in Britain and on the continent, marries Guinevere, and holds his court at Camelot, where his most famous knights were Kay, Bedivere, and Gawain.

A: ***The Canterbury Tales***
Q: What Chaucer poem describes a band of pilgrims setting out from an English inn?
W: *The Canterbury Tales*, by Geoffrey Chaucer, is set in the framework of a pilgrimage to the Shrine of Thomas Becket at Canterbury. Each pilgrim is to tell four tales and the best storyteller is to have dinner at the others' expense when the party returns to the Tabard Inn, Southwark.

A: **Captain Hook**
Q: Who commanded the *Jolly Roger* in J.M. Barrie's *Peter Pan*?
W: Wendy, Michael, and John Darling are whisked away to Never-never Land by an elfin boy named Peter Pan and Tinker Bell, a fairy. There they have remarkable adventures and meet unforgettable characters including the pirate Captain Hook, Tootles, Nibs, Smee, and Tiger Lily.

A: **Captain Nemo**
Q: Who commanded Jules Verne's *Nautilus*?
W: Verne's fantastic plots took advantage of the widespread interest in science in the 1800s. *Twenty Thousand Leagues Under the Sea*, published in 1870, tells of the adventures of Captain Nemo, a mad sea captain who cruises beneath the oceans in a submarine, the *Nautilus*.

A: **Captain Queeg**
Q: Who commanded the *Caine*?
W: *The Caine Mutiny*, by Herman Wouk, is a gripping account of Navy life during World War II. After a college boy begins his service on the mine sweeper *Caine*, he takes part in a desperate mutiny of the officers against their inefficient and cowardly commander. The story became an immediate best-seller and later a play and a movie.

A: **Capulet**
Q: What is Juliet's last name?
W: William Shakespeare's *Romeo and Juliet* is the 15th century love story of Juliet, the only daughter of old Capulet, and Romeo, the only son of old Montague. The Capulets and the Montagues have a long-standing feud. The attempt to avoid Juliet's forced marriage resulted in the suicide deaths of both lovers.

A: **Carlos Castaneda**
Q: Who wrote *Tales of Power*, *Journey to Ixtlan* and *Separate Reality*?
W: Carlos Casteneda, an American anthropologist, is noted for a series of best-selling books that report the nonrational wisdom of the Mexican "Brujo" called Don Juan, under whom Casteneda claims to have studied. His first book, *The Teachings of Don Juan: a Yaqui Way of Knowledge* relates his introduction to the visionary reality of Don Juan by means of hallucinogens. His later works, *Tales of Power*, *Journey to Ixtlan*, and *Separate Reality*, continue to develop his mystical themes.

A: **Carl Sandburg**
Q: What 20th-century American poet wrote a four-volume biography of Abraham Lincoln?
W: Carl Sandburg set out to make himself an authority on Abraham Lincoln, whose personality and achievements attracted the poet. His biography of the Civil War president appeared in two volumes entitled *Abraham Lincoln: The Prairie Years* and in four volumes entitled *Abraham Lincoln: The War Years*, which won a Pulitzer Prize.

A: *Casino Royale*
Q: What novel did Ian Fleming introduce James Bond in?
W: The 1953 book *Casino Royale*, was the first of Ian Fleming's adventures of James Bond. Bond takes on the first of his archvillains, Le Chiffre, who is trying to regain misappropriated S.M.E.R.S.H. (a Russian murder organization) funds at a gambling casino in northern France.

A: **cast of characters, The**
Q: What's the *dramatis personae* of a play?
W: "Dramatis personae" are the characters or actors in a play, or even a novel or poem. It also includes the participants in an actual dramatic event.

A: **cat and a goldfish, A**
Q: What kinds of animals were Pinocchio's pets Cleo and Figaro?
W: *Pinocchio*, created by Carlo Lorenzini, is the tale of a puppet, created by Geppetto from a piece of wood, that laughs and cries like a child. Because of his reckless adventures, Pinocchio learns wisdom through trouble and with wisdom achieves reformation from a puppet into a boy.

A: *The Catcher in the Rye*
Q: What book does Holden Caulfield appear in?
W: *The Catcher in the Rye*, the 1951 novel by J.D. Salinger, deals with two days in the life of Holden Caulfield, an adolescent boy on the verge of a nervous breakdown, who runs away from prep school just before Christmas vacation and drifts about in New York, getting himself into a series of wryly humorous adventures.

A: *Catch-22*
Q: What novel contains the line: "Who promoted Major Major?"
W: Major Major Major, whose tragedy is that he resembles Henry Fonda, is a character in Joseph Heller's *Catch-22*. The story is set in the closing months of World War II, in an American bomber squadron on a small island off Italy. Its hero is bombardier Yossarian, who is furious because thousands of people he hasn't even met are trying to kill him.

A: **"Catch-22"**
Q: What novel features the character Lieutenant Milo Minderbinder?
W: Lieutenant Milo Minderbinder is a dedicated entrepreneur. He even bombs his own airfield when the Germans make him a reasonable offer: cost plus 6 percent.

A: **Catskills, The**
Q: What mountains did Rip Van Winkle nod off in?
W: Rip Van Winkle is the central character of a short story by Washington Irving, first published in *The Sketch Book of Geoffrey Crayon, Gent*. Van Winkle was a ne'er-do-well in a village in the Hudson River Valley, who slept for 20 years after drinking from a keg. He awoke to find his wife dead, and to discover that no one in the village recognized him and that he had slept through the American Revolution.

A: **Cedars of Lebanon, The**
Q: What did 80,000 men cut to build Solomon's Temple?
W: King Solomon built the first temple of Jerusalem to house the ark holding the sacred "Tablets of the Law," which the Lord had given to Moses. It was built from the cedars of Lebanon, evergreen trees that attain great age and height. A celebrated grove on Mount Lebanon is called locally the "Cedars of the Lord."

A: **Charles Darwin**
Q: Who is the subject of Irving Stone's *The Origin*?
W: *The Origin* is a biographical novel about Charles Darwin. Irving Stone's other subjects have included Michelangelo, Van Gogh, and Freud.

A: **Charles Dickens**
Q: Who left *The Mystery of Edwin Drood* unfinished at his death?
W: *The Mystery of Edwin Drood*, Dickens' 15th novel, is about the murder of a nephew by his uncle, who reviews his own career in a condemned cell as though it were somebody else's. The uncle was to learn the utter needlessness of his act soon after its commission, and was to be discovered by means of a gold ring found uncorroded in quicklime.

A: **Charles Dickens**
Q: Who wrote: "Darkness was cheap, and Scrooge liked it?"
W: This is from Charles Dickens' *The Christmas Carol*, the story of Ebenezer Scrooge, an old miser and survivor of the partnership of Scrooge and Marley. On Christmas Eve Marley's ghost visits Scrooge to tell him that he will be visited by three ghosts who will give him the chance to escape Marley's fate—wandering around the world in chains.

ART AND LITERATURE

A: **Charles Lindbergh**
Q: Who was *Time's* first Man of the Year for 1927?
W: Charles Lindbergh created a world sensation when he flew solo across the Atlantic Ocean on May 20-21,1927. As *Time* magazine's first Man of the Year, he wrote an account of his flight with Fitzhugh Green. It was entitled *We*, which referred to Lindbergh and his plane, *The Spirit of St. Louis.*

A: **Charles Lindbergh's**
Q: Whose 1954 Pulitzer Prize-winning autobiography was titled *The Spirit of St. Louis?*
W: Besides *We*, the account of Lindbergh's first solo flight across the Atlantic, he also wrote *Of Flight and Life* in 1948 and his autobiography *The Spirit of St. Louis* in 1953, which was awarded the Pulitzer Prize.

A: **Charles M. Schulz**
Q: Who wrote *Charlie Brown, Snoopy and Me?*
W: Charles Monroe Schulz began his career lettering cartoons for a religious publication. He continued as an art instructor and cartoonist, with his now famous *Peanuts* cartoon making its debut on Oct. 2, 1950. Drawn from childhood memories, Peanuts, though unnoticed at first, has become the most successful comic feature of all time.

A: **Charlie Chan**
Q: What detective lives on Punchbowl Hill and has 11 children?
W: Considered the best detective on the Honolulu Police Force, Chan is very stout, with ivory-tinted skin and the chubby cheeks of a baby. His hair is black and closely cut. The Chinese-Hawaiian-American sleuth wears Western clothes but speaks broken English. He is considered lovable by all who know him.

A: *Charly*
Q: What film was inspired by Daniel Keyes' novel *Flowers for Algernon?*
W: *Charly* was the 1968 film for which Cliff Robertson won an Academy Award. It is the tale of a mentally retarded baker who becomes a genius after submitting to a new surgical technique.

A: **Chester Gould**
Q: What cartoonist created a two-way wrist radio?
W: Chester Gould devoted most of his life since 1931 to his creation *Dick Tracy*. He spent a great deal of time in research with the Chicago police as well as with the crime laboratories of Northwestern University. This research was revealed in "Crime Stoppers," small vignettes designed to draw attention to some small facet of of police procedure or crime prevention inserted near the cartoon's title in the Sunday paper.

A: *The Children's Hour*
Q: What Lillian Hellman play sends rumors of lesbianism through a boarding school?
W: *The Children's Hour* was based on an actual case in Edinburgh. Tragedy resulted when a child at a boarding school maliciously started a rumor that the two heads of the school were lesbians. After an attempt to suppress the 1934 Hellman play, it was filmed successfully in 1936, without the lesbian theme.

A: **Chinese**
Q: What nationality was Aladdin?
W: Aladdin was a boy in the *Arabian Nights* who was able to cause one genie to appear whenever he rubbed a magic lamp and another to appear whenever he rubbed a magic ring.

A: *A Christmas Carol*
Q: What book did Dickens call "a ghostly little book, to raise the ghost of an idea?"
W: Ebenezer Scrooge is visited by three spirits who offer him a last chance to escape his life of avarice. With the Ghost of Christmas Past he sees his boyhood. The Ghost of Christmas Present takes him to the homes of his nephew and his clerk, Bob Cratchit. The Ghost of Christmas Yet to Come shows Scrooge his own death.

A: **Christopher Robin**
Q: Who had a teddy bear named Winnie-the-Pooh?
W: The Pooh stories tell of the adventures of the little boy Christopher Robin and his animal friends. Winnie-the-Pooh is a bear who is fond of eating honey and hasn't many brains; Piglet is his close friend; Elyore is the melancholy donkey; and Rabbitt, Kanga, and Baby Roo are other forest friends.

A: **Cinderella**
Q: Who was Anastasia and Drizella's stepsister?
W: Anastasia and Drizella Tremaine were Cinderella's stepsisters in the cartoon feature movie by Walt Disney. Their voices were by Lucille Bliss and Rhoda Williams, respectively.

A: **Cinderella**
Q: What children's tale contains the line: "Come, Cinderslut, and hold this skein of wool for me?"
W: This line is typical of the unkindness and degradation that the wicked and lazy stepmother and her two daughters showed Cinderella.

A: **Clifford Irving**
Q: Who was imprisoned for faking Howard Hughes's autobiography?
W: McGraw Hill and *Life* magazine announced in December 1971 that Clifford Michael Irving was writing an authorized autobiography of Howard R. Hughes, American billionaire and aviator. On Jan. 7, 1972, Hughes himself in his first interview to the press in 15 years, by phone from Paradise Island, Nassau, squashed Irving's claim. Within a month, Irving confessed his hoax and subsequently went to prison for a short term.

A: **Cocaine**
Q: What drug did Sherlock Holmes take at the start of his career?
W: When tall, slender, hawk-nosed Sherlock Holmes was considering sharing an apartment with Dr. John H. Watson, the two first aired their respective shortcomings. Holmes confessed that he gets in the dumps at times and doesn't open his mouth for days, smokes a vile tobacco, and conducts experiments with loathsome-smelling chemicals. He failed to mention, however, his affection for cocaine.

A: **Columbia's**
Q: What U.S. university's trustees award the Pulitzer Prize?
W: The Pulitzer Prize, named after its originator, newspaper reporter and publisher Joseph Pulitzer, is awarded "for the encouragement of public service, public morals, American Literature, and advancement of education." The prizes are made annually under the control of the School of Journalism at Columbia University and the university Trustees.

A: **comma, The**
Q: What is the most commonly-used punctuation mark?
W: The comma is a punctuation mark that is used to indicate separation in ideas or construction within a sentence. Unlike the period, it can be used a number of times within a sentence resulting in the comma being the most commonly used punctuation mark.

A: ***The Complete Scarsdale Diet***
Q: What diet book was named for a town in New York state?
W: *The Complete Scarsdale Diet* was written by Herman Tarnower, a distinguished cardiologist and internist at Scarsdale, New York, Medical Center. The book was written with Sinclair Baker and describes a diet that has helped many take off up to 20 pounds in 14 days. It was originally developed to enable Tarnower's overweight patients to reduce merely to survive. Yes, it's the same Tarnower who was shot and killed by his scorned lover, Jean Harris.

A: ***The Confessions of Nat Turner***
Q: What William Styron book is about a black preacher who leads a slave revolt?
W: The 1967 story of *The Confessions of Nat Turner* recreates the 1831 revolt of Virginia slaves led by an educated Negro minister who was dedicated to the destruction of the white man. Styron's novel won the 1968 Pulitzer Prize.

A: **Constance**
Q: What was Lady Chatterley's first name?
W: *Lady Chatterley's Lover*, a novel by D.H. Lawrence, has been one of the most controversial books of the 20th century. Lady Constance Chatterley is the wife of a British industrialist who is paralyzed below the waist by war wounds. She finds fulfillment in a sexual union with Mellors, her husband's gamekeeper.

A: **Cordelia**
Q: Who was King Lear's favorite daughter?
W: King Lear favors his youngest daughter, Cordelia. Endowed with her father's stubbornness, she refuses to flatter him as her sisters have done. In his adversity she returns to him with love and forgiveness, restoring to him his sanity and redeeming him from bitterness. Her untimely death brings about her father's death.

A: **Count of Monte Cristo, The**
Q: What count did Alexandre Dumas write about?
W: *The Count of Monte Cristo* is a swashbuckling, romantic tale of a young man's revenge on the people who had him unjustly condemned to prison. The hero, Edmon Dantes, escapes from prison through courage, cunning, and improbable events. On the island of Monte Cristo he discovers a fortune that enables him to plot his revenge.

A: **Craig Claiborne**
Q: Who's the food editor of *the New York Times*?
W: Craig Claiborne has been the food editor for *the New York Times* for over 25 years. He was influenced by the southern cooking of his home state, Mississippi; by the exotic dishes of Casablanca that he tasted as a Yeoman in the Navy; and by the Professional School of The Swiss Hotelkeepers Association, where he studied cooking.

A: ***The Crash of '79***
Q: What financial collapse did Paul Erdman write about?
W: Paul Erdman is an American writer of financial crime stories and ex-president of a Swiss bank. He was tried in absentia in Switzerland and sentenced to eight years imprisonment after $40 million of depositors' funds were illegally used by some of his employees for speculation in commodity futures. His best work, *The Crash of '79*, is a frighteningly topical and realistic story about oil and the demise of the west.

A: **Croquet**
Q: What game does the Queen of Hearts order Alice to play?
W: When Alice can see the obvious order and logic in absurdity, she accepts politely and with interest the part allotted to her. While playing croquet with the queen in Wonderland, she is puzzled by the way her flamingo mallet behaves, but is willing to play because the game clearly has rules, strange as they are.

A: *The Crucible*
Q: What Arthur Miller play has the 1692 Salem witch trials as its setting?
W: *The Crucible*, a 1953 play by Arthur Miller, deals with the Salem witchcraft trials of 1692 and the question of freedom of conscience. There are parallels to the McCarthyism era in American during the early 1950s.

A: C.S. Forester
Q: Who created Horatio Hornblower?
W: Cecil Scott Forester, biographer and novelist, was an English writer who settled in California as a member of the British Information Service in 1940. He is best known for his novels about Horatio Hornblower, which follow the hero from midshipman to admiral in the British navy.

A: Curds and whey
Q: What was Little Miss Muffet eating when she sat on her tuffet?
W: Curds are the coagulated portion of milk, from which cheese is made. Whey is the clear, straw-colored liquid that separates from the curd when milk is curdled. Now, what's a tuffet?

A: Curfew
Q: What English word comes from the Old French *covrefeu*, meaning "cover fire?"
W: This term is from the French word *coubre-feu*, *covrir* means "to cover" and *feu* means "fire." Originally, in Europe in the Middle Ages, a bell was rung indicating that

fires should be covered or extinguished at a fixed hour in the evening. It is now used to indicate a time in the evening beyond which children, or possibly others, may not appear in the streets. How many of you had a curfew of "when the street lights come on?"

A: Cyclops
Q: Who is the one-eyed giant of Greek mythology?
W: According to Homer, the Cyclops is a race of one-eyed giants who live without laws or government in a distant country. In the *Odyssey* they make thunderbolts for Zeus and are skilled craftsmen who work in the forge of Hephaestus. The Greeks also credited them with making the walls found in pre-Greek cities.

D

A: Dagwood Bumstead
Q: Who did Blondie Boopadoo marry?
W: *Blondie*, created in 1930 by Murat (Chic) Young, began with Blondie Boopadoop, a bird-brained flapper, pursued by Dagwood Bumstead, playboy and son of a railroad tycoon. In 1933 Blondie married Dagwood, who was promptly disinherited by his father. Blondie became the devoted wife, mother, and affectionate companion, as well as the actual head of the Bumstead household. She often had to rescue Dagwood from the many jams he got into.

A: Damon Runyon
Q: What writer-journalist made his mark describing colorful Broadway and underworld characters?
W: Damon Runyon, born in 1884 in Kansas, wrote a column for the Hearst syndicate from 1918 until his death in 1946. Many of his stories about Broadway characters appeared in the *Saturday Evening Post* and other popular magazines. His style, so individual that it is often referred to as "Runyonesque", relies upon Broadway slang, outrageous metaphor, and the constant use of the present tense.

A: Dan Rather
Q: What TV journalist wrote *The Camera Never Blinks*?
W: CBS correspondent Dan Rather was known to millions of TV viewers as a co-editor of "60 Minutes." In his 1977 book, *The Camera Never Blinks* he brings alive the fascinating world of the TV reporter. Not only does he tell the behind-the-scenes stories of recent stormy events, but he also gives his insightful views on such vital topics as checkbook journalism.

ART AND LITERATURE

A: **Dashiell Hammett**
Q: Who wrote *The Maltese Falcon*?
W: Dashiel Hammett is best known as the creator of the "hard-boiled" detective story. In *The Maltese Falcon*, published in 1930, he created his most famous sleuth, Sam Spade.

A: *David Copperfield*
Q: What Dickens novel has David carrying the message "Barkis is willin" to Peggy?
W: When David Copperfield fails to satisfy his stepfather in the learning of his lessons, he is beaten and imprisoned in his room before being sent away to a boarding school. The carrier who takes David to the school, Mr. Barkis, is struck by the devoted servant of David's mother and sends her the message "Barkis is willin" by David. Clara Peggotty accepts Barkis' marriage proposal.

A: **David Niven**
Q: What actor wrote *The Moon's a Balloon*?
W: *The Moon's a Balloon* and *Bring on the Empty Horses* are the two best-selling autobiographies of English actor David Niven. His best acting performances were in *Bachelor Mother*, *A Matter of Life and Death*, *Around the World in 80 Days*, and *Separate Tables* for which he won an Academy Award.

A: *Day of the Triffids, The*
Q: What John Wyndham novel features triffids killing humans?
W: "The Day of the Triffids" is a 1951 science fiction novel by John Wyndham, the pen name of John Beynon Harris. This fantastic story is a gripping account of how mobile and deadly plants threaten a population blinded by a radiation storm. It was filmed by Security Pictures in 1963.

A: *Death of a Salesman*
Q: What play recounts the last hours of Willy Loman?

W: *Death of a Salesman*; winner of the 1949 Pulitzer Prize for Drama, is Arthur Miller's best known and most important problem play. It challenges the American values concerning success held by the aging Willy Loman. Fired, Willy tries to understand why he has failed as a traveling salesman, husband, and father. Still holding onto false values of success that have both sustained and destroyed him, Willy Loman ultimately commits suicide.

A: **Deerslayer, The**
Q: What was the James Fenimore Cooper character Natty Bumppo also known as?
W: In *The Deerslayer* Natty Bumppo, called Deerslayer, is a young hunter. In *The Last of the Mohicans*, as Hawkeye, he is a frontier scout. In the *Pathfinder*, as Pathfinder, he is a frontier scout in his prime. In *The Pioneer*, Natty, called Leatherstocking, is a 71 year old woodsman, and in *The Prairie* Natty is an old independent woodsman of 82.

A: *Delilah*
Q: Who betrayed Samson to the Philistines?
W: Delilah was Samson's Philistine mistress who betrayed him to the Philistines by cutting off his hair while he was asleep, thus depriving him of his strength

A: *Deliverance*
Q: What James Dickey novel tells the story of an ill-fated canoe trip?
W: *Deliverance*, Dickey's first novel, is the story of four men who embark on a three-day canoe trip down a particularly wild section of a river in the South. The canoe trip turns into a nightmare of horror and murder. The leader of the group must call upon all his resources to try to achieve deliverance.

A: **Della Street**
Q: Who turned down five marriage proposals from Perry Mason?
W: In *The Case of the Stuttering Bishop*, Della says, "I wouldn't want to live unless I could work for a living." Knowing that Perry Mason would not permit his wife to work, she has, on five separate occasions, refused his proposal of marriage. So much for Perry's enlightenment.

A: **Della Street**
Q: Who took dictation from Perry Mason?
W: Della Street, the most famous secretary in fiction, was steadfastly loyal to Perry Mason. She risked her life and freedom on his behalf. She was arrested five times while performing her job.

A: **Denmark**
Q: What country is home to Shakespeare's Hamlet?
W: Hamlet, the Prince of Denmark, is generally agreed to be Shakespeare's most fascinating hero. Torn by grief for his dead father and disappointment in the conduct of his beloved mother, Hamlet desires revenge from his villainous uncle, who has murdered Hamlet's father and married his mother. Hamlet gains revenge but loses his life.

A: **Desdemona**
Q: Who is Othello's wife?
W: Desdemona is an innocent idealistic girl who gives her love completely to her warrior husband. Othello becomes unjustly jealous of Desdemona and his loyal lieutenant, Cassio. After killing his wife with his own hands, he learns of her innocence and executes himself.

A: **"Desiderata"**
Q: What work begins: "Go placidly amid the noise and haste, & Remember what peace there may be in silence"?
W: "Desiderata" is the 1927 philosophical poem by Max

ART AND LITERATURE

Ehrmann. Its last three lines are: "With all its sham, drudgery and broken dreams, it is still a beautiful world. Be cheerful. Strive to be happy."

A: D.H. Lawrence
Q: Who wrote *Sons and Lovers*?
W: *Sons and Lovers*, published in 1913 when Lawrence was in his twenties, is to some extent autobiographical. It is the story of the emotional crises of a son growing to manhood in the Nottingham coalfields amid the conflict between a possessive and strong mother and a weak coalminer father.

A: D.H. Lawrence
Q: Who wrote *Women in Love*?
W: David Herbert Lawrence was born in Eastwood in the Nottingham coalfields. His father was a miner, his mother a former schoolteacher who set up as a small shopkeeper. His most famous works are *Sons and Lovers*, *Women in Love*, *The Rainbow*, and *Lady Chatterley's Lover*.

A: dish, The
Q: When the cow jumped over the moon, what ran away with the spoon?
W: In this nursery rhyme the cat was paired with the fiddle, and the little dog laughed to see such sport.

A: Dogpatch
Q: Where did Evil-Eye Fleagle, General Bullmoose, and Tobacco Rhoda all live?
W: These are all characters in the comic strip *L'il Abner*. They live in Dogpatch along with Abner, Daisy Mae and Pansy Yokum, and Lucifer Ornamental Yokum.

A: Dogpatch
Q: Where do L'il Abner and Daisy Mae live?
W: L'il Abner, who is 19 years old, lives in Dogpatch, somewhere in the Appalachian Mountains, with his wife Daisy Mae Scraggs and his Mammy and Pappy Yokum.

A: *Dogs of War, The*
Q: What Frederick Forsyth novel chronicles the toppling of an African government by mercenaries?
W: In *The Dogs of War* mining magnate Sir James Manson schemes a coup d'etat in Zangara, a small West African dictatorship where a secret source of platinum lies waiting to be exploited. He enlists the aid of Cat Shannon, an Anglo-Irishman, late of Nigeria and the Congo. Author Forsyth experienced what he wrote about when he was on assignment for the BBC during the Biafran War.

A: *Don Quixote*
Q: What book opens: "At a certain village in La Mancha, which I shall not name..."?
W: *Don Quixote* is Miguel de Cervantes Shavedra's great Spanish novel, a classic of world satire. It describes the adventures of Don Quixote who imagines himself a knight. The novel served as the model for the popular Broadway musical, *Man of La Mancha*.

A: dove and raven, A
Q: What two birds did Noah send out from the Ark?
W: When the waters receded enough after the "deluge," the ark was able to rest on top of Mount Araat. Noah let loose a raven, which did not return. He then sent forth a dove, which returned because it could find no place to perch. On its third flight it returned with an olive branch in its mouth.

A: Dracula
Q: Who was Bram Stoker's most infamous character?
W: Bram Stoker's *Dracula*, the most famous vampire story ever written, was published in 1897 and became an instant success. It later became a film classic and stage hit, with Bela Lugosi in the title role.

A: Dr. Benjamin Spock
Q: Who wrote the *Common Sense Book of Baby and Child Care*?
W: Spock, an American doctor, became famous for his books on child care. His best known book, *Common Sense Book of Baby and Child Care*, was translated into more than 25 languages.

A: Dr. Dolittle
Q: What Hugh Lofting character lived in Puddleby-on-the-Marsh and had a pet duck named Dab Dab?
W: Hugh Lofting was the creator of Dr. Dolittle, a well-known character in children's fiction. He first wrote about the doctor in letters to his children during World War I, when he served in the British Army. Because *The Story of Dr. Dolittle* won such popularity when it was published in 1920, Lofting continued the adventures of Dr. Dolittle and his animal friends in *The Voyages of Doctor Dolittle*.

A: Dr. Frankenstein
Q: Who created the monster in Mary Shelley's novel *Frankenstein*?
W: *Frankenstein*, which was written by Mary Shelley when she was 20, is the most famous Gothic story ever written. In the movie version Boris Karloff played the monster, although he had, up to that point, only had bit and character parts. Though he was not considered important enough to be invited to the world premiere, Karloff became a major star after the movie's release.

A: Dr. Seuss
Q: Who created Yertle the Turtle?
W: Dr. Seuss wrote delightful nonsense fantasies and accompanied them with his own illustrations. Other books by Seuss include *Horton Hatches the Egg*, *The Cat in the Hat*, and *Green Eggs and Ham*. Yertle the Turtle appears in *Yertle the Turtle and Other Stories* which consists of three fables about a dictator turtle, an envious young lady bird, and two animal braggarts.

A: Dr. Seuss
Q: What's the pen name of Theodor Geisel?
W: Seuss was his middle name!

A: Dr. Watson
Q: Who narrates the Sherlock Holmes stories?
W: The Sherlock Holmes stories make up the history of an amateur consulting detective of England, told by his friend and far less keen associate, Dr. John Watson. Watson believed that the affairs, if told at all, should be presented to the public as straightforward exercises in cold logic and deductive reasoning.

A: *Dr. Zhivago*
Q: What Boris Pasternak book sold 500,000 copies to become the fiction best-seller of 1958?
W: *Doctor Zhivago*, a novel by Russian Boris Pasternak, records the life of a physician and poet reminiscent of Pasternak himself. It is a tragic demonstation of how fragile the qualities of intimacy, poetry, and individuality can be in the wake of destructive historical forces such as the Russian Revolution. In 1965, *Dr. Zhivago* was created as a movie.

A: Dublin
Q: What city is the setting of James Joyce's novel *Ulysses*?
W: Joyce lived in poverty and obscurity until the 1922 publication of *Ulysses* made him one of the most celebrated novelists of the 1900s.

The adventures of his main character, Leopold Bloom, parallel the wanderings of Ulysses, the hero of the *Odyssey*. Bloom is ridiculed because he is both Jewish and has peculiar sexual tastes and because his wife is unfaithful.

A: Duke Ellington's
Q: Whose biography by Derek Jewell is titled *Duke*?
W: Derek Jewell's 1977 *Duke: The Portrait of Duke Ellington* is the biography of Edward Kennedy "Duke" Ellington, a composer, pianist, and orchestra leader. He is considered by many to be the most important figure in the history and evolution of jazz. Ellington wrote over 1,000 short pieces, with his first hit being the 1930 *Mood Indigo*.

A: Dulcinea
Q: Who was Don Quixote's imaginary love?
W: Don Quixote, the lean elderly hero of *Don Quixote*, is inflamed by a diet of romantic reading and thinks himself a knight. He sets out on his emaciated horse, Rosinante, to fight giants, rescue damsels, uplift the oppressed, and court the approval of his so-called lady, Dulcinea del Toboso.

A: Duncan Hines
Q: What gourmet wrote *Adventures in Good Eating*, a 1935 restaurant guide?
W: Duncan Hines, an American businessman and author, became an authority on eating and lodging establishments from his extensive traveling. His first book, *Adventures in Good Eating*, gave information on eating establishments. He continued to write books on similar subjects.

A: dustman, A
Q: What do the English call a garbageman?
W: In England, a dustman is a person whose job is to remove dirt and refuse. In folklore, the dustman is the genius of sleep, whose coming is marked by blinking and rubbing the eyes as if to remove dust.

A: E
Q: What letter accounts for one of every eight used in written English?
W: *E*, the fifth letter of the English alphabet, is called *epsilon* in the Greek alphabet. The Romans gave the capital *E* its present form. *E* is the most frequently used letter in books, newspapers, and other printed material in English.

A: "East is east and west is west"
Q: What precedes: "And never the twain shall meet?"
W: "Oh, east is east, and west is west, and never the twain shall meet," is a quote from Rudyard Kipling's "The Ballad of East and West."

A: *Ebony*
Q: What's the biggest-selling U.S. magazine aimed at a black audience?
W: *Ebony*, a general illustrated magazine for Black Americans, was created in Chicago in 1945 by John H. Johnson, later a black publishing leader. It was inspired by *Life*, the photojournalism magazine, and is similar in size and plan. Its opinions on racial issues are moderate.

A: Edgar Allan Poe
Q: Who wrote "The Purloined Letter?"
W: "The Purloined Letter" is usually regarded as the greatest of Poe's three detective stories. A woman of royal rank has been blackmailed by a cabinet minister; she appeals to the police and they to Poe's detective C. Auguste Dupin. After Dupin visits the blackmailer and finds the blackmail letter "hidden" where everyone can see it, he manages to retrieve the letter by substituting a facsimile.

A: Edgar Allan Poe
Q: Whose epitaph reads: "Quoth the Raven nevermore?"
W: Late in September 1849, Poe supposedly attended a birthday party in Baltimore, pledged his hostess in wine, and went on a spree. His whereabouts were unknown from then until October 3, when he was found in great distress. He was brought to the hospital and died without ever becoming completely conscious. He was buried Oct. 8, 1849.

A: Edgar Allan Poe
Q: Who's credited with writing the first detective story, "The Murders in the Rue Morgue?"
W: "The Murders in the Rue Morgue," if not the first detective story, certainly set the form. Poe made an attempt to solve a real crime in "The Mystery of Marie Roget" in 1842; he dismissed the crime itself as of no interest in "The Purloined Letter" in 1844.

A: Edgar Degas
Q: What French impressionist is famed for his paintings of ballet dancers?
W: Degas, son of a rich banker and a Creole mother, lived from 1834 to 1917. He originally painted portraits and compositions in a severely classical style. Later he turned to painting dancers, the races, town life and portraits in an environment, which established his reputation.

A: Edward G. Robinson's
Q: What actor's autobiography is titled *All My Yesterdays?*
W: This 1975 book was written by Edward G. Robinson and Leonard Spigelfass. Robinson became one of the major figures of Hollywood films of the 1930s. Although he specialized in gangster roles, he was also adept at comedy or benevolent character roles. His most important films include *Little Caesar*, *Double Indemnity* and *Key Largo*.

A: Eeyore
Q: What's the name of the old gray donkey in *Winnie-the-Pooh?*

W: Eeyore is a friend of Pooh. In the A.A. Milne story, "Eeyore Has a Birthday," the old donkey is quite gloomy on his birthday until Pooh and friends bring him presents and cheer him up.

A: E. Howard Hunt
Q: What Watergate figure was the author of numerous spy novels?
W: For his part in Watergate, Hunt was originally convicted of burglary and sentenced to two and a half years in prison. He had served 21 years in the CIA, not only in the U.S. but also in Paris, Vienna, and Latin America. All of his experiences were used as material for his spy stories, of which he has written 43 under various pseudonyms.

A: Eight
Q: How many reindeer pull Santa's sleigh?
W: In Clement Clarke Moore's poem "A Visit from St. Nicholas" (1823), Santa's sleigh was pulled by Dasher, Dancer, Prancer, Vixen, Comet, Cupid, Donner, and Blitzen.

A: Eight
Q: How many people took refuge on Noah's Ark?
W: Noah's ark measured 300 by 50 by 30 cubits (a cubit equaling 18 inches). It carried eight human passengers: Noah and his wife; their three sons Ham Shem and Japheth; and the wife of each son.

A: Eight o'clock
Q: What time does Wee Willie Winkie run through the town?
W: He "runs upstairs and downstairs in his nightgown, Rapping at the windows, crying through the lock, Are the children in their beds, for now it's eight o'clock."

A: Eleanor Roosevelt's
Q: Whose biography is titled *Eleanor: The Lonely Years?*
W: Eleanor Roosevelt, niece of Theodore Roosevelt and wife of Franklin D. Roosevelt, was probably the most active First Lady in American history and won fame for her humanitarian work. She worked with young people and the underprivileged and fought for equal rights for minority groups. Her books include *This Is My Story*, *This I Remember*, *On My Own*, and *Tomorrow Is Now*.

A: elephant, An
Q: What kind of animal is Babar?
W: The stories of Babar were originally written and illustrated by Jean de Brunhoff. After his death, his son Laurent continued the saga. Babar the elephant escaped from the hunter who shot his mother and fled to town. He was befriended by a rich old lady who knew he was longing for a new suit. Soon the mature, well-dressed Babar decided to return to his homeland where he became "king of the elephants."

A: Elizabeth Taylor
Q: What actress holds the record for the most appearances on the cover of *Life?*
W: Elizabeth Taylor, a violet-eyed actress, achieved stardom with her fourth Hollywood movie *National Velvet*. She has gained as much attention for her glamorous personal

life and numerous marriages as for her acting ability. Her best acting performances were in *A Place in the Sun*, *Cat on a Hot Tin Roof*, *Butterfield 8*, and *Who's Afraid of Virginia Woolf*.

A: **Ella**
Q: What was Cinderella's real name?
W: Ella's cruel stepmother and her two stepsisters made her wear rags, sweep the hearth, and sleep in the kitchen, so she was always covered with soot. Thus they came to call her "cinder Ella."

A: **Emerald City, The**
Q: Where did The Wizard of Oz live?
W: The Wizard of Oz, an insignificant old man with a bald head and a wrinkled face was blown to Oz from Omaha in a balloon and taken for a powerful king by the inhabitants of Oz. Toto, Dorothy's dog, discovers the "man" behind the "Wizard" when he draws back the curtain on the man and the machine he uses to create a "bigger than life" image.

A: **"Emperor's New Clothes, The"**
Q: What Hans Christian Andersen story has a monarch bamboozled by the tailor?
W: The "clothes horse" emperor, always wanting new clothes that are finer and finer, is taken in by two rogues who promise they will make him a special outfit that only the wise and pure of heart can see. There are of course no clothes at all, but everyone goes along with the charade for fear of looking stupid until a little child declares that the king is not wearing any clothes. Out of the mouths of babes!

A: **end, The**
Q: What does the term "30" mean to a newspaper editor?
W: "30" is a symbol that means the end of a newspaper story: "and that's 30." The number was used as the title for a 1959 Jack Webb and William Conrad movie.

A: **England**
Q: What country is the setting of John Fowle's *The French Lieutenant's Woman*?
W: The setting of *The French Lieutenant's Woman* is the village of Lyme Regis on Dorset's Lyme Bay. The major characters in the love triangle are Charles Smithson, his fiancee Ernestina Freeman, and Sarah Woodruff, who was deserted after a brief affair with a French naval officer a short time before the story begins.

A: **English**
Q: What language evolved from Latin, Norman-French and Anglo-Saxon?
W: The English language is used by over 400 million people in almost every part of the world. The only language spoken by more people is Chinese.

A: *Equus*
Q: What Peter Shaffer play is about a boy who blinds six horses?
W: *Equus* examines the relationship between an analyst and one of his patients, a young boy named Alan Strang, who has committed an extraordinary and grotesque crime. He has speared the eyes of six horses in a riding stable where he worked as a groom. In his attempt to understand why this has happened, the analyst discovers the boy has almost a religious obsession with the horses.

A: **Erle Stanley Gardner's**
Q: Whose novels all begin with: *The Case of the...*?
W: Erle Stanley Gardner wrote more than 100 detective novels under his own name and under the pen name of A.A. Faire. In most of his stories, the lawyer Perry Mason brilliantly solves a mystery. The first Mason story, "The Case of the Velvet Claws," was also Gardner's first novel.

A: **Erle Stanley Gardner's**
Q: Whose first book was titled *The Case of the Velvet Claws*?
W: This 1933 novel was rejected by several publishers before it was accepted by William Morrow and Company, the firm that subsequently published the hardcover edition of all Gardner's books. Thayer Hobson, then President of Morrow, suggested that Perry Mason, the hero of the book, become a series character.

A: **Ernest Hemingway**
Q: What American writer used Nick Adams as the narrator in his short stories?
W: Nick Adams was the narrator of Ernest Hemingway's short stories. James Dean was to have played Nick Adams in Hemingway's TV production of "The Battler," but because of his death was replaced by Paul Newman.

A: **Ernest Hemingway**
Q: What author landed a 468-pound marlin without harness in the early 1930s?
W: Hemingway's last major work, *The Old Man and the Sea*, was also a story of man's struggle with a marlin. It describes the fight that an old fisherman has to catch a giant marlin, only to have it eaten by sharks after he lands it. Hemingway received the 1954 Nobel Prize for Literature for this work.

A: **Ernest Hemingway**
Q: Who wrote *A Farewell to Arms*?
W: *A Farewell to Arms*, a pessimistic novel that questions many traditional values of western society, is a tragic story of an American Army Lieutenant who is "defeated" in love and by World War I.

A: **Ernest Hemingway**
Q: Who wrote 1935's *Green Hills of Africa*?
W: The nonfictional work *Green Hills of Africa* was based on Hemingway's adventures on a big game safari in Kenya and Tanganyika. This African experience also provided material for the short story "The Snows of Kilimanjaro."

ART AND LITERATURE

A: Ernest Hemingway
Q: Who wrote "Across the River and into the Trees?"
W: This 1950 novel, which was more widely attacked than praised, used a Venetian locale to tell a story of love and war.

A: Ernest Hemingway
Q: What writer was nicknamed Papa?
W: The nickname "Papa" was given to him by Marlene Dietrich.

A: Errol Flynn's
Q: Whose autobiography is titled *My Wicked, Wicked Ways*?
W: This 1959 book is the story of Leslie Thomas Flynn, better known as Errol Flynn. Flynn was known principally for his roles as a swashbuckling romantic hero. *Captain Blood* and *The Sea Hawk* are two of his adventure films.

A: Erskine Caldwell
Q: Who wrote *Tobacco Road* and *God's Little Acre*?
W: *Tobacco Road* describes the physical hunger of Jeeter, the sexual appetites of Ellie May and sister Bessie, and the sterile marriage of Pearl and Tom as they try to survive on land made sterile by the cultivation of tobacco. Ty Ty Walden, the digger after gold, is a character in *God's Little Acre*. Considered by some to be a masterpiece, it was originally censored as being comic pornography.

A: Esperanto
Q: What's the best known artificial international language?
W: Esperanto was invented by Ludwig Zamenhof, a Russian scholar, and was published in 1887. Its vocabulary consists of words common to every important European language and is spelled more or less phonetically. The language was named for Dr. Esperanto (Dr. Hopeful), the pen name of the inventor.

A: Eugene O'Neill's
Q: Whose autobiographical masterpiece was entitled *Long Day's Journey into Night*?
W: Eugene Gladstone O'Neill was the first native-born American to achieve international prominence as a dramatist. He wrote more than 45 plays ranging in length from single scenes to some of the most monumental dramas of the 20th century. *Beyond The Horizon*, *Anna Christie* and *Long Day's Journey Into Night* all won Pulitzer Prizes for O'Neill.

A: Exempli gratia, or for example
Q: What does the abbreviation *e.g.* stand for?
W: The Latin *exempli gratia* means "by way of example." It is abbreviated *e.g.* or *ex*. Other derivations of the words are *exemplar*, *exemplary*, *exemplification*, and *exemplify*, all indicating a model or example.

A: Exodus
Q: What Leon Uris novel recounts the birth of Israel?
W: Leon Uris, an American novelist and screenwriter, is famous for his massive best-selling adventure novels in which a fictitious protagonist is placed in a semifactual historical context. *Exodus* is about the founding of the Israeli state; *Armageddon* is about the Berlin Airlift; and *Topaz* concerns the Cuban missile crisis.

A: Exorcist, The
Q: What Peter Blatty novel recounts the horrors of Regan MacNeil's possession by the devil?
W: The idea for *The Exorcist* came to William Peter Blatty first in 1950. Since then he has read every book in English on the subject. He spent almost a year writing the novel. His particular interest is in the fact that psychiatrically we know no more about the phenomenon of possession that we did in 1921.

F

A: F. Lee Bailey's
Q: Whose autobiography is titled *The Defense Never Rests?*
W: F. Lee Bailey has become one of the best known criminal lawyers of his day due in part to his aggressive courtroom tactics. In 1977 he represented Patricia Hearst at her trial for involvement in the bank robbery conducted by the Symbionese Liberation Army.

A: F. Scott Fitzgerald
Q: Who created Nicole in *Tender is the Night?*
W: *Tender is the Night* is a beautifully written account of the general decline of a few glamorous Americans in Europe. The book fail-

ed because readers during the Great Depression of the 1930s were not interested in jazz age "parties."

A: F. Scott Fitzgerald
Q: What Jazz Age writer said: "I have drunk too much, and that is certainly slowing me up?"
W: Critics generally agree that Fitzgerald's early success damaged his personal life and marred his literary production. His success led to extravagant living and a need for a large income, which probably contributed to Fitzgerald's alcoholism and the mental breakdown of his wife Zelda.

A: F. Scott Fitzgerald
Q: Who was the chief spokesman for the "Lost Generation?"
W: The "Lost Generation" refers to the generation of men and women who came to maturity during World War I. It specifically refers to their experiences in the war itself and to their rootlessness and disillusionment. Gertrude Stein is said to have coined the term in conversation with Ernest Hemingway, who together with F. Scott Fitzgerald wrote novels considered to typify the attitudes of the lost generation.

A: *Fahrenheit 451*
Q: What Ray Bradbury novel is named for the temperature at which paper catches fire?
W: *Fahrenheit 451* describes a future world in which all books are banned. The hero is a member of the Fire Brigade who first questions the regime, then rebels totally, incinerating the fire chief instead of the books. He joins a rural community whose members are memorizing a book in order to preserve it.

A: Faith, hope, charity
Q: What are the three cardinal virtues?
W: Hey, there are four! The four cardinal virtues are justice, temperance, prudence, and fortitude. The Christian Scholastic Moralists added the three *theological*

virtues of faith, hope, and charity or love. The latter three are sometimes called the Supernatural or Christian Virtues, the former are the Natural Virtues. All seven are in opposition to the Seven Deadly Sins.

A: "Fall of the House of Usher, The"
Q: What Edgar Allen Poe tale has a friend visiting Roderick Usher in his ancestral home?
W: "The Fall of the House of Usher," which contains the poem "The Haunted Palace," describes the visit of a childhood companion to a sick friend, Roderick Usher. Usher, who has not seen his friend for many years, summons him to the gloomy House of Usher, where he and his twin Madeline, the only surviving members of the family, live. Both Usher and Madeline suffer from serious physical and nervous maladies.

A: Falstaff
Q: Who's the clown in Shakespeare's *Henry IV* and *The Merry Wives of Windsor*?
W: Sir John Falstaff is one of William Shakespeare's most famous comic characters. He is the bragging self-indulgent knight who first appeared in the two parts of *Henry IV*. He was so popular with audiences that Shakespeare wrote *The Merry Wives of Windsor* to feature him.

A: *Fanny*
Q: What Erica Jong novel is about the adventures of a lusty 18th century Englishwoman?
W: As an infant, Fanny Hackabout Jones is discovered on the steps of a great house in Wiltshire. She is raised by Lord and Lady Bellars but forced "by circumstances" to run away to London to seek her fortune. Before long she ventures around the world. The novel *Fanny* describes the adventures of this 18th century woman who has contemporary aspirations.

A: Father Time
Q: What mythical figure carries an hourglass and a scythe?
W: Father Time was time personified, especially in old almanacs. He appeared as an old man, bald and bearded, holding a scythe and water jar (or sometimes an hourglass).

A: *Fear of Flying*
Q: What Erica Jong novel deals with Isadora Wing's fear?
W: Isadora Wing is a compulsive daydreamer, a seeker of saviors and psychiatrists, and an author of a book of supposedly erotic poems. She has a phobia about flying but does not allow that fear to keep her off aiplanes. She forces herself to keep traveling, at the risk of her marriage, in pursuit of her liberation.

A: fear of the Lord, The
Q: What does the Bible call the beginning of wisdom?
W: This is from the Bible, Proverbs 9:10 "The fear of the Lord is the beginning of wisdom; and the knowledge of the holy is understanding."

A: Fearless Fosdick
Q: What dutiful detective does L'il Abner worship?
W: "Fearless Fosdick," Al Capp's strip-within-a strip, is a parody of the cartoon strip *Dick Tracy*. Fosdick was not only Abner's favorite "comical paper" character but his also heroic "ideal."

A: Feedback
Q: What's the shortest word in English that contains the letters A,B,C,D,E and F?
W: Funk and Wagnalls describes *feedback* as the return of part of the output of a system into the input for purposes of modification and control of the output. And, we can think of no shorter word to make with these six letters!

ART AND LITERATURE

A: **Felix Leiter**
Q: Who is James Bond's CIA contact?
W: In the movies, Felix Leiter was played by R.K. Van Nutter in *Thunderball*, Cec Linder in *Goldfinger*, David Hedison in *Live and Let Die*, Jack Lord in *Dr. No*, and Norman Burton in *Diamonds are Forever*.

A: *Fellowship of the Ring, The*
Q: What was the first part of J.R.R. Tolkien's *Lord of the Rings* trilogy?
W: Tolkien, who was profoundly interested in philosophy, created the environment of Middle Earth within which the Elvish language that he had devised could exist. With this created world he set *The Hobbit* and his trilogy consisting of *The Fellowship of the Ring, The Two Towers*, and *The Return of the Rings*.

A: **Fifteen cents**
Q: What was the price of the first issue of *TV Guide*?
W: Costing 15 cents in 1953 when it was founded in Radnor, Pennsylvania, this weekly magazine gives the listings of TV programs for the week along with short articles on current popular television topics and personalities. It is printed in 79 separate editions, and over 17 million copies are distributed each week.

A: **fifth step, The**
Q: Where is the key hidden in the play *Dial M for Murder*?
W: The play, written by Frederick Knott, is a mystery about an ingenious murder conceived as the perfect crime. This story of a man plotting his wife's murder and the police investigation following was made into a 1954 film directed by Alfred Hitchcock and starring Grace Kelly, Ray Milland, and others.

A: **Fifty cents**
Q: How much did the first issue of *Playboy* cost?

W: *Playboy*, the "entertainment for men" magazine, was founded by Hugh Marston Hefner in December 1953. The Big Bunny, which appears on every cover, was designed by Arthur Paul. Marilyn Monroe was the first playmate of the month.

A: **Five**
Q: How many lines are there in a limerick?
W: A limerick takes its name from the city of Limerick, Ireland. Although no one knows how or where the form originated, it was made popular by Edward Lear's *A Book of Nonsense*. The first two lines rhyme with the fifth, and the third and fouth lines also rhyme.

A: **Five cents**
Q: How much did Lucy Van Pelt originally charge for psychiatric sessions?
W: This is from the cartoon strip *Peanuts* with Linus and Snoopy. Remember the poster? Psychiatrist In 5 cents; Psychiatrist Out.

A: **Flo**
Q: What's the name of Andy Capp's wife?
W: Flo, or Florrie, is the name of Andy Capp's wife, in the comic strip. They call each other "Pet."

A: **Florence**
Q: Where are the Pitti and Uffizi art galleries?
W: Uffizi Palace, a famous palace in Florence, Italy, contains one of the finest art collections in the world. Built between 1560 and 1576, it was originally used by the Grand Dukes of Tuscany as a government office. Also housing a fine collection of paintings is the Pitti, the largest palace in Florence and once a home of Italian kings.

A: **Florence**
Q: What city is graced by Michelangelo's *David*?

W: Michelangelo's marble statue *David* was commissioned in 1501 by the authorities of the Cathedral of Florence. For political reasons it was erected in front of the main entrance to Palazzo Vecchio, instead of the Cathedral. In 1873, the statue was moved to Galleria dell' Accademia in Florence. A copy now stands in front of the Pallazzo Vecchio.

A: **flying school, A**
Q: What kind of school did Pussy Galore run?
W: Pussy Galore, Goldfinger's lesbian accomplice, ran a flying school for female pilots. In the 1964 movie *Goldfinger*, Pussy was played by Honor Blackman.

A: *For Whom the Bell Tolls*
Q: What Ernest Hemingway novel focuses on the Republican side of the Spanish Civil War?
W: *For Whom the Bell Tolls*, Hemingway's best sustained work since the 1920s, implies a return to the values of the western society. It describes the adventures of an American guerilla in combat and love during the Spanish Civil War

A: **Four**
Q: How many attended the March Hare's tea party?
W: The table for the tea party in *Alice in Wonderland* was set out under a tree in front of the house. Attending the party were the March Hare, the Hatter, the Dormouse, and Alice.

A: Four
Q: How many ghosts appear to Scrooge in Dickens's *A Christmas Carol?*
W: The four ghosts who appear to Scrooge are the chained ghost of his dead partner, Jacob Marley; the Ghost of Christmas Past; the Ghost of Christmas Present; and the Ghost of Christmas Yet to Come.

A: Fourteen
Q: How many lines are there in a sonnet?
W: The sonnet, an enduringly popular and extemely flexible verse form with 14 lines, originated in 13th-century Italy. The sonnet has normally been written in the characteristic meter of the poet's language – with 11 syllables in Italian, 12 in French, and 10 in English.

A: fox, The
Q: What Aesop animal assumed the grapes he couldn't reach were sour anyway?
W: "The Fox and the Grapes" is the story of a fox who spies a tempting bunch of grapes hanging over a high branch on a hot summer day. After repeated attempts to reach them he finally gives up. The moral of the fable: "It is easy to scorn what you can't get."

A: *Frankenstein*
Q: What novel was written by Mary Shelley at the age of 19?
W: This novel by Mary Wollstonecraft Shelley was published in 1818 under the title *Frankenstein, or The Modern Prometheus*. It tells the story of a monster that has been created from parts of dead bodies by a scientist named Count Frankenstein.

A: French
Q: What was Paul Cezanne's nationality?
W: Cezanne, born in Aix en Provence, was the son of a well-to-do banker. He devoted himself entirely to painting at the age of 22. His original paintings tended to be clumsy and coarse in texture, painted with a palette-knife in dark colors. His later work was more controlled with more use of primary colors.

A: French
Q: What language was *Babar* written in?
W: Babar is the little elephant in a series of French children's books. They were written and illustrated from 1899 to 1937 by Jean de Brunhoff. They became very popular in the United States after being translated into English.

A: French poodle, A
Q: What was John Steinbeck's traveling companion Charley?
W: *Travels with Charley in Search of America* was one of the two works of nonfiction that Steinbeck wrote in the 1960s. It is an account of his travels across the U.S. in a camper with his French poodle, Charley.

A: French Revolution, The
Q: What revolution did the Scarlet Pimpernel show his colors in?
W: "The Scarlet Pimpernel" written by Baroness Orczy, is an adventure story of the French Revolution. The apparently foppish young Englishman, Sir Percy Blakeney, is discovered to be the daring Scarlet Pimpernel, rescuer of the distressed French aristocracy.

A: Friday
Q: What day did the rabbi sleep late, according to Harry Kemelman?
W: Harry Kemelman is an American writer of mystery stories, whose detective is a quietly thoughtful Boston Rabbi. In *Friday the Rabbi Slept Late*, Rabbi David Small is a suspect in the murder of a young woman whose body is found on the grounds of the temple. By practicing deductive reasoning, he exonerates himself.

A: Friedrich Nietzsche
Q: What German author first proposed the idea of the superman?
W: Friedrich Wilhelm Nietzsche was among the most influential figures of German philosophical thought. He formed the concept of "Superman," whose creative impulses were initiated by the "Will to Power," asserting that humans must live in the material world without their gods.

A: *From Here to Eternity*
Q: What's the first book in James Jones's World War II trilogy James
W: James Jones, an Illinois-born author, served in the Pacific with the army. His experiences furnished background for *From Here to Eternity*, a naturalistic novel about army life in Hawaii on the eve of the Pearl Harbor attack.

A: Fu Manchu
Q: Who was the sinister doctor of Sax Rohmer's novels?
W: Dr. Fu Manchu, the ultimate villain, is a Chinese master criminal of untold weath, intellect, and occult powers whose goal is world conquest. He is believed to be a Chinese noble descended from the Manchu Dynasty.

A: Galahad
Q:Who was Lancelot's son in Arthurian legend?
W: Galahad, the noblest and most vitrious knight in the legend of King Arthur's Round Table, was the illegitimate son of Sir Lancelot and Princess Elaine of Astolat. He was also supposedly the last descendent of Joseph of Arimathea, a follower of Christ.

A: Gary Gilmore's
Q:Whose story was told by Norman Mailer in *The Executioner's Song*?
W: Gary Gilmore was a convicted murderer who was put to death on Jan. 17, 1977, in front of a firing squad in Utah. He was the first person to be executed in the United States in ten years. Gilmore was the illegitimate grandson of magician Harry Houdini, and the subject of Norman Mailer's 1979 Pulitzer Prize winning book, *The Executioner's Song*.

A: Gary Trudeau
Q:Who created *Doonesbury*?
W: *Doonesbury* was originally created as *Bull Tales* in the *Yale Record* when Trudeau was an undergraduate. The strip moved up to the *Yale Daily News* where it attracted wide notice. Universal Press syndicate gave the feature its new title when it started distributing the strip nationally in 1969. In 1975 Garry Trudeau received the Pulitzer Prize for cartooning.

A: gate of Hades, The
Q:What gate does the three-headed dog Cerberus guard?
W: Cerberus is the three-headed hound that guarded the Greek underworld of Hades. He admitted anyone who wanted to enter but devoured those who tried to get out.

A: Gaylord
Q:What's the name of Broomhilda's buzzard buddy?
W: Broomhilda, from the comic strip of the same name, is a tame and even endearing creature despite her repulsive appearance. Her black magic sometimes misfires on her, and her spells, more often than not, do not work. Even her pet buzzard, Gaylord, seldom heeds her commands.

A: General Douglas MacArthur
Q:Who's the subject of William Manchester's book *American Caesar*?
W: William Manchester is a World War II combat veteran who later served as a foreign correspondent and war correspondent with the French Foreign Legion. Besides *American Caesar*, his biography of the legendary General MacArthur, he has also written biographies of the Rockefellers and John F. Kennedy.

A: Genesis
Q:What is the first book of the Old Testament?
W: Genesis, the first book of the Bible, comes from a Greek word meaning "birth" or "beginning". The first part of Genesis describes God's creation of the world and relates the stories of Adam and Eve in the Garden of Eden and of Cain and Abel. It then tells of the "deluge", or great flood, from which only Noah and his family escaped.

A: Geoffrey Chaucer
Q:Who wrote *The Canterbury Tales*?
W: Geoffrey Chaucer was an administrator and diplomat by vocation, who described 14th century life in his masterpiece *Canterbury Tales*. He was keenly observant of human nature and used this ability in his vivid portraits of the Canterbury Pilgrims.

A: George Bernard Shaw
Q:Who wrote *Man and Superman*?
W: Shaw, an Irish born dramatist, critic, and essayist ranks as one of the most important literary figures of the 1900s. He won the Nobel Prize for Literature in 1925. His play *Man and Superman* introduced Shaw's theory of *Life Force*, the energy that dominates man biologically. However, when harnessed by man's will, the "Life Force" can lead to a higher, more creative existence.

A: George Eliot
Q:What was the pen name of English novelist Mary Ann Evans?
W: Much of George Eliot's fiction reflects the middle-class rural background of her childhood and youth. Three of her more well-known works include *Middlemarch: A Study of Provincial Life*, *The Mill on the Floss*, and *Silas Marner*.

A: George Plimpton
Q:What writer quarterbacked the Detroit Lions and boxed three rounds with Archie Moore?
W: George Plimpton, the "Professional Amateur", wrote *Out of My League* and the *Paper Lion*. Other professional amateur feats include performing as a trapeze artist with the circus, driving in an auto race, acting as a guard at Buckingham Palace, and participating in an African safari. He only practiced with the Lions and also with the Baltimore Colts.

A: Georgie Porgie
Q:Who ran away when the boys came out to play?
W: But not before Georgie Porgie, Pudding and Pie, kissed the girls and made them cry.

A: Geppetto
Q:What was Pinocchio's father's name?
W: Geppetto, Pinocchio's creator, lived in a small ground floor room that was only lighted from the staircase, with the simplest of furniture — a bad chair, a poor bed, and a broken-down table.

A: German
Q: What language is *Stern* magazine published in?
W: *Der Stern* is a German weekly news and photo-feature magazine published in Hamburg. It was established in 1947 and has achieved a circulation of about two million. It was modeled after the former U.S. weekly magazine *Life*.

A: German
Q: What is considered the sister language of English?
W: German is the official language of Germany, Austria, and Liechtenstein, and an official language of Switzerland and Luxembourg. It is the fourth most widely used European language following English, Russian, and Spanish. German and English have many close connections, being related to an older Germanic, or Teutonic, language once used by tribes of north-central Europe.

A: Gertrude Stein
Q: Who wrote: "Rose is a rose is a rose is a rose"?
W: This quote of Gertrude Stein's is from *Sacred Emily*. She is also the originator of the phrase "the Lost Generation", referring to those disillusioned by the World War I.

A: Gertrude Stein
Q: What 1920s female writer is credited with the term "the Lost Generation"?
W: "The Lost Generation" is the name applied to the disillusioned intellectuals of the years following World War I, who rebelled against former ideals and values but could replace them only with despair and cynicism. Gertrude Stein's remark, "You are all a lost generation", was addressed to Ernest Hemingway.

A: G.K. Chesterton
Q: Who wrote the Father Brown crime stories?

W: Father Brown is a quiet, gentle Roman Catholic priest who views wrongdoers as souls needing salvation, not criminals to be brought to justice. He uses a psychological approach, aided by his deep understanding of human nature. *The Father Brown Omnibus* contains all 51 Father Brown stories.

A: *Glass Menagerie, The*
Q: What Tennessee Williams play features a girl who collects glass animals?
W: Williams is an American playwright whose dramas portray the loneliness and isolation of man. In *The Glass Menagerie*, the narrator, Tom Wingfield, relates his memories of his sister, Laura, and mother, Amanda. Laura, a cripple, lives in a make-believe world of the glass animals in her toy menagerie. Amanda withdraws into delusions about her girlhood.

A: Gloria Steinem
Q: Who founded *Ms.*?
W: Gloria Steinem is best known as the editor of *MS* magazine, the country's most widely read feminist journal. She has campaigned for liberal democratic party candidates, the United Farm Workers, black civil rights, the anti-war movement, and the ERA.

A: God bless us, everyone
Q: What's the last line of Dickens' *A Christmas Carol*?
W: What a wonderful end to a beautiful story. This tale was published in 1843 and is a Christmas classic about Scrooge, an old curmudgeon, who is visited by ghosts on Christmas Eve. Upon awakening Christmas morning he is a changed man. He finally understands the real meaning of Christmas and extends himself to his poor clerk Bob Cratchit and his family including Tiny Tim, Cratchit's crippled son.

A: Godfather, The
Q: What book ends with the line: "..she said tle necessary prayers for the soul of Michael Corleone"?
W: Kay Corleone, wife of Michael, said the necessary prayers for her husband's soul as she received communion and "emptied her mind of all thought of herself, of her children, of all anger, of all rebellion, of all questions".

A: Godfather, The
Q: What's the secret identity of Don Vito Corleone?
W: In *The Godfather*, a novel by Mario Puzo, Don Corleone is the founder of a vastly influential crime syndicate. His values are contradictory: he maintains a domestic life, that of a family man, and at the same time an anti-social life, often killing off his opposition.

A: Godzilla
Q: What radioactive, 164-foot Tyrannosaurus Rex made the covers of *Time* and *Newsweek*?
W: Created by Troshira Honda and Eiji Tsuburuya, the fire breathing Godzilla was originally called Gojira in the 1954 movie named after a workman at the Toho Studios. The voice of the narrator in the English dubbing in the original movie was Raymond Burr. He also played a reporter.

ART AND LITERATURE

A: **Gold, myrrh, frankincense**
Q:What three gifts were brought to Jesus by the Magi?
W: Besides gold, the Magi brought myrrh and frankincense to the baby Jesus. Myrrh is a spice produced from the gum resin of a large bush or small tree. Frankincense is a genuine incense. It is a fragrant gum resin occurring in the form of large tears of a light yellowish-brown color.

A: *Gone with the Wind*
Q:What was the only book Margaret Mitchell wrote?
W: Margaret Mitchell, a Georgia author and journalist, wrote her one book, *Gone with the Wind*, from 1926 to 1936. This long romantic novel of Georgia during the Civil War and Reconstruction was told entirely from the point of view of the middle class in the Old South.

A: *Gone with the Wind*
Q:What book originally weighed three pounds, ran 1,037 pages and sold for $3?
W: *Gone with the Wind* had a sales record of 50,000 copies in one day and approximately 1,500,000 during its first year. By May 1941 the sales reached 3,368,000 in the English language; of the 18 translations, the German was the most popular.

A: **Goodbye**
Q:What word was on the lower right-hand corner of *Life's* last weekly issue?
W: It is certainly missed; however, special issues are still published. This New York weekly picture magazine was founded in 1936 by Time, Inc. and was a new venture in pictoral journalism that became very popular.

A: **Good Earth, The**
Q:What 1932 novel won Pearl Buck a Pulitzer Prize?
W: *The Good Earth* tells the story of the Chinese farmer, Wang Lung, and his wife, O'Lan. It follows the tale of their family life, their religion, and their love of the earth.

A: **Gordon**
Q:What's the name of Dick Tracy's brother?
W: In the 1937 movie serial, Gordon Tracy was played by both Richard Breach and Carleton Young. Dick Tracy's sidekick are Sam Catchem and Pat Patton. Gordon married his true love on Dec. 24, 1949, and their adopted son is Junior.

A: **Gotham City**
Q:Where do Batman and Robin live?
W: Batman and Robin travel though the alleys of Gotham City by night, striking fear into the hearts of criminals. In his civilian identify, Batman is millionaire Bruce Wayne who, as a child, vowed revenge on all criminals because of the murder of his parents. Wayne took on a ward, Robin, the Boy Wonder, a young circus performer named Dick Grayson who was also orphaned.

A: **Graffito**
Q:What is the singular of graffiti?
W: Graffito is any design or scribbled motto drawn on a wall or other exposed surface. In archaeological terms it is a pictograph scratched on an escarpment, wall, or any other surface.

A: **Graham Greene**
Q:Who created Harry Lime?
W: Harry Lime was the third man in Graham Greene's story *The Third Man*. In the 1949 movie directed by Carol Reed, Lime was played by Orson Welles.

A: **Grand National, The**
Q:What horse race is *National Velvet* centered on?
W: *National Velvet*, Elizabeth Taylor's fourth Hollywood movie, propelled her to stardom. It's based on the horse race the Grand National, also called the Grand National Steeple Chase. The race was instituted in 1830 by a Liverpool innkeeper, William Lynn.

A: **Grandma Moses**
Q:What female painter produced primitives of rural New England life?
W: Grandma Moses, Anna Mary Robertson, lived from 1860 to 1961. She took up painting in her old age and rapidly gained widespread attention in the U.S. In 1951 an exhibition of her work was held in Paris.

A: **"Grapes of Wrath, The"**
Q:What John Steinbeck novel portrays the Joad family, driven from the Oklahoma dust bowl?
W: John Steinbeck's concern with the problems of the landless farm laborer received greatest emphasis in *The Grapes of Wrath*. This 1940 Pulitzer Prize winner is the saga of a refugee family from the dust bowl that migrates to California and struggles to find work.

A: **Great Dane, A**
Q:What kind of dog is Marmaduke?
W: Marmaduke is a large, loveable dog in a cartoon strip created by Brad Anderson.

A: *Great White Hope, The*
Q:What Pulitzer Prize-winning play dramatized the life of black boxing champ Jack Johnson?
W: John Arthur Johnson was an American heavyweight boxer who became the first black to hold the world prize. Because he was outspoken and black, he incurred much hostility when he won the title by defeating Tommy Burns in Australia in 1908. The white-controlled boxing world began its search for a "Great White Hope" to regain the title from the champion. This was achieved when Johnson was knocked out by Jesse Willard in Havana in 1915.

A: **Greece**
Q:Where was El Greco born?
W: El Greco, Domenikas Theotokopoulos, was a Spanish painter born in Crete. There were three main phases in his development: *The Holy Trinity* belongs to the first period, *The Burial of Count Orgaz* to the second, and *View of Toledo* belongs to the third period.

A: *Green Berets, The*
Q: What was the title of Robin Moore's book about the Green Berets?
W: *The Green Berets* narrates the stories of a group of true-life heroes, the men of the U.S. Army Special Forces, who have made their distinctive green berets a badge of courage in the jungles of South Vietnam and in other parts of the world. Robin Moore went through guerilla training and fought along with the Green Berets to research his book.

A: Grimy Gulch
Q: What town is *Tumbleweeds* set in?
W: Grimy Gulch is the Western town where Tumbleweeds and the gang live in the cartoon *Tumbleweeds*. Their favorite saloon is The Nugget.

A: Grinch, The
Q: What Dr. Seuss character steals Christmas?
W: The Grinch is the green-skinned Dr. Seuss creature who steals Christmas. The TV adaptation was narrated by Boris Karloff.

A: Groucho Marx's
Q: Whose autobiography is titled *Groucho and Me?*
W: Groucho Marx, the stage name of Julius Marx, was named for Groucho Monk, a comic strip character. He debuted in movies at the age of 33. Some of his movies include *The Cocoanuts, Animal Crackers, Duck Soup,* and *A Day at the Races.*

A: Guinevere
Q: Who was King Arthur's queen and Lancelot's lover?
W: In the movies, Guinevere was played by Ava Gardner in *King of the Round Table*, by Jean Wallace in *Sword of Lancelot*, and by Vanessa Regrave in *Camelot.*

A: Guinness Book of World Records, The
Q: What book did the McWhirter twins originate to settle arguments in English pubs?
W: Born in London in 1925, the McWhirter twins founded the *Guiness Book of World Records*, originally called *The Guiness Book of Superlatives*. Both joined the British Navy in World War II, which was the first time in their lives that they were separated. They were united when the two ships they were on collided in the Malta Harbor.

A: Gutenberg Bible, The
Q: What was the first book set in type?
W: The Gutenberg Bible was the first book set in movable type, from 1450 to 1455. There are only 49 known Gutenberg Bibles remaining in the world.

H

A: H.G. Wells
Q: Who envisioned "The Invisible Man" and "The Time Machine"?
W: "The Time Machine" was the first scientific fantasy on which Wells built his early reputation. It is a serious story with a political message concerning relations between the future ruling and working classes in industrial society.

A: H.G. Wells
Q: What professional cricketer's son wrote *The War of the Worlds* in 1898?

W: *The War of the Worlds* concerns an invasion of earth by Martians who terrorize England with their superior technology and thirst for human blood. The English are saved only by the Martians' inability to resist bacteria. The 1898 novel was instantly popular and continues to be read and enjoyed.

A: Halley's Comet
Q: What phenomenon appeared the day Mark Twain was born and the day he died?
W: Halley's Comet, a recurring, highly visible comet, has been tracked as far back as 240 B.C. It was named for Sir Edmund Halley, astronomer royal, who calculated its 76-year appearance cycle and predicted its return in 1758. It appeared the year of Mark Twain's birth (1835) and also the year of his death (1910).

A: Hamelin's
Q: What German town's problem with rats was handled by the Pied Piper?
W: Hamelin is the town in Germany from which the Pied Piper led the rats. In the 1957 movie, *Pied Piper of Hamelin*, the piper is played by Van Johnson.

A: Hamilton Burger
Q: Who is literature's losingest district attorney?
W: Burger faced Perry Mason many times and only won once! This crime drama created by Erle Stanley Gardner, was made into a TV series, "Perry Mason", that ran from September 1957 to September 1966 starring William Talman as Burger. In "The New Adventures of Perry Mason", September 1973 to January 1974, Burger was played by Harry Guardino.

A: *Hamlet*
Q: What Shakespearean play contains the line: "Something is rotten in the state of Denmark"?
W: One of Shakespeare's greatest tragedies, *Hamlet* is regarded by

ART AND LITERATURE

many to be his finest work. It was probably written in 1601, performed by July 1602, and published in 1603. The story of Hamlet first appeared in the *Historia Danica*, a Latin work by the 12th century Danish chronicler, Saxo Grammaticus.

A: **Hamlet**
Q: What Shakespearean character has the most lines, with 1,422?
W: Hamlet is the Prince of Denmark, son of the former king and nephew to the present monarch. The need to avenge his father's death, which is acting contrary to his nature, is only one aspect of Hamlet's dilemma. He is also faced with the possibility of his mother's adultery. He had a lot to talk about!

A: *Hamlet*
Q: What Shakespearean play features Rosencrantz and Guilderstern?
W: Rosencrantz, former university friend of Hamlet, and his close companion Guildenstern, are induced by Claudius to stay at the Danish court to spy on Hamlet. Later they are both sent to England with Hamlet, carrying sealed orders from the king ordering Hamlet's death. During the voyage, Hamlet substitutes a forged letter requesting the bearers be killed, and they are subsequently put to death.

A: **Hank Ketcham**
Q: Who created Dennis the Menace?
W: Inspiration for Hank Ketchum's comic strip, which debuted on March 12, 1951, was Ketchum's own son, Dennis. Dennis the Menace, son of Alice and Henry Mitchell, is about six or seven years old. His girlfriend is Margaret and his favorite sandwich is peanut butter.

A: **Hannibal**
Q: What Missouri town was Mark Twain's boyhood home?
W: Born Samuel Langhorne Clemens in 1835, Mark Twain led a most exciting and adventuresome lives. Raised in the river town of Hannibal, Missouri, he had to leave school at age 12 to seek work. He was successively a journeyman printer, a steamboat pilot, a halfhearted soldier for a few weeks, a prospector, a miner, and a reporter in the western territories.

A: *Hans Brinker*
Q: What's the alternate title of *The Silver Skates* by Mary Dodge?
W: One of the best known and most popular children's books is by American author Mary Mapes Dodge. *Hans Brinker* is the story of a brother and sister in Holland, Hans and Gretel, their Dutch life, and the exciting ice skate races.

A: **Hans Christian Andersen**
Q: Who wrote "The Ugly Duckling"?
W: The story of the ugly little duckling, who was really a beautiful swan, teaches us that "beauty is in the eye of the beholder". Also, that sometimes not-so-pretty babies grow into beautiful adults and vice cersa.

A: **Hans Christian Andersen**
Q: What writer is Copenhagen's Little Mermaid a memorial to?
W: The Little Mermaid is a statue by Edward Ericksen at the water's edge in Copenhagen Harbor. It depicts the heroine of one of Hans Christian Andersen's stories.

A: **Happiness**
Q: What's a warm puppy, by Charles Schultz's reckoning?
W: This is from Schultz's comic strip *Peanuts*. Snoopy, Charlie Brown's dog, is a beagle. Another of our favorite Schultz quotes is, "Life is like an ice cream cone, you have to learn to lick it".

A: **Harold Pinter's**
Q: What playwright's works include *The Collection* and *The Caretaker*?
W: Pinter was an English playwright and actor who had an ability to create an atmosphere of menace from ordinary and often very funny dialogue/situations. Other plays include *The Birthday Party*, *A Slight Ache*, and *The Tea Party*.

A: **Harold Robbins'**
Q: Whose novels include *The Betsy*, *The Pirate* and *The Carpetbaggers*?
W: Set for the most part in high society, Robbin's lengthy books are about personal empire building and the dramas involved. Although brief, sexually explicit passages account for some of his success, he writes fluently and paces his cleverly contrived plots with precision. His first big seller was *The Carpetbaggers*.

A: **Harry Truman's**
Q: What former president's daughter has written a book titled *Murder in the White House*?
W: Margaret Truman wrote *Murder in the White House*, which was published in 1980. She also wrote *Murder on Capitol Hill*, *Murder in the Smithsonian* and *Murder in the Supreme Court*. All of her murder mysteries are set in Washington, D.C.

A: **Harvard**
Q: What university is *Love Story* set at?
W: Erich Segal's first novel and best-seller relates the unlikely love story of Oliver Barrett IV, who went to Harvard, and Jenny Cavilleri, who attended Radcliffe. He was rich; she was poor. He was a jock; she enjoyed serious music. Despite their differences they fell in love and married.

A: **He was a shepherd**
Q: What did Moses do for a living before he was called by God?
W: While Moses was keeping his father-in-law's flock, God spoke to him and commissioned him to lead Israel out of Egypt. In the 1250 B.C. exodus, Moses led the ancient Hebrews out of Egypt, mediated the Covenant between them and Yahweh at Sinai, and guided them through the desert to the borders of Canaan.

A: **Headless Horseman, The**
Q: Who chases Ichabod Crane in "The Legend of Sleepy Hollow"?
W: "The Legend of Sleepy Hollow", a short story by Washington Irving, was published in *The Sketch Book*. Ichabod Crane, a lanky schoolmaster, is frightened by a headless apparition that rides after him and throws a round object at his head. Ichabod is never again seen in Sleepy Hollow, although the next morning the round object is discovered to be a pumpkin.

A: **Healthy, wealthy, and wise**
Q: What does early to bed and early to rise make one?
W: "Early to bed and early to rise, makes a man healthy, wealthy, and wise" is a 1639 quote of John Clarke. This proverb, in slightly different forms, is very old. Benjamin Franklin copied Clarke's wording in *Poor Richard's Almanack*, and as a result most Americans credit the saying to Franklin.

A: *Heart of Darkness*
Q: What Joseph Conrad book was *Apocalypse Now* derived from?
W: *Apocalypse Now*, a 1979 movie directed by Francis Coppola, is a Vietnam War epic based on the novel by Joseph Conrad. *Apocalypse Now* is a story about a special agent who journeys up river into Vietnam with orders to find and kill an errant officer. It is a mesmerizing odyssey of turbulent and surreal encounters. *Heart of Darkness* is a two-fold adventure into deepest Africa to bring home a madman and into the darkness of the unknown regions of the human heart.

A: **Heaven**
Q: What did God call the firmament?
W: In the Bible (Genesis 1:14), heaven is called the starry firmament as in, "Let there be lights in the firmament of heaven".

A: **Heaven and earth**
Q: What does God create in the first sentence of the Bible?
W: The First Book of Moses, commonly called Genesis, states that "In the beginning God created the heavens and the earth. The earth was without form and void, and darkness was upon the face of the deep; and the Spirit of God was moving over the face of the waters". It goes on to tell us that light was next thing created.

A: **"Heidi"**
Q: What Johanna Spyri story is about a little Alpine lass?
W: When Heidi is five years old her Aunt Dete decides that it is time for the child's grandfather to take his turn caring for the orphan. Although the calm uncle takes in the child grudgingly, Heidi's affectionate ways thaw his reserve and also win the friendship of Peter the goat boy and his blind old grandmother.

A: **Helen Gurley Brown**
Q: What author of *Sex and the Single Girl* went on to edit *Cosmopolitan* into a money-making magazine?
W: Helen Gurley Brown, the publisher of *Cosmopolitan* magazine, is loosely protrayed in the 1964 movie *Sex and the Single Girl* by Natalie Wood. The movie's title was taken from Brown's 1962 book.

A: *Helter Skelter*
Q: What's the title of prosecuting attorney Vincent Bugliosi's account of the Manson murders and trial?
W: *Helter Skelter* was written by Vincent Bugliosi with Curt Gentry. At the time of the Manson case, Bugliosi was the Deputy District Attorney in Los Angeles and a professor of criminal law at the Beverly School of Law. Curt Gentry is a successful

writer of nonfiction. Two of his most recent books are *The Last Days of the Late, Great State of California* and *Frame-Up*.

A: **Henri de Toulouse-Lautrec**
Q: What French painter gained renown for his posters?
W: Toulouse-Lautrec, born of an aristocratic family, was crippled after he broke both his legs in accidents. He studied the exotic silhouettes of the race courses, music halls, and cabarets. His reputation as a graphic artist was established with his earliest posters and lithographs of 1891 and 1892.

A: **Henry**
Q: What's Dr. Jekyll's first name?
W: In Robert Louis Stevenson's *Dr. Jekyll and Mr. Hyde*, Dr. Henry Jekyll is the "good" side. Edward Hyde is the "evil" side of the split personality.

A: **Henry David Thoreau**
Q: Who wrote the essay "Civil Disobedience" in 1849?
W: The famous essay "Civil Disobedience" elaborated Thoreau's theory of passive resistance and belief in the superiority of the individual conscience to the majority or the state.

A: **Henry David Thoreau**
Q: What philosopher-author lived on the shores of Walden Pond?
W: In 1844 Thoreau cleared the land, built a cabin, and lived for two years next to Walden Pond, Concord, where he practiced his doctrines of self-sufficiency and closeness to nature. These were the most fruitful years of his life, providing material for his later work.

A: **Henry Fielding**
Q: Who wrote about a foundling named Tom who marries Sophia?
W: *The History of Tom Jones, A Foundling* is an exciting, humorous story of an orphan and his adventures. The novel begins when Tom is a baby, but follows the hero as a young man for most of its adven-

ART AND LITERATURE

tures, including a variety of love affairs ranging from passing fancies to his true love for Sophia Western.

A: Henry Kissinger
Q: What U.S. secretary of state wrote a book of memoirs titled *The White House Years*?
W: Henry Alfred Kissinger was chief foreign policy adviser and Secretary of State to Presidents Richard Nixon and Gerald Ford. His doctoral dissertation was later published as *A World Restored*. His *Nuclear Weapons and Foreign Policy* brought him recognition as an expert on nuclear strategy. His memoirs, *White House Years*, appeared in 1979.

A: Hercule Poirot
Q: Who solves the crime in *Death on the Nile*?
W: In *Death on the Nile* a wealthy beautiful bride on a honeymoon cruise through Egypt is shot to death. The ship is crawling with suspects, and there are as many motives as there are passengers. Hercule Poirot must solve the crime before another murder is committed.

A: Hercules
Q: Who was assigned to steal the girdle of the Amazon queen Hippolyta?
W: Hercules is the greatest of the Greek heroes, with a large number of stories about him. The most important are the "Twelve Labours" which he performed for King Eurystheus of Tiryns. One of these labours was to steal the Amazon queen's girdle, which gave her strength in battle.

A: Herman Melville
Q: Who created Billy Budd?
W: *Billy Budd* was published after Melville's death. This short novel, published in 1924, is considered Melville's finest book after *Moby Dick*. It is a sybolic story about the clash between innocence and evil and between social reforms and individual liberty.

A: Herman Wouk
Q: Who wrote *Marjorie Morningstar*?
W: In his best-selling novel *Marjorie Morningstar*, Marjorie rebels against the constricting life of her hard working Jewish parents only to discover that her freedom is without substance.

A: Herman Wouk
Q: Who won a Pulitzer Prize for his novel *The Caine Mutiny*?
W: This Pulitzer-Prize winning novel describes the cruelties and cowardice on a minesweeper in the Pacific during World War II. It was adapted by Wouk as a play, *The Caine Mutiny Court-Martial*.

A: Hiawatha
Q: Who lived on the shores of Gitchee Gumee?
W: "The Song of Hiawatha" is a narrative poem by Longfellow. Hiawatha is reared by his grandmother Nokomis, daughter of the moon, among the Ojibwas on the southern shore of Lake Superior. He becomes defender and civilizer of his people.

A: Hiawatha
Q: Who was Minnehaha's husband?
W: Hiawatha married Minnehaha, the lovely daughter of an arrow-maker of the once hostile Dakotahs. The wedding feast and "Song of the Evening Star" inaugurated an idyllic time of peace and culture.

A: His mother's cow
Q: What did Jack exchange with the butcher for a handful of beans?

W: Jack went to the market at the request of his widow mother to sell their cow, Milky-white. He exchanged the cow for a handful of beans which, if planted overnight, would grow up to the sky by morning. Jack got more than just "beans" in exchange of the cow!

A: His right heel
Q: What was the bulls-eye on Achilles?
W: Achilles was dipped into the River Styx by his mother and thus made invulnerable except for the heel by which she held him. Achilles was killed by an arrow shot by Paris into his vulnerable right heel. Ergo, the "Achilles Heel" syndrome!

A: *Hobbit, The*
Q: What J.R.R. Tolkien book features Bilbo Baggins as the central character?
W: In *The Hobbit*, Bilbo Baggins, a Hobbit, acquires an evil magic ring sought by Sauron, the Dark Lord of Murder, that would give him absolute power. In the trilogy, Frodo inherits the ring and, counseled by the Wizard Gandalf, makes the journey to the Crack of Doom in Mordor, the only place where the ring can be destroyed.

A: Hockey
Q: What sport was *Love Story's* Oliver a letterman in?
W: Oliver Barrett IV and Jenny Cavileri's first date was at the hockey game in which Oliver's Harvard team played Dartmouth. Harvard won with a score of 7-0.

A: Honolulu's
Q: What city's police force did Charlie Chan work for?
W: Charlie Chan was a detective with the Honolulu police. He was the father of 11 children, begnning with "No. 1 son". He was created by Earl Derr Biggers in 1925, with the intention of providing a positive image after so many years of the Chinese being portrayed as evil. Chan was featured in six novels and many spin-off movies.

A: **Horton**
Q: What's the name of Dr. Seuss's egg-hatching elephant?
W: Dr. Seuss, who also uses the pen name of Theo Le Seig, authored more than 50 children's books from the 1930s through the 1970s. He uses a distinctive style of writing, consisting of the use of nonsense words and rhyme, to instill word recognition in prereaders and to encourage them to pronounce words. *Horton Hatches the Egg*, *The Cat in the Hat*, and *Why the Grinch Stole Christmas* are his best known works.

A: *Hotel*
Q: What Arthur Hailey novel recounts efforts to save a New Orleans hotel?
W: This is the story of the trials and tribulations and human interest stories that occur in running an aging hotel. It was made into a 1967 movie and recently into a TV series.

A: *Hotel*
Q: What best-selling novel catapulted Arthur Hailey to fame?
W: Hailey writes documentary fiction, or what has been called "faction", a mixture of the real and the fictitious. After spending a year of research for each novel, Hailey is prepared to give his readers as much information as he can in a novel. Consequently only his characters and situations are imaginary, and they are only "slightly fictitious".

A: **Huey, Dewey, Louie**
Q: What are the names of Donald Duck's nephews?
W: The *Donald Duck* comic strip became a solid hit when Donald's tormenting nephews, Huey, Louie, and Dewey, appeared on a visit from Donald's cousin, Della Duck. Other regulars include Goofy, Horace Horsecollar, Pluto, and Daisy Duck.

A: **Hugh Hefner**
Q: Who's the editor-publisher of *VIP* and *Oui* magazines?
W: Hugh Hefner, editor and publisher of *Playboy*, was also editor and publisher of *VIP* and *Oui*. *VIP* was the magazine for Playboy Club keyholders that featured news and social events from the various clubs. *Oui* ran from October 1972 to August 1981 and was designed for the 18 to 34 year-old male reader. *Oui* concentrated on photos and sexual interest with very little literary content.

I

A: **I came, I saw, I conquered**
Q: What's the meaning of: "Veni, vidi, vici?"
W: This famous statement was written by Caesar in a letter announcing his victory over the Pharnaces at Zela in Pontus in 47 B.C.

A: **Ian**
Q: What's the Scottish equivalent of John?
W: The name John is a favorite in many countries throughout the world. The French equivalent is *Jean*, German is *Hans*, Italian is *Giovanni*, Spanish is *Juan*, Russian is *Ivan*, Welsh is *Evan*, and the Irish is *Sean* and/or *Shane*.

A: **Ian Fleming**
Q: What British spy novelist wrote the children's story "Chitty Chitty Bang Bang?"
W: This story of a flying car was made into a children's musical movie in 1968. (Stick with James Bond books!)

A: **Ian Fleming**
Q: Who created James Bond?
W: Ian Fleming did espionage work as the personal assistant to the director of British Naval Intelligence during World War II. He won fame for his creation of James Bond, a British secret service agent who meets old-fashioned, fantastic adventure in the modern world.

A: *Iberia*
Q: What James Michener book is subtitled *Spanish Travels and Reflections*?
W: Master storyteller Michener first traveled to Spain in 1932 and returned many times. This in-depth book about Spain from prehistoric to present times was published in 1968.

A: **Icarus**
Q: Who flew too near the sun wearing wings attached with wax?
W: In Greek mythology, Icarus attempted to escape from Crete with his father, Daedalus. During this attempt he flew too near the sun, melting the wax that fastened his artificial wings, resulting in his drowning when he fell into the sea. "Icarian" is a term describing someone who is rash or adventuresome.

A: *I Kid You Not*
Q: What's the title of Jack Paar's autobiography?
W: "I kid you not" is the favorite expression of Jack Paar and the title of his autobiography. The line was used by Captain Queeg (Humphrey Bogart) in the movie *The Caine Mutiny*.

A: *Iliad, The*
Q: What Homerian epic chronicles events toward the end of the Trojan Wars?
W: *The Iliad*, the oldest surviving Greek poem, was, according to

tradition, written by the ancient Greek poet Homer probably in the 700s B.C. It describes the final year of the Trojan War, which was fought between Greece and the City of Troy. The war was fought over Helen, the beautiful wife of King Menelaus of Sparta, who was captured by Paris and taken to the City of Troy.

A: *I'm OK, You're OK*
Q: What 1960s self-help book was based on people not feeling OK?
W: *I'm OK, You're OK* was written by Thomas A. Harris, a practicing psychiatrist and one of the pioneers in the application of transactional analysis to the treatment of psychiatric patients. His self-help book is the culmination of the experience of a 25-year medical career. "T.A." distinguishes three active elements in each person's makeup: the parent, the adult, and the child.

A: **In a pumpkin shell**
Q: Where did Peter, Peter, Pumpkin Eater, put his wife?
W: This is from the Mother Goose rhyme: Peter, Peter, pumpkin eater, Had a wife and couldn't keep her; Put her in a pumpkin shell; And there he kept her very well.

A: **In bed**
Q: Where does a librocubicularist read?
W: Librocubicularist comes from "librarious" which means pertaining to books, and "cubicular" meaning pertaining to bedroom. Thus, one who reads books in bed.

A: **In the beginning**
Q: What are the first three words in the Bible?
W: These words are the first three in the first book of *The Bible*, commonly known as the *Book of Genesis*. "In the beginning God created the heavens and the earth."

A: **inn An**
Q: What's an *auberge* in France?
W: In France an *auberge* is an inn. One who keeps the inn is called a *aubergiste*.

A: **In prison**
Q: Where did Adolph Hitler write *Mein Kampf*?
W: Hitler was born in Austria in 1889 and rose to become leader of the German Nazi Party from 1933 until his death in 1945. He was imprisoned for trying to overthrow the German government in 1923. He served nine months of his five year sentence in the fortress of Landaberg where he wrote *Mein Kampf*, a crude, disorganized, unoriginal but still important book.

A: **Ireland**
Q: What country was *A Terrible Beauty* to Leon Uris?
W: Ireland, *A Terrible Beauty*, was the setting of Leon Uris' novel *Trinity*. It takes place during the period from the famine of the 1840s to the Easter rising of 1916. The Trinity consists of the Larkin family, generations of Catholic hill farmers; the Hubbles, representing three generations of British aristocracy; and the MacLeods, a family of devout Presbyterian shipyard workers.

A: **Irwin Shaw**
Q: Who wrote *The Young Lions* and *Rich Man, Poor Man*?
W: *The Young Lions* was a best-selling World War II novel. *Rich Man, Poor Man* traces a family through

three generations, questioning many fundamental American beliefs.

A: **Isaac Asimov**
Q: Who wrote the sci-fi trilogy *Foundation*, *Foundation and Empire* and *Second Foundation*?
W: "The Foundation Trilogy" was originally conceived by Isaac Asimov as a single story. The idea of the fall of the Roman Empire, written as science fiction, eventually evolved into the trilogy that won a Hugo Award in 1966 as Best All-Time Series

A: *Islands in the Stream*
Q: What Ernest Hemingway novel was published after his death?
W: This novel was left among Hemingway's writings at the time of his death. The book is divided into three parts, each describing a stage in the life of Thomas Hudson. The first describes his life as a painter, the second follows his adventures in secret anti-submarine activities, and the third part describes his assignment to hunt down survivors of a German submarine.

A: *"It was the best of times"*
Q: What are the first six words of Dickens's *A Tale of Two Cities*?
W: *A Tale of Two Cities*, set during the French Revolution, contains three strong themes: the imprisonment and recurrent amnesia of Doctor Manette; the heartless behavior of the women spectators at the guillotine; and the self-sacrifice of Sydney Carton. The first sentence of the book begins: "It was the best of times, it was the worst of times, it was the age of wisdom, it was the age of foolishness."

A: **Ivory**
Q: What was Captain Ahab's peg leg made of?
W: Captain Ahab, Captain of the whaler *Pequod* in Herman Melville's *Moby Dick*, lost his right leg to the white whale and replaced it with one of whalebone. In the movies, Captain Ahab was played by John Barrymore and Gregory Peck.

ART AND LITERATURE

J

A: J
Q: What letter was used as a pseudonym by the author of *The Sensuous Woman*?
W: *The Way to Become the Sensuous Woman* was published in 1969 and is described as the "first how-to book for the female who yearns to be all woman." The *J* stood for Joan Garritz who wrote this book.

A: Jack
Q: What's the most common name in nursery rhymes?
W: The most memorable of the nursery rhymes about Jack include "Jack and Jill," "Jack Sprat Could Eat No Fat," "Jack Be Nimble," and "Little Jack Horner."

A: Jack
Q: What was the name of Mother Goose's son?
W: Mother Goose was said to be the nickname of Mrs. Isaac Goose of colonial Boston. Her daughter Elizabeth married Thomas Fleet in 1715 and made "Mother" Goose a grandmother! We don't know if son Jack ever married.

A: Jack Kerouac
Q: Who defined "the Beat Generation?"
W: Kerouac and others, including William Burroughs, created the legend of the "Beat Generation." His sprawling *On the Road* influenced a generation by preaching "spontaneous" life and indulgence in drugs, drink, and whatever else you feel like. A victim of his own preaching, he died of drink.

A: Jack London
Q: Who wrote *The Call of the Wild*?
W: *The Call of the Wild* is the story of Buck, offspring of a St. Bernard and Scotch Shepherd dog, who lives on a California estate until he is stolen and shipped to the Klondike where he is trained as a sled dog. After his master is murdered, Buck responds to the call of the wild and abandons human civilization to lead a wolf pack.

A: Jackson Pollock
Q: What non-conformist abstract painter was dubbed "Jack The Dripper" by *Time*?
W: Pollock's early work is characteristic of the American romantic realism of the 1930s. By 1936, he was influenced by surrealism. In 1947 he painted his first "drip painting," in which the paint was allowed to fall from the brush to a canvas laid on the floor. He describes his work: "The painting has a life of its own. I try to let it come through."

A: Jacob Marley
Q: Who was Scrooge's dead partner in Dickens's *A Christmas Carol*?
W: Jacob Marley, in the form of a chained ghost, visits Scrooge to warn his former partner that three spirits will visit him to offer him a last chance to escape from his life of greed.

A: Jacqueline Kennedy Onassis
Q: Who's the most famous editor at Doubleday and Co.?
W: Prior to being First Lady of the United States during the administration of her first husband, John F. Kennedy, Jacqueline Bouvier Kennedy Onassis had been a newspaper reporter and photographer. After the death of her second husband, Greek shipping millionaire Aristotle Onassis, she worked as an editor for book publishing companies.

A: Jacqueline Susann's
Q: Whose second novel was *The Love Machine*?
W: Jacqueline Susann achieved fame and fortune on the strength of several novels dealing with the seamy side of life among the rich and famous. *The Valley of the Dolls*, which was later filmed, proved to be the world's all time best-seller. *The Love Machine* and *Once is Not Enough* were also successful as both books and movies.

A: James Baldwin
Q: What black author wrote *Another Country* and *Nobody Knows My Name*?
W: James Baldwin is an American author noted for his books on racial conflict in the U.S.; homosexuality is another major theme of his fiction. *Nobody Knows My Name* is an autobiographical essay. *Another Country*, perhaps Baldwin's most powerful novel, describes the agonies of homosexuality and racial interbreeding in a hostile society.

A: James Beard
Q: What rotund cook wrote on bread and a cook's catalogue?
W: Twenty-five years ago Beard started giving cooking lessons in what later became the kitchen of the restaurant Lutece; this was the beginning of his famous cooking school. He is now well-known as a cooking authority, having written 19 books on food, including *Hors d'Oeuvre and Canapes*, *The James Beard Cookbook*, *Beard on Bread*, and *Beard on Pasta*.

A: James Bond
Q: What literary character was tossed out of Eton and graduated from the University of Geneva?
W: Ian Fleming created the most famous spy in literature with his first book about Bond, *Casino Royale* in 1953. Bond, the son of a Swiss mother and Scottish father, is deeply patriotic to England. Good thing he graduated from the University of Geneva, because a good secret agent needs an education.

ART AND LITERATURE

A: James Bond
Q: Who's the archenemy of Ernst Stavro Blofeld?
W: Blofield, an employee of SPECTRE, appears in *For Your Eyes Only, Thunderball, On Her Majesty's Secret Service,* and *You Only Live Twice.*

A: James Bond's
Q: Whose cover is that of an employee of Universal Import and Export?
W: Delaney Bros. Ltd. was another company used as a cover for James Bond in the 007 episodes. The novel *Moonraker* tells us that Miss Twinning was a real person who sat at the front entrance and politely brushed off people who wanted to have their radios checked or something exported by Universal.

A: James Earl Ray's
Q: Whose life is depicted in George McMillan's *The Portrait of an Assassin?*
W: Incorrect, the title is *The Making of an Assassin: The Life of James Earl Ray.* It is the biography of the killer of civil rights leader Martin Luther King, Jr. The author submits that Ray's hatred of blacks and other minorities supports the premise that he was not part of a conspiracy.

A: James Fenimore Cooper
Q: Who's considered the first important native American novelist?
W: Cooper, the most significant American novelist before Nathaniel Hawthorne, achieved a wide international audience. He is best known for the five novels known collectively as *The Leatherstocking Tales.*

A: James Fenimore Cooper
Q: Who wrote the so-called *Leatherstocking Tales?*
W: The American life on the frontier is the theme of Cooper's Leatherstocking saga. His heroes are Natty Bumppo, the skilled white hunter refusing urban life, and Chingachgook, the American gentleman in the form of the noble savage, the Red Indian.

A: James Joyce
Q: What renowned Irish writer wore an eye patch?
W: In 1917, while Joyce was at work on *Ulysses,* he had his first attack of glaucoma, the eye disease that troubled him for the rest of his life. At times he was reduced to total blindness as a result of the disease.

A: James Michener
Q: Who won the 1948 Pulitzer Prize for *Tales of the South Pacific?*
W: Michener's first and most famous work, *Tales of the South Pacific,* is a collection of short stories, loosely unified by the invasion of Kuralei during World War II. In this book he focuses on one or two characters in each of his brief glimpses into life in the Pacific atolls, including Tony Fry, Bloody Mary, and the Remittance Man.

A: James Thurber
Q: Who wrote "The Secret Life of Walter Mitty?"
W: James Thurber, an American humorist and cartoonist, is especially associated with the *New Yorker* where his work appeared regularly for many years. One of his most famous stories, "The Secret Life of Walter Mitty," is about a man whose failures and frustrations have forced him to escape into a drown identity.

A: James Whistler
Q: Who painted *The Artist's Mother?*
W: *Whistler's Mother* is the popular title of James McNeil Whistler's painting *Arrangement in Grey and Black.* His mother, Anna McNeil, posed for the picture when she was 65 years old. The painting hangs in the Louvre in Paris.

A: Jane Austen's
Q: Whose novels include *Emma, Pride and Prejudice* and *Northanger Abbey?*
W: Jane Austen's works slowly became established as classics. They all center around a young heroine and end in a happy marriage. The plots depend little on exciting events but instead show how much meaning and drama can result from misunderstood feelings, the neglect of social obligations, and all the ordinary human weaknesses.

A: Jane Austen
Q: Who was only 21 when she wrote *Pride and Prejudice?*
W: Jane Austen is usually considered the first great woman novelist. Although she began writing as a girl, she did not publish until late in her life. Four of her six novels had been published and she was winning wider recognition when she died in 1817.

A: Japan
Q: What country was the setting of *You Only Live Twice?*
W: Another episode in the "ho-hum" life of agent 007, James Bond. The movie starred Sean Connery, with the theme song performed by Nancy Sinatra.

A: Jason
Q: Who led the Argonauts in search of the Golden Fleece?
W: The Argonauts were a group of heroes in Greek mythology who sailed with their leader Jason on the ship *Argo* to search for the Golden Fleece. Jason was sent by King Pelias, his wicked uncle, to fetch the Fleece from a grove guarded by a dragon. The King's daughter, Edea, fell in love with Jason and helped him perform the tasks her father had assigned to him.

A: Jaws
Q: What novel opens with: "The great fish moved silently through the night water?"
W: *Jaws,* the best seller and major motion picture, was written by Peter Benchley, who belongs to one of

America's most celebrated literary families. His grandfather was the humorist Robert Benchley, and his father was the novelist Nathaniel Benchley.

A: Jay
Q: What was The Great Gatsby's first name?
W: Jay Gatsby, who was rumored to be everything from ex-German spy to murderer, was born James Gatz. Of poor midwestern background, he had gained tremendous wealth through bootlegging and other criminal activities.

A: Jay Gatsby
Q: What fictional character had a mansion at West Egg, Long Island?
W: Gatsby lived mysteriously in an expensive Long Island colony in 1922, playing host to hundreds of people. As a poor Army lieutenant he had fallen in love with Daisy, who later married Tom Buchanan, a crude but wealthy man. Through a mutual friend Gatsby and Daisy are brought together again, but with tragic results.

A: Jayne Mansfield
Q: What buxom blonde appeared on the cover of more than 500 magazines Jayne Mansfield was born Vera Jane Palmer in 1933. Her figure was 40-21-35, and she claimed to have an IQ of 163. She died of decapitation in a car accident on June 29, 1967. Pink — her favorite color — was the color of her home and her car; in fact, her Hollywood home was called "The Pink Palace."

A: J.D. Salinger
Q: Who created the fictional character Zooey?
W: Zen Buddhism is central to the story of the Glass family in J.D. Salinger's *Franny and Zooey*. Franny Glass, a college student dissatisfied with life around her, seeks divergence from her own ego. Her older brother, Zooey, is an actor and intellecutal who feels alienated from his family and from society.

A: Jean Harlow
Q: Who was the first female star to appear on the cover of *Life*?
W: Hollywood actress Jean Harlow was born Harlean Carpentier in 1911. She died in 1937. The name Harlow was actually her mother's maiden name. In 1965 two biographical moves were made, both titled *Harlow*.

A: Jeeves
Q: Who was Bertie Wooster's butler?
W: P.G. Wodehouses' caricatures of English life, especially Bertie Wooster, Jeeves, and Psmith, have become famous. His works include *Leave It to Psmith*, *The Code of the Woosters*, *Carry on Jeeves*, and *Stiff Upper Lip, Jeeves*.

A: Jeeves
Q: What famed butler did P.G. Wodehouse create?
W: Wodehouse, a famous novelist and short-story writer, wrote books that became popular for their rich and outlandish humor and for their caricatures of English types. He became an American citizen in 1955 and was knighted by Queen Elizabeth II in 1975.

A: Jekyll and Hyde
Q: What were the last names of Dr. Henry and Mr. Edward?
W: In Robert Louis Stevenson's *The Strange Case of Dr. Jekyll and Mr. Hyde*, a respectable physician, Dr. Henry Jekyll chemically transforms himself into an unscrupulous alter ego. Mr. Edward Hyde is the embodiment of Dr. Jekyll's "lower nature." Jekyll is fatally attracted to his alter ego, with Hyde eventually winning control.

A: Jerry Rubin
Q: Who wrote the 1960s revolutionary journal *Do It!*?
W: Jerry Rubin authored the best-seller *Do It!*. He was co-founder, with Abbie Hoffman, of the Yippies; a member of the "Chicago Seven"; and one of the organizers of the first Berkeley anti-war

demonstrations. His 1976 book *Growing Up at 37* depicts the changes that he has gone through.

A: Jesus Christ
Q: Who said: "He that is without sin among you, let him cast a stone?"
W: People who live in glass houses... Actually this was in reference to the stoning of a sinner.

A: Jesus wept (John 11:35)
Q: What's the shortest verse in the Bible?
W: This statement was in reference to the death of Jesus' close friend Lazarus, whom Jesus eventually brings back to life.

A: Jim
Q: Who accompanied Huck Finn on his Mississippi River raft ride?
W: *The Adventures of Huckleberry Finn*, a sequel to ark Twain's *Adventures of Tom Sawyer*, is a more adult treatment of the Mississippi River region. The "immorality" of Huck's decision that he would rather go to hell himself than be the means of sending Nigger Jim back into slavery is what caused the book to be banned from the public libraries of Concord, Massachusetts, Brooklyn, Omaha, and Denver.

A: Jimmy Breslin
Q: What newspaper columnist wrote *The Gang That Couldn't Shoot Straight*?
W: Jimmy Breslin, whose work typifies the colorful muckraking style of the "New Journalism," began as a sportswriter while still in his teens, switching to political subjects in the 1960s. His fiction includes *The Gang That Couldn't Shoot Straight*, *World Without End*, and *Amen*.

A: Jimmy Carter
Q: Who was the only future U.S. president to be the subject of a *Playboy* Interview?
W: Presidential candidate Jimmy Carter was interviewed in *Playboy* by Robert Scheer for their Nov. 1976 issue. Carter spent more time with

Playboy than with any other interview. The interview is best remembered for his unpolitician-like admission of having experienced lust in his heart.

A: Jimmy Carter
Q: Who was *Time's* Man of the Year for 1976?
W: James Earl Carter, Jr., became the 39th president of the U.S. by defeating Gerald R. Ford, Jr., on Nov. 2, 1976. *Time* magazine selects "some person or group as Man of the Year" and places that picture on the cover of the first issue of the next year. Carter, as Man of the Year for 1976 appeared on the cover of the first *Time* magazine of 1977.

A: Joe and Frank Hardy
Q: What detective duo are featured in *Viking Symbol Mystery* and *Mystery at Devil's Paw*?
W: Eighteen-year-old Frank and 17-year-old Joe are sons of Detective Fenton and Laura Hardy in the stories written by Franklin W. Dixon. There were two TV series about the Hardy Boys, the earlier one starring Tim Considine and Tommy Kirk and the more recent show starring Parker Stevenson and Shawn Cassidy.

A: John Dean III's
Q: Whose Watergate revelations are titled *Blind Ambition*?
W: John W. Dean was White House Counsel to President Richard Nixon. Dean was portrayed in the 1979 TV mini-series, Blind Ambition by Martin Sheen; his wife, Maureen, was played by Theresa Russell.

A: John D. MacDonald
Q: Who created detective Travis McGee?
W: Travis McGee is a combination detective-thief who makes a living recovering stolen property. Although he works outside the law, his "victims" are invariably criminals. McGee's standard "contract" permits him to keep half of what he recovers, but profit is not his only motivation.

A man of deep loyalty to his friends, he has been described as "more the private avenger than the private eye."

A: John Dos Passos
Q: Who wrote the Trilogy U.S.A.?
W: Dos Passos great work, the *Trilogy U.S.A., consisting of The 42nd Parallel, 1919*, and *The Big Money*, deals with the social classes and conflicts within American capitalist society.

A: John Ehrlichman
Q: What aide to Richard Nixon wrote a political novel titled *The Company*?
W: Domestic Council Chief John Ehrlichman was indicted on charges of conspiracy in covering up the Watergate break-in. As a result of the cover-up trial, which lasted from October 1974 to January 1975, Ehrlichman was convicted of conspiracy, obstruction of justice, and perjury and was sentenced to a prison term of 2.5 to 8 years.

A: John F. Kennedy
Q: Who's the only U.S. president to have won a Pulitzer Prize?
W: Like his earlier book on English foreign policy, Kennedy's 1957 Pulitzer Prize-winning novel, *Profiles in Courage*, revealed his admiration of forceful political figures.

A: John F. Kennedy
Q: What later U.S. president wrote *Profiles in Courage*?
W: During Kennedy's first Senate term, his back caused him severe pain. While recovering from operations to correct the injury, he wrote a book about some of the brave deeds performed by U.S. senators. He was awarded the Pulitzer Prize for Biography for this book in 1957.

A: John Keats
Q: Who wrote: "A thing of beauty is a joy forever?"
W: John Keats was an English poet of the Romantic Period. "Endymion," a long mythological story in

verse, opens with the famous line, "A thing of beauty is a joy forever." In this poem, Keats retold the classic story of the shepherd who loved and won the goddess of the moon. The reviews for this work ruined Keat's reputation.

A: John Le Carre
Q: Who created British master spy George Smiley?
W: Le Carre's novels are not romantic tales of adventure and sex. His characters are weary victims of espionage, antiheroes trying to play the game according to the rules and blundering into situations in which they are merely pawns Master spy George Smiley was featured in Le Carre's first novel *Call for the Dead*.

A: John Le Carre
Q: Who wrote *The Spy Who Came in from the Cold*?
W: The central figure in this book is Alec Leamas, who willingly becomes a martyr, even though he dies for a cause with which he has no sympathy. The financial rewards from this novel allowed Le Carre to resign from his civil service job, admit that his real name is Cornwell, and devote full time to writing.

A: Johnny Appleseed
Q: What was American folk hero John Chapman's nickname?
W: John Chapman, a Massachusett's born orchardist, is known as "Johnny Appleseed" because of the fruit trees he planted for frontier settlers in Pennsylvania, Ohio, Indiana, and Illinois. He is the subject of a ballad by W.H. Venable and of many poems by Vachel Lindsay, including "In Praise of Johnny Appleseed."

A: Johnny Carson
Q: What comedian wrote *Happiness Is a Dry Martini*?
W: Johnny Carson, best known as the host of NBC's "Tonight Show," describes his life in his 1965 autobiography *Happiness is a Dry Martini*. As a child in Nebraska he performed magic tricks under the name "The Great Carson." He was a gag writer for "The Red Skelton Show," followed by "Who Do You Trust." He achieved fame when he replaced Jack Paar as host of the "Tonight Show" in 1962.

A: Johnny Cash's
Q: What singer's autobiography is titled *The Man in Black*?
W: In his 1975 autobiography, *The Man in Black*, Johnny Cash describes his life as a famous country singer and guitarist. Prison songs are an important part of his repertoire, and he regularly performs in prisons. He has won three Grammy Awards. Many of his songs were written in collaboration with his wife, country singer June Carter Cash.

A: Johnny Hart
Q: Who created the comic strip *B.C.*?
W: Johnny Hart's first comic strip creation, "B.C.," was a far-out feature about a weird assortment of cavemen, talking animals, and plants. In 1964 Hart developed a new strip idea and teamed up with cartoonist Brant Parker to produce *The Wizard of Id*.

A: John Sirica
Q: What judge told his side of Watergate in *To Set the Record Straight*?
W: John Joseph Sirica presided as judge at the 1973 trial of the seven original Watergate defendants. He played a key role in gradually uncovering evidence of the far-ranging scandal.

A: John Steinbeck
Q: Who wrote *East of Eden*?
W: *East of Eden*, published in 1952, was Steinbeck's first major novel since *The Grapes of Wrath*. It is a long family saga taking place from the Civil War to World War I, partly set in the Salinas Valley. Using the theme of Cain and Abel, the story is both symbolic and realistic of man's struggle between good and evil.

A: John Steinbeck
Q: Who won a Pulitzer prize for his novel *The Grapes of Wrath*?
W: *The Grapes of Wrath* is a realistic novel tracing the Joad family, one of the many Oklahoma dust bowl dwellers driven from the land by poverty and drought. Enticed by leaflets advertising employment in California, they make the long trip in a dilapidated car, only to find a more oppressive economic system.

A: John Steinbeck
Q: Who wrote the 1937 novelette *Of Mice and Men*?
W: *Of Mice and Men* is the tragedy of three itinerant workers who dream of a ranch of their own. George Milton is the self-appointed guardian of the simple-witted giant Lennie Small. On a Salinas Valley ranch they meet Candy, a broken old man whose meager savings seem enough to buy a piece of land for the three of them.

A: John the Baptist's
Q: Whose head did Salome demand?
W: John, who baptized Jesus, was imprisoned by Herod, ruler of Galilee, because he condemned Herod for having married his half brother's wife, Herodias. Herodias, determined for revenge, asked her daughter Salome to dance for Herod at a feast. He was so pleased by her dance that he offered her any reward she wanted. Salome demanded the head of John the Baptist.

A: John Wayne's
Q: Whose biography by Maurice Zolotow is titled *Shooting Star*?
W: *Shooting Star: A Biography of John Wayne* is Maurice Zolotow's 1974 version of Marion Michael Morrison's life. Wayne epitomized the archetypal hero of the American western frontier. He appeared in more than 150 films, winning an Academy Award for his role as the aging westerner in *True Grit*.

A: "Jonathon Livingston Seagull"
Q: What was Richard Bach's best-selling adult fairy tale?
W: Richard Bach's best-selling novel was made into the 1973 movie of the same name. It featured the voice of James Franciscus and was scored by Neil Diamond.

A: Joseph
Q: Who wore the coat of many colors?
W: Joseph's favored status and his coat of many colors, a gift from his father, caused jealousy among his brothers, with the resulting staged accidental "death." He was actually taken to Egypt where his ability to interpret dreams brought him the Pharaoh's favor, and he became a high Egyptian official. When his unsuspecting brothers sought grain in Egypt during a famine, the forgiving Joseph arranged a family reunion.

A: Joseph Conrad
Q: What renowned English author had been a Polish sailor?
W: Joseph Conrad, a Polish born novelist, visited England for the first time in 1878, after four years at sea. He became a British citizen in 1886. His first novel, *Almayer's Folly*, was begun during a voyage to the Congo and was published after he left the Merchant Service.

A: Joseph Conrad
Q: Who wrote *The Nigger of the Narcissus*?
W: "The Nigger of the Narcissus" tells the story of James Wait, a huge West Indian Negro who is dying of tuberculosis. His destiny is followed from the moment he boards the *Narcissus* at Bombay. His physical disintegration, which is accompanied by curses at life and mankind, is watched with compassion and terror by his crew mates.

A: **Joseph Heller**
Q: Who wrote *Catch-22*?
W: Heller established his reputation with the comic novel, *Catch-22*. The title describes the absurdities that characterize some complex organizations, which in "Catch-22" is the military. The novel portrays the misadventures of Yossarian, a U.S. officer, during World War II. His ways of retaining his identity depend on his ability to maneuver within an absurd and illogical system.

A: **Joseph Stalin**
Q: Who was *Time's* Man of the Year for 1939 and 1942?
W: It isn't easy to find these covers to verify this information or the reasons why! However, we did verify that Stalin was *Time's* Man of the Year in 1939 and 1942. Stalin was leader of Russia and the Communist Party from the death of Lenin in 1924 until his own death in 1953.

ART AND LITERATURE

A: **Joseph Wambaugh**
Q: What best-selling novelist was once a Los Angeles Police Department detective?
W: Joseph Wambaugh is an American writer of police procedural novels. A former Los Angeles policeman, he shows brutality, corruption, perversion and evil in his cops, as well as courage, dedication and honor. Two of his novels are *The Onion Field* (1973) and *The Choirboys* (1975).

A: **Joy Adamson**
Q: Who wrote of the lioness Elsa in the books *Born Free, Living Free* and *Forever Free*?
W: Joy Adamson's *Born Free* tells the story of the African lioness Elsa. The other two books are follow-up volumes telling about Elsa. *Born Free* was made into a 1966 movie, and for her role, Elsa was the winner of the 1967 and 1975 TV Patsy.

A: **Joyce Kilmer**
Q: Who wrote: "Poems are made by fools like me but only God can make a tree?"
W: Alfred Joyce Kilmer wrote many poems and essays, but is remembered for one short poem, "Trees." It first appeared in *Poetry Magazine* in 1918, and was the title poem in his collection *Trees and Other Poems.*

A: *Joy of Cooking, The*
Q: What best-selling cookbook was compiled by Irma Rombauer and Marion Rombauer Becker?
W: The *Joy of Cooking*, which is now published in two volumes, was first copywrighted in 1931. It was written by Marion Rombauer Becker and her mother Irma S. Rombauer.

A: *Joy of Sex, The*
Q: What illustrated sex guide did Alex Comfort write?
W: The 1972 book *The Joy of Sex: A Gourmet Guide to Love Making* was edited by Alex Comfort, MB, PhD. It is divided into four sections: "Starters," "Main Courses," "Sauces and Pickles" and "Problems."

A: *Jules Verne*
Q: Who wrote *Around the World in Eighty Days*?
W: Jules Verne, a French novelist, wrote some of the first science fiction stories. He forecast the invention of airplanes, submarines, television, guided missiles, and man-made space satellites, and even predicted their uses accurately. In his 1873 novel, *Around the World in Eighty Days*, Phileas Fogg travels around the earth in the then unheard of time of 80 days, just to win a bet.

A: **Julius Dithers**
Q: Who is Dagwood Bumstead's boss?
W: Blondie and Dagwood Bumstead are the main characters of the comic strip *Blondie*. There are many colorful characters revolving around the Bumsteads, the most important being their neighbors, Herbert and Tootsie Woodley; Mr. Dithers, Dagwood's boss; the mailman, Mr. Beasley; not to mention Daisy the family dog and her five pups.

K

A: **Kal-El**
Q: What was Superman's name on Krypton?
W: Clark Kent, alias Superman, was born Kal-el. Metropolis, Illinois was his hometown on Earth. He lived in Smallville where he was Superboy until age 26.

A: *Kamikaze*
Q: What is the Japanese word for "divine wind?"
W: Kamikaze, or Divine Wind, is derived from the two words *Kami* meaning "a God" and *Kaze* meaning "the wind." In World War II, a Japanese Kamikaze pilot pledged to die by crashing his bomb-laden plane against the target.

A: **Karamazov**
Q: What's the last name of brothers Dmitri, Ivan, Alyosha, and Smerdyakov?
W: *The Brothers Karamazov* was written by Russian novelist Fyodor Mikhailavich Dostoyevsky. The central drama of the novel is the struggle between the repulsive father and his four sons. Each son represents a universal trait of humanity: Alyosha, Saintliness; Dmitri, Passion and Sexuality; Ivan, the Intellect; and Smerdyakov, Ugliness of Body, Mind, and Spirit.

A: **Kate Millett**
Q: What feminist wrote *Sexual Politics* and *Flying*?
W: Kate Millet came to national prominence on the publication of her first book, *Sexual Politics*, which argues that nearly all relations between men and women are determined by the male establishment's need to preserve its power over women. She also published a memoir, *Flying*, that deals with the emotional traumas of celebrity and bi-sexuality.

A: **Kathryn Kuhlman**
Q: What female faith healer wrote the inspirational book *I Believe in Miracles*?
W: Kathryn Kuhlman, who died in 1976, cured thousands of people of terrible afflictions by her power of healing through the Holy Spirit. She was a Christian minister who spread her faith through personal appearances, radio and television. As of 1976 her television program was the longest running half hour series that CBS ever had. In 1962 her book *I Believe in Miracles* was published.

A: **Katzenjammer Kids, The**
Q: What comic strip kids with German accents did Rudolph Dirks create in 1897?
W: The oldest comic strip in existence, *The Katzenjammer Kids* depicts the guerilla war conducted by the twins Hans and Fritz against any form of authority. Their more popular targets include die Mama (the mother of the Katzies), der Captain (their surrogate father) and der inspector (representative of the school authorities).

A: **Ken Kesey**
Q: What former ward attendant in a mental hospital wrote *One Flew Over the Cuckoo's Nest*?
W: This 1962 novel was made into a film in 1975 and cleaned up at the Academy Awards: 1. Best Picture; 2. Best Actor, Jack Nicholson; 3. Best Actress, Louise Flecher; and 4. Best Director, Milos Forman.

A: **Kickapoo Joy Juice**
Q: What did the 12-member Polecat Indian tribe sell in Dogpatch?
W: A short-lived soft drink called Kickapoo Joy Juice was marketed for a time in the 1950s but failed.

A: *Kidnapped*
Q: What Robert Louis Stevenson sea adventure features the ship the *Covenant*?
W: Robert Louis Stevenson describes the contents of his 1886 novel *Kidnapped* as "memoirs of the Adventure of David Balfour in the Year 1751; how he was kidnapped and cast away, his sufferings on a desert isle, his journey in the wild highlands, his acquaintance with Alan Breck Stewart and other notorious highland Jacobites, with all that he suffered at the hands of his uncle, Ebenezer Balfour of Shaws, falsely so called."

A: **Killing a king**
Q: What is regicide?
W: Regicide means the killing or killer of a king or sovereign. *Regis* means "king," and *cide* means "killing" or "killer."

A: **King Arthur**
Q: Who wielded a sword named Excalibur?
W: King Arthur is a legendary king of the sixth century. He was the hero of the Round Table and subject of many romances. In Arthurian legend, "Excalibur" or "Caliburn" was the sword of King Arthur.

A: **King Midas**
Q: Who turned all he touched to gold?
W: Midas once found Silenus asleep on the banks of a river where he had been tied up by some peasants while he was drunk. Midas released him and was offered a wish by Dionysus, who was grateful for Midas' kindness to his follower. Midas asked that everything he touched be turned to gold, but soon regretted this because even his food turned to gold. After Midas washed in a sacred river, the spell was lifted.

A: *King Rat*
Q: What James Clavell novel was filmed with George Segal as its star?
W: James Clavell, an Australian-born film director and novelist, was captured by the Japanese when he was 18. He was imprisoned at the notorious Changi Jail, where his first book *King Rat* was set. It is the powerful study of the relationships and characters of the prisoners, British and American, in the face of cruelty and imminent death.

A: **Korak**
Q: Who was Tarzan's son in the books by Edgar Rice Burroughs?
W: Korak was also Tarzan and Jane's son in the 1920 movie *The Son of Tarzan*. He was played by Gordon Griffith as a boy and by Kamuela Searle as a man. Searle was killed by an elephant named Tantor while filming the movie.

A: Kris Kringle
Q: Who's the hero of Valentine Davie's *Miracle on 34th Street*?
W: *Miracle on 34th Street* is the story of an old man who thinks he is Santa Claus. His name is Kris Kringle, and not only do children love him, but reindeer eat out of his hand. Because certain practical people refuse to believe he is Santa Claus he is taken to court and tried for lunacy. The lives of many people are affected by Judge Harper's verdict.

A: Krypto
Q: What's the name of Superman's dog?
W: Krypto was Superboy's Superdog, "Dog of Steel." Krypton was Superman's planet of birth. Kryptonite is a metal that affects Superman's power.

A: Krypton
Q: What planet gave birth to Superman?
W: Superman was born on the doomed planet Krypton. He landed on earth after being launched into space just before the collapse of the planet. His adoptive parents were Jonathan and Martha Kent.

A: Kurt Vonnegut Jr.'s
Q: Whose books include *Breakfast of Champions, Cat's Cradle* and *Slapstick*?
W: *Cat's Cradle* revolves around the confrontation of opposing philosophies. Following his book *Slaughterhouse Five*, Vonnegut's work showed a sharp decline in quals and *Slapstick* were published.

A: Kurt Vonnegut Jr.
Q: Who created Billy Pilgrim, a survivor of the Dresden firestorm?
W: Kurt Vonnegut, Jr., born in Indianapolis, was a prisoner of war in Dresden during the saturation bombing of the city and its subsequent firestorm. *Slaughterhouse Five* follows the career of Billy Pilgrim, also a survivor of the Dresden firestorm, who finds peace of mind after being kidnapped and learning the secret of life is to live only in the happy moments.

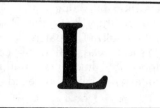

A: L.L.
Q: What are the most common initials of Superman's friends and enemies?
W: Friends: Lois Lane, Lana Lang, Lori Lemaris, Lightning Lad, Luma Lynai, Linda Lee. Enemies: Lorraine Lewis, Lee Luthor.

A: *La dolce vita*
Q: What's the soft life in Rome?
W: *La dolce vita* means "the sweet life" or a life devoted to luxury and pleasure.

A: Lady Godiva
Q: Who did Peeping Tom peep at?
W: According to one story, during Lady Godiva's historic ride, a tailor named Tom peeped through a shutter and was struck blind. This traditional incident is the origin of the phrase "Peeping Tom."

A: Lady Godiva
Q: Who rode naked through the streets of Coventry?
W: Lady Godiva, the wife of Earl Leofric of Chester, England, lived during the 1000s. She asked her husband to reduce the heavy taxes he had imposed, and he agreed to do so if she would ride naked through town. She asked all the townspeople to remain indoors, and, clothed only in her long hair, she mounted a horse and rode through the streets. Let's all get naked and reduce taxes!

A: *Lampoon, The*
Q: What's the name of Harvard University's satirical newspaper?
W: A "lampoon" refers to any piece of pointed mockery of an individual or institution. Its use is seen in the name of Harvard University's humor magazine, *The Harvard Lampoon* .

A: Larry Flynt
Q: Who's the controversial publisher of *Hustler*?
W: I'll say he's controversial! He pushes the first amendment to its limits and sometimes beyond.

A: last, The
Q: What chapter of *Gone with the Wind* has Rhett Butler leaving Scarlett O'Hara?
W: *Tomorrow Is Another Day* was the book's original title. *Gone With The Wind* came from Ernest Dowson's poem "Cynara," in particular, the 13th line: "I have forgot much, Cynara! gone with the wind, /Flung roses, roses riotously with the throng."

A: *Last Tycoon, The*
Q: What book was F. Scott Fitgerald working on when he died in Hollywood in 1940?
W: After a life of extravagance and mental and physical deterioration, Fitzgerald made an enormous effort to pull himself together and found work in Hollywood. But he did not live to complete *The Last Tycoon*. He died of a heart attack at the age of 45.

A: Latin
Q: What subject did Mr. Chips teach?
W: *Goodbye, Mr. Chips* is the best-selling short novel by James Hilton that deals sentimentally with the life of an English schoolteacher, Mr. Chips. Hilton also wrote *Lost Horizon* and *Random Harvest*.

A: Lean
Q: What couldn't Jack Sprat's wife eat?
W: And Jack could eat no fat, and so betwixt them both, you see, they licked the platter clean.

A: Lee Harvey Oswald's
Q: Whose mother was the subject of Jean Stafford's *A Mother in History*?
W: Stafford wrote the book after three days of extensive, candid interviews with Mrs. Marguerite Oswald in Fort Worth, Texas. It relates the

biograpy of Mrs. Oswald, the mother of the man who killed John F. Kennedy. Her quotes and feelings about her son are included.

A: **Lee Harvey Oswald's**
Q: Whose biography, written by his brother, was titled *Lee*?
W: Robert L. Oswald attempts to shed light on his brother Lee's life and the unanswered questions concerning the assassination. The book was published in 1967.

A: **left, The**
Q: Which ear did Vincent Van Gogh partially cut off?
W: Vincent Van Gogh, one of the most famous painters in modern art, received no recognition and sold only one painting during his life. He failed in every career and felt unloved and friendless throughout his lifetime. During an epileptic seizure in 1888, he threatened to kill the French painter, Paul Gauguin, who was visiting him. During this seizure, he cut off one of his own ears. In 1890 he committed suicide.

A: **left, The**
Q: Which side of a book are the even-numbered pages usually on?
W: Books generally begin with a right-hand page numbered 1; thus the even pages will always be the left-handed ones.

A: **Len Deighton**
Q: Who wrote *Funeral in Berlin*?
W: Len Deighton is the author of several best-selling books of international espionage, beginning with the *Ipcress File*. *Funeral in Berlin* is a tale of the nightmare world where double and triple crosses are common practices. It is set in Europe from London to Berlin, the divided city where enemies become friends and friends enemies.

A: **Leningrad's**
Q: What city's siege is chronicled in Harrison Salisbury's *The 900 Days*?
W: Salisbury chronicles the seige by Hitler's army of the Russian city, Leningrad, a seige endured by more than three million people of whom just under one half died. It is a history of the bravery and suffering of these people during World War II. Salisbury, an American correspondent, wrote his book after going to Leningrad in January 1944 after the seige was lifted.

A: **Lenny Bruce's**
Q: Whose autobiography is titled *How to Talk Dirty and Influence People*?
W: Lenny Bruce, born Leonard A. Schneider in 1926, died on Aug. 3, 1966. He was a nightclub comedian, monologist, and author of two books. *How to Talk Dirty and Influence People* was his autobiography, published in 1965. *The Essential Lenny Bruce*, his other book, was published in 1967.

A: **Leonardo da Vinci**
Q: Who painted the *Mona Lisa*?
W: Leonardo da Vinci, 1452-1519, was an Italian artist, scientist, inventor, and creative genius — one of the most multi-faceted original thinkers of all ages. The *Mona Lisa*, painted in 1503 and one of his most famous paintings, was the portrait of the wife of a Florentine merchant. The painting hangs in the Louvre, Paris. It is considered the most valuable painting in the world, assessed at $100 million for insurance purposes.

A: **Leon Uris's**
Q: What author's first novel was *Battle Cry*, in 1953?
W: Uris was born in Baltimore in 1924. He wrote this popular novel about the World War II U.S. Marines with whom he served as a private from 1942 to 1946.

A: **library, A**
Q: What's a *bibliotek* in Frankfurt?
W: The *Deutsch Bibliotek* in Frankfurt is one of the main libraries of the Federal Republic of Germany. Public libraries in West Germany report holdings of more than 30 million volumes with 80 million lendings a year.

A: **Library of Congress, The**
Q: What's the largest library in the world?
W: The Library of Congress in Washington, D.C., was founded in 1800, initially to make books available to congressional members. It is the largest library, and has perhaps the greatest collection, in the world, exceeding 74 million pieces of material. It is housed in two buildings opposite the Capitol.

A: **license to kill, A**
Q: What does the double-O indicate in 007?
W: It is taken from Ian Fleming's character James Bond in the series of thriller, secret agent novels.

A: *Life*
Q: What magazine paid $50,000 for an eight-millimeter film of John F. Kennedy's assassination?
W: In the tradition of *Time* magazine, after its change of ownership in 1936, *Life* became more a news magazine than a humorous weekly. These color pictures were taken at the assassination scene by Abraham Zapruder using a home movie camera and were published in *Life* the week of the president's funeral.

A: *Life*
Q: What magazine hit the newsstands on Nov. 23, 1936?
W: It was founded by J.A. Mitchell and E.S. Martin, young Harvard graduates, in 1883. It was intended to be a satirical weekly. In 1936 *Time* magazine publishers purchased the name *Life* and began its publication.

A: *Life on the Mississippi*
Q: What's the title of Mark Twain's autobiography?
W: Mark Twain, pen name for Samuel Clemens, gives a brief history of the Mississippi River along with his life history in this vividly descriptive book.

A: *Li'l Abner*
Q: What comic strip inspired the observance of Sadie Hawkins Day?
W: *Li'l Abner*, the comic strip by Al Capp, began Aug. 12, 1935. Li'l Abner and his father and mother, Pappy and Mammy Yokum, live in Dogpatch, somewhere in the Appalachian mountains. Sadie Hawkins Day is the first Saturday after Nov. 11, when girls chase boys to catch husbands. Sadie is the daughter of Hekgebiah Hawkins, one of the founders of Dogpatch.

A: **Lillian Hellman**
Q: What authoress had a 30-year love affair with Dashiell Hammett?
W: Hellman was a New York dramatist who was born in 1905 and who died in 1984. Hammett was an American writer of detective stories, perhaps best known for *The Maltese Falcon* (1930) and *The Thin Man* (1932).

A: **Lilliput**
Q: Where did Gulliver find a race of tiny people?
W: Lilliput was an imaginary country peopled with little characters in the book *Gulliver's Travels* by Jonathan Swift. The book, published in 1726, was a satire on man and human institutions and a wonderful travelogue of adventures that still appeals to young and old.

A: **limerick, A**
Q: What type of humorous verse might begin: "There once was a man from Nantucket?"
W: A limerick is said to have been a custom at convivial parties, during which each member sang and extemporized "nonsense verse." It is hard to establish who first applied this term to the nonsense verse, although it is thought that the term comes from the city of Limerick, Ireland.

A: **Linus**
Q: What Peanuts character clings to a security blanket?
W: *Peanuts*, the most real comic strip in the world, was created by Charles Shultz. It debuted Oct. 2, 1950. All characters live in Sabastopal, California. The four original members were Charlie Brown, Snoopy, Patty, and Sherman. Lucy Van Pelt is a militant little girl whose brother, Linus, is always carrying a security blanket made of flannel.

A: *Little Annie Fanny*
Q: What comic strip is featured in *Playboy*?
W: Little Annie Fanny is the very sexy heroine appearing in a comic stip adventure in *Playboy* magazine. It was created by Harvey Kartzman and Will Elder and first appeared in October 1962.

A: **Little Black Sambo's**
Q: Whose parents were Black Mumbo and Black Jumbo?
W: *Little Black Sambo* was first printed in London in 1899. Author Helen Bannerman wrote this story for her two daughters, but it is considered by some to be racist. The story has also been known as *Little Black Mingo*. Do you remember that Black Sambo ate 169 pancakes, his dad 55, and his mom 27?

A: **Little Boy Blue**
Q: What nursery rhyme character was warned that the cow was in the corn?
W: This is from the classic Mother Goose rhyme: "Little Boy Blue, come blow your horn, The sheep's in the meadow, the cow's in the corn." Little Boy Blue was under the haystack fast asleep!

A: *Little Women*
Q: What Louisa May Alcott novel is subtitled *Meg, Jo, Beth, and Amy*?
W: Alcott portrays herself as Jo in the novel, her sister May is Amy, her sister Elizabeth is Beth, and her sister Anna is Meg.

A: *Little Women*
Q: What 1868 Louisa May Alcott novel sold millions?
W: This cheerful account of Alcott's early life in New England brought financial security to the family portrayed.

A: **"Lloyd's Register"**
Q: What's the annual list of all ships of various classes called?
W: "Lloyd's Register of Shipping," although separate from Lloyd's of London, maintains close liaison. "Lloyd's Register" supervises and sets rules for ship construction, inspects and surveys ships in use, and issues comprehensive registers for seagoing merchant vessels and yachts.

A: *Lolita*
Q: What Vladimir Nabokov novel features Professor Humbert in love with a 12-year-old girl?
W: Nabokov was born in Russia in 1897 and came to the U.S. in 1940, where he was a professor at Cornell and an author. *Lolita* was a farcical and satirical novel of the passion of a middle-aged man and a young girl and their wanderings across the U.S.

A: **London**
Q: Where did Phileas Fogg begin and end his trip around the world?
W: London, the capital of the United Kingdom, is Britain's chief port and major industrial and cultural center. The seaport is the mouth of the Thames River. Jules Verne's classic

Le Tour du Monde en Quatre-vingts jours was published in 1873 and translated to English *Around the World in Eighty Days*. It is the story of Phileas Fogg's daring travel feat, just to win a bet.

A: London and Paris
Q: What were the cities of Dicken's *A Tale of Two Cities*?
W: Dickens wrote *A Tale of Two Cities* in 1859. It took place in Paris and London at the time of the French Revolution.

A: *Longest Day, The*
Q: What Cornelius Ryan book chronicles the events of D-Day?
W: *The Longest Day* was the story of the Normandy landings on D-Day during World War II. It takes place in France, England, and Germany for a brief, yet significant, time in history, June 4 to 6, 1944.

A: Long John Silver
Q: What peg-legged pirate had a parrot named Captain Kidd?
W: Robert Louis Stevenson, author of *Treasure Island*, wrote this book for the amusement of his stepson, Lloyd Osbourne. *Treasure Island* contained the colorful main character Long John Silver, and his shoulder-riding parrot Captain Kidd.

A: *Looking for Mr. Goodbar*
Q: What Judith Rossner novel was made into a film starring Diane Keaton   Rossner's novel about a teacher of deaf children who leads a sordid, secret life was filmed in 1977.

A: Lot's
Q: Whose wife was turned to a pillar of salt   Lot, from the Old Testament, was a son of Harman and the nephew of Abram. In Sodom, Lot was visited by two angels in the form of men. The evil men of Sodom attempted to abuse the visitors sexually and were struck blind by the angels. Lot and his family were warned to flee from the impending doom of Sodom without looking back. Lot's wife, however, looked back and was turned into a pillar of salt.

A: Louvre, Paris; The
Q: Where does the *Venus de Milo* stand?
W: The *Venus de Milo*, the ancient statue of Aphrodite, now stands at the Louvre, Paris. The Louvre, located on the right bank of the Seine River, is one of the world's greatest museums of art. Itself a museum of architectural design, having evolved over a period of 400 years, it covers over 48 acres and contains treasures by da Vinci and many others.

A: Love
Q: What means never having to say you're sorry?
W: This famous quote is from the 1970 film, *Love Story* written by Eric Segal. Two students marry; she dies. (I'm sorry.)

A: Love is never having to say you're sorry
Q: What line did the dying Jenny Cavilleri say to Oliver Barret IV?
W: In Eric Segal's cliche-ridden, but popular, film *Love Story*, Ali MacGraw said these words to Ryan O'Neal.

A: love of money, The
Q: What is the root of all evil?
W: From the New Testament (1 Timothy) the quote is often misquoted as "money is the root of all evil." Mark Twain amended it to read "lack of money is the root of all evil."

A: love letter, The
Q: What's a *billet-doux*?
W: From the French *billet*, "letter" or "message," and *doux*, "affable" or "amiable."

A: *Love Story*
Q: What was the title of Erich Segal's 1970 tearjerker?
W: This touching story was described by Alexander Walker as "*Camille* with bullshit."

A: Lucille Ball's
Q: What comedienne's baby appeared on the first cover of *TV Guide*?
W: Lucille Ball married Cuban band leader Desi Arnaz Oct. 15, 1951. She became perhaps American TV's biggest star with the long-running "I Love Lucy" series. When Ms. Ball became pregnant with Desi, Jr., in 1952, so did the TV Lucy, and the world waited.

A: Ludwig von Beethoven
Q: Who is Schroeder's favorite composer?
W: Beethoven (1770-1827), the German composer, is considered by many to be the greatest composer ever to have lived. He is the favorite of the piano-playing *Peanuts* comic strip character, Schroeder.

M

A: **M**
Q: What letter was the pseudonym of the author of *The Sensuous Man*?
W: This is a cheap spin-off book for men that followed the original book *The Sensuous Woman* by J, published in 1969. Both books concentrate on advice and instructions on how to be a better lover. Both are early sexual "how-to" books in the sexual revolution.

A: *Macbeth*
Q: What's the shortest and bloodiest of Shakespeare's plays?
W: *Macbeth*, written in 1606, was probably meant as a tribute to King James I. It is the story of the bloody, murderous, and unsuccessful attempt by Macbeth to be King of Scotland.

A: **Mad Hatter's, The**
Q: Whose hat featured a sign reading: "In this style 10/6"?
W: The Mad Hatter is one of the strange characters Alice meets in Lewis Carroll's children's story, *Alice's Adventure in Wonderland*, or *Through the Looking Glass*, published in 1865.

A: **Madrid**
Q: Where's the Prado art museum?
W: Madrid, the capital and largest city of Spain, is also the hub of transportation, business, and commerce. The Museo del Prado is considered one of the finest art galleries of the world.

A: *Maltese Falcon, The*
Q: What was the first Sam Spade novel?
W: Written by Dashiell Hammett, *The Maltese Falcon* was made into a movie in 1931 by Warner Brothers. Warner Brothers remade the movie ten years later starring Humphrey Bogart.

A: *Man, The*
Q: What Irving Wallace book is about a black U.S. president?
W: Irving Wallace, born March 19, 1916, is the author of numerous books including *The Prize*, published in 1962, and *The Man*, published in 1964.

A: **Man Friday**
Q: Who was Robinson Crusoe's right-hand man?
W: The *Adventures of Robinson Crusoe*, written in 1719, was the best known work of Daniel DeFoe. For his film portrayal of Robinson Crusoe, Dan O'Herlihy was nominated for best actor in 1954, but lost to Marlon Brando for *On the Waterfront*.

A: *Man Who Came to Dinner, The*
Q: Who was Sheridan Whiteside?
W: This is Julius J. and Philip G. Epstein's story of an acid-tongued radio celebrity who breaks his hip while on a lecture tour and terrorizes the inhabitants of the suburban home where he must stay for several weeks. It was made into a movie in 1941, starring Monty Woolley as Sheridan Whiteside.

A: **Margaret Mitchell**
Q: What woman won the 1937 Pulitzer Prize for fiction?
W: Mitchell wrote *Gone with the Wind*, her only novel, from 1926 to 1936. It is a long, romantic novel of Georgia during and after the Civil War. The book had unprecedented popularity that was boosted by a lavish motion picture production first released in 1939.

A: **Marilyn Monroe**
Q: Who appeared on the first cover of *Playboy*?
W: For $200 Hugh Hefner purchased from a calendar printer the two color plates and one-time reproduction rights of a picture of Marilyn Monroe in the nude. Based on this, a few risque jokes, and a few articles from known writers, he was able to borrow money on his 1950 Studebaker, get 45 days credit from the printer, and the rest is history!

A: **Marilyn Monroe**
Q: What movie star did Norman Mailer write about?
W: Norman Mailer is a popular American writer born in 1923. He wrote a speculative biography of film star Marilyn Monroe in 1973. He also wrote *Of Women and Their Elegance*, an imaginary memoir of Marilyn Monroe in 1982.

A: **Marilyn Monroe**
Q: Who was *Playboy*'s first centerfold model?
W: No centerfold ever received less. Hefner paid $200 for the picture, which he bought from a calendar printer. Marilyn Monroe made not a cent, and Hefner went on to earn millions.

A: **Mario Puzo**
Q: Who wrote *The Godfather*?
W: Mario Puzo wrote the novel on which the 1971 movie was based. It is the story of the Mafia in America, although the word *mafia* is never spoken.

A: **Mark Lane**
Q: What New York City lawyer wrote *Rush to Judgment*, criticizing the Warren Commission Report?
W: Mark Lane wrote the critique of the Warren Commission's inquiry into the murders of President John F. Kennedy, Officer J.D. Tippet, and Lee Harvey Oswald after a two-and-a-half year investigation of his own, including reading the 26 volumes of testimony, trips to Dallas, and interviews with witnesses. He said he wrote it because of grave and inexplicable contradictions in the Warren Report that made it unclear that Oswald acted alone as the Commission concluded.

A: **Mark Twain**
Q: Who wrote about a frog called Dan'l from Calaveras county?
W: "The Celebrated Jumping Frog of Calaveras County" was published in the New York Saturday Press in the autumn of 1865 and won Twain fame as a humorist. It was written during Twain's few years spent in

California. He fled there when a verbal duel with a rival journalist in the East became a challenge to duel with pistols.

A: Mark Twain
Q: Who wrote *The Prince and the Pauper*?
W: Twain wrote *The Prince and the Pauper* in 1881. It was his first attempt at historical romance and at a children's story.

A: Mark Twain
Q: What 19th-century humorist cabled home from Europe: "The report of my death was an exaggeration"?
W: Twain sent the above cable to the Associated Press from Europe in response to erroneous reports of his death. Other quotes from Twain include: "A Classic is something that everybody wants to have read but nobody wants to read"; "When angry count to a hundred; when very angry, swear"; and "There ain't no way to find out why a snorer can't hear himself snore".

A: Mark Twain
Q: Who was the first novelist to present a typed manuscript to the publisher?
W: Twain, always interested in business and inventions, supported himself for a time as a printer. The first typewriter, the Remington, appeared on the market in 1874. The machine was named the Remington. Mark Twain purchased a Remington and became the first author to submit a typewritten manuscript.

A: Mark Twain
Q: What author did Hal Holbrook portray in his one-man Broadway show?
W: Hal Holbrook was born Harold Rowe Holbrook on Feb. 17, 1925. He first appeared in New York at the Purple Onion (nightclub) in February 1955 in his original one-man show *Mark Twain Tonight!* Holbrook made his broadway debut on April 6, 1959.

A: Marquis de Sade, The
Q: What French writer served 27 years in prison for sexual offenses?
W: He was the author of obscene writings that have linked his name to the term "sadism." His life of debauchery led him to be imprisoned in 1772 where his death sentence was commuted by the king. The Revolution freed him, but Bonaparte had him committed to an insane asylum, where he died. He is today considered a psychologist and analyst a century ahead of his time.

A: Mars
Q: Where does Ray Bradbury's *Chronicles* take place?
W: Bradbury was born in Illinois in 1920. He is known for works of fantasy and science fiction, including *Martian Chronicles* in 1950, which was titled *The Silver Locusts* in England. It is a story about Mars, a century hence.

A: Marshall McLuhan
Q: Who gained fame with the book *The Gutenberg Galaxy*?
W: *The Gutenberg Galaxy* attempted to demonstrate how the structure of modern western society evolved from the invention of movable type. Marshall McLuhan (1911-1980), a Canadian, was a communication theorist. He is best known for his book *The Medium is the Message*.

A: Martin Luther King, Jr.'s
Q: Whose assassination is probed in a book by Mark Lane and Dick Gregory called *Code Name "Zorro"*?
W: This book asks the question: was James Earl Ray the solitary assassin or a "jackal-like hired killer"? Or was he an unwitting pawn in a far-reaching conspiracy to murder Martin Luther King, Jr.? Mark Lane is a lawyer, author, former member of the New York State legislature and director of Citizens Committee of Inquiry, an organization that urged Congress to investigate the murders of Martin Luther King, Jr., and John F. Kennedy. Dick Gregory is a political activist, civil rights worker, and a famous black comedian.

A: martini, The
Q: What cocktail inspired John Doxat to write the book *Stirred – Not Shaken*?
W: John Doxat's book, subtitled *The Dry Martini* was published in London in 1976. It is a 192-page book on the martini, with an introduction by Kingsley Amos.

A: Marvel Comics
Q: What company published *The Fantastic Four*, *The Incredible Hulk*, and *The Mighty Thor*?
W: Marvel comics also published such greats as *Cyclops*, *Human Torch*, and *Submariner*. Remember those?

A: Mary Poppins
Q: What's the name of P.L. Travers's magical nanny?
W: P.L. Travers's book was about a "practically perfect" nanny who brings profound change to the Banks family of Edwardian London. It was made into a four-star film in 1964, starring Julie Andrews.

A: Matthew, Mark, Luke, John
Q: What four evangelists wrote the Gospels?
W: The Gospels are four narratives covering the life and death of Jesus Christ. They were written, according to tradition, by Matthew, Mark, Luke, and John, respectively. The Gospels occur at the beginning of the New Testament and comprise about half of the total text.

A: *Mayor of Casterbridge, The*
Q: What Thomas Hardy novel centers on a Wessex county mayor?
W: Published by Hardy in 1886, it is a novel about a hay-tresser who gets drunk and sells his wife and child. When he regains his senses, he vows not to drink for 20 years. Although he becomes the rich, respected mayor in his sobriety, the trials and tribulations continue for Michael Hinchard, Mayor of Casterbridge,.

ART AND LITERATURE

A: **medium, The**
Q: What's Marshall McLuhan's message?
W: McLuhan was best known for his ideas about the ways in which the various media of communication and the devices of technology shape society and even perception itself.

A: *Merchant of Venice, The*
Q: What Shakespearean play featured Shylock?
W: This play, a comedy, was probably written in about 1596. Shylock is a moneylender who claims that he is owed a pound of flesh from Bassanio, an honest but poor debtor. Portia, Bassanio's wife, cleverly argues successfully that he is entitled to not one drop of blood and can collect his flesh only if he can do so bloodlessly.

A: **Merlin**
Q: What magician dazzled at King Arthur's court?
W: Merlin, the magician in the Authurian legend of the Knights of the Round Table, may have actually had some place in ancient English history. He is supposed to have helped bring the great stones to Stonehenge from Ireland.

A: **Methuselah**
Q: Who lived to the ripe old age of 969?
W: Methuselah, mentioned in the Old Testament, was the father of Lamech, grandfather of Noah, and a descendant of Seth. He was said to be the oldest person to have ever lived.

A: **Mia Farrow**
Q: Who was on the first cover of *People*?
W: On March 4, 1974, *People Weekly* published its first issue with actress Mia Farrow on the cover. Mia was married twice, to Frank Sinatra and then to Andre Previn with whom she had twins. In 1973 she starred in the film, *The Great Gatsby*.

A: **Michael**
Q: What's Doonesbury's first name?
W: Michael J. Doonesbury and cohorts were comic strip characters who appeared in over 500 daily strips and 80 color Sunday features. In 1975, for the first time in the history of journalism awards, the Pulitzer Prize for Editorial Cartooning went to Garry Trudeau's nationally syndicated *Doonesbury*.

A: **Michelangelo**
Q: Who painted the Sistine Chapel?
W: Michelangelo, Italian sculptor, architect, painter, and poet, was born March 6, 1475. From May 1508 to October 1512, he worked to complete the fresco of the vault of the Sistine Chapel.

A: **Michelangelo**
Q: Who carved the famed Medici tombs in Florence?
W: The tombs were done at intervals between 1521 and 1534 and are considered to be the most melancholy of all Michelangelo's works. The architecture and statues immerse spectators in a gray and introspective world.

A: **Mickey Spillane**
Q: Who created detective Mike Hammer?
W: Mickey Spillane (real name Frank Morrison) was born in 1918 and is the prolific author of tough detective stories published in the 1940s through the 1960s.

A: *Midnight Cowboy*
Q: What James Leo Herlihy novel recounts the story of Joe Buck and Rico Rizzo?
W: Herlihy was born in Detroit in 1927 and wrote *Midnight Cowboy* in 1965. It is the story of an ingenuous cowboy who goes to New York City, participates in the seamy nightlife, and takes up with a crippled pickpocket. It was made into a movie in 1969, starring Dustin Hoffman and Jon Voight.

A: *Midsummer Night's Dream*
Q: What Shakespearean play features a character named Puck?
W: It was a comedy probably written about 1595 or 1596. Set in Greece, it includes Puck, a mischievous sprite who is sent to fetch magic flower juice which, when placed on sleeping eyelids, causes the subject to fall in love.

A: **Miguel de Cervantes**
Q: What classical Spanish writer warned: "All that glitters is not gold"?
W: Miguel de Cervantes Soavedra, a Spanish writer born in 1547, is best known for his book *Don Quixote*, from which comes this quotable quote.

A: **Miguel de Cervantes and William Shakespeare**
Q: What Spanish and English writers died on the same day—April 23, 1616?
W: Cervantes, born in 1547 in the province of Madrid, and William Shakespeare, born at Stratford-on-Avon, England, in 1564, both died in 1616.

A: *Mila 18*
Q: What Leon Uris book compelled Joseph Heller to change his title from *Catch-18* to *Catch-22*?
W: Heller, a New York author born in 1923 and a contemporary of Uris, wrote *Catch-22* in 1961, the same year Uris wrote *Mila 18*. Heller was in the air force in World War II, and *Catch 22* is a comic account of a

madcap bombardier's resistance to his fanatic commander's desire for promotion at the expense of his American squadron.

A: *Mila 18*
Q: What Leon Uris novel deals with the Warsaw Ghetto uprising?
W: *Mila 18*, written in 1961, is a novel about the revolt of the Warsaw Jewish Ghetto against the Nazis.

A: **Minesweeper**
Q: What class of ship was the *Caine*?
W: *The Caine Mutiny* is a novel by Herman Wouk published in 1951. It is the story about Willie Keith, a wealthy, spoiled Princeton grad who entered the navy in 1942 as a midshipman and grows to manhood through his experiences in the South Pacific aboard the *Caine*.

A: **Miss Moneypenny**
Q: Who is M's secretary?
W: Miss Moneypenny is the secretary to M, who is British Secret Service agent James Bond's boss. Bond is the super agent in the series of novels by Ian Fleming. The movie series started with *Dr. No* in 1962.

A: **Miss Piggy**
Q: What puppet was featured on the August 1980 cover of *Life*?
W: Jim Henson's "The Muppet Show" was an award winning series in the late 1970s. Some of the adorable characters are also featured on "Sesame Street". Kermit the Frog and Miss Piggy are two of the favorites.

A: **Miss Piggy**
Q: What superstar porcine character has her own *Guide to Life*, as told to Henry Beard?
W: The famous Muppet, Miss Piggy, who constantly refers to herself as "moi" and is in love with Kermit the Frog, has her own tongue-in-cheek *Guide to Life*, published in 1981. Some chapters include: Body Language, Depressed, Exercise, Food, Manners, and Success. In instructions on makeup she says:

"Never wear yellow lipstick, never put anything blue on your cheeks, and never purchase beauty products at a hardware store".

A: **Mississippi**
Q: What southern state is the setting of William Faulkner's *The Sound and the Fury*?
W: It's the story of a once proud southern family that has sunk low in financial and moral stature and a stern elder son who tries to do something about it. It was made into a film in 1959 starring Yul Brynner and Joanne Woodward.

A: **Mitchell**
Q: What's Dennis the Menace's last name?
W: *Dennis the Menace* was a 30-minute comedy show on CBS from September 1959 to September 1963. The Mitchell family lived at 627 Elm Street, Hillsdale. Henry, an engineer, and wife Alice had only one child, the mischievous Dennis. Dennis's real name was Jay North; Henry was played by Herbert Anderson, Alice by Gloria Henry, George Wilson by Joseph Kearns, and Martha Wilson by Sylvia Field. And don't forget Freemont, the dog. The TV show was based on the original comic strip of the same name.

A: *Moby Dick*
Q: What book do Stubb, Starbuck and Queequeg appear in?
W: In Herman Melville's 1851 novel *Moby Dick*, Stubb is the happy-go-lucky second mate; Starbuck is the earnest, prudent first mate; and Queequeg is a Polynesian prince. It was made into a movie in 1930, starring John Barrymore, and again in 1956, starring Gregory Peck.

A: **Mock Turtle**
Q: What character encountered by Alice never stops sobbing?
W: Mock Turtle is one of the strange characters in *Alice's Adventures in Wonderland* (1865) by Lewis Carroll.

A: *Mommie Dearest*
Q: What Christina Crawford book was originally titled *The Hype*?
W: Christina Crawford's book was about growing up as the adopted and abused daughter of movie queen Joan Crawford. It was made into a film in 1981 starring Faye Dunaway as Joan Crawford.

A: *Mona Lisa, The*
Q: What's the alternate title of the masterpiece painting *La Giaconda*?
W: It is a portrait painted by Leonardo da Vinci. The subject was the seond wife of Francesco Bartolommeo del Giacondo, a Florentine merchant. The painting is also called *La Giaconda*.

A: *Mona Lisa, The*
Q: What was stolen from the Louvre on Aug. 21, 1911?
W: The *Mona Lisa*, painted by Leonardo da Vinci in 1503, was stolen by Vincenzo Peruggia in order to return the masterpiece to its native land. If you're going to steal a painting why not steal one of the world's best known works? A bit difficult to fence, don't you agree?

A: *Mona Lisa, The*
Q: What's the most looked-at painting in the Louvre?
W: This painting, which Leonard da Vinci began in 1503, has been a fascination to people the world over because of the subject's enigmatic smile, which some art critics consider not a smile at all but the outer expression of inner life that Leonardo had defined as the aim of portraiture.

A: **Mongooses**
Q: What's the plural of mongoose?
W: Mongooses are any of various small furry animals that are noted for their ability to kill mice, rats, and snakes. When confronting a snake, the mongoose deliberately induces it to strike. When the snake does so, the mongoose steps smartly aside, then pounces on the snake's head from above, cracking the skull with one bite. Who would want mongooses around the house?

A: Moo
Q: What prehistoric kingdom does Alley Oop live in?
W: This comic strip was introduced by its creator, Vince T. Hanlin, on Aug. 7, 1933. The prehistoric kingdom of Moo is ruled by King Gug (or Guzzle), whose daughter Wootie is enamored of Alley Oop, who in turn loves (and later marries) Oola.

A: Moscow and New York
Q: What two cities were destroyed in the novel *Fail Safe*?
W: In this novel by Eugene Burdick, an American bomber is accidentally sent to destroy Moscow, and the president then has to agree to destroy New York in compensation. It was made into a movie starring Henry Fonda in 1964.

A: Mothers-in-law
Q: What did Mark Twain put last on a 27-item list of things to be rescued in the event of a boardinghouse fire?
W: This is from a short work entitled "At a Fire" that appeared in the book *Mark Twain's Letters from the Earth*. Twain has methodically planned what you should save in the case of a boardinghouse fire: Fiancees are first, followed by relatives, including third cousins, and everyone else you could possibly imagine, then possessions such as furniture (item 26), and finally mothers-in-law!

A: *Mousetrap, The*
Q: What Agatha Christie play features Molly Ralston, Major Metcalf, and Detective-Sergeant Trotter?
W: Agatha Christie was born on Sept. 15, 1890. She was a prolific writer of detective fiction and plays. *The Mousetrap*, which opened in London in 1952, became the longest-running legitimate play in history. Christie died Jan. 12, 1976.

A: Mudville
Q: Where did the baseball game take place in the poem "Casey at the Bat"?

W: The hometown of Casey's baseball team in "Casey at the Bat", a poem by written Ernest L. Thayer in 1888, was said to be Boston.

A: Mrs. Hudson
Q: Who's Sherlock Holmes' landlady?
W: Mrs. Hudson was played by Mary Gordon in the film adaptation of Arthur Conan Doyle's mystery novel series. The earliest movie was made in 1932 starring Clive Brook as Holmes. Most other Sherlock Holmes movies starred Basil Rathbone as the super sleuth.

A: Munchkins
Q: What's the name of the little people in Frank Baum's *The Wonderful Wizard of Oz*?
W: It is the story of a Kansas girl who goes "Over the Rainbow" to a land of colorful characters and spirited adventure. In the 1939 film version of this genuine American classic, the Munchkins were played by the Singer Midgets.

A: *Murder in the Cathedral*
Q: What T.S. Eliot play is set in Canterbury Cathedral?
W: *Murder in the Cathedral*, written by Eliot in 1935, is a latter-day morality play about the assassination of Thomas Becket that affirms the value of the Church as a medium for social action. Eliot was a loyal Anglo-Catholic.

A: *Mutiny on the Bounty*
Q: What was the first book of the trilogy that ended with *Pitcairn's Island*?
W: Charles Nordhoff and James Hall lived in Tahiti and wrote popular novels including *Mutiny on the Bounty* (1932), *Men Against the Sea* (1934), and *Pitcairn's Island* (1934), a trilogy about the 18th-century mutiny against Captain Bligh.

A: Mutt
Q: Who met Jeff in 1908?
W: Mutt is from the comic strip created by Bud Fisher, which debuted Nov. 15, 1907.

A: *My Friend Flicka*
Q: What's the name of Mary O'Hara's classic tale of a boy and his colt?
W: This story takes place on the Goose Bar Ranch in Montana during the 1880s and concerns the McLaughlins, their son Ken, and a once wild stallion named Flicka (Swedish for Little Girl).

A: Mycroft
Q: What was the name of Sherlock Holmes' smarter brother?
W: Mycroft Holmes, Sherlock Holmes brother, was supposed to have been even more clever than Sherlock. Mycroft is 7 years older than Sherlock; he appeared in three stories: "The Great Interpreter", "The Final Problem", and "The Adventure of Bruce-Partington Plans."

A: *Myra Breckenridge*
Q: What Gore Vidal novel traces the life of a transvestite?
W: Myra Breckenridge is the main character in Gore Vidal's 1964 satire about the lurid adventures of a transsexual. It was made into a movie in 1970 starring Raquel Welch, and it bombed.

N

A: N
Q: What letter ends all Japanese words not ending with a vowel?
W: Remember *A, E, I, O, U*, and sometimes *Y* are vowels. Now check out the Japanese restaurants, food products, autos, etc. and see for yourself!

A: *Naked Came the Stranger*
Q: What best-selling 1969 sex spoof had a different author for every chapter?
W: Twenty-five writers, all editors and reporters for *Newsday* magazine, contributed to this book by Penelope Ashe. Published in 1969, it is about the seduction of a wife mad at her spouse. Critics rated the erotic fantasies in this book at a "C."

A: Narcissus
Q: What beautiful youth pined for the love of his reflection?
W: In Greek mythology, Nemesis caused Narcissus to fall in love with his own image in a pool of water and to pine away for it until he died. Narcissus was then changed into a flowering plant, the narcissus.

A: Narnia
Q: What's the fairy tale world in C.S. Lewis' "The Lion, the Witch, and the Wardrobe?"
W: Well-known as a poet and author, C.S. Lewis created for children the strange new world of Narnia, which they first enter through an old wardrobe. In this adventure story the children become kings and queens of Narnia. They engage in endless conflict between good and evil, symbolized by the benevolent Lion, Aslam, and the malicious witch.

A: *Negro*
Q: What's the Spanish word for "black?"
W: Translated from Spanish *negro* means "black," "jet-black," "blackish," "murky," "gloomy," "dismal," "melancholy," "unfortunate," "wretched," "sablel;" also a black person of the color.

A: Neil Simon
Q: What playwright blitzed Broadway with four simultaneously-running plays in the 1966-67 season?
W: Neil Simon is the only playwright in history to have four Broadway plays running simultaneously. They were *Barefoot in the Park*, *The Odd Couple*, *Star-Spangled Girl*, and *Sweet Charity*.

A: Nelson Rockefeller's
Q: Whose life story is titled *I Never Wanted to be Vice-President of Anything*?
W: Nelson Aldrich Rockefeller (1908-1979) was a U.S. political leader and art collector. He was elected governor of New York state in 1958, 1962, 1966, and 1970. In 1974 he became the 41st U.S. vice-president, after being nominated by Gerald R. Ford. He retired to private life in 1977 having never attained the presidency, as he had so desired for many years. His biography, co-authored with Sam Roberts and Michael Krames, was published in 1976.

A: Never-Never Land
Q: Where would you arrive by going second to the right and straight on till morning?
W: Sir James Matthew Barrie, British journalist and author, gained immense popularity with his dramatic children's fantasy *Peter and Wendy*, published in 1911. Peter Pan, the boy who wouldn't grow up, along with his fairy friend Tinker Bell, visits the three children of the Darling family – Wendy, John, Michael, and their nurse Nana (a dog). He takes them all to Never-Never Land where they encounter Captain Hook, pirates, Redskins, and adventure.

A: New York *Daily News*, The
Q: What newspaper carried a column by Ed Sullivan for more than 40 years?
W: The New York *Daily News*, founded in 1919, was the first successful tabloid newspaper in America and still has the largest daily circulation, over two million. It carried Ed Sullivan's column on entertainment. Ed also hosted a successful TV variety show from 1955 to 1971.

A: New York subway train, A
Q: What was taken in *The Taking of Pelham 123*?
W: *The Taking of Pelham 123* was a 1974 movied based on a novel by John Godey. Four ruthless gunmen hold a New York subway train for ransom and have an ingenious plan for escape.

A: New York *Times*, The
Q: What newspaper has the largest Sunday circulation in North America?
W: The *Times* was founded on Sept. 18, 1851, by Henry J. Raymond and George Jones as the New York *Daily News*. In 1857 the word *daily* was dropped. It was developed into a larger paper by Adolph Oaks when he purchased it in 1896, and today it remains a giant.

A: New York *Times*', The
Q: What newspaper's motto is: "All the news that's fit to print?"
W: Adolph Oaks bought the paper in 1896 and developed it into one of the largest in the world with the above slogan. Oaks was publisher until his death in 1935. Arthur O. Sulzberger is now publisher.

A: New York *Times*, The; and The Washington *Post*
Q: What two newspapers first published *The Pentagon Papers*?
W: *The Pentagon Papers* were a Defense Department history of U.S. involvement in Vietnam. The papers were published in the New York *Times* in its issues of June, 13, 14, and 15, 1971. Publication was temporarily interrupted by a restraining

order, but a Supreme Court decision on June 30th upheld the right of the *Times* and the Washington *Post* to publish the documents. Controversy reigned over the contents and the publication of this secret history of the Vietnam War.

A: *New Yorker, The*
Q: What magazine did S.J. Perelman write for?
W: Sidney Joseph Perelman was born in Brooklyn in 1904. For 45 years he was a contributor to *The New Yorker* of short humorous and satirical pieces lampooning the world of advertising, motion pictures, and other popular fiction subjects.

A: **Niccolo Machiavelli**
Q: What Florentine philosopher wrote *The Prince*?
W: Machiavelli was a political theorist and statesman. His best known work was *The Prince*, which was written in 1513. He teaches that the lessons of the past should be applied to the present and that the acquisition and use of power may necessitate unethical methods not in themselves desirable. (The end justifies the means?)

A: *Nineteen Eighty-Four*
Q: What novel has Big Brother watching?
W: In the novel, Europe has become the fascist state of Oceania, ruled by Big Brother. The novel, published in 1949, and the film adaptation of 1955 are well-known for the prophecy of a dehumanized future. What do you think of the prophecy so far?

A: *Nineteen Eighty-Four*
Q: What George Orwell book forsees Oceania, Eurasia, and Eastasia?
W: These three places are settings for Orwell's second political novel. His first was *Animal Farm*. *Nineteen Eighty-Four* was Orwell's last major work. The book exposes Orwell's fear, the horror of totalitarianism.

A: **Noah Webster**
Q: Who compiled the first American dictionary?
W: He was called the "Schoolmaster to America." *A Compendious Dictionary of the English Language* was published in 1806 and continues to be updated to this day as the language changes.

A: **Noah's Ark**
Q: What measured 300 by 50 by 30 cubits?
W: As Bill Cosby said in a skit about Noah and the Ark, "What the hell is a cubit?" It turns out that a cubit is an ancient measurement of length, originally represented by the length of the forearm; usually it was about 18 to 20 inches.

A: **Noel Coward**
Q: Who observed: "Mad dogs and Englishmen go out in the mid-day sun?"
W: Coward, an English actor, dramatist, and composer was born in 1899. His plays of the 1920s established his popularity, and his continued production of plays, musicals, operettas and films added to it. Best known plays include: *Private Lives* (1930), *Cavalcade* (1931), *Design for Living* (1933) and *Blithe Spirit* (1941).

A: **Norman Mailer**
Q: What Pulitzer Prize-winning novelist ran for mayor of New York City?
W: Mailer was born in New Jersey in 1923 and reared in Brooklyn, New York. He is a prolific author of fiction and non-fiction. Two of his well-known works are: *Why Are We in Vietnam?* published in 1967 and *The Executioner's Song* about Gary Gillmore, the convicted and confessed murderer who was executed in 1977, the first such execution in the U.S. in over a decade.

A: **Norman Mailer**
Q: What Pulitzer Prize-winning writer's first novel was *The Naked and the Dead*?
W: After serving in the army in the Pacific he wrote *The Naked and the Dead* in 1948. It was a realistic and naturalistic novel of the fates of 13 men in an infantry platoon who survive the invasion of a Japanese-held island. It was a popular and critical success.

A: **Norman Rockwell**
Q: Who painted more than 300 covers for *The Saturday Evening Post*?
W: Rockwell was an American artist and illustrator, born in New York City in 1894. His first *Post* cover appeared in May, 1916. He contributed regularly to the magazine on an average of about ten illustrations per year. Most of his illustrations were humourous pictorials of family life in America.

O

A: O
Q: What vowel do all Esperanto nouns end in?
W: Esperanto is an artificial language invented in 1887 by Dr. L. Zamenhoff, a Russian scholar. It has a vocabulary based on words in the major European languages with a simple, regularized phonetic and inflection system.

A: Oddjob
Q: Who was Goldfinger's bodyguard?
W: One of the best of the James Bond series of thrillers, *Goldfinger* was filmed in 1964. In it, James prevents an international gold smuggler, Goldfinger, from robbing Fort Knox. This big budget, lively, and amusing film starred Sean Connery and Honor Blackman.

A: "Ode on a Grecian Urn"
Q: What Keats poem contains the observation: "Beauty is truth, truth beauty?"
W: John Keats was born in London in 1795. He acquired a knowledge of Latin, history, and some French, but (what?) no Greek. Other works include "To a Nightingale," "To Autumn," "On Melancholy," and "On Indolence."

A: *Odessa File, The*
Q: What Frederick Forsyth novel has a German journalist searching for a Nazi war criminal?
W: It was made into a mediocre movie in 1974. The story, which takes place in 1963, is about a reporter who tracks down a gang of neo-Nazis. It is an elaborate, but uninvolving suspenser, with several cliff-hanging sequences, but the climax is a letdown.

A: *Of Human Bondage*
Q: What Somerset Maugham novel has been filmed three times?
W: It was first filmed in the U.S. in 1934 and starred Bette Davis. This story of a well-to-do Englishman who is brought down by his infatuation with a sluttish waitress brought Miss Davis to prominence. The film was remade in 1946 by Warner Brothers and remade again by MGM/Seven Arts in 1964 – but neither remake compares to the original adaptation by Bette Davis.

A: *Official Preppy Handbook, The*
Q: What college handbook edited by Lisa Birnbach described how to be really top drawer?
W: This humorous, tongue in cheek book is a guide to being preppie even if you don't have a cute nickname like "Muffy," "Missy," "Skip" or "Chip." It tells you not to feel like a loser even if you've never been to a Harvard-Yale game, Bermuda, or Martha's Vineyard. And it says you can succeed as "preppy" even if you're not rich, Caucasian, or an ace tennis player — but all that helps.

A: Ogden Nash
Q: What U.S. poet penned: "Candy is dandy, but liquor is quicker?"
W: He was a New York author of light verse, ranging from satire to good humor to mildly mad.

A: Oliver Twist
Q: Who was the pupil of Dickens' Fagan?
W: *Oliver Twist*, a novel published in 1837-38 by Charles Dickens, is the story of Oliver, who runs away from cruel treatment to London where he falls in with a gang of thieves headed by Fagan. Every effort is made to make Oliver into a thief.

A: Oliver Twist
Q: What Dickens character said: "Please, sir, I want some more?"
W: Oliver was a boy of unknown parentage, born in a workhouse. He was brought up under cruel conditions and suffered at the hand of Bumble, the character from whom he asked more food.

A: Oliver Twist
Q: What Dickens novel features the Artful Dodger?
W: The Artful Dodger is an impudent young pickpocket in the employ of Fagan, the crook.

A: *Oliver's Story*
Q: What was Erich Segal's sequel to *Love Story*?
W: This sequel showed how Oliver succumbed to depression after the death of his wife, but finally found another girl friend. Love means never having to watch this trendy rubbish! The sequel starred Ryan O'Neal and Candice Bergen and was released in 1978.

A: Omar Khayyam
Q: What Persian astronomer-poet wrote a celebrated collection of quatrains?
W: Translation of his quatrains (*The Rubaiyat*) made him famous as a poet. The common themes of *The Rubaiyat* are: "Life is fugitive and vain; the quest for truth is elusive; joy can be found in the pleasures of wine, love, and contemplation of nature."

A: "On the Beach"
Q: What Nevil Shute novel is about the doomed survivors of a nuclear war?
W: This novel by Nevil Shute takes place when most of the world has been devastated by atomic waste. An American atomic submarine sets out to investigate whatever is left. This gloomy prophecy was made into a movie in 1959 starring Gregory Peck, Ava Gardner, Fred Astaire, and Anthony Perkins.

A: "On the Road"
Q: What book is termed "the Bible of the Beat Generation?"
W: It was written by Jack Kerovac in 1957. The characters are morally hedonistic, finding fullfillment in camaraderie, sex, physical speed,

uninhibited speech, and philosophical generalizations. They refuse to join the "rat race" of the work-a-day world in a time of fear of nuclear war and desperate clinging to economic security.

A: One o'clock
Q: What time was it when the mouse ran up the clock?
W: This is from the classic Mother Goose rhyme: "Hickory, dickory, dock; the mouse ran up the clock; the clock struck one; the mouse ran down; hickory, dickory, dock."

A: Open Sesame
Q: What is the magic phrase in "Ali Baba and the Forty Thieves?"
W: This oriental tale is generally regarded as one of the stories in *The Arabian Nights*. It's the story of two brothers, Ali Baba and Kassim, in a town in Persia. Ali Baba, while collecting wood in the forest, observes 40 robbers gain access to a cave with the words "Open Sesame." Ali Baba speaks the same words and wins access to the cave and their treasure.

A: opossum, An
Q: What kind of animal is Pogo?
W: Pogo is an opossum that lives in Okefenokee Swamp in Ware County, Georgia. He is from the satirical cartoon strip by Walt Kelly. An opossum is an American marsupial of largely arboreal and nocturnal habits, having prehensile paws and tail.

A: *Orca*, The
Q: What was the name of Quint's boat in Peter Benchley's novel *Jaws*?
W: Benchley's novel was made into a film in 1975. It was about a man-eating shark causing havoc off the coast of Long Island. One of the money makers of the exploitation–hungry 1970s films, it contains some suspenseful and frightening sequences. Lest we forget, the *Orca* and its captain were lunch for Jaws in the closing sequence of the film.

A: Oscar Wilde
Q: What Irish-born playwright was sentenced to two years at hard labor for homosexuality?
W: *The Importance of Being Ernest*, proved to be the most successful of his plays. It was in its first year of production when Wilde, married and with two young sons, was imprisoned. When released, with his health and future broken, he went to Paris. Shortly thereafter he died.

A: Othello
Q: Who's Shakespeare's Moorish general in the service of Venice?
W: Othello was the Moore of Venice. In this tragedy by Shakespeare, Othello is married to Desdemona. He is manipulated to question her fidelity and smothers her. Upon finding evidence of her innocence, he kills himself.

A: *Overload*
Q: What Arthur Hailey novel describes the world of electric power production?
W: Hailey's other novels include *Wheels, Airport* and *Hotel*. *Overload* contains fascinating glimpses inside the world of power production and the drama leading up to a power crisis–not short term but a really (lights out) long one.

A: owl, The
Q: What creature is Athena, Greek goddess of wisdom, associated with?
W: In Greek mythology, Athena is the virgin goddess of wisdom, war, arts, and crafts. Owls are seen as predatory, thus the war-like association, and "wise as an owl," thus the association with wisdom.

A: owl, The
Q: Who eloped with the pussycat?
W: Edward Lear (1812-1888) wrote "The Owl and the Pussycat." After a courtship voyage of a year and a day, Owl and Pussy finally buy a ring from Piggy and are blissfully married.

P

A: Pablo Picasso
Q: Who was the only living artist to have his work displayed in the Grand Gallery of the Louvre?
W: Picasso, Spanish painter, sculptor, printmaker, ceramicist, scene designer, and giant of 20th-century art, adapted and created more styles than any other artist. The Louvre, a great museum of art covering 48 acres in Paris, displays most of its painting in the Grand Gallery, and examples of Picasso's paintings were displayed there even before his death in 1973. Picasso lived in Paris during World War II.

A: Pan
Q: What shepherd god was the legendary inventor of the flute?
W: In Greek mythology, Pan was the God of all nature and originally the patron of shepherds and hunters. Enchanted by the musical rustling of the reeds, Pan joined several together to produce the Panpipe. It produced mysterious sounds that startled travelers, thus originated the word *panic*.

A: Panama Canal, The
Q: What canal did Gaugin help build as a laborer?
W: He was one of the 35,000 men who worked on the Canal. It is 51.2 miles long, 38.8 feet deep and 500 feet wide at its narrowest point.

A: *Papillon*
Q: What Henri Charriere best-seller describes his escape from Devil's Island?
W: The book was made into a film in 1973 starring Steve McQueen and Dustin Hoffman. The film was based on Charriere's best-seller

autobiography of life on Devil's Island, a rocky island off the coast of French Guiana, formerly a penal colony. It is filled with detail and torture and "man's inhumanity to man."

A: **Paprika**
Q: What's the Hungarian word for pepper?
W: Paprika is a condiment made from the ripe fruit of a mild variety of red pepper. It has a mildly spicy taste and is red-orange in color.

A: **Papyrus**
Q: What Egyptian writing material gave us the word *paper*?
W: Papyrus is a swamp plant of the sedge family that grows in standing water. A sheet of writing paper, in ancient times, was made by pasting together thin sections of the Egyptian sedge.

A: **Paradise**
Q: What was lost and regained by poet John Milton?
W: *Paradise Lost* was an epic poem by British author John Milton published in 1667. Originally in ten books but rearranged into 12, it is about man's disobedience of God and subsequent loss of Paradise and banishment from it. *Paradise Regained* was published in 1671, as an epic poem sequel. It was arranged in four books and deals with the temptation of Christ in the wilderness.

A: **Paris**
Q: Who was Helen of Troy's Trojan lover?
W: In Greek mythology, Paris, son of Priam and Hecuba, carried off Helen, wife of Menelaus, thus causing the Trojan War.

A: **parrot, A**
Q: What kind of bird taught Dr. Dolittle to talk to the animals?
W: In a Victorian English village, Dr. Dolittle is a veterinary surgeon who talks to his patients. Escaping from a lunatic asylum, he travels with friends to the South Seas in search of the Great Pink Sea Snail. A parrot taught him the tricks of the trade.

A: **Pat Nixon**
Q: Who was the subject of Lester David's *The Lonely Lady of San Clemente*?
W: David's book is a compassionate, full-scale biography of Thelma Ryan Nixon, a California farm girl, movie extra, teacher, and First Lady of President Richard Nixon. In developing the story of this remarkable woman, David interviewed over 300 people who knew her.

A: **Paul**
Q: What apostle is Taylor Caldwell's *Great Lion of God*?
W: Janet Taylor Caldwell, Mrs. J. Marcus Reback, was born on Sept. 7, 1901, near Manchester, England. She published *Great Lion of God* in 1970.

A: **Paul Drake**
Q: Who is Perry Mason's private investigator?
W: Paul Drake is the private eye that Mason uses to help find clues and evidence to present in his always melodramatic courtroom scenes. The original Erle Stanley Gardner dramas were made into a very popular TV series that was first telecast in the late 1950s. Raymond Burr starred as Perry Mason; Paul Drake was played by William Hopper. Did you know that William was the son of Hedda Hopper?

A: **Paul Gauguin**
Q: What French stockbroker fled his homeland to paint in the Pacific?
W: Gauguin, at the age of 23, began a successful but brief career as a stockbroker in Paris. The financial success allowed him to pursue painting to which he devoted himself to full-time in 1883. After his money dwindled, his marriage failed, and he traveled to such places as Martinique, he realized the need for a natural remote setting. He auctioned paintings off in 1891 to raise funds to go to Tahiti in the south Pacific where he lived and painted.

A: **Paul Gauguin**
Q: What French painter was the subject of Somerset Maughm's *The Moon and Sixpence*?
W: William Somerset Maugham wrote *The Moon and Sixpence* in 1919 about a stockbroker who leaves his wife and family, spends some selfish years painting in Paris, and finally dies of leprosy on a South Sea island. It was made into a three-star 1943 movie. Maugham also wrote *Of Human Bondage*, which was largely autobiographical.

A: *Peanuts*
Q: What's the world's most-read comic strip?
W: As seen in newspaper comic strips and animated cartoons, the Peanuts gang consists of Charlie Brown, Linus, Lucy, Schroeder, Pig Pen, Frieda, Peppermint Patty, and Sally. This popular series of misadventures was created by Charles Schultz.

A: **Pegasus**
Q: What's the name of the winged horse of Greek mythology?
W: Pegasus sprang from the neck or the blood of Medusa after her head was cut off by Perseus. The Romans considered this winged horse to be the symbol of immortality.

A: *Penthouse*
Q: What monthly is subtitled *The International Magazine for Men?*
W: The first issue of *Penthouse* magazine came out in September 1969. It is edited and published by Bob Guccione. This chic magazine for men now boasts sales in excess of five million copies worldwide. *Penthouse* features attractive pictures of nude women, articles, essays, satire, and humor. Guccione created a furor when he published nude photographs of the 1984 Miss America.

A: *Penthouse*
Q: What magazine is the cornerstone of Bob Guccione's publishing empire At $30 per year for a subscription and worldwide sales in excess of 5,000,000 copies, one can see how a publishing empire is built. *Penthouse* features excellent quality photography of attractive, young, provocatively posed naked women as well as interesting articles and humor.

A: **Perry Mason loses**
Q: What is the distinction of Erle Stanley Gardner's *The Case of the Terrified Typist?*
W: Perry Mason was the sharp Los Angeles lawyer-detective created by Erle Stanley Gardner. All his novels begin with *The Case of the ...* In 84 cases, Mason loses only once in *The Case of the Terrified Typist.* After the guilty verdict, attorney Mason convinced Judge Hartley that a retrial was in order since there were two Duane Jeffersons, one his client and the other the accused!

A: **Perry White**
Q: Who was the editor of *The Daily Planet?*
W: Perry White was the editor of *The Daily Planet,* a crusading newspaper in Metropolis. He employed Clark Kent (alias Superman), "a mild-mannered reporter for the great metropolitan newspaper, who fought the never-ending battle for truth, justice and the American way." In the TV series "Superman," Kent/Superman was played by George Reeves, and Perry White was played by John Hamilton.

A: **Peter**
Q: What was Rubens' first name?
W: Peter Paul Rubens, a Flemish artist, was born in Westphalia on June 19, 1577. He is known for many fine paintings including the *Raising of the Cross* and the *Descent from the Cross,* which are in the Cathedral of Antwerp.

A: **Peter Pan**
Q: Who decided never to grow up and ran off to live with the fairies?
W: Peter Pan, title character of Barrie's play, decided to live in Never-Never Land, where lost children live in the underground and in the trunks of trees. Peter lives in the treetops. His best friend is Tinker Bell, the fairy.

A: *Peter Pan*
Q: What J.M. Barrie play features John, Michael, and Wendy?
W: John, Michael, and Wendy are the Darling family children whom Peter drops in on, teaches to fly, and then travels with to Never-Never Land for adventures.

A: **Peter Pan**
Q: Who was famous for saying: "All you need to fly are lovely thoughts and fairy dust?"
W: When Peter Pan drops in on the Darling children in their nursery he wants to take them to Never-Never Land, but first he must teach them to fly. And fly they do, after Tinker Bell sprinkles them with fairy dust and Peter has them thinking lovely thoughts.

A: *Peter Pan*
Q: What's the alternate title of the play *The Boy Who Would Not Grow Up?*
W: Peter Pan was the boy who would not grow up. The play captures the essential child each of us hopes to hold throughout our days. The play will never grow old. Mary Martin and Sandy Duncan are two of the American actresses who have performed the title role for audiences in America.

A: *Peter Pan*
Q: What play explains the beginning of fairies?
W: During the adventures in Never-Never Land, Tinker Bell (represented by a spot of light) drinks poison that mean old pirate Captain Hook prepared for Peter. Peter turns to the audience to save her by "applauding if you believe in fairies." The applause makes her light grow brighter. Peter Pan explains that "when the first baby laughed for the first time, the laugh broke into a thousand pieces and they all went skipping about, and that was the beginning of fairies. And now when every new baby is born, its first laugh becomes a fairy."

A: *Peter Pan*
Q: What was the first English play written exclusively for children?
W: Sir James Matthew Barrie wrote this charming dramatic fantasy about Peter Pan, the boy who wouldn't grow up, in 1909. It was published as a play in 1911 under the title *Peter and Wendy.* Wendy was one of the three children of the Darling family who adventure to Never-Never Land with Peter and Tinker Bell, the fairy. Filled with Indians and pirates, it is still popular today with children of all ages.

A: **Peter Principle, The**
Q: What's the doctrine that every employee tends to rise to the level of his incompetence?
W: Author, educator, and consultant Dr. Lawrence J. Peter is best known for his writings on the Peter Principle. His best-selling book expands upon the principle that an employee in a hierarchy tends to rise to the level of his incompetence.

A: **Peter Sellers**
Q: Who was the first man to appear on the cover of *Playboy*?
W: Peter Sellers was the first male to appear on the cover of *Playboy* magazine. Marilyn Monroe was the first female. What more is there to say?!

A: **Peyton Place**
Q: What 1956 Grace Metalious novel was on the best-seller list for two years?
W: Grace Metalious' novel is about the fermentation of sex, frustration and violence under the placid facade of a small New England town. The novel was made into a 1957 film starring Mark Robson, Lana Turner, Hope Lange, Arthur Kennedy, and Lloyd Nolan, to name just a few.

A: *Peyton Place*
Q: What 1958 best-seller claimed to lift the lid off a small New England town?
W: *Peyton Place* is a novel by Grace Metalious written in 1956, which was followed by *Return to Peyton Place* in 1959. Beneath the exterior propriety of life in a small town lurks vice, perversion, and crime.

A: **Phileas Fogg**
Q: Who made the lofty claim that he could fly around the world in 80 days?
W: Phileas Fogg, a Victorian gentleman, and his valet won a bet that they could go around the world in eighty days. This novel by Jules Verne was made into a three-star movie in 1956.

A: **Philip Roth**
Q: Who wrote *Goodbye Columbus*?
W: Roth was born March 19, 1933, in Newark, New Jersey. He authored *Goodbye Columbus* in 1957 and *Portnoy's Complaint* in 1969. Richard Benjamin and Ali McGraw starred in the movie *Goodbye Columbus*, which was the story of a young Jewish librarian who has an affair with the willful daughter of a nouveau riche family.

A: **Phoenix, The**
Q: What fabled bird sprang to new life from the ashes of its nest?
W: In Egyptian mythology the Phoenix is purported to be a bird of great beauty. It is said to live for 500 to 600 years in the Arabian Desert, then consume itself by fire, rising from its ashes to live through another cycle. Often it is used as a symbol of immortality or to describe a person of matchless beauty or excellence: a paragon.

A: **Picasso**
Q: What name did Pablo Picasso sign to his paintings?
W: Picasso was born Oct. 25, 1881, in Malagor, Spain to Jose Ruiz and Maria Picasso. Ruiz being a rather common name, he took his mother's name. He was a painter, sculptor, printmaker, ceramicist, and scene designer and is considered the unchallenged giant of 20th century art. He lived several artistic lifetimes and died April 8, 1973, in France.

A: **pig, A**
Q: What did Tom, Tom, the piper's son, steal?
W: This is a strange Mother Goose rhyme: "Tom, Tom, the piper's son Stole a pig and away he run; The pig was eat, And Tom was beat, And Tom ran crying down the street."

A: **Pigeon sisters, The**
Q: Who live upstairs from Felix Unger and Oscar Madison in Neil Simon's *The Odd Couple*?
W: Neil Simon's story about the two divorced men living together features Oscar Madison, the sloppy sportswriter and Felix, the neatnik photographer. Their upstairs neighbors were sisters, Cecily and Gwen Pigeon.

A: *Pilgrim's Progress*
Q: What John Bunyan story opens in the City of Destruction?
W: *Pilgrim's Progress*, published in 1678, is an allegory that takes the form of a dream by the author. In this dream he sees Christian, the main character, reading a book from which he learns that the city in which he dwells will be burned by fire. Christian flees the City of Destruction and begins his pilgrimage through various places including the Valley of the Shadow of Death.

A: **Pills**
Q: What were the dolls in Jacqueline Susann's *Valley of the Dolls*?
W: *Valley of the Dolls* was the 1966 best selling novel about the sexual adventures of various women and their reliance on pills and prescription drugs to keep their lives in order. Made into a movie in 1967, it starred Barbara Parkins, Patty Duke Astin, and Sharon Tate.

A: **Pipe tobacco**
Q: What did Sherlock Holmes keep in the toe of a Persian slipper?
W: It's not surprising that a brilliant detective, who solves baffling acts of criminal injustice through deductive reasoning and scientific evaluation uses cocaine and morphine, plays a Stradivarius, and retires as a beekeeper, should keep pipe tobacco in his Persian slipper.

A: **pitchfork, A**
Q: What is the man holding in the painting *American Gothic*?
W: Grant Wood was an American painter, best known for his penetrating renderings of the landscape and people of the midwestern U.S. *American Gothic*, painted in 1930, made him famous as it was a purely American painting. It is a stark portrait of a farmer and his wife, unsmiling. The farmer is holding his pitchfork.

A: **Plato**
Q: Who is known as "the Father of Western Philosophy?"
W: Plato, Greek philosopher and educator, was born in Athens in 427 B.C. and lived to be 80 or 81. He was a friend of Socrates. His views and theories of ethics, reason, and nature are multitudinous, but one basic concept was that man has a soul and is good by nature and that there is an order to the world.

A: *Playboy*
Q: What magazine debuted in December 1953?
W: Founded and published by Hugh Marston Hefner in 1953, *Playboy* magazine was not an instant success. The publishing venture lost $25,000 its first year. Originally planned to be called *Stag Party*, its name was changed at the last moment to *Playboy*. Because it emphasized sexual activity, the rabbit was chosen for its symbol.

A: *Playboy*
Q: What monthly is subtitled *Entertainment for Men*?
W: Because of *Playboy*'s sexual nature in photographs and articles, it was originally and still currently subtitled *Entertainment for Men*. *Playboy* is mostly variations on a single theme: sex. In later years, it has published serious articles on subjects of contemporary interest.

A: **Plural of new**
Q: What's the origin of the word *"news*?
W: New is defined in the dictionary as "having recently been made or developed." The idea that this word derives from the four directions of the compass (north, east, west, south) has been generally discredited.

A: **Poetry**
Q: What is "the Gay Science?"
W: Perhaps best described by the French poet Valery, who said that prose was walking and poetry dancing.

A: *Pogo*
Q: What comic strip is set in the Okefenokee Swamp?
W: Pogo is a possum that lives in the Okefenokee Swamp in Ware County, Georgia. This character was created by Walt Kelly as part of the satirical comic strip that ran from May, 1949 to July 1975.

A: **Polly**
Q: What's the name of Tom Sawyer's aunt with whom he lives?
W: *The Adventures of Tom Sawyer* was published in 1876 by Mark Twain. The story is set in the drowsy Mississippi River town of Petersburg, Missouri. Tom, mischievous and imaginative, and his priggish brother Sid live with their simple, kind-hearted Aunt Polly.

A: **Pop's Choklit Shoppe**
Q: What soda fountain do Archie and his friends hang out at?
W: Archie Andrews and his friends, Jughead, Betty, Veronica, Reggie, and Moose are all originally comic strip characters who attended Riverdale High School and hung out after school or while cutting classes at Pop's Choklit Shoppe. The comic strip was created by Bob Montana and premiered in Pep Comics No. 22.

A: **Porridge**
Q: What food of the three bears did Goldilocks eat?
W: Porridge, a chiefly British food, is made by boiling oatmeal or other meal in water or milk until it thickens. As the children's story "Goldilocks and the Three Bears" goes, the bears had left their bowls of porridge sitting on the table to cool when Goldilocks came along.

A: **Postscript**
Q: What does P.S. stand for at the end of a letter?
W: "P.S." is a sentence or paragraph added to a letter after the writer's signature, a supplment or addition to a written or printed document. Sometimes it's the best part of the whole letter!

A: **Prince Valiant**
Q: Who is Queen Aleta's husband?
W: This is a long standing comic strip by Hal Foster. It tells a continuing saga about Prince Valiant, one of King Arthur's Knights of the Round Table. His wife, Queen Aleta, is Queen of the Misty Isles. She and Prince Valiant have five children.

A: **press, The**
Q: What's the fourth estate?
W: According to Webster, the fourth estate is a group other than the clergy, nobility, or common that wields political powers, specifically the public press.

A: **prince, A**
Q: What does the beast become in *Beauty and the Beast*?
W: *Beauty and The Beast* by Le Prince de Beaumont, features a human-turned-animal whose bewitchment is broken by the love and constancy of a human.

A: **Professor Henry Higgins**
Q: Who taught Eliza Doolittle to be a lady?
W: *My Fair Lady* is the musical version of the George Bernard Shaw play *Pygmalion*. It is about a girl who peddles flowers, Eliza Doolittle, and who trained by an arrogant elecutionist, Higgins, to pass as a lady. In the 1964 film of the same name, Rex Harrison portrays Higgins, and Audrey Hepburn is Eliza.

A: **Professor Moriarity**
Q: Who was Sherlock Holmes's archenemy?
W: In the series of mystery books about the character Holmes, his adversary, Professor Moriarty, is almost as cunning and smart as Holmes, but not quite. Still, he is a worthy opponent for Holmes to match wits with.

A: **Prometheus**
Q: What figure of Greek mythology gave fire to man?
W: Prometheus was a titan in Greek mythology, who stole fire from heaven for mankind. As punishment he was chained to a rock where an eagle devoured his liver daily, but it became whole again each night. Prometheus was released by Hercules

A: *Prophet, The*
Q: Which of Kahlil Gibran's books is considered his masterpiece?
W: Of all his books, *The Prophet* has perhaps the widest appeal. It has been immensely popular since its publication in 1923, because it is "filled with truth, beauty, and idealism, vibrant with feeling and majestic rhythm," according to the Chicago *Post*. *The Prophet* is a series of 28 visionary prose poems on such subjects as love, marriage, work, beauty, religion, and death. It has sold several million copies and been translated into more than 20 other languages.

A: **Psalm 23**
Q: What psalm begins: "The Lord is my shepherd…?"
W: The Book of Psalms in the Old Testament is a collection of ancient Israel's poetry of faith. The term "Psalm" refers to oral music accompanied by stringed instruments. The Twenty-third Psalm is a song of confidence.

A: **Puff**
Q: What's the name of Dick and Jane's cat?
W: Dick and Jane and their little sister, Sally, were the children in the primary reader that has been used for decades in elementary schools. Spot was their dog and Puff was the beloved cat.

A: **Pun**
Q: What's the literary term for a play on words?
W: A pun is the humorous use of two words having the same or similar sounds but different meanings; or of two different, more or less incongruous meanings of the same word. Groucho Marx was a master of the pun. He once said of a safari he was on in Africa: "We shot two bucks, but that was all the money we had."

A: **Pupils and irises**
Q: What features are missing from Little Orphan Annie's face?
W: This ageless, pupil-less little girl is a cartoon character created by Harold Gray. The comic strip debuted in the New York *Daily News* on Aug. 5, 1924. Her adopted parents were Mr. and Mrs. Silo. Her faithful companion was a dog named Sandy.

A: **Pussy**
Q: What did Little Johnny Green put in the well?
W: The original version of this Mother Goose rhyme had Little Tommy Lin putting pussy in the well and Johnny Stout pulling her out; over the years the names were changed (to protect the innocent?) to Johnny Green putting her in and Tommy Stout pulling her out.

A: **Pygmalion**
Q: What George Bernard Shaw play inspired *My Fair Lady*?
W: Shaw was born in Dublin in 1856 and went to London in 1876 where he lived and wrote til his death in 1950. He wrote *Pygmalion* in 1912.

A: **Q**
Q: What letter is used least in the English language?
W: The 17th letter in the English alphabet alphabet is *Q*. In English usage it is always followed by a *U*.

A: **Quasimodo**
Q: Who was the humpbacked bell-ringer of Notre Dame?
W: The deformed bell-ringer, Quasimodo, rescues a gypsy girl from the evil intentions of her guardian in Victor Hugo's *Notre Dame de Paris*, written in 1931. It was made into a silent movie in 1923 and a talkie remake in 1939.

A: **queen, The**
Q: Who was in the parlor eating bread and honey?
W: This is another Mother Goose rhyme! You probably remember the opening line, "Sing a song of sixpence, a pocket full of rye; four and twenty blackbirds baked in a pie…" Later we're told "The king was in the counting house counting out his money; the queen was in the parlor eating bread and honey."

A: **queen of diamonds, The**
Q: What playing card put Raymond Shaw into a hypnotic trance in Richard Condon's *The Manchurian Candidate*?
W: A Korean War "hero" comes back a brainwashed zombie. He is triggered to kill a liberal politician, his control being his own monstrously ambitious mother. It was made into a 1962 film based on the Condon novel.

ART AND LITERATURE

A: **Queen's Bench No. 7**
Q: What does QB VII refer to in Leon Uris's title?
W: *QB VII* is a novel about the trial of an American novelist in Queen's Bench 7 (a court). He is accused of libeling a Polish surgeon by contending he performed experimental sterilizations of Jews in concentration camps.

R

A: **R**
Q: What letter does Archie wear on his sweater?
W: It stands for Riverdale High School.

A: **Rachel Carson**
Q: Who shocked the pesticide industry with the 1962 *Silent Spring*?
W: Carson was born May 27, 1907, and died April 14, 1964. She was a zoologist, scientist, and writer. Her sensitive interpretations of scientific data made her books popular. *Silent Spring* was a sensation because it described the potentially dangerous effects of misued pesticides.

A: **Ralph Nader**
Q: Who wrote *Unsafe at Any Speed*?
W: Ralph is a lawyer, author, and consumer advocate. He was born Feb. 27, 1934, in Connecticut, and wrote *Unsafe at Any Speed* in 1965. The book was an indictment of the automobile industry for being more concerned with outward appearance than with safety.

A: **Raymond Chandler**
Q: Who created private detective Philip Marlowe?
W: Chandler is American author who was born in Chicago on July 23, 1888. He was reared in England, then moved to southern California in 1912. He did not begin to write his famous hard-boiled detective and mystery fiction until he was in his 40s. His tough sleuth, Marlowe, became a cult figure.

A: ***Reader's Digest***
Q: What's the second-biggest selling magazine in America?
W: In February 1922 DeWitt Wallace, founder and editor, along with his wife, Lila Acheson Wallace, co-owner and co-chairman, published the first issue of 5,000 copies of *The Reader's Digest*. According to latest figures, *Reader's Digest* now has the largest circulation of any magazine in the world.

A: **Rembrandt**
Q: What Dutch master painted 64 self-portraits?
W: Rembrandt was a Dutch artist who lived from 1606 to 1669. His special genius was expressed in portraits because of the character and emotion he expressed therein. His self-portraits are a candid record of his youth, maturity, and later years.

A: **Rembrandt**
Q: Who painted *The Night Watch*?
W: This painting is associated with the beginning of Rembrandt's nature period. *Night Watch*, painted in 1642, hangs today in Rijksmuseum, Amsterdam. Misnamed, it actually represents the assembly of Captain Frans Banning Cocq's militia company in broad daylight.

A: ***Return of the King, The***
Q: What's the third part of J.R.R Tolkien's *Lord of the Rings*?
W: John Ronald Reuel Tolkien was born in 1892. Popularly known for mythological novels, he wrote *The Fellowship of the Ring*, a sequence in three volumes: *The Lord of the Rings* (1954), *The Two Towers* (1954), and *The Return of the King* (1955).

A: ***Return to Peyton Place***
Q: What was the sequel to *Peyton Place*?

W: *Peyton Place*, written by Grace Metalious in 1956, was a novel about life in a small town. It was followed in 1959 by *Return to Petyon Place*, a sequel about more of the vices, perversions, and crimes of the residents. We guess one novel didn't cover all the vice, perversion, and crime.

A: **Rev. Jim Jones, The**
Q: Who is James Reston, Jr.'s book *Our Father Who Art in Hell* about?
W: Jim Jones founded a commune in Guyana, on the north coast of South America. U.S. Representative Leo J. Ryan was ambushed and killed as he and others were investigating mistreatment of Jones' followers. This triggered a mass suicide in November 1978.

A: **Revised Standard Edition of *The Holy Bible*, The**
Q: What was the non-fiction best-seller of 1952, 1953, and 1954?
W: The Bible is the best-selling book of all times.

A: **Rex Stout**
Q: Who created detective Nero Wolfe?
W: Rex Stout is best known for his detective novels about Nero Wolfe, gourmet and connoisseur, who solves crimes without leaving his desk. From 1935 until his death, Stout produced these novels at the rate of one or two a year. He died in 1975 at the age of 89.

A: **Rhett Butler**
Q: Who was Bonnie Blue Butler's father?
W: Rhett was finally married to Scarlet O'Hara in Margaret Mitchell's novel *Gone With the Wind*. They had one child, Bonnie, who was killed in a riding accident. The character Rhett Butler was supposedly based on Mitchell's first husband.

A: **Richard Nixon**
Q: What later U.S. president wrote *Six Crises*?
W: Nixon, born in 1913 in California, entered politics after law school and naval service. He was the 37th president of the U.S. from 1969 until 1974, when he resigned following the Watergate scandal. In 1962, he wrote *Six Crises* about earlier involvements in critical situations. Everything was a crisis in Tricky Dick's life!

A: **Riddle of the Sphinx, The**
Q: What riddle asked: "What is it that walks on four legs, then on two legs, and then on three??"
W: The Sphinx destroyed those unable to guess her riddle. The answer to the above riddle is "man" – crawling, walking, using a cane.

A: **right, The**
Q: Which hand does God give life to Adam with on the ceiling of the Sistine Chapel?
W: Michelangelo, Italian painter, sculptor, architect, and poet was commissioned by Pope Julius II to paint the ceiling of the Sistine Chapel in Rome. He did so in a period of four years, from 1508 to 1512.

A: *Right Stuff, The*
Q: What Tom Wolfe book is about the Mercury astronauts?
W: Thomas Kennerly Wolfe, Jr. was born in Virginia in 1931. He is known for his treatment of contemporary life, from its popular heroes to its alternative lifestyles.

A: **"Rime of the Ancient Mariner, The"**
Q: What Samuel Taylor Coleridge poem tells of a sailor who kills an albatross?
W: This English romanticist (1772-1834) wrote "Mariner," which appeared in a volume jointly published with Wordsworth called *Lyrical Ballads* in 1798. The theme of the poem seems to be one of despair and grace, sin and redemption by acceptance of the blessedness of life.

A: **Riverdale**
Q: What high school does Archie attend?
W: Archie Andrews, comic strip hero of *Archie* attended Riverdale High School along with his sidekicks Jughead, Reggie, Moose, Betty, and Veronica.

A: *RN*
Q: What's the title of Richard Nixon's presidential memoirs?
W: Richard Milhous Nixon, born in 1913, was the 37th president of the United States. A Republican, he was also vice-president under President Eisenhower from 1952 to 1960. He was elected president in 1968, defeating Hubert Humphrey, and re-elected defeating George McGovern in 1972. Nixon resigned the presidency on Aug. 9, 1974 as a result of his revealed involvement in the famous Watergate scandal. Most Americans will most likely remember that day.

A: **Robert Browning**
Q: Who was Elizabeth Barrett in love with?
W: Elizabeth Barrett (1806-1861) married Robert Browning (1812-1889) in 1846. She wrote to Robert the famous lines,... *"How do I love thee, let me count the ways..."*

A: **Robert Frost**
Q: What poet wrote: "...I have promises to keep, and miles to go before I sleep?"
W: Robert Frost was an American poet who drew his inspirations and symbols from the New England countryside. Single words and basic ideas were his materials for his eloquent and profound works of poetry. The above quote is from perhaps his most famous poem, "Stopping By Woods On a Snowy Evening."

A: **Robert Frost**
Q: Who wrote the poem "The Road Not Taken"
W: Robert Lee Frost was born in San Francisco but moved at the age of ten to the New England farming country with which his poetry is identified. *Mountain Interval*, a book of poems published in 1916, contained the poem "The Road Not Taken." From the poem: "Two roads diverged in a wood and I – I took the one less traveled by, and that has made all the difference."

A: **Robert Frost**
Q: What American poet won the Pulitzer Prize four times?
W: Frost won four Pulitzer Prizes with the following books: *New Hampshire* in 1923; *Collected Poems* in 1930; *A Further Range* in 1936; and *A Witness Tree* in 1940. His verse was as simple and honest as an axe and hoe.

A: **Robert Frost**
Q: What American poet wrote: "Good fences make good neighbors?"
W: From the poem the "Mending Wall:" "My apple trees will never get across And eat the cones under his pines, I tell him He only says, "Good fences make good neighbors.""

A: **Robert Heinlein**
Q: Who wrote the sci-fi blockbuster *Stranger in a Strange Land*?
W: Robert Heinlein was an American author born in 1907. The most popular of his longer novels, *Stranger...*, is about a human born of space travelers from Earth and raised by Martians and is considered in

some ways a satire of the U.S. in the 1960s. The plot tells how the hero creates a Utopian society in which people preserve their individuality but share a brotherhood of community. Heinlein's novel, published in 1961, became a cult object for young people dedicated to a counterculture.

A: **Robert Louis Stevenson**
Q: Who created Dr. Jekyll and Mr. Hyde?
W: In 1886, Stevenson wrote *The Strange Case of Dr. Jekyll and Mr. Hyde*. The story is of a Victorian research chemist who finds a formula that separates the good and evil in his soul. When the latter predominates, he becomes a rampaging monster.

A: **Robert Ludlum**
Q: Who wrote *The Scarlatti Inheritance*?
W: Author Robert Ludlum, an American born in 1927, also writes as Jonathan Ryder and Michael Sheppard. *The Scarlatti Inheritance* was published in 1971. A most recent best-seller is *The Parsifal Mosaic*, published in 1982.

A: **Robin**
Q: Who exclaimed: "Holy Barracuda!?"
W: Robin is the sidekick of Batman, the mysterious caped crusader against criminals in Gotham City. Bruce Wayne, millionaire, is secretly Batman, and the orphaned teenager Dick Greyson is Robin. Only Dick and the Wayne family's butler, Alfred, know the true identity of Batman. Batman was created by Bob Kane and first appeared in Detective Comics in 1939 and then later in Batman comics, on the radio in the 1940s and in a 15-chapter serial released to theaters in the 1940s. It became a popular 30-minute TV program starring Adam West and Burt Ward from January 1966 to March 1968.

A: **Robin Hood's**
Q: Whose band did Will Scarlet belong to?
W: Robin Hood was a legendary outlaw and leader of a band of outlaws such as Will Scarlet, Little John, and Friar Tuck. The facts behind this English folk hero of legends is uncertain. The band supposedly robbed from the rich and gave to the poor. The story of Robin is probably based on a real person born about 1160 in Nottinghamshire and the Earl of Huntington. This is what researchers can glean from ballads, songs and stories.

A: **Robinson Crusoe**
Q: Who was shipwrecked for 28 years, two months, and 19 days?
W: Crusoe is the main character of a book written by Daniel Defoe and published in 1719. *The Life and Strange Surprising Adventures of Robinson Crusoe* is a fiction adventure about a shipwrecked sailor and the life he makes for himself on an uninhabited island until rescued by an English ship.

A: **Robinson Crusoe**
Q: What Daniel Defoe character had everything done by Friday?
W: Friday is the name of a savage that Crusoe saved from death when cannibal savages visited "his" island. After rescuing the grateful savage, Crusoe named him Friday and made him his manservant.

A: **Roman Empire's, The**
Q: What empire's decline is described by Edward Gibbon?
W: A great historical work was conceived by Gibbon while visiting Italy from England. Volume I of the *Decline and Fall of the Roman Empire* was published in London in 1776, Volumes II and III in 1781, and the last three volumes in 1788. It covers a period of about 13 centuries and traces the connection of the ancient world with the modern.

A: **Romeo**
Q: Who pined: "But soft! what light at yonder window breaks??"
W: In Shakespeare's romantic tragedy, probably written about 1595, the young man Romeo says these words while hiding under the window of Juliet, the young woman he has fallen in love with. He has hidden there in hopes of catching glimpses of her. (Peeping Tom Romeo?)

A: *Romeo and Juliet*
Q: What Shakespearean play features the line: "A plague on both your houses?"
W: *Romeo and Juliet* is a tragic story of two prominent families in Verona, Italy. Juliet's family, the Capulets, and Romeo's family, the Montagues, are bitter enemies. Romeo and Juliet fall in love at a party that Romeo has crashed at Juliet's house. The "plague on both houses" sees the tragic deaths of the young lovers after trying to be together. The families then finally end their bitter feud.

A: **Ronald Reagan's**
Q: Whose autobiography is titled *Where's the Rest of Me??*
W: Reagan's autobiography, written with Richard G. Hubler, was published in 1965. The title is a classic line from the movie *King's Row*, which marked the peak of his movie career. He gives glimpses of other stars of his era but few political views. The book is dedicated "To Honey With Love."

A: **Ronson, A**
Q: What make of lighter does James Bond light his ladies' cigarettes with?
W: You know, the kind that when overfilled and placed in your pants pocket after you've lit something causes your thigh to burn for hours. If Bond were smart, he'd change to a Ronson butane!

A: **Root beer**
Q: What is Dennis the Menace's favorite drink?
W: "Dennis the Menace" was a 30-minute TV show on CBS from September 1959 to September 1963. Dennis Mitchell, played by Jay North, is the mischievous little boy and only child of Henry and Alice. Dennis is a particular pain in the neck to the next door neighbor, George Wilson. Dennis isn't really a bad little boy, but stories depict his disastrous attempts to assist people he believes are in trouble. *Dennis the Menace* is also a cartoon strip.

A: **rope, A**
Q: What did Hans Christian Andersen always travel with in case of fire?
W: Hans Christian Andersen was a Danish poet and author. He traveled widely, once spending 16 months on a journey in Germany, France, Switzerland, and Italy. Since these were the days before smoke alarms, we assume he was assuring his safe escape!

A: **Rose Kennedy**
Q: What U.S. presidential mother wrote an autobiography titled *Times to Remember*?
W: Rose Fitzgerald Kennedy, mother of John Fitzgerald Kennedy, was born in 1890. Her memoirs, published in 1974, are filled with photos of the whole Kennedy clan. Royalties from the book go to the Joseph P. Kennedy, Jr., Foundation to aid the mentally retarded.

A: *Rosy Crucifixion, The*
Q: What's the name of the trilogy consisting of "Sexus, Plexus, and Nexus?"
W: These were written by Henry Miller. "Sexus" was the story of his first marriage, and "Plexus" was about his early years with his second wife. Other books by Miller were *Tropic of Capricorn* and *Tropic of Cancer*.

A: **Rudyard Kipling**
Q: What British author created Gunga Din?
W: Gunga Din, in Rudyard Kipling's poem of the same name, is the regimental water carrier, a Hindu lad whose singleminded devotion to duty leads to a heroic death on the battlefield. Rudyard Kipling (1865-1936) was a novelist, short story writer, and poet, noted for his tales and poems of British soldiers in Burma and India.

A: **Rudyard Kipling**
Q: Who wrote the *Jungle Book* series?
W: Kipling was a British subject born in Bombay in 1865. He wrote *The Jungle Book* in 1894 and *The Second Jungle Book* in 1895. They contained stories about a child, Mowgli, brought up by wolves and taught the law and business of the jungle by Baloo, the bear, and Bagheera, the black panther.

A: **Rudyard Kipling**
Q: Who won England's first Nobel Prize for literature, in 1907?
W: He was awarded the Nobel Prize in 1907 for *Jungle Book* and *Captains Courageous*. At the age of 42, he was the youngest person to win the literature award.

A: **Rudyard Kipling**
Q: What Bombay-born writer was called "the Bard of the Empire?"
W: Kipling, English poet and fiction writer and one of the great masters of the short story, was born in India when his father was director of a museum in Bombay. A minstrel (bard) of the British Empire, he was

famous mostly for short stories dealing with India, the sea, the jungle and its beasts, the army, and the navy.

A: **Ruff**
Q: What's the name of Dennis the Menace's dog?
W: Dennis Mitchell of 627 Elm Street, Hillsdale, was the main character of the TV series "Dennis the Menace" and the cartoon strip of the same name. His dog Ruff was afraid of cats! Mr. Wilson, next door, had a dog named Freemont.

A: **Rugby**
Q: What school does Tom attend in *Tom Brown's School Days*?
W: Thomas Hughes considerably influenced English ideas on public schools when he published *Tom Brown's School Days* in 1857, the story of an ordinary schoolboy at Rugby with its schoolboy cruelties and loyalties. Hughes himself was educated at Rugby and Oriel College, Oxford.

S

A: **Sally**
Q: What's the name of Dick and Jane's little sister?
W: And of course there was their dog Spot, but do you remember Sally's teddy bear's name? Tim!

A: **Salt**
Q: What seasoning is mentioned more than 30 times in the Bible?
W: Here's perhaps the most remembered reference to salt: Lot's wife was turned to a pillar of salt for looking back at her burning city.

A: **Salvador Dali**
Q: What Spanish artist painted *Crucifixion*?

W: In the period of the 1950s to 1970s, Dali's most important works were concerned with religious themes, notably *The Crucifixion of St. John of the Cross* in 1951, now in the Museum and Art Gallery, Glasgow.

A: **Salvador Dali**
Q: Who painted *Soft Self-Portrait with Grilled Bacon?*
W: Sigmund Freud's writings had a great influence on Dali's art as did his association with the Paris Surrealists, a group of artists and writers who sought to establish the "greater reality" of man's subconscious over his reason. He painted images suggestive of hallucinations and dreams such as the above mentioned self-portrait.

A: **Salvation Army, The**
Q: What army publishes the newspaper *The War Cry?*
W: *The War Cry* is a weekly newspaper published by the Salvation Army in New York.

A: **Salvation Army, The**
Q: What army did Shaw's Major Barbara serve in?
W: Shaw was one of the most influential figures of modern literature. In several of his plays, he explored the nature of the "great man," such as Napoleon in *Man of Destiny* (1895) and the rich munitions-maker Sir Andrew Undershaft in *Major Barbara* (1905).

A: **Sam McGee**
Q: Who was cremated on the marge of Lake Lebarge?
W: This is from "The Cremation of Sam McGee," a poem by Robert Service. The last line: "Was that night on the marge of Lake Lebarge I cremated Sam McGee."

A: **Sammy Davis, Jr.'s**
Q: Whose autobiography is titled *Yes I Can?*
W: The autobiography about the popular black, Jewish performer covers his boyhood as Silent Sam, the dancing midget to his membership as part of the team of the Will Mastin Trio and his number 1 record *Candy Man*. Sammy tells of his struggle in his youth, his days in the Army, his marriage, and the endless work to achieve fame as a performer and happiness as a man.

A: **Samuel Langhorne Clemens**
Q: What was Mark Twain's real name?
W: Clemens, born in Missouri in 1835, was an American author and humorist well-known for the books *Tom Sawyer* and *Huckleberry Finn*. He first used the pseudonym "Mark Twain" first in a contribution to the Virginia City *Territorial Enterprise* on Feb. 3, 1863. The phrase "mark twain" means "measure two fathoms deep" and was the command given to the crew by riverboat captains on the Mississippi. Clemens had experience as a riverboat pilot.

A: **Samuel Pepys**
Q: Who kept the most famous diary in the English language?
W: Pepys was the son of a London tailor. He began his diary Jan. 1, 1660, and discontinued it May 31, 1669, because of failing eyesight. It is of extraordinary interest because of the light it sheds on the author's own lovable character and the vivid picture that it gives of everyday life at that time, of the administration of the navy, and of the ways of the court. The diary remained in cypher, a form of shorthand, until 1825.

A: **Sancho Panza**
Q: Who rode a donkey named Dapple?
W: Sancho Panza was the squire of Don Quixote. He accompanied him in his adventures and shared some of their unpleasant consequences. His conversation is full of common sense and pithy proverbs.

A: **Sancho Panza**
Q: Who was Don Quixote's sidekick?
W: *Don Quixote de la Mancha* is a satirical romance by Spanish writer Cervantes, published in 1605. It is about a poor gentleman of La Mancha, amiable and sane, who sets out in search of adventure with his friend Sancho Panza. They are involved in some absurd adventures and chivalrous exploits. Quixote's horse is named Rosinante.

A: **Sandy**
Q: What's the name of Little Orphan Annie's dog?
W: In Harold Gray's cartoon strip *Little Orphan Annie*, which debuted in the New York *Daily News* in 1924, Annie had a faithful dog named Sandy.

A: **San Francisco**
Q: What city does Sam Spade work in?
W: Sam Spade is the detective hero of adventure novels by Dashiell Hammett. Hammett went to San Francisco as a Pinkerton detective and drew upon the city's atmosphere and his own business for the novels he soon began to write. His books were cool, tough, and hard-boiled, and Sam Spade was cynical and tough.

A: **Santiago**
Q: What was the name of the fisherman in Hemingway's *The Old Man and the Sea?*
W: Ernest Miller Hemingway won a 1954 Nobel Prize for *Old Man and the Sea*. It is a novelette, published in 1952, about a Cuban fisherman (Santiago) who is aged but nevertheless goes out in search of marlin.

He hooks a great one that tows his boat for days before he finally harpoons it and returns home.

A: Saturday
Q: What day of the week did Solomon Grundy die?
W: This was a real tricky one! We tried every encyclopedia in the library, and the closest we came was a Mrs. Grundy. Then Mother Goose reappeared! "Solomon Grundy Born on Monday Christened on Tuesday Married on Wednesday Took ill on Thursday Worse on Friday Died on Saturday Buried on Sunday This is the end of Solomon Grundy."

A: Saul Bellow
Q: Who won the 1976 Nobel Prize for his novel *Humboldt's Gift*?
W: Saul Bellow was born in Canada in 1915 and educated in Chicago. He began writing after teaching at Princeton and other colleges. *Humboldt's Gift* depicts a crisis in the life of the narrator that is resolved by his friend, the poet Humboldt.

A: *Scampo*
Q: What's the singular of *scampi*?
W: *Scampo*, a noun, is the Italian zoological word for shrimp. *Scampo* also means "a means of escape or way out." *Shrimp* is singular or plural, and *shrimps* is another acceptable plural form."

A: Scarlett O'Hara
Q: What literary character marries Charles Hamilton out of spite?
W: In Margaret Mitchell's epic novel *Gone With the Wind*, Scarlett is in love with a neighbor, Ashley Wilkes. She learns Ashley is going to marry Melanie Hamilton, so Scarlet marries Melanie's brother, Charles, who had been courting Ashley's sister. The Civil War is just beginning, and Charles is killed in the war.

A: Scarlett O'Hara
Q: Who was Mrs. Hamilton, Mrs. Kennedy, and Mrs. Butler but failed to become Mrs. Wilkes?

W: After the Civil War in which Scarlett loses her first husband, Charles Hamilton, she becomes determined to keep *Tara*, the family estate, and marries Frank Kennedy. Frank is killed in an incident avenging an insult to Scarlett, and she then marries Rhett Butler. During all three marriages, she continues her infatuation for Ashley Wilkes who consistently rejects her romantic advances.

A: Science fiction
Q: What category of writing are the Hugo and Nebula Awards given for?
W: The Hugo is the one award for the year's outstanding science fiction writing. It was first presented in 1953 at the Eleventh World Science Fiction Convention in Philadelphia to Alfred Bester for *The Demolished Man*. The Nebula Award is the annual award given out by Tirst presented in 1965 to Frank Herbert for *Dune*.

A: Scotland
Q: What country is the setting for Shakespeare's *Macbeth*?
W: *Macbeth*, a tragedy by Shakespeare, was probably finished by 1606. It was first printed in 1623, no doubt as a tribute to King James I. It is the bloody tale of Macbeth's quest to be king of Scotland, and the murders he commits in this attempt.

A: Scrooge McDuck
Q: Who's the world's richest duck?
W: Scrooge McDuck, Donald Duck's uncle, appears in the Donald Duck cartoons along with Donald's three nephews Huey, Dewey, and Louie, the offspring of Donald's sister, Dumbella. Scrooge is definitely the world's richest duck; you will often see his vault, which is in his house. In spite of his tremendous wealth and all of his relatives, upon whom he could very well shower gifts, he is also the world's stingiest duck!

A: *Sea-Wolf*, The
Q: What Jack London novel is about a dreaded sea captain named Wolf Larsen?

W: *The Sea-Wolf* is a novel published in 1904 by Jack London. Wolf Larson is the ruthless captain of a sailing schooner, *Ghost*, that rescues literary critic Humphrey Van Weyden from a ferry boat accident. Later, the *Ghost* saves some refugees from an ocean disaster, and a struggle develops between Van Weyden and Larsen over poet Maude Brewster. In the end, Wolf Larsen dies a slow death from cerebral cancer.

A: septic tank, The
Q: What does Erma Bombeck say the grass is always greener over?
W: Bombeck is today's reigning humorist of the foibles and frustrations of everyday life. Besides this famous book, which is an expose of the suburbs, she is the author of several other best-sellers and a syndicated newspaper column titled "At Wit's End." Erma frequently appears on the nationwide talk show "Good Morning, America."

A: Seven
Q: How many voyages did Sinbad make?
W: "Sinbad the Sailor" is one of the tales in *The Arabian Nights*, a collection of stories written in Arabic, probably in the 14th to 16th centuries. Sinbad, a rich, young man of Baghdad, having wasted much of his wealth in prodigal living, undertakes seven sea voyages as a merchant and meets with various marvelous adventures.

A: Seven Deadly Sins, The
Q: What are lust, pride, anger, envy, sloth, avarice, and gluttony?
W: The Seven Deadly Sins also listed as pride, lechery, envy, anger, covetousness, gluttony, and sloth are frequently personified in medieval literature, as in Chaucer's *Parson's Tales* and Spencer's *Faerie Queen*.

A: Seventeen
Q: How many steps are there to the second-story flat at 221B Baker Street?
W: That's the address of Sherlock Holmes' residence.

A: Shaken, not stirred
Q: How does James Bond like his martinis?
W: In each of Ian Fleming's novels featuring Agent 007, Bond could always tell by taste when he had ordered a martini whether it had been stirred instead of shaken, as he preferred. Bond had quick wit, reflexes, and very discriminating taste.

A: *Shalom*
Q: What's the Hebrew word for peace, used as both a greeting and a farewell?
W: *Shalom* is Hebrew and used as a traditional Jewish greeting and farewell. It can also be spelled *Sholom*.

A: shamrock, The
Q: What plant did St. Patrick use to explain the Trinity?
W: The shamrock, with three leaves (trifoliate) on each stem, and was used by St. Patrick to explain the concept of three beings (Father, Son and Holy Ghost) in one (God): the Trinity. The shamrock is the national emblem of Ireland.

A: Shangri-La
Q: What was the mythical utopia of James Hilton's *Lost Horizon*?
W: Shangi-La was the imaginary mountain land depicted as a utopia in James Hilton's 1933 novel *Lost Horizon*. Shangri-La is now a common term for any remote beautiful imaginary place where life approaches perfection.

A: Shazam
Q: What was Captain Marvel's magic word?

W: *Shazam* is the magic word that changes Billy Batson into Captain Marvel and back again. Here's what the letters stand for: S = wisdom of Solomon; H = strength of Hercules; A = stamina of Atlas; Z = power of Zeus; A = courage of Achilles; and M = speed of Mercury.

A: Sheilah Graham
Q: Who wrote *Beloved Infidel* about her relationship with F. Scott Fitgerald?
W: Graham's book, co-authored with Gerald Frank, was published in 1958. A musical comedy star and columnist, Ms. Graham tells about her life and her love with Fitzgerald, the literary giant, near the end of his life.

A: Shelley Winters's
Q: What actress's autobiography is titled *Shelly: Also Known as Shirley*?
W: Shelley Winters, born Shirley Schrift in St. Louis, Missouri, in 1927, is an American stage and screen actress best described as blowzy, effusive, brash, and maternal, neither voluptuous nor drab. In her autobiography one learns more one they ever wanted to know about her life, loves, and career.

A: Sherlock Holmes
Q: What detective retired to become a beekeeper?
W: Sherlock Holmes retired to his home Windlesham in Crowborough, Sussex, where he raised bees until his death on Jan. 6, 1930.

A: Sherlock Holmes
Q: Who lived at 221B Baker Street?
W: Detective Sherlock Holmes lived at 221B Baker Street in London, England. He lived with Dr. John Watson before and between Watson's marriages and with Mrs. Hudson as landlady.

A: Sherlock Holmes
Q: What detective débuted in a *Study in Scarlet*?
W: Sherlock Holmes was the detective created by Sir Arthur Conan Doyle who was, himself, a doctor of medicine practicing in England at Southsea. *Study in Scarlet* was published in 1887, followed later by many stories of the clever, eccentric detective and his able assistant Dr. Watson.

A: Sherlock Holmes
Q: What detective could distinguish 140 forms of tobacco ash?
W: Sir Arthur Conan Doyle's creation, detective Sherlock Holmes, is perhaps the best known fictional character in the world. He was incredibly clever, indulged in cocaine and morphine, and had an uncanny way of solving all of his cases. To a man possessing his characteristics, identifying 140 forms of tobacco ash was probably a snap!

A: Sherlock Holmes's
Q: Whose brother Mycroft was a founder of the Diogenes Club?
W: Sherlock Holmes's older brother, Mycroft was supposed to have been even more clever and witty than Sherlock. The Diogenes Club was a reserved London club in which talking was allowed only in the Strangers Room.

A: Sherwood Forest
Q: What forest was home to Robin Hood?
W: Robin Hood, a legendary outlaw of England, supposedly robbed from the rich and gave to the poor. The facts behind the legend are unclear, but writings, songs, and ballads place him in various places such as Yorkshire, Sherwood, Plumpton Park (Cumberland), and also as Earl of Huntington. He was perhaps a real man born in Nottinghamshire in the year 1160.

ART AND LITERATURE

A: **Shirley Temple**
Q: Who was the youngest person listed in *Who's Who*?
W: Shirley Temple, born April 23, 1928, first attracted attention when she starred in the film *Baby Burlesks* at the age of four. At age six she received a Special Academy Award for recognition of her outstanding contribution to screen entertainment during the year 1934.

A: *Shoes of the Fisherman, The*
Q: What Morris West novel deals with a Russian bishop who becomes Pope?
W: The novel was made into a movie in 1968 starring Anthony Quinn, David Janssen, and Lawrence Olivier. It is the story of a Russian bishop who, after 20 years as a political prisoner, becomes Pope.

A: *Shogun*
Q: What James Clavell novel recounts John Blackthorne's adventures in 16th-century Japan?
W: Clavell's 1975 novel is set in Japan around 1600. John Blackstone, the principal figure, dreams of being the first Englishman to circumnavigate the globe, to wrest control of trade between Japan and China from the Portuguese, and to return home wealthy. Foranaga is the most powerful feudal lord in Japan, who strives to seize ultimate power by becoming Shogun, supreme military dictator. Lady Mariko is a Catholic convert who falls in love with Blackstone.

A: **siesta, The**
Q: What mid-day nap takes its name from the Spanish word *sexta*, meaning "sixth?"
W: A siesta, a nap taken during the hottest part of the day, is taken from the word *sexta*, an ancient Roman division of the day meaning "afternoon."

A: **Simon Templar**
Q: What fictional detective was created by Leslie Charteris?

W: Simon Templar, the Saint, is a dashing daredevil, freelance trouble-shooter who is wealthy, young, handsome, suave, and sophisticated, possessing rich and fancy tastes in wine and women.

A: **Simon Templar's**
Q: What literary character's other identity is the Saint?
W: "The Saint" was a 60-minute TV series in the 1960s starring Roger Moore (who also played James Bond in the movies). The Saint is cunning, ingenious, and a master among thieves. Considered a criminal by police, he actually assists them in his quest to aid people in distress.

A: **Sinbad**
Q: Who met Cyclops on his third voyage?
W: Sinbad the sailor's adventures as a merchant at sea included meeting Cyclops, a giant with one eye in the middle of his forehead. The stories of his adventures are told in the tales of *The Arabian Nights*, which describe his meetings with other adversaries such as Roe, a huge bird that can lift elephants with its claws. There are a total of seven voyages described.

A: **Sinclair Lewis**
Q: Who was the first American to win the Nobel Prize for Literature, for his novel *Babbit*?
W: Lewis published this novel in 1922. It is about George Folansbee Babbit, an enterprising, stereotyped, moral, and prosperous real estate broker in a typical midwestern city, trained to believe in the virtues of homelife, the Republican party, and middle class conventions. The book tells about his straying from these values and his wife, as well as his eventual return to them.

A: **Sir Arthur Conan Doyle**
Q: What author named his main character for Oliver Wendell Holmes?

W: Doyle was an English physician and author. He created the series of stories about the amateur detective Sherlock Holmes. Actually the main character was also named after a popular cricket player of the time, Sherlock.

A: **Sir Freddie Laker's**
Q: Whose life story is titled *Fly Me, I'm Freddie*?
W: Sir Freddie's book, co-authored with Roger Eglin and Berry Ritchie, is about the life and times of the man who broke the airline cartel and made air travel available to everyone. The book is an interesting account of Laker's six-year battle with British and American aviation authorities to bring cheaper fares to trans-Atlantic flights.

A: **Six**
Q: How many times a year is a bimonthly periodical published?
W: Bimonthly means occuring once every two months. A bimonthly publication is printed once in two months, therefore six times in a year.

A: *Six Days of the Condor*
Q: What book was the 1975 film *Three Days of the Condor* based on?
W: Based on the book by James Grady, *Six Days of the Condor* is about an innocent researcher for a branch of the CIA, who finds himself marked for death by assassins employed by another branch. The 1975 movie starred Robert Redford and Fay Dunaway.

A: *Sleeping Beauty*
Q: What Tchaikovsky ballet do Red Riding Hood and Cinderella appear in?
W: This ballet is only one of many composed by Russian Peter Illyich Tchaikovsky (1840-1893). He is known for his colorful romantic music and unusual melodic gifts. *Sleeping Beauty* was orchestrated during the summer of 1889 and produced early in 1890.

ART AND LITERATURE

A: *Sleuth*
Q: What Anthony Shaffer two-man play opens in the living room of Andrew Wyke's Norman manor house?
W: Anthony, twin brother of Peter Levin Shaffer, also a playwright, was born in 1926 and presented *Sleuth*, his first play, to audiences in New York and London in 1970. In 1972 it was released as a film starring Laurence Olivier and Michael Caine. It is about a successful thriller writer who invents a murder plot that rebounds on himself.

A: **Smallville**
Q: What Illinois town was Superman's boyhood home He was raised by Mr. and Mrs. Kent on Main Street in Smallville, which had a population of 5,012. Clark left Smallville for Metropolis at the age of 26.

A: **Snakes, snails, puppy dogs' tails**
Q: What are little boys made of?
W: From the poem obviously written by a woman because "little girls are made of sugar and spice and everything nice."

A: **Snoopy**
Q: Who's Woodstock's beagle buddy?
W: Charles Schultz, the creator of the comic strip *Peanuts*, was going to call him Sniffy, but he found out that the name was being used in another comic strip.

A: **Snoopy**
Q: Who plays shortstop for Charlie Brown's baseball team?
W: Snoopy, Charlie Brown's clever and witty beagle, besides playing shortstop on the forever losing baseball team, spends much of his time pretending to fly a Sopwith Camel against the Red Baron. Snoopy hates coconut candy and suffers from weed claustrophobia.

A: **Sodom and Gomorrah**
Q: What's destroyed in Genesis 19:24?
W: In the Bible, Sodom, a city on the Dead Sea, is destroyed along with the neighboring city of Gomorrah because of the wickedness of the people who live there. Sodomy, unnatural sexual relations between humans or between humans and animals, is so named after the people of Sodom who supposedly practiced this.

A: **Solomon Grundy**
Q: What nursery rhyme character was rich on Monday but broke on Saturday?
W: This is from an old Mother Goose rhyme. It was changed over the years, and the most best known version says "Born on Monday," and "Died on Saturday."

A: **Somerset Maugham**
Q: Who wrote *The Razor's Edge*?
W: Maugham wrote *Razor's Edge* in 1944. Released in 1946 as a movie, it is about a well-to-do young man who spends the years between the wars first idling, then looking for essential truth.

A: **Son of**
Q: What do Mc and Mac mean when used in surnames?
W: Mac or Mc is a prefix in Scottish and Irish names that means "son of …"; hence, McDougal means "son of Dougal." I wonder if Donald knows that his son *Mc*Donald makes billions of burgers!

A: **Son of Sam Killings, The**
Q: What inspired Jimmy Breslin's novel *.44*?
W: Jimmy Breslin is a New York journalist and author born in 1930. His novel is based on the shootings of young lovers in parked cars in New York by David Berkowitz with a .44 caliber revolver. Berkowitz claimed the "Son of Sam" was responsible for the killings.

A: **Spain**
Q: What country is the setting for Edgar Allan Poe's "The Pit and the Pendulum?"
W: This story, a tale of horror by Poe published in the book *The Gift* in 1842, is about a prisoner of the Spanish Inquisition at Toledo who describes his imprisonment. His tortures include waking to find himself strapped to a wooden framework while a giant pendulum with a sharp crescent swings over him slowly descending and rats crawl all over him. He is rescued moments before falling into the pit by General LaSalle. WOOOOO - spooky!!

A: **Spanish**
Q: What nationality was Pablo Picasso?
W: Picasso was born Oct. 25, 1881, in Malaga, Spain, to artist Jose Ruiz and Maria Picasso. Pablo took the less common name of his mother. This unchallenged giant of 20th century art studied in Barcelona and Madrid and lived and worked in Paris. He died April 8, 1973, in France.

A: **Spanish**
Q: What nationality was Goya?
W: Francisco Jose Goya y Lucientes was born March 30, 1746. He was a revolutionary Spanish court painter and etcher, perhaps best known for his portraits of the royalty and nobility of Spain. His etchings satirized customs and evils of the time. He was one of Spain's outstanding artists.

ART AND LITERATURE

A: Spanish Civil War, The
Q: What war is the background to George Orwell's *Homage to Catalonia*?
W: George Orwell is the pen name of Eric Blair, born in Bengal and brought to England at an early age. *Homage to Catalonia* (1938) is an autobiographical record of the Spanish Civil War, in which Orwell fought for the Republicans and was wounded.

A: Spanish Civil War and World War I, The
Q: What two wars did Ernest Hemingway cover as a correspondent?
W: Ernest Miller Hemingway was an American journalist and prolific author. After working as a Kansas City reporter, he joined a volunteer ambulance unit in France, then transferred to the Italian infantry until the close of World War I. After this war he reported on battles in the Near East for the Toronto *Star*. He settled in Paris where he was encouraged by Gertrude Stein and Ezra Pound to become a creative writer.

A: sparrow, The
Q: Who killed Cock Robin?
W: The opening stanza from "The Death and Burial of Poor Cock Robin": "Who killed Cock Robin 'I' said the sparrow, "With my little bow and arrow.'"

A: Spiderman
Q: What's comic strip photographer Peter Parker's secret identity?
W: Peter Parker lives with his Aunt May. A bite from a radioactive spider gies him his powers, and when his Uncle Ben is killed by a burglar, Parker decides to become a crime fighter. The comic strip *Spiderman* first appeared in *Amazing Fantasy Comics No. 15* in August 1962.

A: *Sports Illustrated*
Q: What magazine paid Ernest Hemingway $15 a word to write a bullfighting article?
W: Because of Hemingway's 1932 novel on bullfighting *Death in the Afternoon* and his 1954 Nobel Prize, what better way was there for a new magazine to capture readers' attention than with an article by Hemingway! *Sports Illustrated* was founded in 1954.

A: Sports writer
Q: What's the occupation of Oscar Madison in Neil Simon's *The Odd Couple*?
W: Neil Simon's play was made into a film in 1968 starring Jack Lemmon and Walter Matthau. It is about a fussy divorce-shocked photographer who moves in with his sloppy sportscaster friend. As is to be expected they get on each others nerves.

A: Spring
Q: What season is the setting for Shakespeare's *Midsummer Night's Dream*?
W: This is a comedy written by Shakespeare in 1595 or 1596 and printed in 1610. As a young lover's fancy turns to thoughts of love in spring, this play is about two pairs of lovers who sort out their problems with the help of fairies in the woods outside Athens, Greece.

A: St. Nicholas
Q: Who is considered the patron saint of children?
W: A popular saint honored in the Greek as well as the Latin Church on Dec. 6, St. Nicholas belongs to the 14th century of the Christian era. As the patron saint of Russia, Greece, and many cities in Europe, he is regarded as the special guardian of maidens, merchants, sailors, as well as of children. The American Santa Claus is an adaptation of the Dutch St. Nicholas.

A: St. Peter's, Rome
Q: Where is Michelangelo's *Pieta*?
W: The *Pieta*, one of his early marble sculptures, is an example of one of the two main themes that characterize much of his work; love-pity of Christ and exultation of

the male nude. Michelangelo was one of the architects responsible for building St. Peters Basilica, central church of Roman Catholicism. This Italian church in Vatican City, Rome, is on a site believed to be the grave of St. Peter.

A: *Stars and Stripes, The*
Q: What's the U.S. military's newspaper?
W: This newspaper was originally published by the American Expeditionary Force in France, founded February 1918. The newspaper expired in 1919, but was revived in Washington, D.C., from 1919 to 1926 and again in 1942 in London as a weekly, then as a daily. During the course of World War II, other editions appeared in other cities abroad. Bill Maudlin's cartoon *Up Front* appeared in it as well as George Backer's cartoon *Sad Sack*.

A: steam launch, A
Q: What was the *African Queen* in C.S. Forester's novel?
W: Forrester's novel was made into a 1951 movie of the same name starring Humphrey Bogart, who won an Academy Award, and Katherine Hepburn, who was nominated for an Academy Award. The story is set in Africa in 1915 and is about a gin-drinking river trader and a prim missionary who make odd companions on his little steam powered boat down the dangerous river. The characters finally fall in love.

ART AND LITERATURE

A: Stephen Crane
Q: Who wrote *The Red Badge of Courage*?
W: Crane wrote *Red Badge of Courage*, which was published in 1895, with no personal experience of war. However, the book is a very realistic study of the mind of an inexperienced soldier trapped in the fury and turmoil of battle.

A: *Steppenwolf*
Q: What Hermann Hesse book gave its name to a rock group?
W: German novelist Hermann Hesse wrote *Der Steppenwolf* in 1927 and later translated it into the English *Steppenwolf* in 1929. The story is a severe indictment of our present cultureless age. A 1960s rock group later took on the name "Steppenwolf" and became known for two hit singles entitled "Born To Be Wild" and "Magic Carpet Ride."

A: Sterling Hayden
Q: What movie actor has written a novel of the sea called *Voyage*?
W: Hayden, born John Hamilton on March 26, 1916, was a leading man of Hollywood films in the 1940s and early 1950s. Drawn to the sea in his early teens, he became a mate on a schooner. This love of the sea eventually led him to write *Voyage: A Novel of 1896*, published in 1976.

A: Steve Martin
Q: What wild and crazy guy wrote a book called *Cruel Shoes*?
W: Steve Martin is the brilliantly witty and crazy comedian whose appearances on "Saturday Night Live" first brought him fame. *Cruel Shoes*, published in 1979, is a collection of humorous short stories. Martin is best known for his portrayal of a "wild and crazy guy!"

A: Straw
Q: What did Rumpelstiltskin's daughter spin into gold?
W: Rumpelstiltskin is a passionate, deformed dwarf of German folklore. The story is one of a miller's daughter enjoined by a king to spin straw into gold. The little dwarf does this deed for her, but only on the condition that she give him her first child. The daughter marries the king, a child is born, and Rumpelstiltskin takes possession of the child. He tells the mother that he will relinquish the child if she can find out his name in three days. She does so, the child is reunited with its parents, and the dwarf kills himself with rage.

A: Straw, sticks, bricks
Q: What materials did the three little pigs use to build their houses?
W: In this classic folk tale, three little pigs each set out to build a house of different materials to ward off the Big Bad Wolf. The straw and sticks obviously do not withstand the "huffing and puffing," but the pigs are saved by the sturdy brick house.

A: *Streetcar Named Desire, A*
Q: What Tennessee Williams play features Blanche Dubois and the Kowalskis?
W: Williams' Pulitzer Prize-winning play is about a repressed southern widow who is raped and driven mad by her brutal brother-in-law. It was made into a movie in 1951, starring Vivien Leigh and Marlon Brando, and was nominated for an Academy Award for Best Picture. Marlon Brando was nominated for an Award, and Vivien Leigh won an Oscar.

A: Sugarplums
Q: What visions dance in children's heads in the poem "A Visit from St. Nicholas?"
W: Sugarplums are small balls or disks of candy.

A: sultana, A
Q: What's a sultan's wife called?
W: A sultan is the ruler of a Moslem country. A sultana or sultaness is the wife, daughter, sister, mother, or a royal mistress of a sultan.

A: *Sun Also Rises, The*
Q: What novel established Ernest Hemingway's reputation?
W: Hemingway was encouraged to become a creative writer by Gertrude Stein and Ezra Pound while he was in Paris. He returned to New York and wrote *The Sun Also Rises* in 1926, which carried over the style and attitude of his short stories into a novel. It depicts the moral collapse of a group of expatriated Americans and Englishmen broken by the war, who turn toward escape through all types of violent diversions.

A: *Sunshine Boys, The*
Q: What Neil Simon play tells the story of two retired vaudeville partners?
W: The play was made into a movie in 1975 starring George Burns and Walter Matthau as the two old feuding vaudeville comedians who come together for a TV spot and ruin it. Simon and Matthau received Academy Award nominations; Burns won an Oscar.

A: Superman
Q: Who made his debut in *Action Comics* No. 1?
W: Superman debuted in *Action Comics* in June 1938. The creator of this character was Jerry Siegel, and Joe Shuster added his artistry as the illustrator.

A: Surfing
Q: What was the favorite sport of Tom Wolfe's *The Pump House Gang*?
W: *The Pump House Gang* was written in 1968 by Thomas Kennerly Wolfe, Jr., who was born in Virginia in 1931. He is a journalist known for his treatment of contemporary American culture from its popular heroes to its alternative lifestyles.

A: Swiss
Q: What was William Tell's nationality?
W: William Tell was a legendary Swiss hero in the struggle for independence from Austria. Because he refused to salute the governor's cap, he was forced to shoot an apple off his own son's head with a bow and arrow.

ART AND LITERATURE

A: **Swiss Family Robinson's, The**
Q: Whose adventures are told in a book subtitled *Adventures in a Desert Island*?
W: *The Swiss Family Robinson* is the romance of a family wrecked on a desert island, written in German by Johann Rudolf Wyss, a Swiss author and professor of philosophy at Bern. It was published in two parts in Zurich (1812–13) and translated into English a year later.

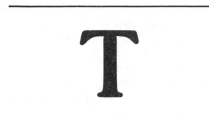

A: **"Tales of Peter Rabbit"**
Q: What story features Flopsy, Mopsy and Cottontail?
W: This tale was created by Beatrix Potter in 1902 and features Peter Rabbit and his brother and sisters, Flopsy, Mopsy, and Cottontail.

A: **Tara**
Q: What was the name of Scarlett O'Hara's mansion?
W: This is from Margaret Mitchell's novel *Gone With the Wind*, which was set in Georgia around the time of the Civil War. The main character, Scarlett O'Hara, is the daughter of Gerald O'Hara, an Irish immigrant, who is the owner of a large plantation, Tara. Upon her father's death, Scarlett inherits Tara.

A: **Tarts**
Q: What did the Knave of Hearts steal?
W: Originally this was a Mother Goose rhyme. It was used by Lewis Carroll in *Alice in Wonderland* for the courtroom scene: "The Queen of Hearts, she made some tarts, All on a summer day. The Knave of Hearts, He stole those tarts, And took them quite away."

A: **Tattoos**
Q: What is Ray Bradbury's illustrated man illustrated with?
W: Ray Douglas Bradbury, born in Illinois in 1920, wrote *The Illustrated Man* in 1951. "Illustrated" refers to the tattoos. Tattooing is the production of patterns on the face and body by inserting dye under the skin. It is an old custom known around the world and was reportedly practiced in Egypt before 1300 B.C.

A: **T.E. Lawrence's or Lawrence of Arabia's**
Q: What British officer's autobiography is titled *Seven Pillars of Wisdom*?
W: Lawrence was a British archaeologist who traveled and excavated in Syria. In World War I, he was one of the British officers sent from Egypt to help the Sharif of Mecca in his revolt against the Turks. After gaining a position of influence with the Arabs and performing many daring exploits, he entered Damascus in 1918 with the leading Arab forces. *Pillars of Wisdom* narrates these experiences.

A: **Telephone exchange 288**
Q: What is Butterfield 8 in *Butterfield 8*?
W: John O'Hara's novel *Butterfield 8*, was made into a 1960 movie starring Elizabeth Taylor. Taylor won an Academcy Award for her role. This coy sex drama, mildly daring in the 1960s, was the story of a society girl who has a complex love life.

A: ***Tempest, The***
Q: What Shakespearean play opens with a storm at sea?
W: *The Tempest* is a romantic drama by Shakespeare printed in 1623. It is about Prospero, Duke of Milan, and his daughter Miranda who are cast adrift at sea and beach on a lonely island inhabited by Sycorax the witch. Prospero, with the help of magic, finally defeats the brother who has usurped his throne.

A: **Ten**
Q: How many days shook the world in a book by John Reed?
W: Reed was an American writer and journalist. His eyewitness stories of the Russian Revolution are "Red Russia" (1919) and *Ten Days That Shook the World* (1919). This graphic account was approved by the Soviets, and Lenin even wrote an introduction to it.

A: **Ten cents**
Q: What was the price of the first *Mad* magazine?
W: *Mad* magazine is published monthly in New York. It was founded in 1952 by Harvey Kurtzman and is noted for its topical humor and satire, especially its lampoons on the whole area of mass culture and communications.

A: **Tennessee Williams**
Q: Who wrote *The Night of the Iguana*?
W: This play was made into a 1964 movie starring Richard Burton, Deborah Kerr, Ava Gardner, and Sue Lyon. It is the story of a disbarred clergyman who becomes a travel courier in Mexico and is sexually desired by a teenage nymphomaniac, a middle-aged hotel owner, and a frustrated itinerant artist.

A: **Tennessee Williams**
Q: Who won a Pulitzer Prize for his play *Cat on a Hot Tin Roof?*
W: This play is an intense drama of family relationships set on a plantation in the Mississippi delta. It was a 1958 movie starring Burl Ives, Paul Newman, and Elizabeth Taylor. A rich plantation owner, dying of cancer, finds his two sons lacking; one is a conniver, the other a neurotic who refuses to sleep with his wife.

A: **Tennessee Williams's**
Q: What playwright's works include *The Glass Menagerie* and *The Rose Tattoo?*
W: Tennesse Williams wrote *The Glass Menagerie* about his own mentally retarded sister, changing the affliction to a clubfoot in the play. *The Rose Tattoo* is the story of a Sicilian woman on the gulf coast who is tormented by the infidelity of her husband (now deceased), but a brawny truck driver makes her forget her husband.

A: **Tevye**
Q: Who's the principal character in *Fiddler on the Roof?*
W: In a pre-revolutionary Russian village, Tevye, the Jewish milkman, survives family and political problems and, when the pogroms begin, cheerfully emigrates to America. It is a celebration of a vanished way of life. It was a 1971 movie from the play by Joseph Stein. You must remember the song "If I Were a Rich Man..."

A: **The**
Q: What is the most-used word in written English?
W: The word *the* is a definite article, as opposed to the indefinite *a* or *an*, and is used especially before nouns to render the modified word more particular or individual. It is used specifically: 1. when reference is made to a particular person, thing, or group; 2. to give an adjective substantive force or render a notion abstract; 3. before a noun to make it generic; 4. with the force of a possessive pronoun; 5. to give distributive force; and 6. to designate. That about covers it!

A: **Their mittens**
Q: What did the three little kittens lose?
W: "What! Lost your mittens, you naughty kittens! Then you shall have no pie." Another of the Mother Goose rhymes!

A: **Their tails were cut off**
Q: What was the fate of the Three Blind Mice?
W: From the classic Mother Goose rhyme: "Three blind mice! See how they run! They all ran after the farmer's wife, Who cut off their tails with a carving knife; Did you ever see such a sight in your life As three blind mice?"

A: **Theodore Roosevelt**
Q: What U.S. president wrote 37 books?
W: Teddy Roosevelt was the 26th president of the U.S. (1901-09). He was born in New York City, graduated from Harvard, and became president when McKinley was assassinated. He wrote books of an historical nature that promoted his beliefs and told of his adventures in and out of politics.

A: **They were miners**
Q: What did the Seven Dwarfs do for a living?
W: In this famous fairy tale, Snow White is a fair princess left in the woods to die by her wicked stepmother. She is found and cared for by the Seven Dwarfs, who "hi-hoed" their way off to work in the mines while she kept their house.

A: **They're twin sisters**
Q: How are Ann Landers and Abigail Van Buren related?
W: Ann Landers, Mrs. Esther P. Lederer, and Abigail Van Buren, Pauline Friedman Phillips, were born July 4, 1918. They are both nationally syndicated columnists and authors.

A: *Third Wave, The*
Q: What book is the follow-up to *Future Shock?*
W: Alvin Toffler published *Future Shock* in 1970, followed by *The Third Wave* in 1980. Both books explore and illuminate the civilization of tomorrow and analyze the forces creating our future.

A: **Third World War, The**
Q: What future was described in a 1978 best-seller by General Sir John Hackett and others?
W: General Sir John Hackett, former commander of the British Army of the Rhine, and other top ranking NATO generals and advisers wrote this gripping and astonishing narrative about the Third World War, beginning August 1985. It is compelling and realistic.

A: **Thirteen**
Q: How many people appear in da Vinci's *The Last Supper?*
W: In Leonardo da Vinci's famous painting, the first major painting of the High Renaissance (1497), there are 13 people pictured: Jesus and his 12 disciples. It depicts the moment after Christ says, "Verily I say unto you that one of you shall betray me."

A: **Thirty-nine**
Q: How many steps are there in John Buchan's novel?
W: The novel, *The Thirty-nine Steps*, was written by Buchan in 1915. It outlines the "the Thirty-nine Articles of Religion in England," which are the statements to which those who take orders in the Church of England subscribe. These were sanctioned by Parliament in 1571.

A: **Thirty-seven**
Q: How many known plays did William Shakespeare write?
W: William Shakespeare was an English actor and playwright who wrote romances, comedies and dramas, probably beginning with *Henry VI* about 1590-91. It is believed that *The Tempest* was the last drama he completed about

1611-12. Shakespeare is considered to have been the greatest of authors in any language, ancient or modern.

A: *This Side of Paradise*
Q: What was F. Scott Fitzgerald's first novel?
W: F. Scott Fitzgerald was born in St. Paul, went to Princeton in 1913, and joined the Army in 1917. While being trained, he wrote the first draft of *This Side of Paradise*, set at his alma mater and an expression of a new generation and its jazz age. The book, pubished in 1920, caught the flavor and interests of a changing era and placed his stories in demand.

A: Thomas Gainsborough
Q: Who painted *The Blue Boy*?
W: Gainsborough was the British painter known for his landscapes and portraits. One of his best known portraits is *Blue Boy*. It's not Boy George in a blue dress either!

A: Thomas Stearns
Q: What did the T.S. stand for in Eliot's name?
W: Eliot was born in St. Louis, graduated from Harvard, and studied at the Sorbonne and Morton College, Oxford. In 1927 he became a British subject because of his interest in the English Church and state. This interest was reflected in his prose, but it is for his poetry that he is better known.

A: Thor
Q: Who's the god of thunder and war in Norse mythology?
W: In Norse mythology, Thor was the god of war, thunder, and strength who destroyed the enemies of the gods with his magic hammer.

A: Thou shalt not kill
Q: What does Exodus give as the sixth Commandment in the King James Version of the Bible?
W: The Ten Commandments appear in two different places in the Old Testament: Exodus 20:1-17 and Deuteronomy 5: 6-21. The phrasing is similar but not identical. In Exodus "Thou shalt not kill" is the sixth commandment and in Deuteronomy it is the tenth.

A: Three
Q: How many fiddlers did Old King Cole have?
W: A legendary British king, described in the nursery rhyme as "a merry old soul," was "fond of his pipe, fond of his bowl, and fond of his fiddlers three"

A: Three
Q: How many children did Adam and Eve have together?
W: This is from the Bible, Genesis 4: "And Adam knew Eve his wife; and she conceived, and bore Cain... And she again bore his brother Abel... And Adam knew his wife again, and she bore a son, and called his name Seth..."

A: Three
Q: How many volumes make up J.R.R. Tolkien's *Lord of the Rings"*
W: In 1954 and 1955, Tolkien published *The Fellowship of the Ring*, as a sequence in three volumes: *The Lord of the Rings*, *The Two Towers*, and *The Return of the King*. Another of his well-known works is *The Hobbit* published in 1937.

A: Three
Q: How many Ss are there in the word misspells?
W: It is probably "mispelt" more than any other word!

A: Three Musketeers, The
Q: What heroic group did D'Artagnan lead?
W: *The Three Musketeers* was written by French dramatist and novelist Alexandre Dumas, known generally as "Dumas pere." One of the most popular of his romances, the story deals with the life of a poor Gascon gentleman, d'Artagnon, who comes to Paris in the reign of Louis XIII to join the king's musketeers. He gets involved in duels with three valiant members of that force (Athos, Porthos, and Aramis) and thereafter becomes their friend and shares their fortunes and their many heroic adventures.

A: *Through The Looking Glass*
Q: What's the sequel to *Alice's Adventures in Wonderland*?
W: In *Alices' Adventures in Wonderland*, Alice is a little girl who dreams that she pursues a white rabbit down a rabbit hole and there meets with strange adventures and odd characters (published 1865). In the 1872 sequel, Alice walks in a dream through the looking glass into "Looking-glass House" where she finds that the chessmen, particularly the red and white queens, are alive.

A: *Through The Looking Glass*
Q: What Lewis Carroll book introduced Humpty Dumpty to the world?
W: Charles Lutwidge Dodgson, an English author whose pseudonym was Lewis Carroll, wrote this sequel to *Alice's Adventures in Wonderland*. In it she meets more strange characters such as Tweedledum, Tweedledee, and Humpty Dumpty.

A: *Time*
Q: What weekly magazine features a column called "The Presidency?"
W: *Time*, the New York weekly news magazine, presents concise and comprehensive summaries of current news and relates it to its larger background. Articles are grouped in various general and specialized departments such as the above mentioned column.

ART AND LITERATURE

A: *Time*
Q: What news magazine did Henry Luce and Briton Hadden found?
W: Founded in 1923 by Luce and Hadden, *Time* is a pioneer in deft, incisive condensation of news in a tone that is factual, but that also expresses attitudes.

A: *Time Machine, The*
Q: What was H.G. Wells's first novel?
W: Herbert George Wells, an English author of great imagination, wrote *Time Machine* in 1895. It is about a Victorian scientist who builds a machine that transports him into the distant future.

A: **Tinker Bell**
Q: Who was the fairy in *Peter Pan*?
W: In the dramatic fantasy about the "boy who wouldn't grow up," Tinker Bell is Peter Pan's fairy friend. She lives with him in the treetops in Never-Never Land, and her fairy dust is one of the ingredients needed by the three children of the Darling family in order to fly.

A: **To arms, To arms**
Q: What's the meaning of the Latin battle cry: *Ad arma, ad arma*?
W: *Ad* is a preposition expressing primarily direction toward, to a point. *Arma* is a noun meaning "defensive arms, armour," especially "shield," but in a wider sense "weapons of war."

A: **To the fair**
Q: Where was Simple Simon going when he met a pieman?
W: From the classic Mother Goose rhyme: "Simple Simon met a pieman Going to the fair; Says Simple Simon to the pieman: "Pray let me taste your ware.' Says the pieman to Simple Simon "Show me first your penny' Says Simple Simon to the pieman: "Indeed I have not any.'"

A: **Tom Sawyer**
Q: Who was Becky Thatcher's boyfriend?

W: Mark Twain's 1876 book *The Adventures of Tom Sawyer* takes place in a quiet Mississippi river town, Petersburg, Missouri. Young Tom's friend is Huck Finn, and his sweetheart is Becky Thatcher. Adventurous Tom, besides running away from home and getting into trouble, spends several days lost in a cave with Becky.

A: **Tom Sawyer**
Q: Who's the orphan – Huck Finn, Tom Sawyer or Becky Thatcher?
W: In *The Adventures of Tom Sawyer* Becky Thatcher is the sweetheart of Tom Sawyer who, along with his priggish brother Sid, live with their kindhearted Aunt Polly. Huck Finn, Tom's buddy, is the orphan who is adopted by the Widow Douglas of Petersburg, Missouri.

A: *Torrents of Spring, The*
Q: What was Ernest Hemingway's first novel?
W: Although Hemingway had published several short stories, his first novel was not published until 1926.

A: **Travel guides**
Q: What kind of books does Fodor's publish?
W: Eugene Fodor was editor and publisher of Fodor's Modern Guides, Inc., from 1949 to 1965 and executive chairman of the board of Fodor's Modern Guides, Ltd., London.

A: **Travis McGee series, The**
Q: What John D. MacDonald detective series has a color in every title?
W: Some of the McGee mysteries are titled: *Tan and Sandy Silence*, *Dress Her in Indigo*, *Deep Blue Goodbye*, *Free Fall in Crimson*, and *The Turquoise Lament*.

A: *Treasure Island*
Q: What Robert Louis Stevenson novel follows the adventures of cabin boy Jim Hawkins?

W: *Treasure Island*, the novel of romance by Stevenson, was published in book form in 1883. Jim Hawkins is the narrator of the story and the main character. Jim comes into possession of a treasure map and sets sail for Treasure Island with Squire Trelawney, Dr. Livesey, and crew.

A: *Treasure Island*
Q: What adventure tale introduced: "Yo-ho-ho-, and a bottle of rum!"?
W: This book centers around the struggle of William Long John Silver to take over possession of the treasure map owned by Jim Hawkins and his crew.

A: **Troy**
Q: What city fell to the Wooden Horse?
W: The fall of the city was caused, according to Greek mythology, by the elopement of Helen, wife of Menelaus, King of Sparta, to Troy with Paris causing the Trojan War. Spartan soldiers filled the large hollow wooden horse that was left at night outide the city walls. When the Trojans brought the horse inside, the Spartans emerged and conquered Troy. Isn't divorce easier?

A: **Truman Capote**
Q: Who wrote *In Cold Blood* about the murder of a Kansas family?
W: The work, published in 1966, was described by its author as "a non-fiction novel." It is the story of the murder of a farmer, his wife, and two children in Holcomb, Kansas, by ex-convicts robbing their home. This event did happen in 1959, and the book follows the criminals' escape, capture, trial, and hanging in April 1965. Capote died in August 1984.

A: **Truth**
Q: What does the name of the Russian newspaper *Pravda* mean?
W: Truth is what the Soviets would like to have you to believe they are reporting. Lenin launched publication of the Russian daily newspaper on May 5, 1912.

A: *TV Guide*
Q: What's America's best-selling weekly magazine?
W: *TV Guide* was founded in 1953. It consists, essentially, of a weekly listing of TV programs, with short articles on current, popular television topics and personalities. It was acquired by the Philadelphia *Inquirer* in 1969 and has a current weekly circulation of over 17 million copies.

A: *Twelfth Night*
Q: What Shakespeare play begins: "If music be the food of love, play on?"
W: *Twelfth Night* or *What You Will*, a Shakespearean comedy probably produced about 1600, is about Sebastain and Viola, twin brother and sister who are separated in a shipwreck off the coast of Illyria. Viola is brought to shore and disguised as a boy and takes service as a page for a duke, with whom she secretly falls in love. The confusion and fun begin when her brother arrives in Illyria, but the "right" lovers finally get together and are married.

A: **Twelve**
Q: How many deeds did Hercules perform to free himself from bondage?
W: In classical mythology, Hercules was the son of Zeus and Alcmena, renowned for his great strength and endurance. He is also known for his performance of the twelve gigantic labors imposed upon him by Eurystheus, King of Argo, at the urging of Hera, queen and wife of Zeus.

A: **Twenty**
Q: How many years did Rip Van Winkle sleep?

W: "Rip Van Winkle" was a tale published in *The Sketch Book* by Washington Irving in 1819-20. Rip is an indolent, good-natured Dutch American in a village on the Hudson. Hunting with his dog Wolf one day, he meets a dwarf-like stranger whom he helps carry a hog. He joins a party of dwarfs and after drinking with them falls asleep for 20 years, during which the Revolutionary War takes place and his wife dies. He is finally remembered when he returns to town and goes to live with his grown-up daughter.

A: **Twenty-eight**
Q: How many years was Robinson Crusoe shipwrecked on his island?
W: *The Life and Strange Surprising Adventures of Robinson Crusoe* was written by Daniel Defoe and published in 1719. Crusoe was shipwrecked on an uninhabited island until an English ship finally came by. His adventures and survival were based on the real life story of Andrew Selkirk who ran away to sea and was, at his own request, put ashore on the uninhabited island of Juan Fernandez from 1704 to 1709.

A: **Twenty-four**
Q: How many letters are there in the Greek alphabet?
W: Modern Greek has been the language of Greece since 1500, and its literary form retain many classical features. It is also called "Romaic," especially in its spoken form. College fraternities and sororities in the U.S. are designated by Greek letters.

A: **Twelve Oaks**
Q: What's the name of the Wilkes plantation in *Gone With the Wind*?
W: The 1936 Pulitzer Prize winning novel by Margaret Mitchell is set in Georgia during the Civil War and Reconstruction and is a long romantic tale about young Scarlett O'Hara who lives on the plantation, Tara. She is in love with Ashley Wilkes who lives on the neighboring plantation, Twelve Oakes.

A: **Twenty-one**
Q: How many Gutenberg Bibles are there?
W: Johann Gutenberg was a German printer and the inventor of moveable type. A Gutenberg Bible is an edition of the Vulgate, printed in Mainz before 1456 and regarded as the first large work printed from moveable type.

A: **Two**
Q: How many years before the mast did Richard H. Dana write about?
W: Richard Henry Dana, Jr. (1815-82) had eye trouble as a Harvard law school student and took time out to regain his health. He sailed for California as a common sailor, and in 1840, the year he was admitted to the bar, he published his account of the voyage, *Two Years Before the Mast*. The book immediately became popular.

A: **Two**
Q: How many guns of Navarone were there?
W: *The Guns of Navarone* was a 1961 movie of Alistair Maclean's novel. It is about a sabotage team sent in 1943 to destroy two giant guns on a Turkish island. Full of lots of noise and self-sacrifice, it received an Oscar nomination for Best Picture.

A: **Two**
Q: How many genies appear to Aladdin in the *Arabian Nights* tale?
W: "Aladdin and the Wonderful Lamp" is an oriental tale generally regarded as belonging to the *Arabian Nights* collected tales, but that is questionable. Aladdin, son of a poor tailor in China, is hired by a Moorish sorcerer to obtain for him a magic lamp. Discovering the powers of the lamp, Aladdin keeps it himself, becomes wealthy, marries, and with the lamp's help constructs a palace. The sorcerer recovers the lamp and whisks bride and palace off to Africa. Aladdin pursues, regains the lamp, and has the genie in the lamp take bride and palace back to China.

ART AND LITERATURE

A: two-headed llama, A
Q: What kind of animal is Dr. Dolittle's Pushmi-Pullyu?
W: This animal is from the Hugh Lofting novel, *Dr. Dolittle*, which became a 1967 movie. In a Victorian English village, Dr. Doolittle is a veterinary surgeon who talks to his patients. The song "Talk to the Animals" won an Academy Award. How many of you asked for your own talking "pushmi-pullyu" stuffed animal from Santa that year?

A: *Two Towers, The*
Q: What was the second book in J.R.R. Tolkien's trilogy *The Lord of the Rings*?
W: Tolkien's trilogy, *The Fellowship of the Ring* was released in three volumes: *Lord of the Rings* (1954); *The Two Towers* (1954); and *The Return of the King* (1955).

U

A: U.S. Civil War, The
Q: What war was the subject of Bruce Catton's *The Coming Fury*?
W: Bruce Catton was an American journalist who wrote a centennial history of the Civil War in three volumes: *The Coming Fury* (1961), *Terrible Swift Sword* (1963), and *Never Call Retreat* (1965).

A: U.S. Civil War, The
Q: What war killed Brent and Stuart, the Tarleton twins?
W: These boys are from *Gone With the Wind*. This classic saga begins with Miss Scarlett O'Hara seated on the front porch of Tara, exchanging promises for secrets with the Tarleton twins. It was Brent and Stuart who told Scarlett about Ashley Wilkes marrying Melanie Hamilton. When the twins died in the Civil War, Scarlett was shocked because their parents bought extravagant tombstones when the money was desperately needed for food.

A: U.S. Supreme Court, The
Q: What court does Bob Woodward describe in *The Brethren*?
W: Woodward co-authored with Carl Bernstein *All the President's Men* and *The Final Days*. *The Brethern*, which he co-authored with Scott Armstrong, is a detailed, behind the scenes account of the Supreme Court in action. It candidly reveals the politicking, compromising, and maneuvering that go into the decisions that shape our lives.

A: Ulysses
Q: What was Odysseus called by the Romans?
W: Odysseus was, in Greek legend, King of Ithaca, one of the Greek leaders of the Trojan War, and hero of the *Odyssey*. Ulysses is the Latin name for Odysseus.

A: *Uncle Remus*
Q: What Joel Chandler Harris book tells the stories of Br'er Fox and Br'er Rabbit?
W: Joel Chandler Harris was an American author devoted from childhood to English literature. He possessed much knowledge of Negro myth, customs, dialect, and idiom that he reproduced in his famous *Uncle Remus* series of tales. These contain a number of folklore tales relating to a variety of animals, including the rabbit and the fox, that are told by a Negro man to a little boy.

A: *Uncle Tom's Cabin*
Q: What Harriet Beecher Stowe novel is about slavery?
W: Stowe's 1852 novel described the life of Uncle Tom, a noble, high-minded, devoutly Christian black slave, and his death by flogging because of the fury of his cruel master, Simon Legree. It was a powerful book in the cause of abolition.

A: *Uncle Tom's Cabin*
Q: What was the biggest-selling American novel before *Gone With the Wind*?
W: *Uncle Tom's Cabin* or *Live Among the Lowly*, a novel by Harriet Beecher Stowe, was published in book form in 1852. During it's first publication it sold 300,000 copies and had a powerful antislavery influence. It is the story of a nobel black slave who gets sold at auction to a cruel master, Simon Legree. Tom's courage and religious fortitude impress his master but Legree has him flogged to death when Tom refuses to reveal the hiding place of two female slaves.

A: Utopia
Q: What imaginary island did Sir Thomas More create in a 1516 work?
W: More was a member of the English parliament and devoted his leisure to literature. His description of the imaginary island Utopia was published in 1516. Sir Thomas was imprisoned and beheaded for not taking an oath that would impugn the Pope's authority or assume the justice of the king's (Henry VIII) divorce from Queen Catherine.

A: Under-25 Generation, The
Q: What group was *Time*'s Man of the Year for 1967?
W: The baby-boom generation was coming into its own at this time, and taking an active role in political rallies and anti-war demonstrations.

A: Unto
Q: What does the *U* stand for in the abbreviation I.O.U.?
W: The letters I.O.U. stand for "I owe unto you." A paper that has on it the letters I.O.U., a sum of money, and a signature is an acknowledgement of debt and is sometimes used as the equivalent of a promissory note.

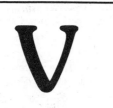

A: V.I. Lenin
Q: Who founded *Pravda*?
W: Vladimir Ilyich Lenin or N. Lenin are two pseudonyms of Vladimir Il-yich Ulyanov, Russian Communist leader. He was born April 22, 1870. Lenin launched publication of of the Bolshevik daily newspaper in St. Petersburg on May 5, 1912. On Jan. 21, 1924, Lenin died after a series of stokes, and his body is still on display in Red Square.

A: Van Pelt
Q: What's the last name of Lucy and Linus?
W: Lucy and her younger brother Linus are characters in Charles Schultz's cartoon stip *Peanuts*. Lucy, the militant, is in love with Schroeder; and Linus is the one who is always dragging around his flannel security blanket.

A: Van Rijn
Q: What was Rembrandt's last name?
W: Rembrandt Harmenszoon van Rijn was born in Holland on July 15, 1606. He was a master artist, best appreciated for his portraits, especially his series of self-portraits that show the progress of his skills as well as his life story.

A: *Variety*
Q: What's the leading newspaper of the entertainment industry?
W: *Variety*, weekly journal of the entertainment world was founded in New York in 1905 by Sime Silverman. It is noted for its slang and theatrical jargon, and some of its articles are unintelligible to persons not familiar with the slangy speech of Broadway. For example, the headline "Stix Nix Hix Pix" means that rural areas do not care for pictures depicting farm life.

A: Vassar
Q: What school did the eight members of Mary McCarthy's *The Group* attend?
W: Mary Therese McCarthy, American author born in 1912, wrote *The Group* in 1963. It's about the misadventures of eight Vassar alumnae, Class of '33, in the 30 years since their graduation from the prestigious co-ed college in Poughkeepsie, New York.

A: Veterinarian
Q: What is British novelist James Herriot's other occupation?
W: Practicing veterinary surgery before becoming a writer and since, Herriot is a beloved storyteller who has authored such books as *All Things Bright and Beautiful*, *All Creatures Great and Small*, and *All Things Wise and Wonderful*. All three titles are from the verse of a hymn.

A: Victor Hugo
Q: Who penned *The Hunchback of Notre Dame*?
W: *Notre Dame de Paris* (1831) is a novel of 15th century Paris by Victor Marie Hugo. Quasimodo is the grotesque hunchback bellringer of Notre Dame and central character of the book, which is a vivid picture of medieval Paris. Hugo, French poet and novelist, was the leader of the French Romantic movement.

A: Vincent
Q: What name did Vincent Van Gogh sign to his paintings?
W: Van Gogh was a Dutch artist and the first of the great modern expressionist painters. Many of his paintings are intense and emotional. His life seemed to be driven by a great need for self-expression.

A: Vincent Van Gogh
Q: Who painted *Self Portrait with Bandaged Ear*?
W: His art was always an expression of his life, and this portrait was probably painted after a visit with Paul Gauguin. Van Gogh, who was sub-ject to periods of insanity, attacked Gauguin during a heated discussion, mutilating his own ear.

A: Vincent Van Gogh
Q: Who's the subject of Irving Stone's *Lust for Life*?
W: Stone is a California-born author of widely popular fictionized biographies that include *Lust for Life* about Van Gogh. The book was written in 1934.

A: Vincent Van Gogh
Q: Who shot and killed himself while painting *Wheatfield with Crows*?
W: Van Gogh's last canvases, painted after some months at the asylum at Saint-Remy, were views of endless wheat fields under hot and troubled skies in which he tried to express "sadness and exteme loneliness." On July 27, 1890, he shot himself and died two days later.

A: Vincent Van Gogh's
Q: What painter's works include *Potato Eaters*, *Cypress Road* and *Starry Night*?
W: *Potato Eaters* (1885), Van Gogh's first major painting, is a large and somber picture of peasants at their evening meal. His empathy with the working people is reflected in his art. He spent much of his life in poverty, and his art is inseparable from his life. *Cypress Road* was painted while he was hospitalized for mental illness and depression.

A: violin, The
Q: What musical instrument did Sherlock Holmes play?
W: Sherlock Holmes, the renowned detective created by Sir Arthur Conan Doyle, has appeared in individual films and a series, in adaptations of the original stories, and in manufactured plots that would certainly have impressed Doyle. Whether fighting criminals or matching wits with his arch enemy, Professor Moriarty, Holmes was known to relax and "fine tune" his mind with the violin.

ART AND LITERATURE

A: **Virgin Mary, The**
Q: What woman has made the most appearances on the cover of *Time*?
W: The Virgin Mary is the mother of Jesus who is believed to be the son of God in Christian theology.

A: **"Visit from St. Nicholas, A"**
Q: What poem begins: "Twas the night before Christmas…?"
W: The poem that has become popularly known as "Twas the Night Before Christmas," was written by Clement Clark Moore, a professor of Biblical learning. It was published anonymously in the *Frog Sentinel* Dec. 23, 1823, and reprinted in the author's book of *Poems* published in 1844.

A: **Volkswagen, A**
Q: What does a CBer refer to as as "pregnant roller skate?"
W: This small German economy car first imported into the U.S. in the late 1940s is referred to as a "pregnant roller skate" because of its small size and unusually rounded shape. The Volkswagen has also been known as "the bug," "the beetle," and "the V dub."

W

A: *Walden*
Q: What Thoreau work is subtitled *Life in the Woods*?
W: Henry David Thoreau, American author and individualist, described himself as "a mystic, transcendentalist, and a natural philosopher to boot." Born in Concord, Massachusetts, Thoreau built a hut at nearby Walden Pond where he lived from July 4, 1845 to Sept. 6, 1847, a period about which he wrote in his most famous book *Walden*.

A: **Wallaces, The**
Q: What family compiled the book *The Intimate Sex Lives of Famous People*?
W: The authors were Irving Wallace, his wife Sylvia, their daughter Amy, and son David (Wallechinsky). The book was published in 1981. Irving and son David are also the authors of the famous *People's Almanac* that now has three volumes.

A: **walrus, The**
Q: What animal dined on bread and oysters with a carpenter?
W: This is from the poem "The Walrus and the Carpenter" in Lewis Carroll's *Through the Looking Glass*. The walrus and the carpenter invite a bed of oysters to take a walk with them. The oysters follow hand in hand only to find that they are the main course at their friends' picnic!

A: *War and Peace*
Q: What Russian novel embracing more than 500 characters is set in the Napoleonic Wars?
W: This masterpiece of Leo Tolstoy is one of the two or three greatest novels of world literature. This vast work was carefully planned and slowly written over the course of some six years. It is essentially an historical novel concerned with family life and war in Russia between the years 1805 and 1814. The work concentrates on five major families, but scores of other characters appear.

A: *War and Remembrance*
Q: What's the sequel to Herman Wouk's *The Winds of War*?
W: *The Winds of War* (1971) and *War and Remembrances* (1978) are lengthy novels comprising a saga of World War II in its vast scope, often concentrating on Pacific operations, but also vividly depicting the Holocaust.

A: **Washington Irving**
Q: What author was appointed U.S. ambassador to Spain in 1842?

W: Author Washington Irving was probably best known for "Rip Van Winkle" and "The Legend of Sleepy Hollow," both from his most successful work *The Sketch Book*. Irving became minister to Spain in 1842, but resigned in 1845 because of the Spanish insurrection.

A: *Washington Post*, **The**
Q: What newspaper returned a Pulitzer Prize for the fraudulent story "Jimmy's World?"
W: Janet Cooke, reporter with the Washington *Post*, received the Pulitzer Prize for "Jimmy's World," a story of a very young drug addict. It was later found to be more story than truth, and Cooke lost both her Pulitzer Prize and her job.

A: *Washington Post's*, **The**
Q: What newspaper's two reporter team exposed the Watergate cover-up?
W: The Washington, D.C., newspaper exposed the Watergate cover-up through the work of the investigative reporters Carl Bernstein and Bob Woodward under editor Ben Bradlee. The 1976 movie, *All the President's Men* is a reconstruction of the discovery of the White House link with the Watergate affair. Robert Redford and Dustin Hoffman play Woodward and Bernstein.

A: *Watership Down*
Q: What Richard Adams book includes an account of Bigwig's encounter with a fox?
W: Bigwig's encounter with a fox takes place in Richard G. Adams thought-provoking novel *Watership Down*. The story chronicles the adventures of a group of rabbits searching for a safe place to establish a new home where they can live in peace.

A: **Wendy**
Q: What Good Little Witch is Casper's girlfriend?
W: Introduced in 1953 by Harney Publications, Casper was known as "the friendly ghost," who had the

ability to become invisible at will. His friends include Wendy, the Witch, Spooky, and Nightmare. Casper also became a popular animated TV series.

A: **whale, A**
Q: What was Simple Simon fishing for in his mother's pail?
W: Another Mother Goose rhyme! Simple Simon went fishing to catch a whale but the only water he could find was in his mother's pail.

A: **What, me worry?**
Q: What is Alfred E. Neuman's motto?
W: Alfred E. Neuman is *Mad* magazine's" "What me worry?" hero. He first appeared on a *Mad* cover in 1956. The original drawing of Alfred is an undated, traceable "comic" postcard of many years before.

A: **Where are you going?**
Q: What does the Latin *quo vadis* ask?
W: *Quo* is the Latin adverb of place, "to what place," "at what place." *Vadere* is a verb meaning "to go." Hence, where are you going?

A: **Where is everybody?**
Q: What did Carl Sandburg reply to the question: "What did the last man on Earth say?"W: Carl Sandburg was an American author who sought to describe the distinctive flavor of American idiom and thought.

A: **White**
Q: What color was Moby Dick?
W: Born in New York City in 1819, Herman Melville is best known today for his novel *Moby Dick* or *The Whale*, published in 1851. The story concerns Captain Ahab, a monomaniac whose one purpose is to capture the fierce, cunning white whale, Moby Dick, that had torn away Ahab's leg during an earlier encounter.

A: **White**
Q: What was the color of Christ's hair in St. John's vision?
W: This is from the Bible in "The Revelation of St. John the Divine," Chapter I, verse 14: "His head and his hair were white like wool, as white as snow; and his eyes were as a flame of fire…"

A: **White Rabbit, The**
Q: Who does Alice follow down the hole?
W: In the opening pages of *Alice in Wonderland*, Alice spots a white rabbit while she's sitting outdoors with her sister. She follows the rabbit down its hole and finds, at the other end, the beautiful and confusing "Wonderland."

A: ***Who's Afraid of Virginia Woolf?***
Q: What was Edward Albee's first full-length play?
W: Produced in 1962, this play concerns Martha, the middle-aged daughter of the president of a small New England college, and her husband, George, an unsuccessful professor in its history department. They entertain a new faculty member, Nick, and his wife, Honey, in an evening of drunken antagonism, much of it devoted to Martha's game "humiliate the host."

A: ***Who's Afraid of Virginia Woolf?***
Q: What Edward Albee play centers on George and Martha, a childless couple?
W: In the better known 1966 film version of Edward Albee's play, Martha is played by Elizabeth Taylor and George, her husband, is played by Richard Burton. The film broke Hollywood taboos for adult material because of the language in the many bitter conversations.

A: **William F. Buckley Jr.**
Q: Who's the founder and editor of *The National Review*?
W: *The National Review* is a New York biweekly founded in 1955 by Buckley and edited by him. It is the chief organ of conservatism as an intellecutal, social, and political movement.

A: **William L. Shirer**
Q: Who wrote *The Rise and Fall of the Third Reich*?
W: William Lawrence Shirer was born in 1904 in Illinois. He is a journalist, war correspondent, and commentator on radio, but is best known for his firsthand studies of Germany. In addition to the *Rise and Fall of the Third Reich* written in 1960, he wrote *Berlin Diary*, *The Collapse of the Third Republic*, and several other novels.

A: **William Manchester**
Q: Who did Jackie Kennedy commission to write *The Death of a President*?
W: William Raymond Manchester, American author born April 1, 1922, has written such books as *Rockefeller Family Portrait* (1959), *Portrait of a President* (1962) and *Death of a President* (1967). The latter was written after the assassination of President John F. Kennedy.

A: **William Peter Blatty**
Q: Who wrote *The Exorcist*?
W: Blatty is best known for his novel *The Exorcist*, which was made into a successful movie in 1973 starring Linda Blair, Ellen Burstyn, and Max von Sydow. It was the story of a small town girl who is unaccountably possessed by the devil and turns into a monster who causes several violent deaths before she is rid of the devil.

A: **William Shakespeare**
Q: Who penned: "Neither a borrower nor a lender be?"
W: "Neither a borrower nor a lender be; For loan oft loses both itself and friend, And borrowing dulls the edge by William Shakespeare.

A: **woman scorned, A**
Q: What does "hell hath no fury like?"
W: This quote is from "The Mourning Bride" by William Congreve. "Heaven has no rage like love to hatred turned, Nor Hell a fury like a woman scorned."

ART AND LITERATURE

A: **wooden shoe, A**
Q: What did Wynken, Blynken, and Nod go out to sea in?
W: In this wonderful Eugene Field poem, Wynken, Blynken, and Nod go to sea to fish for herring. The moon laughed and sped them along while the stars were the fish in the sea. "Wynken and Blynken are two eyes, and Nod is a little head; And the wooden shoe that sailed the skies is a wee one's trundle bed."

A: **Woodstock**
Q: What's the name of Snoopy's secretary?
W: Snoopy's bird, friend, and secretary are all one and the same: Woodstock. These characters are from Charles Schulz's *Peanuts* cartoon strip introduced in 1950.

A: **Woody Guthrie's**
Q: What singer's autobiography is titled *Bound for Glory*?
W: Woodrow Wilson Guthrie was a ballad composer, folk singer, and author of *Bound for Glory* (1943). He was the composer-lyricist of numerous songs including "This Land is Your Land" and "This Train is Bound for Glory." Woody is the father of songwriter and performer Arlo Guthrie.

A: *Working*
Q: What Studs Terkel best-seller consists of people's feelings about their jobs?
W: Louis "Studs" Terkel published *Working* in 1974. In this book people tell about what they do all day and how they feel about what they do.

A: **World War I**
Q: What war added *camouflage, scrounge* and *zero hour* to the English language?
W: *Camouflage* is action or material used to conceal or disguise the identity of something; *scrounge* is a slang term meaning to hunt about in order to take or pilfer; *zero hour* is the time set for attack or other military operations.

A: **World War II**
Q: What war added *jeep* and *quisling* to the English language?
W: The word *jeep* came from Eugene the Jeep, a small fanciful wonder-working animal in the comic strip *Thimble Theatre* by Elzie C. Segar. A *quisling* is a traiterous national who aids the invader of his country, then often serves as the agent or puppet governor. The term comes from Vidkun Quisling, a Norwegian politician in 1945, who aided the Nazies.

A: **Writer**
Q: What was the occupation of Herman Wouk's Youngblood Hawke?
W: *Youngblood Hawke* was written by Herman Wouk in 1962. It's the story of a young Kentucky author who is commerically successful but destroyed as an artist and person in New York.

A: *Wuthering Heights*
Q: What novel has the ghost of Catherine appearing to Mr. Lockwood?
W: An Emily Bronte novel published in 1847, this is a somber and imaginative tale of love and romance. Heathcliff, a gypsy orphan who has been raised with Catherine Earnshaw and her family, loves Catherine passionately. Catherine dies giving birth to her daughter Cathy.

A: *Wuthering Heights*
Q: What Emily Bronte novel features Heathcliff?
W: Heathcliff is the young orphan gypsy boy who grows up with the Earnshaw family and falls passionatley in love with Catherine Earnshaw. They never marry but his love endures for her even after her death.

A: **X**
Q: What letter begins the fewest words in the English language?
W: There are 237 words, prefixes, and usages starting with the letter *X*, the 24th letter in the alphabet. The letter *S* begins the most words, several thousand!

A: **Xaviera Hollander**
Q: What former New York madam writes a column in *Penthouse*?
W: Xaviera Hollander draws from her vast sexual experiences as Madam and call girl to write a column called "Call Me Madam." The column counsels, answers questions, and gives advice on any and all sexually related problems. Her column appears monthly in *Penthouse* magazine."

A: **Yellow stars**
Q: What does Wonder Woman have all over her blue shorts?
W: This comic strip was created in 1941 by psychiatrist Dr. William Moulton Marston. Wonder Woman, a superheroine with extraordinary abilities, has the secret identity of nurse Diana Prince. As Wonder Woman she wears blue shorts with yellow stars, a red top, and red boots. She was played by Lynda Carter in the former TV series.

A: **Yokum**

Q: What's L'il Abner's last name?

W: L'il Abner Yokum was from the hillbilly town of Dogpatch, tagged the most useless town in America. *L'il Abner* is the cartoon character created by Al Capp. *L'il Abner* was also a movie made in 1959 with Peter Palmer as L'il Abner.

A: *Your Erroneous Zones*

Q: What 1970s self-help book by Wayne Dyer divided behavior into zones?

W: First printed in September 1977, this number 1 best-seller by Dr. Wayne W. Dyer contains two central themes. The first involves one's ability to make choices about one's emotions. The second theme emphasizes taking charge of one's present moments. The ultimate goal is to create happiness in one's life. The author is a practicing therapist and counselor.

A: **Zane Gray**

Q: Who wrote *Riders of the Purple Sage*?

W: Zane Gray was an author born in Zanesville, Ohio in 1875. He wrote dozens of novels about the old west, fishing, and the romance of surviving in the great outdoors. *Riders of the Purple Sage* was his first book, published in 1912

A: **Zane Gray**

Q: Who wrote a total of 54 western romances?

W: Zane Gray, author, was born Pearl Grey in Zanesville, Ohio, on Jan. 31, 1875. His immense popularity began with the 1912 novel *Riders of the Purple Sage*, which has sold over a million copies. He has produced over 60 volumes, some published posthumously.

A: **Zelda Fitzgerald's**

Q: Whose biography by Nancy Milford is titled *Zelda*?

W: Nancy Mitford's biography, published in 1970, explored the life of Zelda, the wife of F. Scott Fitzgerald. Zelda was a talented young woman from Montgomery, Alabama. The biography details their marriage in 1920, the flair with which the Fitzgeralds lived, and the struggles that Zelda endured with mental illness.

A: **4-2**

Q: What was the final score after Casey struck out in "Casey at the Bat?"

W: This mock-heroic poem by Ernest Lawrence Thayer was first published in the San Francisco *Examiner* June 5, 1888. This enormously popular poem tells of the dramatic defeat of the Mudville baseball team when its hero, Casey, strikes out. No, it wasn't Casey Stengel!

A: **100**

Q: How many years did Sleeping Beauty sleep?

W: This is the lovely old story about the Princess Rosamund who was cursed at birth by a slighted, wise woman. When the princess was 15, she pricked her finger and fell into a deep sleep for 100 years. It all ends happily though!

A: **1876**

Q: What Gore Vidal book tells the story of Aaron Burr's son, Charlie Schuyler?

W: This historical novel followed the book *Burr*, a novel about Aaron Burr. *1876* is an absorbing look at our history during the lifetime of Burr's son Charlie and Charlie's daughter Emma. While Charlie and Emma in this book are fictional characters, the story gives a lucid picture of the U.S. at the centennial.

A: **1970s, The**

Q: What did Tom Wolfe call the "Me Decade?"

W: Thomas Kennerly Wolfe, Jr., was a journalist and the author of such well-known books as *The Kandy-Kolored Tangerine – Flake Streamline Baby* and *The Electric Kool-Aid Acid Test*. The phrase the "Me Decade" refers to a period in which people were cocentrating on themselves through self-awareness and self-improvement.

A: *2001: A Space Odyssey*

Q: What film is based on Arthur C. Clarke's novel *Sentinel*?

W: *2001: A Space Odyssey* is the 1968 film adaptation of A.C. Clarke's novel *Sentinel*. This milestone film was about space travel placed into the context of man's history, from first confrontation with a Greater Power to a future time warp where life has no meaning. Man vs. machinery of his own making, in an unforgettable journey with computer HAL in control.

A: *20,000 Leagues Under the Sea*

Q: What Jules Verne novel features scientists held captive in the submarine *Nautilus*?

W: In *20,000 Leagues Under the Sea*, Victorian scientists are wrecked and captured by the mysterious, power-hungry Captain Nemo, who operates a futuristic submarine. It was made into a four-star film in 1954.

ART AND LITERATURE

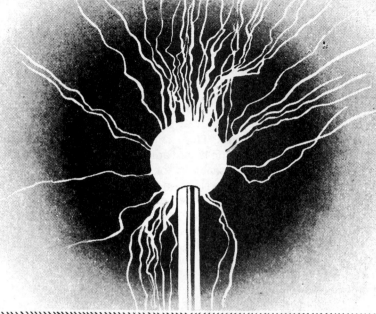

SCIENCE & NATURE

A

A: **A**
Q: What letter is on the left end of the middle row of letters on a typewriter keyboard?
W: Yes, it's right there alright!

A: **A, B, AB, O**
Q: What are the four major blood types?
W: In 1901, American pathologists classified blood types. Type O is considered the universal donor, and AB is considered the universal recipient.

A: **A, B, C**
Q: What letters appear over the number 2 on a telephone dial?
W: Dial phones, push button phones, any make and any model — it's all the same!

A: **A.D. 1**
Q: What year followed 1 B.C.?
W: Years before the birth of Christ (B.C.) are counted backward from the first Christmas. The years are then dated consecutively from the year of Christ's birth (A.D. from the Latin *Anno Domini*, "Year of the Lord").

A: **aardvark, The**
Q: What's also known as an earth pig, antbear, and Cape anteater?
W: The aardvark's tubular snout with which he burrows in the ground for his diet of termites and ants accounts for the first two names. He is found in Africa from the northern tip to the Cape of Good Hope.

A: **"Abominable Snowman, The"**
Q: What's the more familiar name of the Himalayas' Yeti?
W: Tibetan tribesmen believe these bizarre creatures have lived there for centuries. Several sightings have been reported, the most descriptive of which is the creature is 12 to 14 feet long and quite broad, with long brownish hair that hangs over his eyes, pointed head, and deeply sunken reddish eyes. Sounds like only another Yeti could love one of these!

A: **Absolute zero**
Q: What's the better known identity of minus 273.15 degrees Celsius?
W: This is the lowest temperature theoretically possible and represents the absolute absence of heat. It is not obtainable experimentally and can only be mathematically extrapolated.

A: **Acid**
Q: What turns blue litmus paper red?
W: Litmus is a vegetable dye made from lichens. The paper turns pink in an acid and blue in an alkaline solution.

A: **adder, The**
Q: What's the only venomous British snake?
W: These venomous snakes are found throughout Europe and Asia and feed on small rodents. Lucky for the Queen's subjects it grows no longer than two feet!

A: African, The
Q: Which elephant can't be domesticated, the African or Indian?
W: In recent history, African elephants have not been domesticated. However, historically, Hannibal led 37 elephants captured in Ethiopia across the Alps. Another difference: African elephants sleep standing up!

A: Agate
Q: What is June's birthstone?
W: Others say pearl or alexandrite. The flower for June births is honeysuckle.

A: air, The
Q: What do trees get 90 percent of their nutrients from?
W: Utilizing the chlorophyll of its leaves, a green plant absorbs water from the soil and carbon dioxide from the air to form a sugar. Oxygen is given off as a waste product. The process is called photosynthesis.

A: Alan B. Shepard, Jr.
Q: Who was the first American in space?
W: On the morning of May 5, 1961, Shepard, aboard *Freedom 7*, roared into space. He splashed down in the Atlantic Ocean 302 miles from Cape Canaveral. His 15-minute flight earned him the title "America's first astronaut."

A: Alan B. Shepard, Jr.
Q: Who was the first man to hit a golf ball on the moon?
W: As a member of the Apollo 14 crew in 1971, Shepard spent over nine hours on the lunar surface. God only knows how far the ball went with no resistance or gravity!

A: Alan B. Shepard, Jr.
Q: Who went into space aboard *Freedom 7* on May 5, 1961?
W: A commander in the U.S. Navy, Alan Shepard reached an altitude of 115 miles in the first manned suborbital space flight in U.S. history.

A: albatross, The
Q: What sea bird is also known as the gooney bird?
W: The albatross is known for its tameness on land; it is also referred to as Mollymawk, from the Dutch for "stupid gull."

A: albatross, The
Q: What's the largest aquatic bird?
W: The seabirds of the family Diomedeidae sleep on the ocean surface, drink seawater, and fuel on the refuse from ocean-going ships.

A: albatross, The
Q: What's the largest web-footed bird?
W: The wandering albatross is a seabird with white and black plummage, orange or pink markings, and a wing span of 12 feet.

A: Albert Blake Dick
Q: Who invented the mimeograph machine?
W: Actually, the first duplicating process to employ a wax stencil was developed by Thomas Edison in 1875, and he patented it. Albert Blake Dick bought the patent in 1886 and improved on Edison's process to make it useful for office purposes. The A.B. Dick Company sold the first machine in 1887. The first duplicating machine, regarded as the first offset printing press, was patented in February 1780 by James Watt in England.

A: Albert Einstein
Q: Who said of his quantum theory: "God does not play dice"?
W: The quote is from the book, *Einstein, His Life and Times* by Philipp Frank (1947). The entire quote is, "I shall never believe that God plays dice with the world."

A: Albert Einstein
Q: Who wrote President Roosevelt in 1939 proposing the feasibility of an atomic bomb?
W: The possibility that such a weapon might first be developed by Nazi Germany alarmed many scientists and was drawn to the attention of FDR by Einstein who was then living in the U.S.

A: Alcohol
Q: What does a dipsomaniac crave?
W: Dipsomaniacs have an insatiable, often periodic, craving for alcohol.

A: Alexander Fleming
Q: Who discovered penicillin?
W: Fleming discovered penicillin in 1928. He shared the 1945 Nobel Prize for Physiology or Medicine with Ernst Boris Chain and Howard Walter Florey who carried Fleming's discovery to the point of quantity production.

A: Alexander Graham Bell
Q: Who transmitted the first telephone message: "Watson, come here, I want you"?
W: In September 1875, Bell began to write the specifications for the telephone. He received Patent No. 174,465 on March 7, 1876. Thomas Watson was a young repair mechanic and model maker who assisted Bell in developing the multiple telegraph and the telephone.

A: Alfred Kinsey
Q: What zoologist wrote *Sexual Behavior in the Human Male* in 1948, based on more than 18,000 personal interviews?
W: The study started in 1938. Our sources indicate that he interviewed 5,300, but any way you look at it, that's a lot of verbal sexual intercourse!

A: Alfred Nobel
Q: Who invented dynamite?
W: Nobel became one of the richest men in the world as a result of this invention. To ease his conscience after inventing the deadly explosive and to avoid leaving his millions to relatives, he decided to leave his fortune to persons most benefiting mankind. He signed a brief homemade will on a torn sheet of paper in the presence of four witnesses on Nov. 27, 1895, establishing the Nobel Prizes. He died two weeks later.

A: All Saint's Day
Q: What religious day follows Halloween?
W: Also known as All Hallows or Hallowmas, the festival is a celebration of God and all the saints. November 1 was established for this celebration in 835 A.D., in hopes it would supplant the major heathen holiday held on that day.

A: All the tea in China
Q: What did a United Nations organization say consisted of 356,000 metric tons in 1978?
W: The Boston Tea Party, in which 342 chests of tea were sent overboard, was nothing compared to this!

A: Alligators
Q: Which have a better chance of running you down on land, alligators or crocodiles?
W: Although it would be best not to challenge either animal, alligators are better constructed to operate on land. Stay away from both in the water!

A: Almonds
Q: What nuts are used in marzipan?
W: Ground pieces of this nut are mixed throughout the confection, along with egg whites and sugar. Sounds delicious, don't you agree?

A: Amber
Q: What yellow, fossilized resin did the Greeks and Romans use in jewelry?
W: In prehistoric times this resin was exuded from now extinct trees. In ancient times it was mined on the Baltic Sea Coast, and this continues today.

A: Amelia Earhart
Q: Who was the first woman to fly solo across the Atlantic?
W: She first achieved fame on June 17 to 18, 1928, as the first woman to cross the Atlantic (but only as a passenger). Determined to justify the fame that her 1928 crossing brought her, she crossed the Atlantic alone on May 20 to 21, 1932.

A: American
Q: What kind of women gave Sigmund Freud erotic dreams?
W: *Wrong!* Freud confided to Dr. Carl Jung one morning during breakfast at Clark University, "I haven't been able to sleep since I came to America, I continue to dream of prostitutes".

A: Amethyst
Q: What's known as "the Bishop's Stone"?
W: It is also the birthstone of those born in February. The name is derived from the Greek *amethystos* meaning "not intoxicated", because their folk belief was that the stone protects its owner against drunkenness! This stone is mentioned in the Bible as one of 12 stones on the breastplate of the high priests of Yahweh.

A: Andromeda
Q: What is the nearest galaxy to our own?
W: Andromeda is about 1.5 million light years distant from earth and appears to us as the largest constellation visible from the northern hemisphere.

A: Animal, vegetable, mineral
Q: What are the three kingdoms of nature?
W: But who are the kings?

A: Animals
Q: What do humans catch zoonose diseases from?
W: This word is taken from the Greek *zoion* meaning "animal" (as in zoo!) and *nosos* meaning "disease".

A: Animals
Q: Are barnacles plants or animals?
W: A barnacle is considered to be a true, but odd, crustacean covered with shells. In its development it must eventually attach itself by its front end to some surface – rock, pier, living creature, or ship – where it will remain for the rest of its life.

A: *Anno Domini*
Q: What does A.D. stand for in the Christian Calendar?
W: From the Latin words *Anno*, "year"; and *Domini*, "Lord".

A: anode, The
Q: What's the positive electrode of a battery called?
W: In an electrolytic cell the anode is the positively charged electrode toward which the current flows.

A: *Ante meridiem*
Q: What's A.M. an abbreviation for, as in 10 A.M.?
W: This term comes from the Latin *ante* meaning "before", and *meridianus* meaning "midday."

A: Ants
Q: What creatures live in a formicary?
W: A formicary is an anthill or ant nest; ants generate formic acid.

A: aorta, The
Q: What's the largest artery in the human body?
W: The aorta is the great vessel that exits from the left ventricle of the heart and from which all other arteries branch.

A: ape, The
Q: What mammal ranks next to man on the *evolutionary* scale?
W: Next to man apes are the most advanced primates, and some believe that ape and man had a common ancestor 20 million years ago.

SCIENCE AND NATURE

A: **Apollo 8**
Q: What was the first Apollo mission to orbit the moon?
W: On Dec. 21, 1968, the journey to the moon began. It took two days and 18 hours to cover the 234,000 miles. Apollo made ten orbits of the moon at a distance of 70 miles from the surface.

A: **Apollo 8's**
Q: What Apollo mission's crew read from Genesis in lunar orbit at Christmas, 1968?
W: On this day Apollo 8, with a crew consisting of Frank Borman, William Anders, and James Lovell, began its trip back to earth after orbiting the moon.

A: **Apollo 11**
Q: What was the name of the mission that landed Armstrong and Aldrin on the moon?
W: The *Eagle* landed on the moon at 4:17 P.M. eastern daylight time on July 20, 1969. And don't forget Michael Collins who remained in an eliptical orbit around the moon in the *Columbia* as Armstrong and Aldrin walked around on the moon.

A: **Apples**
Q: What fruit does the Stackspur Golden Delicious produce?
W: Delicious apples are the most widely grown apples in the U.S. They are particularly adapted to the northwest, but are grown commercially in all apple areas.

A: **Apricots**
Q: What kind of fruit were the golden apples of Greek mythology?
W: The golden fruit, related to the plum and peach, is widely grown in the Mediterranean.

A: **Apricot's**
Q: What fruit's pit does Laetrile come from?
W: By crushing the pit of the apricot, a fine powder is created that in some circles is regarded as a cancer cure. The U.S. Food and Drug Administration (FDA) has denied these claims and forbidden its use in the U.S. as a cancer treatment.

A: **Aquarius**
Q: What constellation is known as the Water Bearer?
W: The name of the constellation was probably chosen because when the sun is in the Aquarius (Latin: Water Bearer) position from Jan. 21 to Feb. 20, it is the rainy season in southern Europe.

A: **Aquarius**
Q: What sign is the Water Carrier the zodiacal sign for?
W: The 11th sign of the zodiac rules those born Jan. 21 to Feb. 20. The world today is supposedly entering the auspicious age of Aquarius as immortalized in the musical *Hair*.

A: **arc, An**
Q: What's the curved line between any two points on a circle?
W: An arc is any curved line. Since a circle is one continuous curved line, pick your points!

A: **Archer, The**
Q: What's the zodiacal symbol for Sagittarius?
W: The centaur shooting an arrow is representative of the ninth sign of the zodiac governing those born from Nov. 23 to Dec. 21.

A: **Arctic Circle, The**
Q: What rings the globe 23 1/2 degrees south of the North Pole?
W: It marks the southern limit of the area within which, for one day or more each year, the sun does not set (about June 21) or rise (about Dec. 21).

A: **Argon**
Q: What inert gas is used in fluorescent lights?
W: Argon is produced commercially by the fractional distillation of air. When used in a neon lamp, argon causes the pure neon, which is red, to turn blue, and when amber glass is added, the neon light is green.

A: **Aries**
Q: What's the first sign of the zodiac?
W: The "ram" governs those born from March 21 to April 19.

A: **artesian well, An**
Q: What was the first dug at Artois, France?
W: By definition this type of well is drilled down to the point at which water pressure is so great that the water is forced out at the surface. The first one was dug in 1126.

A: **Arthur C. Clarke**
Q: What science fiction writer played a part in the development of radar?
W: Clarke was born in 1917. In 1941 he joined the Royal Air Force and became a radar instructor. In 1945 he wrote *Extra-Terrestrial Relays*, which predicted a satellite system that would relay radio and TV signals all over the world. The first such satellite was launched in April 1965! He collaborated with Stanley Kubrich in making *2001: A Space Odyssey*, based on "The Sentinel," a short story by Clarke.

A: **Ash Wednesday**
Q: What's the first day of Lent?
W: Ash Wednesday is 40 days before Easter, not counting Sundays. Ashes obtained from the burned palm leaves of the previous Palm Sunday are blessed and placed on the foreheads of members of the Christian faithful as a sign of penitence. The custom was originated with Pope Gregory I (590-604).

A: **Aspirin**
Q: What was introduced commercially by Bayer, A.G. of Leverkusen, Germany in 1899?
W: Acetylsalicylic acid (ASA) is the full name of this compound. The word aspirin was formerly the trade name of the compound made by Bayer Co., Inc.

A: **Aspirin**
Q: What's the common name for acetylsalicylic acid?
W: The compound, used to reduce fever and pain, is also considered to be an anti-inflammatory agent. Americans swallow 17 billion aspirin per year!

A: Astrology
Q: What, in 1975, did 18 Nobel laureates claim has no basis in fact?
W: But not everybody listened or cared! We wonder what their signs were?

A: Atmospheric pressure
Q: What does a barometer measure?
W: The barometer measures the force exerted on a unit area by the atmosphere, either with a column of mercury or in the aneroid form in which the pressure bends the elastic top of a drum actuating a pointer. The barometric pressure at sea level ranges between 29 and 30.5 inches of mercury.

A: Au
Q: What is the chemical symbol for gold?
W: That's right, and Au-H_2O means Goldwater!

A: August
Q: What month were you born in if your birthstone is sardonyx?
W: August also claims peridot as a birthstone and a poppy as its flower.

A: Aurora borealis
Q: What's the Latin name for the Northern Lights?
W: Aurora, in Roman mythology, was Goddess of the Dawn, and *boreal* means "pertaining to the north."

A: Australia
Q: What country did Skylab hit?
W: The Skylab was a space laboratory that was sent into space on May 14, 1973. It was damaged during launch and was later repaired in orbit by astronauts of a later Apollo mission. But the repairs were not enough to keep pieces of Skylab from falling to earth.

A: avocado, The
Q: What fruit is packed with the most calories?
W: Also known as the Alligator Pear, it has a high fat content containing 10 to 20 percent oil. However, it is also rich in protein and contains 11 vitamins and 17 minerals.

B

A: B. F. Skinner
Q: Who invented the box that psychologists use to shock rats?
W: Burrhus Frederick Skinner was the foremost exponent in the U.S. of the behaviorist school of psychology. His experience with rats sought to prove that there can be patterned psychological response to external stimuli.

A: baboon, A
Q: What is a mandrill?
W: The mandrill is one of the most distinctive monkeys because of its brightly colored face markings, which are repeated around the sex organs. Some zoologists feel the purpose of the markings is to confuse predators as to which end is which!

A: back, The
Q: Where is the human skin the thickest?
W: Maybe to thwart back stabbers!

A: ball point pen, The
Q: What writing instrument did Hungarian brothers Laslo and Georg Biro invent in 1938?
W: The brothers were impressed by the quick drying ink used in printing and constructed a prototype ball point pen to use this kind of ink. During World War II, Britain's Royal Air Force (RAF) found it to be extremely useful during flight. The brothers didn't patent it in the U.S. It was sold for the first time at Gimbel's department store in New York in 1945, and over 10,000 were sold on the first day!

A: Ballistics
Q: What science deals with the motion of projectiles?
W: Ballistics usually deals with projectiles fired from small firearms, but it may also concern itself with bombs and rockets.

A: Balsa
Q: What kind of wood was the *Kon-Tiki* raft made of?
W: This craft was used by Thor Heyerdahl on his 4,300 mile voyage from Lima, Peru, to the Tuamotu Islands (Polynesia) in 1947. It was constructed as the ancient Peruvians might have done, because Heyerdahl was attempting to prove that such a migration would have been possible by the prehistoric American Indians.

A: banana, The
Q: What's the most widely eaten fruit in America?
W: World banana exports usually exceed 5,500,000 tons per year. The U.S. imports more bananas than any other country — each U.S. household consumes an average of 20 pounds of bananas per year!

A: Barrels
Q: What does a cooper make?
W: The word "cooper" comes from the Latin *cupa*, meaning a "cask."

A: Bartlett pear, The
Q: What fruit was named for Enoch Bartlett?
W: The Bartlett pear is the only variety of pear that is harvested dur-

ing the summer to ripen off the tree. The pear named for Mr. Bartlett, an early 19th century American merchant, constitutes three quarters of the American pear crop. The first pears were planted in America by John Endicott in 1630.

A: **base of the brain, The**
Q: Where's the pituitary gland?
W: The pituitary sits in the bone depression known as the sella turcica just behind the nose. It is frequently called the ""master gland" because of its control over other endrocrine glands.

A: **base of the nails, The**
Q: Where will you find the 20 moons that grace the human body?
W: The physiologic reason for this is that near the root of the nail, the nail is thinner, there are fewer blood vessels, and the nail and skin are less adherent.

A: **base of the spine, The**
Q: Where's the coccyx?
W: It is the curved, semi-flexible lower end of the backbone, which is thought by evolutionists to be the remainder of our tail!

A: *Beagle*, **The**
Q: What was the name of Charles Darwin's survey ship?
W: The *Beagle* was a British naval vessel in which Darwin served as naturalist on a surveying expedition in the Pacific and elsewhere from 1831 to 1836. His observations, especially in the Galapagos Islands, led him toward the theory of evolution.

A: **Beat their chests**
Q: What do gorillas do when they get nervous?
W: And they stamp their feet and roar, too—in hopes of scaring off whatever it is that's making them nervous. No one asked the guy who made them nervous what he did.

A: **beaver, The**
Q: What animal lives in a lodge?
W: The lodges of the beaver are dome-shaped stick and mud structures which may be over five feet high. There are also tunnel entrances that open beneath the frozen water. And there are three types: the island lodge, the pond lodge, and the lake lodge, depending on where the colony lives...or what credit cards they accept!

A: **Bees**
Q: What creatures call an apiary home?
W: This word is from the Latin *apiarium*, meaning "beehive." This term is usually used to describe an artificial beehive where bees are kept for their honey, usually consisting of several hives.

A: **Beetles**
Q: What order of insects contains the most species?
W: At least 200,000 kinds of beetles are known. Beetles make up more than one quarter of all types of animals.

A: **Beetroot**
Q: What's the common name of the vegetable *Beta vulgaris*
W: *Better known to those who eat them as "beets."*

A: *Being alone*
Q: *What does a monophobe fear?*
W: *Monophobia is excessive fear of solitude. From Greek monos, "single" or "alone."*

A: **Belladonna**
Q: What plant takes its name from the Italian for "beautiful lady"?
W: Belladonna is a poisonous plant that is the source of the drug atropine. If it doesn't kill you, it will dilate your eyes, and in ancient times it was consequently used as a cosmetic because of this property.

A: **Benjamin Franklin**
Q: Who invented the bifocal lens in 1780?
W: He accomplished this by cutting away the lower part of the weaker distance lens and cementing in a section of greater strength glass. He thereby eliminated the need to change glasses all day.

A: **Benjamin Franklin**
Q: Who invented the lightening rod?
W: Franklin's experiments with the kite and key in a thunderstorm resulted in his theory that the positive and negative aspects of electricity were in fact "one fluid", that when a body with an over-quantity approached one with an under-quantity, a discharge equalized the two. He suggested that buildings might be protected from lightening by placing iron rods on them. He was right.

A: **Big Dipper**
Q: What cluster of stars is also known as the Plow or the Wagon?
W: To the Greeks it was the Bear and the Wagon, to the Romans it resembled Ursa Major (Great Bear) and a seven plow oxen. In Europe it is known as the Plow or the Wagon.

A: **big toe, The**
Q: What toe is the foot reflexology pressure point for the head?
W: Correct. Pressure on the web space between the big toe and second toe will alleviate your headache!

A: **Binary digit**
Q: What term does the computer word "bit" derive from?
W: The word "bit", used in information theory, is a shortened word for *bi*nary digit.

A: **binary system, The**
Q: What's the name of the number system using only the symbols 1 and 0?
W: The system was developed in the 1940s with the coming of digital computers because the two digits

could be made to correspond to "off" and "on" positions of a switch. The first five numbers in the binary system are 1, 10, 11, 100, and 101.

A: **bird, A**
Q: What's a yellow-shafted flicker?
W: It is the most common North American dwelling woodpecker. Let him flick your yellow Bic!

A: **Black**
Q: What color is diamond dust?
W: Diamond dust is black because a diamond is the purest form of carbon. Therefore the dust of the substance would be nothing more than black carbon dust.

A: **Black**
Q: What color is produced by the complete absorption of light rays?
W: When light strikes an object with a rough surface, it is either absorbed or scattered depending on the frequency of the light. White surfaces scatter light in all frequencies equally, while black absorbs all wavelengths. The easy way to remember this (should you choose to accept this mission) is by the color of your tennis outfit — white will keep you cooler longer because it reflects the light.

A: **Black and white**
Q: What two colors is a magpie?
W: The common magpie or Pica Pica is black except for its white breast and white wing patches. Most famous magpies? Heckle and Jeckle, of course!

A: **Black, green, blue**
Q: What three colors of ink are used to print a U.S. dollar bill?
W: On the off-white paper, the back of the bill is printed entirely in green; on the front the majority of the printing is in black ink, while the seal and serial numbers are printed in green. On silver certificates the seal is blue.

A: **black hole, A**
Q: What is believed to be created when a star collapses?

W: A black hole is composed of densely packed neutrons that have a gravitational pull so powerful that no matter, or even light, can escape them. Another acceptable answer could have been "a break for the understudy"!

A: **Blarney Stone, The**
Q: What do you kiss to be endowed with great powers of persuasion?
W: It's at Blarney Castle, County Cork, Ireland, below the parapets of the southern wall of the castle. You can test the theory after hanging head first in a very precarious position in order to kiss the stone.

A: **Blood**
Q: What does the horned toad squirt from its eyes when it's angry?
W: The more correct name for this animal is the horned lizard. The blood squirting from his eyes is thought to be caused by a rise in blood pressure causing the capillaries near the corners of the eyes to rupture, therefore squirting blood. Don't ever get one of these guys angry with you!

A: **Blue**
Q: What color are a scallop's 35 eyes?
W: True blue or do they use tinted contact lenses?

A: **Blue**
Q: What's the most common color of "lapis lazuli"?
W: They are opaque, azure-blue to deep-blue gemstones of lazulite (mineral).

A: **Blue**
Q: What's the most popular contact lens color?
W: Old Blue Eyes are back.

A: **blue moon, A**
Q: What's a second full moon in a month called?
W: It happens so seldom that the expression "once in a blue moon" originates here.

A: **blue whale, The**
Q: What's the fastest-growing thing in the plant and animal kingdoms?
W: The blue whale is the largest animal alive today. A blue whale usually reaches a maximum length of 110 feet. The largest recorded weight is 300,707 pounds. These animals may double their length in the first year of life and reach full maturity in two or three years.

A: **blue whale, The**
Q: What's the largest mammal ever to have lived?
W: Actually, the blue whale is the largest animal to have ever lived. Yes, it's even larger than the largest dinosaur skeletons, which measure 87.5 feet compared to the whale's 110. The largest dinosaur weighed no more than 50 tons while the largest whale weighs over 150 tons!

A: **blue whale, The**
Q: What's the world's largest and heaviest mammal?
W: The blue whale has been known to reach a maximum length of 110 feet and a weight of 300,707 pounds.

A: **Bodies from graves**
Q: What does a resurrectionist steal?
W: So that makes Dracula a self-resurrectionist!

A: **Bonsai**
Q: What's the common name for a Japanese dwarf tree?
W: This art of dwarfing originated in China about a thousand years ago; the Japanese have pursued and developed the art. *Bonsai* is the Japanese word for "tray-planted".

A: **brain, The**
Q: What organ did Aristotle think the blood cooled?
W: Hence the expression to "keep a cool head"!

A: **brain, The**
Q: What organ is inflamed in the condition encephalitis?
W: This word is taken from the Latin *cephala* meaning "head" and *itis* meaning "inflammation of." There are a variety of causes of encephalitis, including complications from measles and chicken pox.

A: **brain, The**
Q: Where are the convolutions of Broca?
W: They are located in the frontal lobe and are responsible for the motor segment of speech.

A: **brain, The**
Q: Where would you find the medulla oblongata?
W: The medulla is the part of the brain that connects it to the spinal cord. It is the most vital part of the brain since it controls heart action and breathing.

A: **Brandy**
Q: What's the pure spirit distilled from wine?
W: The distilled wine is aged in wooden casks, giving it its light brown tint. The most famous brandy, cognac, is made by distilling white wine and aging it in oak casks.

A: **brassiere, The**
Q: What did Otto Titzling invent?
W: We figured this had to be wrong, but no...Titzling was the first! Unfortunately he did not obtain a patent, and when Philippe de Brassiere glamorized the "chest halter" about 1929, Titzling was only able to win minor damages when he sued for infringement.

A: **Bravo**
Q: What's the international radio code word for the letter *B*
W: Bravo Yankee Echo, Bravo Yankee Echo – bye bye!

A: **Breasts**
Q: What's missing from a woman suffering from amazia?
W: An extrapolation from the folk tales of the Amazon women who cut off their right breasts to facilitate their archery skills.

A: **British Museum, London, The**
Q: What museum houses "the Elgin Marbles" and "the Rosetta Stone"?
W: The "Elgin Marbles", a collection of Greek marble sculptures, were acquired by the museum in 1816 from the seventh Earl of Elgin. The "Rosetta Stone," the key to the deciphering of Egyptian hieroglyphics, was found in 1799 in Rosetta, Egypt.

A: **Bronze**
Q: What alloy do copper and tin form?
W: This alloy is of exceptional importance and historical interest. It was made as early as 3000 B.C., although its appearance in artifacts is rare until much later.

A: **Brown**
Q: What color is demerara sugar?
W: Demerara sugar is a coarse light brown raw sugar that is produced in the sugar refining process.

A: **Bubonic plague**
Q: What disease was "the Black Death"?
W: This disease was referred to as "Black Death" in the 14th century. The number of deaths was enormous in some parts of Europe; two thirds to three quarters of the population was lost in the first pestilence.

A: **Buckminster Fuller's**
Q: What architect's story was told in *Wizard of the Dome*
W: Fuller was the pioneer in the use of metal alloys to build unconventional structures. He designed the the U.S. Pavilion at Expo '67 in Montreal.

A: **Bulb**
Q: What does the camera shutter speed B stand for?
W: The shutter speed is adjusted for the use of a flash bulb, which increases the available light.

A: **bull, The**
Q: What's the symbol for the zodiacal sign Taurus?
W: The bull is the symbol for the second sign of the zodiac governing those born April 20 to May 20.

A: **By flying**
Q: How did pterodactyls get from one place to another?
W: Probably better gliders than flyers because of underdeveloped musculature, they were small dinosaurs, some no larger than sparrows.

A: **By the scruff of the neck**
Q: What's the best way to pick up a rabbit?
W: The loose skin of the rabbit allows this to be done without pain to the animal as proven by the fact that they do not wiggle or seem frightened when picked up this way. But we know of no rabbit who will attest to this assumption!

C

A: Cabbage
Q: What were broccoli and cauliflower developed from?
W: Both broccoli and cauliflower are members of the cabbage family, and all were probably developed from the wild cabbage native to the coasts of Europe.

A: Cabbage
Q: What's shredded to make sauerkraut?
W: Sauerkraut is shredded whhte cabbage fermented in salt brine.

A: cabbage, The
Q: What vegetable yields the most pounds of produce per acre?
W: Cabbage is the heaviest vegetable by weight. Makes sense that it would yield the most produce per acre, given other options! The record weight for a cabbage was reputedly 123 pounds!

A: calf, A
Q: What do you call an infant whale?
W: And the largest calf was born of a blue whale. It was 25 feet long and weighed 6,000 pounds — Mama Whale immediately demanded a hysterectomy!

A: California
Q: What U.S. state raises the most turkeys?
W: We assume they mean Thanksgiving-type turkeys and are not casting aspersions on the California lifestyle! In 1981 there were 25 million turkeys raised in California; Minnesota was a close second.

A: calorie, The
Q: What unit of heat will raise the temperature of one gram of water by one degree Celsius?

W: But did you know that the "calories" you count are really called kilocalories? The "kilo" has been dropped in modern usage, but not the value.

A: *Calypso*, The
Q: What's the name of Jacques Cousteau's research ship?
W: The name was chosen from Greek mythology. Calypso was a sea nymph who kept Odyssus captive for seven years. She could not overcome his desire to return home and finally released him.

A: camel, The
Q: What's known as "the Ship of the Desert"?
W: The camel can subsist without water for several days, and the humps store flesh and fat to be absorbed as nutrition when food is unavailable. For these reasons, and because of the camels strength (they can carry up to 1,000 pounds), they are valuable, although not speedy (1.5 miles per hour) beasts of burden in the desert.

A: Camels
Q: What animals were crucial to Lawrence of Arabia's campaigns in the 1924-1928 war?
W: Correction, the campaigns were in 1914-1918, but he did use camels! His book, *The Seven Pillars of Wisdom*, presents his own version of the events that occurred during these years when he headed a hit-and-run guerrilla operation designed to create an Arab nation again by crushing the Turks. It was also a ploy to keep the Turks busy at home and to decrease their ability to aid their ally, Germany.

A: Cancer
Q: What disease is carcinomaphobia the fear of?
W: Carcinoma is a malignant tumor of the membranous tissue covering most internal body surfaces, organs, and the body's outer surface. From *kar*, "things with hard shells" and *phobos*, "fear or flight."

A: Cancer
Q: What disease is the second-biggest killer of North Americans?
W: The largest killer of North Americans is heart disease.

A: Cancer
Q: What's your zodiacal sign if your're born on July 15?
W: The sign of the crab is the fourth constellation of the zodiac and governs those born between June 21 and July 21.

A: Cannibals
Q: Who might refer to humans as "long pig"?
W: This expression may come from the true story that when missionaries came to the Hawaiian Islands they convinced the cannibals there to change from human feasts to the now famous method of preparing a luau of roast pig.

A: capillary, A
Q: What tiny vessel connects an artery with a vein?
W: The walls of the capillaries are very thin and extremely permeable. It is through these walls that oxygen and carbon dioxide are exchanged and the processes of nutrition and elimination are carried out at the cellular level.

A: Capricorn
Q: What was Christ's zodiacal sign?
W: Zodiacal sign of Capricorn is from Dec. 22 to Jan. 22, we celebrate his birthday on Dec. 25th.

A: Capricorn
Q: What's your zodiacal sign if you're born on New Year's Day?
W: The sign of Capricorn is from Dec. 22 to Jan. 22. The name Capricorn (from Latin "goat horn") is derived from Greek myths about Pan who was often represented as a goat-like figure.

SCIENCE AND NATURE

A: **Captain Robert Scott**
Q: Who reached the South Pole in January 1912, only to find Amundsen had gotten there first?
W: Scott's expedition started overland from Cape Evans on Oct. 24, 1911, and reached the pole on Jan. 17, 1912, only to find Roald Amundsen had preceded them by about a month. Scott died about March 29, 1912, during a blizzard eleven miles from his base. Frozen bodies of Scott and two others were found Nov. 12, 1912.

A: **Carat and color**
Q: What are the two Cs of a diamond apart from clarity and cut?
W: Carat is the metric carat or about .007 ounce (a point is equal to .01 carat), and the color of a diamond is best determined by looking through the thickest portion of the stone at a piece of white paper. The fifth, and other essential C of the diamond – CASH!!

A: **Carbon**
Q: What element do all organic compounds contain?
W: Carbon atoms have the peculiar ability to attach themselves to one another and thereby create a great many different types of organic compounds.

A: **Carbon dioxide**
Q: What puts the fizz in soda water?
W: When dissolved under a pressure of 2 to 5 atmospheres in H_2O, CO_2 causes effervescent bubbles.

A: **Carcinogen**
Q: What's the term for a cancer-causing substance?
W: The word is from Latin or Greek *karkinoma*, "cancer" and *-gen*, "bearing" or "producing." And, it would be easier for us to list NON-carcinogens (if there are any) than to list carcinogens.

A: **caribou, The**
Q: What's the only female animal that has antlers?
W: These undomesticated reindeer live in North America.

A: **Carl Sagan**
Q: Who wrote *The Dragons of Eden* and *Broca's Brain*?
W: He is best known for his research on the possibilities of extraterrestrial life. He won the 1978 Pulitzer Prize for *The Dragons of Eden* and in his spare time was associated with the Viking and Mariner space missions.

A: **Cartilage**
Q: What is a shark's skeleton made of?
W: This probably explains their agility and speed in the water, because cartilage is a very elastic tissue.

A: **castrated rooster, A**
Q: What's a capon?
W: And now do you want to know how it's done?

A: **cat, The**
Q: What animal was revered by the ancient Egyptians?
W: The exalted status probably arose from the cat's importance in rodent control in the granaries of Egypt. Cats were even mummified after death...with a few mice mummies for food along their way.

A: **Cats**
Q: What kind of animals was Napoleon terrified of?
W: Napoleon's ailurophobia may be explained by a hoax played by an Englishman. In 1815 when Napoleon was to depart for St. Helena's, the jokester sent out hand-bills saying that the French government would pay for cats to solve the rat problem in St. Helena's. When the hoax was discovered a riot ensued and at least 1,000 cats escaped their owners and went wild. The wild cats became such a menace that a regiment of soldiers was dispatched to kill them. Napoleon's hatred of cats is also explained by their refusal to obey his commands – a very dangerous thing to do.

A: **Caviar**
Q: What delicacy is known indelicately as pickled roe?
W: Because that's what caviar is! – salted roe or fish eggs that are loosened from the ovaries of the female fish by beating the her.

A: **CD**
Q: What is 400 in Roman numerals?
W: If the symbol on the left is smaller than the one on the right, it is subtracted, i.e., D (500) minus C (100).

A: **Cerebral palsy**
Q: What disease is the greatest American childcrippler?
W: Cerebral palsy (CP) is a term for various nonprogressive disorders of motor function resulting from brain damage prenatally, at birth, or shortly after birth. Prevalence is estimated at 6 per 1,000 births.

A: **Charles Lindbergh**
Q: Who flew an N-X-211 Ryan Monoplane into history?
W: This was the type of plane piloted by Lindbergh on his transatlantic flight on May 20, 1927.

A: **Charles Richter**
Q: Who wrote *Elementary Seismology* in 1958?
W: The book describes the basics of earthquake origins and measurement. He is perhaps better known for his development of the Richter Scale that measures the magnitude of earthquakes on a scale of 1 to 9.

A: Charles Rolls
Q: Who was Sir Frederick Royce's partner?
W: In 1902 Rolls became a motor dealer and in 1906 merged his firm with that of Sir Frederick Henry Royce to form Rolls-Royce, Ltd. Rolls died in a flying accident, becoming the first British pilot fatality.

A: Cheese
Q: What food comes blue-veined, soft, or hard-pressed?
W: Cheese is hard or soft depending on the amount of water left in it and the character of curing. Blue veins are found in bleu cheese. The average American eats a half ton of cheese during his lifetime!

A: cheetah, The
Q: What's the fastest land animal?
W: The cheetah is able to attain speeds of 70 mph.

A: Chewing gum
Q: What's made from chicle?
W: Chicle is the milky juice of the Sapodilla tree of Central and South America. It was first produced in the U.S. in 1872 by Thomas Adams (New York) while he was experimenting with the gum from the chicle tree trying to create a substitute for rubber.

A: chicken, The
Q: What's the most common fowl on earth?
W: It is believed that with the exception of dairy products, more food of animal origin for man is derived from the chicken than from any other source. Each American eats an average of 48.6 pounds of chicken each year!

A: chihuahua, The
Q: What dog is named for a Mexican state?
W: The dog is descended from an ancient breed of dogs of the Toltec Indians in the ninth Century. The breed as we know it was found in 1850 in Chihuahua, Mexico.

A: chihuahua, The
Q: What's the smallest breed of dog?
W: You are also correct if you guessed the Yorkshire terrier or the Toy poodle; miniature versions of these have been known to weigh less than a pound!

A: chimpanzee, The
Q: What's the most intelligent subhuman primate?
W: The chimpanzees are generally regarded as man's closest ape relative. Their complex behavior indicates they are highly intelligent and social animals. Some have been taught to recognize vocabularies of 100 to 200 words.

A: China
Q: What country saw the origin of the Asian Flu?
W: The 1957 flu pandemic was started in China by the mutant vir1s, A2. The next pandemic began in Hong Kong in 1968 and was caused by another mutant virus, A3.

A: China
Q: What country would you come up in if you drilled a hole straight through the earth from Buenos Aires?
W: And the distance you would have to drill is about 7,900 miles.

A: Chinook, The
Q: What dry wind blows down the eastern slopes of the Rockies?
W: It blows from a westerly direction, primarily in winter. The word Chinook was first used at Astoria, Oregon to describe the moist wind blowing off the Pacific Ocean, because it came from the direction of the Chinook Indian Camp near the mouth of the Columbia River.

A: Chlorophyll
Q: What makes plants green?
W: The importance of chlorophyll is that it is necessary for photosynthesis to take place. The interesting thing is that its molecular structure is like that of hemin in human hemoglobin, and it generally serves the same oxygen carrying purposes in a more simplistic manner.

A: Chocolate, strawberry, vanilla
Q: What are the three usual flavors in Neapolitan ice cream?
W: Since they couldn't make stripes of 31 flavors to please everyone, they chose the three favorites. The origin of ice cream as we know it was the court of British King Charles I. George Washington spent $290 in two months on ice cream in the summer of 1790!

A: chow, The
Q: What's the only dog that doesn't have a pink tongue?
W: This dog, of ancient Chinese origin has a blue-black tongue and was first brought to the U.S. in 1890. They look like a smaller version of the lion in the *Wizard of Oz*.

A: Christopher Wren
Q: What astronomer-architect designed the present St. Paul's Cathedral in London?
W: Wren is considered England's greatest architect. After the fire of 1666, which destroyed the oldest part of London, Wren designed the new St. Paul's Cathedral that took 35 years to complete. Wren was buried in St. Paul's in 1723.

SCIENCE AND NATURE

A: **Christ's**
Q: Whose image is alleged to be on the Shroud of Turin?
W: The cloth is believed to be the burial shroud of Christ. Testing has indicated that the cloth probably dates to the first 100 years A.D. It has been preserved in the cathedral of Turin, Italy, since 1578.

A: **circle, A**
Q: What flat area do you get by cutting a solid sphere vertically, horizontally, or on a slant?
W: By definition, a sphere is a round body having its surface equidistant from the center at all points. Therefore, any dissection of it which intersects the center would create a circle, a plane figure bounded by a single curved line that is equidistant from the center point.

A: **clavicle or collar bone, The**
Q: What's the most frequently broken bone in the body?
W: The position of the clavicle and its relative thinness account for this statistic, as well as the frequency of shoulder injuries in children and athletes. It is also the most commonly broken bone during the birth process.

A: **Coal, oil natural gas**
Q: What are the three main fossil fuels?
W: These fossils were formed by the remains of once living organisms. While at present oil and natural gas supply more than half of the energy consumed in the world, they take millions of years to form, and when the reserves are used up they cannot be replaced. Coal is much more abundant, and it is expected that there is a 450-year supply of coal versus a 30-year supply of oil.

A: **Coca-Cola's**
Q: What product's secret formula is 7X?
W: Coca-Cola was invented by Dr. John S. Pemberton of Atlanta, Georgia, in 1886. It was first sold at Jacobs Pharmacy on May 8,1886, and launched as "Esteemed Brain Tonic and Intellectual Beverage" on March 29th. Only seven men have ever known the formula for Coca-Cola. Today only two are living, and they fly in separate airplanes as a precaution. Incidentally, 90 million bottles of Coca-Cola are drunk each day throughout the world!

A: **Cocaine**
Q: What by-product of the manufacture of Coca-Cola is sold to pharmaceutical companies?
W: The coca plant, used in the manufacture of Coca-Cola, yields the bitter, colorless powder known as cocaine. The by-product is chiefly sold to foreign pharmaceutical companies.

A: **codfish, A**
Q: What's a "Cape Cod turkey" to a fisherman?
W: Probably so named because of the tasty white meat they provide. In Colonial America they became a mainstay of the diet and were even dried and shipped back to Europe.

A: **Coffee**
Q: What's the world's most popular nonalcoholic organic beverage?
W: In a 1973 survey the daily rate of coffee consumption in America by people over ten was 2.3 cups per day. Wouldn't Mrs. Olsen be proud!

A: **Coffee and chocolate**
Q: What two flavors make mocha?
W: Mocha is a choice grade of coffee grown in Arabia. Mocha can mean a flavoring made with coffee, or made with coffee and chocolate.

A: **cold, A**
Q: What common ailment can't you catch at the North Pole?
W: Perhaps because of the low temperatures the cold virus cannot proliferate, because exposure to cold does not cause the common cold, only exposure to the virus. It's too cold for anything there, even the cold!

A: **colony, A**
Q: What's a community of ants called?
W: All ants are social and live in groups. In most species ant colonies contain males winged through life, females who are winged until mating, and wingless barren females who are workers. Their colonies usually have many chambers and galleries for specific purposes.

A: **Color**
Q: What do goldfish lose if kept in dimly-lit or running water?
W: The goldfish is actually a kind of carp and if put in a large body of water will grow to tremendous size, lose its color, and look very much like carp. It has been reported that some have grown to two feet in length.

A: **comma, The**
Q: What butterfly has the same name as a punctuation mark?
W: If you answered question mark you're also right! The *polygonia interrogationis* and the *polygonia comma* are distinguishable by the punctuation marks on their wings.

A: **Competitive and aggressive behavior**
Q: What do pointed letters mean to a handwriting analyst?
W: Psychologists still argue about the validity of handwriting analysis; however, there is evidence that the slant, size, letter form, and tendencies to the left and right can be directly correlated to personality.

A: **computer, A**
Q: What is a Univac I?
W: Univac I stands for Universal Automatic Computer and was built by Remington-Rand. It is generally credited as being the first commercially available stored-program electronic digital computer, and it was used by the U.S. Census Bureau in 1951.

A: **Computer languages**
Q: What are Cobol, Fortran, and Pascal?
W: Cobol was designed for business programming and Fortran for scientific and engineering programs. All three are designed to convince a computer to follow human instructions!

A: **Concorde, The**
Q: What plane did Aerospatiale of France and the British Aircraft Corp. develop?
W: The Concorde is a supersonic jet transport capable of speeds of 1,200 miles hour.

A: **Condensed milk**
Q: What did Gail Borden give to the world in 1853?
W: Condensed milk has about 60 percent less water than whole milk. The process of evaporation in a vacuum was patented in 1856, and Borden's product was used extensively by the troops in the Civil War. And yes, Daisy Borden was his cow.

A: **contour line, A**
Q: What line on a map connects all points of the same elevation?
W: Each such line passes through points of the same elevation. Such a map is called a topographic map.

A: **Copper**
Q: What metal makes up 10 percent of yellow gold?
W: The addition of copper to gold increases its yellow color and decreases its value. The name "copper" comes from the Island of Cyprus where it is found in abundance.

A: **Corduroy**
Q: What fabric derives its name from the French for "cord of the king"?
W: Or it could come from the English *cord*, "ribbed fabric" and *duroy* a "coarse woolen cloth

A: **Corn**
Q: What's the largest U.S. agricultural crop by weight?
W: But it is ranked behind rice and wheat as the world's largest grain crop. The U.S. production of corn makes up over half of the total world production.

A: **corona, The**
Q: What's the outermost part of the sun's atmosphere called?
W: The residual light seen during a solar eclipse is caused largely by the sun's corona. This is the only time it is visible. It consists of rarefied gases and shines by reflecting ordinary sunlight.

A: **Corvair, The**
Q: What was unsafe at any speed, by Ralph Nader's reckoning?
W: Ralph Nader, the chief consumer advocate in the U.S. maintained that the Chevrolet Corvair was poorly constructed and none too safe once it was turned on.

A: **Cosmology**
Q: What science deals with the structure of the universe and its origin?
W: It's a branch of philosophy dealing with origin, processes, and structure of the universe. From Greek *kosmos*.

A: **crocodile, The**
Q: What African animal kills the most people?
W: One investigator believes that the African or Nile crocodile kills about 1,000 people a year. He cites one crocodile who was thought to be singly responsible for the death of almost 400 people over several years. When eventually killed he was over 15 feet long.

A: **Cub or kit**
Q: What's the term for a young fox?
W: And what's the term for a female fox? Vixen!

A: **cubit, A**
Q: What ancient measure is the distance from the elbow to the tip of the middle finger?
W: The term is from the Latin *cubitum* meaning "elbow." A cubit measures approximately 18 to 20 inches in length.

A: **Cud chewer**
Q: What's the meaning of the zoological term ruminant?
W: And what the cud chewers are chewing is the regurgitated food that they have swallowed. The three to four-chambered stomach allows for this enviable skill! Ruminants include the camel, llama, sheep, giraffe, and cow.

A: **Cusps**
Q: What are the transitional periods of the zodiac called?
W: These periods usually cover the 20th to 24th of each month, and, as an avid sign reader explains, the person born on the cusp possesses traits of the two signs.

A: **Cyclamates**
Q: What artificial sweeteners got the ax in 1969?
W: Their short but widespread use in food and drink in the late 1960s came to a screeching halt when a university study indicated they were linked to cancer in rats.

A: **cygnet, A**
Q: What's a newly-hatched swan called?
W: You've all heard of the "ugly cygnet"! The word comes from one branch of the swan family tree – Cygnus.

SCIENCE AND NATURE

SCIENCE AND NATURE

A: **DDT**
Q: What was the first manmade insecticide?
W:
Dichloro-diphenyl-trichloroethane was first synthesized in 1874 and found to be a valuable insecticide in 1939. Its great toxicity and its persistence in the soil and water it touches have made it a dangerous substance. It is stored in the fatty tissues of animals, including man, and is toxic in large amounts.

A: **dandelion's, The**
Q: What weed's name derives from the French for "tooth of the lion"?
W: Although we in the U.S. see it only as a weed, parts can be used in salads, as a laxative, as a coffee extender, and, of course, in wine making.

A: **Dark**
Q: Which meat on a roast turkey has more calories, white or dark?
W: In a 4 by 4.75 inch piece of turkey, the white meat has 183 calories and the dark meat has 205.

A: **Davy Jones' Locker**
Q: What's the resting place of those buried at sea?
W: In American and British sealore, Davy Jones' Locker represented the domain that received drowned sailors or seashore dwellers. The origin of the term is unclear, but may come from *Deva Lokka*, the Hindu goddess of death.

A: **December**
Q: What translated literally is the tenth month?
W: From Latin *December* the "tenth month", from *decem*, "ten." (Roman calendar)

A: **Dec. 21 or 22**
Q: What is the date when the sun is directly over the tropic of Capricorn?
W: The ancient Greeks named the tropic of Capricorn after the constellation Capricornus because the sun entered the constellation at the winter solstice (Dec. 22).

A: *Deja vu*
Q: What do you call the feeling of having experienced something before?
W: This is from the French meaning "already seen".

A: **Density**
Q: What's the term for mass per unit volume?
W: Density is usually expressed as specific gravity, which is the ratio of the density of a body to the density of water (1.0). Osmium is the densest substance on earth; it is used in pen points, phonograph needles, and instrument pivots.

A: **Deoxyribonucleic acid or DNA**
Q: What molecule did James Watson and Francis Crick unravel in 1944?
W: Typo here – it should be about 1954. Determination of this structure is widely regarded as the most important discovery of 20th century biology. DNA is the chemical substance ultimately responsible for hereditary control of life functions.

A: **Depth and time**
Q: What are the two dimensions apart from length and width?
W: And the fifth dimension is "Up, Up and Away".

A: **dew point, The**
Q: What's the name of the point at which condensation begins?
W: The liquification of vapor occurs when saturated air cools, and therefore the vapor content is more than the maximum possible for the lower temperature.

A: **diameter, The**
Q: What line divides a circle into two semicircles?
W: The diameter is a line that passes through the center of the circle connecting any two points on the perimeter of the circle.

A: **Diamond**
Q: What is April's birthstone?
W: Correct again, and the flower for that month is the daisy.

A: **Diamond**
Q: What was the name of Sir Isaac Newton's dog?
W: Poor Isaac was a lonely man, and he needed a dog. His first experiments dealt with the dispersion of light into colors of the spectrum using prisms and diamonds. We assume this is where he came up with the name for his favorite spaniel.

A: **Diamond**
Q: What's the simplest gem in chemical composition?
W: A diamond is made of pure carbon that has been under pressure for millions of years.

A: **Diamonds**
Q: What are "the Star of Africa" and "Cullinan II"?
W: Both of these cut diamonds are from the world's largest gem diamond, Cullinan, which weighed 3,106 carats in rough form when found Jan. 25, 1905. "The Star of Africa," largest cut diamond known, is a 530 carat pear-shaped gem set in the English sceptre. The "Cullinan II" is 317 carats and is part of the imperial state crown of the Queen of England.

A: **Dissolved salt**
Q: What makes up 3.5 percent of the oceans?
W: There is some variation – for example the Red Sea has 4.4 percent salt content, while continental waters have nearly zero percent salinity.

A: **dog, A**
Q: What is a Mexican hairless?
W: The Mexican hairless is a breed of toy dog native to Mexico that is bald except for the end of its tail and a patch of hair on its head.

A: **doldrums, The**
Q: What is the belt of low pressure around the equator called?
W: And even if you haven't been there geographically you probably know what it feels like spiritually! From Old English *dol* meaning "dull". This is an area characterized by calms or light winds.

A: **dolphin, The**
Q: What's the most intelligent creature on earth after man?
W: This assumption is probably based on the dolphins' sophisticated form of language and the fact that they like to play just for the fun of play.

A: *Double Eagle II*, **The**
Q: What was the name of the balloon three Americans piloted across the Atlantic in 1978?
W: The huge helium craft was named after Charles Linbergh's *Lone Eagle*. The *Double Eagle I* was the 1977 attempt to cross the Atlantic that failed. *Double Eagle II* rode a high pressure ridge from Presque Isle, Maine, to a barley field near Miserey, France in six days.

A: **dove, The**
Q: What bird's a symbol of peace?
W: The dove was sacred to ancient Israelites, became a Christian symbol of simplicity and gentleness, and is now a symbol of peace. The dove's meaning is probably also related to the appearance of the dove after John the Baptist baptized Christ.

A: **Dr. Benjamin Spock**
Q: Who said: "Feed 'em, love 'em, and leave 'em alone"?
W: Spock is an American pediatrician and author who in 1946 published *Common Sense of Baby and Child Care*, in which he essentially told parents of the baby-boom generation to sit back, relax, and watch their children grow.

A: **Dr. Christiaan Barnard**
Q: Who performed the first successful human heart transplant?
W: On Dec. 3, 1967, in South Africa, he performed the first heart transplant, putting the heart of a 25-year-old woman into the body of a 53-year-old grocer. His first transplant patient lived 18 days. His second transplant was done in 1968, and the patient lived 563 days.

A: **Dr. Jonas E. Salk**
Q: Who developed the first polio vaccine?
W: The American physician and epidemiologist prepared the vaccine by means of tissue culture, a technique developed by Nobel Prize winner John Enders. The vaccine was made from killed virus and was widely distributed in 1955. Were you one of the first to receive the vaccine during "Operation Lollipop"?

A: **Dr. Michael DeBakey**
Q: What Texas surgeon performed the first artificial heart transplant?
W: In 1966 he implanted the DeBakey device, which was a booster pump that aided the left ventricle while the heart continued to function.

A: **drone, A**
Q: What nonworking, stingless bee mates with the queen?
W: There are three casts within the bee system: the queen, who lays the eggs; the workers, who are sterile females and who do all the work of maintaining the hive; and the drones, who simply mate with the queen.

A: **Drugs**
Q: What does a narcomaniac crave?
W: And aspirin is not the drug they crave.

A: **duckbilled platypus, The**
Q: What mammal has a bill, webbed feet with claws, and lays eggs?
W: Perhaps the most confusing mammal because the platypus doesn't follow all the guidelines used to define mammals. A mammal has fur and mammary glands and usually gives birth to live offspring. The duckbill and the spiny anteater are the only two mammals that lay eggs.

A: **DuPont**
Q: What's the world's largest chemical company?
W: The company was founded in 1802 and since then has supplied the U.S. with nearly all the explosives used in its wars. After 1918 explosives became a minor interest, and DuPont diversified into chemicals, synthetic fibers, and film.

A: **During a total solar eclipse**
Q: When do Bailey's Beads appear in the sky?
W: The phenomenon was first described in the 19th century by English astronomer Francis Bailey. Just before the moon entirely covers the sun and as the sun emerges after a total eclipse, the thin slice of sun visible looks like a belt of bright separable beads. The illusion is caused by the irregular surface of the moon and its shadow over the sun.

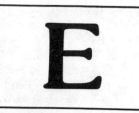

A: *Eagle,* **The**
Q: What was the name of Armstrong and Aldrin's lunar module?
W: On July 20, 1969, at 10:56 EDT, "the *Eagle* has landed" was heard from the moon over live television on earth. The lower half of the *Eagle* was used as a launch pad for the return to the mothership, Apollo 11, and remains on the moon next to the American flag.

A: **eaglet, An**
Q: What's an infant eagle called?
W: Easy enough, but how about a baby oyster? It's a "spat".

A: **ear, The**
Q: What organ contains the smallest bones?
W: The malleus (hammer), the incus (anvil) and the stapes (stirrup), the bones of the middle ear, are the smallest bones in the body.

A: **Eardrum**
Q: What's the common term for the tympanic membrane?
W: It stretches across the inner end of the ear's outer canal, separating it from the middle ear. Sound waves cause vibration of this membrane that in turn sets in motion a series of mechanical transmitters, which finally reach the brain through the auditory nerve.

A: **ears, The**
Q: What features of the African elephant are larger than those of the Indian elephant?
W: The African elephant's ears usually measure 2.5 to 4 feet wide, even though its hearing is poor. The African elephant also differs from the Indian in that it has an upper and lower finger-like projection at the end of its trunk that it uses like a finger and thumb.

A: **Ears and legs**
Q: What two features are longer on a hare than on a rabbit?
W: Zoologists differentiate between the rabbit and hare because the newborn offspring of the rabbit are born naked and blind while hare offspring are born furred and with vision. Also, the rabbit is a very social animal living in underground colonies while hares rarely live in groups.

A: **Earth**
Q: What does the Greek *geo* denote?
W: Hence geography and geophysics.

A: **Earth**
Q: What travels through space at 66,700 miles per hour?
W: At that speed it takes the earth 364.5 days to travel its orbit of 583,400,000 miles.

A: **Earth**
Q: What weighs 6,600 billion billion tons?
W: We're not sure who weighed it. And the barysphere, or interior of the earth, below 25 miles from the surface, makes up 99.6 percent of this weight.

A: **Earth, air, fire, water**
Q: What did the ancients call the four great elements?
W: From these great elements evolved the gods of ancient Greece: Persephone, goddess of earth; Hera, queen of the heavens; Hephaestus, god of fire; and Poseidon, god of the sea.

A: **Easter**
Q: What holiday is on the first Sunday after the first full moon after March 20?
W: The celebration of the resurrection of Christ was set by the Council of Nicea in 325 A.D. convoked by Constantine I, Emperor of Rome. Acceptance of the Gregorian calendar, adopted in 1582 by Pope Gregory XIII, eliminated much of the confusion about the date of Easter, although not all Eastern religions have accepted this calendar.

A: **Eaten grass**
Q: What have you done if you've eaten timothy?
W: You probably wouldn't enjoy it, but it is considered one of the most valuable hays and is used as the standard by which to compare other hays. It gets its name from Timothy Hanson who carried it for seeding from New England to Maryland in 1720.

A: **Eau de Cologne**
Q: What did Jean Marie Farina of Cologne, Germany, invent in 1850?
W: If you guessed farina, you were wrong! The term means water of Cologne and consists of alcohol mixed with aromatic oils.

A: **Ebb tide**
Q: What's the term for the outward flow of water following high tide?
W: When the moon is directly over a point on the earth, its gravitational pull on the water causes a net rise in the normal level of the water. In most areas of the world two high waters and two low waters (ebb tide) occur during a lunar day (24 hours, 50 minutes).

A: **edible fungus, An**
Q: What's a truffle?
W: Actually truffles are non-poisonous mushrooms that are grown in subterranean areas of Europe. They have a distinctive odor and are usually found by trained dogs or pigs who sniff them out. Truffles and goose liver are the major ingredients of pate de foie gras.

A: **Edsel, The**
Q: What automobile flop was named for the only child of Henry Ford?
W: Edsel Bryant Ford (1893-1943), father of Henry Ford II, was president of the Ford Motor Company from 1919 to 1943. Edsel himself was definitely not a flop; he inherited a good portion of his dad's $700 million fortune.

A: **Edward H. White II**
Q: Who was the first American to take a walk in space?
W: On June 3, 1965, White spent 21 minutes outside *Gemini 4* tethered to the spacecraft. White was killed three years later in a flash fire during a routine test on Cape Kennedy.

A: **Edward Teller**
Q: Who's called "the Father of the H-bomb"?
W: Teller was born in Budapest, Hungary, in 1908, and emigrated to the U.S. in 1935. He worked with Enrico Fermi's team that produced the first nuclear chain reaction. He then worked on the secret weapons project at Los Alamos weapons lab in New Mexico. He and others developed the first H-bomb in 1949.

A: **Edwin Aldrin**
Q: Who was the second man on the moon?
W: Neil Armstrong was first out of the *Eagle*, the lunar module. Before coming out Aldrin asked, "Is it OK to come out?" Do you suppose he wouldn't have if Armstrong said "No"?

A: **Eggs**
Q: What does the typical American eat 263 of each year?
W: With that kind of average consumption, it's a wonder we all don't cluck!

A: **Eight**
Q: How many engines does a B-52 bomber have?
W: The B-52 bomber, which weighs over 225 tons, is capable of delivering large atomic bombs with great accuracy from altitudes much higher than most aircraft.

A: **Eight**
Q: How many points are there on a Maltese cross?
W: The Maltese Cross originated as the emblem of the Knights of Malta, a military and religious order founded in 1113 as a segment of the Knights of St. John of Jerusalem. It is a white cross with eight points on a black background and is also now used as the emblem of firefighters.

A: **Eight minutes**
Q: How long does it take sunlight to reach earth?
W: It takes light that long to travel the 92.9 million miles between the sun and the earth. During that time, the light is spread in so many directions that we receive only five ten-billionths of the light that originated from the sun.

A: **Eighteen**
Q: What age is adolescence considered to end at?
W: And in some people it never ends! Our sources say that in women it theoretically begins at 12 and ends at 18; for men it runs from 14 to 21. This is based on the physiologic changes that occur in adolescence.

A: **Eighteen**
Q: How many claws does a housecat have?
W: There are five retractable claws on each front paw and four retractable claws on the back paws.

A: **electric shaver, The**
Q: What did Colonel Jacob Schick patent on Nov. 6, 1928?
W: And King Camp Gillette (1855-1932) introduced the safety razor a few years earlier.

A: **Electrocardiogram**
Q: What does ECG stand for?
W: Often abbreviated EKG, it is the curve traced by an electrocardiograph. It is used to diagnose heart disease by measuring the electrical conductivity in the heart muscle.

A: **elephant, The**
Q: What's the longest living land mammal after man?
W: Authorities believe that it is possible some elephants may live to 100, but it has only been verified that one elephant lived to an age over 70. One killer whale seen near Australia was known to be over 90 years of age.

A: **elephant, The**
Q: What's the only mammal that can't jump?
W: We can believe it, can you? But the Klipspringer, a small African antelope, can jump the highest of all animals at heights of about 25 feet.

A: **elephant, The**
Q: What's the only mammal with four knees?
W: This honor is bestowed by the definition of what does and does not define a knee. Many mammals have four legs and a mid-joint in all four extremities. A knee is a hinge joint, and the elephant is, therefore, the only mammal with hinges on each of his four legs.

A: **Eleven**
Q: What's the square root of 121?
W: The only additional information we can come up with is to define "square," which is the product of a number multiplied by itself.

A: **Eli Whitney**
Q: Who invented the cotton gin?
W: But do you know why it is called a cotton *gin*? Because the machine separates the seeds from the cotton plant and cleans the cotton with GIN! This quick process, which was first used in 1793, made cotton the profitable crop it became in the rise of the South's economy.

A: **emerald, The**
Q: What gem did Roman Pliny say out-greened nature itself?
W: The green color of the mineral beryl is caused by the presence of chromium.

A: Emerald
Q: What is May's birthstone?
W: That's right, and May's flower is the hawthorne.

A: Enamel
Q: What's the hardest substance in the human body?
W: Now how many of you guessed that? Enamel is calcified tissue, which in the embryo occurs in the second month after conception.

A: Energy
Q: What does the E stand for in the equation $E = mc^2$
W: ...and the M stands for mass, and c stands for the velocity of light.

A: English Channel, The
Q: What did Bryan Allen cross in the *Gossamer Albatross*
W: In June 1979, he pedaled his 70-pound "airplane" across the channel, flying a few feet above the water. He landed, after almost three hours "aloft," on two wheels that weighed one ounce each.

A: epicenter, The
Q: What's the point on the earth's surface directly above an earthquake's focus?
W: The point of origin of an earthquake is underground and the distance from the focus to the epicenter is called focal depth. The more shallow the focal depth, the more destructive the earthquake. And the further away you can get from the epicenter the less severe the intensity of the quake.

A: epidermis, The
Q: What is the outermost layer of skin called?
W: Actually what we see of the epidermis is dead, flattened cells. The lower layers of the epidermis are the living part of this organ.

A: equator, The
Q: What imaginary line encircling the earth is 90 degrees from both poles at every point?
W: The circumference of the earth at the equator is 24,902 miles, and the diameter of the earth is 7,926 miles.

A: eucalyptus tree's, The
Q: What tree's leaves make up most of the diet of the koala bear?
W: Koala bears feed, very selectively, on eucalyptus leaves – about three pounds per day! The koala has an intestinal pouch 23 feet long to aid in digesting this delicacy!

A: Euclid
Q: Who is known as "the Father of Geometry"?
W: This Greek mathematician is the genius whom we have to thank for our high school agonies with plane geometry!

A: "Eureka"
Q: What did Archimedes say upon discovering the principle of buoyancy in his bath?
W: The principle of hydrostatics, known as Archimedes' Principle, is said to have occurred because he misjudged the fullness of his bathtub.

A: Everything
Q: What does a panophobe fear?
W: This word is from the Greek *pan* meaning "all", and the Greek *phobia* meaning "fear."

A: eyebrow, An
Q: What facial feature typically contains about 550 hairs?
W: We assume this means unplucked eyebrows! And they do have a function; they are positioned to absorb or deflect rain or perspiration before it runs into the *eyes*.

A: eyes, The
Q: What part of the body does glaucoma strike?
W: Glaucoma, one of the leading causes of blindness in the U.S., occurs when there is an increase in pressure in the eyeball caused by failure of the fluid in the anterior chamber of the eye to drain properly.

A: eyes, The
Q: What part of the body does lacrimal fluid lubricate?
W: This salty secretion lubricates the eye and through its drainage system washes away foreign particles.

A: eyes, The
Q: What's it impossible to keep open while sneezing?
W: And can you believe there is a sneezing *center* in the brain! It is located in the medulla oblongata.

F

A: F
Q: What letter is to the left of G on a typewriter?
W: One of three places on the typewriter where the letters are actually in alphabetical order: O-P, F-G-H, J-K-L!

A: F
Q: What musical key do most American car horns beep in?
W: This difference in musical keys explains why you can so clearly tell the home-grown models from the foreign ones!

A: Fall
Q: What season ends with the winter solstice?
W: The winter solstice, Dec. 21, is the time when the equator is farthest from the sun. Fall begins on September 23rd, the autumnal equinox.

A: Fallopian tubes
Q: What tubes carry eggs from the ovaries to the womb?
W: The egg travels through these four-inch tubes on its way to the uterus (womb). Fertilization by a sperm usually occurs in the tube. They were named after Gabriel Fallopius, an Italian physician who first described them.

A: **Fallow**
Q: What's the term for arable land left unseeded for one season?
W: Land may be left fallow for one or more seasons to allow the soil to enrich itself or to allow undesirable weeds or growth to die.

A: **Fe**
Q: What is the chemical symbol for iron?
W: This is from the Latin *ferrum*, "iron." Iron is the most used and cheapest metal and is essential to biological life. Iron makes up about 35 percent of the earth as a whole; the core of the earth is largely iron, but in the crust the metal is rare.

A: **Fear**
Q: What does a phobophobe fear?
W: And we have nothing to fear but fear itself? One of every 20 Americans suffers from a phobia, and there are 700 different kinds!

A: **Fear of the number thirteen**
Q: What is triskaidekaphobia?
W: We all have a little "triskaidekaphobia" — who isn't a little wary on Friday the 13th, and who wants 13 at a dinner table! Try to find the 13th floor in most high rises!

A: **Fear of strangers or foreigners**
Q: What is xenophobia?
W: A xenophobe is unduly fearful or contemptuous of strangers or foreigners, especially as reflected in cultural or political views.

A: **Feb. 2**
Q: When is Ground Hog Day?
W: The tradition of making the groundhog the weather prophet probably originated in England, where they use the hedgehog for similar purposes. Finding no hedgehog in America, the Pilgrim Fathers transferred the responsibility to the groundhog. Probably the most famous is Punksatonne Phil.

A: **February**
Q: What's the only month that can have fewer than four moon phases?
W: First, a four moon phase means new moon (completely in shadow), first quarter, full moon, then last quarter. For the moon to complete one full four moon phase takes 29 days, 12 hours, and 44 minutes. So when February only has 28, or even 29, days the phase will not be complete.

A: **female, The**
Q: Which mosquito's bite draws blood, the male or female?
W: And she is built to draw blood with her long mouth parts. The male on the other hand, has short rudimentary mouth parts suitable for his diet of water and nectar. The female cannot reproduce without the blood.

A: **female, The**
Q: Which sex has the shorter human vocal cords?
W: These shorter cords result in higher frequency sound waves and thus a higher voice.

A: **female fox, The**
Q: What's a vixen?
W: The vixen doesn't stay with one mate too long, usually only long enough to produce a litter of cubs. The slang term, vixen, undoubtedly comes from this cunning but fickle lady.

A: **femur, The**
Q: What's the longest bone in the human body?
W: The thigh bones are also the heaviest in the body. The head of the femur forms the hip joint, while the condyles form the knee joint.

A: **fifteenth, The**
Q: What is the Crystal Anniversary?
W: The tradition of naming anniversaries probably came from an ancient custom of giving particular gifts for good luck. In today's world the appropriate gift is a watch on the fifteenth anniversary and crystal and glass for the third. So if you guessed third, you are also correct.

A: **fifth, The**
Q: What is the Wood Anniversary?
W: In modern times the appropriate gift is considered to be silverware, although the traditional wood is also proper.

A: **Fifty percent**
Q: What percentage of alcohol constitutes 100 proof whisky?
W: Proof is the standard by which alcohol content is measured and it represents twice the volume percentage of alcohol. Proof reflects the amount of water and the degree of distillation in an alcoholic beverage.

A: **Fifty percent**
Q: What percentage of the population has an IQ above 100?
W: And fifty percent are below! That's why 100 is considered the average IQ.

A: **fingerprint, A**
Q: What's a dactylogram?
W: This word is from the Greek *daktulos*, "finger," and *gramma gramme*, "letter and line."

A: **Firearms**
Q: What's the most popular form of suicide among American males?
W: Correct, however nine out of every ten suicide victims are female.

A: **Fireworks**
Q: What is a pyrotechnic display?
W: Pyrotechnics include substances that when ignited produce sound, color, smoke, and/or motion. The Chinese are credited with the first fireworks after the invention of gunpowder in the tenth century.

A: **first, The**
Q: What is the Paper Anniversary?
W: Probably best to send paper plates and napkins, and let the newlyweds take a break from washing their wedding china! Paper is the traditional gift for the first anniversary; a clock is the modern gift.

A: **fish, The**
Q: What's the zodiacal symbol for Pisces?
W: The twelfth sign of the zodiac rules those born from Feb. 20 to March 20. The sign is usually two fish with their tales bound together. It is from the Latin *piscis* meaning "fish."

SCIENCE AND NATURE

A: **Fission**
Q: What's the process of splitting atoms called?
W: By definition nuclear fission is the splitting of an atom by bombardment with neutrons. Neutrons released during this process can cause a chain reaction to occur by bombarding other atoms and causing their fission. The result is an energy release that can be used as a source of power like electricity.

A: **Five**
Q: What number is represented in Morse Code by five dots?
W: It is the only number that is represented by a corresponding number of dots; e.g., four is four dots and a dash, six is a dash and four dots, and zero is five dashes.

A: **Five**
Q: How many sides are there on a pentagon?
W: The most familiar pentagon, besides home plate, is the building that houses the U.S. Department of Defense. It covers 29 acres and was completed in 1943.

A: **Five**
Q: How many varieties of twins are there?
W: This is five combinations of the two sexes. Identical twins are two boys or two girls. Fraternal twins can be two boys, two girls, or one boy and one girl.

A: **Flight**
Q: What ability has the silkworm moth lost through domestication?
W: And this poor guy is the only useful species of moth. To add insult to injury, most silkworm caterpillars are killed before they become moths so they won't damage their valuable silk cocoon by emerging from it.

A: **flush toilet, The**
Q: What's the great and proud claim to fame of Thomas Crapper?
W: Now this is not a joke! Think of the colloquialisms with which this man has provided us. Then think of the cold walks to the outhouse he saved us. As a statistical fact we offer the following: each flush of the toilet consumes seven gallons of water.

A: *Flyer*
Q: What was the name of the Wright brothers' plane?
W: On Dec. 17, 1903, Orville and Wilbur made the first powered flight at Kitty Hawk, North Carolina. The plane weighed 750 pounds and had a 12.5 horsepower engine.

A: **foot, The**
Q: What part of the body goes to sleep when you experience taresthesia?
W: We're not sure this is a real medical term but... *tar* refers to the tarsal bones that comprise the ankle and top of the foot, and *esthesia* is from the Greek meaning "lack of feeling." Taresthesia would be caused by compression of the nerve feeding this area and would most commonly occur from crossing your legs for awhile.

A: **foot, The**
Q: What part of the human body is most commonly bitten by insects?
W: That statistic should keep you from going barefoot!

A: **Forty**
Q: How many times more than the brain does the human body typically weigh?
W: In most adults the brain weighs about three pounds. So if you guessed fifty times and you weigh 150, you have a correct answer, too! The brain contains about 12 billion cells and is 85 percent water. The brain of a sperm whale weighs 20 pounds. And then there's the stegasaurus who weighed 6.5 tons but had a brain weighing 3.5 ounces. No wonder they're extinct!

A: **Forty-five**
Q: How many degrees is northeast on a compass with north at zero degrees?
W: With the compass needle pointing toward the magnetic north or North Pole, east and west would be at 90 degree angles on the circle face of the compass and south at 180 degrees. Therefore, any halfway designations between the 90-degree angles would be 45-degree angles.

A: **Forty-nine**
Q: What's 70 percent of 70?
W: There's just no way to make this **any** more interesting or informative; it just *is* 49.

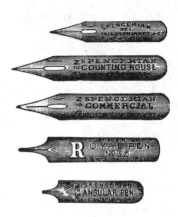

A: **fountain pen, The**
Q: What did Lewis E. Waterman invent?
W: He didn't really invent it. It was used as early as 1656 in Paris. Waterman, an insurance saleman, did however produce the first practical fountain pen that would hold the ink. Angered by the loss of an insurance customer because the ink from his pen spilled all over the policy, he refined the fountain pen in 1884.

A: **Four**
Q: How many chambers are there in the human heart?
W: The heart is divided into two upper atria and two lower ventricles. The right atrium receives blood from a vein and sends the blood to the

right ventricle. The right ventricle pumps the blood out of the heart into the lungs. The refreshed blood returns to the left atrium, wihch pumps it into the left ventricle. The left ventricle has the largest muscular wall since it is responsible for pumping blood to the whole body.

A: **Four**
Q: How many compartments does a cow's stomach have?
W: The true ruminants, including the cow, deer, and giraffe, have the enviable ability to regurgitate and chew their food after it has been swallowed. The four chambers lie between the esophagus and intestine, and are the rumen, reticulum, omasum, and rennet bag. Nice names don't you think? "I have a rennet bag ache, Mom."

A: **Four**
Q: How many manned Apollo flights preceded the first moon landing?
W: Apollo 7 circled the earth 163 times; Apollo 8 orbited the moon ten times; Apollo 9 tested the lunar module maneuvers; and the Apollo 10 crew separated the lunar module, descended to within ten miles of the lunar surface, and returned to the mother craft. These four missions occurred between October 1968 and May 1969.

A: **Four**
Q: How many noggins are there in a pint?
W: A noggin is a unit of liquid measure equal to one quarter of a pint. It is most commonly used as a measure for ale or liquor.

A: **Four**
Q: How many pecks are there in a bushel?
W: And there are eight quarts in a peck. So if someone loves you a bushel and a peck, you are loved 40 quarts worth!

A: **Four**
Q: How many rows of whiskers does a cat have?
W: You're lucky if you had a cat around to help you answer this one.

A: **Four**
Q: How many teats does a cow have?
W: These are more often called udders — is that what threw you off? In most cases the poor calf only gets to nurse for up to three days after birth, then he is given diluted whole milk or skim milk. But, even if the calf were allowed to nurse, cows produce much more milk than their offspring could use.

A: **Four**
Q: How many times is the capacity of a pipe increased if the diameter is doubled?
W: The formula for determining the volume of a cylinder is "radius squared times the length times pi (3.14)." Doubling the diameter would therefore quadruple the capacity.

A: **Four**
Q: How many tines are there on a standard dinner fork?
W: A service of table silver often has four kinds of forks: the dinner fork; the entree fork similar to, but smaller than, the dinner fork; the broader salad fork, with three or four tines, the outermost left tine being wider than the others with a cutting edge; and the three-tined oyster fork.

A: **Four**
Q: How many wings does a bee have?
W: And when flying he beats his wings 250 times per second.

A: **Four**
Q: How many wisdom teeth are there in a normal set of teeth?
W: There are two on the bottom and two on the top, and they are also called third molars. They derive their name from the age at which they appear. The wisdom teeth usually erupt after the age of 17, hopefully the same time at which wisdom appears.

A: **Four**
Q: What's the cube root of 64?
W: Cubed means to the third power of a number. Therefore the cube root is that number which multiplied by itself three times equals the desired number. Need another example? Three is the cube root of 27.

A: **Fourteen**
Q: How many calendars are needed for a perpetual calendar?
W: A perpetual calendar is one in which a means has been derived of finding the day of the week for any date in a wide range of years. It takes into consideration all the inconsistencies of both the Julian and Gregorian systems. In the Gregorian system a perpetual calendar shows 14 years.

A: **Fourteen**
Q: How many pounds are there in a stone?
W: A stone is a British unit of measurement. Translate your weight from pounds to stones and you'll lose weight delightfully!

A: **fox's, The**
Q: What animal's tail is called a brush?
W: The gray fox's tail is perhaps most deserving of this name since it has a crest of concealed stiff hairs on its tail.

A: **Foxtrot**
Q: What's the international radio code word for the letter *F*?
W: Correct! Our favorite is the word for *Z*: "Zulu".

A: **France**
Q: What country has the third-most satellites in orbit?
W: Surprised? In fact, France was the first nation other than the U.S. and USSR to launch its own spacecraft, A-1, on Nov. 26, 1965.

A: **Freckles**
Q: What appear when the sun activates your melanocytes?
W: Melanocytes are specialized cells found in the deepest layers of the epidermis. Their skin darkening powers are stimulated by sunlight. Howdy Doody had 48 freckles, one representing each of the then 48 states.

SCIENCE AND NATURE

A: **Frequency modulation**
Q: What does FM stand for?
W: ...and AM stands for amplitude modulation. The two refer to the method by which a radio signal is impressed in the carrier of the wave. Radio signals using low or medium frequency use AM, and higher frequencies may use FM.

A: **Frogs**
Q: Which move faster, frogs or toads?
W: Frogs are skilled and agile jumpers, while the uglier warty toad has clumsy short hops.

A: **front, A**
Q: What's the boundary between two air masses called?
W: Fronts are actually very narrow zones of active weather change. When air masses come together there is usually a great temperature contrast with resultant weather turbulence.

A: **Frozen food**
Q: What did Clarence Birdseye perfect in 1924?
W: He first learned these skills from the natives of Labrador, as he observed them catching and freezing fish during the winter months. He first froze vegetables by putting them in a tub of water and freezing them in the cold Labrador winter.

A: **Fusion**
Q: What nuclear process takes place in an H-bomb?
W: The fusion process involves the fusing together of the nuclei of atoms like hydrogen (hence the H-bomb). The process is the opposite of that of the A-bomb in which atoms of uranium are split to create energy. The energy released from one pound of hydrogen fuel is three times that released from one pound of uranium.

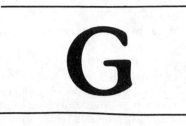

A: **Gabriel Fahrenheit**
Q: Who invented the mercury thermometer?
W: In 1714 in Holland he developed the first thermometer using mercury instead of alcohol. He developed the corresponding temperature scale that bears his name.

A: **Galileo**
Q: What Italian astronomer wrote *The Starry Messenger*?
W: His last name was Galilei! The poor man went blind a few years before his death, probably from years of looking at the sun through his telescope.

A: **Galileo**
Q: Who discovered Saturn's rings?
W: He improved on telescopes that had been previously invented and saw not only Saturn's rings, but the mountains of the moon as well as Jupiter's moons and sunspots.

A: **Garlic**
Q: What plant is revered by the Lovers of the Stinky Rose?
W: The garlic we use in cooking is actually the bulb of a plant that has small six-part white flowers, almost resembling a rose in appearance, but not in fragrance!

A: **Garnet**
Q: What is January's birthstone?
W: ...and its flower is the snowdrop.

A: **Gasohol**
Q: What's 10 percent alcohol and 90 percent unleaded gasoline?
W: Gasohol is a mixture of gasoline and ethyl alcohol that became widely available in the late 1970s as oil prices rose and supplies dwindled. Standard cars could use gasohol containing up to 17 percent alcohol. Gasohol burns more slowly and cleanly than gasoline but can damage the engine's rubber seals and diaphragms.

A: **gauge of railroad tracks, The**
Q: What in North America is four feet, eight and half inches wide, approximating the width of chariot tracks?
W: The traditional gauge of the track in America probably came from the necessity of accomodating wagons with a standard five foot axle.

A: **Geese**
Q: What travel in gaggles?
W: And imagine if they laughed instead of honked, there would be a giggling gaggle of geese overhead each spring.

A: **Gemini**
Q: What constellation contains the twins Castor and Pollux?
W: *Gemini* is Latin for "twins." Castor and Pollux are the two brightest stars. Ancient astronomers used different symbols for this constellation: Egyptians used two goats, Arabians used peacocks, and the Greeks used young children. It is the third sign of the zodiac.

A: **Genetics**
Q: What science did Gregor Mendel establish in 1866?
W: Mendel was a botanist and priest. Using the peas in the garden of his monastery, he developed the tenets of Mendel's Law of the hereditary transmission of physical characteristics. He published his work in 1865, but no one cared much until 1900, 16 years after his death.

A: **genius, A**
Q: What must a Mensa member be?
W: Mensa International is an organization whose members have scored higher in recognized intelligence tests than 98 percent of the population in general. It was formed in 1946 and has about 18,000 members currently.

A: **George M. Pullman**
Q: Who invented the railroad sleeping car in 1859?
W: He invented the first modern railway sleeping car, including fold-down upper berths and seats that converted into lower berths. In 1838, however, the first railway car was put on the rails with bunk beds; there was no bedding, and the travelers slept in their clothes.

A: **George Washington Carver**
Q: Who invented peanut butter?
W: In 1896 at Tuskeegee Institute, he began a long series of experiments with peanuts. He found hundreds of industrial uses for peanuts, potatoes, and soybeans in an effort to encourage southern farmers to grow crops in addition to cotton. But...who invented the jelly?

A: **German measles**
Q: What is rubella better known as?
W: In 1961 the virus responsible for German measles was identified. Since then a vaccine has been developed that is given in the same injection with the measles and mumps vaccines, hence the name the MMR. Rubeola is the medical name for measles.

A: **giant panda, The**
Q: What endangered animal is the symbol of the World Wildlife Fund?
W: This bear-like animal, of the raccoon family, inhabits Tibet and western China. They are extremely rare in the U.S. – we only have two, and they are in a zoo. At birth a panda is smaller than a mouse and weighs about four ounces.

A: **giant tortoise, The**
Q: What animal has the longest lifespan in captivity?
W: Some of the family have lived to over 100 years. And what makes a tortoise different from a turtle, you ask? A tortoise has a telescoping neck that pulls back into the shell, while a turtle has one that moves sideways into the shell.

A: **Gibraltar**
Q: What's the only place in Europe where monkeys live free?
W: This southernmost tip of the Iberian Peninsula is connnected to Spain by a small narrow isthmus. It is 2.75 miles long and .75 miles wide and is home to the Barbary Ape. These tailless monkeys, covered with greenish brown fur, are also abundant in parts of north Africa.

A: **Giraffe**
Q: What animal is considered to have the highest blood pressure?
W: The giraffe's heart weighs 25 pounds, has walls up to three inches thick, and is two feet long. This size is necessary to pump the blood up the ten to twelve foot neck to the brain. It's blood pressure is two to three times that of a healthy human.

A: **Giraffe**
Q: What's another term for a camelopard?
W: Apparently Europeans once thought the parents of the giraffe were a camel (its long neck) and a leopard (its spots)!

A: **Glaciation**
Q: What process forms drumlins, eskers, and cirques?
W: A drumlin is an oval-shaped hill or long ridge caused by glacial erosion. An esker is a long narrow ridge of gravel caused by a stream running under a glacier. The cirque is the semicircular form caused by the erosion of a glacier in a valley. Now that's trivia!

A: **gladiolus, The**
Q: What flower was named for a Roman gladiator's sword?
W: This member of the iris family is so named because of its sword-like leaves and tall spikes of funnel-like flowers. Trivia: gladiolus is also the name for the central part of the breastbone.

A: **goat, The**
Q: What animal has been called "the Poor Man's Cow"?
W: It has been so named because goat's milk is very similar to cow's milk, but the cost of keeping a goat is significantly less than that of feeding and tending a cow. Actually goat's milk is superior to cow's milk because it is more easily digested.

SCIENCE AND NATURE

A: **goat, The**
Q: What four-legged creature did a Cornell University study say would make man's best companion in space?
W: The first animal in space was a Russian dog named Laika, who orbited the earth for 162 days in 1957 in Sputnik II. Chimpanzees have been sent too, but no one seemed to care for the goat suggestion.

A: **goat, The**
Q: What's the zodiacal symbol for Capricorn?
W: This stellar constellation supposedly resembles the outline of a goat. It is the tenth sign of the zodiac ruling those born Dec. 22 to Jan. 21.

A: **Gold**
Q: What metal was Danish astronomer Tycho Brahe's nose made of?
W: Brahe, the most prominent astronomer of the late 16th century, was quite arrogant. Over a point in mathematics he challenged a fellow scientist to a midnight duel. At the age of 19 he lost his nose.

A: **Gold and silver**
Q: What two metals form the alloy white gold?
W: Actually white gold can also contain zinc and nickel or platinum. These metals are added to increase the hardness of the product for jewelry or coins.

A: **goose, The**
Q: What was the first domesticated bird?
W: The first domesticated goose was probably a gaylag, a wild gray European goose. But...one of the most important famous geese is the Toulouse goose from France.

A: **Graham crackers**
Q: What crackers were named for a U.S. doctor who promoted them to combat alcoholism?
W: Sylvester Graham preached against the evils of liquor, coffee, tobacco, tea, meat, featherbeds, and corsets. He developed his own diet

in the 1930s (years before Scarsdale!) that included "graham" flour and "graham" crackers.

A: **grape, The**
Q: What fruit is used in the dye for government inspectors' meat stamps?
W: We all know what a stain the fruit of the vine makes on clothes; it works even better on meat.

A: **Grapefruit**
Q: What food got its name from the way it hung in bunches like grapes?
W: A grapefruit tree is a tropical or semi-tropical evergreen tree cultivated for its edible fruit.

A: **Grapefruit**
Q: What's the common name for the fruit *Citrus grandis*?
W: The grapefruit is also called the *Citrus maximus*. The fruit was brought to Florida from Jamaica by the Spanish.

A: **Great Bear**
Q: What's the common name for the constellation Ursa Major?
W: The Great Bear is also known as the Big Dipper. To the Greeks it was the Bear and Wagon, and to the Romans it was Seven Plowing Oxen. It is situated over the North Pole.

A: **Great Wall of China, The**
Q: What's the only manmade structure visible from space?
W: In 1971 Captain Alan Bean, the astronaut, reported to Doug Baker, columnist for the Portland *Oregon Journal*, that in fact the only thing you can see from the moon is "a beautiful sphere with some white, some blue, some yellow, and once in a while some green...at only a few thousand miles away, no manmade object is visible". And that's the truth!

A: **Green**
Q: What color is a Granny Smith apple?
W: And you can eat it without fear of a stomachache. Ripe or unripe, green, gold, or red, the stomach does not know the difference. If you

want to see one look at the label on the front of the Beatles album from Apple Records.

A: **Green**
Q: What color is the inside of a pistachio nut?
W: The pistachio nut grows wild in Turkey, Lebanon and Afghanistan. Very few domestic groves have proven successful. The varieties vary from light tan shell with light green nut, to red shell with dark green nut. Most U.S. distributors dye the shell red.

A: **Greenwich Mean Time**
Q: What does G.M.T. stand for?
W: The original site of the Greenwich observatory in Great Britain was chosen as 0 degrees longitude, the point of departure for time zones, because the British were the naval leaders of the day, and when they suggested this, the other maritime nations agreed. The observatory was originally built in 1675 to keep track of the position of the moon for use in nautical calculations for English trading ships.

A: **Grenadine**
Q: What nonalcoholic syrup is made from pomegranate juice?
W: This virtually tasteless syrup is used for coloring cocktails and, when mixed with a little sugar, to frost the rim of a glass.

A: **greyhound, The**
Q: What's the world's fastest dog?
W: The greyhound is an ancient breed of hunting dog who only in recent years has been used as a racer. Fast as he can go, his motivation is an electrically propelled replica of a rabbit. He can reach speeds of up to 41.7 mph.

A: **Gulf Stream, The**
Q: What will carry a message in a bottle at an average of four miles an hour?
W: This warm current of the Atlantic Ocean flows from Florida to Newfoundland in a northeasterly direction. The surface current runs about 2.7 to 5 mph depending on the location you place the bottle and the prevailing winds.

H

A: Hair
Q: What is a rhinoceros' horn made of?
W: Rhinos have one or two horns made of a solid mass of agglutinated hairs that grow from the skin of the nose, but originate in the bones of his nose. That is one heck of an ingrown hair!

A: Hairy
Q: What are you if you're hirsute?
W: Hirsute means covered or coated with hair. It is from the Latin *hirsutus*, "bristly" or "shaggy."

A: Haiti
Q: Where did voodoo originate?
W: This religion combines beliefs of Roman Catholicism and tribal religions of West Africa. The gods resemble the Saints of Catholicism (e.g. the snake god is likened to St. Patrick), and they use the sign of the cross, candles, bells, and the crosses of the Catholic Church. From the African religions come the drums, dancing, and worshiping of ancestors.

A: Halley's comet
Q: What can Earthlings see every 76 years?
W: In 1704 the English astronomer Halley noticed that the comet he observed in 1681 followed the same paths described earlier in 1531 and 1607. He predicted the return of the comet in 1758. It returned in 1759, 1835, 1910 and is expected in 1987.

A: hands and feet, The
Q: What does a chiropodist treat?
W: This is from the Greek *kheir*, "hand"; and *pous*, "foot"; and *logos*, "word" or "speech."

A: Hawaii
Q: What has *Science Digest* called the most healthful U.S. state to live in?
W: This may be substantiated by the fact that it has the highest average male lifespan, 73.6 years. The District of Columbia has the lowest, 65.7. But if you're a female, try North Dakota with the highest average female lifespan of 80.3 years.

A: He invented the safety razor
Q: What was the claim to fame of King Camp Gillette?
W: ...and it took him eight years! He said after years of perfecting and marketing it, "If I had been technically trained, I would have quit".

A: He took the first space walk
Q: What's the claim to fame of Aleksei Leonov?
W: On March 18, 1965, Leonov left the Voskhod 2 spacecraft and floated in space for ten minutes while attached to the craft by a tether.

A: Head, Heart, Hands, Health
Q: What do the Hs stand for in 4-H Club?
W: Founded in 1914, its purpose was to educate young farmers between nine and 19 in agriculture, home economics, and citizenship. The sign is a four leaf clover with an *H* on each leaf. The pledge reads: "I pledge my head to clearer thinking, my heart to greater loyalty, my hands to larger service, and my health to better living for my club, my community, and my country".

A: Hearing
Q: Which of the five senses are you most likely to lose if hit by lightning?
W: This phenomenon may occur because of the overloading of the sensitive electrical circuitry of the hearing process in the brain.

A: Hearing
Q: Which of the five senses is less sharp after you eat too much?
W: Hence the expression, "I'm full up to my ears!"

A: Heart disease
Q: What's the Number 1 killer in industrialized countries?
W: In 1981, 758,100 people in America died of heart disease. The second most common cause of death was cancer, causing 422,720 deaths that same year.

A: heel, The
Q: Where is the human skin least sensitive?
W: That is probably because the skin there is one sixth of an inch thick.

A: heifer, A
Q: What do you call a female calf?
W: A heifer becomes a cow when she has borne her own calf. The word comes from the Old English *haifre* meaning "full grown oxen."

A: Helium
Q: What gas makes little Johnny's balloon rise?
W: Almost all naturally occurring helium in the world originates from natural gas wells in the United States. Want to sound like Donald Duck? Suck in the helium from a balloon and start talking...

A: Hemophilia
Q: What's known as "the Royal Disease"?
W: It is an hereditary coagulation (clotting) disorder characterized by excessive bleeding. It principally affects males, but is transmitted by females. Queen Victoria's son and several of her daughters' male descendants were hemophiliacs as was Alexis, the son of Nicholas II, last czar of Russia. Frequent marriages between the royal families of Europe accounted for the high rate of the disease among royalty.

SCIENCE AND NATURE

A: **Hibernation**
Q: What's the winter counterpart to estivation?
W: The almost "suspended animation" of hibernation is best illustrated by the change in the woodchuck. When active the woodchuck breathes 2,100 times per hour; when hibernating he breathes ten times per hour.

A: **Himself**
Q: What does an autophobe avoid referring to?
W: From *auto*, "self" or "same"; and *phobia*, "strong fear.'

A: **hip, The**
Q: What is the fruit of the rosebush called?
W: The hip is actually the fleshy false fruit that contains the true fruit. This fruit is edible, quite rich in Vitamin C, and can be made into preserves.

A: **Hippocrates**
Q: What Greek physician is known as "the Father of Medicine"?
W: He was the first physician to reject the idea that disease was caused by evil powers. He believed it was the result of an imbalance in the body. His high ethical standards and scientific approach to patient history made him a cornerstone of the medical profession.

A: **The Hippocratic oath**
Q: What oath begins with: "I swear by Apollo, the Physician…"?
W: The oath was believed to have been written by Hippocrates, but research indicates that it was probably written 500 years after his death. It is the oath taken by physicans.

A: **hippopotamus, The**
Q: What's the hog's largest living relative?
W: They are the largest non-ruminating, even-toed, hoofed animal of that family. The mammalian order includes pigs, giraffes, antelopes, sheep, goats, camels, and cattle.

A: **His head**
Q: What does the male praying mantis lose to the female after mating?
W: …and the human male usually loses his *before*!

A: **Homo sapiens**
Q: What genus and species is man classified as?
W: Modern man is Homo sapien. The family of man is *Hominidae* of the suborder *Anthropoidea* of the order of *Primate* of the subclass *Eutheria*, of the class *Mammalia* of the subphylum *Vertebrata* of the phylum *Chordata* of the *Metazoan* group. All of this means that man is a many-celled animal with a spinal cord and backbone, which suckles its young who use a placenta in gestation, which has five-digited extremities and a collarbone, which has a single pair of mammary glands in its chest, and which has eyes at the front of the head as well as stereoscopic vision and a relatively large brain. And you thought we were unique!

A: **Hops**
Q: What gives beer its distinctive bitter flavor?
W: Commercial hops are covered with lupulin, a bitter powder which is used as a sedative in medicine.

A: **Horses**
Q: What animal does a hippophobe fear?
W: This word is from the Greek *hippo* meaning "horse", and *phobia* meaning "fear." A hippophile is a horse lover.

A: **Horses**
Q: What does a farrier put shoes on?
W: This word is from the Latin *ferrum* meaning "iron," and *ferrare* meaning "to shoe horse." In earlier times farriers also served as veterinarians.

A: **hot Saharan wind, A**
Q: What is a sirocco?
W: It is a hot, humid south or southeast wind of southern Italy, Sicily and other Mediterranean islands that starts dry over the Sahara and picks up moisture as it crosses the sea. AKA a Volkswagen!

A: **Houston, Tranquility Base here; the *Eagle* has landed**
Q: What were the first words spoken from the moon?
W: These words were spoken from the Lunar Module *Eagle* of the Apollo 11 spacecraft that landed on the moon on July 20, 1969.

A: **Howard Hughes**
Q: Who built the *Spruce Goose*
W: From 1942 Howard Hughes worked on the design of this, the world's largest aircraft. It is an eight-engine wooden flying "boat" intended to carry 750 passengers. In 1947, he piloted the *Spruce Goose* on its only flight – one mile.

A: **hummingbird, The**
Q: What's the smallest bird in the world?
W: The tiniest hummingbird is the bee hummingbird of Cuba, which from beak tip to tail tip is two inches long. By the way, hummingbirds are only found in the Western Hemisphere.

A: **Hundredweight**
Q: What does the abbreviation cwt. stand for?
W: Back to the Roman numerals: *c* stands for one hundred, from the Latin *centum* meaning "hundred." It is equal to 100 pounds in the U.S. and 112 pounds in Great Britain.

A: **Hydrogen**
Q: What's the most abundant element in the sun?
W: Most of the sun is composed of elements that are found on earth, including hydrogen, helium, and calcium. The difference is that because of the temperatures and pressures of the interior of the sun, the atoms of the elements are in a high state of excitation.

A: **Hydrogen**
Q: What's the most common atom in the universe?
W: It is also the lightest and simplest of the chemical elements.

A: **Hydroponics**
Q: What's the science of growing plants in liquid nutrients rather than soil?
W: Plants need carbon, hydrogen, and oxygen from water and air, and the mineral salts they need from the soil can be supplied with liquid preparations. The advantage of hydroponics is that plants can be grown more quickly and out of season in greenhouses and will produce more blooms if given a scientifically designed diet of the minerals they need.

A: **Hypoxemia, or lack of blood to the brain**
Q: What has caused every human death?
W: Whatever the cause of the lack of blood to the brain, and cardiac arrest is usually the most immediate, it is the cessation of brain function that causes the vital functions of the body to cease. Death is also defined in medicine as the cessation of brain function.

A: *I Ching*
Q: What is the Chinese book of changes called?
W: *I Ching* means "Classic of Changes" in Chinese. It is an ancient Chinese text, one of the five classics of Confucianism. *I Ching* enthusiasts have claimed that the book is a means of understanding and even controlling future events.

A: **Iceland**
Q: What was the first country to legalize abortion?
W: Iceland was the first country to allow abortion for medico-social reasons. On Jan. 28, 1935, Law Number 38 declared that abortion might be done within the first 28 weeks of pregnancy if the mother's physical or mental well-being would be threatened by continuation of the pregnancy. In 1920 the USSR allowed abortion on demand, rescinded it in 1936, and reinstated it in 1955.

A: **idiot, An**
Q: What are you if your IQ is below 25?
W: You are definitely not playing this game!

A: **Igneous, metamorphic, sedimentary**
Q: What are the three major causes of rock?
W: Igneous rock results from the solidification of materials from molten substances like lava; sedimentary rock results from the consolidation of substances deposited by water or wind; metamorphic rock is produced through changing of existing rock by pressure and heat.

A: **Impotence**
Q: What sexual problem is grounds for divorce in 24 U.S. states?
W: The other grounds are incompatibility, cruelty, desertion, non-support, alcohol or drug addiction, felony, and insanity. Alabama, North Dakota, and Oklahoma are the only states to accept all grounds.

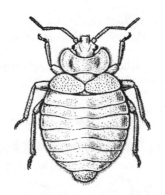

A: **In the bones**
Q: Where are the haversian canals?
W: You didn't guess Venice, did you? These are the small tunnels running through bones, through which the blood vessels pass.

A: **In the fall**
Q: When do you plant winter wheat?
W: You harvest it in the summer. Spring wheat is planted in the spring and harvested in late summer.

A: **Incisors**
Q: What are the front cutting teeth called?
W: Just in case you wanted to know: the incisors cut the food in your mouth, the cuspids further reduce it in size, and the molars grind it to a digestible mass before it leaves your mouth on its way to your stomach.

A: **index finger, The**
Q: What's the most sensitive finger on the human hand?
W: This is because of the Meissner's Corpuscle (a specialized nerve receptor) that shoots the information from the finger to the brain to tell you whether you've touched silk or sandpaper.

A: **Influenza**
Q: What caused 20 million deaths in 1918?
W: Most people died because of the complication of bacterial pneumonia. There have been 31 flu pandemics since the 16th century, the most recent were the Asian flu pandemic of 1957 and 1958 and the Hong Kong flu pandemic in 1968.

A: **Insects**
Q: What class of animals makes up more than two thirds of known species?
W: Animals of the class *Insecta* have three body parts, three pairs of legs, and an external skeleton and by far outnumber any other class. They range in size from 0.01 inch in length to one type of moth that has a wingspread of one foot. How would you like *him* flying around your lamppost some summer night!

A: **Insects**
Q: What's the oldest and most numerous class of animals?
W: At present 800,000 separate species of insect have been identified. The oldest known fossil insects date back to 300 million years ago, but they probably existed long before then.

A: **Insulin**
Q: What substance did Charles Best and Frederick Banting discover in 1922?
W: The name insulin comes from the fact that this hormone is produced by islands of cells (Latin *insula* meaning "island") in the pancreas known as the islands of Langerhans. These islands were discovered by Paul Langerhans. Insulin was isolated in July 1921 and first administered to a patient, a 14-year-old diabetic, six months later in January 1922.

A: **Intelligence**
Q: What does the Binet test measure?
W: Alfred Binet (1857-1911) was a French psychologist. From 1905 to 1911, he developed scales for measuring intelligence and educational achievement, inspired by his interest in mental differences between subnormal and normal children.

A: **Intelligence quotient**
Q: What does IQ stand for?
W: It is a ratio or quotient designating an individual's rate of mental development.

A: **iris, The**
Q: What membrane controls the amount of light entering the eye?
W: The iris is the colored portion of the eye. It is actually a smooth muscle with fibers arranged in a circle. Its opening and closing, regulating the light to the eye, is controlled by the third cranial nerve, the oculomotor nerve.

A: **Irish Wolfhound, The**
Q: What's the world's largest dog?
W: It is the world's tallest dog, but not necessarily the heaviest. It is up to 39 inches tall at the shoulder and weighs up to 135 pounds. It almost became extinct in the 1800s, but was reestablished by Scottish dog breeder G.A. Graham. The Great Dane is the other tallest dog, so you are correct if this was your answer. If you thought "largest" was "heaviest" and guessed the St. Bernard, you are also correct – they can weigh over 250 pounds.

A: **Isaac Newton**
Q: Who invented the reflecting telescope?
W: As a result of his experiments with light, in which he drew an erroneous conclusion that the dispersion of light into colors could not be prevented, he invented the reflecting telescope in 1668. The problem with this telescope was that the eyepiece and head of the observor get in the way of the object. It was refined by James Gregory by using two reflecting mirrors.

A: **It was the first U.S. satellite**
Q: What was the claim to fame of Explorer I, launched Feb. 1, 1958?
W: The 31-pound spacecraft sent back information about meteorites, radiation belts, and cosmic rays for 112 days.

A: **Its eyes**
Q: What does a frog close when it swallows?
W: In swallowing, both toads and frogs close their eyes, press down with their eyeballs, and thereby lower the roof of their mouth against the tongue. This pushes their food down to the stomach.

A: **Its head**
Q: Where are a snail's reproductive organs?
W: So they always use their heads when having an affair!

A: **Its mouth**
Q: What does a baby elephant suck with?
W: His trunk, which may have been your answer, is essentially his nose. He can suck up water with it and spray it into his mouth, but the baby elephant uses its mouth when nursing.

A: **Its trunk**
Q: What goes up when an elephant senses danger?
W: Because the nostrils are at the tip of his trunk, he lifts it to detect the scent of oncoming danger. Elephants can pick up the scent of a human being from an amazing distance. Since his hearing and sight are not particularly good, he depends on his huge nose to warn him.

A: **It's the humerus**
Q: Why is the funny bone so called?
W: So when someone tickles your funny bone they are stimulating your upper arm!

A: **It's the largest muscle in the body**
Q: What's the claim to fame of the gluteus maximus?
W: ...and in some of us it is a little larger than we'd care to discuss! This muscle is responsible for the major movements of the hips and it also makes it comfortable to sit on bleachers for extended periods of times as it protects (pads) the underlying pelvic bones.

A: **Ivan Pavlov**
Q: What Russian physiologist went to the dogs to write *Conditioned Reflexes*"?
W: In 1889 he explored the conditioned reflexes in dogs, the most famous of which is stimulating salivation by ringing a bell. He influenced 20th century psychology with his physiologically based theories of behavior.

A: **Ivory**
Q: What are walrus tusks made of?
W: These huge elongated canine teeth are used by the walrus to rake the ocean bottom for his food, as a weapon and as a pick while climbing ice. They have also served as a disservice to him because man has greatly reduced his multitudes in an effort to secure his valuable tusks.

SCIENCE AND NATURE

J

A: **J. Robert Oppenheimer**
Q: Who oversaw the design and assembly of the first atomic bomb?
W: During a leave of absence from the University of California, he served as director of the atomic bomb project at Los Alamos, New Mexico, in 1943 to 1945. He received the Atomic Energy Commission's Enrico Fermi Award in 1963, despite his suspension from the Atomic Energy Commission in 1954 for supposed Communist ties.

A: **jack rabbit, The**
Q: What rabbit got its name because its ears resembled those of a jackass?
W: His ears don't slow him down though; he is the fastest member of his family achieving speeds of 45 mph and leaping up to 20 feet.

A: **jaguar, The**
Q: What's the largest cat in the Americas?
W: The jaguar is about six feet long and two feet high at the shoulder. He is clearly the most powerful cat, and is an accomplished swimmer.

A: **Jan. 1, 2001**
Q: What will be the date of the first day of the 21st century?
W: That's correct, the end of the 20th century will be Dec. 31, 2000.

A: **January**
Q: What month is showing on the calendar when the earth is nearest the sun?
W: In its slightly elliptical 583,400,000 mile orbit around the sun, the earth comes closest to the sun in our month of January. The warmth of the month depends on whether your hemisphere is tilted toward the sun (summer) or away from the sun (winter).

A: **Janus**
Q: What Roman god is January named for?
W: As the first month of the year it seemed fitting to be named for the Roman god of doors and beginnings. In ancient Rome, Janus was publicly invoked on the first day of January, and in every home the morning prayer was addressed to him.

A: **jawbone, The**
Q: What's the hardest bone in the human body?
W: Unless you have a glass jaw!

A: **jellyfish, A**
Q: What is a Portuguese man-o-war?
W: He is a spineless, quivering jellyfish but don't push him around! Dead or alive his 100-foot long tentacles contain a poison 75 percent as powerful as cobra venom.

A: **jukebox, A**
Q: What was the 24-disc John Gabel Entertainer the first example of in 1906?
W: It was the first disc-playing preselective jukebox. The first jukebox was placed in the Palais Royal Saloon in San Francisco in 1889. It had a phonograph with four listening tubes you could pay a nickel to listen through.

A: **July 2**
Q: What's the middle day of a non-leap year?
W: It's the 183rd day of the year. A non-leap year has 365 days. Think about it! There are 182 days before and after July 2nd in a non-leap year.

A: **July 20, 1969**
Q: What date did man first land on the moon?
W: The first man on the moon was Neil Armstrong, mission commander of Apollo 11. The second man to set foot on the moon was Colonel Edwin Aldrin, the pilot of the Lunar Module *Eagle*.

A: **July and August**
Q: What two months are named for men?
W: Gaius Julius Caesar was born in the fifth month of the Roman calendar, which is now July. When he was assassinated in 44 B.C., the month was named after him. The emperor Augustus gave his name to August, until then the sixth month; and in order to make his month as important as Julius' a day was taken from February to make August 31 days long!

A: **June, July, August**
Q: What are the three winter months in the Southern Hemisphere?
W: Hard to envision Christmas as the highpoint of the summer season!

A: **June 21 or 22**
Q: What date is it when the sun is directly over the tropic of Cancer?
W: The tropic of Cancer at 23 degrees 27 minutes north latitude is so named because when the sun is directly over it on June 21, the summer solstice, the sun enters the constellation Cancer. The corresponding zodiac sign rules those from June 21 to July 21.

A: **June 21 or 22**
Q: When is the summer solstice in the Northern Hemisphere?
W: The solstices are two points at which the sun is farthest from the celestial equator. Solstice means "sun stands still," and at these points the sun changes little in its position on the celestial equator. The winter solstice is December 21 or 22.

A: **Juniper berries**
Q: What berries give gin its flavor?
W: The berries of this evergreen also yield oil of savin which is currently used in perfumery and, in earlier times, was used as a stimulant.

A: **Jupiter**
Q: What celestial body is the center of the Jovian system?
W: Jove is another name for Jupiter, the mythological Roman ruler of the gods, son of the god Saturn. Isn't Jovian easier to say than Jupitarian?

SCIENCE AND NATURE

A: **Jupiter**
Q: What is the largest planet in the solar system?
W: The mass of this giant planet is 2.5 times the combined mass of all the rest of the solar system excluding the sun.

A: **Jupiter**
Q: What planet boasts the Great Red Spot?
W: The spot covers an area several times the size of earth. The spot varies in color from blood red to intense pink for yet unknown reasons, and it moves. It was once believed to be the reflection of a surface lava flow, but this notion has been disregarded since the temperature of Jupiter is 225 degrees below zero.

A: **Jupiter's**
Q: What planet's moons include Io, Ganymede, and Hades?
W: These three moons, and a fourth, Gallista, were the first celestial bodies to be discovered by means of a telescope. Galileo discovered them in 1610. There are eight other known Jupiter moons, also called Galilean satellites.

K

A: **kangaroo, A**
Q: What's a wallaby?
W: Smaller kangaroos are often called wallabies. They are commonly the size of a rabbit and are usually brighter in color than the larger species of kangaroos.

A: **Karl Benz**
Q: Who invented the automobile in 1885?
W: The original Benz car is a three-wheeled vehicle. It was the first practical auto powered by an internal combustion engine.

A: **key, A**
Q: What did Benjamin Franklin tie his kite to?
W: The kite and key apparatus was sent to him from an Englishman, Peter Collinson. Actually the experiment, which proved the conductivity and electricity of lightening, was performed in England before Ben's 1752 experiment.

A: **kid, A**
Q: What is the goat's offspring called?
W: Two kids are usually produced at birth and are sexually mature at six months. Their mother is a doe and the father a buck.

A: **kilogram, The**
Q: What's the only base unit of measure still defined by an artifact?
W: The correct answer is the kilo*meter*. A kilogram is actually 1000 grams, a gram being the weight of 1 cubic centimeter of water at 4 degrees Centigrade. A kilometer, however, is 1,000 meters. A meter is defined as the length between two lines on a bronze bar made in *1845* in Great Britain. In 1960 it was redefined in the U.S. as 1,650,763.73 wavelengths of the reddish orange light emitted by Krypton 86 at -210 degrees Centigrade!!

A: **kindle, A**
Q: What's a group of kittens called?
W: This word is from the German *kind* meaning "offspring." And who can resist a cute, cuddly kindle of kittens?

A: **Kitty Hawk, North Carolina**
Q: Where did the Wright brothers make their first flight?
W: After they had flown four times on that day in 1903, a gust of wind turned over and wrecked their *Flyer*. They packed up the pieces in barrels and sent them back to their Ohio bicycle shop.

A: **Knock-kneed**
Q: What are you if you suffer from baker's leg?
W: So called baker's leg because the length of time a baker spends on his feet was thought to cause this deformity of the legs.

A: **Kodak**
Q: What company is the world's largest user of silver?
W: The Kodak Company uses most of its silver in producing photographic film. Minute particles of silver are suspended in gelatin, and this solution is used to coat the cellulose base of the film.

L

A: **L**
Q: What letter is to the right of K on a typewriter keyboard?
W: It sure is!

A: **L**
Q: What's the Roman numeral for 50?
W: Could also be written XX plus XXX, or LX minus X!

A: **Larynx**
Q: What's the anatomical term for the voice box?
W: This hollow chamber serves as an echo chamber to increase the sound formed by the vibration of the vocal cords. Inflammation of the larynx results in laryngitis.

A: **laser beam, A**
Q: What kind of beam derives its name from "light amplification by stimulated emission of radiation"?
W: The acronym stands for a light consisting of a well-defined frequency in which the waves reinforce one another. The light is a narrow and nearly parallel beam as opposed to an ordinary light bulb which emits a jumble of many high frequencies and directions.

A: **Lassie**
Q: What was the first animal named to the Animal Hall of Fame in 1969?
W: The famous collie first appeared in Eric Knight's classic *Lassie Come Home.* Rudd Weatherwax's dog, Pal, played the first Lassie in the 1943 movie, and Pal, Jr., played Lassie in the TV series.

A: **Late afternoon**
Q: What's the best time of day to buy a pair of shoes?
W: Reasoning: this is the point at which your feet reach their average size because of fluid accumulation and balance after a day of supporting your body.

A: **lb**
Q: What abbreviation comes from *libra,* meaning "pound" in Latin?
W: We didn't believe this one, but it is in Webster's under "lb"!

A: **Lead poisoning**
Q: What kind of poisoning is known as plumbism?
W: The word *plumbism* comes from the Latin word for "lead", *plumbum.* Since the elimination of lead from interior house paint, cases of plumbism in children have been greatly reduced.

A: **Lead's**
Q: What element's chemical symbol is Pb?
W: This is from the Latin *plumbum* meaning "lead."

A: **leaves, The**
Q: Where in a tree does photosynthesis occur?

W: It is in the leaves where the chlorophyll containing chloroplasts gathers light from the sun or artificial light and combines water and carbon dioxide to form a hexose sugar with a by-product of oxygen.

A: **left, The**
Q: Which is more tender, the left or right leg of a chicken?
W: In a right-handed chicken this may be true because the right leg gets more exercise and therefore contains a larger tougher muscle, the edible part of the leg.

A: **left, The**
Q: Which shoulder should you throw spilled salt over?
W: This tradition refers to evil spirits emanating from the sinister (left) side. Spilling salt is bad luck unless you throw salt in the face of the evil spirits.

A: **left, The**
Q: Which side of the bed does superstition say is the wrong side?
W: The left is always the evil side of everything. In earlier times even left-handed people were burned as witches. For some of us, either side is the wrong side of bed until the first cup of coffee.

A: **lens, The**
Q: What part of the eye continues to grow throughout a person's life?
W: The lens, the flattened sphere that sits in the anterior portion of the eye, is constructed of layers of transparent fibers. It is through changes in the shape of the lens that the eye focuses on distant or near objects.

A: **Leo**
Q: What's your zodiacal sign if you're born on Aug. 9?
W: Leo's the lion, people born between July 23 and Aug. 22 claim this as their zodiacal sign.

A: **Leukemia**
Q: What is the medical term for cancer of the blood?
W: More specifically, leukemia is a

disease that affects the leukocytes (white blood cells) and the organs that produce them. Leukemia affects birds and many mammals in addition to man.

A: **Libra**
Q: What zodiacal sign is represented by the balance, or scales?
W: Those of you born between Sept. 24 and Oct. 23 can weigh this answer!

A: **Life, heart, fate, head**
Q: What are the four main lines in palmistry?
W: The left hand reflects the inbred traits and the right hand the acquired characteristics of a personality. Aside from the lines, the mounts are also of interest indicating success, financial interests, honor and happiness, as well as several other aspects of the future.

A: **Ligaments**
Q: What are looser than normal in a double-jointed person?
W: Ligaments are a type of connective tissue that are responsible for some of the strength or stability of a joint, because they connect the bones in a joint one to another.

A: **Liger**
Q: What's the term for the hybrid offspring of a lion and tiger?
W: Careful here: if it's a male tiger and female lion, it is a liger; however, if it's a male lion and female tiger, it's a tigron! These are zoo-bred hybrids.

A: **Lightning**
Q: What natural phenomenon kills more people than any other?
W: An average of 400 deaths and 1,000 injuries are due to lightning each year...including golfers.

A: **Lightning**
Q: What strikes the Empire State Building more than 50 times a year?
W: Lightning strikes the earth about 100 times every second, emanating from the 1,800 thunderstorms occurring at any moment. The height of

SCIENCE AND NATURE

the Empire State Building in comparison to the surrounding structures, and the height of its radio tower, make the building a sitting duck!

A: **Light-year**
Q: What's the astronomical term for the distance light travels in a vacuum in one year?
W: Light travels at a rate of 186,000 miles per second. At that speed one light year is equal to 5,800,000,000,000 miles.

A: **lion, The**
Q: What's the zodiacal sign for Leo?
W: The fifth sign of the zodiac, ruling those born July 23 to Aug. 22, corresponds to the northern constellation, Leo, east of Cancer and containing the star Regulus.

A: **Little America**
Q: What Antarctic base was established by Richard Byrd?
W: During his first expedition to Antarctica from 1928 to 1930, he established the base on the Bay of Whales and later made four trips back to it.

A: **Little Dipper**
Q: What constellation embraces Polaris, the North Star?
W: Polaris, or Ursa Minor, marks the end of the handle of the Little Dipper. The star is situated less than 1 degree from the North Pole.

A: **Little Miss Muffet**
Q: What nursery rhyme character was arachnaphobic?
W: Arachnaphobia is the fear of arachnoid, which the little spider who sat down beside her is.

A: **liver, The**
Q: What part of the body is inflamed in hepatitis?
W: *Hepaticus* is Latin for "liver." The inflammation of the liver, in the case of hepatitis, is caused by a virus and occurs in two forms, infectious and serum.

A: **liver, The**
Q: What's the largest gland in the human body?
W: And...if 80 percent of your liver were removed, the remaining part would function and in a few months regenerate to the original size!

A: **llama, The**
Q: What branch of the camel family is found only in the Andes?
W: He is the largest member of the camel family and spunky, too! When weary he will spit at his driver and then lie down and refuse to move.

A: **Loch Ness, Scotland**
Q: Where does Nessie live?
W: More specifically Nessie resides in the long narrow lake, Loch Ness, in Iverness County, Scotland. The lake has a depth of 754 feet and could accommodate a large monster.

A: **Lockjaw**
Q: What's another name for tetanus?
W: This disease of the nervous system, with symptoms of severe muscles spasms, is caused by the *Clostridium tetani* bacteria. The bacteria are found almost everywhere, and it is worth your while to be vaccinated!

A: **Locksmith**
Q: What was Linus Yale's occupation?
W: Linus Yale began the Yale Lock Company that supplies us with the now famous Yale combination and key locks.

A: **low-frequency speaker, A**
Q: What's a woofer?
W: And a tweeter is the high-frequency speaker in your **stereo** system.

A: **LSD**
Q: What's the secret identity of lysergic acid diethylamide?
W: It is probably the most **potent** of the hallucinogenic drugs **derived** from the ergot fungus.

A: **LXIX**
Q: How do you write 69 in **Roman** numerals?
W: L = 50, X = 10, IX = 9, add them up and there you have it!

A: **magician, A**
Q: What is a prestidigitator?
W: This is a person manually skilled in execution of tricks, sleight of hand. It is from the Latin *praestigiator* meaning "juggler's tricks."

A: **Magnetic north**
Q: What does a compass needle point to?
W: Because the magnetic **compass** points toward the north *magnetic* pole it seldom points to the true North Pole at the same time, **as the** actual location of the magnetic **poles** vary from year to year. To understand the compass, one should consider the earth as a large permanent magnet with magnetic lines of **force** flowing between the two **magnetic** poles.

A: **Maharishi Mahesh Yogi**
Q: Who taught the Beatles transcendental meditation?
W: Patty Harrison, George Harrison's wife, first introduced the Beatles to the Maharishi in 1967,

and their first meditation course took place in Bangor, Wales. Their stay was cut short by the news that their manager, Brian Epstein, had died. In February 1968 the Beatles had planned to go to the Maharishi to study for three months. With them were their wives, Donovan, Mike Love of the Beach Boys, and Mia Farrow. Their devotion soon turned to disdain when it was learned that the Maharishi desired sexual relations with some of the female members of their group. When the Maharishi asked why they were leaving, Lennon said, "You're the cosmic one, you should know."

A: **male, The**
Q: Which sex is twice as likely to contract leprosy?
W: Leprosy is also known as Hansen's Disease because G. Armauer Hansen discovered the bacterium that causes the disease in 1874. It is a contagious disease that attacks the skin and nerves and causes the skin to swell and become lumpy and discolored. The worldwide incidence in males is three times greater than that in females. It usually occurs in tropical and subtropical regions.

A: **Malted milk**
Q: What product did William Horlick discover and produce?
W: Malted milk was developed by Horlick in 1887 in Racine, Wisconsin. It was originally known as "diastoid."

A: **Man**
Q: What mammal lives the longest?
W: Few non-bacterial creatures live longer than man. It appears, however, that the tortoise is such a creature. The longest-lived was 152 years old. The average life expectancy of man is now 74 years.

A: **Man**
Q: What is the only mammal that can't fly that can fly?
W: Pretty tricky. Not unassisted, however!

A: **manatee, The**
Q: What uncomely creature inspired sailors' tales of mermaids?
W: The manatee has a stout, tapered body ending in a rounded flipper. Adult manatees range in length from eight to 15 feet. Our guess is that the manatee in deep water could look like a mermaid to some sailors, after too much grog!

A: **March and September**
Q: What are the two hottest months at the equator?
W: The equator is the great imaginary circle around the earth, equally distant from the North and South Poles, that divides the earth into the Northern and Southern Hemispheres. At noon on the days of March 20 or 21 and September 22 or 23, the sun at the equator is 90 degrees above the horizon, which means directly over the equator.

A: **March and September**
Q: What two months contain equinoxes?
W: The equinoxes take place when the sun crosses the celestial equator. This occurs twice yearly. First, the vernal (spring) equinox occurs when the sun crosses into the Northern Hemisphere on March 20 or 21. The second occurs on September 22 or 23 when the sun crosses into the Southern Hemisphere and is known as the autumnal equinox. On dates when the equinox takes place, the days and nights are of equal time.

A: **March 21**
Q: What's the first day of the astrological year?
W: Aries is the first sign of the zodiac and commences on March 21. Symbolized by the Ram, it covers people born between March 21 and April 19 and is associated with the energetic forces of spring.

A: **Margaret Mead**
Q: What anthropologist wrote *Coming of Age in Samoa*?
W: Her field work in 1925 on adolescence in Samoa provided

material for her first major work, *Coming of Age in Samoa*, published in 1928.

A: **Mars**
Q: What's the red planet?
W: The surface of Mars is the only planet that can be seen from earth. Its name comes from the Roman God of War. It's the planet fourth closest to the sun and second closest to earth.

A: **Mars**
Q: What planet did Viking I land on?
W: Viking I, launched on Aug. 20, 1975, and Viking II, launched on Sept. 9, 1975, were designed to find biological artifacts on the martian surface. Other instruments aboard were for geochemical and geophysical investigation.

A: **Meltdown**
Q: What's the term for the physical disintegration of a nuclear reactor's core?
W: Another term that could be used is "the end." We all learned this term on March 28, 1979, with the accident at the Three-Mile Island nuclear reactor in Pennsylvania.

A: **Men**
Q: What does an androphobic maiden fear?
W: This is from the Greek *andro*, "man"; and *phobia*, "strong fear."

A: **Mercury**
Q: What is quicksilver?
W: It's called quicksilver because it takes the form of a silver-white liquid at room temperature. Its existence has been documented back to ancient times. It's found in ore deposits, usually as mercury sulfide.

A: **Mercury**
Q: What planet is nearest the sun?
W: At an average distance of 36 million miles from the sun, Mercury is still some 30 million miles closer than the next closest planet, Venus. It is 60 million miles closer to the sun than Earth. Mercury, however, does not have the highest surface temperature. Its maximum is estimated at 648 degrees Fahrenheit, while Venus is estimated at close to 850 degrees.

A: **Mercury**
Q: What planet has the shortest year?
W: Mercury orbits the sun on an average of 88 earth days, translating into 30 miles per second. Its period of rotation on its axis, similar to part of one 24 hour earth day, takes 59 days. You win some, you lose some!

A: **Michael Collins**
Q: What Apollo 11 astronaut minded the store while Armstrong and Aldrin made history?
W: While Armstrong and Aldrin were on the lunar surface collecting 48.5 pounds of soil and rock samples during their stay of 21 hours, 36 minutes, and 21 seconds, Collins was in the command module minding the store.

A: **middle finger, The**
Q: What finger boasts the fastest-growing nail?
W: Don't stop to look at it now; other people in the game may get the wrong idea!

A: **Milk**
Q: What's the most popular beverage in America?
W: Consumption of major food commodities are given in pounds per person. Fluid milk and cream is listed at about 247 pounds per person; coffee at approximately 7.5 pounds per person.

A: **Milky Way, The**
Q: What's the earth's galaxy called?
W: From end to end, it's 100,000 light years long. And that's a long time!

A: **MM**
Q: How is the year 2000 written in Roman numerals?
W: In Roman numerals, *M* stands for 1,000. The way to express two or three of any power of ten is to simply place them side by side. For example, 3,000 would become MMM or 20 becomes XX. Simple, huh?

A: **Mobile Army Surgical Hospital**
Q: What does MASH stand for?
W: And millions of laughs in the 4077th!

A: **Molasses**
Q: What's the syrup drained from raw sugar?
W: It's the syrup remaining after sugar is crystallized out of cane or beet juice.

A: **Monday**
Q: What day of the week will January 1, 2001, be?
W: There are 14 patterns of days that make up a perpetual calendar. The current *Almanac* will help you find the first day of a year up to the year 2080!

A: **mongoose, The**
Q: What animal was barred live entry to the U.S. in a 1902 law?
W: One species of mongoose was introduced into Hawaii and the West Indies to control rodents and snakes. The results were disastrous, however, as the mongoose caused severe damage to the population of native animals.

A: **monkey wrench, The**
Q: What tool did Charles Moncke invent?
W: Moncke was a London blacksmith. Tradition has it that he first invented the wrench that had moving jaws adjusted by a screw. Because of popular ignorance as to the origin of the word, it became known as the monkey wrench, which is the pronunciation of the inventor's name.

A: **Monosodium glutamate**
Q: What does MSG stand for?
W: Monosodium glutamate is used as a flavor enhancer in many seasonings. It is a simple salt comprised of sodium and glutamate acid. Although the jury hasn't reached a verdict, the sodium in MSG is believed to be a possible factor in causing hypertension.

A: **monsoon, The**
Q: What seasonal south Asian wind is characterized by heavy rains?
W: Monsoons are seasonal winds that blow onshore in summer and offshore in winter between large land masses and adjacent ocean surfaces. Monsoon circulation is strongest along tropical coastal regions, especially in southern and eastern Asia, where planetary circulation is weak and thermally induced pressures are at a maximum.

A: **moon, The**
Q: What's receding from earth by half an inch a year?
W: This is occurring because of tidal frictions in the earth's oceans. Because of the tidal bulges caused by the moon's gravitational force on the earth, the displacement of water causes a new gravitational force to act on the moon. There is now a force that acts along the moon's path, causing the moon to spiral slowly outward. If none of this makes sense, who cares — its only a half inch anyway!

A: **moon, The**
Q: What's the largest satellite orbiting the earth?
W: A satellite, by definition, is any small solid body moving in an orbit around a planet. By this definition, the moon, being smaller than the earth and revolving around it, qualifies it as a satellite.

A: **moon, The**
Q: Where's the Sea of Showers?
W: The dark patches on the moon were originally thought to be bodies of water by the early astronomer, Galileo. The "seas" are actually

lowlands on the moon formed from lava 3.3 to 3.8 billion years ago. The Sea of Showers contains the largest crater, 700 miles wide. It forms one of the eyes of the "Man in The Moon."

A: **Morphine**
Q: What drug was named for Morpheus, the Greek god of dreams?
W: Morphine is an organic compound extracted from opium. The soluable salts are used as a light anesthetic or sedative causing a sleeplike state.

A: **mosquito, The**
Q: What insect transmits yellow fever?
W: Yellow fever is an acute infectious disease of subtropical and tropical areas caused by a virus transmitted by mosquitoes of the genus *Aedes*. *Aedes*, from the Greek, translates into "not pleasant."

A: **Mosquitoes**
Q: What's the favorite food of dragonflies?
W: The dragonfly is one of the fastest flying and most predacious insects. In 30 minutes it can eat its own weight in food.

A: **Mother's Day**
Q: What is observed on the second Sunday in May?
W: In 1890 Miss Mary Sasseen suggested to a group of teachers that annual homage be paid to mothers every April 20th, her own mother's birthday, but nothing came of the suggestion. The actual creator of the modern Mother's Day observation was a Philadelphia spinster who reached the age of 84 having only cared for her own mother. Upon her mother's death, she brooded over the loss for two or three years, and her obsession led to the creation of the day as we know it.

A: **Motion sickness**
Q: What do you take Dramamine for?
W: Motion sickness drugs frequently produce blurred vision and drowsiness. So, in our minds, it's a toss-up as to which is worse.

A: **Mount St. Helens**
Q: What did *Esquire* name Ash Hole of the Year for 1980?
W: Our vote for 1984 is a tie between Mauna Loa and Kilauea who are blowing their tops now!

A: **mule, The**
Q: What hybrid do an ass and horse produce?
W: That's a cross between a male ass and female horse. When a female ass and male horse mate, a hinny is the offspring. It's smaller than a mule but just as cute!

A: **murder, A**
Q: What's a row of crows called?
W: The non-crow version of Murder's Row is: Babe Ruth, Lou Gehrig, Tony Lazzeri, and Bob Meusel of the 1927 New York Yankees.

A: **mushroom, The**
Q: What fungus has a crown, spores, gills, and a stalk?
W: Mushrooms, which often grow from the ground like small umbrellas, are among the best known of the plants called fungi. They have thin bladelike gills on the underside of the cap from which spores are shed. The body consists of the cap and stalk.

A: **My son**
Q: Who's this man: "Brother and sisters I have none, but this man's father's my father's son"?
W: Think of it this way: "My father's son" is either yourself, hypothetically, or your brother. Now taking this into account, if "this man's father" is either myself or my brother, "this man" could be my son or my nephew. "Brothers and sisters I have none" is not just there to confuse you, but to help you.

N

A: **NaCl**
Q: What's the chemical formula for table salt?
W: Common table salt, also known as sodium chloride, is a simple ionic compound formed from the bonding of the positively charged sodium and the negatively charged chloride. All we know is that it's great on french fries, with catsup, of course!

A: **Napalm**
Q: What do gasoline and napthenic and palmitic acids combine to form?
W: It becomes a thickened mixture that burns more slowly and can be propelled more precisely and to much greater distances than can gasoline in flame throwers. It was developed by U.S. scientists during World War II.

A: **Napoleon's**
Q: Whose army were canned foods developed to feed?
W: The principle whereby perishable foods could be preserved in sealed containers was discovered by Parisian confectioner, Nicholas Appert. He developed the process in response to an offer made by the French government in 1795 of a 12,000 franc prize. He did not use metal containers; rather, he employed glass bottles.

A: **Narcissism**
Q: What's the psychiatric term for self-love?
W: In Greek mythology Narcissus was a youth who pined away in love with his own reflection in a pool of water. He was turned into a flower that now bears his name.

A: **narwhal, The**
Q: What tusked creature helped embellish sailors' tales of unicorns?
W: The narwhal is a small whale that lacks a dorsal fin and has only two teeth, both at the tip of the upper jaw. The left tooth of the male develops into a straight tusk that protrudes forward from the upper lip.

A: **National Audubon Society, The**
Q: What U.S. society arose in 1905 to protect wildlife?
W: State audubon societies arose in the late 1800s for the protection of native birds. In 1905 the National Association of Audubon Societies was incorporated, and in 1940 it became the National Audubon Society. It is one of the oldest conservation organizations in the U.S. Headquartered in New York, it has expanded its purpose to preserving a unified natural environment of animal and plant life.

A: **National Geographic Society, The**
Q: What's the world's largest non-profit scientific and educational organization?
W: By the 1970s, it boasted a membership of more than 5,500,000. That's a lot of people paging through magazines looking at naked African tribal women!

A: **Near-sighted**
Q: What are you if you're myopic?
W: Myopia is caused by an eyeball that is longer than normal from front to rear, thereby causing the image of a distant object to focus at a point in front of the retina, where it should normally focus.

A: **neck, The**
Q: Where's the thyroid gland?
W: More precisely, it's the endocrine gland in the throat below the voice box that secretes hormones vital to metabolism and growth.

A: **Nectar**
Q: What do bees collect?
W: Nectar is the raw material used by the honeybee to produce honey. It is mainly a watery solution of the sugars fructose, glucose, and sucrose. The sugar content varies from 3 to 80 percent, but bees rarely gather nectars having less than 15 percent sugar content.

A: **Neil Armstrong**
Q: Who said: "The surface is fine and powdery"?
W: Following his famous "One small step for man...one giant step for mankind" line, Armstrong commented on the moon's surface, observing that his foot sank into the fine, powdery substance.

A: **Nescafe**
Q: What was the first instant coffee?
W: Nescafe was introduced by Nestle's of Vevey, Switzerland in 1938 after eight years of research. The process of reducing coffee beans to a soluble powder was undertaken at the suggestion of the Brazilian Institute of Coffee in 1930.

A: **neutron bomb, The**
Q: What's called a radiation enhancement weapon by the Pentagon?
W: Couldn't verify this one, and no one at the Pentagon was available for comment!

A: **Never**
Q: How often are brain cells replaced?
W: Alcohol and old age deplete your brain cells. This way an old drunkard can barely remember his own name!

A: **New York**
Q: What was the first city with more than one TV station?
W: In 1936 RCA, which owns NBC, installed televisions in 150 homes in New York City and broadcast a cartoon of *Felix the Cat* as its first program. All the national networks based themselves in New York and resumed broadcasts shortly after World War II, at first to the eastern seaboard, then coast-to-coast in 1951. The first city with two educational channels was Pittsburgh.

A: **New York and San Francisco**
Q: What were the first U.S. cities linked by a transcontinental phone line?
W: This demonstration occurred on Jan. 25, 1915, when Alexander Graham Bell, in New York, made a historic call to his assistant, Thomas Augustus Watson, who was in San Francisco.

A: **Nicolas Copernicus**
Q: What Pole is considered the father of modern astronomy?
W: He was the first astronomer to challenge Ptolemy's view that the earth was the center of the universe. By observing the heavens and employing his great mathmetical skill, he demonstrated that the earth revolved around the sun, not the other way around.

A: **Nicolas Copernicus**
Q: What Polish astronomer demonstrated in 1512 that the sun is the center of the solar system?
W: In 1512 Copernicus distributed a manuscript that briefly described his explanation of the planet's revolutions. It was not until 1543, one week before his death, that his definitive masterpiece became published and his name public. He did, however, restrict himself to the ancient theory that planetary orbits were circular or perfect. Not until Galileo did the framework of our solar system did it become fully understood.

SCIENCE AND NATURE

A: **Nine**
Q: How many sides does a nonagon have?
W: That's right! It's a closed plane figure having nine sides and nine angles.

A: **Nine**
Q: How many zeros are there in a billion?
W: A billion is a thousand million. If you have that much of anything, who's going to care how many zeros there are?

A: **Nine**
Q: What's considered the luckiest number worldwide?
W: The reasons are unending! It symbolizes the absolute completeness and end of a cycle. It is also symbolic of truth as it ever produces itself, i.e., twice $9 = 18$, $1 + 8 = 9$; 3 times $9 = 27$, $2 + 7 = 9$; 4 times $9 = 36$, $3 + 6 = 9$; and so on. Early Egyptians identified nine celestial spheres, and a Christian choir of angels is nine.

A: **Nine**
Q: What's the minimum number of bars on an abacus?
W: The abacus is a calculating device of Babylonian origin. An expert practioner can compete against many modern calculating machines.

A: **Ninety**
Q: How many degrees are there in a right angle?
W: In a triangle the other two angles must add to 90 because all triangles must total 180 degrees. In a four sided figure, the angles total 360 degrees.

A: **No**
Q: Is a spider an insect?
W: They are not insects and are no nearer to insects than reptiles are to birds. Spiders belong to the class of Arachnida, which includes scorpions, mites, and ticks, and differ from insects. Although they have feelers or antennae as do all insects, they also have four pairs of legs and two pairs of jaws, while insects have three pairs of legs and three pairs of jaws.

A: **No**
Q: Do beavers eat fish?
W: Beavers are rodents that never eat fish or any other animal food. They subsist entirely on a vegetable diet consisting principally of bark and tender roots.

A: **Noise**
Q: What does a phonophobe fear?
W: *Phono* indicates "sound" or "voice," *phobe* is the Greek word for "fear."

A: **North Pole, The**
Q: Where's the hub of the world, according to the International Flat Earth Society?
W: ...And the "contrasting" hub, if you flipped the flat earth over, would be the South Pole. We wonder if everybody would fall off?

A: **North Pole, The**
Q: Which pole gets more sunlight, the North Pole or South Pole?
W: The North Pole experiences six months of complete sunlight and six months of total darkness each year.

A: **North Pole, The**
Q: Which Pole tilts toward the sun between June 21 and Sept. 21?
W: Summer begins in the Northern Hemisphere when the summer solstice occurs on June 20 or 21, and this is the day when there are more hours of sunlight in this hemisphere than on any other day of the year. The sun is directly over the equator on the vernal and autumnal equinoxes, Mar. 20 or 21 and Sept. 22 or 23, respectively. The North Pole is tipped toward the sun from the beginning of spring, the Vernal Equinox, through the beginning of fall, the Autumnal Equinox, which is about Mar. 20 through Sept. 22.

A: **nose, The**
Q: Where are cows' sweat glands?
W: A cow will sweat freely on the end of her nose. The perspiration that appears on her body is usually slight and almost imperceptible.

A: **nose and paws, The**
Q: What are the only two places that dogs have sweat glands?
W: Dogs sweat very little. The limited amount of sweating occurs almost wholly on the soles of the feet where the largest sweat glands are located. The popular notion that dogs perspire through the muzzle is incorrect. There are no sweat glands in that region. The secretion on the muzzle comes from the lateral nasal gland.

A: **Nose prints**
Q: What prints are used by breeders and trainers to identify dogs?
W: This is still done to some degree; however, a more common practice is to tattoo a number inside the dog's ear.

A: **Nothing**
Q: What does a nihilist believe in?
W: Nihilism is a metaphysical doctrine that states that nothing exists, is knowable, or can be communicated. It is from the Latin *nihilum*, "nothing."

AND NATURE

A: **November**
Q: What, translated literally, is the ninth month?
W: This is from the Latin *novem*, "nine," the ninth month of the Roman calendar.

A: **Oil pollution**
Q: What did Thor Heyerdahl report seeing on 43 of 57 days at sea aboard the *Ra II*
W: Thor Heyerdahl sailed the *Ra II* from Safi, Morocco, to Barbados in July 1970. Madami Ait Ouhanni, one of the crew, collected samples of the oil clots floating all over the Atlantic.

A: **Omnivorous**
Q: What adjective describes an animal that eats both plants and animals?
W: The bear, the brown rat, and the opossum are examples of omnivores. A carnivore is an animal that eats chiefly meat. Most carnivores prey on herbivores, animals that eat plants.

A: **On a map**
Q: Where might you find Mercator's Projection?
W: Mercator was the 16th-century Flemish cartographer who put the lines on the map that became known as meridians and parallels of latitude running at right angles. As you move away from the equator in either direction, the distance between latitudes increases.

A: **One**
Q: How many astronauts manned each Project Mercury flight?
W: Project Mercury flights began March 5, 1961, and ran through 1963. There were six Mercury flights in all, involving these astronauts: Alan Shepard, Virgil Grisom, John Glenn, Scott Carpenter, Wally Schirra, and Gordon Cooper.

A: **One**
Q: How many days does a typical mayfly live?
W: The mayfly is a dainty insect with lacy wings and a slender tail. It is not a true fly, because it only has two wings instead of four. The adult mayfly survives only a few hours or days; however, it lives as a nymph or young mayfly for a few months to two years in the water. When it leaves the water, it sheds its skin and becomes a subadult. After a few hours as a subadult, it sheds its skin and becomes a full-fledged adult!

A: **One**
Q: How many humps does an African camel have?
W: True, but the backbone of the single-humped camel is not curved upward in the middle, as many people suppose. It is as straight as the backbone of a horse. Humps on camels are composed chiefly of fat.

A: **One**
Q: How many months does it take the moon to revolve around the earth?
W: Close...the actual time is 29 days, 12 hours, and 44 minutes. The moon rotates on its own axis every 27 days, 7 hours, and 43 minutes. Its days and nights are about 14 earth days each.

A: **One**
Q: How many queen bees reign in a hive?
W: A good colony, roughly estimated, may contain as many as 50,000 workers, a few hundred drones, and only one queen. The queen bee lays the eggs that hatch into the workers. The queen does not rule the colony but is the force that holds it together. The workers are small females that do all the work. The drones, male honeybees who do no work and have no sting, develop from unfertilized eggs. The only function of the drone is to mate with the queen.

A: **One**
Q: How many times a year does a penguin have sex?
W: The largest penguin, the emperor, begins the ritual of courtship and marriage early in April. After finding the right mate and waiting a month, they consumate the marriage and an egg hatches 25 days later after their one and only coition. They never leave one another until the eggs are laid. Most species lay their eggs on bare ground or in grass. The female emperor penguin lays one egg on land at the start of the Antarctic autumn and returns to the water. The male keeps it warm for two months until it hatches, then feeds it with a milk-like substance produced in his throat. The female returns after the chicks are hatched and takes over caring for them. Within six months the chicks can take care of themselves.

A: **One and seventeen**
Q: What are the only two numbers that will divide into seventeen evenly?
W: Seventeen is one of the prime numbers, that is, numbers only divisible evenly by themselves and one. Other examples are 2, 3, 5, 7, 11, 13, 17, etc. The number 2 is the only even prime number.

A: **One and zero**
Q: What two numbers on a telephone dial don't have letters?
W: Dial zero for operator. The number one has no letters assigned. Do you know which letters do not appear on the telephone dial? They are Q and Z. All other letters in the alphabet are present.

A: **One day**
Q: What do you gain by crossing the international date line to the east?
W: The international date line is an imaginary line on the earth's surface

that marks the spot on the earth's surface where each new calender day begins. It follows the 180th meridian in the Pacific Ocean for the most part. There is a 24-hour difference between the two sides of the date line. Saturday is just beginning on the eastern side and just ending on the western side, and it's noon at the prime meridian in Greenwich Village.

A: One percent
Q: What percentage of the earth's water is drinkable?
W: Ninety-seven percent of the earth's water is in the oceans and is too salty to be used for drinking, farming, or manufacturing. Of the 3 percent that is fresh water, over 2 percent is locked in glaciers and icecaps, and about half of one percent is below the earth's surface. Rivers and lakes contain about one fiftieth of one percent of the earth's water.

A: One year
Q: How long does it take the typical hen to lay 19 dozen eggs?
W: Hens and some ducks can lay up to 350 eggs in a single year, which is a few more than 19 dozen! Egg production in domestic hens today continues all year whereas their ancestors laid only during the spring months.

A: One-billionth of a minute
Q: What is a nanominute?
W: *Nano-* means "dwarf, extreme smallness," and is now used as one billionth of a measure, e.g., nanominute. This is from the Greek *nanna*, "aunt," to *nannas*, "uncle" to *nan(n)os*, "little old man, dwarf."

A: One half
Q: What's the square root of one quarter?
W: The square root is a number that when multiplied by itself produces the given number. In this case, .5, or one half, multiplied by .5 is .25, or one quarter.

A: One ninth
Q: What fraction of an iceberg shows above water?
W: One eighth to one tenth of the total mass of the iceberg is above water. Icebergs form where chunks of ice break away from a glacier as it flows into the sea. The sun and wind melt the top, while the bottom under water melts more slowly. Icebergs are formed by frozen fresh water; thus, they have often been used by sailors as an emergency supply of fresh water.

A: One sixth
Q: What fraction of the earth's gravity is the moon's?
W: The earth's gravity is the force that causes objects to fall when they are dropped. The surface gravity of the moon is one sixth that of the earth. Newton and Einstein both expounded on the theory of gravitation.

A: One third
Q: What fraction of a person's life passes in sleep?
W: That's assuming you sleep an average of eight hours a day over the period of your lifetime.

A: opium poppy, The
Q: What plant is opium derived from?
W: Processors near poppy farms make poppy juice into raw opium, a brownish powder also known as refined opium. They also extract a yellowish powder called morphine base from the opium. Poppy farms can be found in India.

A: opossum, The
Q: What's the only native North American marsupial?
W: Marsupials are those animals that have pouches. The most easily recognized marsupials are the Australian kangaroos and koala bears.

A: optic nerve, The
Q: What nerve carries signals from the retina to the brain?
W: The optic nerve is the second cranial nerve in man and serves the sense of light. The two optic nerves, one from each eyeball, converge at the optic chiasma on the undersurface of the brain. The retina is the light sensitive membrane lining the inner eyeball and connected to the brain by the optic nerve.

A: orchid, The
Q: What plant does natural vanilla flavoring come from?
W: The aromatic vanilla beans can be found in any of various tropical American orchids.

A: *Origin of the Species, The*
Q: What book is subtitled *The Preservation of Favoured Races in the Struggle for Life*
W: Obscure! This book was written by Charles Darwin and published in 1859. Darwin served as a naturalist with the HMS *Beagle* expedition from 1831 to 1836. The study of specimens collected during this time convinced him that modern species had evolved from earlier ones.

A: Orion
Q: What constellation represents a hunter with club and shield?
W: Traditionally, when Orion rose at dawn, it was taken as a sign of summer approaching. If Orion arose in the evening, it was a sign of winter and storms. Grape picking season was signaled by Orion arising at midnight.

A: Orville
Q: Which of the Wright brothers flew their plane, based on the toss of a 50-cent piece?

W: According to our information, both of the Wright brothers had flown the first heavier-than-air plane on the historic day of Dec. 17, 1903, near Kitty Hawk, North Carolina. Orville was first, covering a distance of 120 feet in about 12 seconds. Wilbur made the longer flight that day, covering 852 feet in 59 seconds.

A: **Orville and Wilbur Wright**
Q: Who were the first two members elected to the U.S. Aviation Hall of Fame?
W: The U.S. Aviation Hall of Fame was recently created by an Act of Congress and is located in Dayton, Ohio. Orville and Wilbur were also elected to the Hall of Fame for Great Americans, located on the Bronx campus of New York University. The criteria for election are that the person was an American, lived in America, and has been dead for at least 25 years. Wilbur Wright was elected in 1955, Orville in 1965, setting a precedent for having been dead for only 17 years when elected.

A: **Orville Wright**
Q: Who flew for 43 years without a pilots license?
W: The first pilots licenses were issued on Jan. 1, 1910, to pilots who had flown up to the end of 1909. Sixteen licenses were issued in alphabetical order to avoid any suggestion of precedence. Orville must not have gotten around to taking the test!

A: **Orville Wright**
Q: Who was the pilot in the first fatal plane crash?
W: On Sept. 9, 1908, Orville was piloting a test plane in Virginia. He managed to attain an altitude of 120 feet and remain aloft for one hour and two minutes. Later his right propeller blade struck a wire that attached to the rear rudder. The plane crashed and Orville broke a few bones. His passenger, Thomas Selfridge, however, died three hours after the crash from a fractured skull.

A: **Oscar**
Q: What's the international radio code word for the letter *O*
W: Some more code words are as follows: *Y* = Yankee; *J* = Juliet; *N* = November; *P* = papa; *Q* = Quebec; and *R* = rodeo.

A: **ostrich, The**
Q: What bird has a 46-foot-long small intestine?
W: The ostrich has three stomach segments with a gut up to 14 meters long. One meter is 39.37 inches so we get 45.9 feet. Close, real close and long, very long

A: **ostrich, The**
Q: What bird lays the largest egg?
W: The ostrich's egg averages six inches in length and five inches in diameter and weighs up to three pounds. That would make you cluck, alright!!

A: **ostrich, The**
Q: What's the only bird that gives us leather?
W: The ostrich hide produces a soft, finely-grained leather. But they don't give it up willingly. You have to take it from them!

A: **Oxygen**
Q: What gas did Joseph Priestley discover in 1774?
W: Actually, a Swedish scientist, Carl Scheele, discovered oxygen in 1772. The English scientist, Priestly, made the discovery independently in 1774 and published his findings the same year, three years before Scheele published his discoveries.

A: **Paleontology**
Q: What is the study of fossils called?
W: This word is from the Greek word *palai*, meaning "long ago." Paleozoology is another word for this study of fossils and ancient life forms.

A: **palm, The**
Q: Where is the line of life?
W: Palmistry is the practice of reading hands to gain knowledge about personality and past and future life events. It is believed to have begun in India and spread through Europe via the nomadic gypsies. The life line is said to give an indication of how long a person will live.

A: **Palm trees**
Q: What do dates grow on?
W: Egypt, Iran, and Iraq lead in world production of dates. In the U.S. dates are grown in Arizona and southern California. Indio, California, has a yearly festival at which the many varieties are exhibited. The leaves of the date palm tree are used for the celebration of Palm Sunday.

A: **pancreas, The**
Q: What organ contains the islands of Langerhans?
W: They are a type of secretory tissue named for the 17th-century German pathologist, Paul Langerhans. The pancreas is responsible for the secretion of insulin and glucagon, hormones that control the amount of sugar stored in the body.

A: **Panther**
Q: What's another term for a black leopard?
W: Leopards are often called panthers, especially in India. In black form it is more commonly called a black panther. But the most famous of all is the Pink Panther!

A: Paper patterns for dresses
Q: What did Ellen and Ebenezer Butterick invent and first sell in 1863?
W: These paper patterns for dresses and other clothing were manufactured in Sterling, Massachusetts. Four years later Butterick and Company was formed with official headquarters on lower Broadway in New York City.

A: Parasite
Q: What's the term for an organism that lives on or in another?
W: This word is from the Greek word *parasitos*, meaning "fellow guest." A parasite is a biological term for an organism that grows, feeds, and is sheltered on or in another organism while contributing nothing to the survival of its host.

A: Paris
Q: What city did Jacques Garnerin make the first parachute jump over in 1797?
W: On Oct. 22, 1797, to be precise. He was released from a balloon at a height of 2,230 feet.

A: parking meter, The
Q: What meter was invented by C.C. Magee in 1935?
W: It was developed to provide cities with revenue, but he had difficulty selling the idea. The first one was installed in Oklahoma City, Oklahoma, in July 1935 and caught on elsewhere immediately.

A: Pate de foie gras
Q: What delicacy comes from the fattened livers of geese?
W: The word *pate* is French meaning "paste," *foie* means "liver," and *gras* is "fat or greasy". The literal translation is a "pie of fat liver." And some call it a delicacy!

A: pea, The
Q: What's the oldest known vegetable?
W: Although usually classified with other vegetables, peas are a member of the legume family. It appears that beans, peas, bottle gourds and water chestnuts were grown in North Thailand in 7000 B.C. and pumpkins and gourds in the Americas at the same time. When you go back that far, who knows "oldest"!

A: peacock's, The
Q: What bird's feathers does superstition say should never be in a house as a decoration?
W: This prejudice can be traced to the early days when they adorned the holy temple and only the priest dare touch them. It was not "right" for any custom confined to the priesthood to be carried out by the layman. In Egypt and Rome, the unlucky feathers were considered to be an emblem of the "evil eye."

A: Peahens
Q: What do peacocks mate with?
W: The peacock is the male bird, the peahen is the female, and peafoul is the correct terminology for either. The male has the long train of greenish feathers, growing from its back not its tail, which spreads into a gorgeous fan. The peahen lays ten or more brownish eggs at a time in a nest in a protected spot on the ground.

A: Pekingese, The
Q: What's the royal dog of China?
W: The Pekingese is a toy dog of a breed developed in China. It has a flat nose, long-haired coat, and short, bowed front legs.

A: penguin, The
Q: What bird can swim but can't fly?
W: Penguins, which cannot fly, use their featherless wings like paddles to propel themselves beneath the surface of the water. Most observers describe their wing motion as "flying under water".

A: People
Q: What does an anthropophagist eat?
W: No doubt about it – we're talking cannibalism here!

A: Permafrost
Q: What's permanently frozen subsoil called?
W: This word comes from *perma*(nent)*frost*. It is continuous in the polar regions and occurs locally in perennially frigid areas.

A: perpetual motion machine, A
Q: What invention does the principle of conservation of energy make impossible?
W: Perpetual motion is the hypothetical continous operation of an isolated mechanical device or other closed system without a sustaining energy source. However, a self-generating, self-perpetuating power that overcomes friction would be contrary to physical law. The principle of conservation of energy is that energy is uncreatable and indestructible in the course of nature. The U.S. Patent Office is so convinced that it can't be done that in order to get a patent for a perpetual motion device, one must submit a working model!

A: Pewter
Q: What alloy do tin and lead form?
W: Pewter is a tin base alloy used nearly 2,000 years ago by ancient Orientals and Romans. Old pewter has a dark satin sheen because the lead content causes it to darken with age. Modern pewter, tin hardened with antimony and copper, resists tarnishing. The best grades have no lead.

A: Pi
Q: What did an IBM 7090 computer calculate to 100,265 decimal places in 1961?
W: This word, from the Greek letter of the same name, is used as a symbol for the ratio of a circle's circumference to its diameter. The value is 3.1415, adinfinitum.

A: Pi
Q: What is 3.14159 better known as?
W: In 1873, William Shanks, an English mathematician, calculated Pi to 707 places. It took him 15 years to complete the calculations. In 1949, the first electronic computers

SCIENCE AND NATURE

calculated it to 2,035 places in three days! It found Shank had made a mistake on the last hundred or so figures.

A: **pineapple, A**
Q: What's the fruit of the Ananas comosus?
W: The pineapple, a tropical American plant of the family Bromeliad genus, Ananas, and species A. Comosus, has swordlike leaves and a large fleshy, edible fruit consisting of flowers fused into a whole. The earliest references to this fruit are by Columbus and Sir Walter Raleigh, who found it growing in the West Indies. It was introduced to Africa, India, and other tropical areas by the Portugese

A: **Pink**
Q: What color is yak's milk?
W: We read everything there is on yaks and finally called the Brookfield Zoo near Chicago, Illinois, to confirm this answer. According to the librarian at the zoo, yak's milk is a rich, golden color because of the presence of butterfat. The only likely reason it could be pink is if the liquid portion of the blood were leaking into it! We did find one source that said it had been "advised" that yak's milk was pink…but no scientific source!

A: **Pink or red**
Q: What color does litmus paper turn if a solution is acidic?
W: Litmus is a blue amorphous powder derived from certain lichens that changes to red with increasing acidity and to blue with increasing alkalinity.

A: **placebo's, The**
Q: What pill's name translated from the Latin means "I will please"?
W: This word is from the medieval Latin phrase *placebo domino in regione vivouim*, meaning "I shall please the Lord in the land of the living". In the Roman Catholic church, it is the service of vespers for the dead. In medicine, it is a substance containing no medication and given to humor the patient or to serve as a control in an experiment.

A: **Pluto**
Q: What planet did Percival Lovell discover?
W: Lovell never discovered Pluto. He only predicted the existence of the planet in 1915. He did this by noticing that some unknown and unseen body was acting on and affecting the orbits of Neptune and Uranus. He set out to find this unknown planet by using a telescope to photograph the area where he believed it to be. He died Nov. 12, 1916, years before his assistants "discovered" the planet Pluto in 1930.

A: **Pluto**
Q: What planet travels around the sun every 248 years?
W: The planet named Pluto, after the Roman God of the Dead, has the longest orbit around the sun. It is, however, not always the farthest planet from the sun. Every 248 years, the same amount of time it takes to orbit the sun, Pluto falls within Neptune's orbit of the sun, making Neptune the outermost planet.

A: **polar bear, A**
Q: What kind of animal is a *nanook* in the Eskimo tongue?
W: Eskimos often have one or more words for an animal depending on whether the animal is young or old, in water or on land, etc. For example, *nanuark* is a baby polar bear, *atertak* is the cub polar bear on his way to the sea for the first time. The polar bear is a flesh-eating bear of the far north that lives on ice floats in the cold waters of the Artic Ocean. A full grown bear may be as much as nine and half feet long and weigh as much as 1,000 pounds or more.

A: **Poles**
Q: What are the two ends of a magnet called?
W: In physics, a pole is a force that attracts or pushes away other forces. The law of poles is that like poles repel each other and unlike poles attract each other. Compasses were used for many years before Dr. William Gilbert showed in the 1600s

that the earth itself was one huge magnet and attracted the ends of the magnetic needle of the compass.

A: **Polio**
Q: What does Salk vaccine prevent?
W: Poliomyelitis, also called polio and infantile paralysis, is a disease caused by viruses that results in muscular paralysis. Jonas E. Salk of the University of Pittsburgh was the first to develop a vaccine to prevent polio. It was declared safe and effective in 1955. Albert E. Sabin developed another vaccine that can be taken orally. It was approved for use in the U.S. in 1960.

A: **Poodle**
Q: What's the most popular registered dog in America?
W: The poodle originated in Germany in the 1500s and was once used as a hunter and retriever. In 1978 the American Kennel Club had 101,100 new poodle registrations. More poodles were registered than any other dogs, followed by doberman pinschers.

A: **Post meridiem**
Q: What is P.M. an abbreviation for, as in 5 P.M.?
W: According to the U.S. Naval Observatory, 12 M is almost universally used to designate 12:00 noon. In this connection, *M* comes from the Latin word *meridies*, meaning "midday." The correction abbreviation to indicate after midday is P.M.

A: **potato, A**
Q: What's a California Long White?
W: There are several varieties of potatoes that differ according to the size, shape, and texture of the tuber.

A: **Project Mercury**
Q: What was the name of the U.S.'s first manned space program?
W: The umbrella name for these missions was Mercury. The first mission was named Mercury-Redstone 3 with Alan Shepard aboard as the first American in space. There were six Mercury Project flights, the last also being the longest. The duration of the Mercury Atlas 9 Mission was 34 hours, 19 minutes, and 49 seconds. Gordon Cooper made 22 orbits of earth.

A: **Proof**
Q: What's the standard of strength of distilled alcoholic liquors called?
W: The alcoholic content of some beverages is measured in proof, which is about twice the percentage of alcohol by volume. A 90-proof whiskey contains about 45 percent alcohol.

A: **prune, A**
Q: What's a dried plum?
W: Only a few varieties of plums are capable of being converted into prunes. Most plums, if dried with the pits in them, will ferment and sour in the process. Any plum that has sufficient sugar in its substance to dry without souring is called a prune.

A: **Pulverized tobacco**
Q: What is snuff?
W: Snuff is a fine powder made from the stems and leaves of the tobacco plant. The tobacco is fermented, dried, and ground. At one time, each person carried a snuffbox, and it was considered proper etiquette to offer a "pinch" upon meeting another individual.

A: **Purple**
Q: What's the most common color of amethyst?

W: Amethyst, also known as the "bishop's stone" because of its wide use in the bishop's ring, is a violet-blue variety of crystalline quartz. The word *amethyst* is composed of two Greek words meaning "not to be drunk," because the ancients believed this stone would keep the wearer sober.

A: **python, The**
Q: What's the world's longest snake?
W: Thank heavens this snake lives in the East Indies and southeastern Asia, because its 30-foot body would be a little uncomfortable should it be wrapped around you! The stories about these huge snakes are that they squeeze victims out of shape and break their bones. Actually a python suffocates the prey by wrapping itself around the victim and not allowing it to breathe.

A: **Quadrilateral**
Q: What's the term for any four-sided figure?
W: This term comes from the Latin words *quadri* meaning "four" and *later* meaning "side."

A: **Quasars**
Q: What are quasi-stellar radio sources better known as?
W: The abbreviation is QSRS. A quasi-stellar object is a member of any of several classes of starlike objects having exceptionally large red shifts that are often emitters of radio frequency as well as visible radiation.

A: **Quebec**
Q: What's the international radio code for the letter Q?
W: The International Telecommunication Union is a specialized agency of the UN that developed from the International Telegraph Union established in 1865. Its headquarters are in Geneva, Switzerland, and it establishes regulations for the international use of telegraph, telephone, and radio communications. Quebec is the established code for "Q".

A: **Quinine**
Q: What's added to water to make tonic water?
W: Quinine is a bitter, colorless, amorphous powder derived from certain cinchona barks. Cinchona is a variety of trees and shrubs native to South America.

A: **R. Buckminster Fuller's**
Q: Whose brainchild was the geodesic dome?
W: Richard Buckminster Fuller was expelled twice from Harvard! He developed the geodesic dome, a structure of tetrahedrons or octohedrons assembled to approximate a sphere. It is the only type of large dome that can be set directly on the ground as a complete structure. The U.S. exhibition dome for Expo '67 held in Montreal, Canada, was a geodesic dome.

A: **Ra**
Q: Who was the sun god of ancient Egypt?
W: Also known as Re or Phra, this god of the sun and of creation was one of the most important Egyptian gods. He had a falcon head and became the official god of the Pharoahs.

A: *Ra II*, **The**
Q: What was the name of the craft Thor Heyerdahl sailed from Morocco to Barbados in July 1970?

W: Heyerdahl's first voyage was on *Kon-Tiki* in 1947 when he sailed from South America to Polynesia, proving the possibility that the Polynesians may have originated in South America. In 1969 on *Ra I* he tried to sail from Morocco to South America but failed because of design defects. The following year he made the trip on *Ra II*, a facsimile of an Egyptian reed boat.

A: **Rabies**
Q: What disease do the French call *la rage*
W: Rabies is an infectious viral disease of the central nervous system usually spread among domestic dogs and wild contagious animals by a bite. Infected dogs and animals show a type of restlessness or nervousness; hence, *la rage*.

A: **Ragweed**
Q: What plant is the commonest cause of hay fever?
W: Ragweed is the common name for weedy plants of the genus Ambrosia. The small drooping flower heads produce large amounts of pollen that aggravate hay fever conditions. Hay fever is a seasonally recurrent allergy to the pollen of certain plants, chiefly those depending on the wind for cross-fertilization, including the ragweed of the U.S. and timothy grass in Great Britain.

A: **Rainfall**
Q: What does a pluviometer measure?
W: It is a rain gauge. The word comes from the Latin word *pluvia* meaning "rain."

A: **ram, The**
Q: What's the symbol for the zodiacal sign Aries?
W: The signs of the zodiac were named from the 12 constellations as they coincided with the dates in the time of the astronomer Hipparchus about 2,000 years ago. Aries governs those born between Mar. 21 and Apr. 19.

A: **rattlesnake, The**
Q: What venomous serpent is known as "the Gentleman Among Snakes"?
W: The rattlesnake is the one species of venomous snake that gives warning before it strikes, and because of this characteristic, it is sometimes referred to as "the gentleman among snakes." Some gentleman! His bite will kill ya!

A: **Red**
Q: What's the most common color of garnet?
W: The word *garnet* comes from the Latin word *granatum* that alludes to the resemblance to the red seeds of the pomegranate. Garnets show great ranges of color including colorless, black, and many shades of red and green.

A: **Red**
Q: What's the primary color with the shortest name?
W: Customarily, the primary colors are considered to be as follows: red, green, and blue. Lights of red, green, and blue wavelengths may be mixed to produce all colors.

A: **Red and green**
Q: What two colors does a color-blind person have trouble distinquishing?
W: A color-blind person may also have difficulty distinguishing blue. Blindness to red is called protanopia; confusion in distinguishing red from green is called deuteranopia. Blindness to the color of blue is called tritanopia. Color-blindness affects men more than women, about 20 to 1.

A: **Red and white**
Q: What are the two kinds of blood corpuscles in vertebrates?
W: A corpuscle is a cell that is capable of free movement in a fluid as distinguished from a cell fixed in tissue. The red cells, erythrocytes, permit the blood the carry sufficient oxygen to sustain life. The white blood cells, leukocytes, are primarily concerned with defense mechanisms. There are also platelets, the smallest cells of the blood, which are instrumental in the coagulation of the blood.

A: **Resistance**
Q: What's the term for opposition to an electrical current in a conductor?
W: It is a force that retards the motion of the current. This part of the circuit transforms electric energy into heat energy.

A: **Rhubarb and asparagus**
Q: What are the only two perennial vegetables?
W: Perennials are plants having a life span of two or more years as opposed to annuals, which must be planted anew each year. Try this one: there are two definitions of fruits versus vegetables. Botanically, when you eat that portion of a plant containing seeds, you are eating a fruit. When you eat some other part of the plant, you are eating a vegetable! Popularly, the definition of fruit is what you eat for dessert, whereas what you eat with the meal is a vegetable. Hence, the confusion on the tomato!

A: **Rice**
Q: What grows in a paddy field?
W: Rice is an edible starchy cereal grain, the origin of which has been traced to India around 3000 B.C. Rice is grown in paddy fields that are submerged under two to four inches of water.

A: **Rice**
Q: What's Japanese *sake* made from?
W: Sake is a strong Japanese beverage made from fermented rice. The word *sake* is the Japanese word for "liquor." It is the national beverage of Japan and is sipped warm from a small porcelain cup.

A: **Richard J. Gatling**
Q: Who invented the machine gun in 1862?
W: 1861, by our sources! Gatling developed the gun to assist the North in the Civil War; however, it was four years before he succeeded, so it was too late for effective use in this war.

A: **Richter scale, The**
Q: What scale measures earthquakes?
W: Developed by the U.S. seismologist Charles F. Richter, it has an intensity range of 0 to 10. The largest earthquakes to date have not exceeded 8.6.

A: **right, The**
Q: What bank lies to the left of a canoeist paddling upstream, the left or the right?
W: This comes from the direction of the river. The left bank is on your left going downstream and on your right when you are going upstream.

A: **right, The**
Q: Which ear can most people hear better with?
W: Most people put the telephone to the left ear, possibly because they take notes with the right hand. However, it is a fact that most people hear better with the right ear. Ever notice how a mechanic will cock his right ear toward the engine of your car while listening for the oddball noise that you're trying to explain you keep hearing?

A: **Ripen**
Q: What doesn't a pineapple do after it's picked?
W: Oranges are another of the skinned fruit that does not ripen or improve in taste after being picked.

A: **Robert Fulton**
Q: Who called his steamboat the *Clermont*
W: *Robert Fulton did not* call his steamboat *Clermont*, the name by which it is known in most history books. The vessel that inaugurated passenger service between New York and Albany in 1807 was registered as the *North River Steam Boat*. Her sailing port, however, was Clermont, New York.

A: **Robert H. Goddard**
Q: What American is considered the pioneer of modern rocketry?
W: Robert Goddard launched the first liquid-fueled rocket in the U.S. in 1926.

A: **Roman, The**
Q: What civilization invented the arch?
W: The Egyptians and Greeks knew of the arch but considered it unsuitable for monumental architecture so it was rarely used. The Romans, however, used the semicircular arch widely in bridges, aqueducts, and large-scale architecture.

A: **Roman gods**
Q: What are most of the solar system's planets named for?
W: Here they are: Pluto for the Roman God of the Dead; Neptune for the God of Oceans, Earthquakes, and Tidal Waves; Mercury for the Messenger of the Gods; Venus for the Goddess of Love and Beauty; Mars for the God of War; Jupiter for the Roman name for Zeus, the leader of the Gods; Saturn for the God of Agriculture; and last, but not least, Uranus for the earliest supreme God, a personification of the sky.

A: **Rope**
Q: What was the Bridge of San Luis Rey made of?
W: This bridge was built in 1350 A.D. and crossed the Apurimac River in Peru. It was suspended 118 feet above the river and stretched 148 feet from bank to bank. The bridge collapsed in 1890. This particular bridge spawned Thornton Wilder's book *The Bridge of San Luis Rey*.

A: **Rosetta Stone, The**
Q: What 40-inch piece of black basalt unlocked the secret of Egyptian hieroglyphics?
W: The stone was found in 1799 by an officer in Napolean's army near the village of Rosetta, Egypt. The stone was divided into three separate sections, one being a historical account in Greek and the other two in hieroglyphics and demotics. The Greek account stated it was exactly the same as the Egyptian section thus enabling scholars to decipher the mysterious ancient Egyptian carvings.

A: **roulette wheel, The**
Q: What wheel did Blaise Pascal invent in a search for perpetual motion?
W: *Roulette* is French for "small wheel," and one of several stories about its origin is that it was developed by Blaise Pascal in 1655. Others believe that it was an old Chinese game.

A: **Rubber**
Q: What substance did Joseph Priestly name for its ability to erase pencil marks?
W: Joseph Priestly was the first Unitarian minister and also one of the discoverers of the element oxygen. He was the first to mention the use of the eraser, popularly called rubber or "lead eraser." Hyman Lipman of Philadelphia obtained patent No: 19,783 on March 30, 1858 for the pencil with a groove at one end into which was "secured a piece of prepared rubber".

SCIENCE AND NATURE

A: Saccharin
Q: What did Ira Remsen discover in 1879, perhaps proclaiming: "How sweet it is!"?
W: The discovery of saccharin was reported by Constantine Fahlberg and Professor Ira Remsen at Johns Hopkins University, Baltimore, Maryland, on Feb. 27, 1879.

A: Saccharin
Q: What's 550 times sweeter than cane sugar?
W: This commercial product has 500 times the sweetening power of table sugar. A .25 grain pellet is equal to a teaspoon of sugar. It was used by diabetics and others who needed to avoid sugar intake. Saccharin was banned in the U.S. following laboratory studies showing it caused cancer in rats.

A: Sagittarius
Q: What sign of the zodiac covers Nov. 22 to Dec. 21?
W: The symbol of this sign is a centaur shooting a bow and arrow or an arrow drawn across a bow. This ninth sign of the zodiac governs those born between Nov. 22 and Dec. 21.

A: Sahara, The
Q: What desert has the highest sand dunes?
W: The dunes of the Sahara Desert are the most impressive feature of the desert. Many of them, the Whalebacks, are 100 miles long, two miles wide, and 200 feet high. The Sahara's level varies from the Qattara Depression in Egypt, which is 436 feet below sea level, to the Emi Koussi Mountain in Chad, which is 11,204 feet high.

A: Sailor's heaven
Q: What's fiddler's green?
W: This is from a poem by Marryat: "At Fiddler's Green, where seamen true, When here they've gone." Another source expands on this and defines it as "a place of unlimited rum and tobacco."

A: Salad dressing
Q: What do dilute acetic acid and vegetable oil make?
W: Vinegar is an impure dilute solution of acetic acid obtained by fermentation beyond the alcohol stage.

A: Saliva
Q: What substance must mix with food to give it taste?
W: Saliva has many functions including lubricating and moistening the inside of the mouth to help with speech, and changing food into a liquid or semisolid mass that can be tasted and swallowed more easily.

A: Salt
Q: What's the most widely-used seasoning in the world?
W: Common table salt is sodium chloride. Cakes of salt have been used as money in Ethiopia, elsewhere in Africa, and in Tibet. In Roman times, an allowance of salt was made to officers. Later the salarium, from which the English word "salary" is derived, was converted into an allowance of money for salt.

A: Samuel Colt
Q: Who perfected the first American revolver?

W: Colt carved a wooden revolver that he patented in 1835 but his guns didn't become popular until the 1840s.

A: Samuel Morse
Q: Who sent the first telegraph message, in 1844: "What hath God wrought?"?
W: Samuel Morse developed the first successful electric telegraph in the U.S. and invented the Morse code on May 24, 1844. Morse strung the telegraph line from the U.S. Supreme Courtroom in Washington, D.C., to Baltimore, Maryland, and tapped out on the telegraph his famous message.

A: Sand
Q: What's the main ingredient in glass? W: Glass is made chiefly from sand, soda, and lime. Glassmakers mix together a large amount of sand and small amounts of the other materials to give the glass special qualities. Materials are mixed in a large furnace until it is a syrupy mass. When it cools, it becomes glass.

A: sandstorm, A
Q: What are you caught in if a "haboob" blows up?
W: The wind-driven sand forms a low cloud above the ground. Most of the sand does not rise higher than 20 inches during sandstorms; however, winds reach speeds of up to ten miles per hour or more. Most sandstorms

occur in the sandy areas of deserts and reduce visibility. The sand moves by a jumping or bouncing motion. When the wind gains speed, grains of sand roll forward and collide with other grains causing many of them to bounce upward.

A: Saturday
Q: What day of the week sees the most fatal car accidents?
W: Statistics maintained by the National Safety Council reveal that most fatal car accidents do occur on Saturdays.

A: Saturday
Q: What's the only day named for a planet?
W: Technically Saturday, but Wednesday does come from Old English "Woden", which translated is "Mercurii." Monday = Moon day; Tuesday = Tiw day (god of war); Thursday = Thor's day; Friday = beloved, free, not in bondage; Sunday = day of the sun.

A: Saturn
Q: What's the second-largest planet in the solar system?
W: Saturn's diameter at its equator is 74,600 miles, approximately ten times that of earth. The largest planet, Jupiter has a diameter of 88,700 miles.

A: Saturn, Uranus and Neptune's
Q: What three planets' first letters spell "sun"?
W: Here's another cutie using the first letters of planets: *V*enus, *E*arth, *N*eptune, *U*ranus, and *S*aturn – you get Venus!

A: Scales
Q: What reptilian feature evolved into feathers?
W: A scale is a small plate that forms part of the skin of an animal. Feathers, unique to birds, apparently evolved from the scales of the bird's reptilian ancestors. The many different types of feathers are variously specialized for insulation, flight, and sensory reception.

A: Scurvy
Q: What sailors' disease resulted from a deficiency of Vitamin C?
W: Scurvy is one of the oldest nutritional disorders. It became a major cause of disability and mortality among sailors on long sea voyages. In 1753, Scottish naval surgeon James Lind showed that scurvy could be cured and prevented by the use of citrus juice. That's why British sailors are sometimes called limeys.

A: Seat belts
Q: What became mandatory equipment on U.S. cars on March 1, 1968?
W: Although seat belts are mandatory equipment, few states have laws making it mandatory to use them. A Swedish study showed that an 85 to 90 percent reduction in fatalities occurred when a combined lap and seat belt were used.

A: Seeds
Q: What's missing from a navel orange?
W: They have an "outie" navel. That's how they got their name!

A: September
Q: What month features the harvest moon?
W: Harvest moon is the name given to the full moon that occurs nearest the autumnal equinox of the sun around Sept. 23. The moon rises at about the same time for several nights and shines with such brightness that farmers in northern Europe and Canada can work until late at night to take in the fall harvest.

A: September
Q: What month were you born in if your birthstone is chrysolite?
W: Chrysolite (olivine) is the ancient birthstone for September while sapphire is the modern stone.

A: Sequoya
Q: What Cherokee Indian gave his name to a tree?

W: The Cherokee Indian, Sequoya, invented a system of writing for his people after 12 years of work. The large trees found in Sequoia National Park in California are named after him.

A: Seven
Q: How many colors are there in a rainbow?
W: Rainbow colored arcs are seen in the skies when the sun or moon is illuminating large numbers of falling raindrops. The seven colors are violet, indigo, blue, green, yellow, orange, and red.

A: Seven
Q: How many colors are there in the spectrum?
W: The term spectrum is applied to any class of similar entities or properties strictly arrayed in order of increasing or decreasing magnitude. The seven colors are violet, blue, green, indigo, yellow, orange, and red.

A: Seven
Q: How many minutes does it take the typical person to fall asleep?
W: When a person falls asleep all activity decreases, the muscles relax, and the heartbeat and breathing rate slow down. Sleep is a period of rest in which the sleeper loses awareness of his or her surroundings.

A: Seven
Q: How many sides does a heptagon have?
W: A heptagon is a seven-sided polygon. A polygon is a closed plane figure bounded by three or more line segments.

A: Seven
Q: How many stars are there in Big Dipper?
W: The Big Dipper is part of the constellation known as Ursa Major or Great Bear, consisting of seven stars. Four stars form the bowl of the dipper while the remaining three stars form the handle.

SCIENCE AND NATURE

A: **Seven**
Q: How many tenths of the earth's surface lie under water?
W: Our sources say .75 so if you guessed eight tenths, you could be correct as well.

A: **Seven**
Q: How many years of bad luck follow breaking a mirror?
W: The superstition can be traced back to the days when there were no looking glasses. Each house had a pool set in a marble frame in the courtyard that served as a looking glass. A vicious rival wishing to bring bad luck upon a girl would throw a pebble at the reflection. This superstition carried through to the breaking of a mirror.

A: **Seven**
Q: What number did Adolf Hitler believe possessed supernatural power?
W: He favored this number so much that he planned major military battles for the 7th of the month. More trivia: an ancient Buddhist symbol that represents, among other things, the wheel of life was the basis for the Nazi swastika.

A: **Sex "a trois"**
Q: What is troilism?
W: Troilism is sexual play or an activity practiced by a group of three persons, either by two men and a woman or by two women and a man.

A: **shark's, The**
Q: What fish's skin was once used commercially as sandpaper?
W: The internal skeletons of sharks are comprised of cartilage. Bony parts are found in the scales. When stroking the skin of a shark, one generally has the impression of rubbing sandpaper because of the many pointed teeth protruding from the skin of many species.

A: **She was the first dog in space**
Q: What was the claim to fame of Laika, the Russian bitch?
W: Laika flew aboard Sputnik 2, the USSR's second space shot that took place Nov. 5, 1957. Laika was the first earth creature to inhabit a space capsule.

A: **She was the first test tube baby**
Q: What was the claim to fame of Louise Joy Brown, born July 25, 1978?
W: Louise weighed 5 pounds, 12 ounces and was delivered by cesarian section in Oldham General Hospital, Lancashire, England.

A: **She was the first woman in space?**
Q: What's Valentina Tereshkova's claim to fame?
W: She was also the first person in space who was not trained as a pilot. She was aboard Vostok 6, part of the Soviet Union's first "manned" space flight program. Her flight lasted about 70 hours as she orbited the earth 48 times.

A: **sheep's, The**
Q: What animal's fleece yields lanolin?
W: Lanolin is wool fat or wool grease, especially in a refined condition. It is much used as a basis for ointments, lotions, and cosmetics.

A: **shell, The**
Q: What constitutes 12 percent of an egg's weight?
W: The shell consists of 98 percent calcium carbonate and phosphate and 2 percent organic matter. The white or albumen of the egg makes up nearly half the total weight. The shell *does* account for 12 percent!

A: **Shellac**
Q: What resin used in varnish is a secretion of the lac insect?
W: Lac is an important ingredient of sealing wax, dyes, varnishes, and lacquers. The lac insects are cultivated in northern India and secrete this resinous substance. The word *lak* means "hundred thousand" in Persian, referring to the vast number of insects required to produce lac.

A: **Shells and mollusks**
Q: What does a conchologist study?
W: This is from the Greek *konkho*, "shell." What more is there to say?

A: **Shredded wheat**
Q: What was the first ready-to-eat breakfast cereal?
W: Shredded wheat was produced in Denver, Colorado in 1893 by Henry Perky. He began manufacturing it in a factory in Worchester, Massachusetts, in 1895.

A: **shrew, The**
Q: What's the smallest mammal?
W: A shrew is mouselike in form, but is most closely related to moles. Some shrews are only two inches in length. They are chiefly nocturnal, feeding mostly on worms and insects.

A: **Shrove Tuesday**
Q: What's the day before Ash Wednesday?
W: On this day it was formerly customary in England for people to confess their sins to a priest and afterward to dine on pancakes. This custom of eating pancakes and ringing a bell is still kept up in parts of England. The pancakes seem to have become particularly associated with Shrove Tuesday because people wanted to use up the grease, lard, and other goods they had on hand that were forbidden during Lent. *Mardi Gras*, the French name of Shrove Tuesday, literally means "Fat Tuesday."

A: **Siamese**
Q: What kind of cats are seal points and blue points?
W: Siamese cats are a short-haired breed of cat originally from Siam. The cat is born white or cream colored and later develops the dark

points on its ears, face, legs and tail. If the points are dark brown, they are called seal point; if they are blue-gray they are called blue points.

A: Sigmund Freud
Q: Who founded psychoanalysis?
W: During the years 1892 to 1895 Freud developed his psycho-analytical method using the technique of free association. It is the process of revealing the subconscious thoughts of an individual by inducing him to relate without restraint the complete details of his life's experiences, in order to detect hidden mental conflicts that may produce disorders of mind or body.

A: Sigmund Freud
Q: Who published *The Ego and the Id* in 1923?
W: Sigmund Freud's last major contribution to psychoanalytic theory was *The Ego and The Id*, in which he elaborated on the concept of the superego. In the project, he had assumed that the inhibiting ego processes were conscious and that those of id were unconscious. The superego was a part of the ego that did not involve consciousness. The superego, the result of parental criticism and prohibitions, was Freud's version of conscience.

A: silkworm, The
Q: What worm prefers the mulberry?
W: The silkworm is a moth whose larva spins a large amount of strong silk in constructing its cocoon. Its cultivation was introduced into western Asia and Europe early in the Christian era and into America during the colonial period. The leaves of the white mulberry are fed to the silkworm in China.

A: Sirius, or the Dog Star
Q: What's the brightest star in the night sky?
W: Sirius is a star whose rising and setting with the sun gives name to the dog days, July to early September, when the hot sultry weather of summer occurs in the Northern Hemisphere. The ancient Egyptians

noted that the time between the first rising of Sirius each year occurred at intervals of 365.25 days, not 365. A correction in the length of a year was later incorporated into the Julian Calendar (leap year).

A: Six
Q: How many feet are there in a fathom?
W: Fathom is used for measuring the depth of water by soundings. Fathom also is used to measure by extending the arms for cables and cordage.

A: Six
Q: How many more weeks of winter are there if a groundhog sees his shadow?
W: Groundhog Day is February 2. If the groundhog sees his shadow, superstition has it that there will be six more weeks of winter; however, statistics don't bear this out. The tradition stems from the English Candlemas.

A: Six
Q: How many sides does a cube have?
W: A cube is a solid body with six equal sides.

A: Six
Q: How many sides does a hexagon have?
W: A hexagon is a polygon (plane) of six angles and, therefore, six sides.

A: Six
Q: How many sides does a snowflake have?
W: It is said that no two snowflakes are identical. Most recognizable as a typical snowflake is a six-pointed star. Other common shapes are the column, the needle, and the hexagon.

A: Six
Q: How many times a day does the typical person go to the bathroom?
W: This doesn't even include the times that a person goes to the comfort station, rest room, washroom,

lavatory, water closet, latrine, can, johnny, head, loo, and toilet! Our sources say a man goes six times during an average workday. Could be he doesn't like his job!

A: Six
Q: How many times thicker than water is blood?
W: Red cells form about 45 percent volume of the blood's volume and plasma about 55 pecent. The color of red cells is due to the iron-containing respiratory pigment, hemoglobin. If all the iron was extracted from the hemoglobin in a man's body, there would be enough to manufacture a 2.5 inch nail. And yes, blood is indeed six times thicker than water!

A: Sixteen
Q: What's 40 percent of 40?
W: Any way you see it, it still comes up 16.

A: Sixtieth
Q: What is the diamond anniversary?
W: In case you missed getting an engagement ring, ladies, hang in there! Diamonds are the hardest natural substance. The most valued diamonds are colorless and made of pure carbon.

A: Sixty
Q: How many nautical miles are there in one degree of longitude?
W: The earth is not a perfect sphere; therefore, the nautical mile is any of various units of distance used for sea and air navigation based on the length of a minute of arc of a great circle of the earth.

A: Sixty-eight degrees Fahrenheit
Q: What's room temperature?
W: If you like a cool room!

SCIENCE AND NATURE

A: **Skin**
Q: What is shed when you des-quamate?
W: A human being sheds skin con-tinually, replacing it with a new outer layer once every 28 days.

A: **skin, The**
Q: What is by far the largest organ of the human body?
W: Skin protects the soft, watery protoplasm found in all living cells. There are two layers, an inner layer and an outer layer. They are a shield against germs, cuts, and bruises. Skin is also a message center, picking up sensations of touch, pressure, pain, heat, and cold. The skin is the largest single organ measuring 2,800 square inches on the average per-son.

A: **Skull features**
Q: What does a phrenologist feel and interpret?
W: A phrenologist believes the con-formation of the skull is an indication of mental faculties and character. Franz Joseph Gall, Viennese physiologist, assumed that the bumps on the skull represented areas of the brain that were particularly well-developed.

A: **skunk, The**
Q: What's the smelliest member of the weasel family?
W: The skunk is known for its power of ejecting an offensively odorous secretion produced in two muscular walled perineal glands. When a skunk is alarmed, it stamps its forefeet, then raises its tail with the tip hanging down. Finally, it raises the tip of the tail and ejects the fluid for which it is well-known. The skunk is also referred to as the polecat or zorrino.

A: **sleepwalker, A**
Q: What's a somnambulist?
W: A somnambulist is a person who is asleep but performing actions ap-propriate to the waking state.

A: **sleuth, A**
Q: What's a group of bears called?
W: Bears have heavy bodies and short, strong legs and are able to stand upright and grasp things with their front paws. Because bears are so large, their only enemies are other bears and man. They do not normal-ly attack man unless provoked or in-jured, or if their young are in danger. A group of bears is also referred to as a sloth.

A: **Smell**
Q: What sense is most closely linked to memory?
W: The sense of smell is heavily in-volved with taste. The loss of the sense of smell is called anosmia, while hyperosmia is the increased sensitivity to odors. There is also a condition called parasmia, that relates to someone who has a distorted sense of smell. Some men-tally ill people complain of olfactory hallucinations, meaning they smell substances that are not present. As far as the link with memory is con-cerned, think about the advertising slogan "Let Windsong whisper your name!"

A: **Smell**
Q: Which of the five senses develops first?
W: ...but as early as the third month of life in the uterus, the fetus has been shown to react to a touch.

A: **Smoking is a health hazard**
Q: What did the U.S. surgeon general conclude on Jan. 11, 1964?
W: Federal laws require all cigarette packages to contain a warning, and cigarette advertising has been bann-ed from radio and television for some years now.

A: **sneeze, The**
Q: What bodily function can reach the breakneck speed of 200 miles an hour?
W: Sneezing is a reflex act, a sud-den, violent spasmodic and audible expiration of breath, chiefly or wholly through the nose.

A: **Someone choking on food**
Q: Who would you use the Heimlich maneuver on?
W: Using the Heimlich maneuver, you stand to the victim's back, reach around and thrust inward and up-ward with your locked hands just below the ribs below the breastbone. By squeezing the upper abdomen and lower chest, you are forcing the diaphragm – the band of muscle bet-ween the chest and abdomen – up so that air is pushed out of the lungs. This will pop the object out of the air-way. If no help is near by, a victim should attempt to perform this maneuver on himself by pressing his own fists upward into the abdomen.

A: **South**
Q: What direction is the Sahara ex-panding in by half a mile a year?
W: Buy land now!!

A: **Southern Lights, The**
Q: What's another name for the Aurora Australis?
W: The Aurora Australis is a luminous phenomenon in the Southern hemisphere. This light usually appears in ascending streamers, often in a fan shape. When this phenomenon assumes a waving appearance, the streams of light are called "Merry Dancers." *Australis* is the word for "southern," as opposed to *borealis*, which is "northern"; Aurora borealis is the northern lights.

A: **Space Shuttle *Columbia*, The**
Q: What did John Young and Bob Crippen take into orbit   On April 11 and 12, 1980, the space shuttle *Col-umbia* succeeded in its first flight. Since then, it has changed from an experimental research vehicle to an operational space transport. The main objective of *Columbia*'s first four missions was to prove that a reusable manned spaceship could in-deed work.

A: speed of light, The
Q: What does the c stand for in the equation $E = mc^2$?
W: In 1675 Olaus Roemer of Denmark had the theory that light has finite velocity. The speed of light was then established for the first time with a value of about 140,000 miles per second. The equation is "energy equals the mass times the speed of light squared." This law of physics was put forth by Albert Einstein in 1905.

A: speed of sound, The
Q: What must be exceeded to produce a sonic boom?
W: Sonic means having a speed approaching or equalling that of sound in air, approximately 738 miles per hour at sea level. A sonic boom is a loud transient explosive sound caused by the shock wave preceding an aircraft traveling at supersonic speeds.

A: speed of sound at sea level, The
Q: What is Mach 1?
W: The Mach scale is used to express speeds faster than sound, with Mach 1 equal to the speed of sound. The speed of sound is not constant since it depends on the substance through which the sound waves are passing and on temperatures.

A: spleen, The
Q: What's removed in a splenectomy?
W: And the doctor that removes it then proceeds with an even more delicate surgery — a walletectomy, the removal of the dollars from your wallet!!

A: Spring
Q: What season begins with the vernal equinox?
W: When the sun is vertically above the equator the day is of equal length all over the earth. This happens twice a year. The vernal equinox is in March, the start of spring, and September brings the second equinox.

A: Sputnik I
Q: What was the first manmade satellite put into orbit?
W: Sputnik I was launched Oct. 4, 1957. At the time, Soviet scientists released no details about the launch except for the fact that it had been accomplished. It wasn't until 1967 that the basic launch vehicle was displayed. It had a total of 16 rockets.

A: Sputnik's
Q: What satellite series' name is Russian for "Fellow Traveler"?
W: Sputnik was a series of Soviet earth-orbiting satellites. Sputnik I, launched Oct. 4, 1957, was the first of the series. The satellite was the size of a beachball, about 23 inches. Sputnik is the Russian word for "traveling companion.'

A: Stainless
Q: What type of steel did Englishman Harry Brearley invent in 1913?
W: Stainless steel is any of a large and complex group of corrosion-resistant iron-chromium alloys, containing 10 percent or more chromium. It also occasionally contains other elements, such as nickel, silicon, molybdenum, tungsten, and niobium.

A: Stalagmite
Q: What's the term for a limestone deposit rising from the floor of a cave?
W: Stalagmite is a conical structure, usually composed of calcium carbonate, formed upward from the floor of a cave by the action of dripping water.

A: Stanley Steamer, The
Q: What automobile was known as "The Flying Teapot"?
W: More than 100 American companies manufactured steam automobiles. The most famous steam auto was made by Abner Dobe and by the Stanley twins, Francis and Freelan. Their later models were popular American cars until the mid-1920s. In 1906, the brothers built a steam car that broke the world's record for the fastest mile — 28.2 seconds...a "flying teapot."

A: "Star of India, The"
Q: What's the world's largest sapphire?
W: "The Star of India" is a blue-gray sapphire that weighs 563 carats. The "Star of Asia" is a blue sapphire that weighs in at 330 carats. However, the largest we found is a 1,318 carat head of President Abraham Lincoln. It was carved from a 2,302 carat stone found in Australia in 1935.

A: steer, A
Q: What is a castrated bull called?
W: Castration is the removing or inhibiting the function or development of the testes. A steer is a male bovine animal castrated before sexual maturity.

A: Stomach
Q: What's tripe on a menu?
W: Tripe is the first or second stomach of a ruminant, especially an ox, prepared as food. Tripe is the light-colored rubbery lining of the stomach often used for food. Sounds delicious!

SCIENCE AND NATURE

A: Stonehenge
Q: What is widely considered to be man's first celestial observatory?
W: In the 18th-century B.C., Stonehenge, a celebrated stone circle on Salisbury Plain in Britain, was erected on some unknown astronomical rationale.

A: Stones
Q: What do Englishmen weigh themselves in?
W: Stones, a unit of mass in common use in the United Kingdom, equal 14 pounds.

A: Straight
Q: What's the shape of a camel's spine?
W: The bumps of camels are fatty tissues, not bone. As a pack and saddle animal, the camel has no equal and has been used since early times.

A: styptic pencil, A
Q: What kind of pencil writes "finis" to bleeding?
W: A styptic pencil has the power of contracting organic tissues and contains an ointment that arrests bleeding, especially after shaving!

A: Sugar
Q: What's the main ingredient in Coca-Cola after water?
W: There are five teaspoons of sugar in each small bottle of Coca-Cola. Coca-Cola is a registered trademark of the company, but only the first half of the Coca-Cola is protected. Other soft drink companies are free to use the "cola" part

A: Sugar cane
Q: What plant is rum made from?
W: Sugar cane, the source of more than 50 percent of the world's annual sugar production, is a stout, perennial grass plant characterized by two ranked leaves and a many-jointed stalk with a terminal inflorescence in the form of a silky panicle.

A: Summer
Q: What season is hail most prevalent in?
W: Hail is precipitation in the form of balls or irregular bumps of ice, always produced by convective clouds, nearly always cumulonimbus. Hail can range from the size of a pea to that of a grapefruit.

A: Summer
Q: What season is statistically the most hazardous?
W: You are most active in the summer season, and more things can go wrong as a result of this increased activity.

A: Summer
Q: When are shadows shorter, in summer or winter?
W: In summer the sun shines most directly upon any region. Shadows are caused by the sun coming at an angle toward an object; thus, they are shortest in the summer.

A: sun, The
Q: What celestial body has a diameter of 864,000 miles?
W: Our sun is the nearest star. Stars are composed of intensely hot gasses deriving their energy from nuclear reactions going on in their systems. The sun's fuel supply, hydrogen, is estimated to last another five billion years. It is the most massive body in our solar system.

A: sun, The
Q: What does a heliologist study?
W: The sun seems to have been formed over six billion years ago from a cloud of hydrogen mixed with small amounts of other substances that had been manufactured in the bodies of other stars before the sun was born. This word *heliologist* comes from the Greek word *helios*, meaning "sun."

A: sun, The
Q: What's the nearest star to Earth?
W: The surface area of the sun is approximately 12,000 times that of the earth. Compared to other stars, the sun is just a bit below average in size and temperature. Stars are self-luminating, self-contained masses of gas, whereas planets are non-luminous bodies, illuminated by a star, such as the sun, around which they revolve.

A: Sunday
Q: What's the first day of the week?
W: The week was often merely the interval between market days and varied between four days in West Africa to ten days with the Incas. The seven-day week is of Jewish origin. The word Sunday comes from the Old English *sunnandaeg*, meaning "day of the sun." It is the weekly memorial of Christ's resurrection from the dead on the first day of the week.

A: sundial, A
Q: What is a shadow clock?
W: A sundial is an instrument used for telling time by the sun. It is composed of a stylus that casts a shadow and a dial plate on which hour lines are marked and upon which the shadow falls.

A: Swallow
Q: What does the typical person do 295 times during the dinner hour?
W: Swallowing is the passage of chewed food from the mouth through the throat and esophagus into the stomach. It is a complicated reflex that begins by muscular action under the control of the brain and then is continued the rest of the way automatically. Next time you eat, try to count your swallows!

A: Swallows
Q: What are supposed to return to the San Juan Capistrano mission every March 19?
W: A professor of zoology at UCLA, and others, indicate that the swallows are merely following a typical pattern of bird migration. The swallows have been recorded as arriving at this southern California mission anywhere from the last week in February to the last week in March! So much for the song!

A: **swan, A**
Q: What bird is the offspring of a cob and a pen?
W: A swan is any of several species of large waterfowl comprising the subfamily Anatidae. They are herb eaters with stout bodies, long necks and spatulated bills. A male swan is the cob, a female the pen. In some species, the cob takes his turn at brooding. The young offspring are called cygnets.

A: **Sweet, sour, salt, bitter**
Q: What four tastes can a human distinguish?
W: These four tastes are distinguished by the tongue; the other flavors we taste are detected by our noses. Although all normal people can taste the four basic flavors, some persons are unable to taste substances that to others have a very distinct flavor. This is governed by inherited characteristics. Some scientists claim so little is known about taste that it may well be that we do taste more than these four with our tongues.

A: **Syphilis**
Q: What disease did August von Wassermann develop a specific test for in 1906?
W: Syphilis is a highly contagious venereal disease, worldwide in incidence. The greatest rate of increase of the disease in the U.S. is among teenagers and adults with casual sexual habits. Congenital syphilis can be transmitted during pregnancy by an infected mother to the unborn child and can result in spontaneous abortion, stillbirths, or death. The test developed by Wasserman, a German bacteriologist, is still used today.

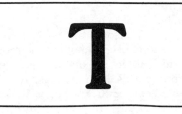

A: **tail, The**
Q: What section of an airplane gives you the bumpiest ride?
W: Our research only indicated that seats in the rear have a higher noise level, but anyone who has ridden in the tail section will attest to the fact that the ride is bumpiest there. Why else would they put first class in the very front!

A: **Tango**
Q: What's the international radio code word for the letter T?
W: In the International Telecommunication Union phonetics, some other letters are: *A*, alpha; *B*, bravo; *C*, Charlie; *D*, delta; *E*, echo; *F*, foxtrot; *G*, golf; and *H*, hotel.

A: **Tarot cards**
Q: What deck of cards includes the Wheel of Fortune, the Lovers, and Death?
W: Tarot cards, a set of 22 pictoral playing cards, are used for fortune-telling and as trump to the card game tarok, an old popular card game played in central Europe. The modern tarok game uses 32 suit cards, 21 tarots (permanent trump), and a joker.

A: **Teeth**
Q: What do frogs have in their mouths that toads don't?
W: Teeth on the jaws of some frogs enable them to grasp and subdue their prey. Most frogs do not use their forelimbs to force the morsel into the mouth. Whenever toads, all of them toothless, manage to snare any animal that does not readily fit into the mouth, however, their forelimbs invariably hasten the operation.

A: **telephone, The**
Q: What bears U.S. patent No. 174,465?
W: Which matches the number of pages on the new phone bills! The patent was issued to Alexander Graham Bell on March 7, 1876. He started to write the specifications for the telephone in September 1875. The telephone was the subject of the most involved patent litigation in history.

A: **Temperature**
Q: What does the Kelvin scale measure?
W: The Kelvin scale was developed by William Thomsom, Lord Kelvin, in 1848 and is a scale based on the assumption that absolute zero, the state of no thermal energy, could be attained. The scale is primarily used in thermodynamics. A little trivia: Thomson entered the University of Glasgow at age ten and published two mathematical papers at the ages of 16 and 17!

A: **Ten**
Q: How many grams make up a dekagram?
W: Ten grams, or a dekagram, in the metric system equals approximately 0.035 ounces in U.S. measure.

A: **Ten**
Q: How many sides does a decagon have?
W: A decagon is a ten-sided polygon, it has ten angles and ten sides.

A: **Ten**
Q: How many tentacles does a squid have?
W: Some squid are active predators of the high seas. The horny rings around some of the suckers on the tentacles have been modified into arranged hooks of various lengths. Two rows of their hooks on the terminal end of each tentacle are effective grasping organs.

A: **Ten**
Q: What is statistically the safest age of life?
W: The safest period of life is from age five to age 15. Persons in this age group are too young for drinking, driving, and heart attacks; most of them have been vaccinated against the typical childhood diseases such as rubella and mumps; and the infectious diseases, e.g., smallpox and measles, that claimed so many lives years ago have been virtually eradicated.

A: **Testicles**
Q: What does a polyorchid man have at least three of?
W: This is from the Greek *polus*, "much or many, more than one or more than usual"; and the Greek *orkhis*, "testicle." The orchid plant also takes its name from *orkhis* because of the shape of its root.

A: **Testicles**
Q: What does a stallion have that a gelding used to?
W: The stallion is a mature male horse. A gelding has been castrated.

A: **They were the original Siamese twins**
Q: What's the claim to fame of Chang and Eng Bunker?
W: Chang and Eng Bunker, born April 15, 1811, in Bangesaco, Siam, were joined at the waist by a cartilaginous band about four inches long and eight inches in circumference. They grew to be about 5'2" in height, and since they faced the same direction, they could walk, run, and swim. They were married to Misses Sarah and Adelaide Yates in 1843. Chang fathered ten children and Eng had nine children. They died within three hours of each other on Jan. 17, 1884. Siamese twins are twins born with their bodies joined together in any manner.

A: **They're webbed**
Q: What's distinctive about a palmiped's feet?
W: Webbed feet have a membrane between digits and are found in many birds and amphibians.

A: **Think**
Q: What is IBM's motto?
W: T.J. Watson, Sr., IBM's first president, chose "Think" as the motto. He insisted on a "rah-rah" atmosphere at sales meetings, which included company fight songs! IBM is the acronym for International Business Machines.

A: **third, The**
Q: What is the leather anniversary?
W: In the Modern Wedding Anniversary Gift List the third anniversary means crystal or glass. Leather is considered a gift for the ninth anniversary. However, in the traditional guide to gifts, leather is appropriate for the third anniversary.

A: **Thirteen**
Q: How many people seated at a table is considered bad luck?
W: Fear of number 13 is called tredecaphobia. It is said to come from the Last Supper where 13 dined, one of whom later betrayed Christ.

A: **Thirty**
Q: How many degrees are there in each house of the zodiac?
W: The zodiac is a band around the celestial sphere, including the apparent annual path of the sun as seen from the earth and also the orbit of the moon and principal planets apart from Pluto. The band was divided by the ancient Greeks into twelve parts, each 30 degrees wide, known as the sign of the zodiac.

A: **Thirty**
Q: What's the square root of 900?
W: The square root of a number is a number that times itself gives you the desired figure. 30 times 30 is 900; pull out your calculator if you don't believe us!

A: **Thirty-two**
Q: How many compass point names are there?
W: The compass is a device for determining directions by means of a magnetic needle or group of needles turning freely on a pivot and pointing

to the magnetic north. The four major points are north, south, east, and west, which are further divided into northwest, southwest, then north-northwest, etc.

A: **Thirty-two degrees**
Q: What's the Fahrenheit equivalent of zero degrees centigrade?
W: ...and the boiling point of water, which is 100 degrees centigrade, is 212 degrees Fahrenheit. The freezing point of water is 32 degrees Fahrenheit or 0 degrees centigrade. Absolute zero is the lowest possible temperature at which all molecular motion would cease.

A: **Thomas Edison**
Q: What creative genius said: "Everything comes to him who hustles while he waits"?
W: He also said "Nothing that's good works by itself, you've got to make the damn thing work." Edison wasn't investigating just for the sake of inventing. In his own words: "Anything that won't sell, I don't want to invent."

A: **Thomas Edison**
Q: What inventor said: "Genius is one percent inspiration and 99 percent perspiration"?
W: Hard work was Edison's credo; it is reported that he lived on not more than five hours of sleep a night. In fact he collapsed working in his laboratory at the age of 84 and died two months later. As far as perspiration goes, Edison would sleep in his clothes; he believed that changing them or taking them off would cause insomnia. We bet he worked alone, often!

A: **Thomas Edison**
Q: What inventor was known as "the Wizard of Menlo Park"?
W: After discovering an electrical phenomenon, now called the "Edison Effect" in 1875, he moved to Menlo Park, New Jersey, to start a new laboratory. The "Edison Effect" led to creation of the wireless radio in 1876 in his new lab. He invented the

microphone, the telephone transmitter, and the first phonograph (1877). With the invention of the phonograph, Edison became known as "the Wizard of Menlo Park".

A: **Thomas Edison**
Q: Who died with more than 1,000 U.S. patents to his credit?
W: We can't list them all here, but some were the automatic telegraph, improved stock ticker, improved typewriter, microphone, phonograph, light bulb, electric generators, storage battery, motion picture camera...to name only a few!

A: **Thomas Edison**
Q: Who filed for the first patent in America for a motion picture camera?
W: In 1891 Edison obtained patents for his kinescope. He bought the patent for the film projector from another inventor. On April 23, 1896, Edison showed his first motion pictures to the public in a New York City music hall. In 1913 Edison showed the first synchronized sound film.

A: **Thomas Edison**
Q: Who invented the stock ticker in 1870?
W: Edison didn't invent the stock ticker tape machine. It was invented

by Edward A. Calahan in 1867, who was given $100,000 for the purchase of its patent. Edison was living in the boiler room of the Stock Exchange at the time, he repaired the broken tape machines and eventually improved their design.

A: **Thomas Edison**
Q: Who patented the first phonograph?
W: It was his favorite accomplishment. Edison was partially deaf, because of an explosion from an experiment he was working on at the age of *six*! He had little knowledge of music and had originally planned that the phonograph would be used as a dictaphone and for education. It was even hoped to be used to record telephone messages.

A: **Thomas Edison**
Q: Who spoke the first recorded message: "Mary had a little lamb"?
W: These words were "recorded" on a fine piece of tinfoil wrapped around a cylindrical drum.

A: **Thomas Edison**
Q: Who was known as "the Prince of Light"?
W: After years of effort, Edison invented the light bulb on Oct. 21, 1879. Edison wintered in Fort Myers, Florida, and offered to install the first streetlights there at no charge. The City Fathers refused Edison's offer, because they thought it would keep the cows awake and they wouldn't give milk.

A: **Thor Heyerdahl**
Q: Who led the *Ra I, Ra II*, and *Kon-Tiki* expeditions?
W: Thor Heyerdahl was a Norwegian explorer who substantiated the diffusionist theory of anthropology with these trans-Pacific raft journeys. He won fame sailing the balsamwood raft *Kon Tiki* in 1947, from Peru to the Tuamotu Islands in eastern Polynesia. *RA II*, a papyrus red boat, sailed from Morocco to Barbados in the West Indies.

A: **Three**
Q: How many astronauts manned each Apollo flight?
W: Apollo space flight projects were designated as the U.S.'s efforts to land a man on the moon and return him safely to earth. The goal was completed successfully with Apollo 11 in July 1969. Six Apollo flights followed. The Apollo program closed with the rendezvous and docking of an Apollo spacecraft with the Russian Soyuz craft in earth orbit on July 18, 1975.

A: **Three**
Q: How many dimensions does a solid have?
W: A geometrical figure or element such as a cube has three dimensions: length, width, and depth.

A: **Three**
Q: How many dots are there in the symbol for "therefore"?
W: Correct, they are placed in the form of a triangle with two dots on the bottom and one on the top.

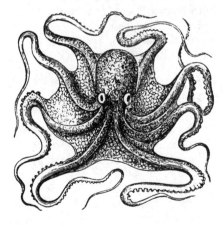

A: **Three**
Q: How many hearts does an octopus have?
W: Here's another interesting fact about them: a female octopus occasionally may look after a brood of up to 150,000 eggs. She circulates the water around the eggs, touches and cleans them and doesn't leave them the entire brooding time of one month. The female then usually dies, because she does not feed during the brooding process!

A: **Three**
Q: How many land miles are there in a league?
W: A league is a unit of measurement equal to three statute miles. So the story *20,000 Leagues Under the Sea* took place *way* down there!

A: **Three**
Q: How many pedals does a grand piano have?
W: Grand pianos vary in length from a five-foot baby grand to a nine-foot concert grand. It sits horizontally on legs and has a wing shape derived from the harpsichord. The metal pedals are suspended in a wooden frame known as a lyre. They provide further control over the damping mechanism and create infinite possibilities for modifying the timbre of the sound. The three pedals are the left pedal(soft), right pedal(loud), and the middle pedal(sustaining).

A: **Three**
Q: How many stars make up Orion's belt?
W: Orion was a hunter of Greek mythology. The constellation Orion represents a figure of a man with a sword by his side. Three stars in a line form his belt.

A: **Three**
Q: How many teaspoons make up a tablespoon?
W: The tablespoon is used as a cooking measure and consists of three teaspoons or four liquid drams.

A: **Three**
Q: How many times did John Glenn orbit the Earth?
W: The same number of months that he sought the Democratic nomination for president in 1984!

A: **Three**
Q: What's the cube root of 27?
W: The cube root is that number that multiplied by itself three times gives you the desired number: 3 times 3 times 3 equals 27.

A: **Three-dimensional**
Q: What kind of image does a hologram slide produce?
W: A hologram is a three-dimensional picture that is made on a photographic film or plate without the use of a camera. The picture consists of a pattern of interference produced by a split coherent beam of light; for viewing it is illuminated with coherent light from behind.

A: **Three dots, three dashes, three dots**
Q: What is SOS in international Morse code?
W: Morse code is either of two codes consisting of dots and dashes or long and short sounds used for transmitting messages by audible or visual signs.

A: **Three-quarters**
Q: What fraction pure is 18-carat gold?
W: Pure gold is 24 carats; 18 carat gold is six parts of alloy. A carat is a measure used to weigh precious stones and pearls.

A: **Three times a day**
Q: What does T.I.D. mean on a doctor's prescription?
W: This is from the Latin term *ter in die*, meaning "three times a day."

A: **Tiger**
Q: What's the largest feline?
W: The largest of the cat family is the long-furred Siberian tiger. Adult males average ten feet, four inches in length, stand 39 to 42 inches at the shoulder, and weigh about 585 pounds. (Don't call them, "Here, Kitty, Kitty"!)

A: **Time**
Q: What does a horologist measure?
W: Horology is the science of measuring time; a horologist is a person skilled in the practice or theory of horology.

A: **"Tin Lizzie," The**
Q: What was the nickname of the Model T Ford?
W: The Model T, a trademark for Ford automobiles produced from 1908 to 1928, was referred to originally as a symbol of simplicity, economy and dependability, and later as a symbol of the old-fashioned.

A: **TNT**
Q: What's the abbreviation for trinitrotoluene?
W: Trinitrotoluene is a high explosive made by treating toluene with nitric acid.

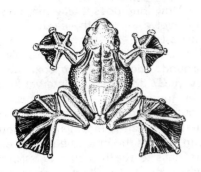

A: Toads
Q: Which have warts, frogs or toads?
W: That's accurate. The frog is a smooth-skinned, high leaper. But people having one tossed into their laps have been known to leap higher than either the frog or the toad!

A: toes, The
Q: What do vampire bats usually go for on sleeping humans?
W: Vampire bats have 20 teeth, all of which have razor sharp edges with which they cut into the skin of their prey, usually a warm-blooded animal. After drinking the blood, the bats retreat to their hiding places to digest their meal.

A: Toilet paper
Q: What was first marketed as Gayetty's Medicated Paper?
W: "…a perfectly pure article for the toilet and for the prevention of piles." Sold in 500 sheet packages for 50 cents in 1857, each sheet had Gayetty's name watermarked on it!

A: Tomatoes
Q: What are love apples?
W: Tomatoes are a tropical American plant of the potato family. It is a nutritious fruit that is pulpy, acidic, and usually red. Tomatoes are classified as fruits by botanists and sometimes called "love apples" because of a superstition that eating them made people fall in love.

A: tongue, The
Q: What's the strongest muscle in the body?
W: The tongue is the organ of taste and speech that also assists in chewing and swallowing of food. The tongue is composed mostly of muscle covered by mucous membrane. It is attached to the hyoid bone in the back of the throat and tapers forward to end loosely at the tip. Taste buds are located on the rear one third of the back of the tongue.

A: Tooth decay
Q: What's the most common non-contagious disease in the world?
W: Dental diseases are the most common noncontagious diseases in the world. Within the category of dental diseases, it is periodontal disease (disease of the gum and other supporting tissue) that ranks first as the cause of tooth loss, not tooth decay!

A: Topaz
Q: What is November's birthstone?
W: Topaz is a gem harder than quartz, transparent to translucent, and colored yellow, white, green, or blue.

A: Tortoises
Q: What creatures do the Galapagos Islands take their name from?
W: The really huge land tortoises live on two quite isolated and widely separated groups of islands: the Galapagos Islands off the western coast of South America and the Seychelles, north of Madagascar in the Indian Ocean. *Galapago* is the old Spanish word for these giant land tortoises.

A: Touch
Q: What is commonly considered the fifth sense?
W: The other four are sight, hearing, smell, and taste.

A: traffic light, The
Q: What first appeared at the corner of Euclid Avenue and East 105th Street, Cleveland, on Aug. 5, 1914?
W: It was erected by the American Traffic Signal Co. and was 15 feet tall. Red and green lights were used in association with a warning buzzer. The first traffic signal with red, green, and amber lights was brought into use in New York four years later.

A: Tuberculosis
Q: What disease was known as "the White Plague"?
W: This was probably suggested in contrast to the "black plague" because of the pallor associated with TB in its advanced stages and the great toll of life. During most of recorded history, TB has been among the most feared of human ills. It is one of the few human diseases that can be traced with certainty far back into antiquity, the infection having been found in the bones of Egyptian mummies. Now, because of better nutrition and living standards along with the use of modern drugs, it is no longer a major threat to life in the developed regions of the world.

A: turkey, The
Q: What's the dumbest domesticated animal?
W: The domestic turkey cannot survive without human care. Wild turkeys have larger brains and are livelier than domestic turkeys. A newborn domesticated turkey chick has to be taught to eat or it will starve. Domesticated turkeys tend to look up with their mouths open during rainstorms, and as a result, many drown. Now that's dumb!!

A: TWA
Q: What airline operates the tours at the Kennedy Space Center?
W: On the east coast of Florida is one of the most historic sites in the world, Kennedy Space Center. This is the site of the launchings and landings of the Space Shuttle. The Center also is the place from which men left the earth to walk and drive vehicles on the moon.

A: Tweed
Q: What fabric are Harris, Lewis and Donegal the leading examples of?
W: Tweed was originally called

SCIENCE AND NATURE

tweels, that is twills, but this name was mistakenly written "tweeds" by a London clerk in 1826. Tweed is a twilled woolen fabric used principally for suits and coats. Other examples of tweed fabrics are Scottish, Welsh, and Saxony. The names are often determined by the place of manufacturing and describe the color and weave.

A: **Twelve**
Q: How many sides does a dodecagon have?
W: A dodecagon is a regular figure or polygon consisting of twelve equal sides and angles.

A: **Twelve**
Q: How many zeros are there in a trillion?
W: In the U.S. and France a trillion is a thousand billions, in Great Britain and Germany a trillion has eighteen zeros. The U.S. trillion is 1,000,000,000,000 (it goes thousand, million, billion, trillion).

A: **Twelve**
Q: What's the base number in the duodecimal system?
W: Duodecimal is computing by twelves, or an arithmetical method of ascertaining the number of square feet and square inches in a rectangular area or surface whose sides are given in feet and inches.

A: **Twelve volts**
Q: What's the voltage of most car batteries?
W: Correct. Volt is the practical unit of electromotive force. Volt is named for Count Alessandro Volta, an Italian physicist.

A: **Twenty**
Q: How many matches are there in a standard book of matches?
W: Match books were invented by Joshua Pusey, a Philadelphia lawyer in 1892. His packages held 50 matches and the striking surface was on the inside cover, dangerously near the heads of the matches. The Diamond Match Company purchased Pusey's patent and made the book matches safe and usable.

A: **Twenty**
Q: How many times larger than life size is the Statue of Liberty?
W: Twenty times in height maybe, at 152 feet including the raised arm, but the weight is a little off at 225 tons! This statue represents liberty as a woman with a torch upraised in one hand and a tablet in the other. It is located in the Statue of Liberty National Monument, which includes Liberty Island and Ellis Island in New York Harbor.

A: **Twenty**
Q: How many years make up a vicennial period?
W: Vicennial is a period of 20 years; it comes from the Latin *vicies* meaning "20 times".

A: **Twenty-four**
Q: How many days will it be before a clock, losing 30 minutes a day, shows the right time again?
W: 30 minutes a day for 24 days will equal 12 hours lost, but the time will still be wrong if the clock has an AM-PM indicator!

A: **Twenty-four**
Q: How many letters appear with the numbers 2 through 9 on the telephone dial?
W: Correct; the two letters omitted on the phone are Q and Z.

A: **Twenty-one months**
Q: What's the gestation period of the elephant, within three months?
W: The female carries her baby for 20 to 22 months, longer than any other animal. A newborn calf weighs about 200 pounds at birth and stands three feet tall. A typical life span of an African elephant is 60 years. The largest reaches an average height of 10'6" for a male and 9'2" for a female. A 30-year-old male weighs nearly four and one half tons, and one about 60 years old was reported to weigh six tons.

A: **Twenty-seven days**
Q: How long does it take the moon to revolve around the earth, to the nearest day?
W: Although the moon revolves around the earth approximately every 27.33 days, the interval from new moon to new moon is two extra days. This delay is due to the fact that the earth is moving around the sun, so that the moon needs two extra days to reach a spot in its orbit where no part is illuminated by the sun, as seen from earth.

A: **Twenty-three**
Q: How many pairs of chromosomes does a normal human have?
W: Chromosomes are any of the small, elongated bodies in the cell nucleus that control the activity of the cell and play an important role in inheritance. Man has 22 pairs of autosomes and one pair of sex chromosomes for a total of 23 pairs of chromosomes.

A: **Twins, The**
Q: What's the symbol for the zodiacal sign Gemini?
W: Gemini is the third sign of the zodiac. People born between May 21 and June 21 are ruled by Gemini.

A: **Two**
Q: How many astronauts manned each of the Project Gemini flights?
W: Gemini was America's multi-manned space flight program. Gemini 3 was flown by Virgil Grissom and John Young. Grissom became the first man to go into space twice with this flight. There were nine shots made in the Gemini series. All of the astronauts aboard Apollo 11 (the first moon landing) flew in the Gemini series: Aldrin on Gemini 12, Collins on Gemini 8, and Armstrong on Gemini 10.

A: **Two**
Q: How many cups of butter are there in a pound?
W: One pound is 16 ounces, and each cup is eight ounces. Remember the cooking adage, "two cups in a pint, two pints in a quart, four quarts in a gallon"? Well, now you can add "two cups in a pound…of butter."

A: **Two**
Q: How many daily tides are there?
W: Tide is the rise and fall of ocean waters on a definite time schedule. Tides follow the moon in its apparent motion around the earth and rise and fall in the time between two rising moons, about 24 hours and 50 minutes. The moon's gravity pulls the water nearest the moon slightly away from the solid part of the earth. At the same time the moon pulls the solid earth slightly away from the water on the opposite side of the earth, hence, the two daily tides.

A: **Two**
Q: How many engines does a Boeing 737 have?
W: The Boeing 737-100 holds approximately 112 passengers, weighs about 111,000 pounds and can exceed 586 miles per hour. The 737-200 carries 115 passengers, weighs 116,000 pounds, and also goes up to 586 miles per hour. The 737-220 advanced also carries 115 passengers and can go up to 586 miles per hour; however, it weighs 125,000 pounds.

A: **Two**
Q: How many equal angles are there in an isosceles triangle?
W: The word isosceles comes from the Greek *isoskeles* meaning "having equal legs." The isosceles triangle has two sides of equal length and two equal angles.

A: **Two**
Q: How many eyes does a bat have?
W: It is believed that bats can see only a short distance and only moving objects. Most bats are nocturnal and hunt in the twilight.

A: **Two**
Q: How many front toes does a parrot have?
W: The fourth (lateral) toe is reversed, like the first, so that the two function opposed to the second and third. This gives them a pair of pincers that are useful in climbing and grasping objects.

A: **Two**
Q: How many legs does an oyster catcher have?
W: We thought this meant "man," one who "catches oysters," but research showed that in fact there is a bird known as the "oyster catcher"! It is a British shorebird that feeds on small molluscan. These birds have stout legs, a heavy wedge-shaped bill, and often black and white plumage.

A: **Two**
Q: How many logarithmic scales are there on a slide rule?
W: The slide rule is an instrument consisting in its simplest form of a ruler and a medial slide that are graduated with similar logarithmic scales, labeled with the corresponding antilogarithms, and used for rapid calculations.

A: **Two**
Q: How many pints are there in a quart?
W: There are two cups in a pint and two pints in a quart, so there are also four cups in a quart.

A: **Two**
Q: How many tons of gem diamonds are mined every year?
W: According to the Department of Commerce, Bureau of the Census, Foreign Trade Division, in 1981 $2,201 million worth of gems were imported. In 1982, $1,917 million were imported.

A: **Two**
Q: How many tusks does an Indian rhinoceros have?
W: The Indian rhinoceros can be traced back approximately 25 million years. Skillfully carved cups of rhinoceros horn were used by Indian and far eastern potentates to test beverages for the possibilities of containing poison. Today these horn cups are rare collector's items.

A: **Two**
Q: What's the only prime number that's even?

W: A prime number is a positive integer having no divisors except itself and the integer 1.

A: **Two fathoms, or twelve feet**
Q: How deep is "mark twain"?
W: This does not refer to the pen name of Samuel Langhorne Clemens, but to the expression from which he took his pen name! Twain is the two-fathom mark on a sounding line, used by riverboats to determine water of navigable depths. Samuel Clemens worked on Mississippi riverboats at one point and used their call to "mark (measure) twain" as his pen name.

A: **Two penises**
Q: What does a man suffering from diphallic terata have?
W: This non-dictionary term can be dissected as follows: *terata* from the Greek meaning "monster"; *phallic* from the Greek meaning "penis"; and *di* from the Greek meaning "two." Diaphallus is a double penis or more correctly, a penis that appears to be split longitudinally, because of the failure of the cylindrical shafts that form the body of the penis to unite.

A: **Two square miles**
Q: What's the difference between two miles square and two square miles?
W: Two miles square means each side is two miles long, for an area of four square miles (2x2); two square miles is any shape which when the area is calculated equals two square miles (an area 1x2, or an area 1/2 x 4, etc.). When you get done, the difference is still two square miles!

A: **Typhoid fever**
Q: What disease did Mary Mallon carry?
W: The most notorious carrier of typhoid was Mary Mallon of New York, known as Typhoid Mary. She was responsible for nine outbreaks of typhoid fever and was eventually confined from 1915 until her death in 1938.

SCIENCE AND NATURE

U

A: universe, The
Q: What's the Big Bang said to have created?
W: The Big Bang is a theory in astronomy that states that the universe originated billions of years ago from the explosion of a single mass of material and that the pieces are still flying apart.

A: U.S., The
Q: What country is plagued by the most tornadoes?
W: Tornadoes are dangerous whirlwinds associated with the cumulonimbus clouds of severe thunderstorms and winds up to 300 MPH.

A: U.S., The
Q: Which is larger, the U.S. or British fluid ounce?
W: An ounce is the sixteenth of a pound in the U.S. An ounce is the twelfth part of a pound troy.

A: Uri Geller
Q: Who gained fame as a mind-over-matter spoon-bender?
W: He was an Israeli pyschic who made a name for himself in the mid-1970s by apparently using pyschic energy to bend spoons and keys on television talk shows. Geller warns that in 50 years the Russians will be able to use psychic powers to seriously jeopardize the U.S.' security.

A: uterus, The
Q: What is removed in a hysterectomy?
W: Disorders of the uterus include prolapse, lacerations at childbirth, fibroid tumors, and cancer.

A: uterus, The
Q: What organ gave us the word hysterical?
W: *Hysteria* in German means "the uterus, or the womb"; the Latin term for uterus is *hysteria* as well.

A: uvula, The
Q: What dangles over the tongue from the palate?
W: The uvula is a small, fleshy conical mass that hangs loosely from the soft palate at the back of the mouth. It rarely causes any trouble except that it may be implicated in snoring, but generally that does not trouble the snorer, only his auditors!!

V

A: Vacuum
Q: What term applies to space devoid of matter?
W: A vacuum is a space devoid of all matter or an enclosed space from which air is completely removed.

A: Valhalla
Q: What's heaven to fallen Norse warriors?
W: Valhalla in Scandinavian mythology is the palace of Adin, inhabited by souls of heroes slain in battle.

A: Valium
Q: What's the most widely-used tranquilizer in America?
W: A drug that is used by many people to relieve nervousness or tension is Valium. It is effective for this purpose, but it is important to try to remove the causes of the tension and anxiety as well.

A: vampire, A
Q: What has no reflection, no shadow, and can't stand the smell of garlic?
W: Vampires are a kind of spectral being or ghost believed to suck the blood of living men and women while they are asleep.

A: Venus
Q: What is the brightest planet seen from Earth?
W: Venus is a planet having its orbit between Mercury and the earth. It is the most brilliant of all planetary bodies.

A: Venus
Q: What planet did the Mariner spacecraft explore?
W: Actually, Mariners II and V explored Venus exclusively. Mariner X went to Venus and Mercury, while Mariners IV, VI, VII, and IX were sent to Mars.

A: Venus
Q: What planet has the longest day?
W: It takes 117.4 "earth days" for Venus to rotate on its own axis just one time!

A: Venus
Q: What planet is best known as both the morning and the evening star?
W: Venus is listed as the morning and evening star only in June; Mercury is the morning and evening star in March, June, August, October, and December.

A: Venus
Q: What planet is considered the earth's twin in size and mass?
W: The Earth is 7,926 miles in equatorial diameter, while Venus is 7,700 miles in diameter.

A: Vertical Take-Off and Landing
Q: What does VTOL stand for?
W: This is a flight technique in which an aircraft rises directly into the air and settles vertically onto the ground.

A: Video Cassette Recorder
Q: What does VCR stand for?
W: There are two formats for recorders: Beta and VHS. Although it is generally conceeded that Beta produces better quality, VHS outsells Beta three to one.

A: Video Display Terminal
Q: What does VDT stand for?
W: The video display terminal is also known as visual data processer.

A: Virgil Grissom
Q: Who was the first man to return to space?
W: Grissom's first trip was aboard Liberty 7, one of the Mercury series, in July 1961. He returned to space in March 1965 on Gemini 3, America's first multi-manned mission.

A: Virgil Grissom
Q: Who was the third man in space?
W: Preceding Grissom into space was Yuri Gagarin of the Soviet Union and Alan Shepard of the U.S.

A: Virgin, The
Q: What's the zodiacal symbol for Virgo?
W: Virgo is one of the twelve signs of the zodiac, which the sun enters about August 22.

A: Vitamin B
Q: What vitamin complex includes thiamine, niacin, and riboflavin?
W: Vitamin B is essential to normal metabolism and nerve function. Riboflavin is a growth-promoting member of the Vitamin B complex.

A: Vitamin C
Q: What vitamin is also called ascorbic acid?
W: The anticarbutic vitamin, Vitamin C is abundant in citrus fruits, tomatoes, and green vegetables. Some animal products also contain this vitamin.

A: Vomit
Q: What are rats unable to do, making them extra vulnerable to poison?
W: Rats do not have a vomiting center and consequently may be poisoned by substances that vomitory mammals get rid of with relative ease.

A: Vulcanized rubber
Q: What did Charles Goodyear invent by accident in 1839?
W: It happened like this: one day, Goodyear spilled his mixture on a stove, and when he picked up the hot rubber sulfur mixture, he found that he had something that was dry and flexible at all temperatures. He patented the discovery in 1844, but his process was too simple and many infringed upon it.

A: Walking distance
Q: What does a pedometer measure?
W: Pedometers are instruments often resembing a watch by which paces are numbered as a person walks, and the distance is then ascertained.

A: Walking or standing erect
Q: What does a chairbound basophobic fear?
W: Basophobia is the fear of walking without any justifiable reason. Sasiphobia is the fear of standing up.

A: warlock, A
Q: What's a male witch called?
W: A warlock is a male witch or demon who supposedly, according to mythology, practices black magic and sorcery. Remember Samantha and her warlock and witch relatives?

A: Warm-blooded
Q: What term describes an animal with a constant blood temperature?
W: The mammal has the ability of maintaining constant blood and body temperature independent of outside temperatures. Additional characteristics of mammals include four-chamber hearts, the unique shape of the lower jaw joint, and the female mammary glands.

A: Water
Q: What drink is the best thirst-quencher?
W: Water is a clear, odorless, colorless and tasteless liquid essential for most plant and animal life. It is also the most widely used solvent.

A: Water
Q: What inside corn makes it pop?
W: A variety of corn, Zea Mays Everta, has hard kernals that burst to form white, irregularly shaped puffs when heated hence, the name "popcorn."

A: Water
Q: What's known as the universal solvent
W: Water, also known by its scientific formula, H_2O, is the fluid that dissolves other bodies and makes them fluid or more fluid.

A: Water
Q: What's the common name for hydrogen hydroxide?
W: Approximately 97 percent of the water on earth is in the salty ocean. A person who drinks only seawater would die because the kidneys cannot get rid of all the salt. Distillation is the oldest and most common method of turning seawater into fresh water.

A: Water
Q: What's the world's most common compound?
W: Water consists of tiny particles or molecules. A drop contains millions of molecules, each consisting of even smaller particles called atoms. Water molecules consist of atoms of hydrogen and oxygen. Hydrogen and oxygen by themselves are gases, but when two atoms of hydrogen combine with one atom of oxygen, they form the chemical compound water, or H_2O.

A: Wave
Q: What's the term for oscillation of water particles in the oceans?

W: A wave is a swell or ridge on the surface of water or other liquid resulting from the oscillation motion of its component particles when disturbed from their position of rest by any force. Waves are most thought of as occurring on large bodies of water such as lakes, oceans, and seas.

A: **Weather**
Q: What does a meteorologist study?
W: A meteorologist studies the science of the atmospheric phenomena, or weather and all elements relating to or affecting the weather.

A: **Werner von Braun**
Q: Who oversaw Hitler's rocket program?
W: Werner von Braun became an American rocket engineer, but he was born in Germany in 1912 and first served Hitler. He died in 1977.

A: **West**
Q: What direction do the best surfing beaches face?
W: Some of the great beaches for surfing are along the Australian seashore and off the South African coast of the Indian Ocean. The best U.S. beaches seem to be concentrated on the island of Oahu in Hawaii and at Huntington Beach in California, which holds an annual surf board riding classic.

A: **whale, The**
Q: What's considered the most highly-specialized mammal?
W: Whales are forced to come to the surface of the water in order to breathe. This process of exhaling and inhaling lasts only one to two seconds. The whale carries only 9 percent of its oxygen in its lungs. However, it carries 41 percent in its muscles, 41 percent in its blood, and 9 percent in the remaining body tissues.

A: **Whales**
Q: What mammals travel in pods?
W: A small herd of seals or whales that travel in clusters are referred to as pods.

A: **Wheat**
Q: What's the most extensively grown and eaten food?
W: Wheat is a cereal grain that yields a fine flour. It is the chief breadstuff of temperate climates and is used also in pastas and animal feeds. The embryo of a kernel of wheat, wheat germ, is a great source of vitamins.

A: **Whiskers**
Q: What does the typical man have 13,000 of?
W: Whiskers are hairs growing on the sides of the face, the chin, and the upper lip. We are still counting them!

A: **White**
Q: What color are a cherry tree's flowers?
W: Sweet cherry trees have white, scented flowers that grow in umbels with a long stalk. Sour cherry or dwarf wild cherry trees also produce white flowers.

A: **wild turkey, The**
Q: What's the heaviest land bird in North America?
W: The wild turkey has a larger brain than the domesticated turkey and is also smarter and more vigilant.

A: **Wiley Post**
Q: Who made the first solo round-the-world flight?
W: Wiley Post was an American pioneer high-altitude pilot and the first man to fly around the world alone. He set many intercity speed records in the *Winnie Mae*, an advanced airplane for its time. He helped prove that high-altitude flight was possible. He died in a plane crash with Will Rogers in Atlanta in 1935.

A: **Winds**
Q: What are the Roaring Forties?
W: A prevailing westerly is a wind that blows in the north or south middle latitude from west to east. In the Southern Hemisphere, the prevailing westerlies over the ocean blow with such force that sailors call this region the "Roaring Forties." The prevailing westerlies make flying from west to east faster than flying in the opposite direction.

A: **windshield wiper, The**
Q: What glass-cleaning device did Mary Anderson invent in 1902?
W: Not according to our research she didn't! The first mechanically operated windscreen wiper was introduced in 1916. The first manually operated wiper was patented in 1921. The first automatic wiper came out that same year, and the first electric windscreen wiper was produced in the U.S. in 1923. Maybe Mary wiped windshields by hand with paper towels!

A: **Wink at them**
Q: What do nictitating women do to men?
W: To shut one eye briefly as a signal or in teasing is known as a wink. A hint or sign can be given by doing this.

A: **wolf, A**
Q: What is a *Canis lupus*
W: *A wolf is any of various large predatory mammals that resembles the related dogs. They are destructive to game and livestock and may very occasionally attack man, especially when provoked or in a pack.*

A: *Women*
Q: *What does a gynephobic man fear?*
W: *Not in Webster's, but if it were, it would probably be gynophobic! This is from the Greek gyne, "woman", and phobia, "strong fear."*

A: **Woody Guthrie**
Q: What folk singer died of Huntington's chorea?
W: Chorea is a nervous disorder marked by spasmodic movements of limbs and facial muscles and by severe incoordination.

SCIENCE AND NATURE

X

A: **XCIX**
Q: How do you write 99 in Roman numerals?
W: X = 10 and C = 100 so X before C is 90. I = 1 and X = 10, thus giving you 9.

A: **X rays**
Q: What did Wilhelm Roentgen discover in 1895?
W: The X-ray was discovered by accident when Roentgen set a Crookes tube (cathode rays) on a book that contained a key and was resting on photographic film. When he later developed the film, he found the image of the key.

A: **XXI**
Q: What does C minus LXXIX equal?
W: C = 100, LXXIX = 79, XXI = 21, therefore, C-LXXIX-XXI! Easy, huh?

Y

A: **yak, the**
Q: What mammal lives at the highest altitude?
W: The yak is a kind of ox with long silky hair, a bushy mane, and horselike tail. Yaks inhabit Tibet and the Himalayas.

A: **Yankee**
Q: What's the international radio code word for the letter *Y*
W: *As part of the International Telecommunication Union*

phonetics, some letters are: I, India; *J*, Juliet; *K*, kilo; *L*, Lima; *M*, Mike; *N*, November; and *O*, Oscar.

A: **Yeast**
Q: What causes baker's itch?
W: Baker's itch is an eruption on the hands and arms of bakers because of an allergic reaction to yeast and other substances handled.

A: **Yeast**
Q: What fungus is used in making bread?
W: Yeast is a unicellular fungus. It is also used in the fermentation of alcoholic beverages.

A: **Yellow**
Q: What color on black produces the most visible combination?
W: Because yellow has good visibility qualities, it is commonly used to denote caution, e.g., the yellow light before red traffic lights and also traffic dividers. But yellow doesn't always denote caution. How about the numerous advertising signs in yellow and what about McDonald's golden yellow arches!

A: **Yellow**
Q: What's the most common color of topaz?
W: Topaz is also white, green and blue in color. Topaz happens to be the birthstone for the zodiac sign of Scorpio.

A: **Yes**
Q: Do mosquitoes have teeth?
W: Their bite is potentially more dangerous than a tarantula because of the likelihood of malaria. Here's an interesting tidbit: research indicates that mosquitoes tend to bite persons who have recently eaten a banana!

A: **Yes**
Q: Do sea gulls drink sea water?
W: In the winter at sea, the gull plunges into the ocean for fish and does drink the water.

A: **Yes**
Q: Does Uranus have an aurora?
W: Observations of Uranus indicate nine narrow, nearly opaque rings circling the planet.

A: **Yes**
Q: Is the thumb considered a finger?
W: It is one of the five digits of the hand, but it is usually set at an angle distinct from the other digits—as if you didn't know!

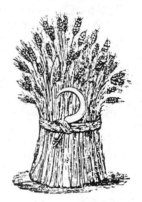

A: **Yew trees**
Q: What trees are commonly found in English churchyards?
W: Yews are an evergreen tree allied to the conifers. Yielding a hard and durable timber, yew trees are often used for cabinetry and, years ago, for making bows. Yews are frequently planted in churchyards and associated with death, perhaps because of its poisonous leaves.

A: **Yogurt**
Q: What do you get by adding "Lactobacillus bulgaricus" to milk?
W: Yogurt is a thick, acidic milk food made from fermented milk. It is often flavored with fruit.

A: **You sneeze**
Q: What happens if you get pepper in your proboscis?
W: Pepper, or any other material for that matter, irritating the membranes of the proboscis, commonly known as the nose, causes an audible involuntary convulsive force of air.

SCIENCE AND NATURE

A: **Your fingers and toes**
Q: What can't you stop moving if you suffer from athetosis?
W: Athetosis is a condition marked by constant, slow, involuntary writhing movements of the hand, fingers, and sometimes the toes.

A: **Your hair**
Q: What falls out when you suffer from phalacrosis?
W: Webster's dictionary defines the word *phalacrosis* as "baldness – alopecia". *Alopecia* is defined as "baldness; loss of hair from the head; partial or complete loss of hair due to any causes."

A: **Yuri Gagarin**
Q: Who was the first man to orbit the earth?
W: Gagarin, a Soviet cosmonaut, was the very first man, preceding even the U.S. astronauts, to orbit the earth. He flew aboard the Vostor I on April 12, 1961, and orbited the earth once on a flight that lasted one hour and 48 minutes.

A: **Yuri Gagarin**
Q: Who was the first man to return safely from space?
W: As Gagarin was the first man ever to fly in space, it makes sense that he also was the first to return safely from space, fortunately for him! Gagarin was the Soviet cosmonaut who flew aboard the Voster I on April 12, 1961, and orbited the earth once in a flight which lasted one hour and 48 minutes.

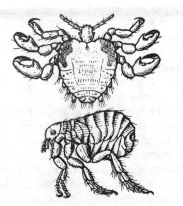

Z

A: **Z**
Q: What letter is at the left end of the bottom row of a typewriter keyboard?
W: The bottom row of letters only on a typewriter going from left to right read as follows: Z, X, C, V, B, N, M, and your punctuation marks.

A: **Zero**
Q: How many calories are there in a glass of water?
W: If we could live only on water!

A: **Zero**
Q: How many equal sides are there on a scalene triangle?
W: A scalene triangle is a triangle having three sides of unequal length.

A: **Zero**
Q: How many eyes does an earthworm have?
W: An earthworm lives in wet soil and has a long cylindrical body tapering at each end, which bristles in movement. It also has a digestive system that ingests organic material obtained from the soil. Earthworms do not have eyes or ears, but they do have a mouth and are sensitive to heat, light, and touch. They have no lungs or gills but breathe through their thin skin.

A: **Zero**
Q: How many Russians have landed on the moon?
W: Although they have launched more manned space flights than the U.S., the Soviets have never yet attempted a moon landing. The great majority of their work has been dedicated to the development of "long-term" inhabitance of space stations.

A: **Zero**
Q: How many tiles did the Space Shuttle *Columbia* lose on its second flight?
W: Heat-dissipating tiles line the underside of the *Columbia* spaceship. Without them, the orbiter would burn up when re-entering the earth's atmosphere. Approximately 34,000 tiles cover about 70 percent of the orbiter's surface.

A: **Zero**
Q: How many wings does a flea have?
W: A flea has no wings. Characteristics of the flea include a small body, long legs adapted for jumping, and a fondness for blood. Fleas are the champion jumpers in the animal world; many can jump as high as ten inches. If man could jump this high relative to his size, he would be able to jump over 200 feet.

A: **Zero**
Q: What number can't be represented in Roman numerals?
W: The Roman numerals are built up of seven basic symbols as follows: I, V, X, L, C, D, and M.

A: **Zero**
Q: What number is represented in Morse code by five dashes?
W: – – . ./ . / – . / – – – / This spells zero.

A: **zipper, The**
Q: What fastener did Whitcomb Judson patent in 1893?
W: He developed it to speed up fastening of boots and high button shoes. In 1896 a friend suggested it could be a "Universal Fastener", but consumer response was poor. Judson simplified the fastener, renamed it C-Curity, and sold it for 35 cents in 1910. Several more improvements followed, and finally the U.S. military ordered large quantities and the company made its first profit. An anonymous employee of the B.F. Goodrich Company remarked that it was quite a "zipper," and the name was immediately adopted and registered.

A: **Zulu**
Q: What's the international radio code word for the letter *Z*
W: *According to the International Telecommunication Union phonetics some other letters are: P, papa; Q, Quebec; R, rodeo; S, Sierra; T, tango; U, uniform; V, Victor; W, whiskey; X, X ray; Y, Yankee; and Z, Zulu.*

# #

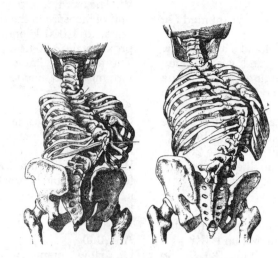

A: **2.2**
Q: How many pounds are there in a kilogram?
W: In a kilogram, there are 1,000 grams, the U.S. equivalent of 2.2045 pounds.

A: **100**
Q: What number does the Roman numeral C represent?
W: Roman numerals are still far from extinct. They are used to differentiate popes, monarchs, and even artificial satellites. The Roman numerals are also used on coinage, statutes, formal documents, and buildings to denote dates or the years of origin.

A: **100 degrees**
Q: What's the boiling point of water on the centigrade scale?
W: The centigrade thermometric scale takes the interval between the two standard points, the freezing and boiling points of water, and divides it into 100 degrees, with 0 degrees representing the freezing point and 100 degrees as the boiling point.

A: **120 miles**
Q: What's the thickness of Earth's atmosphere, within 20 miles?
W: The upper limit of the atmosphere is usually given as 120 miles. No definite figure is possible as there is no boundary line between the incredibly attenuated gases 120 miles up and space.

A: **140**
Q: What IQ level is considered to be the beginning of genius?
W: The initials "IQ" stand for intelligence quotient, which is a number used to express the apparent relative intelligence of a person. This number is determined by dividing the person's mental age as reported on a standarized test by his chronological age and then multiplying by 100.

A: **144**
Q: What's a gross?
W: Or a dozen dozen!

A: **144**
Q: What's the square of 12?
W: Or a gross. The square of a number is the value that results when you multiply the number by itself, e.g. 12 x 12 = 144.

A: **150 years**
Q: How old is a town celebrating its sesquicentennial?
W: *Sesqui-* is a prefix meaning "one and a half times," *centennial* means "100."

A: **206**
Q: How many bones are there in the human body?
W: Some bones protect the skull, heart, and lungs. Other bones enable us to move by being attached to muscles; thus these bones are used as "levers." The most common

disease that afflicts the skeletal system is arthritis, which can be very painful as well as crippling.

A: **212 degrees**
Q: What's the Fahrenheit equivalent of 100 degrees centigrade?
W: A centigrade thermometer divides the interval between the freezing and boiling points of water into 100 degrees, while a Fahrenheit thermometer takes the same interval and divides it into 180 degrees. Freezing in centigrade is 0 degrees while the Fahrenheit equivilent is 32 degrees.

A: **366**
Q: How many days were there in 1976?
W: It was a leap year! A leap year occurs when the number of the year can be divided evenly by four, except those that are divisible by 100 but not by 400. Leap year occurs every four years and can cause some distress for persons born on February 29, the extra day during leap year. They only have birthdays every four years!

A: **500**
Q: How many sheets of paper are there in a ream?
W: A ream is a bundle or package of paper always consisting of 500 sheets of paper. A ream also equals 20 squires.

SCIENCE AND NATURE

A: **737, The**
Q: What Boeing jet is nicknamed *Fat Albert*?
W: The Boeing Model 737 first flew on April 9, 1967, and was designed as a twin engine short-range transport. The model 737-300 is a stretched version, seating up to 128 passengers. It is a low-cost structure of an aircraft with new technology turbofans that will burn some 20 percent less fuel than the present turbofans. It looks like a pot belly!

A: **991**
Q: What's the Arabic answer to the Roman subtraction M minus IX?
W: Simple: M = 1000, IX = 9. So 1000-9 = 991.

A: **1,000**
Q: How many kilograms are there in a metric ton?
W: The word, *tonne*, is defined as "a unit of measure in the metric system, equal to 1,000 kilograms or to approximately 2,204.62 pound mass." The ton is also known as the metric ton, millier ton, and tonneau.

A: **1,000**
Q: How many times is a Roman numeral's value increased if it has a line over it?
W: For instance, the Roman numeral for 5,000 would be V with a line over it, or one million would be M with a line over it.

A: **1,000**
Q: How many watts make a kilowatt?
W: The kilowat is a unit of power equal to 1,000 watts or about 134 horsepower.

A: **1,000**
Q: How many years are there in a millenium?
W: A millenium is a period of 1,000 years. It can mean the 1,000th anniversary or its celebration.

A: **1,760**
Q: How many yards make a mile?
W: 5,280 feet in a mile divided by 3 is 1,760!

A: **5,280**
Q: How many feet make a mile?
W: 1,760 yards in a mile, multiplied by 3 feet in a yard is 5,280!

A: **555-1212**
Q: What seven digits follow the area code in the number for long distance information?
W: Now they are charging you for that, too!!

SCIENCE AND NATURE

SPORTS & LEISURE

A: **Ace, two, three, four, six**
Q: What five cards constitute the lowest possible poker hand, with aces low?
W: Talk about lousy hands. The only worse possibility would be to have been dealt this mess with a large pot on the table.

A: **ace of spades, The**
Q: What playing card symbolizes death?
W: In fortune-telling, the ace is a card of ill omen, misfortune, or death.

A: **Aces**
Q: What cards are bullets?
W: The term is used in poker because, like a bullet, no player can argue with an ace! Not to mention the resemblance of the marking to a bullet hole!

A: **Adolf Hitler**
Q: Who refused to shake Jesse Owens' hand at the 1936 Summer Olympics?
W: Too much has been made of Hitler's alleged refusal to shake Owens' hand. The German leader had stopped congratulating visitors publicly two days before the black champion began competing, perhaps because he anticipated embarrassment.

A: **Advantage**
Q: What is the point scored immediately before deuce in tennis?
W: The advantage is to the player who just scored. If he or she scores the next point, he or she wins that game.

A: **Akron, Ohio**
Q: What's the site of the annual All-American Soap Box Derby?
W: The All-American Soap Box Derby is a national contest held yearly in which boys and girls between the ages of ten and 15 design, build, and drive their own motorless race cars. The first contest took place in

Dayton, Ohio, in 1934. In 1935 it was changed to Akron, where it has been held since with the exception of 1942 to 1945 when the contest was suspended because of World War II.

A: **Alabama**
Q: What college did Joe Namath play football for?
W: Broadway Joe played his college football for the Crimson Tide and Bear Bryant from 1961 to 1965. He led the Crimson Tide to the National Championship in 1964 with a Sugar Bowl victory over Mississippi, 12-7.

A: **Alleys**
Q: What are marbles made from alabaster called?
W: Alley is short for alabaster! These large marbles are often used as the shooters in marbles.

A: **Amaretto**
Q: What Italian liqueur is made from bitter almonds?
W: This, like other cordials is made by mixing spirits with fruits, seeds, nuts, plants, or juices to which a

sweetener has been added. Most liqueurs and cordials are sweet and colorful.

A: **American**
Q: What nationality is tennis star Vitas Gerulaitis?
W: Vitas, the son of a Lithuanian immigrant, was born in Brooklyn, New York, on July 26, 1954.

A: **America's Cup, The**
Q: What's the most illustrious trophy in yachting?
W: One of the Carnival features of the 1851 London Exposition was a contest to establish a World Yachting Championship. It became known as the "America's Cup" because it was first won by the United States yacht *America*. Twenty-four successive attempts to win the cup by British and Australian yachtsmen had failed, until Sept. 26, 1983 when *Australia II* beat *Liberty* 4 out of 7, the first time America has ever lost.

A: **anchor man, The**
Q: What's the end man on a tug-of-war team?
W: Usually the largest individual on the team, he is considered the "anchor" or "rock" of the team.

A: **Anchorage, Alaska**
Q: Where is the world championship sled dog race held each February?
W: It is part of the Anchorage Fur Rendezvous Carnival.

A: **Ante**
Q: What's the term for a bet before cards are dealt?
W: Comes from the Latin word *Ante* meaning "before."

A: **Any queen**
Q: What card is removed from the deck in Old Maid?
W: When using standard playing cards, remove any Queen. The remaining Queen of the same color as the one removed is the "Old Maid".

A: **apron, The**
Q: What is the closely-cut grass that surrounds a golf green?
W: It is also known as fringe, or frog hair, and is generally the same variety of grass as the fairway but cut a little shorter.

A: **Archie Moore**
Q: What light-heavyweight boxer was known as "the Mongoose"?
W: Moore scored 141 knockouts during his nearly 30-year career. He held the light-heavyweight crown for almost ten years, from December 1952 until May 1962. A mongoose is an active, bold predator who depends on speed and agility to defeat his enemy. Sound like Archie?

A: **Archie Moore**
Q: Who was the oldest man to hold a world boxing title, at 44?
W: Our records indicate that Archie Moore was the oldest man to hold a title. He held the world light heavyweight title in 1961 at the age of *48*.

A: **Arkansas Razorbacks, The**
Q: What's the only Southwest Conference football team not based in Texas?
W: Here's the rest of the conference: Baylor Bears, Houston Cougars, Rice Owls, SMU Mustangs, Texas Longhorns, Texas A&M Aggies, TCU Horned Frogs, and the Red Raiders of Texas Tech.

A: **Arnie's Army**
Q: What are Arnold Palmer's fans called?
W: Perhaps no one man has done as much to popularize the game of golf as Arnold Palmer has. When Arnie joined the PGA Tour in the late 1950s, golf was still considered a game for the rich. Arnie's mass appeal and charisma changed that. People came by the thousands to watch Arnie play, and now for the first time millions were viewing at home. The gallery would cheer Palmer's every shot, which was in-

timidating to his opponents. When paired with Palmer you not only had to fight the course but also Arnie's Army.

A: **Arnold Palmer**
Q: Who set a record for golf earnings in 1963 without winning a national title?
W: Arnold earned $128,230 in 1963. It was his last year as the leading money winner. Jack Nicklaus was second with $100,040. The following year Arnie was second to Nicklaus falling $81 short of Nicklaus's record $113,284. Arnie won seven titles in 1963: L.A. Open, Phoenix Open, Pensacola Open, Thunderbird Classic, Cleveland Open, Western Open, and Whitemarsh Open.

A: **Arnold Palmer**
Q: Who was the first golfer to win $100,000 in one year?
W: In 1963, Arnold Palmer broke the $100,000 barrier by earning $128,230. From that year on, the leading money winner on the PGA tour has never won *less* than $100,000.

A: **Arnold Palmer**
Q: Who was the first million-dollar winner in golf?
W: Arnie Palmer, the 1970 Associated Athlete of the Decade and Golfer of the Decade, hit the million dollar mark in 1968.

A: **"Arrivederci Roma"**
Q: What was the theme song of the Rome Olympics?
W: It was the home of the 1960 Summer Games.

A: **Arthur Ashe**
Q: Who was the first black to win the U.S. men's national tennis title?
W: In 1968, Ashe defeated Torn Okker in the final round.

A: **Arthur Ashe**
Q: Who was the first black to win the Wimbledon men's singles tennis title?
W: In 1975 Ashe defeated Jimmy Conners in the final round.

A: **Athens**
Q: What was the site of the first modern-day Olympic games?
W: The first modern-day Olympics were in 1896, the result of efforts by Baron Pierre de Coubertin. The first ancient Olympics were said to have consisted merely of a 200-yard foot race near the small city of Olympia. Nine nations sent athletes to this competition.

A: **Atlantic City, N.J.**
Q: What's the actual location of all the streets found on a *Monopoly®* board?
W: *Monopoly®* is a real estate board game invented in 1933 by Charles Darrow, a heating engineer. There is one street that is misspelled – Marvin Gardens. It is actually Marven Gardens in Atlantic City.

A: **Australia**
Q: What continent is considered the easiest to defend in the game of *Risk*?
W: Through a throw of the dice, players try to conquer adjacent countries without dangerously diminishing the strength of their forces. Australia is the easiest to defend because you need only occupy four territories to control the continent, and you may be "attacked" from only one adjacent territory, Siam.

A: **Australia, Britain, Canada**
Q: What are the only three countries to have challenged the U.S. for yachting's America's Cup?
W: In the 25 times the U.S. has been challenged for the America's Cup, they have only lost once: that was in September of 1983 when the Australian yacht *Australia II* bested the U.S. entry *Liberty* in the seventh and final race 4 to 3.

A: **Auto racing**
Q: What sport confronts participants with hairpins?
W: This is a turn that carries a car through a 180-degree turn.

A: **Auto racing**
Q: What sport does FISA govern?
W: Our records show four governing bodies: Federation Internationale de l'Automobile (FISA-France); United States Auto Club (USA); Royal Automotive Club (UK); and International Rally Drivers Club (UK).

A: **Auto racing**
Q: What sport is Andy Granatelli associated with?
W: As founder of STP, a company that produces auto oils and lubricants, Andy, himself a former racer, sponsored Mario Andretti in the 1969 Indy victory.

A: **automobile, An**
Q: What's a Stutz Bearcat?
W: The Ideal Motor Car Company was renamed the Stutz Motor Car Company in 1913. It produced the Bearcat until the 1930s in its plant in Indianapolis, Indiana.

A: **Avery Brundage**
Q: Who was International Olympic Committee chairman at the 1936 Summer Games?
W: He also represented the U.S. in the decathlon of the 1912 games. He was president of the U.S. Olympic Association from 1929 to 1953 and president of the International Olympic Committee from 1952 to 1972.

B

A: **B and O, The; Pennslyvania; Reading; Short Line**
Q: What are the four railways in *Monopoly®* ?
W: ...and you can buy them each for $200, about the same as what some railways are worth today. The Short Line was not a railroad in Atlantic City, the town the game is based on: actually the Short Line was a freight-carrying bus company that had a depot in Atlantic City.

A: **Babe Ruth**
Q: What athlete earned $70,000 in 1927?
W: In 1930 Babe earned $80,000. When told that President Hoover made only $75,000, the Babe snorted, "Yeah, but I had a better year than he did."

A: **Babe Ruth**
Q: What baseball player was walked the most times?
W: In 1923 the Babe was walked 170 times with the New York Yankees in 152 games. Would you want to pitch to him?

A: **Babe Ruth**
Q: Who slammed a three-run homer in Yankee Stadium's first opening day game?
W: OK, everyone knows it was Babe who christened the "house" named in his honor, but did you know what his favorite snack was? Pickled eel and chocolate ice cream...together (yucko bucko!)

A: **Babe Ruth**
Q: Who was known as "the Sultan of Swat"?
W: Also "the King of Swat", "the Colossus of Clout", "the Behemoth of Bust", "the Slambino", and "Bambino" are all names used to describe George Herman "Babe" Ruth — followed in the line-up by the "Crown Prince" Lou Gehrig.

A: **Babe Ruth's**
Q: Whose 44-ounce baseball bat was called "Black Betsy"?
W: It was made by Hillerich and Gradsy of Louisville, Kentucky (Louisville Slugger).

A: **back of the head, The**
Q: Where does a rabbit punch land in boxing?
W: No fair hitting there! A punch to the back of the head or neck could severely injure or kill your opponent, and it is grounds for disqualification.

A: **backstretch, The**
Q: What's the straightaway opposite the one with the finish line in horse racing?
W: The one where the finish line is referred to as the stretch. Here they come spinning out of the turn, heading for home.

A: **balk, A**
Q: What's an illegal move by a baseball pitcher called?
W: It's only in effect if a player is on base. Once a pitcher starts a delivery to either home plate or a base, he must complete his delivery. If he does not, it is ruled a balk, and the base runner(s) is (are) allowed to advance one base.

A: **Baltimore Colts, The**
Q: Who won the first overtime championship game in NFL history?
W: In 1971 the Colts beat Dallas 16-13 at the Orange Bowl in Miami.

A: **Baltimore Orioles, The**
Q: What team did baseball's St. Louis Browns become?
W: This team is known for the antics of owner Bill Veeck, such as the use of a three foot, seven inch midget pinch hitter on Aug. 19, 1951. The St. Louis Browns played their last game Sept. 27, 1953, against the Chicago White Sox. Six and one-half months later they became known as the Baltimore Orioles.

A: **Baltimore Orioles, The**
Q: Who did the Miracle Mets defeat to win the 1969 World Series?
W: They did it in five games. MVP was Donn Clendenon and the most notable saying was by Tug McGraw: "You gotta believe!"

A: **Bank notes**
Q: What does a notaphile collect?
W: A bank note was the form of currency issued by individual banks, similar to a cashier's check or bank draft.

A: **bar, The**
Q: What's the center division of a backgammon board called?
W: Each side of the board is called a table; the inner table and outer table. The object is to be the first player to move all your pieces to the inner table and then off the board. The game of backgammon is thousands of years older than chess. If you get "bumped," your piece sits on the bar till you can get back in on the outer table.

A: **Bart Starr**
Q: Who was the Most Valuable Player in the first two Super Bowls?
W: In 1967 and 1968, the Green Bay Packers' quarterback, Bart Starr, received the MVP award. He led the team to five NFL titles and two Super Bowl victories. He was later hired as coach of the Packers, then fired at the end of the 1983 season.

A: **Baseball**
Q: What did "the Gas House Gang" play?
W: The St. Louis Cardinals of the 1930s included such greats as Pepper Martin, Leo Durocher, and Dizzy and Daffy Dean. This team was known for their baserunning and progressive style of play, as well as for their nickname, "the Gas House Gang."

A: **Baseball**
Q: What sport did the Homestead Grays and Kansas City Monarchs play?
W: The Homestead Grays played in the Negro National League; the Kansas City Monarchs played in the Negro American League.

A: **Baseball**
Q: What sport do you shag flies in?
W: ...And you get bit by a few also. The term "shagging flies" refers to catching or chasing fly balls in the outfield.

A: **Baseball**
Q: What sport is featured in the movie *Bang the Drum Slowly*?
W: This 1973 film is about a baseball player stricken with leukemia who wants to play another season before he dies. It starred Michael Moriarty and Robert DeNiro.

A: **Baseball**
Q: What sport is known as "the Grand Old Game"?
W: Baseball, as we know it today, traces its roots back to Cooperstown, New York, in 1839. However, baseball grew out of the English games of cricket and rounders and was probably played in the United States in the 1700s. That's pretty old!

A: **Baseball**
Q: What sport was pictured on the first cover of *Sports Illustrated*?
W: The first issue of *Sports Illustrated* was published on August 16, 1954.

A: baseball, A
Q: Which is heavier, a baseball or softball?
W: We don't think so...we weighed several of each and a regulaton softball weighed an average 7 ounces and had a circumference of 12.125 inches. An official major league baseball weighed 5.25 ounces with a circumference of 9.25 inches.

A: Baseball and bridge
Q: What two games have a "rubber" and "a grand slam"?
W: The rubber in baseball is the spot on the mound from which the pitcher throws the ball; baseball's grand slam is a home run with bases loaded. A grand slam in bridge is the winning of all 13 tricks by one side; a rubber is the winning of the first two out of three games by one side, or the winning of a series of deals in four-suit bridge.

A: baseline, The
Q: What's the back boundary line in tennis called?
W: A server must serve from behind the baseline and all returns must land before the baseline.

A: Basketball
Q: What ball game did James Naismith invent at Springfield, Massachusetts?
W: Naismith was a physical education instructor at the International Young Men's Christian Association, now called Springfield College. He was asked to devise a game to keep students active indoors between football and baseball seasons.

A: Basketball
Q: What sport features a fullcourt press?
W: A fullcourt press is a defensive attack that begins as soon as the offensive team gets the ball. The press usually is a result of a rebound in your backcourt.

A: basketball, A
Q: What kind of ball do you play Free-Throw Twenty-One with?
W: Free-Throw Twenty-One is an informal variation of basketball usually found in one-against-one play.

A: Batting average, home runs, runs batted in
Q: What are the three components of baseball's Triple Crown?
W: In 1921 Babe Ruth had a .378 average, 59 home runs, and 179 runs-batted-in; however, he did not win the Triple Crown. Ty Cobb batted .389, and Harry Heilmann batted .394.

A: Be prepared
Q: What's the motto of the Boy Scouts?
W: The Boy Scouts were established in 1907 by Robert Baden-Powell, a retired British colonial officer. His objective was to give boys varied experiences so they would be prepared for various life situations.

A: Bee's Knees, A
Q: What drink does gin, honey, and lemon juice make?
W: The *Bee's Knees* was a popular term of the Roaring Twenties meaning "good" or "great." This obscure cocktail was named for this term.

A: Beer
Q: What do you chase whiskey with in a boilermaker?
W: A boilermaker is a jigger of whiskey dropped into a glass of beer. When the jigger is dropped it fizzes the beer and gives the illusion of a boil. The boil in your stomach after a few of these is no illusion!

A: Ben Hogan
Q: Who was the only golfer to have his life story made the subject of a movie?
W: *Follow the Sun* was the 1951 movie with Glenn Ford as Ben. It told the story of Ben's tragic automobile accident and subsequent comeback to golfing prominence.

A: Benedictine and brandy
Q: What is mixed in B-and-B?
W: Benedictine is a secret herb formula first produced by Benedictine monks. Added to brandy, this becomes the bottle name of a popular liqueur.

A: Berlin
Q: Where were the 1936 Summer Olympics held?
W: It was perhaps best known for Hitler's refusal to shake hands with black athlete Jesse Owens, winner of four Gold Metals.

A: Bicycles
Q: What vehicles are raced in Tour de France?
W: It's the most drawn out, non-mechanical sporting event. In 1926 this event was over 3,569 miles long and lasted 29 days. This annual event has been reduced now to only 2,315 miles!

A: Bill Bradley
Q: What U.S. senator once played basketball for the New York Knicks?
W: In 1967 the Rhodes Scholar from Princeton signed with the New York Knickerbockers and played until 1977. He played in 742 games. He was elected to the U.S. Senate in 1978 for a six-year term commencing Jan. 3, 1979, representing New Jersey.

A: **Bill Russell**
Q: Who was the first black to be head coach of a major league pro sports team?
W: Bill Russell, the Boston Celtics center, led the team to 11 NBA titles; he was MVP five times, and the first black coach of a major pro sports team, the Boston Celtics. In 1966 his role became that of player/coach until he retired in 1969.

A: **Billiards**
Q: What sport do you rack your balls in?
W: No comment. Actually, in billiards or pool you use a rack to position the balls at the beginning of the game.

A: **Billiards**
Q: What sport uses rubber cushions and slate beds?
W: Also pool or pocket billiards. The bed and cushions are traditionally covered with green baize (felt) but may be a shade of orange.

A: **billiards room, A**
Q: What game room is on a *Clue* board?
W: Here are the other "rooms" on the board: library, kitchen, ballroom, study, dining room, conservatory, lounge, and hall. Don't shoot pool with Colonel Mustard!

A: **Billie Jean King**
Q: What woman holds the record for most Wimbledon tennis championships?
W: She holds six championsips: 1966, 1967, 1968, 1972, 1973, and 1975, not counting doubles championships.

A: **Billie Jean King**
Q: Who was *Sports Illustrated*'s first female Sportsman of the Year?
W: In 1977 she shared the honor of Sportsman of the Year with basketball coach John Wooden.

A: **Bjorn Borg**
Q: Who led Sweden to its first Davis Cup victory, in 1975?

W: Sweden beat Czechoslovakia 3-2, the only time Sweden has won the Davis Cup.

A: **Bjorn Borg**
Q: Who was first to win five straight Wimbledon singles tennis titles?
W: Here's when and against whom: 1976, Ilie Nastase; 1977, Jimmy Conners; 1978, Jimmy Conners; 1979, Roscoe Tanner; 1980, John McEnroe.

A: **Black**
Q: What color is the eight ball in pocket billiards?
W: The eight ball is the dividing ball of the 15 in the set. The first seven (1-7) are solid colors. The second seven (9-15) are striped. In the game of eight ball, the act of knocking the eight ball in the pocket out o sequence means instant loss or sudden death.

A: **Black**
Q: What color moves first in checkers?
W: At the beginning of a game, lots are cast for choice of colors. The first move is made by the player of the black pieces. Thereafter, the colors alternate with each succeeding game. This is in accordance with standard tournament rules.

A: **Black**
Q: What color shirts must table tennis players wear in official competition?
W: The reason for black is that the white ball will show up best. If you wear a light color the ball might blend in the background and make it difficult for your opponent to see the ball and return it.

A: **Black**
Q: What color square does the white king start a chess game on?
W: And the black king on the white so they are in the same file. The black king starts on K1 and the white on K8.

A: **Black**
Q: What color were 14 of the 15 jockeys in the first Kentucky Derby?
W: It was run on May 17, 1875. Aristides, the winner of the first Derby was ridden by the black jockey Oliver Lewis. The winning purse was $2,850. Today it would cost an owner more than that just to start a horse! There was no prestige associated with riding race horses, and no fees were paid to the jockeys at that time. Most of the riders in the first Derby were stable hands!

A: **Black, blue, red, green, yellow**
Q: What are the colors of the five Olympic rings?
W: Each ring represents one of the five continents: Europe, Asia, America, Australia, and Africa.

A: **Black, green, red**
Q: What are the three colors on a roulette wheel?
W: The American wheel has sections 1 to 36 alternately colored red and black with two additional green sections 0 and 00. The French wheel differs from the American wheel in that it only has one green section, 0.

A: **Black Label**
Q: What do you say after: "Hey, Mabel"?
W: This was the advertising slogan for Carling's Black Label beer.

A: **Black or red**
Q: What color belt does a tenth-degree dan wear with his karate garb?
W: *Any color he wants!* The white is the lowest color, sixth through eighth can wear a red and white, ninth and tenth can wear a solid red. But only a tenth can wear solid black.

A: **Blackjack**
Q: What's the better known name of the card game Twenty-one?
W: If you are dealt a black Jack (i.e., a jack of either clubs or spades) and a ten, you automatically win and are paid double your bet.

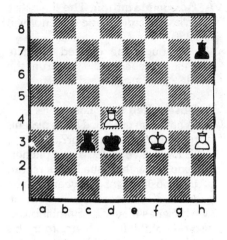

A: **Blackjack, or Twenty-one**
Q: What game is fatal to anybody over 21?
W: If the total of the cards dealt to you is over 21 in point value, you lose.

A: **Blindman's buff**
Q: What game is known in various countries as blind fly, blind cow, and blind buck?
W: This is the popular children's game in which a player is blindfolded and tries to catch and identify another player.

A: **Bloody Mary, The**
Q: What's known as "the Queen of Drinks"?
W: This hangover reliever consists of 1.5 ounces of vodka, 1.5 ounces of tomato juice, a dash of lemon juice, and celery salt, optional!

A: **Bob Mathias**
Q: Who's the only man to have won the Olympic decathlon twice?
W: Mathias won the decathlon in 1948 at London and in 1952 at Helsinki.

A: **Bobby Fischer**
Q: Who was the first American world chess champion?
W: Bobby was the U.S. champion from 1962 to 1968. He beat Boris Spassky, the Russian, in 1972 to claim the World Championship. By the way Bobby, has an IQ of 187 and at the age of 15 became the youngest ever International Grandmaster.

A: **Bobby Fischer and Boris Spassky**
Q: Who battled for the world chess championship at Reykjavik, Iceland, in 1972?
W: Bobby won. However, his reign was ended in April 1975 by default after his refusal to accept International Chess Federation rules for a championship match.

A: **Bobby Jones**
Q: What golfer was nicknamed Emperor Jones?
W: Bobby won his first major championhhip at the age of 21. He won 12 more by the time he retired from competition at the age of 28. All this was done as an amateur. He won the British American, the British Open, the USGA Open, and the USGA Amateur. That feat had never been accomplished before or since. All hail to the Emperor!

A: **Bobby Jones**
Q: Who was the only golfer to win the U.S. and British Opens and Amateurs in the same year?
W: In 1930 Bobby won golf's Grand Slam: British Amateur at St. Andrews Country Club; British Open at Hoylake Country Club; U.S. Open, at Minneapolis Interlochen Golf Club; and U.S. Amateur, at Marion Golf Club. In November 1930 Bobby retired saying, "It just isn't fun any longer."

A: **Bobby Orr**
Q: What hockey player was Sports Illustrated's Sportsman of the Year for 1970?
W: He started with the Boston Bruins at the age of 18. Bobby finished his career with the Chicago Blackhawks in 1977 when he played 18 games.

A: **Bobby Orr**
Q: Who was the first defenseman to win the NHL scoring championship?
W: In 1970 Bobby Orr won the Ross trophy as leading scorer in the NHL. He assisted in the scoring of 102 points in the 1970-71 season.

A: **Bobby Riggs**
Q: What tennis star wrote the book *Court Hustler*?
W: Bobby's biggest hustle was the "Battle of the Sexes" in a $100,000 winner-take-all match with Billie Jean King in the Houston Astrodome in 1973. Billie Jean beat him 6-4, 6-3, and 6-3.

A: **Bocci**
Q: What's the Italian game that resembles lawn bowling?
W: Two teams of four each play on a boarded field of sand or soil measuring 75 by eight feet. It was first played in Turin, Italy, in 1898. The first world championships were in Genoa, Italy, in 1951.

A: **Body**
Q: What term applies to the consistency, thickness, and substance of a wine?
W: This wine taster's term is often misused. A full-bodied wine is not necessarily high in alcohol, but it is the opposite of watery or thin; it gives an impression of weight, rather than lightness.

A: **Bones**
Q: What do you call the playing pieces in dominoes?
W: Dominoes are thought to have been derived from dice. Bones are the rectangular tiles that are marked with all possible combinations of numbers that can be rolled by dice.

A: **Bonneville Salt Flats, The**
Q: What Utah site are land speed records set at?
W: The last official land speed record was set there by Gary Gabelich on Oct. 23, 1970. His rocket engine "Blue Flame" was clocked at 622.287 mph. The latest record was the jet engine "Thrust-2", driven at 633 mph by Richard Nobel Oct. 3, 1983, at the Black Rock Desert, Nevada.

A: **bonspiel, A**
Q: What's a curling tournament called?
W: Bonspiel denotes a "Grand" curling match or tournament. The largest Bonspiel is the Alcan Employees'. Held in Arvida, Quebec, Canada, the tournament lasts 22 days and involves 200 teams.

A: **Boris Spassky**
Q: Who did Bobby Fischer beat to win the world chess championship?
W: This occurred at Reykjavik, Iceland, in 1972. Bobby held the title until April 1, 1975, losing by default.

A: **Boston Bruins, The**
Q: What was the first U.S. based team in the NHL?
W: In 1924 it took this expansion team all of five years to become league champs.

A: **Boston Celtics, The**
Q: What team did Bob Cousy help to six NBA championships?
W: Orginally passed over by the Celtics he started his career with the Chicago Staggs. He joined the Celtics in 1951 where he played until 1963. Here's the championship seasons: 1956-57, 1958-59, 1959-60, 1960-61, 1961-62, and 1962-63.

A: **Boston Celtics, The**
Q: What team has won the most NBA championships?
W: They have 14 NBA titles. They won their first in 1957 and last in 1981.

A: **Boston Marathon, The**
Q: What race did Rosie Ruiz not win in 1980?
W: Although she crossed the line first, she allegedly did not run the whole 26 mile, 385 yard race!

A: **Boston Red Sox, The**
Q: What team did Babe Ruth play his first major league game for?
W: Babe started in 1914 as a pitcher. Did you know the Babe held a record at that position for 43 years? Babe pitched 29⅔ scoreless innings in World Series Play. The Bambino was also one of the first athletes to try his hand in the movies. He was in three flicks: *Babe Come Home, Speedy*, and *The Pride of the Yankees*.

A: **Bouquet**
Q: What term applies to the aroma of wine?
W: Aroma is one of the qualities of a fine wine!

A: **Bowling**
Q: What did Dick Weber, Steve Nagy, and Don Nagy excel at?
W: For 19 PBA Tournaments held in 1965, Dick Weber posted an average of over 211, leading all bowlers in those competitions. He was also the leading money winner that year. In 1954 Steve Nagy became the first bowler to roll a 300 in a televised match. He was named to the Bowling Hall of Fame in 1963.

A: **Bowling**
Q: What sport features a "railroad split"?
W: Leaving the 7 pin and 10 pin gives you the "railroad split" and acid indigestion!

A: **boxer, A**
Q: What's a pugilist?
W: Pugilism, which derives its name from the Latin *pugil*, "boxer," is the description of "one who fights with his fists."

A: **Boxing**
Q: What activity other than hopping do kangaroos excel at?
W: The largest male in a "mob" of kangaroos will keep the younger rivals at bay by kicking, biting, and "boxing." Boxing kangaroos became a carnival novelty act of the 1800s. But what does the word kangaroo mean? In the Kanaka dialect, "I don't know." Actually, we do know: it means "I don't know." It seems an English explorer asked a native the name of the animal, and he replied, "Kangaroo."

A: **Boxing**
Q: What sport is considered the easiest for gamblers to fix?
W: There are not many sports in which the outcome can be attributed to one individual; boxing is one, however. If a gambler wants to assure the outcome, he has fewer people to persuade!

A: **Boxing**
Q: What sport is known as "the Sweet Science"?
W: It has been called that by romantics, but law enforcement officials call it the most corrupt sport of all!

A: **Boxing**
Q: What sport was standardized under the Queensberry Rules?
W: They were formulated in 1867 for John Sholto Douglas, ninth Marquess of Queensberry.

A: **Boxing gloves**
Q: What were first used by John L. Sullivan and James J. Corbett in 1892?
W: On September 7 of that year Corbett defeated Sullivan in 21 rounds. Sullivan was the last of the bareknuckle champs. This was another in the overused phrase "Battle of the Century" fights.

A: **Brandy**
Q: What, with white "creme de menthe", puts the sting in a stinger?
W: One ounce of each; shake well with cracked ice and strain into a

three-ounce cocktail glass. It's called a stinger because the creme de menthe makes it easy to swallow but the brandy packs a sting!

A: **break, The**
Q: What is the first shot in a billiards game called?
W: In billiards the break shot requires that you hit the red ball first before hitting the white target ball. In pocket billiards it means literally to break the formation the balls were racked in.

A: **Break it in half**
Q: What does Emily Post say you do to your donut before dunking it?
W: Emily was the author of a nationally syndicated column, "Doing the Right Thing." We guess it's hard to get a whole donut into a cup of coffee!

A: **breaststroke, The**
Q: What's the oldest stroke used in competitive swimming?
W: Perhaps because it is swum with the face out of the water, and thus the swimmers are able to see and breathe more easily. It is one of the most popular strokes for distance and survival swimming.

A: *Brian's Song*
Q: What TV movie dramatized the death of the Chicago Bears' Brian Piccolo?
W: The film first aired on ABC's Movie of the Week on Tuesday, Nov. 31, 1971. It is the story about the relationship between Piccolo and his roommate, the great Chicago running back, Gale Sayers, and Brian's battle with cancer.

A: **Bricklaying**
Q: What's the traditional trade for aspiring Spanish bullfighters?
W: Even matadors had to moonlight! Aspiring matadors had to pay fees to fight. After they developed a following, they could find a sponsor and direct their talents to the ring. But before the fame came some backbreaking work like bricklaying.

A: **Bridge**
Q: What card game derived its name from *biritch* or Russian whist?
W: *Biritch* is a Russian word meaning "declarer." The game is thought to be of either Levantine origin or to have come from India. A historic four-page pamphlet, thought to be the earliest publication of the rules of bridge, was authored by John Collinson of London on July 14, 1886.

A: **Bridge**
Q: What was Dwight Eisenhower's favorite card game?
W: As an officer in the Army Ike used bridge to relax during invasions of Europe. As president he was the host of many World Class games. Ike also contributed greatly to the promotion of golf.

A: **Bridge**
Q: What world championship is called the Bermuda Bowl?
W: The first World Team Championship was played in Bermuda in 1950 on the initiative of Norman M. Bach. In 1974 the World Bridge Federation voted to hold the championship on alternating years. The Bermuda Bowl is not always played in Bermuda.

A: **Bridge**
Q: What's the most popular card game in the English-speaking world?
W: More than 5,000 books have been written on the subject, with those still in print selling a million copies annually. A majority of newspapers in the western world carry bridge columns or articles.

A: **Bridge**
Q: What's the most popular four-player game of all time?
W: By the 1970s, 80 million people were playing bridge in every part of the world. There are 5,500 bridge clubs in North America alone.

A: **Broadway Joe**
Q: What's Joe Namath's nickname?
W: The media made much of his swinging lifestyle. The nickname applies now, since Joe has taken up acting and has appeared on Broadway.

A: **Brooklyn Dodgers, The**
Q: What baseball team was routinely called "dem bums" by its frustrated fans?
W: Long before they moved to L.A. and became "like, totally awesome."

A: **Brown**
Q: What color bottles do good Rhine wines come in?
W: It's basically just a tradition. Red wines, white wines, and roses are usually in green glass. White bordeaux, such as sauterne, are usually in flint glass.

A: **Bulldogs**
Q: What's the nickname of the University of Georgia football team?
W: ...or, as they are known in the South, "Dem Dawgs", with colors of red and black. They are members of the Southeast Conference.

A: **Bullfighting**
Q: What sport is central to Hemingway's *Death in the Afternoon*?
W: The book was published in 1932. Hemingway spent five years researching this book on bullfighting.

A: **bullseye, The**
Q: What part of a dartboard must be five feet, eight inches above the floor?
W: In this traditional English pub game, five feet, eight inches was considered the average eye level of the player.

A: Buster Crabbe
Q: What movie Tarzan won the 400-meter freestyle at the 1932 Olympics?
W: Me Clarence, you Jane. He won the event as Clarence Crabbe with a time of 4:48.4. Buster sounds more like a Tarzan than Clarence, don't you think?

A: Butterflies and moths
Q: What does a lepidopterist collect?
W: What's the difference? Butterflies have smooth antennae with knobby ends; moths have feathery antennae. Butterflies hold their wings vertically when resting; moths horizontally. Most moths fly at night, while butterflies fly during the day.

A: By knockout, technical knockout, or decision
Q: What three ways, apart from a disqualification, can a boxer win a fight?
W: A knockout means exactly that. A technical knockout means the referee has stopped the fight because he feels physical harm would come to one of the boxers if the contest continues. A decision is a tallying of rounds won by a point method.

C

A: Calais and Dover
Q: What two cities usually mark the extremes of English Channel swims?
W: The first to swim the English Channel from shore to shore (without a life jacket) was Merchant Navy Captain Matthew Webb, who swam breastroke from Dover, England, to Calais Sands, France, in 21 hours, 45 minutes on Aug. 24-25, 1875.

A: Calgary Stampede, The
Q: What's the largest rodeo in the world?
W: It is officially referred to as the "Calgary Extinction and Stampede." The record attendance was 1,069,830 on July 8 to 17, 1977. The single day attendance record was 141,670 on July 13, 1974.

A: California
Q: What U.S. state grants the most fishing licenses?
W: According to an official of the State of California, Department of Fish and Game, the projection of sport fishing licenses issued for the period of July 1, 1983, through June 1984 is 4,918,210. Beginning in January 1984 the state switched over to a single license with stamps for various types of fishing. The basic license carries a price tag of $13.50. With almost five million licenses issued, California leads all other states in fishermen!

A: Canada
Q: What country has won the most Olympic hockey gold medals?
W: Canada has won six Gold Medals in hockey: 1920, 1924, 1928, 1932, 1948, and 1952. But as a result of the 1984 Olympics there is now a tie with the USSR, which also holds six Golds in the following years: 1956, 1964, 1968, 1972, 1976, and 1984.

A: Canada
Q: What's the only host country not to win gold at its own Summer Olympics?
W: Canada came up "empty" during the 1976 Olympics in Montreal.

A: Canada
Q: Who beat Denmark 47-0 at the 1949 world hockey championships?
W: In this, the highest scoring game, Canada defeated Denmark in Stockholm, Sweden.

A: Candlestick, knife, lead pipe, revolver, rope, wrench
Q: What are the six murder weapons in the game of *Clue*?
W: Watch out for any of these culprits carrying one of those weapons: Professor Plum, Colonel Mustard, Mr. Green, Mrs. White, Mrs. Peacock, or Miss Scarlet.

A: canoe, a; or kayak
Q: What would you be in if you did an Eskimo roll?
W: An eskimo roll is a stunt roll in which the kayaker leans over to one side causing the kayak to capsize and then rights the kayak with a movement of the hips so that he surfaces on the other side, completing a full circle in one continuous motion. Easy, huh?

A: Captain Morgan
Q: What Jamaican rum is named for a Welsh pirate?
W: It is a spiced rum with the primary flavoring being vanilla, produced by Seagram Distillers Company. Rum is one of the spirits of which consumption has been rising in recent years.

A: car, A
Q: What's approaching when a cyclist shouts, "Oil"?
W: This term is used by bicycle racers to warn others of an oncoming vehicle.

A: *Careers*
Q: What board game asks you to create a success formula from money, fame, and happiness?
W: In real life the formula has not been working so well, according to the PhD who pumped gas into my car yesterday!

A: Carl Yastrzemski
Q: Who won the Triple Crown in leading the Boston Red Sox to the 1967 American League pennant?
W: Yaz had 121 RBIs, tied with Harmon Killebrew of Minnesota with 44 HRs, and hit for a .326 batting average to win baseball's Triple Crown by leading the American

League in all three categories. The Red Sox won the American League Pennant but lost the World Series to St. Louis four games to three.

A: Casey Stengel
Q: What New York Mets manager asked: "Can't anybody here play this game?"?
W: In the same statement he added, "This team has shown me ways to lose I couldn't believe. You've got to look up and down the bench and say 'can't anyone here play this game?'" Another of Casey's comments about the Mets of the early 1960s was, "Look at that guy, can't hit, can't run, can't catch. Of course, that's why they gave him to us."

A: Cassius Clay
Q: Who was known as "the Louisville Lip"?
W: Clay, better known as Muhammad Ali, was the 1960 Olympic Gold Medalist in boxing. He would tout, "They all must fall in the round I call."

A: Cassius Clay
Q: Who won the 1960 Olympic light-heavyweight boxing gold medal?
W: Clay became known as Muhammad Ali. He's also the only professional fighter to have won the world's heavyweight championship three times.

A: Castle
Q: What's the other term for the rook in chess?
W: The rook is in the shape of a castle. There is also a move called "castling" that is a compound move of the king and one rook. The rook is the second most valuable fighting piece, preceded only by the Queen (the King is not considerd a fighting piece).

A: catcher, The
Q: What player squats an average of 300 times during a baseball doubleheader?
W: No wonder nobody wants to be a catcher. Imagine the wear on the knees; that's over 16 squats an inning.

A: Caves
Q: What do spelunkers explore?
W: These hobbyists are also known as speleologists!

A: center, The
Q: What player on a basketball team usually plays the post, or pivot, position?
W: Post, or pivot, is when the player holding the ball steps one or more times in any direction with the same foot while keepping the other foot in contact with the floor.

A: Champagne
Q: What sparkling French wine is best served at between 41 and 45 degrees Fahrenheit?
W: Iced before or after a meal, the true champagne is made only in France from a certain variety of grape. All others are just expensive imitations.

A: Champagne
Q: What's bottled in jeroboams?
W: A jeroboam is an oversized wine bottle, holding as much as six ordinary bottles. Think of the hangover if you polish one off.

A: Champagne and stout
Q: What two ingredients make a Black Velvet?
W: Stout is a dark beer brewed from full-flavored malts, often with the addition of caramel sugar. Hint, don't use Dom Perignon champagne!

A: Champagne Tony Lema
Q: What late golfer was renowned for passing out the bubbly in the press tent?
W: Tony was the Number 2 money winner in 1965 with $101,816 in prizes. He was killed while flying his own plane in 1966.

A: Charles Atlas
Q: What strongman was the original 97-pound weakling?
W: His real name was Angelo Siciliano. When he came to the U.S. with his mother at the age of 11, he began to sicken and grow spindly. At the age of 16 he saw a statue of Hercules in a Brooklyn museum and marveled at its muscles. A week later he joined the YMCA and began to lift weights. He developed a chest that expanded to 54.75 inches and biceps of 17 inches. But he really did start out as a 97 pound weakling!

A: Charles Atlas
Q: Who claimed to be the world's most perfectly developed man?
W: After constant workouts in the YMCA where he started weight training, Angelo Siciliano started a program of pitting muscle against muscle. By means of this exercise he doubled his weight and acquired a mighty form: 54.75-inch expanded chest, 17-inch biceps. His friends took note of his development and compared his physique to the statue of Atlas at a nearby corner bank building. The name stuck and eventually Angelo legally changed his name to Charles Atlas.

A: Charles Goren
Q: Who devised the point count bidding system for bridge?
W: This Philadelphia lawyer-turned-bridge-authority is known to millions as "Mr. Bridge." This point system made it easier to learn the game and helped increase its popularity.

A: Checkers
Q: What board game is called draughts in Britain?
W: William Payne wrote an introduction to the rules of the British game of draughts. It is one of the world's oldest intellectual pastimes. Checkers derived its name from the design of the board.

A: Chestnuts
Q: What's the game of conkers played with?
W: This is a popular game with British children. Two players each have a conker (chestnut or hazelnut) threaded on a knotted string. Players take alternate hits at their opponent's conker with theirs. The game is won when one player destroys the other's conker.

A: Chess
Q: What board game derives its name from the Persian word for "king"?
W: *Shatranj* is the Persian word understood to mean "the play of kings."

A: Chess
Q: What board game did Humphrey Bogart excel at?
W: Move it again, Sam! Bogie was known as a moody actor, but you could often find him behind a chessboard during downtime on the set.

A: Chess
Q: What is "the Royal Game"?
W: Chess originated in India or China about the sixth century and was later known by the Persian name *shatranj*, which some have understood to mean "play of the kings." The term may also have come from the fact that the pieces each represent members of the royal court: king, queen, bishop, knight, etc. Another version is that the game was so termed because it was popular among the intellectual upper class.

A: Chicago Black Hawks, The
Q: What team did Bobby Orr play his last NHL game for?
W: Bobby played in his last game with the Black Hawks on Jan. 22, 1977, against the Detroit Red Wings. He was originally sold to the Black Hawks in 1976 for a reported $600,000.

A: Chicago Cubs, The
Q: What baseball team did Ernie Banks play his entire career for?
W: In 19 years with the Cubs "Mr. Cub" hit 512 home runs for a lifetime batting average of .274. He was twice MVP and inducted into the Hall of Fame in 1977. And what did he say when he saw *Trivial Pursuit®* ? "Hey, let's play two today!"

A: Chicago Cubs, The
Q: What team has suffered the longest since its last National League baseball pennant?
W: It was 1945 when last a pennant flew over Wrigley Field, and 1908 was the last time the Cubs were world champs. We'll have to see what happens if they get into the playoffs! TV networks will want them to play night games, and there are no lights at Wrigley Field.

A: Chicken and red wine
Q: What are the two main ingredients of *coq au vin*?
W: In French *coq* is "chicken," *au* is "with," and *vin* is "wine." How simple! But we thought you never served red wine with poultry.

A: Chitlins
Q: What's the Southern dish made of pigs' small intestines?
W: ...with some corn bread and greens, it's a lot better than it sounds.

A: Chocolate
Q: What's the flavor of a Hostess Ding Dong?
W: Definitely...but the real question is how do YOU eat it? Around the filling, or with it?

A: Chuck Conners
Q: What Dodgers and Cubs first baseman dropped baseball to take up acting?
W: Better known for the TV series "The Rifleman", "Luke" played one game for the Brooklyn Dodgers in 1949 and 66 games for the Chicago Cubs in 1951, batting .239 in 201 times at bats with two home runs.

A: Churchill Downs
Q: What racetrack is home to the Kentucky Derby?
W: It has been home to the Derby since 1875. The Derby is probably the single most famous thoroughbred race in the U.S.

A: Cigar bands
Q: What does a brandophile collect?
W: It is a hobby that for the large part died out in the 1930s. In the past cigar bands were brightly colored and detailed. Expense has limited the band of today and also limited its worth as a collectible item.

A: Citation
Q: What was the first thoroughbred racehorse to win $1 million?
W: Our records show Citation to have won $709,470; the first to win a million was Spectacular Bid in 1979 with total winnings of $1,279,334.

A: *Citius, Altius, Fortius,* or "Faster, Higher, Stronger"
Q: What's the Olympic motto?
W: The original Latin meant "Faster, Higher, Braver", and the modern interpretation is "Swifter, Higher, Stronger." The motto was coined by Father Didon, a French educator, in 1895.

SPORTS AND LEISURE

A: Clay
Q: What are the targets in skeet and trap shooting made of?
W: They are 25 to 27mm high and weigh 100 to 110g each. The color may vary from black, white, or yellow.

A: Cleveland Browns, The
Q: What NFL team was named for its first coach?
W: Their first head coach was Paul Brown.

A: Cleveland Browns, The
Q: What's the only NFL team without decorations on the sides of its helmets?
W: The helmet is orange with a white stripe down the middle.

A: clubhouse, The
Q: Where's the 19th hole on a golf course?
W: It is also known as the hole that takes the longest to play out. There are usually many hazards: scotch, whiskey, and gin, to name a few. Many have been known to go out of bounds there.

A: Clubs
Q: What's the lowest-ranking suit in bridge?
W: From lowest to highest they are: clubs, diamonds, hearts, and spades.

A: Cockfighting
Q: What blood sport originated the word "crestfallen"?
W: This sport, now illegal in most countries, consists of two gamecocks that fight with beak and spur in a small arena until one is killed.

A: Coco Chanel
Q: Who named a perfume for her fashion shows on the fifth of each month?
W: Gabrielle Chanel, a French fashion designer who was tops in the 1920s and 1930s, was better known for her perfume business. She developed the perfume Chanel Number 5. She used to sell her fragrances in her own boutique in France.

A: Coffee
Q: What's the basic flavoring of Kahlua?
W: Kahlua is a popular liqueur from Mexico and is 56 proof. It is similar to the Jamaican liqueur Tia Maria at 63 proof.

A: Coin collecting
Q: What's the most popular hobby in America?
W: Numismatics became so enormously popular in the U.S. after World War II that it created a shortage of many coins. Silver coins prior to 1964 are worth many times their face value; hence, most coins in circulation are not more than several years old.

A: College football bowl games
Q: What are the Liberty, Gator, Hula, Pecan, and Bluebonnet?
W: The Liberty Bowl is played in Memphis, Tennessee; the Gator Bowl is played in Jacksonville, Florida; the Hula Bowl is played in Honolulu, Hawaii; and the Blue Bonnet is played in Houston, Texas. The Pecan Bowl must be played under a nut dish somewhere, because we couldn't find it. The Pelican Bowl, however, *was* played in New Orleans.

A: Colonel Mustard
Q: What suspect in the game of *Clue* holds a military rank?
W: The only other professional title by any other suspect is Professor Plum.

A: Color blindness
Q: What eye problem does Jack Nicklaus suffer from?
W: One color he can see is green: he owns five green "Masters Blazers", more than anyone else, and was golf's leading money winner for eight years. A fellow golfer once said about Jack that "when he (Jack Nicklaus) plays well, he wins. When he plays badly, he finishes second. When he plays terrible, he finishes third."

A: Continents
Q: What do the five Olympic rings represent?
W: Five rings or circles are linked together to represent the sporting friendship of all peoples. The rings also symbolize the five continents: Europe, Asia, Africa, Australia, and America. Each ring is a different color—blue, yellow, black, green, and red.

A: Contract bridge
Q: What card game was invented by Harold S. Vanderbilt in 1925?
W: Contract bridge has an added element that auction bridge does not. In contract bridge the goal is to make or defeat the contract, rather than simply to win as many tricks as possible. This is called the Plafond principle, after a French game. Vanderbilt successfully got this principle, a decimal system of scoring and slam bonuses, incorporated into the game formerly called auction bridge. In 1928 the Whist Club of New York passed rules accepting these changes, and contract bridge, as we know it, was born.

A: **Contract bridge**
Q: What's the most popular form of bridge?
W: By the 1970s it was being played by 80 million people in every part of the world. There are more than 5,500 clubs in North America alone.

A: **Cooperstown, New York**
Q: Where is the Baseball Hall of Fame?
W: It was founded in 1936 and dedicated on June 12, 1939, in the same town in which Abner Doubleday invented the game. Ty Cobb was the first inductee into the Hall in 1936.

A: **Corn and beans**
Q: What two vegetables are combined in succotash?
W: As Sylvester the cat, in his futile pursuit of Tweety-Bird would say, "Sufferin' Succotash"! Succotash is from the Narraganset Indian word *meseseckquatash*. It was originally a boiled stew containing fish, corn, and beans.

A: **Counterclockwise**
Q: Which direction are greyhound races run in, clockwise or counterclockwise?
W: All U.S. sporting races are run counterclockwise.

A: **Craps**
Q: What game is the biggest money-maker for Las Vegas casinos?
W: History's biggest and fastest action gambling game, craps is undoubtedly the most widely played dice game in the U.S. today. More money is won and lost at craps every day that at any other form of casino gambling.

A: **Craps**
Q: What Las Vegas casino game gives the best odds?
W: Bank craps is the version of the game found in all Nevada casinos and in most legalized establishments throughout the world. Good chance you'll roll a seven on your first turn and win.

A: **Crazy Legs**
Q: What was football star Elroy Hirsch's nickname?
W: Lean and likable, Elroy Hirsch of the Los Angeles Rams had the speed of a sprinter and the elusiveness of a cake of soap in a bathtub. He is regarded as one of pro football's most spectacular receivers of the 1950s.

A: **Cribbage**
Q: What game can you peg out in?
W: Scoring is called pegging, because it is done by moving pegs on the cribbage board. The final point of the game is marked by pegging into an extra game hole at the head of the board.

A: **Cricket**
Q: What sport uses stumps, bails and bats?
W: This is English baseball. The bat is paddle-shaped, and the wicket consists of three stumps or stakes 28 inches high. Two pieces of wood called bails are set on top of the stumps. A further explanation of cricket could become a "sticky wicket."

A: **Crickets and rounders**
Q: What two English games did baseball derive from?
W: Both these games have a similarity to baseball in that there is a batting team and a pitching team. The objective is to score runs. Cricket is traditionally the male sport of Britain, while rounders is a female sport.

A: **crossbow, The**
Q: What stringed weapon fires a bolt?
W: The crossbow was the leading hand missile weapon of the Middle Ages prior to the introduction of firearms. A square-headed bolt known as a "quarrel" was the standard ammunition. About ten inches long, it could be fired up to 300 yards. The crossbow is of Italian origin.

A: **Cross-country and jumping**
Q: What are the two Nordic skiing events?
W: In men's cross-country competition there are the 15-, 30-, and 50-kilometer cross-country; 40-kilometer relay; and combined cross-country and jumping events. In addition there are 70- and 90-meter ski jumping events. Women's events are the 5- and 10-kilometer cross-country and the 15-kilmometer cross-country relay.

A: **Cross-country skiing and target shooting**
Q: What two skills make up the winter biathlon?
W: The biathlon was introduced at the 1960 games in Squaw Valley with a 20-kilometer event. There is now additional competition in 10 and 40 kilometers.

A: **Croquet**
Q: What sport begins in front of the south stake?
W: The predecessor to lawn jarts! Originating in France during the 13th century, it is a game in which you hit a wooden ball with a mallet through a series of hoops until you hit the stake at the end of the course.

A: **Cuba**
Q: Where did the rumba originate?
W: In the 1950s Cuba was the vacation place to be. It was known for great weather, gambling, and entertainment. Rumba, anyone?

A: **Curling**
Q: What sport sees stones thrown at a house?
W: This Scottish game is similar to shuffleboard played on ice. The object is to slide stones down a rink to a fixed point called the tee. The house is the 12-foot circle around the tee.

A: **Cyclones**
Q: What's the nickname of the Iowa State football team?
W: The team colors are cardinal and gold. The team is a member of the Big Eight Conference.

D

A: Daiquiri, The
Q: What rum, lime, and sugar cocktail is named for a town near Santiago, Cuba?
W: After the Spanish-American War of 1898, a group of American engineers were invited to Santiago, Cuba, to help develop the Daiquiri Iron Mines. They would relax after a hard hot day of work at the Venus hotel where the bartender made this cooling drink. The chief engineer, Jennings S. Cox, suggested the cocktail be named after the mines, and the name stuck.

A: Dallas
Q: Where is the Cotton Bowl played?
W: The first Cotton Bowl was played in 1937, and Texas Christian University beat Marquette 16-6.

A: Darts
Q: What game challenges you to double in and double out?
W: Actually it would be triple in, double out. Each sector of the board is given a point value. There are two rings on the board, an outer ring in which the point value is doubled and an inner ring in which the point value is tripled.

A: Davis Cup, The
Q: What's the International Lawn Tennis Challenge Trophy usually called?
W: The Davis Cup began with a series between the British and the Americans. Played on the courts of the Longwood Cricket Club, Chestnut Hill, Massachusetts, in 1900, the U.S. won 3-0.

A: Dead Man's Hand, The
Q: What do you call a poker hand including the black aces and eights?
W: This was the hand held by Wild Bill Hickok when he was shot and killed by Jack McCall in Deadwood, Dakota Territory, on August 2, 1876.

A: Dean Brothers, The
Q: What brothers nicknamed Dizzy and Daffy pitched for the St. Louis Cardinals?
W: While pitching for the St. Louis Cardinals on Sept. 21, 1934, in a double header against Brooklyn, the brothers limited the opponents to a total of three hits. Dizzy tossed a three-hitter in the opener, and Daffy pitched a no-hitter in the nightcap.

A: decathlon's, The
Q: What Olympic event's winner is considered the world's greatest athlete?
W: The decathlon was made an Olympic event in 1912. It was won by American Jim Thorpe. but his medals were taken away because Jim had played semi-professional baseball and thus was considered a professional athlete. His medals were restored in 1982.

A: deck of cards, A
Q: What was a "California prayer book" to an Old West gambler?
W: Cards came into use about 1855 and were also known as a California Bible. Many fortunes of gold prospectors were won and lost in card games.

A: defender, The
Q: Which *Risk* player wins tied dice rolls, the attacker or defender?
W: *Risk* is a pleasant board game in which the object is to rule the world. Wonder if it's popular in Russia?

A: Denver
Q: What city was chosen to host and then refused the 1976 Winter Olympics?
W: The games were transferred to Lake Placid in New York.

A: Denver
Q: Where is Mile High Stadium?
W: This stadium is the home of the Denver Broncos and has a seating capacity of 75,123.

A: Detroit Red Wings, The
Q: What team did Ted Lindsay, Gordie Howe, and Alex Delvecchio play together on?
W: All three of these athletes played hockey for Detroit in the 1950s and 1960s

A: Dice
Q: What loaded gaming devices were found in the ruins of Pompeii?
W: Modern looking dice from 1500 B.C. have been found in the tombs of Egypt. King Henry VIII of England staked and lost the bells of old St. Paul's Church.

A: Dice
Q: What were "ivories" to an Old West gambler?
W: Don't feel bad if you said piano keys. That's the most popular use of the term, but an old west gambler wasn't much interested in music.

A: **Dick Fosbury**
Q: Who flopped to win the 1968 Olympic gold medal in the high jump?
W: Dick used the "Fosbury Flop" to clear the 7 foot ¼ inch bar and win the gold medal. The "Fosbury Flop" was a new style of jumping in which you approach on a curved angle and at point of takeoff, you turn and go over the bar backward. I guess you could say this is one of the most successful "flops" in history!

A: **Die**
Q: What's the singular of dice?
W: A die is a cube having faces numbered from one to six that is used in many games.

A: *Diplomacy*
Q: What is Henry Kissinger's favorite board game?
W: Only God knows why!

A: **Direction**
Q: What is changed when you tack your yacht?
W: In common usage, a tack refers to a heading toward the direction of the wind

A: **Dizzy Dean**
Q: What play-by-play man once said: "They woulda had 'im at second, but he slud"?
W: Dizzy spent a total of two years in grade school. "If I'da' went to third grade," he once joked, "I'd of passed up my old man. I didn't want to show Paw up." Dizzy also quotes Will Rogers in explaining his grammar: "A lot of people who don't say 'ain't' ain't eating. I'm gonna keep on saying 'ain't' and keep on eating."

A: **Don Larsen**
Q: Who pitched a perfect game for the New York Yankees in the 1956 World Series?
W: On Oct. 8, 1956, Larsen needed only 97 pitches to beat the Brooklyn Dodgers 2-0. New York went on to win the series in seven games.

A: **Double fault**
Q: What's the tennis term for missing on first and second service?
W: A double fault consists of two successive faults committed while serving either by an inability to hit the ball over the net, by having the serve land outside the service box, or by having your foot cross the service line.

A: **Double sixes on a dice roll**
Q: What are boxcars?
W: The highest number in craps is 12. The term "boxcars" is used at the racetrack and means "high" or "long odds."

A: **Downhill, giant slalom, slalom**
Q: What are the three Alpine skiing events?
W: Downhill is, as the name expresses, leaving a starting point and seeing how fast one can reach the finish, a true race against time. A slalom course is defined by pairs of flags through which a contestant must ski from start to finish. A slalom course is at least 500 feet long while the giant slalom measures 1,000 feet.

A: **dribble, The**
Q: What basketball maneuver did Bert Loomis invent?
W: A dribble ends when a player touches the ball with both hands simultaneously, tries for a basket, or otherwise loses control, or when the ball is declared "dead." The dribble was first used as a defensive measure against losing possession of the ball. Players realized that by dribbling they could control the ball longer without passing.

A: **Dry**
Q: What does the French word *brut* mean on a wine bottle?
W: The term is applied to champagnes and other sparkling wines. Properly, it means "unmodified", a champagne to which no sweetening has been added.

A: **Duke Snider**
Q: Who was "the Duke of Flatbush"?
W: This American baseball player, born Edwin Donald Snider, was also known as the "Silver Fox."

A: **E**
Q: What letter appears on the most *Scrabble®* board crossword game tiles?
W: There are 12 *e*'s in a *Scrabble®* game and nine *A*'s along with nine *I*'s.

A: **Earthball**
Q: What game features the largest ball?
W: Earthball uses a six-foot ball and any number from two to 200 can play. The object is simply to push the ball over the other team's goal.

A: **Eddie Arcaro**
Q: What five-time winner of the Kentucky Derby lost his first 250 races?
W: When this came to Eddie's ears, he had the record books checked and they showed that he had 45 mounts before his first win on Jan. 14, 1932, the first of almost 5,000 wins.

A: **Eddie Arcaro**
Q: What jockey was nicknamed Banana Nose?
W: *Sports Illustrated* called him "the most famous man to ride a horse in America since Paul Revere." Didn't you ever hear the term winning by a nose? Actually Eddie's nose doesn't look like a banana at all.

A: **Eddie Arcaro**
Q: Who was the first jockey to ride two Triple Crown winners?
W: Eddie won the Triple Crown of racing in 1941 aboard Whirlaway and again in 1948 aboard Citation.

A: **Eddie Rickenbacker**
Q: What flying ace was the first man to wear a helmet in the Indianapolis 500?
W: In World War I Eddie was the leading American combat pilot. He shot down 22 German planes and four observation balloons. He drove in the 1911 and 1912 Indy 500 and at one point owned the track. In 1921 he opened Rickenbacker Car Company, but closed in 1925. In 1938 he purchased Eastern Airlines. During World War 2 he returned to the service and flew missions for the U.S. in both Europe and the Pacific.

A: **Eight**
Q: How many lanes does an Olympic swimming pool have?
W: An Olympic pool is 50m. (55 yards) long and 21m. (23 yards) wide. Each lane is 2.5m. (8ft. 2in.) wide.

A: **Eight**
Q: How many nail holes are there in a standard horse shoe?
W: Yup! And pitching these shoes in the form of a game was first done by the Roman soldiers around 150 A.D.

A: **Eight**
Q: How many pawns does each player have at the start of a chess game?
W: The pawns are basically used for protection of the more vital pieces. A pawn can only capture an adversary's piece by moving in a diagonal direction.

A: **Eight**
Q: How many seconds must a cowboy stay aboard a rodeo bronc?
W: Eight seconds to ride a jumping, twisting horse while holding on with one hand to a rope attached to a band around the bull's chest...nice, real nice!

A: **Eight**
Q: How many triple-word-score spaces are there on a *Scrabble*® brand crossword game board?
W: Yes, we counted them.

A: **Eight**
Q: How many warmup pitches does a reliever get coming into a baseball game?
W: That's eight on the mound, but he can toss as many as he wishes in the bull pen prior to being called into the game.

A: **Eight**
Q: What's the point value of the letter *J* in *Scrabble*® brand crossword game?
W: ...and there's only one of them in the game, so use it well!

A: **Eighteen inches**
Q: What's the diameter of a basketball hoop?
W: The hoop or basket must be ten feet high. It is bright orange with a white net attached. With some of the high scores you would think it was bigger!

A: **Eight feet**
Q: How high is a soccer goal?
W: ...and 24 feet wide, now I know why the goalie is the only one who can use his hands.

A: **Eighty-seven**
Q: How many diamonds appear in a standard deck of cards?
W: When you go to count them don't forget the two in the diagonal corners of each card. This number is also the same for hearts, clubs, and spades.

A: **El Cordobes**
Q: What was bullfighter Manuel Benitez Perez's professional name?
W: El Cordobes retired in 1977. He received $15,000 per half hour for his endeavors. Not bad, huh?

A: **Eleven**
Q: How many players are there on a cricket side?
W: This English form of baseball originated in the 13th century. Unlike baseball, there is no bench and all players are actively involved with the game at all times.

A: **Eleven**
Q: How many players are there on a soccer team?
W: One of the eleven is a goalkeeper. He is the only player who is allowed to touch the ball with his hands.

A: **England**
Q: What country has the best defensive position in the board game *Diplomacy*?
W: We used to be able to tell you why, but we've forgotten since all we play is *Trivial Pursuit*® .

A: **England**
Q: What country is considered the cradle of horse racing?
W: The first public racecourse was the Smithfield Track in London, built about 1174 A.D. The date of its opening is generally regarded as the birthday of organized racing under saddle.

A: **England**
Q: What country saw the origin of lawn tennis?
W: Major Walter C. Wingfield, a British Army officer, invented lawn tennis, introducing it at a lawn party in Wales in 1873. He had patented the name "Sphairistike" for the game.

A: **England**
Q: What country saw the origin of rugby?
W: In 1823 William Ellis at Rugby College in England was playing in an interclass football (soccer) game. The only action then was kicking. Ellis, frustrated over not being able to kick the ball, picked it up and carried it down the field. Although critized for his act, players felt the option of running with the ball added zest to a contest, and it became adopted as part of the game.

A: **Eric Heiden**
Q: What speed skater won five gold medals at the 1980 Winter Olympics?
W: In Lake Placid, New York, Eric had the following times: 500 meters in 0:38.03; 1,000 meters in 1:15.18; 1,500 meters in 1:55.44; 5,000 meters in 7:02.29 and 10,000 meters in 14:28.13.

A: **Evonne Goolagong**
Q: Who was the first Australian aboriginal to play international tennis?
W: Aborigines, descendents of the original Australians, didn't have much of a shot in the country that originally belonged to them. The odds against any of them making it in tennis are so great that only one has succeeded – Evonne. She was the winner at Wimbledon in 1971.

A: **Extra weight**
Q: What's a racehorse burdened with when handicapped in a race?
W: When a five-year-old runs with a group of three-year-olds, they must carry the extra weight in or under the saddle.

A: **FA Cup soccer final**
Q: What's played at Wembley Stadium, London, every May?
W: The Football Association Challenge Cup has been played at Wembley every year since 1923. The first finals were played in 1872 and the stadiums varied from year to year.

A: **Falconry**
Q: What's the practice of training hawks called?
W: Actually falconry is the sport of hunting with trained birds. The evidence shows that falconry was practiced by the Chinese as early as 2000 B.C.

A: **Fannie Farmer**
Q: What culinary expert was known as "the Mother of Level Measurements"?
W: Miss Farmer was born in Boston on March 23, 1857 and opened Miss Farmer's School of Cookery in 1902. She was one of the first to stress the importance of using standard measurements and following recipes exactly. She authored many cookbooks and cooking columns.

A: **Federation Cup, The**
Q: What's the women's tennis equivalent to the Davis Cup?
W: Originated in 1963, it is an annual worldwide women's tennis competition among nations.

A: **Felipe, Jesus, Matty**
Q: Who were baseball's three Alou brothers?
W: Not only were they brothers, but they all were the first to bat at new stadiums. Felipe (Atlanta) was the first batter at Bush Memorial Stadium on May 12, 1966; Jesus (Houston) at San Diego Stadium on April 8, 1969; and Matty (Pittsburgh) in Atlanta Stadium on April 12, 1966.

A: **Fencing**
Q: What sport was Boris Onishchenko caught cheating at in the Montreal Olympics?
W: Onishchenko was the Russian Silver Medalist in the 1972 Munich Olympics in the modern Pentathlon. He was disqualified in 1976 when it was discovered that his epee was wired illegally to score a hit without making contact with his opponent.

A: **Fifteen**
Q: How many numbered colored balls are there in pocket billiards?
W: The first seven are solid colors, the eight ball is black, balls 9 to 15 are striped with one color. The complete rundown: 1 = yellow, 2 = blue, 3 = red, 4 = purple, 5 = orange, 6 = green, 7 = maroon, 8 = black, 9 = yellow/white, 10 = blue/white, 11 = red/white, 12 = purple/white, 13 = orange/white, 14 = green/white, 15 = maroon/white.

A: **Fifteen**
Q: How many playing pieces does each Backgammon player start with?
W: It's what you finish with that counts (against you that is!).

A: **Fifteen**
Q: How many yards is a football team penalized for clipping?
W: Clipping is an illegal block by a player who throws his body across the back of an opponent's leg or hits him from behind.

A: **Fifteen feet**
Q: How far is the free throw line from the backboard in basketball?
W: Just far enough for Ted St. Martin of Jacksonville, Florida, who scored a record 2,036 consecutive free throws on June 25, 1977.

A: **Fifty**
Q: How many points is a bullseye worth in darts?
W: The inner eye is worth 50 points and the outer eye is worth 25 points.

A: **Fifty**
Q: How many sticks are used in jackstraws, or pickup sticks?
W: You mean there is a game you play with those? We thought they were giant toothpicks or fondue sticks!

A: **Fifty-four**
Q: How many colored squares are there on a Rubik's Cube?
W: Nine on each of the six sides. We would rather play *Trivial Pursuit®*

A: **Fifty-nine minutes**
Q: How long does it take to complete a 15-round boxing match?
W: That depends on who's fighting, but each round lasts three minutes with one minute between rounds. (That adds up to 59, doesn't it?)

A: **Fifty-two**
Q: How old was Gordie Howe when he retired from hockey for the second time?
W: In 1980 Howe, at the age of 52, retired from the Hartford Whalers. During his career, which spanned 34 years, Howe received no less than 500 stitches to his face alone but in the process set records too numerous to mention here.

A: **Figure skating**
Q: What sport uses the term "double axel"?
W: An axel is a jump from the outside edge of one skate to the back outside of the other, making a 540 degree turn. A double axel is the immediate repetition of this movement.

A: **Filly**
Q: What's a young female racehorse called?
W: A filly is a thoroughbred of age four or less or a standardbred of age three or less.

A: **final out, The**
Q: When's a baseball game never over until?
W: ...or as Yogi Berra put it, "It's not over until it's over."

A: **first automobile race, The**
Q: What did an Oshkosh steamer win?
W: The first automobile race occurred in 1878 and was a 201-mile race from Greenbay, Wisconsin, to Madison, Wisconsin.

A: **Fishing**
Q: What does a piscatologist excel at?
W: This word is from the Latin term *piscarius*, meaning "fish" or "hunting."

A: **Fishing**
Q: What sport uses plugs and leaders?
W: A plug is a lure that consists of a solid wood, plastic, or cork body with one or more hooks. The leader is the length of line or wire between the end of the main fishing line and the hook or lure. Sorry, Charlie!

A: **Five**
Q: How many dice are used to play Yahtzee?
W: It is a dice game invented by E.S. Lowe in which you roll five dice to score for certain combinations akin to poker hands, such as straights and twos and threes of a kind.

A: **Five**
Q: How many innings constitute an official baseball game?
W: ...more than half of the regulation game.

A: **Five**
Q: How many innings must a starting pitcher work to gain credit for a victory?

W: Five out of the nine innings of a regulation game must be worked by the starting pitcher in order to gain a victory. He can also gain a win with a majority of the game whether he starts the game or relieves the starting pitcher.

A: **Five**
Q: How many sets are there in a full-length men's championship tennis match?
W: You must win three of five games to claim the victory. Women's championships are best of three games.

A: **Five**
Q: How many yards is a football team penalized for going offside?
W: After the teams line up, a player that moves across the line of scrimmage is offside.

A: **Five**
Q: What age does a filly become a mare at?
W: Considered an "older" female racehorse, a filly becomes a mare at age five or older. A standardbred is a mare at age four or older.

A: **Five**
Q: What's the point value of the letter K in *Scrabble®* Brand Crossword Game?
W: That's correct...and there is only one piece with the letter K so go for the triple word square!

A: **Five aces**
Q: What's the highest hand in five-card draw poker with wild cards?
W: If you draw this hand, bet the moon.

A: **Five-card poker**
Q: What card game has 2,598,960 possible hands?
W: ...with more losers than winners!

A: **Five of a kind**
Q: What's the only poker hand that has to include a wild card?
W: Because there are only four of any card in a deck, to get five you have to have a wild card.

A: Five P.M.
Q: What's the traditional hour for a bullfight to begin?
W: In most countries in which bullfights are held, the events take place in the late afternoon of the summer season. In Mexico, bullfights are held thoughout the year. The reason for 5pm is that it is too hot to fight during the middle of the day.

A: Floyd Patterson
Q: Who did Sonny Liston succeed as world heavyweight boxing champion?
W: On Sept. 25, 1962, Sonny knocked out Patterson in the first round in Chicago. A rematch between the two was held on July 22, 1963, – deja vu, Liston won in the first round again.

A: Floyd Patterson and Ingemar Johansson
Q: What two boxers met in title bouts in June 1959, June 1960, and March 1961?
W: In 1959 Johansson knocked out Patterson in the third round. In 1960 Patterson became the first heavyweight to regain his title by knocking out Johansson in the fifth. Johansson tried again and this time he did better, but not much – Patterson won in the sixth round.

A: flush, A
Q: What do you call a poker hand with five cards of the same suit?
W: Any five cards of the same suit but not is sequence is a flush. If you have them in sequence it's a straight flush.

A: flush, A
Q: What's the lowest hand that beats a straight in poker?
W: A straight is five consecutive cards but not of the same suit. Five consecutive cards in the same suit is a straight flush. A flush is five nonconsecutive cards of the same suit.

A: Football
Q: What North American field sport has the most rules?
W: ...and they seem to add new ones every year. Who says football players are dumb?

A: Football
Q: What professional sport did the Canton Bulldogs and Providence Steamrollers play?
W: In 1904 an Ohio newspaperman, looking for something to fill the sports season void, hit upon the idea of pro football. And so were born the Canton Bulldogs. In 1928 one of the first teams formed, the Providence Steamrollers, won their first and only title.

A: Football
Q: What sport did Burt Reynolds play at Florida State University?
W: Burt "Buddy" Reynolds, Number 20, was a running back for the Seminoles in 1954 and 1957 before a knee injury ended his career. Another FSU football alumnus that made it big in Hollywood was Robert "Vegas" Urich.

A: Football
Q: What sport did John Wayne play at the University of Southern California?
W: The Duke was a tackle for the Trojans in 1925 and 1926. In 1927, with the help of his coach, he got a bit part in a movie that ended his college days but started his illustrious movie career.

A: Football
Q: What sport do you throw bombs in?
W: A bomb is a forward pass of considerable length. It is a low precentage pass but when complete results in a large gain, lots of cheering and usually wild dances if it makes it to the end zone.

A: Football
Q: What sport features slotbacks, tailbacks, and touchbacks?
W: A slotback is a running back positioned between the outside of the tackle and the split end. A tailback is also a running back, the farthest back in the formation. A touchback occurs when a ball is dead behind a team's own goal line, providing the impetus came from the opponent and it is not a touchdown or missed field goal.

A: Football
Q: What sport sees striped-shirted men working on the chain gang?
W: The chain which is exactly ten yards long is used to determine first downs. The men in the striped shirts are the referees.

A: footrace, A
Q: What ends when the winner breasts the tape?
W: Breasting the tape refers to the racer breaking the tape at the end of the race with his or her chest. The runner must not reach out with hands or arms to break the tape.

A: Forty
Q: How many feet apart are the stakes in men's horseshoe pitching?
W: Yes, but the throwing line is to be marked two feet in front of each peg in regulation play, so you "pitch" the shoe 38 feet not 40!

A: Forty
Q: How many spaces are there on a *Monopoly®* Brand Crossword board?
W: All the streets are actual streets that can be found in Atlantic City. There are spaces for four railroads, two utilities, one jail , one go to jail, one go collect $200, one free park-

ing, three community chests, one income tax, three chances, one luxury tax, and 22 streets.

A: **Forty-four**
Q: How many points does the word *quiz*, without blanks, score if it's the first played in *Scrabble* Brand Crossword Game?
W: Q = 10 points, U = 1 point, I = 1 point, Z = 10 point. That equals 22 points; however the first word played is worth double the letters' point value.

A: **Forty-two**
Q: How many dots are there on a pair of dice?
W: Really there are better things to do with your time. But 21 dots a die is 42 a pair. What is interesting is that if you add up the opposite sides of a die the total will always total be seven.

A: **Forty-two**
Q: How many eyes are there in a deck of 52 cards?
W: Nine of the court cards have four eyes each; the jacks of spades and hearts are "one-eyed," and so is the king of diamonds, so that's 42.

A: **Four**
Q: How many gold medals did Jesse Owens win in the 1936 Olympics?
W: Jesse won golds in the following: 100-meter sprint (10.3 seconds); 200-meter sprint (20.7 seconds); broad jump, (26ft-5/16 inches); and the 400-meter relay (39.8 seconds).

A: **Four**
Q: How many horses are there on a polo team?
W: Basically, polo is soccer on horses. This game must be gaining popularity; we see so many people with polo players on their shirts.

A: **Four**
Q: How many Olympic Games were canceled because of World War II?
W: The 1940 summer games were to be held in Tokyo, and preparation began until Japan became involved in the Indo-China war. The Olympic

Committee looked toward Helsinki, but the Finns were overtaken by war. The 1940 winter games were proposed for Garmisch-Partenkirchen, the 1944 summer games were to have been in London, and the 1944 winter games were to have been in Cortina d'Ampezzo.

A: **Four**
Q: How many pins form the back row in tenpin bowling?
W: The pins are placed in a triangle; the back row pins are numbered 7, 8, 9, and 10.

A: **Four**
Q: How many rings are there on a five-zone archery target?
W: One bull's eye and four rings make five zones. Tricky!

A: **Four**
Q: How many seams are there on a football?
W: The ball is an inflated rubber bladder enclosed in leather. Other specifications vary from league to league. But generally it is 11 to 11.25 inches in length, 28 to 28.5 inches along the long circumference, 21.25 to 21.5 inches around the short circumference, and 14 to 15 ounces in weight.

A: **Four**
Q: How many umpires handle a regular season major league baseball game?
W: One at each base: first, second, third, and home plate. Good eyesight, however, has never been a prerequiste!

A: **Four**
Q: What dice roll in craps is nicknamed "Little Dick"?
W: It is also referred to as "Little Joe", "Little Joe from Baltimore", and "Little Joe from Kokomo."

A: **Four**
Q: What's men's par on a 455-yard golf hole?
W: Usually, but not always the case. The USGA rules state that a par four hole must not exceed 470 yards and

generally be over 451 yards. But there are many par five holes that measure less than 455 yards.

A: **Four and a quarter inches**
Q: What's the diameter of a golf hole?
W: It must also be four inches deep. But it sure looks smaller than four and one quarter inches across sometimes!

A: **Four Horsemen of Notre Dame, The**
Q: Who did the Seven Mules block for?
W: The great football backfield was otherwise known as Harry Stuhldreher, Don Miller, Jim Crowley, and Elmer Layden.

A: **four-minute mile, The**
Q: What was broken at Oxford, England, on May 6, 1954?
W: Dr. Roger Bannister first broke the four minute mile with a time of 3:59.4.

A: **four of clubs, The**
Q: What playing card was once known as "the devil's bedposts"?
W: The term is used in contract bridge, and the nickname came into use about 1930.

A: **Fourteen**
Q: What's the maximum number of clubs a golfer may use in a round?
W: It's a two-stroke penalty for each additional club in your bag, and, yes, a ball retriever is considered a club.

A: **France**
Q: What country did roulette originate in?
W: *Roulette* is French for "small wheel." This casino gambling game is said to have been invented by French scientist Blaise Pascal in 1655 in his search for a perpetual motion machine! Others believe the wheel is from an ancient Chinese game.

A: **Frank Robinson**
Q: Who was the first black major league baseball manager?
W: Frank was the MVP in both the American and National leagues, the Triple Crown winner in 1966, and the coach of the Cleveland Indians in 1975. In his first game as player/manager, April 8, 1975, Frank slugged a home run as the designated hitter. (Nice managerial decision, Frank!)

A: **Fred Perry**
Q: Who was the first man to win three consecutive Wimbledon singles tennis titles?
W: Here's when and against whom: in 1934 he defeated Jack Crawford; in 1935 he defeated Gottfried von Cramm; in 1936 he again defeated Gottfried von Cramm.

A: **Friday**
Q: What night of the week was Fight Night at Madison Square Garden in the 1950s?
W: However, in the 1950s fights were on television four to five nights a week. This overexposure almost wiped out the sport in the U.S.

A: **Fried chicken**
Q: What's the most commonly ordered sit-down meal in U.S. restaurants?
W: Where's the beef?! On the average, each American eats almost 63 pounds of chicken a year.

A: **Frisbee, The**
Q: What was originally called the Pluto Platter?
W: The Pluto Platter is the basic design for all succeeding Frisbees. Credit Fred Morrison, the inventor, for hitting on plastic instead of the old pie tins originally tossed about.

A: **front crawl, The; or freestyle**
Q: What's the fastest stroke in swimming?
W: Since the crawl is the fastest competitive stroke, it is invariably used in freestyle competition.

A: **full house, A**
Q: What poker hand comprises three of a kind and a pair?
W: In evaluating two or more competing full houses, the hand with the highest three-of-a-kind wins, regardless of the rank of the pair.

A: **full house, A**
Q: What's the lowest hand that beats a flush in poker?
W: The standard rank of poker hands, without use of wild cards, is as follows: 1) royal flush; 2) straight flush; 3) four of a kind; 4) full house; 5) flush; 6) straight; 7) three of a kind; 8) two pairs; 9) one pair; and 10) high card.

G

A: **Galliano**
Q: What yellow Italian liqueur goes into a Harvey Wallbanger?
W: What's a Harvey Wallbanger? A drink, and here's how you make one: Mix one ounce of Vodka with four ounces of orange juice, then float one half ounce of Galliano on top. The sweetness of the Galliano makes them go down easy — beware!!

A: **Gary Player**
Q: Who was the first non-American to win the Masters golf title?
W: A native of South Africa, Gary won the 1961 Masters by carding a score of 280 edging out Arnold Palmer by one stroke. Arnie gained revenge the following year by beating Player in a playoff for the 1962 Masters Title.

A: **Gene Autry**
Q: What cowboy star is part-owner of the California Angels baseball team?
W: There's no truth to the rumor that when Reggie Jackson dies, Gene will have him stuffed and placed next to Champion!

A: **Gene Tunney**
Q: Who was the only boxer to defeat Jack Dempsey twice?
W: On Sept. 23, 1926, Tunney outpointed Dempsey. The rematch was on Sept. 22, 1927. It was this rematch that had the long count controversy. Tunney was knocked down in the seventh round but got up to win a decision over Dempsey. Film shows Tunney was actually down for 16 seconds.

A: **General Motors**
Q: What company makes the Corvette Stingray?
W: This two seat fiberglass sports car was introduced in 1953 by the Chevrolet Division of General Motors. They want a lot of money for a plastic car with only two seats and no trunk!

A: **Gentlemen, start your engines**
Q: What words signal the start of the Indianapolis 500?
W: That was the traditional line that started all of the Indy 500 races until 1977 when the line had to be altered a bit to recognize Janet Guthrie. The line then became "Lady and Gentlemen, start your engines!" Janet didn't finish the race; mechanical difficulties forced her out of the race after 27 laps.

A: **George Blanda**
Q: Who played for the Chicago Bears, Houston Oilers, and Oakland Raiders in a 26-year pro football careeer?
W: George started his career as quarterback with the Bears in 1949-50 and ended it as a kicker with the Raiders. In 26 years as an active player, he scored 2,002 points. He holds the records for playing in the most games, most seasons, and most consecutive games as well.

A: **George Herman**
Q: What were Babe Ruth's Christian names?
W: In 1914, Jack Dunn, owner of Baltimore's International League Club, signed a 19-year-old, gawky, left-handed pitcher and tagged him with the nickname "Babe". Before the 1914 season was over he was sold to the Boston Red Sox. As a pitcher his credentials are 94 wins and 46 losses with a 2.28 ERA.

A: **George Plimpton**
Q: Who was "the Paper Lion"?
W: In this 1966 book, author George Plimpton practiced as a quarterback with the Detroit Lions and Baltimore Colts as research. In 1968 *Paper Lion* was made into a movie and Alan Alda portrayed the "Paper Lion."

A: **Germany, Italy, Japan**
Q: What three International Olympic Committee countries weren't invited to the 1948 Summer Games?
W: It was punishment for their actions during World War II.

A: **Gil Hodges**
Q: Who managed the New York Mets to the 1969 World Series title?
W: The Miracle Mets bested the Baltimore Orioles by sweeping four consecutive games after losing the opener.

A: **Glenfiddich**
Q: What's the best known brand of straight, or single, malt scotch?
W: The most preferred brand is Macallan, but since it is rarely available, the best known is Glenfiddich, established in 1869.

A: **glider, A**
Q: What kind of aircraft could you use a bungey launch or a car tow on?
W: Although resembling an airplane, a glider has no engine for sustained flight and could easily be towed by a car.

A: **glove, A**
Q: What baseball equipment was first baseman Charles Waite the first to wear?
W: A skin tight glove with the fingertips cut off was reputedly first worn by Charles C. Waite while playing first base for St. Louis in 1875. This was 25 after the organization of the first baseball team.

A: **go-kart, A**
Q: What did Stan Mott drive around the world?
W: Twenty-eight-year-old Stan Mott, a free-lance illustrator and go-kart enthusiast, departed New York City in the spring of 1961 and began a round-the-world trip on his go-kart. After three years of traveling through dozens of countries, Stan arrived on the west coast and traveled across the U.S. to end this record-setting event in New York City in the spring of 1964. Some of the more notable experiences included over 160 traffic citations, crossing the Sahara Desert, and getting hepatitis in Japan. There was one major crash in the Swiss Alps that required the rebuilding of Stan's cart by Italkart in Italy. The most frequently asked question was, believe it or not, "Hey, mister, do those tires have air in them?" (Source: Robert (last name withheld), Stan's best friend.)

A: **Golf**
Q: What sport did George Plimpton write about in *The Bogey Man*?
W: George joined the PGA tour to get first-hand experience for this book: an in-depth look at the life of a professional golfer.

A: **Golf**
Q: What sport do competitors play for the Ryder Cup in?
W: Samuel A. Ryder, a wealthy seed merchant, offered a solid gold cup to the winner of matches between British and U.S. professionals. This competition has been held on alternating years at alternating sites in the U.S. and Britain since 1927, except 1938 to 1946 because of World War II. New rules now state a professional born in any European country can compete against the U.S.

A: **Golf**
Q: What sport features Scotch foursomes?
W: Two partners play the same ball while alternating shots.

A: **Golf**
Q: What sport used the term "mashie-niblick"?
W: It is an earlier term used for an iron-headed club, comparable to a seven-iron.

A: **Golf and tennis**
Q: What two ball sports use the term ace?
W: In golf a hole-in-one constitutes an ace. An ace in tennis occurs when your opponent fails to return your serve and you are awarded the point. This answer does not take into account any personal references to another player in any other sport, for example, "Nice shot, Ace!".

A: **golf ball, A**
Q: What did Floyd Rood drive across the U.S.?
W: He played from the Pacific surf to the Atlantic surf Sept. 14, 1963 to Oct. 3, l964. It took him 114,737 strokes to complete the 3,397.7 mile course. Duffers take heart – Rood lost 3,511 balls!

A: **golf ball, A**
Q: What has 336 dimples?
W: This is a matter of controversy among avid golfers. Although 336 was the industry standard at one time the number of dimples and configuration now vary from manufacturer to manufacturer. The USGA places no requirements as to the number of dimples, but it does state a ball must not weigh over 1.62 ounces, cannot measure less than 1.68 inches, or travel with a velocity of over 250 feet per second. (Much ado about nothing!)

A: **Gordie Howe**
Q: Who's played in the most NHL all-star games?
W: Gordie Howe leads all other players with 20 all-star games to his credit. Bobby Hull is next with 12.

A: **Gordie Howe**
Q: Who's the NHL's all-time leading goal scorer?
W: Playing for the Detroit Red Wings, Gordie had 786 goals to his credit.

A: **Gorgeous George**
Q: Who had Chanel No. 5 sprayed in the ring before he wrestled?
W: He was a 1950s wrestler who wore his blonde hair in rollers! Born George Raymond Wagner in 1915, he died in 1964. George was ever the showman, having his valet douse the ring with Chanel No. 10 before each bout! (*10* is correct.)

A: **Grand Prix auto racing**
Q: What sport did Juan Fangio win five world championships in?
W: He won world championships in 1951, 1954, 1955, 1956, and 1957. He retired in 1958 at the age of 46.

A: **Grass**
Q: What kind of surface are the Wimbledon tennis championships played on?
W: In 1877 the first championship was held at the All England Croquet Club at Wimbledon on the turf of Worpole Road. Although today most courts are of clay composition, Wimbledon has stuck with grass.

A: **Gravity**
Q: What provides the power in a soap box derby?
W: This annual contest is held in Akron, Ohio. The final race is run on a 975.4-foot coasting track known as "Derby Downs." The total weight of the car and driver must not exceed 250 pounds in the Senior Division and 210 pounds in the Junior Division. Since the soap box is a motorless vehicle, gravity is the only force!

A: ***Greatest, The***
Q: What's the title of Muhammad Ali's autobiography?
W: What else would he title it? After all, it *is* an autobiography!

A: **Green**
Q: What color is displayed on the starboard side of a boat?
W: The starboard is the right side; the left side is the port side, and the red light is displayed there.

A: **Green Bay Packers, The**
Q: What team won the first Super Bowl?
W: Green Bay beat the Kansas City Chiefs 35-10 at the Los Angeles Coliseum in 1967.

A: **Green Bay Packers, The**
Q: What's the only community-owned franchise in the NFL?
W: Almost 50 different cities have been affiliated with the NFL in its 40 year history. Only two, Green Bay and Chicago, have been represented from the beginning in 1919 up until today. The population of Green Bay was about 30,000 in 1919 when "Curly" Lambeau talked the Indian Packing Company into sponsoring a professional football team.

A: **Green and white**
Q: What are the team colors of the Boston Celtics?
W: Always have been, probably always will be! Let us not forget another characteristic of their uniforms – black shoes!!

A: **greyhound, The; and whippet**
Q: What two breeds of dog are used in parimutuel racing?
W: It is believed that a whippet is actually a breed of greyhound; however, a whippet is smaller, 18 to 22 inches tall and ten to 28 pounds. A greyhound is about 26 inches tall with an average weight of 65 pounds.

A: **Ground-rule double**
Q: What's the umpire's ruling if a line drive hits the third base bag and bounces into the stands?
W: A ground-rule double is also awarded when a fair fly ball goes under, through, over, or lodges in a fence. Now if the ball were to bounce at least 250 feet from the home plate and continue over the fence, it would be a home run. However, we think the powers that be would question a ball being able to do that!

A: **Gymnastics**
Q: What sport did Olga Korbut excel at?
W: Born in 1956, this Soviet gymnast won three Gold Medals in the 1972 Summer Olympics held in Munich.

H

A: hand, The
Q: What's the unit of measure for a racehorse's height?
W: It is a unit of measurement that is equal to four inches.

A: Hank Aaron
Q: Who holds the career record for the most major league home runs?
W: Hank has 755 in total. He broke Babe Ruth's record of 714 by hitting number 715 on April 8, 1974, in Atlanta off Los Angeles Dodgers' pitcher Al Downing. But the all-league record of 800 in a lifetime has been claimed by Josh Gibson, one of the Homestead Greys in the old Negro League.

A: Hank Aaron
Q: Who retired with 755 home runs to his credit?
W: Hank retired in 1976 from the Milwaukee Brewers and baseball at the age of 43.

A: Harlem Globetrotters, The
Q: What team did Abraham M. Saperstein establish and send on the road in 1927?
W: This native of London, England, formed the Harlem Globetrotters, an all black basketball team. They played their first game on Jan. 7, 1927, in Hinckley, Illinois.

A: Harlem Globetrotters, The
Q: What's the most-traveled sports team?
W: This trick-shooting comedic basketball team has played over 12,000 games in nearly 100 countries.

A: Harness racing
Q: What form of horse racing boasts the Little Brown Jug?

W: The first leg of harness racing's Triple Crown is held in Delaware, Ohio. The Little Brown Jug is also the trophy awarded to the winner of the Minnesota-Michigan football game.

A: Harness racing
Q: What sport can a free-legged pacer compete in?
W: A pace is a lateral, swaying gait in which the legs on one side (of the horse) are thrust forward in unison followed by the other side. Pacers are faster than trotters.

A: Harvard, Princeton, Yale
Q: What are the Big Three colleges of the Ivy League?
W: The question here is do they play two-handed touch above or below the waist. Big time football escaped the Ivy League years ago, although the annual Harvard-Yale game is referred to as "The Game".

A: Havana cigar, A
Q: What's a Rafael Gonzalez Vitola E?
W: It's probably very expensive and likely not imported into the U.S. because of the embargo. But to be honest we couldn't find one.

A: He pitched a perfect game
Q: What did Jim Bunning do on June 21, 1964?
W: Bunning, of the Philadelphia Phillies, won 6-0 over the New York Mets in New York. This was Jim's second no-hitter, the first being on July 20, 1958, while with the Detroit Tigers, beating Boston 3-0.

A: He refused miliary induction
Q: Why was Muhammad Ali stripped of his title and barred from boxing in 1967?
W: Because of religious beliefs Ali (Cassius Clay) refused to be drafted. He was allowed to return to boxing by a ruling of the Supreme Court. In 1974 he knocked out George Foreman to regain the title. He lost to Leon Spinks on Feb. 15, 1978, but the "Louisville Lip" came back to

beat Spinks Sept. 15, 1978, and retired as champion in 1979. Ali was the only heavyweight to win the title three times.

A: He turned a triple play
Q: What did second baseman Billy Wambsganss do all by himself in a 1920 World Series game?
W: The Cleveland Indians' second baseman turned the only unassisted triple play in World Series history. Cleveland won the series beating Brooklyn.

A: Hearts
Q: What suit is "the Suicide King"?
W: In a regular deck of 52 playing cards all four kings are holding weapons; however, the king of hearts has his weapon (a dagger) stuck in his head. Get the Excedrin!

A: Hearts and spades
Q: What two suits are the one-eyed jacks in a deck of cards?
W: That's right. We looked and so can you, just to make sure!

A: Hedonism
Q: What's the term for pleasure-seeking as a way of life?
W: It's the way the author will live if this book sells! Actually it comes from the Greek word *hedone* meaning "pleasure".

A: Heisman Trophy, The
Q: What trophy goes to the outstanding U.S. college football player of the year?
W: It's given by the Downtown Athletic Club of New York and was first awarded in 1935 to Jay Berwanger of the University of Chicago. Notre Dame has produced the most Heisman Trophy winners.

A: Helsinki
Q: Where were the 1952 Summer Olympics?
W: The United States was the unofficial winner of the games held in Helsinki, Finland.

A: **high jump, The**
Q: What track and field event can you use the scissors in?
W: But now more athletes use the Dick "Fosbury" flop style in the high jump.

A: **higher, The**
Q: Which point value counts when an arrow cuts two colors of an archery target, the higher or lower?
W: That's nice, not often does the advantage go to the player.

A: **His own**
Q: Whose record did Babe Ruth break when he hit 60 home runs in 1927?
W: The Bambino slugged 47 round-trippers in 1926 and 46 in 1924. He also held the major league home run record in three consecutive years, 1919 to 1921.

A: **Hits a single, double, triple, homer**
Q: What does a baseball player do in a game if he "hits for the cycle"?
W: Meaning to hit safely for all the possible types of hits in a single game.

A: **Hockey**
Q: What sport gives you 24 square feet to shoot at?
W: The goal net opening is six feet wide and four feet high.

A: **Hockey**
Q: What's the only major sport that allows substitutions while play is in progress?
W: Substitutes may be introduced into play whenever the game is stopped (when the puck is dead) but no substitution may be made unless the player to be relieved has left the ice. Substitute players are considered essential because of the fast speed at which the game is played.

A: **Holy Bible, The**
Q: What did Forrest Smithson carry for inspiration while running the hurdles at the 1908 Olympics?
W: I guess it helped the U.S. track star who took the gold in the 110-meter hurdles in London.

A: **home run, A**
Q: What's a ball that hits the foul pole called?
W: A foul pole, either of two vertical poles placed at or near the boundary of the field on the foul line, serves as a vertical extension of the foul line to aid the umpire in determining whether a ball hit to the outfield is fair or foul.

A: **Horn**
Q: What's the first word played in the *Scrabble*® Brand Crossword Game rules demonstration game?
W: Correct, and to continue the example: *farm* is the second word, linked by the *R*.

A: **horse race in the rain, A**
Q: What's a good mudder likely to win?
W: When it rains a horse track becomes quite sloppy and muddy and many horses perform better under these track conditions.

A: **Horse racing**
Q: What's known as "the Sport of Kings"?
W: England is considered the birthplace of horse racing under saddle. The first public racecourse was the Smithfield Track in London, built about 1174 A.D.

A: **Horse racing**
Q: What's the most attended sport in the U.S.?
W: Racing is a billion dollar industry that gives jobs to more than 60,000 persons and has a payroll of almost $250,000,000 each year.

A: **Horses**
Q: What were raced in Greek and Roman hippodromes?
W: The origin of horse racing is lost in time, but it was evidently derived from warfare chariot racing and the chase. A hippodrome, from the Greek *hippos*, meaning "horse," was a large open-air stadium with an oval course for horse and chariot races.

A: **Houston Astrodome, The**
Q: What stadium did Bobby Riggs and Billie Jean King battle it out in?
W: On Sept. 20, 1973, Ms. King defeated Mr. Riggs 6-4, 6-3, 6-3 before 30,492 spectators. Riggs had swept the 1939 Wimbledon championships four years before Billie Jean was born!

A: **Howard Cosell**
Q: What sports broadcaster graduated Phi Beta Kappa from law school?
W: Howard studied English literature at New York University, where he received his Phi Beta Kappa key. He then entered law school and was admitted to the bar at the age of 21 in 1940. He practiced law until 1956 when he entered broadcasting.

A: **Howard Cosell**
Q: Who tells it like it is?
W: The wide wide mouth of sports was the only personality to be both first and last in a poll of sports commentators.

A: **hula hoop, The**
Q: What was the biggest-selling toy of 1957?
W: We show the hula hoop being invented in 1958 by two California toymakers. Their company, Wham-O, began selling the plastic rings for $1.98. Within six months they sold almost 30 million hoops.

A: **Hurling**
Q: What sport uses a ball called a slitter?
W: Hurling is the national sport of Ireland, similar to field hockey. The ball is called a sliothar, which means "ball" in Gaelic.

I

A: **Idi Amin**
Q: What former African leader held his country's boxing title for nine years?
W: He was the heavyweight champ of Uganda from 1951 to 1960.

A: **Illinois Avenue**
Q: What is the most landed-on *Monopoly®* property?
W: The 24th spot on the board, it is a red property with a price of $240.

A: **In a plane crash**
Q: How did golfer Champagne Tony Lema die?
W: Tony was known for setting up champagne for the press after every victory. He died on July 24, 1966.

A: **In a plane crash**
Q: How did Rocky Marciano die?
W: Rocky Marciano, the undefeated heavyweight champion from 1952 to 1956, died in a 1969 plane crash on an Iowa farm. He was flying in a private plane to a party to celebrate his 46th birthday.

A: **Indianapolis Motor Speedway, The**
Q: Where is "Gasoline Alley"?
W: "Gasoline Alley" is a term that refers to the two buildings in which Indy participants store and work on their cars. There are 88 garage stalls, but the numbers go up to 89 because there is no stall number 13.

A: **India rubber**
Q: What's a lacrosse ball made of?
W: In our book if you said sponge rubber, you would also be correct.

A: **Ingemar Johansson**
Q: Who was the last white man to hold the world heavyweight boxing championship?

W: In 1959 Ingmar of Sweden beat Floyd Patterson who returned the favor in 1961.

A: **Ingemar Johansson**
Q: Who was the only Swede to hold the world heavyweight boxing championship?
W: On June 26, 1959, as a one to four underdog, the "wooden shoe" defeated Floyd Patterson with a third round knockout.

A: **Inside the penalty area**
Q: Where must a soccer goalie stand to be permitted to handle the ball?
W: In soccer you are not permitted to touch the ball with your hands unless you are the goalie; but if the goalie leaves the penalty area (the area around the goal), he also is not allowed to touch the ball with his hands.

A: **In the shade**
Q: Where are the most expensive seats at a bullfight?
W: The seats of the bullring are uncovered, except for the *palcos* (boxes) and the *grada* (first gallery). Not only is the temperature better, but you can see the whole ring better because the seats are higher. The seats on the west walls of the bullring building are called *sombra* (shade). They are the most expensive because they are in the shade when the fight commences.

A: **Israel's exclusion**
Q: What averted an Arab boycott of the 1948 Summer Olympics?
W: The International Olympic Committee ruled that the new state of Israel could not compete because it was not yet a member of the International Olympic Committee.

A: **Italy**
Q: What country has won the most contract bridge world championships?
W: The world championship, known as the Bermuda Bowl, has been dominated by *suadra assurra*, Italy's blue team. They have won over 50 percent of all championships to date.

A: **It's the oldest in North America**
Q: What's the claim to fame of the Royal Montreal Golf Club?
W: It was established in 1873 and later followed by the Foxburg Golf Club in Foxburg, Pennsylvania.

J

A: **J and X**
Q: What two *Scrabble®* Brand Crossword game letters have eight-point values?
W: If you used the word *juxtapose*, you would amaze your friends and get lots of points too!

A: **Jack Dempsey**
Q: What heavyweight boxing champion was nicknamed "the Manassa Mauler"?
W: This term was coined by Damon Runyon because Dempsey was born in Manassa, Colorado. A little more trivia: Jack kept some pretty rich company. In fact, one of his sparring partners was J. Paul Getty.

A: **Jack Dempsey and Gene Tunney**
Q: What two boxers were involved in 1927's long-count bout?
W: This match took place on Sept. 22, 1927, in Soldier Field, Chicago, Illinois. It was the largest gate ever for a professional boxing match. Tunney, the champ, was knocked down in the seventh round. The referee started the count but noticed Dempsey was not in his corner. So he advised Jack to return to his corner and then resumed the count. Tunney got up and won the fight by a decision.

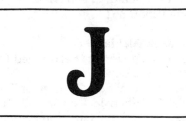

A: Jack Daniels
Q: What renowned sour mash whiskey is made in Lynchburg, Tennessee?
W: ...and the next time you are in the neighborhood you can stop in for a tour: Jack Daniels Distillery, Route 1, Lynchburg, Tennessee, 37352; population 361.

A: Jack Nicklaus
Q: What golfer has been called Ohio Fats and Blobbo?
W: What about "Whaleman" and "Jelly"? When Jack embarked on the first tour, the Ohio State graduate weighed over 200 lbs. Many of these names were used by the soldiers of Arnie's Army who were witnessing this youngster regularly beating their general, Arnold Palmer.

A: Jack Nicklaus
Q: What golfer is nicknamed "the Golden Bear"?
W: OK, you can't continue to call the greatest player of modern golf Blobbo. Once this blonde kid started tearing up the tour and attacking the course like an angry bear, the name had to change. It has also been said that in Jack's weight loss process, he went on a bear meat diet.

A: Jack Nicklaus
Q: Who won the U.S. Open golf title "washed up at 40"?
W: He won at Baltusrol Country Club scoring 272, three shots better than the last time he won in the U.S. Open on the same course. As Jack put it "the longer you play, the better chance the better player has of winning".

A: Jack Nicklaus, Arnold Palmer, Gary Player
Q: What golfers were once known as "the Big Three"?
W: Of course this was B.T. (before Trevino). In the 1960s this threesome was responsible for winning a total of 16 major championships, including the Masters, U.S. Open, British Open and PGA. To this day they are three of the most popular players on the tour.

A: Jack Nicklaus, Arnold Palmer, Gary Player
Q: What three golfers corralled the Masters title for seven years starting in 1960?
W: Here is a detailed breakdown for all you golf fans: 1960, Palmer with a 282; 1961, Player with a 280; 1962, Palmer in a playoff with Player; 1963, Nicklaus with a 286; 1964, Palmer with a 276; 1965, Palmer with a 271; 1966, Nicklaus in a playoff with Jacobs and Brewer. Since then Nicklaus has won again in 1972 and 1975; Player in 1974 and 1978.

A: Jai-alai
Q: What sport features the fastest moving ball?
W: During play speeds of more than 150 mph or 220 feet per second are not uncommon. This game was imported from Spain by way of Cuba. However, a professional golfer's drive from the tee averages 155 mph.

A: jai-alai player, A
Q: What player uses a *cesta* to hurl a *pelota*?
W: The *cesta* is the wicker basket strapped to the players hand and used to throw the *pelota* (Spanish for "ball").

A: Jake LaMotta's
Q: What boxer's life story is titled *Raging Bull*
W: It's the story of the middleweight champ from the Bronx who held the title from 1949 to 1951.

A: James J. Corbett's
Q: What boxer's nickname was Gentleman Jim?
W: Gentleman Jim fought heavyweight from 1886 to 1903. He had 33 professional bouts, winning 20, nine by knockouts. He was World Champion from Sept. 7, 1892, when he knocked out John L. Sullivan in 21 rounds at New Orleans, Louisiana, until March 17, 1897, when he was knocked out by Bob Fitzsimmons in 11 rounds at Carson City, Nevada. He fought suc-cessfully under Queensbury Rules, and his tasteful dress and personality added to his being called "Gentleman Jim". He also had the lead in several stage plays and was considered a competent actor.

A: James Michener
Q: What Pulitzer-Prize-winning author wrote *Sports in America*
W: Michener won the Pulitzer for *Tales of the South Pacific* in 1948. Other works of Michener's include *Hawaii* published in 1959 and *Bridges at Toko-Ri* published in 1953.

A: Janet Guthrie
Q: Who was the first woman to race in the Indianapolis 500?
W: Janet drove in the 1977 classic; however, she didn't finish the 500 miles. Mechanical difficulties forced her out of the competition after 27 laps.

A: Jarry Park
Q: What was the Montreal Expos' home before they moved to Olympic Stadium?
W: The Expos, who joined the National Baseball League in 1969, moved into the stadium built for the 1976 Summer Olympics following the conclusion of the games.

A: javelin, The
Q: What's usually thrown the farthest in a track and field competition?
W: True, in men's Olympic competition, javelin throwers consistently outdistance discus throwers. However, the reverse is true in women's competition.

A: Jean-Claude Killy
Q: Who swept the men's Alpine skiing events at the 1968 Winter Olympics?
W: Jean-Claude Killy, from France, took the gold in the downhill, giant slalom, and slalom. Jean-Claude was only the second man ever to sweep the three events, the first being Anton Sailer in 1956.

A: **Jersey Joe Walcott**
Q: What boxer lost the most heavyweight title fights?
W: Prior to his win over Ezzard Charles, Jersey Joe tried and failed on four previous occasions. This is a record for the most times challenging for the title.

A: **Jersey Joe Walcott**
Q: Who's the oldest man to have held the world heavyweight boxing title?
W: Jersey Joe's real name was Arnold Raymond Cream. He defeated Ezzard Charles by a knockout in the seventh round in a bout held at Pittsburgh's Forbes Field on July 18, 1951. At the age of 37, Walcott was the oldest man to have won the world heavyweight title.

A: **Jesse Owens**
Q: What Olympic track star was nicknamed "The Ebony Express"?
W: What else are you to call a man who could beat racehorses in 100-yard sprints?

A: **Jets**
Q: What name did football's New York Titans adopt in 1963?
W: The year 1960 saw the organization of the American Football League with the Boston Patriots, Buffalo Bills, Houston Oilers, New York Titans, Dallas Texans, Denver Broncos, Los Angeles Chargers, and Oakland Raiders. The Chargers moved to San Diego in 1961 while the Titans became the Jets in 1963.

A: **Jim Bouton**
Q: Who told all in *Ball Four*
W: Jim Bouton's book was published in 1970. It infuriated many because it treated baseball players as human beings rather than athletic idols.

A: **Jim Brown**
Q: Who was named football back of the decade for 1950-1960?
W: To suggest that Jim Brown is the greatest running back who ever lived is like suggesting the universe is pretty big! Here's some of his NFL records: most yards gained in a lifetime – 12,312; led league in rushing eight years; highest average gain in a lifetime – 700 attempts, 5.22 yards per carry; most touchdowns in a lifetime – 126; and most touchdowns rushing in a lifetime – 106. And he was at his peak when he quit!

A: **Jim Brown**
Q: Who was the first NFL running back to gain 10,000 yards rushing?
W: The Cleveland Browns's fullback ran for 12,312 yards from 1957 to 1965.

A: **Jim Thorpe**
Q: Who was forced to return his Olympic gold medals after it was learned he had played semi-pro baseball?
W: Jim dominated the 1912 Olympics in Stockholm. In addition, he was a football All-American in 1911-12. He was forced to return his medals, but they were finally reinso was the hero of the 1912 Olympics at Stockholm?

A: *Jim Thorpe*
Q: *Who was the hero of the 1912 Olympics at Stockholm?*
W: Jim won the pentathlon and decathlon and came in fourth in the high jump and seventh in the long jump.

A: **Jim Thorpe**
Q: Who was voted the greatest athlete of the first half of the 20th century in an Associated Press poll?
W: He received this recognition in a 1950 AP poll. At the Olympics in Stockholm in 1912, he won the gold medals in the decathlon and pentathlon and was named the "World's Greatest Athlete" by King Gustav V of Sweden.

A: **Jimmy the Greek**
Q: What's the nickname of oddsmaker Jimmy Snyder?
W: This gambling and sports oddsmaker can be seen along with his buddy Brent Musberger on CBS sports giving commentary on football.

A: **Joe DiMaggio**
Q: What baseball great flogged Mr. Coffee?
W: New York Yankee outfielder DiMaggio hit safely in 56 consecutive games in 1941 and was voted Most Valuable Player three times. He was once married to Marilyn Monroe.

A: **Joe DiMaggio**
Q: Who was known as "the Yankee Clipper"?
W: Team mates tagged Joe with this nickname in reference to his large schnozz (nose).

A: **Joe DiMaggio's**
Q: Whose nickname was "Joltin' Joe"?
W: This nickname was given to DiMaggio by song writer Paul Simon in his song from the movie, *The Graduate*. It went as follows: "Where have you gone, Joe DiMaggio? A nation turns its lonely eyes to you..Ooh Ooh Ooh; What's that you say, Mrs. Robinson? Joltin' Joe has left and gone away...Hey Hey Hey.

A: **Joe Frazier**
Q: Who fought Muhammad Ali in the Thrilla in Manila?
W: A rematch of their 1971 New York fight was held in Manila, and Frazier bested Ali in 15 rounds. But both ended up in the hospital. In the Manila match Ali knocked out Frazier in the 14th round.

A: **Joe Frazier**
Q: Who won the Fight of the Century on March 8, 1971?
W: In New York, Smokin' Joe handed Muhammad Ali (Cassius Clay) his first professional defeat after a string of 34 victories.

A: **Joe Louis**
Q: What heavyweight boxer defended his title the most?
W: He successfully defended his title seven times in 1941. Actually, Ali had more successful defenses with five in 1966 and four in 1976, but Joe did it all in the the same year.

A: **Joe Louis**
Q: Who was world heavyweight boxing champion from 1937 to 1949?
W: Joe, at the age of 23, was also the youngest man to hold the title. He retired March 1, 1949. Louis came out of retirement in 1950 at the age of 36, 20 pounds heavier than his prime, and lost to the reigning champ, Ezzard Charles by a decision in 15 rounds.

A: **Joe Namath**
Q: Who did the New York Jets sign to a $427,000 contact on Jan. 2, 1965?
W: Broadway Joe was drafted by the New York Jets of the AFL and the St. Louis Cardinals of the NFL when the rival leagues were outbidding each other for the services of college stars. Joe signed the highest contract ever negotiated until that time in professional team sports. The package, covering three years and an option for a fourth, totaled $427,000.

A: **Joe Namath**
Q: Who said of Super Bowl III in 1969: "We'll win – I guarantee it"?
W: And they did...in a 16-7 victory over Baltimore in the Orange Bowl in Miami, Florida. The year 1969 was not a good year for Baltimore teams to play any New York teams. The Mets also beat the Orioles in baseball's World Series.

A: **John L. Sullivan**
Q: Who was the last bareknuckle heavyweight boxing champion?
W: He was the last champ of the bareknuckle heavyweight champs and the first of the new era. He became champion in 1882 by knocking out Paddy Ryan. In 1892, he lost after 21 rounds to Gentleman Jim Corbett and surrendered the title.

A: **John McEnroe**
Q: What tennis star earned the nickname "Superbrat"?
W: At the age of 20, John McEnroe said "My greatest strength is that I have no weaknesses". Humility wasn't John's strong suit.

A: **John McEnroe**
Q: Who stopped Bjorn Borg's string of Wimbledon singles titles at five?
W: In 1981 McEnroe defeated Bjorn in the final round.

A: **Johnny Weissmuller**
Q: What later actor was the first to swim 100 meters in less than one minute?
W: Johnny Weissmuller did the 100-meter freestyle in the 1924 Olympics in a time of 59 seconds. In the 1928 games he took the gold with a time of 58.6 seconds. He also anchored the American team in the 800-meter freestyle to two golds and won the 400-meter free style in 1924. It was said that in ten years of racing competition, he never lost a race from 50 to 880 yards. He later went on to Hollywood where he played Tarzan.

A: **Johnny Weissmuller**
Q: Who was the first person inducted into the U.S. Swimming Hall of Fame?
W: Weissmuller won 52 national championships, five Olympic gold medals, and set 67 world records during his swimming career.

A: **Jokers and twos**
Q: What cards are wild in canasta?
W: Wild cards may be melded with natural cards (maximum of two wild cards to each meld) or by themselves in a set of from three to seven cards.

A: **Jousting**
Q: What ancient sports event galloped into action with the command: "Charge, sir knight"?
W: Jousting is a simulation of warfare in which mounted combatants fight each other. Occasionally they would fight to death but most times the contestants were not injured. The term *joust* was derived from *juster*, meaning "bring together, unite, engage on horseback".

A: **Judo**
Q: What combat sport did Dr. Jigoro Kano devise in Japan in 1882?
W: *Judo* is Japanese for "gentle way". Kano borrowed heavily from jujitsu to create judo. The philosophy of judo is a harmony of brain, body, and state of mind.

A: **Julius Caesar**
Q: What Roman emperor does the king of diamonds represent?
W: Diamonds refer to tiles in building. Julius Caesar was considered a great builder and possessor of wealth. The king of diamonds does not show a sword, but pictures a battle-ax similar to the Roman *fasces*.

A: **Justerini and Brooks**
Q: What does the J and B stand for on the scotch?
W: J&B is a blended scotch whiskey bottled by Justerini and Brooks, Ltd., in London, England. The scotch is a product of Scotland.

K

A: **Kahlua or Tia Maria**
Q: What makes a Black Russian black?
W: Don't forget the ounce and a half of vodka!

A: **Kansas City Chiefs, The**
Q: What team lost the first Super Bowl?
W: Kansas City lost to the Green Bay Packers 35-10 in the Los Angles Coliseum, Los Angeles, California, in 1967.

A: **Kathy Whitworth**
Q: Who was the first woman golfer to earn a million?
W: Kathy has won more professional tournaments and more money than any other woman golfer in history. She turned professional when she was 19 and after six months on the tour she finally placed among the prizewinners. For placing 16th in the tournament, she won $33.00. She became a million dollar winner in July 1981.

A: **Ken**
Q: What's the name of Barbie Doll's boyfriend?
W: Ken Thurston, Barbie's long-standing beau, was created by Jack Ryan, Zsa Zsa Gabor's sixth husband. I guess Jack must have given Ken some advice on women and marriage because Ken hasn't popped the question in all these years!

A: **Kennesaw Mountain Landis**
Q: Who was the first commissioner of baseball?
W: He was commissioner from 1920 until his death in 1944. When baseball's image sank after the "Black Sox" scandal, baseball owners hired Judge Landis. Landis was named for

a mountain on which his father was struck by a Confederate cannon-ball – Kennesaw Mountain.

A: **Kentucky Derby, The**
Q: What's known as "The Most Exciting Two Minutes in Sports"?
W: It's the average time for the winners of this classic race among the best three-year-old thoroughbreds. The two-minute mark was only broken once, by Secretariat in 1973.

A: **Kentucky Derby, The**
Q: What's run on the first Saturday in May?
W: The Kentucky Derby was founded in 1875. It's run over a course of 1.25 miles at Churchill Downs in Louisville, Kentucky.

A: **Kentucky Derby, The**
Q: What's the first leg of horse racing's Triple Crown?
W: It's followed by the Belmont Stakes and Preakness Stakes.

A: **Kentucky Derby's, The**
Q: What race's winner is draped with a blanket of roses?
W: Bill Corum coined the phrase "Run For The Roses" while he was a New York sportswriter. He later came on board as president of Churchill Downs. Story has it that Colonel Lewis Clark, founder of the Churchill Downs, would pluck roses on his way to the track.

A: **Kentucky, Illinois, Indiana**
Q: What are the red *Monopoly*® properties?
W: They are properties on spaces 21, 23, and 24 of the board game that was invented in 1933. Kentucky costs $220.00, Indiana costs $240.00, and Illinois costs $220.00.

A: **Kick-the-can**
Q: What hide-and-seek game is played around a tin can?
W: The object of the game is to keep from being captured by the player designated as "it" and to release those already caught. For further information, simply ask a six-year-old!

A: **king, The**
Q: What's the tallest piece on a chessboard?
W: The second tallest is the queen.

A: **king, The; and rook**
Q: What two pieces are moved in chess' castling maneuver?
W: The move is executed by moving the king two squares toward the rook and then placing the rook on the square passed over by the king. There are many rules surrounding this move, and it is not commonly used.

A: **Kings, queens, jacks**
Q: What are the court cards in a deck?
W: They are more commonly referred to as "face cards".

A: **knight, The**
Q: What chessman makes an L-shaped move?
W: This is not a line move, but a move from point to point; therefore, it cannot be obstructed by any neighboring pieces. The knight thus can jump over other pieces.

A: **Knitting**
Q: What are you doing if you "yarn over" or "pop corn"?
W: Yarn over and popcorn are both forms of stitches used in knitting. Each of the stitches has many variations of its own.

A: **Knitting**
Q: What hobby uses the term "cast on"?
W: This is a beginning stitch or setting up stitch used to attach the yarn to a knitting needle.

A: **knot, A**
Q: What's a Fisherman's Bend, or Bucket Hitch?
W: It is a knot made by passing the end twice through a ring and then back under twice. It is understood to be the knot used primarily to tie the bait bucket to the boat while fishing.

A: **knuckleball, The**
Q: What was Hoyt Wilhelm's pet pitch?
W: Hoyt played for various teams from 1952 to 1972 with a record of 143 wins and 122 losses. A knuckleball is a ball actually gripped by the pitcher's knucles or fingertips. It has unpredictable results; it may break to the right or left or drop sharply. Not even the pitcher knows what it will do!

A: **Knute Rockne**
Q: What football coach popularized the forward pass?
W: Forward passing had been outlawed until 1906. In the seasons prior to World War I, Knute Rockne, a youthful assistant coach at Notre Dame, became influential in football through his use of the then novel forward pass.

A: **Knute Rockne**
Q: Who's credited with saying: "When the going gets tough, the tough get going"?
W: Rockne was a great motivational speaker. He once said, "A team in an ordinary frame of mind will do ordinary things. In the proper emotional stage, a team will do extraordinary things".

L

A: **Lacrosse**
Q: What's the national sport of Canada?
W: This game, originated by the Algonquin tribe of Indians who lived in the St. Lawrence valley in Canada, is similar to curling and field hockey.

A: **Ladbrokes of London**
Q: What's the world's largest legal bookmaking firm?
W: …with yearly gambling turnover of almost 100 million! They control 1,249 betting parlors in the United Kingdom.

A: **Lake Placid**
Q: What U.S. city has hosted two Winter Olympics?
W: Lake Placid first hosted the Winter Olympics in 1932. They got the call again in 1980 after Denver snubbed the Olympics.

A: **Large-yacht racing**
Q: What's the most expensive sport to compete in?
W: The most expensive of all sports is the racing of large yachts–J" type boats and international 12-meter boats. The owning and racing of these is beyond the means of individual millionaires and is confined to multimillionaires or syndicates.

A: **Larry Holmes**
Q: Who spoiled Muhammad Ali's 1980 comeback?
W: Holmes and Ali fought at Caesar's Palace Hotel in Las Vegas in a specially built arena on Oct. 2, 1980. Ali did not answer the bell in the 11th round and Holmes was awarded the knockout. Ali got $8 million, Holmes got $6 million. The fight drew the largest gate in boxing history to that date – $6 million.

A: **Las Vegas**
Q: Where is the annual World Series of Poker held?
W: Some of the odds in this game are astronomical. In the World Series of Poker in 1982, Jack "Treetop" Straus won $957,000 on the last hand with a pair of 10s and an ace to beat Dewey Tomko, a Florida kindergarten teacher, who was holding a pair of 4s with an ace. This annual championship was held at Binion's Horsehoe Club in Las Vegas, Nevada.

A: **Las Vegas casinos**
Q: What are the Golden Nugget, Horseshoe, Lucky Strike, and Jackpot?
W: They are actually located in "Lost Wages", Nevada!

A: **last, The**
Q: What shot is the hammer shot in a shuffleboard end?
W: There is an advantage to shooting second in shuffleboard, a game originally called "shove a penny." In the second position you have the last opportunity to knock your opponent's discs off of the point positions. It is called a "hammer" shot because it can "smash" a good score.

A: **Lee Elder**
Q: Who was the first black golfer to tee off in the Masters?
W: Lee qualified for the 1975 Masters by winning the Monsanto Open on April 21, 1974, at Pensacola, Florida.

A: **Lee Trevino**
Q: What golfer is nicknamed "Super Mex"?
W: Known for his jovial personality and crowd pleasing antics, Lee has done as much for Mexico as the taco. He was the U.S. Open Champ in 1968 and 1971 and British Open Champ in 1971 and 1972. In 1970 he was the leading money winner with $157,037!

A: left, The
Q: What's the "near" side on a horse?
W: It's the side from which a horse is led, mounted, or dismounted.

A: left-field wall, The
Q: What's "the Green Monster" at Boston's Fenway Park?
W: The wall is 37 feet high with a 23-foot screen extension. The "monster" is 315 feet from home plate. It takes a good poke to hit one over that obstacle.

A: Leo Durocher
Q: Who said: "Nice guys finish last"?
W: "Leo The Lip" was the manager of various baseball teams. He used to yell at his pitchers who were hesitant to use a brushback pitch "accidentally" thrown at the batter to scare him. *Nice Guys Finish Last* was the title of Leo's book.

A: Lew Alcindor
Q: What was Kareem Abdul-Jabbar's name before he became a Muslim?
W: Born and raised a Roman Catholic, Lew Alcindor says he became a Sunnite Muslim because of the hate-filled, so-called Christians he saw in L.A. in the 1960s.

A: Lines or scratches
Q: What does "scotch" refer to in hopscotch?
W: This seems clear since the object is to jump over the lines or hop scotch.

A: London
Q: Where is Wembley Stadium?
W: It's one of the most famous stadiums in the world. First used April 29, 1923, for the FA Cup final, it has also been used for other sports and was the site of the football tournament in the 1948 Olympics.

A: Lord Killanin
Q: Who succeeded Avery Brundage as International Olympic Committee chairman?
W: Avery Brundage, of the Avery Brundage Company in Chicago, Illinois, known for the construction of some of the first skyscrapers in Chicago, was president from 1952 to 1972. Shortly after the 1972 Olympic Games in Muncich, Lord Killanin was named president of the International Olympic Committee.

A: Los Angeles, Mexico City, Montreal, St. Louis
Q: What four North American cities have hosted the Summer Olympics?
W: St. Louis in 1904; Los Angeles in 1932 and 1984; Mexico City in 1968; and Montreal in 1976.

A: Los Angeles Rams, The
Q: What NFL team do the Embraceable Ewes cheer for?
W: There is sometimes more to see on the sidelines these days at pro football games. The Ewes are the official cheerleaders of the Rams.

A: Lose
Q: What didn't Rocky Marciano do in his pro boxing career?
W: He was champ from 1952 to 1956, and he defended his title six times. Rocky died in a plane crash in 1969.

A: Lou Gehrig
Q: What New York Yankee was known as "the Iron Horse"?
W: Lou Gehrig, 1903–1941, New York Yankees' first baseman, played a record 2,130 consecutive games. He was the American League's MVP in 1936. He had 14 full seasons to his credit.

A: Lou Gehrig
Q: Who played 2,130 consecutive baseball games for the New York Yankees?
W: Known as "the Iron Horse", he played his last game on April 30, 1939. He died of amyotrophic lateral sclerosis, a disintegration of the spinal cord. This disease has since become known as Lou Gehrig disease.

A: Lou Gehrig
Q: Who was the first major league baseball player to have his number retired?
W: Lou wore number 4 on his Yankee uniform, and his number was retired in 1939.

A: Lou Gehrig
Q: Who was "the Pride of the Yankees"?
W: It was also the title of the 1942 movie starring Gary Cooper and Babe Ruth as himself. Lou was always polishing the Yankee image. He never appeared in public without a coat and tie, and would often scold teammates who did not adhere to a dress code, "You're a big leaguer, look and act like one."

A: Louis Firpo
Q: What heavyweight boxer was known as "The Wild Bull of the Pampas"?
W: Firpo was born in Buenos Aires, Argentina. He knocked Dempsey out of the ring but Dempsey won by a knockout in the second round in 1923.

A: Love
Q: What tennis term is said to come from the French word for "egg"?
W: When you have love you have no points – but a song in your heart!

M

A: Mah-Jongg
Q: What Chinese parlor game swept America in the 1920s?
W: This game is a Chinese version of dominoes with similarities to rummy. An American businessman and traveler in China, Joseph P. Babcock, made a study of the game, devised a set of rules for occidental play, and added Arabic numerals to the tiles. In 1920 he imported sets under the trademark of Mah-Jongg.

A: Manhattan, A
Q: What cocktail do you concoct with whisky and sweet vermouth?
W: One and one half ounces blended whiskey, one half ounce sweet vermouth, and one dash bitters. This drink was named after the Manhattan club, which first mixed it in 1870.

A: Man o'War
Q: What racehorse won an Associated Press poll as the greatest horse of the 20th century?
W: He was defeated only once in 20 starts.

A: Manuel Benitez Perez, or El Cordobes
Q: What bullfighter earned more than $3 million a year at the height of his career?
W: He retired in 1977 and was earning an average of $15,000 for each half hour of bullfighting.

A: map, A; and compass
Q: What are the two basic aids in the sport of orienteering?
W: Orienteering is a cross-country race in which each participant uses a map and a compass to navigate his way between checkpoints along an unfamiliar course.

A: marathon, The
Q: What race was increased by 385 yards so Edward VII could see the finish line better?
W: That's why it's 26 miles, 385 yards — for good seats. It pays to be King! In the 1908 Olympics, the race began on the grounds of Windsor Castle and ended at White City Stadium.

A: Marbles
Q: What game does the New York Institute for the Investigation of Rolling Spheroids specialize in?
W: A rolling stone gathers no moss, and neither do spheroids. They have apparently rolled elsewhere as New York City information has no record of the institute

A: Margarita, A
Q: What do you get when you mix tequila, triple sec and lime juice?
W: You can also get "wasted away in Margaritaville," according to Jimmy Buffet.

A: Mario Andretti
Q: What American won the world Grand Prix driving championship in 1978?
W: Driving for the Lotus Team, Mario, from Nazareth, Pennsylvania, was the first American to win the championship since Phil Hill won in 1961.

A: Mark Spitz
Q: Who holds the record for the most gold medals in a single Olympic Games?
W: Mark won a record seven gold medals in the 1972 games. They were the 100-meter freestyle, 200-meter freestyle, 100-meter butterfly, 200-meter butterfly, 400-meter freestyle relay, 800-meter freestyle, and the 400-meter medley relay.

A: Mark Spitz
Q: Who predicted he would, but didn't win six gold medals at the 1968 Summer Olympics?
W: In Mexico City he had to "settle" for two gold, one silver and one bronze. They were gold in the 400-meter freestyle relay; gold in the 800-meter freestyle relay; silver in the 100-meter butterfly; and bronze for the 100-meter freestyle.

A: marked deck, A
Q: What were "doped cards" to a cowboy in the Old West?
W: Many a gambler has ended up in Boot Hill for the use of illegit cards.

A: marksman, A
Q: What is an expert rifle shot called?
W: In a basic proficiency test over a prescribed course with target distances ranging from 50 to 300 meters and the possibility of 100 hits, you need to score in the following ranges to achieve the listed status: 75-100, expert; 66-74, sharpshooter; 54-65, marksman; and 53 or below, unqualified.

A: Martina Navratilova
Q: Who was the first Czechoslovakian to win the Wimbledon women's singles tennis title?
W: Four times so far: 1978, 1979, 1982, and 1983.

A: martini, A
Q: What do you get by mixing gin and vermouth?
W: Use vodka and vermouth if you happen to be making it for .007, James Bond. He likes it very dry and shaken, not stirred.

A: martini, The
Q: What's the most popular cocktail in the U.S.?
W: Providing you don't count beer as a form of cocktail, especially among the younger set. It's hard to find a martini drinker in that crowd.

A: **Maryland, My Maryland**
Q: What song is played as the horses parade to the post for the Preakness Stakes?
W: This makes sense: "Maryland, My Maryland" is the state song. The Preakness Stakes, third jewel in racing's Triple Crown, is run at Pimlico Race Track in Baltimore, Maryland.

A: **Master's, The**
Q: What golf tournament's winner needs to know his jacket size?
W: A green blazer is presented each year to the victor of this, the first leg of the modern Grand Slam. The Masters tournament was first held in 1934 and is played each spring at Augusta National Country Club in Augusta, Georgia.

A: **Masters, The; PGA; and U.S., British Opens**
Q: What four tournaments make up golf's Grand Slam?
W: Actually this is the modern Grand Slam, and to date has never been successfully completed by any one player in the same year. In 1930 Bobby Jones won the old Grand Slam by winning the U.S. and British Opens and the U.S. and British Amateurs.

A: **Maureen Connolly**
Q: What women's tennis star was affectionately called "Little Mo"?
W: Precious "Little Mo" won the women's Tennis Grand Slam in 1953 with wins in the American, British, French, and Australian Opens.

A: **Maurice Richard**
Q: Who was the first NHL player to score 50 goals in a season?
W: Maurice "Rocket" Richard scored 50 goals in 50 games during the 1944-45 season with the Montreal Canadiens. His feat of 50 has been duplicated, however, by players in 70 game seasons.

A: **Maximum Time Aloft**
Q: What does MTA stand for among Frisbee freaks?
W: A Frisbee is that brightly colored disc that keeps hitting you while you are tanning on the beach. It has also been seen attached to a dog.

A: **Max Schmeling**
Q: What boxer was hailed by Hitler as a paragon of Teutonic manhood?
W: Schmeling was born in Klein-Luckaw, Germany. He was the first German to have held the world heavyweight crown, and Hitler saw another chance to tout his homeland.

A: **Max Schmeling**
Q: Who kayoed Joe Louis in 1936 and was kayoed by him in 1937?
W: We have it as 1936 and 1938. Louis was defeated by Schmeling in the 12th round of their first match. It was Louis' first professional loss. A June 22, 1938, rematch resulted in "the Brown Bomber" knocking out Schmeling in the first round.

A: **Max Schmeling**
Q: Who's the only German to have held the world heavyweight boxing championship?
W: On June 20, 1930 he defeated Jack Sharkey in the fourth round to take the title in New York.

A: **Mel Allen**
Q: Who was known as "the Voice of The Yankees"?
W: Mel was the radio announcer for the boys in pinstripes during the 1940s and 1950s. "It's going...going...gone! How about that!"

A: **Melbourne**
Q: What's the only Australian city to have hosted the Olympic Games?
W: Melbourne was the site for the 1956 Summer Olympics, but because op the Australian government's strict laws on quarantine, the equestrian events had to be held in Stockholm.

A: **Melbourne**
Q: Where were the 1956 Summer Olympics held?
W: That is with the exception of the equestrian events, which were held in Stockholm.

A: **Memorial Day**
Q: What holiday is the Indianapolis 500 run on?
W: It began on Memorial Day, 1911. It was decided that the race be 500 miles because that was the longest possible race for a crowd to watch during daylight.

A: **Mexico City**
Q: What's the highest city to have hosted the Summer Olympics?
W: The altitude of Mexico, at approximately 7,000 feet, caused quite a problem for athletes who were not used to the conditions. Competitors coming from countries with high elevations had a clear advantage in the games.

A: **Mexico City**
Q: Where's the world's largest bullfighting ring?
W: It's the Plaza with a seating capacity of 48,000. However, it was closed in March of 1976!

A: **Miami**
Q: What was the first major U.S. city to present jai-alai?
W: In 1935 a law was passed in the Florida State Legislature permitting parimutuel wagering on the sport.

A: **Miami Dolphins, The**
Q: What was the last NFL team to go through a season unbeaten?
W: In 1972 the Miami Dolphins posted 17 consecutive victories under head coach Don Shula, a 1951 graduate of John Carroll University in Cleveland, Ohio.

A: **Mickey Mantle**
Q: What New York Yankees star struck out 1,710 times in his career?
W: In 18 years with the Yankees, he was at bat 8,102 times.

A: **Mickey Mantle**
Q: Who's played the most games for the New York Yankees?
W: Mickey played in 2,401 games over 18 seasons for the Yankees.

A: **Middleweight**
Q: What's the weight classification of a 159-pound boxer?
W: The World Boxing Association provides the following list of weight classes: heavyweight – over 175 pounds; light heavyweight – 175 or less; middleweight – 160 or less; junior middleweight – 154 or less; welterweight – 147 or less; junior welterweight – 140 or less; lightweight – 135 or less; junior lightweight – 130 or less; featherweight – 126 or less; bantamweight – 118 or less; and flyweight – 112 pounds or less.

A: **Milk**
Q: What do Indianapolis 500 winners traditionally drink in the winner's circle?
W: According to the Indianapolis Motor Speedway officials, the tradition began shortly after World War II. The American Dairy Association is a major sponsor of the Indy 500.

A: **Milwaukee**
Q: What city did the Atlanta Braves transfer from for the 1966 baseball season?
W: They get around. The Boston Braves played their last game as Boston on Sept. 28, 1952, before moving to Milwaukee where they stayed until Oct. 3, 1965. They currently play in Atlanta and are owned by Ted Turner.

A: **Milwaukee Brewers, The**
Q: What team did home-run king Hank Aaron play his last major league game for?
W: "Hammerin' Hank" played his last game in 1976 at the age of 43 with 755 home runs to his credit.

A: **Milwaukee's**
Q: What city's baseball park boasts the world's largest beer barrel?
W: "Ya, hey der!" – Vere else but de home of de Brewers?

A: **Minnesota Fats**
Q: What pool shark did Jackie Gleason portray in *The Hustler*?
W: Jackie was in good company for the movie. Also starring was Paul Newman and George C. Scott. However, Jackie was the only one to do all of his own shots.

A: **Minnesota Twins, The**
Q: What baseball team retired Harmon Killebrew's Number 3?
W: Harmon's number was retired in 1975.

A: **Minnesota Vikings, The**
Q: What team has lost the most Super Bowls?
W: The Vikings were bridesmaids on four occasions. They lost in 1970 to the Kansas City Chiefs 23 to 7 in Tulane Stadium, New Orleans; in 1974 to the Miami Dolphins 24 to 7 in Rice Stadium, Houston, Texas; in 1975 to the Pittsburgh Steelers 16 to 6 in Tulane Stadium, New Orleans; and in 1977 to the Oakland Raiders 32 to 14 in the Rose Bowl Stadium, Pasadena, California.

A: **mint julep, The**
Q: What's the traditional drink at the Kentucky Derby?
W: Fill a Tom Collins glass with shaved ice, add two and one half ounces of straight bourbon whiskey, one teaspoon of powdered sugar, two teaspoons of water and stir. Add sprigs of fresh mint leaves, close your eyes, imagine millions of people screaming and thundering hooves – you're there!

A: **Miss Scarlet**
Q: What female suspect in the game of Clue is single?
W: Other suspects are Professor Plum, Colonel Mustard, Mr. Green, Mrs. White, and Mrs. Peacock.

A: **Monopoly®**
Q: What board game is banned in the Soviet Union?
W: Strange, the Soviet government seems to have a philosophy of monopoly! I guess they don't want you to even pretend that you "own" any real estate.

A: **Monopoly®**
Q: What board game's tokens include a thimble, shoe, top hat, and dog?
W: Also a race car, steamship, and cannon.

A: **Montreal Canadiens, The**
Q: What team has won the most Stanley Cup championships?
W: Since 1928 the Montreal Canadiens have won the championship 20 times.

A: **Moses Fleetwood Walker**
Q: Who was the first black to play major league baseball?
W: In 1884 Fleetwood Walker caught 41 games for the Toledo Mudhens of the American Association. In 1888 the National League adopted an anti-Negro rule. In the long years between the late 1880s and the mid-1940s, dark-skinned Americans played ball in a world of their own.

A: **Motor vehicles**
Q: What are raced at Brands Hatch?
W: This English race track opened in 1928.

A: **Mountain climbing**
Q: What sport uses a piton hammer and nylon rope, with a crash helmet optional?
W: A hammer to dig in with, rope to hold on to, and a helmet to protect your head in case neither of the previous items works.

A: **Mr. Boddy**
Q: Who is the victim of the murder in the game of Clue?
W: Is it possible that from the millions of times he has been killed in the game, Mr. Boddy gives us the phrase "habeas corpus"? We doubt it, but what else is there to say.

A: **Mrs. Peacock**
Q: What suspect in the game of Clue has the same name as a bird?
W: No other birds among the suspects: Professor Plum, Miss Scarlet, Colonel Mustard, Mr. Green, and Mrs. White.

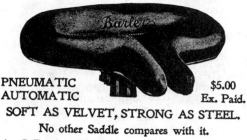
A: **Muhammad Ali**
Q: What boxer played the lead in the Broadway musical *Buck White*?
W: Ali has also hammed it up in the movies; e.g. *The Greatest* of 1976, *Freedom Road* of 1980, and *Freedom Road* for television of 1978.

A: **Muhammad Ali**
Q: Who was said to float like a butterfly, sting like a bee?
W: Cassius Clay, "the Louisville Lip", used this as a motto describing how light he was on his feet, as well as how hard he could hit. It was first touted by Clay's cornerman Drew Brown, before Clay's 1964 fight with Sonny Liston.

A: **Muhammad Ali**
Q: Who was the first boxer to hold the world heavyweight championship three times?
W: Also known as Cassius Clay, he won the title on Feb. 25, 1964, by knocking out Sonny Liston in the seventh round; on March 3, 1974, by knocking out George Foreman in the eighth round; and on Sept. 15, 1978, by a decision over Leon Spinks after 15 rounds.

A: **Muhammad Ali's**
Q: Whose famed jaw did Ken Norton break?
W: Although Ken did quiet "the Louisville Lip" on Sept. 28, 1976, Ali was the victor that evening in New York, winning a decision in 15 rounds.

A: **My Old Kentucky Home**
Q: What song is heard as the horses parade to the post for the Kentucky Derby?
W: That's the state song of the "Bluegrass State," appropriately sung at the Louisville, Kentucky Churchill Downs Race Track, first leg of horse racing's Triple Crown.

N

A: **Nadia Comaneci**
Q: Who received seven perfect scores in gymnastics at the 1976 Montreal Olympics?
W: The tiny Romanian gymnast won three gold medals and achieved seven perfect scores in Montreal.

A: **Nadia Comaneci**
Q: Who stole the show at the Montreal Olympics?
W: Nadia was the first to achieve a perfect score of 10 at the Montreal Olympics in July 1976. She did it seven times!

A: **National Football League, The**
Q: What league requires the home team to provide 24 balls?
W: According to an official of the Chicago Bears of the NFL, each team must supply 24 new Wilson footballs. They must be inspected before the game by the officials. We checked local sporting goods stores and the cost of that ball averages $33.00. That's almost $800.00 a game just for balls!

A: **National Football League, The**
Q: What professional sports league originated the college draft?
W: The draft is a method of choosing collegiate seniors for pro teams, based on won-lost records with the last-place team picking first. Bert Bell introduced the draft in 1935 with the first actual draft taking place in 1936. The first player picked was Jay

Berwanger of the University of Chicago by the Philadelphia Eagles. Berwanger's contract was sold to the Chicago Bears, but Bears owner George Hallas was unable to come to terms with Berwanger who never did play pro football.

A: **National Football League, The**
Q: What was the first major league to feature wild-card playoff teams?
W: The team with the best conference record, excluding divisional champs, qualifies for the playoffs.

A: **Needles**
Q: What tools do you use to crewel?
W: Crewel is a type of loosely twisted worsted yarn used for fancywork and embroidery.

A: **New Orleans**
Q: Where is the Sugar Bowl played?
W: It was first played in 1935 when Tulane beat Temple 20-14.

A: **New York and Paris**
Q: What cities were the start and finish of the first intercontinental auto race in 1908?
W: Our research indicates the race took place in 1906. It was sponsored by the New York *Times*. There were six team entrants: one American, three from France, one from Italy, and one from Germany. Each team consisted of three drivers. The Germans drove into Paris four days ahead of the American car, but because the Americans were given a 30-day allowance, they were proclaimed the winners by 26 days.

A: **New York Mets, The**
Q: What team lost a record 117th game of the season on Sept. 15, 1962?
W: The New York manager Casey Stengel was once overheard telling his players, "Can't anyone here play this game?"

A: **New York Yankees, The**
Q: What team has played the most World Series games?
W: They have won the penant 28 times since 1901, and the World Series 22 times. Go ahead count 'em: 1923, 1927, 1928, 1932, 1936, 1937, 1938, 1939, 1941, 1943, 1947, 1949, 1950, 1951, 1952, 1953, 1956, 1958, 1961, 1962, 1977, and 1978.

A: **New York Yankees, The**
Q: What 1927 baseball team had a crew of heavy hitters called "Murderers' Row"?
W: The nickname was coined by writer Arthur Robinson. "Murderers' Row" was the group of heavy hitters of the 1927 New York Yankees consisting of Babe Ruth, Lou Gehrig, Bob Meusel, and Tony Lazzeri. Each member had over 100 RBIs that year with a total of 544 collectively.

A: **New York Yankees, The**
Q: Who are "The Bronx Bombers"?
W: Ruth, Gehrig, DiMaggio, Mantle, Jackson, Munson, etc. Not to mention that Yankee Stadium sits in the Bronx. Need we say more?

A: **Niagara Falls**
Q: What did Charles Blondin cross on a tightrope in 1855 and 1860?
W: We find Chuck crossing Niagra several times in 1859, once with his manager An his back.

A: **nickel, The**
Q: What coin did the first slot machine take?
W: The slot machine was first called the Liberty Bell. It was built by German immigrant Charles Frey in San Francisco in 1889.

A: **Night baseball**
Q: What baseball innovation first occurred on May 24, 1935, in Cincinnati?
W: The first night game was played in 1880 at Nantucket Beach, Massachusetts. Edison's incandescent bulb paved the way for night ball; however, the two amateur teams playing suffered "innumerable" errors because of imperfect light.

A: **"Night Train"**
Q: What was football player Dick Lane's nickname?
W: Dick was a defensive back for the Los Angeles Rams, Chicago Cardinals, and Detroit Lions during his career which ran from 1952 to 1965. Dick had all the skills needed to be an offensive player; however, he preferred to dole out the punishment rather than receive it. Lane set a season record for most interceptions with 14 and shares the record for most seasons leading the league in interceptions with two.

A: **Nine**
Q: How many pins are used in skittles?
W: Skittles was a popular sport in Britain and Europe during the Middle Ages. In America this game developed into bowling as we know it now. Ever hear the expression "life's not all skittles and beer"?

A: **Nine**
Q: How many rooms are there on a *Clue* game board?
W: They are: library, kitchen, ballroom, billiard room, study, hall, conservatory, lounge and dining room. Watch out for Professor Plum if he invites you to a candlelight dinner!

A: **Nine**
Q: How many strokes make up a quadruple bogey on a par five golf hole?
W: Here's some other bad scores on a par five: one over par (6) is a bogey; two over par (7) is a double bogey; three over par (8) is a triple bogey; four over par (9) is a quadruple bogey. Any more and you have to move on to the next hole

A: **nine of diamonds, The**
Q: What playing card is called "the Curse of Scotland"?
W: There are many stories suggesting why the nine of diamonds is the curse of Scotland. The earliest reference we can find is that a Colonel Packer (1650), who was in command of the Parliament Army at Dunbar, had nine diamonds on his coat of arms. Colonel Packer was known as "the Curse of Scotland."

A: **nine of hearts, The**
Q: What playing card is the symbol of love?
W: Our research indicates the nine of hearts to be the card of money or wishes. The seven of clubs seems to refer to love.

A: **Nineteen**
Q: How many cherubs are there on a *Trivial Pursuit®* board?
W: All you can do is sit there and count 'em. They're the cute little winged characters, and when you get to 18 (those are easy), check the game

A: **Ninety minutes**
Q: How long is a regulation soccer game?
W: Better be in good shape, though; there are no timeouts! Play stops only when the ball goes out of bounds, when there's a blatant foul or when someone is injured – like having a heart attack after running around chasing a ball with your feet for 90 minutes!

A: **Notre Dame**
Q: What college football team did Knute Rockne build into a power?
W: Rockne coached from 1918 to 1931. He revolutionized the game by stressing the forward pass. He had a record of 105 wins, 12 losses, and five ties.

O

A: O.J. Simpson
Q: What football player rushed for 2,003 yards in 1973?
W: O.J. was the AFC leading rusher four times. The "Juice" had a severe case of rickets and wore leg braces as a child.

A: O.J. Simpson
Q: Who holds the NFL record for most touchdowns in a season?
W: The "Juice" held the record with 23 in the 1975 season with the Buffalo Bills. But in 1983 John Riggins of the Washington Redskins scored 24 TDs.

A: Oak
Q: What are the barrels used to age Bordeaux made of?
W: The Bordeaux district in France is the most famous in the production of red wines. There are thousands of vineyards in this region who sell their wines by the barrel to clearinghouses or wine merchants who bottle it under their names. Rarely will the vineyard owner bottle and market his own wine.

A: Olympic Games, The
Q: What international amateur sports spectacle was first telecast in 1956?
W: The 1956 games in Melbourne were the first televised, and the telecast helped greatly in financing the Olympics. In 1964 the TV coverage was live for ten-12 minutes a day. It wasn't until 1968 that live color pictures were transmitted on a regular basis. Now you can overdose on Olympic coverage!

A: Olympic Games, The
Q: What modern competition was founded by Baron Pierre de Coubertin?

W: The Olympics were first held in Athens, Greece, in 1896 to promote interest in education and culture and also to foster international understanding through the universal medium of a youth's love for athletics. This French educator enlisted nine nations to send athletes to the first modern Olympics.

A: Omar Sharif
Q: What actor is one of the world's top professional bridge players?
W: Sharif, known for films such as *Lawrence of Arabia, Dr. Zhivago,* and others, has a passion for bridge and horse racing.

A: On your marks
Q: What's the first instruction given runners by the starter of a race?
W: ...get set, go!

A: One
Q: How many daily doubles are run on each racing card?
W: In the daily double you pick the winners of the first and second race in either horse racing or dog racing, or the winners of the first and second games in Jai-alai.

A: One
Q: How many masts does a sloop have?
W: A sloop is a fore-and-aft rigged boat with one mast and a single headsail jib.

A: One
Q: How many Olympic Games were canceled because of World War I?
W: The sixth Olympiad, scheduled for 1916, was not held.

A: One
Q: How many referees work a soccer game?
W: Talk about being all over the field!

A: One
Q: What number wood is a driver in golf?
W: It is generally used off a tee for the first shot of the hole. It is also the longest club in the bag.

A: One
Q: What's the point value of standard vowels in *Scrabble®* Brand Crossword Game?
W: A = 1, E = 1, I = 1, O = 1, U = 1. What about the "sometimes y"? Well, it equals four points.

A: One and a quarter miles
Q: What distance is the Kentucky Derby run at?
W: From its inauguration in 1875 until 1896, it was 1.5 miles, but today it's run at 1.25 miles at Churchill Downs.

A: One and three
Q: What two pins is the pocket between for a right-handed bowler?
W: If you roll a straight ball or hook, that's where you want to hit the pocket. Beware of coming too high on the headpin. You'll end up with a railroad split (7-10).

A: One foot
Q: What must remain on the floor in pocket billiards?
W: You are allowed to lift one leg while trying to complete a shot that is difficult to reach.

A: One inch
Q: How thick is a hockey puck?
W: A puck is made of vulcanized rubber and is one inch thick and three inches in diameter. Before being played with, it is frozen to reduce resiliency.

A: One jack and four fives
Q: What five cards make up a perfect cribbage hand?
W: This 29-point score can only be attained when holding a jack and three fives with the starter being a five of the same suit as the held jack.

A: One lap to go
Q: What does the bell rung during the 1,500-meter race mean?
W: This is done to help the runners remember at which point in the race they are. As if they couldn't tell by how tired they already have become.

A: One minute
Q: How long is the rest between rounds in boxing?
W: Sometimes it's not long enough!!

A: One or two
Q: How many ride a luge?
W: It depends on whether you're riding a one- or a two-man luge!

A: Orange
Q: What color of *Monopoly*® Brand Crossword Game properties are landed on most often?
W: The orange-colored properties are St. James Place, Tennessee Avenue, and New York Avenue.

A: Orange
Q: What flavor is Grand Marnier?
W: A French liqueur, Grand Marnier was first made in 1880 with a fine cognac base. It comes in two varities: Cordon Rouge and a slightly weaker strain, Cordon Jaune.

A: Organist Gladys Gooding
Q: Who played for the New York Rangers, Brooklyn Dodgers, and New York Knicks in a single season?
W: Tricky, very tricky!

A: Oscar Bonavena
Q: What Argentine boxer was shot dead outside a Nevada brothel in May 1976?
W: Oscar was born in 1942. His record, over 53 professional bouts, was 46-6-l. Thirty-six wins by knockout, nine by decision, and one by disqualification.

A: Oscar Robertson
Q: What basketball player was known as "the Big O"?
W: "The Big O" stood 6'5" tall and weighed 220 pounds. He played 14 consecutive seasons in the NBA, beginning in 1960. He played ten with the Cincinnati Royals and the last four with the Milwaukee Bucks. He retired as the NBA's all time leader in assists and free throws and was second in scoring to Wilt Chamberlain

A: "Ouija"
Q: What board game features a three-legged planchette that points to letters and numbers?
W: Ouija is a combination of the French *oui* and the German *ja* words, both meaning "yes." Participants place their fingers lightly on a small heart-shaped device (planchette) that moves across the board to spell messages answer questions.

A: outfield, The
Q: What baseball position are you playing if you're in the corn?
W: As Dizzy Dean said, "That lazy, high fly ball to the outfield is a tall can o'corn." The outfield is also called "the orchard."

A: Oxford and Cambridge
Q: What schools race their boats from Putney to Mortlake on the Thames every year?
W: This, the University Boat Race, is the oldest event of world renown in rowing. It was first rowed in 1829, but this course was not used until 1845. It became an annual event in 1856, interrupted only by World War I and World War II.

P

A: Paavo Nurmi
Q: What six-time Olympic champion was known as "the Flying Finn"?
W: In the Olympics of 1920, 1924, and 1928, Nurmi won six individual gold medals and three team gold medals, more than any other track athlete in history. From 1921 to 1931, he broke 23 world outdoor records in 16 events ranging from 1,500 to 20,000 meters. He could really fly!

A: Pacific, North Carolina, Pennsylvania
Q: What three *Monopoly*® properties are green?
W: How can you be expected to know all this trivia about *Monopoly*® since you sold your game at a garage sale a week after you played *Trivial Pursuit*® for the first time?

A: Pacing and trotting
Q: What are the two categories of harness racing?
W: Pacers have a lateral, swaying gait in which the legs on one side are thrust forward in unison followed by those on the other side. Trotters have a high-stepping diagonal gait, in which the right front and left hind legs are thrust forward in unison, followed by the left front and right hind legs.

A: Painting by numbers
Q: What hobby was developed by the Palmer Paint company of Detroit?
W: Color them gone. No listing and no forwarding address. If not a lost art form, it's certainly a lost company. At least we couldn't find them!

A: pair of twos, A
Q: What's the lowest hand that beats ace-high in straight poker?
W: When hands like this win, you wonder what you have done to deserve "these lousy cards."

A: **Pancho**
Q: What was Richard Alonzo Gonzales' nickname?
W: Pancho was the Men's Singles Champion of the United States Tennis Association in 1948 and 1949. He beat Eric Sturgess in 1948 and F.R. Schroeder, Jr. in 1949.

A: **Paper**
Q: What's better than stone in the paper, stone, and scissors game?
W: A children's game in which on the count of three you make either the shape of paper, stone, or scissors with your hand. A paper covers stone, scissors cuts paper, and stone dulls scissors.

A: **Paper, stone, and scissors**
Q: What game has the winner striking the loser's wrist with two extended fingers?
W: What can we say other than we hope the players don't strike each other too hard.

A: **par five, A**
Q: What's the only kind of golf hole you can shoot a double eagle on?
W: Wrong! A double eagle means playing a hole in three shots under regulation, so a hole-in-one on a par four would also constitute a double eagle. Believe it or not this feat happens frequently. The longest ace on record is 480 yards, which is a "triple eagle."

A: **Parimutuel**
Q: What type of betting is used in horse racing?
W: The term "parimutuel" is a corruption of the term "Paris Mutual," which was the system invented by Pierre Oller and used first at Longchamps Race Track in Paris in 1872.

A: **Paris**
Q: Where were the 1900 Olympics held?
W: Paris was the site of the second modern-day Olympics. The first were held in Athens in 1896. The first Winter Olympics were held in Cahmonix, France, in 1924.

A: **Paris**
Q: Where's the Longchamps racetrack?
W: It's where parimutuel betting was first introduced in 1872.

A: **Parsley**
Q: What herb is most often used as a garnish?
W: It also serves the purpose as a breath freshener! But it usually ends up just sitting on your plate.

A: **Pasadena**
Q: Where is the Rose Bowl played?
W: The first competition took place in 1902 when Michigan beat Stanford 49-0!

A: **Paul Hornung and Alex Karras**
Q: What two NFL stars were suspended for the 1963 season for gambling?
W: Paul Hornung of the Green Bay Packers and Alex Karras of the Detroit Lions were suspended for the 1963 season as a result of investigations that revealed they had gambled on football games.

A: **Peggy Fleming**
Q: What woman won the only gold medal for the U.S. at the 1968 Winter Olympics?
W: She won the women's singles event in figure skating at the tenth Winter Olympics held in Grenoble, France.

A: **Pele**
Q: What soccer player was known as "the Black Pearl"?
W: To the countrymen and countrywomen of his native Brazil, he is a demigod. He is Pele, the world's most famous athlete.

A: **Pele**
Q: What's the better known name of Edson Arantes do Nascimento?
W: He is probably the world's best known soccer player. When three Italian soccer teams pooled $2 million in an effort to buy his contract from Santos (the Brazilian team), the president of Brazil blocked the sale by declaring him a national treasure.

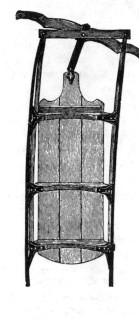

A: **Pepper**
Q: What do chefs call "the Master Spice"?
W: Pepper is a herbaceous or woody plant belonging to the genus piper. The spice is obtained from the seeds.

A: **Peppermint**
Q: What was the first Lifesaver flavor?
W: The world's most popular candy came into production in 1913. Now owned by the Nabisco Company, Lifesavers have sold almost 30 billion rolls to date.

A: **perfect surfing wave, The**
Q: What was being sought in the film *The Endless Summer*?
W: It was a superior documentary on surfing, filmed on location around the world. The 1966 film was directed by Bruce Brown and featured Mike Hyson and Robert August.

A: **Peru**
Q: What country has the world's highest golf course?
W: This course, located at the Tuctu Golf Club in Morococha, Peru, is 14,335 feet above sea level at its lowest point.

A: Pete Rose
Q: What baseball player is known as Charley Hustle?
W: Pete Rose hustled his way to National League Rookie of the Year for 1963, Most Valuable Player of 1973, and five batting crowns. He's been hustling ever since!

A: PGA, The
Q: What's the only major golf tournament Arnold Palmer never won?
W: But he came close twice! He was second to Bobby Nichols in 1964 and lost by one shot to Julius Boros in 1968.

A: photofinish, The
Q: What mechanical arbitrator was first used at Hialeah?
W: The first electric eye photofinish camera was installed on Jan. 16, 1936, at the Hialeah race track in Florida.

A: Pigeons
Q: What are the clay targets in trap shooting called?
W: They are in the shape of discs, 4.3 inches in diameter. The pigeons of the world should thank the inventor for not using the real thing to blow out of the sky.

A: Pillsbury Bake-Off, The
Q: What competition did Nan Rob win in 1969 with her Onion Lover's Twist?
W: Nan Rob won in 1970. The 1969 winner was Mrs. Edna Homgren of Hopkins, Minnesota, for her marshmallow crescent puffs. This national baking contest is held annually to locate the best recipe of the year. The contest is sponsored by Pillsbury, and prizes include cash and appliances.

A: Pina Colada, The
Q: What drink is made up of rum, coconut milk, and pineapple?
W: This tropical delight is made with three ounces rum, three tablespoons coconut milk, and three tablespoons crushed pineapple. Place all ingredients in a blender with two cups of crushed ice and blend at high speed for five seconds. Strain and serve with toasted coconut garnish.

A: pipe, A
Q: What's a meerschaum?
W: Meerschaum is a white claylike mineral used for tobacco pipes.

A: Pitcher
Q: What position do baseball's Cy Young Award winners play?
W: The award is named after Cy who won a record 511 major league games, averaging over 23 wins per season from 1890 to 1911.

A: pitcher, The and catcher
Q: What two baseball players make up the battery?
W: …or battery mates. The primary focus of their responsibility is to "serve" the ball to the batter, but not too well done! Get it?

A: Pittsburgh
Q: Where is Three Rivers Stadium?
W: Three Rivers is the home of the Pittsburgh Pirates and Steelers. It has artificial grass with a seating capacity of 54,598. It is so named because Pittsburgh is the point at which the Allegheny and Monongahela Rivers merge to form the Ohio River.

A: Pocket billiards
Q: What was Willie Mosconi famed for shooting?
W: Willie dominated the game from 1941 to 1957. In an exhibition match against a local hotshot in Springfield, Ohio, in 1954, Willie ran 526 balls in a row. That's a little more than 37 racks!

A: pocketknife, A
Q: What is mumblety-peg played with?
W: The object is to flip a knife from various positions so the blade will stick into the ground. Originally the loser had to pull a peg out of the ground with his teeth.

A: Poker
Q: What card game can feature dealer's choice?
W: The dealer has the right to name the variant to be played in his deal.

A: Poker
Q: What card game has variations known as Cincinnati, Chicago, and Lowball?
W: Cincinnati Poker is also known as "Spit in the Ocean" and "Confession." Lowball is especially popular in the western states and is draw poker in reverse

A: Polo
Q: What sport permits three minutes between chukkers to rest the ponies?
W: Chukkers are periods that last seven and one half minutes. A game may last from six to eight chukkers.

A: Polo
Q: What sport's played on the largest field?
W: It is the largest for any ball sport, 300 by 200 yards. But the game of Buzkashi, similar to polo, has a much larger field, up to one quarter mile in length

A: Pool
Q: What's another name for championship pocket billiards?
W: What's in a name anyway? The game with numbered balls began to become standardized around 1890. The greatest exponents were the American's Ralph Greenleaf who won the "world" professional title 19 times between 1919 and 1937 and Willie Moscani who dominated from 1941 to 1957.

A: Port
Q: What was known as "the Englishman's Drink"?
W: Originally from Portugal, port first appeared in England in 1689 and quickly became the favorite drink of the upper class.

A: Postcards
Q: What does a deltiologist collect?
W: This is from *deltion*, the Greek word for "small writing tablets."

A: **Potato**
Q: What's the main vegetable in vichyssoise?
W: Vichyssoise is a cold potato soup that consists also of leeks or onions, cream, and chicken stock. They sure eat funny in France!

A: **Potato chips**
Q: What's North America's most popular snack food?
W: Americans eat 400,000 tons of potato chips a year. That averages four and one half pounds per person! Betcha can't eat just one!!

A: **Pottery**
Q: What craft uses a kiln and a kick wheel?
W: The kiln is the oven used to fire clay to make it hard. A kick wheel spins the clay so the artist can form the pot. The power to spin the wheel is supplied by the artist's foot.

A: **Powdered bone**
Q: What would you add to the clay mixture to produce bone china?
W: Characterized by its whiteness, it is a translucent china made with bone ash or calcium phosphate.

A: **Power boats**
Q: What were *Miss Bardahl, Maverick, Slo-Mo-Shun,* and *Miss Supertest?*
W: The Harmsworth Cup was won three times by the power boat *Miss Supertest.* The sport in general was given impetus by the awarding of the Harmsworth Cup in 1903. These boats reach speeds of about 100 mph! *Miss Bardahl* won the 1963 Gold Cup in a record time: 105.119 mph.

A: **Preakness Stakes, The**
Q: What's the second jewel in horse racing's Triple Crown?
W: It's run at Pimlico race track in Baltimore, Maryland. Inaugurated in 1873, it is a mile and three-sixteenth for three-year-olds. The other two jewels are the Kentucky Derby and the Belmont Stakes.

A: **Princess Anne**
Q: What member of the British royal family competed in the 1976 Summer Olympics?
W: It looks as if the Princess should stay around the Windsor Castle stables and ride for pleasure. She scored so few points that we couldn't find any record of her competing. But we know she competed in the equestrian events.

A: **Princess Anne**
Q: Who was the only female athlete at the 1976 Summer Olympics not given a sex test?
W: Sex tests are given to female athletes to assure they are actually females rather than men in drag because, no offense ladies, men are assumed to have an adavantage in sporting events. This test is not given to males because it is assumed that it is no advantage for a male to compete as a female.

A: **Princeton and Rutgers**
Q: What two schools met in the first football game?
W: The game was played at New Brunswick, New Jersey, on Nov. 6, 1869, by teams of 25 men. Rutgers won by six goals to four. The game was not timed by a watch but was decided when one team scored six goals.

A: **Professional wrestling**
Q: What sport did Mr. Moto, Lou Thesz, and Big Daddy Lipscomb star in?
W: Everyone knows that these were professional wrestlers, but here's a fact nobody pays attention to: there is a little known law in Los Angeles that prohibits a wrestler from making faces during a match!

A: **Professor Plum**
Q: What suspect in the game of *Clue* teaches college?
W: Probably criminology!

A: **purse, The**
Q: What's the prize money in a horse race or a boxing match called?
W: ...and you need a big one to carry the money away these days!

A: **Q and Z**
Q: What are the two highest-valued letters in *Scrabble*® Brand Crossword Game?
W: Each is given a point value of ten. Next are *J* and *X* at eight points each.

A: **quarter-mile, A**
Q: What is the distance of straight-line sprints in drag racing?
W: A drag race is a car race with cars using one or two supercharged engines designed especially for high acceleration. The cars break at the end of the run with assistance of a parachute.

A: **queen of spades, The**
Q: What playing card was called "Calamity Jane" in the Old West?
W: This is also the name that golfer Bobby Jones gave to his putter.

A: **queen of spades, The**
Q: What's the crucial card in the game of Hearts?
W: The queen of spades is also referred to as the Black Queen, Black Lady, Black Maria, Calamity Jane, and the Slippery Bitch. She's yours at the drop of the ace or king of spades.

A: **quiver, A**
Q: What does an archer carry his arrows in?
W: The quiver also carries the bow.

A: Red
Q: What color is Manhattan-style clam chowder?
W: To make Manhattan clam chowder from New England clam chowder, omit milk and add a cup and a half of canned tomatoes.

A: Red
Q: What color light is displayed on the port side of a boat?
W: Green is on the starboard.

A: Red Auerbach
Q: What Hall of Famer coached the Boston Celtics to nine NBA titles?
W: He first led them to the title in 1957 and every year from 1959 through 1966

A: Red Grange
Q: Who was "the Galloping Ghost"?
W: Red Grange, a picture of grace, balance, and speed, became the "Galloping Ghost" in newspaper write-ups of his broken field running. During college he hauled 200-pound blocks of ice to build his physique; hence the nickname "Illinois Iceman."

A: Reggie Jackson
Q: Who hit three home runs in the final game of the 1977 World Series?
W: Only the second player ever to do this, Jackson was preceded only by the "Sultan of Swat", Babe Ruth, who did it twice, in 1926 and 1928. Reggie's came on October 18th at Yankee Stadium. Each homer was the first pitch from Burt Hootun, Charles Hough, and Elias Sosa. The final game score was 8-4, with Jackson accounting for five of the eight runs.

A: Richard Nixon
Q: What U.S. president called himself the nation's Number 1 football fan?
W: "Let me make this perfectly clear. Your president is a fan." Nixon tried out for his college team for four years but only played in his freshman year when only 11 men turned out. His coach said Nixon "had alot of spunk and drive," which usually means no talent.

A: Right
Q: Which way does the jack of hearts face?
W: The other one-eyed jack, the jack of spades, faces left.

A: right, The
Q: Does tennis service begin in the left or right court?
W: You begin on the right, alternating each point.

A: right bower, The
Q: What's the most powerful card in euchre?
W: This is the jack of trumps in the game of euchre. Incidentally, euchre was probably introduced into America by the French in Louisiana.

A: right, The; or starboard
Q: What side would the wind be coming from on a starboard tack in sailing?
W: Starboard means the right side of the ship.

A: ringer, A
Q: What's the horseshoe pitching equivalent of a bullseye?
W: To pitch the shoe so it encircles the stake; that scores three points.

A: *Risk's*
Q: What game's board shows the territories of Irkutsk, Yakutsk, and Kamchatka?
W: These three territories are part of the Asian continent in the game of *Risk*. The others in this continent are Uraq, Siberia, Mongolia, China, Japan, Afghanistan, India, Siam, and the Middle East. Great game for kids as they are instructed to eliminate their opponents and conquer the world!

A: Roberto Clemente
Q: What four-time National League batting champ was killed in a plane crash on Dec. 31, 1972?
W: This Pittsburgh Pirates outfielder won four batting titles and was voted Most Valuable Player in 1966. He was on a mission of mercy to feed the children of Nicaragua following a violent earthquake.

A: Roberto Duran
Q: Who defeated Sugar Ray Leonard in the Brawl in Montreal?
W: Duran defeated Leonard in June 1980. He lost to Leonard in a November rematch.

A: Rob Roy, A
Q: What drink is mixed with scotch, sweet vermouth, and angostura bitters?
W: This is the scotch version of a Manhattan.

A: Rocky Marciano
Q: What heavyweight champion was known as "the Brockton Bomber"?
W: Rocky, from Brockton, Massachusetts, first earned the title with his knockout of "Jersey Joe" Walcott on Sept. 23, 1952. Marciano retired undefeated on April 27, 1956.

A: Rocky Marciano
Q: Who was the only undefeated heavyweight boxing champion?
W: He first won the heavyweight title in 1952 and retired undefeated in 1956 with 46 victories—41 by knockouts! He was killed in an air crash in 1969.

A: **Rodeo**
Q: What sport has a competition for bulldoggers?
W: Rodeo came into being in the early days of the North American cattle industry. Earliest references date back to 1847 in Sante Fe, New Mexico. The fastest time given for overcoming a steer is 2.4 seconds by Jim Bynum in Oklahoma in 1955.

A: **Rodeo**
Q: What sport uses clowns to protect the competitors?
W: The clowns are used to distract the bulls and allow the cowboys to leave the arena.

A: **Roger Bannister**
Q: What runner was *Sports Illustrated*'s 1954 Sportsman of the Year?
W: Dr. Bannister's one mile time of 3:59.4 was run on May 6, 1954, at Oxford, England.

A: **Roger Bannister**
Q: Who was the first man to run the mile in less than four minutes?
W: On May 6, 1954, at Iffley Stadium at Oxford, Bannister and two friends, Chris Brasher and Chris Chataway, challenged the four-minute mile. Bannister was the only one to beat it with a time of 3 minutes, 59.4 seconds.

A: **Roller coasters**
Q: What are the "Texas Cyclone" and "Mister Twister"?
W: These babies will scare you to death. The world's longest is "The Beast" at King's Island, Ohio. "The American Eagle" at Great America in Gurnee, Illinois has the greatest vertical drop, 147.4 feet straight down, and reaches speeds of 66.31 mph!

A: **Roller derby**
Q: What sport did Leo Seltzer develop from the dance marathons and walkathons of the 1920s and 1930s?
W: The first roller derby was on Aug. l3, 1935 at the Chicago Coliseum. At first they were little more than walkathons on wheels. It wasn't until later that the rules were changed to include body contact that roller derby is known for today. Seltzer also was the first to put roller derby on television in 1947.

A: **Roller derby**
Q: What sport features jammers breaking out of the pack?
W: Only the jammers can score as they lap the pack and try to pass opposing players. Each opponent passed up by the jammers is a point.

A: **Roller derby**
Q: What sport was featured in the film *Kansas City Bomber*
W: The movie starred Raquel Welch as the "bomber." In this 1973 film Raquel needed very little padding.

A: **roller skate, The**
Q: What kind of skate did Belgium's Joseph Merlin invent in 1760?
W: Old Joe made quite an entrance wearing his new invention to the celebrated Mrs. Cornelly's masquerade at Carlisle House, Soho Square, in 1760. Mounted on the skates, Merlin came sailing into the ballroom playing a violin. Being unable to control the skates, he crashed into a mirror valued at more than $500, smashed it to smithereens, broke the violin, and severely wounded himself. We hope he went back to being a muscial instrument maker, his original occupation.

A: **Romanian**
Q: What nationality is tennis spoilsport Ilie Nastase?
W: He is locally known as "nasty." Nastase has been an officer in the Romanian army but does more fighting on the tennis court. He's been known to be either obnoxious or cute while baiting opponents or infuriating officials and fans with indecent gestures.

A: **Rome**
Q: Where were the 1960 Summer Olympics held?
W: Many of the events of the XVII Games were held in the ancient buildings. It has been said "the new and the old were never so closely together in Olympism."

A: **Ron Turcotte**
Q: What Canadian jockey, later crippled, rode Secretariat to the Triple Crown in 1973?
W: Secretariat beat Sham in the Derby with a time of 1:59.2 (a record); beat Sham in the Preakness with a time of 1:54.2 (a record later broken by Spectaular Bid in 1979 and Codex in 1980); and beat Twice a Prince in the Belmont with a time of 2:24 (a record).

A: **Rose Bowl, The**
Q: What bowl game began as an East-West contest between Michigan and Stanford in 1902?
W: The first contest final was Michigan 49, Stanford 0. The game is played each year in Pasadena, California, pitting the Big Ten champs against the Pacific Ten.

A: **Roulette**
Q: What game made Monte Carlo?
W: Monte Carlo is considered the Las Vegas of the Mediterranean. Gambling is the main activity of the area and provides a fair percentage of the income of this principality.

A: Rowing
Q: What sport features skulls, strokes, and slides?
W: Stroke... stroke... The use of two oars, one in each hand, is called skulling. You sit on the slide, otherwise known as the thwart.

A: Royal and Ancient Golf Club, St. Andrews, The
Q: What golf club has an 800-year-old bridge leading to one of its 18th holes?
W: There are four main courses at St. Andrews, the most famous of which is the internationally renowned Old Course. We doubt that the bridge ever envisioned golf carts; as a matter of fact, no carts of any kind are allowed on the course.

A: royal flush, A
Q: What's the highest hand in straight poker?
W: This is an ace high straight flush. The most depressing would be to have an ace high straight flush in diamonds, only to find another player has it in spades... so he or she wins since spades outrank diamonds!

A: Rugby
Q: What sport has a hooker in a scrum?
W: William Webb Ellis, while playing soccer at the Rugby School in England, picked up the ball and ran with it. The new game was called Rugby in honor of the school.

S

A: Sadaharu Oh
Q: Who's known as "the Babe Ruth of Japan"?
W: Oh played for the Tokyo Giants and beat Hank Aaron's record for most home runs with number 756 on Sept. 3, 1977.

A: Saffron
Q: What spice do chefs pay the most for?
W: Saffron is an orange-yellow dye obtained from the dried stigmas of the flower of the saffron crocus. It is used to flavor and color food, candy, and medicines.

A: Sailing
Q: What sport has you "hike out" while "close-hauled"?
W: "Hike out" is essentially hanging out over the edge of the boat while "close-hauled" is pulling on the sails to place or bring the boat into a more upright position.

A: Salt
Q: What should a bartender ring the glass with when serving a Margarita?
W: Mix one and one quarter ounce tequila, a half ounce triple sec, and one ounce lemon or lime juice. Rub the rim of the glass with the rind of the lemon or lime, then dip the rim in salt. Shake ingredients with ice and strain into salt-rimmed glass.

A: Salt, tequila, lemon
Q: What's the order of consumption of lemon, salt, and tequila?
W: Don't sniff the salt, throw the tequila over your shoulder, or suck the lemon...you'll be missing something.

A: Sandy Koufax
Q: What southpaw pitcher led the Los Angeles Dodgers to a World Series sweep in 1963?
W: He won the Cy Young award in 1963 as well as being named the league's most valuable player. Sandy was the winning pitcher in two games as the Dodgers swept the Yankees in four straight. Don Drysdale and Johnny Padres won the other two games. Their superior pitching limited the Yankees to a grand total of four runs.

A: Sandy Koufax's
Q: What superstar pitcher's career ended in 1966 because of arthritis?
W: The L.A. Dodgers pitcher won the Cy Young Award three times; had the lowest earned run average in the National League, 1962-66; and pitched four no-hitters, one of which was a perfect game.

A: San Francisco
Q: Where is Candlestick Park?
W: It's home to the Giants of the National League. It has natural grass and can seat 58,000 windblown fans.

A: Sangria
Q: What do you get if you add fresh fruit to red wine?
W: ...and pretty drunk fruit!

A: Sapporo, Japan
Q: What city hosted the first Winter Olympics in Asia?
W: Sappora, which is on Hokkaido, the northernmost island of Japan hosted the 1972 Winter Olympics.

A: Satchel Paige
Q: What timeless ball player counseled: "Avoid running at all times"?
W: He also said, "Never look back, time may be gaining on you."

A: Satchel Paige
Q: Who was the first black to pitch in major league baseball?
W: He starred in the Negro Leagues from 1924 to 1948 and entered the major leagues at the age of 42. He finally retired at the age of 59 from the Kansas City As. Carl Yastrzemski of the Boston Red Sox got the last hit Paige ever allowed.

A: **Schlitz**
Q: What's the beer that made Milwaukee famous?
W: Is Milwaukee really famous? This was a slogan used in the advertisements for Schlitz beer. Ironically, Schlitz is no longer brewed in Milwaukee.

A: **Scotland**
Q: Where did the sport of caber-tossing originate?
W: Caber is the Scandinavian word for pole. The caber is a tree trunk of considerable length and weight. The object is to toss or pitch it farther than other competitors.

A: **Scouts and Guides**
Q: Who meet at World Jamborees?
W: The Boy Scouts hold a world jamboree every four years in a different country. It is organized by the World Scout Bureau in Geneva, Switzerland.

A: *Scrabble®* **Brand Crossword Game**
Q: What board game was originally called *Criss Cross*?
W: An unemployed architest, Alfred Mosher Butts, invented the word game in 1931. He called it *Scrabble®* to reflect the "digging" for letters involved, a key part of the game's strategy.

A: **screwdriver, The**
Q: What drink was invented by oilmen, who used their tools to stir it?
W: This drink consists solely of vodka, orange juice, and ice. We couldn't find any reference to its invention by oilmen, but vodka didn't gain popularity in America until after World War II, with the screwdriver being one of the first drinks made with vodka.

A: **Seafood**
Q: What's the main ingredient in bouillabaisse?
W: Bouillabaisse is a highly seasoned fish stew made of at least two kinds of fish.

A: **Seattle Mariners, The; and Toronto Blue Jays**
Q: What two teams joined baseball's American League in 1977?
W: Seattle joined as part of the Western Division while Toronto became a member of the Eastern Division.

A: **Sea water**
Q: What water is it best to steam or boil lobsters in?
W: Not if you're the lobster, but it is said that the salt from the sea water seasons the meat.

A: **Secretariat**
Q: What Triple Crown-winning horse took the 1973 Belmont Stakes by 31 lengths?
W: With Ron Turcotte aboard, Secretariat left the field in a cloud of dust with a record time of 2:24 for the mile and a half at Belmont.

A: **Secretariat**
Q: What was the first horse after Citation to win the Triple Crown?
W: In 1973 Secretariat won the Triple Crown, the first to do it since Citation had won in 1948. Since then, the Triple Crown has gone to Seattle Slew in 1977 and Affirmed in 1978.

A: **Self-contained underwater breathing apparatus**
Q: What does "scuba" stand for?
W: It was devised in 1942 by Jacques Cousteau and Emile Gagnan.

A: **Seven**
Q: How many gold medals did Mark Spitz win at the 1972 Munich Olympics?
W: Here they are: 100-meter freestyle in 51.22; 200-meter freestyle in 1:52.78; 100-meter butterfly in 54.27; 200-meter butterfly in 2:00.70; 400-meter freestyle relay in 3:26.42; 800-meter freestyle relay in 7:35.78; and the 400-meter medley relay in 3:48.16.

A: **Seven**
Q: How many innings are there in a regulation softball game?
W: This is according to the Amateur Softball Association of America, one of the fastest growing associations in America.

A: **Seven**
Q: How many players make up a water polo team?
W: And you can have up to six substitutes.

A: **Seven**
Q: What do opposite faces of a die always add up to?
W: Correct. The combinations are six and one, five and two, and four and three.

A: **Seven**
Q: What uniform number did Mickey Mantle wear with the New York Yankees?
W: Mickey broke into the majors in 1951 with the Yankees. He played in 2,401 games in 18 seasons, crowned with 536 home runs—all with the number 7 on his back. Who knows how good he might have been if he'd had two good legs to play on!

A: Seven
Q: What's the most frequently rolled number with two dice?
W: Odds are 5 to 1. Next are the totals 6 or 8 (31-5); 5 or 9 (8-1); 4 or 10 (11-1); 3 or 11 (17-1); and 1 or 12 (35-1).

A: Seven and eleven
Q: What two numbers are called naturals and mean a quick win in craps?
W: If you roll a "natural", a 7 or 11, you win automatically, collect your bet and start a new come-out roll if you wish.

A: Seventeen
Q: How many double-word-score spaces are there on a *Scrabble®* Brand Crossword Game board?
W: *Scrabble®* was invented by Alfred Mosher Butts, an unemployed architect in 1931. Butts decided that by having premium squares, the sophistication of the game would increase because the pattern of laying down words would be more crucial.

A: Seventeen
Q: What do Las Vegas blackjack dealers stand on?
W: The rule requiring the dealer to "hit" on 16 or less and to stay on 17 is standard today in all casinos here and abroad. If the dealer holds a "soft" 17, that is, a 17 count with an ace, he must also stay.

A: Seventeen inches
Q: How wide is baseball's home plate?
W: Walter Johnson treated it as if it were 17 feet wide. He posted 3,508 strikeouts in his pitching career.

A: seventh, The
Q: What baseball inning has a stretch in it?
W: The stretch is for the fans during the seventh inning. When your team comes to bat, you get up and stretch your legs to refresh yourself for the last two innings. Don't forget to wave to the camera!

A: Severiano Ballesteros
Q: Who's the youngest golfer to have won the Masters?
W: Ballesteros was also the second youngest to win the British open at the age of 22 in 1979. He won the Masters nine months later at the age 23 and again in 1982. Besides Gary Player, Ballesteros is the only non-American to win the conveted green blazer of the Masters.

A: Shirley Temple, A
Q: What do you get by mixing ginger ale with grenadine and a cherry?
W: This is a popular kiddie cocktail named after the child actress.

A: shoe, A; and top hat
Q: What articles of clothing are tokens in *Monopoly*?
W: Other tokens include a race car, steamship, cannon, and thimble.

A: Shoes
Q: What did Abebe Bikila go without in winning the 1960 Olympic marathon?
W: He was the first man to win the marathon twice, first in 1960 and later in 1964 when he did wear shoes. However, he was lacking his appendix at the time of the second race as it had been removed only 34 days before the event!

A: Shuffleboard
Q: What game became popular aboard ocean liners during the 19th century?
W: It became popular because it could be played in limited space. It has all but died out except in Florida where an annual tournament is held.

A: Shuttlecock
Q: What's another term for a badminton bird?
W: Shuttlecock is the original name given to the bird by the Badminton Association of England.

A: sidecar, The
Q: What drink was named for the mode of transportation used by the inventor?
W: To make this drink: juice of one quarter lemon, one half ounce triple sec, and one ounce brandy. Shake with ice and strain into glass.

A: "The Sidewalks of New York"
Q: What song is heard as the horses parade to the post for the Belmont Stakes?
W: This song was written in 1894 by James W. Blake and Charles B. Lawlor. Since 1905 this race has been run at Belmont Park near New York City.

A: Silks
Q: What is a jockey's uniform called?
W: And rightly so, as the jacket and cap are made of silk in the colors that represent the owner's stable.

A: Silly Putty
Q: What gooey substance that bounced and stretched was sold in a plastic egg?
W: In 1945 General Electric was experimenting looking for a synthetic rubber, and it came up with this compound. Marketing specialist Pete Hodgson thought to sell it as a toy, but he didn't have much money to package it. So he purchased some plastic eggs left over from Easter at a reduced price, which were also easy to ship in egg cartons. The egg package was so popular that he stuck with it.

A: Six
Q: How many bulls are killed in a formal bullfight?
W: Each matador is to kill two bulls in a bullfight, which always has three matadors. Check this: if the first matador is injured his bulls transfer to the next matador and so on. The last matador could get "stuck" with six bulls!

A: Six
Q: How many drops make a dash in cooking?
W: At least that's what Fanny Farmer says!

A: **Six**
Q: How many hoops are there on an Association croquet court?
W: The court measures 84 by 105 feet. It has six hoops and one peg.

A: **Six**
Q: How many points are there on the star on a Chinese checkers board?
W: Chinese checkers is the modern version of the board game Holma, invented in England in 1880.

A: **Six**
Q: How many trials is each competitor permitted in javelin throwing?
W: Javelin throwing is a track and field event in which a spearlike instrument is thrown. You are judged on approach, form, distance, and the manner in which your javelin lands.

A: **six, A**
Q: What was a "Johnny Hicks" to a dice player in the Old West?
W: This is correct, but we can't explain why.

A: **Sixty feet, six inches**
Q: What's the distance between the pitcher's rubber and home plate in baseball?
W: Now imagine a fastball at 90 mph that takes four tenths of a second coming right at you!!

A: **Sixty-four**
Q: How many squares are there on a checkerboard?
W: The game of checkers has been traced back to about 6000 B.C. History reveals that the game was known in Egypt at least as early as that date, if not earlier

A: **Skateboarding**
Q: What sport might you "tick-tack" or "walk the dog" in?
W: "Tick-tack" is a kick turn, a basic method of moving along on a skateboard, much similar to popping a wheelie on a bike. "Walking the dog" was one of the first tricks invented. It is like waddling side to side while on the skateboard.

A: **Skiing**
Q: What sport has you herringboning to get uphill?
W: Cross country skiing especially falls into this category.

A: **Skiing**
Q: What sport would you helicopter to the Bugaboos for?
W: For many skiiers the ultimate experience is helicopter glacier skiing in the Bugaboos in the Canadian Rockies of British Columbia. There are no chair lifts; rather, you are taken by helicopter to your starting point!

A: **skip, The**
Q: What's the captain of a curling foursome called?
W: The sweepers follow the instructions of the "skip" as he directs them in sweeping frost and moisture from in front of the sliding stone. This helps to keep the stone traveling straight and running farther.

A: **Skydiving**
Q: What nonmechanical sport achieves the highest speeds?
W: Speeds of about 185 mph are attained in a head-down free falling position.

A: **Slate**
Q: What stone is used in the manufacture of billiards tables?
W: The slate is covered with felt to make a perfectly smooth playing surface.

A: **slot machine, A**
Q: What's a fruit machine?
W: The first one was the "Liberty Bell" designed and built in 1889 by Charles Frey in San Francisco. The jackpot was 50 cents.

A: **slot machine, A**
Q: What's a one-armed bandit?
W: The world's biggest is Super Bertha that measures 555 cubic feet and is located at the Four Queens Casino in Las Vegas, Nevada.

A: **Slot machines**
Q: What's the most popular form of gambling with women in Las Vegas?
W: It seems as if there are more women tugging on the one-armed bandits, while their husbands go off to blow the "big bucks" at craps and blackjack!

A: **Snowshoes**
Q: What are you wearing if you're shod in beavertails?
W: The snowshoe resembles the shape of a beavertail. They are rounded like a tennis racket, but have a short and wide tail.

A: **Soccer**
Q: What sport is played in more countries than any other?
W: Soccer has evolved from a crude rustic pastime into a sophisated industry. It is now the fastest growing sport in the U.S.

A: **Soccer teams**
Q: What are A.C. Milan, Ajax, and Real Madrid?
W: The countries that these teams represent are as follows respectively: Italy, Netherlands, and Spain.

A: **Solitaire**
Q: What card game has variations called Canfield, Klondike, and Spider?
W: Canfield solitaire takes its name from the celebrated gaming house of Saratoga Springs, New York. Klondike, the most popular of all solitaires, is at the same time one of the most difficult to win. The devotees of Spider, who are legion, claim it as the king of all solitaires.

A: **Solitaire**
Q: What's the most widely played card game in the world?
W: Every person who knows one card from another has a favorite solitaire to which he or she turns from time to time for relaxation. There are many games known by several names, each being identified by its characteristic layout.

A: Solitaire
Q: What's the other name for the card game Patience?
W: It must take patience to choose which one of the many solitaire games you would like to play.

A: Sonja Henie
Q: What female athlete holds the most figure skating titles?
W: Sonja holds ten individual titles for figure skating for the years 1928 to 1936 and three Olympic gold medals from 1928, 1932, and 1936.

A: Sonja Henie
Q: Who parlayed figure skating successes into a film career?
W: She made eleven films between 1938 and 1960.

A: Sonny Liston
Q: Who did Muhammad Ali beat to become world heavyweight champion for the first time?
W: The odds were 10 to 1 in favor of Liston when the challenger, then known as Cassius Clay, went up against him on Feb. 25, 1964. Clay beat Liston by a technical knockout in the seventh round. After the fight Cassius took on the name Muhammad Ali.

A: Southern California Trojans, The
Q: What university football team did O.J. Simpson take to the Rose Bowl?
W: Raised in San Francisco, Simpson graduated from high school with honors in football but a grade point average too low for admission to a four-year college. After two years in junior college, O.J. was accepted by Southern California.

A: Soviet Union, The
Q: What country took part in the 1952 Summer Olympics after a 40-year absence?
W: The Soviet Union had last played in the Olympics in 1912. Although they participated in the 1952 Summer Olympics, the athletes did not stay at the International Village;

rather, they set up their own housing with competitors from Hungary, Poland, Bulgaria, Romania, and Czechoslovakia.

A: Spades
Q: What's the highest ranking suit in bridge?
W: In rank order they are: spades, hearts, diamonds, and clubs (lowest rank).

A: Spain's
Q: What country's lottery, known as "El Gordo", gives the most prize money?
W: Some of our state lotteries make "El Gordo" look like the second prize at the church raffle. Nicholas Jarich, in Pennsylvania, walked off with $8.8 million in 1983!

A: spectator, A
Q: What is a kibitzer in bridge?
W: A nonplaying and most likely nonpaying spectator.

A: spectator's clothes, The
Q: What did a 16th-century Aztec athlete get for putting a rubber ball through a ring?

W: The Aztecs may have actually invented basketball but nobody would watch so it kind of died out.

A: *Sports Illustrated*
Q: What sports magazine has the largest circulation?
W: This magazine has a weekly circulation of over 2,360,000. That's a lot of sports fans!!

A: Squash
Q: What racket sport derives its name from the resilience of its ball?
W: Squash rules are similar to handball or racquetball. It's played with a 27-inch round-headed racket.

A: St. Andrews, Scotland
Q: Where was golf's first first hole?W: There is no documentation as to where the game originated. Golf could be traced back to the Romans who played a game called Paganica. The first official course on record was the Royal Blackheath Golf Club of London, 1608.

A: St. Andrews, Scotland
Q: Where's the world's oldest golf course?
W: Actually this is inaccurate. It is generally conceded that the Royal Blackheath Golf Club of London is the oldest existing golf course in the world, dating from 1608. The Royal Burgess Golfing Society of Edinburgh (1735), and several others preceded the Royal and Ancient Golf Club of St. Andrews formed on May 14, 1754.

A: St. Louis Cardinals, The
Q: What team retired baseball player Stan Musial's Number 6?
W: "Stan the Man" held seven National League batting titles, three Most Valuable Player awards, and a career total of 3,630 hits.

A: St. Moritz
Q: What Swiss town has hosted two Winter Olympics?
W: St. Moritz was the site of the Winter Olympics in 1928 and 1948.

A: **stalemate, A**
Q: What chess outcome results when a player has no legal move?
W: When a player doesn't have a legal move, it is checkmate. A stalemate occurs when neither player has a legal move, or king meets king.

A: **stamp, A**
Q: What is a Canada two-penny black?
W: The penny black was the first stamp issued in 1841 in England. The Canada two-penny black is simply a two cent stamp.

A: **stamp collector, A**
Q: Who would be interested in definitives, overprints, and "tete-beches"?
W: Definitives are regular issue stamps. Overprint is a word, numeral, or inscription on a stamp to change its use or value. And "tete-beches" are adjoining stamps inverted in relation to each other.

A: **Stamp collectors**
Q: Who actively pursue the acquisition of first-day covers?
W: A first-day cover is any envelope bearing a newly issued stamp that is canceled on the first day of issue.

A: **Stamp collectors**
Q: Who buy cornerblocks?
W: A cornerblock is a group of stamps, usually at least two wide and two deep, unseparated. They often have a "piece" of one complete illustration or picture

A: **Stamps**
Q: What does a philatelist collect?
W: This is the collection and study of postage stamps, postmarks, etc. Ho-hum.

A: **Stanley Cup, The**
Q: What's the oldest trophy competed for by professional athletes in North America?
W: This cup (original cost $48.67), first presented by the Governor-General Lord Stanley, became the emblem of world professional hockey supremacy 33 years after the first contest at Montreal in 1893.

A: **Strawberries and cream**
Q: What's the traditional dish served at Wimbledon?
W: Strawberries are a rare treat in England because of their very short growing season; and strawberries and St. Devon cream, from the city of Devon, are an English country tradition. Since Wimbledon is held during the height of the short strawberry season, it has become part of the tradition to serve this dish.

A: **strike zone, The**
Q: What zone varies from batter to batter in baseball?
W: The strike zone is from the center of the batter's chest, known as "the letters", to the knees. The smallest strike zone in the majors would belong to Eddie Gaedel, of the 1951 St. Louis Browns. Eddie stood three feet seven inches tall.

A: **stirrups, The**
Q: What are the "irons" in horse racing?
W: Stirrups are used to hold the jockey's feet.

A: **Stone skipping**
Q: What sport features small hops called pitty-pats at the end of a run of plinkers?
W: Plinkers are the big hops, pitty-pats are the series of small hops, and both are followed by a "kerplunk"!

A: **Stop**
Q: What does a red flag mean in auto racing?
W: Yellow means caution, white means one lap to go, black indicates death on the track, and black and white checkered means the race is over.

A: **sulky, A**
Q: What does a harness racing driver sit in?
W: A sulky is a light two-wheeled carriage or chaise with room for one person.

A: **Sumo wrestling**
Q: What's the national sport of Japan?
W: A Sumo fight takes place today in a 12-foot circle. The object is to force your opponent out of the ring. In ancient times battles or wars were avoided by having two Sumo experts fight to resolve the issue.

A: **Sunday**
Q: What day is the Super Bowl always played on?
W: Wrong, it's "Super Sunday", and it receives TV ratings of almost 50 percent of all households in the U.S.

A: **Super Ball, The**
Q: What high- and long-bouncing spheroid did Norman Stingley sell to the Wham-O toy company?
W: Stingley was a chemist doing research on synthetic materials when he formed this compound that bounced six times higher than a normal rubber ball.

A: **Surfers**
Q: What sportsmen are divided into naturals and goofy-foots?
W: Goofy-foots perform tricks while surfing, as if surfing wasn't tricky enough by itself.

A: **"Sweet Georgia Brown"**
Q: What's the theme song of the Harlem Globetrotters?
W: The "trotters" spread their basketball mastery and trickery to the tune of this Ben Bernie composition.

A: **swimming pool, A**
Q: What's a natatorium?
W: Actually a natatorium is defined as an "indoor" swimming pool.

A: **Swim the English Channel**
Q: What was Gertrude Ederle the first woman to do?
W: The first person to swim the Channel was 27-year-old Captain Matthew Webb in August 1875. Gertrude Ederle, the Olympic medalist, gained fame in 1926 when she became the first woman to swim the English Channel. She covered the distance in 14 hours, 39 minutes, setting a world record at the same time — men's record included!

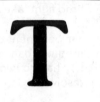

A: Take a card
Q: What must a Las Vegas blackjack dealer do when he reaches 16?
W: If you get lucky, he'll go bust (i.e., receive more than 21 points).

A: Tallyho
Q: What do hunstmen traditionally call out upon sighting a fox?
W: The term has a French origin, *tai aut*, a cry used to excite the hounds in deer hunting.

A: Technical knockout
Q: What does TKO stand for?
W: That's right, and sometimes a technical knockout hurts more than a knockout. When a referee decides a man can no longer continue to fight, he is ruled to be technically knocked out.

A: Ted Turner
Q: What baseball team owner and sailor is known as "the Mouth of the South"?
W: Ted once said "If I only had a little humility, I would be perfect." Modesty has never been a strong point of the Altanta Braves' owner, America's Cup champion yachtsman, and cable television pioneer. Turner also held the post of manager of the Braves for one day, May 11, 1977. The Braves lost to Pittsburgh 2-1, so he stepped down the next day. Before the game Ted said, "Managing isn't all that difficult, just score more runs than the other guy."

A: Ted Turner
Q: Who captained the *Courageous* to the America's Cup championship in 1977?
W: Ted whipped the Aussies that year 4-0! *Courageous* beat the Australian entry named *Australia*.

A: Ted Williams
Q: What baseball player was nicknamed "the Splendid Splinter"?
W: Theodore Samuel Williams was also known as "the Kid", "the Thumper", and "the Terrible Ted", the last to pitchers only.

A: Ted Williams
Q: Who was the last major league baseball player to bat .400?
W: Ted batted .406 in 1941 for the Boston Red Sox. On the last day of the season he had a .39955 average and could have stayed on the bench and been declared a .400 hitter. Ted wasn't much for sitting around, so he played on the last day of the season in a double header against the Philadelphia Athletics. He had six hits in eight at bats and finished with a .406 batting average.

A: tee, The
Q: What golfing accessory was patented by George Grant on Dec. 12, 1899?
W: Prior to that date golfers would carry a small bag of sand. They would pour some out on each hole and fashion a little mound to hit from.

A: Ten
Q: How many cards are dealt to each player in Gin Rummy?
W: The dealer gives the cards, one at a time, face down in an alternating fashion until each player has ten cards. The next card, called the up-card, is placed face up in the center of the table, and the remaining cards are placed face down beside it.

A: Ten
Q: How many events make up the decathlon?
W: These ten events are: 100-meter dash, long jump, 16-pound shot put, high jump, 400-meter dash, 110-meter hurdles, discus throw, pole vault, javelin throw- and the 1,500-meter run.

A: Ten
Q: How many furlongs are there in a mile-and-a-quarter racetrack?

W: A furlong is one eighth mile or 220 yards. It's simple math from there.

A: Ten
Q: How many games are played in a five-team roundrobin tournament?
W: A roundrobin tournament is one in which each team meets each other team in order. So a five-team roundrobin would have ten games.

A: Ten
Q: What dice roll in craps is known as Big Dick?
W: The game craps, as we know it, is of Afro-American origin from the river gamblers of New Orleans. Some of the expressions used in the game have been adopted from their culture.

A: Ten
Q: What do face cards count in gin rummy?
W: Gin rummy is a direct descendent of whiskey poker, a truly American game that first appeared in the Midwest about 1850. These games received their names because they were played for drinks.

A: Ten
Q: What's a perfect score in a gymnastics exercise?
W: Seems like it's becoming more common. Remember Nadia Comeneci and Bo Derek?

A: Ten
Q: What's the point value of the letter *Q* in *Scrabble*® Brand Crossword Game?
W: Points are assigned according to the frequency with which letters occur in the English language. Inventor Al Butts arrived at values by counting up the number of times the letters of the alphabet appeared on the front page of the newspaper and then rating them accordingly.

A: **Ten**
Q: What's the value of face cards in cribbage?
W: Cribbage, known as noddy in its original form, is one of the oldest card games in existence today. Its invention is attributed to the English poet and soldier Sir John Suckling, who lived from 1609 to 1642. The cards rank in their natural order down to ace, which counts as one.

A: **Ten feet**
Q: How high is the crossbar on a football goal post?
W: Whether it be amateur, professional, or Canadian, the bar is always ten feet high. The upper posts for amateur football are twenty-three feet four inches apart while professional and Canadian posts are eighteen feet six inches apart.

A: **Ten feet**
Q: What's the height of a basketball hoop?
W: The object of the game is to score the most points by tossing a ball through a hoop mounted on a backboard ten feet above the court. The hoop is bound to be raised someday. Today's players are so tall, some can stuff the ball in with their elbows.

A: **Tennis**
Q: What sport can a player double-fault in?

W: Two failed attempts to serve the ball over the net is a real faux pas.

A: **Tequila**
Q: What do Mexicans submerge in a glass of beer to make a "submarino"?
W: This is a south of the border version of the boilermaker.

A: **Tequila**
Q: What packs the punch in an Aztec Punch?
W: Tequila is a colorless Mexican liquor made from the mescal plant.

A: **Tequila Sunrise, A**
Q: What drink is formed of tequila, orange juice, and Galliano?
W: Nobody's perfect...but to make a perfect Tequila Sunrise you need grenadine, not Galliano. Try this one: two ounces tequila, four ounces orange juice, three quarter ounce grenadine. Mix tequila and orange juice, pour over ice, then slowly pour in the grenadine. Allow to settle at the bottom of the glass and you will see why it is called a "sunrise." Stir before drinking.

A: **Texas Christian's**
Q: What school's football team is nicknamed the Horned Frogs?
W: The Horned Frogs are members of the Southwest Conference with school colors of purple and white. Purple frogs?

A: **Texas leaguer, A**
Q: What's the name of a baseball hit that falls between the infield and outfield?
W: So called because at the turn of the century, the parks in the Texas League were particularly small. Other names for this type of hit are sea gulls, dying swans, bloopers, and bleeders. (But they look like line drives in the box score.)

A: **Their fists**
Q: What did Tommie Smith and John Carlos raise at the 1968 Summer Olympics?
W: Both of these athletes raised clenched fists covered when receiving their medals with black gloves signifying "Black power." Smith set the Olympic record for the 200-meter run in 19.8 seconds. He took the gold, and Carlos took the bronze.

A: **They finished last**
Q: What did the New York Yankees do in 1966 for the first time in 54 years?
W: ...with a record of 70-89 (a .440 winning percentage), they ended the season 26.5 games out of first place.

A: **thirty-five, The**
Q: What yard line do NFL teams kick off from?
W: Unless there was a penalty assessed on the kickoff, then the ball would be placed farther back!

A: **Thirty-five to one**
Q: What are the highest paying odds on a roulette table?
W: If you put your chip in the center of one of the numbered squares on the table including the 0 and 00 squares and the ball on the wheel lands on your number, you win 35 times what you bet. Pick up your chips and go back to your room!

A: **Three**
Q: How many consecutive misses eliminate a high jumper?
W: You must clear the bar at the set height by your third try or you are eliminated from the competition.

A: **Three**
Q: How many fingers are used to draw a bow?
W: The first and third fingers pull back on the string and the arrow is held between the first and second fingers, with the first above the arrow and the second and third fingers below.

A: **Three**
Q: How many golf balls are there on the moon?
W: Astronaut Alan Shepard hit three balls on Feb. 6, 1976. He used a six iron for the 800-yard approach shot. And you thought Nicklaus hit it far!

A: **Three**
Q: How many golf courses is the Bing Crosby Pro-Am played on?
W: The tournament is played in Monterey, California, Pebble Beach, Spy Glass Hill, and Cypress Point. This tournament has been called the "Crosby Clambake" because of the bad weather that usually prevails during the tournament. The tournament is now hosted by Nathaniel Crosby, Bing's son, a former U.S. Amateur Champ and University of Miami standout.

A: **Three**
Q: How many holes are there in a tenpin bowling ball?
W: Usually three. Some odd balls have more, some less.

A: **Three**
Q: How many layers of tobacco are there in a handmade cigar?
W: They are called the wrapper, the binder, and the filler.

A: **Three**
Q: How many major league baseball teams are named for birds?
W: They are the Baltimore Orioles, Toronto Bluejays, and St. Louis Cardinals.

A: **Three**
Q: How many of the animal's legs must a cowboy tie in a calf-roping contest?
W: Any three legs are tied after chasing down and roping the calf. The first reference to this sport was in Santa Fe, New Mexico, in 1847.

A: **Three**
Q: How many points is a ringer worth in horseshoe pitching?
W: You are awarded three points when the shoe encircles the stake.

A: **Three**
Q: How many rounds are there in an Olympic boxing match?
W: Providing it doesn't end sooner by knockout, the match lasts three rounds with a one-minute rest period between rounds.

A: **Three**
Q: How many stumps are there in a cricket wicket?
W: Wickets are placed opposite and parallel to each other at a distance of 22 yards. Each wicket is nine inches in width consisting of three stumps of equal size and must prevent a ball from passing through.

A: **Three**
Q: How many throws make up each turn in a game of darts?
W: Darts is one of the most exciting indoor sports you can play with your clothes on.

A: **Three**
Q: How many times in a row may a volleyball be struck by one team?
W: On the third hit, the ball must go over the net.

A: **Three**
Q: How many years old are horses that run in the Kentucky Derby?
W: All horses become one year older on Jan. 1st of each year so all horses that run in the Derby are not necessarily three years old chronologically.

A: **Three**
Q: What does the referee count to when a professional wrestler is pinned?
W: Being pinned means that both shoulders must be flush against the mat for the count of three.

A: **Three**
Q: What have you come up with if you roll cockeyes in craps?
W: The term *cockeyed* means "askew, awry, or slightly crazy." With a two on one die and a one on the other, this certainly is a case of cockeyes! Don't throw it on the first roll because you'll lose and have to pass the dice to the next player.

A: **Three**
Q: What is par on a 245-yard golf hole?
W: Usually, but the USGA sets no minimum length in regard to the yardage a hole must be to be classified a specific par rating.

A: **Three**
Q: What number is at 6 o'clock on a dartboard?
W: Curiously, these areas around the board or "clock" appear to increase after a few beers and then progressively diminish as the evening wears on.

A: **Three consecutive strikes**
Q: What's a turkey in bowling?
W: That's three consecutive strikes in a single game.

A: **Three feet**
Q: How high is the center of a tennis net?
W: The same height as the ends of the net. It's sometimes measured by a racket length and head of a racket.

A: **Three of a kind**
Q: Which is the higher poker hand, two pairs or three of a kind?
W: The odds of two pairs are 4 to 52 and the odds of three of a kind are 3 to 52.

A: **Thurman Munson**
Q: What New York Yankee catcher was killed in a plane crash on Aug. 2, 1979?
W: Munson, whose number was 15, was 1970 Rookie of the Year and 1976 American League Most Valuable Player. He died while trying to land his own jet plane at Akron-Canton Airport in Ohio.

A: **Tigers**
Q: What's the most common nickname of U.S. college football teams?
W: There are eleven in Division I alone, followed by "Bulldogs" with seven.

A: **tightrope walker, A**
Q: What's a funambulist?
W: The word funambulist comes from the Greek word *funis*, meaning "rope" and *ambulare*, meaning "to walk."

A: **To the right**
Q: Where are wineglasses placed at a table setting?
W: The wineglasses chosen depend on the menu, but their table setting arrangement is according to size, so that the little glasses are not hidden by the larger. The water goblet is placed directly above the knife at the right of the plate; a little to the right is the champagne glass. In front or between these two is where you place the white or red wine glass. In front or somewhat to the right of the champagne glass is the sherry glass. If you use all the glasses, no one will care what is being served as the main dish.

A: **Tokyo**
Q: What Asian city boasts the world's largest bowling alley?
W: The world'd largest bowling center is the Tokyo World Lanes Center with 252 lanes. Can you imagine the noise!

A: **Tokyo**
Q: Where were the canceled 1940 Summer Olympics to have been held?
W: The games of the twelfth Olympiad were to be held in Tokyo but, as a result of the Indo-China War, were transferred to Helsinki. When Finland was overtaken by war, the games were canceled.

A: **totalizator, The; or tote board**
Q: What's a racetrack's betting board called?
W: The tote board is a display of data in the infield. The board gives such information as approximate odds, total amount bet in each pool, track conditions, post time, time of day, race results, etc.

A: **Touch football**
Q: What was the favorite sport of the Kennedy clan?
W: Next to politics the Kennedy family played touch football more than anything at family get-togethers.

A: **Tour de France, The**
Q: What race has the distinction of being the longest lasting nonmechanical sports event?
W: The 1983 bicycle race was 2,315 miles long!

A: **towel, A**
Q: What does a boxer's second throw into the ring to stop a fight?
W: In the past the manager could end the fight if his boxer was being badly beaten, but it is no longer allowed by most commissions. The referee is the only participant who can end the fight by declaring a technical knock-out.

A: **trampoline, A**
Q: What is spaceball played on?
W: While bouncing up and down on the trampoline, you try to put a ball through a cyclindrical hoop in the center of a net that crosses over the middle of the trampoline, while your opponent tries to catch it and return it to your side.

A: **Trampolining**
Q: What bouncing sport features kabooms and swivel hip seat drops?
W: The swivel hip seat drop is when you land on your bottom, bounce up and do a 180 degree turn, drop back to trampoline on your bottom, and bounce up again.

A: **Trivia**
Q: What does a spermologer collect?
W: If you got this one you are truly a world-class spermologer!

A: **Twelve**
Q: How many men does a Canadian football team field?
W: The wider field encourages both forward and lateral passes. The twelfth man is used in the backfield or as an additional wide receiver. On defense he is used as an additional back or safety.

A: **Twelve**
Q: How many men does each player start a game of checkers with?
W: The checkers come in two contrastingly colored sets of 12 pieces each, usually black and red, but sometimes black and white. The checkers are placed on the dark squares in the first three rows of each player's side of the board.

A: **Twelve**
Q: How many strikes make up a perfect tenpin bowling game?
W: Believe it or not, it's been done hundreds of times in PBA sanctioned tournaments, not to mention those of the amateurs.

A: **Twelve minutes**
Q: How long is each quarter in an NBA game?
W: ...and in 1978 George Gervin scored 33 points in one quarter. That's a record!

A: **Twelve to one**
Q: What are the odds against cutting an ace from a deck of cards?
W: There are four aces in a deck of 52 cards and 48 possibilities other than an ace: ergo, 12 to one against.

A: **Twenty**
Q: How many numbered segments are there on a dartboard?
W: In clockwise order they are as follows: 20, 1, 18, 4, 13, 6, 10, 15, 2, 17, 3, 19, 7, 16, 8, 11, 14, 9, 12, and 5.

A: **Twenty**
Q: What number is at 12 o'clock on a dartboard?
W: Look at the standard dart board. There it is at 12 o'clock – the number 20.

A: **Twenty**
Q: What's the *Scrabble®* Brand Crossword Game point value of the word *jar* on a double-word-score without blanks?
W: J = 8, A = 1, R = 1; that's 10 and doubled is twenty. Simple, huh?

A: **Twenty-eight**
Q: How many properties are there on a *Monopoly®* Brand Crossword board?
W: They are 22 streets, four railroads, and two utilities.

A: **Twenty-five**
Q: What's the point value of the outer bulls-eye on a dartboard?
W: That's right and if you were a little better and hit the center bulls-eye you would be awarded 50 points.

A: **Twenty-four**
Q: How many points are there on a backgammon board?
W: There are six in each of the four sections of the board.

A: **Twenty-four**
Q: How many seconds does an NBA team have to shoot after getting the ball?
W: Hardly any wait that long before shooting. Have you seen some of the scores? They break the hundred mark quite often.

A: **Twenty-four hours**
Q: How long is the Le Mans endurance race?
W: As a tortuous 8.3 mile run over the public roads of France, Le Mans is to road racing what the Indy 500 is to car racing. It is the Grand Prix d'Endurance – The Summit in a series of endurance races for the World Manufacturer's Championship. The prize goes to the car, not the driver!

A: **Twenty-nine**
Q: How many points are there in a perfect cribbage hand?
W: There are 12,994,800 possible cribbage hands.

A: **Twenty-one**
Q: How many balls apart from the cue ball are used in snooker?
W: Snooker is a form of billiards played with 15 red balls and six variously colored balls.

A: **Twenty-one feet**
Q: How far is it from the service line to the net in tennis?
W: That's right, and the net is three feet high. It's four feet six inches from the baseline to the service line.

A: **Two**
Q: How many bails are there in a cricket wicket?
W: Bails are the small pieces of wood that sit upon the stumps.

A: **Two**
Q: How many bottles are there in a magnum of champagne?
W: Since wines, red wines especially, tend to develop and age more slowly in large bottles than in small ones, champagne is occasionally fermented in magnums.

A: **Two**
Q: How many bowling balls does it take to make a spare?
W: Sometimes you would like more, but if you don't "strike" on the first ball, you have only one more shot at the remaining pins for the "spare."

A: **Two**
Q: How many heads are there on a croquet mallet?
W: Association croquet mallets are made of wood. The heads may be round or square and are often bound in brass to prevent splitting. A croquet mallet has one face made of rubber and one made either of aluminum or plastic.

A: **Two**
Q: How many letters long must a word be to collect first-move bonus points in *Scrabble®* Brand Crossword Game?
W: That's the minimum number of letters that need to be used in opening the game. The bonus awarded is "double word score." *Q* and *Z* are ten points each, resulting in 20, double would be 40. One hitch though: *QZ* is not a word.

A: **Two**
Q: How many points are awarded for a safety touch in football?
W: If you are tackled in your own end zone by an opponent, it is called a safety. You must also kick off and give them another chance to score after having suffered the humiliation.

A: **Two**
Q: How many sleds may each country enter in the four-man Olympic bobsled event?
W: Each team may have a backup sled in case one is damaged in a run.

A NEW GAME, PAT. OCT. 21, 1890.

FOUR PLAY AND TEN LAUGH.

For Parlor, Social and Y. M. C. A's

Address NORBURY W. THORNTON
GENESEO, ILL.
Enclose stamp for reply.

A: Two
Q: How many strokes are tournament golfers penalized for slow play?
W: It is considered slow play when the group in front of you is at least one full hole ahead of your group, i.e., if group A is teeing off at the third hole, your group B must have "holed out" on the first green.

A: Two
Q: What's the minimum number of masts on a schooner?
W: A fore-and-aft rigged ship (front and middle to back) is a schooner and may have as few as two or as many as seven masts.

A: Two letters
Q: How long must the first word in a *Scrabble*® Brand Crossword game?
W: It must read either across or down; diagonal words are not permitted. Try this one: *ai* – it's a three-toed South American sloth!

A: Two, three, twelve
Q: What numbers on the first roll of the dice make you crap out?
W: When you roll craps, a two, three, or 12, you've lost the roll, not to mention the money you bet, and you pass the dice on to the next player.

A: Two under par on a hole
Q: What's an eagle in golf?
W: Possible eagles are ace on a par three, deuce on a par four, or three on a par five.

A: Ty Cobb
Q: What baseball player was nicknamed "the Georgia Peach"?

W: Ty was born in Narrows, Georgia, the son of Georgia State Senator Professor W.H. Cobb. Ty was released from his first pro team in Augusta in 1904 but went on to become a baseball immortal.

A: Ty Cobb
Q: Who was the first player elected to the Baseball Hall of Fame?
W: In 1936 he polled 222 of the 226 votes cast. He had 4,191 career hits and a .397 lifetime batting average. Others inducted in 1936 were Babe Ruth, Walter Johnson, John Wagner, and Christy Matthewson.

U

A: U.S., The
Q: What country won the first gold medal in the first modern-day Olympics?
W: James Connolly won the triple jump with 13.71 meters. But in the first Olympics there were no gold medals, first place finishers received a diploma, a silver medal, and a crown of olive branches.

A: U.S., The
Q: What country won the 1960 Olympic gold medal in hockey?
W: At Squaw Valley, in front of a home crowd, the U.S. bested both Canada and the USSR.

A: United States Golf Association, The
Q: What's the governing body of golf in the U.S.?
W: On Dec. 22, 1894 the Amateur Golf Association of the United States was formed by representatives of five of the leading golf clubs of the country. The name was soon changed to the American Golf Associaion and finally to the USGA. In addition to governing the game, it's purpose is to promote golf to the public.

A: Unser brothers, The
Q: What brothers named Bobby and Al have won the Indianapolis 500?
W: Bobby Unser posted victories in 1968, 1975, and 1981, while brother Al took the checkered flag in 1970, 1971, and 1978.

V

A: Vanilla
Q: What's the most popular ice cream flavor in North America?
W: If your consumption is average, you ate 2.5 gallons of ice cream last year, mostly vanilla, followed by chocolate.

A: Very Superior Old Pale
Q: What does V.S.O.P. stand for on a bottle of brandy?
W: ...or Very Special Old Pale. It stems from when cognac changed from a heavier style in flavor and color to the paler type of today. It should contain no brandy that has been aged less than four years in wood.

A: Vida Blue
Q: Who's the only pitcher to start for both leagues in baseball's all-star game?
W: In the 1971 classic, Blue, a member of the Oakland As won 6-4 in Detroit. He was the only American League pitcher to post an all-star win between 1963 and 1982. In 1978, representing San Francisco at San Diego, Blue started for the National League, but was not the pitcher of record in their 7-3 victory. Although he didn't start in the 1981 classic, Blue did earn the win. He's the only pitcher to earn a win in all-star games for each league. Vida Blue is now in jail (at the time of this writing).

A: Vince Lombardi
Q: What football coach said: "Winning isn't everything – it's the only thing"?
W: He said it to the Washington Redskins after he had agreed to coach them in 1969. Washington hadn't had a winning season since 1955. Vince's 1969 Redskins posted a 7-5-2 record. Vince died two weeks before the start of the 1970 season.

A: Vince Lombardi trophy, The
Q: What trophy is awarded to the winners of the Super Bowl?
W: The Super Bowl was first played in 1967 between the Green Bay Packers and the Kansas City Chiefs.

A: Vince Lombardi's
Q: What football coach's story was told in the movie *Run to Daylight*?
W: The film was based on a book written by Vince and first published in 1963.

A: Vodka
Q: What's mixed with Kahlua or Tia Maria to make a Black Russian?
W: Mix one ounce vodka with one half ounce of coffee-flavored liqueur (Tia Maria or Kahlua). For a variation try a White Russian by adding one half ounce of cream.

A: Volleyball
Q: What pro sport did Wilt Chamberlain play after basketball?
W: After one year as player/coach of the new San Diego franchise in the American Basketball Association, Wilt quit to travel, produce movies, play volleyball, and coach his women's track team.

A: Volunteers
Q: What's the nickname of the University of Tennessee football team?
W: The University of Tennessee is a member of the Southeastern Conference with team *colors of orange and white*.

A: Walnuts
Q: What kind of nuts were originally used in the old shell game?
W: Walnuts have the largest, most rounded, and most uniform shape of any nutshell.

A: Washington Redskins, The
Q: What losing team did Richard Nixon support in the 1973 Super Bowl?
W: Tricky Dick could sure pick 'em. Miami beat Washington 14 to 7 in Super Bowl VII.

A: Washington Senators, The
Q: What baseball team became the Minnesota Twins?
W: Did you know there were two Washington Senators teams? The American League's first franchise lost their last game to the Baltimore Orioles on Oct. 2, 1960. They became the Minnesota Twins in 1961. The second Washington Senators, although leading the Yankees 7-5, had to forfeit their last game on Sept. 30, 1971, when souvenir hunters swarmed the field in the ninth inning. In 1972 they became the Texas Rangers. It just goes to show you senators can't stay in Washington for long!

A: Watermelon seeds
Q: What are spit in the annual contest in Paul's Valley, Oklahoma?
W: It's a very sloppy competition!

A: Weaving
Q: What handicraft requires you to interlace your warp and weft?
W: Strands of yarn placed lengthwise are called warp. Crosswise yarns are called weft or filling. The three basic weaves are plain, twill, and satin.

A: Weeb Ewbank
Q: Who coached the New York jets to the 1969 Super Bowl title?
W: Ewbank, with a "little" help from "Broadway Joe" Namath, beat the Baltimore Colts 16-7 at the Orange Bowl in Miami.

A: Weight lifting
Q: What sport features snatches and clean jerks?
W: In the snatch, the lifter must lift the bar in a single continuous movement until his arms are fully extended above his head. As the bar passes chest level, he splits to get beneath it and return to an upright position in his own time. In the "clean-and-jerk," the lifter brings the bar to his shoulders while he splits, recovers to an upright position, splits again to get his arms fully extended above his head, and finally recovers again to the upright position.

A: Whiskey
Q: What did cowboys refer to as "tonsil paint"?
W: Red eye, rot gut, take your pick! The quality of whiskey in the Old West was terrible.

A: White
Q: What color are the Lippizaner stallions used at the Spanish Riding School of Vienna?
W: We would also give you credit if you said gray. Occasionally there have been some colored brown, but rarely. They are bred to complete difficult and intricate movements.

A: White
Q: What color is "bianco" wine?
W: "Bianco" is the common word for "white" in Italian: a vino bianco is any white wine.

A: White
Q: What color is Chablis?
W: Chablis is a little town southeast of Paris that produces the most famous of all white wines.

A: **White**

Q: What color of dry wine should be served with veal roasts and chops?

W: Red wines are usually stronger and can overpower meats with delicate flavoring such as veal, pork, or poulty. In a pinch, a light rose can pass.

A: **White**

Q: Who moves first in chess?

W: The board is placed so that each player has a white square in the corner at his right. In printed diagrams the white player is at the bottom and the black player at the top. Chess must follow the old "smoke before fire" rule!

A: **White-walled tires**

Q: What are "snowballs" to a hot-rodder?

W: Remember the hot-rod, that loud, high-powered car with big tires? Those of us with whitewalls call them "gear heads."

A: **Whitey Ford**

Q: What Hall of Fame pitcher started three World Series Games for the New York Yankees in 1962?

W: Whitey Ford pitched on 11 pennant-winning Yankee teams, was victorious in more World Series games than any pitcher in history, and compiled the highest winning percentage of any hurler with more than 300 career victories.

A: **Willie Mays**

Q: What baseball player was known as "the Say Hey Kid"?

W: Willie greeted everyone with the expression "Say Hey" from his early days in baseball with the New York Giants, later with the San Francisco Giants, and finally with the New York Mets. He addressed his teammates with this expression because he could not remember names! His records are too numerous to mention here, but he won MVP honors in both 1954 and 1965.

A: **Willie Mays**

Q: Who hit his 600th home run on Sept. 22, 1969, for the San Francisco Giants?

W: A total of 660 places him third on the all-time major league home run list. He hit number 600 off of San Diego's Mike Corkins at San Diego.

A: **Willie Mays**

Q: Who was the first black major league baseball captain?

W: In 1964 the "Say Hey" kid was appointed captain of the San Francisco Giants by manager Alvin Dark.

A: **Willie Shoemaker**

Q: What jockey was nicknamed Wee Willie?

W: He was better known as "the shoe." This four foot, 11 inch jockey is horse racing's all-time leading money winner. In 1935 Willie became the first jockey to win 400 races in a single year — out of 485!

A: **Willie Shoemaker**

Q: What jockey won $3,052,146 in 1967?

W: OK, but Braulio Baeza won $3,088,888 the same year to claim first place as leading jockey money winner.

A: **Willie Shoemaker**

Q: Who was the first jockey to ride more than 7,000 winners?

W: Willie is the most successful jockey of all time. From April 1, 1949, to the end of 1977, he rode 7,331 winners.

A: **Wilma Rudolph**

Q: What black U.S. runner, crippled as a child, struck gold at the 1960 Olympics?

W: Wilma set the Olympic record in the 100 meter run and took the gold in the 200-meter as well. She also anchored the 400-meter relay team in the 1960 Olympics to become the first American woman to win three gold medals in track and field events.

A: **Wilt Chamberlain**

Q: What basketball player is credited with 23,924 rebounds?

W: Wilt was busy at the other end of the floor as well, scoring over 30,000 points.

A: **Wilt Chamberlain**

Q: Who scored 100 points in a basketball game on March 2, 1962?

W: Wilt "the Stilt" was playing for the Philadelphia Warriors against the New York Knicks when this happened. That year Wilt averaged 50.4 points a game.

A: **Wimbledon**

Q: What is considered tennis's most illustrious championship?

W: And it all got started with the first tournament winner being S.W. Gore in 1877; 200 spectators paid one shilling each to watch the match. The game was interrupted, however, by the Eaton-Harrow Cricket Match that was scheduled at the same time. (A doubleheader, or time out for strawberries and cream?)

A: **Wimbledon**

Q: What town do the Wimbledon tennis championships take place in?

W: Ever wonder how it started there? Well, in 1877 Julian Marshall, Henry Jones, and C.G. Heathcote persuaded the All England Croquet Club at Wimbledon to allow them to play on the turf of Worpole Road. The first championship was held the same year.

A: **Wimbledon and the French, Australian, U.S. Opens**

Q: What four tournaments make up tennis' Grand Slam?

W: The first man to hold all four simultaneously was Don Budge in 1938. Rod Laver has done it twice, once in 1962 as an amateur and again in 1969 as a professional.

A: **Win, place or show**
Q: What do you want a racehorse to do if you bet across the board?
W: Meaning, you will come out ahead if your horse comes in third or better. Example, if your horse comes in third, you collect the show bet; if your horse comes in second you collect the place and show bet; if your horse wins, you clean up and collect on all your bets. But you would have won more if you had bet it to win — and he did. But cashing in is fun any way you can.

A: **Wine**
Q: What would you be examining if you used a tastevin?
W: A tastevin is a flat, shallow, silver wine taster's cup. It is widely used for sampling burgundy wines, especially young wines.

A: **wink, The**
Q: What's the name of the piece flipped into the cup in tiddlywinks?
W: Think this is silly? In 1955 Cambridge University, England, issued a challenge to Oxford for a "flipoff"!

A: **winners of the first and second race, The**
Q: What do you have to pick to win a daily double at the track?
W: The only time you feel worse than being wrong twice is to have only half of the daily double.

A: **Won a race**
Q: What has a maiden thoroughbred horse never done?
W: And it doesn't matter what the sex of the horse happens to be. Non-winners, male or female, are classified as maidens until they win once. After that, they can move into races classified as nonwinners of two, three, or four races. Further classifications are based on winnings in dollar amounts.

A: **world's largest slot machine, The**
Q: What's "Super Bertha", found in the Four Queens Casino in Las Vegas?

W: No, she's not a hooker but she can cost as much money and on occasion has given as much pleasure. Bertha is a sizable 555 cubic feet.

A: **Wrestling**
Q: What sport can catch you in a half nelson?
W: A half nelson is a wrestling hold in which one arm is thrust under the corresponding arm of the opponent and the hand is placed upon the opponent's neck.

A: **Wrist-wrestling**
Q: What strength-testing world championship is held every October in Petaluma, California?
W: Both men and women compete in this annual display of leverage and strength. The competition is taken quite seriously by the participants, as it should be. On occasion the sound of shattering bones has echoed in the hall.

A: **X**
Q: What symbol goes first in the game of tick-tack-toe?
W: This simple game is actually called Tic-Tat-Toe. There is an advantage in going first, so players alternate having the first move in successive games.

A: **Yachting**
Q: What sport is it recommended that you duck the boom in?
W: When changing direction while sailing, the boom will cross over the deck. Better duck — it could easily knock you overboard.

A: **Yankee Stadium**
Q: What baseball stadium has memorials to three players in center field?
W: The three honored players are Miller Huggins, Lou Gehrig, and Babe Ruth.

A: **Yankee Stadium**
Q: What was "the House that Ruth Built"?
W: The name was coined by sportswriter Fred Lieb. The Yankees would never have had the the need for this stadium if it had not been for the popularity of Ruth. Ruth may have built it, but Gehrig, DiMaggio, Mantle, Jackson, and others have paid the mortgage!

A: **Yankees, The**
Q: What team was called the New York Highlanders before 1913?
W: Their ball park was built on a tract of land that was the highest point in Washington Heights on Manhattan Island. The name wasn't popular, so in 1913 they opted for a more American sounding name!

A: **Yellow**
Q: What color is the bulls-eye on an official archery target?
W: More correctly, yellow or gold. The order of color on the target from the center out is as follows: yellow or gold, red, blue, black, and white.

A: **Yellow**
Q: What color is the danger flag in auto racing?
W: The yellow flag is raised when there is a wreck on the course. Rules state that you are not allowed to pass another auto when the flag is up. In 1982 Al Unser illegally passed on the yellow en route to his victory. The race was temporarily awarded to second place finisher Mario Andretti but later reversed back to Unser.

A: **Yes**
Q: Does the giver receive the basketball back on a give-and-go play?
W: I give it to you; you give it back to me. And I go!

A: **Yes, no, goodbye**
Q: What are the three operative words on a Ouija board?
W: Ouija is a combination of the French *oui* and the German *ja*, both meaning "yes." Participants place their fingers lightly on a small heart-shaped device that moves across the board to spell messages and answer questions.

A: **yo-yo, A**
Q: What toy can you make sleep?
W: Remember how to do it? You make the yo-yo go down and spin without coming back up. Then you could do "walking the dog."

A: **Zero**
Q: How many Olympic medals has gymnast Cathy Rigby won?
W: Although Cathy has never won an Olympic medal, she is perhaps the best known American gymnast. She took the silver at the world games in 1970, but injuries hampered her at the 1972 games. She ended up placing tenth. Rather than trying to compete in the 1976

Olympics, Cathy chose to go professional and has since gone on to become a television personality.

A: **Zero**
Q: How many stitches are there in the seams of a tennis ball?
W: That's right, and the balls must be white, yellow, or orange, weigh between 2 and 2.06 ounces, and be from 2.5 to 2.62 inches in diameter.

A: **zombie, A**
Q: What drink contains as many types of rum as possible?
W: The original recipe is a closely guarded secret of Don the Beachcomber but here's how *we* make it: three quarter ounce lime juice, three quarter ounce pineapple juice, one teaspoon falernum, one ounce light rum, two ounces medium rum, one ounce Jamaican rum, one half ounce 151 Demeraran rum. Shake well, pour into tall glass with shaved ice. Although there are many more kinds of rum, after a few of the above, you won't know the difference anyway!

A: **9-0**
Q: What's the score of a forfeited baseball game?
W: The "winning" team is awarded one run for each of the unplayed nine innings. In softball, a forfeited game score would be 7 to 0, since an official softball game is seven innings.

A: **$10**
Q: How much *Monopoly*® money do you collect for finishing second in a beauty contest?
W: What, no Porsche? No new wardrobe? No life supply of lip gloss? Times were simpler in 1933 when this game was invented.

A: **100**
Q: How many squares are there on a Snakes and Ladders board?
W: We counted them, and it *is* 100.

A: **100**
Q: How many tiles are there in a *Scrabble*® Brand Crossword Game?
W: There are a certain number of tiles for each letter of the alphabet, and there are two blank tiles that are used as "wild" cards, so to speak.

A: **110**
Q: How many yards are there from goal line to goal line in Canadian football?
W: The field is 110 yards or 100 meters long and 195 yards or 60 meters wide. The American field measures 100 yards long and 160 feet wide. Another difference between Canadian and American football is that in Canada you are only allowed three downs; in the American game there are four downs.

A: **121**
Q: How many points does it take to win a cribbage game?
W: And if you are not halfway around the board by the time your opponent wins, you are "skunked."

A: **$150**
Q: What does each of the utilities cost in *Monopoly*® W: That's not a monthly bill! That's the whole price for the electric company or the waterworks. I wonder what they would charge for AT&T.

A: **180**
Q: How many points are there in a perfect three-dart throw?
W: The outer ring is triple the point score, so three darts in the outer ring of the 20-point position would net 180 points. Did you think three bulls-eyes would be the perfect three-dart throw? Nope, that only gets you 150 points.

A: **200**
Q: How many laps make up the Indianapolis 500?
W: The Indianapolis Motor Speedway oval is 2.5 miles around. It's not too hard to figure out from there. One strip of the original "brickyard" still exists on the straightaway.

A: **225**
Q: How many spaces are there on a *Scrabble®* Brand Crossword Puzzle?
W: The board has rows of 15 spaces across and rows of 15 spaces down, so 15 X 15 = 225 spaces. That was easy enough.

A: **$260**
Q: How much does Ventnor Avenue cost in *Monopoly*
W: *If you have been missing a lot of Monopoly® questions, it's understandable; after all, who plays Monopoly® anymore now that we can play Trivial Pursuit® !*

A: **360 feet**
Q: How far do you have to run if you hit a home run?
W: Actually you can walk, but it is 90 feet between the bases.

A: **$400**
Q: What does Boardwalk cost?
W: Boardwalk is the most expensive property in the board game of *Monopoly®*. Rent with a hotel fetches a cool two grand.

A: **450**
Q: How many points make up a perfect five-pin bowling score?
W: That's like a perfect 900 series in ten-pin bowling. This game has only five pins.

A: **1,500 meters, The**
Q: What's the last event in the decathlon?
W: Can you imagine having already run a 100-meter dash, jumped in the long jump, put a 16-pound ball, jumped in the high jump, run in the 400-meter dash, jumped in the 110-meter hurdles, thrown a discus, jumped in the pole vault, thrown the javelin, and all you have left to do is run 1,500 meters. Well, it's only once every four years!

A: **1,500 meters, The**
Q: What's the metric mile?
W: The metric mile is equivalent to 4,921.25 feet. The standard U.S. mile is 5,280 feet.

A: **$1,500**
Q: What's every player's bankroll at the start of a *Monopoly* game?
W: And here's how it goes: two $500 bills, two $100 bills, two $50 bills, six $20 bills, five $10 bills, five $5 bills, and five $1 bills.

A: **1960**
Q: What year did Squaw Valley, California, host the Winter Olympics?
W: A precedent was set in that this was the first center specifically built for the games.

A: **1961**
Q: What year did Roger Maris hit 61 home runs?
W: Maris hit 61 home runs with the New York Yankees, breaking Babe Ruth's record of 60. The record book will always carry the footnote that Ruth hit his in 154 games, and Maris played in 162 games.

A: **1967**
Q: What year was the first Super Bowl played?
W: The Green Bay Packers beat the Kansas City Chiefs 35-10 on Jan. 15, 1967, in Memorial Coliseum at Los Angeles, California, before a crowd of 61,946.

A: **1968**
Q: What year did Mexico City host the Summer Olympics?
W: Mexico City, with an altitude of approximately 7,000 feet, proved to be a poor choice because many of the athletes were not accustomed to the thin air at this altitude.

A: **1980 Olympic hockey victory, A**
Q: What was Mark Johnson referring to when he said: "I still can't believe it – we beat the Russians"?
W: The "miracle on ice" took place in Lake Placid, New York, as the U.S. team beat the Russians for the gold medal, 4-3.

A: **2,000**
Q: How many bonus points does a wild card canasta score?
W: A wild card canasta means all seven cards held must be wild. This give you 2,000 bonus points. A pure canasta with no wild cards gives you a 500-point bonus. A mixed canasta containing one to three wild cards earns 300 bonus points.

A: **$2,000**
Q: What's the rent for Boardwalk with a hotel?
W: Boardwalk is the highest priced piece of property on the board game *Monopoly®*, and it has the highest rent.